GREAT VERSES THROUGH THE BIBLE

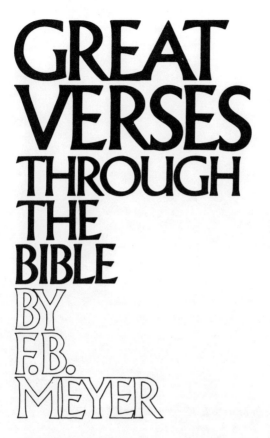

GREAT VERSES THROUGH THE BIBLE

BY F.B. MEYER

A Devotional Commentary on Key Verses

ZONDERVAN PUBLISHING HOUSE
GRAND RAPIDS, MICHIGAN

Contents

THE OLD TESTAMENT

THE NEW TESTAMENT

Foreword

THE ministry of Dr. F. B. Meyer was one of the most widely influential in the twentieth century. He had memorable pastorates in York, Leicester and London, which were sufficient of themselves to establish his lasting fame. But his influence was worldwide. Like John Wesley, he was an incessant traveler. In the course of sixty years he preached in all parts of the British Isles, and in several countries of Northern and South-Eastern Europe. He went ten times to the United States, and also visited Canada, South Africa, Australia, the West Indies, Turkey, Syria and Egypt, India and China.

Everywhere his intimate and memorable presentation of the Gospel brought blessing to multitudes. His biographer, Dr. W. Y. Fullerton, has described Meyer as "one of the greatest heralds of the faith delivered to the saints." His outstanding gifts as preacher, expositor, pastor and administrator were all subordinated to his supreme aim — to win men and women to Christ, and to lead believers into closer fellowship with Him. His chief legacy is the influence he has exerted on two generations which will, in unguessed ways, pass on to generations following.

Since F. B. Meyer passed to his rest he has continued to speak powerfully through the living message of his books, some seventy in number, many of which are veritable classics of the devout life. Amongst these, none has more enduring value than this volume *Great Verses Through the Bible* (formerly published as *Our Daily Homily*) in which Dr. Meyer continues to guide the lives of many Christians in many countries by these expositions of selected passages from every chapter in the Bible.

GREAT
VERSES
THROUGH
THE
BIBLE

THE OLD TESTAMENT

Genesis

The Evening and the Morning were the First Day. Gen. 1: 5.

HOW different is God's method from man's! The creature works from day to night, his best is first; but darkness overshadows his fairest hopes and best-concerted schemes. The Creator's days begin with the preceding eve. He reckons the evenings and night into the days, because out of them the day is born; they usher in the light, and recreate body and brain for the busy hours that follow.

ART THOU DISAPPOINTED IN CHRISTIAN WORK? Remember that God wrought on through long dark ages, ere his schemes were evolved in order and beauty. Human schemes begin with blare of trumpet and roll of drum, but are soon plunged in darkness. The heavenly seed is sown in autumn shadows; the foundation-stone of redemption was laid amid the gloom of Calvary; the work that lasts generally begins amid disappointment, difficulty, and heart-break, but inevitably passes into the day.

ART THOU PASSING THROUGH THE BITTERNESS OF SOUL-TROUBLE? For weeks there has been no ray of comfort, no sign of deliverance. Yet every dark hour is hastening towards the dawn. Thou shalt see thy Beloved walking towards thee in the morning light.

ART THOU IN DESPAIR FOR THE WORLD? The times are dark, and threaten to get darker. But if the first creation began in the dark, can it be wondered at that the second must begin there too? But as the one emerged in daylight, so shall the other. The morning cometh; see the star of day standing sentry! Time is bearing us to a day that shall never go down to night, but shall mount ever towards its meridian.

The Lord God put him into the Garden. Gen. 2: 15.

THUS God started man in an ideal home. Memories of Eden, exquisite as dreams, weave the background of human life. Fellowship with the Creator, who walked its glades; its river, trees, and fruits; its blessed companionship; its light and ennobling toils—how fair the picture!

THE GARDEN OF EDEN. That was God's ideal. When men point thee to the scars on the world's face, left by the trail of the Arab slaver, the march of the army, the decaying glory of human civilization, and ask how such things are consistent with God's love, point to that garden and say, "That is what the love of God meant for man; Satan and sin have wrought this."

THE GARDEN OF GETHSEMANE. When man forfeited Paradise, the Saviour was revealed to regain it. He trod the winepress alone in the shadowed garden of the olive trees, that through its glades He might pass to his cross, and so make the wastes of sin bloom again as Eden. Is it wonderful that another Paradise is possible, when He sowed its seeds and watered the soil with his blood?

TURNING WASTES INTO GARDENS. In Eden man wrought as God's fellow-worker; and we are called each day to do something towards reconstructing the Lost Paradise. Find thy part in delving, sowing, watering, or tending the tender shoots! Seek that thine heart should be an Eden, kept sacred for thy King, and endeavour thy best to plant gardens where hitherto sand-wastes and thorn-thickets have prevailed. Then, "instead of the thorn shall come up the fir tree, and instead of the briar shall come up the myrtle tree; and it shall be to the Lord for a name, for an everlasting sign that shall not be cut off."

Where art thou? Gen. 3: 9.

THE cool of the day, when the breeze steals over the fevered landscape, is an appropriate time for man to hold fellowship with God. We need to have his hand laid on our throbbing temples, stilling, tranquillizing, shedding his serenity throughout our being. What the breath of evening is in summer, fellowship with God will be for thee, my soul; see that thou art not so absorbed with thy sins, thy love, or thy business, as to miss the tryst, when the sun is westering.

GOD MISSES HIS CHILD. That hour of fellowship was much to Adam, and it was more to God. Love, God's love, craves for fellowship. As the musician for his lute, as the hart for the brook, as the mother for the twining arms and babbling talk of her child —so does God long for the free outpourings of his child's heart in prayer; misses them when withheld; is jealous when they are fitful and intermittent.

GOD SEEKS HIS CHILD. He did not wait till Adam found his way back to his side. But He hastened in search of him. So through the glades He comes to seek thee, O truant one! Where art thou, that for these many days thou hast withheld thyself from the hour of prayer? Wilt thou not say with the psalmist, "When thou saidst, Seek ye my face, my heart said unto Thee, Thy face, Lord, will I seek"?

GOD MOURNS OVER HIS CHILD. These words, in one version, are rendered, Alas, for thee: as though the heart of God were wrung with sorrow for our loss, as well as his. But He does not content Himself with regret. By the pang of travail, by the prick of thorns, by the necessity of labour, by sacrifice and gifts of covering for our nakedness, He brings us back to Himself.

Where is Abel thy Brother? Gen. 4: 9.
THE first question God puts to the soul is, "Adam, where art thou?" The next, "Where is Abel thy brother?" We are our brothers' keepers. Each within our reach, all who need our help, all related to us by the ties of the family, have a claim on us. We must not take an advantage over them; their weakness and need are strong claims on our resources of every kind; we are bound to keep them so far as we can; we may at any moment be called to give an account of their whereabouts. To dispute this is to betray the spirit of Cain, who was a murderer.

GOD KEEPS AN INVENTORY OF HIS SAINTS. In his book their names are written. Their names, abode, and circumstances; their fathers, mothers, and brothers; their occupation, whether they keep the sheep or till the land: all are known to Him, because fixed by his providence. Whatever touches them is, therefore, instantly known to Him. It is as though they were part of his very being, and a stab of pain to them thrills his heart.

GOD CALLS US TO HELP HIM IN KEEPING ONE ANOTHER. We are to watch for each other's souls; to consider one another to provoke to good works; to bear one another's burdens; to exhort each other, to convert the wanderer from the path of the destroyer, and to wash stains from his feet. The cure of souls is the work of all the saints. But this is only possible to those who have been baptized into the Spirit of Christ. Remember that you have just as much love towards God, as you are willing to show towards the brother whom you have seen. "This commandment have we from Him, That he who loveth God love his brother also."

Enoch walked with God. Gen. 5: 24.
WHAT an epitaph on this ancient saint! It is as clear-cut to-day as when first recorded here. We know nothing of Enoch but this brief record; but it tells us everything. It was not an act or a number of acts, but a high tone of life constantly maintained. Better to walk with God every day in calm, unbroken fellowship, than to have occasional rapturous experiences, succeeded by long relapses and backslidings. The Hebrew word might be rendered, "Enoch walked and continued to walk."

BE SURE TO GO GOD'S WAY. He will not walk with thee in thy way, but thou mayest walk with Him in his. To this He calls thee. Each moment, and especially when two or three roads diverge, look up to Him, and say, "Which way art Thou taking, that I may accompany Thee?" It will not be so hard to forsake inviting paths and engaging companions, if only the eye is kept fixed on his face, and the track of his footsteps determines thy road beyond hesitation or dispute.

BE SURE TO KEEP GOD'S PACE. Do not run impetuously before Him; learn to wait his time: the minute-hand as well as the hour-hand must point the exact moment for action. Do not loiter behind in indolence or sloth. Be loyal and true to his ideals, and quick to obey his least commands.

BE SURE TO WEAR GOD'S LIVERY. He is in the light; the light is his chosen symbol; it ill becomes thee to wear the unfruitful works of darkness. Put them off, and put on the armour of light. Walk with Him daily in stainless robes, washed in the blood of the Lamb. Then thy fellowship shall be with the Father, the Son, and the Holy Spirit, and with all holy souls everywhere.

Noah was just . . . perfect, . . . walked with God.
Gen. 6: 9.

THE eyes of God went to and fro over the ancient world, where sin reigned unchecked, to discover one grateful spectacle. But they were doomed to disappointment, till they lighted on Noah. He found grace in the eyes of the Lord, because him only had God seen to be righteous in all his generation. Like Antipas, he dwelt where Satan's seat was, held fast the divine name, and was God's faithful witness. Be thou loyal to God, my soul, though thou stand alone. There are three characteristics in the man who finds grace in the eyes of the Lord.

IN HIMSELF HE IS JUST. Not faultless, as judged by the white light of eternity; but blameless, so far as his own consciousness is concerned. He wears ever the white flower of a blameless life. His strength is as the strength of ten, because his heart is pure. He exercises himself to have always a conscience void of offence towards God and man. This condition is only possible to faith, that opens the door of the heart to receive the life of God. Wouldst thou be just, welcome that Just One. Let Him live within thee.

TOWARDS MAN HE IS UPRIGHT. He does not keep his eyes bowing down to the ground in shame, or furtively looking around to gain a secret advantage; he looks the whole world in the face. His eyes reflect the integrity and purity of his soul; they beam with sincerity, unselfishness, and love.

WITH RESPECT TO GOD, HE ABIDES IN PERPETUAL FELLOWSHIP. This were worth our getting, though we parted with all our jewels to win it. To be tuned into one deep accord with the divine nature; to answer to Him with one full, responsive chord; to be always found where God is, and never where He is not—that were life indeed.

As God had commanded. Gen. 7: 9.

THIS is the secret of a Holy and Blessed Life. Most of our sorrows and disappointments have come on us because we have chosen our own path, and done according to our own will.

IN OBEYING, WE MUST SOMETIMES WALK IN THE DARK. When Noah began to walk with God, he knew not that it would lead him into collision with his generation, with the suggestions of common sense and experience, and with much that he held dear as life. But walking on each day, he grew strong to trust in the bare word of his Almighty Guide, and grasped it as men in the catacombs will keep their hand on a tiny string or cord, until the first streak of daylight appear. Obey absolutely the voice that speaks in thy heart; the way is dark, but it is the way.

IN OBEYING, WE MUST LEARN TO WAIT. For one hundred and twenty years the long-suffering of God waited, and during that weary period this true heart failed not. Then for seven days the patriarch waited within the closed doors. It is not easy to bear the long strain of endurance. To rush into the battle, to do something desperate, to strike for liberty—this is the choice of the flesh; but to live in hourly fear, to toil on without result, to see the years stealing away the bank or shoal on which our heart had erected its structures of hope—this is hardest of all, unless our hope is anchored beyond life's ebb and swell.

IN OBEYING GOD OTHERS OBEY US. How came it that these creeping things and flying fowls, these living creatures, clean and unclean, entered the Ark so tamely and submissively? Surely a divine constraint was upon them. When we are under authority, we can say "Go," "Come," "Do this." All things serve the man who serves the divine Master, Christ.

God remembered Noah. Gen. 8: 1.

HE cannot forget thee, though all hearts that loved thee are cold in death, and though floods of trouble surge and break around. He comes nearest when there is none else to intercept his love. The floods but bear us nearer to his heart, above the tops of the highest hills.

HE COULD NOT FORGET BECAUSE HIS HONOUR WAS PLEDGED. There was a tacit understanding between Noah and himself, that if his servant obeyed his mandate He would be responsible for the consequences that obedience might involve. There is no need to make bargains with God, as Jacob did. It is far better simply to obey, sure that whatever the highest honour may demand, God will be equal to it. He will have prepared more than we expected.

HE COULD NOT FORGET, BECAUSE HE RODE THE WATERS WITH HIS CHILD. He said, "Come thou into the Ark," evidently He was inside; and when it is said that God shut him in, it was from inside that the door was locked. Whatever happened to Noah was an experience for his Almighty Friend. They had walked together on the earth; they now shared together the seclusion of the Ark. God is identified in the experiences of his saints. Their pangs, and tears, and waiting-hours are his. He can no more forget, than a mother her sucking child.

HE COULD NOT FORGET, BECAUSE NOAH WAS A TYPE OF HIS BELOVED SON. Across the dark sea of death, the cross of Jesus has brought Him and his own: so that we now belong, not to the old world which is under the curse, but to the world of Resurrection-Life. The dark woes of Calvary were imaged there: how could God forget? Reckon on God's faithfulness: He will not leave thy soul in Hades.

My Bow in the Cloud. Gen. 9: 13.

A COVENANT is a promise or undertaking, resting on certain conditions, with a sign or token attached to it. The rainbow on the raincloud, the Lord's Supper, the wedding-ring, are signs and seals of the respective covenants to which they belong. Whenever we see them we should bethink ourselves of the covenant. Whenever you see a rainbow, recall the covenant into which God has entered with thee; for as He has sworn that the water of Noah should no more go over the earth, so his kindness shall not depart from thee, nor the covenant of his peace be removed. Three things are needed to make a rainbow.

A CLOUD. When man's sin overshadowed Paradise, the bow of promise shone; and when the thunderclouds gathered about the Saviour's path, the divine voice assured Him that as He had glorified the divine name by his life, He should glorify it much more by his death. When the black clouds of conviction, bereavement, soul anguish beset thee, look out for the bow: it is always there, though sufferers do not always perceive it.

RAIN. There are no rainbows unless there be falling drops to catch and unravel the sunbeams. It may be that all evil is worse in its anticipation than in its endurance; but this is certain, that the big drops of sorrow have to patter on our souls before we can realize all that God is prepared to be to us.

SUNSHINE. It is only when God comes into our grief that we can see the treasures of Love and Grace which are stored for us in Him. We never know how great a blessing sorrow may be till we carry it into the light of the King's face. It is the dark canvas on which the artist produces his most marvellous effects.

The Isles of the Gentiles. Gen. 10: 5.

FEW realize the treasures that lie in this heap of names. This chapter is the key to ancient histories and contains many of the names that lie on our modern maps. What teeming myriads are here! We learn three things.

THE ONENESS OF THE HUMAN RACE. "God hath made of one blood all nations of men to dwell on the face of the earth." The slave that crouches in the African wood, the meanest outcast that creeps along in the dark, the veriest ruffian red-handed in crime —are bone of our bone, no less than the kings and sàints, the prophets and martyrs.

THE WEALTH OF OUR SAVIOUR'S NATURE. He loved all; He gave Himself for all; He became the Propitiation for the sins of all; through Him all will rise; and He is able to satisfy all from his royal heart. "My God shall supply all your need according to his riches in glory by Christ Jesus." There is not one child of man who may not find his consummation and bliss in Jesus, the One Man. All men are but broken lights of Him; and of all men that have ever lived He is the one flawless, sinless, perfect Man, the apex of the pyramid of humanity, the Head and Prince.

THE WARRANT FOR FOREIGN MISSIONS. If the races of mankind have sprung from a common stock, the experience of one is the key to all. Each may learn from his own heart to estimate the hopes and fears, the yearnings and temptations, the weariness and sin-consciousness of the rest. The Gospel which has brought the blessing will do as much for each of those who bear, however obliterated, the print-mark of our race. "Go ye into all the world, and preach the Gospel to every creature."

Let us go Down. Gen. 11: 7.

GOD comes down into human life. Though the world is corrupt and full of violence; though his arch-enemy has taught man to dread and hate Him; though attempts are on foot to resist Him in open rebellion, by making a unity apart from Him, and in exclusion of his corner-stone, yet He comes down.

HE COMES DOWN TO SEE. He will not pronounce judgment till He has satisfied Himself by personal inspection how things stand. He comes down to our bedrooms, and overhears the words we speak, the deeds we do there; to our home-life, and is a silent listener and observer of all its incidents; to our shops, warehouses, and bank-parlours, auditing our accounts, casting up the columns, examining our samples, our weights and measures, our advertisements and circulars. From Him no secrets are hid.

HE COMES DOWN TO PUNISH. "Let me alone, that I may destroy." Never forget the punitive side of God's character. How easily He asserts his power! He can disorganize the memory, breathe on the brain, touch one small nerve or muscle, and the best-concerted schemes fail. Why shouldst thou fear every day the fury of the oppressor, when God is at thy side!

HE COMES DOWN TO SAVE. If there be one Lot, He will bring him forth. What was the Incarnation, the descent to Calvary and the grave, but the coming down of the "us" of the blessed Trinity. He that ascended is the same that also first descended. He has come that He may heal our wounds, take us in His arms, and bear us with Him far beyond all principality and power. He is the way, by which we may pass from the confusion of Babel to the love of Pentecost, and the one speech of heaven.

Get thee Out. Gen. 12: 1.

NEVER did a corn of wheat more utterly fall into the ground to die. It seemed as though he were urgently needed in his country and among his kindred; but man's thoughts and ways are not God's. The blessing of Abram's life could only come in the land of promise, and after he had died to the whole life of nature. To every one who is to be richly blessed and made a blessing there is the inevitable command, "Get thee out. Be willing to die."

GET THEE OUT OF THE LAND OF IDOLS. Beyond the flood of the Euphrates, Terah and the rest served other gods. Had Abram remained there, he might have touched the unclean thing; hence God's desire to get him beyond the reach of infection, that he and his race might remain monotheistic. Hast thou had communion with darkness, with Belial, with idols? Get thee out and be separate; touch not the unclean thing. Be clean, thou art to bear the vessels of the Lord. Reckon thyself to have died.

GET THEE OUT IN LONELINESS. "I called him alone, and increased him." If thou art unwilling to abide alone, thou must fall alone into the ground and die. God must reduce us to a minimum before He can work through us to the maximum. But there is no loneliness to the soul who is one with God. Alone against the world, it is still in a majority.

GET THEE OUT IN FAITH. "He went out, not knowing whither." It was what man calls a venture; but as he stepped out on what seemed a void, he found it rock beneath his feet. Day by day a track appeared across the desert, and all his needs were met till he reached the place of blessing. Death was the gate of life. Having died to Haran, he began to bring forth much fruit in every soil of the world.

The Lord said unto Abram, after that Lot was separated from him. Gen. 13: 14.

ABRAM'S life was one of an ever-perfecting separation. But out of these experiences sprang his rarest joys. The separate and obedient soul may reckon on:

FRESH REVELATION. Whenever Abram dared to step out in obedience, the Lord spake freshly to him. But in Egypt we find no trace of the divine voice. If God spake there, it would be in warning and rebuke. Has the voice of God long been silent to thee—no fresh command, no deeper insight into truth? See to it that thou art not in Egypt. Separate thyself, not only from Haran, but from Lot; not only from what is clearly wrong, but from all that is questionable; and the Lord will speak to thee things it is not possible for man to utter.

FURTHER VISION. Lot lifted up his eyes to espy what would make for his advantage and well-being, and beheld only the plain of Sodom, which indeed was well-watered, but the seat of exceeding sin. But when Abram lifted up his eyes, not to search out aught for himself, but to see what God had prepared, he looked northward, and southward, and eastward, and westward—words which remind us of the length, and breadth, and depth, and height of the love of Christ. The single eye is full of light; the far climber gets the widest horizon; if thou wilt do his will, thou shalt know.

HUNDREDFOLD COMPENSATION. Whatever Abram renounced, when he left his home, or gave Lot the right to choose, he received back in the usual measure of God, with an overflowing overplus. God gave him the entire land, including Lot's portion. We can never give up for God, without receiving in this life more than we gave.

God Most High, Maker of Heaven and Earth. Gen. 14: 19 (R.V. *marg.*).

IT was to Melchizedek, the lonely king-priest living outside the busy rush of the world, that this new name of God was given. There are some to whom God gives these direct revelations of Himself, that they may communicate them to others. These are our seers. This title for God, which Abram immediately appropriated, was the source:

OF HUMILITY. To think of God as the Maker and Possessor of heaven and earth induces the profoundest humility of heaven. "They cast their crowns before the throne, saying, Thou didst create all things." How great God is! His greatness is unsearchable. Earth and heaven are his handiwork. Take time to think of this, but never forget that He is Love; then, with the familiarity of the child, thou wilt combine the lowly reverence of the creature.

OF STEADFASTNESS IN THE HOUR OF TEMPTATION. When the king of Sodom desired Abram to share in the spoils of the kings, setting before him a most subtle temptation, and one which might have dragged him from the life and walk of faith, Abram fell back on the revelation of God just vouchsafed to him, and said in effect: "What need is there that I should do this thing, or receive of thy gold? All God is mine; in God all things are mine also. What I need He will assuredly give. What He withholds I will receive from no other source." There is no need for us to get wealth wrongly; God can supply all we need.

OF SECURITY. God owns all; all the earth is his empire; wherever we travel we are within his dominion, breathe his air, are ministered to by his angels. We have a right to the best in all good things, since they are our Father's, and we are heirs of God, joint-heirs with Christ.

Behold, a Smoking Furnace and a Flaming Torch. Gen. 15: 17 (R.V.).

FIRE is the chosen emblem of God; and as these fire-emblems passed slowly between the divided carcases it was as though God accommodated Himself to the method of human oath-taking, and solemnly bound Himself. But in all his dealings with us He is prepared to be both a furnace and a torch.

GOD AS A FURNACE. Take up a piece of iron ore, and see how the metal is scattered amid commoner substances. How can it be disintegrated? The chisel cannot do it, but fire will. Plunge it now into the fire; let it fall in the heart of the glowing furnace, and presently the stream of liquid metal will issue forth, pure and beautiful. It is thus that God deals with human hearts; the blood makes propitiation, but the fire cleanses. The love of God, the purity of God, the spirituality of God brought home to us by the Holy Ghost, search and try us to the innermost fibre of our being, and burn out of us the evils which had long held empire.

> Refining Fire, go through my heart,
> Illuminate my soul;
> Scatter thy life through every part,
> And sanctify the whole.

GOD AS A FLAMING TORCH. The torch guides the footsteps through the dark; and God's Spirit waits to shed light on many dark and hidden things, and to guide us into all the truth. It is one thing to comprehend by the intellect; it is altogether another to apprehend by the heart. There is no such teacher as God; and the mistake of our modern religious life is to receive so much from man, instead of waiting in rapt silence until God Himself communicates his truth to us. The conditions are purity of desire, cleanness of heart, and willingness to obey.

Return to thy mistress, and submit thyself under her hands. Gen. 16: 9.

POOR Hagar! No wonder that she fled. Her proud Arab independence and the sense of coming motherhood made her rebel against Sarah's hard dealings. We have often meditated flight, if we have not actually fled from intolerable conditions. Of course, when God opens the door out of a dungeon we need not hesitate, as Peter did, to rise and follow. But this is very different to flight from the post of duty.

OUR CROSS. For Hagar, Sarah; for Hannah, Peninnah; for David, Joab; for Jesus, Judas; for Paul, Alexander the coppersmith. Life assumes hard and forbidding aspects. Sometimes the cross is not a person, but a trial—the pressure of a slow and lingering disease; the demand for grinding and persistent toil; the weight of over-mastering anxiety for those dearer than life, who have no knowledge of God.

OUR DEMEANOUR. Return and submit. We are apt to suppose that we shall get rest and peace elsewhere. It is not so, however. Nowhere else shall we find the path less rugged, or the pillow less hard. To evade the yoke will not give us heartsease. The Master's advice is that we shall take his yoke, and bear it as He did; remain where God has put us, till He shows us another place; and bear what He ordains and permits, even though it comes through the means of others.

OUR FAITH. We cannot patiently submit to our lot unless we believe that what God permits is as much his will as what He appoints. Behind Sarah's hard dealings we must behold his permissive providence. Through all the discipline of life we must believe that God has a purpose of unfailing love and wisdom. Then our submission is not stoicism, but loving acquiescence in our Father's will.

Walk before Me and be thou Perfect. Gen. 17:1.
GOD precedes his commands with such revelations of Himself, that obedience is rendered easily possible. Before calling Abram to perfection, He described himself as El Shaddai, the Almighty. What may we not do if we learn to avail ourselves of the all-might of God? Oh to know the exceeding greatness of his power toward us who believe! Our lack is that we do not know our God, and therefore fail to perform exploits. "Thus saith the Lord, Let not the wise man glory in his wisdom, neither let the mighty man glory in his might, let not the rich man glory in his riches: but let him that glorieth glory in this, that he understandeth and knoweth Me." Lie on thy face, and let God talk with thee, and tell thee the conditions on which He will make thee exceeding fruitful. First—Walk before Me: Second—Be thou wholehearted.

THERE MUST BE WHOLENESS IN OUR SURRENDER. No part of our nature barred or curtained off from God. Every chamber must be freely placed at his disposal; every relationship placed under his direction; every power devoted to his service. All we have and are must be entirely his.

THERE MUST BE WHOLENESS IN OUR INTENTION. The one aim of our Lord was to bring glory to his Father; and we should never be satisfied till we are so absolutely eager for the glory of Christ that we would seek it though at the cost of infamy to ourselves; and be as glad for another to bring it to Him, as we should be in bringing it ourselves.

THERE MUST BE WHOLENESS IN OUR OBEDIENCE. It was clearly so with Abram. As soon as God left talking with his servant, he took Isaac and performed the rite which had just been enjoined.

And Abraham drew near. Gen. 18:23.
THE patriarch's attitudes are well worthy of note: he sat (1), bowed (2), ran (7), stood by (8), went with them (16), stood before the Lord (22); here, he drew near.

HE DREW NEAR WITH AWFUL REVERENCE. "I have taken upon me to speak unto the Lord, which am but dust and ashes." The place whereon he stood was holy ground; and if he trod or crossed it, in the intensity of his desire, he never forgot that the most intimate fellowship of man with God must be mingled with the reverence of godly fear, which remembers that He is a consuming fire.

HE DREW NEAR IN FAITH. He had enjoyed a blessed prevision of the day of Christ. There had been revealed to Him that one perfect and sufficient Sacrifice, in virtue of which sinners are welcome to draw near to God. They have boldness to enter the holiest, and draw near with a true heart in full assurance of faith, who know the new and living way which Jesus has opened for us.

HE DREW NEAR AS INTERCESSOR. We never get so near God as when we plead for others. At such times we enter the holiest and innermost chamber, and talk to Him with an urgency which we dare not use for ourselves. Whilst the Syrophenician pleaded for her daughter, she came to the very feet of Jesus. Wouldst thou know the inner chamber? Go thither on errands for others.

HE DREW NEAR IN INTENSITY. When Haman pleaded for his life, he fell on the Queen's couch in the anguish of his soul. Sometimes God appears to hesitate; it is only to draw us on, ever further and deeper, till we awake to find ourselves alone in his presence.

Abraham got up early to the place where he stood before the Lord, and looked. Gen. 19: 27.
THERE was not much sleep that night for this loyal heart! With the spring of day he was where, probably, Lot, years before, had looked on the face of the country, and beheld it as a garden of the Lord. But how great the contrast! The smoke of the land went up as the smoke of a furnace!

HAVE A PLACE WHERE YOU STAND BEFORE GOD. It may not always be to speak to Him, but to be spoken to, to be judged, to have the motives and intentions of the heart winnowed and sifted. Well is it to stand each day before the judgment-seat of Christ, and to receive his verdict on our innermost life. Oh that the grass of that trysting-place may be well worn through our frequent intercourse with our beloved Lord!

FOLLOW UP YOUR PRAYERS. Abraham was not content with shooting arrows into the air; he followed them to see how they sped, and where they fell. We do not need to reiterate our petitions with unbelieving monotony, as though they were not safe in God's keeping; but we should remind Him by our upward look that our expectation is from Him.

VIEW THE FATE OF THE UNGODLY FROM GOD'S STANDPOINT. We are apt to consider it from that of our own pity, or commiseration, or tolerance of shortcoming. We judge lightly, because we dread too searching a judgment on ourselves. But we need sometimes to see sin as God sees it. Stand on Calvary and learn what sin is, and how much it has cost the Saviour. There, too, you will learn that God goes further than his servants' prayers. Though He may not be able to discover the ten, yet He will deliver the one righteous man. "His countenance doth behold the upright."

I also withheld thee from sinning against Me. Gen. 20: 6.
AS we review our lives, we can see many occasions on which our feet had well-nigh gone—our steps were on the very brink of the precipice. Another inch, and we should have brought shame on Christ and lasting remorse to ourselves. To what can we attribute our escape but to the grace of God, which withheld us, even though we failed to recognize it?

HE DOES NOT WITHHOLD US FROM TEMPTA-TION. He could not do so without serious and permanent loss. The waves of ink will surge up against the white marble palace of the soul. To us, as to our Lord, fresh from under the opened heavens, the tempter will come. What the fire is in fixing the colour on the porcelain vase, that temptation is in rendering permanent the lessons and impressions made by God's providence and grace.

HE DOES NOT WITHHOLD US FROM OCCASIONS IN WHICH IT WOULD BE EASY TO TRANSGRESS. Abimelech was not hindered from taking Sarah into his palace. The door of occasion and opportunity stood open before him; but he was withheld from the fatal act. We must never infer that occasion confers licence. The fact of an opportunity being present does not warrant indulgence in wrong-doing.

IF GOD WITHHELD ABIMELECH, WHO DID NOT SEEK HIS SPECIAL HELP, HOW MUCH MORE THOSE THAT SEEK HIM! You are not insensible of the perils of your life; but wait earnestly and persistently on God. Are you more eager to be kept than He to keep? Did He not implant that desire? Will He not do exceeding abundantly above what we ask or think? Is not the good Shepherd strong enough to keep one poor trembling sheep? Begone, unbelief! My God whom I serve is able to deliver, and He will! (Dan. 3: 17).

And God opened her eyes, and she saw. Gen. 21: 19.
POOR Hagar! There was no help for it; and she, who a little before had thought she was giving Abraham his heir, found herself and her boy homeless wayfarers on the desert sands. Their one need was water; they little deemed it was so near. No need to create a new fountain, but to open their eyes. We need the opened eye to see:

THE FINISHED WORK OF CHRIST. The work of propitiation for sin is complete. We are not required to add to it one tear, or prayer, or vow. "It is finished." To go to heaven to bring Christ down, or to the deep to bring Him up, is alike superfluous. All we need is the opened eye to see what Jesus has done, and recognize that it is all that was demanded to meet the claims of God's holy law.

THE THINGS FREELY GIVEN TO US OF GOD. God hath given us in Jesus all things that pertain to life and godliness. There is no possible gift or grace, in which we are deficient, that is not stored in Him, in whom the fulness of God abides. But we are blind; the eyes of our heart have not been opened to see the hope of our calling, the riches of our inheritance, the greatness of God's power. Did we know these things, surely not a moment would elapse without our availing ourselves of God's rich provision.

THE ALLEVIATIONS WHICH GOD PROVIDES AGAINST EXCESSIVE SORROW. Hagar's anguish, as Mary's at the sepulchre in after years, blinded her to available comfort. So grief puts a bandage over our eyes. Life is sad, and lonely, and dark, but God is near and if you ask, He will show springs of consolation of which you may drink. There is no desert without its spring; no dying child without the angel of the Lord.

Jehovah-Jireh; In the Mount of the Lord it shall be provided. Gen. 22: 14 (R.V.)

ABRAHAM knew it would be. Probably he never told Sarah what God had asked of him till he and the lad were safely back in the tent. What need to trouble her? Her weak faith could not have stood the ordeal. It was with an unfaltering tone that the patriarch told his young men that they two would presently return. Even though he should actually take Isaac's life, he was sure that he would receive him again from the altar in health. It was only at the very last moment that God indicated the ram as the sufficient substitute. So God's deliverances always come; they are provided in the mount of trial and sacrifice.

WHEN THE FOE SEEMS SECURE OF VICTORY. So it was with Israel. Pharaoh, with his hosts, counted on an easy victory, the precipices around, the sea in front. To the eye of sense it seemed impossible to escape: all hope died. It was just then that the Almighty cleft a path through the mighty deep.

"IN THE FOURTH HOUR OF THE NIGHT." Strength was well-nigh exhausted in long battling with the waves. For hours the disciples with difficulty had kept themselves afloat. It seemed as if they must give in through physical collapse. It was then that the form of Jesus drew nigh unto the ship.

ON THE NIGHT BEFORE EXECUTION. Thus Peter lies sleeping whilst the Church is gathered in prayer. To-morrow he will be a corpse. But the angel comes then to open the prison doors.

So you may have come to an end of your own strength, and wisdom, and energy. The altar, wood, and fire are ready, the knife upraised, your Isaac on the point to die: but even now God will provide. Trust Him to indicate the way of escape.

I am a Stranger and a Sojourner. Gen. 23: 4.

THE minute details of this purchase are recorded to emphasize the fact that, though the whole land was Abraham's by the divine gift, he would not enter on its possession till God's time was come. We may be sure of certain blessings—ours in God's safe keeping —though they are withheld till the moment that his wisdom sees best. It was a touching confession. The aged patriarch had for long years owned no settled dwelling-place. After years in the land of promise he was still without land enough for a grave.

FAITH CANNOT BE SATISFIED WITH THE THINGS OF THIS WORLD. The sons of Heth had goods and lands, but Abraham did not envy them; he had caught a glimpse of the city which hath foundations, and this so satisfied and attracted him that he had no desire for aught that Palestine could yield.

FAITH DETACHES US FROM THE PRESENT. We are content to dwell in tents, because here we have no abiding place. The shows and vanities of the world, in comparison with the vision of eternal realities, are as the glare of the streets compared with the steady glory of the constellations of the night.

FAITH PROMPTS TO CONFESSION. It betrayeth itself. We should be careful and orderly in our business arrangements; but, in our dealings with our fellows, in our justice, fairness, honour, the lightness of our hold on the present world, we should make it manifest that we are seeking a country not our own.

FAITH CANNOT BE ASHAMED. The God who prompted it must satisfy it, else He would have reason to be ashamed of having failed the souls that trusted Him. But now He is not ashamed to be called our God, because He has prepared for us a city.

My Master Abraham. Gen. 24: 12.

THIS worthy man, Eliezer, the steward of Abraham's house, was almost garrulous about his master. Count up the number of times in which he contrives to bring in the two words, "my master." We may learn from him how to speak of our Master, whenever we get the opportunity. 'Rabboni, which, being interpreted, is, My Master."

WE TOO CAN SPEAK OF THE LORD GOD AS OUR MASTER. The servant did not know Jehovah directly; it was enough that he had seen and heard Abraham pray to Him. This encouraged him to draw near for himself. So we are emboldened to draw near, because God is the God and Father of our Master Jesus. We love Him that was begotten, and are attracted to Him of whom Jesus said, "I ascend to my Father, and your Father; to my God, and your God."

WE, TOO, CAN PLEAD FOR OUR MASTER'S SAKE. When asking for good speed to be sent to himself, he alleged as his plea that it would be showing kindness to his master Abraham. So when we ask great things from God, we can plead in the name of Jesus, and urge that in answering our petition God will be showing kindness to his Well-beloved.

WE, TOO, SHOULD BLESS IN OUR MASTER'S NAME. When the answer was given, this reverent soul gave thanks as though the favour had been shown to his master. Indeed, all through his intercourse with Bethuel and Laban he seems to have lost his identity in Abraham. He could talk of nothing else but that one scheme; was only eager to carry his point for his master's sake; and when the errand was done, longed only to get back to his master's side. It is a beautiful lesson for those who call Jesus Master and Lord.

And he sold his Birthright. Gen. 25: 33.
EVERY ONE is born with a birthright, which the devil tries hard to make him barter away for a mess of pottage. In that birthright are included:

INNOCENCE AND PURITY. The child of the vilest ancestry enters this world unsullied by the filthy touch of unclean habit. But how eager Satan is to induce us to part with this for his unsatisfying pleasure.

THE LOVE OF OUR KIND. Few are the children, of all the myriads of our race, that are not loved by some fond heart. In some cases the infant life is cradled in love. But Satan is glad when he can get the soul to break away from all earthly affection, which might possibly soften and refine it, and to renounce mother, sister, wife, child, for the drunkard's cup, the wanton's kiss.

THE REDEMPTION OF JESUS CHRIST. Every one is born into a redeemed world; the propitiation of the blessed Lord, the blood that flowed on Calvary, the cancelment of the effects of Adam's sin, are for all. As all the world was affected by Adam's sin, so all are included in God's love in Jesus. But again Satan is eager to induce men to abjure and cast away these benefits; he blinds the eyes of those that believe not, so that they refuse to "behold the Lamb of God which taketh away the sin of the world."

THE GRACE OF THE SPIRIT. Every one may build up a strong and beautiful character by yielding to the Holy Ghost's gracious promptings. That grace knocks, like sunshine, at the windows of every soul; but how often it is sold for a mess of pottage? The choice between these two is constantly being presented to us. God help us always to choose the divine, the spiritual, the eternal!

Because that Abraham obeyed My Voice and kept My Charge. Gen. 26: 5.
IT is awful to realize how our sins may repeat themselves in our children. Here is Isaac following in the precise steps of Abraham, who had acted in a similar manner towards Sarah when entering Egypt. In each case there was a sad lapse of faith; but it was even worse for Isaac, with Abraham's example to warn him. But a man may pass blessings on to his children, as well as the sad entail of evil habits.

HE LEAVES THE BLESSING OF THE DIVINE COVENANT. God had entered into covenant with Abraham, and was prepared to fulfil its provisions to his son. "I will be a God to thee, and to thy seed after thee." So a godly ancestor may be able to secure for all his seed a share in the divine grace and favour. The spirit that is put on him does not depart from his seed, or his seed's seed for ever.

THE BLESSING OF HIS PRAYER. It is impossible to overestimate the effect of a good man's prayers; they are as streams or trees, which go on flowing and bearing fruit long after they were originated. The legacy of a good man's prayers is of priceless worth. He may have long since passed to his rest; but God remembers them, and answers them in blessings to the next generation. How often in this chapter we read that "God blessed Isaac."

THE BLESSING OF A NOBLE NAME. We may

all leave that, if we can transmit nothing else. To have had a father that knew God, walked with God, pleased God; who was on intimate terms with Him, and could speak to Him, as a man with his friend—illumined the ordinary nature and existence of Isaac with unearthly beauty. Let us live so that our children may be ranked as nobles, because they bear our name.

Esau cried with an exceeding great and bitter Cry. Gen. 27: 34.

ON this incident the writer to the Hebrews founds the impressive lesson, that the choices of the past may cast a bitter and irrevocable shadow on all our future. When he afterwards desired to inherit blessing he was rejected; for he found no place of repentence, though he sought it diligently with tears (Heb. 12: 16, 17, R.V.).

BEWARE OF THE CRAVINGS OF APPETITE. In an evil moment Esau yielded to these, and sold his birthright to secure their gratification; he found afterwards that the choice made in that hour was irrevocable. How needful that we watch and pray, lest we fall into temptation!

There are four facts which, when borne in mind, guard us against the sudden oversetting of passionate appetite.

WE WERE ONCE DEAD IN SINS. Surely we do not want to go back again to the charnel-house with its corruption.

WE DIED FOR SINS IN THE PERSON OF CHRIST OUR REPRESENTATIVE. In Him we have met the demands of God's holy law; but surely that must be an awful thing which cost our Saviour so dearly.

WE DIED TO SIN WITH THE LORD JESUS. We have passed with Him on to Resurrection ground; so that we belong to the new heavens and new earth, wherein dwelleth righteousness.

WE ARE CALLED ON TO RECKON OURSELVES DEAD TO SIN. The nearer we live to God, the more sensitive we shall be to the most distant suggestion of evil, closing doors and windows against its entrance, reckoning ourselves "not at home" to it, and yielding our members as instrument of righteousness unto God.

Behold a Ladder set up on the Earth, and the top of it reached to Heaven. Gen. 28: 12.

ALL men feel that earth and heaven touch at the horizons of the distant past and future; but we ought to feel that the present moment of time and this bit of the world's surface are linked with heaven. This is what the ladder meant for Jacob. The moorland waste, where he lay, and Laban's home, whither he journeyed, were as near God as his father's tent. Earth is linked with heaven:

BY GOD'S DAILY PROVIDENCE. His loving eye is ever upon us, his ears always open to our cry, and his angels go to and fro on our world performing ceaseless ministries.

BY OUR SAVIOUR'S MEDIATION. As He intimated to Nathanael, his own nature as uniting God with man, and especially his Ascension glory as the man Christ Jesus, is the one great connecting link. "Hereafter ye shall see heaven open, and the angels of God ascending and descending upon the Son of Man."

BY DAILY FELLOWSHIP AND HOLY THOUGHT. We should practise the sense of God's presence, often stopping ourselves amid our ordinary avocations and interests to say, aloud when possible, "God is near, God is here." In all likelihood we are daily living amid the glories of the eternal world; but our eyes are blinded. Oh that by humility and purity we may become more sensitive, and awake to the things that are unseen and eternal! Lord, open our eyes, that we may see! (2 Kings 6: 17).

BY HOLY YEARNING. When Jesus ascended, He unrolled a path behind Him, along which we shall one day travel to meet Him. Hope treads that glorious Ascension ladder; and as she does so, again we see the heaven opened, and our destiny unfolded at Christ's right hand.

But a few days, for the love he had. Gen. 29: 20.

THAT touch is enough! We can fill in all the rest. This old-world love was of the same quality as our own. Oh, blessed God! what a priceless inheritance this is! Time itself never tedious, but always too short; labour never hard; distance never long; sacrifice unheard of, the word almost in disuse—where Love is queen. This is how we would feel to our dear Lord: so that the missionary away from home and friends, as well as the invalid suffering for Jesus, might feel years of loneliness and pain but a few days, for love of the beloved Master. We may acquire such love thus:

MEDITATE MUCH ON THE LOVE OF JESUS. Sit with the Apostle beneath his cross, and say, each time with deeper appreciation: He loved me, He gave Himself for me. Do not think of your love to Him, but of his. It is well to take the Lord's Supper frequently, as affording opportunities for remembering his dying love.

BE ON THE ALERT TO DETECT HIS LOVE IN DAILY PROVIDENCE AND TRIFLES. It is amazing how much is ever being arranged by his tender thoughtfulness to alleviate and brighten our lot. If you cannot detect it, dare still to believe it.

ASK THE HOLY SPIRIT TO BREATHE HIS LOVE INTO YOUR HEART. He that is joined to the Lord is one spirit; and when the doors are open between Christ and the soul, the aroma of his love freely enters.

SHOW HIS LOVE TO EVERY ONE. Whether you like people or not, do to them as He would do; let his love flow through you to them; what we manifest to others for his sake we shall come to feel towards Him, and them also. "This commandment have we from Him, That he who loveth God love his brother also."

The Lord hath blessed me for thy sake.
Gen. 30: 27.

LABAN requested the longer stay of Jacob because he felt sure that the divine blessings had been brought by him into his home. It was a selfish, low, motive for desiring the postponement of his departure; and Laban was destined, alas! to be terribly undeceived. He would wake up one day, to find that during his sojourn with him, and under the cloak of religion, Jacob had been ruthlessly plundering his property. It was a shameful betrayal of trust on Jacob's part; and it conveys a searching warning to those who, because of their religious professions, are trusted by their relatives or others:

WITH THEIR PROPERTY. Always do the best possible for your employer or friend, who has entrusted his interests to you, acting towards him as the servant and steward of God. Bear in mind that God has bidden you undertake the office for Himself, and accepts your fidelity as rendered to Him: He will recompense.

WITH THEIR FRIENDSHIP. Be very careful here. God puts us into one another's lives, that we may be the medium through which his love and tenderness may enter them;

but there is such danger of our monopolizing for ourselves the place that He would fill. Sometimes we almost unconsciously deteriorate rather then elevate our friends by the intrusion of our own personality.

WITH THEIR CHRISTIAN INSTRUCTION AND TRAINING. Ministers of God's holy gospel must specially guard against the tendency to make name, fame, money, out of a position which they should occupy only as God's stewards. There is such subtleness in the temptation to attract men to ourselves, instead of attaching them to Christ.

Take heed to thyself that thou speak not to Jacob either good or bad. Gen. 31: 24 (R.V.)
THIS visitation of God made a deep impression on Laban. He refers to it afterwards as restraining him from injuring his runaway son-in-law. Jacob, too, was struck by it. It is very wonderful to find the Holy God casting the mantle of his protection around this crafty and deceitful soul. No doubt it was due to his covenant relationship with the family and race, of which Jacob was a most unworthy member (13, 42). But if God thus interposed for Jacob, will He not much more interpose for those who desire to be his obedient children?

GOD WILL LAY AN ARREST ON YOUR PERSE-CUTORS. Israel was rebuked because the exiles in Babylon thought they would perish before a man that could die, and the son of man who was as grass, and forgot their Maker, the Lord of heaven and earth. All around you the fire may rage; but you shall walk amid it unscathed, if only you trust. No weapon formed against you shall prosper.

GOD WILL LAY AN ARREST ON TRIAL. His finger is always on our pulse; and the moment the pain becomes more than we can bear, He will stay it. His eye is ever upon his own.

GOD WILL LAY AN ARREST ON THE POWER OF THE EVIL ONE. We shall not be tempted beyond that we are able to bear. There is always a thus far and no farther. "The Lord maketh a way in the sea, and a path in the mighty waters." The Only-begotten of the Father keeps the sheep whom his Father has entrusted to Him. Not one of them can be devoured by the lion of hell. If only we believed this, we should be calmer, happier, even though circumstanced as Jacob. No need to altercate with Laban, but to look beyond him to the "Fear of Isaac."

He touched the Hollow of his Thigh. Gen.
32: 25.

OUR greatest victories are wrought out
through pain, and purchased at the cost of
the humbling of the flesh. Jacob learnt that
the secret of prevailing with God and man
was not in the strength, but in the weakness
and suffering of the flesh. It must ever be so.
The victor Lamb bears still the scars of
Calvary, and appears as one who had been
slain.

Had Laban met Jacob that morning, he
would have pointed to that limp as an indication of God's wrath and displeasure; but
if he had looked into his face, he would have
seen all its hardness and cunning gone, and
would have been arrested by the unwonted
tenderness in his voice.

THE SHRUNKEN SINEW COUNTERACTS PRIDE.
So high a spiritual achievement as to prevail
with God might have tempted Jacob to
arrogance and self-esteem. But God anticipated the possible temptation by this physical
infirmity, which was constantly present to
Jacob's consciousness.

THE SHRUNKEN SINEW WAS THE SECRET OF
VICTORY. Had it not been shrivelled by the
angel's touch, Jacob would have continued
to resist in the pride of his strength, and
would never have clung convulsively to the
angel, crying, "I will not let thee go." It was
only in that act that he became Israel, the
Prince.

THE SHRUNKEN SINEW MAKES US THINK
LITTLE OF THIS WORLD AND MUCH OF THE
NEXT. From this moment Jacob takes up
more of the pilgrim attitude. He finds that
for him, at least, the pace will have to be
slower; but it is well, for he relaxes his hold
on the seen to entwine more tenaciously about
the unseen. "The days of the years of my
pilgrimage"—such is his epitome of his life.

*I will lead on softly . . . Until I come unto
my lord unto Seir.* Gen. 33: 14.

THIS was rather unworthy of the man who,
the night before, had seen the face of God,
and learnt to prevail. The man who had
seen God, and prevailed, was doubtful of
his newly-given blessing! He did not realize
that it would carry him through the difficulty
that threatened him. He had not as yet
learnt to apply it to every emergency. It is a
solemn lesson to those who have passed
through some rapturous experience.

AFTER BLESSING, OFTEN TRIAL. When the
fair colours have been laid on, the vessel is
plunged into the furnace, that they may be
burnt in.

THE TRIAL FREQUENTLY PRESENTS ITSELF IN
THE HOME OR ORDINARY LIFE. Some are led
into the wilderness to be tempted; but more
often it is the contact with our Esaus that
furnishes us with the supreme test of the
worth of what we have received.

FAILURE COMES FROM NOT RECKONING ON
GOD. Jacob looked at Esau's four hundred
armed men, and compared his own following
with despair. So Peter looked at the winds
and waves. At such times we must fail, if we
rely on schemes or plans, instead of saying,
God is.

Oh for the peace that floweth as a river,
    Making life's desert places bloom and
        smile;
Oh for the faith to grasp Heaven's bright
        "for ever"
    And the shadow of earth's "little while."

WE MUST ACT FAITH. If Jacob had refused
to use this subterfuge, and had spoken
simply and manfully, he would have found
that Esau would have acquiesced and left him.
The angels who had gone forward to deal
with him (Gen. 32: 2) had done their work
effectively, and God had changed his purpose.

*Ye have troubled me to make me to stink
among the Inhabitants of the Land.* Gen. 34: 30.

THE Bible does not hesitate to hold the
mirror up to our fallen nature, or show us
what we are. Here is Israel, the prince with
God, who had power with man, in a very
sorry plight. His children had involved him
in it; but first, he had involved them.

DINAH. Little did she realize all the evil
which that visit of hers would bring on her
people and on those whose guest she was.
What took her there? Had her upbringing
been unnecessarily strict, and did she want
a little more freedom? There is an inevitable
rebound with young people to the other
extreme, if needless severity has been brought
to bear on them in their early days.

The probability, however, is that the
laxity of her father's home, and the effect of
her mother's gods, had made the line of
separation a very faint one, and she felt no
difficulty in overstepping it.

SIMEON AND LEVI. "Ye have made me to

stink." On his dying bed Jacob remembered this treacherous cruelty and pronounced their scattering in Israel; though Levi undid the effect of that bitter curse by his obedience and devotion. In after days it was said, "My covenant was with him of life and peace," and though scattered, he was as salt. In Simeon's case the curse was not cancelled by any subsequent manifestation of obedience and devotion, and ran out its course. There is encouragement and warning here.

JACOB. The real mistake of it all was that Jacob bought that land, and settled too near the city (33: 18). As a pilgrim he had no right to do this. If Christian parents will settle down in fellowship with the world, they have themselves to thank for all the misery which accrues to themselves and children, and the dishonour to God.

Arise, go up to Bethel, and dwell there. Gen. 35: 1.

GOD had set his hand to make Jacob a saint. He had given him a glimpse of his ideal at the Jabbok ford, but his nature was not then capable of taking in the divine conception; and, as we have seen, both in his subterfuge to Esau and his settling outside Shechem, he had fallen back into the schemer and money-maker. In this chapter God uses several methods of awakening and renewal.

THE DIVINE SUMMONS. "Arise, go up to Bethel." He had been in the lowlands too long: too long had he "lain among the pots." The voice of God spoke words of resurrection life into his grave, as afterwards into that of Lazarus.

THE POWER OF OLD ASSOCIATION. What memories clustered around that name and place of Bethel! It recalled his distress and fear; the angel-ladder, and the comforting assurance which had inspired him with new hope, directly he heard it, he seemed to have felt the incongruity of the life that was being lived in his camp, and he said to his people, "Put away the strange gods. . . Arise, let us go up to Bethel, and I will make there an altar unto God."

A FRESH REVELATION. God appeared to him again. For long there had been no vision of God; but now that the idols were put away, his eyes were opened to see Him who had been beside him amid all his backslidings.

DEATH. Deborah, the beloved Rachel, the old father—one after another were taken from him; and there came the far-away look into his eyes which showed that he had imbibed the pilgrim-spirit and had become Israel the Prince. So God stripped him that he might be better able to run the race set before him.

The Kings that reigned in Edam before there reigned any King over Israel. Gen. 36: 31.

APPARENTLY Esau had the best and happiest lot.

WHAT HE ESCAPED. For him there were no few and evil days of pilgrimage; nor the pressure of famine; nor the going down into Egypt; nor the forty years of wanderings in the desert; nor the vicissitudes of the Judges. All these he escaped—and must have congratulated himself merrily. But he had no vision of God; no communion with Jehovah; no contact with the messengers of heaven.

WHAT HE ENJOYED. A line of dukes; a royal dynasty, which was old when Israel's first king ascended the throne; a rich and fertile territory; peace and comfort. He reminds us of the Psalmist's picture of the man of this world, whose portion is in this life, and who is filled with hid treasure. But Esau never awoke satisfied with God's likeness; nor ever enjoyed the blessedness of the man who is "a prince with God."

HOW HE BORE HIMSELF. His heart was generous, full of good nature, jovial, and free-handed. When the land could not bear both Jacob and himself, he went off into another, and settled down in Mount Seir. It was no hardship with him to leave the land of promise. Most would, doubtless, have preferred his society to Jacob's; but God did not (Mal. 1: 2, 3).

WHAT MADE THE LOT OF THESE BROTHERS SO DIFFERENT. The one lived for the world; the other was a citizen of the heavenly Jerusalem, a pilgrim to the City of God. The one was an ordinary man of the world; the other had been selected of God as the channel of blessing to mankind. The flower and fruit which are to be propagated require the special attention of the gardener's knife. What solemn words! (Amos 3: 2).

They took him and cast him into a pit. Gen. 37: 24.

IT is impossible to read this inimitable story without detecting in the water-mark of the paper on which it is written the name JESUS. Indeed, we lose much of the beauty and force of these early Scriptures if we fail to observe the references to the life, character, and work of the blessed Redeemer. Notice some of these precious analogies:

Our Saviour's shepherd-heart (2).

The love of the Father before the worlds were made (3).

The dreams of empire, which are so certainly to be realized, when we shall see Him acknowledged as King of kings and Lord of lords (7).

Envied by his brethren, to whom he came, though they received Him not (11).

His alacrity to do his Father's will, and to finish his work, in which will we too have been sanctified (13).

Cast into the pit of the grave, as a seed-corn into the ground to die, that He might not abide alone, but bear much fruit (24).

The thirty pieces of silver for which He was betrayed (28).

The indifference of the Jewish people to their great Brother's fate (25).

Rejected of the Jew, and turning to the Gentile (28).

The bitter grief which his rejection has brought on the Jewish people (35),

It is as though the Holy Ghost, eager to glorify the Lord, could not wait for the slow unfolding of history, but must anticipate the story of that precious life and death which were to make the world new again.

Judah. Gen. 38: 1.

THIS was the destined heir of the birthright of which Reuben had shown himself unworthy; and yet this chapter is a dark story of his unbridled passion. O my soul, remember that the possibilities of all these sins are latent in thee! Thou mightest have been as one of these men or women but for the grace of God.

There is nothing so absolutely priceless as the white flower of a pure and blameless life. The pure in heart are the children of the presence-chamber—entrusted with secrets hidden from the wise and prudent—vessels by which God does not hesitate to quench the thirst of men, because the water of the crystal river will not be diluted or contaminated by contact with their natures. Above all other gifts, covet that of a cleansed heart. You may be very conscious of tempta-

tion, and that naturally you are no better than others, and yet if you will constantly live in the Spirit, and walk in the Spirit, you will be kept absolutely pure; and the sea of ink that is sweeping through the world will leave no stain on you.

THE BLOOD CLEANSETH: "The blood of Jesus Christ, his Son, cleanseth us from all sin" (1 John 1: 7).

THE SAVIOUR KEEPETH: "The Lord is faithful, who shall stablish you, and keep you from evil" (2 Thess. 3: 3).

THE SPIRIT FILLETH: "Know ye not that your body is the temple of the Holy Ghost which is in you, which ye have of God, and that ye are not your own?" (1 Cor. 6: 19).

God can take in hand the Judahs amongst us, and so deal with them as to produce such a character as is forthshadowed in chap. 49: 8.

How can I do this great wickedness and sin against God. Gen. 39: 9.

WHAT a contrast between this chapter and the former: that, like a Rembrandt background, throws up the bright colours of this. Where the older brother fell, the younger stood victoriously; and the light of God shone on the young heart, so that even the dungeon gloom could not extinguish it. Who does not know what it is to be misunderstood, misrepresented, accused falsely, and punished wrongfully? Yet God reigns: and in his own time "He shall bring forth thy righteousness as the light, and thy judgment as the noon-day."

GOD ALLOWS STRENGTH TO BE TESTED. We do not know what we are, or where we stand, till we are compelled to choose. Insensibly character is ever forming—unconsciously we are taking sides; but the testing-hour that compels us to declare ourselves causes the solution suddenly to crystallize, and we know ourselves in our choice. The man who has chosen the pure and good once, will choose them more easily next time; and at each choice will become stronger.

GOD ALLOWS VIRTUE TO BE MALIGNED. In all Egypt there was not a purer soul, and yet Joseph lay under a terrible imputation; but he committed his cause to God, sure that He would not leave him in Hades; and the time came when the King's word cleared him, and he stood forth vindicated. "Fret not thyself. Rest in the Lord, and wait patiently for Him."

GOD ALLOWS CONSCIENTIOUSNESS TO BE ILL-REPAID. Of what avail that he had so well cared for his master's goods? Ah, but that dungeon was the subterranean passage to a throne; and through those fetters iron entered into that young soul. We all need more iron in our blood!

Wherefore look ye so sadly to-day? Gen. 40: 7. WE may learn from Joseph the true method of bearing grief. Joseph might have become moody and sullen, absorbed in his own misfortunes, and pessimistic about the course of human life. How far removed from all this was his behaviour!

HE FILLED HIS TIME WITH MINISTRY. The captain of the guard charged him with two state-prisoners, and he ministered unto them. A new interest came into his life, and he almost forgot the heavy pressure of his own troubles amid the interest of listening to the tales of those who were more unfortunate than himself. Do not nurse your grief in lonely brooding: arise and minister to some one; do something in the world; exert yourself to alleviate the sufferings of those close by your side, who have not so clear a conscience or so bright a trust in God.

HE WAS QUICK TO SYMPATHIZE AND COMFORT. Quick to notice traces of sorrow, because he had sorrowed; able to sympathize, because he had wept; adept at comforting, because he had been comforted of God. We gain comfort when we attempt to comfort. Out of such intercourse we get what Joseph got—the key which will unlock the heavy doors by which we have been shut in. Light a fire in another's heart, and your own heart will be warmed.

HE KEPT HIS FAITH IN GOD. Depression, captivity, loneliness, separation from those he loved, could not quench his faith in God. Still God was near and precious to him. The stifling darkness and oppression of the prison were irksome to the free child of the camp; but God was as near as in Jacob's tent. There is no evil to them that love God; and the believer loses sight of second causes in the contemplation of the unfolding of the mystery of his Father's will.

It is not in me; God shall give. Gen. 41: 16. IT is beautiful to notice Joseph's reverent references to God in his first interview with Pharaoh. When the heart is full of God, the tongue will be almost obliged to speak of Him; and all such references will be easy and natural as flowers in May.

These words might have been uttered by the Lord Jesus. They are so perfectly in harmony with the tenor of his life. He loved to say that his words, and works, and plans, were not his own, but the Father's. Once, when a ruler called Him good, He reminded him that only One was good, and that all goodness was derived from God. Men knew little enough of Jesus, because He sought ever to be a reflecting mirror for his Father, and to glorify Him on the earth. But the Spirit reveals Him to those that love.

These words might have been the Apostle Paul's. He delighted to say that he worked, yet not he, but the grace of God in him; that he lived, yet not he, but Christ in him; that he knew and spake the mysteries of God, yet not he, but the Spirit of God.

Thus we should speak. Our light must so shine that men may turn from us to Him from whom we have derived it. Whenever the temptation arises to revert on ourselves, to attract men to ourselves, to lead them to think that we can meet their need, let us count ourselves dead to the suggestion, saying, "It is not in me; God shall give (Acts 3: 12). What strength and comfort come into our hearts, in view of demands which are too great for our weak nature to meet. "It is not in me; God, shall give." If our hearts were inditing a good matter, they would boil over, and we should speak more frequently of the things that touch our King.

The man spake roughly to us. Gen. 42: 30. HE SPAKE ROUGHLY, BUT HE DID NOT FEEL SO. When he had spoken in these harsh tones, he restored their money; turned aside to weep (24); and did his best to alleviate the toils of travel. So sometimes God seems to deal harshly, and speak roughly; but there is no change in the tender love of his heart. It costs Him immeasurably more than it does us. Often when some unusual severity has been evinced, if we could but see his face, it would be full of pity, pain, and pleading on our behalf. He feels yearnings over us which He restrains, and dares not betray till the work of conviction is complete.

HE SPAKE ROUGHLY TO AWAKEN CONSCIENCE. It had slept for twenty years. They had almost forgotten that scene at the pit's mouth; but as he repeated their tones, and words, and treatment, it all came back again, and they cried, "We are verily guilty concerning our brother." There must be repentance and confession before God can take us to his heart. We must confess the wrongs done to our Brother in heaven and our brothers on earth; and many of the roughnesses of God's Providence are intended to awaken us, and bring our sin to remembrance.

HE SPAKE ROUGHLY TO TEST THEM. How did they feel toward each other: was there rivalry or bitterness, or angry feeling? Beneath his biting words, Joseph would mark their behaviour! Would they disown each other, or cling to one another? There was an opportunity for their doing one or the other; and he was glad to notice how their love approved itself. So we are led over stony roads, that God may know what is in our hearts. He gives us opportunities of showing our real feeling towards our brothers, that He may test our love towards Himself.

Every man's money was in the mouth of his sack. Gen. 43: 21.
JOSEPH, who gave corn to save his own brethren and the Gentiles from starvation, is a type of Him who gives the bread of life to Jew and Greek—to all that hunger and come to Him for supplies. And in this return of the full money in the sack's mouth, we are reminded that salvation and satisfaction are all of grace. They are without money and without price. Whatever we yield to Him, He returns in full weight.

We bring Him works of merit as a price of our pardon; but they are not noticed.

We bring Him emotion, tears, anguish of soul; but He will have none of them.

We bring Him our faith as a price, instead of as a hand that accepts; and He refuses it.

How many are our mistakes and misunderstandings! Yet He does not for that reason withhold his blessed gift. We get the corn as an act of his free grace; and afterwards He explains why it was that our careful dues were not accepted.

There is bread enough in God to supply every mouth of desire and hunger in your soul. You may have it for the seeking. The law is—ask, and have. What if you have no money with which to purchase, no earnestness, no merit! Nevertheless the best wheat

of heaven may be yours. Our Father's love is constantly devising means of expressing itself. It puts money into our sacks; it invites us to its home, and spreads banquets before us; it inclines stewards to meet us peacefully; it washes our feet; it takes a tender interest in those we love; it wishes us grace from God; it adjusts itself to our temperaments and puts us at our ease, so that gleams of light as to the love of Jesus strike into our hearts!

And I said, Surely he is torn in pieces. Gen. 44: 28.
THESE are words caught from his Father's mouth by Judah; and here repeated, in his most pathetic intercession, with the hope of softening the Governor's heart, and moving him to spare Benjamin at least. They are very sad, and, without doubt, justified by the vision of that blood-stained coat. Yet there was another interpretation to the sad and dark suggestion which it made: Joseph was alive, and they were soon to know that it was he with whom they were dealing, and that he was conducting them through these strange experiences.

We are often tempted to judge hastily, and by appearances; by our own despondent, sorrowful hearts; or by the reports of others. We may say that certain things are against us, when, if we would only look beyond appearances and circumstances to God, we should find that He had been working, and was working, mightily on our behalf—that all was for our lasting good.

Do not say that you have lost your Joseph; he lives, and will yet be a comfort to you. He was taken from you for a little, to bring blessing to your whole family, but to be given back to you, more yours than ever.

Do not look on the sad, but on the bright side of God's Providence. All things are working for the best. "In all these things is the life of the spirit." Do not judge Him, or try to understand; be still and trust. You will some day be ashamed of your little faith.

Blind unbelief is sure to err,
   And scan his work in vain,
God is his own interpreter,
   And He will make it plain.

God did send me before you. Gen. 45: 5.
THERE was great delicacy in Joseph's command, "Cause every man to go out from me."

He did not want to expose his brethren; yet he wanted to say words which could not be understood by the curious courtiers. Then he made himself known, and said, "Be not grieved, nor angry, for God did send me before you." This was not only a kind way of alleviating their remorse and sorrow, but was the standpoint from which Joseph was wont to review his life-course. It was his habit to trace the working-out of God's plan, and the interposition of his Providence amid and through the malevolence and treachery of men (50: 20).

This was also David's habit, who, in the cursing of Shimei and the revolt of Absalom, saw the evolution of God's permissive purposes.

Thus also Jesus spoke, when anticipating the coming of Judas to betray Him. "The Son of Man goeth, as it was written of Him." "The cup that my Father giveth Me to drink."

It is one of the inexplicable mysteries of Providence that bad men subserve God's purposes and unwittingly execute his plans. It is not for us to explain it, but to consider the perplexities and disaster which we suffer at the hands of evil men as being permitted by God for the furtherance of some divine and hidden purpose. Paul's prayer that he might preach the Gospel at Rome was fulfilled through the hatred of the Jews; and he went to Rome at the Emperor's expense. We may comfort ourselves whenever the storm is high, that God is at the helm, and is making the wrath of man praise Him, whilst the remainder of it shall be restrained. Yes, Joseph, God is sending you through that pit and prison: but there is a way out into sunlight.

Fear not to go down into Egypt. Gen. 46: 3.
PROBABLY the old man, remembering the experiences of Abraham, was very fearful to adventure himself into Egypt. Besides, was it not as though, in going thither, he renounced the Land of Promise? Therefore this special bidding and assurance were the more necessary.

WHEN OUR HEART MISGIVES US, LET US LOOK OUT FOR ONE OF GOD'S FEAR-NOTS. His eye is ever upon the righteous, and his ear open to their cry. One upward glance or tremulous prayer will make Him ride on a cherub to our side, and whisper, "Be not afraid; fear not, I am with thee."

GOD'S PROMISES ARE FULFILLED IN MOST UNEXPECTED WAYS. He had always foretold that the seed of Abraham should outnumber stars and sands; but who would have supposed that the promise would be realized amid the pressure and persecution of Egypt? Yet so it happened. "I will there make of thee a great nation." We must not judge after the sight of our eyes, nor act on what is known as our common sense; faith is led by very uncommon paths. Trust and obey!

GOD'S PRESENCE IN EGYPT ACTED AS AN ANTIDOTE TO ITS EVIL, AND DELIVERED FROM ITS TYRANT'S GRASP. Ah, my soul, thou mightest descend without fear into hell itself if God said, "I will go down with thee, and will surely bring thee up again." The divine Presence is strength to the fearful—security and consolation in life, peace in death. It was probably thus that the Father spake to the Son by the lips of the Angel in Gethsemane: "Fear not to go down into the grave: I will surely bring thee up again." Thus He speaks to us. He is with us, and will deliver.

Thou hast saved our lives: . . . We will be Pharaoh's servants. Gen. 47: 25.
NOTHING less would have extorted such an acknowledgment from those proud Egyptians. They were willing to serve their saviour. No doubt, had there been no provision made by Joseph, the streets would have been filled by emaciated skeletons picking their way feebly amid the heaps of the dying and the dead. Gratitude brought them into the dust before him who held the keys of the granaries.

THE KINGDOM OF CHRIST IS A MATTER OF SUPREME IMPORTANCE TO INDIVIDUALS AND THE WORLD. He is not ambitious of power for its own sake; but that He may be able to exercise it more fully for our benefit, and that He may finally render up the kingdom to God, even his Father, that God may be all in all. He will never, therefore, be perfectly satisfied till He has triumphantly entered all closed gates, as King.

HIS KINGDOM IS GIVEN HIM BY THE GLAD CHOICE OF THOSE WHOM HE HAD BLESSED AND SAVED. The song of heaven reflects this thought: "Thou art worthy, . . for thou wast slain." His empire depends on the sacrifice by which He has saved a multitude whom no man can number. Meditate much on the love of Calvary, and you too will feel that his empire should begin within your heart, and hasten to subdue the kingdoms of the world.

WHEN HE BECOMES KING, HE STILL FURTHER BLESSES US. The first hour of Joseph's supreme power was the beginning of Egypt's brightest days. The Egyptians could not do so well for themselves as he for them. We shall never know the real blessedness of living, its peace and joy and strength, till we have utterly surrendered to Christ's supremacy. To serve such a Master utterly is to drink of the river of perfect blessedness.

Behold, thy son Joseph cometh. Gen. 48: 2.
HOW needful Joseph was to Jacob! The aged patriarch could not die without seeing him. His presence lit the dark valley. His hand closed the tired eyes of the aged pilgrim. And Joseph was as quick to come at the first intimation of his father's desire to see him. There was a perfect sympathy and reciprocity between them, just as there may be between Christ and those who owe all to Him.

JESUS IS EVER LEADING US ON TO NEW AND DEEPER EXPERIENCES. In no true life is stagnation admissible. So the nest is constantly being stirred up, and the trumpets sounded for the striking of our tents. But there is a divine motive in it all. Jesus cannot rest satisfied with less than the best for those He loves, as Joseph could not permit Jacob to remain in Canaan whilst Goshen with its plenty awaited him.

IN ALL THE NEW EXPERIENCES JESUS MEETS us. When his father entered Egypt, Joseph was waiting for him. When he was summoned to stand before Pharaoh, Joseph brought him. When he lay a-dying, Joseph was at his side to receive his last commissions. So, trembling soul, if Jesus presses you into the unknown, He does not leave you there, but keeps coming again, meeting you at every point of anxiety and distress. Yea, He does what Joseph could not do. He stands, not on this side only, but on the other side, of death. Here to calm with his benediction; there to receive into his glory.

JESUS IS CAREFUL FOR BODY AS WELL AS SOUL. The dying man was anxious about the disposal of his body, and Joseph readily undertook to see it buried in Machpelah's cave. So Jesus cares for us. He is the Saviour of the body in this life and in the resurrection.

Until Shiloh come, and unto Him shall the obedience of the peoples be. Gen. 49: 10 (R.V.)
OLD experience is said to attain to something of prophetic strain; but there is more than old experience here. From these aged lips the Holy Ghost is speaking.

THE MISSION AND WORK OF JESUS ARE DESIGNATED. He is Shiloh—the Maker, Giver, and Bringer of Peace. The troubled conscience, smitten with conviction, finds peace when He reveals his all-sufficient sacrifice and atonement. The discordant elements within us settle into a great calm when He enters to reign, bringing every thought into captivity to his rule. Nor is his work for individuals only; it is for man, for the world, the universe. Peace was made at his cross; it is proclaimed by his Spirit; and it will be consummated when God is All in all.

THE TIME OF HIS ADVENT PREDICTED. Not till the Romans came and annexed Palestine as one of the provinces of the empire, did the semblance of the Hebrew monarchy expire. And it was then that the Shiloh came. Surely these words must often have been quoted by the pious Jews, with whom Simeon and Anna consorted, as pointing to the near advent of the Messiah. Let us be wise to discern the symptoms of his second advent.

THE INEVITABLENESS OF HIS DOMINION. Ah, Saviour, it is predicted that all peoples shall obey Thee; and we know well that it is only through obedience that men can enter into thy peace. Teach us to obey, to do all thy commands, to bear all thy burdens, to wait before Thee, that thus we may know the peace that passeth all understanding.

Ponder this well, O my soul; the Peace-giver must be obeyed. Only so can He give thee peace that floweth as a river.

God meant it for good. Gen. 50: 20 (R.V.)
GOD's deeper meanings! We are apt to see a malicious meaning; are we equally apt to detect the divine and benevolent one? Our enemies are many, and they hate us with perfect hatred; they are ever laying their plots, and working their unholy purposes. But there is a greater and wiser than they, who, through all these plottings, is prosecuting his divine purpose. There is another and deeper meaning than appears to the short sight of sense.

LET US BELIEVE THAT THERE IS A DIVINE AND DEEPER MEANING IN THE ADVERSITIES OF OUR

LIVES. Joseph might be forgiven for not doing so; but with his history and that of many others before us, we have no excuse for despair in the face of crushing sorrow. Whether it comes from man or devil, all creatures are under the divine control, holding to our lips cups which the Father's hand has mixed. He has no complicity with their evil, but they unconsciously perform his will. Even if you cannot see the divine meaning, dare to believe that it is there.

AWAIT THE DISCLOSURES OF TIME. Even here we sometimes reach an eminence from which we detect the meaning of the path by which we have been conducted. It may have been rough and circuitous, but there was a reason in it all. Often God rewards patient trust by allowing us to see and know.

AND FOR THE FULL REVELATION OF ETERNITY. One day God will call us to his side in the clear light of eternity, and will explain his meanings in life's most sorrowful experiences; and we shall learn that we suffered, not for ourselves only, but for others, and, as part of his great remedial scheme, "to save much people alive."

Exodus

The more they afflicted them, the more they multiplied. Exod. 1: 12.

IT was a very unequal struggle on which Pharaoh had entered; for he opposed not the Hebrews, but Jehovah. It is thus that the great ones of this world have ever spoken and acted. "Let us build a tower;" "Let us break their bands asunder, and cast away their cords from us." "Against thy holy child Jesus, both Herod and Pontius Pilate were gathered together." In every case, He that sits in the heavens has laughed at the boast of human pride. His cause and his people's are one. Yet times of affliction have always been in times of multiplication.

IN THE HISTORY OF THE CHURCH. When has she made her greatest number of adherents? When her pulpits have been filled with eloquent preachers, and her aisles crowded with fashion and wealth? No, but when she has been driven to the dens and caves of the earth, and her sons have been proscribed outcasts. The real triumphs of the early Church were in the first centuries of opprobrium and persecution; her decline began when Constantine made Christianity the religion of the State.

IN THE HISTORY OF EACH EARNEST SOUL. It is rarely the case that we make much spiritual headway when winds and currents favour us. We do best when all is against us. We grow quickest in the dark. In times of persecution we realize the security, and comfort, and joy, which are in Christ Jesus our Lord; and as God goes the round of the world, it is in chambers of pain, sickness, and bereavement, that He beholds the multiplication of the choice graces of holy character and temper. The affliction, which is for the moment, is working out an exceeding weight of glory.

He Smote the Egyptian. Exod. 2: 12 (R.V.)

THIS was creature-strength, wrought on by creature-passion, and ending in creature-failure. Moses stood on an eminence, and reached down to these poor brethren of his with a passing spasm of pity. He was very careful to look this way and that, so as not to invalidate his own position at court. And fear for himself carried him swiftly from the scene of his people's woes. It was a brief effort to do the divine work of redemption in his own energy. Long years must pass, during which God would drain away drop by drop his strength, his resolution, and his very desire to be an emancipator; that when he had become nothing, God through him might effect his almighty will.

WE SOMETIMES SMITE THE EGYPTIAN WITHIN. We rise up against some tyrant passion, and strike two or three vigorous blows. Our efforts to rid ourselves of its thrall originate and are prosecuted in our own resolve. At first the conflict seems easily our own; finally the dead weight of all the Egyptians within is more than a match for us.

WE OFTEN SMITE THE EGYPTIAN WITHOUT. We make an assault on some giant evil—drink, gambling, impurity. It seems at first as though we should carry the position by our sudden and impetuous rush. But Egypt conquers in the end, and we flee.

No: we need to learn for the inward and outward conflict the lesson that forty years in Midian taught Moses, that only the Spirit of God in man can overcome the spirit of the world. By disappointment and repeated failure, by the silence of the desert, we are taught that we are nothing—then God becomes our all in all: and all things become possible to us as we believe.

I am come down. Exod. 3: 8.

THIS is a marvellous chapter, because it is so full of God. If the previous one, in its story of human striving, reminds us of Rom. 7, this as surely recalls Rom. 8. There is little mention of the part that Moses was to play, but much is said of what God was about to do. "I am come down." "I will bring you up." "I will put forth mine hand." O weary soul, bitter with weary bondage, groaning beneath cruel taskmasters, afflicted and tossed with tempest, the I AM has come down!

GOD COMES DOWN TO OUR LOWEST TO LIFT US TO HIS HIGHEST. This is the theme of the Magnificat, and of Hannah's song. God comes down to the dust for the poor, and to the dunghill for the needy. You cannot be too lonely or broken in spirit for Him to notice and help. In proportion to your humiliation will be your exaltation.

HE COMES DOWN TO OUR SADDEST TO LIFT US TO HIS JOYFULLEST. How great the contrast between the cry of the Hebrews, because of their taskmasters, and the exultant note that smote on the rocks of the Red Sea! Such shall be your experience also. If you suffer in the line of God's will and providence, you are sowing the seeds of light and gladness. Oh, anticipate the harvest!

HE COMES DOWN TO OUR HELPLESSNESS TO SUCCOUR WITH HIS GREAT MIGHT. Israel could not help herself; but the resources of I AM were sufficient for every need, and they will be for yours and mine. This is God's blank cheque; fill it in! Insert after these majestic words, wisdom, or courage, or love, or whatever you need most. And He will be all this, and more also: not for a moment, but always; not spasmodically, but unchangeably.

I am not Eloquent. Exod. 4: 10.

THIS is what we all say. We think more of the words than of the message; more of our eloquence or slowness of speech than of the King's seal and signature. Moses had learnt many wholesome lessons through his long sojourn in Midian; but he had to learn this last one, that God does not want excellency of speech or of language in his messengers, but the unction and power which come on those who speak after direct audience with the Eternal. Aaron, who came to meet Moses, could speak well; but he was a weak man, whose alliance with Moses caused his nobler younger brother much anxiety and pain. However, God determined to send Aaron with him, to be his colleague and spokesman. Better a thousand times had it been for Moses to trust God for speech, than be thus deposed of his premiership.

BE SURE TO GET THY MESSAGE FROM THE KING. Wait before Him in the inner shrine, till He says the word which thou shalt speak. This will give thee the real eloquence of the heart.

LOOK UP FOR THE RIGHT WORDS. The Apostle said that the Corinthians were enriched in all utterance; and he said that he spoke the divine mysteries in words which the Holy Spirit taught. Ask for these, and you will not be disappointed.

RELY ON THE DIVINE CO-OPERATION. There is another force at work, more subtle and penetrating than the most eloquent words of man—the power of the Holy Ghost. Seek for his divine demonstration and co-witness. And it shall come to pass, that mysterious influences shall move over the heart of those that listen to thy words, which shall attest the mighty fellowship and co-operation of One whom the natural man cannot detect.

Why is it that Thou hast sent me? Exod. 5: 22.

BEFORE God can use us, He must bring us to an end of ourselves. When Paul was summoned to the greatest epistles and labours of his life, his strength was drained to utter weakness, and he despaired even of life. So in the case of Moses and Israel.

Moses, for forty years, had been undergoing the emptying process; but perhaps when God called him to this great enterprise, there may have been a slight revival of confidence in himself, in his mission, his miracles, the eloquence of Aaron's speech. So in the rebuff he received from Pharaoh, in the bitter remonstrances of the elders of his people, in the sad consciousness that his efforts had aggravated their condition, the lesson was still further taught him—that of himself he could do absolutely nothing.

ISRAEL also had begun to hope something from his mission. Through the brickfields the story ran of his early years, his uncomprising speech to Pharaoh, of his miracles; and the wretched slaves cherished faith in him and Aaron as their heaven-sent deliverers. They had, however, to learn that all such hopes were vain, and to see that the brothers, at the best, were as weak as themselves. Then the way was prepared to lean only on God.

OURSELVES. By repeated failures all along our life-course God is teaching us the same lesson. We fail to justify and then to sanctify ourselves. Our efforts to serve and please Him only end in increasing perplexity. The tale of bricks is doubled; the burdens augment; the strength of our purpose is broken; we are utterly discouraged; and then, when the soul is utterly desolate, the heavenly Bridegroom draws near and says, "I will do all; I am Alpha and Omega; I am thy salvation."

I am Jehovah, and I Will! Exod. 6: 6.

WHEN all human help has failed, and the soul, exhausted and despairing, has given up hope from man, God draws near, and says, I AM. It is as though He said, "All that can really help you resides in my nature as in its native home. I have weaned you from all beside, that you might seek in Me what you had been wont to seek in men and things and self-help."

Thus God with Israel. The people had come to relish the dainties of Egypt—the leeks and onions, the fleshpots and sensual delights; therefore the need for this cruel bondage to wean them, and prepare them for marriage union with Himself. Moreover, they placed great hopes in Moses, and such appeals as might be made to move Pharaoh's pity; from these too it was necessary to withdraw the people's heart, that they might look for all to their heavenly Lover, and find in Jehovah their infinite supply.

AFFLICTION is always needful in the first stage of the Christian's deepening experience. The world, with its vain glory, pride, and envy; the delights of the flesh; the praise and good opinion of our fellows—these take the place of Christ in his disciples. We must be taught to despise these things, and feel their vanity and insufficiency to satisfy.

FAILURE is often necessary to teach humility and patience; so that we may have no confidence in anything we can call our own, and be prepared to find all our satisfaction and delight in Jesus only.

REVELATION then becomes possible, of all that God can be and do. He draws near with his sevenfold "I will." He looks on us with infinite delight, and commences to bring us into such blessedness that we forget all else, and behold our Bridegroom only.

The Egyptians shall know that I am the Lord. Exod. 7: 5.

IN God's dealings with his people He purposed to reveal Himself to Egypt: so that when He led forth Israel's hosts, in redemption power, from the brickfields of slavery on to resurrection ground, there might be afforded such a display of his love, and pity, and power, as the world had never before witnessed. Egypt and all surrounding nations should know the character of God in the Exodus, as the Lover and Redeemer of his own.

SO WITH THE CHURCH. The Apostle tells us that redeemed men are to be the subjects of angelic contemplation and wonder. In the Church, principalities and powers shall discern the manifold wisdom and grace of God. When God has brought all the ransomed hosts up from the Egyptian bondage of the world to stand in the radiance of the eternal morning, then the universe shall ring with the ascription, "Great and marvellous are thy works. Righteous and true are thy ways."

SO WITH EACH INDIVIDUAL BELIEVER. Each one of us has been formed for Jesus Himself, that we might show forth his praise. In growing purity and sweetness, in our deliverance from the clinging corruptions of the world and flesh, in our patience under tribulation, our submission and steadfast hope, in our willingness to sacrifice ourselves for others, let us be revelations of what Christ is, and of what He can make sinful men become.

Believers are the world's Bibles, by studying which men may come to know the Lord Himself. Let us see to it that we be clear in type, unmistakable in our testimony, pleasant to behold, thoughtful and helpful towards all, commending the blessed Bridegroom whom the world sees not.

I will put a Division between My People and thy People. Exod. 8: 23.

THIS division is as old as eternity. In the council chamber of the Godhead the Father chose Jesus and all who should believe in Him unto eternal life. We cannot understand the reason of that divine choice; we can only affirm it, that in those ages of the unfathomed past, Christ and his seed stood out from the rest of mankind, the people of God's own possession and inheritance.

IT WAS EFFECTED BY THE CROSS OF JESUS. By it we are crucified to the world, and the world to us. The cross, with its outstretched arms, stands sentinel between the Church and the world which cast out her Lord. The grave, like a great gulf, yawns between those who gather round the risen Master on resurrection ground, and all men else. From the moment that Jesus ascended, the rallying centre of the Church was removed from earth to heaven, from the cross to the throne.

IT IS WROUGHT OUT BY THE DAILY GRACE OF THE HOLY GHOST. It is right, of course, to come out and be separate in our outward walk and behaviour. But, deeper than this, if only we will let the Spirit of God work un-hindered, He will effect an inward division. Our tastes and desires, our hopes and aims, will become different, and we shall be aware of a growing dissimilarity between ourselves and the world.

Then to the separate soul the Bridegroom comes. He says tender and loving words. In one hour He teaches more than all human teachers could; and sheds forth by the Holy Ghost the torrent of divine Love. There may be darkness without, but there is light in the dwellings of Goshen: there may be plague and pestilence in the world, but there is peace, joy, and bliss, in the separated soul.

Only in Goshen, where the Children of Israel were, was there no hail. Exod. 9: 26.

THOSE who are included in the provisions of the covenant are sealed. The storm may sweep around them, but the great angel, who ascends from the east, cries with a great voice to the angels to whom it is given to hurt the earth, and the sea, and the trees, saying, Hurt them not till we have sealed the servants of God in their foreheads (Rev. 7: 3).

The only spot in which the soul is safe is within the encircling provisions of the cov-enant. Israel stood there, and was safe—not only from the hail, but from the destroying sword. The invulnerable walls of that sacred enclosure were the oath and promise of God to Abraham. God had bound Himself by the most solemn sanctions to be a God to this people, and deliver them; it was necessary, therefore, that He should be their pavilion and canopy, catching the hailstones on his outstretched wings and securing them from hurt.

The covenant is entered, not by merit nor by works. There was neither the one nor the other in that race of slaves; but they stood there simply because of their relationship to the Friend of God. So we enter the blessed safety of the better covenant, through our relation-ship with the Lord Jesus, who is the Beloved of the Father, the one glorious and blessed Man. Without beauty or merit, the soul attaches itself by faith to Him, and discovers that it was loved before the worlds were made.

Ah, blessed Lover of souls, we see how the storm swept thy heart, that it might never touch us. Thou art our hiding-place, our shield, our deliverer, our strong tower. Without dismay we can anticipate the storms of death, judgment, and eternity, sure that wherever Thou art there can be no hail.

All the Children of Israel had Light in their dwellings. Exod. 10: 23.

WITHOUT, darkness that might be felt; within, light. This should be the condition of each believing heart. The sun may have gone down, and the moon withdrawn herself in the firmament of the world; the darkness of perplexity and trouble may envelop Pharaoh and all his chosen counsellors; all things may wear the aspect of approaching dissolu-tion: but with the Lord as our everlasting Light we walk in the light of life.

LIGHT IS PURITY. The soul which is exposed to the indwelling of God, purifies itself even as He is pure; and walks as Jesus did, with white and stainless robes. He that says he has fellowship with the Holy Ghost, and walks in the darkness of his own lusts, lies. Where God is really hidden in the heart, the beams of his lovely purity must irradiate and beautify the life.

LIGHT IS KNOWLEDGE. There is a wisdom, an insight, an understanding of the divine mysteries, which the mere intellect could never give, but are the product of the divine in-dwelling in the holy soul. All around men may be groping aimlessly after truth, trying to discover the secret of the Universe, whilst to the loving, childlike soul, in which God has taken up his abode, these things, which are hidden from the wise and prudent, are unveiled.

LIGHT IS LOVE. It steals so gently over the world, blessing flowers and birds, little children and invalids. Everywhere it is the symbol of the beneficent work of its Creator. His eldest daughter! Thus amid the selfishness of the world, let Jesus dwell deep in thee, that thou mayest be rooted and grounded in the love of God, which shall illumine thy dwelling, and ray out to the world.

Jewels of Silver and Jewels of Gold. Exod. 11: 2.

THE Egyptians knew very well that they would never see their jewels again; and the people of Israel were thus, to some extent, compensated for their unpaid toils. The Lord gave them such favour with the Egyptians that they gave them whatever they asked; so that "they spoiled the Egyptians."

These jewels were employed afterwards in the adornment and enrichment of the Sanctuary. They flashed in the breastplate of the High Priest, and shone in the sacred vessels. In this they remind us of the treasures which David gathered by his conquests from neighbouring nations, and which were afterwards incorporated in the Temple of Solomon. They recall also the glowing predictions of the prophet, that the kings of the earth shall bring their treasures into the New Jerusalem.

The jewels of the Church, whether they stand for her graces or her choice children, have often been obtained from the midst of Egypt. Was not Saul of Tarsus just such a jewel? The world counted him one of her rarest sons; but God set him as a jewel in the breastplate of Immanuel.

Let us ever seek jewels from the land of our captivity and suffering. It will not do to come away empty. It is not enough merely to bear what God permits to fall on us for our chastisement; but to go further, and extract from all trials, jewels. Let every trial and temptation enrich you with the opposite grace. There are Egyptians in your life, which have grievously tormented you with their heavy whips, yet even these shall yield wealth— "jewels of silver and jewels of gold"; which you shall consecrate to holy service, and

which shall shine in the fabric and worship of the New Jerusalem.

With bitter herbs. Exod. 12: 8.

THE Paschal feast is the emblem of the Christian life. The Blood is ever speaking to God for us; though we see it not, God sees it, and hears its prevalent plea. We in the meanwhile are called upon to feed in faith daily, hourly, on the flesh of the Son of Man, according to his own command. In all Christian life, even in its hours of greatest rapture, there must be a touch of the bitter herb.

WE CAN NEVER FORGET THE COST OF OUR REDEMPTION. Even in heaven, in the full realization of its bliss, whenever we catch sight of the print of the nails in his hand, we shall remember the agony and bloody sweat the cross and passion, and eat the feast with the flavour of the bitter herb. How much more on earth, where we are so constantly requiring the efficacy of his precious death!

THERE WILL ALWAYS BE THE MEMORY OF OUR SINNERSHIP. We cannot forget our unworthiness and sin. He has forgiven; but we cannot forget. Ah, those years of rebellion and perverseness before we yielded to Him; and those years of self-will and pride since we knew his love! They will sometimes come back to us and give us to eat of the bitter herb.

MOREOVER, THERE MUST BE THE CONSTANT CRUCIFIXION OF THE SELF-LIFE. We can only properly feed on Jesus, the Lamb of God, when we are animated by the spirit of self-surrender and humiliation, of death to the world and to the will of the flesh, which were the characteristics of his cross. Deep down in our hearts, the drinking of his cup and being baptized with his baptism, will be the touch of the bitter herbs in the feast. But "the sufferings of this present time are not worthy to be compared with the glory which shall be revealed in us."

By strength of hand the Lord brought us out. Exod. 13: 14.

FOUR times over in this chapter Moses lays stress on the strong hand which God redeemed his people from the bondage of Egypt; and we are reminded of "the exceeding greatness of His power, which is to us-ward who believe" (Eph. 1: 12-20).

GOD'S STRONG HAND REACHES DOWN TO

WHERE WE ARE. It would have been useless if Israel had been bidden to help itself up to a certain point, whilst God would do the rest. The people were so broken that they could only lie at the bottom of the pit, and moan. God's hand reached down to touch and grasp them at their lowest. So God's help is not conditional on our doing something, whilst He will do the rest. When we are without strength, when we have expended our all in vain, when heart and flesh fail—then God comes where we are, and becomes the strength of our heart and our portion for ever.

GOD'S STRONG HAND IS MIGHTIER THAN OUR MIGHTIEST ADVERSARIES. Pharaoh was strong, and held the people as a child may hold a moth in its clenched fist. But a man's hand is stronger than a child's, and God's than Pharaoh's. So Satan may have held you in bondage; but do not fear him any more, look away to the strength of God's hand. What can it not do for you?

WE MUST APPROPRIATE AND RECKON ON GOD'S STRONG HAND. It is there towards them who believe, as a locomotive may be next a line of carriages; yet there must be a coupling-iron connecting them. So you must trust God's strength, and avail yourself of it, and yield to it. Remember that his arm is not shortened, nor his hand paralysed, except our unbelief and sin intercept and hinder the mighty working of his Power.

And Israel saw the Egyptians dead upon the sea-shore. Exod. 14: 30.
WHAT a relief that morning brought from the anxieties of the previous night! Then, as they lifted up their eyes, they saw Pharaoh and the dreaded Egyptian taskmaster in full pursuit; now they beheld the sea-shore strewn with their bodies, stark and cold. They would never see them again, nor hear the crack of their whips.

So in life we are permitted to see the dreaded temptations and evils of earlier days suddenly deprived of all power to hurt us. The Egyptians are dead upon the shore; and we see the great work of the Lord. Let us take comfort in this:

IN THE PRESSURE OF TRIAL. You are suffering keenly; yet remember that no trial is allowed to come from any source in which there is not a divine meaning. Nothing can enter your life, of which God is not cognisant, and which He does not permit. Though the pressure of your trial is almost unbearable, you will one day see your Egyptians dead.

AMID THE TEMPTATIONS OF THE GREAT ADVERSARY OF SOULS. They may seem at this moment more than you can bear; but God is about to deliver you. He can so absolutely free you from the habits of self-indulgence which you have contracted, and from the perpetual yielding to temptation to which you have been prone, that some day you will look with amazement and thankfulness on these things, as Egyptians dead on the sea-shore.

SO ALSO IN THE PRESENCE OF DEATH. Many believers dread, not the after-death, but the act of dying. But as the morning of eternity breaks, they will awake with songs of joy to see death and the grave and all the evils that they dreaded, like Egyptians, strewn on the shores of the sea of glass.

The waters were made Sweet. Exod. 15: 25.
OUR joys and sorrows, like the varied products of nature, lie very close together. One moment we are singing the joyous song of victory on the shores of the Red Sea, and vow we will never again mistrust our God; and then, by a sudden transition, we find ourselves standing beside the Marah water of pain and disappointment inclined to murmur at our lot.

There is, however, a tree, which, when cast into the waters, makes them sweet. It is the tree of the cross. "He bare our sins in his own body on the tree." The cross means the yielding up of the will. Now, it is in proportion as we see God's will in the various events of life, and surrender ourselves either to bear or do it, that we shall find earth's bitter things becoming sweet, and its hard things easy.

WE MUST YIELD OUR WILL TO GOD. The secret of blessedness is in saying "Yes" to the will of God, as it is shown in the circumstances of our lot or the revelations of his Word. It is the will of a Father whose love and wisdom are beyond question.

WE MUST ACCEPT WHAT HE PERMITS. It may be that our pains emanate from the malevolence or negligence of others; still, if He has permitted them, they are his will for us. By the time they reach us they have become minted with his die, and we must patiently submit.

WE MUST DO ALL HE BIDS. The thread of obedience must always be running through our hands. At all costs to our choice and feeling we must not only have his commands, but keep them. Our Lord perpetually lays stress on obeying his words. This is the spirit of the Cross, and the properties of this tree sweeten earth's bitterest sorrows. "Disappointments become his appointments."

A Day's Portion every day. Exod. 16: 4 (R.V.) IT is said that the twenty-four hours should be divided thus: Eight hours for work, eight for rest, eight for recreation, food, etc. There should be a counterpart of this in Christian living. Each day there should be a portion for work, a portion for restful meditation and sitting before the Lord, and a portion for the gathering of God's manna.

EACH DAY BRINGS ITS OWN WORK. God has created us for good works, and has prepared our pathway, so that we may come to them one by one. He has apportioned to each one some office to fulfil, some service to render, some function in the mystical body of our Lord. It is comforting to know that we have not to scheme for ourselves, but to look up for guidance into the divine plan.

EACH DAY BRINGS ITS OWN DIFFICULTIES. God spreads them over our days, giving each day only what we can sustain. The servant girl might be startled were she told that she would have to carry the coals, which it has taken two horses and a great cart to bring to her master's door; but she will be comforted by being reminded that they will be borne upstairs only a coal-scuttle full at a time.

EACH DAY BRINGS ITS OWN SUPPLY. No Israelite could point to his store of manna and congratulate himself that he was proof against any famine that might befall. The lesson of daily trust for daily bread was constantly being enforced; for as the day came the manna fell. Those who followed the cloud were always certain of their sustenance. Where the cloud brooded the manna fell. Whatever any day may bring there always will be within reach of you, lying ready prepared on the sands of the desert, just what you require. Go forth and carry it; there will be no lack.

I will stand before thee upon the rock in Horeb, and thou shalt smite the rock. Exod. 17: 6.
HERE is a beautiful example of the co-operation between God and his servants in providing for the needs of his people. Clearly the smiting of the rock was a very small item in this incident, the main consideration was what God was doing in the heart of the earth. But the two wrought together: Moses in the eyes of the people, God in hidden depths. Similarly we are fellow-workers with God.

One of the greatest revelations that can come to any Christian worker is the realization that in every act of Christian ministry there are two agents, God and man: that God does not need to be implored to help us, but wants us to help Him; that our part is the very unimportant and subsidiary one of smiting the rock, whilst his is the divine and all important part of making the waters flow.

Did Moses go to the rock that day weighted with care, his brow furrowed with the anxiety of furnishing a river of which his people might drink? Certainly not; he had only to smite: God would do all the rest, and had pledged Himself to it. So, Christian worker, you have been worrying as though the whole weight of God's inheritance were upon you, but you are greatly mistaken; smiting is very easy work.

In every congregation and religious gathering the Holy Spirit is present, eager to glorify Christ, and to pour out rivers of living water for thirsty men; believe this. See that you are spiritually in a right condition, that He may be able to ally you with Himself. Keep reckoning on Him to do his share; and when the river is flowing, be sure not to take the praise.

"We are workers together with God."

And God command thee so. Exod. 18: 23.
IT was good and sound advice that Jethro gave his son-in-law. It could hardly have been better. It is always better to set one hundred men to work than attempt to do the work of one hundred men. There is no greater art in the world than to develop the latent capacities of those around us by yoking them to useful service. But good though the advice obviously was, Jethro carefully guarded Moses against adopting it, unless the Lord had been consulted, and had commanded it.

LET US TEST HUMAN ADVICE. There are plenty of voices that advise us, and each has some nostrum for your health, some direction for our path. Some are true guides, whom God has sent to us, as Jethro to Moses.

Often an onlooker can see mistakes we are making, and can suggest something better. But we are wise to get alone into the holy presence of God, and ask what He commands, what is his will.

LET US TEST HUMAN TEACHINGS. So full is the world of voices, so bewildering the din of religious schools and sects! The Apostle was justified in advising us to prove all things and, to try the spirits, whether they were of God. There are four tests for truth: what glorifies Christ; what humbles the flesh; what is in accord with the Word of God; and what has stood the trial of Christian experience in the past.

There is no teacher like God, and we may always detect his voice. It is small and still; it casts down imagination, and brings our thoughts into the captivity of Jesus; it is definite and distinct. When there is an indistinct murmur of many sounds along the wire, you may be sure that you are not in communication with your Father's person. When He speaks, there is no mistaking his voice or his will.

A peculiar Treasure unto Me. Exod. 19: 5.
OUR Saviour told of a man who, in ploughing his field, heard his plough-share chink against buried treasure, and hastened to sell all that he had in order to buy it. In speaking thus, He pictured Himself as well as us. He found us before we found Him. The treasure is his people, to purchase whom He gave up all that He had, even to his throne (Matt. 13: 44). "Ye are an elect race, a royal priesthood, a holy nation, a people for God's own possession, that ye may show forth the excellencies of Him who called you out of darkness into his marvellous light" (1 Peter 2: 9, R.V.).

Where his treasure is, there is a man's heart. If it is in ships on the treacherous sea, he tosses restlessly on his bed, solicitous for its safety. If it is in fabrics, he guards against moth; if in metal, against rust and thieves. And is Christ less careful for his own? Does he not guard with equal care against all that would deteriorate our value in his esteem? Need we fear the thief? Will not the Onlybegotten keep us, so that the evil one shall not touch us (Matt. 6: 19, 20)?

God's treasure is his for ever. "They shall be mine, saith the Lord of Hosts, in the day that I do make, even a peculiar treasure." He will hold his own, as men cling to their treasure, binding it about their loins, in a storm at sea (Mal. 3: 17, R.V.).

Let us mind the conditions: to obey his voice, and keep his covenant; then on eagles' wings He will bring us to Himself. Compliance with these is blessed in its results. God regards us with the ecstasy of a love that rejoices over us with singing; and counts on us as a mother on her child, a miser on his gold.

The thick darkness where God was. Exod. 20: 21.
GOD is light, and dwells in light, but it is mercifully veiled to the weak eye of man. This is why Christ spake in parables—that seeing, they might not see. As Moses veiled his face when he spake to the people, so God veils Himself in the flesh of Jesus, in which He tabernacles; and in the mysteries of his providence, beneath which He conceals a smiling face. The Sun of Righteousness in whose beams we rejoice must needs hide beneath the cloud, else we should fall at his feet as dead. It may be that his light seems to us darkness, because of its excessive brilliance; but God dwells in the thick darkness—clouds and darkness are around about Him.

THE DARKNESS OF MYSTERY. God has still his hidden secrets, hidden from the wise and prudent. Do not fear them; be content to accept things you cannot understand; wait patiently. Presently He will reveal to you the treasures of darkness, the riches of the glory of the mystery. Mystery is only the veil on God's face.

THE DARKNESS OF TRIAL. Do not be afraid to enter the cloud that is settling down on your life. God is in it. The other side is radiant with his glory. "Think it not strange concerning the fiery trial which is to try you, as though some strange thing happened unto you: but rejoice, inasmuch as ye are partakers of Christ's sufferings."

THE DARKNESS OF DESERTION. When you seem loneliest and most forsaken, God is nighest. Jesus once cried "Forsaken," and immediately after, "Father." God is in the dark cloud. Plunge into the blackness of its darkness without flinching—under the shrouding curtain of his pavilion you will find God awaiting you.

With an awl. Exod. 21: 6.
THE Hebrew slave who meant perpetual

consecration of service had to lose a little blood. It was a disagreeable and not wholly painless process, by which his vows were ratified and rendered permanent. But not otherwise could he serve for ever. That awl represents the nail that affixed Christ to the cross, and we must expect it in every true act of consecration. For want of it so many seem to go through that supreme act, and shortly after go back from it, bringing discredit and shame upon the teaching they had eagerly welcomed. There are two stages in the Christian life: that in which we serve with the spirit of a slave, and that in which we freely yield ourselves to serve our Master for ever. This is the service represented by the pierced ear.

The awl spiritually means the humiliation and pain with which we surrender the self-life. We are tempted to consecrate ourselves in our own energy; to resolve on the devout life in the strength of our own resolution; to say, "I will serve Christ utterly." We avoid the awl which deprives us of our own energy, which is applied to us by the hand of another and which makes us helpless and self-emptied, that God may become all in all. In your case the awl may be the daily fret of some uncongenial associate; the pressure of loss and anxiety for the sake of Jesus; the humiliation of your pride by perpetual sense of failure. Whatever it may be, welcome all that binds you to his cross, because through death you live.

"I beseech you therefore, brethren, by the mercies of God, that ye present your bodies a living sacrifice, holy, acceptable unto God, which is your reasonable service."

He shall make Restitution. Exod. 22:5.
THIS chapter is full of restitution, of which there is far too little in ordinary Christian life. We try to make amends for injury done to another by an extraordinary amount of civility; but we are reluctant in so many words to frankly confess that we have done wrong, and make proper reparation for the act or speech. We often excuse ourselves by the thought that we were fully justified in speaking or acting as we did, whereas we may behave ourselves wrongly in courses of conduct which are themselves legitimate.

LOOSING A BEAST INTO ANOTHER MAN'S FIELD (5). We may through our carelessness allow another to suffer detriment. The beast ought not to have been thus allowed to stray; and, as we let it loose, we should make amends for our carelessness in respect to our brother's interests. We wrong another not only by what we do, or permit to be done, but in what we carelessly fail to do.

KINDLING A FIRE (6). The tongue is a spark that kindles a great matter. If we drop firebrands and lighted matches in the inflammable material of a circle of gossip, we should make amends to the person whose character may have been thereby injured.

BORROWED GOODS (14). To return a house, a book, a horse, in the state in which we received it, fair wear and tear excepted, or to make good any injury, should be a commonplace of Christian morality. Trustees are responsible for not making due inquiry into risky investments. Each is his brother's keeper. If we remember at the prayer-hour that he has aught against us, let us seek him, and confess, and restore.

An enemy unto thine enemies. Exod. 23:22.
IT is a most helpful thought that the angel of the covenant in whom is God's name, always precedes us. In our march through the wilderness we perceive his form, which is viewless to others, and realize that his strong hand prepares our path. Let us be very careful not to grieve or disobey Him, lest we lose his mighty championship. Strict obedience to his slightest whisper secures the certainty of his vindication of us from the wrongs we suffer at the hands of our foes. A little further on the same voice promises to send a hornet before the chosen host (28). He who is an angel to the saint is a hornet to his foes. A swarm of hornets is the most relentless and irresistible foe that man can face.

Have you enemies? Be sure that they hate you only for the truth's sake, and because darkness must always be in antagonism to light. "Who is he that will harm you, if ye be followers of that which is good? But and if ye suffer for righteousness' sake, happy are ye: and be not afraid of their terror, neither be troubled." But see to it that you cherish no spirit of hatred or retaliation towards them. Think of the misery of their heart, which is full of jealousy, envy, and bitterness. Pity and pray for them.

When we are right with God we shall have many new enemies. All who hate Him will hate us. But this is rather to our credit than otherwise. Those who have defamed the master of the household will be hostile to his servants. But when our cause is one with God's, and his foes ours, our foes are his, and He deals with them; He stands between us and their hate. He will not leave us in their hands; He will give us vindication and deliverance.

They beheld God, and did eat and drink. Exod. 24: 11.

IT is a beautiful combination, which we should do well to emulate.

SOME EAT AND DRINK, AND DO NOT BEHOLD GOD. They are taken up with the delights of sense. Their one cry, as the children of this world is, What shall we eat, what shall we drink, and wherewithal shall we be clothed? But the God in whose hand their breath is and whose are all their ways, they do not glorify. Let us beware; it was of Christian professors that the Apostle said, Their god is their belly.

SOME BEHOLD GOD, AND DO NOT EAT AND DRINK. They look on God with such awful fear that they isolate Him from the common duties of life. They draw a strict line between the sacred and secular, between Sunday and weekday, between God's and their own. This divorce between religion and daily life is fatal to true religion, which was meant to be the bond between the commonest details of life and the service of God.

SOME BEHOLD GOD, AND EAT AND DRINK. They turn from the commonest avocations to look up into his face. They glorify God in their body as well as in their spirit. They obey the apostle's injunction, "Whether therefore ye eat, or drink or whatsoever ye do, do all to the glory of God." Oh for the grace to be able to combine the vision of God with every common incident—to live always beneath his eye in the unrestrained gladness of little children in their Father's presence!

Never a trial that He is not there,
Never a burden that He doth not bear;
Never a sorrow that He doth not share—
Moment by moment I'm under his care.

According to all that I shew thee, . . . even so shall ye make it. Exod. 25: 9.

IT was clear that God would only be res-

ponsible for the material that was needed for his plan. If Moses, or the people, insisted on putting in more than was in his original plan, they would have to bear the anxiety of securing the stuff. This is our mistake. We incur responsibilities that God does not put on us; we burden our hearts with anxiety and care because we insist on introducing so many items into our daily life, which would not have been there if we had but been content with God's pattern, and acquiesced in his programme.

This injunction is repeated in four different passages, showing the importance with which God regards it. Indeed, to be on God's plan is the only place of rightness, safety, and joy.

GOD'S PLAN IN OUR CHARACTER. It is presented in the human life of Jesus. We are to walk as He walked. Having been called according to his purpose, let us never rest content with anything less than being conformed to the image of God's Son.

GOD'S PLAN IN OUR CHRISTIAN SERVICE. Not seeking to resemble some other devoted life; but endeavouring to be as God would have us, the embodiment of his thought, the expression of his conception. Then our efforts will be crowned with success, and we shall bear much fruit to the glory of God.

GOD'S PLAN FOR EVERY DAY. He has prepared a scheme for the employment of every hour, and will show it to us by the indication of his Spirit, or by the trend of circumstances. Let us abide in Him, doing nothing that He does not teach, doing all He does. So life will become a tabernacle, in which the Shechinah will shine and sacrifices be offered.

The vail shall divide unto you. Exod. 26: 33.

THAT vail was rent when Jesus died, the Holy Ghost signifying that from that moment access was free into the Holiest. All believers are now welcome to draw near and live in the perpetual presence of God, their Father, even as Jesus did in his earthly life, and as He does in the Heaven of Heavens. This is the clear teaching of Heb. 10: 19-22: "Having therefore, brethren, boldness to enter into the holiest by the blood of Jesus, by a new and living way, which He hath consecrated for us, through the vail, that is to say, his flesh; and having a High Priest over the house of God; let us draw near with a true heart, in full assurance of faith, having our hearts sprinkled from an evil conscience and our bodies washed with pure water."

But there is a deeper significance still. The new and living way was opened through the rending of the flesh of Jesus Christ. As his flesh was rent on the Cross, the Temple vail was rent from the top to the bottom. And it is only when we have chosen the cross, with its shame and death, as the lot of our self-life, that we can enter into that immediate fellowship with God, which is described as "within the vail."

How many there are who never get beyond that dividing vail! They know the brazen altar of Atonement, the laver of daily washing, the golden altar of intercession; but they are never admitted to that blessed intimacy of communion which sees the Shechinah glory between the cherubim and blood-sprinkled mercy-seat.

O Spirit of God, apply the blood to sprinkle our consciences, and the water to cleanse the habits of our daily life; and lead us where our Forerunner and Priest awaits us.

Pure olive oil beaten for the Light. Exod. 27: 20.

THE saintly McCheyne used to say, when urging his brother ministers to diligent preparation for the pulpit: "Beaten oil for the sanctuary." And he strove never to present to his people truth which had not been beaten out by careful devout meditation.

But there is yet another thought. That lamp in the Holy Place was an emblem of the testimony of the Church, that is, of believers. As the incense table was a type of their aspect towards God, as intercessors, so the seven-branched candlestick was a type of their aspect towards the world, as luminaries. In the Book of Revelation the Lord compares his churches to candlesticks: "the seven candlesticks which thou sawest are the seven churches."

The oil is, of course, as always in Scripture, a type of the Holy Spirit. He in us is the only source of light-bearing. But the beaten oil reminds us of the chastisement and discipline through which alone our best testimony can be given. The persecutions of the Church have always been the times when she has given her fairest, brightest witness to the Redeemer. The sufferings of believers have ever led to the tenderest, strongest words

for the Master, whether by the sick bed or in the hospital ward. That brokenness of spirit, which is the surest mark of the mature work of God in the heart, is also a rare condition of light-giving. The more beaten and broken you are, in poverty of spirit, the purer will be the heavenly ray of love and light which will shine forth from your life; and it is the purpose of God that you should be "blameless and harmless, the sons of God, without rebuke, in the midst of a crooked and perverse nation, among whom ye shine as lights in the world" (Phil. 2: 15).

A golden bell and a pomegranate. Exod. 28: 34.

THE robe of the high priest's ephod was of blue, the colour of heaven, of deep lakes, of the glacier-crevasse, of the gentian and forget-me-not. On the hem of the robe were these alternate bells and pomegranates.

THOSE SKIRTS MAY ILLUSTRATE OUR OWN POSITION. We dare not take a high place near the head or arm; but, thank God, there is a place for each of us at the skirt, near the foot; and the holy oil will reach us there, for the Psalmist tells us that it descended even to the skirts of the high priest's robe. It is a blessed thought, that we may receive the droppings of each anointing that falls on the head of Jesus.

But the anointing of the Holy Ghost always shows itself in sweetness and fruitfulness; the sweetness of the golden bell, tinkling with every movement, and the fruitfulness of the pomegranate.

WE MUST BE SWEET, AS WELL AS FRUITFUL. Too many Christian workers are overtired and overwrought; they are peevish and fretful. When they come back from meetings on which they have bestowed their last energies, they are neither sweet nor gentle to the home-circle, which has been so lonesome during their absence.

WE MUST BE FRUITFUL, AS WELL AS SWEET. True religion is not a mere sentimentality; it is strong, healthy, helpful, fruit-bearing. Some seem to think that to attend moving meetings, to be profuse in emotional tears and smiles, to make profuse use of the word dear, is to touch the high-water mark; let them learn that the worth of our life is measured by its influence on others, and its bearing fruit, which has in it the seed of reproduction. "Herein is my Father glorified, that ye bear much fruit."

Thou shalt wash them with water. Exod. 29: 4.
THIS chapter tells of the consecration to their high office of Aaron and his sons. The entire family is constantly joined thus together as one in God's sight. Similarly, Christ and his house—which is ourselves, who believe—are one. We too must be sprinkled by the blood on ear and thumb and toe, as those who have been redeemed. We too must be consecrated and anointed; and there must be the cleanliness of which these words speak.

This is where so many have erred; they have sought consecration, anointing, and the priestly office; but have not remembered that their bodies must first be washed with pure water.

WE MUST BE CLEAN IN OUR HABITS. If there is anything in our daily behaviour which is not quite clean, it must be put away. There seems some incongruity between the anointing of the Holy Ghost and the smell of spirits or fumes of tobacco. Any excessive indulgence of the flesh, even in legitimate directions, and all indulgence in wrong ones, are inconsistent with the life of consecration.

WE MUST BE CLEANSED IN OUR THOUGHTS. Whenever temptation is suggested, even though it is still in the far distance, we must turn from it with loathing, and ask that the blood of Jesus may go on cleansing hour by hour. "Cleanse the thoughts of our hearts by the inspiration of thy Holy Spirit, that we may perfectly love Thee."

WE MUST BE CLEANSED IN OUR INTENTIONS. The self-life recedes as it is driven from the outworks of our nature, and goes deeper into the motives and springs of action. We discover that self is the spring of so much of our religious activity. Everywhere we need the laver, the hourly washing of John 13.

Upon the flesh of man shall it not be poured. Exod. 30: 32.
WHAT perpetual references to the work of the Holy Spirit, under the symbol of the Anointing Oil, meet us in these chapters. It becomes us to ask ourselves very seriously whether we lay an equal stress on it in our daily experience. Is it true of us, as of those to whom the Beloved Apostle wrote, that the anointing which we received abideth in us? It is not enough to have the Spirit in us for sanctification; He must be on us for service and ministry.

But He cannot come on the flesh of the natural man; He descends only to those who are washed, consecrated, set apart for God. Many claim the Holy Spirit's anointing, and try to reckon they have received it; but they find it fail, because they desire it for the flesh.

THERE MUST BE NO YIELDING TO FLESHLY APPETITE. When we were in the flesh, sinful passions wrought in our members. But there must be no permission given in these directions. A calm, reverent, self-disciplined nature is alone fitted to be the seat of the Holy Ghost, his nest and home.

THERE MUST BE NO GRATIFICATION TO WORLDLY PRIDE AND AMBITION. Too many are eager for the Holy Ghost, that they may be able to make a name, or gather an audience; but God is not likely to give us his river of throne-water to turn the mill-wheels of personal ambition.

THERE MUST BE NO FLESHLY STRIVING AFTER IT. We wrestle and struggle to win the Spirit, and miss Him. It is only when our hope of attaining this blessing by our own efforts dies down, and we are humbled and broken before God; when we cry out to Him to give what we cannot win, that He draws near and gives the best of all his donations.

I have called by name Bezaleel. Exod. 31: 2.
WE lightly speak of a man's occupation as his calling, and fail to realize the profound significance of the phrase. One man is called to the ministry; another to the bar; others, like Bezaleel and Aholiab, to work in all manner of workmanship. Each should realize, therefore, that faculty, desire, circumstance, constitute a divine call, and that there may be as distinct a vocation in the merchant's office, the tradesman's shop, or in the work of a domestic servant, as in the Church itself.

The morning bell that summons us to daily duty is the call of our Father, bidding us to engage in the toils to which He has assigned us. He, who gave Moses the plan, gave the artificers the power to work it in gold, silver, brass, and wood. Let this be your faith; and each morning, as you go to your work, however distasteful it may be, say, "God has called me to this; and He will fill me with all the strength, wisdom, and grace, that I need for its right doing."

ABIDE IN YOUR CALLING. Unless it is a wrong or dishonourable one, it is better to stay in it than to become restless and changeable;

and if you must leave it, wait for God to open another door.

FIND IN GOD THE MAKEWEIGHT TO ALL THE DEFICIENCIES OF YOUR LIFE. If you are enslaved by daily duty, remember that in Christ you are free; if free from daily toil, in Christ you are a slave. The supply of every deficiency, the rectification of every hardship, is to be found in Jesus.

MIND TO DO ALL FOR GOD. To do all in God and for Him, remembering that He sees and accepts all, not according to the results accomplished, but to the heavenly and holy motives that prompt the worker—this is to be blessed.

Peradventure I shall make an Atonement for your sin. Exod. 32: 30.

THE heart of Moses was full of that great, wonderful new word, Atonement. For many days, God had been telling him about it, and speaking it over and over to his heart. He seemed, however, to feel that no ordinary sacrifices would avail: the blood of goats and bulls would surely be insufficient to put away the black transgression into which Israel had fallen. But there was rising in his heart a resolve, to which he gave expression when he returned to God: "Blot me, I pray thee, out of the book which Thou hast written." He did not realize that his blood would not avail, but that the blood of Christ, who should, in the fulness of time, offer Himself without spot to God, alone could put away sin.

IN EVERY HEART THERE IS A DEEP CONVICTION OF THE NECESSITY OF AN ATONEMENT. This is the source of the temples, altars, and sacrifices, which have marked the history of every nation under heaven. Man has felt as by a natural instinct that some reparation was necessary to the broken law.

THE INSUFFICIENCY OF ANIMAL SACRIFICE. In the Levitical system there was a remembrance of sin made year by year; but the sin itself could not be purged by such rites. The fact that the worshippers so constantly came back to offer their sacrifices shows that they were not assured. The priests always stood: their attitude was an emblem of an unfinished work.

THE SUFFICIENCY OF CHRIST'S ATONEMENT. He was willing to be cut off out of the land of the living for the transgression of his people; and because He died, there is no longer the "—" which in Moses' prayer speaks of

uncertainty; but a blessed assurance that we are at one with God, with each other, and with all holy beings.

In a Cleft of the Rock. Exod. 33: 22.

THAT rock was Christ. In the divine thought the position of Moses, first on the rock, and afterwards in its cleft, was a moving emblem of the position in which alone we can dare to look out on the sublime progress of God's glory.

GOD IS ALWAYS PASSING BY. In the great movements of history which evolve his plans, and are leading to Christ's advent; in the passage of the ages, which are his swift chariots; in storm and catastrophe, which break up old forces and forms of evil; in the goodness of his daily mercy; in the revelation of his character—we are always living in the very midst of God's presence and power.

IN OUR CONDITION OF WEAKNESS AND SINFULNESS WE NEED A POSITION OF STABILITY AND SHELTER FROM WHICH TO LOOK ON GOD. No man can see that face of awful holiness and love and live. Sir John Herschel says that when sweeping the heavens with his telescope the brilliant Sirius suddenly burst on his view, he nearly fainted. Who then could behold God! But in Jesus, we are stable, established in Him, accepted in the Beloved; and in Him we are covered. The full blaze of the divine glory is tempered to our gaze; it comes to us through the medium of the pierced hand. We stand on the rock; we are hidden under the covering hand.

OUR ROCK WAS CLEFT. How scarred are the great Alps! Their sides have been split by the action of tempest, avalanche, earthquake, frost, and glacier. Hence their clefts. But who shall enumerate all that has been borne by our dear Lord for us! What storms have pelted on Him, that we might have a safe hiding. On Calvary, a niche was hollowed in which a world of sinners may take shelter!

Moses wist not. Exod. 34: 29.

UNCONSCIOUSNESS of goodness is always a main element in the highest forms of goodness: in the same way that unconsciousness is characteristic of the worst forms of depravity. "Samson wist not that the Lord had departed from him."

Directly people become conscious of their superiority to others, and boast of it, it is certain that they have never really seen the beauty of God's holiness, and have no clear knowledge of the condition of their own hearts. They see that they have been cleansed from their old sins; but they do not perceive that the spirit of selfishness has retreated into the springs of motive and intention.

We are all tempted to this terrible self-consciousness. We are proud of being humble, complacent for being lowly, self-congratulatory because we take back-seats. In all this we betray the vanity of our pretensions. This sort of goodness is like a thin veneer of mahogany on very common deal.

The real goodness is more conscious of the remaining evil than of the acquired good; of the lingering darkness than of the hill-tops smitten with the dawn; of that which has not been attained. But we can only attain this blessed condition by intimate and prolonged fellowship with God, in solitudes where human voices and interests cease to distract. The brightness of which Moses was unconscious was caught from the Presence-chamber of the divine Loveliness. Ah, what patterns are seen on the Mount! What cries are uttered there! What visions are seen there! What revelations are made there! What injunctions are received there! Oh for the closer access, the nearer view, the more intimate face to face intercourse, such as is open still to the friends of God!

To work all manner of workmanship. Exod. 35: 35 (R.V.)

THERE was an infinite variety in the contributions made to the Tabernacle, from the precious jewels of the rulers to the acacia wood of the poor, and the goats' hair of the women. The completed structure was a monument of the united gifts, handicrafts, and gems of the entire people. But in all there was the unity of the spirit, and plan, and devotion.

IN THE CHURCH AND THE WORLD THERE IS A WORK FOR EACH OF US TO DO. It may be a very humble part in the great factory—like minding the lift, or stoking the furnace, or fetching materials for the more skilled operatives; but there is a berth for each willing worker, if only the will and way of God are diligently sought and followed.

THIS WORK IS SUITED TO OUR SPECIAL POWERS. He who prepares the work for the worker, prepares the worker for the work. Whenever God gives us a task to fulfil, it is because He sees in us faculties for its successful and happy accomplishment, in co-operation with Himself. It is a mistake then to turn back daunted by difficulty and opposition. As Caleb and Joshua said of the possessors of Canaan, "We be well able to overcome them."

WE MUST BRING OUR RESOURCES AND POWERS TO GOD. Willing hearts were summoned to bring their offerings to the Lord. The maker of a musical instrument knows best how to develop its waiting music, and He who created and endowed us can make the most of us. Let us not work for Him; but yield ourselves to his hand, and our members as instruments of righteousness for his service. We may differ from all others in the special character of our work; but it matters not, so long as God effects through us his purpose in our creation.

Much more than enough. Exod. 36: 5.

THIS is always God's way. No words could better express the Imperial measure and standard of his dealings with his people. When he calls us out, as He did Moses, Bezaleel, and Aholiab, and entrusts us with his plan; and when we are careful to work out his specifications; He always makes more than enough provision for all our need.

THE REDEMPTION IN CHRIST JESUS. Where sin abounded grace did much more abound. The topmost hills were covered by the waters of the deluge, and the Apline heights of human rebellion were more than atoned for when Jesus died. Grace overtops sin.

GOD'S ABILITY TO ANSWER PRAYER. He does exceeding abundantly above all that we ask or think. We ask great things, and secretly think that if God were to give only a fraction, we would be thankful. How we straiten Him! He cannot do much because of our unbelief! He yearns to do not only enough, but much more than enough for us. See his prodigality in nature: its enamelled shells, its profusion of flowers, its swarming life.

IN DAILY PROVISION FOR SPIRIT, SOUL, AND BODY. Give, and it shall be given to you, good measure, pressed down, shaken together, and running over. God is not niggard. If He withholds, it is that we may cling to the Giver rather than the gift. But for the most part, He gives all things richly to enjoy. He opens his hand, and satisfies. Whatever thy need, God has much more than enough to meet it. He has riches of grace and of glory. Trust Him, obey Him, appropriate thy share in thy Father's rich provision. Weak and needy as thou art, there is much more than enough strength in God to perfect what concerns thee.

A mercy-seat of pure gold. Exod. 37: 6.
THIS was the Propitiatory. Beneath it lay the tables of the law, which even Moses had broken, almost as soon as they came into his hands, but which had been renewed. Concealing and covering them lay this golden lid, encrusted with the blood which successive generations of priests sprinkled there on the Great Day of Atonement.

There can be no doubt that this golden slab sets forth our Saviour's obedience unto death. God set Him forth to be "the Propitiation for our sins; and not for ours only, but also for the sins of the whole world."

OUR LORD'S OBEDIENCE IS PRICELESS IN THE DIVINE ESTEEM. What pure gold is among metals, that is his advent to do God's will, in comparison with all other endeavours to do it. It takes the first place, and is of peerless beauty and excellence. "Though He were a Son, yet learned He obedience by the things which He suffered."

HIS OBEDIENCE WAS TO BLOOD. His wounds tell the story. He held nothing back; but yielded all to blood-shedding. Blood is life, and life is in the Blood: this He freely poured out to meet the claims of justice, and herein gave the sublimest token of his love.

HIS PERSON AND WORK ARE THE MEDIUM OF OUR APPROACH. In Jesus the Shechinah of God's presence awaits us. On this priceless mercy-seat the Divine Fire trembles, and we may draw near with boldness. We are beloved children; but let us never forget that we are redeemed sinners.

There is a place were Jesus sheds
The oil of gladness on our heads;
A place than all beside more sweet—
It is the blood-stained Mercy-seat.

The laver . . . of the mirrors of the serving-women. Exod. 38: 8 (R.V.)
THIS was a good use to put these mirrors to. The women were so deeply interested in the work which was afoot, that they counted no sacrifice too great. But the main suggestion for ourselves is the wisdom of renouncing self-inspection.

THE MIRROR SPEAKS OF SELF-SCRUTINY. We are constantly holding up the mirror to our inner life, studying its mechanism and operations. Our fingers often on our pulse; the attention of the soul turned back on itself; the study of symptoms carried to the grievous extent of inducing the diseases which we dread. Of course, where there is evident mischief at work, we do well to take heed; but we must guard against a morbid self-anatomy, a perpetual analysis of motive and intention, an inwardness which diverts our attention from the person of Christ and the performance of duty.

THE EVILS OF SELF-SCRUTINY. If we look down into the depths of our own nature, we miss the face of Jesus. To consider self is to become involved in a maze of perplexities and disappointments. The disease cannot be cured by ceaselessly pondering its symptoms. The soul cannot lift the soul. Self can never expel the spirit of self.

ITS CURE. These women became so interested in the service of the Tabernacle that they were weaned from their mirrors. The better expelled the worse; the higher cast out the lower. Go out of yourself, find some work to do for God and man; seek in the laver the removal of the stains of human sin; find your centre in God and his plans; and you will abandon the habit of morbid self-scrutiny. For every look at self, take ten at Christ: He "healeth all thy diseases."

Holy to the Lord. Exod. 39: 30 (R.V.)
ZECHARIAH tells us that these words were to be written on the bells of the horses. The sacred inscription, which stood on the brow of Aaron, designating his separation to his sublime office, was to become incorporated with the business of the farm and city, where burdens were borne and heavy weights drawn with difficulty. The inscription befits all bells that ring in the home, the shop, the factory. We are to be God's priests everywhere.

THE PRIEST WAS SEPARATED FROM ALL IMPURITY. We must be in the world, but separate from its sin. When evil threatens us from a distance, we must be sensitive to its approach, and quick to put the covering presence of Christ between.

THE PRIEST WAS SEPARATED TO HOLY SERVICE.

He was keenly sensitive to the honour of Jehovah, and to the demands of his service. Rather be cut down at his altar, like Zechariah the son of Berachiah, than prove a delinquent. We cannot all do the inner service of offering incense and of blessing men, but we can render every act as a sacred service to God; always treading the holy floor, and within sight of the holy presence, and within earshot of the divine voice; eating, drinking, doing everything for the glory of God. Throughout this chapter we are reminded that all was made as the Lord commanded Moses; this should be the law of our life.

THE PRIEST BORE HOLINESS WRITTEN WHERE ALL COULD READ IT; SO SHOULD WE. It should not be necessary for us to be labelled. For men to need telling that we are Christians, is a sign that we are far from what we should be. But so to live that the first and slightest glance at us should betray our heavenly calling, is to adorn the Gospel and please our Master.

The cloud of the Lord by day, . . . and there was fire therein by night. Exod. 40: 38 (R.V.) THIS was the cloud of the Shechinah, in the heart of which was fire, the symbol of the presence of God. Probably this fire was always present, but only visible against the background of the surrounding darkness. In the New Testament fire is always associated with the ministry of the Holy Spirit; and in Isaiah (4: 5) we learn that in the coming time God would give, on every dwelling-place in Mount Zion, and in all her assemblies, the same cloud of smoke by day, and flaming fire by night, as had been vouchsafed to the Tabernacle where God dwelt. What a glorious revelation is this!

THE HOLY SPIRIT BROODING OVER EACH INDIVIDUAL BELIEVER. It is a symptom of the highest life, when God spreads his tabernacle over the soul. We should march only when He lifts up his enfolding presence, rest under his canopy, and recognize the sanctity of all life.

THE HOLY SPIRIT RESTING ON EACH HOME. "Every dwelling-place in Zion" must stand for the homes of God's people. How blessed it is when the home is a temple, and each inmate of the beloved circle a priest! Such homes are rare, but they are possible. Let those who are founding a new family make this their ideal.

THE HOLY SPIRIT DIRECTING AND FILLING EACH ASSEMBLY AND BELIEVER. As of old the movements of the cloud determined those of the tent and people, so in the Pentecostal Church the Spirit was Guide, Director, Executor. "Separate Me . . . to the work to which I have called them." We must rely most absolutely on Him, waiting for his initiation, his teaching, the settling down of his infinite benediction. Then there will be glory and defence.

Leviticus

A sweet savour unto the Lord. Lev. 1: 9, 13, 17. HOW sweet the offering up of the Son was to the Father! "Christ also hath loved us, and hath given Himself for us an offering and a sacrifice to God for a sweet-smelling savour" (Eph. 5: 2). The burnt-offering was an imperfect type of his entire devotion to his Father's will. When Jesus saw the inability of man to keep the holy law, and volunteered to magnify it, and make it honourable; when He laid aside his glory, and stepped down from his throne, saying, "I delight to do thy will, O my God"; when He became obedient even to the death of the cross—it was as sweet to God as the fragrance of a garden of flowers to us.

Let us never forget the Godward aspect of the cross. The sacrificial fire fed on every part of the sacrifice, on the inwards as well as the carcase; so did the Holy God delight to witness the spotless and entire devotion of the Son to the great work in which the entire Godhead was most deeply interested. The fragrant graces of Christ were made manifest on the cross, and are perpetuated in his intercession.

There is a sense also in which our consecration to God is fragrant and precious. When we see his claims, and yield to them; when we submit to his will, and commit our lives wholly to his direction; when we offer and present ourselves to Him, a living sacrifice, keeping nothing back—his heart is gladdened, and his fire of complacency feeds on our act. Always count on this; you may feel no thrill, and see no light, but reckon on God, believe that He accepts what you give, and will crown your sacrifice with the fire of Pentecost. Who to-day will surrender to God, and become an offering of a sweet savour?

Fine flour, and He shall pour oil upon it and put frankincense thereon. Lev. 2: 1.

THIS type is only true in its fullest extent of the blessed Master; but as we are to be conformed to his image, we may humbly take the ingredients of the meat offering as indicating various qualities in our personal character and behaviour.

FINE FLOUR. There should be nothing coarse-grained or rough to the touch; but all even and tender. So that however great the pressure brought to bear on us, we should meet it with perfect grace and gentleness. Jesus reviled not again, but was led as a lamb to the slaughter. David Livingstone said that the promise of Christ was the word of a perfect gentleman. This should be our character.

OIL UPON IT. We must be mingled with oil—that is, the Holy Spirit must have access into the secret places of the inner life, and we must have the anointing of the Holy Ghost for service. In Christian work nothing is of any value or permanence, useful to man or pleasing to God, in which the Holy Spirit is not first.

FRANKINCENSE. Every act of our life should emit sweet fragrance towards God. Always moving forward in Christ's triumphant procession, bearing aloft the incense—bowls of thought, action, word, filled with love and praise.

SALT. "Let your conversation be always with grace, seasoned with salt." The words of Jesus were full of grace, and also of truth. There was a pungency and purity and un-corruptness in his speech, which have in every age arrested the progress of the world's evil. Let us give Him our lips.

NO LEAVEN—the symbol of the rising of pride and self.

NO HONEY—that which is merely attractive and sensuous.

A sacrifice of Peace-offering. Lev. 3: 1.

IN the burnt-offering the priest burnt all; but in the peace-offering a part only was burnt, "the fat, kidneys, and caul." The inner parts were consumed as God's portion whilst Aaron and his sons fed on the breast and the shoulder. In that feast God and the priests participated; and it is an emblem of our participation in the joy of God, over the person and work of Jesus.

Think of this blessed feast with God. We who were once far off in the wicked and hostile imaginings, are now made nigh; we sit at God's table as his children, and hear Him say, Let us make merry and be glad; this my son was dead, and is alive again.

WE HAVE PEACE WITH GOD. We are justified by faith in Jesus. In Him we stand before God, accepted and beloved. The curse is exchanged for blessing; distance for presence; the husks of the swine for the fatted calf. The past is for ever under the blood; above us is the clear heaven of God's love.

WE HAVE THE PEACE OF GOD. The very peace that fills our Father's heart, undisturbed by the storms of care and strife which sweeps this lower world, is ours also. We sit in heavenly places; his peace, like a sentry, keeps our hearts and minds against molesta-tion; the peace of God rules in us bringing every thought into subjection to itself. We have perfect peace because our mind is stayed on Him.

WE HAVE THE GOD OF PEACE. According to the Apostle's fervent hope and prayer, He is with us. Not the gift, but the Giver; not I, but He; not the river only, but the source. We may well open our doors to admit such a guest, in having whom we receive the Author and Giver of concord, unity, and unbroken rest.

If a soul shall sin through ignorance. Lev. 4: 2.

SIN is something more than that of which our conscience convicts us. Our conscience may excuse or palliate our sins, or may fail to detect them for want of proper enlightenment, or may be misled by the practices and senti-ments of those around. Therefore we may do things which are grievously wrong in God's sight without realizing their evil or bemoaning it.

All such sin must be met and atoned for ere God can admit us into his holy presence. Sin must be dealt with and put away, not only as it appears to us, but as it is in itself and in the sight of the All-Holy. So, in the types of Leviticus, provision was made for sins of ignorance; and the blood of Jesus cleanseth from all sin, whether known to us or not.

There is more sin in us than any of us know. If we think we have passed a day without conscious sin, we have only to wait till an intenser light is flashed on our motives and intentions—for firelight to be exchanged for electric light—and we shall see specks and flaws. If we do not actually violate known commands, there may be a grievous coming short of the infinite standard of the divine perfection. Who shall dare to say that he has loved God with all his heart, and soul, and strength? Besides, there is always the liability to sinfulness; and this needs to be perpetually met and atoned for.

It is very needful, then, for us to be perpetually cleansed in the precious blood of Christ. We must ask to be forgiven for the many sins which we know not, as well as for those we know. The work of confession and forgiveness must therefore go on to life's end, applied to each heart and conscience by the Holy Spirit.

He shall confess that wherein he hath sinned, and bring his Guilt-offering. Lev. 5: 5, 6 (R.V.)
IT is said that sometimes a soldier will come from the battle bleeding from a hidden wound which he has received without knowing it. So in the rush of life we may contract defilement by touching uncleanness, or speaking rashly, which in the sight of God will leave a foul stain upon the white robe of the soul.

The presence of unconscious sin with us is the reason why we are often unable to pray or read the Word of God at night. We are aware of a certain distance, a veil, a cloud, which has settled down between us and the beatific vision. At such times we do well to examine ourselves and the past more critically; for probably we shall be able to detect the hidden cause, which, when we know it, must be confessed and placed on the head of our guilt-offering, whilst we yield ourselves to God as a whole burnt-offering, in a new act of self-surrender.

But confession is all important. We must confess our sins, if the faithful Lord is to forgive them. Confession is taking God's side against ourselves. It is the act of judging evil in the light of the Throne. It is like the unpacking of a box, in which one begins with the lighter things at the top, and works steadily down to the heavy articles underneath. It is the repetition in the heart of Joshua's calling the roll of Israel until Achan, the son of Carmi, was taken.

When the atonement has been made as touching sin "in any of these things," there is forgiveness. Dare to believe that this is so, O penitent soul, who hast made Christ's soul an offering for thy sin. He says: "I have blotted out, as a thick cloud, thy transgressions, and as a cloud thy sins." Go thy way, and sin no more.

Fire shall be kept burning upon the altar continually; it shall not go out. Lev. 6: 13 (R.V.)
THIS is an emblem of the perpetual work of God for man.

THE LOVE OF GOD. There never was a time when God did not love. The bush that Moses saw gave no fuel to maintain the holy flame that trembled around it, because the love of God to Israel and to the human race demands no sustenance. Through the ages it burns and will burn; however much indifference and neglect and rejection are heaped upon it, or poured over it, like barrels of water over Elijah's sacrifice, it never goes out. It is as fresh and vigorous to-day as ever, and waits to consume your sin and mine; for God is a consuming fire.

THE INTERCESSION OF CHRIST. As the ages pass, this sacrifice retains its merit. What He did as Priest on the cross, He does as Priest on the throne. It is always "this same Jesus." What He was, He is, and will be; and as generations of saints bring their gifts to the altar, He takes them, and lifts them up to God, as the fire bears up the substances which are submitted to it. He ever liveth to make intercession; and the fire that burnt through the long night in the Tabernacle bore witness to the undimming, unwaning virtue of our Saviour's work.

THE MINISTRY OF THE HOLY GHOST. The fire that was lit on the Day of Pentecost burns still in the Church. There has been no intermission to its presence from the first day till now. Multitudes of unknown sects and persecuted saints have kept that fire burning in the world. On the perpetuity of its existence in our midst depends the constancy of our own love and purity and prayer. If the fire shall never go out in our hearts; if the life in our spirits is indeed everlasting—it is because He lives and loves always.

Every one that is clean shall eat thereof.
Lev. 7: 19 (R.V.)

IN verse 13, it is admitted that leaven must be present in this holy feast, inasmuch as it stands for the essential principle of evil, which intrudes into our holiest worship. The self-life is an all-pervasive leaven. We may not be conscious of it; there may be no sufficient recognition of its distastefulness to the holy God: but it follows us even into the Holy place.

The worshipper was not allowed, however, to be knowingly unclean. There must be no stain on the conscience, which he might remove by confession and repentance. If there were, he must be cut off; that is, he must be debarred from all participation in holy rites, and suspended from entering the sacred enclosure of the Tabernacle.

This cutting off answers to the suspension of a believer's communion with God, because of unconfessed sin. The presence of the leaven of the self-life is no barrier to the enjoyment of the divine fellowship, for we meet God in Jesus. But permitted sin makes such fellowship impossible, because we have not availed ourselves of the gracious arrangements made by God for the perpetual cleansing of the soul in the precious blood of Jesus Christ. For "it is the blood that maketh an atonement for the soul."

How many excommunicate Christians there are. You can easily see that they have been cut off; their joyless faces and powerless prayers, their inability to bear testimony for God—all tell the sad story. If you have been cut off, search your past history to discover the cause. Put away your sin, and seek the blessed cleansing of John 13; then come to feast with God, in holy communion, as at a common table.

Ye shall not go out. Lev. 8: 33.

FOR seven days Aaron and his sons, newly consecrated by the blood and oil, waited together in the Holy Place. They were prohibited from going beyond the door, but fed on the consecrated food till the eighth day summoned them to begin their priestly duties. Similarly we are shut in with our Great Aaron, the High Priest of our profession. We are in Christ in the purposes of God, for we were chosen in Him before the foundation of the world. We are in Him, as Noah was in the ark, and as the child is in the home; as the member is in the body, and the branch in the vine; as the sponge in the ocean, or the jewel in the sunbeam. We are in Him as a strong enclosure, through which the malice and strength of our foes cannot break —a fortress, a strong tower, a castle keep. We are in Him, as a banqueting-hall, a Tabernacle with its shew-bread, an upper room with its descending fire.

It is highly necessary that we should maintain our walk and experience on this blessed elevation. The great enemy of our souls is perpetually tempting us to leave our abiding-place, and to try issues with him in the plains beneath. What is temptation but his subtle solicitation to come out from the secret place of the Most High. Beware! the bait may be very attractive, but the end is death. Keep the charge of the Lord, and abide day and night in the company of the Great High Priest. "He shall dwell among them."

On what viands do such happy souls feast with Christ! A table is provided before them by the Lord Himself, and they feast on all that pertains to Him in blessed partnership. "Son, thou art ever with Me, and all that I have is thine."

Aaron lifted up his hand toward the people, and blessed them. Lev. 9: 22.

THE eighth day is evidently the type of the bright millennial morning. During the present age we are hidden with Christ in God; the world knoweth us not, as it knew Him not; our hopes, and joys, and aims, are largely secret. But the day is not far distant when He shall be manifested, and then we shall be manifested with Him in glory. That group of priests, following the high priest out from the recesses of the Holy Place, is a picture of the Second Advent, when Christ and his own shall come forth to bless the world. When Jesus was parted in the Ascension from his disciples, He was in the act of blessing them; and in that attitude He will return. Who can doubt that all through the intervening ages those blessed hands have still been outstretched, that heart ever going forth, in blessing.

What a Saviour is ours! In Him are combined meekness that bears all insult and hatred, and mercy that retaliates on wrongdoing in ministries of love. He fulfils his own idea of blessing those that hate, and praying for those that despitefully use. How truly can it be said of Him, as of Archbishop Ussher, that to do him a wrong is to make him your friend for ever!

Let us imitate Him in this, and let the going forth of our lives be one incessant stream of benediction to men, until they shall fall on their faces and acknowledge the overwhelming power of love. But in order to do this we must be much in company with our blessed Lord; gazing on his face we shall reflect his likeness; the lineaments of the divine beauty shall pass into our life, and light it up with a loveliness which is not of earth. Thus shall we bring glory to our God.

Aaron held his peace. Lev. 10:3.

HIS heart must have been rent with paroxysms of grief, as he beheld the bodies of his beloved sons on the floor of the Tabernacle, stretched out in death. He repressed the cry, choked back the sob, staunched the flowing tear, and continued to perform the holy duties with which he was charged. He was no stoic, and tears are not wrong for our dead; but his relationship to God was so overmastering as to still the expressions of nature.

HE SAW THE WRONG FROM GOD'S STANDPOINT. It was of great importance that the divine regulations and enactments should be maintained, and that the ministering priests should always prefer God's work and service above their own ideas. Aaron was able to appreciate that position, and saw the sin of which his children were guilty. They had forgotten the voice which said, Sanctify thou Me. Obedience is the foundation of reverence, honour, and service; and if it were relaxed with the priests, how for the people! How careful they should be who bear the vessels of the Lord! With what fear and trembling must they work, who work with God!

HE ACQUIESCED IN THE DIVINE DEALINGS. To take the yoke, and meekly bear it; to put the hand on the mouth, and bow in the dust—this is rest and peace. In this way we drink Christ's cup and become partakers of his sufferings.

HE FELT THAT HIS WORK AS PRIEST MUST TAKE PRECEDENCE. It was a solemn and awful thing to be God's anointed priest, and the office must come first, even to the denial of the dues of nature, if that were necessary: so always with us, there must be the subordination of everything to our service and work for God.

Whatsoever parteth the hoof and cheweth the cud. Lev. 11:3 (R.V.)

THE animals, in which these two characteristics met, were reckoned clean, and therefore fit for food. It is certain that the minute particularity of these words has some further reference than to the diet of Israel, important though that was, or to accentuate with every meal the necessity of their being a separate people. We, at least, may gather this lesson, that in our daily experience we must combine meditation and separation.

MEDITATION. The cattle do not simply browse on the pastures, but they lie down to chew the cud. It is not enough to peruse our allotted Scripture portion; we must ruminate upon it, comparing spiritual things with spiritual, and scripture with scripture. The Holy Ghost will take of the things of Christ and show them unto us, and He will bring all things to our remembrance.

SEPARATION. "Whosoever doeth not righteousness is not of God." "The Word of God is quick, and powerful, and sharper than any two-edged sword, piercing even to the dividing asunder of soul and spirit, and of the joints and marrow, and is a discerner of the thoughts and intents of the heart." We have not meditated to good purpose unless we have felt its keen edge. Detachment from the world must follow on true attachment to Christ. Love to Naomi will draw Ruth from Moab across the Jordan.

THE TWO MUST BE COMBINED. The swine divideth the hoof, but cheweth not the cud, and was therefore unclean. A man may profess to love his Bible, but the supreme test is his daily separation from evil. On the other hand, our daily life ought to emanate, not from without, which is Pharisaism, but from within, where we chew the cud of holy meditation.

Two young pigeons. Lev. 12:8.

THESE were the offerings of the poor, of those whose means did not suffice to buy a lamb. All these offerings pointed to the one

great Sacrifice which was to be offered on
Calvary.

THE BLOOD OF CHRIST IS WITHIN THE REACH
OF THE POOREST AND FEEBLEST. None can say
that it is beyond them, that they cannot
afford to procure it, that they are too poor.
To the poor the Gospel is preached. The
divine call is to those who have no money.
Salvation is to him that worketh not, but
believeth on Him that justifies the ungodly.
"It is nigh thee."

THE FAITH THAT APPREHENDS BUT A PART
OF THE SAVIOUR'S WORK SAVES. The pigeon
may stand for the meagre apprehension of
Christ that is the portion of the faltering and
timid; but it saves equally with that fuller
conception of his saving work, which might
be compared to the bullock of the priest.
The question is not as to the quantity but the
object of faith. Is it fixed on Jesus? All faith
directed to Him cannot but be genuine. It may
but touch his garment's hem, yet it saves.

THE BENEFICENCE OF GOD'S LAW. What
tender touches there are through this strong
ancient code! There is such a one here,
framed partly in anticipation of the mother
of our Lord, who gladly availed herself of its
provision. What a glimpse into our Master's
humiliation! He owned the cattle on a
thousand hills, yet He so emptied Himself
that his parents were compelled to bring the
poorest offering the law allowed. He stooped
that we might rise; emptied Himself that we
might be full; became poor that we might
be made rich; was made human that we
might be made divine.

*Behold, if the leprosy have covered all his flesh,
he shall pronounce him clean.* Lev. 13: 13.
AT first sight this seems a very extraordinary
provision. When the leprosy was beginning
to show itself, and whilst the marks were
hardly distinguishable, the poor patient was
treated as unclean; but, when it was fully
developed, from the crown of the head to the
sole of the foot, the priest pronounced the
leper clean.

As long as we palliate and excuse our sins,
and dream that there is much in us which is
noble and lovely, we are not fit subjects for
God's saving grace. But when we take our
place as helpless and undone, without one
plea or one redeeming trait, we are in the
position in which the free grace of God can
have its blessed way with us.

We must come to an end of ourselves, and
fall prostrate, in the very helplessness of our
despair, in the very dust at our Saviour's
feet; we must confess that from the crown of
our head to the sole of our foot we are full
of need and sin—then we are nearest Christ,
and in a fit condition to be richly blest, and
made the channel of blessing to others.

Would you rise? then you must humble
yourself before God. God's thrones are
approached, not by steps up to them, but by
steps down to them. It is the publican who
beats his breast, saying, "God be merciful to
me the sinner," that goes down justified to
his house. It is when sin abounds, that grace
much more abounds. He that humbleth
himself shall be exalted. "For thus saith the
high and lofty One that inhabiteth eternity,
whose name is Holy: I dwell in the high and
holy place, with him also that is of a contrite
and humble spirit, to revive the spirit of the
humble, and to revive the heart of the contrite
ones" (Isa. 57: 15).

Shall let go the living bird into the open field.
Lev. 14: 7 (R.V.)
THAT is thou, O trembling soul. Thine
iniquities have come between thee and
freedom, like the bars of a cage to a bird
caught from its native woods and imprisoned.
See the quickly-palpitating breast, beaten
against the bars, pining for the open field—is
not that an apt symbol of thy deep yearning
for deliverance from the tyranny and thrall
of besetting sin?

WE ARE MADE FREE FROM THE PENALTY OF
SIN THROUGH THE BLOOD OF HIM WHO DIED.
One of the birds was killed in an earthen
vessel over running water—here is symbolized
the precious death of thy Saviour, in the
earthen vessel of his human nature, and in
connection with the living power of the Holy
Spirit, which bore forth the tidings into all
the world. We have dipped into the crimson
tide and are freed—as the leper was—from
the taint of our disease. He might go freely
among men, and join the congregation of
worshippers: and we may mingle with the
saints, and enter the very presence-chamber
of God.

WE ARE MADE FREE FROM THE POWER OF
SIN THROUGH THE GRACE OF HIM WHO ROSE.
He has passed into the resurrection life, and
we in Him. When He rose through all the
heavens to his native home, we ascended too.

We are made free from the thraldom of evil by identification with the risen Lord; and the Holy Spirit, entering our hearts from our exalted Head, makes us possessors of all the privileges which are ours in the divine purpose (Rom. 8: 3, 4). Fly away, happy soul, to thy nest in the heart of God! Seek those things which are above! It is your privilege to live in the heavenlies with Christ. Sursum Corda!

He that 'toucheth . . . shall be unclean. Lev. 15: 7.

THERE were doubtless great sanitary reasons for many of these enactments. This book is one of the greatest sanitary codes in existence. God made religious duty enforce regulations essential to the physical health and well-being of his people. But there were deeper reasons yet. The whole of these arrangements were contrived to teach profound lessons to us all of the nature and evil of sin, and of the need of being continually cleansed in the precious blood of Jesus Christ.

THE UNCLEAN SOUL SPREADS UNCLEANNESS. Whatever the ceremonially unclean touched, used, or sat on, was polluted. Even those who came into contact with him were defiled. How wary all true Israelites must have been of their associates, lest they should contract pollution! Let us adopt similar precautions, and not voluntarily associate with the unholy or unclean. And if our business calls us into their daily company, let us seek cleansing for ourselves as we return to our homes, that any adhering germs of evil may be removed.

THE URGENT DEMAND FOR HOLINESS. The ordinary processes of life are not necessarily clean because they are natural. The foul heart may vitiate the most natural functions. We must bring the thought of God into the simplest, the commonest, and the most secret acts. Nothing is outside his jurisdiction. Though hid from sight, yet He is ever near the child of God. His grace, and blood, and cleansing, are always requisite, and ever ready. Amidst and after every act, incident, and episode of life, we should be quiet before God, considering if we have aught to confess, and asking to be ever kept from staining our white robes.

Unto a solitary land. Lev. 16: 22 (R.V.)

THIS chapter is full of Christ in his most precious death for men. Its various aspects are set forth under these diverse sacrifices, as light reflected from the many facets of a diamond. We think now only of the live goat which was led away into the wilderness. We see in it:

CHRIST MADE SIN. With both hands Aaron, in symbol, transferred all the iniquities, sins, and transgressions of the people to the head of the goat, which became so identified with them that it was accounted an unclean thing; and even he who led it away must needs wash his clothes and bathe. This is what the apostle means when he says that Jesus was made sin for us. Our sins met in Him; were assumed by Him; He stood before God as though, in some mysterious sense, they were his own.

CHRIST BEARING SIN AWAY. As the goat went away, the eyes of the people followed it, and they were taught to believe that sin was no longer reckoned to them. Aaron put off his linen garments and arrayed himself in festal robes, and came forth to bless the congregation. What rejoicing must have broken from the crowds! So Jesus, in his matchless grace, has borne away the sin of the world into a land of forgetfulness. "Their sins and iniquities will I remember no more."

CHRIST'S LONELINESS. He was alone in his mediatorial work. None could bear Him company. Loved ones might stand beside his cross, or in after ages suffer, as He did, deaths of martyrdom; but none could do what He did as the sacrifice for sin. Ah, how lonely He was! Even the Father seemed to have forsaken Him! Before the universe in that dread hour, the Saviour stood in awful, unapproachable solitude!

The life of the flesh is in the blood. Lev. 17: 11.

THERE is probably a deeper truth in these words than man has ever fathomed. The R.V. marg. translates "life," soul. Why that reverence for blood; that horror when it is unrighteously shed and gurgles forth; that perpetual reference of Scripture to the blood of Christ? Probably the answer to such questions would be given, if we perfectly understood the affirmation of this remarkable verse.

WHEN JESUS GAVE HIS BLOOD, HE GAVE HIS LIFE, THE LIFE OF HIS HOLY SOUL. We are accustomed often to speak about the blood of Christ, by which we mean the life of Jesus, shed forth for us substitutionally and sacrificially. The sinner takes this blood, this life, in his hands, and presents it to God as his plea. Does the broken law require satisfaction, homage, acknowledgment? Here it is in this priceless, pure, and sinless blood, never infected by pollution, never heated by passion. Let this shed life atone for thee! "God be propitious (because of the sacrifice on the altar) to me the sinner."

> Five bleeding wounds He bears,
> Received on Calvary;
> They pour effectual prayers,
> They strongly plead for me:
> "Forgive him, oh, forgive," they cry,
> "Nor let that ransomed sinner die."

WHEN WE ARE BIDDEN DRINK HIS BLOOD, IT IS OF HIS LIFE THAT WE PARTAKE. At the table of our Lord we symbolically drink of his blood; in doing this we identify ourselves with his death, and give up our self-life to the cross. Yea, we do more; we testify our desire to receive into our natures more and more of the soul and life of our Blessed Lord, so that we may dwell in Him, and He in us.

Therefore shall ye keep My Charge. Lev. 18: 30
(R.V.)
LITERAL obedience was God's perpetual demand of his chosen people. Why should we claim to be exonerated from an equally exact obedience to the commands of Jesus? And yet how few of us do exactly as He has bidden! Let us take some tests.

THE LORD'S SUPPER is a case in point. In the present day there are many who, from year's end to year's end, never go to the Table, though Jesus said that his disciples were to do it in remembrance of Him.

BAPTISM is another. Christians shelter themselves under the excuse that it is not essential, and therefore may be omitted. But what do they mean by essential? It is not essential to salvation, because that has been achieved by our Lord; but it may be essential to show that we love Him, that we have a genuine faith, that we are ready to take Him as King. Surely a soldier is not freed from obeying the command of his officer because he cannot see it to be essential!

GOING TO LAW is another. If there is one thing clearer than others, it is the reiterated charge of the New Testament that we should rather suffer wrong than avenge ourselves. Yet how many professing Christians will this day issue a County Court summons against defaulters!

FORGIVENESS is another. "If ye forgive not men their trespasses, neither will your Father forgive your trespasses.' Yet there are hundreds of Christ's professing followers who are at feud with their relatives or fellow-members.

Let us remember the imperative tone of these words, and ask God to work in us to will and to do of his good pleasure.

I am the Lord your God. Lev. 19: 3.
THIS is the refrain of the entire chapter; count how many times it recurs. Evidently the thought of God should ring out in our lives, as a perpetual chime.

Sometimes as an inspiration to duty. We should seek to be holy because He is holy. "Imitators of God." Or as a remonstrance against yielding to temptation. Lo, God is in this place; his pure eye is upon me: how can I do this great wickedness! Or as an incentive to liberality. We can afford to be generous to the poor and hireling, because we are children of so great and rich a parent. Or as a reason for mercy and gentle kindness. How can we act otherwise than lovingly, when his love encompasses us with its persuasive bands?

Thus the perpetual consciousness of God becomes the source of holy and happy living. But how may it become ours? We may make many resolutions, only to break them. We forget after our most definite purposing. There is no help but in the Holy Spirit, whose office it is to teach us all things, and bring all things to our remembrance. He is able also to help our infirmity: "for we know not how to pray as we ought; but the Spirit Himself maketh intercession for us with groanings which cannot be uttered."

In the morning let the thought of God's presence with you in your secret closet sink well into your heart. Wait till his presence is made real to you, and you cry, Lo, God is here. Then entrust yourself to the Holy Spirit, asking Him to keep you in the current of the love and thought of God. Reckon on Him to do so. Now and then in the course of daily duty stop and remember God. Thus you will live in his fear and love all the day long.

I have separated you from the peoples, that ye should be Mine. Lev. 20: 26 (R.V.)

"SEPARATE me Barnabas and Saul," said the Holy Ghost. And in after days Paul spoke of himself as being separated unto the Gospel of God. It is a mistake to make the act of separation our own resolve and deed. We shall inevitably drop back unless God has come into the transaction, and has set us apart for Himself. We must be separated from sin and sinners unto a holy God.

WE ARE NEEDED FOR A SPECIFIC PURPOSE. God can bless men only through men. As once He used the Jews to be the medium of communicating his truth to men, so now He is eager to use his Church; if only she will allow Him to deliver her from the taint of sin and the world, and separate her for a peculiar possession unto Himself. Let us individually yield ourselves to the blessed influences of the Holy Spirit, that He may realize in us the purpose for which He has called us.

WE ARE REQUIRED TO SATISFY GOD'S HEART. He needs love for love. Throughout the world He seeks for those who can afford Him pleasure, as his enclosed gardens, his sealed fountains, his peculiar treasure.

THIS SEPARATION IS EFFECTED BY THE HOLY GHOST, and is referred to in the word "sealing." "He hath sealed us unto the day of redemption."

What an honour is this! To be for God Himself: to do his errands, to fulfil his behests and give Him pleasure! Rejoice greatly when God says, "Thou art mine." We also can take up his words, and answer back, "Thou also art mine." Let us be glad, if we know that the oil of separation has come on our heads, and let us walk worthily of our high calling, separated to the Holy Ghost, and counting it sacrilege to be used for any unholy purpose.

I the Lord, which Sanctify you. Lev. 21: 8, 15, 23.

THIS chapter is full of restrictions and cautions against anything that might defile the priests, the sons of Aaron. The holiness of God was set in a clear light by the care that there should be no ceremonial pollution or personal defect in those who ministered before his presence. What Aaron and his sons were in the ancient typical worship, that Jesus and his people are in the spiritual dispensation which has taken its place. "Ye are an elect race, a royal priesthood, a holy nation, a people for God's own possession."

How holy we should be "in all manner of living"! What may be innocent and natural for others would be wrong and inconsistent in us. Even the pointing of the beard after the fashion of the nations around, and for appearance' sake, was forbidden them; and contact with death in the home of domestic mourning. These, with many suchlike cautions, indicate that our spiritual separation for the service of God must enter into the minutest details. The clothes we wear, the books we read, the amusements we engage in, the details of the home-life—will all be affected by the thought, "I have been set apart for God; the anointing of the Spirit is on me; I am called to offer Him the bread of a holy life; I may not do as others, who have not realized the sacredness of life, as I do; and who may permit without compunction what I forgo."

This is a high ideal; and it is only practicable to those who realize the thrice-made announcement of our text, that God will sanctify us: setting us apart for Himself—by the precious blood of Christ, by the anointing of the Spirit, and by the separation of our thoughts, and aims, and practices.

He shall not eat of the holy things till he be clean. Lev. 22: 4.

THE holy things referred to here are the offerings made by Israel to Jehovah, a part of which was presented to God in fire, and the rest partaken of by the priests and their families. None, however, might feed on them whilst ceremonially unclean. This suggests some useful precautions for ourselves, if we would fully enjoy the privileges and blessings attending the worship of the holy God.

WE MUST BE CLEAN BEFORE WE CAN ENJOY THE PRIVATE READING OF THE WORD OF GOD. We would wash our hands, soiled with the dust and grime of toil, before opening an exquisitely printed copy of the Scriptures; how much more should we seek cleansing at the hands of Christ before we feed on the holy things of Scripture!

WE MUST BE CLEAN BEFORE ENTERING THE HOUSE OF GOD. It is a holy habit for each intending worshipper to be quiet before leaving the house on the Lord's day; or to use carefully the moment of the bent head at the commencement of the public service, in order that the soul may be made clean from any contracted stain, and resolve henceforth to abstain from all evil.

WE MUST BE CLEAN BEFORE PARTAKING OF THE LORD'S SUPPER. There we feed upon the bread of God; and as we wash our hands before we sit at the table of a friend, so should our hearts be cleansed ere we partake of the emblems of the body and blood of Christ. Holiness becomes God's house. Those that ascend the hill of the Lord must have clean hands and a pure heart. The reason why religious exercises do not profit you, may lie in your failure to comply with this demand. "He shall not eat of the holy things until he be clean."

Ye shall afflict your souls. Lev. 23: 27, 29, 32.
WHILST Aaron was making the solemn atonement for the people, confessing their sins on the victims and sending them away, the camp was pervaded with the atmosphere of the Sabbath rest. No servile work was done on penalty of death. Probably for the most part the people abode in their tents. No sound was heard save sighs, and groans and cries of penitence. The people afflicted themselves for their sins.

SIN IS FORGIVEN BY GOD, BUT IT SHOULD NOT BE FORGOTTEN BY US. We should remember it, in order to refresh our memory of God's great grace in putting it away; in order to deepen our sense of gratitude and to promote our self-humiliation; in order to make us watchful and careful in our daily walk and conversation. Holding the hand of our Saviour, we need not dread to look down into the abyss from which He has redeemed us. We shall turn from it to Him with tenderer love and gratitude.

REPENTENCE IS ONCE FOR ALL; PENITENCE IS PERENNIAL. We repent when we turn from the kingdom of darkness to that of God's dear Son; it is the act of the will, the utter reversal of the course we had been pursuing. But we are penitent after we have seen the face of Jesus: it is the act of emotions; the sense of Christ's love and of our unworthiness together makes us weep, as the forgiven sinner did at his feet.

PENITENCE DOES NOT PURCHASE FORGIVE-NESS, BUT ACCOMPANIES AND FOLLOWS IT. Could our tears for ever flow, they could not bring God's pardon into our souls. That is secured by the offering of our Substitute on Calvary. But being forgiven, we wash his feet with our tears, we break our alabaster boxes on his head, and love much.

Before the Lord continually. Lev. 24: 4-8.
THE light of the candlestick and the twelve cakes of fine flour were to be before the Lord continually, as symbols of the twofold office his people were to sustain, on the one hand to the world's darkness, on the other to God Himself.

WE MUST SHINE AS LIGHTS IN THE WORLD. As a candle in the hand of the housewife, who sweeps her house diligently; as a lamp in the hand of the virgin expecting the bridegroom; or as the lighthouse on a rocky coast. We must dispel the darkness, and guide wanderers through the murky night. Light is soft and still, and is thus a fitting emblem of the influence of a holy life, which burns steadily on before the Lord continually, and is unaffected by the heed or comment of man. If no one seems the better for our consistent testimony, aim to satisfy the Lord. The lamps of the pure candlestick of a holy life are not for man only, but for Him. But they can only be maintained through the constant supply of the pure oil of the Holy Ghost, ministered by Him who walks amid the seven golden candlesticks. "Ye are the light of the world."

WE MUST BE AS BREAD TO GOD. In a blessed sense we feed on God, but God also feeds on us. He finds satisfaction in beholding his people's unity and love, in receiving their sacrifices of praise, and in watching their growing conformity to his will. The two rows of six cakes foreshadow the unity and order of the Church; the fine flour, its holy, equable character; the pure frankincense, the fragrance of Christian love. There is a testimony in all these to the world; but we do not always realize the satisfaction afforded to the great God, who has made such costly sacrifices on behalf of his Church.

His kinsman that is next to him. Lev. 25: 25
(R.V.)
IN the case of Naomi this was Boaz; in our case it is Jesus Christ. Redemption, as described in this chapter, had to do with persons and lands; and each illustrates Christ's work on behalf of believers throughout all ages.

HE HAS REDEEMED OUR PERSONS. It often happened that a Hebrew waxed poor, and was compelled to sell himself to some wealthy Gentile who sojourned in the land. He who had owned his own patrimony now wrought as a bondservant for another. But after he had sold himself he might be redeemed by his next kinsman. So we had sold ourselves for nought; we wrought the will of the flesh; we were enslaved to the fashions of the world; we obeyed the promptings of the prince of the power of the air. Alas for us! But we have been redeemed, not with corruptible things, but with the precious blood of Christ. We have been made free by right, and have only to claim and act upon the freedom with which the risen Christ has made us free.

HE HAS REDEEMED OUR INHERITANCE. What we lost in the first Adam we have more than regained in the second. For innocence, we have purity; for external fellowship with God, his indwelling; for the delights of an earthly paradise, the fulness of God's blessedness and joy.

HE IS OUR NEAREST KINSMAN. "My brother, my sister," He says of each who will do the will of his Father. He has made Himself one with us by taking on Himself our nature, and identifying Himself with our race. We know that Jesus, our Göel and Redeemer, liveth; and that He will come to redeem us from the power of the grave, and receive us to Himself.

None shall make you afraid. Lev. 26: 6.

BUT we are afraid, often very greatly so. How can we be secured from the dread of men and things which so easily besets us?

WE MUST BE ABSOLUTELY RIGHT WITH GOD. To walk in God's statutes, and keep his commandments, was the first condition of Israel's immunity from fear. When we know that there is no cause of controversy between us and God, we feel able to count confidently on his protection and deliverance. "Perfect love casteth out fear."

WE MUST COUNT ON GOD'S FAITHFULNESS. He has put us where we are, and we dare not think He will withdraw from us, as Joab did from Uriah. We are his partners, summoned to co-operate with Him: will He allow us to incur responsibilities in his name, and then leave the burden on our unassisted resources? Fear will yield before a clear sense of God's might; but it is still more likely to yield before a deep sense of God's perfect faithfulness.

WE MUST RELY ON THE ENVIRONMENT OF ANGEL KEEPERS. When David, during his flight before Absalom, slept in the open, he believed that the Angel of the Lord encamped around him. More are they which are for us than those that be against us. The mountain is full of horses and chariots of fire. Lord, open our eyes that we may see!

WE MUST BELIEVE THAT OUR ENEMIES ARE LESS FORMIDABLE THAN THEY SEEM. They surround us with their bluster and threatenings, they come against us in embattled array; but if we dare to go forward and do the right thing in the sight of God, they will vanish like a puff of smoke. "For, lo, the kings assembled themselves. . . . They were arrayed, they were dismayed, they hasted away."

No devoted thing . . . shall be sold or redeemed.
Lev. 27: 28.

THERE is a great principle involved in these words. When once a person or possession had been solemnly dedicated to God, it was not permissible to withdraw from the obligations which had been assumed. Once given, the offering was regarded as God's property, and might not be resumed by the offerer, or placed to any inferior use.

This regulation is specially applicable to our conception and practice of consecration. We are Christ's: by the gift of the Father, by the purchase of the blood of Christ, by the sealing of the Spirit; but a moment often comes in the life of the earnest believer when the Lord appears to claim a more earnest recognition of his rightful claim. Then thoughtfully and earnestly, spirit, soul, and body, are laid upon the altar, and we solemnly declare, "I am thine, O Lord!"

When once this is done, we must reckon that God has accepted us, and that we cannot repeat the gift. We may perpetually refer to it, and acknowledge its abiding obligation, and apply its principle to all those new departments and functions which are perpetually increasing on us; but we can no more repeat it, than could the Israelite give God the firstling lamb, since it was already his (ver. 26).

If we go back from the attitude we have once taken up, we must confess our relapse with tears and deep contrition, asking to be restored, waiting to be put back again into the old place by our merciful and compassionate High Priest. We cannot undo that past; but we may ask Him to restore us to the place we occupied before we went astray. Oh that we might never withdraw from the altar of entire consecration!

Numbers

They declared their pedigrees. Num. 1: 18.
IT was not enough to be a true-born Israelite, a man must be able to show his descent. The genealogical tables were kept with the greatest care; and there was a holy pride in being able to vindicate the claim of having the blood of the patriarchs in the veins.

It is a blessed thing to be sure that we have passed from death unto life, and are the children of God by faith in Christ Jesus. True, our eternal destiny does not hinge on it. Many will doubtless be saved at last, who have spent their lives between hope and fear. But it is very needful for our comfort and growth in grace to be able to declare our pedigree, and to know that we have been translated into the Kingdom of God's dear Son.

The Gospel of John was written that we might believe; the Epistle that we might know. But many seek this knowledge in the wrong way, and are exposed to endless questionings. They try to discover the date, place, or experience in the past, when they were incorporated into the divine family; and because they cannot point to these, they imagine that they are still outside. Now for everyone that has had a definite experience of the new birth, there are perhaps a score who entered the divine family almost as a sailor passes the line of the Equator. Yet it is possible for you to know that you are born again, though you may not be able to tell your birthday.

If you are trusting Jesus, if the Spirit witnesses with your spirit that God is your Father, if you are full of a holy fear of grieving Him, if you are becoming like Him, if you love the brethren—you may certainly declare yourself his child.

The Children of Israel shall pitch every man by his own standard. Num. 2: 2-34 (R.V.)
OUR God is a God of order; and it was needful for the order of the camp, whether at rest or on the march, that each man should know his place, and keep to it. But though there were different standards and positions, there was one centre, the ark, and one host of redeemed men.

Each believer has an appointed place in the great army of God. It is indicated by the voice of God, and by the circumstances of our life; and it should be jealously retained. Repeatedly the Apostle bade his converts abide in the calling wherein they were called. Yours may be towards the bleak north of difficulty, or the warm south of privilege—in the home, the country parish, or the difficult foreign post. But, on the whole, you should stay where you are; unless the Captain of our salvation moves you by some unmistakable indication of his will. The apostle Paul ever lived in such dependence on the Holy Spirit for guidance, and for the unfolding of the divine purpose, that from some apparently trivial circumstance he would "gather" the movements of the pillar of cloud by day, and of fire by night. And interval there was none between his apprehension of the divine purpose and his endeavour to strike his tent and follow wherever it might lead (Acts 16: 6, 7).

The main point with us all is to face the ark, to which the doors of all the tents looked, so that we may ever catch the first symptom of the movement of the cloud. On the whole, we do best to pitch and fight under our own standards. There is a closer bond of brotherhood possible between those who think alike. But whilst we are positive in what we affirm for ourselves, let us not deny that other standards represent necessary aspects of the common faith.

Take the Levites instead. Num. 3: 45.
EACH first-born son was God's. On the day of the Exodus, as the first-born of Egypt were stricken, so the first-born of Israel were hallowed. God claimed the right of their

service in his Temple, to serve there as priests and attendants. But instead of them, He accepted the whole tribe of Levi; and for the overplus of first-born sons above the number of Levites, He accepted redemption money, which went to maintain Aaron and his family. Thus, each first-born son was represented, either by a substitute, or by a money payment.

AN APPEAL TO PARENTS. Would it not be a blessed custom if, in all our churches, the first-born child was, in a special sense, regarded as God's, and trained for some branch of his holy service in the home and foreign field? What a blessing would rest on our homes if this were the custom! It would lead to very definite prayer, that the young soul might be truly converted and led to realize the parents' ideal.

AN APPEAL TO FIRST-BORN CHILDREN. Either go yourself into the service of God, at home or abroad, or send a substitute. Consider yourself under obligation to do some special work for Christ and his Church. And if you cannot, earn money to support your representative. This is laying up treasure in heaven.

AN APPEAL TO FAMILIES. Why should not each Christian family become a missionary society, sending one of its members forth in the name of the rest, who should bind themselves solemnly to "hold the ropes;" and thus obey the Master's parting commission, "Go ye into all the world, and preach the gospel to every creature"?

Every one to his service and to his burden.
Num. 4: 19.

IS this what the Apostle referred to when he said that every man should bear his own burden? There are burdens which we cannot share or depute, to bear which we need special grace, and must continually seek the aid of the divine Spirit.

THE BURDEN OF OUR OWN EXISTENCE. Each of us must give an account of himself to God. We were created for a specific purpose; and our failure to fulfil it cannot be settled on another. God will require each man's soul of himself. "Every one of us shall give account of himself to God" (Rom. 14: 12). You have a charge to keep, a soul to save, and a God to glorify.

THE BURDEN OF OUR LIFE-WORK. What makest thou in the world? The Maker of all waits for thee to enter his great workshop

and become his apprentice and co-worker. To be an idler, or an absentee, will land thee in inevitable disgrace. The appointed place cannot be left vacant, and thy tools untouched, save at thy grave peril.

THE BURDEN OF THE SOULS OF OTHERS. We are our brothers' keepers, liable at any moment to be called upon to give an account of how they fare; and we cannot rid ourselves of this responsibility by annual donations or subscriptions to charitable or missionary institutions.

THE BURDEN OF DAILY INTERCESSION. Jesus bears the burdens of his people as He intercedes for them in heaven; and there is a sense in which we are called to bear up his hands in this holy service. We must consider the work of daily prayer for his Church, for sufferers, and for the world, as part of the burden of the Lord, allotted to us because we are members of his body.

Without the camp, . . . in the midst whereof I dwell. Num. 5: 3.

WHAT a sublime conception!—God dwelt with his people. The Tabernacle was his tent amongst theirs; the cloudy pillar was his ensign. To attack them was to come into collision with Him. All the expense and anxiety of the march rested on his shoulders, as the care of a family of young children on a father. How needful it was that nothing should be permitted which could grieve or offend Him!

What the camp of Israel was in those long-ago days, the Church is now. It is the host of the redeemed, the representative of God, the pilgrimage of the saints. Amongst his people God still walks, and dwells, and tabernacles. Their griefs, conflicts, and experiences, are shared by their ever-present Almighty Friend.

The presence of God in the Church is by the Holy Spirit. "Know ye not that ye are the temple of God, and that the Spirit of God dwelleth in you?" (1 Cor. 3: 16). He is with her and in her as the Body of which the risen Lord is Head. When the one Advocate went up, the other came down; when the Second Person in the Holy Trinity ascended to his throne, the Third Person came down to perpetuate his work in the world, through the Church. "He dwelleth with you, and shall be in you."

How careful should we be in the ordering

of our church-life, as well as of our individual lives, so that there may be nothing to offend Him! "What will the Holy Spirit think of this?" should be always our first inquiry. We must walk in the paracletism of the Holy Ghost, if we would be edified and multiplied, as were the churches throughout Judaea and Galilee, and Samaria (Acts 9: 31).

The former days shall be void. Num. 6: 12
(R.V.)

HOW solemn is the suggestion of these words! If the separation of the Nazarite were broken in upon by his sudden contact with death, he might start afresh; but all the days that preceded that untoward event would go for nothing—they would not be counted.

How many days in our life have been made void! Days in which we have learned no new lesson of God; have had no access into his presence; have done no kind and helpful act; have spoken no loving, tender word. It is all-important that even our days of rest from active engagements should be days of learning deeper lessons, of vision, and of reception from the fulness of God.

Each day comes to us fresh from God, like soft metal, waiting to be stamped with our inscription; or like a piece of yielding clay, to be moulded into some shape of beauty or use. Each morning the slate is brought for us to write on; the canvas on which we may paint. But too often we miss our opportunity, and a blurred, marred, confused result is all we have to show.

If you would avoid this, let God plan each day; follow the guidance of his Spirit; do all you touch with your might and for his glory; put away all known sin, and be separate from evil; in everything learn to submit to his dealings, and to commit yourself to his faithful keeping. Then each day will have something to keep in charge, and resemble a chalice filled to its brim with holy service. We must ever remember that "every man's work shall be made manifest: for the Day shall declare it, because it shall be revealed by fire; and the fire shall try every man's work of what sort it is" (1 Cor. 3: 13).

Moses . . . heard the voice speaking unto him, . . . and He spake unto him. Num. 7: 89.

THE meaning of this verse seems to be that when Moses went into the Holy Place to speak with God he became conscious of the divine voice, that opened out to him the thoughts and purposes of God in such a way that he was caught up on the current and borne back to God.

This is the true conception of prayer. We often go to God with our thoughts and desires, and having uttered them we go our way. We do not wait long enough to see the cherubim and the light of the Shekinah, or hear the divine voice. Thus our prayers fail of their answer. We do not ask what is according to the will and mind of our Heavenly Father; and the heavens seems like brass. We have not because we ask not, or because we ask amiss. We must ask in faith, nothing wavering.

The true conception of prayer is that it originates in the purpose of God, and passes from the Father to the Son, who is also the Head and Representative of his people. From Jesus it is brought into our hearts by the blessed Spirit, who unites the Head with each member of the mystical body; and from the saints it returns to the source from which it came.

If, then, we would pray aright, we should wait before God until the Holy Spirit suggests what we should pray for, and indeed begins to plead within us for the saints. Silence, solitude, waiting before God; the return to God of his own thoughts; the being burdened with the weighty matters that lie heavily on the heart of Jesus—such is the noblest kind of prayer. It is those who wait upon the Lord that renew their strength, that mount up with wings as eagles; that run and are not weary, that walk and are not faint (Isa. 40: 31).

Aaron offered them for a wave offering. Num. 8: 11, 13, 15, 21 (R.V.)

THIS is interesting and instructive. The Levites were substituted for the first-born of Israel. They were first separated from the rest of the people, cleansed, sprinkled, shaven, and finally presented to the Lord by the act of Aaron, who, according to the Hebrew word, waved them before the Lord. This waving must, of course, have been done in symbol and figure. But it was not enough that they were thus waved, they had thereafter to go in to do their service. In other words, they were called to realize actually that which was their position and standing in the sight of God.

There is a precise analogy in all this to the work which the Lord Jesus has accomplished for us all. He said, "I consecrate Myself, that they also may be consecrated." When He offered Himself without spot to God, to do his Father's will, though it cost Him the agony of Calvary, the heavenly Aaron waved us before God to be his. We were separated by his most precious death, that we should be wholly for God. But what is ours in the great deed of Christ, must become ours by our own choice and deed. We must go in to do the service for which we have been chosen and set apart by the Holy Ghost.

This can only be through the grace of the blessed Spirit. Ask Him to realize in you the purposes of God: trust Him to keep you trusting: each morning say, "Holy Spirit, I rely on Thee to keep me in the current of the divine purpose." Then dare to go forth to do the day's duties, believing that you may be always engaged in God's holy service; that in everything, whether you eat, or drink, or whatsoever you do, you do all to the glory of God.

When the cloud tarried. Num. 9: 19.

THIS was the supreme test of obedience. It was comparatively easy to strike the tents, when the fleecy folds of the cloud were slowly gathered from off the Tabernacle, and it floated majestically before the host. Change is always delightful; and there was excitement and interest in the route, the scenery, the locality of the next halting-place. But, ah, the tarrying! Sometimes the cloud tarried for two days, or a month, or a year; then, however uninviting and sultry the location, however trying to flesh and blood, however irksome to the impatient disposition, however perilously exposed to danger—there was no option but to remain encamped. The Psalmist says, "I waited patiently for the Lord, and He inclined unto me, and heard my cry." And what He has done for the Old Testament saints He will do for believers throughout all ages.

Still, God often keeps us waiting. Face to face with threatening foes, in the midst of alarms, encircled by perils, beneath the impending rock. May we not go? Is it not time to strike our tent? Have we not suffered ao the point of utter collapse? May we not txchange the glare and heat for green pastures end still waters? There is no answer. The cloud tarries, and we must remain, though sure of manna, rock-water, shelter, and defence. God never keeps us at a post without assuring us of his presence, and sending us daily supplies.

Wait, domestic servant, before you give notice! Young man, do not be in a hurry to make a change! Minister, remain at your post! Until the cloud clearly moves, you must tarry (8th verse). Wait, then, thy Lord's good pleasure! He will be in plenty of time!

What good soever the Lord shall do unto us, the same will we do unto thee. Num. 10: 32 (R.V.)

HOBAB was a Gentile by race, but he was invited to fellowship with Israel in all the blessing of their covenant. Moses reckoned that Israel was called to a stewardship of the manifold blessings of their lot. Whatever good was entrusted to them, they were called upon to distribute and pass on. As the Lord did them good, they would do Hobab good; making him, Gentile though he were, a fellow-heir, a fellow-member of the body, and a fellow-partaker of the promises of God.

WE GET BY GIVING. If the river-bed were to hoard up its waters, they would become stagnant and noisome. It is only in parting with them that it receives constant supplies from the crystal fountain-head. So, if we keep God's good things to ourselves, we make it impossible to receive more. You cannot put more water into a full glass. But as we part with them we get more and better. Distribute five loaves, and you have twelve baskets of fragments.

WE LEARN BY TEACHING. To stay in a class till you shall feel fully educated, is to miss one prime means of education. There is no way of discovering what we do not know, and getting grounded in what we do, like that of imparting what we have learnt to others. Would you learn, teach. Would you grow in grace, tell of the grace which has saved you.

WE KEEP WHAT WE GIVE AWAY. Hoard your money, and you lose it. Give it away, and it is caught in bags that wax not old, and stored beyond the reach of moth or thief. "There is that scattereth, and increaseth yet more; and there is that withholdeth more than is meet, but it tendeth only to want" (Prov. 11: 24). This is folly to the worldling, but sober fact to the child of the King.

Would God that all the Lord's people were prophets. Num. 11: 29 (R.V.)

THIS one saying proves the incomparable greatness of Moses' character. Little souls are monopolists. They like to be good and gifted, because it gives them a kind of superiority to others; but they dislike to see a levelling-up process at work by which the Eldads and Medads are lifted to stand by their side.

THIS WAS THE MISTAKE OF JOSHUA. When he heard that Eldad and Medad prophesied in the camp, he said, "My lord Moses, forbid them!" But he was immature, a saint in the process of manufacture, and smitten with jealousy, for the sake of his master and friend.

THIS WAS THE COMPLAINT OF JOHN'S DISCIPLES, when they saw the crowds ebbing away from their great teacher.

THIS WAS THE QUARREL OF THE PHARISEES, that Jesus made religion so cheap and accessible to all, that even the publicans and sinners received his priceless wares.

But when a man is really great and good, he longs that all should be as he is, and better; he takes a deep delight in the spread of vital godliness; he is glad when others are endowed with greater gifts than himself, that they may make the Gospel better known than he could ever do; he is content to decrease, if Christ may only increase; he is willing that affliction should be added to his bonds, if only Christ may be magnified; he prays that the Lord would put his Spirit on all his people. This is very unnatural to any of us; but God, the Holy Spirit, waits to baptize us even into this, and to make the glory of God the object of our life. Make haste, O blessed Paraclete, and do this for me!

My servant Moses is faithful: . . . with him will I speak mouth to mouth. Num. 12: 8.

THE meekest of men was vindicated by God Himself. He held his peace, but his Almighty Friend spoke up for him. It is thus that the meek inherit the earth and rejoice themselves in the abundance of peace. Oh, keep still, ye afflicted and tormented souls, God will not let you be trodden underfoot, if only you commit your cause to Him, and are faithful in all that He has committed to you. "That good thing keep which was committed to you: He is able to keep that which I have committed unto Him."

Notice to what faithfulness leads! The vision of God is not given to great intellectual ability or mental gift; but to those who as servants are faithful in the administration of God's Household, and the performance of such duties as are entrusted to them by the Great Householder. Such are they that enjoy the face-to-face fellowship, and the mouth-to-mouth speech.

These words about Moses are quoted in Heb. 3, as though it was pleasant to the Holy Spirit to commemorate in all ages the faithfulness of his servants: and there is this further thought added, that the Household is one, and that all dispensations are included in its precincts. "Whose house are we." It is inspiring to know that we are in the same house with Moses, and may have the same blessing. Are God's dealings with you in dark speeches, in mysterious and perplexing enigmas? Be patient and faithful in well-doing: He is but testing you, and soon He will say, I have called you not servants, but friends; for the servant knoweth not what his Lord doeth: but all things I have heard of the Father I have made known unto you.

We were in our own sight as grasshoppers, and so we were in their sight. Num. 13: 33.

THERE is a good deal of talk in this chapter about giants and fenced cities. But the way of speaking about them was very different on the part of the ten, and on that of the two. The ten said: "The Amalekites dwell in the land of the south: and the Hittites, and the Jebusites, and the Amorites, dwell in the mountains: and the Canaanites dwell by the sea, and by the coast of Jordan." But the two said: "Let us go up at once and possess it; for we are well able to overcome it." They saw the same spectacles in their survey of the land; but the result in the one case was panic, in the other confidence and peace. What made the difference? It lay in this, that the ten spies compared themselves with the giants, whilst the two compared the giants with God. "The Lord is with us, fear them not."

Faith looks away from the greatness of her difficulty to the greatness of her God. "If considered in itself, it is clear that this difficulty is too great for me to combat; but it is nothing to my God. The wall is too solid and high for me; but before God's touch it will fall down like cardboard. These ropes are stout; but before God they are only as tow before flame. I will not consider the man that shall die, and the son of man that shall be made as grass; but will look away resolutely to my Maker, who made heaven and earth, and who can still the roaring of the sea."

Do you want a fearless faith, be careful not to measure the comparative forces of yourself and others; but remember that God is working for you to will and do of his own good pleasure. If He is for you, who can be against you? When compared with Primrose Hill, Snowden is high; but where is it when compared with the Himalayas?

The Egyptians shall hear it. Num. 14: 13.
WHAT a noble concern for the credit of God! Here was a great opportunity for Moses. God was testing him by the proposal, that, the entire nation of Israel being cut off as a judgment for their repeated shortcomings and transgressions, Moses should become the slip or stock of the Hebrew race: "I will disinherit them, and make of thee a nation greater and mightier than they." This was not the settled purpose of God; but a suggestion to test his servant, who would not entertain it for a moment. All thought of the honour to be done to himself was submerged in his great eagerness for the divine credit. "The Egyptians shall hear it: the nations which have heard the fame of Thee will speak, saying, Because the Lord was not able. . . ."

The Egyptians are always around us, watching and listening. They can only judge of God by our behaviour and the course of our experience: and are only too ready to catch up anything which they may interpret to the discrediting of the Eternal. How careful we should be in all our life and conversation so that the ungodly may have, not lower, but loftier conceptions of our God.

When tempted to anything which is not perfectly noble and honourable; when inclined to murmur and complain of God's dealings with you; when an opportunity comes, as it did to Moses, to make gain at the expense of others; then remember the name of God, and the urgency of need that exists, to maintain it unsullied and untarnished. We should be restrained by a double fear: first, lest we should grieve God; second, lest the Egyptians should have a handle against Him, and should be prejudiced against religion.

A cord of blue. Num. 15: 38 (R.V.)
THROUGHOUT their generations the Israelites were bidden to wear it. It is the symbol of depth, of love, of Heaven. The azure sky, the glacier-rift, the deep lake, the far horizon, the eye of the hopeful, buoyant, tender nature —all tell the same story of deep and constant love, which mirrors below God's heaven of love above. Therefore to wear this cord of blue was to be kept in mind of the eternal and unseen. No outward symbol is needed by us. The very best, after a while, becomes tame and commonplace. We get so accustomed to it that it ceases to stir our thoughts. But if we will entrust ourselves to the Holy Spirit, He will teach us all things, and keep us always in mind. He is the blessed Remembrancer, whose mission is to bring Christ to our thought and keep Him there, the prominent object of our soul's vision.

The object of this cord of blue was to restrain the people from going about "after their own heart and their own eyes." We need to be kept from the same, that we may walk not after the flesh, but after the Spirit. In our resolutions, our energies, our acts of consecration, our Christian activities, we are all too apt to go at the dictates of our heart and eyes. May God forgive us! It has been the source of our perpetual failure and defeat. There is a more excellent way. Let us ask the Holy Spirit to keep the blue cord of the Christ-memory ever before our gaze, that we may become utterly absorbed in his beauty and glory, in doing his will, and in executing his commands. Let us seek to be bound to our Master, who is Love, by that same cord, that we may never for a moment forget the demands of the unseen and eternal.

The Lord will show who is holy; and will cause him to come near unto Him. Num. 16: 5.
IT was on these words that the Psalmist founded his exclamation, "Blessed is the man whom Thou choosest, and causest to approach unto Thee." This is what we all need. We often endeavour to approach unto God, but meet with many disappointments. Thomas Welsh said, on one occasion, that he had been wrestling to obtain access from six in the morning until nine! There is something better. If you are his, you may humbly count on God to cause you to come near; believing his promise: "Draw nigh to God, and God will draw nigh to you."

In your morning prayer, or at any other time which you set apart for devotion, let this be the cry of your soul: "My God, cause me to come near." When for long you have been dwelling afar off, and the distance threatens to become chronic or permanent, let this again be your petition: "Cause me to come near." And throughout the rush of daily life, let your dependence be on Him who alone can cause you to come near so that you may dwell in his courts.

But God cannot do this unless the soul is utterly surrendered to be his; for "if we say we have fellowship with Him, and walk in darkness, we lie, and do not the truth." We must be unanchored and unbeached if the tide is to bear us on its bosom. We must be free from the touch of other hands if we are to respond to his. We must sit loosely by the things of the earth to feel the drawing of heaven. This is, in part, the meaning of holiness. "Who are his, and who is holy?" Those who have experienced separation to God and sin. Give us this, O Lord; then draw us near to Thyself, and we will run after Thee!

The man whom I shall choose, his rod shall bud.
Num. 17: 5 (R.V.)

THERE was deep significance in this method of indicating the man of God's choice. Too many have taken God's election as referring exclusively to their enjoyment of God's grace and their preservation to his heavenly kingdom. Here we are taught that one of its chief results will be, and must be—buds, blossoms, and fruit. "The rod of Aaron budded and bloomed, blossomed and bare ripe almonds." It would almost seem that spring, summer, and autumn; the promise, maturity, and fruit—were simultaneously present in that marvellous rod. So should it be in those who have been chosen in Christ to be holy.

THE BUD OF SPRING. There is a perennial freshness in the true saint. He may be old in years, but his leaf is green with vernal tenderness, and there are the budding promises of richer and better things than he has yet attained. The youths faint, and are weary; but he renews his strength. The outward man decayeth, but the inward renews his youth like an eagle's.

THE BLOSSOM OF EARLY SUMMER. There is exquisite beauty in the blossom of orchard and garden. No painter has ever yet learnt God's secret of mixing his colours. Such is the beauty of the character of the believer.

Men say involuntarily, "How attractive, how beautiful!"

THE FRUIT OF AUTUMN. That we should bear fruit is the end of Christ in our redemption and discipline. We can only do it in fellowship with Himself. He must bear it through us. "From Me is thy fruit found." "I have chosen you, that ye should go and bear fruit, and that your fruit should remain."

I am thy Portion and thine Inheritance. Num.
18: 20 (R.V.)

WE are God's portion, and He is ours. The Lord's portion is his people; Israel is the lot of his inheritance; and He says to the soul, I am thy Portion and thine Inheritance. We, with all we have, for God; and God, with all He has, for us. "Heirs of God."

WE ARE LIKE SETTLERS ON THE FRINGE OF THEIR ESTATE. The emigrant to the Far West has a plot of land allotted to him; but how little does he know of its contents!—There may be coal, or iron-ore, or rivers full of fish, or rich soil; he settles on the outskirts, but every year he pushes his fences further back to take in more of the land, which is all his, but it is not yet brought into use, or under cultivation. So each year we should increase in the knowledge of what God is, and of what He is willing to be to us. Not as though we were already perfect; but we follow on to apprehend that for which we were apprehended, and to be filled full with his grace and heavenly benediction.

OUR POSSESSION OF GOD WILL LARGELY DEPEND ON HIS POSSESSION OF US. There are some who wonder that God is so much more to others than to them. Is not the answer to be found in their withholding so much of what they might yield up to his occupation and use? If you would have all from God, you must give all to God. Your enjoyment of God will be in precise proportion to the deepening and widening consecration of your life.

Why should any of us be poor, or strengthless, or fearful, when all the Godhead is stored in Jesus, and awaits our appropriation? Go up and possess his infinite continent that flows with milk and honey; watered by the rain of heaven; and rich in treasure.

For the unclean, they shall take of the ashes.
Num. 19: 17 (R.V.)

IT was very easy to become unclean without

realizing it. To touch a corpse, to be in the same room as the dead, to stumble over a grave, was enough to defile the Israelite, and excommunicate him from the Tabernacle with its holy rites. Could anything more graphically set forth the contagiousness of sin? We cannot be in contact with those who are dead in trespasses and sins, or breathe air defiled by their filthy speech, or read books which contain their thoughts, without suffering in some way by it.

This is the reason why, at the end of the day, we often feel unable to pray, or hold fellowship with God: we are excluded from the Most Holy Place, because of this defilement. Indeed, there is only one way of escaping it, and that is in being covered, hermetically sealed, by the Spirit of God. "In whom ye were sealed unto the day of redemption" (Eph. 4: 30, R.V.).

For this reason also, we should perpetually seek fresh cleansing in the precious blood of Christ. He is represented in this heifer without spot, slain in its prime, whose ashes were mingled in running water to testify their perpetual efficacy and freshness. If the ashes of an heifer availed for the purifying of the flesh, how much more shall the blood of Christ cleanse our consciences! Ask perpetually for the sprinkling of the blood of Jesus Christ, that you may have access with confidence into the Most Holy Place. The red heifer of Numbers answers to John 13. Let us apply the ashes and the water of purification to each other. Jesus said: "If I then, your Lord and Master, have washed your feet, ye also ought to wash one another's feet."

Speak ye to the rock; . . . and Moses smote the rock twice. Num. 20: 8, 11.
WHAT a miracle of grace is here! Nothing could have been more explicit than the divine command that Moses should, on this occasion, simply speak to the rock. We cannot fathom the deep reason; perhaps it was because the Spiritual Rock of our salvation could not be smitten by the soldier's spear twice. "Christ was once offered to bear the sins of many." Moreover, we are taught to wait on God each time we perform duties which appear similar, for the ways in which they should be performed may vary widely. It is clear, whatever the reason, that Moses was to speak, not smite.

However, he grievously disobeyed: largely probably, because he could not believe that mere speech would suffice for the miracle. He thought that he must do something to aid God, not realizing how slight a part man's is in the divine esteem. No flesh may glory in his presence. God must be all in all. We must believe that a word is enough; and that God will do the rest.

But, in spite of his irritation, disobedience, and unbelief, the water gushed out. The sin of the servant did not annul the love and faithfulness of God. "If we believe not, He remaineth faithful." It is a sweet lesson. We are worthless and unprofitable servants; we fail to believe and obey. But God's grace flows over the bank, and inundates the wilderness with crystal streams. The Psalmist says the waters did not trickle, they gushed out. Oh, miracle of Divine faithfulness! But Moses himself had to pay the penalty in later years. Disobedience in God's servants cannot be condoned. In proportion to the saintliness of their character is the rigour of their punishment.

Spring up, O well! Num. 21: 17.
THIS was a sweet song. It must have been a stirring scene, when Israel, in its thousands, sang forth this command to the waters that were under the earth, to show themselves, with the musical accompaniment of the gushing rill.

SPRING UP, O WELL, IN OUR HEARTS. Too long has the soil been arid and bare. A great drought has smitten it, and devoured every green thing. The flowers wither, the fruit falls. But Jesus promised to open in believing hearts a well, the waters of which should spring up unto eternal life. Not a stagnant pool, but a spring. Not a failing Cherith, but a perennial Siloam. Let that promise be realized in us here, and now; and if we have permitted rubbish to accumulate, or the weeds to grow rank, may we have grace to put them away, that there may be a clear course for the living water to flow through us and refresh the lives of all with whom we come in contact.

SPRING UP, O WELL, IN THE CHURCH OF GOD. This is a petition with which we may enter the place of worship where we meet God's people. Spring up, O well, to-day! With this petition, we may plead for distant mission stations, and for the entire Church. Jesus dug the well with the staff of his cross; but we wish that the Spirit, who is as a fountain of living water, fed from eternity and returning to its source, may spring up within it with greater volume and force.

SPRING UP, O WELL, IN THE WORLD. It is weary with sorrow and sin. Too far and long have the desert sands swept their devastations. Hasten the millennial day, when springs shall break out in the desert, and wilderness shall blossom as the rose!

The Angel of the Lord: . . . for an adversary against him. Num. 22: 22.

THE Angel of Jehovah is often referred to as a very present help, and as encamping round about those that fear God; but here, as an adversary with a drawn sword. When we serve God his sword is for us, as for Joshua at Jericho; but when we turn as here from his way to our crooked paths, it is drawn against us. That which seems to be full of menace is, when we look deeper, an angel force seeking to stay our further progress towards destruction.

Look for the Angel with his drawn sword in every pain of body, anxiety of circumstance, or suffering of mind. You were intent on pursuing your own way, and obtaining the rewards of unrighteousness, when suddenly you were stayed in your course. Another step would have brought you to the edge of the precipice; but you were suddenly arrested by that which forbade advance. Do not curse the hindering obstacle. Beneath it is God's gentlest angel, endeavouring to turn you from your evil purpose; and though his sword may be drawn against you, yet he is but keeping you from taking that step which might result in lifelong regret.

Too often our eyes are holden. We fret and chafe against God's kindest providence. Our anger is kindled at the ass which sees the angel, and thrusts herself against the wall. Let this day be one of humble searching of heart. Try to learn the reason why God has frustrated your plans, and blocked your progress. Ask for the opened eyes. Be sure that there is mercy in every broken plan. He sees the end from the beginning. Bow your head, and acquiesce in his appointments. Fall on your face, and bless Him whose kindliest angels sometimes assume the roughest disguise.

He hath blessed, and I cannot reverse it. Num. 23: 20.

BALAAM would have reversed the blessing into a curse, had he been able. Large rewards were depending on his doing so. But he was restrained. The current of blessing was running too strong for him to stem: the music was too overpowering for him to alter the air. Is not this also the despair of Satan? God hath blessed us with all spiritual blessings in Christ Jesus, and he cannot reverse them.

THE BLESSING OF ADOPTION. When the soul believes in Jesus, it is adopted into the family of God; the new life begins to throb within; it is constituted an heir of God, a joint-heir with Christ (John 1: 12). This position is irreversible. We may be tempted and overthrown, we may go for a season into the far country, we may even bring the family-name into contempt; but Satan cannot untie the knot with which God has bound us to Himself.

THE BLESSING OF ACCEPTANCE IN THE BELOVED. We are in Him, chosen in Him before the foundation of the world, risen and ascended and seated in Him in the heavenlies; and as our God views us in Jesus, He cannot behold iniquity or see perverseness in Him, and He accepts and blesses us as his wellbeloved. This, too, is irreversible by the arts and machinations of the great Accuser.

THE BLESSING OF THE COVENANT. God has taken us to be a people for his own possession. His name is named on us, his character is implicated in our ultimate deliverance from evil, and glorification. If we could be cast away, He would suffer irreparable dishonour. Therefore, though Satan do his utmost to discredit us, as he did the patriarch Job, he cannot reverse the covenant in which God and we are for ever and indissolubly joined.

The Spirit of God came upon him. Num. 24: 2.

THIS is a solemn warning for us all. Balaam saw truly, but he perished miserably. He heard the words of God, and saw the vision of the Almighty; but because he loved the wages of unrighteousness, and taught Balak to cast the stumbling-block of licentiousness before the children of Israel, he was slain in battle by the people whom he had blessed. He wished to die the death of the righteous, but was overtaken in that of the apostate. How near we may come to the gates of salvation, and yet perish miserably without!

DISTINGUISH BETWEEN UNCTION AND UNION. Hooper, the greatest of English divines, says: "We are not to confuse the grace of union with the grace of unction." It is possible to be united to the Lord Jesus in regeneration, without receiving the enduement of the Holy Spirit for service; and it is possible like Saul, to be anointed for high office, without being truly regenerate. Official position may be worthily filled, and yet the heart be all awry.

DISTINGUISH BETWEEN GIFT AND GRACE. We may be able to speak with the tongues of men and of angels, and have the gift of prayer, and know all mysteries and all knowledge; and yet be without love. The most gifted souls are by no means the most gracious. Desire earnestly the greater gifts, if you will; but be very sure that your heart is established with grace.

DISTINGUISH BETWEEN VISION AND REALIZATION. To see the fair land from afar, as Balaam did, is not enough; we must place our foot down on its soil, and go into it to possess. It is not enough to have intellectual appreciation of the blessed life and the way to enter it; not enough to extol or proclaim it. We must make it ours by humility and faith.

Israel joined himself unto Baal-Peor. Num. 25: 3.

THE margin of the Revised Version gives the alternative, yoked. The people were attracted by the charms of the women of Moab; but what they entered for pleasure, became clasped on them as a yoke. "Every one that committeth sin is the bond-servant of sin" (John 8: 34, R.V.).

SIN IS SLAVERY. The drunkard loathes his chains, vows not to yield again; but sinks deeper into the mire with every ineffectual struggle. The libertine is bound with passions, his heart is a dungeon, his conscience a scourge. We are promised pleasure and gratification; but when once the syrens have prevailed and got us in their power, they cast off their disguise, and work their horrid will.

THE ONLY DELIVERANCE IS THROUGH THE ANOINTED PRIEST. Phinehas interposed, and he was Aaron's grandson, on whom the anointing oil rested. And this illustrates a remarkable expression in Isaiah 10:27, "The yoke shall be destroyed because of the anointing." Is not that the anointing of the Holy Ghost? It is only through the Holy Spirit that we can be made free with the freedom of the Son of God. Where He is there is liberty. "Walk in the Spirit, and ye shall not fulfil the lusts of the flesh. For the flesh lusteth against the Spirit, and the Spirit against the flesh."

WE MUST DIE TO THE SIN THAT ENCHAINED US. There could be no half-measures. Phinehas took a spear. Whatever the cursed thing is which has crept in to enslave, it must be slain before the Lord. Is there some secret evil in your soul, eating out its strength? Ask the Faithful High Priest to deal with it, that your soul may cast off its bondage, and rise into the liberty of the sons of God.

There was not left a man of them. Num. 26: 65.

TWICE Moses numbered the people: on the first occasion Aaron was his colleague, at the beginning of the forty years; on the second occasion Eleazar, and this was at the end of the wanderings, on the threshold of Canaan. But only two had survived, Joshua and Caleb, because only they followed the Lord. God deals with a nation by dealing with individuals. He misses no one.

HIS LOVE MISSES NONE. The little sick child put her love hand outside the coverlet before falling asleep, in the hope that the Good Shepherd would notice it, and not miss her, as He passed down the hospital ward. But there is no need to fear his missing us, whose eyes are like a flame of fire, bringing the light with which they see. He tasted death for every man; He seeks each missing sheep, each lost coin. "He loved me, and gave Himself for me."

HIS SPIRIT MISSES NONE. If thou hast faith as a grain of mustard seed, it will attract his notice. If thou yieldest thyself to his Spirit, though thy lung be weak and diseased, He will fill it. If thou desirest to be endued with the gift of Pentecost, it will fall upon thy head, though thou art as obscure as the shepherd-psalmist of old.

DEATH AND JUDGMENT MISS NONE. On each of these unbelieving men the divine sentence was executed. One or two might linger, as autumn leaves on the topmost boughs of stripped trees; but ultimately they shared the fate of their companions. Unless Christ come first, our turn will come. In Adam all die. We must all appear before the judgment-seat of Christ. Each was born alone, must die alone, and alone give an account to the King. Prepare, my soul, to meet Him!

At his word shall they go out, and at his word they shall come in. Num. 27: 21.

THE emphasis is on the word his. Moses had asked God to indicate a successor to lead out and bring in the people. But Jehovah drew a distinction. Joshua was to receive the divine direction from Eleazar, the priest, who should inquire of the Lord; and at his word, i.e., God's word through Eleazar, the people were to go out and come in.

OUR GOINGS-OUT SHOULD BE DETERMINED BY THE WORD OF GOD. We never waste time when we stand before the true Priest, who has the Urim of divine direction, especially when we are considering some call to duty. Very often we have gone out at the instigation of pride, or emulation, or fussy activity; we have gone out because others have done so, and we were eager not to be left behind. Under these circumstances the out-goings of our mornings have not been made to rejoice; we have encountered disappointment and defeat. When we go forth at God's bidding, He becomes absolutely responsible; otherwise we pierce ourselves through with many sorrows, and bring discredit on the cause we would fain serve.

OUR COMINGS-IN MUST BE DETERMINED BY THE WORD OF GOD. When we should come in to rest, to pray, to fill again our souls with his Spirit, to suffer in secret, or to die, must be left to the determination of his will. It is easier to go out than to come in. Activity is pleasanter than passivity; the stir and rush of the world preferable to lying still to suffer. But our times are in his hand, and as soon as we recognize the decisions of the Urim in the appointments of divine Providence, the speedier shall we be at peace. If we are fully surrendered to God, both our going-out and our coming-in shall be ordered aright by his Spirit.

My food. Num. 28: 2 (R.V.)

GOD speaks as though He fed, through the sacrificial flame, on the offering of his people. There can be no doubt that the obedience of the blessed Lord to the death of the cross was very satisfying to the hunger of the Father's heart (Eph. 5: 2); and there is a sense in which our prayers and praises, the offering of ourselves in consecration, the gifts we lay before Him, are, when laid upon the altar of Christ, very pleasing to God. They are his food (Heb. 13: 15, 16).

We often speak of ourselves as hungering for God. Do we sufficiently realize that He hungers for our love, our whole-hearted devotion, our fellowship with Him? May it not sometimes act as an incentive to prayer to reflect that we may be passing from our chamber in the morning leaving God's desire unsatisfied? He was longing for the uplifting of our soul in devotion and praise which was not forthcoming. Still, as of old, in the morning the hungry Lord comes to seek fruit on his trees. Too often there is nothing but leaves. Too seldom does He have the opportunity of saying: "I have eaten my honeycomb with my honey."

If we really loved Jesus, we should be eager to give Him food in our prayers, and yearnings, and activities; and we should long with intense desire for Him to be satisfied, though we were not primarily concerned in spreading his banqueting table. It were enough for us to know that his hunger was feeding on the love of saints, or on the joy of new converts, though we were not the medium of the one or the other. Oh for this unselfish love for Jesus, which looks at things from his standpoint, altogether irrespective of ourselves!

Ye shall do no servile work. Num. 29: 1, 7, 12, 35.

THERE was a good deal of work to be done, but it was not servile work. Throughout the seventh month, the work centred around the Tabernacle and the service of God, rather than around the tents and occupations of Israel as at other times. The same distinction is clearly made by the Apostle; our faith and salvation are not of works, lest any man should boast; but we are created in Christ Jesus unto good works (Eph. 2: 9, 10).

DO NOT WORK UP TO THE CROSS, BUT DOWN FROM IT. We must come empty-handed to the Cross, and receive forgiveness and eternal life; but these will immediately begin to vindicate their presence in the fruits of righteousness. None work like those who have been saved by the grace of God—but their work is not servile work; not that of slaves, but of sons. Many confuse these, trying to work for salvation, instead of receiving it first and then working.

DO NOT WORK UP TO UNION WITH CHRIST, BUT FROM IT—We cannot unite ourselves to the true Vine by any activity of ours; our only resort is to lay ourselves at the feet of the great Husbandman, that He may graft us into living union with Jesus. When once that union is consummated, through our yielded nature, the Root begins to pour his mighty energy. Fruit-bearing is not servile work; but easy, natural, blessed.

DO NOT WORK UP TO PENTECOST, BUT OUT FROM IT. We cannot win the gift of the blessed Paraclete. No tears, prayers, agonies of soul, can purchase it. It must be received by a single act of faith. But when once He is in us in his fulness, then tears, and prayers, and strivings for the salvation of men flow out without effort. But there is no servility, no strain, no restraint, save that of love.

The Lord shall forgive her. Num. 30: 5, 8, 12.
IF the father or husband disallowed the vow a woman made, it would not stand, nor would she be held responsible for its fulfilment. God would not keep her to a promise which was hindered from execution by causes over which she had no control. This is a profound principle.

You may feel that a certain step is required of you by Christ; that indeed you are bound by your allegiance to Him to take it; nay, you have already promised Him that you will take it; but, suddenly and most unexpectedly, you are prevented from taking it. The express prohibition of those who have a right to determine your action, or the verdict of the physician, or the evident call of duty in another direction, makes it needful for you to relinquish your project. What then: is God grieved and angry? Not so; He understands the whole of the case perfectly, and accepts your will for the deed, and bids you go in peace. This, however, does not affect matters in which conscience is clear in demanding or prohibiting a certain line of conduct.

Sometimes God's silence is consent. You made your solemn dedication in His holy presence: there was no answering voice, or rush of emotion, or witnessing seal; He held his peace from day to day. But in that silence He established all your vows, all your bonds.

If parents capriciously forbid their children carrying out solemn resolutions and vows, the burden of blame must rest on their shoulders. They must render their account to God, and give answer for their action. It will go hard with those who put needless hindrances and obstacles in their brother's pathway.

Everything that may abide the fire, ye shall make to through the fire. Num. 31 : 23.
THE great aim of this enactment was to render these articles ceremonially clean. They had been in the use of the Midianites, and required cleansing, before they could be appropriated by Israel. But the cleansing processes were to be determined by their texture. Fire for what would stand fire; water for what could not stand fire.

WE MUST BE THOROUGHLY CLEANSED. If a man will purge himself, he shall be a vessel unto honour, meet for the Master's use. Not cleverness, but cleanliness, is the prime condition of service. Jesus will not put throne-water into impure and polluted receptacles. What fellowship hath Christ with Belial?

WE SHALL NOT BE PASSED THROUGH FIRE, UNLESS WE CAN STAND IT. Our faith is too precious to God to be exposed to risk. He will not let us be tempted beyond what we are able, lest we be discouraged, and make shipwreck. If, then, you are called at this time to pass through an unusually searching ordeal, be sure that your Heavenly Father knows that you can endure it. "That the trial of your faith, being much more precious than of gold that perisheth, though it be tried by fire, might be found unto praise and honour and glory at the appearing of Jesus Christ."

WE MUST GO THROUGH WATER, IF NOT THROUGH FIRE. The law provided also that "all that abideth not the fire, ye shall make go through the water." The one is negative, the other positive; the first appertains to John the Baptist, the second to the Holy Spirit. The latter is the best; but be thankful, if you cannot endure it, that there is a discipline more tempered and gentle, which will yet render you meet for the handling of the Holy Saviour.

Be sure your sin will find you out. Num. 32: 23.
SIN is like the boomerang of the savage, it comes back on the hand that has launched it forth. The brethren accused Joseph of being a spy, and cast him into the pit; and on the same charge they were cast into prison. King

David committed adultery and murder; so Absalom requited him. The Jews crucified the blessed Lord; and they were impaled around Jerusalem till room and wood for their crosses failed.

There is a divine order in society. God has so constituted the world, that as man deals with his neighbour, so he is dealt with. The consequence does not always follow immediately. There is often a long interval between the lightning flash and the thunder-peal. The sentence against an evil work is not executed suddenly. But though God's mills grind slowly, they do grind, and to powder. It is impossible to deceive God; for it is his immutable law, "whatsoever a man soweth, that shall he also reap. For he that soweth to his flesh shall of the flesh reap corruption; but he that soweth to the Spirit shall of the Spirit reap life everlasting" (Gal. 6: 7, 8).

When sin comes to find you out, like a sleuth-hound on the track of the criminal, be sure that it finds you in Jesus. "That I may be found in Him." Nothing will avail to intercept the awful execution of sin's vengeance, except the blood and righteousness of Jesus. Put Him between you and your sins, between you and your past, between you and the penalty of a broken law. Be sure that only when the blood of Jesus speaks for you through earth and heaven, there can be a cutting off of sin's terrible entail.

They journeyed from Marah, and came unto Elim: and in Elim . . . Num. 33: 9 (R.V.)

IN his enumeration of the halting places of Israel, Moses mentions Marah and Elim. In the case of the former, he does not dwell on the murmuring of the people over the bitter stream: but in the case of Elim, he loves to dilate on the twelve springs of water, and the three-score and ten palm trees, under which they pitched. Years of weary travel had not obliterated the memory of the refreshment afforded by those seventy palms.

WE SHOULD REMEMBER THE BLESSINGS OF THE PAST. God has so made us that we soon forget pain; but memory is willing to keep the fresco-pictures of sunny scenes unobliterated upon the walls of her galleries. Thus we may encourage our faith and comfort our hearts, by musing on the hand of the Lord which has been upon us for good. You have had many hard tracks of desert sand to traverse; but never forget those three-score and ten palm trees. Let their gracious shade and fruit still refresh you. And remember that God will restore them, whenever needed. If not, you can always find your palm trees and wells in Himself.

GOD DOES NOT REMEMBER THE SINS OF THE PAST. There is no word of their murmurings, either at Marah or Rephidim. It is thus that God deals with us. "I, even I, am He that blotteth out thy transgressions for mine own sake, and will not remember thy sins." When God forgives, He forgets. He erases the record from his book, and deals with us as though no sin had been committed. When we get to heaven and study the way-book we shall find all the deeds of love and self-denial carefully recorded, though we have forgotten them; and all the sins blotted out, though we remember them.

This is the land which ye shall inherit. Num. 34: 13.

IT is important that we should know the limits and possibilities of our lives. We must beat the bounds, first to know how far we may go; and secondly where we must stop, in our inheritance.

HOW FAR WE MAY GO. It is our privilege to know God and the hope of his calling, and the riches of the glory of his indwelling in our hearts, and the power of the Resurrection throbbing within us, lifting us to share the risen life of Jesus. Day by day we may be kept from yielding to known sin; day by day, though keenly conscious of temptation, we may be more than conquerors; day by day, the Holy Spirit may work in us perfect love towards God and man, to the limit of our light; day by day the Lord Jesus may be more perfectly formed within us.

WHERE WE MUST STOP. We may expect to be blameless, but not faultless, till He present us to Himself: to be delivered from temptation, but not freed from its assaults: to be kept in perfect peace, but not secured from the pressure of adversity: to be dead to sin and self, but not daring to say that either is dead within us: to be delivered from this present evil world, as to spirit and temper, though still called to inhabit it as its salt and light. Take possession of every inch of God-given territory in Jesus, but beware of going beyond it.

It is a solemn question to all who have been

appointed leaders in God's hosts, whether they are rightly dividing their heritage. We must hold back nothing that is profitable: nor must we shun to declare the whole counsel of God. Let our preaching and teaching include all God's provision for his children.

The Death of the High Priest. Num. 35: 25, 28, 32.

ONE after another they passed away. They were not able to continue by reason of death. Their offices, and garments, and ministry, passed from each in turn, as from Aaron, whom Moses stripped with his own hands on Nebo. But their death only brings into greater prominence the encouraging contrast in the case of our blessed Lord, who ever liveth, and hath, therefore, an unchangeable priesthood.

CHRIST EVER LIVES: WHAT AN ENCOURAGE-MENT TO THE PENITENT! All that He ever was, He is; all that He ever did for others, He is willing to do for thee. The records of his earthly life, with his tenderness for those who were out of the way, are leaves and specimen pages of the diary of his life. Therefore, there need be no hesitation in applying to Him.

CHRIST EVER LIVES: WHAT A BLESSING TO THE SAINT! "I am He that liveth." He bent over his fainting apostle, and said in effect, You remember what I was when you leant on my bosom, followed Me to the shore on which I had prepared your repast, and assured you of my never-altering affection. I am all that still; through death I have come to a life which can never decay; because I live, ye shall live also. Let us rest our souls on this sweet word—from his heart there will ever stream to us rivers of incorruptible life. Let us keep all the channels of our being open towards the fountains of eternal life, that there may be no stint or restraint to our reception.

CHRIST EVER LIVES: WHAT A WARNING TO THE CHURCH! There is no need, therefore, of the human priest to transact matters between man and God. The Son is Priest and King in his own house, in the power of an endless life; and human mediators are no more necessary than flickering night-lights at noon.

The inheritance of Zelophehad unto his daughters. Num. 36: 2.

FROM the earliest, the germ-principle of the emancipation of woman, and her right to stand on an equality with man, is recognized in Scripture. These women were heiresses in their own right, and might marry as they thought best. Christianity in this respect, as in so many others, is the fulfilment of the divine thought in the older dispensation. Ruth was the prototype of Mary of Bethany; Rahab of the Syrophenician woman; Hagar of Lydia.

THE INHERITANCE OF WOMAN IN THE NATURE OF CHRIST. There are certain qualities in the Son of Man peculiarly adapted for the heart of woman. Tenderness for her many tears— "Woman, why weepest thou?" Sympathy in her quest for a love that will not fail— "Mary." An answer to her many questions— "Woman, believe Me." Strength for her clinging weakness—"Forbid her not" Hope for her despair—"If thou couldest believe, thou shouldest see the glory of God." O woman, remember Him who is the counter-part of thy need, and offers thee Himself. "The same is my sister."

THE INHERITANCE OF WOMAN IN THE WORK OF CHRIST. She is called to enrich men by bringing to them her inheritance. So the daughters of Zelophehad brought their land to their husbands, and the women bore the tidings of the risen Lord to the disciples. Thus women, receiving much from fellowship with Christ, come to men, steeped in materialism and sense, telling of a purer, fairer life, and summoning them to inherit it. Well is it for the home where this principle is recognized, and where the wife and mother is ever feeding her soul with noble ideals, to correct the false estimates that too much contact with men of the world are apt to induce in those she loves!

Deuteronomy

The Lord thy God bare thee. Deut. 1: 31.

A SAFE carriage was that! In his love and in his pity God redeemed them, and bare them, and carried them all the days of old. When the little lad was tired and complained of his head, his father bade a servant carry him to his mother; but God does not hand over his children to his servants, He carries them Himself. When we realize that his everlasting arms are underneath, it is safer riding than any the ingenuity of man can devise; and here we need fear no ill.

"IN ALL THE WAY." There are great varieties in the way—sometimes the sleepers are badly laid, and the carriage rocks and jolts; sometimes the gradient is steep, and the progress tedious; sometimes the pilgrim has to go afoot, climbing with difficulty from ridge to ridge; sometimes the route lies through a territory infested with enemies, and haunted by miasma; but we can each rejoice in the fact that the Lord "knoweth the way that I take," and that all the way, those gentle and unwearied arms bear us up and on.

"ALL THE DAYS." Never a day without its cross, its lesson, its discipline, its peril; but never a day that God does not bear us up in his hands, as some mighty river bears up the boat of the missionary explorer. Through wilds, past villages of infuriated savages, over reefs and rocks, the patient river bears the voyager and his goods. Thus does God carry us. The Good Shepherd carries the lambs in his bosom. Why, then, should we dread the future, or quail before the faces of our foes? "The eternal God is thy refuge; and underneath are the everlasting arms." So strong: so tender! Let yourself go, and trust.

Wheresoever the Lord our God forbad us. Deut. 2: 37 (R.V.)

THIS chapter is full of restrictions and prohibitions. There were territories which Israel was forbidden to enter at that time; though afterwards, in the days of David, Solomon, and Hezekiah, they were all included in the possessions of the chosen people.

There are temporary limitations in all lives. Paul was forbidden to preach the Word in Asia, when first he came on its frontiers; though two or three years after he so filled it with his teaching that the trade of the silversmiths, who made shrines for Diana, was affected.

LIMITATIONS IN OUR USEFULNESS. Provinces of holy endeavour seem shut against you, as the Gentile world from the public ministry of Jesus. Nevertheless, do your best in what is open, as He did for the Jews, and the rest will be unbarred; but if not, in God's good time,

the field will be cultivated by hands specially instructed and prepared.

LIMITATIONS IN KNOWLEDGE. There are mysteries which, in the earlier stages of their experience, are not made known to the saints; but which we come to know, as we follow on to know the Lord. And while there may be much in God's providence that is difficult to understand, yet our knowledge of Himself may increase as the years go by, until we glory in this, that we understand and know Him (Jer. 9: 23).

LIMITATIONS IN EXPERIENCE. Not to every one is it given to feel Christ's love as Rutherford did. Some are excluded from the sunny realms, as Cowper was. Such is the choice of God for them, and it must be best; but they shall all attain one day to the stature of the perfect man, and possess the blessedness from which they are now restrained.

Speak no more unto Me of this matter. Deut. 3: 26.

WE are to pray without ceasing; always praying, never fainting; asking, seeking, knocking. But there are some subjects concerning which God says, "Speak no more unto Me of this." In some cases these topics have to do with others, but more often with ourselves, as in the case of the Apostle Paul (2 Cor. 12: 9).

It is an awful thing when God says of certain individuals, Ephraim is joined to idols, let him alone; and when the conviction is wrought within us that the sin unto death is being committed, concerning which even the Apostle John said, "I do not say that he should pray for it." Such times come comparatively rarely; and so long as you feel able to pray for another, so long as no negative has been spoken, you may be sure that God waits to be entreated, and that your prayer will assuredly be answered.

But have you not realized at times that God has said about some earthly boon you were craving?—"Child, do not ask Me more, leave it with Me. I know what you want, and what is best for you. Seek first my kingdom, and all these things, literally or in their equivalent, shall be added." It is well when we have been praying eagerly, to allow God's winnowing-fan to pass over our petitions, to winnow away all that is not in his mind to give; so that only those desires may remain which his Spirit has indicted, and which He is therefore pledged to bestow. If He does not give the exact thing you ask, He will give the Pisgah view and more grace. He will say to you, as to Paul, "My grace is sufficient for thee: for my strength is made perfect in weakness."

The Lord hath taken you to be unto Him a people of inheritance. Deut. 4: 20.

THE Apostle prays that we may know the riches of the glory of God's inheritance in his saints. God is our inheritance, and we are his. We are called to possess Him; He desires to possess us. His nature will yield crops of holy helpfulness to those who diligently seek Him; and He demands crops of holy love and devotion from ours.

WHAT SOVEREIGN GRACE IS HERE! There was nothing in us to distinguish us from others. We were but part of the great moorland waste, when He fenced us in, and placed us under his tillage and husbandry. It is by the grace of God that we are what we are. "To the praise of the glory of his grace, wherein He hath made us accepted in the Beloved: in whom we have redemption through his blood, the forgiveness of sins, according to the riches of his grace."

WHAT RESPONSIBILITY! Three times over in this chapter we are bidden to take heed to ourselves. It is no small thing to have been the subjects of God's special workmanship; because He is a jealous God very quick to mark the least symptom of declension and very searching in his dealing and discipline. As we learn here, our God is a consuming fire, a jealous God.

WHAT HOPE! We cannot derive much from ourselves, however we toil and strive. Self cannot discipline self to any advantage. The field is worked out. The divine Husbandman must put into us what He would take out of us; He needs therefore to have almost infinite resources. But these are God's, and if we yield ourselves to Him, He can make all grace abound towards us, that we, always having all sufficiency in all things, may abound unto every good work.

That it might be well with them. Deut. 5: 29.

HERE is a sigh from the divine heart. It recalls the tears of the Lord Jesus over Jerusalem. The people insisted on their willingness to do all that was required of them, but they were destined to learn and teach that the will may be present, without the power; just as a sick man may have the will to walk across his bedroom, and will fall to the floor because he has no strength.

GOD'S COMMANDMENTS ARE FOR OUR WELFARE. We find men shrinking from consecration to complete obedience because they fear that it will mean loss and pain. There may be loss and pain; but only in the excision of things which they would be the first to put away, if they understood their nature and out-working as God does. Those who obey God most literally find the most blessedness in life, whether now or hereafter.

WE APPROVE THEM WITH OUR WILL. More than once the people insisted that they would do as God commanded. We are not so destitute of moral perception as not to see the beauty of a life wholly yielded to God; but let us not rest content with this, or we may have yet to cry with the Apostle, The law is holy, just, and good; but I am carnal, sold under sin.

GOD WANTS THE HEART. He will not trust Himself to us, so long as the heart is a stranger to the indwelling of the divine Spirit. "Oh, that there were such a heart in them!" We need to cry to Him to create in us a clean heart, to ask that He would exchange the heart of stone for one of flesh, to entreat that his love may be shed abroad in our heart, that we may perfectly love Him. "My son, give me thy heart!"

Thou shalt Love. Deut. 6: 5.

"LOVEST thou Me?"

"Who art Thou, Lord, that I should love Thee?"

"I am He that liveth, but I died; I loved thee, and gave Myself for thee; I have made thee mine for ever in a bond that even death cannot break; I have loved thee with an everlasting love; I shall never be at rest till thou art with Me where I am."

"Indeed I would love Thee; but how?"

"Thou shalt love Me with all thine heart, and with all thy soul, and with all thy might."

"This were impossible unless Thou give me the love Thou requirest."

"This I will do for thee, since love is of God. Only obey these simple directions:

"1. Abstain from all wrath, anger, malice evil speaking, and all else that would grieve my Holy Spirit.

"2. Yield thyself to the Spirit, that He may produce in thee his choice fruit—Love. 'The fruit of the Spirit is love.' 'He sheds love abroad in the heart.'

"3. Consider my love to thee, especially that I died for thee when thou wert yet in thy sins. Meditate much upon the sacrifice I made for thee, that thou mightest have thy sins blotted out, and enjoy the peace which passeth all understanding.

"4. Believing that thou hast received the love of the Spirit, begin to let it work through thy life to all around thee.

"5. If thy heart is unwilling to love any, put thy will on my side, and confidently believe that I am able to work in thee to will and do to of my own good pleasure."

They will turn away thy son from following Me. Deut. 7: 4.

THE question of marriage is repeatedly considered in these chapters, and never once is it supposed that the Israelites might bring a heathen partner to the faith of God's elect; but it is always insisted that the heathen husband or wife will subvert the faith of the child of Abraham. "Thou shalt not make marriages with them; for they will turn away thy son from following Me, that they may serve other gods. . . . For thou art an holy people unto the Lord thy God."

The same law holds still. You may suppose that by marrying the ungodly and irreligious you will be able to convert them to your way of thinking; but you must remember that regeneration is the work of the Holy Ghost, and He is not likely to lend his aid in regeneration whilst you are acting in defiance of his distinct prohibitions. The command of Christ is so clear and positive against his followers entering into an unequal yoke with unbelievers, that it simply leaves no option for the obedient. With the child of God, marriage must be "only in the Lord."

In order to make these marriages impossible, Israel was bidden to destroy the nations of Canaan. Separation from their society and practices was thus enforced. The slaughter seemed ruthless; but there was no other way of preserving intact the chosen race, as a peculiar people unto the Lord. Our separation also must be strict even to the extreme. If we would keep our young people from worldly alliances, we must begin with their amusements and companionships. There should be

every endeavour to promote their happiness and interests; but we must very carefully guard the young plants from the blight of worldliness.

He suffered thee to hunger. Deut. 8: 3.

THERE was a divine intention, then, in the hunger and thirst and weariness of the desert march. God suffered these hardships to come to the chosen people, in order to teach them dependence on Himself. The daily gift of manna was a perpetual evidence of his loving thought and care for the pilgrim host; they came to learn that sin and backsliding could not alienate his compassions; they found that the Word of God was life. But none of these lessons could have been acquired if the supplies of food had been as regular and plentiful as in Egypt. They were suffered to hunger that God might make them know.

YOU ARE SUFFERED TO HUNGER FOR HUMAN LOVE, that you may know what the love of Jesus can be to his own. Open your heart to it, until it flood you as the sunshine does the south windows of a house.

YOU ARE SUFFERED TO HUNGER FOR RECOGNITION AND GRATITUDE, that you may know what the "Well done!" of Jesus is, and to lead you to look for that only. What do the words of men amount to unless He smile?

YOU ARE SUFFERED TO HUNGER FOR EASIER CIRCUMSTANCES, for money, that you may know the tender provision which Jesus can make for those who are wholly dependent on Him. In the absence of all human help, you will learn the sweet taste of his manna.

Glory to God, to God, he saith,
Knowledge by suffering entereth,
And life is perfected in death.

These seasons of hunger are necessary for the discipline of life. But, thank God, He is able to satisfy us; and out of his riches in glory in Christ Jesus He can and will fulfil every need of ours (Phil. 4: 19, R.V.).

Not for thy righteousness. Deut. 9: 5.

IT is well to be reminded that we have no claim on God. All He does for us and gives us is of his own free grace. By grace have we been saved, through faith, and that not of ourselves—it is the gift of God. There certainly was nothing in us to merit eternal life, before our conversion; and it is equally sure that there has been nothing since to merit the continuance of his favour. Indeed, as we remember and review the past, to us belong shame and confusion of face for our repeated acts of disobedience. Oh the depth of the riches of his grace!

IF WE WERE NOT SAVED FOR OUR GOODNESS WE SHALL NOT BE LOST FOR THE LACK OF IT. When we have been betrayed into sin, in the keenness of our remorse the fear is suggested lest God should put us utterly away. And there would be ground for the fear if we had been chosen because of our righteousness.

But since our original acceptance with God did not depend on works of righteousness which we had done, but on his mercy in Jesus Christ, it will not be undone by our failures. This thought does not lead to carelessness and indifference, but to a holy fear of sinning.

IF OUR JUSTIFICATION WAS APART FROM OUR MERIT, OUR SANCTIFICATION WILL BE. The one was a gift, so must the other be; the hand of faith must receive each from Christ, and her voice must render thanks for each, as the unmerited gift of divine Love. Where is boasting, then? It is shut out. We can claim nothing but emptiness and need. Handfuls of withered leaves! The Lord Jesus is our only hope, pleading for us in heaven, and living within our hearts. Of ourselves we are nothing: only in Him are we complete.

He doth execute the judgment of the fatherless and widow. Deut. 10: 18.

IN the gate of the Eastern town, at early morn, the judge sits, and any suppliant has a right to appeal to him. The word Porte, or Gate, as applied to the Turkish Government, alludes to this. So to the thought of the inspired writers, behind the flimsy vail of sense, God sat within the shadow, "keeping watch upon his own," waiting to answer every plea, and to avenge the innocent and oppressed against high-handed wrong.

INDIVIDUALS MAY APPEAL TO THAT TRIBUNAL. David, Jeremiah, and other sufferers, lodged their complaints there. Their cry was not for revenge, but for avengement. There is a great difference between the two. The one is vindictive and retaliatory; the other is magisterial and passionless.

Whenever an affront or wrong is inflicted on thee, avoid vindicating, or answering for thyself. Be still towards man, unless it be to induce thy brother to repent; but turn instantly to thy righteous Judge asking Him to right the wrong and vindicate the right. He shall bring forth thy righteousness as the light, and thy judgment as the noonday. When Christians go to law, and seek to maintain their cause against wrong-doing, they miss this. The weaker you are, the more certainly will the Lord judge for you.

THE CHURCH MAY APPEAL. Our Lord depicted her as a widow pleading to be avenged of her adversary. Her martyrs cry from under the altar, "How long, O Master, holy and true? Dost Thou not judge and avenge our blood?" To us the delay is long; but we know that He has no complicity with evil, and that He is faithful. Give us the white robe, that we may wait!

If ye shall keep all this Commandment, then will the Lord drive out. Deut. 11: 22, 23 (R.V.).

WE wonder why the Lord does not drive out and subdue our besetting sins. We do not possess them, but they us. The explanation is to be found in our lack of consecration. We do not keep all his commandments, or walk in all his ways.

GOD CANNOT DELIVER US FROM BESETTING SIN UNLESS WE YIELD OURSELVES TO HIM ENTIRELY. It is only when He is Judge, Lawgiver, and King, that He can save us. The great surgeon will not undertake a case unless he have its entire management. The general cannot protect a town until it has passed over its government entirely into his hands. If you would give yourself utterly and unreservedly to God, you would find how strong He is for those whose heart is perfect towards Him.

UNLESS WE OBEY ALL HIS COMMANDMENTS; because they contain his precise direction as to what we should, or should not do. If you want your medical man to heal you, you must abstain from things he forbids, and do those he prescribes. You cannot expect God to save you unless you utterly and reverently obey all his commandments; that, for instance of not having fellowship with the world and its ways.

UNLESS WE CLEAVE UNTO HIM. There must be the daily walk with God, the abiding in Him, the holy and unbroken communion. "He that saith, I know Him, and keepeth not his commandments, is a liar, and the truth is not in him. But whoso keepeth his word, in him truly is the love of God perfected." "He that abideth in Him sinneth not." The anointing of the Holy Spirit will teach us this sacred habit (1 John 2: 27). But entire consecration must precede entire deliverance.

Thou shalt rejoice before the Lord thy God.
Deut. 12: 7, 12, 18.

THE presence of God is an incentive to true joy. We rejoice before Him. There is some mistake in our religious life when it is not a joy to us to stand in the presence of God. He that feareth, and rejoiceth not, is not made perfect in love. Note the elements of true joy.

First. THE PUTTING AWAY OF ALL KNOWN EVIL. "Ye shall surely destroy." The permission of evil habits, books, companionships, and unlawful methods of obtaining money, are destructive of peace and joy. The prodigal son went away for merriment; but he only found real joy when he had given up his evil ways and returned to his father, a true penitent, and resolving upon a better life.

Second. THE SENSE OF ACCEPTANCE WITH GOD THROUGH JESUS CHRIST. "Unto the place which the Lord shall choose shall ye come." This refers, of course, to the brazen altar and the altar of incense. We have a better heritage in the finished work of Jesus, whose blood is more precious than that of bulls and goats and lambs, and in whom we are accepted and beloved.

Third. FEEDING ON CHRIST. "Ye shall eat and rejoice." A part of the meal-offerings and other sacrifices was reserved for the worshippers. We have an altar of which we, too, eat. His flesh is meat indeed; his blood drink indeed.

Fourth. ENTRANCE ON THE REST OF OUR INHERITANCE. We which believe do enter into rest; not the rest of heaven, but the heavenly places which those enjoy who have learnt to cast every load of anxious care on the great Burden-bearer. "There remaineth a Sabbath rest for the people of God. . . Let us give diligence to enter into that rest" (Heb. 4: 9, 11, R.V.).

The Lord your God proveth you. Deut. 13: 3.

HOW much happens to us for this reason! God proves us—not that He may learn aught of us which He did not know before, but that He may reveal us to ourselves. We need to know ourselves, that we may be prompted to know and use his infinite resources and that,

we may be led to avail ourselves of his grace.

GOD PROVES US BY OPPORTUNITIES OF CHRISTIAN SERVICE. We think we are fitted for some great sphere, and chafe because it is withheld: but the reason is not far to seek. We have been tested in some very little service, as a class in the Sunday-school, and have been found careless and unpunctual; is it likely that we shall be entrusted with the greater?

GOD PROVES US BY THE MONEY WITH WHICH HE ENTRUSTS US. Money resembles the counters with which children play. It greatly tests us. It is described as the unrighteousness mammon, and as not being our true riches; but it is entrusted to us that we may be proved, before God entrusts us with the real treasures of his Kingdom. Be wary how you use money; on this may turn the responsibilities of the eternal world of which we now know nothing.

GOD PROVES US BY OUR ACTIONS WITH REGARD TO DOUBTFUL THINGS. Not in the things which are clearly right or wrong, but in those which lie in the debatable ground of the twilight, is our true character tested. What you are in matters which must be viewed in relation to others is all-important, as the true gauge of character. By currents of opinion, by winds of doctrine, and by the many voices that are speaking in the world, the Lord your God proveth you.

If the way be too long for thee, so that thou art not able to carry it. Deut. 14: 24.

GOD'S pitifulness is very manifest here. If the pious Jew found it impossible to transport all his tithes in kind, he might change them into money, and bind it in his hand. It was far from God's thought that his service should become irksome, or the soul faint in performing it. An alleviation was suggested, of which the worshipper might take advantage, if he would. This principle may be applied in several directions. We are not to make God's service a toil, but esteem it a delight. "Thou shalt rejoice, and thine household."

THE LORD'S DAY should be the gladdest of the week; full of love and joy and holy song. We should carefully guard against anything approaching to slavish observance: and be very careful that our children and servants should look forward to it with delight.

CHRISTIAN WORK should not be carried to the point of exhaustion. There is a mistake somewhere if it so breaks down the health and spirits that the worker is not able to carry it. At such a time, we need to avail ourselves of any assistance or alleviation that may be possible.

ACTS OF DEVOTION, ALSO, should be for our enjoyment and refreshment. It seems sometimes as though God's children relied more on length than strength, in their prayers. They are not at ease or natural in the Father's presence. The forms of their devotion are so numerous and prolonged, that they are not able to carry them. By all means maintain the salutary form, but not for form's sake. Let the joy of the Lord, taking pleasure in his presence and in communion with Him, be always the first thought.

Thy bondman for ever. Deut. 15: 17 (R.V., marg.).

THIS is what we desire to be to Christ. We have forfeited our own natural inheritance, and have taken refuge in his house. For six years we have enjoyed all that Jesus could do to make us happy; has not the time come when we should say to Him, "We do not want to go out from Thee again, but to remain with Thee for ever"? Paul delighted to call himself "a bond-servant of Jesus Christ" (Rom. 1: 1; Gal. 1: 10; Phil. 1: 1, R.V.; etc.).

There are two stages, so to speak, in our dealings with Him. First, we come driven by fear; the produce of our own efforts has failed; we have no other resort. Like the bird fleeing from the hawk, we have made for his breast; like the sailor driven by the tempest, we have taken the first harbour that offered. But when we have tested the blessed Master, and found Him so sweet and strong, we elect to remain with Him, not for his gifts or even his salvation, but for Himself. We do not wish to go out free; we love Him so dearly that we would rather go anywhere with Him than remain without Him.

This resolve of ours is ratified by Him. He nails our ear to his cross. Through the blood of self-sacrifice, and self-surrender; through our deeper appreciation of the meaning of his cross, as separating us from the old selfish life; through our identification with Him in death and resurrection; through our sacrifice of all that would hinder us—we come into deeper and closer oneness with Himself. As the Father bored through his ear, in accepting his glad delight to do his will, so does Jesus make real and permanent the consecration we lay at his feet (See Psa. 40: 6, 7).

Thou shalt remember that thou wast a bondman. Deut. 16: 12.

THIS gave the touch of gentle tenderness to Israel's treatment of the stranger, the fatherless, and the widow. They knew what loneliness and desperate suffering were; and from their own experience could speak to the heart. Without tenderness and sympathy, what are our gifts to the poor worth? It is as important to give graciously and kindly as to give at all. None are so sensitive as sufferers, whether in mind, body, or circumstance; they are quick to notce the slightest roughness or harshness in our manner of bestowing relief; they would prefer a pittance given with tender sympathy to a larger gift flung at them grudgingly. But what can give this thoughtful sympathetic manner like the memory of our own sufferings, when we were bondmen in Egypt!

It may be that God is passing thee through some fiery ordeal, to teach thee and fit thee to be his almoner, touching and soothing as his outstretched hand of pity. Soon thy present sorrow shall be but a memory; but thou wilt be called to minister to the fatherless, the widow, the stranger. Always say in thine heart, God is passing me through this sorrow, and comforting me, and delivering me, that I may be able to comfort those who are in any trouble with the very accent, caress, and tender word which He hath spoken to me. "Blessed be the God of all comfort; who comforteth us in all our affliction, that we may be able to comfort them that are in any affliction through the comfort wherewith we ourselves are comforted of God."

In heaven itself we shall never quite forget that we were bondmen once, but were redeemed with the precious blood of Christ. This will give a new meaning to the song of adoring gladness.

That his heart be not lifted up. Deut. 17: 20.

BEWARE of pride! By that sin fell the angels. If they fell by it, how much more may we! When a man is raised from some lowly sphere to a position of commanding influence, he is greatly tempted to arrogance and pride. The adulation which he receives on every hand makes it all the harder to live humbly and unassumingly. But when once pride enters, it seems to close the heart to God. The proud man multiplies to himself chariots and horses, with the intention of making his position more secure; but he shuts out the help of the Most High. How necessary, therefore, that our hearts should not be lifted up!

The corrective suggested here is meditation on the Word of God. The king was to write out a copy with his own hand, and meditate on it all the days of his life; this would keep him in the lowlands of humility. The Bible is so true in its analysis of the heart; like a mirror it reveals a man to himself. It gives such exalted views of the greatness and holiness of God, compared with which the greatest human state is like the royalties of an ant-heap. It assures us that we must receive everything as the gift of God's grace. "Where is boasting then? It is excluded. By what law—of works?" No, but by the grace of God which bringeth salvation, apart from merit.

May God make us humble, with a transparent humility, which is not conscious that it is humble, like the utter unconsciousness of the little child, who does not bend back on herself. Still and quiet your soul, dear child of God, as a child weaned from its mother; and be sure to feed humility on the sincere milk of the Word.

With all the desire of his soul. Deut. 18: 6 (R.V.).

HERE is the inspiration of a noble purpose taking a man out from his quiet life in some distant village, far removed from the great sacred city, and plunging him suddenly into the very midst of its holy engagements and services. Other men were happy there. What more did they want than the quiet routine of buying and selling cattle, tending vines, and cultivating their fields? But for this man these could not suffice. There was a light that excelled beckoning him on; a voice, which only he could hear, calling to him. He was not asked to come; his name did not appear on the rota of the Temple servitors; the great Temple might seem perfectly able to dispense with him; yet because with all the desire of his soul he longed to be one of the Temple Levites, he might minister in the name of the Lord, as the others did; and be supported, as they, from the Temple funds.

It is a blessed thing to feel an impulse like this. It may prompt to home or foreign missions, to some enterprise of self-denying ministry to the helpless and sad, to service for God or man. It may come on you like a strong current, fresh from the ocean, sweeping up into some quiet river or harbour basin, and lifting the ponderous barges. But when it comes, be true to it, nurse it, reverence it, thank God for it, trust and follow it where it leads. You will find a niche awaiting you, and the portions by which life will be nourished and maintained; and the Holy Spirit will not fail to be your Guide and Teacher, leading you into all the truth. Until it come, wait upon God in prayer; commune with Him in the Holy of Holies; and spend much time in reading and meditating upon his Holy Word.

Then shall ye do unto him as he had thought to do to his brother. Deut. 19: 19.

THERE is a Nemesis in wrong-doing; evil comes home to roost; what we meditate against others returns on ourselves. They that take the sword shall perish with the sword. The publican who sells drink to debauch sons and fathers, lives to see the drink curse his own family. The man who is treacherous to women lives to see his own sons fall beneath their wiles. Haman erects a gallows for Mordecai, but is hanged upon it himself. Adoni-bezek cut off the toes and thumbs of captive princes, and confessed the rightness of the fate which overtook himself. England imposes opium on China, but presently discovers that it is eating out the heart of her own subjects in India and Burmah. "Whoso causeth the upright to go astray in an evil way, he shall fall himself into his own pit."

And why is all this? Because God sits behind the slight curtain of the present, judging the acts of men. It is not necessary to wait for the conclusion of the present age to see the sentence inflicted. Now the Son of Man sits on the throne of his glory, and before Him the nations are gathered. Nineveh, Babylon, Capernaum, Tyre, Pompeii, the power of Spain, the Empire of Napoleon, have already been condemned to Hades. Now the judgment is set, now the books are opened, now the "Come, ye blessed," and "Depart, ye cursed," are being uttered. God has so made the moral world that the seed of punishment lies hid in each unkind word, each unchristian act; and it is only necessary to give time enough to show that the man who has sown to his neighbour's hurt will reap that hurt in his own life. To every man will be rendered according to his deeds, even in this life.

When ye draw nigh unto the battle, the priest shall approach Deut. 20: 2.

WHEN Abraham returned from the slaughter of the kings, the priest of the Most High appeared to welcome him, and to prepare him for the still more subtle encounter which awaited him with the king of Sodom. As Abraham drew nigh to that battle the priest approached.

WHENEVER A BATTLE IS IMMINENT, LOOK OUT FOR THE PRIEST. Do not go to the war at your own charges you cannot stand against the mighty power of your arch-adversary. Look around, and see the Priest stand. What Priest? The Apostle and High Priest of your confession. He will offer prayer for you, and anoint your shield with the precious oil, and put his hand upon your hand as you feebly draw the bow.

"What makes you so bold, my lad?" the captain asked of a stripling as he went into the fight. And the answer came quickly, "My mother put her hands on my head and blessed me ere I left our home."

WHENEVER THE PRIEST HAS BEEN NEAR, ANTICIPATE A BATTLE. The best hours come to prepare us for the worst. The dove descends that we may be able to stand for forty days against the devil. Do not be surprised at this. And whenever some experience of unusual radiance and helpfulness has visited you, say to yourself, "This is God's sweet way of preparing me against coming trial. Let me walk warily, for danger is near. The Priest has been with me; I am drawing nigh to the battle. I know not what lies before me: but He is acquainted with the difficulties I have to face and the fierceness of the adversary I have to encounter. He alone can equip me for the fight."

He that is hanged is accursed of God. Deut. 21: 23 (R.V.).

THIS law on the Jewish statute-book hastened the awful tragedy of Calvary. No body must be left to rot on the cross on which it had been impaled. The corpse of the malefactor must be taken down at nightfall. But how little did the Pharisees and Scribes realize that the remainder of this verse had so pertinent a reference, and was having so remarkable a fulfilment. The Apostle quotes this verse as giving the inner rationale or meaning of the death of the blessed Lord (Gal. 3: 13). "Cursed is every one that hangeth on a tree." On Jesus fell the reduplicated curses, that were deserved by the race, and by each.

THE CURSE OF THE BROKEN LAW. "Cursed is every one that continueth not in all things written in the Book of the Law." None had kept, all had broken that law. None was righteous, no, not one. Man's lot was cast under Mount Ebal. The race was guilty and silent before the bar of infinite justice. But Jesus, by virtue of his relationship with the entire human family, was able to stand before God charged with that sin, bearing that curse, and put them away for ever. There is no barrier therefore, now to the outflow of God's free grace.

THE CURSE DUE TO INDIVIDUAL TRANSGRESSION. The whole race had broken away from God, and was under the curse; so that each of us shared in the solemn accountability to God, for the whole and for our part. But He became sin for us; cursed, that we might be blessed; cast out, that we might be for ever welcomed; naked, that we might be clothed; hungry, that we might feed on his flesh; poor, that we might be enriched; dying, that we might live beyond the range of the curse for evermore.

Thou shalt make a battlement for thy roof. Deut. 22: 8.

THE householder was not to be content with what would be safe for himself; he must see to it that the undefended roof of his house should not be a source of danger to little children, the weak, or the careless. He might be able to walk on the roof of his house with so sure a foot as not to need the parapet or trellis-work, warning him from the edge; but what he could do might be impossible for feet less sure than his. Hence the need of the battlement! Each new house must have its battlement around the margin of its roof.

THIS SHOULD BE THE LAW FOR EACH NEW HOME. Wherever a household is constituted, battlements should be built to protect, as far as possible, the weak and tempted. The pace of the household should be that of the feeblest of its members. You are careful to have the balustrade and the little swing gate, not that the grown-up require them, but for the protection and safety of young and feeble life. Similarly build the battlement of total abstinence, of the discountenance of worldly amusement, of the habit of family worship. Guard against exposure to needless temptation, and occasions for falling.

THIS SHOULD BE THE LAW IN OLDER HOUSEHOLDS. It becomes the master of the home sometimes to go around his household, to study his own character, to inspect the condition of the battlements. Is there laxity, inconsistency, need of precaution? Let us search our hearts and lives, our habits, and the ordering of our homes, that the battlements may be strengthened where they are weak, or erected where they are wanting. "Look not every man on his own things, but every man also on the things of others."

The Lord thy God walketh in the midst of thy camp to deliver thee. Deut. 23: 14.

AT all times Israel needed to keep from evil, but especially when her embattled hosts went forth to war; for in the conception of her prophets and saints her battles were not to be fought or won by herself. The Lord God of hosts was there. It was a joint campaign. This was specially revealed to Joshua, when he beheld the captain of the Lord's host, with a drawn sword, beside him. So, Christian soul, remember, in thy war against the evil of the world, and the solicitations of thine own wicked heart, that the battle is not yours, but God's. He is in the midst of thee; thou needest not be moved! He has sworn to deliver thee by his own right hand, and by his holy arm, and to give up thine enemies before thee.

There was one condition, however, on which the presence of God amongst his people was possible—the camp must be holy. No unclean thing might be seen in any of its borders. The vail of mother-earth must cover all impurity. Thus, as God went up and down the long avenues of the tents, He would see nothing to offend his gaze and make Him turn away. How deep a lesson! God is ever patrolling the avenues of our life. The most secret processes of our daily existence, our innermost relationships, the thoughts and intents of our heart, are all manifest to Him.

There must be nothing to make Him turn away in holy abhorrence, else we cannot count on Him to deliver us, to give up our enemies before us.

"Search me, O God, and know my heart:
Try me, and know my thoughts:
And see if there be any wicked way in me,
And lead me in the way everlasting."

The man to whom thou dost lend shall bring forth the pledge without unto thee. Deut. 24: 11 (R.V.).

WHAT courtesy and respect for the feelings of another prompted this injunction! The poor man needs a loan, and for this purpose goes to his rich neighbour. It would be possible for the latter, in the pride of his purse and position, to go ruthlessly across the threshold of the poor man's house, look contemptuously around its penury, and lay his hand with indelicate haste on the treasure of the poor man's family life. This, which had been dear to his father! That, associated with happier, better days! Such conduct might not be, said the divine precept. If the poor man asked a loan, he must choose his own pledge, and fetch it from his house with his own hand; it must be his act.

GOD RESPECTS THE NATURE WITH WHICH HE HAS ENDOWED US. He will not force an entrance on any man. Though He made us, He waits for us to give Him right of entrance. He stands at the door and knocks. He asks for our consecration, that we should give Him our whole being in pledge, and in return for the loan of infinite grace; but He will not take till we give, or count on aught belonging to us as his property, until we have surrendered spirit, soul, and body, at his invitation.

GOD EXPECTS US TO RESPECT THE NATURE OF OTHERS. Let us reverence that wonderful soul-life which is the perquisite of each individual. We have no right to break in with the mailed foot of the politician, or the furtive tread of the priest. The father-confessor has no right to stand within the sacred precincts of conscience. No man has a claim on his brother save that which love supplies. If we have partaken of the grace of God, we must be gracious to our fellows.

Thou shalt not muzzle the ox when he treadeth out the corn. Deut. 25: 4.

"GOD taketh care of oxen," is Paul's comment on this text; and so God did. These pages are filled with tokens of his thought— for the ass that might not be overtaxed by being set to plough with an ox; for the ass or ox which were to be helped up if they had sunk on the road overpowered with their burdens; or for the bird sitting on her nest. Here the ox, as it went around the monotonous tread of the mill, was to be allowed to take a chance mouthful of corn.

The care for dumb creatures is part of our religious duty. It is one of the elements of religion to think for the dumb creatures, who are not able to speak for themselves, but suffer so patiently the accumulated wrongs heaped on them by man. "A righteous man regardeth the life of his beast: but the tender mercies of the wicked are cruel." Oh, when will the travail of creation cease! Man's sin has indeed worked woe for the lower orders of creation.

The Apostle used this injunction to remind his converts of the necessity of caring for their spiritual teachers. Some are called to plough, others to thresh; but "he that plougheth should plough in hope; and he that thresheth in hope should be partaker of his hope" (1 Cor. 9: 10). They that serve the altar should live by the altar; and those who proclaim the Gospel should live of the Gospel.

But there is sweet encouragement here for those who are anxious about their daily bread. God takes care for oxen; will He not for you? Shall the oxen browse on the wolds and pasture-lands, and be nourished to fatness, and will He leave to starve the soul that really trusts and serves Him?

Thou shalt rejoice in all the good the Lord thy God hath given unto thee. Deut. 26: 11 (R.V.).
DO not be afraid of joy! There are some who only sip of the sweet draughts which God puts to their lips, afraid of drinking long and deeply. When good things come into their lives, they are always thinking of some bitter make-weight, possibly some impending trouble. This is a mistake. We must be prepared to learn the lessons of dark hours when God sends them; but we need not hesitate to learn those of bright and happy ones, when they, too, are meted out to us. As we give ourselves up to sorrow, we should give ourselves up to joy! As the soul descends into the grave, it should have great joy in its resurrection and ascension! If the soul-planet must travel to a wintry distance, let us hail those halcyon hours when it returns to stand in the summer spheres of joy! In the life of consecration our joy is considerably enhanced by sharing it with our Lord. Just as our burden of care is lightened by rolling it upon Him, in the same proportion our joy will be increased when He is permitted to partake of it.

We cannot always be on the strain. It is not possible to live on one side of our nature without impairing the health of all. David must bring his harp, and play in the presence of the soul, when its fits of depression return. There is necessity that we should cultivate tracks of our soul that lie towards a southern aspect, filling them with flowers, and fruits, and beehives, and things that children love.

Open you heart to joy, when it comes in the morning with jocund voice; by the back-door weeping will steal away. She only came to sojourn for a night.

Thou shalt build the altar of the Lord thy God of unhewn stones. Deut. 27: 6.
THE obvious intention of this precept was to prevent idolatry, lest the people should think more of the altar than of Jehovah who has worshipped there. Beware of anything that would divert men's thoughts from God.

BUILD YOUR ADDRESSES OF UNHEWN STONES. When speaking to men, Paul determined to erect structures of unhewn stones, eschewing worldly wisdom, that the power of God might burn more conspicuously on the altar of his words. He knew that his speech and his preaching could never be in persuasive words of human wisdom, and it was his fixed determination to know nothing among men but Jesus Christ and Him crucified. If you spend too much time in cutting the stones of your address, your hearers will probably be more occupied with their artistic grace than with the divine fire that should burn upon them.

BUILD YOUR PRAYERS OF UNHEWN STONES. The expressions of some men in prayer are so exquisitely chiselled that you keep wondering what they will say next, and how. Their prayers stand as beautiful altars on which there is no fire. Oh for the strong cryings and tears of a Spirit-taught man, expressing the real need of his nature, rather than the exquisite beauty of an oration to God!

BUILD YOUR INNER LIFE OF UNHEWN STONES. Do not keep looking to see how you are performing the acts of consecration, confession, devotion. The least you think of these the better, that your entire thought may be concentrated on the great God and his Presence. There must be sincerity in our acts of consecration. One inch of rising flame is better than yards of chiselled stone!

Because thou servedest not the Lord with joyfulness and with gladness. Deut. 28: 47, 48.
WE must serve. It is our nature. Our Lord never suggested a third course as an alternative to the service of God or mammon, as though it were possible to escape all service whatsoever. We either yield ourselves servants of righteousness unto holiness, or of iniquity unto iniquity; and to whom we yield ourselves servants to obey, his we are.

It is a solemn thought: if we are not serving God with joyfulness and gladness of heart, we are serving things which are our worst enemies. A man has no worse foe than himself when he lives to serve his own whims and desires. These habits, and appetites, and fashions, are luxurious and pleasant just now; but their silken cords will became iron bands.

On the other hand, if we would be secure from the service which hurts us, let us give ourselves to the Lord to serve Him with joyfulness and gladness. Do you ask the source of these? Remember, He will put gladness into thy heart; joy is the fruit of his Spirit. When thou art in a healthy state, joyfulness and gladness rise spontaneously in the soul, as music from song-birds. When the sacrifice begins, then will the song of the Lord begin.

The heart finds the well-spring of perennial blessedness when it has yielded itself absolutely and unconditionally to the Lord Jesus Christ. If He is Alpha and Omega; if our faith, however feebly, looks up to Him; if we press on to know Him, the power of his resurrection, and the fellowship of his sufferings; if we count all things but loss for the excellency of his knowledge—we may possess ourselves in peace amid the mysteries of life, and we shall have learnt the blessed secret of serving the Lord "with joyfulness and with gladness of heart."

I shall have peace, though I walk in the stubbornness of mine heart. Deut. 29: 19 (R.V., marg.).
SO man's foolish heart reasons. He hears the curse pronounced against sin; he knows that the man who turns from God is threatened with gall and wormwood, and yet he persists in his evil ways, secretly blessing himself, and laying the flattering unction to his heart that he at least will come off scot free. Such an one is an abomination to the Lord, and shall not escape: "The Lord will not pardon him, but his anger shall smoke against him." It is still true of the wicked, "that every imagination of the thoughts of his heart is only evil continually."

The only way to peace is by abjuring the stubbornness which sets up its own will and way against God's. Is not this the secret of the unrest of your soul—that you have never perfectly yielded to God? You know that if others did as you do, and cherished the dispositions that you permit, you would instantly condemn them, and assure them of the incompatibility of soul-rest and such things as these; but you bless yourself, and say, "I shall have peace, though I walk in the stubbornness of my heart."

Ask God to take the stubbornness out of you, to rid you of your hard heart, to bring you into loving, gentle subordination to Himself; to fulfil his promise in your experience, "I will take the stony heart out of their flesh, and will give them a heart of flesh." Return and submit. Take his yoke and learn of Him. Bow down at his feet. Let every step of your daily walk be taken in the track of his holy will. So shall you find rest unto your soul; and the peace of God, which passeth all understanding, shall guard your hearts and your thoughts in Christ Jesus" (Phil. 4: 7, R.V.).

The Lord thy God will circumcise thine heart, to love the Lord thy God. Deut. 30: 6.
CIRCUMCISION is the sign of separation. It was enjoined on Abraham and his children that they might be God's peculiar people, chosen from all the nations of the earth. Similarly, the circumcision of Christ, which is made without hands, of which the Apostle speaks, is a putting off, a separation from the sins of the flesh, a participation in the grave and burial of Christ (Col. 2: 12).

We must be separated from the spirit and temper of the world. Between us and its sins, ambitions, methods, there must be not only an outward, but a heart severance. We were separated in the purpose of God when Jesus was cast without the camp to die. But we must be separate in our personal behaviour. Wouldst thou have this? Then claim that this promise should be fulfilled, and ask that God would circumcise thine heart—the seat of thine affections, the hearth of thy soul-life.

Then thou wilt love the Lord with all thine heart. This is why we love God so little. The force of our love is spread over too wide a surface—it is like the river Orinoco, which is lost in swamps as it approaches the sea. If only we were really separated from all that is alien to God, and given up to Him wholly, we should find all the capacity of our hearts becoming filled with his love. We should love all things and people with a tenderness and glow which were steeped in colours obtained from his.

You will never succeed in overthrowing the strongholds of Satan, Christian workers, till God has taken away your self-reliance, and has brought you down into the dust of death: then, when the sentence of death is in yourself you will begin to experience the energy of the divine life, the glory of the divine victory.

Thou shalt cause them to inherit it. Deut. 31: 7.

JOSHUA is ever the type of our blessed Jesus. Joshua not only won Canaan for his people by his faith in the gift of God, coupled with his strenuous efforts, but he caused them to inherit it. Jesus not only won the wealth of the heavenlies for his Church by his death and resurrection, but He waits to cause us to inherit it through the Holy Spirit which He gives.

How great is our heritage! Heirs of God and joint-heirs with Christ! All things that pertain to life and godliness await our appropriation! All spiritual blessings in Christ Jesus! There is no conceivable grace or virtue, no fabric of the divine looms for the soul's dress, no ornament of heavenly jewellery for the soul's adorning, no weapon of celestial temper for the soul's equipment, no salve or balm of divine comfort for the soul's healing, which is not ours in Jesus. The Father has given Him to have life in Himself that He might give us life more abundantly. He is full of grace and truth, that out of his fulness we all may receive. He received of the Father the promise of the Holy Ghost, that He might pour Him forth

in Pentecostal fulness. But we do not possess our possessions. We are like people who have sent all their valuables to the strong-room of a bank, and never by any chance make use of them.

This is a lack which Jesus can also supply. He can cause us to inherit: first, by his Spirit He reveals the lavishness of the divine possession; next He excites an appetite of desire; next, He begets the expectant faith that claims; and, lastly, He becomes to us each one of these things, so that we are enriched in Him, and possessing Him, find that all things are really ours.

As an eagle stirreth up her nest, that fluttereth over her young. Deut. 32: 11.

THREE references are made to the eagle in this passage.

SHE STIRS UP HER NEST. When her fledglings are old enough to fly, but linger around the few bits of stick, dignified as a nest, the mother-bird breaks it up, and scatters them. How much better this, than that they should miss the luxury of flight on outspread pinions in the blue vault, and of basking in the eye of the sun. So when the Father sees his children clinging to earth's bare rocks, captured and held by the poor sticks they have gathered, and missing the ascension-glory, He breaks up the nest. The fortune is dispersed, the home broken up, the aspect of the life changed. We are then able to enjoy the bliss of life in the heavenlies with Christ Jesus.

SHE FLUTTERS OVER HER YOUNG. They stand scared and wretched on the edge of the rock, but she careers gently above them, now edging around, now mounting, then dropping far below to rise again. So would she allure them to follow her example. Here again we have an emblem of God's efforts to make us imitators of Himself, to teach us the possibilities that await us in Jesus.

SHE SPREADS FORTH HER WINGS AND TAKES THEM. Incited by the mother's endeavours, the eaglet may venture on the untried air, and lo! the unaccustomed wings fail beneath its weight. It falls, but not far, for the mother swoops beneath, and bears it up and away. Trembling soul, God is beneath thee. If thy faith fails, and thou art falling, like another Peter, into a bottomless abyss, He will catch thee, and bear thee up, and teach thee the mystery of the more abundant life.

Thy Thummim and thy Urim are with Him whom thou lovest. Deut. 33: 8 (R.V., marg.).

WHAT a contrast between the blessings of Jacob and of Moses! In Jacob's farewell charge, we find the ominous words, "Cursed be Levi"; and he foretells that this tribe should be divided and scattered in Israel. But here the curse is turned into a blessing; and the scattering is transformed into a holy ministry for the whole of Israel, "They shall teach Jacob thy judgments and Israel thy law." See to what a place of privilege they are exalted! "They shall put incense before thee, and whole burnt-offering upon thine altar."

If ever there was an illustration of the power we have to turn a curse into a blessing, it is here. Step by step the results of that awful sin, for which Jacob cursed his sons, are changed into benedictions. Where sin abounded, grace has much more abounded; indeed, it has reigned, it has broken out into radiant and royal glory. Do not sit down hopeless, because of the consequences of an early sin that threaten to follow thee to thy grave. Thou mayest yet get honey out of the lion's carcase.

The way to this was by entire devotion to the call of God. After the sin of the golden calf, Levi said of his father and of his mother, I have not seen them; neither did he acknowledge his brethren, nor know his children. The cause of God, which Aaron had so ruthlessly betrayed, was dearer to him than the tenderest ties of blood. So he came into God's secret counsels of love, and knew the Urim and Thummim answers of the One whom he loved. "The secret of the Lord is with them that fear Him." It is only to those with whom He dwells that He can communicate his blessed will and purposes. Oh, may such bliss be mine!

His eye was not dim, nor his natural force abated. Deut. 34: 7.

THIS was true of Moses as a man. He had seen plenty of sorrow and toil; but such was the simple power of his faith, in casting his burden on the Lord, that they had not worn him out in premature decay. There had been no undue strain on his energy. All that he wrought on earth was the outcome of the secret abiding of his soul in God. God was his home, his help, his stay. He was nothing: God was all. Therefore his youth was renewed.

But there is a deeper thought than this. Moses stood for the law. It came by him, and was incarnated in his stern, grave aspect. He brought the people to the frontier of the land, but would not bring them over it: and so the Law of God, even when honoured and obeyed, cannot bring us into the Land of Promise. We stand on the Pisgah-height of effort, and view it afar in all its fair expanse; but if we have never got further than "Thou shalt do this and live," we can never pass into the blessed life of rest and victory symbolized by Canaan.

But though the law fails, it is through no intrinsic feebleness. It is always holy, just, and good. Though the ages vanish, and heaven and earth pass away, its jots and tittles remain in unimpaired majesty. It must be fulfilled, first by the Son, then by his Spirit in our hearts. Let us ever remember the searching eye of that holy Law detecting evil, and its mighty force avenging wrong. Its eye will never wax dim, nor its natural force abate. Let us, therefore, shelter in Him, who, as our Representative, magnified the law and met its claims, and made it honourable.

Joshua

Every place that the sole of your foot shall tread upon. Josh. 1: 3.

ALL the land was given, but every inch of it had to be claimed. Israel had to put her foot down upon the land, whether wilderness or Lebanon, plain or hill, and say, "This is mine by the gift of God." And as the right was asserted, God made it good. The land had

been covenanted to them through Abraham, but it awaited conquest and appropriation by the Israelites. No man was able to stand with them in the lot of their inheritance.

The settler who has purchased a plot of land in the Far West claims it to its furthest borders; and, if needs be, invokes the aid of the Government to make good his purchase.

So with our possessions in Christ. All spiritual gifts are ours in the Risen Saviour. From the wilderness of the earth even to the river that makes glad the city of God, and unto the glassy sea on which the sun never goes down, is our border. But we must put the foot of faith down and say, "All things are ours; we have been blessed with all spiritual blessings in the heavenlies in Christ. He hath given us all things that pertain to life and godliness."

Let this be the beginning of a new life for thee. Reckon that thou art on the resurrection side of death. Do not look at temptation or difficulty, but claim by steadfast faith whatever God has taught thee to feel the need of. Dost thou ask how that strong courage may be thine? The answer is at hand. Meditate on the Word of God day and night, and depart not from it to the right or left. The strength of the inner life finds nourishment in the Word of God. Only in this way can we behold the broad expanse of territory that is ours by right, and obtain strength to go up and possess it.

This line of scarlet thread. Josh. 2: 18.
IT speaks of the precious blood of Christ. Scarlet is the colour of Calvary. Twine it round the window through which thou lookest out on thy foes, and away to the river of death. Nothing can hurt the soul which has put the precious blood of Christ between it and condemnation or alarm. Let every outlook to the future be associated with a remembrance that his blood was shed for thee, and be thou thankful.

Rahab is the type of Gentile sinners who are permitted to share in the unsearchable riches of Christ, and to sit with Him in the heavenlies. That scarlet thread had been the means of salvation to the spies. By it they had been let down to the ground and saved from death. It must have been strong. So the blood of Christ avails, not only for us, but for all who shelter with us in the household of faith, and for others who find it the means of life as they receive it from our hands.

Let us see to it that, like Rahab, we gather father and mother, brethren and friends, to share with us the shelter and safeguard of the precious blood.

But, after all, it was not the cord that saved—that was only the emblem and type. Behind it on the one hand was God's oath, spoken through the spies, and on the other

was Rahab's faith. The true safety of that house on the wall stood in the moral attitude of one woman in it. Rahab believed God who had dried up the water of the Red Sea, and who was God in heaven above and in earth beneath. This faith raised her afterwards from her life of shame to become the ancestress of Christ. Such wonders does the blood of Christ work in outcasts from the commonwealth of Israel, bringing them nigh.

When the soles of the feet of the priests . . . shall rest in the Jordan. Josh. 3: 13 (R.V.)
THE floods of the Jordan were high: so may be the floods of trial and sorrow that sometimes overflow their banks; so the floods of conviction of sin; and so, to some at least, the waters of death. Possibly this overflowing is needed for the time of harvest; the width of golden grain in the Jordan valley was no doubt to a large extent dependent on the far-spreading of those waters. How the heart trembles, as we hear the gurgling and rushing of the floods. Hark, how they lift up their voice!

But when the priest's foot touches them, they shrink away. Jesus has stepped down into these floods as our High Priest. In Gethsemane their overflowing tide washed around Him. At Calvary the water-spouts went over his head. In the grave He seemed momentarily to have succumbed. But since then they have been cut off. Through the ages He has stood, bearing the ark of propitiation, and arresting the tumultuous floods. "Thus far, and no further."

Sinful soul, deeply convicted, "Look for the Priest," on whose person the storm broke, and by whom it has been checked and stayed! Tried believer, be sure that the water-floods cannot pass Jesus, to reach or drown thee! His promise to thee is: "When thou passest through the waters, I will be with thee; and through the rivers, they shall not overflow thee: when thou walkest through the fire thou shalt not be burned; neither shall the flame kindle upon thee" (Isa. 43: 2). And when death approaches thee, O fearful and trembling one, thou wilt find Jesus standing between thee and its might, making a path by which thou shalt pass over dry-shod.

Those twelve stones did Joshua set up in Gilgal. Josh. 4: 20 (R.V.)
NOT content with pitching a cairn of stones

on the river's bank, Joshua, at God's command, set up twelve stones in the midst of Jordan, in the place where the feet of the priests that bare the Ark of the Covenant stood. And often, as he came back to Gilgal, he must have gone out by himself to walk and muse beside the river, turning the outward and the inner gaze to the spot where beneath the flow of the current those stones lay hidden. They were a perpetual memorial of where the people had been, of the grace which had brought them forth, and of the position to which God had conducted them. Children in after days would gather round those mighty boulders and be instructed, and it is a great matter that the deliverances of God should be graven as with a pen of iron on the soft and yielding surface of the child's heart; thus the coming generation shall revere and love the name of Jehovah.

The story of these stones is told again by the Apostle Paul in Ephesians 2. We were dead in trespasses and sins, and lay hopelessly in the grave, like stones in the heart of the river of death. But we were brought forth by God's mighty hand and outstretched arm. We were raised up together with Christ. The resurrection of Jesus is the memorial stone of our position in the sight of God; from this we should never recede, How those old stones would have cried out, if Israel had gone back over the Jordan! And does not Christ's empty grave protest against our living amid the pleasures and cares of the world from which He has gone, and going, has taken us also? This is not our rest; let us make good our standing in the risen Christ.

Behold, there stood a Man. Josh. 5: 13.
WHEN Jericho, its fortifications looming dark through the night, must be assailed, then the divine Man may be looked for. Only let circumcision do its keen work of separation, so that there be nothing of the flesh with its energy and pride to vaunt itself before God; then, as we stand face to face with some imminent peril, God will be revealed as our very present help. Not weeks before our need, not before the Jordan has been crossed in faith, not before circumcision has been performed; but when all God's demands have been met, and to-morrow calls for action, then behold there will stand the Man Christ Jesus, not by Himself, but as Captain of the Lord's host, awaiting with

mightly legions on the wing for his least word.

It is sometimes thought that the Divine Warrior had come to supersede Joshua; this is not so. He was Prince of another host than Israel. His host was the celestial armies, which were going forth to war against Canaan. As long as Israel was true to God, these were its allies. Look up, Christian soul! Thou thinkest thyself alone; or countest sorrowfully thy poor array; but in very deed the Man of Calvary and of the throne is beside thee. All heaven owns his authority, and will supplement thine efforts. Be reverent, obedient, full of faith and prayer. Keep step with the goings forth of God. Thou shalt have light work to do. Before the impact of his might, thy Jericho shall fall. The battle is not to the strong, nor the race to the swift; but each to those who are living lives separate from the world, and dedicated to God. The vessels which are meet for the Master's use are pure ones. Cleanness, rather than cleverness, is the prime condition of successful service.

Every man straight before him. Josh. 6: 20.
GOD required of the Israelites only to wait, obey, and trust, whilst the divine Captain led his celestial hosts to the assault, and achieved the victory. "And the Lord said unto Joshua, See, I have given into thine hand Jericho, and the king thereof, and the mighty men of valour. And ye shall compass the city, all ye men of war, and go round about the city once. Thus shalt thou do six days." We must be sure that our way lies through and beyond Jericho, and that God has called us to take it. When that is ascertained, we may be perfectly certain that the frowning walls of difficulty, which rise between us and the further land of promise, will fall down flat.

There must be times of Waiting. Israel waited a whole week. We may have to wait still longer. Let patience have her perfect work. There is no such teacher as she is; her pupils become perfect and entire, wanting nothing.

There must be times of Obedience. The people could not understand the meaning of these repeated marchings around the walls. They were not, however, asked to understand, but simply to obey. First the priests and ark, then the warriors. We must subordinate our armed activities to the slow and reverent pace of faith, hope, and love.

There must be time of exultant Faith. There was no quaver or hesitation in that cry. The

Word of God, as communicated by Joshua, hushed every doubt and misgiving. In confident assurance the people shouted, and according to their faith, so it was to them. "By faith the walls of Jericho fell down." There are no walls of superstition and sin strong enough to resist Faith's shout, when God says that her shouting time is come.

The Lord said unto Joshua, Get thee up. Josh. 7: 10.

THERE was something very beautiful and impressive in that prostrate form. And as the awed people gathered around in silence to contemplate their leader thus prone upon his face, it must have greatly touched them.

There was cause for soul-anguish. Joshua had counted on unbroken victory through the might of his covenant-keeping God; but here it appeared, either that God had deserted his people, or that He could not cope with the gods on which the Canaanites depended. In either case, Israel was in awful peril; obviously she had not strength sufficient to cope with the seven nations of Canaan. If left to herself, she must inevitably be cut off. But even this prospect alarmed Joshua less than the discredit that would attach to the name of Jehovah.

There are hours in our life when we are called from the exercises of devotion, good and God-honouring though they may be, to deal with the sin of our people, or to cut out some source of failure and defeat. Our place is no longer before the ark; but arraigning the people by their tribes, casting lots for the offender, or consigning the accursed thing to fire. Child of God, do not be content with weeping and praying before God; diligently ascertain and put away the accursed thing which has hidden his face from you. When defeat befalls you at the hands of Satan, you may always be sure that there is some flaw in your consecration. You have taken some of the devoted thing back from God. The course of the Christian warrior should be as the sun when he goeth forth in his strength, and in regular gradients drives his chariot from the eastern wane up the steep of heaven.

He wrote a copy of the law of Moses. Josh. 8: 32.

IF we view this act typically, it is very significant. These things happened to Israel as a type and foreshadowing of great spiritual realities. Canaan is an emblem of the heavenlies, that blessed condition of joy and peace and spiritual power which is ours in Jesus, and becomes ours to enjoy, when we receive the gift of the Holy Ghost. It might have been supposed that in the land of promise there would have been no need for the holy law of God, as given at Sinai, and repeated in Deuteronomy. But it was not so. So, even in the heavenlies, the law must be written again.

JESUS SAID, I CAME NOT TO DESTROY, BUT TO FULFIL (Matt. 5: 17). Not to abrogate, or set aside, or supersede the holy law, but to re-enact it after a more spiritual sort, and to secure, not an outward, but an inward compliance with its precepts. Our Lord complied, not only with the moral, but with the ceremonial law; and his great aim and purpose was to honour and magnify it in the hearts of his people.

THE APOSTLE PAUL SAYS THAT THE ORDINANCE OF THE LAW WILL BE FULFILLED BY THOSE WHO WALK AFTER THE SPIRIT (Rom. 8: 4). It is holy, just, and good; and they who are carnal and sold under sin cannot by their own resolutions and efforts comply with its demands; but when the soul is yielded to the Holy Spirit, He works in us the will and the power.

THE EPISTLE TO THE HEBREWS SAYS THAT IT WILL BE WRITTEN ON OUR HEARTS (Heb. 8: 10). This is the provision of the new covenant; God's law written, not on stone, whence it might be obliterated; not on metal, whence it might be melted; not on the memory, whence it might fade: but on the tablets of the heart, where we shall love it.

They asked not counsel at the mouth of the Lord. Josh. 9: 14.

WHAT an ominous sound there is in those words! They portend disaster—and it befell. Up to this moment the initiative had always been taken by the Lord. Now for the first time it is taken by Joshua and the people. It was a bad business! Certainly the Gibeonites did their work with guile, and were more than a match for the chosen race. Probably they would not have dared to attempt such a piece of imposition on men of their own sort; but the Israelites seemed a likely prey. They had so recently come into the land, that they might be supposed to be unfamiliar with the guile of Canaan. Yet how astute they fancied themselves!

So the children of God are imposed upon still! Women get married to unconverted husbands, supposing all the while that they are converted. Ministers of churches admit ravening wolves into their midst, deceived by the device of the sheepskin. Young converts get seduced from the simplicity and purity of the faith by lying spirits, that seem as lovely as God's angels. This is due to their relying on their own judgment, and not asking counsel of God. We must try the spirits, whether they be of God, for many false spirits are gone into the world.

Yet God held Israel to the covenant that their leaders had struck, and in after years their breach of this promise was awfully avenged (2 Sam. 21: 1, 2). When we have taken a false step we may be forgiven, but we shall be held to its results. O souls, be sure to call in the Priest, with the Urim and Thummim, that He may give you counsel. Seek the purged eye and the pure heart, to be able to see people and things as they really are.

There was no day like that after it. Josh. 10: 14.
THE sun seemed to stay its course in mid-heaven, and hasted not to go down; but there has been no day like that, and there will be none. You may bid the westering sun of another's life stay its downward track toward the western sea, but in vain. It may be some revered minister, some sainted parent, some life dearer to you than your own; but it obeys not your bidding. Surely and inevitably the little daughter of Jairus fades like a flower plucked from its stalk: and Lazarus sinks into his death-sleep, despite the eager message of the sisters to the Life-giver.

So with the sun of your own life. Slowly and steadily it descends. Work while it is called to-day; for the night cometh, in which no man can work. Finish the work that your Father has given you to do; there is only just time enough for it to be done within the span of your days. Our one anxiety should be that nothing divert us from his path, or intercept the communication of his grace.

But there is one Sun that goes not down. "Thy sun shall no more go down, neither shall thy moon withdraw herself; for the Lord shall be to thee an everlasting light, and the days of thy mourning shall be ended." Ah, precious Sun of Righteousness, when once Thou hast risen upon the soul, Thou shalt know no setting, ever higher and higher shalt Thou rise until the perfect day; no twilight or night can come where Thou art; no darkness draw its vail across the sky! Neither life nor death, nor principalities, nor powers, nor things present, nor things to come, shall be able to separate us from the love of God, which has broken upon our hearts, through the wall of cloud.

So Joshua took the whole land, . . . and Joshua gave it . . . Josh. 11: 23.
THIS is almost an exact parallel of the words addressed by Peter to the crowds on the day of Pentecost: "Having received of the Father the promise of the Holy Ghost, He hath shed forth this." In his representative capacity, as the Head of his Church, and the Forerunner of the great host of the redeemed, it was necessary that Jesus should first receive from God the Father all that spiritual inheritance which He was to communicate to those who should afterwards believe in his name: and having received, He is prepared to give. "Ye shall receive power, when the Holy Ghost is come upon you."

The whole land of spiritual blessing is now in the hand of Jesus. The prince of this world is cast out. The power of the Anakim is broken. The seven nations of Canaan and all the power of the enemy is under his feet. His are the rivers of the fulness of the Holy Ghost, and his the mountains of fellowship; his the slopes where the vines of Eshcol ripen and the corn of Canaan goldens; his the green pastures and the still waters of communion, as well as the rocky defile of death. Whatever, then, you desire, you must seek at his hand, in whom it is vested for thee, and me, and every believer: and He will give it.

The land had rest from war. Cease, then, from strife. You will not win by sore wrestling. The lame take the prey. Learn to take; let Him cause you to inherit; let Him give according to the division allotted you in the providence and determination of God. "It shall be given to those for whom it is prepared." "They that receive the abundance of grace shall reign."

Moses, the servant of the Lord, gave it. Josh. 12: 6.
WE must not press a type, or analogy, un-

duly, though we may employ it to illustrate a doctrine well established from other parts of Scripture. Such an illustration is here. It is remarkable that the two tribes and a half which Moses settled beyond the Jordan took little part in the national life, and were soon wiped out of their inheritance. They were apparently absorbed by the nations whom they were supposed to have superseded.

This was partly due to the devotion of the people to their material prosperity. In the words of Deborah, Reuben preferred to sit among the sheepfolds, to hear the piping of the flocks, rather than to take part in the emancipation of Canaan from Midian. But, looked at typically may we not say that whatever Moses gives will ultimately evade our grasp and slip from our possession? Like the tables of stone, it will fall from our hand and be broken in pieces. All that you try to be or do in the power of your own resolution and energy will inevitably fail and deceive you. The land looks fair and the tenure seems good, but you will not be able to retain it.

The deepest blessings of the spiritual life cannot be won or held in the strength of our own purpose, even though it be a holy and earnest one. These things can be ours only in so far as we abide in Christ, in whom our inheritance is vested, and from whom we receive it as we need, by faith. We can hold nothing apart from abiding fellowship with Jesus. And this is our privilege. Let us lift our hearts to the blessed Spirit, asking that He would reveal to us that which eye hath not seen, nor ear heard, nor the heart of man conceived, but which God hath prepared for those that love Him.

There remaineth yet very much land to be possessed. Josh. 13: 1.

THIS is true in many directions:

OF THE BIBLE. How many pages of our Bibles are unpossessed! We have not underlined any verses in them, or put any marks in the margin to indicate that God has spoken through them to our souls. They are as clean as when they came from the printers. It is well sometimes to consider this, and to resolve to master some unfamiliar portions of God's Word, believing that no word of God is devoid of power. To many believers the Bible, which God intended for their possession, is yet an unexplored continent.

OF DOCTRINAL TRUTH. Doctrine groups texts, and compares them. Doctrine is to isolated texts what natural laws are to particular facts. We should know the doctrines of the Bible. We should understand what is meant by Predestination; the unction of the Holy Ghost; and the Second Advent. How much unoccupied land there is is here which, if brought under cultivation, would yield grapes, and corn, and other produce for the refreshment and strength of the soul!

OF SPIRITUAL EXPERIENCE. Talk with some deeply-taught saint, and you will see how little you have traversed of the good land beyond the Jordan, or know of its blessed extent. To know the length, and breadth, and depth, and height, of the love of Christ seems given to but few; but it need not be. There is no favouritism in the Kingdom which excludes some poor souls from the richer portions, and shuts them up to barrenness and a northern aspect. Rise, go through the land in the length and breadth of it; it is all yours; the gift of God in Jesus Christ; claim and possess it.

As my strength was then, even so is my strength now. Josh. 14: 11.

MEN sometimes lose heart as they grow old. They say: My intellect will become impaired, my physical strength will abate, my power for service will wane. Yes: but if the outward man decays, the inward man shall be renewed day by day.

Those that wait on the Lord shall renew their strength: whether to war, to go out for service, or to come in for fellowship and rest. Be of good courage, and He shall strengthen thine heart. He shall satisfy thy mouth with good things, so that thy youth shall be renewed as the eagle's. God's angels are always young. The drain of the years is amply met by the inflow of his all-sufficient grace. There is no reason why we should decline in usefulness and fruit-bearing with the increase of years; but the reverse. The last sheaves that fall beneath thy sickle shall be the heaviest; and the width of thy swathe shall be greatest as the angel of death touches thee and bids thee home. The secret lies in wholly following the Lord.

But Caleb did not rely on his strength to win Hebron. Very modestly and humbly he said, "It may be that the Lord will be with me." Not that he for a moment doubted it. Could it be for one moment supposed that the God whom he had wholly followed for eighty years would desert him in the supreme crisis of his life? But he put it thus in the sweet lowliness of his soul, because he counted not himself worthy. The strongest men are they who count that they are helpless as worms; and who put their weakness at the disposal of God's might. To each of us comes the promise of God: "My grace is sufficient for thee; for my strength is made perfect in weakness."

He gave her the upper springs, and the nether springs. Josh. 15: 19.

CALEB had conquered his giants, and so he was able to give his daughter an inheritance of land and springs of water. It was when Jesus had overcome the sharpness of death that He opened the Kingdom of Heaven to all believers; it was as He trampled under his victorious feet the principalities and powers of darkness that He gave to his Church the upper and the nether springs.

There are two departments in our life, which are closely related and yet one. We occupy the one in our contact with men and our work in the world; the other, in our holy moments of meditation and prayer. Christ's sheep go out to their manifold activities, and come in to feed on the green pastures beside waters of rest. In each of these we stand in daily need of the springs that are fed from the River which proceeds from the Throne of God, and which is an emblem of the Holy Ghost.

On the Lord's Day, in the House of God, or in private prayer, we climb the hills and stand on the margin of the upper springs that rise there; in the solemn hush we hear the murmur of their waters. On Monday we descend into the valley amid the clang of the battle and the cries of human need; but, thank God! plentiful springs are there also. Upper springs from the Mount of Transfiguration; nether springs for the Valley of Humiliation. Upper springs for the days of health and abounding activity; nether springs for days of depression, and pain, and death. Upper springs in praise, adoration, and rapture; nether springs for taking the yoke, bearing the burden, and drinking of his cup. Let us partake freely of the refreshing water which flows from the River of God.

And the children of Joseph took their inheritance. Josh. 16: 4.

WHAT a wonderful wealth of blessing these children of Joseph came into! There were the precious things of heaven, the dew, and the deep that couched beneath; the precious fruits of the sun and of the growth of the moons; the metals of the ancient mountains and the everlasting hills; the precious things of the earth, and the fulness thereof: and, above all, the goodwill of Him that dwelt in the bush (Deut. 33: 13-16). Surely they were blessed with all manner of blessings—more than they had asked or thought! The rich gifts of God's grace! An inheritance which could not have been won by their prowess or arms, but was the free gift of God's love—to be taken and enjoyed!

These things happened to them as types; the spiritual counterparts of all are ours in Christ. He is precious—nay, priceless: his promises are exceeding great and precious. The blood by which we were redeemed is precious, has meanings not yet explored; the very trial of our faith is precious as the gold taken from the everlasting hills. How much preciousness there is for us who believe! (1 Pet. 2: 7, R.V.). But we are poor, and wretched, and miserable, and blind, and naked, because we have not taken our inheritance.

We need to do more than ask for it. He that asketh should not rest till he receiveth. We must take by a faith which claims, appropriates, employs. Open your heart to the Lord Jesus Christ, that He may cause you to receive and enjoy all his precious gifts. In Christ all things are yours: go in and possess; take your inheritance; believe that you do receive; thank Him, and go on your way rejoicing.

The hill country shall be thine. Josh. 17: 18 (R.V.).

THE hills were steep, irregular, covered with forest. "These shall be yours," said Joshua to the children of Joseph; "you are a great people, and have great power; cut down the forest, terrace the slopes, turn their bare declivities into cornfields and vineyards; fill these vast untenanted spaces with life and song."

THERE IS ALWAYS ROOM HIGHER UP. When the valleys are full of Canaanites, whose iron chariots withstand your progress, get up into the hills, occupy the upper spaces. If you can no longer work for God, pray for those who can. If you cannot move earth by your speech, you may move Heaven. If the development of life on the lower slopes is impossible, through limitations of service, the necessity of maintaining others, and such-like restrictions, let it break out towards the unseen, the eternal, the divine.

FAITH CAN FELL FORESTS. Even if the tribes had realized what treasures lay above them, they would hardly have dared to suppose it possible to rid the hills of their dense forest-growth. But as God indicated their task, He reminded them that they had power enough. The visions of things that seem impossible are presented to us, like these forest-covered steeps; not to mock us, but to incite us to spiritual exploits which would be impossible unless God had stored within us the great strength of his own indwelling. Difficulty is sent to reveal to us what God can do in answer to the faith that prays and works. Are you straitened in the valleys? Get away to the hills, live there; get honey out of the rock, and wealth out of the terraced slopes now hidden by forest.

Joshua charged them that went to describe the land. Josh. 18: 8.

IN every age of the Church's story, God has sent forth men to walk through and describe the land of our spiritual inheritance. They have become dissatisfied with the low attainments of their brethren, and with great desire have followed the divine suggestions which pointed to a wider knowledge and enjoyment of the possibilities of Christian living. In the first ages, this was the work of men like Chrysostom and Augustine; in later ones, of the Reformers; in later ones still, of men whose names are still fresh in the memory of the Church.

But there is a sense in which all the experiences of life, all our walkings through the land of promise, all our discoveries of springs and valleys and far-stretching champaigns of territory, are not intended for ourselves alone, but for others. We are led by a certain path, that we may know how to direct a poor wanderer on his way. We are comforted, that we may be able to comfort those who are in any trouble. Our Father has blessed us with all spiritual blessings in Christ, that we may communicate those blessings to our fellows. We are shown the mysteries of the Kingdom of Heaven, that we may be able to unfold their joy and helpfulness to others. We are saved that we may become workers together with God.

The books which come to us from holy men who have traversed the land are of priceless value, like this Domesday book which Joshua prepared. But we who cannot write books should yet describe the land. "Come and hear, all ye that fear God; and I will declare what He hath done for my soul." There is a divine warrant for experience meetings of the right sort, where the form is subordinate to the fresh and living Spirit.

In the midst of them. Josh. 19: 49 (R.V.).

SINCE Joshua prefigures the Lord Jesus, we are led to think of his inheritance in the midst of his brethren.

IN THE MIDST ON THE CROSS. "They crucified Him, and with Him two others, on either side one, and Jesus in the midst." Forasmuch as we partook of flesh and blood, He shared the same; and since we were under the curse of a broken law, He also bowed beneath its weight, and was made a curse for us. He took the mid-current of pain; where the pressure was heaviest, there the Lamb of God bore the sin of the world. On Him God made to meet the iniquities of us all; alike of those who refuse, as did the one thief, and of those who accept, as did the other.

IN THE MIDST, IN THE GATHERINGS OF HIS PEOPLE. "Where two or three are gathered together in my name, there am I in the midst of them." He is the centre of unity. We come from different quarters with our peculiar prepossessions and preconceptions, with no special affinity to each other; but touching Him, we become one with all who touch Him also. See that, not the sermon, nor the supper, nor the form of worship, is the centre of fellowship; but Christ always and in all. Then let Him be the centre of thy home life and thy business life under all circumstances.

IN THE MIDST IN HEAVEN. "In the midst of the throne, and in the midst of the elders, a Lamb standing." All the circles of the redeemed, of angels, and of all other things, revolve around Jesus, as their common centre. They thus become concentric. Jesus is the Heart of Heaven; the Sun of Paradise; the Essence of its bliss; the Centre of its love; the innermost Soul of its life.

And for the stranger that sojourneth among them. Josh. 20: 9.

IT is interesting to note this provision, made

in the Land of Promise, for the passing over of sins which were not sins of presumption. In this verse there is that great word "Whosoever." These cities of refuge were not for Hebrews only, but for whosoever had killed any person, without malice or forethought, but quite unintentionally, and had fled thither. Some poor Gentile might be sojourning among the chosen people, and suddenly find himself liable to the pursuit of the avenger of blood; but the gates of the refuge city were open to him, and the elders of the city were bound to give him a place that he might dwell among them (4), not only safely, but in rest and peace.

Herein there was a foreshadowing of the days when God should open the door of faith unto the Gentiles. "For there is no distinction between Jew and Greek, since the same Lord is Lord of all, and is rich unto all them that call upon Him."

There were two mysteries made known to the Apostle Paul: one he unfolds in the Epistle to the Ephesians, the other in the Epistle to the Colossians. First, he teaches us that the Gentiles may be fellow-heirs and fellow-members of the body, and fellow-partakers of the promise of Christ through the Gospel. Next, he expatiates on the riches of the glory of this mystery, among the Gentiles, that the living Saviour is prepared to dwell in their hearts also, as the Hope of Glory. It is a serious question how far we are participating in our inhieritance. The gates of the promises made to Abraham and his seed are open for us to enter in and dwell there; but there is too much backwardness and hesitancy in us all. "Whosoever will, let him take."

There failed not aught of any good thing which the Lord had spoken. Josh. 21: 45.
SUCH will be the summary of our lives, as we review them from the land of the sunset. We shall see plenty of our own failures, shortcomings, and sins, and sadly acknowledge them. We shall see that our unbelief and disobedience have deprived us of the enjoyment of much that God intended for us. We shall see that whatever was lacking was in no wise due to Him, but to ourselves. The land of our inheritance had been all given us in Jesus; but we suffered the lack of much, because of our failure to enter in.

THERE MAY BE LONG DELAYS IN THE FULFIL-MENT OF PROMISE. But delays are not denials; and it is better to let the fruit ripen before you pluck it. Wait till God drops it into your hand; it will be ever so much sweeter.

THERE MAY BE ENEMIES AND OBSTACLES. But they will give back, before the will of God, as the gates of night roll back before the touch of the dawn. Do not scheme, or fret, or be impatient; God is doing all to make thy life full of favour and blessing. Wait on Him, and keep his way; He will exalt thee to inherit the earth. Thou art as safe as if the gate of pearl were behind thee; thy joy cannot rust or be stolen; every wind is a south wind; every shore thy native land; every circumstance a rough packing-case containing the gifts of thy Father's love.

THERE MAY BE IGNORANCE AND WEAKNESS. But God can deal with this also. Take to Him thine imperfect apprehension, thy faltering faith, He can make right what is wrong, and adjust thee to receive all He waits to give. Heaven will be full of wonder at the way in which God has kept his word, and done all that He had promised, and more.

A witness between us and you. Josh. 22: 27.
THE two tribes and a half made the mistake which all Christendom has made since. They endeavoured to erect an outward symbol of unity in this altar. They hoped that it would secure them for excision from the rest of Israel. They sought to make a unity, instead of accepting this as a fact, and endeavouring to manifest it by three pilgrimages a year to God's altar at Shiloh.

Similarly, some Christians set up a church, a system, a creed, and mode of worship, and maintain that the divine unity can only be realized in connection with one or other of these. You must be a votary at their altar of Ed, or you run the risk of their accusing you of the sin of schism. They substitute an outward for an inward unity, and a mechanical for a vital spiritual fellowship.

If we belong to Christ, we belong to one another. The Church, with all its members, is one vine, one body, one family; and therefore we have to manifest, rather than to make the unity, concerning which our Lord thought so much in his intercessory prayer. "That they all may be one; as Thou, Father, art in Me, and I in Thee, that they also may be One in us; that the world may believe that Thou hast sent Me."

We are one in the thought of the Father,

one in the redemption of the Son, one in the possession of the indwelling Holy Spirit. Let us be one in our relation to others, pitying, loving, aiding each other, forgiving and restoring, avoiding unkind comparisons and criticisms, remembering that the failure or success of one is that of all, and endeavouring to hasten the hour when the manifested oneness of the Church shall compel the world to believe that the Father sent the Son.

Take good heed unto yourselves, that ye love the Lord your God. Josh. 23: 11.

LOVE is the crown of human nature; its regal chaplet of flowers; the bond by which the sentient universe is made one; the trait in which we most nearly resemble God—for God is love. We may love God from four parts of our nature (Luke 10: 27). From the heart, the seat of the emotions: from the soul, the seat of individuality or will; in the strength of our activities; and in the mind, the organ of thought and intelligence. Some natures are more prone to one, and others to another. Each is a gate into the metropolis of Love, or by which the love of God may enter us. And it is of small consequence which gate you use, so long as you use one, and in this way enter the city.

Many people are accustomed to impute love to the heart only, instead of associating it also with other departments of the inner life. Because you have no emotion of love, you therefore conclude that you do not love. But there may be the love of soul, wherein the will crowns Christ as King; or the love of the strength, wherein all the energy of life revolves around Jesus; or the love of the mind, in which all thought is brought into captivity to the obedience of Christ. Choose which you will.

But we must take heed to ourselves. The love of God will come naturally and easily in us as the fruit of the Spirit, unless we do anything to mar or hinder it. Love begets love; think then how much He loved you,

when He gave Himself for you. Take heed to your speech, acts, intentions, volitions, affections; watch as well as pray; keep yourselves in the love of God; love one another and so abide in his love; and in you also the love of God will be perfected.

Ye cannot serve the Lord. Josh. 24: 19.

IT seemed as though Joshua sought to damp down the enthusiasm of the people. They were all on fire to serve, but he repressed their ardour, crying, "Back, back! This is no place for you." We are reminded of a precise analogy in the Gospels, where our Saviour said to Peter and the rest, "Ye cannot follow Me now" (John 13: 31–38). Why this divine reluctance?

The answer is clear, when we consider the sequel in each case. In the one, we have only to turn a page in our Bibles, to come on all the disobedience, anarchy, and backsliding of the Book of Judges; in the other we see that Peter denied and the rest forsook Him. How obviously it was shown that there was a moral incompatibility between their self-confident assertions and the service of the Holy God. But this incompatibility was present to the Spirit's discernment when these strong asseverations were made, first by the Israelites, and secondly by the Apostles.

So it becomes us to speak very reverently and leniently of our ability to obey. We are probably overestimating our powers. Created might wanes and fails beneath the searching demands of the Holy One. Perpetual failure has weakened us; for when once a door has been broken through a wall, that spot is always weaker. A fallen ancestry has predisposed us to fail. To will is present with us, but how to perform that which is good we find not. No one can look thoughtfully into the workings of his own nature without realizing the terrible paralysis which has befallen it. We need then that God should counteract our fickleness by upholding us with his steadfast, or constant, Spirit (Psa. 51: 10).

Judges

The Canaanites would dwell in that land. Judges 1: 27.

HOW persistent evil habits are! They have

dwelt in our lives so long that they dislike being dislodged. Why should they quit their dwelling-place and go out into the void?

Sometimes, at the beginning of our Christian life, we make a feeble effort against them, and hope to cast them out; but they stubbornly resist. Whenever a remonstrance is addressed to us, we are apt to reply, "Do not find fault; we couldn't help it. These Canaanites are self-willed and persistent, they would dwell in the land."

But the one point that Israel should have borne in mind was that they had no right there. The land was not theirs, it had become Israel's. And, moreover, God was prepared to drive them out; so that his people would have no fighting to do, but only to chase a flying foe. One man was to chase a thousand (Josh. 23: 10).

So these evil habits have no right to persist in the believer's life. The whole soil of his heart has been made over to the Son of God, and there should be no part left to weeds. "Sin shall not have dominion over you," said the Apostle. Nor is this all. The Holy Spirit is prepared to lust against the flesh, that we may not fulfil it in the lusts thereof, or do the things we otherwise would. The hasty temper may be natural to you: but seeing that your position in Christ is supernatural, this Canaanite must be conquered. There is a complete deliverance possible to all who will open their hearts to the might of the Spirit of God. Talk no more of these Canaanites who would stay in the land; but say of the blessed Spirit, "He is well able to drive them out."

The Lord raised them up judges. Judges 2: 18.
THIS was better than nothing. It was better to have even the fitful gleam of deliverance than to settle down under a monotony of servitude; but how much better it would have been if their national history had been a steady progression from one degree of prosperity to another, like the sun rising towards the perfect day! It was of God's kindness and grace that the judges created these temporary respites; it was the fault of their own infidelity and sin that they were not always delivered.

This fitful life is too often the experience of the believer. We have our Gideons, and Baraks, and Samsons; times of revival, times of deep and blessed experience, followed by backsliding and relapse; times when the flood-tide of grace rises high in our soul, to be succeeded by the ebb, with long stretches of desert sand. Thank God for the judges; but be on the alert for the reign of the kings, for David and Solomon, Josiah and Hezekiah —for the reign of the King.

The days of the judges were those in which there was no king over Israel. The fitfulness of our experience is often attributable to our failure to recognize the kingship of Jesus. We worship other gods—the gods of the nations around; the idols of the market-place, the studio, the camp, and the bar. The aims and practices of the worldly and ungodly too much engross our thoughts, and sway our behaviour. Alas for us! Is it strange that God leaves us to reap much bitterness, recalling us when He can, but longing to be able to do some permanent work of salvation and edification? Oh, let us gladly accord Him what is his right, to "sit and rule upon his throne."

I have a message from God unto thee. Judges 3: 20.
GOD'S MESSAGES ARE OFTEN SECRET. When Eglon was assured that Ehud had brought a divine message, which could only be delivered in secret, "a secret errand" (19), he fearlessly bade all his retinue go forth from the audience chamber. And in utter loneliness the one passed to the other the message of death. So there are crises in our lives when God's messengers bring us the secret message, in which none can intrude or interfere.

GOD'S MESSAGES MUST BE RECEIVED WITH REVERENCE. When Ehud said, "I have a message for thee," Eglon rose out of his seat. This was a mark of respect, the attitude of attention. It is with similar awe that we should ever wait for the revelation of the divine will. "What saith my Lord unto his servant?"

GOD'S MESSAGES LEAP OUT FROM UNEXPECTED QUARTERS. Ehud was left-handed; his sword was therefore on his right side, and he appeared unarmed. No one dreamed of looking for his sword, except on his left side; he was therefore allowed to pass unchallenged into the presence of the king. So Nathan strode into David's presence, who thought his sin was undiscovered, and said, "Thou art the man." Cultivate this surprise with sinners.

GOD'S MESSAGES ARE SHARP AS A TWO-EDGED SWORD, AND CAUSE DEATH. A scimitar is sharp at the edge, and blunt at the back to strike; whilst a two-edged sword is made to pierce. God's Word pierces as a two-edged sword to the dividing of soul and spirit in the recesses of the being, and is a discerner of the thoughts and intents of the heart. When the Eglon of self has received its death-wound, the glad trumpet of freedom is blown on the hills.

The journey that thou takest shall not be for thine honour. Judges 4: 9.

BARAK preferred the inspiration of Deborah's presence to the invisible but certain help of Almighty God. It was Jehovah who had commanded him to draw his forces towards the River Kishon, and had promised to deliver Sisera into his hand. But he seemed unable to rise to the splendour of the situation. If only he could have Deborah beside him he would go, but otherwise not. He is mentioned in Heb. 11 as one of the heroes of faith; but his faith lay rather in Deborah's influence with God than in his own. Thus he missed the crown of that great day of victory.

It is the mark of the carnal Christian that he has no direct dealings with God for himself, but must needs deal with Him through the medium of another's prayers, and words, and leadership. Barak must have Deborah. It is faith, though greatly attenuated and reduced by the opaqueness of the medium through which it passes. Such do not attain "unto the first three." God cannot honour them as He does those who have absolutely no help or hope save in Himself. "Them that honour Me I will honour; and those that despise Me shall be lightly esteemed."

If God tells you to go alone to a work, be sure and obey. Go, at whatever cost. Dare to stand by yourself if God is with you. In such hours we realize what Jesus meant when He said, "Whosoever shall say unto this mountain, Be thou taken up and cast into the sea; and shall not doubt in his heart, but shall believe that what he saith cometh to pass, he shall have it." Yet if you are unbelieving, your unbelief cannot make God's faith of none effect. He abideth faithful. He cannot deny Himself. He will still deliver Israel.

Let them that love Him be as the sun when he goeth forth in his might. Judges 5: 31.

SO sang Deborah; and we may take up her strain, making it our prayer for all that love the Lord Jesus Christ in sincerity.

WE DESIRE IT FOR HIS SAKE. It cannot be for his glory that his followers should be weak-kneed and decrepit, waning and flickering, backsliding and inconstant. Men will judge Him by them, and will count his light a vanishing luminary if He cannot maintain the glow and fire in those that follow Him. Besides, how great the anguish of his heart must be when those on whom He has expended pains and care deceive and fail Him!

WE DESIRE IT FOR THEIR SAKES. Think of the beneficent ministry of the sun—awakening bird and blossom; painting the rich colours of natural beauty; ripening fruits; gladdening children and grandsires; carrying everywhere healing with his beams. If he were conscious of the good he imparts, what blessedness would be his! Would he grudge the expenditure of his vitalizing forces, when from millions of upturned lips he heard himself blessed? Such may the bliss of the Christian worker be if, without diminution of light and heat, his life grows to the perfect day. Blessed are they who bless. If it is happy to receive, it is far happier to impart. "Remember the words of the Lord Jesus, how He said, It is more blessed to give than to receive."

WE DESIRE IT FOR THE SAKE OF OTHERS. The world is sunless enough! Many are perishing for a bath of sunshine! Darkness broods chill and deathly. Let no clouds dim your pathway, or, if they do, transmute them to gold. Shine forth, ye righteous, in the kingdom of your Father, satellites of the greater central Sun of Righteousness!

And the Lord looked upon him and said, Go in this thy might. Judges 6: 14.

THE strength-giving power of a look from the eyes of Christ! Gideon was weak enough. He said, quite naturally, "My family is the poorest in Manasseh, and I am the least in my father's house" (ver. 15, R.V.). But from the moment of that look, accompanied by that summons, he arose in a strength that never afterwards faltered. How truly "God hath chosen the foolish things of the world to confound the wise; and the weak things of the world to confound the things which are mighty."

IT WAS A LOOK OF EXPECTATION. Gideon felt that the angel expected him to save Israel. It is a great matter to excite hope in a man. Tell him that you are anticipating some noble deed from him, and you may light a spark that will set his whole soul aglow. It is of immense importance to stir the timid and retiring with fresh conceptions of the possibilities of their lives.

IT WAS A LOOK OF ENCOURAGEMENT. Those gentle, loving eyes said, as though they spoke, "I will be with thee; do not hesitate to look for Me in every hour of need." Such looks Christ still gives us across the battlefields of life; and if our eyes are fixed upon Him, we shall surely hear Him saying to us, "My grace is sufficient for thee: go in this thy might!"

IT WAS A LOOK OF STRENGTH-GIVING MIGHT. It carried help with it. On its beam new spiritual force sped from the speaker to the listener; from captain to cadet. So from the excellent glory one look from Jesus will bring reinforcement. As He looks on us He imparts his strength to us, and says, Go in this thy might. "Be strong in the Lord, and in the power of his might."

A cake of barley bread. Judges 7: 13.

LIKE most dreams, incoherent and grotesque! Who ever heard of a cake of barley bread upsetting a tent! To the dreamer and his comrade, there was no sense in it. But how much it meant to the two Hebrews, who had crept up to the other side of the curtain, in the thick darkness, and were drinking in each word!

THE DREAM WAS VERY HUMBLING. It brought Gideon back to the simplicity and helplessness of his own resources. In the gathering of these crowds of warriors, in the notoriety he had achieved, in the loyalty of the three hundred, there was much to inflate his pride. Therefore God brought him face to face with himself. He was only a cake of barley bread at the best. Before God can uplift, use, and anoint us, He must show us what we are, humbling and emptying us, bringing us into the dust of death. Before God can use thee to work a great deliverance, He must convince thee of being only a cake of barley bread. "Five barley loaves, and two small fishes."

IT WAS FULL OF HOPE. A cake of barley bread might be a worthless thing; but if God were behind it, it would upset a tent! So when the weakest life is placed at the disposal of the Almighty, and taken in hand by Him, it becomes mighty to the pulling down of strongholds.

IT IS FULL OF TEACHING. How much has to

be learnt by us on these lines! We are too strong for God. We vaunt our might, we count our warriors, we magnify our generalship. This may not be! So God brings us down to the brook and tests us there; and reduces our force to three hundred men, and ourselves to barley-cakes, and there gets the victory with his right hand, and his holy arm.

As thou art, so were they; each one resembled the children of a king. Judges 8: 18.

IT was a magnificent tribute to the royal bearing of this illustrious family. All the children had the stamp of kingliness on them, which had impressed even these barbaric princes. Would that a similar confession could be extorted from those who behold the members of the royal house of Jesus!

The children of a king! It is within the reach of any who aspire to it. By the second birth we become the children of God, jointheirs with Christ, and the Spirit witnesses to our sonship, teaching us to cry, Abba, Father. As children of the great King we should bear the sign of our high lineage in our bearing and walk.

ROYALTY OF DEMEANOUR. There is an aristocratic bearing in the scions of noble houses among men. The head is lifted high, the mien is proud, the manner distant and reserved. But in the family of God, meekness and lowliness, humility and contriteness, are marks of family likeness. We walk as Jesus walked, of whom the Baptist said, "Behold the Lamb of God!"

ROYALTY OF DRESS. The king is marked by the brilliant orders glittering on his breast. Purple and ermine become those who date their descent from a line of kings. But the emblem of our family is the cross; our colour is scarlet; our insignia is the towel and basin that speak of lowly service.

ROYALTY OF OCCUPATION. The earthly king does nothing servile. He is waited on with lowly obeisance. But they who are of the same family as Jesus are found performing the lowliest acts of service, in gaols, hospitals, and slums. In this they follow closely on the steps of Him who went about doing good.

Their hearts inclined to follow Abimelech; for they said, He is our brother. Judges 9: 3.

IS not this the reason why God has set us in families? Had He so chosen, each of us might have been created alone as Adam was, and sent out with no special connection with others of our race. But instead, we are closely connected. It is very rarely that a man is so utterly bereaved as to be destitute of some relative.

Between a man and his brother there is a special tie. It may be truly said, in the case of brothers, that a doorway has been made through the walls which ordinarily part men, which may be bricked up or filled with debris; but the wall there will always be thinner than anywhere else, and some day the doorway may be opened for the passage of the messenger of peace. Men are always more inclined to follow the man of whom they can say, "He is our brother." Brotherhood, sisterhood, relationship of any kind, is therefore a very precious talent; and it becomes us solemnly to ask ourselves whether it has been put to use. Have you ever spoken or written to your brother or sister about Christ?

As soon as Andrew had found Jesus, he started off to find his own brother Simon; and Simon was glad to follow him because he was his brother. Had another tried, it is as likely as not that he would have repelled him. But what could he say to the man who had shared his childhood's sports, and had helped him haul in a net of fish many a time after a night of hard work?

This is the reason that Jesus has so strong a hold on human hearts. He is our brother, bone of our bone; not ashamed to call us brethren; and this constitutes a moving argument why we should be inclined to follow Him.

His soul was grieved for the misery of Israel. Judges 10: 16.
THIS is a very strong way of stating the pitifulness of God. It is applying to Him terms borrowed from our own experiences as men; and in no other way we realize the tender love and compassion of our Heavenly Father. Israel's miseries were due to the sins with which their history was marked; but God's love brooded over them, longing to deliver.

THIS IS THE EXPLANATION OF GOD'S FIRST WORDS TO ADAM. One of the versions substitutes for "Where art thou?" the words "Alas for thee!" as though God were treading the glades of Eden with a broken heart, grieved for the misery of his children.

THIS WAS THE LAMENT OF GOD'S SPIRIT THROUGHOUT THE OLD TESTAMENT. "How shall I give thee up, Ephraim? Mine heart is turned within me; my compassions are kindled together." "O Israel, thou hast destroyed thyself!"

THIS LED TO THE INCARNATION AND PASSION OF OUR LORD. He looked, and there was no man; He wondered that there was none to help, therefore his own arm brought salvation.

THIS CHARACTERIZED OUR LORD'S EARTHLY LIFE. When He beheld the city, and foresaw all the evil that would accrue to it, He could not hold back his tears. "His soul was grieved." In all likelihood, you, my reader, may be suffering keenly the result of your own mistakes and sins in earlier life. The troubles that hem you are the direct outcome of your having forsaken God. He could, and would, have saved you; but you made it impossible, because you withdrew yourself from his care. And now He grieves over you. If only you would forsake your sins and turn to Him, He would assuredly raise up a Jephthah for your help.

And Jephthah sent messengers unto the king of the children of Ammon. Judges 11: 12.
JEPHTHAH'S procedure was admirable in his quiet expostulation, before resorting to force in the defence of home and country against the aggression of Amalek. It was quite clear that Ammon had no right to the lands of which Israel, at God's command, had dispossessed the Amorites. "Thou doest me wrong to war against me." But before repelling the invasion, Jephthah did his best to show the unreasonableness of Ammon's pretext.

Thus our Lord expostulated with the servant that smote Him. "If I have spoken evil, bear witness of the evil; but if well, why smitest thou Me?"

It is in this way that we are to act still. "If thy brother sin against thee, go, show him his fault between thee and him alone: if he hear thee, thou hast gained thy brother."

In the Master's judgment, the wrongdoer injured himself much more than any one else; and therefore earnest words of expostulation were desirable to stay him from his own destruction.

How admirable it would be if we would act in such a spirit of meek conciliation! Then our cause might fairly be submitted to the Judge of all (27); and we should be strong in after-times to stand for the sacred rights of others.

There is no need to bribe God's help, as Jephthah did, by his rash promise. He will give gladly and freely out of his own heart of love the help and deliverance we need, if only our cause is rightly ordered before Him. "Who delivered, . . and doth deliver; . . He will yet deliver" (2 Cor. 1: 10). When we are right with our fellow-men, we can confidently count on God's almighty helpfulness.

And he said, Sibboleth.   Judges 12: 6.

IT was only the omission of "h," but it meant the death of the man who missed it. One little letter, and the whole wonder and beauty of a human life was forfeited. It is only recently that the peace of an empire was in jeopardy, because a full-stop was misplaced. This scene has become proverbial of those who exact compliance with · some arbitrary test, before admitting their fellows into their sect or church. But how thankful we should be, that our admission to the privilege of the Kingdom of God does not depend upon our pronunciation; that the reality of the new-birth is not tested by the accuracy with which we utter the creed; that we shall not be excluded from the gates of the New Jerusalem because we fail in the utterance of an "h"!

Our acceptance with God does not depend on how much we believe. The woman who was healed had very inadequate notions of faith and Christ. She thought that his garment would communicate blessing, yet she was cured. The dying thief had but a glimmering ray of knowledge of the majesty and power of Jesus, but he entered Paradise in His company. The prime necessity with us, is not faith in the sense of creed, but as standing for TRUST. It is not our belief about Christ, but our trust in Him; not our ability to answer the questions of the Catechism, but our coming to Him, and finding rest to our souls—this only is necessary to pass us across the fords of Jordan. "If thou shalt confess with thy mouth the Lord Jesus, and shalt believe in thine heart that God hath raised Him from the dead, thou shalt be saved. For with the heart man believeth unto righteousness; and with the mouth confession is made unto salvation" (Rom 10: 10).

If the Lord were pleased to kill us, He would not have received an offering.   Judges. 13: 23.

MANOAH was a pessimist, given to dark foreboding, fond of anticipating misfortune. So soon as he realized that he had seen the face of God, he made sure that his wife and he would die. His wife, on the contrary, was prone to look on the bright side of things, and she must have been an admirable help-meet. How much some of us owe to the temperament of those with whom we live! Many a time would Christian sit down to die, and succumb in the dark waters of the river, if it were not for Hopeful, who pierces the gloom, and beholds the light shining beyond the cloud.

Often enough Foreboding whispers, "We shall surely die." It is the voice of conscience, dreading the result of sin. It is the voice of mistrust, which fails to look beyond the hills for help. It is the voice of human frailty. At such times let us look back and recount the blessings of the past. Did not God receive our burnt-offering? Did He not conspicuously answer our prayers? Did He not give his only begotten Son? Has He not led us by his right hand and holy arm? Has He not delivered us in seven troubles? Besides, has He not pledged Himself for the future? Has He not showed us "all these things"? It is impossible to believe that He will allow us to be overwhelmed.

His love in time past forbids me to think,
He'll leave me at last in trouble to sink.

Trust Him, O suffering saints, doing his will in the teeth of opposition and hate! Fear not the faces of men; be not dismayed before their threats—He is with you to deliver you. They may fight against you, but they shall not prevail; their proudest threats shall fail of their fulfilment.

Out of the eater came forth meat.   Judges 14: 14.

YOUNG lions roar at the saints. The lion of hell gives them no little trouble. Though he may not come upon the path of holiness—for no lion shall be there—yet he comes very near it. "He goeth about like a roaring lion." Temptation may well be compared to the attack on Samson by the young lion of Timnath.

The lion's carcase lying where Samson had rent and cast it, became the home of honeybees. And as the hero went back to look at it in after-days, he obtained meat and sweetness.

How apt the parable! Every conquered temptation yields these two things—strength and sweetness. We are more than conquerors, not only vanquishing the foe, but dividing the spoils of victory.

IT YIELDS STRENGTH. Each time we overcome sin, the strength of the temptation passes into our hearts; as the Indian warrior supposes that the might of each warrior whom he levels to the dust, enters into himself. To resist impatience, makes us more patient in proportion to the strength of the temptation we resist. "Blessed is the man that endureth temptation: for when he is tried, he shall receive the crown of life, which the Lord hath promised to them that love Him."

IT GIVES SWEETNESS. There is a new gentleness to those who have been tempted; a humility, a modesty, a consciousness of the presence of God, through whom the victory has been secured; a new zest for the Word of God. How sweet are thy words to my taste! sweeter than honey and the honeycomb. The life that is hid with Christ in God is full of sweetness and gentleness. "The fruit of the Spirit is gentleness."

And now shall I die for thirst? Judges 15: 18.
IT had been a great victory. With the jawbone of an ass Samson had smitten a thousand men. But he knew where to attribute the glory. It was not he, but the Spirit of the Lord which had come mightily upon him. This is distinctly recognized when he called unto God, and said, "Thou hast given this great deliverance by my hand." It was because he had been expending his strength for God, had been, so to speak, burnt up by the divine fire, that he was able to claim God's interposition for his thirst.

This is the great law of prayer. We have no right to count on God in the agony of a crisis, unless we have been walking in fellowship with Him previously, or are exhausted in fighting his battles. There is nothing that we may not claim of Him when we are living in the current of his life, or when we are exhausted in his service. "Thou hast given this great deliverance by the hand of thy servant; and now shall I die for thirst?"

God's springs burst out in unlikely spots. He is never at a loss. If there is no natural spring, He can create one. If all around the mighty rocks reflect the sultry heat, and our spirit seems on the point of exhaustion, then in the wilderness He will cause streams to break out. Be of good courage, fainting warrior! The God who made thee, and has used thee, knows thy frame, and what thou needest before thou askest. Hereafter the place shall be known as "the spring of him that called!" He can cause the refreshing stream to pour forth from the flinty rock; He can turn the bitter water sweet for thee to drink thereof; He quenches thy soul-thirst with the water of life.

He wist not that the Lord was departed from him. Judges 16: 20.
BEWARE of unconscious deterioration! Grey hairs may be here and there upon us without our knowing it. The Lord may be gone out on feet so noiseless, that we are not aware that his Spirit has glided along the corridor, and through the doorway, whispering, Let us depart.

Deterioration is unconscious because it is so gradual. The rot that sets in on autumn fruit is very gradual. The damp that silences the violin or piano does its work almost imperceptibly. Satan is too knowing to plunge us into some outrageous sin at a bound. He has sappers and miners engaged long before the explosion, in hollowing subterranean passages through the soul, and filling them with explosives.

Spiritual declension blunts our sensibility. The first act of the burglar is to gag the voice that might alarm, and poison the watch-dog. So, sin blinds our eyes, and dulls our keen alertness to the presence of evil. Thus, the stages of our relapse are obvious to all eyes but our own. We are drugged as we are being carried off captives.

The progress of evil within us is a matter of unconsciousness, largely because we are quick to discover reasons to justify our decadence. We gloze over the real state of affairs. We call sins by other names. We insist on considerations which in our eyes appear to justify our conduct. We still attend to our religious duties, and try to persuade ourselves that it is with us as in time past. To avoid deterioration we must ever watch and pray, and realize that we are the temple of the Holy Ghost. Then shall the peace of God as a sentry guard our hearts and our thoughts in Christ Jesus.

Dwell with me, and be unto me a priest.
Judges 17: 10.

MEN crave for a priest. In every age of the world's history, where there has been a tent indicating the presence of human life, there has been an altar indicating man's consciousness of God, and a priest suggesting his consciousness of unworthiness to enter into the divine presence. Man has perpetually taken one of his fellows whose character seemed less blemished than that of others, and after setting him apart with special rites from the ordinary engagements of life, has promised him maintenance and honour, if only he will act as priest. Be my priest; say for me to God what I cannot say. The sacrifices offered by thy hands are more likely to avail with Him than those rendered by mine.

(1) LET US BEWARE OF THE RELIGION WHICH IGNORES MAN'S CRAVING FOR A PRIEST. The world abounds with attempts at religious systems, from which the conception of the priest is eliminated. These reduce the worship of God to a system of high-thinking, but fail to deal with man's consciousness of sin, and his yearning for a settled basis of peace.

(2) LET US REMEMBER THAT ALL HUMAN PRIESTS MUST ULTIMATELY FAIL. God has put them all aside, setting up the priesthood of the blessed Lord. "We have such a High Priest, who is set on the right hand of the throne of the Majesty in the heavens; a minister of the sanctuary, and of the true tabernacle which the Lord pitched, and not a man." Stars are needless when the sun has arisen. The human priesthood is rendered unnecessary since the Son of God has passed into the heavens to be a priest after the order of Melchizedek. No one has a right to pose as priest to others, except in the sense that all Christians are such.

Ye have taken away my gods, and the priest.
Judges 18: 24.

WHATEVER can be taken from us has the mark and signature of man upon it. Since the Jewish priests were not permitted to continue, by reason of death, it was evident that they were men at the best; and nothing that man makes is adequate to supply the immortal cravings of the soul which, having come from God, craves for God.

CHANGE CANNOT TAKE AWAY OUR HIGH PRIEST. All around us is a state of flux. No two days in the most brilliant summer are quite the same. The hues are deepening towards autumnal decay. But He continueth ever, and hath an unchangeable priesthood. All that He was years ago, He is still, and will be. What to our forefathers, that to us—"the same yesterday, and to-day, and for ever."

THE CONCERNS OF OTHER SOULS CANNOT TAKE HIM AWAY. It is not difficult to conceive of the attention of a human priest being diverted from those who once claimed all his help, to fresh interests and younger generations. But, however many they be who flock as doves to the windows of Christ's mercy, they will never be able to divert an atom of his love and sympathy from us.

SINS AND FAILURE CANNOT ROB US OF HIM. Indeed, they make Him nearer, dearer, more absolutely necessary. The bands of Danites left Micah wailing: when he wanted the comfort of his priest most, lo, he was gone; but neither principalities, nor things present, nor things to come, nor powers, nor height, nor depth, nor any other creature, can separate us from Him who ever liveth to make intercession. "Having a High Priest over the house of God, let us draw near with a true heart in full assurance of faith."

And it came to pass in those days when there was no king in Israel. Judges 19: 1.

IT will be sufficient to ponder these words, which occur four times in this book, without reading further in this terrible chapter, which shows the depths of depravity to which man may sink apart from the grace of God. Where Christ is not enthroned as King, drunkenness, impurity, cruelty, selfishness, are supreme, and pursue their ravages unchecked. How different where He reigns in righteousness, and where his will is done as it is done in heaven!

The Book of Judges depicts the State of the heart which has not admitted the Kingship of our Saviour. Where there is no recognition of this, and a man does as he likes, then the heart breeds all manner of uncleanness; and sin when it is finished bringeth forth death.

In connection with the present marvellous movement afoot in our colleges, five hundred Japanese students met recently under the motto, "Make Jesus King." Oh that this might be our life-motto! We must crown Him lord of all.

Let young men and women, who may read these words, specially ponder this suggestion. Perpetual failure in life indicates failure in consecration. If you are continually broken in upon by raids of evil, it is certain that you have never enthroned the Son of God. He is never Saviour in the fulness of his power till He is acknowledged King. Directly the coronation has taken place, He assumes the responsibility of putting down all rule, authority, and power; overcoming the evils that had held sway; and bringing every thought into captivity. Such are the warnings and appeals of this chapter and the next. "Make Jesus King."

And put away evil from Israel. Judges 20: 13. THE earnestness and promptness with which Israel dealt with and put away this evil thing were very commendable. They had gathered from all the land, even from Gilead beyond the Jordan. They were knit together in a perfect unity of feeling and action. They resolved to subordinate all things beside to the excision of this evil.

So must it be in the Church. The Lord Himself took Ananias and Sapphira out of the infant Church, and the Apostle very earnestly besought and commanded the Corinthians to put away from among them the wicked person, who had committed a sin that would not be named among the Gentiles. "Christ our Passover is sacrificed for us; therefore let us keep the feast, not with old leaven, neither with the leaven of malice and wickedness; but with the unleavened bread of sincerity and truth" (1 Cor. 5: 7, 8).

At the close of this age God will send forth his angels, to sever the wicked from among the just, and to cast them into the furnace of fire.

In our own life it is impossible altogether to avoid contact with such people. Indeed, to do so, as the Apostle says truly, we must got out of the world. But we can abstain from their friendship and company. It is an altogether different thing to have dealings with a worldly man in business, and to admit him into bosom fellowship and comradeship in our leisure hours. The first is permissible, but not the second; else our companions will seduce us from our loyalty to God. Beware of taking on the colour of the ground on which you lie. "I pray not that Thou shouldest take them out of the world, but that Thou shouldest keep them from the evil."

We have sworn by the Lord. Judges 21: 7. AMID the gross evils of this time, the people of Israel were very tenacious of their vows, which had been ratified in the presence of God, and under the solemn sanctions of the Tabernacle. Because they had sworn not to give their daughters in marriage to Benjamin, they had to devise an expedient to obtain wives for the six hundred who had escaped massacre, that the tribe should not become extinct.

The same spirit was manifested by Jephthah, when he said, "I have opened my mouth to the Lord; I cannot go back." No doubt there was the implied conviction that God would avenge the violation of an oath solemnly taken in his name.

What new emphasis is added by this conception to the words of the Epistle to the Hebrews: "God, willing to show unto the heirs of promise the immutability of his counsel, confirmed it by an oath." Since He could swear by no greater, He swore by Himself, that He would bless and multiply Abraham and his seed. If then you are of the faith of faithful Abraham, you have the right to claim the fulfilment of God's promise in this double aspect: He will bless and multiply. And it is impossible for Him to alter or fail in the word He hath spoken.

The Psalmist said that God's statutes, i.e. the things which He established, were his songs. Surely we have every reason to sing, who know that the covenant of God's love is as steadfast as his throne. Let us turn his statutes into songs. He has given us exceeding great and precious promises; and we can rejoice that "All the promises of God in Him are yea, and in Him Amen, unto the glory of God by us." "The word of the Lord endureth for ever."

Ruth

Call me not Naomi, call me Mara. Ruth 1: 20. SO she spoke, as many have spoken since, not knowing that God's ways are ways of pleasant-ness and all his paths peace, when they are not isolated from the plan of our life, but considered as parts of the whole. We cannot pronounce on any part of God's dealing with us until the entire plan has been allowed to work itself out. How grieved God's Spirit must be, who is lovingly doing his best, when He hears these words of murmuring and complaint! Let us lift the vail, and notice the pleasant things in Naomi's life.

True, her husband and sons were dead; but their deaths in a foreign land had left her free to come back to her people and her God; to nestle again under the wings of Jehovah; and to share the advantages of the Tabernacle.

True, Orpah had gone back. Mahlon and Chilion were both buried in Moab; but she had Ruth, who was better to her than seven sons.

True, she had no male child to perpetuate her name; but the little Obed would, within a few months, be nestling in her aged arms, and laughing into her withered face.

True, she was very poor; but it was through her poverty that Ruth was brought first into contact with that good man, Boaz; and, besides, there was yet a little patrimony which pertained to her.

Yes, Naomi, like thousands more, thou must take back thy words. Thou didst deal bitterly with thine own happiness in leaving the Land of Promise for Moab; but God dealt pleasantly with thee in thy return and latter end. "Behold, the eye of the Lord is upon them that fear Him, upon them that hope in his mercy."

Under whose wings thou art come to trust.
Ruth 2: 12.
IN after-days this was a favourite image with David in his wanderings and escapes among those same hills. Perhaps he had received it as a fragrant legacy from the life of his good ancestor, Boaz. At least on one occasion Jesus employed it in saying that He had wished to gather Jerusalem as a hen her chicks.

How warm, cosy, and safe, the chickens are when they have gathered under the wings of the brooding hen! It must be a very heaven for them. The storm may roll through the sky, the heavy raindrops fall, the hawk may hover above, poising itself on its wings; but the body of the parent-bird is interposed between them and all that threatens. What wonder that the Psalmist said that he would hide under the shadow of God's wings till all his calamities were overpast!

Are you sheltering there? Have you come out of the storm and tempest to hide there? Can you say of the Lord, "He is my refuge and my fortress: my God; in Him will I trust"? If so, remain in happy confidence. God is between you and all evil or alarm. Be still; yea, be still.

If you have not come to trust under the outspread wings of the Cherubim, do as Ruth did. Leave the land of your nativity, the far country of Moab; leave your people and your gods; tear yourself away even from some twin-soul, dear as Orpah; come across the border-line, and glean in the fields of the Gospel. There you will meet with the true Boaz, who will show kindness unto you, and you will become affianced to Him, and live at home for evermore in the house of bread, where you will be blessed indeed.

The man will not be in rest, until he have finished the thing this day. Ruth. 3: 18.
BOAZ had many good traits—his religious demeanour and speech, his courtesy in greeting his servants, his refusal to take advantage of Ruth's trust; but none are more satisfactory as an index of a noble character than this well-known and acknowledged promptness of action, when he had once taken in hand the cause of the needy. From of old, Naomi had recognized this quality in her kinsman, and knew that he was a man of his word, who would assiduously complete what he had undertaken to perform.

It is a characteristic that we should do well to cultivate. Let us not arouse hopes, and finally disappoint them; let us not make promises to forget them. Our words should be yea, yea. Those who commit their cause to us should feel perfectly at rest about our executing what we have promised.

How true this is of Jesus! If we have put our matters into his hands, we have no further need of worry or fear, but may sit still in assured trust. For Zion's sake He does not hold his peace, and for Jerusalem's sake He will not rest. He has undertaken the cause of the Church, albeit that it is so largely composed of Gentiles, and He will not be in rest until the marriage-feast is celebrated. He has made Himself responsible for thee and me; and He will not rest until He has played the part of a Goel to the furthest limit, and accomplished our redemption. When we have fully yielded ourselves to Him, and have tasted the joys of complete rest, we may assuredly say with the Apostle, "I know whom I have believed, and am persuaded that He is able to keep that which I have committed unto Him against that day."

Ruth have I purchased to be my wife. Ruth 4: 10.

SO this exquisite idyll, which began with three deaths and famine, ends with marriage rejoicings. Shall not all God's idylls end thus? Shall it be left to the dream of the novelist only to make happy for ever after? God has eternity at his disposal, as well as time. Only trust Him; "thy darkest night shall end in brightest day."

It is impossible not to read between these lines and see the foreshadowing of another marriage, when the purchase of the Church shall issue in her everlasting union with the Son, in the presence of God the Father. Let us, however, apply these words to ourselves as individuals.

THE LORD JESUS HAS PURCHASED US TO BE HIS OWN, not with corruptible things, as silver and gold, but with his precious blood.

HE HAS ALSO WON BACK OUR PATRIMONY; this earth is his; and shall be yet rid of all intruding evil, to shine as the brightest jewel in his crown.

HE HAS RECEIVED THE SHOE, the symbol of dominion and authority. He is not only our lover, but our Lord.

HE WAITS TO TAKE US TO HIMSELF, in a love that shall not cease, and compared to which all the love we have ever known is as moonlight compared with sunshine.

1 Samuel

I have poured out my soul before the Lord. 1 Sam. 1: 15.

HANNAH'S soul was full of complaint and grief, which flowed over into her face and made it sorrowful. But when she had poured out her soul before the Lord, emptying out all its bitterness, the peace of God took the place of her soul-anguish, she went her way, and did eat, and her countenance was no more sad. What a glad exchange! How great the contrast! How much the better for herself, and for her home!

Is your face darkened by the bitterness of your soul? Perhaps the enemy has been vexing you sorely; or there is an unrealized hope, an unfulfilled purpose in your life; or, perchance, the Lord seems to have forgotten you. Poor sufferer, there is nothing for it but to pour out your soul before the Lord. Empty out its contents in confession and prayer. God knows it all; ye tell Him, as if He knew nothing. "Ye people, pour out your hearts before Him. God is a refuge for us." "In everything, by prayer and supplication make your requests known unto God."

As we pour out our bitterness, God pours in his peace. Weeping goes out of one door whilst joy enters at another. We transmit the cup of tears to the Man of Sorrows, and He hands it back to us filled with the blessings of the new covenant. Some day you will come to the spot where you wept and prayed, bringing your offering of praise and thanksgiving.

His mother made him a little coat. 1 Sam. 2: 19.

WHAT happy work it was! Those nimble fingers flew along the seams, because love inspired them. All her woman's art and wit were put into the garment, her one idea and ambition being to make something which should not be only useful, but becoming. Not mothers only, but fathers, are always making little coats for their children, which they wear long years after a material fabric would have become worn out. How many men and women are wearing to-day the coats which their parents cut out and made for them long years ago!

Habits are the vesture of the soul. The Apostle bade his converts put off the old man, "which is corrupt, according to the deceitful lusts," and to put on the new man, "which after God is created in righteousness and true holiness"; to put off anger, wrath, and malice, whilst they put on mercy, humility, and meekness. What words could better establish the fact that habits are (as the name indicates) the clothing of the inner life? Where and how are habits formed? Not in the mid-passage of life, but at its dawn; not in great crises, but in daily circumstances; not in life's arena, but in the home, amid the surroundings of earliest childhood. Oh that the spotless robe of Christ's righteousness may ever be exhibited before those with whom we daily come in contact!

By their behaviour to each other and to their children; by the ordering of the home-life; by their actions, more than by their words; by the way in which they speak, and spend their lesure hours, and pray—men and women are making the little coats which, for better or worse, their children wear ever after, and perhaps pass down to after generations.

And the Lord came, and stood, and called as at other times, Samuel, Samuel! 1 Sam. 3: 10.
SEE the urgency of God! Four times He came and stood, and called. Mark how He stands at the door to knock. At first He was content to call the lad once by name; but after three unsucessful attempts to attract him to Himself, He uttered the name twice, with strong urgency in the appeal, Samuel! Samuel! This has been called God's double knock. There are seven or eight of these double knocks in Scripture: Simon, Simon; Saul, Saul; Abraham, Abraham.

How may we be sure of a divine call?

WE MAY KNOW GOD'S CALL WHEN IT GROWS IN INTENSITY. If an impression comes into your soul, and you are not quite sure of its origin, pray over it; above all, act on it so far as possible, follow in the direction in which it leads—and as you lift up your soul before God, it will wax or wane. If it wanes at all, abandon it. If it waxes follow it, though all hell attempt to stay you.

WE MAY TEST GOD'S CALL BY THE ASSISTANCE OF GODLY FRIENDS. The aged Eli perceived that the Lord had called the child, and gave him good advice as to the manner in which he should respond to it. Our special gifts and the drift of our circumstances will also assuredly concur in one of God's calls.

WE MAY TEST GOD'S CALL BY ITS EFFECT ON US. Does it lead to self-denial? Does it induce us to leave the comfortable bed and step into the cold? Does it drive us forth to minister to others? Does it make us more unselfish, loving, tender, modest, humble? Whatever is to the humbling of our pride, and the glory

of God, may be truly deemed God's call. Be quick to respond, and fearlessly deliver the message the Lord has given you.

Let us fetch the Ark of the Covenant of the Lord. 1 Sam. 4: 3.
ISRAEL had been defeated with great loss. Their only hope of being able to hold their own against the Philistines and the people of the land was in the protection and help vouchsafed to them by God. They knew this, and thought that they would be secured, if only the Ark of the covenant were on the field. They forgot that it was only the material symbol of a spiritual relationship; that it was useless unless that relationship was in living force; and that the bending forms of the cherubim, emblematic of the divine protection, would not avail if their fellowship with the God of the cherubim had been ruptured by backsliding.

There is a sense in which we are always sending for the Ark. The reliance on outward rites, such as Baptism and the Lord's Supper, on the part of those who are alienated from the life of God; the maintenance of the forms of prayer and Scripture-reading which no longer express the passionate love of the soul; the habit of church-going, which so many practise, not because they love God, but because they think that it will in some way secure his alliance in life's battle—all these are forms in which we still fetch the Ark of the covenant, whilst our hearts are wrong with the God of the covenant.

It should never be forgotten that nothing can afford to us protection and succour but vital union with Christ. We must hide in his secret place if we would abide under his shadow. We must dwell in the most holy place if we would be shadowed by the wings of the Shekinah. There must be nothing between us and God, if we are to walk together, and enjoy fellowship with the Father and with his Son, Jesus Christ.

Dagon was fallen upon his face to the earth before the Ark of the Lord. 1 Sam. 5: 3.
THE idols of the heathen represent demons who are their accepted gods, just as the Ark was the symbol of the presence of Jehovah. In the one case there was a material representation of the demon; but in the case of the Ark there was only a throne, the Mercy

Seat; and no attempt was made to represent the appearance of the God of Israel. When placed in the Holy of Holies, the Shekinah shone between the cherubim; this alone spoke of the divine Spirit who filled the apparently vacant throne. When the effigy of the fish-god was confronted by the Sacred Ark, it was as though the demon spirit and the divine Spirit had come into contact, with the in-evitable result that the inferiority of the one ensured the crash of its effigy to the ground.

What a lesson this must have been to the Philistines—similar to that given Pharaoh in the plagues of Egypt, and with the same object of leading them to see the superior greatness of Jehovah! How great the encouragement to Israel—to know that God could defend his superiority! And how striking the prognostica-tion for the future, when all the Dagons of the world shall be broken before the symbol of divine power and love!

Bring the Ark of God into your life. Set it down in your heart, and forthwith the Dagons which have held sway for so long will one after another succumb. "The idols He will utterly abolish." Let Christ in—that is the one need of the soul; and let Him take full possession of you. Then He will do his own work. Darkness cannot abide light; nor the defilement of the Augean stable the turning in of the water of the river.

And the kine went along the highway, lowing as they went. 1 Sam. 6: 12.
THAT two milch kine which had never borne the yoke should move quietly along the high road, turning neither to the right nor to the left, and lowing for the calves they had left behind, clearly indicated that they were possessed and guided by some mysterious power, which we know to have been God's. And if He were able thus to overpower the instincts of their nature, and to compel them to do his will, may we not infer that all circumstances, and all men, however un-wittingly, and against their natural instinct, are subserving the purposes of his will, and bearing on the Ark? The fish yields the tribute money; the colt of the ass waits where two ways meet to bear the Redeemer; the man with the waterpot leads to the upper room; the Roman soldiers enable Paul to fulfil the mission of his life, in preaching the Gospel without hindrance in the very heart of Rome.

As we go forth into the world, let us believe that the movement of all things is towards the accomplishment of God's purpose. Herein is a fulfilment of the Psalmist's prediction about man, which can only be perfectly fulfilled in Jesus Christ, the second Adam—that all things are under his feet, all sheep and oxen, yea, and the beasts of the field. Every-thing serves Christ, and those who serve Christ. In a true sense all things are ours; they minister to us, even as Christ to God.

And against our natural inclinations let us always regard the claims of God as para-mount; and dare to go his way, though our heart pines for those we leave behind. "He that loveth father or mother, son or daughter more than Me, is not worthy of Me."

Cease not to cry unto the Lord our God. 1 Sam. 7: 8.
SAMUEL was famous for his prayers. They are repeatedly referred to in the brief record of his life. In the Psalms he is spoken of as the one "who called upon God's name." Indeed, he fought and won Israel's battles by his strong intercessions. Mary of Scots said that she dreaded the prayers of John Knox more than the battalions of the King of France. So his people were accustomed to think that if the prophet's hands were held out in importunate prayer, their foes must be restrained.

In the Life of Mr. Reginald Radcliffe, one who contributes a reminiscence interjects a remark which deserves to be carefully pon-dered: "The great secret of the blessing which came from God to the awakening of whole districts, the quickening of Christians, and the salvation of multitudes, was prayer, continued, fervent, believing, expectant. There was never anything striking in the addresses; but through communion with the living Christ, the word came forth with living and life-giving power. Often would the forenoon be spent in continuous prayer." This may well convict some of us of the cause of our failure. We have expected the Lord to thunder and discomfort our Philistines, and with a great deliverance; but we have ceased to cry unto the Lord.

Ye that are the Lord's remembrancers, cease not to cry unto Him. If the judge avenged the unfortunate widow, shall not God avenge his own elect, who cry day and night? It is recorded of our Lord that He prayed early and late, and all night. He prayed when He was about to be transfigured; for his disciples; in the Garden of Gethsemane; and for his murderers. How much more do we need to "pray without ceasing"!

But the thing displeased Samuel. . . . And Samuel prayed unto the Lord. 1 Sam. 8: 6.

A LITTLE further down in the chapter we learn that Samuel rehearsed the words of the people unto the Lord. His prayer, to a large extent, was a rehearsal of all the strong and unkind things that the people had said to him; and in this way he passed them off his mind, and found relief. There is a suggestion of close communion with God in the expression, "He rehearsed them in the ears of the Lord." It had been the habit of his life to be on intimate terms with his God.

Things do not always turn out as we had hoped, and we get displeased for our own sakes and God's. We had planned in one direction, but events have issued in another; and the results have threatened to become disastrous. There is but one resource. If we allow vexations to eat into our heart, they will corrode and injure it. We must rehearse them to God—spreading the letter before Him, as Hezekiah did; making request like Paul; crying like Samuel.

Surely it is the mistake of our life, that we carry our burdens instead of handing them over; that we worry instead of trusting; that we pray so little. The grass grows thick on the pathway to our oratory; the cobwebs hang across the doorway. The time we spend in prayer is perhaps better spent than in any other way. It was whilst Samuel prayed thus, that he saw the divine programme for Israel:

"And he who at the sixth hour sought
The lone house-top to pray,
There gained a sight beyond his thought—
The dawn of Gentile day.

Then reckon not, when perils lour,
The time of prayer mis-spent;
Nor meanest chance, nor place, nor hour,
Without its heavenward bent."

Behold, there is in this city a man of God. 1 Sam. 9: 6.

THERE is a street in London, near St. Paul's, which I never traverse without very peculiar feelings. It is Godliman Street. Evidently the name is a corruption of godly man. Did some saint of God once live here, whose life was so holy as to give a sweet savour to the very street in which he dwelt? Were the neighbours who knew him best, the most sure of his godliness? Would that our piety might leave its mark on our neighbourhoods, and the memory linger long after we have passed away!

A generation or two ago in the Highlands, there were earnest and holy men who were known by the significant title of "the men." No great religious gathering was deemed complete without them. Their prayers and exhortations were accompanied by an especial unction.

In such manner Samuel's godliness was recognized far and wide. The fragrance of his character could not be concealed. And this gave men confidence in him. They said, "He is an honourable man; all that he saith cometh surely to pass." How much credit redounds to godliness, when it is combined with trustworthiness and high credit amongst our fellows!

Let us seek to be God's men and women. Let us live not only soberly and righteously, but godly, in this present world. Let us remember that God hath set apart the godly for Himself. The godly are the godlike. They become so by cultivating the fellowship and friendship of God. Their faces become enlightened with his beauty; their words are weighty with his truth. After being for a little in their company, you detect the gravity, serenity, gentleness, beauty of holiness, which are the court manners of heaven.

Thou shalt do as occasion serve thee. 1 Sam. 10: 7.

THIS is an example of how God demands of us the use of our sanctified common sense. Samuel sketches to Saul the course of events during the next few days; showing how clearly our lives lie naked and open to the eyes of God, and how easily He can reveal them when necessary. But whilst the various incidents are told, the prophet does not feel it incumbent to tell this goodly young man how he should behave in any given instance. "When these signs are come upon thee, thou shalt do as occasion serve thee."

We are reminded of a parallel in the life of Peter. The angel of God unbarred the prison-doors, and led him forth, because nothing short of divine power would avail. He led the dazed Apostle through one street, because he was too bewildered to realize what had happened. But, as soon as the night-air had brought him to his senses, the angel left him "to consider the matter"—to use his own judgment. The result of which was, that he went to the house of Mary.

One of the divinest of our faculties is the judgment, before which the reasons for and against a certain course of action must be adduced, but with which the ultimate decision lies. It is a tendency with some to depreciate the use of this wonderful power, by looking for signs and visions to point their path. This is a profound mistake. God will give these when there are complications in which the exercise of judgment might be at fault; but not where it is sufficient. Where no sign is given, carefully divest yourself of selfish considerations, weigh the pros and cons, ask for guidance, dare to act; and having acted in faith, never look back or doubt.

Come, let us go to Gilgal, and renew the Kingdom there. 1 Sam. 11: 14.
IT is good to have days and occasions for renewing the kingdom. Already Saul had been anointed king. It was a recognized matter that he should inaugurate the days of the kings, as distinguished from those of the judges. But his great victory at Jabesh-Gilead seems to have wrought the enthusiasm of the people to the highest pitch, and to have presented a great opportunity for renewing the kingdom. They went to Gilgal to do this, because there, on the first entrance into Canaan, Israel had rolled away the reproach of uncircumcision, which symbolized their lack of separation.

Jesus is our King. The Father hath anointed Him, and set Him on his holy hill; and we have gladly assented to the appointment, and made Him King. But sometimes our sense of loyalty and devotion wanes. Insensibly we drift from our strenuous endeavour to act always as his devoted subjects. Therefore we need, from time to time, to renew the kingdom, and revently make Him King before the Lord.

Go over the old solemn form of dedication; turn to the yellow leaves of the diary; bring under his sceptre any new provinces of influence that have been acquired; tell Him how glad and thankful you are to live only for Him. Let this be done at Gilgal, the place of circumcision and separation, with the Jordan of death flowing behind, and the Land of Promise beckoning in front. There is a sense in which we can consecrate ourselves only once; but we can renew our vows often.

"Blessings abound where'er He reigns;
The prisoner leaps to burst his chains;
The weary find eternal rest,
And all the sons of want are blest."

The Lord will not forsake his people for his great Name's sake. 1 Sam. 12: 22.
THE certainty of our salvation rests on the character of God. Moses, years before, had pleaded that God could not afford to destroy or forsake Israel, lest the Egyptians and others should have some ground for saying that He was not able to carry out his purpose, or that He was fickle and changeable. "What wilt Thou do for thy great Name?" Samuel uses the same argument. We also may avail ourselves of it for our great comfort.

God knew what we should be—how weak and frail and changeful—before He arrested us and brought us to Himself. Speaking after the manner of men, we might say He counted the cost. He computed whether his resources were sufficient to secure us from our foes, keep us from falling, and present us faultless before the presence of his glory with exceeding joy. He foreknew how much forbearance, pity, consolation, and tenderness, we should require. And yet it pleased Him to make us his people. He cannot, therefore, now run back from his purpose; otherwise it would seem that difficulties had arisen which either He had not anticipated, or was not so well able to combat as He had thought. What an absurd suggestion! In the former case there would be a slur on his omniscience; on the other, upon his omnipotence.

"What if God should cast you into hell?" was asked of an old Scotswoman. "Well," she answered, "If He do, all I can say is, He will lose mair than I will."

The gracious promise given to Joshua may be appropriated by every trembling saint of God: "I will never leave thee nor forsake thee." To the poor and needy He says, "I the God of Israel will not forsake them."

I forced myself, therefore, and offered a burnt-offering. 1 Sam. 13: 12.
THIS was wholly outside Saul's province. Samuel had engaged to arrive within the

seven days: they had nearly expired, and still there were no signs of the prophet; and Saul, yielding to the promptings of his impetuous nature, took the matter into his own hand, and rashly assumed an office to which he had no right. He protested that he had been very unwilling to add the function of priest to that of king. But this was notoriously contrary to the truth. For some time he had chafed against Samuel's prerogative, and now sought to supersede the divine order.

It seemed but a small act, and, to superficial judgment, not enough to warrant the loss of his kingdom; but it was symptomatic of a great moral deficiency. He had not learned to obey the commandment of the Lord: how could he rule? He could not control the hasty suggestions of his own nature, in favour of the deliberate movements of the divine order: how could he be God's chosen agent? He acted on the showings of expediency, rather than of faith: how could he be a man after God's own heart? The restlessness and haste which characterize the present age must not be allowed to affect our service for God; for thereby the progress of the Gospel will be hindered rather than helped.

We must learn to wait for God. He may not come till the allotted time has almost passed; but He will come. He waits for the exact moment in which He can best succour you. Not till patience has been exercised, but before it has given out. In the meanwhile, be sure that your safety is secured; He will see to it that the Philistines shall not come down to overwhelm you.

His eyes were enlightened. 1 Sam. 14: 27.
THE Philistines were in full flight. The Israelites followed hard at their heels through the wood. It was there that the honey dropped in rich abundance on the ground, and there Jonathan tasted a little, dipping the end of his rod into it. It made all the difference to him, warding off the excessive exhaustion which paralysed the rest of the army.

THE WORD OF GOD IS SWEETER THAN THE HONEYCOMB. Luscious to the sanctified taste; enlightening to the dimming eyes; strength-giving to the weary. It drops in abundance to the ground, as though inviting the hand of the Christian warrior or wayfarer to take it freely. If there is no taste for the written Word, it may be assumed that the living Word has not been enthroned in the heart;

for where He reigns supreme, there is a longing for the food which alone can fit us for the Christian life.

WHERE WE CANNOT TAKE MUCH, LET US TAKE SOME. There was not time for Jonathan to sit down and take his fill. He could only catch up some as he hastily passed through the forest-glade; but that little made all the difference to him. So, in the early morning, or at mid-day, if we cannot fill our hearts with Scripture, we may catch up a morsel, which will minister untold refreshment, and clear our spiritual vision.

WE SPECIALLY NEED TO DO THIS WHEN FLUSHED WITH SUCCESS. Too often, when we have had success in the battles of the Lord—a good time in preaching or teaching—we are apt to congratulate ourselves, and suppose that we can live on the emotions excited. But, probably, there is no time when we need more absolutely to turn to the Word of God. In victory, as in defeat, we must be fed and nourished.

To obey is better than sacrifice, and to hearken than the fat of rams. 1 Sam. 15: 22.
THIS is a great principle, which is repeatedly enforced throughout the Bible. Men have always been apt to divorce religion and morality, and to suppose that a certain tribute of sacrifice to God will be sufficient compensation for notorious evil-doing. But in every age God's servants have protested against the notion, and have insisted, as Samuel did with Saul, that it were better to obey, although there should be no spoil from which to select victims for sacrifice. This was Christ's perpetual protest against the Pharisees.

LET THE RITUALIST BEWARE. There is a grave fear lest extreme attention to the outward rite may be accompanied by carelessness to the inward temper. Where the outward observance is the expression of the attitude of the soul, it is to be respected even by those of us who feel that excessive symbolism is hostile to the devout life; but where the rite takes the place of the soul's devotion, or condones a lax morality, it cannot be too sternly deprecated. Though all the Levitical rites should be observed without flaw, they could not compensate for the persistent neglect of the least item of the decalogue. "God is a Spirit; and they that worship Him must worship Him in spirit and in truth."

LET US ALL BEWARE. We are apt to make

sacrifices of time and money and energy for God, and to comfort ourselves with the reflection that such as we are may be excused if in small lapses of temper, or disposition, we come short of the divine standard. No; it cannot pass muster. One sin mastered, one temptation resisted, one duty performed, is dearer to God than the most costly sacrifices that were ever piled upon the altar.

The Spirit of the Lord came upon David from that day forward. 1 Sam. 16: 13.
WHAT may not a day bring forth! Here was a shepherd lad, summoned hastily from his sheep, and anointed king. But an even greater blessing came into his life that day, for he was mightily endued with the Holy Spirit. Without doubt, during his early years the Spirit of God had dwelt within him, moulding his character, inditing his songs; but, henceforth, the Spirit was to abide on him, as a divine unction.

Why should not this day witness a similar transformation for you; not in the change of earthly position, but in your reception of the "power from on high" through a renewed enduement? Why should not the Spirit of the Lord come mightily upon you from this holy hour, even as your eyes glance down this page? Though it is quite possible that you have been empowered once, there is no finality in God's bestowals; the apostles were filled and filled again (Acts 2 and 4).

The age of Pentecost in which we live is distinctly one of divine anointing. It awaits all who will separate themselves to God, and receive it for his glory. The characteristic preposition of this age is on. If you have not received power, seek it; he that seeketh findeth; nay, receive it—to ask is to get. If the Master, though begotten of the Holy Spirit, forebore to preach the Gospel, and bind up broken hearts, till He had been anointed as the Christ by the Spirit, who descended on Him at his baptism; how foolish it is for us, who were born in sin, to attempt similar work, apart from similar enduement! The promise to each child of God is: "Ye shall receive power after that the Holy Ghost is come upon you; and ye shall be witnesses unto Me" (Acts 1: 8).

The armies of the living God. 1 Sam. 17: 26, 36.
THIS made all the difference between David and the rest of the camp. To Saul and his soldiers God was an absentee—a name, but little else. They believed that He had done great things for his people in the past, and that at some future time, in the days of the Messiah, He might be expected to do great things again; but no one thought of Him as present. Keenly sensitive to the defiance of the Philistine, and grieved by the apathy of his people. David, on the other hand, felt that God was alive. He had lived alone with Him in the solitude of the hills, till God had become one of the greatest and most real facts of his young existence; and as the lad went to and fro among the armed warriors, he was sublimely conscious of the presence of the living God amid the clang of the camp.

This is what we need. To live so much with God, that when we come amongst men, whether in the bazaars of India or the market-place of an English town, we may be more aware of his overshadowing presence than of the presence or absence of any one. Lo, God is here! This place is hallowed ground! But none can realize this by the act of the will. We can only find God everywhere when we carry Him everywhere. The miner sees by the candle he carries on his forehead.

Each of us is opposed by difficulties, privations, and trials of different sorts. But the one answer to them all is faith's vision of the Living God. We can face the mightiest foe in his name. If our faith can but make Him a passage, along which He shall come, there is no Goliath He will not quell; no question He will not answer; no need He will not meet.

David behaved himself wisely. 1 Sam. 18: 5, 14, 15, 30.
THERE must be some strong reason for the fourfold repetition of this phrase in so short a space. It is as though the Holy Ghost would lay very distinct stress on the divine prudence and circumspection, which must characterize the man whose life is hid in God. Let us walk with God, abiding in Him, subjecting our thoughts and plans to his, communing about all things with Him, talking over our lives with Him, before we go out to live them in the presence of our fellows. Then we too shall have this gracious wisdom, which is more moral than intellectual—the product of the grace of God rather than of human culture.
OUR LIFE SHALL COMMEND ITSELF TO MEN (5).

David's was good in the sight of all the people, and more wonderful still, in the sight of Saul's servants, who might have been jealous. A life lived in God disarms jealousy and envy. He who, as a boy, did his Father's business, increased in wisdom, and in favour with God and men.

OUR LIFE SHALL REBUKE AND AWE OUR FOES (15). Saul stood in awe of him. When traps and snares are laid for us we shall be enabled to thread our way through them all, as Jesus did when they tried to entangle Him in his talk. We shall have a wisdom which all our foes together shall not be able to gainsay or resist.

OUR NAMES WILL BE PRECIOUS (30). People loved to dwell on the name of David; it was much set by; they noticed and were impressed with the beauty and nobility of his character. We must always view our lives, amusements, and undertakings, in the light of the result which will accrue to Him whose name it is our privilege to bear.

And Saul hearkened unto the voice of Jonathan.
1 Sam. 19: 6.

IT was a noble act of Jonathan. He might have withdrawn from his friendship with David when it threatened his relations with his father; but, instead, he stepped into the breach, and pleaded for his friend, endeavouring to eradicate the false and ungenerous conceptions of which Saul had become possessed. It is an example we do well to study and copy. For his love's sake, as well as for his father's, he was extremely eager to effect a reconciliation between him to whom he owed allegiance of son and subject, and this fair shepherd-minstrel-warrior, who had so recently cast a sunny gleam upon his life.

Men often misconceive of one another. Jealousy and envy distort behaviour and actions which are in themselves as beautiful as possible. Misrepresentation will blind us to the true excellences of one another's characters. Wrong constructions are often put on the most innocent incidents. We cannot help these things they are part of the sad heritage of the Fall; but we may often take up the cause of a misunderstood man, and at the risk of losing our own reputation, and diverting to ourselves some of the odium which attaches to him, we may stand as his sponsors.

Even if we dislike another, as Saul did David, let us give scope to the good Spirit to plead his cause at the bar of our hearts, as Jonathan did for his friend. Let us consider all the kind and loving things that may be said of him; let us put ourselves in his position; let us be willing to believe and hope all things. Let us plead for others, since this is a work in which Christ's followers most closely approximate to Him who ever liveth to intercede.

Thou shalt be missed, because thy seat will be
empty. 1 Sam. 20: 18.

JONATHAN and David had entered into a covenant, each loving the other as his own soul. Anxious to shield his friend from the wrath of his father, Jonathan discloses to David the plan by which he shall know how matters fared in the royal palace. David's vacant seat suggests a lesson for us.

There are a good many empty seats in our houses. Those that occupied them can never do so again; they have gone never to return again, and we miss them sorely.

Let us see to it that we do not leave our seats in the home circle needlessly vacant. Let not the mother be away at the dance, or even at the religious meeting, when she should be at home, joining in her children's evening prayers. Let the father be very sure that God has called him elsewhere, before he habitually vacates his place in the evening family circle. Let each of us avoid giving needless pain to those we love by leaving empty seats. But if God calls us away to his service, then for those who miss us, another Form shall glide in, and sit in the vacant chair; and they will become conscious that the Master is filling the gap, and beguiling the weary moments.

Above all, let not your seat be empty in the house of God, at the ordinary service, or at the Lord's Table. We are too prone to allow a trifle to deter us from joining in the sacred feasts. At such times we are missed, our empty seat witnesses against us; there is a lack in the song and prayer, which cries out against us; there is a distinct loss to the power of the service, which is in proportion to the number of earnest souls present. Oh that there may be no empty seats at the marriage supper, vacated through our unfaithfulness!

There is none like that; give it me. 1 Sam.
21: 9.

WHAT David said of the sword of Goliath

we may say of Holy Scripture—the sword of the Spirit—"There is none like that."

THERE IS NO BOOK LIKE THE BIBLE FOR THOSE CONVINCED OF SIN. The Word of God assures the sinner of God's love in Christ, whilst it refuses to condone a single sin, or excuse one shortcoming. The Bible is as stern as conscience herself against sin, but as pitiful as the heart of God to the sinner. It, moreover, discloses the method by which the just God becomes the justifier of those who believe.

THERE IS NO BOOK LIKE THE BIBLE FOR THE SORROWFUL. It tells of the Comforter; it reminds us that in all our sorrow God also is sad; it points to the perfect plan according to which God is working out our blessedness; it insists that all things are working together for good; it opens the vision of the blessed future, where all the griefs and tears of men shall be put away for ever.

THERE IS NO BOOK LIKE THE BIBLE FOR THE DYING. "Read to me," said Sir Walter Scott, on his dying bed, to his friend. "What shall I read?" "There is only one book for a dying man," was the answer; "read to me from the Bible." The Book which tells of the Lord, who died and rose again; of the mansions which He has gone to prepare; of the reunion of the saints; of the fountains of water of life—is the only pillow on which the dying head can rest softly.

In these days of debate and doubt there is no such evidence for the divine authority of the Bible as that which accrues from its perpetual use, whether in our own life, or in the conviction of the ungodly.

Till I know what God will do for me. 1 Sam. 22: 3.

WE shall never get to the end of all that God will do for us, if only we perfectly give ourselves up to Him. David had a very imperfect vision of all that was in God's plan for him; he had an inkling, but that was all. And we have still less. Yet let us recapitulate some of the things which God will do for us.

He waits to give us the spirit of Sonship: so that we may ever be conscious of his Fatherhood, and look up into his face in the garden of Gethsemane, and on the Mount of Transfiguration alike, calling Him Abba, Father.

He longs to lead us to full consecration; to lead us into such close association with Jesus in his redeeming purpose, that we may become his willing bond-servants, with no other purpose and aim in life than his service and glory.

He desires to deliver us from all known sin: that we may be blameless and harmless, his children without rebuke in this sinful world, who walk before Him in holiness and righteousness all our days.

He wants to anoint us with the Holy Spirit: so that our ministry to men may have more of the savour of Christ; may plough deeper furrows in human hearts; may have more abiding results.

He desires us to come into partnership with his Son—here in his redemptive purpose, yonder in his throne. To this indeed He calls us.

Who can know all that God waits to do, not here only, but yonder, when life has entered upon its eternal stage! "Now are we children of God; and it is not yet made manifest what we shall be" (1 John 3: 2, R.V.).

He said to Abiathar the priest, Bring hither the ephod. 1 Sam. 23: 9.

DAVID was passing through one of the most awful experiences of his life, when his men spoke of stoning him instead of taking up his cause. How many times in this chapter we are informed that David inquired of the Lord! Some three or four times the appeal for direction was renewed, as though he were fearful to stir one step by the light of his own unaided wisdom. In that changeful life of his, it must have been extremely difficult to set the Lord always before him, and await divine direction. Many a time his circumstances might seem to demand immediate action rather than prayer; and the rude soldiery must have insisted on their voice being heard rather than a priest's; but David was not deterred by one or the other, and still held to his practice of consulting the Urim and Thummim stone, set in the ephod; which was probably a splendid diamond, flashing with God's distinct "Yes," or growing cloudy and dark with his definite "No."

Let us inquire of the Lord. The answer will surely come, if we wait for it. If we are not sure of it, let us still wait, for it will come— not so early as to save us from using our faith, not so late as to permit us to be overwhelmed. Direction will come in the growing conviction of duty, in the drift of circumstances, in the advice of friends, in the perceptions of a sanctified judgment. None that wait on God can be ashamed. Whether our duty be to arise and pursue, to sit still, or to escape—"the meek He will guide in judgment; the meek He will teach his way." He gives us a white stone in which a name is written, which only they know who receive.

And David's heart smote him. 1 Sam. 24: 5.

IT is well to have a tender conscience, and to obey its least monitions, even when men and things militate against it. Here was an opportunity for David and his band to end their wanderings and hardships by one thrust of the spear; but though it was a very small thing that he had done, David was struck with remorse for having taken advantage of Saul's retirement in the precincts of the cave, where his men and he were hiding, and cut off a piece of his robe.

IT WAS A TRIFLING MATTER, and yet it seemed dishonouring to God's anointed king; and as such it hurt David to have done it. We sometimes in conversation and criticism cut off a piece of a man's character, or influence for good, or standing in the esteem of others. Ought not our heart to smite us for such thoughtless conduct? Ought we not to make confession or reparation?

CIRCUMSTANCES SEEMED TO FAVOUR IT. Of all the scores of caves in the neighbourhood, the king had happened to choose the very one, in the dark recesses of which David and his men were sheltering. What more natural than to obtain some token to convince the king how absolutely he had been in his young rival's power? But favouring circumstances do not justify an act which is not perfectly healthy and right. Opportunity does not make a wrong thing right.

HIS MEN UNANIMOUSLY APPROVED THE ACT, nay, they wanted him to go further. Their standard was a very low one, not only in this case, but in others. How wonderful that David kept such a high ideal amid such comrades! We shall not be judged hereafter by the standard which obtained among our comrades.

This shall be no grief unto thee. 1 Sam. 25: 31.

THERE was an inimitable blending of woman's wit with worldly prudence in the words of the beautiful Abigail. Poor woman, she had had a sorry life of it, mated to such a man as Nabal was! An ill-assorted pair certainly, though probably she had had no hand in bringing about the alliance. Like so many Eastern women, she was the creature of another's act and choice. But she succeeded in averting the blow which David was hasting to inflict, by asserting her belief that the time was not far distant when he would no longer be a fugitive from his foes, and by suggesting that when that happy time came it would be a relief to feel that he had not allowed himself to be carried to all lengths by his hot passion.

It was very salutary advice. Let us always look at things from the view-point of the future, when our passion shall have subsided, when time shall have cooled us, and especially when we review the present from the verge of the other world—how then?

We can well afford to do this since God is with us, and our life is bound up with Him in the bundle of life. Abigail reminded David that God would do to him all the good of which He had spoken, and would sling out his enemies as from a sling. So God will do for us; not one good thing will fail of all that He hath promised; no weapon that is formed against us shall prosper. Within a little, Nabal was dead, and David's wrong righted. So shall the evil that now molests us pass away. God will deal with it. Let us leave it to Him: before Him mountains shall melt like wax; and we shall have nothing to regret.

Then said Saul, I have sinned. 1 Sam. 26: 21.

THE Apostle makes a great distinction, and rightly, between the sorrow of the world and the sorrow of a godly repentance which needeth not to be repented of. Certainly Saul's confession of sin belonged to the former; whilst the cry of the latter comes out in Psalm 51, extorted from David by the crimes of after years.

The difference between the two may be briefly summarized in this, that the one counts sin a folly and regrets its consequences; whilst the other regards sin as a crime done against the most Holy God, and regrets the pain given to Him. "Against Thee, Thee only, have I sinned, and done this evil in thy sight."

Obviously Saul's confession was of the former description, "I have played the fool." He recognized the unkingliness of his behaviour, and the futility of his efforts against

David. But he stayed there, stopping short of a faithful recognition of his position in the sight of God, as weighed in the balances of eternal justice.

Many a time in Scripture do we meet with this confession. The Prodigal, Judas, Pharaoh, David, and Saul, uttered it; but in what differing tones, and with what differing motives! We need to winnow our words before God; not content with using the expressions of penitence, unless we are very sure that they bear the mint-mark of heaven, and deserve the master's Beatitude, "Blessed are they that mourn, for they shall be comforted."

When sin is humbly confessed, the Saviour assures us: "Thy sins, which are many, are forgiven thee, go in peace." "If we confess our sins, He is faithful and just to forgive us our sins, and to cleanse us from all unrighteousness."

And David said, I shall now perish one day by the hand of Saul. 1 Sam. 27: 1.
WHAT a fit of despondency and unbelief was here! We can hardly believe that this is he who in so many psalms had boasted of the shepherd care of God, who had so often insisted on the safety of God's pavilion. It was a fainting fit, brought on by the bad air he had breathed amid the evil associations of Adullam's cave. Had not God promised to take care of him? Was not his future already guaranteed by the promises that he should succeed to the kingdom? But nothing availed to check his precipitate flight into the land of the Philistines.

Bitterly he rued this mistake. The prevarication and deceit to which he was driven; the anguish of having to march with Achish against his own people; the sack and burning of Ziklag: these were the price he had to pay for his mistrust. Unbelief always brings many other bitter sorrows in its train, and leads the soul to cry,

"How long, O Lord? Wilt Thou forget me for ever?
How long wilt Thou hide thy face from me?"

Let us beware of losing heart, as David did. Look not at Saul, but at God, who is omnipotent; not at the winds and waves, but at Him who walks across the water; not at what may come, but at that which is—

for the glorious Lord is round about thee to deliver thee. He shall deliver thy soul from death, thine eyes from tears, and thy feet from falling. He that has helped will help. What He has done, He will do. God always works from less to more, never from more to less. Dost thou not hear—hast thou not heard—his voice saying, I will never leave thee, nor forsake thee? What, then, can man do unto thee? Every weapon used against thee shall go blunt on an invisible shield!

Because thou obeyest not the voice of the Lord, therefore . . . 1 Sam. 28: 18.
THUS unforgiven sin comes back to a man. We cannot explain the mysteries that lie around this incident; but it is clear that in that supreme hour of Saul's fate, that early sin, which had never been confessed and put away, came surging back on the mind and heart of the terror-stricken monarch. "Because thou obeyedst not the voice of the Lord, and didst not execute his fierce wrath upon Amalek, therefore hath the Lord done this thing unto thee this day. Moreover the Lord will deliver Israel also with thee into the hands of the Philistines" (R.V.). But Saul did not realize that even then the gates of God's love stood open to him, if only he would pass through them by humble penitence and faith. If instead of applying to the witch, he had sought God's mercy, light would have burst on his darkened path, and he had never perished by his own hand on Mount Gilboa.

In strong contrast with this, let us put the assurance of the new covenant: "Their sins and iniquities will I remember no more." When God forgives, He blots out from the book of his remembrance. The sin is gone as a pebble in the ocean; as a cloud in the blue of a summer's sky.

Saul's was a sin of omission. The question was not what evil he had done, but the good he had failed to do. Let us remember that we need pardon for the sad lapses and failures of our lives, equally as for the positive transgressions. And if such things are not forgiven, they will lie heavy on our consciences when the shadows of death begin to gather around us. The New Testament especially judges those who knew and did not do— the slothful servant, the virgin without the oil, the priest that passed by on the other side.

What do these Hebrews here? 1 Sam. 29: 3.
IT was a very natural remark. The Philistines
were going into battle with the Hebrew king
and his troops, and it was very anomalous
that a strong body of Hebrews should be
forming part of the Philistine array. They had
no business to be there. The annoyance of the
chief captains and lords that surrounded
Achish was natural enough. For long,
probably, it had been smouldering; now it
broke out into flame.

It is very terrible when the children of the
world have a higher sense of Christian propriety and fitness than Christians themselves,
and say to one another, "What do these
Hebrews here?" The word "Hebrew" means
one that has passed over—a separatist. The
death of our Lord Jesus was intended to
make all his followers separatists. Through
Him they have passed from death unto life;
they have been delivered out of the power of
darkness and translated into the kingdom of
God's dear Son. The appeal of his cross to us
all is, "Come out from among them, and be
ye separate." Too often, however, that call is
unheeded; and, for fear of man, we mingle
with the ranks of the enemies of our Lord.

If Christians attend the theatre; if Sunday-
school teachers, elders or deacons of a church,
are found participating in the pleasures of the
ungodly; if the young Christian man is
found loosely consorting with the card-
players of the smoking-room of an ocean
steamer—may not the sneer go round,
"What do these Hebrews here?" "What doest
thou here, Elijah?" is the remonstrance of
God. "What do these Hebrews here?" that
of the world, which not unfrequently has a
truer sense of propriety than God's professing
followers.

David encouraged himself in the Lord his God.
1 Sam. 30: 6.
HIS God! Doubtless the chronicler heard
him say repeatedly, as he was so fond of
saying, "My God, my God." "I will say unto
God, my rock, why hast Thou forsaken me?"
Though he had seriously compromised God's
cause, by the failure of his faith, by consorting
with Achish and the Philistines, by a tortuous
and treacherous policy, yet God was still his
God; and, in the supreme crisis which had
overtaken him, he naturally betook himself
to the covert of those loving wings.

HE ENCOURAGED HIMSELF. He would go
back on promises of forgiveness and succour,
which had so often cheered him in similar
straits. He would recall his songs in former
nights as black as this, and therefore would
have hope. He would remember that he had
been brought through worse trials; and
surely He who had helped him against
Goliath and Saul would not fail him against
the Amalekites. Besides, he had probably left
his dear ones in the protection of the encamping angel; and though his faith might be
tried, it could not be entirely disappointed.
In this way he encouraged himself. All
around was tumult and fear; but in God
peace and rest brooded, as swans on a tranquil
lake. His men might speak of stoning him;
his heart be greatly distressed for wives and
children; his life be in jeopardy: but God was
a very present help. "Why art thou cast
down, and disquieted, O my soul? Hope thou
in God."

In similar circumstances, let us have resort
to similar sources of comfort; hide in God,
and encourage ourselves in Him. It was in
this spirit that John Knox, when about to face
death, said to his wife, "Read to me where I
first cast anchor."

All the valiant men . . . 1 Sam. 31: 11, 12.
THIS was a noble and generous act. At the
beginning of his reign, in the early dawn of
youthful promise and prowess, when he was
the darling of the nation, Saul had interposed
to deliver their beleagured city. And now, as
the awful tidings of his defeat and suicide
spread like fire through the country, the men
whom he had succoured remembered his
first kingly act, and showed their appreciation
for his kindness by doing a strong and
chivalrous deed in rescuing his remains from
dishonour. They could not help him, but they
could save his honour. When David heard of
this act, he sent messengers to the men of
Jabesh-Gilead, thanking them for their
chivalrous devotion to the memory of the fallen
king, and promising to requite the kindness as
one done to the entire nation, and to himself.

Are we careful enough of the honour and
name of our dear Lord? He has done for us
spiritually all that Saul did for Jabesh-Gilead,
and more. He has delivered our soul from
death, our eyes from tears, and our feet from
falling. Let us be swift to maintain the honour
of his name among those who are so apt at
making it their scorn.

It was well that these men did not wait for others to act. Had they done so, the body of Saul might have rotted piecemeal on the walls of the temple at Bethshan. If they had left this act of reparation for Abner, or Ish-bosheth, it would never have been done.

There is no order of precedence, when a wrong has to be righted, or a friend vindicated. The man who is next must act. Let us strike into the fray, and count that our opportunity is warrant enough. He who can, may.

2 Samuel

Saul and Jonathan were lovely and pleasant in their lives. 2 Sam. 1: 23.

IT was very lovely and pleasant of David to say so. He had no hesitation, of course, in saying this of his beloved Jonathan, every memory of whom was very pleasant, like a sweet strain of music, or the scent of the spring breeze; but he might have been excused for omitting Saul from the graceful and generous epithets he heaped on the kindred soul of his friend. But death had obliterated the sad, dark memories of recent days, and had transported the Psalmist across the dream of years to Saul as he was when he was first introduced to him. All that could be said in praise of the first Hebrew king was crowded into these glowing lines—the courage, martial prowess, swiftness to aid those who required help, his pleasantness and courtesy in address.

This is the love of God, which He breathes into the hearts of his children. They become perfect in love, as He is. "God commendeth his love towards us, in that, while we were yet sinners, Christ died for us." It is God-like for his children to love their enemies, bless those who curse them, and pray for all who despitefully use and persecute them. Is such love ours? Do we forbear from thinking evil? Do we look on the virtues more often than the failures of our friends? Do we cast the mantle of forgiveness over the injuries done to us, and dwell tenderly on the excellences of our foes? Such is the love which never fails, but endures when faith has turned to fruition, and hope has realized its dreams.

We need most of all a baptism of love. A piece of clay will become fragrant if placed in contiguity to attar of roses. Let us lie where John did, on the bosom of incarnate love, till we begin to love as he.

The men of Judah came, and there they anointed David king. 2 Sam. 2: 4.

THUS was David anointed a second time. Hitherto he had been the leader of a troop; now he became king of his own tribe: and his kingdom clustered around the ancient city of Hebron.

TYPICALLY, we learn that our blessed Lord will be acknowledged King of his own people, the Jews, before He is accepted by the world at large. Now, his kingdom is in mystery— it is in the Adullam stage. Men are gathering to Him from all quarters; but as yet the world does not recognize it in their political calculations. But ere long the Jews will recognize Him as King, and then we may begin to expect his enthronement over the populations of the globe. When they repent and are converted, times of repenting will come to all the world.

EXPERIMENTALLY we are taught, that as each new department of our life unfolds, we should give Christ a fresh coronation. The attitude which we took up years ago, of complete consecration, must be applied perpetually to each fresh development of experience. Each new step should be characterized by a definite waiting on God, that there may be a fresh enduement of power, a recharging of the spirit with his might. Was He King in the cave, then be sure to acknowledge Him as such, now that you are called from obscurity into the glare of noon. Whenever God says, by the circumstance of your life, Go up; always kneel at the feet of Jesus, "Lord, in the very little I found my joy and strength in serving Thee only; and now, amid the greater responsibility and publicity of my life, I desire to be thy earnest, simple-minded, whole-hearted follower."

Have you anointed Jesus as your King? Do not fail. Remember how near of kin He is.

David waxed stronger and stronger, and the house of Saul waxed weaker. 2 Sam. 3: 1.

THE war between the flesh and the Spirit is long, but the end is sure. As the Baptist said of Jesus, so must the flesh say of the Spirit, He must increase; I must decrease. Sometimes in the long strain of the war, our spirit dies down. Will the bugle never cease to ring out its alarm? Will the assaults never come to an end? When shall we be able to lay aside sword and breastplate, and to enter the land of rest? Oh to be able to say with the Apostle, "I have fought the good fight, I have finished my course, I have kept the faith"!

Yet take heart. The assaults diminish in frequency and strength in proportion as they are faithfully resisted. Each time you resist successfully you will find it easier to resist. The strength of the vanquished foe enters the vanquisher.

Moreover, ultimate victory is secured. "Whatsoever is born of God overcometh the world; and this is the victory that overcometh the world, even our faith. Who is he that overcometh the world, but he that believeth that Jesus is the Son of God?" (1 John 5: 4, 5). It makes a great difference to the soldier, when he belongs to an All-Victorious Legion, and serves under a Captain that never lost a fight. And there can be no doubt as to the issue in your heart or mine. "He must reign till He has put all enemies under his feet."

At any moment we may look for the sudden collapse of a great portion of the confederacy of evil, which has so long menaced us; as when Abner suddenly came to Hebron to give in his adhesion to David. What a huge piece of cliff fell that day into the sea! Expect the sudden collapse of evils which have long troubled you.

As the Lord liveth, who hath redeemed my soul out of all adversity. 2 Sam. 4: 9.

IT was the midday of David's life, and, looking back, he saw how good the Lord had been to him. Step by step God had brought him up out of a horrible pit, and from the miry clay, setting him upon a rock, and establishing his goings. What need was there, then, that men should interfere to hasten the unfolding of the divine purposes? It had been his lifelong habit to wait. Whatever he needed he looked to God to supply. Whatever difficulties blocked his path, he looked to God to remove. Whatever men stood in his way, he looked to God to deal with them. Twice in the wilderness he refused to take Saul's life. He had executed the Amalekite because he claimed to have slain Saul on Gilboa. And, in pursuance of the same policy, he could have no complicity in the act of the murderers of Ishbosheth, even though they made his way clear to the throne of Israel.

Let God redeem thee out of all thine adversities. Do not lose heart or hope. Do not put forth thy hand to snatch at any position or deliverance by an act which might afterwards cause thee shame or sorrow. "Trust in the Lord, and do good. Roll thy way upon the Lord. Trust also in Him, and He shall bring it to pass. Rest in the Lord, and wait patiently for Him" (Psa. 37: 3–7, R.V.). He who turns glaciers to rivers that pass away, will remove all thy difficulties and perplexities. He shall cause thee to inherit the land. He will promote thee in due time, and give thee to see thy desire upon thine enemies. He who redeemed thy soul by his most precious blood cannot fail thee, however long he may tarry. Remember that He ever liveth, and loveth, and reigneth.

And David took him more wives out of Jerusalem. 2 Sam. 5: 13.

THIS is terribly disappointing! According to the ideas of the surrounding nations, the greatness of a monarch was gauged by the extent of his harem. But the law of Moses put severe restraint on the multiplication of wives, "that his heart turn not away" (Deut. 17: 17). It seems as though the soul of David sank into sensual indulgence and luxuriance. It lost much of its early hardihood and strength in consequence; and at this period of his life those seeds were sown, which in after years brought forth such a plentiful and terrible harvest of anguish, murder, and impurity, in his family.

Few of us realize how much our character owes to the stern discipline to which God subjects us. The only way to keep us healthy and vigorous is to send us many a nipping frost, many a keen northern blast. The bleak hillside breeds stronger natures than the warm sheltered valley. The difference between Anglo-Saxon and Negro is largely wrought by temperature and soil. The campaign, with its strain on every power of endurance, trains better soldiers than the barracks. As David was a stronger, better man, when hunted like a coney in the rocks of Engedi, so are we braced to a nobler life, when all things seem against us.

Few of us can be trusted with unbroken happiness. God is compelled to withhold what the flesh craves. But where prosperity has shone on your path, be very careful not to abuse it. Consider it as indicating God's loving trust in you. He would rather convey his lesson in sunshine than in storm. But walk carefully and humbly, looking to Him constantly for daily grace, and never relaxing the girdle about the loin.

They set the Ark of God upon a new cart.
2 Sam. 6: 3.

THIS was their mistake. The divine directions were explicit that the Ark of the living God must be carried on the shoulders of living men. There would have been no stumbling of oxen, no swaying of the Ark to falling, no need for Uzzah to reach out his hand, if only this simple direction had been obeyed. This breaking forth of God was to recall men to simple absolute obedience to the rules and regulations that had been so explicitly laid down in the Levitical code. It would not fall into disuse without grave loss to the entire people. Better that one life should be sacrificed for disobedience than that the whole nation should be impoverished for the relaxation of that ancient law.

We are fond of bringing new carts to God. At every birthday we build the new cart of good resolution, and place thereon the Ark of God. We will be different, and on our fresh endeavours the Lord of Hosts shall ride; but we must drive, and if needs be, steady the Ark. Ah! it is not long before the oxen stumble, and Uzzah who drives is smitten to the dust of death.

God wants, not new carts, but the living shoulders of consecrated men. We must live for Him, surrendering ourselves to his service; not driving, but being driven; not conducting, but being impelled; not imposing our thoughts on Him, but being willing to submit ourselves to Him. There is no need to fear God, if only we will obey Him, and in obedience discover the laws by which we may approach and serve Him. Then the power which otherwise flames forth to destroy will become the useful servant of our faith, and we shall be able to undertake great things for God.

Do as Thou hast said. 2 Sam. 7: 25.

THIS is the voice of a childlike faith.

NOTE WHAT LED TO THESE WORDS. Nathan had just unfolded to the king all the purposes of God's heart towards him. That He would establish his throne, deliver him from his enemies, and set up his dynasty to succeed him—this and much else. David's heart was full of joy and gladness—he knew that God would not run back from his word; but he felt none the less the duty of claiming the fulfilments of these guarantees. So it is with all the promises of God; though they are Yea and Amen in Christ, it is requisite for us to put our hand on them; plead them before God; and claim their fulfilment with appropriating faith.

NOTICE THE ATTITUDE IN WHICH DAVID UTTERED THESE WORDS. "He sat before the Lord." Was not this the position of rest and trust? On another occasion, he lay all night upon the earth (12: 16), in an agony of prayer, because not sure of God's purpose, and hoping to turn God by the extremity of his anguish. But there is a marvellous alteration in the tone of our prayer, so soon as we can base it on the declared purposes of God. We enter into his rest; we put ourselves in the current of his purposes; we sit before the Lord.

MARK THE BLESSEDNESS OF COMMUNION WITH GOD. It is as a man talks with his friend. We are not required always to kneel when we pray, or to con over a certain form of words; we can sit and talk with God, catching up his words as they fall on our hearts, and reflecting back on Him in praise, and prayer, and happy converse. All true prayer originates in the declarations of God's love, to each of which we answer, Do as Thou hast said.

The silver and gold he had dedicated of all nations which he subdued. 2 Sam. 8 :11.

DAVID might not build the temple, but he was bent on making provision for it. Indeed, Solomon had never been able to do as he did, unless his father had gathered these stores of gold and silver. Thus other men labour, and we enter into their labours; but the accomplished building is credited by God to each. He does not forget David when Solomon's temple stands complete. The reward is proportioned to each man's service, according to his share.

It is a glorious thing when we not only

defeat our foes, but get spoils out of their overthrow which we can use for the service of God and man. It is as possible for us as for David. Out of our failures, temptations, mistakes, let us get the power of helping and directing others. In death Jesus won the keys of death and Hades, and the power to become a merciful and faithful High Priest; and now He ever liveth to make intercession for his people. (Heb. 7: 25).

But the main lesson of this chapter is the foreshadowing of God's purpose, that Gentiles should contribute to the building of his Temple. What was literally true in the case of the temple of Solomon, is spiritually true of the heavenly Temple, the Church. From every nation, and kindred, people and tongue, souls are being gathered, who form a spiritual house, a holy Temple in the Lord. The whole world is destined to contribute to that structure, which is being prepared secretly and mystically, but shall ere long be manifested in its full glory. It is very interesting to get this suggestion from the chronicles of a nation so exclusive and haughty as the Jews. "They shall come from the East and West. . . ."

Thou shalt eat bread at my table continually.
2 Sam. 9: 7.
FOUR times in this chapter we are told of the lame man eating bread at the royal table. But what are these facts recorded and repeated for, save to accentuate the infinite blessings which come to us through the divine love?

Mephibosheth had done nothing to merit the royal favour. Not a word is said of his being well-favoured and attractive. So far from that, he was lame on both his feet, and probably a sickly invalid. In his own judgment he was worthless as a dead dog. His state was impoverished; no deed of prowess could win David's notice; he was almost entirely at the mercy of his servant, Ziba. In these respects there are many analogies to our own condition in the sight of God. We are lame indeed; and, so far as we are concerned, it is quite impossible that we should ever win the divine regard, or sit at his table among his sons.

But between David and Jonathan a covenant had been struck, which had provided for the children of the ill-fated Jonathan (1 Sam. 20: 14-16). It was because of this sacred obligation that Mephibosheth fared as he did. Look away, child of God, to the covenant struck between God and thy representative, the Son of his love. It is idle of thee to seek to propitiate the divine favour, or earn a seat at his table; but if thou art willing to identify thyself with thy Lord, and to shelter thyself in Him by the living union of faith; if thou canst base thy plea on the Blood of the everlasting covenant—then the provisions of that covenant between Father and Son shall be extended to thee: and because of God's love to Jesus thou shalt sit at the divine table, and be regarded as one of the heirs of the great King.

The Lord do that which seemeth Him good.
2 Sam. 10: 12.
ISRAEL was arrayed against overwhelming odds. To human sight it must have appeared very improbable that Joab would be able to hold his own. However, he made the best arrangements he could; exhorted his men to be of good courage and do their utmost; and then piously left the issue to the God of battles.

There are times in all lives when the case seems desperate. How can we meet with ten thousand him who cometh against us with twenty thousand! Heart and flesh fail. What resource is there, then, save in the flight of the lonely man to the only God? It is for God to act, since the help of man is vain.

IN YOUR PERSONAL STRAITS. When patience is exhausted; when the last handful is taken from the barrel; when complicated trials meet and hem you in; when the iron gate and the keepers before the door appear to render escape impossible—then look up, God is marching with reinforcements to your aid.

IN YOUR WORK AND WAR FOR GOD IN THE WORLD. We too often act and speak as if success were to be won by the forces that we may be able to bring into the field, whereas God asks us for nothing more than fidelity and the right disposition of such forces as we can command; He will do all the rest.

IN YOUR OUTLOOK ON THE CONFLICT BETWEEN GOOD AND EVIL. It is quite true that there appears to be an infinite disparity between the one and the other. But there are other forces in the field than appear. There is another host of which God Himself is captain. When the enemy comes in like a flood, the Spirit of the Lord lifts up the standard. "There is none like unto the God

Jeshurun, who rideth upon the heaven to thy help."

David tarried still at Jerusalem. 2 Sam. 11: 1.
AH! fatal dalliance in the arms of sensual ease! It led to David's undoing. It was the time of the year when kings generally went forth to the fight; and in earlier days David would never have thought of leaving to Joab or others the strain and stress of conflict when there were hard knocks to give and take. Indeed, on more than one occasion his followers had remonstrated against his exposing the Light of Israel to the risks of the battlefield. But now he sends Joab and his mighty men to fight against Ammon, while he tarries securely at Jerusalem. In this fatal lethargy he betrays the deterioriation of his soul. Already the walls were broken down, and entrance into the citadel was easy. We are not surprised to learn that as he sauntered lazily on his palace roof in the sultry afternoon he was swept away before the rush of sudden passion, and took the poor man's ewe lamb to satisfy the vagrant, hungry impulse which suddenly came to him.

Beware of hours of ease! Rest is necessary; times of recruiting and renewal must come to us all; nature positively demands re-creation; but there must be no neglect of known duty, no handing over to others of what we might and could do ourselves, no tarrying behind the march of the troops when we should go forth with them to the battle. Watch and pray, that ye enter not into temptation. Be most on guard when not actively engaged against the enemy. One unlocked gate may admit the foe to the citadel of the life, and rob you of peace for all after-days. The luxury of the plains of Capua was more fatal to the soldiers of Hannibal than the passage of the Alps.

And David went to Rabbah, and fought against it, and took it. 2 Sam. 12: 29.
VICTORY might seem to have been for ever forfeited after so great a fall. We could not have been surprised had we been told that from this time onward the course of David's conquests had stayed. And yet this thought would be a misconception of God's dealing with the penitent. Where there is true contrition, confession, and faith, He not only forgives, but restores; He not only restores to the enjoyment of his favour, but reinstates in opportunities of usefulness. So Jesus not only met the apostle who had denied Him, and put him back into the old position of happy fellowship, but gave him a commission to feed his sheep and lambs.

We have sometimes met backsliders who have doubted the possibility of their forgiveness; or, if they have realized this, they have never dared to hope that they could ever be what they had been. And so long as faith refuses to believe in the perfect work of God's love, it must inevitably take a back seat. Let us seek for such an entire faith in God's forgiving and restoring love as to dare to believe that we are put again into the old place, and allowed to anticipate the same victories as aforetime. "If we confess our sins, He is faithful and just to forgive us our sins, and to cleanse us from all unrighteousness' (1 John 1: 9).

Directly David said, "I have sinned," in the flash of a moment Nathan said, "The Lord hath put away thy sin"; and when Joab sent tidings that Rabbah was about to fall, David was permitted the honour of its final capture, though it had been associated so closely with Uriah's death. Where sin abounds grace superabounds, and reigns through righteousness. Dare to believe this.

Then the king arose, and tare his garments, and lay on the earth. 2 Sam. 13: 31.
THROUGHOUT the incidents of this chapter, the soul of David touched the bottom of the sea of anguish and remorse. The circumstances narrated were in themselves sad enough; but there was a more bitter element in them for David, because he knew that they were the harvest of which his own sin was the seed. Here began to be fulfilled the sentence of God through Nathan, "The sword shall never depart from thine house."

He had broken up the peace of another's home, and peace had quitted his home, never to return. He had defiled the purity of Uriah's wife, and the purity of his own daughter had been trampled underfoot. He had smitten Uriah, and now Absalom had murdered Amnon. Through those awful hours when the entire fate of the whole of his family seemed trembling in the balance, he drank to the dregs the cup of bitterness. Oh, how true are the apostle's words: "Whatsoever a man soweth, that shall he also reap. For he that soweth to his flesh shall of the flesh reap corruption; but he that soweth to the Spirit shall of the Spirit reap life everlasting."

Sin resembles the Australian weed, which when once it is sown in the waters will spread with such rapidity as to spoil their beauty, and choke their flow. We must distinguish between the penal and natural results. The penal were borne by Christ for us all, and are remitted for evermore; but the natural remain even to forgiven penitents, as they did to David. Still, God's grace may transmute them into blessings, and cause pearls to grow where before there had been gaping wounds. Ask God to take in hand the natural consequence of yours sins, and make them means of grace and ennoblement.

Yet doth He devise means that his banished be not expelled from Him. 2 Sam. 14: 14.
THE means that David devised were really inadequate. He allowed his heart to dictate to his royal sense of justice and rectitude, and permitted Absalom to return to his country and home without one word of confession, one symptom of penitence. The king was overmastered by the father; and the result was disastrous. It shook the respect of his people, undermined the foundations of just government, slackened the bands of every family in the land, and confirmed Absalom in his wilful and obstinate career. "What!" said he to himself, "does my father bid me come back without conditions? Does he demand no confession or reparation? Then he condones my sin."

Let parents be warned. If your children disobey, and violate the rules of your home, you have no right to treat them as you did before, until they have owned their sin. You must insist on penitence, confession, and reparation, though it take hours or days or even weeks of suffering and pleading to bring it about.

Into what relief does David's mistake throw God's way of forgiveness and salvation! Had he acted as David, and as so many wish us to believe, He would have reinstated the human family in the Paradise of his love without waiting for the work of the Mediator, or the confession of the prodigal. By the arbitrary exercise of his sovereign will He might have wiped out the record of our sins without our concurrence. But it would have been to the irreparable undoing of man. Hence it behoved

Christ to suffer, by his blood making an atonement for our sins, and by his Spirit bringing us to penitence and confession.

Here am I, let Him do to me as seemeth good unto Him. 2 Sam. 15: 26.
THERE is the patience of hope. We love to gird ourselves in the vehemence of our self-will, to go where we choose, to rule the lives of others; but as the years pass and our pride is humbled, the sinews of our strength slackened, and the radiance of early prospects overcast, we are willing to hand ourselves over to our Father, saying, "Behold, here am I; let Him do to me as seemeth good unto Him."

It was thus that Isaac was passive in the hands of Abraham. It was thus that Jesus spoke to his Father, "I come to do thy will, O my God." It was thus that the maiden who was blessed above women, answered the angel's message. It was thus that Paul, when urged not to go up to Jerusalem, avowed his willingness to live or die, as the Lord might choose.

God is ever working upon us through circumstances; and, as in the present case, sometimes He overrules the plottings of wicked men to fulfil his Divine purpose. His will is sometimes brought to us in a cup which a Judas holds to our lips. How blessed to be able to say, as we go forth to meet our Father's will, Behold, here am I! and to look beyond the plottings and machinations of our enemies to One who loves us infinitely. Whatever He permits must be good. Good, if driven as an exile from our home; good, if exposed to the revilings of a Shimei; good, if the heart breaks in bitter tears. All must be good which the good Lord permits or appoints. Many were the afflictions of David, but out of them all he was delivered. When he had learnt the lesson, the rod was stayed. God did not take away his mercy from him. Thou too art in his hands, and He will certainly bring thee again, and show thee the city and his habitation.

The king and all the people came weary, and refreshed themselves there. 2 Sam. 16: 14.
A GREAT weariness falls often on our souls. We are wearied because of the greatness of our way, and inclined to say there is no hope. Memory tires us, perpetually casting up the

record of past unfaithfulness and transgression. The bitter way of the natural
consequences of sin is toilsome and difficult
to the feet. We faint before the averted eye of
former friends and the pitiless criticism of
foes. Longings for a vanished past, for life
and love, for purity and peace, grind heavily
in the soul. Our King has known something
of human weariness, though not from all the
sources that cause it in his subjects.

But amidst the presence of our weariness
the voice of God may be heard saying, "This
is the rest wherewith ye may cause the weary
to rest, and this is the refreshing." There is
rest for weary souls beneath the shadow of
the cross, in the sight of which the burden
rolls away. There is rest and refreshment as
we sit in the banqueting house of Christ's
manifested and realized affection. There is
refreshment as we eat of his flesh and drink
of his blood; as we yield our will to his; as
we sit with Him in heavenly places. We
assuredly find Him to be "a hiding place
from the wind, and a covert from the tempest;
as rivers of water in a dry place, as the shadow
of a great rock in a weary land" (Isa. 32: 2).

There is no hill Difficulty without its
arbour; no desert without its oasis; no sultry
heat without its shadow of a great rock; no
weariness without its pillow; no intolerable
sorrow without its solace; no weariness
without its refreshment; no failure of man
without a very present help in God.

Arise, and pass quickly over the water. 2 Sam.
17: 21.

THE water of Jordan may serve as an illustration for our position. Our David has
passed over the waters of death, and in doing
so has taken us with Him. There is a sense
in which in the morning light of Easter Day
all who believed passed over with Him, so
that "by the morning light there lacked not
one of them that was not gone over Jordan."
We all hold the doctrine of Substitution.
Do we sufficiently realize that of Identification? Not only did Jesus die for us, but we
died with and in Him. In Him, as the true
Naoh's Ark, the whole Church passed over
the Jordan of death from the old world to
the new. There are some who do not understand that in the purpose of God we are
already standing on resurrection ground.
Across the water we can hear the murmur
of the world, and detect its corruption; but

we are the inheritors of the world in which
there is no death nor corruption nor the
dominion of sin. When a man realizes this
he no longer braces himself up to meet death,
because he knows that in the person of Christ
he has left it behind for ever.

What is true, however, in God's purpose
should be the aim and goal of our daily
striving. To us there comes the unceasing call,
"Arise, and go over Jordan." There is always
a thither and a hither side for every experience
and act. We may always do as the world does;
this is to stay on the death side. We may
always do as Christ does; this is to pass over
to the risen and living side. Reckon that you
have died, and mortify the deeds of your
body. "And if Christ be in you, the body is
dead because of sin; but the spirit is life
because of righteousness."

*Wherefore wilt thou run? . . . Come what may,
said he, I will run.* 2 Sam. 18: 22, 23 (R.V.).

JOAB did not love David, as Ahimaaz did,
and could not understand what made the
young man so eager to carry the tidings.
Doubtless Ahimaaz and Cushi entirely mis-
interpreted the heart of David, and thought
he would be glad to hear that the rebellion
was stamped out, and Absalom was dead.
And it was because of the pleasure which he
thought to give his king that the swift-footed
son of Zadok pleaded for permission to run.
What though there would be no reward, or
that it would fall to the lot of Cushi, who had
already started at Joab's command—that
mattered not, the love of David constrained
him.

How often that question of reward is thrown
at the servants of God! It is one of the
favourite taunts of the world; as Satan said
of Job, that we do as we do because we are
paid. "Doth Job serve God for nought?"
And nothing so startles men as disinterested
service. They cannot account for it; but it
wins their respect. "Reward or no reward;
recompense or none; smiles or tears, come
what may, let me run." That is the spirit
that becomes a Christian, and convinces the
world. "The love of Christ constraineth us."

Ahimaaz outran Cushi. The one was a
volunteer for love's dear sake; the other, a
bond-servant, doing as he was told. Love
lent wings to his feet, and speeding past his
fellow bore him first into David's presence.
So God's will is done in heaven: "The

cherubim ran and returned like a flash of lightning." So God's will is done on earth: "They departed quickly from the tomb with fear and great joy, and ran to bring his disciples word. And behold, Jesus met them, saying, All hail!"

The King is near of kin to us. 2 Sam. 19: 42.
THERE are two derivations for the word king: one from the word can—the king is the man that can do things; the other from the word kin—the king is closely related to us, of our kith and kin. In either case, there is a beautiful meaning, as touching our Lord and Savour. He is King, because He has overcome our enemies, and can overcome. He is King, because He has taken on Himself our flesh and blood, and has for ever made us one with Himself. The King is our kinsman. Our kinsman is King.

It is very comforting to know how really our Lord has identified Himself with us. The Gospels are full of the wonderful story. His kinship was manifested in:

HIS PRAYERS. He bade us speak to God as our Father; in that marvellous possessive pronoun, not only linking us all to one another, but including Himself in our petitions, save when we ask for forgiveness.

HIS INFIRMITIES. "We have not a high priest who cannot be touched with the feeling of our infirmities." His hunger and thirst; his weariness and exhaustion; his suffering unto death—all accentuate the closeness of the tie between us.

HIS TEMPTATIONS. "In all points tempted like as we are, yet without sin." The avenues through which the tempter could approach Him were those by which He assails us also. No temptation took Him, but such as is common to man. So to every lonely soldier of his He draws near, saying, "Be of good cheer; I have passed through it all. I am your brother in the fight; I feel for you with a quick sympathy; the glories of my throne do not alter my true-hearted love."

The men of Judah clave unto their King.
2 Sam. 20: 2.
WE are reminded of the exhortation of the good Barnabas, that with purpose of heart the converts of Antioch should cleave unto the Lord. This is the test of a true faith. We often come to the dividing of the paths. We stand on the watershed of the hills: that way leads back to Moab with its fascinations; this on to Canaan with its spiritual attractions. Orpah and Ruth must choose. Each is equally profuse in speeches and tears; but the ultimate test of love is whether they will stay or go. Which will cleave to the widowed Naomi? She is the truest lover; her fidelity will attest the fervour and strength of her affection. Orpah kissed her mother-in-law, and returned to her people and her gods, while Ruth "clave unto her."

We must cleave to Jesus, in spite of the derision of the multitude. We must be prepared to stand with Him when He stands alone, or goes forth alone to die. We must be willing to stem the mighty tide of the world which has left Him and pours past us. Though all forsake Him, yet we must cleave.

We must cleave to Jesus, in spite of the rebellion of the flesh. Our whole nature may sometimes rise in insurrection, demanding some forbidden fruit. It is no child's play then for the lonely will to stand by itself in unshaken fidelity and loyalty; but it must.

We must cleave to Jesus when He seems to rebuff us. Only those who can stand so sharp an ordeal, are exposed to it. But sometimes we are called to pass through it as Job, that angels may learn how Christ's lovers cling to Him, not for his gifts, but for Himself.

Because he slew the Gibeonites. 2 Sam. 21: 1.
THE Gibeonites were under the protection of a special covenant, which had been entered into between them and Joshua. That covenant was the outcome of a ruse on their part. But since it had been most solemnly made by the leaders of Israel, it held good. The fact of their deceit and chicanery could not absolve Israel from the oath which had been passed for their safety. For centuries the provisions of this covenant had been observed, till Saul invaded them, and slew the Gibeonites. This was a grievous sin, which, according to the religious light of the time, seemed to demand blood; and David proposed to atone for blood by blood. Nothing but blood could atone for sin so black and dark.

We are also protected by a covenant, into which the Father has entered with the Son, not for our worthiness or merit, but only because He would. The provisions of that covenant engage to take us to be his people, to remember our sins no more, and to make the divine law the object of our love (Heb. 8). And the argument is irresistible, that if man is so mindful of a covenant as to feel that its infraction is a sin which can only be expiated by blood-shedding, it is impossible to suppose that God will ever run back from his.

O my soul, thou mayest rest secure in this: here is an everlasting rock; this foundation shall suffice thee for evermore. Thou art in the Son of his love. Though thou art sinful and evil, yet thou art included in the covenant which is more lasting than that of day and night. Jesus has met its conditions on thy behalf, and has undertaken to secure thy obedience and holiness.

Thy gentleness hath made me great. 2 Sam. 22: 36.

THE triumph of God's gentle goodness will be our song for ever. In those far distant ages, when we look back on our earthly course, as a grown man on his boyhood, and when the words of this Psalm shall express our glad emotions, we shall recognize that the Hand which brought us thither was as gentle as our mother's; and that the things we craved, but failed to receive, were withheld by his gentle goodness. Our history tells what gentleness will do.

The Apostle besought the Corinthian converts by the gentleness of Christ (2 Cor. 10: 1). Though there were abuses amongst them that seemed to call for stringent dealing, he felt that they could be best removed by the gentle love which he had learned from the heart of Christ. The wisdom which is from above is gentle as well as pure; and in dealing with the sin that chokes our growth, it is probable that gentleness will do more than severity. The gentleness of the nurse that cherishes her children; of the lover to her whom he cherishes above himself; of the infinite love which bears and endures to the uttermost—is the furnace before which the foul ingredients of our hearts are driven never to return. We might brave the lion; we are vanquished by the Lamb. We could withstand the scathing look of scorn; but when the gentle Lord casts on us the look of ineffable tenderness, we go out to weep bitterly.

That He has borne with us so lovingly; that He has filled our lives with mercy even when compelled to correct; that He has never altered in his tender behaviour towards us; that He has returned our rebuffs and slights with meekness and forbearance; that He has never wearied of us—this is an everlasting tribute to the gentleness that makes great.

As the light of the morning when the sun riseth, a morning without clouds. 2 Sam. 23: 4.

THE dealings of God with man are compared to morning light, and the sprouting of tender grass in the sunshine that follows rain. The one may refer to youth, and the other to age. In each there is sunlight: in the one case it is before the clouds have gathered; in the other after they have dispersed.

CLOUDS. There are may different sorts: the cirrus, like platines in the sky; the cumulus, in heaps, like the summits of distant mountains; the strata, or long bars; the nimbus, heavy with showers. There is a counterpart for each human life, without which we should miss much of those experiences of light and shade that so frequently reveal the nature of the light. We should not know God's comfort and very present help, if it were not for the clouds which are born in the marsh-lands of trouble. Who does not prefer the changeful beauty of an English spring to the unclouded blue of Italian skies?

THE LIGHT OF THE MORNING. The love of God steals over hearts as the dawn. He is the Rock; but his advent breaks gently as light. So God's love came to Lydia, whose heart opened as a flower its petals. This makes it difficult for some of us to decide the moment of our regeneration; only we know that, once darkness, we are now light in the Lord.

CLEAR SHINING AFTER RAIN. We all know something of cloud and rain. If we did not, our lives would be arid as a desert. Rain is necessary to fructify the seeds that lie buried in the soil; but clear shining is needed too. Times of joy are needed equally as those of sorrow. The tender grass is the child of rain and sun. Hast thou had tears, thou shalt have smiles! Hast thou had clouds and rain, thou shalt have clear shining!

Neither will I offer burnt offerings . . . of that which doth cost me nothing. 2 Sam. 24: 24.

GOD'S love to us cost Him something. He spared not his own Son, and that Son spared not his blood. But how little our love to Him costs us! Let us understand that where there is true, strong love to Jesus, it will cost us something. Love is the costliest of all undertakings.

It will cost us Self-denial. Christ and self are perfectly incompatible; to have the one we must be prepared to surrender the other. The heart subtly schemes to hold both; but it does not deceive Christ. He knows in a moment when we have preferred to spare ourselves and to sacrifice Him, or to obey Him and sacrifice ourselves. We know it also. At first we may find it an effort to count all things but loss for Him; but as we go on doing it, and drink in the fresh air that breathes about the mountains of self-denial—above all, as we see the smile of pleasure on his face— our hearts leap with joy, and we love to give Him everything, not thinking of the cost, any more than Mary did when she broke the alabaster box of very precious ointment. After all, it is but fitting that we offer our bodies "a living sacrifice, holy, acceptable unto God."

It will cost us Companionships. Those who knew us will pass us with averted faces. It will cost us hard-earned money; for we shall realize that we have no property in anything that we possess. It will cost us high repute amongst our fellows. But what shall we mind if we gain Christ? You cannot give up for Him without regaining everything you have renounced, but purified and transfigured. Did not the Lord say so? And did He not add a hundredfold, with persecution. Let us heartily respond, "Lord, Thou knowest all things: Thou knowest that I love Thee!"

1 Kings

As the Lord liveth, that hath redeemed my soul out of all distress. 1 Kings 1: 29.

"IN my distress I called on the Lord, and cried to my God." Never let there be distress without its cry. He will hear your voice out of his temple, and your cry will come before Him even into his ears. He will answer, and set you in a large place. There is even a gain to be won from distress, because it brings out new phases of Christ's redemptive help.

God redeemed David from the calumny of those who maligned him without cause. In so many of his psalms he refers to the unjust and cruel hatred which misrepresented him and his doings. But God, to whom he committed his cause, vindicated him, so that his righteousness shone as the light, and his judgment as the noonday. So He will do for you. Those who now lay all manner of unkind charges to your door, will be compelled to admit your innocence. Only leave your cause with God, and be still.

God redeemed David from all the afflictions that shadowed his early days: from his wanderings in the wilderness; from his hairbreadth escapes in the caves; from meeting his death on many a terrible battlefield. We hardly realize, just now, how much we owe to the Angel of God's redemption, who is ever beside us, environing us with careful love, so that no evil may approach us, or snare take our feet. Our pathway is thick with snares and dangers, as the pilgrims found it when journeying through the valley of the shadow; but there is a way out, and in the morning we shall marvel to see how we escaped.

God redeemed David's life from destruction. This was the greatest miracle of all, when we consider the strong passions that slumbered within him, breaking out whenever he broke loose from God's grace.

That the Lord may continue his word. 1 Kings 2: 4.

HOW strongly David held to God's promise! It was deeply graven in his soul. How could he forget the word which guaranteed the succession of his race upon the throne of Israel! At the same time he distinctly recognized that the fulfilment was conditional. There was an if in it. It was only in so far as his children took heed to walk before God in truth that God was bound to place them on the throne of Israel; therefore he urged Solomon to keep the charge of the Lord, that the Lord might continue his word. We also must obey the threefold condition if we would enjoy a continuance of God's helpful care.

1. BE THOU STRONG. The strength which is in Jesus Christ waits to make us strong. In the Lion of the tribe of Judah there is the boldness which will not swerve in the face of the foe. Timid women and little children in the days

of persecution have waxed valiant in the fight, and have not flinched from death, because Jesus was beside them.

2. KEEP THE CHARGE OF THE LORD THY GOD. He has committed to our care many a sacred deposit, in return for our deposit with Him (2 Tim. 1: 12, 14; R.V., marg.). They are his holy Gospel, the Rest Day, the doctrines of the Evangelical Faith, and the Inspired Word. Let us watch them until we see them weighed out in the temple as were the sacred vessels which Ezra committed to the priests for transport across the desert (Ezra 8: 33).

3. KEEP HIS STATUTES AND COMMANDMENTS. We must obey with reverent care the one great law of love, which includes all the rest. Acting thus, we shall put ourselves in the way of enjoying a continuance of that favour which God has promised.

I have also given thee that which thou hast not asked. 1 Kings 3: 13.
THE understanding heart was Solomon's supreme request, and it was given him before the morning light had broken over Jerusalem. But God did exceeding abundantly beyond what he asked or thought. Riches and honour, victory and long life, were thrown in as part of the divine gift; as paper and string are given by the tradesmen with the goods we purchase. It seems as though our Lord's words were anticipated, "Seek first the kingdom of God and his righteousness, and all these things shall be added unto you."

PUT FIRST THINGS FIRST. One of the most important lessons of life is to discern the relative value of the objects within our reach. The child will take the handful of glass beads, and leave the heap of diamonds in the rough. It is the terrible mistake of men that, perplexed by earth's cross-lights, they put evil for good and good for evil; they make earth rather than heaven their centre; time rather than eternity their measurement.

SEEK GOD AND ALL THINGS IN HIM. Things without God cannot satisfy the craving of the soul. To know God, and to be known by Him, is to possess all things. All that is lovely, strong, or right, in any human being was in the Creator before it entered the creature; having God, you possess all things in Him.

BE MORE CAREFUL OF WHAT YOU ARE THAN WHAT YOU HAVE. A man's life consisteth not in the abundance of things that he possesseth; but in his purity, truth, tenderness, and the properties of his soul. The fruit of the Spirit must ever be manifest in the life of the believer—"Love, joy, peace, long-suffering, gentleness, goodness, faith, meekness, temperance."

Largeness of heart. 1 Kings 4: 29.
WE must all admit that our soul is too narrow. It holds too little, knows too little, is deficient in will-power, and, above all, in capacity of love; and when we are called to run in the way of God's commandments, we break down in despair, and cry, "If I am to be a runner, Thou must first enlarge my heart."

How little we know of the experience which Madame Guyon describes when she says: "This vastness or enlargedness, which is not bounded by anything, increases every day; so that my soul in partaking of the qualities of her Spouse seems also to partake of his immensity."

"There is," remarks one of the old Puritans, "a straitness, slavery, and narrowness, in all sin; sin crumples up our souls; which, if they were freely spread abroad, would be as large and wide as the whole universe. No man is truly free; but he that hath his will enlarged to the extent of God's will, by loving whatsoever God loves, and nothing else, he enjoys boundless liberty, and a boundless sweetness." God's love embraces the universe. He "so loved the world that He gave his only-begotten Son." We who have partaken of the divine nature must also love as He does.

Thomas à Kempis says, finally: "He who desires glory in things outside of God, or to take pleasure in some private good, shall many ways be encumbered and straitened; but if heavenly grace enter in, and true charity, there will be no envy, neither narrowness of heart, neither will self-love busy itself, for divine charity overcometh all things, and enlargeth all the powers of the soul." Give unto us, O God, this largeness of heart, even as the sand that is on the sea-shore!

Now the Lord my God hath given me rest on every side. 1 Kings 5: 4.
GOD is the Rest-Giver. When He surrounds us on every side with his protecting care, so that our life resembles one of the cities of the Netherlands in the great war—inaccessible to the foe because surrounded by the waters

of the sea, admitted through the sluice—then neither adversary nor evil occurrent can break in, and we are kept in perfect peace, our minds being stayed on God.

"Hidden in the hollow of his blessed hand, Never foe can enter, never traitor stand.

Have you experienced the rest which comes by putting God round about you, on every side—like the light which burns brightly on a windy night because surrounded by its four panes of clear glass? Ah! what a contrast between the third and fourth verse: Wars on every side; Rest on every side. And yet the two are compatible, because the wars expend themselves on God, as the waves on the shingle; and there are far reaches of rest within, like orchards and meadows and pasture-lands beyond the reach of the devastating water.

Out of such rest should come the best work. We are not surprised to find Solomon announcing his purpose to build a house unto the name of the Lord. Mary, who sat at the feet of Jesus, anointed Him. Out of quiet hearts arise the greatest resolves; just as from the seclusion of country hamlets have come the greatest warriors, statesmen, and patriots. Men think, foolishly, that the active, ever-moving souls are the strongest. It is not so, however. They expend themselves before the day of trial comes. Give me those who have the power to restrain themselves and wait; these are they that can act with the greatest momentum in the hour of crisis.

There was neither hammer, nor axe, nor any tool of iron heard. 1 Kings 6: 7.

IN absolute silence, like the growth of a palm in the desert, that noble building arose in the symmetry of its fair proportions. But there was plenty of quarrying and hammering and chiselling before the materials were brought to the site.

The absolute silence with which the Temple rose is a meet emblem of the progress of the Church, from its foundations laid in the Apostolate towards the top stone, which before very long will be laid upon the completed structure. Amid the rise and fall of dynasties and empires, the Church is being built. Soul after soul, as so many added bricks, is being quietly placed upon the walls. Some day the world will be amazed when it sees the New Jerusalem descend out of

heaven from God. The mightiest works of God are the fruit of silence

You and I are now in the quarry, hewn, chipped, chiselled: or are we in the saw-pit, being sawn, planed, pierced by nails. Be of good cheer! It will not be long, the preparatory work will be over, and we shall become part of the eternal structure. Into heaven there can enter neither hammer, nor axe, nor any tool of iron. The trial will have done its work. Sorrow and crying will flee away. The apostle Paul, who knew more than any man what trial and pain meant, could confidently declare: "I reckon that the sufferings of this present time are not worthy to be compared with the glory which shall be revealed in us." Then shall the city of God shine forth in completed beauty, her walls Salvation and her gates Praise; and the triumphant song of the redeemed shall ring forth: "Blessing, and honour, and glory, and power, be unto Him that sitteth upon the throne and unto the Lamb for ever and ever."

In the plain of Jordan did the king cast them. 1 Kings 7: 46.

THE Apostle tells us to obey from the heart that mould or form of doctrine to which we were delivered (Rom. 6: 17). What a mould is to the metal which is wrought into various forms of utensils, that the form of sound doctrine is to believers who desire to resemble Christ. When our hearts, melted in contrition and penitence, are poured into the teaching of the Apostles, to ponder it in memory, and to carry it out in life, they are, so to speak, cast into the pattern of Jesus Christ, which they wear for evermore. Thus we are conformed to the image of his Son.

We differ as widely as the vessels named here. Some are lavers, and some bases; some shovels, and some basons. It matters little what shape we bear; so long as we are cleansed and meet for the Master's use. Each vessel in Solomon's temple filled its own niche. The machinery of the whole would have been hindered if one had been missing. Be content with the shape which the Great Designer hath intended for thee. Yield to it. Dare to pour thyself into the dark passages of the mould. Do not ask the intention of this or that. Obey from the heart, otherwise thou mayest have to be broken up, and put back again into the furnace to go through the process once more. This is the Plain of the Jordan for us, the place of death; but soon we shall be remitted to the Palace and Temple of God.

There is no clue to the understanding of the mysteries of our mortal life, save the hypothesis, that we are being prepared for the position which has been prepared for us in the eternal world. "And we know that all things work together for good to them that love God."

That He maintain the cause of his servant, as every day shall require. 1 Kings 8: 59 (R.V.).
THE marginal (R.V.) reading is, "The thing of a day in its day." What rest would come into our lives, if we really believed that God maintained the cause of his servants! Men hate you, and say unkind or untrue things about you; on your part, though you are quite prepared to admit that you have made mistakes, yet you know that you desire above all things to act as God's servant should, that your motives are sincere, and your hands clean —be of good courage then: God will maintain your cause, as every day may require.

Or, you are beset by strong competition; and, in order to hold your own, you have been tempted to do what is not perfectly the best—to spice your teaching with a little heterodoxy, puff your wares with misleading titles, to adulterate your goods. But there is no need to do this; if only you are faithful to God, He will maintain your cause, as every day may require.

Or, you are tempted almost beyond endurance, and think that you must yield. The seductions are so insidious, the pitfalls so carefully concealed, the charm of evil so subtle. But, if you will only look away to God, you will find Him a very present help to maintain your cause. Oh, trust Him; for none of them that do so can be so desolate. Daily strength for daily need; daily manna for daily hunger; daily maintenance for daily temptation. These are assured.

As we stand on the hill-top in the morning and look across the valley of the coming day, its scenes are too closely veiled in heavy-hanging mists for us to specify all our requests. We can breathe the comprehensive petition, "Give us this day our daily bread." And God will suit his help to each requirement. As the moment arrives "the thing" will be there.

I have hallowed this house which thou hast built.
1 Kings 9: 3.
MAN builds; God hallows. This co-operation between man and God pervades all life. Man performs the outward and mechanical; God the inward and spiritual. Paul plants, Apollos waters; but God gives the increase. We elaborate our sermons and addresses, building them up with careful, eager thought; but God must work in and through them for his own glory in the salvation and upbuilding of souls. We must be careful to do our part with reverence and godly fear, remembering that God must work in realms we cannot touch, and to issues we cannot reach, before our poor exertions can avail.

May we not apply this especially to the education of a child's life? Many who read these lines are engaged in building structures which will outlive the Pyramids. The body is only the scaffolding, behind and through which the building of the soul is being upreared. The materials with which we build may be the gold, silver, and precious stones, of our example, precept, careful watching, and discipline; but God must come in to hallow. Our strenuous endeavour must be supplemented by the incoming of the Holy Spirit.

God hallows by his indwelling. Holiness is the result of his putting his Name into a place, a day, a human soul; for his Name is his nature, Himself. Each day may be a building, reared between sunrise and sunset, with our activities; but it were vain to hope to realize our ideal unless the structure become a Temple filled with God. Build what you will; but never be satisfied unless God sets his eyes and heart upon your life, hallowing and sanctifying each day and act to Himself.

Blessed be the Lord thy God, which delighted in thee. 1 Kings 10: 9.
THERE were two reasons why Solomon was on the throne. First, because of God's love to him; secondly, because of God's love to Israel. May we not address our Saviour with similar expressions of gladness as those which the queen addressed to a less than He?

How well it is, now and again, to let ourselves go in exuberant adoration! Prayer is good, but it may revolve too largely about our own needs and desires: thanks are right, when we have received great benefits at his hands; but praise is best, because the heart forgets itself and earth and time, in enlarged conceptions of its adorable Lover and Saviour.

We are reminded in this connection of a noble hymn by old John Ryland:

"Thou Son of God, and Son of Man,
    Beloved, adored Emmanuel,
Who didst, before all time began,
    In glory with thy Father dwell:

"We sing thy love, who didst in time,
    For us, humanity assume,
To answer for the sinner's crime,
    To suffer in the sinner's room.

"The ransomed Church thy glory sings,
    The hosts of heaven thy will obey;
And, Lord of lords, and King of kings,
    We celebrate thy blessed sway."

We can never praise Him enough. Our furthest thoughts fall short of the reality. His wisdom and prosperity exceed his fame. No question He cannot answer; no desire He cannot gratify; no munificence He cannot excel. Happy are they who stand continually before Him. Let us see that this is our happy privilege; not content to pay Him a transient visit, returning to our own land, but communing with Him always of that which is in our heart.

His wives turned away his heart. 1 Kings 11: 4.
EVERY man is vulnerable at one point of his character. Strong everywhere else, and armour-plated, he is weak there; and our great enemy knows just where to strike home. It would have been useless to argue with Solomon for the claims of idols. He could at once, by his wisdom, have annihilated all infidel arguments, and have established the existence and unity of God. But, step by step, he was led by silken cords, a captive, to the worship of other gods. It is a solemn warning; and Nehemiah was perfectly justified when, in his contention with the Jews who had married wives of Ashdod, of Ammon, and of Moab, he said, "Did not Solomon, king of Israel, sin by these things? Yet among many nations there was no king like him who was beloved of his God."
Let young people beware where they let their hearts go forth in love. Whom we love we resemble; and in the marriage tie it is almost inevitable that seductions to the lower will overcome the drawings to the higher. When a Christian disobeys God's distinct command against intermarriage with the ungodly, he begins to sink to the level of his ungodly partner whom he had thought to raise to his own religious standing.

Our associates determine the drift and current of our life. It is so easy to launch upon the current that flows past our feet; it seems impossible that the laughing, enticing water should ever carry us against sharp, splintering rocks, or over breaking cataracts. When we are compelled to associate with the ungodly, let us maintain a strict self-watch, and pray that the breath of the heavenward gale may more than counteract the tendency of the earthward current.

The month which he had devised of his own heart. 1 Kings 12: 33.
JEROBOAM acted on expediency. It did seem reasonable to argue that the constant going up to Jerusalem to worship might alienate the people from his throne, and awaken a desire for the old national unity; and without doubt a mere worldly wisdom extolled his setting-up of idol-gods at Bethel and Dan; but his policy in this respect led to the downfall of his kingdom. Had he trusted God's promise, made through the prophet Ahijah, the Divine purpose would have ensured the continuance of his rule; but the prompting of expediency resulted in ultimate disaster (ch. 14).

How prone we all are to devise out of our own hearts! We take counsel with ourselves, and do what seems prudent and far-seeing, with the inevitable result of being betrayed into courses of action that God cannot approve, and of which we have reason to repent bitterly. It is infinitely better to wait on God till He develop his plan, as He most certainly will, when the predestined hour strikes. He who trusts in his own heart, and takes his own way, is a fool. To run before God is to sink knee-deep into the swamp. We must make all things after the pattern shown us on the Mount, and take our time from God's almanack. What a contrast to the course of Jeroboam was that of the Son of Man! He would do nothing of Himself. His eye was always on His Father's dial-plate, and thus He knew when his time was not yet fulfilled. He was always consulting the movement of his Father's will, and did only those things which He saw his Father doing. Similarly make God's will and way thy Pole-star. Oh to be able to say with our blessed Lord, "I seek not mine own will, but the will of Him that sent Me."!

Forasmuch as thou hast been disobedient, . . . but camest back. 1 Kings 13:21, 22 (R.V.).
WE are inclined at first sight to pity this unknown prophet, and to justify his return; but as we look closer into the story, we not only discover the reason for the severe penalty that overtook him, but we are warned lest we make a similar mistake. When we have received a direct command fresh from the lips of Christ, we must act on it, and not be turned aside by a different suggestion, made to us through the lips of professing Christians. God does not vacillate or alter in the thing which proceeds from his mouth. When we know we are in the line of his purpose, we must not allow ourselves to be diverted by any appeal or threat, from whomsoever it may emanate. Deal with God at first-hand.

The rule for determining the true worth of the advice which our friends proffer us, is to ask, first, whether it conflicts with our own deep-seated conviction of God's will; and, secondly, whether it tends to the ease and satisfaction of the flesh, as the old prophet's suggestion certainly did. Beware of any one who allures you with the bread and water that are to break your fast. That bait is likely enough to disturb the balance of your judgment. When a voice says spare thyself, be on the alert; it savours the things that be of man, not of those that be of God.

Learn to deal with God at first-hand. Do not run hither and thither to human teachers, or to the Church. Be still before God, and what He says in the depths of thy soul, do. His Holy Spirit shall guide you into all truth; and when once his way has been revealed to thee, go straight on, listening to no other voice, however much it professes Divine inspiration.

I am sent to thee with heavy tidings. 1 Kings 14:6.
HOW foolish! Jeroboam thought that the old prophet could penetrate the vail that hid the future, but not the disguise in which his wife wished to conceal herself. As we might have expected, the aged prophet's inner sight read her heart. From God no secrets are hid. Immediately on his accosting her by her name there came the dread announcement of inevitable disaster.

We must not hesitate to unfold all the consequences of sin. As watchmen on the walls, we are bound to tell men of the certain fearful looking for of fiery indignation which shall devour the transgressors. None of us should flinch from declaring the whole counsel of God. We should specially insist on the guilt side of sin. Not only that it is a misfortune, a mistake, an error, a disease, a tyranny; but a crime. The sinner is a criminal, who has incurred the just wrath and anger of a holy God: for which he must suffer a due recompense.

Oh for more tenderness that we may with tears warn men of their doom! We are so self-possessed, so stolid; we need to ask that our eyes, like Jeremiah's, should be fountains of tears, that we might weep day and night. If the tidings are heavy, let us first feel their pressure on our own hearts; let us bend over the regions of despair and darkness, and hear the bitter weeping, wailing, and gnashing of teeth, and come back to warn our brethren, lest they also come to that place of torment. Though it was with fear and much trembling that Paul preached the Gospel, yet he did not shun to declare the whole counsel of God. And while we go to men with the good tidings of salvation, we must not withhold the heavy tidings from those who persist in unbelief.

Asa did . . . right in the eyes of the Lord, as did David his father. 1 Kings 15:11.
IT is a great thing to have such a testimony as this. We may do right in our own eyes; yet the eye of the Lord may detect evil which neither our associates nor we have seen. We may deceive ourselves, we may deceive others; but we cannot deceive God. In the home or business, in situation or factory, let us live as under the searching gaze of God.

Asa's life was one of religious activity: he destroyed the idols of his father, and even deposed his queen-mother, "because she made an idol in a grove." It needs Divine courage so as to live for God that at home or afield men shall take knowledge of us that we have been with Jesus. This is what the world is languishing for—reality, consistency under all circumstances, and before all men.

There are, however, two clouds overhanging this otherwise bright life. "The high places were not removed" (14). Though idols were destroyed, the groves in which they were erected remained. They were no snare to him;

and he took care that during his life they
should not ensnare others; but after his
death, in the reign of Jehoshaphat his son,
"the people offered and burnt incense" in
them (22: 43). We must not only cleanse our
way before the Lord, but remove any evil
thing which may cause others to stumble.

The other cloud is indicated in 2 Chron.
16: 12: "He was diseased in his feet. . . . Yet
in his disease he sought not to the Lord, but
to the physicians." Strange that in affliction
he should not have turned to the Great
Physician. The enemy of souls is ever on the
watch. Pray that amid the pains of death you
may not act unworthily.

*Ahab did more to provoke the Lord to anger
than all the kings. 1 Kings 16: 33.*
HIS sin was very aggravated, largely through
the influence of Jezebel, his young and
beautiful wife, who introduced the abominations of Phœnician idol-worship. This is why
he is said to have exceeded his predecessors
in wickedness. They broke the second commandment, and worshipped Jehovah under
the form of a calf. Ahab and Jezebel broke
the first, and chose other gods—Baal, the
sun, and Ashtoreth, the moon. The inveterate love for this idolatry was connected
with licentious rites with which these deities
were served. What wonder that the land became corrupt when the fountains of its
religious life were polluted at the source?

The connection between the indulgence of
impurity and the declension of the spiritual
life, is very close. As the apostle Paul tells us
in Romans 1, the men that refuse to retain
God in their knowledge are given up to the
working of passion; and as they yield to
passion they lose the sweet, clear impression
of the truth and nearness of the Christ. The
first, second, and third thing to be said to
young people on venturing out into the world,
corrupt through many deceitful lusts, is, Be
pure. Wear the white flower of a blameless
life. If you cannot be faultless, be blameless.
If you cannot realize all the good you know,
at least refrain from all the evil. Keep your
robes unspotted from the world. Then
through purity of heart and obedience in life,
you shall see God. As the living Christ enters
the heart, He will drive before Him the brute
forms of evil, overthrow the tables of the
money-changers, and will sit to teach of God.
Give yourself unreservedly into his keeping,
that He may govern and control every avenue
of your life.

*I have commanded the ravens . . . a widow
woman . . . there. 1 Kings 17: 4, 9.*
WE MUST BE WHERE GOD DESIRES. Elijah spoke
of himself as always standing before the Lord
God of Israel. He deemed himself as much
a courtier in the royal palace as Gabriel
(Luke 1: 19). And he could as distinctly stand
before God when hiding beside Cherith, or
sheltering in the widow's house at Zarephath,
as when he stood erect on Carmel, or listened
to the voice of God at Horeb. Wherever
you go, and whatever ministry you are called
to undertake, glory in this, that you never
go to any greater distance from God.

If we are where God wants us to be, He
will see to the supply of our need. It is as easy
for Him to feed us by the ravens as by the
widow woman. As long as God says, Stay
here, or there, be sure that He is pledged to
provide for you. Though you resemble a
lonely sentinel in some distant post of missionary service, God will see to you. The
ravens are not less amenable to his command
than of old: and out of the stores of widow
women He is as able to supply your need as
He did Elijah's, at Zarephath.

How often God teaches best in seclusion
and solitude! It is by the murmuring brooks
of nature that we have our deepest lessons.
It is in the homes of the poor that we are
fitted for our greatest tasks. It is beside
couches where children suffer and die, that
we receive those preparations of the heart
which avail us when the bugle note summons
us to some difficult post.

GOD LEADS THROUGH DEATH TO LIFE It was
needful that the child should die, that sin
might be remembered and dealt with; but
through Death's portal the trio entered a
richer, fuller life. Fear not that gateway!

*So Ahab went up to eat and drink. And Elijah
went up to the top of Carmel. 1 Kings 18: 42.*
SUCH differences obtain still. The children
of this world and the children of light are
manifest. What though the bodies of four
hundred and fifty prophets lay slain in the
gorge of the Kishon; or that by one great
act Elijah had hewn down the upas tree, the
deadly influence of which had corrupted
Palestine; or that the long-expected rain was

in the air—yet Ahab must eat and drink. These are the things which the children of the world seek after. Watch and pray, lest you enter into this temptation. Let appetite be kept well in hand—your servant, not your master; and see to it that you are capable of such profound and absorbing interest in the things of the Kingdom of God, as to count the gratification of physical desire unworthy to be compared with the high delights of service, prayer, and communion with the unseen.

Though he must have been exhausted with the excitements and efforts of the day, Elijah must spend the evening hour with God. Though he knew that the rain was near, he felt that his prayers were a needful condition for its bestowment. Though any part of Carmel might have become his oratory, he sought the lonely solitudes of the summit with the outspread sea before him, that his soul might hold undisturbed vigil, and that he might see over the wide expanse of the ocean the first tokens of the coming answer. His attitude denoted his humility. His repeated injunction to the lad, his perseverance. His success approved his faith.

Stand, O suppliant soul, on the highest point of expectant hope; see the hurrying answer, which was being prepared from pools and lakes and seas, long ere thy prayer began. "Before they call, I will answer."

Behold, an angel touched him. 1 Kings 19: 5.
IN all probability the angels often touch us when danger is near, threatening our health and life, or when foul fiends step up to us with hideous temptation. They find us out, especially when, like Elijah, we are alone and depressed; when nervous depression has crept about our hearts; when we seem to have failed in the conflict against evil, and long for death to end our long and weary strife. It was the lament of a holy soul on the verge of eternity, that he had made so little of the ministry of God's holy and tender angels.

It was very gracious for God to deal thus with his servant. We might have expected rebuke or remonstrance, chiding or chastisement; but we would hardly have expected such loving, gentle treatment as this. Is this the man who defied Ahab and all his priests? He is as frail and impotent as any! Nay, but God looked beneath the surface depression, and detected the strong fountains of courage and devotion that lay beneath, only capable of being called again into intense manifestation. He knew his servant's frame, and recognized that he was dust. He knew how to distinguish between the passing overstrain of the body and the heroic temper of the spirit. So, He understands us in our fits of depression and despair.

Whenever these angel-fingers touch you, whether directly or through the medium of loving mortal hands, you will always find the cake and the cruse of water. God never awakens to disappoint. It is an infinite pleasure to Him to awaken his loved ones to good things, which they had neither asked nor thought. Will not dying be something like this? The angel of life will touch us, and we shall awake to see what love has prepared.

As thy servant was busy here and there, he was gone. 1 Kings 20: 40.
THIS was likely enough to happen on a battlefield. It would not be possible to hold your prisoner, and to busy yourself about other things at the same time. This man, in the prophet's parable, made a great mistake to concern himself about a number of trifles, when so serious a matter as his own life depended on giving all his attention to the custodianship of the prisoner entrusted to his care. But is it not thus that men miss the main end of life?

BUSY HERE AND THERE, AND LIFE IS GONE. Many spend their days in mere trivialities. Like children they dig in the sand; like the butterfly, they flit from flower to flower. A round of visits, a few novels, a good many hours of light gaiety; vanity, fashion, and amusement—these fill their hours, the days flash by, and life is gone. They have nothing to show for it.

BUSY HERE AND THERE, AND THE CHANCE OF SAVING OTHERS IS GONE. Lives touch lives, for the chief purpose that one should influence the other. But too often we deal only with superficialities, busying ourselves in the slightest interests, but not seeking the salvation of those with whom we associate. The dance, the game, the business relationship, monopolise our thought, and our friends are swept from us in the eddying whirl of life's battle, and are gone.

BUSY HERE AND THERE, AND THE KNOWLEDGE OF GOD IS GONE. Remember how the birds caught away the seed of the Kingdom; and be sure that, in the same way, the cares and riches of this world, and the lusts of other things may enter in, and destroy the impression made on the heart. The ephemeral interests of life press hard on its real interests. Like boys, we squander in trifling the hours given to prepare for an examination on which all the future must turn.

And Ahab said to Elijah, Hast thou found me, O mine enemy? 1 Kings 21: 20.

AHAB got his garden of herbs, but he had Elijah withal, who stood at the gate like an incarnate conscience. Men may get the prize on which they have set their heart; but if they have obtained it wrongfully, the conscience of the wrong done will haunt them, and take away the pleasure on which they counted, and ultimately bring them like a quarry to the ground.

We turn our best friends into enemies, as Ahab did Elijah. The cloud that lights Israel is darkness to Pharoah; the angel that protects Jerusalem, slays the host of Sennacherib; the gentle love which anoints the Saviour, instigates in Judas a jealousy which ends in murder. The God who shows Himself merciful to the merciful is froward to the froward. The cause of the alteration is to be sought within ourselves. The sun that melts wax hardens clay, but the difference is in the clay. To the widow of Zarephath Elijah was an angel of light; whilst to Ahab he was an enemy. The difference lay in their hearts; the one being holy and loving, the other dark and turbid. What you are, determines whether Elijah will be your friend or your enemy.

This word "sold thyself" is very awful. It underlies Goethe's tragedy of Faust, in which the soul sells itself to the devil for so many years of worldly pleasure. A few promises which are never kept; a mirage that is dissipated in thin air when we approach it; a bribe of gold or silver that burns the hands which receive it—such are the price for which men sell themselves. "They sell themselves for nought." Truly the devil drives a hard bargain. When he gets the soul into his power, he laughs at his former promises, and pays as wages, death.

A certain man . . . smote the king of Israel between the joints of the harness. 1 Kings 22: 34.

EVERY man we meet is clothed in armour; in other words, we all cover ourselves with plates on which to receive the thrust of accusation and reproach. "I only do as others." "I do not see any special harm in it." "My father did it before me." "I cannot help it." Such are some of the plates in the armour of the soul; and our work as Christian workers becomes abortive in so many instances, because we are content to belabour the plates, instead of striking home to the one place where the armour-joints are. Successful soul-winning depends on discovering the vulnerable part of a man, and striking there. But all this demands a very special discernment of spirits, and anointing of the Holy Ghost. Only so can we detect where best to bring about conviction, and make men know their need of the Gospel of God's grace. The great need of the present day is a sharper and more searching analysis of sin. Men need to be shown how they are violating the laws of God. They assent generally to the Scriptural statements of what God requires, but fail to realize how greatly they have come short. You are almost sure to hit, if you begin to show the various ways in which respectably-living people are coming under the divine sentence.

But several conditions must be fulfilled. (1) Study well your own heart. (2) Be a deep student of the biographies of Scripture; because every type of human character is delineated in Holy Writ. (3) Open your heart to the Holy Ghost, through whom alone you can discern spirits. He is a discerner of the thoughts of the heart, and will teach you to cut to the dividing asunder of the soul and spirit, and of the joints and marrow.

2 Kings

Thou man of God! 2 Kings 1: 9, 11, 13.

OH that thou and I might so live before God and men, that they should recognize us as men of God, as God's men! See how these ungodly captains at once recognized this, in the case of Elijah. They fretted and chafed against his holiness; but they were forced to admit it. They tried to impose their orders, or those of their king; but they realized that Elijah was the servant of Him whom they set at nought, so far as their own lives were concerned.

If we are really men of God, we shall be the last to assume the title. Notice that Elijah puts an 'if' before the title with which he was saluted: "If I be a man of God." Paul counted himself the least of all saints.

WE MUST BE OF GOD. All our goodness must originate in Him. We can no more boast of goodness than a chamber can boast of the light which irradiates each corner of its space. The faith that takes his grace, as well as the grace it takes, is his. We are absolutely debtors; and happy are they who love to have it so, and lie always at the Beautiful Gate of God's heart, expecting to receive alms at his hand.

WE MUST BE FOR GOD. This is the only cure for self-consciousness, for that perpetual obtrusion of the self-life which is our bane and curse. Ask that the Holy Spirit may fill you with so absorbing a passion for the glory of Jesus, that there may be no room to think of your own reputation or emolument.

WE MUST BE IN GOD, AND GOD IN US. This is possible, when we love perfectly. He that dwelleth in love, dwelleth in God, and God in him. Oh, sea of light, may we lie spread out in thy translucent waves, as the sponges in southern sapphire seas, till every fibre of our being be permeated and infilled!

Elisha, tarry here, I pray thee. 2 Kings 2: 2, 4, 6.

THRICE Elijah spoke thus to his friend and disciple, to test him. Perseverance, tenacity of purpose, a refusal to be content with anything short of the best, are indispensable conditions for the attainment of the highest possibilities of experience and service. And perpetually in our life's discipline these words come back on us, Tarry here! Not that God desires us to tarry, but because He desires each onward step to be the choice and act of our own will.

TARRY HERE IN CONSECRATION. "You have given so much; it is not time that you refrained from further sacrifices? Ungird your loins, sit down and rest, forbear from this strenuous following after. Spare thyself; this shall not come to thee."

TARRY HERE IN THE LIFE OF PRAYER. "It is waste time to spend so much time at the footstool of God. You have done more than most, desist from further intercession and supplication."

TARRY HERE IN THE ATTAINMENT OF THE LIKENESS OF CHRIST. "It will cost you so much, if all that is not Christ-like is to pass away from your life."

Such voices are perpetually speaking to us all. And if we heed them, we are at once shut out of that crossing the Jordan, that rapturous intercourse with heaven, that reception of the double portion of the Spirit, which await those who have successfully stood the test. The law of the Christian life is always Advance; always leaving that which is behind; always reckoning that you have not attained; always following on to know the Lord, growing in grace and in the knowledge of the blessed Saviour, and saying to the spirit of God, as Elisha to Elijah, I will not leave thee.

Ye shall not see wind, neither shall ye see rain; yet that valley shall be filled. 2 Kings 3: 17.

THIS is God's way of fulfilling the desire of them that fear Him. We like to see the clouds blown forward through the sky, and hear the moan of the rising wind; in other words, we like to see God's gifts on their way, or to have the sensible emotion of receiving them. Sometimes we have symptoms and signs that fill us with rapture; at other times, these are lacking, and we surrender ourselves to despair. Yet when we see neither wind nor rain, God may be most mightily at work.

IT IS SO IN CHURCH WORK. How often we make our valleys full of ditches! Our machinery is complicated and perfect; we have spared neither pains nor care. Then we ardently desire the signs of a powerful revival, and break our hearts if they are not apparent; while, all the time, if we only knew it, the divine blessing is welling up in the ditches, doing more than would be the case if our highest wishes were gratified. Here and there tears are falling silently, hearts are being cleansed, lives are becoming yielded to God.

IT IS SO IN CHRISTIAN EXPERIENCE. We expect to have our Pentecost as the early Church received hers. We desire to see wind and rain, and to know that God is baptizing us; but this is not granted. There is no footfall of hurrying clouds, no coronet of flame, no gift of tongues. But, deep down, the ditches are being filled up, yearnings are being satisfied, the capacity for God within us is being met, though it grows apace. God be praised that the success of his work is not gauged by outward signs!

A well may be filled as completely by the percolation of water, a drop at a time, as by turning a river into it.

And the oil stayed. 2 Kings 4: 6.

WHAT a sorrowful confession! There was no reason why it should stay. There was as much oil as ever, and the power which had made so much could have gone on without limit or exhaustion. The only reason for the ceasing of the oil was in the failure of the vessels. The widow and her sons had secured only a limited number of vessels, and therefor there was only a limited supply of the precious oil.

THIS IS WHY SO MANY OF GOD'S PROMISES ARE UNFULFILLED IN YOUR EXPERIENCE. In former days you kept claiming their fulfilment; frequently you brought God's promises to Him and said, "Do as Thou hast said." Vessel after vessel of need was brought empty and taken away full. But of late years you have refrained, you have rested on your oars, you have ceased to bring the vessels of your need. Hence the dwindling supply.

THIS IS WHY YOUR LIFE IS NOT SO PRODUCTIVE OF BLESSING AS IT MIGHT BE. You do not bring vessels enough. You think that God has wrought as much through you as He can or will. You do not expect Him to fill the latter years of your life as He did the former. You can trust Him for two sermons a week, but not for five or six.

THIS IS WHY THE BLESSING OF A REVIVAL STAYS IN ITS COURSE. As long as the missioner remains with us, we can look for the continuance of blessing. But after awhile we say, Let the services stop; they have run their course, and fulfilled their end. And forthwith the blessing stops in mid-flow. Let us go on pleading with the unsaved, and bringing the empty vessels of our poor effort for God to fill them up to the full measure of their capacity.

Like unto the flesh of a little child. 2 Kings 5: 14.

IS there any fabric woven on the loom of time to be compared in perfect beauty to the flesh of a little child, on which, as yet, no scar or blemish can be traced? So sweet, so pure, so clean. It was a wonderful combination, that the strong muscles and make of the mighty man of war should blend with the flesh of a child. But this may be ours also, if we will let the hand of Jesus pass over our leprous-smitten souls. At this moment, if you let Him, He will touch you and say, "Be clean," and immediately the leprosy will depart, and you will return to the days of your youth—not forgiven only, but cleansed; not pardoned only, but clad in the beauty of the Lord your God, which He will put on you.

We do not count a little child to be free from the taint of sin. It is conceived in sin, and inherits the evil tendencies of our fallen race. Its innocence of evil is not holiness. Jesus gives us more than innocence, He makes us pure and holy. But there are other childlike qualities which our Saviour gives. The humility of a little child, who is unconscious of itself, and who is not perpetually looking for admiration. The unselfishness of a little child, who seeks its companion to share its luxuries and games. The trust of a little child, which so naturally clings to a strong and loving heart, will to follow anywhere, to believe in anything. The love of a little child, who responds to every endearment with sunny laughter and soft caresses.

There is a great difference between childish and childlike. The former is put away, as we grow up into Christ: the latter we grow into, as we become more like our Lord. The oldest angels are the youngest: the ripest saints are the most childlike.

Behold, the mountain was full of horses and chariots of fire round about Elisha. 2 Kings 6: 17.

SO it is with each of God's saints. We cannot see, because of the imperfection of mortal vision, the harnessed squadrons of fire and light; but the Angel of the Lord encampeth round about them that fear Him, and delivereth them. If our eyes were opened, we should see the angel-hosts as an encircling fence of fire; but whether we see them or not, they are certainly there.

GOD IS BETWEEN US AND TEMPTATION. However strong the foe, God is stronger. However swift the descending blow, God is swifter to catch and ward off. However weak we are, through long habits of yielding, God is greater than our hearts, and can keep in perfect peace. "Trust ye in the Lord for ever; for in the Lord Jehovah is the Rock of Ages."

GOD IS BETWEEN US AND THE HATE OF MAN. Dare to believe that there is an invisible wall of protection between you and all that men devise against you. What though the heathen rage, and the people imagine a vain thing! No weapon that is formed against you shall prosper, and every tongue that shall rise in judgment shall be condemned.

GOD IS BETWEEN YOU AND THE DELUGE OF CARE. What thousands are beset with that dark spectre! They have no rest or peace either day or night, saying, "Where will the next rent, the next meal, come from?" How different the life of birds, and flowers, of children, of Jesus, and all holy souls. Oh, rest in the Lord, and put Him between you and black care.

GOD IS BETWEEN YOU AND THE PURSUIT OF YOUR PAST. He is your reward; and as He intercepted the pursuit of Pharaoh, so He stands at Calvary between your past and you. The assayer of retribution is arrested by that divine Victim—what more can we ask!

This day is a day of good tidings. 2 Kings 7: 9.
IT was indeed. The enemy that had so long hemmed them in had dispersed, leaving a great spoil behind. The famine which had driven the people to awful straits was at an end, and there was now plenty of everything. It was inhuman for these four lepers to be content with eating and drinking, and sharing out the spoil, when hard by a city was in agony. Common humanity bade them give information of what had happened.

Let us take care lest some mischief befall us, if we withhold the blessed Gospel from a dying world. We know that Jesus has died and risen again, and that his unsearchable riches wait for appropriation. We have availed ourselves of the offer; but let us see to it that so far as we can, we are making known that the wine and milk may be obtained without money and without price.

Mischief always overtakes a selfish policy; whereas those who dare to share with others what they have received, not only keep what they have, but find the fragments enough for many days afterwards.

Let us tell men that the Saviour has over-come our foes, and has opened the kingdom of heaven to all who believe. Let us speak from a full heart of all that He has proved to be. Let us invite men to share with us the grace which hath neither shore nor bound.

One ounce of testimony is worth a ton weight of argument, and overpowers all objection. The Lord, on whom the king leaned, derided the possibility of the prophet's prediction; and no doubt had plenty of adherents. But the leper's report swept all his words to the winds. They had known, tasted, and handled. Let us remember that we are called to be witnesses of what God hath done for us.

And the Man of God wept. 2 Kings 8: 11.
ELISHA foresaw all the evil that Hazael would inflict on Israel, and it moved him to tears. Though he was a strong man, able to move kingdoms by his message and prayer, yet he was of a tender and compassionate disposition. This was he who one moment upbraided the king of Israel for his crimes, and the next called for a minstrel to calm his perturbed spirit with strains of music. The men that can move others are themselves very susceptible and easily moved.

The nearer we live to God, the more we deserve to be known as men and women of God, the more will our tears flow for the slain of the daughters of our people. Consider the ravages that drink, and impurity, and gambling, are making among our people; enumerate the homes that are desolate, the young life that is wrecked as it is leaving the harbour, the awful dishonour done to woman; and surely there must come times when tears well up for very humanity's sake, to say nothing of the pity which they acquire who look at things from God's standpoint.

Jesus beheld the city and wept over it. Give us this day, O Son of Man, thy compassion, thy love, thy tears, that we may speak of thy grace graciously, of thy love tenderly, and even thy judgments with brimming eyes.

"A broken heart, a fount of tears:
Ask, and it shall not be denied."

Wouldst thou avert such issues; begin with the cradled babes of your homes. Win them for God; teach them how to curb passion and subdue themselves. Tenderness and wisdom may arrest the making of Ben-hadads.

*Is it peace, Jehu? And he answered, What
peace?* 2 Kings 9: 22.

WE all want peace. Of every telegraph
messenger, as he puts the buff-coloured
envelope into our hands, we ask almost
instinctively, Is it peace? If there is a rumour
of war, a depression in trade, a bad harvest,
a sudden calamity in our neighbourhood,
we instantly consider the effect it may have
on the tranquillity and prosperity of our life.

By peace we too often mean the absence
of the disagreeable, the unbroken routine of
outward prosperity, the serene passage of the
years: not always eager for anything deeper.
And if other and profounder questions
intrude themselves, we instantly stifle or evade
them. Like Herod, we shut up the Baptist in
the dungeon. Like the Roman general, we
make a desert and call it peace. Men will flee
from a Gospel ministry which pursues them
into close quarters, and arouses unwelcome
questions that break the peace.

There cannot be true peace so long as we
permit the infidelities and charms of some
Jezebel of the soul-life to attract and affect
us. Jezebel may stand for the painted world,
with its wiles and snares, or for the flesh,
or for some unholy association of the past
life, like that which clung to Augustine. But
there must be no quarter given to the unhallowed rival of our Lord. Whatever its
charms, it must be flung out of the window
before we can be at peace.

"Then, and not till then, we shall see
Thee as Thou art;
Then, and not till then, in thy glory
bear a part;
Then, and not till then, Thou wilt satisfy
each heart."

If you are entirely surrendered to the Lord,
"the peace of God, which passeth all understanding, shall guard your hearts and your
thoughts in Christ Jesus."

*Jehu took no heed to walk in the law of the
Lord God of Israel.* 2 Kings 10: 31.

JEHU was the Cromwell of his time. He swept
away the symbols of idolatry with ruthless
destruction. Nothing could withstand his
iconoclastic enthusiasm. But he failed to keep
his own heart, and therefore his dynasty
lasted for but one generation. It is a deep
lesson for us all.

We may keep other people's vineyards,
and neglect our own. We may give good advice
to our friends, but fall into the very faults
against which we warn them. We may pose
as infallible guides, but fall into the crevasses
and precipices from which we had carefully
warned our companions. Jehu avenged the
idolatries of Ahab, but he departed not from
Jeroboam's calves.

Before you rebuke another, be sure that
you are free from the faults that you detect
in him. When you hear of the failings of some
erring brother, ask yourself whether you are
perfectly free from them. And never attempt
to cast out the mote from your neighbour's
eye till you are sure that the beam has been
taken from your own.

Take heed to your heart. Its complexion
colours all the issues of life. Do not be content
to be strong against evil; be eagerly ambitious
of good. It is easier to be vehement against
the abominations of others than to judge
and put away your own secret sins. But while
we keep our heart with all diligence, we cannot
afford to be independent of the keeping
power of God. We must yield ourselves to
Him, reserving nothing. The King must have
all. The light of his face must fill every nook
and corner of the soul. And every power
that opposes itself to his dominion, must be
dragged beyond the barriers and ruthlessly
slain.

They made him king, and anointed him.
2 Kings 11: 12.

THIS dexterous overthrow of Athaliah by the
bringing of the youthful king, who had been
hidden in the secret chambers of the Temple,
accommodates itself so obviously to a reference to the inner life, that we must be pardoned for making it.

Is not the spiritual condition of too many
children of God represented by the condition
of the Temple, during the early years of the
life of Joash? The king was within its precincts,
the rightful heir of the crown and defender of
the worship of Jehovah: but, as a matter of
fact, the crown was on the head of the
usurper Athaliah, who was exercising a cruel
and sanguinary tyranny. The king was limited
to a chamber, and the majority of the priests,
with all the people, had not even heard of
his existence. So, unless we are reprobates,
Jesus is within the spirit, which has been
regenerated by the Holy Ghost; but in too
many cases He is limited to a very small

corner of our nature, and exercises but a limited power over our life.

There needs to be an anointing, an enthroning, a determination that He shall exercise his power over the entire Temple of our Being; the spirit, which stands for the Holy of Holies; the soul, for the Holy Place; the body, for the outer court.

Holiness or Sanctification is not a quality or attribute which can be attributed to us apart from the indwelling of the Holy One. If we would be holy, we must be indwelt by Him who is holy. If we would have holiness, we must be infilled by the Holy One. But there must be no limiting of his power, no barrier to his control, no veiling or curtaining of his light. The veil, if such there be, must be rent in twain from the top to the bottom.

The money that cometh into any man's heart to bring into the house of the Lord. 2 Kings 12: 4.
THE margin suggests that the thought of giving for God's house would ascend in a man's heart, till it became the royal and predominant thought, swaying the whole man to obedience. It is a beautiful conception!

For the reconstruction of the Temple there were two classes of revenue: the tribute money which each Israelite was bound to give, and the money which a man might feel prompted to give. Surely the latter was the more precious in the eye of God.

Does it ever come into your heart to bring some money into the house of God? Perhaps the suggestion comes, but you put it away, and refuse to consider it. The thought begins to ascend in your heart, but you thrust it down and back, saying, Why should I part with what has cost me so much to get! Beware of stifling these generous promptings. To yield to them would bring untold blessing into heart and life. Besides, the money is only yours as a stewardship; and the thought to give it to God is only the Master's request for his own.

The great mistake with us all is, that we do not hold all our property at God's disposal, seeking his directions for its administration and that we forget how freely we have received that we may resemble our Father in heaven, and freely give. Too many, alas! are anxious to hoard up and keep themselves that which God has given them, instead of counting themselves and all they have as purchased property, and using all things as his repre-

sentatives and trustees. Let us make a complete surrender to our Lord, and from the heart sing,

"Take my silver and my gold,
Not a mite would I withhold."

He smote thrice and stayed. 2 Kings 13: 18.
A STRIKING spectacle. The dying prophet, with his thin hands on the muscular hands of the young king, as he shoots his arrow through the eastern window; the exhortation to smite the remaining arrows on the ground; the bitter chiding that the king had struck thrice only, instead of five or six times. What lessons are here! The Lord Jesus put his hands upon ours. Here is the reverse to the incident referred to. Ours are weak, his are strong; ours would miss the mark, his will direct the arrows, if only we will allow Him, with unerring precision. We shoot, but the Lord directs the arrow's flight to the heart of his foes.

Our success is commensurate with our faith. If we strike but thrice, we conquer but thrice. If we strike seven times, we attain a perfect victory over the adversary. Is not this the cause of comparative failure in Gospel effort? Souls are not saved because we do not expect them to be saved. A few are saved, because we only believe for a few. It is one of the most radical laws in the universe of God, and one which our Lord repeatedly emphasized that our faith determines the less or more in our own growth, and in the victories we win for Christ. Do not stay, O soul-winner, but smite again and yet again in the secret of thy chamber, that thou mayest smite Satan, and compel him to acknowledge thy might.

Let us not stay, though the energy of earlier days may be ebbing fast. The sanctified spirit waxes only stronger and more heroic, as Elisha's and Paul's did, amid the decay of mortal power. The Lord will say to us, as He did to Paul, "My grace is sufficient for thee: for my strength is made perfect in weakness."

Every man shall be put to death for his own sin. 2 Kings 14: 6.
SO ran the law of Moses. It forbade the imposition of punishment on the relatives of the wrong-doer, but it had no mercy on him. "The soul that sinneth, it shall die," was the

succinct and conclusive verdict of the older law, in this reflecting the spirit and letter of one yet older, which ran, "The day that thou eatest thereof thou shalt surely die."

FIRST, WE WERE DEAD IN OUR SINS. Eph. 2: 5 puts this beyond all doubt. In the sight of God, all who walk according to the course of this world, and obey the prince that now worketh in the children of this world, are dead in trespasses and sins. However much they may be alive as to their souls, they are dead as to their spirits, entirely destitute of the life of God.

SECOND, WE HAVE DIED FOR OUR SINS. 2 Cor. 5: 14, 15 (R.V.) establishes this fact, and shows that in Jesus, we who believe in Him, are reckoned to have died in Him when He bore our sins in his own body on the tree. In God's estimate, his death is imputed to us; so that we are reckoned as having satisfied, in Jesus, the demands of a broken law. It has no more to ask.

THIRD, WE MUST DIE TO OUR SIN. Rom. 6: 11. Reckon that you have died, and whenever sin arises, to menace or allure you, point back to the grave, and argue that since you died in Christ, you have passed altogether beyond its jurisdiction, for you have yielded your members as weapons of righteousness unto God. And having been crucified with Christ, you now no longer live, but Christ liveth in you. Let it become your daily habit to place the grave of Jesus between yourself and all allurements of the world, the flesh, and the devil.

The sins of Jeroboam, the son of Nebat, who made Israel to sin. 2 Kings 15: 9, 18, 24, 28.
THIS chapter anticipates the final overthrow of the kingdom of the tribes. It describes the corruption and disorganization of the people which made them the easy prey of Assyria. One puppet-king after another was set upon the throne to fall after a brief space of rule, and four times over it is said that they followed in the steps of Jeroboam, "who made Israel to sin." The seed sown two hundred years before had at last come to maturity, issuing in the ruin of the nation. What a comment on the inspired words, "Sin, when it is finished, bringeth forth death."

Twelve times in the story of the kingdom of Israel are we told that Jeroboam, the son of Nebat, made Israel to sin. The institution of the calves on his part seemed to be a piece of political wisdom, but it was an infraction of the divine law; and what is morally wrong can never be politically right. The house cannot stand unless the foundation can bear the test of the Divine plummet. The kingdom of Israel fell, to prove to all after-time that the disregard of God's law is a foundation of sand, which can never resist the test of time.

Why is Jeroboam so frequently called "the son of Nebat"? Why should the father be for ever pilloried with the son, except that he was in some way responsible for, and implicated in, his sins? There was a time when perhaps Nebat might have restrained the growing boy, or led him to the true worship of God; or perhaps his parental influence and example were deadly in their effect. How important that parents should leave no stone unturned to promote the godliness of their children, bringing them up in the nurture and admonition of the Lord.

King Ahaz sent to Urijah the fashion of the altar and the pattern of it. 2 Kings 16: 10.
THE fashion of this world passeth away like a fleeting dream; or like the panorama of clouds that constitute a pavilion of the setting sun, but which, whilst we gaze, tumbles into a mass of red ruin. And yet we are always so prone to imitate King Ahaz, and visit Damascus with the intention of procuring the latest design, and introducing it, even into the service of the sanctuary.

Man naturally imitates. He must get the pattern of his work from above, or beneath; from God or the devil: hence the repeated injunction to us all, to make all things after the pattern shown on the mount. If we would be rid of the influence of worldly fashion, we must conform ourselves to the heavenly and divine. The pattern of the Body of Christ—of the position of each individual believer among its members, and of the work which each should accomplish—was fixed before the worlds were made. The best cure for worldliness is not unworldliness, but other-worldliness. The best way of resisting the trend of people around us is to cultivate the speech, thought, and behaviour of that celestial world to which we are bound by the most sacred ties, and whither we are travelling at every heart-throb.

This introduction of the altar of a heathen shrine into the holy temple of Jerusalem, reminds us of the many rites in modern religious observances which have been borrowed from paganism, and warns us that the Church has no right to go to the world for its methods and principles. Let the world do as it may in its discussions about truth, its efforts to attract attention, and its organizations; our course is clear—not to build altars after its fashion, nor model our life on its maxims.

These nations feared the Lord, and served their graven images. 2 Kings 17: 41.

IT was a curious mixture. These people had come from Babylon, Hamath, and Sepharvaim, and were settled in the land from which Israel was deported. In their desire to propitiate the God of the country, they added his worship to that of their own gods (ver. 32), though they did not really fear Him (ver. 34). There was an outward recognition of the God of Israel, which was worse than useless. Are you sure this is not a true description of your own position? You pay an outward deference to God by attending his house, and acknowledging his day, whilst you are really prostrating yourself before other shrines. The one originates in a superstitious fear, a desire to stand well with your fellows; but it is in the direction of the other that your heart really goes. You come as his people come, sit as his people sit, kneel as his people kneel; but your heart is far apart, and you only do as you do that you may follow your own evil ways with less fear of discovery.

With all of us there is too much of this double worship; but let it be clearly understood that it is only apparent, not real. No man ever really serves two masters, or worships two gods. Whatever conflicts with God in heart or life is our chosen god. Whatever appears to share our heart with God really holds our heart. God will never be in competition with another. He must either be all or none.

The soul that endeavours to divide its service between Jehovah on the first day, and its graven images all the other days of the week, might as well discontinue its religious observances, for they count for nothing: except to blind it to its true condition.

Now on whom dost thou trust? 2 Kings 18: 20.

IT was no small thing for Hezekiah to rebel against the proud king of Assyria. Hamath and Arpad, Samaria and Sepharvaim, Hena and Ivah, reduced to heaps of stones, were sufficient proofs of the might of his ruthless soldiers. How could Jerusalem hope to withstand? Rabshakeh could not comprehend the secret source of Hezekiah's confidence. It was of no use for him to turn to Egypt. Pharaoh was a bruised reed. And as for Jehovah! Was there any likelihood that He could do for Israel more than the gods of the other nations had done for them? Not infrequently does the puzzled world ask the Church, "In whom dost thou trust?"

Our life must to a large extent be a mystery, our peace pass understanding, and our motives be hidden. The sources of our supply, the ground of our confidence, the reasons for our actions, must evade the most searching scrutiny of those who stand outside the charmed circle of the face of God; as it is written, "Eye hath not seen, nor ear heard . . . what God hath prepared."

We all ought to have the secrets which the world cannot penetrate. Doubt your religion if it all lies on the surface, and if men are able to calculate to a nicety the considerations by which you are actuated. We must be prepared to be misunderstood and criticised, because our behaviour is determined by facts which the princes of this world know not. We do not look up to the hills, because we look beyond them to God; we do not trust in silver or gold, or human resource, because God is our confidence. We cannot but seem eccentric to this world, because we have found another centre, and are concentric with the Eternal Throne.

And Hezekiah spread it before the Lord. 2 Kings 19: 14.

AMID the panic that reigned in Jeruslaem, the king and the prophet alone kept level heads, for they alone had quiet, trustful hearts. We hardly realize the crisis unless we compare it with the march of 200,000 Kurds or Turkish soldiers upon some peaceful Armenian community. Israel had no earthly allies. Her only reinforcements could reach her from heaven, and it was the care of these two saintly men to implicate their cause with that of the living God (ver. 4). This is the faith that overcomes the world, which realizes that God lives here and now in our home and life and circumstances. His cause is implicated in our deliverance; his name will be disgraced if we are overwhelmed, and honoured, if preserved.

He is our Judge, Lawgiver, and King, and is therefore bound by the most solemn obligations to save us, or his name will be tarnished.

When therefore letters come to you, anonymous or otherwise, full of bitter reproach; when unkind and malignant stories are set on foot with respect to you; when all hope from man has perished, then take your complaint—the letter, the article, the speech, the rumour—and lay it before God. Let your requests be made known unto Him. Tell Him how absolutely you trust. Then malice and fear will pass from your heart, whilst peace and love will take their place: and presently there will come a swift message of comfort, like that which Isaiah, the son of Amoz, sent to Hezekiah, saying on the behalf of God, "That which thou has prayed to Me, I have heard."

God knew the contents of the missive before you did; but He likes to read it again in the company of his child.

Let the shadow return backward ten degrees.
2 Kings 20: 10.
IT is impossible for us to understand how this could be. The shadow of the declining day waxes ever longer, and only a miracle could change its appearance on the dial. It may suggest some significant thoughts about shadows that may still go back.

THE SHADOW OF A WASTED LIFE. Of course, there is a sense in which the wasted years will never come again; they have passed beyond recall. But the shadow may go back on the dial of our life when we truly repent, and turn again to God, for He hath promised: "I will never leave thee, neither forsake thee." And "I will give back the years that the canker worm and caterpillar have eaten."

THE SHADOW OF HAPPIER DAYS. These seem to have gone. For long you have noticed the growing twilight, and it seemed impossible ever again to have the lightsomeness and spring of one or two decades back. But be of good cheer, for when a man comes into that fellowship with God which sorrow and temptation teach, when with growing years he attains added grace, we are told that he shall return to the days of his youth.

THE SHADOW OF EARLY AFFECTION. Have you lost loved ones, so that your life is like a house the windows of which, one after another, have become shuttered and dark? But love is not forfeited for ever. Those who forsake all for Christ's sake shall get all back again in Him.

His love comprehends all human love. The relationships of his kingdom surpass in tenderness and tenacity those of the warmest earthly ties. Thy brother shall rise again, and thou shalt hear him call thy name, and shalt sit with him in the Home of Life.

And his mother's name was Hephzi-bah.
2 Kings 21: 1.
HEPHZI-BAH means, "My delight is in her" (Isa 62: 4). How strange, supposing that her name was any indication of her character, that such a woman should have borne such a son; for "Manasseh did wickedly above all the Amorites did which were before him." A godly ancestry, however, does not guarantee a holy seed. Hezekiahs and Hephzi-bahs may be the parents of Manassehs. That this may not be so:—

LET US GUARD AGAINST THE INCONSISTENCIES OF OUR PRIVATE LIFE. The child of religious parents becomes habituated to their use of expressions in public which betoken the highest degree of holiness, and is therefore quicker to notice any inconsistency in temper or walk. Is there not a subtle temptation also for those who work much for God in public to feel that a certain laxity is permissible in the home? Will not late after-meetings at night compensate for indolence in the morning; and will not protracted services be the equivalent for private prayer? May not irritatibility to servants or children be accounted for by the overstrain of our great work? Hence, inconsistency and failure to realize our lofty aims, which are quickly noticed, beget distaste for our religion.

LET US GUARD AGAINST ABSORPTION IN PUBLIC RELIGIOUS DUTY TO THE NEGLECT OF THE HOME. Does it never happen that the children of religious parents are put to bed by nurses who are heedless of their prayers, because their mothers have undertaken a mission? Do not boys sometimes grow up without the correcting influence of the father's character, because he, good man, is so taken up with committees?

LET US GUARD AGAINST AN AUSTERITY OF MANNER, WHICH PREVENTS US BEING THE COMPANIONS, PLAY-FELLOWS, AND ASSOCIATES OF OUR CHILDREN.

Thou shalt be gathered into thy grave in peace.
2 Kings 22: 20.
As a matter of fact, Josiah's death was not a

peaceful one. He persisted in going into conflict with Pharaoh-necho, king of Egypt, against the latter's earnest remonstrance (see 2 Chron. 35: 20–22); and, in consequence of his hardihood, met his death. His servants carried him in a chariot dead from Megiddo (ch. 23: 30). Is there, then, any real contradiction between the prophet's prediction and this sad event?

Certainly not! The one tells us what God was prepared to do for his servant; the other what he brought on himself by his own folly. There are many instances of this change of purpose in the Word of God. One of them is known as "his breach of promise" or "altering of purpose" (Num. 14: 34, marg.). He would have saved his people from the forty years' wandering in the wilderness but they made Him to serve with their sins, and wearied Him with their iniquities. He would have gathered Jerusalem as a hen gathers her brood, but she would not.

Let us beware lest, a promise being left us, we should seem to come short of it lest there be in any of us an evil heart of unbelief in departing from the living God, and frustrating some blessed purpose of his heart. "Eye hath not seen, nor ear heard, neither have entered into the heart of man the things which God hath prepared for them that love Him"; but we may limit the Holy One of Israel, and so restrain Him by our unbelief as to stay the mighty works which are in his plan for us. He may desire for us a prosperous life and a peaceful death; but we may close our dying eyes amid disaster and defeat, because we wilfully chose our own way.

Like unto Josiah was there no king before him.
2 Kings 23: 25.
THIS chapter is a marvellous record of cleansing and purging. We are led from one item to another of drastic reform. Nothing was spared that savoured of idolatry. Priests and altars, buildings and groves, came under the searching scrutiny of this true-hearted monarch; and, as the result, it was possible to keep such a Passover as had not been observed during the days of the judges or the kings (ver. 22).

How much our enjoyment of the solemn feast depends upon our previous efforts to put away from our lives all that is inconsistent with the law of God. We hardly realize how insidiously evils creep in. Before we are aware,

we have fallen beneath God's ideal, and adopted the customs of our neighbours, or of those with whom we come into daily contact. All such declension hinders our joy in keeping the Passover. It is needful, therefore, that there should be times when we turn to God with fresh devotion, and in the light of his holy truth pass the various departments of our life under review, testing everything by the Book of the Law. In Josiah's case, the sacred volume was recovered from long neglect; in our case it needs to be re-read in the light of higher resolves. This would be like a new discovery. Our ultimate rule must always be the will of God, appreciated with growing clearness, and used as a standard by which to judge the habits and tenets of our life. We read the Bible for purposes of a truer knowledge of God and his ways, and for spiritual quickening; but let us also use it more frequently as the bath of the spirit. Let us bathe in it. Let us revel in it as the grimy children of the slums in the laughing wavelets of river and sea.

He carried out thence all the treasures of the House of the Lord. 2 Kings 24: 13.
AMONGST these deported treasures must have been much of the sacred furniture of the Temple, and the holy vessels; because, in the days of Belshazzar, we find them brought out to grace the royal banquet. Belshazzar drank wine from them with his lords, wives, and concubines, whilst they praised the gods of Babylon, who had given them victory over their foes. Amongst the rest was the golden candlestick, whose flame afterwards illuminated the inscription of doom, written by God's hand upon the palace wall. By the command of Cyrus these precious vessels were finally restored (Ezra 5: 14), and carried back to Jerusalem, by a faithful band of priests (8: 33).

THE WHOLE STORY OF THE CAPTIVITY IS FULL OF SOLEMN LESSONS. The Church of God must make her choice between one of two courses: either she must keep from all entangling alliances, and from vying for temporal power; or she must face the liability of being brought under the power with which she would fain assimilate. Israel wanted to be as the other nations around her, imitating their organization, and allying herself now with one, and then with another; in consequence she was swept into captivity to the very nation whose fashions she most affected (Isa. 39).

HAVE WE NEVER TASTED THE BITTERS OF CAPTIVITY? Borne away from our happy early homes to live among strangers, set to repugnant tasks, removed from all that made life worth living, we have known the exile's lot. Alas! if it be so; yet, even in our captivity, where the Lord's song is silenced, and our harps hang from the willows, if we repent, and put away our sins, and turn again to the Lord, He will not only have mercy, but abundantly pardon, and bring us again that we may be as we were in times past.

Every day a portion, all the days of his life.
2 Kings 25: 30 (R.V.).

IS it to be supposed that the king of Babylon took more care of Jehoiachin than God will take of us? Jehoiachin had resisted his suzerain, and cost him a great expenditure of men and treasure; but nothing which had transpired in the past hindered this provision of a daily supply. Will God do less for you, his child? Would it not come as a relief if you were to be told that, from this moment till you die, you could always have a sufficient provision of all the necessaries of life? But

if you are a child of God, that promise has already been made! Do not be anxious, but believe that God's word is at least as sure and as efficient as man's.

THE ALLOWANCE WAS CONTINUAL. It did not begin with plenty, and gradually dwindle to scraps. The supply was maintained year after year. Will God drop off your supplies, think you, because He forgets, or because his power is exhausted? You know that each supposition is alike untenable. What He has done, He will do. The storehouses of nature open to his key. His are the cattle on a thousand hills.

EVERY DAY A PORTION. Jehoiachin had not the provisions of a year or a month put down at his door; but as each day broke he was sure of the day's portion. It may be that God is dealing thus with you. Only manna for the day: daily strength for daily need.

ALL THE DAYS OF HIS LIFE. Jesus is with us "all the days"; and He is the Bread of God, in whom is every property necessary for life. All the days are included in God's care for us, of birth and death, of sunshine and shadow. Surely goodness and mercy shall follow you all the days of your life, and you shall dwell in the House of the Lord for ever.

1 Chronicles

Adam, Seth, Enosh. 1 Chron. 1: 1.

THIS is an ancient graveyard. The names of past generations who were born and died, who loved and suffered, who stormed and fought through the world, are engraven on these solid slabs. But there is no inscription to record their worth or demerit. Just names, and nothing more.

How strange to think that if Christ tarry, our names will be treated with the same apathy as these! So far as this world is concerned, we and all our generation shall pass away. As the flowers of the field, so we shall perish from the earth.

But each of these lives fulfilled a necessary part in the progress of the race. Each was in turn father and son; each passed on the torch of life; each contributed something to the fabric of humanity rising like a coral island from unknown depths. The hill-tops

would not be possible but for their lower courses which touch the valleys. We could not have the somebodies without an immense number of nobodies. The flowers of the race were prepared for by the slow progress of the plant through years of growth.

But each was the object of the love of God. Each was included in the redemptive purpose of our Lord; each contributed some minute particle to his nature; each is living yet somewhere; each will have to stand before the judgment-bar of God; each is pre-destined to live in the unknown world that lies on the other side. It is a stupendous thought to imagine the whole race, rooted in Adam, like one vast far-spreading tree. Ah, reader, be sure that thou art taken out of the first Adam, and grafted into the second—the Lord Jesus; and abiding in Him, see that thou bring forth much fruit to his glory.

These are the sons of Israel. 1 Chron. 2: 1.

IT is noticeable how irrevocable the divine sentence is on a human life. Of Er, the grave, impartial voice of Scripture says, he was "wicked in the sight of the Lord"; of Achan, he was the "troubler of Israel, and committed a trespass in the accursed thing." These sentences are recorded with such precision as to admit of no dispute, no appeal; and they sum up the life.

But was there not much else in each of these men? Were there not tender or chivalrous moments? Did they never shine for a moment in some transfiguring ray? Was all their life dyed with these sad and sombre hues? Ah, it may have been so—still the one thing that the Scripture tells of them is the sin in which all their life seemed to culminate and express itself. With unerring accuracy God can distinguish the one act or word by which the character is revealed. He may forgive it, but He holds it up as the epitome or summary of what the life was.

Let us see how we live, walking before God with reverent fear, watching and praying, because any moment may give birth to a word or act which may characterise our life in all coming time. It must be remembered, however, that all these things emanate from the heart. The heart is deceitful above all things, and desperately wicked; but the issues of life proceed thence: it therefore must be watched with all diligence and care. What a man thinks, that he is. The chance word or act is a true indication of the inner life. Therefore it is preserved for all after-time by the voice of God. See that your heart is perfect before God. There is forgiveness; but there is also the unerring verdict.

These were the sons of David. 1 Chron. 3: 1

BUT how different they were to the Son of David. Contrast any one of these with our blessed Lord, and what an infinite chasm lies between them! Solomon was the most reputable of them, but a greater than Solomon was born in Bethlehem, and cradled in a manger. Surely the least earnest must be struck with the difference in these sons and that Son. But in this difference, is there not the most conspicuous proof of his miraculous conception? Even though the story of his wondrous birth had never been preserved for us by the evangelists, we should have felt convinced that something like it must

have happened, in virtue of which He should be the Man of men, the one absolutely flawless and perfect flower on the stem of humanity. With new emphasis we read the familiar words, "The Holy Ghost shall come upon thee, and the power of the Highest shall overshadow thee; therefore that Holy thing which shall be born of thee shall be called the Son of God."

We, too, who have been born once, need to be born again. To be born of a David does not ensure perfectness of heart and life. Though born of parents, who were after God's own heart and are passed into the skies, we need to be born again, or we may repeat the sins of an Ammon, an Adonijah, an Absalom. It is a serious question to ask whether, like David, we have called his greater Son our Lord. This the true mark of the new birth. Those who are born of the Holy Ghost call Jesus Lord, and none other. The recognition of the supreme lordship of Jesus is imperative for the peace and right ordering of the heart and life. So we pass to our true stature in Jesus.

Because I bare him with sorrow. 1 Chron. 4: 9.

THE products of sorrow have been the rarest gifts to mankind. The books, hymns, discoveries, deeds, to which men and women have been urged by sorrow, or which have been born into the world amid heart-rending soul-travail, are those which will never be allowed to die, because perennial sources of inspiration and comfort. It was thus with the child of whom we have this brief record. We might becomingly weave the four petitions of the prayer of Jabez into the supplications of each new morning hour.

TO BE BLESSED INDEED. Not the lower springs only, but the upper ones also; not life alone, but life more abundantly; not those blessings only which pertain to the body or worldly circumstance, but those spiritual ones of the heavenlies, that are the best donation man can receive or God bestow.

A LARGER COAST. There is a godly ambition which may be reverently cherished for wider influence over men, not for its own sake, but for the Master's. You may feel that you have fulfilled the measure of your present possibilities, but have unexhausted powers and talents. Tell God so, and ask for a wider extent of territory to bring under cultivation for Him.

THINE HAND WITH ME. The father puts his hand on the boy's hand as he draws back the bowstring, strengthening the thin arms of youth. So will the mighty God of Jacob do for you.

KEEP ME FROM EVIL. You cannot keep your heart door shut when a tumult of temptation or care assaults it from without; but God's peace and grace, like angel sentries, can avail you. Though tempted, you may be kept in the temptation and delivered from the evil. Thus your spirit, and the Holy Spirit, shall be ungrieved.

They cried to God in the battle, and He was entreated of them. 1 Chron. 5: 20.

WHETHER they cried to God before they went into the battle we are not told; but probably they did, because we read that the war was of God, and it is hardly likely that they would have prayed to Him in the midst of the fight, when the foemen's blows fell like hail on their armour, if they had not prayed before they entered the bloody fray. Men often excuse themselves for neglecting their morning devotions by saying that they will surely look to God, as they may require his gracious help, in the midst of the day's temptations and needs; but, as a matter of fact, when once they are plunged into its war they forget to look up. You must direct your prayer in the morning, and look up whilst the early shadows lie long on the dewy grass, if you would keep looking off to Jesus, amid the din of the fight.

It is very lovely to contract and preserve this habit of looking upward, and crying to God in the battle. When our feet are slipping, when the foe seems about to overmaster, when heart and flesh fail—how refreshing and strengthening to fling one eager look or cry to heaven, and say, "I am thine, save me." There can be no doubt as to the issue. God is always intreated of those who put their trust in Him. Sooner might a mother forget her sucking child than God be unmindful of one sigh, or tear, or upward glancing look from his own. Oh, child of God, put thou thy trust in God, and go through this tempestuous world as one who is confident of a Divine Ally. At any moment He will ride on the heavens to thy help. "Let us therefore come boldly unto the throne of grace that we may obtain mercy, and find grace to help in time of need."

Heman the singer. 1 Chron. 6: 33.

THIS is a very brief record to put on a man's grave, but a very expressive one. To decipher that epitaph about Heman is to learn a good deal about him. From this clue we might almost construct his entire personality and character. And it would be well if it could be said of us that we had ministered with song before the tabernacle of the Lord.

Would you be a singer—not on Sundays only, but always; not with your voice only, but in your heart; not only when the sunshine pours into the open casement through the swaying boughs of honeysuckle, but when the shutters tell of bereavement and removal— then remember these rules:—(1st) God must put the new song into your mouth; (2nd) You must be fully consecrated to Him; for the song of the Lord only begins when the burnt-offering is complete. (3rd) You must not go into a strange land, for it is impossible to sing the Lord's song there.

Sing on, dear heart, sing on. There is nothing that scares off the devil so quickly as a hymn. Luther said, "Let us sing a hymn, and spite the devil." There is nothing that so well beguiles the pilgrim's step, and quickens his pace, when the miles are growing long and weary. There is nothing that brings so much of heaven into the heart. Singing makes every movement rhythmic, every service praise, every act thanksgiving. Sing when times are dark, you will make them bright; sing when the house of life is lonely, it will become peopled with unseen choristers; go down into the valley of shadow with a song, and you will find yourself singing the new song of Moses, and the Lamb when you awake on the other side.

It went evil with his house. 1 Chron. 7: 23.

IT is an old-world tale, and those tears have long since been wiped away. What led to the death of so many of the stalwart sons of Ephraim is not quite clear; but apparently they made a raid from the hill-fastnesses on the men of Gath to lift their cattle, and were repelled with great disaster. At any rate, they were slain by men of Gath, that were born in the land. They were part of the early nations of Canaan that should have been destroyed. This suggests a significant train of thought. We must beware of the tendencies and impulses which were born in us, which we have inherited.

They are strong in all of us. Parents transmit to an awful extent their own passions. What a reason this is for carefully curbing them! I have known the children of drunkards, grown to middle-life, who have confessed that they have never spent a day without the conscious craving for alcohol. These are the men of Gath, born in the land, who will slay us unless we are on our guard.

There will be irremediable sorrow if we yield to them. Many days of mourning will not avail to wipe out the sad and bitter memory of the disaster, when once they have wreaked their wild will on us. If permitted within, they will, like traitors, open the door to Satan without.

But faith is the victory. He that believeth that Jesus is the Son of God; he in whom Jesus lives by the Holy Spirit; he who knows the Stronger than the strong man armed, shall be kept from falling, and preserved unto God's heavenly kingdom. "Walk in the Spirit, and ye shall not fulfil the lust of the flesh. For the flesh lusteth against the Spirit, and the Spirit against the flesh."

Esh-baal, . . . Merib-baal. 1 Chron. 8: 33, 34.
BAAL was the idol-god of Zidon and of many surrounding nations. This idol, representing the sun in his productive force, was worshipped with impure and scandalous rites. The introduction of this name into the appellation of one of Saul's sons indicates the secret root of the declension and consequent misfortunes of that ill-fated monarch. In the earlier part of his reign he was perfect in his allegiance to Jehovah—Jonathan means "Gift of Jehovah"—but as the years went on, he became proud and self-sufficient; he turned to Baal, the Spirit of the Lord departed from him, and an evil spirit rushed in to take His place, as wind rushes in to fill a vacuum.

The name which Jonathan gave his son had another significance. Merib-baal is one who opposes Baal. It is as though he would undelibly stamp upon his child an undying hatred and opposition to that idolatry which was undoing his father's character and kingdom. In this choice of his child's name we also gather the deep-seated piety and devotion of that noble soul, whose heart was true to God amid the darkening shadows of his father's reign. It was this that probably drew David and him so closely in affinity.

How absolutely necessary it is for the peace of a household that there should be a oneness of devotion to God! Where that is the first consideration, there is peace and blessedness; and that it may be so, it is of the greatest importance that the parents should be constant in their godly allegiance. The ruin of Saul's home, family, and realm, began in his personal disloyalty to God; and how far he influenced the nation for evil it is difficult to estimate.

Chosen to be porters . . appointed over the furniture; . . the singers. 1 Chron. 9: 22, 29, 31, 33.
WHAT a busy scene is suggested in these words! When the morning broke, it called to duty first the porters who opened the House of God; and then, after due ablution, each band of white-robed Levites began its special service. There was no running to and fro in disorder, no intrusion on one another's office, no clashing in duty, no jealousy of each other's ministry. It was enough to know that each had been appointed to his task, and was asked to be faithful to it. The right ordering of the whole depended on the punctuality, fidelity, and conscientiousness of each.

So it is in the Church of Christ, each is specially gifted for some post to which he has been set apart. One to see to the gates, admitting souls to the kingdom; one to the baking in pans, attending to the feeding of the household of God; some are appointed to the furnishing and maintaining of the House of Prayer; others to the psalmody, as the hymn-writers of our praise and holy song. How beautiful it is when we dwell together in this unity, not envying one another, nor interfering in each other's ministry. "He gave some, apostles; and some, prophets; and some, evangelists; and some, pastors and teachers: for the perfecting of the saints, for the work of the ministry, for the edifying of the body of Christ." Whatever is successfully done by the Church is accredited by Christ to each faithful servant, just as the impression produced on the audience by an orchestra is the result of each instrument, even to the piccolo, doing its part. Whatever is done by the whole, is done by each part of the whole. Be content with the position to which thy Master has assigned thee, and let thine eye be single unto Him. So shall each have praise of God.

So Saul died for his trespass. 1 Chron. 10: 13
(R.V.).

IT is suggestive to ponder the threefold analysis of Saul's trespass as given here. He kept not the word of the Lord—this probably refers to his failure to execute the sentence on Amalek; he asked counsel of one that had a familiar spirit—this errand had taken him to Endor on the eve of the battle; he inquired not of the Lord—this was conspicuously the case in his persecution of David.

Do we sufficiently inquire of the Lord? We ask the advice of our friends and religious teachers; we sometimes use doubtful methods of ascertaining God's will, as allowing the Bible to drop open, or interpreting some coincidence in the way we secretly desire to follow; besides which there is an increasing tendency in society to use the crystal, to consult spiritualistic mediums, to employ palmistry. These latter, of course, repeat the sin of Saul, in going to Endor; and the resort to them on the part of children of this world shows that the heart of man must have something exterior to itself for worship and trust; if it has forsaken God, it will deal with the devil rather than drift on alone. But let us all cultivate more carefully the blessed habit of waiting on God. If we ask Him for guidance, He will be sure to impart it; only we must put aside all selfish and personal ends, desiring to know his will, with a single purpose, and an unalloyed determination to follow it at any cost.

Christ has told us that willingness to do his will is the sure organ of spiritual knowledge. "He that wills to do his will, shall know." Be of good cheer, beloved: God hath chosen thee that thou shouldst know his will, and see that Just One, and shouldst hear the voice of his mouth.

Oh that one would give me drink of the water of the well of Bethlehem. 1 Chron. 11: 17.

DAVID had often drunk of this well. As a boy he had gone with his mother to draw its clear, cold water. It was, therefore, associated with the happy days of childhood and youth that lay behind the haze of the years. In the sultry afternoon, as, from the cave in which he was hiding, he looked across the valley where his ancestress Ruth had gleaned in the fields of Boaz, to the long straggling town of his birth, it seemed as though nothing could stay his passionate longing for a draught of the water of the well of Bethlehem that was at the gate.

Sometimes longings like his take possession of us. We desire to drink again the waters of comparative innocence, of childlike trust and joy; to drink again of the fountains of human love; to have the bright, fresh rapture in God, and nature, and home. But it is a mistake to look back. Here and now, within us, Jesus is waiting to open the well of living water which springs up to eternal life, of which if we drink we never thirst.

Purity is better than innocence; the blessedness which comes through suffering is richer than the gladsomeness of childhood; the peace of the heart is more than peace of circumstances. We have solace in Jesus, which even the dear love of home could not equal; and before us lies the reunion with the blessed dead. How shall we thank Him who, at the cost of his own blood, broke through the hosts of our foes, and won for us the river of life; and who for evermore will lead us to the fountains, where life rises fresh from the heart of God! Listen to his voice as He bids us drink abundantly: "Let him that is athirst come; and whosoever will, let him take the water of life freely."

All these men of war, that could keep rank, came to make David king. 1 Chron. 12: 38.

THE crowning of David secured the unity of Israel. Because all these men of war converged on the chosen king, they met each other, and became one great nation. The enthroning of David was the uniting of the kingdom. Herein is the secret of the unity of the Church. We shall never secure it by endeavouring to bring about an unity in thought, or act, or organization. It is as each individual heart enthrones the Saviour that each will become one with all kindred souls in the everlasting kingdom.

Is your heart perfect to make Christ king? We read in verse 33 of Zebulon, whose warriors were not of a double heart; the margin says they were "without a heart and a heart." The double-minded man is unstable in all his ways; he is not to be relied upon in his loyalty or service to his king. The only blessed life is that of the man whose eye is single. It is only such an one that receives anything from the Lord. Let us ask that the thoughts of our hearts may be cleansed by the inspiration of God's Holy Spirit, that our hearts may be perfect towards Him, and so perfect to all who hold Jesus as King and Head, though they differ from us in minor points. Different regiments, but one army, one movement, one king.

Let us learn to keep rank, shoulder to shoulder, and in step, with our brethren. Too many like to break the ranks, and do God's work independently. Fifty men who act together will do greater execution than five hundred acting apart. There is too much of this guerilla fighting. Unity is strength; and in their efforts to overthrow the kingdom of Satan it is most essential that the soldiers of Christ move in rank and keep step.

And David was afraid of God that day.
1 Chron. 13: 12.

THERE was no reason for David to be afraid of God, if he conformed to the rules laid down in Leviticus. There it was expressly ordained that the Ark should be carried on the shoulders of the priests, because the cause of God must proceed through the world by the means of consecrated men, rather than by mechanical instrumentality. David ignored this provision when he placed the Ark on the new cart. He disobeyed the distinct law of the Divine procedure. What wonder that Uzza was struck dead! Fire will burn if you persist in violating its law. Obed-edom, on the other hand, studiously obeyed, so far as he knew them, the Divine regulations, and to him the Ark was a source of blessing; just as fire will toil for us in our furnaces and grates, and be the greatest possible benediction to human life, if only we carefully conform to its ascertained and immutable law.

God is to us what we are to Him. To Pharaoh, blackness and darkness; to Israel, light and help. To the froward, He is froward; to the merciful man, merciful. To one of the thieves, the cross of Christ was the savour of death unto death, because his heart was impenitent; to the other, the savour of life unto life, because his heart was soft and believing. You need not fear God so long as you walk in his ways and do his will. He is to be feared only by those who violate his law. God is a consuming fire. He will make a breach on those who disobey Him. He will consume the evil of our inner life. But let Him be welcomed into your life and home; let the Ark, which is the symbol of his presence, dwell within; bring up your children to minister unto Him; and you will be blessed, with all that you have.

Then thou shalt go out to battle; for God is gone forth before thee. 1 Chron. 14: 15.

WHAT was this "going"? It was not merely a fitful breeze stealing through the leaves; it was not the going of the wind; but of angel squadrons who were proceeding against the enemies of Israel. This thought often occurs in Scripture—as when Jacob met God's host; and the warrior-Saviour told Joshua that He was captain of a host whom God had commissioned to take Jericho; so also the horses and chariots of fire surrounded Elisha. Hearken to the measured footfall of God's host, beneath which the mulberry trees sway, though no wind stirs the sultry air

God's hosts go forth against his foes and ours. Perhaps we should feel less oppressed with the burden of the fight if we realized this. The battle is not ours, but God's. He will deliver the Philistines to us so that we shall have to do little else than fight and spoil. Oh, believe in the co-operation of the Holy Spirit. Lonely missionary in some distant station of the foreign field, listen for the moving in the tops of the mulberry trees! God is stirring for thy succour. Thou art a co-worker with Him in making known his salvation; and He will prosper thee.

Let us wait for our instructions. David inquired of the Lord; let us not anticipate Him. It is useless to go up until He has gone out before us. We may as well save ourselves from disappointment by quietly waiting for the salvation of our God. But oh, be sure that those who wait for God shall not be long before the God for whom they wait shall go forth before them to smite the host, whether it be the hosts of temptation that oppress the inner life, or the hosts of spiritual foes that oppose the progress of God's work.

And Chenaniah, chief of the Levites, was for song. 1 Chron. 15: 22.

THE carrying of the Ark to its right place was associated with every expression of gladness on the part of king and people; but there were some who were specially set apart as the exponents of the general joy. In the old time such were David, Heman, Asaph, Chenaniah; in our time, Watts and Doddridge, Wesley and Toplady, Keble, Havergal, and Bonar.

It is good to be for song. Many a heart that cannot rank as a musician or poet, may yet be susceptible to the joy of the Lord, which is ever passing through creation, catching it up so as to express it. As the Ark of the Lord comes to its place within you, sing.

Song is harmony with the life of God. The will of God sometimes enters life as a sigh, as David's first attempt to move the Ark; but afterwards it becomes a song, as in the second attempt. Enshrine the Ark of God with its tables of stone, its mercy-seat of fellowship, its worshipping Cherubim in the Holy of Holies within; and you will find sighs turned to song, tears to thanks, mourning to the garment of praise.

Worship the will of God. Conform your life with it. Draw on the ground a circle to represent God's will, and step into it, resolving never to step out of its blessed precincts again. Dare to believe and confess that Paradise lies within, though it may be veiled to sight and sense. According to your faith it shall be unto you. If you believe that heaven is there, you will find heaven. The Ark of God is ever a provocative of song. His statutes seem awful in the distance; but so soon as we begin to practise them, they turn to songs.

Talk ye of all His wondrous works. 1 Chron. 16: 9.

WE do not talk sufficiently about God. Why it is so may not be easy to explain; but there seems a too great reticence among Christian people about the best things. In the days of Malachi, "they that feared the Lord spake often one to another, and the Lord hearkened and heard." We talk about sermons, details of worship and church organization, or the latest phase of Scripture criticism; we discuss men, methods, and churches; but our talk in the home, and in the gatherings of Christians for social purposes, is too seldom about the wonderful works of God. Better to speak less, and to talk more of Him.

But probably the real cause of our avoidance of this best of topics, is that our hearts are filled with so much which is not of God, and they speak out of their abundance. You may judge the contents of a shop by what is put in the windows; and you may judge of the inner life of too many Christians by the subjects which are most familiar to their lips. The heart does not seek for God and his strength, nor his face continually; and therefore we find it hard to talk of all his wondrous works.

But go back in thought to the day of Pentecost. One of the first signs of the descent of the blessed Spirit was that the crowd heard every man speaking in his own tongue the wonderful works of God. What God has done in the past, as recorded on the page of Scripture; what He is doing day by day in the world around, and in our hearts; what He has promised to do on the horizon where heaven and earth shall blend in the Second Advent—yield fit themes on which his children may beamingly talk to each other, till He goes beside and talks with them till their hearts burn.

Do as Thou hast said, that thy name may be magnified for ever. 1 Chron. 17: 23, 24.

THIS is a most blessed phase of true prayer. Many a time we ask for things which are not absolutely promised. We are not sure therefore until we have persevered for some time whether our petitions are in the line of God's purpose or no. There are other occasions, and in the life of David this was one, when we are fully persuaded that what we ask is according to God's will. We feel led to take up and plead some promise from the page of Scripture, under the special impression that it contains a message for us.

At such times, in confident faith, we say, "Do as Thou hast said," There is hardly any position more utterly beautiful, strong, or safe, than to put the finger upon some promise of the Divine Word, and claim it. There need be no anguish, or struggle, or wrestling; we simply present the cheque and ask for cash, produce the promise, and claim its fulfilment; nor can there be any doubt as to the issue. It would give much interest to prayer, if we were more definite. It is far better to claim a few things specifically than a score vaguely.

David's argument was not simply that his house might be established, but that God's name might be magnified for ever. It is good when we can lose sight of our personal interests in our keen desire for his glory; when we are so delivered from egotism, that Christ is all and in all. Let the attitude of your soul be more towards the glory of God; and as you quote promise after promise for the enthroning of Christ, the saving of men, and the sanctification of your soul, dare in humble faith to say, Do as Thou hast said, that thy Name may be magnified for ever.

He put garrisons in Edom; and all the Edomites became servants to David. 1 Chron. 18: 13. EDOM and Israel were closely related, but there was constant rivalry and war between the two peoples. Sometimes Israel held the upper hand for a little; but Edom soon broke loose again, and resumed the old independence, with the border forays (2 Chron. 21: 10; 25: 11-14; Psa. 137: 7). Now, as Edom stands for the flesh, which hungers for the savoury dish, and is willing to give even its birthright of spiritual power to secure it—this long feud is full of interest to us. It reminds us of the strife of Rom. 7, between the will of the renewed man and the law of the members, ever striving for mastery.

We turn on the pages of our Bibles to Isa. 63, where a mighty Conqueror is seen coming towards the southern frontier of Palestine, with his back on Bozrah and Edom. His garments are dyed with the blood of Israel's foes; and behind Him cities are desolate and depopulated, territories are laid waste without inhabitant, and Edom's hostility is for ever quenched in blood. What a portraiture is here of Jesus, "mighty to save," who in his cross triumphed over principalities and powers, and made a show of them openly. He has overcome the world, the flesh, and the prince of the power of darkness; and stands for evermore between us and our former oppressors.

Let us resign the conflict wholly to Him. We have sought in vain for victory by resolutions and endeavours; by close attention to religious duties; by occupying our mind with various interests, so that we had no leisure to be tempted; by diet and exercise. Now, hand the conflict absolutely over to Jesus: do not even try to help Him: just let Him do all: be quite still, and when temptation comes, let Him meet it.

Let us behave ourselves valiantly for our people, and for the cities of our God. 1 Chron. 19: 13. THOSE were days in which rough soldiers, like Joab, did not hesitate to speak freely of God to their companions in arms. It is a sorry thing that it is considered a breach of etiquette to mention God's name in polite society. "It is not good form!"

We are reminded in these words of Joab of Cromwell's memorable advice to trust in God and keep the powder dry. David's General felt that the ultimate issue of the battle must be left to God; but that nothing could absolve him and his soldiers from doing their best. They, at least, must make careful dispositions for the fight, and show themselves valiant.

This balance of statement and thought between God's work and ours is an evidence of fine Christian sanity. We must believe that God is the ultimate arbiter, but we must ever speak and act as though the responsibility were entirely on ourselves. To believe that God will do all, and therefore to do nothing, is as bad as to believe that God leaves us to our unaided endeavours. We believe in the strength and sufficiency of God's purpose; but we know that there is a link in the chain of causation which we must supply.

The servant of God who counts most absolutely on the communion and co-operation of the divine Spirit will be most careful in making all needful dispositions for the fight. He will leave no stone unturned to secure the victory, though he knows that the ultimate decision rests with God. The conquests of the cross recorded in the Acts of the Apostles were the result of the united action of the Holy Spirit and the men who were sent forth with the message of the gospel. "We are labourers together with God."

The time when Kings go out to battle. . . . But David tarried at Jerusalem. 1 Chron. 20: 1. THERE are times and tides in the affairs of men. Favourable moments for doing and daring, for attempting and achieving. Hours when the ship must be launched, or it will have to wait for another spring tide. Days when the seed must be sown, or it will have to tarry till another autumn. Royal natures show their quality by taking advantage of times like these, when God and circumstances favour a great attempt.

Alas, if long-continued prosperity has robbed the kingly soul of its desire or power to use its sacred opportunity! Once missed, it may never recur; and the soul that has missed it contemns itself, and loses heart, and surrenders itself to lower and ever lower depths of temptation.

Beware of moments and hours of ease. It is in these that we most easily fall into the power of Satan. The sultriest summer days are most laden with blight. There is no such guard against temptations—next to the keeping power of Jesus, which is all-sufficient

—as occupation to the full measure of time and capacity. If we cannot fill our days with our own matters, there is always plenty to be done for others. You think that no one has hired you, but it is not so; the Master has sent you into his vineyard. If you cannot do one thing, you can another. There is the ministry of intercession for those who are in the field. There is the exercise of worship, in which you take your place amongst the priests. There is the ministry of comfort to some of the sad hearts within your own circle. Redeem the time, because the days are evil. Watch and pray in days of vacation and ease, even more than at other times.

And David said unto God, I have sinned greatly in that I have done this thing. 1 Chron. 21: 8 (R.V.).

HIS sin lay in the spirit of pride and display. He vaunted in the growing numbers of Israel, and credited them to himself, as the result of his own prowess and prudence. All such boasting is very abhorrent to the all-holy God, who will not give his glory to another. It was the sin of Nebuchadnezzar, when he said, "Is not this great Babylon which I have built?" It was the sin of Herod Agrippa when the people shouted, saying, "The voice of a god, and not of a man"; and immediately the angel of the Lord smote him, "because he gave not God the glory."

We are all tempted to it when we count up the number of our adherents and converts; when we unroll our securities and vouchers; when we count up our assets; when we display our jewels. All these are gifts entrusted to our care by our Father and Saviour, to be held in trust as a matter for gratitude rather than for pride.

How greatly David had fallen from the level of his own sweet sonnet!—"Lord, my heart is not haughty, nor my eyes lofty." Oh, let us ask our Master Christ to teach us how to be meek and lowly in heart, that we may find rest unto our souls; let us endeavour to be as little children, devoid of self-consciousness; and let us be careful, as we survey the growing treasures and power of our lives, to remember the Apostle's words: "Who maketh thee to differ? and what hast thou that thou didst not receive? But if thou didst receive it, why dost thou glory, as if thou hadst not received it?"

How well John the Baptist parried the temptation to jealousy, when he said, "A man can receive nothing unless it be given him from heaven."

A man of rest . . . he shall build. 1 Chron. 22: 9, 10.

THE men of rest are the builders of the most lasting structures. Solomon builds the Temple, not David. Mary's deed of anointing, learnt in much sitting at the Lord's feet, fills the world with its aroma. What is needed to make us men and women of rest?

FIRST, A PROFOUND CONVICTION THAT GOD IS WORKING. Never despair of the world, said the late Mrs. Beecher Stowe, when you remember what God did with slavery: the best possible must happen. This serene faith, that all things are working out for the best —the best to God, the best to man—and that God is at the heart of all, will calm and still us in the most feverish days. There is a strong and an experienced Hand on the helm.

NEXT, AN ENTIRE SURRENDER TO HIS WILL. God's will is certain to mean the destruction of the flesh, in whatever form He finds it; but it is our part to yield to Him; to will his will even to the cross; to follow our leader Christ in this, that He yielded Himself without reserve to execute his Father's purpose.

THIRDLY, A CERTAIN KNOWLEDGE THAT HE IS WORKING WITHIN TO WILL AND DO OF HIS GOOD PLEASURE. What a blessed peace possesses us when once we realize that we are not called on to originate or initiate, nor to make great far-reaching plans and try to execute them; but just to believe that God is prepared to work through our hands, speak by our life, dwell in our bodies, and fulfil in us the good purposes of his will. Be full of God's rest. Let there be no hurry, precipitation, or fret; yield to God's hands, that He may mould thee: hush thy quickly throbbing pulse! So shalt thou build to good and lasting purpose.

Aaron was separated, he and his sons for ever, to minister unto Him. 1 Chron. 23: 13.

THE threefold office of Aaron suggests our own. When we are prepared to follow Jesus, through the rent vail of his flesh, living a truly separated life, cleansing ourselves from all filthiness of the flesh and spirit, we also, as chosen priests, may exercise these functions of intercession, ministry, and blessing.

INTERCESSION. The fragrant incense stealing heavenward is a beautiful emblem of intercessory prayer. Let us pray more, not for ourselves so much as for others. This is the sign of growth in grace, when our prayers are fragrant with the names of friend and foe, and mingled with the coals of the golden altar. This is one of the best gifts; oh to exercise it more persistently!

MINISTRY. We have many things to engage our attention, but they may be unified and elevated by the one threading purpose of doing all for the King. Whether we eat, or drink, or whatever else we do, we may do all to his glory. Go up and down in the Temple, O priests; engage in song, or sacrifice, or whatever ministry you will: but be sure that all is of Him, and through Him, and to Him for ever.

BLESSING. As Aaron came forth from the most Holy Place to bless the congregation that waited for him, so we should bless that little portion of the world in which our lot is cast. It is not enough to linger in soft prayer within the vail, we must come forth to bless mankind. He who is nearest God is closest man. Let our smile, our touch, our words, our life, be the greatest blessing possible to those who know us best.

Blessed Spirit, realize through each of us this threefold ideal, and separate us from sin and the world, that we may be prepared for it.

Princes of the Sanctuary. 1 Chron. 24: 5 (R.V.).

IT is not enough for us to be in the sanctuary, we must be princes there. There must be the regal mien, which is a meek humility; the regal largesse, which is peace and blessing; and the regal might, which is self-restraint and self-control. None can be princes of the sanctuary without two things: they must be priests, come of the priestly line; and kings, royal not because of deeds of war, but because they are related to the King Himself, and are regal in their holy and blameless character.

There is only one power that can make us princes of the sanctuary—the hand of the exalted Lamb, who is Himself a Priest-King, after the order of Melchizedek. He it is who makes us kings and priests unto God his Father.

HE MAKES US PRIESTS. This is your position, not now to offer propitiatory sacrifices, but to present yourselves a living sacrifice; to have compassion on the ignorant, and on those who are out of the way; to swing the censer of prayer between the living and the dead, so that plagues may be stayed; and to plead for the dark sad world, with its load of wretchedness, need, and sin. See that your garments are ever white and stainless.

HE MAKES US KINGS. We reign with Him. Sin and Satan, the world and the flesh, are beneath our feet. Ours the life of overcoming power, of unbroken victory, of identification with Jesus in the glory that the Father has given Him. They that receive the abundance of his grace reign. It is there for us all, but many do not know, or knowing do not appreciate. It is on our reception by faith of God's abundant grace, that we reign in this life, and the next.

All these were under the hands of their father for song. 1 Chron. 25: 5, 6.

WHAT a glorious family was here! The household was a band of choristers! From morning to night their home must have been full of holy song and psalm, or talk about the order of the Temple service, in which they were all so deeply interested. Surely no jarring note, no unholy discord, would live in such an atmosphere! The common occupation and worship must have welded the brothers and sisters into the tenderest union.

How one would like to have seen Heman coming into the Temple with his children! It was largely owing to him and their mother that they were what they were. We shall read the Psalms ascribed to him with more interest, now we know of the holy family life out of which they emanated. What interest there would be when the father had produced a new psalm, to know what music would suit it best!

Parents! Be sure that you look on your children, as these Hebrews did on theirs, as the gifts of God; and remember that if He gives you many mouths to feed, He will send the wherewithal to feed them. Be careful also that your own hearts and lives are full of praise and prayer; what you are, the children will become. Would that mothers especially realized how they transmit their characters. But remember that you must be obeyed in the home. Heman's children were "under the hands of their father." Young people must not get the upper hand.

But if you would rule well, you must obey. Asaph, Heman, and Jeduthun, were under the king (6, R.V.). The man who is himself under authority, can say, Go, come, do this or that, with the calm assurance of being obeyed.

For the courses of the doorkeepers. 1 Chron. 26: 1 (R.V.).

MIGHTY men of valour were needed for this, just as sweet singers were for the service of song. Entrance to the House of God was restricted to a privileged few. Gentiles were excluded from certain courts, and women from another. It was incumbent also to look out for those who, like the publican in the Lord's parable, might shrink from intruding, and encourage them to enter. Doorkeepers had to combine many qualities, which would be of the greatest service if they could be repeated in each church and chapel of our great cities, for welcoming old and young.

But chiefly we are concerned with the temple of the heart. We surely need the doorkeeper there, for in the history of the inner life there is so much going and coming; such troops of thoughts pour into the shrine of the soul, and pour out. And often, in the crowd, disloyal and evil thoughts intrude, which, before we know it, introduce a sense of distance and alienation from God, as though a cloud had veiled the shining of the Shekinah. Whenever the sky is overcast within, we should question whether some traitor, some excommunicate, has entered. Our native wit is not quick enough to detect, and our strength not mighty enough to withstand, the entrance of all these evil things. Hence the necessity not only to live in the Spirit, but to walk in the Spirit, i.e., to submit everything to the Spirit's scrutiny.

It is necessary also that strict supervision should be exercised over those who unite with the visible Church, lest her holiness become diluted, and her fences broken down. Nothing is more important than the function of doorkeeping for the Church's purity.

All these were the rulers of the substance which was King David's. Chron. 27: 31.

THERE was great variety in office and gift. He who cared for the work of the field could not have known how to care for the flocks. The overseer of olive-yard and vineyard would have been a poor hand with the camels and asses. One sort of talent was needed for the herds, and another for the wine cellars; and yet there was unity in the common service of the king. We are reminded of the words of the Apostle, describing the variety in unity which must obtain in every healthy church: "There are diversities of gifts, but the same Spirit; diversities of ministrations, and the same Lord; diversities of operations, but the same God."

Each of these different men had his distinct sphere for which he was doubtless specially qualified; and it was his duty—not to be jealous of others, nor eager to imitate them, but—to be faithful in his own province. How much happier we should all be if we recognized our specific work in God's house and kept to it, being content to serve the King as He has seen fit to determine, rendering Him the produce in due season.

How great an error it would have been had any of these begun to account the produce of cattle or ground as his own! He had nothing that he had not received, and whatever he controlled had been entrusted to his care for the emolument and advantage of his sovereign. Yet, how few of us realize that we are put in business with God's capital, for God's use. We take all and give Him a percentage, instead of using all for Him and keeping a percentage for ourselves. In this we rob God, and greatly err. We must acknowledge that both we and all we possess belong to Him.

The Lord God, even my God, . . will not fail thee, nor forsake thee. 1 Chron. 28: 20.

IT is very comforting to take these words to our hearts; especially when we connect them with the foregoing ones about the pattern, and apply the whole passage to the temple-building of our own lives. For each of us, too, there is a pattern, an ideal, a design, based on the possibilities which God sees to be within our reach; for each, too, there is abundance of stored provision; but we are not always strong to do. In Jesus there is the complete ideal of human life; of the Child at Nazareth; of the Servant in the workshop; of the Lover in his affection for his church; of the Friend, the Sufferer, the Patriot, the Saviour. Go forth and imitate Him!

Sometimes our heart and flesh fail us in the mid-passage of life. Once the energy and vigour of youth promised to sustain and carry us to the end of life, without fear or failure; but these die down, and we wonder how the remainder of the life-plan can be fulfilled. And the one sufficient answer is—God. He who helped our fathers to the very end will help us: He who did not fail or forsake them, will never leave nor forsake us, until all the work of life which He has planned, is finished.

It is probable that you will do better and more enduring work henceforth than you have ever done in the heyday and plenitude of youthful power, if you let God work all through you to his own glory. You have no need for despondency, God is sufficient. Oh to write this down on the tablets of the heart—God is; God is here; God is all-sufficient; God has begun and will finish! God has promised that He will never leave nor forsake us; therefore we may boldly say, "God is my helper, I will not fear what man shall do unto me."

Our days on the earth are as a shadow, and there is no abiding. 1 Chron. 29: 15 (R.V.). ALL life has been compared to the shadow of a smoke-wreath; a gesture in the invisible air; a hieroglyph traced for an instant on the sand, and effaced a moment after by a breath of wind; an air-bubble vanishing on the river. Pilgrims and sojourners, as were all our fathers—such is the universal confession. But even such may do a work that will last for ages. David and the men of his time, though transitory their stay on our planet, left behind them a standing evidence that they had been here.

Our life is nothing, but it may be divine: our days are as a breath, but they may affect unborn generations: the tent of the body is laid aside, but the soul, which had dwelt in it, is immortal in its touch: it leaves traces of its own immortality behind in its works, and it lives in them. In one sense, the answer to the ancient prayer is certain: "Establish Thou the works of our hands upon us." But we may well ask, that they may be such that we shall have no need to be ashamed of.

But, for this, God must live mightily within us. Abide in Me, said our Lord. . . . I have appointed you that ye may bring forth fruit, and that your fruit may abide. It is impossible to be in true union with Christ without feeling the pulse of his glorious life; and where it enters like a tidal river, it can have but one result—it must manifest itself in fruit. It is only in proportion as our works are done in God, and God permeates our works, that they become sources of enduring blessing to coming time. Pilgrims though we be, yet, if our lives are spent before Him, we may build temples which will outlast the wreck of matter.

2 Chronicles

I will give thee riches. 2 Chron. 1: 11, 12. SOLOMON had chosen wisdom and knowledge that he might honour God in the sight of his people. And in return God honoured him, and supplemented his choice with abundant wealth.

This reminds one of the constant teaching of Jesus. He who seeks his life loses it; but to lose it is to save it in the best and deepest sense. Seek first the kingdom of God and his righteousness, and all these things shall be added.

The conception of life given in the Bible differs by a whole heaven from the maxims and practices of some good and earnest people. Their notion is that they must work for their living, "keep the wolf from the door," educate their children for successfully meeting the demands of life. These objects are legitimate; but they were never meant by God to be the supreme aim of his servants.

His object in our creation, redemption, and regeneration, was that we might serve his redemptive purposes in the world, manifest his character, do his will, win souls for his kingdom, administer the gifts with which He had entrusted us. He asks us to rise to this high calling, and give our whole life to its realization. He will be responsible for all else. It is surely his will that we should give ourselves to useful trades, and fill our days with honest toil; but the main purpose should ever be his glory, and the exemplification in word and act of his holy character. If we ask for wisdom to do this well, we shall get all else into the bargain. God is a Being of perfect honour and integrity. And if we dare to make his service the main end of life, we shall find that no good thing will fail. He paves the streets of heaven with gold, and will not withhold it from his children, if they really need.

Because the Lord loveth His people, He hath made thee King over them. 2 Chron. 2: 11 (R.V.).

HOW truly might these words be addressed to our blessed Lord! Because God loved the world, He gave his only-begotten Son, his well-beloved, to be both Prince and Saviour. And it is in knowing, loving, and serving Him that we can realize our supreme blessedness.

God's loving appointment in making Jesus King will be apparent when we remember how beautiful He is in his personal character; how closely He is identified with our nature; the might of his arm with which He shields, the patience wherewith He bears, the redemption which He has wrought out and brought in for all who believe. What could God's love have done better to approve itself?

Is He your King? Never till He is so, will you know the fulness of God's love. Those who question or refuse his authority are always in doubt about the love of God to themselves and to the world. Those, on the other hand, who acknowledge his claims, and crown Him as King, suddenly find themselves admitted to a standpoint of vision in which doubts and disputations vanish, and the secret love of God is unfolded. Then they experience the wise and gentle tendence of the divine love in its most entrancing characteristics. All is love where Jesus reigns.

Nothing is more indicative of God's benevolence than his incessant appeal to men to make Jesus King. The demand may sometimes involve severe agony and suffering for those who have acknowledged other lords too long; but God persists in his demand, because only in serving Jesus can the human heart be truly blessed.

"Go, spread your trophies at his feet,
And crown Him Lord of all!"

*He set up the Pillars before the Temple, . .
Jachin and Boaz.* 2 Chron. 3: 17.

THE meaning of these names is significant—

He shall establish, and In it is strength. Each speaks of Him of whom the whole temple was a type. The Lord Jesus has established the work of redemption so that it shall never be removed; has established the covenant, ordered in all things and sure; has established his Church, so that the gates of Hades shall not prevail against it; has established us before the face of his Father for evermore.

There is much in the New Testament about the established life. It is the desire of Peter that the scattered saints should be perfected, established, and strengthened. Paul desires to see the Roman Christians, that he may impart some spiritual gift so that they may be established: he desires that the Colossians may be built up in Christ, and established in the faith. The Epistle to the Hebrews says that it is good for the heart to be established with grace. Let us ask that Jesus should establish us in the divine life, rooting and grounding us in love and faith, so that we may not be moved away from the Gospel, but abound therein with thanksgiving.

It is only as we abide in Jesus, that we shall become steadfast, unmovable, and always abounding.

But Christ is also our strong Helper. We have no strength of our own; but He is strong; and in Him we have righteousness and strength. Let us make our refuge in Him, as the conies, who are a feeble folk, do in the rock. They who abide in Jesus derive from Him fresh supplies of strength for each moment's need. They hear Him saying, "Fear not, I will strengthen, yea, I will help thee"; and they learn to say with Paul: "I can do all things in Christ that strengthened me."

The Weight could not be found out. 2 Chron. 4: 18.

THIS was as it should be. There was no attempt to keep an accurate account of what was given to the service of God. Even Solomon's left hand did not know what his right hand did. There is a tendency in all of us to keep a strict account of what we give to God. We note it down in our ledgers; we rigorously observe the compact into which we have entered with Him; but the loftiest form of devotion overleaps such calculation.

This liberality of the people reminds us of Mary's. She never thought of the great cost of the precious spikenard which she broke over the Master's person. It was her joy to give her all; and it was only when Judas came on the scene, that we learn how many hundred pence it was worth. Thus the churches of Macedonia abounded from their deep poverty unto the riches of their liberality, so that, beyond their power, they gave to the cause of God.

This lavish generosity is the reflection of God's. There is no measure in his bounty. It is heaped up, pressed down, and running over. He never says, I will give up to a certain amount, and hold my hand; but He continues to give like the overflowings of the river of Egypt, or the abundance of the spring flowers which cover the earth as with a carpet. Ah, what a God is ours, who loves with a love that passeth knowledge; and when He gives, exceeds abundance, however much we may have asked or thought. How truly we may say with the psalmist, "Many, O Lord my God, are the wonderful works that Thou hast done, and thy thoughts which are to us-ward. They cannot be reckoned up in order unto Thee; if I would declare and speak of them, they are more than can be numbered."

Then the House was filled with a Cloud. 2 Chron. 5: 13.
THIS was the bright Shekinah cloud, the symbol of the divine Presence, which had shone for Moses in the bush, and led the march through the desert. It was as though God had found a rest. And as it settled upon the Most Holy Place, it was as though God said, This is my rest for ever; here will I dwell, for I have desired it.

The Most Holy Place is the symbol of our spirit, meant to be the abiding-place and home of God; and shall we not invite the blessed Shekinah cloud to enter thither, addressing it in the words of the Psalm, "Arise, O Lord, into thy resting-place, Thou and the ark of thy strength." Because where He comes to abide He abundantly blesses the provision, and satisfies the poor with bread; He clothes his priests with salvation, and makes his saints shout aloud for joy; He erects the horn of strength and prepares the lamp of light. What were the conditions of this incoming?
FIRST, *Unity.* "The trumpeters and singers were as one." We must put away strife, divisions, variance, and evil-speaking. Our heart and life must be full of love. When the disciples were with one accord, in one place, the Spirit descended.

SECOND, *Heartiness.* "They lifted up their voice." There was every symptom of sincerity and fervour.
THIRD, *Thanksgiving and Praise.* "They praised the Lord, saying, He is good, for his mercy endureth for ever." No refrain occurs oftener in the Bible than this. It is an exquisite expression of the heart's joy and rest in God. Let us sing it in our darkest, as well as gladdest hours, full of trust, thanksgiving, and praise.

When Thou teachest them the good way wherein they should walk. 2 Chron. 6: 27 (R.V.).
THIS sentence is exactly parallel with the previous one, When Thou dost afflict them. The obvious meaning then is, that God sometimes taught Israel the good way wherein they should walk, by afflicting them and shutting up the heavens so that there was no rain. This was notably the case in the days of Elijah. Possibly, these words were in his heart, when he prayed earnestly that it might not rain, and it rained not for the space of three years and six months. Perhaps the prophet felt that in no other way could the people be brought back to their senses, and reconciled to God, except by learning the futility of idol-worship. So he asked God to teach them the good way, by shutting up the bad one.

What a lesson for ourselves: God often teaches us by bitter disappointment and pain. Our familiar paths are barricaded by thorns, our familiar hiding-places are blocked up, our fountains are poisoned, and all our pleasant things are laid waste. We sometimes suppose that this is in wrath; may it not rather be in love? God is teaching us the good by showing us the evil; is urging us to tread in the pleasant ways of wisdom, by allowing us to prove the sharp flints and thorns of transgression. Then Ephraim bemoans himself thus: Thou hast chastised me, and I was chastised, as a calf unaccustomed to the yoke: turn Thou me, and I shall be turned. Then the soul cries, I will go and return to my first husband, for then was it better with me than now.

Sit in God's school, and learn from his Word and Spirit, that He may not be compelled to have recourse to such severe measures as these. Why shouldst thou be afflicted, when He is willing to instruct and teach thee in the way that thou shouldst go!

*The Fire came down from heaven, and consumed
the Burnt-Offering.* 2 Chron. 7: 1.

IT was a very gracious and immediate
response to the prayer of King and people.
If we make room for God, He always comes
and fills. If we seek Him, He is instantly with
us. Directly the soul confesses, it is forgiven;
or consecrates itself, it is accepted; or claims
deliverance from the power of sin, it is
cleansed. Do you really want the Lord to come
to you? His glory has even now begun to
shine in on you, to grow and enlighten you
for evermore.

The fire stands for the Divine Presence.
Oh to have always a consciousness of it!
Nothing would so soon arrest and destroy
the impurity and evil within; as sunshine
does fungus-growth. We are told that the
fire was to be kept burning on the altar: it
was never to go out. Thus, we should always
perpetuate and practise the presence of God,
feeding the fire with the fuel of prayer and
meditation.

Fire also stands for the Divine Purity. As
the Plague of London was stamped out by
the Great Fire which destroyed the nests
where it had bred; and as the furnace rids the
ore of dross—so the Holy Spirit in thy heart
and mine is a guarantee of holiness and
righteousness all our days.

Fire also stands for Divine Fellowship. It
consumed that part of the offering which was
placed on the altar; and it seemed as if the
Divine nature was therefore feeding upon the
sacrifice, whilst the remainder of it was
consumed by the offerer. Thus, also, we have
communion with God, as we eat the bread
and drink the wine in the Lord's Supper. We
feed on Christ in adoration, faith, and
identification. God feeds on the completeness
of Christ's obedience, and the glory of his
character. Thus we have fellowship with the
Father and the Son, by the Holy Ghost.

*The places are holy, whereunto the Ark of God
hath come.* 2 Chron. 8: 11.

ON this account Solomon said, My wife
shall not dwell in the house of David, king
of Israel. What a fatal admission! She was
the daughter of Pharaoh, and therefore it was
no doubt considered a splendid match for the
young king; and yet she could not dwell within
the precincts of the old city of David, hallowed
by the presence of the Ark. "He brought her
out of the city of David, into the house that
he had built for her." So from the very outset
there was division of interests, making way
no doubt for much of the waywardness of
Solomon's character in after life, so that we
are told "his wives turned away his heart."

One of the first questions that youth and
maiden should put in considering the question
of marriage is, whether there can be perfect
sympathy in the best and deepest things;
for how can two walk together except they
be agreed?

The blessedness of the marriage tie depends
on whether the twain are one in spirit, in a
common love for Christ, and endeavour for
his glory. Nothing is more terrible than
when either admits in the secrecy of the heart,
concerning the other, My husband or my wife
cannot accompany me into the holy places
where I was reared, and in which my best life
finds its home.

All friendship should follow the same law.
We must abide together in the secret place of
the Most High, if our friends and we are to
be friends indeed. All places may be made
holy where the Ark of God's covenant comes.
Where it goes, love may safely follow; but
woe to the love that cannot! Its inability
proves its lack of elements of permanence
and perfect satisfaction.

She came to prove Solomon with hard questions.
2 Chron. 9: 1.

SHE came to the right place, for Solomon
passed all the kings of the earth in wisdom;
and all the kings of the earth sought his
presence, to hear the wisdom that God had
put into his heart. Bring your hard questions
to Christ; He is greater than Solomon. To
Him is given riches and wisdom, and He is
made unto us wisdom. Before the touch of
his light the darkest perplexities must resolve
themselves. Though He speak no audible
word, the hardest questions are answered to
the eyes and ears of such as wait before Him.

She came in the right spirit, bringing him
gold and spices and precious stones. Those
who would get from Christ must be willing
to give to Him. There must be a reciprocity;
and if we hope to receive from Him from those
infinite stores of which He has the key, we
must count all things but loss for the excellency
of the knowledge of Christ, and must be
prepared to count them as refuse if only we
may win Him.

She came to a right conclusion. He answered

all her questions, and she returned congratulating his servants and blessing God. To each of us life is full of perplexities, to which we can find no solution, however much we strain our eyes and weary our minds. But away there in the light Christ stands, with the perfect plan of every maze in his possession, with a key for every riddle, and solution for every enigma. Wait patiently. Each tough knot will be untied; and there will come into our hearts a radiancy, a bounding joy like that with which the Queen of Sheba turned to go to her own home. The half of the greatness of thy wisdom, O Word of God, can never be told!

For it was brought about of God. 2 Chron. 10: 15 (R.V.).

THIS revolt must have seemed to be the result of an unfortunate mistake on the part of the ill-advised young king. He and the young men that gathered around him thought that the best way of ruling people was by showing a strong hand, and adopting a policy of non-compliance with their very natural requests. But as the result, the Ten Tribes, never very closely bound to David's line, sprang away from it, leaving, as Ahijah had foretold, only two out of the twelve pieces of the rent garment. Here, however, a deeper explanation is given: "It was brought about of God." It seemed to be altogether a piece of human folly and passion; but now we are suddenly brought into the presence of God, and told that beneath the plottings and plannings of man He was carrying out his eternal purpose.

To detect this divine purpose lying beneath the cross-currents of human affairs is the prerogative of the saints. In a recent book, the Duke of Argyll has argued from the purposiveness of nature. With as much certainty we may apply that word to history, politics, the course of current events. All is under law. God doeth according to his will among the armies of heaven and the inhabitants of the earth. "And we know that all things work together for good to them that love God, to them who are the called according to his purpose." Without contravening the action of man's free choice He carries out his great designs and works his sovereign will. Let us trust in this Almighty Providence, which underlies all events and catastrophes and pursues its beneficent objects undeterred by our sins. He makes the wrath of man to praise Him, and weaves the malignant work of Satan into his plans.

Such as set their hearts to seek the Lord God of Israel came to Jerusalem. 2 Chron. 11: 16.

ALL the tribes were represented in those great convocations around the Temple and Ark of God. The territory of the northern tribes was now under Jeroboam; the gulf between the two kingdoms was marked and distinct. Everything was done by the son of Nebat to make it difficult for his people to cross the frontier; but their spiritual affinities prevailed. They were stronger than the antipathy which Rehoboam's haughty behaviour had excited; stronger than the fear of incurring odium with their own king; stronger than the inconvenience of the long journey. In spite of everything, those whose hearts were set on seeking the Lord God of Israel, came to Jerusalem to sacrifice to the Lord God of their fathers.

Does not this foreshadow the unity of the Church of Christ? Territorial distinctions, the risk of incurring disfavour, the necessity of making a sacrifice—these things are as nothing compared with the attraction of our common Lord. Amid wide disunion and disparity of every kind, there is one mighty bond which draws believers of every nation, kindred, tribe, and people together. Each morning we all ascend the steps of the same temple of prayer; each evening we join in one great hymn of praise; at each Lord's Supper we sit at the same table. Eating of one Bread, we know that we are one Loaf; drinking of one Cup, we profess our indebtedness to the same precious Blood for our hope and ground of acceptance (1 Cor. 10: 17, R.V., marg.).

We must set our hearts, if we desire to execute any great purpose in our life: otherwise we shall be daunted and checkmated by the strong opposition of men and things.

He did evil, because he prepared not his heart to seek the Lord. 2 Chron. 12: 14.

IN the margin of the A.V. for prepared the alternative rendering fixed is suggested. The R.V. gives set, "he set not his heart to seek the Lord." This is very true of all of us. Before temptation comes we almost always have a warning of some kind. The barometer falls; the sea birds come in to the shore; the leaves of the trees are bent back. The Spirit of God contrives to give the soul some signal that at any moment it may expect an assault. The question always is at such a time, Is the heart set on seeking and doing the will of God? If it be, if without reserve the whole nature is determined to do God's will at any cost, there is no fear of the enemy effecting an entrance. All day the thunder of its artillery may boom around, but from every side the foe will be repelled, until presently the storm will roll far down the wind.

If, on the other hand, there is any vacillation; if, whilst ostensibly avowing our determination to do the right thing, we secretly whisper in our deepest consciousness that we intend to go as far as we can in self-indulgence, and would be almost thankful if circumstances compelled us to yield—we are almost certain to fall. The will must be whole in its resolves; the heart must be consecrated in its most secret determinations; no traitor may be harboured, who may open the postern gate. Oh to say with David, "My heart is fixed, O God, my heart is fixed"! But this steadfastness is one of those preparations of the heart which can only be obtained through the gracious indwelling of the Holy Spirit. Hence we pray with David, "Renew a steadfast spirit within me." And while we pray, we must never forget our Lord's command to watch also.

Behold, the battle was before and behind.
2 Chron. 13: 14.

ABIJAH'S address is full of true and noble utterances, especially when he describes God as being the Captain of the Host; and this spirit soon permeated his people, so that when the battle was sorest, and they were hemmed in by their foes, it was natural for them to turn to the Lord, and for the priests to give a blast on the trumpets, like that with which the new moon and the solemn feasts were inaugurated.

The point for us to remember is that our enemies may shut us in on all sides, preventing reinforcements from north, south, east, and west; but no earthly power can ever shut off God from above us. The way upwards is always kept clear; the ladder which links the beleaguered soul with God and heaven can never be blocked, except by transgression and sin.

The Priest is always with thee, child of God. His help is always at hand. Neither death, nor life, nor height, nor depth, nor principalities, nor powers, can ever separate thee from the down-coming of God's love.

The battle is often before and behind. From behind come memories of past failure, the consequences of mistakes, the misunderstandings which have alienated us from others, and made it difficult for us to live as we would; on the other hand perplexities and anxieties seem to bar our future path. But when the battle is before and behind, remember that God besets his people behind and before, and covers them with his hand. The invisible film of his protection makes the soul invulnerable. The life that is hid with Christ in God is beyond the reach of harm.

Lord, there is none beside Thee to help.
2 Chron. 14: 11 (R.V.).

REMIND GOD OF HIS ENTIRE RESPONSIBILITY. "There is none beside Thee to help." The odds against Asa were enormous. There were a million of men in arms against him, beside three hundred chariots. It seemed impossible to hold his own against that vast multitude. There were no allies who would come to his help: his only hope therefore was in God. There was none beside to help. It may be that your difficulties have been allowed to come to so alarming a pitch that you may be compelled to renounce all creature aid, to which in lesser trials you have had recourse, and cast yourself back on your Almighty Friend.

PUT GOD BETWEEN YOURSELF AND THE FOE. To Asa's faith, Jehovah seemed to stand between the might of Zerah and himself, as one who had no strength. Nor was he mistaken. We are told that the Ethiopians were destroyed before the Lord and before his host, as though celestial combatants flung themselves against the foe in Israel's behalf, and put the large host to rout, so that Israel had only to follow up and gather the spoil. Our God is Jehovah of Hosts, who can summon unexpected reinforcements at any moment to the aid of his people. Believe that He is there between you and your difficulty, and what baffles you will flee before Him, as clouds before the gale.

IDENTIFY YOUR CAUSE WITH HIS. "In thy name are we come. . . . Let not man prevail against Thee." It is a great matter when a small State is so identified with a strong European power, as that an insult to one of its officials is deemed a *casus belli* by the more powerful Government; and whenever we are so delivered from selfish aims, as to be able to show that our cause and God's are one, we are invincible.

They entered into a covenant to seek the Lord God of their fathers. 2 Chron. 15: 12.

WE hear but little talk in the present day of the covenant, the mention of which was dear to God's people of olden time. There is this difference between it and the covenants which we make with God. That is permanent, these evanescent. That is founded upon the oath and promise of God; these on the resolutions and endeavours of man. That is full of promises of what God will be and do; these recount what we are prepared to sacrifice and suffer. And though we sign them with blood drawn from our veins, they will disappoint and fail.

Do not think too much of entering into and keeping a covenant with God; but remember that the Lord Jesus, on our behalf, has entered into covenant relation with the Father, and the Father with us in Him. This is the new covenant. It is drawn out at length in Hebrews 8. Very little is said about our side, but it is full to overflowing of God's. Nothing is said of our fidelity to our obligations, because man has been too often weighed in the balances and found wanting; and because the Lord Jesus Christ, as our representative, has already fulfilled all the conditions of obedience and devotion on which its provisions depend. He has also graciously undertaken to realize those conditions by the Holy Spirit in us.

Every time we put to our lips the cup of the new covenant, we humbly remind God of all He has promised, and ask Him to do as He has said. At the same time we may confidently ask the great Surety of the covenant to accomplish in us such a mind as may love and keep our Father's law. And what He did for our fathers, who were naturally just such as we are, He will certainly do for us.

To show Himself strong in the behalf of them whose heart is perfect toward Him. 2 Chron. 16: 9.

THE emphasis is clearly on the word perfect. That was the point between Hanani the seer and Asa the king. Asa's mistake and sin lay in his resorting to Benhadad, king of Syria,

as an ally against Baasha. Evidently he did not perfectly trust the delivering power of God; and in this failure of his faith, he forfeited the all-sufficient help which would have more than availed. As the seer said very truly, simple trust in God had brought deliverance from the Ethiopians and Lubim, though they were a much huger host than Baasha's; and the same attitude in respect of Baasha would have secured a like result. God was only awaiting the appeal of Asa's faith, to show Himself strong. What a mistake to send to Syria!

Now, dear reader, this is very pertinent for your life and mine. We often complain that we are bereft of help, and send off for Benhadad. And all the while the eyes of the Lord are looking pitifully and longingly at us. Nothing would give Him greater pleasure than to show Himself strong on our behalf. This, however, He cannot do until renouncing all other confidants and helpers, our heart is perfect in the simplicity and frankness of its faith. What an exquisite thought is suggested by the allusion to the eyes of the Lord running to and fro throughout the whole earth! At a glance He takes in our position; not a sorrow, trial, or temptation visits us without exciting his notice and loving sympathy. In all the whole wide earth there is not one spot so lonely, one heart so darkened, as to escape those eyes. Oh for the perfect confidence which will allow Him to act! It is for lack of this that we remain unhelped, and spend our days in the midst of wars and tumults.

His heart was lifted up in the ways of the Lord. 2 Chron. 17: 6.

SURSUM corda! Lift up your hearts! How beautiful is this ejaculation in the Communion Service of the Church of England, and the response, "We lift them up unto the Lord." I never hear it without the thrill of a holy impulse passing through me. It is possible, and it is meet and right, to lift up our hearts from the sordid cares and pressing responsibilities of daily life, into the calm, serene presence of God our Father.

Lift up your heart to God, as a child its face to be kissed. Lift it up free from mistrust and sinful stain, and unkind feeling towards any. Lift it up in holy joy and inspiration. Lift it up as a censer filled with the hot coals, from which sweet fragrance exhales. And God will bend down to lift it higher, and fill it with his peace and joy and purity.

In hours of depression look up, be lifted. Sursum corda! When the foe is pressing you most severely, look up, your redemption draweth nigh. When the river has to be crossed, when the last farewell must be said, when the flesh fails, let your mind and heart thither ascend, and there continually dwell where Jesus has entered as your Forerunner.

If you would lift up your heart, you must be in the ways of the Lord, as the good Jehoshaphat. You must seek the Lord God, and walk in his commandments. You must take away the high places and groves of idolatry and impurity. Beware of the world's birdlime! Shake yourself from the bands and bonds that would detain you. Oh, heart of mine, why is thy flight so low? Lift thyself up and sit down with Christ in the heavenly places! "Unto Thee, O Lord, do I lift up my soul. Let not mine enemies triumph over me!"

I hate him; for he never prophesied good unto me, but always evil. 2 Chron. 18: 7.

THIS was a very naïve confession. Of course, Micaiah could not speak good of Ahab, whose life was diametrically opposed to all that was God-like and holy. Micaiah had no animosity towards the king of Israel; it was not a personal matter with him. He simply read from the page of the future as God opened it to his eyes, and in which the out-working of the king's evil life was disclosed in gloomy characters. It was as absurd to hate him because he read such dark lessons from the inevitable future, as for a house-holder to shoot his dog, that bays all night, to warn his master against the burglar engaged in rifling his home.

The Bible, the pastor, the whole Church of God, are hated by worldlings for the same reason, because they cannot speak hopefully of their future. It as as though a card-playing crew were to hate the watchman who told them that the course of their vessel was straight for the surf and rocks of the shore. If men will persist in violating God's law, in breaking through the hedge of thorns, and in pursuing their own wild ways, they cannot possibly expect the blessedness of the Beatitudes. However, their hatred against those who warn them is really directed towards God. They are indignant that they cannot have their way; their proud spirit would like to overturn the very order of the universe

rather than that it should be thwarted. They cannot endure the contrast between God's children and themselves. Do not be surprised if the world hate you. It shows that you are no more of the world than your Master was. Jesus said: "If they have persecuted Me, they will also persecute you; if they have kept my saying, they will keep yours also."

Shouldst thou help the ungodly, and love them that hate the Lord? 2 Chron. 19: 2.

THIS looks back to 18: 1, where we learn that Jehoshaphat, though he had riches and honour in abundance, joined affinity with Ahab. Riches and abundance are dangerous things. They usually weaken our character, and incline us to worldly alliances; and it was to their subtle and pernicious influences that Jehoshaphat fell a victim. Ah! what a fall it was to hear him saying, "I am as thou art, and my people as thy people." Well might Jehu take up the role which his father had filled before Asa, and protest. But let us seriously question whether, though there are good things found in us, we may not be falling into the same mistake, and sin. Are there not ways in which we say to men of the world, with whom we mix, "I am as thou art"?

There is a great tendency in the present day to boast in the closeness with which we can approach the world without injury. We join in the social life, read the same books, go to the same amusements, talk of the same themes; and it is almost impossible in a drawing-room to tell the difference between the Jehoshaphats and the Ahabs. So also, in our methods of doing good. The real difficulty lies away back in our want of engagedness with Christ. It is of little use to find fault with the outward, as long as the heart is wayward. Love to the Lord Jesus is our only safeguard. The love of Christ must constrain us. Personal attachment to Christ will wean us away from this close identification with the world. But if we persist in identifying ourselves with the world, which God has doomed, we must not be surprised to find that wrath is on us from the Lord: and He will chasten us for love's sake.

He appointed singers unto the Lord, that should praise the beauty of holiness. 2 Chron. 20: 21.

DOST thou praise the beauty of holiness? Is

holiness beautiful to thee? Art thou in love with it as it is presented in the glorious Lord? Canst thou turn from the noise and anxiety of life's battle to dwell on the loveliness of God and of the devout life, and to praise Him whose mercy endureth for ever? It is a rare accomplishment, acquired only through the indwelling of the Holy Ghost. In each of us there should be the priest-side of character as well as the warrior: the love for what is beautiful in holiness as well as for the strong and active in service.

But the special characteristic of this battle was that the good king put the singers in the forefront of the army, and praised for a victory which was only assured to him by faith. Yet so sure was he of it, that he could praise before he entered into the battle.

There is much to help us here in our daily combat for God and truth. Let us fill the morning hour with holy song, in the heart, if not with the voice; let a psalm or hymn be part of the daily reading; let there be the confidence that God is going to bless, which cannot restrain its jubilant expression. So in all prayer, wait on God till you feel that you can praise Him for what you have asked Him to bestow.

When they began to praise, the Lord did all the rest. Before the onset of his divine reinforcements the enemy fled. His people had but to gather spoil, and then the praise which had anticipated the battle was consummated as they returned, in the valley of blessing.

"There's a song in the valley of blessing
  so sweet,
And angels would fain join the strain,
As with rapturous praises we bow at his
  feet,
Crying, 'Worthy the Lamb that was
  slain!' "

The same time also did Libnah revolt from under his hand. 2 Chron. 21: 10.
AS long as the kings of Judah remained true to their allegiance to God, they were able to keep in subjection the surrounding nations; but just so soon as they revolted from God these peoples revolted from them. It was as though power descended into them from the source of all power; and when the link between themselves and God was broken, that between them and their subordinates was broken also.

This applies very widely: TO OUR PASSIONS. If they master you, rebelling against and revolting from your hand, it is because there is some flaw in your consecration, and you have forsaken to some extent the Lord God.

TO OUR FAMILIES. When the heads of a home are in perfect unity with each other and God, they may generally expect that their children will grow up submissive and obedient. Their authority will be recognized and honoured. Revolt in the home indicates very often some lapse in obedience and loyalty to God.

TO OUR INFLUENCE OVER MEN. When the soul is in blessed fellowship with God power flows into it from Him, before which strongholds are overthrown. "I am full of power by the Spirit of the Lord," said the prophet. "I am a man under authority, and have soldiers under me," said the centurion.

Give yourself entirely to Jesus. Obey Him absolutely; receive by faith from Him living power and grace; be a channel through which He may pour Himself; and you will find that men and things will fall into line at your bidding, and you shall receive power. Our Libnahs will not revolt, unless we forsake the Lord God of our fathers.

Hid in the House of God. 2 Chron. 22: 12.
SAFE from Athaliah, who would have ruthlessly destroyed him if she had had an inkling of his existence, the young Joash was reared beneath the care of Jehoiada and his wife within the precincts of the house of God. He was hidden in the secret place of the Most High, and abode under the shadow of the Almighty. There let us also live. Let us know what it is to dwell in the house of the Lord all the days of our life, and all this day. Let us cultivate the life which is hid with Christ in God.

It is well often to remind ourselves that we are in God, and that the film of his environing presence is about us like a wall of thick-ribbed steel. We are in Him as the jewel in the casket; as the chick under the feathers of the hen; as the child in the warm embrace of its mother. And so long as we stay there we are invulnerable. Therefore our great enemy is continually endeavouring to allure us into the open; he knows he can do as he likes with us, if only he can induce us to venture beyond our hiding-place. Therefore, beware of any temptation to worry, to amass this world's goods, or to seek the indulgence of appetite; it is by such lures and baits that Satan seduces unwary souls from their safe hiding.

If a day in God's courts is better than a thousand, what must it be to dwell in the house of the Lord all one's days, to behold his beauty, and inquire in his temple. The rarest visions, the fairest fellowship, the most entrancing joys, the most confident outlook on life and the hereafter, are the accompaniments of such a residence. The altar of incense, the laver of daily cleansing, the light of the Shekinah, the holy psalm and song, the great altar of sacrifice, are familiar objects to the hidden soul.

And the city was quiet after they had slain Athaliah with the sword. 2 Chron. 23: 21.

THIS was a great revolution, admirably planned and carried into effect. It was intolerable that such a woman as Athaliah should desecrate the throne and temple. Jehoiada, by his prudence and courage, deserved well of the entire nation in ridding the world of her presence. No half measures would have availed to meet the case.

There are times in every life when strong and strenuous action is inevitable if the cause of God is to be promoted and saved. In many of us there is a willingness to tolerate evil, rather than arouse ourselves to grasp it with a firm hand, and, if needs be, drag it up by its roots. Be strong, yea, be strong, is an injunction that has to be emphasized even to men who are greatly beloved. The easiest thing for Jehoiada would have been to shut himself up in the temple, and leave things to take their course. The noblest thing was to come forth, and boldly confront the rampant, evil of his time. So God's call rings out for helpers in the great fight against sin. Its notes penetrate into the retirement of Christian homes, to noble women and devoted men, demanding that they should come forth to resist impurity, the love of strong drink, the strong tendency towards extravagance, luxury, and waste. The world is full of Athaliahs, and it is not befitting that the Jehoiadas should remain at their holy rites and services if there is a paramount need for action in the world's battlefield, in the strife against wrong.

The children of God are citizens of the New Jerusalem, but they are also certainly citizens here; and they must not stand aside from great public issues, allowing them to be decided by ungodly and wicked men.

The Spirit of God clothed itself with Zechariah the son of Jehoiada. 2 Chron. 24: 20 (R.V. marg.).

AS we put on a cloak or dress, so does the Spirit of God, as it were, hide Himself in those who surrender themselves to Him, so that it is not they who speak and act, but He within them. Have you at any time been conscious of having become the clothing of the Holy Spirit? Remember that cloth or leather must yield itself easily to the movements of its wearer, and not less pliable and supple must we be to the Spirit of God.

When the Spirit of God is thus within us, and speaks or acts for us, we may expect, as Zechariah found it, to come into collision with the entire drift and current of society around us, and to incur odium and hatred. Men do not like to be told that they cannot prosper because they have forsaken God; but we have no alternative than to witness against their sins. Does the Spirit clothe Himself with you my friend, as you anticipate the work of to-day? Are you using Him, or is He to use you? Are you seeking to clothe yourself with his power for some personal ambition, or are you desirous that He should array Himself in you, so that the glory may evidently be his? In the agony of battle, when great deeds are to be done, no one stops to think of the uniform of the soldier, but only of the might beneath it.

But for this you must be prepared to pay the cost, and be willing to cross the cherished purposes of men, as the Spirit of God by your voice or deed witnesses against them. They stoned Zechariah at the command of the king; but years after the Lord Jesus referred to it, for no faithful martyr seals his witness with his blood without some quick glance of recognition from the Master, and some record on the imperishable tablets of his heart.

The Lord is able to give thee much more than this. 2 Chron. 25: 9.

AMAZIAH had many good qualities, but he did not clearly see how impossible it was for Israel to be allied with Judah without invalidating the special divine protection and care on which Judah had been taught to rely.

We must understand that God cannot be in fellowship with us if we tolerate fellowship with the ungodly. We must choose between the two. If we can renounce all creature aid, and trust simply in the eternal God, there is no limit to the victories He will secure; but if, turning from Him, we hold out our hand toward the world, we forfeit his aid. O child of God, let not the army of Israel go with thee! Do not adopt worldly policy, methods, or partnership. However strong you make yourself for the battle in alliance with these, you will fail. Indeed, God Himself will make you fall before the enemy, that you may be driven back to Himself.

But you say that you have already entered into so close an alliance that you cannot draw back. You have invested your capital, you have gone to great expenditure. Yet it will be better to forfeit these than Him. Without these aids, and with only God beside you, you will be able to rout Edom, and smite ten thousand men. Would that men knew the absolute deliverance which God will effect for those whose hearts are perfect towards Him!

The soldiers of Israel committed depredations on their way back. This was the result of the folly and sin of Amaziah's proposal. We may be forgiven, and delivered, and yet there will be after-consequences which will follow us from some ill-considered act. Sin may be forgiven, but its secondary results are sometimes very bitter. We must expect to reap as we sow.

He was marvellously helped, till he was strong.
2 Chron. 26: 15, 16.

GREAT and marvellous are thy works, O God; that our soul knoweth quite well. Thou hast showed marvellous loving-kindness. We must sing to Thee; for Thou hast done marvellous things. It is marvellous that Thou shouldst have set thy love upon us; that Thou shouldst have watched over our interests with unwearied care; that our sins, or unbelief, or declensions, have never diverted thy love from us. "Marvellous" is the only word we can use, as we think of the condescension of the well-beloved Son to the manger-bed; of the agony and bloody-sweat; of the cross and passion—and all for us who were his enemies. But it is most marvellous of all that Thou hast made us children, heirs, and joint-heirs with Christ. To think that we shall

shine as the sun in thy kingdom, that we are to sit upon his throne, and be included in that circle of love and life of which the throne of God and the Lamb is the centre! Surely the marvels of thy grace will only seem the greater when eternity with its boundless ages gives us time to explore them.

The danger, however, is that we should become strong in our own conceit, and credit ourselves with the position which is due to the grace of God alone. Oh for the truly humble spirit of the little child, that we may never vaunt ourselves! The laden ship sinks in the water; the fruit-burdened bough stoops to the ground; the truest scientist is the humblest disciple. Oh to be submerged and abashed for the marvellous help of God!

God cannot trust some of us with prosperity and success, because our nature could not stand them. We must tug at the oar, instead of spreading the sail, because we have not enough ballast.

Jotham became mighty, because he ordered his
ways. 2 Chron. 27: 6 (R.V.).

THERE is a lower sense in which this holds good in daily and business life. You can hardly imagine a really successful man being untidy and disorderly. Method is the law of success; and a truly holy soul is sure to be orderly. I do not remember ever meeting one who really walked with God who did not make orderliness one of the first principles of life.

The Lord Jesus would have the men sit down in rows before He broke the bread; and He wrapt together his grave-clothes before He left the sepulchre. It was, therefore, in keeping with the whole tenor of his example when the apostle prescribed that all things should be done decently and in order.

Clear handwriting, especially the direction of an envelope, to give the postman as little trouble as possible; the careful folding of our cast-off garments, to save the maids needless work; the leaving our room that we have been occupying as little disturbed in its arrangements as may be; the gathering up of luncheon fragments from the green banks, where we have sat to view the entrancing prospect; the arrangement of papers, and accounts, and magazines, so that we can readily lay our hand upon whatever is required; the adopting of mental order in prayer and conversation, and in the thinking out of plans and purposes; neatness in dress

—these are all part of the right ordering of life which makes for its success and comfort, and greatly for peace in the home. They are the habits of the soul that walks before God, and which is accustomed to think of Him as seeing in secret, and as considering all our ways. In this way we may become mighty, and by being faithful in that which is least come to great charges.

They clothed all that were naked, and gave them to eat and drink. 2 Chron. 28: 15.

A GREAT burst of generosity was here, for Israel had every reason to be incensed against Judah for the raid made on their territory. But, instead of pushing their advantage to the uttermost, they returned good for evil, and anticipated the words of the apostle, "If thine enemy hunger, feed him; if he thirst, give him drink: for in so doing thou shalt heap coals of fire on his head."

Have you in your life people who have done you injury, and against whom you entertain hard thoughts? You do not injure them in return, but you cannot pray for them. So far as you can, you avoid them; you make no attempt to overcome the evil that is in them. But to act thus is to come short of Christ's standard. It is your duty, not merely to keep at a distance and give a wide berth, but by love to destroy the evil, to transform the enemy into a friend, and to create love and friendship where hostility and alienation had reigned. It is God's way, and in this we are bidden to be perfect, as our Heavenly Father is perfect.

Will you try it? Will you begin by doing kind acts to those who have harmed you? Not because as yet you feel as you would, but because it is right. Then as you dig the trench in right doing, look up to God, and He will pour into your heart the warm gush of affection. If you sincerely will his will in this matter, and act as the Good Samaritan did to the Jew, and exercise faith, God will come to your aid whilst you clothe others and minister to them, you will find their hard heart melted, and yourselves clothed with the beautiful garments of salvation, and of a meek and quiet spirit, which in God's sight is of great price.

When the burnt-offering began, the song of the Lord began also. 2 Chron. 29: 27:

THIS chapter contains a parable of the cleansing of the heart, meant to be a temple for God; but the doors of prayer are unopened, the lamps of testimony unlit, the burnt-offerings of self-sacrifice neglected; and, as the result, grass grows thick in courts which should have been trodden by the feet of Levite minstrels engaged in holy song. If ever that song is to break out again, it can only be after a thorough cleansing and renovation of the inner shrine. You tell me that you cannot sing the Lord's song; then I know you have gone into the strange land of backsliding. You acknowledge that for some time now you have taken no delight in God or his service; then I am sure that the temple is badly in need of renovation.

Cleanse the house of the Lord. Bring out all the uncleanness. By self-examination, confession, and repudiation, be clean of all the filth which has accumulated through months and years of neglect. Resume the position of entire devotion, as a prepared and sanctified soul. Offer the sin-offering for the past, and prepare the burnt-offering of entire consecration for the future. And when that is offered, when you determine to be wholly God's, lay yourself, with all the interests of your life, at the feet of Jesus, for his disposal; then the song of the Lord will begin again.

The music of your life is still, because you are out of accord with the will of God; but when by surrender and consecration there is unison, your heart will be filled with songs without words, and love like an ocean in the fulness of her strength. When the rich, selfish bachelor suddenly finds himself compelled to care for his dead brother's little children, he is startled to find a new song has begun in his life.

The good Lord pardon every one that prepareth his heart to seek God. 2 Chron. 30: 18, 19.

A VERY touching prayer, that opens up deep thoughts as to the progress of the true knowledge of God in Israel, and of the comparative value of heart preparation and ceremonial cleansing. Here were crowds of well-meaning people who had come from all parts of the land in answer to Hezekiah's invitation. Unaccustomed to temple usage, strangers to the temple rites, they had participated in the festivities of this great Passover without submitting first to the necessary ablutions. Their heart was prepared to seek God, they were proud of the great past, they desired to stand right with the Lord God of their fathers; but they were sadly ignorant and careless. The only thing to be done was to pray that their ignorances and negligences might be forgiven.

It is thus that Jesus pleads in heaven; and there are many that obtain mercy on the ground of his merit, because when they sin they do so ignorantly, and from want of knowledge rather than from want of heart. The devout ritualist who lays an excessive stress on outward forms; the man who has sensuous and distorted views of Christ, but sincerely desires to be accepted through Him; the soul that touches the hem of the garment as though the healing power were independent of the will-power of the Redeemer; the dying malefactor, who, in his last hours, catches at some distorted representation of Christ which is filtered through to him from the chance word of an uninstructed preacher—these are included in the fruitful pleading of the Great High Priest, who has compassion on the ignorant and on those who are out of the way. You may not understand doctrine, creed, or rite; but be sure to seek God. No splendid ceremonial nor rigorous etiquette can intercept the seeking soul.

He did it with all his heart and prospered.
2 Chron. 31: 21.

THE man who does his business with all his heart, is sure to prosper. To put your heart into your work is like genius manipulating common materials, till their worth becomes priceless, just because of what has been put into it.

The heart stands for the emotions and affections. What the furnace is to the factory or steamship, that the heart is in the economy of our nature. It is a great thing to love our life-work, to have an aim that kindles us whenever we think of it. Those who are so happily circumstanced, cannot be sufficiently thankful. But what of those who are bound to a work which they did not choose and do not like, who find their daily toil irksome and distasteful—is there any help for them? Can they possibly learn to do such work from their hearts? Certainly: because of Him who set it, and for whom it may be done.

Love performs the most onerous duties with all its heart, if they conduce to the comfort and help of those whom it loves more than itself. Does not a mother or wife perform tasks from which the hireling would shrink? She does them with all her heart, not considering for a moment the loathsomeness and hardness of the demand. So if we look at our life-work as God-appointed; if we realize that He has fixed it for us, who determined the orbits of the stars; if we can hear the voice of Jesus saying, "Do this for Me"—there is no further thought of hardship or distaste. Remember to do all your life-work for Jesus; do all in his name and for his glory; ask Him to fill your heart with submissive, loyal obedience, and you will find that when you introduce the personal element of Christ-service into the meanest acts, they will glisten like a piece of gold-tapestry.

Hezekiah the king, and the prophet Isaiah, prayed and cried to heaven. 2 Chron. 32: 20.
IT was the indignity done to Jehovah that stirred these two holy men to the heart. Not that their lives, and the lives of their people, and the beautiful holy city, were in danger; but that Sennacherib spake against the God of Jerusalem, as against the gods of the people of the earth, which were the work of the hands of man. Oh that we were possessed with a similar zeal for God, so that we might look at sin as it affects Him, and lament over the awful wrongs which are continually being perpetrated against his holy, loving nature! What an argument this would give us in prayer!

This constitutes a special reason why we should plead for a revival of religion throughout our land. Men speak and act so shamelessly, as though God had abdicated his throne, and was hardly to be taken account of. They sin against Him with so high a hand, and treat his laws with so much contumely. Are there no Hezekiahs and Isaiahs who will pray and cry to the God of our fathers to do again the great works He did in their days, and in the old time before?

Then the Lord would save us, and guide us on every side (22). There never was a more conspicuous and glorious deliverance than when the angel of God wrought for Israel against Assyria. The Lord became a place of broad rivers and streams across which the enemy could not pass. As the mother bird settling down on her nest, He covered the city with his outspread wings. And the rich spoils of the foe were left for the beleaguered garrison. Pray on, beloved; the Lord is our Judge, the Lord is our Lawgiver, the Lord is our King; He will save us.

When he was in affliction, he besought the Lord his God. 2 Chron. 33: 12.
SO long as this story stands on the page of revelation, no sinner need despair of mercy. There was hardly a sin possible to man that Manasseh did not commit. "He did that which was evil in the sight of the Lord, like unto the abominations of the heathen, whom the Lord had cast out before the children of Israel." And he made his people do worse than the heathen.

Then came awful sorrow. Bound in fetters, exposed to consummate cruelty and disgrace, he was carried to Babylon, and thrust into the dungeons, where other captive princes were immured, with little chance of liberation or permission to revisit his native land. But there the Spirit of God did his work. He humbled himself greatly, and prayed. What tears, and cries, and bursts of heart-broken penitence, were his! How those walls were saturated with the breath of confession, and those stone floors indented by his kneeling at perpetual prayer! And God came near to his low dungeon, and graciously heard his supplication, and brought him back again.

Yes, and He will do as much for you. The blood of Jesus Christ his Son cleanseth from all sin; the grace of God is exceedingly abundant with faith and love; all sins and blasphemies may be forgiven to the sons of men. Turn to Him with brokenness of soul, and He will not only forgive, but bring you again; and give you, as He did Manasseh, an opportunity of undoing some of those evil things which have marred your past. For the rest, it is good not to wait for affliction to stir us up to seek God, but to abide in Him for love's dear sake.

I have found the book of the law in the house of the Lord. 2 Chron. 34: 15, 18.
IT is supposed that this was the Book of Deuteronomy; though we have no sympathy whatever with a modern notion with respect to its discovery. In our judgment that book is rightly ascribed to Moses. Apparently, however, it had long been missing, and the young king was filled with horror when he heard the list of evils that were associated with apostasy. "He rent his clothes."

We should read the Bible with a particular application to the days in which we live. It is well enough to accept its statements as being generally true and credible; but it is better to realize their pertinence to ourselves and our circumstances. The book of the law had been sadly neglected in the years preceding Josiah's accession; and through the neglect of God's Word the people had become indifferent to his commands, and deaf to the appeals of his prophets. Josiah turned the lantern on the evils of his time, and saw how God was feeling with respect to them.

The Bible is a book for all time. What it said, it says. What it was, it is. You tell me it was written so many centuries ago; but I reply the ink is still wet on its immortal pages. They have been read and pondered by generations; but the light of its eye is not dim, nor its natural force abated. Sin is the same, man the same, God the same, in all ages. And the Bible's claim to be God's Word is substantiated by the fact that it is possessed of living power, and of the same perennial freshness as the sun, or the spring, or the ocean, or the faces of the little children. Would that we might daily read it as we read the newspaper, damp from the press, realizing that it is our Father's great message for the life of every day!

Prepare. 2 Chron. 35: 4, 6, 10, 14, 15, 16.
NO great court function can be carried through successfully, without careful preparation. And Josiah's passover was so vast and rare a success because of the large amount of previous preparation, as is described in this chapter. The priests and Levites were prepared by careful washings and ceremonial rites. The course of the sacrifices was ordered according to the law of Moses. The routine of sacred song and praise was also provided for. Nothing was left to haphazard or chance.

We are taught to rely on the promptings and inspirations of the Holy Spirit; and it is certain that He would use us more on special errands, if we were to trust and obey Him better. But these extraordinary ministries should not lead us to a life of haphazard. We should prepare ourselves for service so far as we may, laying our plans, anticipating the calls and exigencies of coming days, and preparing for the demands which almost certainly will be made on us. We may have to give our special words and addresses and arrangements to the winds; but we shall always need that preparedness of heart which is necessary for those who are to be used of God.

Remember what is said of the vessels that were purged from uncleanness, sanctified, meet for the Master's use, and prepared unto every good work. Be always in your own place, clean so far as you can be, filled with the Holy Ghost, with the handle of your life turned towards the Master's hand, that at any moment He may take hold of you, and use you for his holy service. By the diligent study of his Word, as well as by earnest prayer and waiting upon God, you will be prepared to do his will.

Rising up betimes. 2 Chron. 36: 15.
WHAT a touching and graphic phrase! How did God yearn over that sinful and rebellious city! Sending his messengers, "rising up betimes, and sending"—like a man who has had a sleepless night of anxiety for his friend or child, and rises with the dawn to send a servant on a mission of inquiry, or a message of love. How eager God is for men's salvation!

From God's eagerness, may we not learn a lesson of anxiety for the souls of men? We do not long after them enough, or rise betimes to urge them to repent. Did we realize what heaven is, or hell, what men are missing or incurring, what our duty is, as saved ourselves, we should rise up betimes to seek their eternal interests.

But if God rises betimes to seek men, should they not do the same to seek Him? Think you not, that when Adam heard the voice of the Lord God walking in the garden at morning prime, he would be up and away to meet Him on the upland lawns of Paradise? Can we wonder that our Master would rise up a great while before day, to meet his Father on some unfrequented height? Let us not cling to beds of sloth when God is awaiting us; let us heed his loving remonstrances, that we may be saved in the overthrow of the world; and let us, like Lot, pass on the word to others enwrapt in fatal slumber around us, bidding them to escape to the mountains, before the sun rise on the earth, lest they be consumed.

It was the practice of Sir Henry Havelock, during his campaigns in India, always to have two hours for prayer and Bible study before the march. If the camp was struck at 6.0 a.m., he would rise at 4.0.

Ezra

The Lord stirred up the spirit of Cyrus. Ezra 1: 1.
THERE were many rays focussed on this spot. In the first place, it had been definitely foretold by Jeremiah that the captivity would only last for seventy years. In the next place, Daniel, having learned from comparison of dates that the allotted time had nearly expired, had set himself to pray. Also, if Josephus be credited, the aged prophet had shown the young king the predictions of Isaiah in which his own name was clearly mentioned: "Thus saith the Lord to his anointed, to Cyrus, whose right hand I have holden: . . . he shall build my city, and he shall let go my captives, not for price nor reward, saith the Lord of hosts" (Isa. 45: 1, 13).

God is the fountain-head and source of all spiritual blessing, and of all those great movements for the uplifting and enlighten-ment of mankind which have swept from time to time over the world. Go to Him when you want to reach the heart of kings, prophets, and people. Oh for the faith of Samuel, Elijah, Daniel, and other stalwart men of God, that through Him we may stir up the spirits of those who will not listen to our appeals! For the fervent prayer of a righteous man still availeth much. In prayer you can touch the spring of all the stirrings that the world needs.

But it is not enough for God to stir men, they must obey. It appears that only a comparatively small number of captive Jews obeyed the divine stirring and came out of Babylon with the chief of the fathers. The call resounds for volunteers, but only a few respond; the inspiration breathes over us, but only some are susceptible to it. God works to will and to do, but only certain of the children of men work out what He works in.

Whenever there is a divine stirring abroad, let us rise up and go.

Till there stood up a priest with Urim and with Thummim. Ezra 2: 63.

IT must have been a great disappointment to these people who found themselves excluded from sharing as priests. Their names were not on the register, and so they had to wait until a properly-qualified authority could adjudicate their case. The mere inference of reason was not enough; they needed the direct corroboration of the anointed priest with Urim and with Thummim.

So in our life it is not enough to rely on the inference of reason, or to allow our Christian standing to be determined by the evidence of a document. We must seek the direct witness and testimony of the Holy Spirit. How many Christians there are who have no experimental knowledge of what the Apostle meant when he said that the Spirit witnesseth with our spirit that we are born again. They are always referring to inference, and the testimony of others; and therefore their consciousness varies, and they cannot eat of the holy bread of God. But when the Spirit of God speaks through the Urim and Thummim, and certifies that we are the children of God, giving us the white stone with its new name, and revealing Christ as dwelling within us, we have, immediately, boldness to enter into the holiest of all, and eat of the holy things.

Assurance is needful before we dare to appropriate the things which are freely given to us of God. Who of us is not able to verify this from his personal experience? We could not enjoy the Father's table, so long as there was a doubt about our sonship. But the assurance of faith may be ours as we wait in the presence of our great High Priest, speaking to us by the Holy Spirit, who witnesses with our spirits that we are the children of God.

And they set the altar upon its bases. Ezra 3: 3.

THIS is the first thing that must be done before our temple-building or other undertakings can be crowned with success. It was well that the returned remnant made this their care; it augured well for their future. The new start that God Himself was giving would have been invalidated without that altar, which meant forgiveness for the past, and renewed consecration for the future.

Where is the altar in your life? Where the burnt sacrifice which betokens entire surrender of consecration? It cannot be too often insisted on, that since Christ died for all, all died in Him. We were not only saved by his death, we were included in it, but we must appropriate and identify ourselves with it. We must look up to God and say, "I desire that this death should be mine, to the world, to sin, to the flesh; make it so by the power of the Holy Ghost, that in Jesus I may be truly dead unto sin, but alive unto Thee."

Perhaps that last clause will help some souls most. Do not perpetually dwell on the dying side, but think much of the living side. Yield yourselves to receive God's life, which is the life of the Son of God in the surrendered nature. Be very sensitive, and "quick of scent," to every movement and prompting of the Holy Spirit. Seek the things which are above, where Christ, your life, is seated. So you will find your energy drained away from self to Christ. Because He lives you will live also. A maple tree planted on a barren soil sent out one of its rootlets to a richer patch not far away, and ultimately all its roothold was there, till finally it was bodily moved and transferred from its first position to this more salubrious one.

Let us build with you. Ezra 4: 2.

AT first the world does its best to intimidate the Church; then it asks to be permitted to join with it. A most subtle temptation this. The child of God is greatly inclined to yield; the proposal seems so harmless, and so likely to be a means of blessing to the poor, hungry, weary world. But there is only one condition on which the world may be admitted; it must yield a true and humble submission to the cross, and be willing to give up all for Jesus—conditions which the world will not consider for a moment; and so its heart is filled with bitterness and gall, and it sets itself to hinder where it had professed willingness to help.

There are five things of which we are expressly bidden to beware—they are five phases of an unequal yoke: fellowship with unrighteousness; communion with darkness; concord with Belial; part with an unbeliever; agreement with idols. Let us beware of these things, and cleanse ourselves from all filthiness of the flesh and spirit. There may seem to be great loss and needless sacrifice in dispensing with the help of Rehum and Shimshai; but if once we accepted their help, we should discover to our cost that they were adversaries still, and that their only desire was to retard our efforts.

We sometimes shrink from some great undertaking for God, and are inclined to accept the proffered aid of wealthy but ungodly men. But their help may be purchased by the cost of all that makes our work worth doing. "Be ye not unequally yoked together with unbelievers; for what fellowship hath righteousness with unrighteousness?"

"Yea, with one mouth, O world, though thou deniest
Stand thou on that side, for on this am I."

The eye of their God was upon the elders of the Jews. Ezra 5: 5.
IT was a delightful thought amid obloquy and opposition, like that which the Jews were at this moment encountering, to know that God was watching them with jealous care. We are reminded of the words of the Psalmist, quoted and authenticated by the Apostle Peter, "The eyes of the Lord are upon the righteous, and his ears are open to their cry; but the face of the Lord is against them that do evil." And he goes on to argue, "Who is he that will harm you, if ye be followers of that which is good?" The Jews certainly found it so; for the efforts of their enemies to induce them to desist from their work of temple-building were rendered nugatory and ineffectual by the special care exercised over them by their Almighty Friend.

It may be that you will have to encounter hatred and opposition in doing God's work; but be sure not to look at these things, but steadfastly to Jesus. Must you not watch the foe? No; you could not make a greater mistake. You must look away to the face of Jesus, and you will find that, He, like a good shepherd, is looking carefully and lovingly down on you, and watching the stealthy movements of your foe. Even when we are not directly conscious of that watchful eye, it still follows us. He knoweth the way that you take; and He is acquainted with the varied circumstances of your life. He has pledged Himself to be with you for ever; as Wordsworth once said of his beloved daughter Dora:

"Dear child, fair child, that walkest with me here,
Though thou appear untouched by solemn thought,

Thy nature is not therefore less divine;
Thou liest in Abraham's bosom all the year,
Thou worshippest at the temple's inner shrine,
God being with thee when thou knowest not."

The Lord had made them joyful, and turned the heart of the King unto them. Ezra 6: 22.
YES, the hearts of men are in the hands of God, and He can turn them whither He will. There are many instances of this in Scripture. God gave Joseph favour with Pharaoh; Moses with the Princess; and Daniel with the King of Babylon. If certain matters can only be settled by reference to great men, kings or men of affairs, make the application; and then betake yourself to prayer, believing that as He inclined the heart of Darius, in the instance before us, so He can do as He will among the armies of heaven, and the inhabitants of earth.

That unkind overseer, that vexatious member of your home-circle, that great man whose help you so greatly need—these are accessible to God's Spirit, if only you are intent on seeking his glory, and doing his will. But you must be able to show, as these Jews could, that your cause is identical with the cause of God, before you can claim, with unwavering faith, his interference on your behalf.

Then when the answer comes, let us thank Him, separating ourselves still further from the filthiness around us, so as to keep the feast with joy. Do not be afraid of joy; when God makes you joyful, do not think it necessary to restrain your songs or smiles, for fear that an equivalent of sorrow will presently be meted out as a make-weight. Our blessed Lord was desirous that his joy might be in his disciples; it was for the joy that was set before Him that He endured the cross, despising the shame, and is set down at the right hand of the throne of God; it is with exceeding joy that He will present us faultless before the presence of his glory. "Thou shalt rejoice in every good thing which the Lord thy God giveth thee."

I was strengthened, as the hand of the Lord my God was upon me. Ezra 7: 28.
IT was no small work that the good Ezra had undertaken. To lead a great expedition

across the inhospitable desert; to convoy the sacred vessels and a large treasure of gold and silver; to set magistrates and judges over all that great district beyond the river—this was no slight task, and he needed strength. But in the simple language of his heart the good hand of his God was upon him, and that was sufficient to nerve and strengthen him.

It is wonderful what resistless might comes to the soul, when it realizes that it is treading the path and working out the career determined for it from all eternity by the Almighty. The thought imparts the same kind of impulse to the soul, as the touch of love or authority on the arm. We are reminded of the veteran, who, when charged by the Duke of Wellington to take a difficult position, turned to him and said, "I will go, sir; but first give me a grip of your conquering hand."

Think, soul, of what that hand is which holds the waters in its hollow, and spreads the curtains of the sky, and was nailed to the cross; that brought blessing with its touch to so many weary sufferers, and now holds the mysterious book, sealed with seven seals; that caught Peter, and lay lightly on the heads of the little babes. That hand is strengthening thee for a work for which by nature thou art unequal, but to which thou hast been evidently called. Go forward: it holds, guides, empowers thee. It can lead thee before kings, princes, and nobles, so that thou shalt not fear; it can preserve thee from dangers innumerable; it can shield thee from the fire of the enemy; and none, man or devil, can pluck you out of the Father's hand.

Watch ye, and keep them, until ye weigh them at Jerusalem. Ezra 8: 29.
THEY were protected by God, whose presence with them across the wild desert made it needless to ask for an escort of soldiers; but they had to take care of the precious vessels of his house. It was a reciprocal trust. So it must be with us, as we are taught in 2 Tim. 1: 12, 14. There are two deposits, as the margin shows. We deposit ourselves, and all we are and have, with God; whilst He deposits with us his sacred Gospel, the vessels of which we must "guard through the Holy Ghost which dwelleth in us," and be prepared to defend with our blood.

OUR DEPOSIT WITH GOD. How safe are they who commit their all to God! Faraday was asked, when dying, on what supposition he depended as he contemplated the other world; and he replied, "I am relying on no supposition, but on a certainty; I know in whom I have believed, and am persuaded that He is able to keep that which I have committed to Him."

GOD'S DEPOSIT WITH US. But let us be true to our trust. The Holy Bible, the Doctrines of the Christian Church, the Day of Rest, the House of God, the ordinances of the Lord's Supper and Christian Baptism—these are some of the vessels which have been passed down to us, and we must hand on intact. Be ye clean that carry them! Oh, what joy it will be when we reach our destination, and can resign our trust, and weigh out the deposit, and hear the Master's "Well done!" But, in the meanwhile, whilst marching across the yellow sands, where wild dangers lie in wait, let us not seek the escort of creature or worldly might; but boast of the Hand of our God, which is for good upon all them that seek Him.

The people have not separated themselves. Ezra 9: 1.
THIS was only too true! There had been, on the part of princes and rulers, gross intermarriage with the people of surrounding lands. The holy seed had become mixed and diluted. And it was the more sad that this should have taken place, when it was to cleanse his people from such alliances, and the evils to which they inevitably led, that God had passed them through the purging fires of the seventy years' captivity. It afflicted the good Ezra sorely. With every sign of Oriental grief he poured out his soul before God. And this is the lesson we should carry with us. It has been truly said that communion with the Lord dries many tears, but it starts many more. We no longer sorrow with the sorrow of the world; but we become burdened with some of the griefs that still rend the heart of the Lord in the glory.

This fellowship between the Lord's people and the world is becoming increasingly close as we near the end of the age. In the appointments of our homes, our amusements, books, and practices, there is very little to choose between the one and the other. If there is any distinction, it lies in a certain sadness with which Christians take their pleasures, as though remembering a something better. But the rest of us do not grieve over it; we do not rend our clothes: we do not take these things to heart, as though they specially concerned us.

Let us at least separate ourselves after the manner of Christ, who frequented the temple, acknowledged the State, accepted invitations to great houses; but his heart and speech always revolved about his Father. What if it led to our being cast out without the camp!

We also will be with thee: be of good courage, and do it. Ezra 10: 4.

THIS narrative reminds us of the story of Achan, who took of the accursed thing, and kindled the anger of the Lord against the children of Israel. There must be confession and the putting away of evil ere communion with God can be re-established.

It is not given to everyone to be an Ezra. There are abuses to deal with, and wrongs to right, on every side; but they require to be dealt with by those who are specially adapted or qualified for the work. Be always ready to do such work, if there should be no one else. It was the life motto of a great man always to act as though there were no one else who would. Still, Nehemiahs and Ezras are not given very largely to the Church or the world; and, for the most part, we must be content to be of those who say, "Be of good courage, and do it; we also will be with thee." But though this seems but a little thing, it may lead to great results. Many a man has been urged to a noble deed by the encouragement he received at a critical hour from some unknown and obscure disciple.

If you cannot do a great thing, identify yourself with one who can. Stand by him, identify yourself with him in public or private, by sympathy and prayer. Though the strongholds of evil are great and high, they may be swept away before an avalanche of snowflakes, any one of which would melt in the warm hand of a child.

Oh for more of that magnanimity, which is quick to recognize the matters that belong to certain elect souls—not envying, nor disparaging, but frankly confessing their eminent qualifications, and falling in to further and accelerate their success, which will be the gain of all!

Nehemiah

I was the king's cupbearer. Neh. 1: 11.

THE post was an important one. It gave its occupant the opportunity of coming into close contact with the king; it implied a character of unusual trustworthiness, since Oriental despots were very afraid of poison. But no one expected a royal cupbearer to do anything very heroic. He lived in the inner part of the palace, and was necessarily excluded from the great deeds of the stirring outward world. Nehemiah also was evidently a humble and retiring man. His response to the story of the ruined condition of Jerusalem was just a flood of tears and prayer to the God of heaven. And had you seen those tears and heard that prayer, you might have thought that just another flower was drooping, another seed falling into the ground to die.

But this was not all. These prayers and tears were supplemented by an earnest purpose, which was maturing with every hour. He gave himself to God to be used, if God would have it so, as an instrument in the execution of his recorded purpose. He was a man of faith. It mattered little enough that he was only a cupbearer, for that was no barrier to God; indeed, God might work more efficiently through a frail, weak man, than through the prince, the soldier, or the orator, since He cannot give his glory to another. What a glorious faith was his, which dared to believe that through his yielded life God could pour his mighty rivers! Why do we not yield ourselves in our helplessness to God, and ask Him to work through us, to fulfil his mighty purposes?

"We kneel, how weak! We rise, how full of power!
Why therefore should we do ourselves this wrong,
Or others—that we are not always strong!"

So I prayed to the God of Heaven. Neh. 2: 4.

ALL around the apartment in which this

interview took place were effigies of idol gods: perhaps incense was burning before a shrine, and filling the air with its aroma. But Nehemiah, though standing amid these heathen emblems, and in the presence of the greatest king on earth, thought little of either one or the other, and prostrated himself in spirit before the throne of heaven. Remember that thou hast within thee a shrine, a temple into which at any moment, even amid the excitement of an earthly court, thou mayest retire and ask direction of thy King and Friend.

He had been sorely startled by the king's question; he did not know that his face had betrayed him. He had, doubtless, intended to seek an interview with the king, and formally state the whole case (see 1: 11). But to be taken thus at unawares, to have to state his case on the spur of the moment, appeared to take him at a great disadvantage; and he instinctively turned to prayer.

How little the king knew what was transpiring, or what had happened between his question and the reply which was given, apparently, without the loss of a moment. But how beautiful is the example for ourselves! You cannot acquire this habit of ejaculatory prayer unless you spend prolonged periods in holy fellowship. But when you are much with God in private, you will not find it difficult at any moment to step aside to ask Him a question. The busy mart or the crowded street may at any time become the place of prayer.

"A touch divine
And the scaled eyeball owns the mystic rod;
Visibly through His garden walketh God."

Every one over against his house. Neh. 3: 28.
THIS is the way to deal with the evil of this world. We are all fonder of starting schemes, forming committees, and discussing methods of work, than in setting definitely to work for ourselves. There is a lack of definiteness, and we hardly know where to begin. But this verse suggests that every one should begin over against his own house. Try and make your own neighbourhood a little more like what God would have it. It may be that you have gone too far afield in search of work; you are applying to the Foreign Missionary Society, or are waiting for a sphere of service;

yet, all the time, there is that wretched neighbourhood, like a piece of ruined wall before you. Arise and repair it!

Meshullam repaired over against his chamber (ver. 30). Perhaps he was not rich enough to have a whole house; he lived in a single room, but he discovered that there was a little bit of the wall just opposite his window, which would not be built unless he set to it. Is not that a hint for college students, and for those who live in flats, or industrial dwellings?

The best way is not immediately to begin giving tracts, good though that is in its place. Ask God to give you an opportunity of showing kindness to your neighbours, so that they get to understand and trust you; and wait upon God until the answer comes— until He shall show you what step He would have you take next. This is the foundation of your bit of wall. Then plod on step by step, tier by tier. God will show you how. You may be unpractised in wall-building; but He is the Architect and Builder, and you are but a bricklayer's labourer at the best. Do as He tells you.

Remember the Lord. Neh. 4: 14.
IT was uncommonly good advice. Amid all the wise precautions taken by this man of sanctified common sense, he kept bringing the people back to God. God was amongst them. God would fight for them. God was going to bring the counsel of their enemies to nought.

This would make a good motto for daily living. If in all circumstances we would remember the Lord, the way would be brightened; the burdens would fall; our spirits would never droop; and songs of joy would take the place of sadness. Whenever enemies assail and difficulties gather like storm-clouds, look away from them and remember the Lord. When hemmed in on every side, be sure that He can help you from his holy heaven; remember the Lord. When heart and flesh fail, and you do not know what to do for the best, be sure to remember the Lord, and act as in his most holy presence. What a comfort and strength it is to see a friend, when standing amid a crowd of adversaries intent on your destruction, and to know that he will act and speak for you! But remember that Jesus is always like that.

You say that your forget so soon; that you

would remember, though at the critical moment you are betrayed into forgetfulness. But you must recall His precious promise, that the Holy Spirit will bring all things to remembrance. If only you will trust the difficulty into his hands, you will find that He will gladly undertake it; and as long as you leave it with Him, you will hear his voice rising in your heart, and saying, "Remember the Lord."

"Watch with me, Jesus, in my loneliness,
Though others say me Nay, yet say
  Thou, Yea;
Though others pass me by, stop Thou to
  bless."

So did not I, because of the fear of God. Neh. 5: 15.

THESE were great words. Nehemiah had a perfect right to take this money. Not a word could be said even by his critics, if he did. He was doing a priceless work, and might justly claim his maintenance. On the other hand, the people were very poor, and he would have a larger influence over them if he were prepared to stand on their level, and to share with them. It was just so that the Apostle argued in 1 Cor. 9. And from both we learn that often we must forgo our evident rights and liberties in order to influence others for Christ. Do not always stand on your rights; but live for others, making any sacrifice in order to save some— even as Christ loved us, and gave Himself for us.

If Nehemiah did so much for the holy fear of God, what ought not we to do for love? Love is more inexorable than law. Its exactions are more stringent and searching. Are we doing as much for love of Jesus as generations before did simply on the score of duty? It is much to be questioned if Jesus does not get less, of outward service at least, out of his followers, than Mahomet or Buddha does. But what He does get is infinitely sweet to Him, in so far as love prompts it.

All around you people are doing things that they say are perfectly legitimate; they call you narrow and bigoted because you do not join with them; they are always arguing with you to prove you are wrong. But your supreme law is your attitude to your Master. "I cannot do otherwise for the love of Jesus."

"Not I, because of the fear of God."
"Not I, but the grace of God that was with me."
"Not I, but Christ liveth in me."

I am doing a great work, so that I cannot come down. Neh. 6: 3.

IT was a sublime answer. Below was the Plain of Ono, where Nehemiah's foes awaited him. Let him once descend into it and he would become their easy prey; but he withstood their fourfold solicitation by considering the greatness of the work he was doing and the responsible position he was called to fill. Other-worldliness is the best cure for worldliness. Those whose affections are set on things above will have no difficulty in refusing the appeals of sense. Get your heart and hands deeply engaged in the great work of building God's Temple, and you will be proof to the most flattering proposals ever made by Madam Bubble.

Oh, children of the Great King, let us pray that we may know the grandeur of our position before Him; the high calling with which we have been called; the vast responsibilities with which we are entrusted; the great work of co-operating with God in erecting the city of God. Heirs of God and joint heirs with Christ! Called to sit with Christ in the Heavenlies! Risen, ascended, crowned in Him! Sitting with Christ, far above all principality and power! How can we go down—down to the world that rejected Him; down to the level of the first Adam, from which, at so great cost, we have been raised; down to the quarry from which we were hewn, and the hole of the pit whence we were digged! No, it cannot be; and as we make our choice, let us look to the living and ascended Christ to make it good. Put your will on his side, and expect that the energy of the power that raised Him from the dead will raise and maintain you in union with Him. For "your life is hid with Christ in God."

It was not found. Neh. 7: 64.

CERTAIN claimed the maintenance of the priests, and were challenged to show their name in the register of the priestly line. In all likelihood they were descended from the sons of Aaron, but through marriage outside the priestly clan, and through the fact also of the name of the mother's father being adopted, their names were not reckoned in the priestly genealogy; consequently, their claim for priestly maintenance and service could not be established.

Is there not something like this still? Men, who were called to be God's priests, drop out of the register of those who serve before Him. It may be they are not sure of their genealogy, and have lost the assurance of sonship; their spirit is no longer filled with the blessed co-witness of the Holy Ghost. God is afar from them; and, being out of harmony with Him, they are out of sympathy with their fellows. They are, therefore, rightly put out of the priesthood.

Now trace this matter back to its beginning. As likely as not you will find it originated in some worldly alliance. He that will be a friend of the world is necessarily an enemy with God. For a mess of pottage Esau loses his birthright.

But all this can be put right. There has arisen a Priest, who holds the Urim and Thummim in his hand: God's own Priest after the order of Melchizedek. "Wherefore it behoved Him in all things to be made like unto his brethren, that He might be a merciful and faithful High Priest in things pertaining to God." He waits to reinstate the erring soul, restore it to the priestly office, and give it priestly food and maintenance.

The joy of the Lord is your strength. Neh. 8: 10.

"THE sad heart tires in a mile," is a frequent proverb. What a difference there is between the energy of the healthy, joyous heart and the forced activity of the morbid and depressed one! The one leaps to its task, the other creeps to it. The one discovers its meat and drink in self-sacrifice, the other limps, and stoops, and crawls. If you want to be strong for life's work, be sure to keep a glad heart. But, be equally sure to be glad with the joy of the Lord. There is a counterfeit of it in the world, of which we must beware— an outward merry-making, jesting, and mad laughter, which hides an aching and miserable heart. Solomon compares the joy of the world to the crackling of thorns under a pot, which flare up with great speed, but burn out before the water in the pot is warm.

Ours must be the joy of the Lord. It begins with the assurance of forgiveness and acceptance in the Beloved. It is nourished in trial and tribulation, which veil outward sources of consolation, and lead us to rejoice in God through our Lord Jesus. It is independent of circumstances, so that its possessors can sing in the stocks. It lives not in the gifts of God, but in God Himself. It is the fruit of the Spirit, who begets in us love, joy, peace, long-suffering. Get the Lord Himself to fill your soul, and joy will be as natural as the murmur of a brook to its flow.

And such joy will always reveal itself to others. You will desire to send portions to those for whom nothing is prepared. Your joy will be contagious; it will shed its kindly light on sad and weary hearts. As Rutherford said, we have a new heaven in the heaven of every soul we bring there.

The seed of Israel separated themselves. Neh. 9: 2.

THIS is the beginning of the true life. Turn to the story of creation, and you learn, first, that God divided the light from the darkness; next, the waters of the clouds from those on the earth; and next, the seas from the land. It was only thus that He could effect his purpose of substituting kosmos for chaos. So, in the development of the inner life, there must be separation and judgment; the discrimination of the false from the true, the evil from the good. "Separate Me . . . for the work whereunto I have called them."

When God put his hand to man's highest culture, He separated Shem from his brethren; Terah's house from other kindred clans; and Abraham from his people. What weight this gave to those solemn words, "I am the Lord your God, which have separated you from other people. And ye shall be holy unto Me; for I the Lord am holy, and have severed you from other people that ye should be mine" (Lev. 20: 24, 26). It was not that God had no care for the great world; but that He desired to concentrate his attention on a few, that when they had fully caught his thought they might pass it on to mankind.

This accounts for the cry of the Holy Ghost through the Apostle, "Wherefore, come out from among them, and be ye separate, and touch not the unclean thing." We must be separate in our practices, cleansing ourselves from all filthiness of the flesh and spirit; in our pursuits, going with Christ without the camp; in our pleasures; and in our alliances. "Follow the Christ—the King! Live pure! Speak true! Right wrong! Follow the King! Else, wherefore born!"

The children of Israel and the children of Levi shall bring the offering. Neh. 10: 39.

IT was about this time that Malachi wrote the memorable words, "Bring ye all the tithes into my storehouse that there may be meat in my house; and prove Me now herewith, saith the Lord, if I will not pour you out a blessing." When a people has separated itself to God, there will be no lack in its house, no failure in its supplies, no lack for its ministers. So with the individual. All they that had separated themselves entered into an oath to charge themselves yearly for the service of the house of God. Separation is the negative side of consecration.

How does this touch you, my friend! What proportion of your income are you setting apart for the service of God? The amount that a man gives in proportion to his income is a sure gauge of the genuineness and depth of his religious life. The Jew gave about a third of his yearly income to God; do we come up to this standard? Yet we speak of the Jews with contempt, as hard-fisted and miserly. These old Jews might set an example to us newer Christians. How often we reverse our position from God's ideal! He puts us over his estate that we should send Him all the produce, after deducting what is necessary for our maintenance, and that of our families. But we engross the entire proceeds for ourselves, sending Him an odd guinea, or half-crown, when we can easily spare it. Let us see that we give at least a fixed proportion of our income, and as much more as we can. Do not forsake the House of your God; so shall the heavens be opened in blessing. "There is that giveth and yet increaseth; there is that withholdeth more than is meet, and it sendeth to poverty."

A certain portion should be for the singers. Neh. 11: 23.

IT was the king's command, and it was very right and sensible, because they enlivened and quickened the life of the entire community. A mere utilitarian spirit might have refused to maintain them, because they did not contribute to the handicrafts of the community. They only sang the praises of God; but they fulfilled a very important part in the life of the city, and they deserved the portion which was regularly contributed to them.

You sometimes feel your life to be comparatively useless. You can only say a kind word to those who are doing the main business of the world. When the brothers had wrought all day at the clearing for the farm; their sister Hope sang through the evening hours to cheer them and drive away their sense of fatigue. That was all she could do; but was she not deserving of maintenance? You can only sing your song of hope, and keep the heart of the toilers sweet and fresh. You can only get inspiration from God's heart and pass it on. You can do little but learn to detect, and translate into music that men love, the deep undertones of God's creation. But it is well. You are needed in God's world.

There are invalids, who lie on their back through weary months and years, that are the inspiration of their homes, and to their side the elders and the children come for counsel and comfort. Sing on, ye sweet choristers, that alleviate our depressions and start our hearts to high endeavour! Ye that by night, in sleepless hours, stand in the house of the Lord, praise ye the Lord when all the busy life of men is hushed! The King will see to it that ye do not miss your maintenance, your portion day by day.

David, the man of God. Neh. 12: 24, 36, 37, 45, 46.

HOW long the influence of David has lingered over the world, like the afterglow of a sunset! Mark the characteristic in him which laid the foundation of his supremacy over the hearts of his countrymen. He was pre-eminently "a man of God." Notwithstanding his terrible fall, his people recognized that his salient characteristic was Godward. Would you be one of God's men?

(1) GIVE ALL TO GOD. Too many live lives of piecemeal consecration, giving a bit here and a bit there, but never all. David surrendered himself to do God's will utterly, and in all, and so became a man after God's own heart. With what joy God's voice seems to quiver, as He says, "I have found David, the son of Jesse, a man after mine own heart, who shall fulfil all my will" (Acts 13: 22). Without reserve, holding nothing back, yield yourself to God, to be, and do, and suffer his will, whatever it may be.

(2) TAKE ALL FROM GOD. "It is not what we give to Jesus, but what we take from Him, that makes us strong, helpful, and victorious

day by day." Accept this as a fact, that in Jesus God has made all his fulness dwell. There is nothing we require, for life or godliness, that is not stored in Him; but the terrible loss of our lives is that we take so little. We have ourselves to blame if we are poor, and miserable, and blind, and naked.

(3) USE ALL FOR GOD. It sometimes appears as though Christian people were urged to yield themselves to God only that their lives might be more comfortable. But the supreme and final end in all surrender must be that his will be done, his glory promoted, and Himself magnified whether in life or death.

Remember me, O my God! Neh. 13: 14, 22, 31. THRICE in this chapter this humble man asks to be remembered. We cannot think that he expected to purchase God's favour because of his sacrifices and endeavours. Of this he was already assured. But being a redeemed soul, he desired that his works might come up in remembrance before God, and secure a reward. There is no harm in keeping the eye fixed on the reward for faithful toil in the Lord's service. It was a constant incentive in the life of the great Apostle that he might so run as to obtain; so finish his work that he might win the crown.

Note the three departments of service mentioned in this chapter, in connection with which Nehemiah breathed this petition. He had turned all Tobiah's household stuff out of the temple, so that the whole structure should be given up to the service of God. He had secured the Sabbath from desecration, so that its holy rest and calm were preserved intact. And he insisted on the purity of the holy seed being untainted by foreign alliances. Consecration to God, the Rest of Faith in the inner life, and the separation of God's children from the world, are the counterparts of these in our own time.

Shall we not humbly set ourselves to seek them for the professing Church? Nehemiah was an ungifted, simple-hearted man, but he was able to secure them as the instrument and channel of God's purposes. Why should not God work through us for the same ends. But, first, let us see to it that each of these particulars is being realized in our own personal character and life. Let every room of the heart be for God; let no voice break the inner peace. Then what God has done for us, we may confidently plead as within his scheme for others.

Esther

That every man should bear rule in his own house. Esther 1: 22.
ONE of the prerequisites in choosing a presiding officer in the early Church was that he should rule well his own house; "for if a man know not how to rule his own house, how shall he take care of the Church of God?" (1 Tim. 3: 4, 5).

When a man bears rule as husband and father in the love of God, there is no issue of commands which conflict with primary obligations; rather than that, his authority represents the divine authority. As Christ received his authority from the Father, so does a man derive and receive his from Christ; and in the recognition of his delegated right and ability to lead, the entire household becomes well ordered. The relaxation of the bonds of authority and government in our homes is one of the saddest symptoms of national decay, as it is among the predicted signs of the end (2 Tim. 3: 2, 3).

But, on the other hand, you must show yourself worthy to lead and rule your home. Your character must be such as to command respect. Those whom God has put into your charge require that you do not use your authority for selfish or capricious ends. Above all, love is the source of the truest authority. We count nothing hard or irksome that we do for those we love. Show love, and you will win love; and on love will be built respect, reverence, and obedience.

One of the most eloquent of modern Italians has said truly: "You can only obtain the exercise of your rights by deserving them, through your own activity, and your own spirit of love and sacrifice!" Christ's golden rule holds good in every phase of life— "In all things, whatsoever ye would that men should do to you, do ye even so to them."

Hadassah, that is, Esther. Esther 2: 7.

THROUGH this one girl-life God was about to save his people, though He was all the while hidden from view. The peculiarity of this book is that there is no mention of the name of God; but there is no book in the Bible more full of the presence and working of God for his own. His name is clearly in the water-mark of the paper, if it do not appear in the print.

We know that the meshes of evil plotting were laid for the hurt of Israel long before the fatal decree was made for the destruction of the entire nation; but here we find that God has begun his preparations for deliverance long before. In the beauty of Esther, in the position her uncle held at court, in the favour she won with the king, in the discovery through Mordecai of the plot against the king's life, there are the materials of a great and divine deliverance. God was clearly beforehand to the devil. The angels of light were on the ground before those of darkness were marshalled.

It is a sweet thought to carry with us always: God prepares of his goodness for the poor. He prepares the good work in which we are to walk, and the deliverances by which He will succour us in the hour of need. Do not dread the foe, be not fearful nor dismayed, as he draws his net around thee; God has prepared a way of escape, so that thou shalt be able to bear it. In the meanwhile, rest in the Lord, and wait patiently for Him; trust in the Lord; wait for the Lord; be silent to the Lord. He is more far-seeing, his plans more far-reaching, his help more certain, than all the stratagems of evil. God laughs at them. Into the pit they have dug, thine enemies shall fall.

But Mordecai bowed not. Esther 3: 2.

THERE was stern stuff in this old Jew. He was not going to prostrate himself before one so haughty and so depraved as Haman, albeit that he was the king's favourite. To be the only one in a city office that does not laugh at the questionable story; to stand alone on shipboard against the gambling mania; to refuse to countenance cleverness which is divorced from cleanness, and genius which is

apart from goodness—this is to do as Mordecai did in the gate of the king's palace.

Only God can give this power, since of ourselves we are as reeds shaken by the wind. Sooner might a single ear of wheat resist the breeze that bends all its companions in the same direction, than we stand alone, whilst all our associates bow, unless God Himself enable us. But God is prepared to enable us. Listen: "I will strengthen thee; yea, I will help thee; yea, I will uphold thee with the right hand of my righteousness." But the mistake we are so apt to make is to brace ourselves up by resolution and firm determination, in anticipation of some impending struggle. To do this is to fail. Live in Christ, look up into his face, derive from Him strength for the moment and at the moment; and often wrap about thee that exceeding great and precious promise, "I will make him to become a pillar in the temple of my God; and he shall go no more out; and I will write on him the name of my God." Oh to stand pillar-like amid men, bearing up the temple arch of truth, and inscribed with God's name, whilst the crowds go and come on the pavement beneath!

> "Greatly begin! though thou have time
> But for a line, be that sublime—
> Not Failure, but low aim, is Crime!"

Who knoweth whether thou art come to the Kingdom for such a time as this? Esther 4: 14.

WHAT grand faith was here! Mordecai was in God's secrets, and was assured that deliverance and enlargement would come to his people from some quarter—if not from Esther, then from some other; but he was extremely anxious that she should not miss the honour of being her people's emancipator. Therefore he suggested that she had come to her high position for this very purpose.

We none of us know, at the first, God's reasons for bringing us into positions of honour and trust. Why is that young girl suddenly made mistress over that household? Why is that youth taken from the ranks of the working-people, and placed over that great City church? Why is that man put forward in his business, so that he is the head of the firm in which he served as an office-boy? All these are parts of the divine plan. God has brought them to the Kingdom that He may work out through them some great purpose of salvation. They have the option, however, to serve it or not. They may use their position for themselves, for their own emolument and enjoyment, that they may surround themselves with strong fortifications against misfortune; but in that case they court destruction. Their position and wealth may vanish as suddenly as it came; or ill-health and disaster may incapacitate them.

If, on the other hand, all is used for God, though at the risk of perishing—for it seemed to Esther as though the action to which Mordecai urged her meant that—the issue is blessed. Those that love their lives lose them; those that are prepared to forfeit them keep them. The wheat grain which is buried in the soil bears much fruit.

The King held out to Esther the golden sceptre that was in his hand. Esther 5: 2.
WHAT a beautiful type this is for each of us in our approaches to God!

FOR THE REPENTANT SINNER. You may have said with Esther, "I will go into the king's presence, and if I perish, I perish." But it is impossible for you to perish. None ever perished at the footstool of mercy. God is faithful to his promises, and just to his Son; and He can do no other—He wants to do no other—than forgive. As you stand amid the throng that surrounds his throne, He will espy you, and accept you graciously, because of the God-Man who sits at his right hand, and ever lives to intercede. In his name you may come boldly and obtain mercy.

FOR THE SUPPLIANT. You have a great boon to ask for yourself, or another. The King's court stands open; enter and lodge your petition. He will be very gracious at the voice of your cry: the golden sceptre extended, his word passed, that He will answer with the whole resources of his kingdom. The answer may not come at once, or in the way you expected; but no true suppliant was ever turned away without his complaint or cause being graciously considered, and in the best way met and adjusted.

FOR THE CHRISTIAN WORKER. Surely Esther represents a Paul prepared to be himself accursed, a Luther, a Brainerd. It is a lovely sight when the child of God is so oppressed with the burden of other souls as to sacrifice all else in order to plead their cause. Surely such find favour with God; they are kindred spirits with his own, and He bids them share his throne. God will do anything for those who are consumed by his own redemptive purpose.

As thou hast said, do even so to Mordecai the Jew. Esther 6: 10.
HERE indeed was a turning of the tables! Haman doing honour to the humble Jew, who refused to do honour to himself. Surely that day the old refrain must have rung through Mordecai's heart: "He raiseth up the poor out of the dust, and lifteth up the beggar from the dunghill, to set them among princes, and to make them inherit the throne of glory: for the pillars of the earth are the Lord's." And there was an anticipation of yet other words: "For thou hast a little strength, and hast kept my word, and hast not denied my name: behold, I will make them to come and worship before thy feet, and to know that I have loved thee."

How evidently God was working for his child. The gallows, indeed, was being prepared, but it would be used for Haman; whilst the triumph that Haman thought to be preparing for himself was to be used for Mordecai.

This is not an isolated case. Anyone who has lived a few years in the world and has observed the ways of God could duplicate it with instances that have come under his own notice. Dr. Gordon told us once of a church in Boston that would not admit coloured people; and after a few years it broke up, and the edifice is now occupied by a flourishing coloured church.

Trust on, beloved friend, amid scorn, hate, and threatening death. So long as thy cause is God's, it must prevail. He will vindicate thee. Them that honour Him He will honour; whilst those that despise Him shall be lightly esteemed.

"Though the mills of God grind slowly,
    Yet they grind exceeding small;
Though with patience He stands waiting,
    With exactness grinds He all."

What is thy petition, and it shall be granted thee: and what is thy request? Esther 7: 2.
AMID the sensual conceptions of marriage that obtained in this heathen empire there was doubtless a consciousness in the king's breast of the essential unity between himself and his beautiful queen. She was his better self, and in her pleading he heard the voice of his own higher nature. To nothing less than

this could he have made so far-reaching a promise. It was not so much Ahasuerus pledging himself to Esther, as Ahasuerus, the king, awakening to the appeal of a nobler Ahasuerus, for the most part buried. Such is the power of a pure and noble character awakening a nobler life. Will you try by your unselfishness and purity to awaken those around you to see and follow an ideal, which shall presently assume the form of the living Christ?

In these words of the king we are reminded that God is willing to do beyond what we ask or think. Not to the half of his kingdom, but to the whole extent of it, has God pledged Himself, "according to the power that worketh in us." But our prayer must be in the name, or nature, of Christ; that is, the nature of Christ must pray in us, and God must recognize Himself come back through the circle of our intercession to Himself. The Spirit must make intercession in us, according to the will of God. When the unselfish, lovely, and holy nature of Jesus pleads in us by the Holy Ghost, there is nothing that God will not do for us, even to the whole of his kingdom.

"If ye abide in Me, and my words abide in you, ye shall ask what ye will, and it shall be done unto you."

"Whatsoever ye shall ask the Father in my name He will give it you."

Sealed with the king's ring. Esther 8: 8.
IN chap. 3: 10 the king took the ring from his hand, and gave it to Haman. It is evident that he had resumed it from his chief officer's finger before sending him to execution. It was now entrusted to Mordecai, because it gave validity to the documents that proclaimed liberty to the Jews. Notice those words: "The writing which is written in the king's name, and sealed with the king's seal, no man may reverse," and apply them to that sealing with the Holy Ghost, of which we read so often in the New Testament.

On the molten wax the ring, with its royal device or perhaps the cutting of the royal profile, was pressed, giving sanction, validity, and irreversibleness; so on the tender heart of the believer in Christ, the Holy Spirit impresses the likeness of Jesus. The seal does not leave an impression of itself, but of the sovereign; and the Holy Spirit reveals not Himself, but Christ Jesus the Lord, and aims only to leave the mark and superscription of

Christ on the character. The word character is used in Hebrews 1: 3 (see Greek). How wonderful, that as the image or character of the Father was impressed on Christ, so the Saviour's image and character are impressed on us! "Him hath God the Father sealed," says the evangelist. "Grieve not the Holy Spirit of God, by whom ye were sealed," says the Apostle.

This sealing us with the likeness of Jesus is God's attestation. It is his witness that we are born from above, and are become his sons and daughters. It is God's sign manual of his intention and decree that we should inherit an irreversible portion; and when God has once passed and sealed it, neither man nor devil can reverse it.

The Jews had rule over them that hated them. Esther 9: 1.
YES, my reader, a similar reversal awaits us in the near future! Now, the god of this world and his followers bear rule over us, and work their way with the servants of God. They butcher them like sheep, and scatter the ashes of their homes to the winds; and sometimes its seems as though God had forgotten to avenge the cause of his saints. But the hour is coming when the Almighty will arise on our behalf; and to him who has patiently kept his works unto the end, He will give authority over the nations. Listen to these great words: "Behold I will make them of the synagogue of Satan, which say they are Jews, and they are not, but do lie; behold, I will make them to come and worship before thy feet, and to know that I have loved thee." Words more applicable to the case of the Jews in the days of Mordecai, and to the history of the Church, it would be impossible to find.

But mark a notable distinction. In the case of the enemies of the Jewish people, there was no quarter. Destruction and death were meted to those who had breathed out persecution and slaughter. But in the case of Christ and his Church, power is viewed only as an opportunity of securing salvation and life. The Saviour said, after his resurrection, "All power is given unto Me in heaven and on earth; go ye, therefore, and make disciples of all the nations, baptizing them into the name of the Father, and of the Son, and of the Holy Ghost: and lo, I am with you alway." And the Church says, as through suffering she passes to the right hand of power, "Lay not this sin to their charge; but out of our persecutors raise apostles to carry the Gospel to the confines of the earth."

Seeking the good of his people, and speaking peace to all his seed. Esther 10: 3 (R.V.).

THIS epitaph on the life of a simple-minded, true-hearted man, might be yours also. Why should you not from this moment adopt these twin characteristics? Go about the world seeking the good of people. It does not always mean that you should give them a tract, or a little book. It is much easier to do this than to sacrifice your own good in order to seek theirs. You may be quite sure that some little act of self-sacrifice or thoughtfulness for a weary mother, or crying child, for a sick friend, or for some person who is always maligning and injuring you, would do a great deal in the way of preparing an entrance for the Gospel message. It is thus that the genial spring loosens the earth and prepares the way for the germination of multitudinous life. Count the day lost in which you have not sought to promote the good of someone Adopt as your own the pious Quaker's motto, "Do all the good you can, to all the people you can, in all the ways you can."

SPEAK PEACE TO PEOPLE. Soothe agitated and irritated souls. Throw oil on troubled waters. There are worried and anxious hearts all around us; a word of sympathy and earnest prayer with them will often remove the heavy load, and smooth out the wrinkles of care. Let the law of kindness be on your lip. Do not say sharp or unkind things of the absent, or allow your lips to utter words that will lead to bitterness or wrath. Seek peace and pursue it. And in order to this, let the peace of God that passeth all understanding keep your mind and heart.

"Come, my beloved! We will haste and go
To those pale faces of our fellow-men!
Our loving hearts, burning with summer-fire,
Shall cast a glow upon their pallidness."

Job

Job said, It may be that my sons have sinned and renounced God in their hearts. Job 1: 5 (R.V.).

TIMES of festivity are always full of temptation. The loins are relaxed, the girdle of the soul is loosed. Amid the general hilarity and the passing of the merry joke, words are said and thoughts permitted which are not always consistent with the character of God and his glorious kingdom and service. Job was not wrong, therefore, in supposing that his children might have contracted some defiling stain.

It is necessary for some of us to move in society, and to attend festive gatherings. As the Lord went to the wedding feast, and accepted Simon's invitation, so must we. The sphere of our life lies necessarily in the world. But when we are entering scenes of recreation and pleasure we should be more than ever careful to put on our armour, and by previous meditation and prayer prepare ourselves for the inevitable temptation; and when it is all over, and the lights are down, we should quietly review our behaviour under the light that streams from the Word of God. If we then are made aware of frivolous or uncharitable words, of jealousy because others have outshone us, or of pride at the splendour of our dress and the brilliance of our talk, we must confess it, and obtain forgiveness and restoration.

What a beautiful example is furnished by Job to Christian parents! When your girls are going among strangers, and your boys into the great ways of the world, and you are unable to impose your will upon them, as in the days of childhood, you can yet pray for them, casting over them the shield of intercession, with strong cryings and tears. They are beyond your reach; but by faith you can move the arm of God on their behalf.

A perfect and an upright man. Job. 2: 3.

EVEN God spoke of Job as perfect. Not that he was absolutely so, as judged by the perfect standard of eternity, but as judged by the standard of his own light and knowledge. He was living up to all the requirements of God and man, so far as he understood them. His whole being was open and obedient to the divine impulses. So far as he knew there was no cause of controversy in heart or life. Probably he could have adopted the words of the Apostle, "I know nothing against myself." He exercised himself to have always a conscience void of offence toward God and man.

Satan suggested that his goodness was pure selfishness; that it paid him well to be as he was, because God had hedged him around and blessed his substance. This malignant suggestion was at once dealt with by the Almighty Vindicator of the saints. It was as if God said, "I give thee permission to deprive him of all those favouring conditions, for the sake of which thou sayest he is bribed to goodness; and it shall be seen that his integrity is rooted deep down in the work of my grace upon his heart."

But the book goes on to show that God desired to teach Job that there were flaws and blemishes in his character which could only be seen by comparing it with the more perfect glory of his own divine nature. His friends sought to prove him faulty, and failed; God revealed himself, and he cried, "Behold, I am vile, and abhor myself, and repent in dust and ashes."

How often God takes away our consolations, that we may only love Him for Himself; and reveals our sinfulness, that we may better appreciate the completeness of his salvation!

Job opened his mouth, and cursed his day.
Job. 3: 1.
THAT is, the day of his birth. Probably there have been hours in the majority of lives in which men have wished that they had never been born. When they have stood beside the wreck of all earthly hope, or entered the garden of the grave they have cried, "Why died I not from the birth!" The reason for this is, that the heart has been so occupied with the transient and earthly, that it has lost sight of the unseen and eternal; and in finding itself deprived of the former, it has thought that there was nothing left to live for.

One of the greatest tests of true religion is in bearing suffering. At such a time we are apt, if we are professing Christians, to exert a certain constraint over ourselves, and bear ourselves heroically. We have read of people

in like circumstances who have not shed a tear or uttered a complaining word; and we have braced ourselves to a Christian stoicism. "I am sure you cannot find fault with my behaviour," said one such to me. And yet beneath the correct exterior there may be the pride and haughtiness of an altogether unsubdued self.

There is a more excellent way: to humble oneself under the mighty hand of God; to search the heart for any dross that needs to be burnt out; to resign oneself to the will of the Father; to endeavour to learn the lesson in the black-lettered book; to seek to manifest the specific grace for which the trial calls; to be very tender and thoughtful for others; to live deeper down.

"Nearer, my God to Thee!—Nearer to Thee!
E'en though it be a cross that raiseth me,
Still all my song shall be—Nearer, my God, to Thee! Nearer to Thee!"

But now it is come unto thee, and thou faintest.
Job 4: 5 (R.V.).
IT is much easier to counsel others in their trouble than to bear it ourselves. Full often the soul, which has poured floods of consolation on others, feels sadly in need of a touch, a voice, a sympathizing companion, as the chill waters begin to rise towards the knees, and the shadow of the great eclipse falls around. The fact of our having consoled so many others seems at such a moment to leave us the more solitary and lonesome. People have been so wont to be helped by us that they hardly dare approach us; besides, they suppose that all the fund of comfort from which we have succoured others must be now available for us. What can they say that we have not said a hundred times? and if we have said it, of course we must know all about it; but they do not know how wistful the heart is to hear it said to us with the accent of a sympathetic voice and the touch of a ministering hand.

Ah, it will come unto thee at last. The pain and sorrow of life will find thee out. The arrow will at last fix itself quivering in thy heart. How wilt thou do then? Thou wilt faint unless thy words have sprung from a living experience of the love and presence of Jesus. Thou must have a better hope than "the integrity of thy ways," as suggested by Eliphaz. But there awaits thee the personal fellowship of Jesus, a brother born for the hour of trial. He is the never-failing Friend, who sticketh closer than a brother. Put Him and his will and his choice between thee and thy sorrow, whatever it may be. Hide thee in his secret place, and under the shadow of his wings thou shalt enjoy sweet peace.

"Only heaven is better than a walk
With Christ at midnight over moonlit seas."

He maketh sore, and bindeth up: he woundeth, and his hands make whole. Job. 5: 18.

HAS this been your experience lately? Have you been made sore by the heavy scourge of pain, and wounded by the nails of the cross? Do not look at second causes. Men may have been the instruments, but God is the Agent. The cup has been presented by a Judas, but the Father permitted it; and it is therefore the cup that the Father hath given you to drink. Shall you not drink it? How much He must love you, to dare to inflict this awful discipline, which makes your love and trust, that He values so infinitely, tremble in the scale! "Despise not thou the chastening of the Lord, nor faint when thou art rebuked of Him; for whom the Lord loveth He chasteneth, and scourgeth every son whom He receiveth."

But do not look back on what you have suffered; look on and up! As surely as He has made sore, He will bind up; as soon as He has wounded, his hands will begin to make whole. Consider the reparative processes of nature. So soon as the unsightly ruin or chasm yawns, nature begins to weave her rich festoons, to cover it with moss and lichen; let the flesh be punctured or lacerated, the blood begins to pour out the protoplasmic matter to be woven into a new fabric. So when the heart seems bleeding its life away, God is at work binding up and healing. Think of those dear and tender hands, that fashioned the heavens, and touched the eyeballs of the blind, as laid upon you to make you whole. Trust Him; He loves infinitely, and will suffer none that trust in Him to be desolate.

We must be careful, however, that nothing on our part shall hinder the life of the Son of God from flowing through us, as the sap of the vine through every branch.

As a brook, as the channel of brooks that pass away. Job 6: 15 (R.V.).

JOB complains of his three friends. He was glad when they first came to his side, as likely to yield him comfort in his sore distress. Instead of this, however, they began probing his heart and searching his life, to find the secret sin on account of which his heavy troubles had befallen him. Their philosophy was at fault. They held that special misfortune is always the result of special sin; and since there was nothing in Job's outward conduct to account for his awful sufferings, they felt that he was hiding some secret defection, which they urged him to confess. Job felt that in all this they cruelly misunderstood him, and compares them in these words to one of the desert streams that are choked with ice and snow in the time of the winter rains, but dwindle and dry up on the first approach of summer. And when the weary caravans come to their banks, lo, their bed is a mere heap of stones. "They come thither and are confounded."

Is it not so with human friendships? We hoped that they would quench the raging thirst of our souls; this hope increases when they draw nigh us in days of sorrow; but how often they fail us—stones for bread, scorpions for fish, and scorching pebbles instead of water-brooks. How great a contrast to the love and friendship of Jesus! Not like a brook that dries in the time of drought, but like a well of water springing up within the heart for ever. He does not merely give consolation and sympathy, but He is what He gives. He imparts Himself. His promise chases away our fears as his Spirit reminds us of the words, "I will never leave thee, nor forsake thee." Nothing gives Him greater joy than to be the perfect circle of which earth's friendships are broken arcs.

What is man . . . that thou shouldst visit him every morning? Job 7: 17, 18.

GOD visits us with mercy every morning. Before we are awake He is at work in the world, baptizing it with dew, feeding the birds and wild things, taking pleasure in the jasmine and heliotrope, the honeysuckle, and the rose; and with all his care for his world, He does not forget man, whom He has placed there to be its tenant. There is no life so mean and abject, so suffering and wretched, that He does not visit in order to comfort and relieve it. No heart so forlorn that He does not knock at the door: no window so selfishly curtained and shuttered, at which He does not tap. "Open to Me!" the heavenly visitor entreats, "my love, my dove, my spouse!" Alas for us! that we keep the doors and windows closed to Him—as the poor widow to a beneficent friend, who called to relieve her, but she mistook him for the rent-collector.

But probably Job meant that God visits us in discipline, training, education. He is the watcher of men; not to detect their failures, but to discover opportunities of leading them on to richer, fuller experiences of his grace and life. Surely, as we consider all the time and pains which God has expended on us, we too may cry, with the patriarch, "What is man?" Man is more than we guess, else God would never take such time and pains with him. When a lapidary spends years over a single diamond, the most careless observer begins to appraise properly its intrinsic value.

Every morning God visits thee, with holy thoughts and warnings, with miracles and parables, with anticipations and forecasts—oh, realize how much thou art to Him; give Him love for love, thanks and loving recognition, a child's welcome and trust.

If thou wert pure and upright, surely now He would awake for thee. Job 8:6.

SO Bildad spoke, suggesting that Job was not pure and upright, since God did not appear to deliver him. The premises from which he argued were that God always delivers and prospers pure and upright men, and that therefore, if a man were not delivered and prospered, he was proved to be neither pure nor upright. The fallacy lay in the premise. It is not universally true that God delivers his saints from adverse circumstances, or prospers them with outward good. There have been in all ages thousands of devoted servants of God who have been destitute, afflicted, and tormented; and there are thousands of such to-day in prisons, in hospital wards, in every condition of privation and trial; but in none of these cases can there be the least imputation on the love and righteousness of God, nor necessarily on their fidelity and goodness.

God's arrangements for us are not governed by the superficial philosophy which would make material prosperity a sign of his favour, and adversity of his displeasure. There are many considerations besides. Our privations in the outward strengthen and ripen the inward. As the outward man decays, the inward is renewed day by day. We have to learn and manifest those passive virtues which can only mature in silence and sorrow. We must be taught to be largely independent of circumstances, and to find in God Himself the springs of unfailing supply. We must learn to carry the sentence of death in ourselves, that we may not trust in ourselves, but in the living God. We have to suffer with and for others. All these things worketh God with us to make us partakers of his holiness. But amid all our sorrows, He is always awake for us.

Yet wilt thou plunge me in the ditch, and mine own clothes shall abhor me. Job 9:31.

WE shall never get beyond the need of using daily the Lord's prayer. He has bound by the conjunction and the prayer for forgiveness with that for daily bread, as though to teach us that we shall need the one as long as we need the other. At the end of the best day that we ever spent, when we are not aware of having consciously sinned in act, or speech, or thought, we shall still have need of the precious blood. We may know nothing against ourselves, yet we shall not be thereby justified; because He that judgeth us is our holy Lord, and the standard by which we are judged is his own perfect character. A piece of cambric looks extremely fine to the eye, but how coarse to the microscope! Sheep look white against the dark ground of the early spring; but how dark if there should be a fall of snow! Our characters seem stainless, only because we compare ourselves with ourselves, or with others.

But, when our eyes are opened to see God, to behold the whiteness of the great white throne, and we stand in the searching light of heaven, we are as those who have just emerged from a ditch. I heard the other day of a woman being proud of having lived without sin for ten years! So we deceive ourselves. No, at the best we are sinful men and women, needing constant cleansing; even though we may be kept from known sin by the grace of Christ. It was at an advanced period in the life of the great Apostle, and when he lived nearest God, that he realized himself to be the chief of sinners.

"I know not what I am, but only know
I have had glimpses tongue may never speak:

No more I balance human joy and woe,
But think of my transgressions, and am
　　meek."

The land of darkness and the shadow of death.
Job 10: 21.

THIS represented the highest thinking of that
age about the future. There were gleams now
and again of something more; but they
were fitful and uncertain, soon overtaken by
dark and sad forebodings. How different to
our happy condition, for whom death is
abolished, whilst life and immortality have
been brought to light! The patriarch called
the present life Day, and the future Night.
We know that in comparison the present is
Night, and the future Day. "The night is far
spent, the day is at hand; let us put on the
armour of light."

For us, too, there is something better. We
wait for his Son from heaven; we look for
that blessed hope, the glorious appearing of
our Great God and Saviour Jesus Christ.
"As the waters of the sea are held between
two mighty gravitations, the moon now
drawing them towards itself, and the earth
drawing them back again, thus giving the
ebbing and flowing tide, by which our earth
is kept clean and healthful, so must the tides
of the soul's affection move perpetually
between the cross of Christ and the coming
of Christ, influenced now by the power of
memory and now by the power of hope."
It is said of the late Dr. Gordon: "Hardly a
sermon was preached without allusion to the
glorious appearing. Never a day passed in
which he did not prepare himself for it, in
which its hastening was not sought for with
prayer." "Yet a little while [Greek, how little!
how little!] and He that shall come will
come." The attitude of every believer should
be that of waiting: with loins girt and lamp
burning, let us be ready to meet our Lord.

"The Best is yet to be,
The Last for which the First was made."

Canst thou by searching find out God. Job 11: 7.
THERE is but one answer to that question.
No one can. The very angels veil their faces
before the insufferable glory of his face.

"The firstborn sons of light
Desire in vain his depths to see;
They cannot reach the mystery,
The length, and breadth, and height.

Do not be surprised, then, if there should be
matters in the Bible, in your own life, and in
the Providential government of the world,
which baffle your thought. Remember you
are only a little child in an infant class, and
it is not likely that you can comprehend the
whole system of your instructor. God would
cease to be God to us, if we by searching
could find Him out.

But though we cannot find out God by the
searching of the intellect, we may know Him
by love. "He that loveth, knoweth God; for
God is Love." There is a way of knowing
God, which is hidden from the wise and
prudent, and revealed to babes. Seek to be
strengthened with might by his Spirit in the
inner man. Let Christ dwell deep in your
heart by faith. Take care to obey all his
commandments, and then the Holy God will
come into you, and abide. He will give you
Himself, and you will know Him as a little
child knows its parent, whom it cannot grasp
with its mind, but loves and trusts and knows
with its heart. We cannot find out God by
searching, but we can by loving.

We can also find Him in the character and
life of Jesus. He that hath seen Him hath
seen the Father; why then ask to be shown
the Father? "What is Thy name, O mystery
of strength and beauty?" "Shiloh, Rest-
Giver," is the deep response.

Doth not the ear try words, even as the palate
tasteth its meat. Job 12: 11 (R.V.).
THERE is no appeal from the verdict of our
palate. We know in a moment whether a
substance is sweet or bitter, palatable or
disagreeable. Now what the taste is to articles
of diet, that the ear is to words, whether
of God or man. More especially we can tell
in a moment whether the fire of inspiration
is burning in them. This is the test which Job
proposed to apply to the words of his friends;
and it would be well for all of us to apply
the same test to Holy Scripture.

The humble student of the Word of God
is sometimes much perplexed and cast down
by the assaults which are made on it by
scholars and teachers, who do not scruple
to question the authorship and authority of
large tracts of Scripture. We cannot vie with
these in scholarship, but the humblest may
apply the test of the purged ear; and it will
detect a certain quality in the Bible which is
absent everywhere beside. There is a tone

in the voice of Scripture, which the child of God must recognize. This is the interesting characteristic in the quotations made in the New Testament from the Old. All the writers in the later Revelation detect the voice of God in the Old; to them, it is the divine utterance through holy lips. Hearken, they cry, "the Holy Ghost saith." God is speaking in the prophets, as He spake in his Son.

It is one of the characteristics of Christ's sheep that they know his voice, and follow Him, whilst they flee from the voices of strangers. Ask that the Lord may touch your ears, that they may discern by a swift intuition the voice of the Good Shepherd from that of strangers; and for grace to follow immediately He calls you.

Though He slay me, yet will I trust in Him.
Job 13: 15.

THIS was a noble expression, which has been appropriated by thousands in every subsequent age. In every friendship there is a probation, during which we narrowly watch the actions of another, as indicating the nature of his soul; but after a while we get to such intimate knowledge and confidence, that we read and know his inner secret. We have passed from the outer court into the Holy Place of fellowship. We seem familiar with every nook and cranny of our friend's nature. And then it is comparatively unimportant how he appears to act; we know him.

So it is in respect of God. At first we know Him through the testimony of others, and on the evidence of Scripture; but as time passes, with its ever-deepening experiences of what God is, with those opportunities of converse that arise during years of prayer and communion, we get to know Him as He is and to trust Him implicitly. And when that point has been reached and passed, nothing afterwards can greatly move us. Instead of looking at God from the standpoint of his acts, we look at his dealings with us and all men from the standpoint of his heart. Though He put us on the altar, as Abraham did Isaac, and take the knife to slay us, we trust Him. If we die, it is to pass into a richer life. If He seem to forget and forsake us, it is only in appearance. His heart is yearning over us more than ever. God cannot do a thing which is not perfectly loving and wise and good. Oh to know Him thus!

"Leaving the final issue in His hands
Whose goodness knows no change, whose love is sure,
Who sees, foresees, who cannot judge amiss."

All the days of my warfare would I wait, till my release should come. Job 14: 14 (R.V.).

THE Lord Jesus has chosen us to be his soldiers. We are in the midst of a great campaign: let us endure hardness, as good soldiers of Jesus Christ, and strive above all things to please Him (2 Tim. 2: 4). Amongst other things, let us be sure not to entangle ourselves in the affairs of this life. What purpose could a soldier serve who insisted on taking all his household goods with him on the march!

There is no pause in the warfare. We can never, like Gideon's soldiers, throw ourselves on the bank and quaff the water at our leisure. Every bush may hide a sharp-shooter; every brake an ambuscade. It becomes us to watch and pray; to keep on our harness of armour; to be on the alert for our Captain's voice. We wrestle not against flesh and blood, but against the hosts of wicked spirits in the heavenly places; we need to be strong in the Lord, and in the power of his might, and to take unto ourselves the whole armour of God, that we may be able to withstand in the evil day, and having done all to stand.

But the release will come at last. When the soldier has fought the good fight, the time of his departure will come, and he will go in to receive the crown which the Lord, the righteous Judge, shall give in that day. "Come," said the dying Havelock to his son, "and see how a Christian can die." Sometimes it demands more of a soldier's courage to wait than to charge. Remember that long waiting on the field at Waterloo, when the day passed from morning to evening. If you can do nothing else, wait. Be steadfast, immovable: lying still to suffer, to bear, to endure. This is fighting of the noblest sort.

Thou restraineth prayer before God. Job. 15: 4.

JOB'S friends were bent on discovering the cause of his sufferings in some secret failure and declension. This is why Eliphaz accused him so groundlessly. They did not know of those secret habits of intercession described in the first chapter. But this charge is eminently true of some professing Christians.

THEY RESTRAIN PRIVATE PRAYER. The closet door is too seldom shut behind them, or it is kept shut for too brief a period. They do not give themselves time to get into the mid-current of intercession and be borne forward by it whither it will. The voice of the Holy Spirit is barely able to assert itself amid the hubbub of voices within. They are so taken up with speaking of the Lord, or working for Him, that they slur over private audiences with Himself.

THEY RESTRAIN SOCIAL PRAYER. Their minister never sees them in the gatherings for intercession on behalf of the work of the Church and the salvation of the lost. They forsake the assembling of themselves with the saints. Like Thomas, they are absent from the gathering in the upper room, and miss the smile of the Lord.

THEY RESTRAIN FAMILY PRAYER. Surely we ought to gather at least once a day around the family altar. Where Abraham pitched his tent he erected the altar. A prayerless home is apt to become a worldly and unhappy one. There is no such keystone to the arch of home-life and home-love, as the habit of family worship.

How foolish, how short-sighted, how sinful, it is to restrain prayer! What wonder that your soul is famished when you fail to feed it, or impoverished when you neglect intercourse with heaven!

I was at ease, and He brake me asunder.
Job 16: 12 (R.V.).

THE other day, it was the Lord's Day morning, two sparrows fell from the leads of my church into the vestry, which has a lofty glass skylight. As soon as they had recovered from their astonishment at finding themselves prisoners, they flew up against this skylight as though to break through it to the open heaven, and then round and round the room. They were desperately afraid of myself and the verger, whom I had called, not realizing that we were as anxious as they to get them out again into the air. The only thing we could do to help them was to keep them from alighting to rest; so with long brooms and soft missiles we constantly drove them from every cornice and picture-frame on which they were alighted, till they fell exhausted, and with panting breasts, to the ground. Then we captured them and set them free. They might have said many a time, in the course of that encounter, "We were at ease, and they brake us asunder; they also set us up for their mark." But if they could review that episode now, they would doubtless see that it was love which forbade them to rest anywhere in the vestry, because it desired to give them their fullest liberty.

So with Job. God would not allow him to rest in anything short of the best, and therefore He broke up his nest. Is not this the key to his dealings with you? Oh, believe that behind the perpetual change and displacement of your life God is leading you into the glorious liberty of his children!

"Therefore to whom turn I but Thee, the
    ineffable Name?
Builder and Maker Thou of houses not made
    with hands!
What? have fear of change from Thee
    who art ever the same?
Doubt that Thy power can fill the heart that
    Thy power expands?
There shall never be one lost good."

Yet shall the righteous hold on his way.
Job 17: 9 (R.V.).

WHEN the real life of God enters the soul, it persists there. Genuine religion is shown by its power of persistence. Anything short of a God-given faith will sooner or later fail. It may run well for a time, but its pace will inevitably slacken till it comes to a stand. The youths faint and are weary, and the young men utterly fall. The seed sown on the rock springs up quickly, and as quickly dies down and perishes. But where there is the rooting and grounding in God, there is a perpetuity and persistence which outlives all storms and survives all resistance.

You shall hold on your way because Jesus holds you in his strong hand. He is your Shepherd; He has vanquished all your foes, and you shall never perish.

You shall hold on your way because the Father has designed through you to glorify his Son; and there must be no gaps in his crown where jewels ought to be.

You shall hold on your way because the Holy Spirit has deigned to make you his residence and home; and He is within you the perennial spring of a holy life.

It is said that there was once a debate in heaven, as to which kind of life needed most of God's grace. That of a man who after a lifetime of gross sins was converted at the eleventh hour, or of a man that for his whole career had been kept from destruction. And finally the latter was agreed to be the most conspicuous miracle. And there is no doubt that this is so. Yet for this also shall God's grace avail: and He shall enable thee to hold on thy way till heaven open to thee.

The king of terrors. Job. 18: 14.

SO the ancients spoke of death. They were constantly pursued by the dread of the unknown. Every unpeopled or distant spot was the haunt and dwelling-place of evil and dreadful objects. But the grave, and the world beyond, were above all terrible, and death the King of Terrors. It is difficult for us, who inherit centuries of Christian teaching, to realize how dark and fearsome was all the realm that lay under the dominion of death and the grave. What a shiver in those words, King of Terrors!

But for us how vast the contrast! Jesus has abolished death, and brought life and immortality to light. He has gone through the grave, and come again to assure us that it is the back door into our Father's house, with its many mansions. At his girdle hang the keys of death and Hades; none can shut the door when He opens it, and none open when He keeps it shut. He was Himself dead; but He lives for evermore, and comes to the side of each dying saint to escort him through the valley to his own bright abode.

There is something better. In the case of immense numbers, who shall be alive and remain when He comes again, death will be entirely evaded. "He that liveth and believeth in Him shall never die." They shall be caught away to meet the Lord in the air. Suddenly, in the twinkling of an eye, this mortal shall put on immortality, this corruptible incorruption. At his coming the grave shall be despoiled of its treasures, and death shall miss its expected prey.

"O death, where is thy sting! O grave, where is thy victory! Thanks be to God which giveth us the victory through our Lord Jesus Christ."

I know that my Redeemer liveth. Job 19:25.

THOSE words express the deepest and most radiant conviction of believing hearts. "He lives, the great Redeemer lives!" Man did his worst; the nail, the cross, the spear, were

bitter; but He liveth! Death stood over Him as a vanquished foe; but He liveth; Captain Sepulchre and his henchman Corruption held earnest colloquy together about the best method of detaining Him; but He liveth! He ever liveth: and because He continueth ever, He hath an unchangeable priesthood.

But it is not probable that his words meant all this to Job. The word translated "Redeemer" is Goël—the nearest kinsman, sworn to avenge the wrongs of blood relations. This conception of the kinsman avenger has been always in vogue in the East, where the populations are scattered and migratory, and our system of law impossible. Beyond the heavens Job thought there lived a Kinsman, who saw all his sufferings, and pitied, and would one day appear on earth to vindicate his innocence and avenge his wrongs. He was content to leave the case with Him, sure He would not fail, as his friends had done.

Beyond the sorrows and anguish of time he should yet see God; and he longed to see Him, that he might learn the secret purpose, which explained the sorrow of his lot. He had no dread of that momentous event, since his Göel would be there to stand beside him.

"Sudden the Worst turns the Best to the
  brave,
  The black minute's at end!—
And the Elements' rage, the fiend voices
  that rave,
  Shall dwindle, shall blend,
Shall change, shall become—first a Peace
  out of Pain,
  Then a Light, then thy breast."

This is the portion of a wicked man from God.
Job. 20: 29.

REPEATEDLY in reading this book we are reminded of the strong convictions entertained by thoughtful men among these Eastern peoples, of the sure connection between wrongdoing and its bitter penalty. The friends of the sufferer express their opinions in cold-blooded and unfeeling words; but we can detect their intense convictions beneath all—that special suffering indicates the presence of special sin, and that all wickedness is sooner or later brought to light and punished.

We are less able to follow the track of God's providences in these crowded, hurrying days; but there can be little doubt of the connection between wrongdoing and punishment. The law is immutable. As a man soweth, so shall he also reap. The triumphing of the wicked is short, and the joy of the godless but for a moment. He shall disgorge his wealth; he shall suck the poison of asps in the remorse and bitterness of his soul; the heavens shall reveal his iniquity; and his descendants shall seek favour of the poor. These things are still to be seen among us, in the rise and fall of proud men and their families.

Let us go into the sanctuary of God, and consider their latter end; and as we contrast it with that of the poorest of his children, we shall find no reason to envy them. Even though no human tribunal sentence them, they carry the harpoon in their heart, and sooner or later it will bring them to a certain and awful doom. It cannot be otherwise whilst God is God. The psalmist said:

"I have seen the wicked in great power,
And spreading himself like a green bay tree;
Yet he passed away, and, lo, he was not."

Shall any teach God knowledge? Job. 21: 22. WE cannot tell God anything He does not know already. The most fervent and full of our prayers simply unfold in word all that has been patent to his loving, pitying eye. This does not make prayer needless; on the contrary, it incites to prayer, since it is pleasant to talk with one who knows the whole case perfectly; and it is a relief to feel that God's answers depend—not on the information we bring Him, or even on the specific requests we make, but—on his infinite and perfect acquaintance with circumstances and conditions of which we are altogether ignorant.

"Your Father knoweth." Quicker than lightning is his notice of every transition in your inner life—of your downsittings and your uprisings; of every thought in your heart; every word on your tongue; of the fretting of that inward cross; of the anguish of that stake in your flesh; of the enemy that, like a sword in your bones, reproaches you with the derisive challenge. "Thou compassest my path and my lying down, and art acquainted with all my ways. For there is not a word in my tongue, but, lo, O Lord, thou knowest it altogether." Yes, He knows it all, and loves you better than you know.

Do not presume to dictate to Him; do not dare to say that some other way would be better, some other lot more likely to develop your best self. He knows every track by which to bring sons to glory; and that He has chosen this one is a positive proof that it is the best, the one most adapted to your idiosyncrasies and needs. His ways are higher than your ways, and his thoughts than your thoughts. You could not teach Him knowledge, or increase his love—then trust both.

If thou return to the Almighty. Job. 22: 23. THESE words introduce a most exquisite picture of the blessings consequent on return to God. They do not fit the case of Job, to whom they were addressed, because he had not left God; and they sound strange as coming from the mouth of Eliphaz. Still they are full of sublime truth.

THERE ARE THREE CONDITIONS. We must retrace the steps of our backsliding and wandering lives. We must put away unrighteousness from our home-life and business engagements, so that the tent may be free from idols. We must be content to lay our most treasured possessions in the dust at God's feet for Him to deal with as He pleases.

THERE ARE FOUR CONSEQUENCES. Whatever we give up for God, we shall find again in Him; He shall become our treasure. Prayer shall have new zest, new success; be full of delight; become the interchange of face-to-face fellowship. There shall be more certainty and permanence in our decisions and achievements. Our decrees shall stand, our work shall last, our path shall be illumined with light. Trouble and trial shall depress us for only a brief space, like the passing of an Atlantic breaker over a lighthouse rock, whilst a glad relief shall always follow close on disaster.

Let us ask for all this in our daily prayer. O God, be my precious silver; give me delight in Thee; hear my prayers; may I decree that Thou canst establish; let Thy light shine on my ways; lift me up above all my depressions and fears—that I may stretch out a strong hand to those who are in trouble.

"O, strengthen me, that while I stand
    Firm on the Rock, and strong in Thee,
I may stretch out a loving hand
    To wrestlers with the troubled sea."

Oh that I knew where I might find Him, that I might come even to his seat! Job. 23: 3. POOR tempest-driven man, he knew not that God was intimately near, nearer than breathing. There was no need for him to go forward and backward, on the right hand or the left. The Lord his God was nigh him, even in his heart; for his throne was pitched there on the sands of the desert, between Job and his pitiless accusers.

Thou needest not speak like this. Thou knowest where to find Him; thou canst find the way to his seat. He is to be found in Jesus, seated on the mercy-seat; in that room where thou sittest reading these words; in that railway train or store. No need to ascend into heaven, or descend into the abyss. Thou couldst not be nearer God, if thou wert in heaven. True, the obscuring vail shall be then removed.

"And without a screen,
At one burst shall be seen,
The Presence in which we have ever been";

but the dropping of the scales from our eyes will not make us nearer God than we are at this moment.

Now go to his seat, just in front of thee. Order thy cause before Him, and argue it. Wait to know the words with which He shall answer thee, and understand his reply. Only be sure that He will not contend against thee with his great power. Sometimes we are so bewildered and perplexed that we lose the realizing sense of God's presence; but there is no real difference. God is not really farther away; and nothing glorifies and pleases Him more than for us to go on speaking with Him as though we could see his face, and realize his embrace. Be still for a moment, and say, reverently and believingly: Lo, God is in this place.

Yet a little while, and they are gone. Job 24: 24 (R.V.).

JOB here describes the insecurity of the wicked. He may have raged against the poor and innocent; but in a moment he comes down to Sheol, is hurried to stand before his Maker to receive his sentence. As he had treated the poor, so he is treated. As he had devoured the houses of the innocent, so he is devoured. "How are they become a desolation in a moment! They are utterly consumed with terrors. As a dream when one awaketh; so, O Lord, when Thou awakest, Thou shalt despise their image."

For those who fear God there is a greatly contrasted lot. They receive a kingdom that cannot be moved. Zion may be a desolation, and Jerusalem a wilderness; the holy and beautiful institutions in which their early religious impressions were made may crumble; but they are come to the heavenly Jerusalem. The removing of those things that are capable of being shaken only makes more apparent those which cannot be shaken.

Where do you build your nest? In the trees of this world, that sway in the tempest, or may be hewn down by the woodman's axe; or have you learnt to build in the clefts of the Rock of Ages? Is your treasure in human friendships, which may change or be cut in twain by the sharp shears of death; or is it in the love of God, the unchangeable and everlasting Lover of souls? Let us look off from ourselves; from that diseased introspection that so confuses and dims our life; from the old fears that made us tremble and the old matters of which we must speak no more. And let us look upward and forward to that near future, which is so much larger and better than the past has been, and where we shall attain more than the heights of our dreams.

How then can man be just with God? Job 25: 4 (R.V.).

THIS is the question of the ages. Man knows that he is as a worm, and worse. For no animal, however humble, has consciously and determinedly broken the law of God, and defiled its nature.

Our first effort is to go about to establish a righteousness of our own. Repeated failure only aggravates our misery and chagrin, till we fall helpless at the foot of Sinai. Our vows are broken, the law of God lies shivered around us, the thunders and lightnings make us afraid. Then God in the Person of Jesus comes to our help. First, He meets and satisfies the demands of the broken law, so that it can ask no more. With his own hands He works out, and brings in, everlasting righteousness. And finally, He produces in us that faith by which his finished work is applied to our conscience and heart.

By the works of the law shall no flesh be justified in his sight; for by the law is the knowledge of sin. But we are justified freely by his grace through the redemption that is in Christ Jesus, whom God hath set forth to be a propitiation. God is Himself the Justifier of the ungodly. "Whom He called, them He also justified." He takes off the filthy garments, and clothes us in change of raiment.

But the condition is faith. We must believe in Him who justifieth the ungodly. They who believe are justified from all things. Being justified by faith, we have peace with God, through our Lord Jesus Christ. We are not saved by believing about his work, but in Himself. The Greek of John 3:16 might be rendered, Whosoever even believeth into Him. The motion of faith is ever towards the heart of Him who died, and rose, and lives. Then through our faith the Spirit produces a holy character.

How small a whisper do we hear of Him!
Job 26: 14 (R.V.).
JOB in thought passes through the universe. Sheol stands for the grave and the unseen world; Abaddon, for Satan, or for the great reservoirs in which the destructive agencies of creation have their home. With a marvellous anticipation of the conclusions of modern science, he speaks of the world as pendant in space. He passes to the confines of light and darkness, rides on the wings of the wind, discourses of the clouds, skims the mighty surface of the sea. All this, however, he deems as the outskirts of God's ways. It is but a whisper compared to the mighty thunder of his glory and power. If this is a whisper, what must the thunder be! If this universe is but a flower on the meadows of God's life, what must not God Himself be!

Perhaps we know something more of the thunder of his power than Job could, because we have stood beneath Calvary and seen Jesus die, and He is the wisdom and power of God; yea, we have witnessed the exceeding greatness of his power, according to the working of the strength of his might, which He wrought in Christ, when He raised Him from the dead.

Who of us can fathom or understand the power of God? But what a comfort to know that it is an attribute of his heart. God is not power, but He is love, and his love throbs through and commands his power. Be reverent when you kneel before the great and mighty God; but believe that all his power is engaged on the side of his weakest, neediest child. And more: cease not to wait upon God until He endue you with his mighty power, for service and for daily living. A Nasmyth hammer can break a nutshell without crushing or touching the kernel.

My righteousness I hold fast, and will not let it go. Job 27: 6.
JOB had an ideal and clung to it. Have you such? A vision of what you may be, and, by the grace of God, will aim at being. Bishop Westcott says: "The vision of the ideal guards monotony of work from becoming monotony of life." Bitter indeed is life for those who have not seen the heavenly vision, or heard the calling upward of the voice that says, Come up hither. Any life looks more interesting and attractive when the light of our ideal falls on it, and we realize that every yard leads somewhere, and every step is one nearer the goal. So someone has suggested that "If we cannot realize our ideal, we may at least idealize our real."

But there are many hindrances, many adverse influences to combat, many suggestions that we should let go our ideal. We have so often failed, slipped where we thought we should stand, limped where we thought to overcome by wrestling. The crags are so steep, the encouragment we receive from fellow-climbers so scant, the dissuasions and misconstructions—like those Job had from his friends—so many. But Jesus who inspired the ideal waits to realize it, if only you will open your heart and let Him enter. Do you hunger and thirst? then He will satisfy. He does not tantalize and disappoint the seeking soul.

"Have we not all, amid life's petty strife,
Some pure ideal of a noble life
That once seemed possible? It was.
    And yet
We lost it in this daily jar and fret,
And now live idle in a vague regret.
But still our place is kept, and it will wait,
Ready for us to fill it, soon or late:
No star is ever lost we once have seen—
We always may be what we might have been."

The deep saith, It is not in me: and the sea saith, It is not with me. Job. 28: 14 (R.V.).
IN this sublime chapter the holy soul goes in quest of wisdom, which is the perfect balance of the moral and intellectual attributes of the soul; that knowledge of God,

and life, and truth, which is only possible when the eyes of the heart have been enlightened to know; that radiancy of spirit which is enlightened and illuminated with God who is Himself the Light.

In a marvellous description of mining operations, which would arrest any company of miners in the world, if read from the Revised Version, Job declares it is not to be found in the deep. From one quarter of the universe after another, he receives the intelligence that it is not there. God alone has the secret; He only can communicate it, or give the dispostion to appreciate and receive.

We must deal with God. Looking away from every other source of illumination and satisfaction, we must have close and searching fellowship with Him. Dr. Gordon was wont to say that evangelical faith consists not in a glance alone, but in a gaze. "We live in a very busy, perspiring time, when a thousand clamant calls assail us on every side; but we must have more time for visions if we would be well equipped for our tasks." Let us then turn from the quarters where we have been accustomed to draw our supplies—broken cisterns, with uncertain and brackish water—and let us come to God, the eternal source of life and peace. Love and rest we want. Thy love and rest, oh, give us! From men and things; from the mine, the deep, and the sea; from the murmur of human voices, and the crosslights of human interests, we come back to Thee, our Home.

Oh that I were as in the months of old! Job 29: 2 (R.V.).
WE are irresistibly reminded of Cowper's sad complaint:

> "What peaceful hours I once enjoyed!
> How sweet their memory still;
> But they have left an aching void
> The world can never fill."

We are all prone to think that the earliest days were the best; and it is quite possible they were. But we must carefully distinguish between the exchange of the freshness and novelty of our first love for a deepening and maturing love, and the loss of love. The streamlet may not babble so cheerily, but there may be more water in the river. We lose the green Spring, but is it not better to have the intense light of Autumn in which the fruits ripen? There may not be so much

ecstasy, but there may be stronger, deeper experience. We should not reckon our position in God's sight by our raptures, and count ourselves retrograding because they have gone; there is something better than rapture: the peace of a settled understanding and unvarying faith.

Still, if it be really so, that you have left the old place on the bosom or at the feet of Christ, that your love is cooling and your spirituality waning, I beseech thee, get back! Remember whence thou art fallen, and repent, and do the first works. Jesus yearns to reinstate thee, and has permitted this restless longing for the past to come, that it may be with thee as in the months of old. Again his lamp shall shine above thy head, and the secret of the Lord shall be upon thy tent; thy steps shall be washed with butter, and the rock pour out rivers of oil; thy roots shall spread to the waters, and the dew shall lie all night upon thy branch.

I cry unto Thee, and Thou dost not answer me.
Job 30: 20 (R.V.).
IT may have seemed so to the sufferer; but there is not a cry that goes from the anguished soul which does not ring a bell in the very heart of God, where the Man of Sorrows waits, touched with the feeling of our infirmities.

I have sometimes gone to a telephone office, and have rung the bell, asking to be put in connection with my friend, but it has seemed impossible to get at him; either he has been engaged or absent, and one has found oneself speaking to a stranger, and the voice which replied has been unfamiliar. Thoroughly disappointed, one turns away. But this is never the case with God. And the comfort is, that He is most quick to succour those whose cry is lowest. As a mother goes about her work, she is less sensitive to the trains that thunder past, and the heavy drays, and the laughter of boisterous health, than to the stifled cry of her little invalid; and if there could be one thing more sure than another of awakening God's immediate response, it would be such broken cries as pain elicited from Job.

But the answer will come—nay, it is on its way, timed to arrive in the fourth watch of the night. Perhaps the delay is the answer, because the heart needs to be prepared to receive the great gift when it comes. Perhaps, like the Syrophenician woman, you have to give Christ his right place as Lord, and take yours amongst the dogs. Perhaps the answer is coming all the time by one door, whilst you are looking for it through another; but you cannot and must not say that God is not answering. All the time you are crying, the answer is to your hand, awaiting your appropriation. Go to the post-office for the letter: hasten to the landing-stage for the ship—it is in.

Mine integrity. Job 31: 6.

INTEGRITY is from the Latin word *integrita*, wholeness. It means whole-heartedness. It is interesting in this chapter to see what, in Job's estimation, it involved.

v. 1. Purity in the look.

v. 7. Cleanliness of the hands.

v. 13. Thoughtfulness for domestic servants and underlings.

v. 16. Justice to the poor and the widow.

v. 17. Willingness to share morsels, and to be a father to the fatherless.

v. 19, 20. Clothing for the naked.

v. 21. The refusal to depute to others help which one might render.

v. 24. The heart weaned from the love of gold.

v. 26. Refusal to turn aside to idols.

v. 29. Inability to rejoice at the destruction of those who had derided and hated.

v. 33. The frank confession of wrongdoing.

It becomes us prayerfully to go over these items, and use them as the catechism of our soul; for if this was the standard of character for one who lived so many centuries before the full revelation of Christ, what should not our standard be! How impossible, however, it is to live like this from without! We must enshrine within us the blessed Spirit of God, who alone originates and maintains that perfect love to God and man which compared to Job's maxims is as the heart to the body. Law is given as the expression of God's will for the regulation of life: but it is impossible to keep the law till we have the love; and it is impossible to have the love until we have the Lord Jesus Christ, through the Holy Ghost.

There is a spirit in man, and the breath of the Almighty giveth understanding. Job 32: 8 (R.V.).

ELIHU had waited whilst the three elder men said all that was in their hearts. He now excuses his youth and demands audience, because so conscious that the breath of inspiration had entered his soul. Wisdom is not with age; but wherever the heart is freely open to God, He will make it wise. We have received not the spirit which is of the world, but the Spirit which is of God, that we may know.

George Fox tells us that though he read the Scriptures which spoke of Christ and of God, yet he knew Him not till He who had the key did open. "Then the Lord gently led me along and let me see his love, which was endless and eternal, surpassing all the knowledge that men have in the natural state, or can get by history or books. I had not fellowship with any people, priests or professors, but with Christ, who hath the key, and opened the door of life and light unto me. His one message was the necessity of the Inner Light, the inward witness of the Spirit, his secret revelations of truth to the soul."

This distinction needs to be deeply pondered. We have been trying to know God by the intellect, by reading the Bible intellectually, by endeavouring to apprehend human systems. There is, however, a deeper and truer method. "There is a spirit in man!" Open your spirit to the divine Spirit as you open a window to the sunny air. Instantly God enters and fills. The Spirit witnesses with our spirit. The inbreathed life of God gives us light. We know by intuition, by fellowship with God, by direct vision, what the wise of this world could never discover.

If there be with him a messenger, an interpreter. Job. 33: 23.

GOD is greater than man, and by his love seeks to hold man back from his purpose. Sometimes He comes in the visions of the night; sometimes in pain and sickness. But we are too dull to understand the inner reason of God's endeavours to deliver us from the brink of destruction; and therefore we need an interpreter, one among a thousand, to explain the meaning of his dealings, and to show us the way in which we should amend our ways. How often has the sick visitor, the minister, the friend, interpreted God's purpose, enabling us to see light in his light. There are few higher offices in this world than to act in this way between God and our fellows.

To perform this function, however, we

need to understand two languages; the one of the throne, obtained from deep and intimate converse with our Father, while the other is man's native language of pain and sorrow. Each must be spoken perfectly before we can interpret:

"And to the height of this great argument
Assert eternal Providence,
And justify the ways of God to man."

But, as Bunyan truly says, the best Interpreter is the Holy Spirit. As soon as the Pilgrim has passed the Wicket-gate, he is conducted through the Interpreter's House by the Interpreter Himself. Are you perplexed as to the meaning of God's Word, the dealings of God's providence, the mystery of God's moral government? Ask the Holy Spirit to lead you through chamber after chamber, unfolding to you the mysteries of the kingdom of heaven. They are for babes—for the child-like and pure in heart. He will show you wondrous things out of his law.

He giveth quietness. Job. 34: 29.

QUIETNESS AMID THE ACCUSATIONS OF SATAN. The great accuser points to the stains of our past lives, by which we have defiled our robes and those of others; he says that we shall fall again and again; he imputes evil motives to our holiest actions, and detects flaws in our most sacred services; he raises so great a hubbub that we can hardly hear another voice within our souls. Then the great Intercessor arises and saith, "The Lord rebuke thee, O Satan; the Lord that hath chosen Jerusalem rebuke thee: I have loved with an everlasting love, I have paid the ransom." So "He giveth quietness."

QUIETNESS AMID THE DASH OF THE STORM. We sail the lake with Him still, and as we reach its middle waters, far from land, under midnight skies, suddenly a great storm sweeps down. Earth and hell seem arrayed against us, and each billow threatens to overwhelm. Then He arises from his sleep, and rebukes the winds and the waves; his hand waves benediction and repose over the rage of the tempestuous elements. His voice is heard above the scream of the wind in the cordage and the conflict of the billows. Peace, be still! Can you not hear it? And there is instantly a great calm. "He giveth quietness."

QUIETNESS AMID THE LOSS OF INWARD CONSOLATIONS. He sometimes withdraws these, because we make too much of them. We are tempted to look at our joy, our ecstasies, our transports, or our visions, with too great complacency. Then love, for love's sake, with-draws them. But, by his grace, He leads us to distinguish between them and Himself. He draws nigh, and whispers the assurance of his presence. Thus an infinite calm comes to keep our heart and mind. "He giveth quietness."

None saith, Where is God my Maker, who giveth songs in the night? Job 35: 10.

DO you have sleepless nights, tossing on the hot pillow, and watching for the first glint of dawn? Ask the divine Spirit to enable you to fix your thoughts on God, your Maker, and believe that He can fill those lonely, dreary hours with song.

IS YOURS THE NIGHT OF DOUBT? A holy man tells us that once as he was sitting by the fire, a great cloud came over him, and a tempta-tion beset him to think that all things came by nature; and as he sat still under it, and let it alone, a living hope arose in him, and a true voice said, "There is a living God who made all things." And immediately the cloud and temptation vanished away, and life rose over it all. His heart was glad, and he praised the living God. Was not this a song in the night?

IS YOURS THE NIGHT OF BEREAVEMENT? Is it not often to such God draws near, and assures the mourner that the Lord had need of its beloved, and called "the eager, earnest spirit to stand in the bright throng of the invisible, liberated, radiant, active, intent on some high mission"; and as the thought enters, is there not the beginning of a song?

IS YOURS THE NIGHT OF DISCOURAGEMENT AND FANCIED OR ACTUAL FAILURE? No one understands you, your friends reproach; but your Maker draws nigh, and gives you a song—the song of hope, the song which is harmonious with the strong, deep music of his providence. Be ready to sing the songs that your Makers gives.

"What then? Shall we sit idly down and say
'The night hath come; it is no longer day'?
. . . . . .
Yet as the evening twilight fades away,
The sky is filled with stars, invisible to day."

Behold, God is mighty, and despiseth not any. Job 36: 5.

WHAT entrancing assurances are contained

in this and the preceding sentence! To think that in all our wayfarings through this world One that is perfect in knowledge is always with us, and One that is mighty is pledged to bring us through! Nothing could be desired beside. This makes prayer new. It is a child's confidential whisper to the One who is attent to the lowest murmur, who cannot forget, who will not relinquish a purpose which He has formed though years pass, and who is able to do exceeding abundantly.

It is because God is so great that He despises none. If He were less than infinite, He might overlook. The boundlessness of his being has no ebb, fails of no soul He has made, and is as much at any one point as if He had no care or thought beside. In fact, those that man despises stand the best chance with God. Just because no one else cares for them, He must; just because no one else will help them, He will. This is necessary to his nature.

When a philanthropist adopts a certain lapsed section of the community, he does so because no one else will. It becomes a matter of honour with him that none of these, outcast by all else, should miss his help. And God has constituted Himself Champion, Guardian, and Saviour, of all who have no help from their fellows. Friendless, forlorn, helpless, despised, He recognizes and meets the claim of their urgent necessity. Bruised reeds, bits of smoking tow, half-consumed fire-brands, lost sheep, prodigal sons, waifs and strays, homeless, destitute, neglected— these have a first claim on the Almightiness of the living God.

Men see not the bright light which is in the clouds. Job 37: 21.

THE world owes much of its beauty to cloud-land. The unchanging blue of the Italian sky hardly compensates for the changefulness and glory of the clouds. Clouds also are the cisterns of the rain. Earth would become a wilderness apart from their ministry. There are clouds in human life, shadowing, refreshing, and sometimes draping it in blackness of night; but there is never a cloud without its bright light. "I do set my bow in the cloud!"

If only we could see the clouds from the other side where they lie in billowy glory, bathed in the light they intercept, like heaped ranges of Alps, we should be amazed at their splendid magnificence. We look at their under side; but who shall describe the bright light that bathes their summits, and searches their valleys, and is reflected from every pinnacle of their expanse? Is not every drop drinking in health-giving qualities, which it will carry to the earth?

O child of God! If you could see your sorrows and troubles from the other side; if instead of looking up at them from earth, you would look down on them from the heavenly places where you sit with Christ; if you knew how they are reflecting in prismatic beauty before the gaze of heaven, the bright light of Christ's face—you would be content that they should cast their deep shadows over the mountain slopes of existence. Only remember that clouds are always moving, and passing before God's cleansing wind.

"Green pastures are before me, which yet I
    have not seen;
Bright skies will soon be o'er me, where
    the dark clouds have been:
My hope I cannot measure, my path of
    life is free;
My Saviour hath my treasure, and He will
    walk with me."

Canst thou bind the cluster of the Pleiades?
Job 38: 31 (R.V.).

THE seven stars of the Pleiades always stand for the sweet influences of spring; Orion for the storm and tempest. In this sublime catechism, Jehovah asks Job if he has any control over the one or the other. As it is with the year, so with our life.

There are times when the PLEIADES are in the ascendant. The winter is over and gone, the time of the singing of birds is come. Doves coo their love notes in the trees, and the flowers gem the soil. Days of hope, of radiant light, of ecstatic joy! Days in which God seems to be making a new heaven and a new earth within us! Days when our Beloved shows Himself through the lattice-work, and says, "Come, my beloved!" Oh, tender influences of the Pleiades, we would that ye might ever stay, filling us with immortal youth! When God bids them shine, no one can bind them. When He gives joy, none can give sorrow. No mortal man can restrain the outburst of Nature's spring. You might as well stay the resurrection of the Son of God and his saints!

But ORION has his work as well. Storms

come; the drenching rain veils the landscape; the mighty billows are lashed to fury. But all works for good. The blast in the forest snaps off dead wood. The rain fills up the wells. Frost pulverizes the earth. When God binds Orion, man cannot unloose him; "no weapon that is formed against thee shall prosper." But when the Almighty unlooses Orion, like another Samson, he does his work of devastation, before which we must find refuge in the cleft of the Rock.

"God sendeth sun,
He sendeth shower,
Alike they're needful for the flower."

Knowest thou? Job 39: 1.
THE catechism of this chapter is designed to convince man of his ignorance. How little he knows of nature! Even though centuries of investigation and research have passed, there are still many questions which baffle us. And if we know so little of the Creator's handiwork, how much less do we know of Himself, or the principles on which He acts!

The knowledge of God is not intellectual, but moral and spiritual. Things which eye saw not, and ear heard not, are made known to Love and Obedience. Let the Love of God be shed through the heart, and the will of God be the ruling principle of life, and there will be given a knowledge of God which the research of the investigator could never gain. "We have received, not the spirit of the world, but the Spirit which is of God, that we might know the things that are freely given us of God . . . they are spiritually discerned." Knowest thou?

Dost thou know the exceeding greatness of his power, which He wrought in the Resurrection of thy Lord—that it is all around thee waiting to do as much for thee also; lifting thee, dead weight as thou art, to sit in the heavenlies?

Dost thou know the hope of his calling to a life within the vail, with the vail behind thee, and the light of the Shekinah ever on thy face?

Dost thou know the riches of his glorious indwelling, that He is prepared so to infill thee, that thou shalt partake of the very life wherewith He liveth and reigneth evermore?

Dost thou know the length, and breadth, and depth, and height, of the love that passeth knowledge; and Christ Jesus the Lord?

I am of small acount; what shall I answer Thee? I lay mine hand upon my mouth. Job. 40: 4.
WHAT a different tone is here! This is he who so vehemently protested his innocence, and defended himself against the attacks of his accusers. The Master is come, and the servant who had contended with his fellows takes a lowly place of humility and silence.

The first step in the noblest life, possible to any of us, is to learn and say that we are of small account. We may learn it by successive and perpetual failures which abash and confound us. It is better to learn it by seeing the light of God rise in majesty above the loftiest of earth's mountains. "When I was young," said Gounod to a friend, "I used to talk of 'I and Mozart.' Later I said, 'Mozart and I.' But now I only say 'Mozart.'" Substitute God, and you have the true story of many a soul.

The next step is to choke back words, and lay the hand on the mouth. Silence and meditation! Not arguing or contending! Not complaining or murmuring! Not cavilling or criticizing! But just being still—still, that you may feel God near; still, that you may hear Him speak. "Take heed of many words," said George Fox; "keep down, keep low, that nothing may reign in you but life itself."

The greatest saints avoided, when they could, the society of men, and did rather choose to live to God, in secret. A certain one said, "As oft as I have been among men I returned home less a man than I was before. Shut thy door upon thee, and call unto Jesus, thy Beloved. Stay with Him in thy closet, for thou shalt not find elsewhere so great peace." How good it would be to lay our hands on our mouths rather oftener, whether in silence with our fellows, or in the hour of secret prayer!

Who then is he that can stand before Me? Job. 41: 10 (R.V.).
THE first catechism had been on Job's knowledge; now it turns on his power. The pivot of the one was, Knowest thou? of the other, Canst thou? If a man cannot stand before one of God's creatures, how much less before the Creator! If we dread the wrath of the enraged crocodile, what should not be our dread before the wrath of the Eternal? Canst thou stand before Him? Canst thou strive against Him, with any hope

of success? Canst thou force thyself, unbidden and unfit, into the presence of the Most Holy? Thou couldst not intrude on an earthly sovereign; how much less on Him, in whose sight the heavens are not clean?

> "Eternal light! eternal light!
> How pure the soul must be,
> When placed within thy searching sight,
> It shrinks not, but with calm delight
> Can live, and look on Thee!"

But Jesus can make it possible. Through Him we draw nigh to God. We have boldness to enter into the Holiest of All by his Blood. We may, through Him, be able to say, with Elijah, "Thus saith Jehovah, before whom I stand." Jesus is the minister of the heavenly sanctuary, and in virtue of his office He is able to bring us into, and maintain us within, the Most Holy Place. He comes out to take us by the hand; and then, having fulfilled in us the good pleasure of his will, He brings us in and places us before the face of God for ever. Like Solomon's servants, we evermore stand before the king, see his face, and hear his words.

> "The sons of ignorance and night
> May dwell in the Eternal Light,
> Through the Eternal Love."

Now mine eye seeth Thee: wherefore I abhor myself, and repent in dust and ashes. Job 42: 5, 6.

THIS is the clue to the entire book. Here is a man, who was universally known as perfect and upright, one that feared God, and eschewed evil; who abounded in beneficent and loving ministries to all who were in need; to whom respect and love flowed in a full tide. He was not conscious of any failure in perfect obedience, or of secret sin; indeed, when his friends endeavoured to account for his unparalleled calamities by suggesting that there was some discrepancy between his outward reputation and inward consistency, he indignantly repelled the charge, and repudiated the impeachment.

But there were inconsistencies and failures in him that needed to be exposed and put away before he could attain to perfect blessedness and enjoy unbroken peace. If man could not discover them, and if Job were unconscious of them, they were, nevertheless, present, poisoning the fountain of his being; as a hidden cesspool, whose presence is undetected, may be doing a deadly work of undermining the health of an entire household. So God let the man into his presence; and, like Isaiah, Ezekiel, Peter, and many others, he at once confessed himself vile. The light of the great white throne exposes all unsuspected blemishes. Have you ever seen God! Oh, ask for that vision, that you may know yourself! In proportion as we know God, we abhor ourselves. Then Jesus becomes unspeakably precious. Through his death we pass into the true life, and begin to intercede for others. We never have such power for the blessing of the world as when we lie most humbly at the feet of God.

The Psalms

Whose leaf also doth not wither. Psa. 1: 3 (R.V.).

"IF a man abide not in Me," said our Lord, "he is cast forth as a branch, and is withered." The same thought is here. Thrust down your rootlets to the oozy river bed, and there is no doubt about your continuing earnest, patient, God-filled. The sun of temptation may strike you with sword-like beams, but you will have a source of supply which they cannot exhaust. The secret of an unwithering beauty is in the Word of God, delighted in and meditated upon day and night. And what is the Word of God, but the life of God translated into human speech?

Wean yourself from all beside, and learn to feed on God. Withdraw your rootlets from men and things, and let them travel to the river of God, which is full of water. Close other doors, and open those that lead out on to the terrace, whence you may behold the far-spread landscape of what He is, and says, and is willing to be to us all.

Note that word meditate. The root must lie in contact with the stream, and the soul must steep itself in the Word of God. We must give the truth time to enter and pervade our souls. We must have retreats, shut away from the rush of life, up and down the glades of which we may tread. These retreats are oftener found within the soul than without. Just as in the temple of old, there was Solomon's porch, where Jesus walked, so in the temple within there are closes and cloisters, where we may commune with our heart, and be still.

This day have I begotten Thee. Psa. 2:7.
THE Holy Ghost tells us that this was addressed by the Father to the Son in his Resurrection (see Acts 13:33). It was from the grave that our Lord stepped up to his mediatorial throne, whence all the hatred of his foes has had no power to dislodge Him, and never shall have. Death is a birth into the true life. Jesus was the Firstborn from the dead; we too are to be born out of the darkness of the grave into the Life Immortal.

"There is a beyond, and he who has once caught a glimpse of it is like a man who has gazed at the sun. Wherever he looks, he sees everywhere the image of the sun. Speak to him of finite things, and he will tell you that the finite is impossible and meaningless without the infinite. Speak to him of death, and he will call it birth; speak to him of time, and he will call it the mere shadow of eternity."

But is it not wonderful that He has begotten us also unto a living hope by the Resurrecton of our Lord Jesus Christ from the dead to an incorruptible inheritance? We are the sons of the resurrection. In Jesus we are already on resurrection-ground. Our sun shall no more go down, nor our moon withdraw herself. For us, at least, God hath destroyed "the vail that is spread over all nations."

Do not wonder, then, at the hate of men. They will rage, and imagine vain things; they will take counsel together. It cannot be otherwise.

Thou mayest expect, then, to be bruised by thy brethren, and hated by the world. But at such times Christ will come to thee, and give thee fresh accessions of his resurrection life, carrying thee into the hidden house of his abiding, and confirming the weak knees and the heart that faints.

But Thou, O Lord, art a shield for me; my glory, and the lifter up of mine head. Psa. 3:3.
OH, my soul, hast thou made God thy glory?

Others boast in their wealth, beauty, position, achievements: dost thou find in God what they find in these? Thou needest safety from the shocks of time and change: is He thy shield? Thou must have something outside of thee, to complete thy blessedness: is He thine ideal? Thy head is drooping like a flower-cup—it sadly needs the dexterous hand of the Gardener: is it busy with thee?

"Nothing resting in its own completeness
Can have worth or beauty: but alone—
Because it leads and lends to further
sweetness,
Fuller, higher, deeper than its own—
Life is only bright when it proceedeth
Towards a truer, deeper life above;
Human love is sweetest when it leadeth
To a more divine and perfect love."

God around us as a shield, God above and within us as an ideal, God lifting up the tired and sorrowful face—this was David's three-fold conception of his relation with God. All around men were filled with wrath at him. He heard their harsh voices, and what they said. Nevertheless he comforted, and stayed his heart with the words, But Thou, O Lord. Ah, what an instant change they make!

"We kneel, and all around us seems to lower;
We rise, and all, the distant and the near,
Stands forth in sunny outline, brave and
clear;
We kneel, how weak—we rise, how full of
power!"

Ah, these Buts! What a difference they make in our lives. There is always the hedge of God's care, always an illimitable reserve of power and help within our reach, of which we may avail ourselves; and we are so sure of it, that we lay ourselves down in peace to sleep, though the foe in thousands encamps around.

Know that the Lord hath set apart him that is godly for Himself. Psa. 4:3.
THE LORD SETS APART FOR HIS OWN ENJOYMENT. "A garden enclosed is my sister." Out of the wild prairie Christ encloses favoured bits of land, that they may become fair gardens in which to walk. God must have spirits with which He can commune; and therefore He shuts selected ones away in sick chambers, in loneliness, and in prisons, that there may be nothing to divert them

from the holy intercourse with Himself which is his refreshment and delight.

THE LORD SETS APART FOR FELLOWSHIP IN INTERCESSORY PRAYER. He leads three of the apostles into the shadows of Gethsemane, that they may add their intercessions with his. In each church there is a favoured band to whom He tells his secret anxiety for other souls, and whom He leads out in prayer on the behalf of them and of the world.

THE LORD SETS APART FOR SERVICE. Those that separate themselves from evil become vessels unto honour, sanctified and meet for the Master's use. Do not be surprised if you are withdrawn from the madding crowd, from the ambitions and interests of earlier years; it is the Lord's way of engaging you for special service.

We can never forget how the Holy Ghost bade the early Church separate Barnabas and Saul to their appointed ministry. They were separated unto the Holy Ghost. A similar separation may become ours. Let us live in the world as those who are set apart for God, like the Temple vessels that might not be put, as Belshazzar attempted to put them, to idolatrous and lascivious purposes. Oh to know what God means when He puts his reserve on the soul, and says, This is my rest for ever, here will I dwell!

In the morning will I order my prayer unto Thee. Psa. 5: 3 (R.V.).

IT is very important to consider the order of our petitions. No man would approach an earthly sovereign without taking time to consider how best to present his requests. He would consider the pleas on which to rely, the arguments to present, and the method in which he would be most likely to carry his case. Upon entering the presence of the great King, our Father, would it not well repay us to stay on the threshold for a moment to ask what petitions we are about to proffer, the order in which we should arrange them, and the reasons we should adduce?

It is manifestly a mistake to pray at haphazard. There is too much random praying with us all. We do not return again and again to the same petition, pressing it home with all humility and reverence, and arguing the case, as Abraham did his for the cities of the plain.

Study the order of the Lord's prayer—the adoration and prostration of soul before God prior to supplication for definite gifts; the acquiescence in the divine will before the prayer for daily bread; the entreaty for forgiveness before there can be a thought of deliverance from evil. Or consider the order of the High Priest's intercession for his own in John 17 before He pours out his soul in prayer for the world. Lay the wood "in order." Enter the temple of prayer through successive courts—Confession, Absolution, Ascriptions of Praise, the Te Deum, the broken sentences, the outburst of intercession, as suggested by the Church of England liturgy. At the same time, do not forget to be perfectly natural. Whilst the soul ascends the temple by regular steps, let there be the glad conviction of the tender love of the waiting Father.

And Thou, O Lord, how long? Psa. 6: 3 (R.V.).

YOU have been long in coming, love says. So miserly are we of the minutes, so leaden-paced is the beat of the pendulum, when our heart stands on the tiptoe of expectation. Moments lengthen to hours when we suffer and await deliverance, just as hours contract to moments when the heart is young and gay.

HOW LONG, LORD, ERE THE TRIAL CEASE? When we are entering into the furnace, we like to make bargains with God that it shall not last beyond a certain hour; but He never tells us, lest patience might miss her perfect work. He says simply, It is enough to suffer one moment at a time.

HOW LONG, LORD, ERE DELIVERANCE ARRIVE? Long ago we sent for reinforcements; and since then the battle has been waxing more fierce. We have looked eagerly to the horizon to see the relieving column, clear-cut on the skyline; but in vain. We think we can hold out no more. We have strained at the oar to the last degree of strength, and if some deliverance does not come to us, the fourth watch of night will see us drifting helplessly to destruction. "Where is thy God?" the enemy cries; and we are tempted to think ourselves forsaken and forgotten.

HOW LONG, LORD, ERE THE ADVENT BREAK? He said that He would come quickly—but the weary centuries pass; and, strain our ears as we may, we cannot detect his princely footfall along the corridor of time.

Cease, fond heart, thy complaining. Delay is not denial. He counts a thousand years as a day. He is coming on the wings of every wind; already He is nigh, even at the doors. Never a moment too early—but not a moment too late.

Judge me, O Lord, according to my righteousness, and according to mine integrity. Psa. 7: 8.
SPECIFIC charges were being made against David, of which he knew himself to be absolutely innocent, He would not have dared to challenge God thus, if the whole of his life were passing under review. In that case there would have been no hesitation in confessing that, taken generally, he was a sinful man. Similarly, God's children are often accused of wrongs of which they are absolutely innocent. In such case they have a right to declare their innocence before their fellows; then if this avail not to procure their acquittal, they must turn to God, and ask Him to interpose.

But what a question this suggests! Are you able, child of God, to declare that, as far as you have the light, you are living righteously, soberly, godly, in this present world? Is your life right-wise—that is, four-square with the demands of God's law, able to bear the test of his line and plummet? Can you assert your integrity? Integrity is derived from the Latin integer, a whole, a number unbroken by fractions. Are you whole-hearted? or, to use the grand old word, is your heart perfect before God? If it be, it matters very little what men shall say of your character. If a man suffer as a Christian, let him not be ashamed, but glorify God on this behalf. What is said is aimed rather at the Master than the servant. God becomes responsible for your vindication. He will arise and show Himself strong, putting to silence the enemy and avenger. Trust your reputation with God, and, in the meanwhile, go on doing his will. There is no harm in calmly and temperately attesting your innocence; but if this avails not to stay the storm, bend before it. Do not appeal to law. God will vindicate you.

Thou madest him to have dominion. Psa. 8: 6.
YES, broken, beaten, fallen, O child of man, thou wast made to have dominion. Not only over cattle, birds, and fish, but over thine own wonderful nature. Within thee there is a realm as full of multitudinous life as Paradise was when God brought the animals to Adam that he might name them; and over all this

thou wast meant to rule. Yea, thou wert made to have dominion also over the wicked spirits that are thy sworn foes. A royal, regnant, victorious life was that which thy Creator inbreathed. There is no reason, on God's side, or in thy original constitution, why thou shouldst not exercise thy dominion. Remember, thou wast made to have dominion.

We see not yet all things put under us. There is open revolt and anarchy within. The will resembles the ancient kings whose sway was limited by proud and strong barons. The animal creation largely defies us, and is in this the symbol of our loss of authority everywhere. But look away to Jesus. This old psalm is fulfilled in Him. His glorious nature rose, by its inherent glory, to the right hand of power. All authority is his in heaven and on earth. And in proportion as we identify ourselves with Him, and receive his life, we regain our lost dominion. He makes us kings and priests unto God. We share a life which neither death nor the devil can master.

What shall we say of the excellency of his name, who is not only our Creator, but our Redeemer, and who at such great cost to Himself has replaced on our brows the crown that sin tore from them? He made us to have dominion by the word of creation. He made us kings unto God by his blood. His name shall, therefore, be honoured through all the earth.

They that know thy Name will put their trust in Thee. Psa. 9: 10.
WE do not trust, because we do not know. If we were once to know God, it would seem as absurd to doubt Him as to fear that we should fly off at a tangent from the surface of the earth. Men complain of their little faith: the remedy is in their own hands; let them set themselves to know God. We may know about God, and yet not know Him. We may hear what others say about Him, but have no direct and personal acquaintance. "That I may know Him," said the Apostle.

The materials for the knowledge of God are all around thee; make use of them. Think of the promises by which God has bound Himself to succour those that come to Him; of the record of his gracious interpositions for his saints; of the necessity that He should maintain his character and reputation in the face of the universe.

Above all, argue, as Jesus bade, from your own heart. Would you give stones to hungry babes, and scorpions into childish hands? Would you desert a forlorn and hunted soul that trusted? Would you insist on a certain measure of agony before stepping in to deliver? Would you take delight in inflicting needless anguish? And will God? Trust may be read as the superlative of true. To trust is to count God true, though circumstances belie; to count Him truer than the melancholy forebodings of our hearts; to count Him our truest and tenderest Friend. "Yet let God be true, though every man is proved to be a liar."

But for all this, you must make time. You cannot know a friend in hurried interviews, much less God. So you must steep yourself in deep, long thoughts of his nearness and love.

Why standest Thou afar off, O Lord. Psa. 10: 1.

MEN in sorrow do not always speak wisely; and they ask many questions which God does not answer. Here is one. God does not stand afar off and hide Himself in times of trouble. As the psalmist sings, in a happier mood, "He is a very present help in time of trouble." But He permits trouble to pursue us, as though He were indifferent to its overwhelming pressure; that we may be brought to an end of ourselves and led to discover the treasures of darkness, the unmeasurable gains of tribulation. No cross, no crown. No pain, no gain.

We may be sure that He who permits the suffering is with us in it. The form of the Fourth may be hard to distinguish, but it is there in the fire. It may be that we shall only see Him when the trial is passing; but we must dare to believe that He never leaves the crucible. Our eyes are holden; and we cannot behold Him whom our soul loveth. It is dark —the bandages blind us so that we cannot see the form of our High Priest. But He is there, deeply touched. Let us not rely on feeling, but on faith in his unswerving fidelity; and though we see Him not, let us talk to Him in whispers as though we could detect Him.

> "I take the pain, Lord Jesus, from
>   thine own hand,
> The strength to bear it bravely, Thou
>   wilt command."

Directly we begin to speak to Jesus, as being literally present, though his presence is veiled, there comes an answering voice which shows that He is in the shadow, keeping watch upon his own. Do not be afraid of the darkness. Behind the cloud, the sun is shining. Little child, your Father is as near when you journey through the dark tunnel as when under the open heaven! Go nearer, and you will feel Him!

The Lord trieth the righteous. Psa. 11: 5.

DO not be surprised if you are passing through trials. The righteous Lord is exercising you towards righteousness, that your face may ever behold his in unswerving communion. As the trainer of a young athlete will place him, now in one position, and again in another, to call certain muscles into play, to strengthen them by use, and to make the whole organization supple and subservient to the impulses of the soul, so God tries us—to call into operation, and test by use, each faculty of our being.

> "Trials make the promise sweet,
>   Trials give new life to prayer;
> Trials bring us to his feet,
>   Lay us low, and keep us there."

There is a great difference between the temptings of Satan and the tryings of the Lord. The former are intended to make us fall; the great adversary takes pleasure in showing how weak and sinful we are, and in casting us down to destruction. The latter, that we may be led out towards faith, patience, courage, meekness, and other-worldliness. "Tribulation worketh patience, and patience experience, and experience hope." Whatever spiritual power is latent within us, we may be unaware of its value or helpfulness till it is called into exercise by trial. But when once it has been summoned into manifestation, it becomes the invaluable possession of all after time.

There is this consolation in trial, that at least we are not reprobates. The Lord trieth the righteous. The lapidary does not waste his time in cutting common pebbles. If we endure chastisement, we are clearly not bastards, but sons. Our Father loves us too much to let us miss the rich fruit that is to reward us when all the pruning is over.

The words of the Lord are pure words, as silver tried in a furnace of earth. Psa. 12: 6.
WHAT a contrast is presented in this Psalm between God's words and man's! "They speak vanity, with flattering lip and double heart." God never flatters; his words are absolutely pure because they have passed through the furnace of his holiness, but they are therefore absolutely reliable and trustworthy.

As silver enriches its owner, so does the Word of God enrich its lovers. Nothing so strengthens the intellect, clears the judgment, enlarges the views, purifies the taste, quickens the imagination, and educates the whole man. The humblest day-labourer who imbibes the Bible becomes rich in thought and speech, and able to dispense his riches to others.

As silver is beautiful to the eye, so fair is the Word of God. After a boy born blind had been suddenly possessed of sight through an operation by a skilful oculist, his mother led him out-of-doors, took off the bandages, and gave him his first view of sunshine, sky, and flowers. "Oh, mother," he cried, "why did you never tell me it was so beautiful?" With starting tears, she said, "I tried to tell you, my dear, but you could not understand me." We need opened eyes, and then the Bible is more to be desired than fine gold.

As silver is pure, so is the Word of God; and it purifies. It has been the main purifying agent of the world. Though it deals with the corruptions of the human heart, it does so in such a delicate and holy manner as to excite within us something of the abhorrence of the Holy God. Like the passage of water through a sieve, it cleanses the heart and life.

I will sing unto the Lord, because He hath dealt bountifully with me. Psa. 13: 6.
HERE is the man who had sorrow in his heart all the day breaking into song! We do not find that his troubles were any less. The enemy was still exalted over him, and boasted of having prevailed; it seemed indeed as though he must soon sleep the sleep of death. But he never let go his trust. Whatever were his outward discomforts and trials, he clung to his God and waited patiently for Him; with the result that out of his stormy griefs he built a Bethel, and in the midst of his anguish broke out into song.

When we are sitting under the shadow of severe trial, God can wrap us about with the garment of praise, and fill our mouths with singing. Although the fig-tree does not blossom, and there is no fruit in the vines, yet the soul may rejoice in the Lord, and joy in the God of salvation. You cannot starve a man who is feeding on God's promises; and you cannot make that man or woman wretched who has a clean conscience, the smile of God, and the love of Jesus in the soul.

When brave old Thomas Halyburton lost his much-loved son, he made this record: "This day has been a day to be remembered. O my soul never forget what this day I reached. My soul had smiles that almost wasted nature. Oh, what a sweet day! About half an hour after the Sabbath, my child, after a sharp conflict, slept pleasantly in Jesus, to whom pleasantly he was so often given. . . . Jesus came to me in the third watch of the night, walking upon the waters. . . He stilled the tempest in my soul, and lo! there was a great calm." When God is bereaving us of all else, He may so fill us with Himself that we shall magnify his bountifulness.

When the Lord bringeth back the captivity of his people. Psa. 14: 7.
IT is good to have an eye on the future, even though we get sometimes a little weary of waiting, and impatient of delay. Here a captive soul transports itself to the hours when its captivity shall be ended; and although it cannot altogether suppress the "Oh!" of longing desire, it dilates with ecstasy, as it anticipates the outburst of joy that shall hail the divine deliverance.

Let us look on and up. Bunyan tells us that the heart of the Pilgrim "waxed warm about the place whither he was going." A real lover of Christ, who knows something of the law of sin in his members, and of the dull weight of this mortal tabernacle, is apt to have, at times, eager desires for his home and his glorious inheritance. Paul was one of the most eager of workers, but he was ever dwelling on the blessed hope.

"When," exclaimed Baxter, "when, O my soul, hast thou most forgot thy wintry sorrows? Is it not when thou hast got above, closest to Jesus Christ, and hast conversed with Him, and viewed the mansions of glory, and filled thyself with sweet foretastes, and talked with the inhabitants of the higher world?" Such devout anticipations do not slacken our work down here during this little while. It is said of Samuel Rutherford that he was always studying, always preaching, and always visiting the sick; but it was he who exclaimed, "Oh, time, run fast! Oh, fair day, when wilt thou dawn? Oh, shadows, flee away! Oh, well-beloved Bridegroom, be Thou to me like the roe or the young hart on the mountains!"

"The best is yet to be—
The last, for which the first was made."

Lord, who shall sojourn in thy tabernacle? who shall dwell in thy holy hill? Psa. 15: 1 (marg.).

THIS holy soul was not content to stand in the outer court without the sacred tent; he coveted to enter where the High Priest entered, and to live there. It was impossible then; the way into the Holiest was not made manifest. No ordinary worshipper might pass the Vail, and the high priest who passed it once a year remained but a few moments.

How marvellously different our experience may be! We have boldness to enter into the holy place, and remain there, by the blood of Jesus; and, by the enablings of his Priesthood, we may spend our entire lives under the consciousness of the presence and favour of God. It is much like the servants of Solomon, to stand before our King, and to hear Him speaking, bidding us either to perform his errands, or fold the wings of activity in rapt communion.

This is not your experience? Then look carefully through the conditions which this Psalm enumerates. Perhaps you are not transparently truthful; or your tongue is not carefully controlled; or you are not perfectly honourable in your business dealings; or you do not know the power of the blood of Christ, as it cleanses from dead works to serve the living God.

It is worth any sacrifice to maintain this habit of indwelling the Most Holy Place. Ask that it may become your second nature. The Lord Jesus will secure this, since He was appointed for us in things that pertain to God. Whenever anything in the inner life seems faulty and deficient, we may turn with unabated confidence to our High Priest, asking Him to adjust it, to bring us into the presence of God, and to keep us there.

Thou wilt not leave my soul in Hades. Psa. 16: 10.

THIS hymn is for ever sacred because of its application by the Holy Ghost to our Saviour's resurrection (Acts 2). It was as though our Lord had stayed his soul upon these words as He left this world and entered the unseen. The last words He uttered were of committal to his Father, and then He commenced to traverse the land of shadow. "He that ascended is He that first descended into the lower parts of the earth." The Apostle Peter says that He went to visit the spirits in prison. Whither He went is not material—it is enough for our purpose that He sang, as He went, this hymn of immortal hope. Sure that He was the Father's beloved, He knew that He would not be left in Hades, nor suffered to see corruption. He knew that there was a path of life somewhere, which God would show.

Whenever you are stepping down into the dark, unable to see a hand's-breadth before you, and just letting the foot fall from step to step—it may be because of some act of obedience to conscience, or because you are called to enter the unknown and untried, or even death itself—cheer your heart with this holy Psalm. God will never desert the soul that absolutely honours and obeys Him. His way leads to the light through the dark, to the deathless through death, to the abounding fruit-bearing through desertion and loneliness. How lonely the vine-stock is through the winter! Follow Him, He will show.

"She is sinking very fast," whispered an attendant in the dying chamber of a godly woman, "No, no," was the quick response of the departing saint, who had overheard the words: "no; I am not sinking; I am in the arms of my Saviour."

I shall behold Thy face in righteousness. I shall be satisfied when I awake. Psa. 17: 15.

TO a good man, then, this is the world of dream and shadow, and death is the awakening. We are like men asleep in some chamber that looks towards the eastern sky. Outside is the day with its revealing beams, but our heavy eyes are closed to it all. "Here and there, some lighter sleeper with thinner eyelids or face turned to the sun is half conscious of a vague brightness and feels the light, though he sees not the wealth of colour it reveals. Such souls are our saints and prophets; but most of us sleep on unconscious." But the moment is at hand when we shall awake and start up and declare ourselves fools for having counted dreams as realities, whilst we were oblivious to the eternal realities.

When we awake we shall behold the face of God. Likeness is properly "form," and is the same word employed in reference to Moses, who saw the similitude of the Lord. We shall see Him as He is. There will be an outward revelation and manifestation of his lovely and holy character, and it will satisfy us completely. "The glory of God in the face of Jesus Christ." And we shall be satisfied. The mind will be satisfied with his truth, the heart with his love, the will with his authority. We shall need nothing else. Heaven itself, with its outspread mystery of beauty, will not divert our gaze from God, nor contribute to our satisfaction. To know God, to stand before Him, to realize that we are accepted in the righteousness of the Well-beloved— this will be enough for evermore.

"This life's a dream, an empty show;
But the bright world to which I go
Hath joys substantial and sincere:
When shall I wake, and find me there?"

Thy gentleness hath made me great. Psa. 18: 35.

THE Nasmyth hammer which can pulverize blocks of tough metal, will break the shell of a nut without hurting the kernel. In this it resembles this Psalm, in the earlier part of which there is one of the grandest descriptions that words can give of God's mighty interposition on behalf of his threatened child. But here we are told that it is the divine gentleness which has made him great. It is as though God's power were exerted against our foes, whilst our education is undertaken by his love.

Review your life. See the perils from which you have been rescued; the process of your education; the slow degrees by which you have climbed to any eminence of Christian character; the method by which you have attained the power of influencing others: is it not all attributable to the gentleness of the Good Shepherd? Not by sudden cataclysms and catastrophes; not by the earthquake, the fire, or the hurricane; not even by the stringent requirements of law; but by a succession of tenderest, gentlest movements of the Divine Spirit. He has remonstrated in whispered accents; He has seemed grieved and sad; He has turned and looked; He has sent a message by a woman's lips; He has put a little child into your life to lead you; He has poured on you one continual stream of sunshine. Now, it has been the distilling of dew; and again, soft showers on the mown grass; and through all, the purpose has run of eliminating the self-life, and leading you to the full stature of the perfect man. The strongest soul I ever knew, one who seemed to have been fashioned by God's mightiest strokes, was wont, in life's eventide, to attribute all to the effect of God's gentleness.

Cleanse Thou me from secret faults. Psa. 19: 12.

IT is not likely that we shall be kept from the great transgression unless we are preserved from presumptuous sins; and these in turn will befall us unless we have been cleansed from hidden faults. Just as the germ of disease taken into the system will presently reveal itself in an outburst of malignant fever, so hidden faults flower out into presumptuous sins, and these into great transgression. "Then lust, when it hath conceived, beareth sin; and the sin, when it is full-grown bringeth forth death."

FIRST, we need forgiveness for secret sins. The Jewish law made large provisions for sins of ignorance. A man might unawares walk across a grave, or touch some article of furniture which was ceremonially unclean, and so become defiled. Even though unconscious of actual transgression, he would find his communion with God broken. Thus, after the holiest day we have ever spent we need to ask for cleansing in the precious blood, for sins which God has discerned, but which in the twilight of our ignorance, and because we compared ourselves with those beneath us in spiritual attainment, have escaped notice.

NEXT, we need deliverance from the love and power of sin, in lower depths than we have ever realized. We desire to pass muster at the bar, not only of our neighbours and ourselves, but of God. We desire that the Spirit should antagonize the flesh in depths below the reach of the plumb-line of our consciousness. We desire the inner purity of heart. But this is peculiarly God's prerogative. It is his work to cleanse the thoughts of our hearts by the inspiration of his Holy Spirit. "Cleanse THOU me."

Now know I that the Lord saveth his Anointed.
Psa. 20: 6.

THIS was no doubt true of David as the anointed king of Israel, and of the Lord Jesus for whom the Father hath promised that He will subdue all things under Him; but it is also true of every saint who has been anointed with the Holy Ghost. Christian means an anointed one. Alas, that in so many cases the name is a misnomer! And men cannot claim the saving strength of God's right hand because they have not bent head and heart beneath the chrism of the Holy Spirit. How is it with thee? Art thou included in what Paul said, "He that anointeth us is God"; and in what John said, "The anointing which has once been received, abideth"? If so, there can be no doubt that Jehovah will ever save thee with a present-tense salvation. He saveth those whom He anointeth with the saving strength of his right hand.

Dost thou doubt this? Sayest thou that the annoyances and solicitations, the pitfalls and snares, the antagonisms and temptations of thy life, are so great as to offer an insuperable obstacle to thy entire deliverance from fret, irritation, and failure? Then turn to the marvellous phrase that follows, and tell me, if thou canst, the meaning of the saving strength of God's right hand. Is not God's right hand strong enough? And notice that its strength is pledged not to destroy, but to save. All the strength of God's right hand goes forth to save unto the uttermost. Look away from adversary and temptation, and keep murmuring to thyself, "He shall save me to-day, and always, with the saving strength of his right hand." And is not the right hand of the Most High the place where Jesus sits? Is not the right hand of God moved by the love that died on Calvary? "He laid his right hand upon me, saying, Fear not."

Thou preventest him with the blessings of goodness. Psa. 21: 3.

GOD is always beforehand with us. The word "prevent" is not as familiar to our modern English as it was when the Bible was translated. Then it meant "that which comes or goes before." And the idea is that God goes before us, preparing our way, and laying up supplies of grace to anticipate our need. This is the meaning of the prayer: "Prevent us, O Lord, in all our doings."

Go into the chamber where the mother is preparing for the advent of a little babe. You have no difficulty in telling what the wants of the child will be by all the articles which her tender forethought is providing; and when presently the little one opens its eyes in this strange, new world, it finds that it has been prevented with the blessings of goodness.

For ages prior to the appearance of man on the earth, the great heart of God was exercised in preparing for him. To please his ear, Music tuned her lyre; to satisfy his eye, the Great Artist wrought variety of colour and form; to warm him, seams of coal were laid down; to give him drink, rivers poured from crystal urns of snow-clad peaks; and Adam might have adored God's prevenient grace. Think, for instance, of the colour, the light and scent and driving-power in rock-oils!

Still more is this the case in the kingdom of redemption. God has stored all the blessings of goodness in Jesus. In eternal ages, in the incarnation, the cross, the ascension, He has prepared beforehand for every possible need of our spiritual life. Whenever you pray, remember that you are not to procure unthought-of help; but to avail yourself of the blessings of goodness with which God has anticipated your coming.

He hath done it. Psa. 22: 31 (R.V.).

THIS is the Hebrew equivalent for the words, "It is finished." Surely it was meet that the Psalm of the Cross, which our Lord must have recited to Himself during those hours of anguish, should close with this triumphant outburst.

FINISHED, THE CEREMONIAL LAW. It had served its purpose in prefiguring the person and work of Jesus; but now the rending of the vail betokened the abolition of the forms of the earlier dispensation. The things which could be shaken passed, that those which could not be shaken might remain.

FINISHED, THE FULFILMENT OF PROPHECY. Very diverse predictions had met, and were closed, as gates are when the king has passed through. That He should be a King and a Sufferer; a Priest and a Victim; a Lion of the tribe of Judah, and a Lamb for substitution.

FINISHED, THE WORK WHICH WAS GIVEN TO HIM TO DO. The Messiah was to be cut off, not for Himself, to finish transgressions, to make an end of sins, to make reconciliation for iniquity, and to bring in everlasting righteousness. And each of these great ends was realized.

FINISHED, THE WORK OF ATONEMENT. As the Substitute and Sin-bearer, the Lord Jesus stood with the sins of the race meeting on Him; but when He died He put them away by the sacrifice of Himself. They were borne into the land of forgetfulness, from which they can never be recovered. The demand of divine justice was satisfied. Mercy and truth had met. Righteousness and peace embraced. And this cry of a finished redemption shall be finally crowned by a cry of complete restitution (Rev. 21: 6).

Surely goodness and mercy shall follow me all the days of my life. Psa. 23: 6.

WE are well escorted, with a Shepherd in front and these twin angels behind! Someone called them watch-dogs; but I prefer to think of them as angels. Do you not see the special beauty of these fair, strong angel-forms following? We make such mistakes, give unnecessary pain, leave work ill-done and half-done, often succeed rather in raising dust than cleaning the rooms which we would fain sweep! It is good to think that two such angels follow close upon our track as we go through life, putting kind constructions on our actions, disentangling knots, making good deficiencies, and preventing the consequences of ill-advised and inconsiderate action pursuing us to the bitter end.

There are mothers who are always tidying up after their children. The little ones have had a rare time, which have left confusion and disorder; but the mother comes, mending the broken toys, stitching the rent garments, making everything neat and tidy. As the ambulance corps goes over the battlefield; as time festoons with verdure ruins and decay; as love puts the most tender construction on word and act—so the love of God follows us.

His goodness imputes to us the noble motive, though the act itself has been a failure; credits us with what was in our heart; reckons us the full wage, though we have only wrought one hour. His mercy forgives, obliterates the traces of our sins from his heart, undoes their ill-effects so far as possible towards others, and treats us as if we had never transgressed. Do not fear the future. God's angels do not tire. What has been will be, in all worlds, and to all eternity. All the days, even those in which Satan seems to have obtained permission to sift.

And the King of Glory shall come in. Psa. 24: 7, 9.

THIS is what we all want. We must have the King of Glory within. To have Him without, even though He be on the Throne, will not avail. He must come in to abide, to reign, to sway his sceptre, to keep the everlasting doors through which He has passed. This has been our difficulty, that those doors have so often been forced. We want one who is strong and mighty to keep them strongly barred against our mortal foe.

This Psalm was first realized in the entrance of the Ark into Mount Zion, when God went up with a merry noise. It is supposed that the first part of the verse was a challenge from the warders of the ancient gates, whilst the second was a reply from the escorting band that accompanied the sacred emblem. It was a moment of vast triumph when the Ark of the King of Glory passed to the ancient city of the Jebusites.

A still greater fulfilment took place when Jesus, having overcome the sharpness of death, victor over sin and the grave, mighty in battle, vanquished principalities and powers, and entered the city of God. Then to and fro these challenges and answers flew between the angels that awaited Him, and those who accompanied.

But the most vital fulfilment is when the heart opens to receive Him, and He enters, to go out no more, and to hold it against all comers. Oh, beaten and baffled saint, it is impossible for thee to fail when Jesus, all-victorious, garrisons thy heart! He is strong and mighty. Dost thou want strength? It is in the strong Son of God. Dost thou want might? He is all-mighty. Dost thou want deliverance from thy foes? He is mighty in battle.

The secret of the Lord is with them that fear Him. Psa. 25: 14.

WHAT marvellous words! They remind one of the sapphire work which the elders saw at the foot of the throne, and which was like "the body of heaven for clearness." Three different renderings are suggested by the R.V.

THE SECRET OF THE LORD. To some it is permitted to know the mysteries of the Kingdom of Heaven. To these the white stone is given, on which is engraven a name, which only he knows that receives it. There are secret passages of love between Christ and the believing soul, which it would not be lawful for it to utter. High fellowship: deep blessedness. Things which eye hath not seen. Jesus revealed his secrets when Judas had gone forth. "Wherefore askest thou after my name," He said to Manoah, "seeing it is secret?"

THE COUNSEL OF THE LORD. "His Name shall be called . . . Counsellor." He draws near to those that fear to grieve Him, and gives them counsel. He instructs them in the way that He chooses for them; He guides them in his truth and teaches them; He guides them in judgment; and tells them, as He did Abraham, what He is about to do.

THE FRIENDSHIP OF THE LORD. "Ye are my friends," said Jesus, "if ye do whatsoever I command you." He longs for friends—those to whom He can tell his desires, on whom He may impose implicit confidence, and who will be so taken up with Him as to be indifferent to everything else, their one purpose to do his least bidding. Oh to be honoured with the personal friendship of Jesus! It were a rare privilege to be entrusted with his secrets, and to hear Him say, "I have not called you servants, but friends."

I will wash mine hands in innocency. Psa. 26: 6.

THE Psalmist realized that he could not avail himself of all that was typified by the altar, unless, so far as he knew himself, he had washed his hands in innocency. But he also knew that the washing, to be effective, must be in costlier waters than those of his own innocency. The soul requires a Saviour who comes by water and blood, not by water only.

The compassing of the altar is probably a picturesque way of describing the joyous or penitent circle of worshippers that gathered around the altar; and which needed to be prepared for by the usual lustrations, "The baptisms and laying on of hands." We must separate ourselves from known sin, and wash our hands in innocency, if we are to enjoy the blessings of the altar and its sacred associations.

There is the sacrifice of the burnt-offering, which stands for Christ's perfectness and entire devotedness to God on our behalf. But how can we be utterly given up to God unless, so far as we know, we are innocent of presumptuous and cherished sin?

There are the sacrifices of the meal-offering and the peace-offering. But how can we feed on Christ, or feast with Him in holy rapture, whilst we are concealing the stains of the hands that take the food?

There is the sacrifice of the sin-offering. But is it not a sacrilege to claim a share in its blessing if we permit those very sins which cost the Saviour agony and tears? No; we must come out and be separate; we must be willing for God to examine and prove us; we must hate the congregation of the wicked, their conversation and ways; we must occupy ourselves perpetually with the Divine loving-kindness and truth. So only can we encompass the altar of God, and taste its comfort and help.

One thing have I desired of the Lord, that will I seek after. Psa. 27: 4.

ONE purpose dominated prayer and life. It was never long absent from the Psalmist's thought. The men of one idea are irresistible. The arrowy stream will force its way through the toughest soil. See that all the prayers, incidents, and circumstances of life subserve one intense purpose. String all the beads on one thread. When the eye is single, the whole body is full of light.

THE PSALMIST'S PURPOSE. What a blessing that the Psalmist's purpose may be ours! To dwell in the house of the Lord is to live within the vail in fellowship with God, in the habitual recollection of his presence. To behold his beauty is to keep looking off unto Jesus. To inquire in his Temple is to commune with the Lord about all the concerns of home and business, of church and commonwealth. In senses of which the material Temple could give but a faint conception, we may dwell in the house of the Lord all the days of our lives.

THE PSALMIST'S SEARCH. Let us seek after this as well as pray for it. Let it be the fixed purpose and resolution of every day. Let us begin with it in the morning, and at every

spare moment remember that we have boldness to stand in the Most Holy Place. Oh to
be as intent on this high quest as the man of
science to discover nature's secrets; as the
businessman to make a fortune; as the
brave explorer to extort the secret from the
Polar Seas!

True prayer will never be presumptuous.
It will not ask God to do for us what we may
do for ourselves. It will ask as though all
depended on asking, but it will seek as
though all depended on seeking.

"Thrice blest, whose lives are faithful
    prayers:
What souls possess themselves so pure?"

Feed them also, and lift them up for ever.
    Psa. 28: 9.
THE people of God are here compared to a
flock, scattered over many hills, marked by
differing brands, sheltering in varied folds,
but under the care of one Shepherd, and
being conducted to one Home.

The holy soul is as eager for the welfare of
the Lord's "beautiful flock" as He is. Whatever is dear to the loved one is dear to the
lover. You cannot love the pastor without
taking a keen and constant interest in all
that interests him, and especially in the sheep
of his pasture, and the people of his hand.
Hence when you are nearest the Lord, you are
almost certain to begin pleading for his inheritance, and saying: "Save thy people; bless
them, feed them, and lift them up for ever."

There is an exquisite suggestion in the
R.V., "Bear them up for ever." The Good
Shepherd bare his flock through the desert,
and carried them all the days of old. It is as
easy for Him to bear a flock, as a single
lamb. Jesus does not simply lead us to green
pastures and still waters, He bears us, and
He bears us up, and He does so for ever.
Never tiring, though He imparts infinite rest;
never ceasing for a moment his shepherd-
care. Are you depressed to-day? Are there
strong influences dragging you down? Does
your soul cleave to the dust? Let those strong
arms and that tender breast lift you up for
ever. A dying child asked her father to place
his arms beneath her weary, emaciated body.
"Lift me," she said. He did so. "A little
higher." He did so. "Higher, father." And
when he had lifted her as high as he could,
the convulsive movement proved that Christ
had come to lift her up for ever.

In his temple every thing saith, Glory. Psa
    29: 9 (R.V.).
THIS psalm describes a thunderstorm gathering over the Mediterranean, passing with
devastating fury over Palestine, and finally
dissolving in floods of rain on the pasture-
lands of Bashan and Gilead. But how differently such a scene is regarded! To the
man of the world it presents an interesting
study, or awakes spasms of fear: to the man
of God, contemplating the scene from his
safe hiding in the Temple, it seems as though
nature, with a myriad voices, were pro-
claiming the glory of God. Many storms are
sweeping athwart the world just now. Our
standpoint for watching them must be God's
presence-chamber.

Somehow, everything that has been, is,
and shall be; all that seems startling and
dreadful; all that excites fear and foreboding
—shall conduce to the glory of God. Wait,
O child of God, in patient trust; Jehovah is
King, and He shall sit as King for ever; all is
under law. "Of Him and through Him and
to Him are all things"; and to Him shall be
the glory for ever.

Our body is the temple of the Holy Ghost:
does every whit of it say, Glory? I know of
few things that stir my heart more than the
repeated ascription of "Glory be to the
Father, and to the Son, and to the Holy
Ghost." But is that the refrain of our life?
Outside there may be confusion and storm,
wild chaos and desolation; but see to it
that from your heart's shrine there rises
moment after moment the ascription of
"Glory be to Thee, O Thou most High."

"Glory to God, to God, he saith.
Knowledge of suffering entereth,
And life is perfected in death."

*Weeping may endure for the night; but joy
    cometh in the morning.* Psa. 30: 5.
THE Hebrew might be rendered, "Weeping
may come in to lodge at even" (R.V., MARG.).
See, at nightfall, a black-vestured guest
comes to thy heart. Thou must let him in;
he brings a warrant from your King for his
quartering and entertainment. But he is only
a lodger; he has no abiding-place with thee;
at daybreak he must be gone. Canst thou not
bear with him for these brief hours? It is only
for the brief space of an Eastern summer-
night. Let the first tint of the dawn flush yon

sky, he will go. Like the ghosts of fable, he dies in the light.

Now, see, the morning breaks! Who is this hurrying up the hill, and knocking at the door? Hark to his joyous shout! Who is this? Ah! It is Joy. The child of the morning light! The first-born of Resurrection! And he comes not as a lodger, but as the Lord and Master of Life, to abide for ever. Oh, welcome him in the name of the Lord, and throw open each chamber and each closet in your heart, that all may be filled with joy unspeakable and full of glory. And as he enters, sorrow and sighing flee away. They have passed out at the back as he came in at the front.

Joy in the morning at the resurrection of Jesus: Joy in the coming of the Saviour for his bride: Joy as the Millennium breaks on the world: Joy when the Eternal Day comes to gladden those who have drunk of Christ's sorrow, and shall share his bliss.

Child of God, be on the outlook to welcome Joy. Do not fear his advent, nor thrust him away. Milton's *L'Allegro* is a truer presentation of Christian experience than *Il Penseroso*. "Thou shalt rejoice in every good thing which the Lord thy God giveth thee."

Thou hast known my soul in adversities.
Psa. 31:7.

MEN have a way of forgetting their companions when they fall into adversity. They do not know them or visit them, or recognize them if they meet them in the street. But the love of God is always most tender and considerate then. He seeks us out when the sky is shadowed, and life is overcast with sombre tints. Adversity, so far from alienating Him, draws Him closer, and brings out his tenderest, loveliest traits. He knows us in adversity.

It is only when we are overtaken by adversity that we are revealed in the innermost depths of our nature. God knows us in adversity. "Thou shalt remember," said Moses, "all the way which the Lord thy God hath led thee these forty years in the wilderness, that He might humble thee, to prove thee, to know what was in thine heart." What revelations of unsubdued pride and imperious self-will are afforded, when we are searched and tested by the fiery trial of pain!

But the margin (R.V.) suggests another rendering: "Thou hast known the adversities of my soul." Is it not enough that God should know? Need we go to all our friends and explain to them all we are called to endure? Is not this a needless addition to their sorrow, and the sorrow of the world? What a glorious piece of advice the Master gave, when He said, "Anoint thine head and wash thy face, that thou appear not unto men to fast, but to thy Father which seeth in secret."

"Thou know'st our bitterness!—our joys
    are thine!
No stranger Thou to all our wanderings
    wild!
But yet Thou call'st us Brethren! Sweet
    repose
Is in that word;—the Lord who dwells
    on high
Knows all, yet loves us better than He
    knows."

I will instruct thee and teach thee in the way
which thou shalt go. Psa. 32:8.

"LEARN of Me," said the Master: and indeed there is no teacher like Him; no school like his. We stand at the door of the school-house, saying, "What I know not, teach Thou me"; and He does not hesitate to undertake our case. But there are several points of difference from our methods. In Christ's school there is but one Master for all the scholars, and they all learn from the same books; the pupils begin with the upper classes and end with the lowest; and those that are most proficient, and have been longest under his tuition, are most conscious of their ignorance. There are no holidays; but every day is a holy day. The school never breaks up; but the students leave it for Home, and the prizes are sent after them, and given when they arrive.

We need more than personal instruction; we are travelling through an unknown land, and require direction for the way. This also is guaranteed; but not as in the cases of tourists, who extract all information from their friends before they start from home, as to the places they are about to visit. Our Guide accompanies us. He counsels us with his eye upon us, detecting every pitfall and chasm, and warning us; perhaps even guiding us by the movement of his eye.

How greatly then are we in need of the quickened sense! The eye fixed on his eye;

the ear open to his slightest whisper; the foot quick to place itself down in his footprints. The horse and mule need bit and bridle; but it is enough for us if the heart fears to miss the least indication of the Master's will. Be willing to know; it then becomes his part to make thee know somehow. If not in one way, then in another.

The earth is full of the loving-kindness of the Lord. Psa. 33: 5 (R.V.).

THE Psalmist means that there is no spot in it where the traces and footprints of God's love may not be discerned, if only the eyes and the heart are opened. Just as every corner of a room which faces the south is filled with the morning sunlight, unless artificial and violent means are adopted to keep it out, so every part of human life is full of God's loving-kindness, unless it is blocked out by sin. You think that your lot is absolutely destitute of God's loving-kindness; but may not your eyes be blinded? May there not be more than you suppose? May you not be so occupied with the one irksome thing in it as to be oblivious to ten thousand marks of tender compassion and unobtrusive mercy?

Your chamber is very bare and comfortless; but it is part of the earth, and it is therefore full of God's loving-kindness: look around for it. Your home seems uncongenial and trying; but it must be full to the brim of loving-kindness. Your daily life is hard and difficult; but there is as much loving-kindness in it as if it were easy and prosperous. There is indeed more loving-kindness in these trying and difficult surroundings than in happier ones. It costs God more to give us pain. We need more love, and we get it. We should rejoice in it if our eyes were opened.

The loveless heart can detect nothing but disappointment and unkindness. But the heart that loves, and sings, and rejoices in the Lord, detects the evident tokens of God's love; just as the child of nature knows when friend or foe has passed through the forest-glade, by indications which would be unintelligible to our unpractised eye. Echo always answers in the same key in which we address her!

The Lord is nigh unto them that are of a broken heart. Psa. 34: 18.

WHAT broke your heart? Unkindness?

Desertion? Unfaithfulness on the part of those you trusted? Or did you attempt to do something which was beyond your power, and in the effort, the heart-strings snapped? A bird with a broken wing, an animal with a broken leg, a woman with a broken heart, a man with a broken purpose in his life—these seem to drop out of the main current of life into shadow. They go apart to suffer and droop. The busy rush of life goes on without them. But God draws nigh. The great Lover of man is always at the best when the lights burn low and dim in the house of life. He always comes to us then. He shall sit as the Refiner.

Where do you see love perfected? Not between the father and his stalwart son who counts himself independent, or between the mother and the girl in whom love is awakening in its first faint blush: but where the crippled child of eleven years lies in the truckle-bed, pale and wan, unable to help herself. There the noblest fruits of love ripen and yield refreshment. The father draws nigh to the little sufferer, so soon as he gets home at night, and the mother is nigh all the time to sympathize and comfort and minister. So brokenness attracts God. It is dark; you think yourself deserted; but it is not so. God is there—He is nigh; call to Him—a whisper will bring response.

"There, little one, don't cry;
They have broken your heart, I know
And the rainbow gleams
Of your youthful dreams
Are things of the long ago;
But heaven holds all for which you sigh—
There, little one, don't cry."

Them that are quiet in the land. Psa. 35: 20.

A SIGNIFICANT title for the saints, which has been adopted at least by one great religious body. In every age God has had his quiet ones. Retired from its noise and strife, withdrawn from its ambitions and jealousies, unshaken by its alarms; because they had entered into the secret of a life hidden in God. We must have an outlet for the energies of our nature. If we are unfamiliar with the hidden depths of eternal life, we shall necessarily live a busy, fussy, frothy, ambitious, eager life, in contact with men and things. But the man who is intense on the eternal, can be quiet in the temporal.

The man whose house is shallow, but one

room in depth, cannot help living on the street. But directly we begin to dwell deep—deep in God, deep in the watch for the Master's advent, deep in considering the mysteries of the kingdom, we become quiet. We fill our little space; we get our daily bread and are content; we enjoy natural and simple pleasures; we do not strive, nor cry, nor cause our voice to be heard in the street; we pass through the world, with noiseless tread, dropping a blessing on all we meet; but we are no sooner recognized than we are gone.

Get quiet, beloved soul; tell out thy sorrow and complaint to God. Let not the greatest business or pressure divert thee from God. When men rage about thee, go and tell Jesus. When storms are high, hide thee in his secret place. When others compete for fame and applause, and their passion might infect thee, get into thy closet, and shut thy door, and quiet thyself as a weaned babe. For if thy voice is quiet to man, let it never cease to speak loudly and mightily for man in the ear of God. Oh to be a Quietist in the best sense!

In thy light shall we see light. Psa. 36: 9.
THERE are many dark things around us in which we detect light only when we behold them in the light which streams from the face of Jesus. In his light we see light in them. Yonder lies a bit of charcoal, black and opaque; and even when it has been changed by chemistry to crystals, it is dull and dense, so long as it is in the dark. Who could guess that such depths and fountains of light exist in that insignificant atom? But let it be brought into the rays of the morning sun, and as it flashes and glistens, in that light we see its light; fountains of light welling up; caverns of light, where the elves and fairies of childish story hide.

SO IT IS OF THE BIBLE. Its pages seem devoid of help and comfort, till we open them under the light on Jesus. Cleopas and the other learnt this on the road to Emmaus.

SO IT IS OF NATURE. The Greek, lover of nature though he was, never saw in her face the loveliness which has been the theme of Christian poetry and art. In the light of Christ's parables and allusions we see light.

"Heaven above is softer blue,
Earth around is sweeter green;

Something lives in every hue,
Christless eyes have never seen.
Birds with gladder songs o'erflow,
Flowers with deeper beauties shine,
While I know, as now I know,
I am his, and He is mine."

SO IT IS OF HUMAN LOVE. There is a new preciousness, tenderness, thoughtfulness, blessedness, where the love and light of Jesus reign in home and heart. We see a loveliness and beauty in our dear ones that had eluded us till we beheld them in the love of Jesus.

Delight thyself also in the Lord. Psa. 37: 4.
ONE of Tauler's hymns is a lovely specimen of how a man delights in the Lord. He takes a number of familiar instances of close affinity and interdependence, and applies them to the intimacy subsisting between him and his beloved Lord:

"As the bridegroom to his chosen,
As the king unto his realm,
As the keep unto the castle,
As the pilot to the helm,
So, Lord, art Thou to me."

But we cannot delight thus without effort. We must withdraw our eager desires from the things of earth, fastening and fixing them on Him. The current of our being must set towards God. We must cultivate the habit of holy intimacy with Him, whom the heaven of heavens cannot contain. We must accustom ourselves to hold up before us the successive attributes and works of God, till they strike our admiration, and elicit our homage.

Then we shall find rest unto our souls, because He will give us the desires of our hearts. When God Himself is our desire we shall be for ever delivered from disappointment, because we can always have Him; we shall be removed from risk of penury and want, because we can have as much of Him as we need; we shall be beyond the fear of loss, because He changes not. They who want God possess Him. To long for God is to have that for which you long. To delight in God is to delight in One, of whom there is an infinity for everyone, so that there need be no stint, no jealousy, no envy, no satiety. Everyone can have as much as he can hold. "He giveth not his Spirit by measure," that is, by metre. There is no gauge of our consumption!

Lord, all my desire is before Thee. Psa. 38: 9.
GOD knows our desires. We cannot always put them into words; we dare not trust them to the ears of our dearest, but they lie open to Him—the ideal we desire in our holiest moments; the thorn in the flesh from which we long to be delivered; the prayer for one who is dearer to us than life. "Lord, all my desire is before Thee."

Think of the desires of the saints—for the realization of their ideals; for the salvation of men; for the glory of the Redeemer; for the Divine answer to the scoff, the sneer, the taunt of infidelity; for the coming of the King, the restoration of his ancient people, the setting up of the millenial reign.

"Lo, as some ship, outworn and overladen,
   Strains for the harbour, where her sails
      are furled;
Lo, as some innocent and eager maiden
   Leans o'er the wistful limit of the world:
"So even I, and with a pang more thrilling;
   So even I, and with a hope more sweet,
Yearn for the sign, O Christ! of thy ful-
      filling,
   Faint for the flaming of thine advent
      feet."

And remember, He who implanted the desire does abundantly above all we ask or think. There is always a defect in every earthly joy, a something which shows itself for a moment to elude us.

"It blossoms just beyond the paths I
      follow,
   It shines beyond the farthest stars I see;
It echoes faint from ocean caverns hollow,
   And from the land of dreams it beckons
      me."

But it never can be thus with any desire that God has taught us to cherish. Of these, as the ages pass, we shall say: It was a true report that I heard, but the half was not told. The desire which is directed to God cannot miss gratification.

I am a stranger with Thee, and a sojourner. Psa. 39: 12.
SORROW and pain had taught the Psalmist some deep lessons touching the life of men around him—they seemed to be shadows pursuing shadows. They walked in a vain show, and were disquieted in vain. At their best estate, i.e., when most firmly rooted,

they were only a breath, curling from lip or nostril into the chill morning air, and then gone for ever. The outward life and activity of man seemed to him as the shadow which darkens for a moment a whole mountain-side, and, whilst you look, it has been chased away by the succeeding sheets of sunshine.

Amid all these vanities, the child of God is a pilgrim to the Unseen. He passes through Vanity Fair, with his eyes steadily fixed on the Eternal City, whose Builder and Maker is God. Abraham first described himself as a stranger and sojourner, when he stood up from before his dead, and craved a burying-place from the sons of Heth. All his children, those who inherit a like faith, must say the same. Faith cannot find a home on this side of the stars. It has caught a glimpse of the Infinite, and it can never be content with anything less.

But we are sojourners "with God." He is our constant companion. What Greatheart was to the women and feeble ones, God is to each of his saints. We may be strangers; but we are not solitary. We may be compelled to relax our grasp from the hands of beloved ones; but never alone—the Father is with us. Good company, safe escort, is it not? In the strength of it, we may obey without reluctance or fear the old motto—*Habita, ut migraturus:* Live as about to emigrate. "There is nothing greater than God; nothing less than I. He is rich; I am very poor, but I want for nothing."

I delight to do thy will, O my God. Psa. 40: 7, 8.
THE writer of the Epistle to the Hebrews (chap. 10) lays great stress on these words. He says that this yielding up of Christ's will to his Father's was consummated on the cross, and was the inner heart of our Saviour's passion. "By which will (surrendered and given back to God) we have been sanctified." He then proceeds to suggest that it is only as we enter into a living oneness with Jesus in this that we can pass from the outer court and have boldness to enter into the Holiest of all. This, he says, is the new and living way. Jesus entered into the Holiest because He gave Himself absolutely to his Father. We cannot expect to go thither till we have become possessed of the same spirit.

It is a solemn question for each. Have we all stood at the cross, as the slave of old at the doorpost of his master's house, and said, "I love my Master. I will not go out free"? Have we been united to that cross, as by the boring of the awl? Have we so embraced the will of God that we are prepared to follow it, though it lead to the Cross and grave? Then one condition at least is fulfilled for our standing unabashed where angles veil their faces.

But there is yet another condition. We can have no right to stand within the Holiest, except through the blood of Jesus, shed for sin on the cross. This is necessary ere sinners can have boldness in the presence of Divine Purity.

When Rutherford was like to die of sore illness, instead of a martyr's death, he said, "I would think it a more glorious way of going home, to lay down my life for the cause at the cross of Edinburgh or St. Andrew's; but I submit to my Master's will. Oh for arms to embrace Him!"

Blessed is he that considereth the poor. Psa. 41: 1.

THE realm of Blessedness is all around. It may be entered at any minute, and we may dwell in it all the days of our life. Our enjoyment of blessedness is totally undetermined by outward circumstances. If you stand in some great retail emporium and watch the faces of the women, you will be greatly instructed. Yonder sits a richly-dressed lady with society and fashion, dress and money at her command, but her manner and tone are utterly weary and dissatisfied; whilst across the counter a girl waits on her, whose thin face and simple attire tell their own story, but her expression and bearing betoken the possession of an inner calm and strength, an inexhaustible fund of patience and sweetness. Such contrasts meet us everywhere. The realm of blessedness dips down into humble and lowly lives on every side of us. Have we entered it?

Christ's beatitudes give us eight gates, any one of which will immediately conduct us within its confines. But here is another: "Blessed is he that considereth the poor." Even if you cannot help or relieve them to any appreciable extent, consider them; let them feel that you are thinking of and for them; do not hurry them when they recite their long, sad story; put them at their ease; treat them with Christian courtesy and consideration. Begin at once. There are plenty around you, who, if not poor in the things of this world, are poor in love and hope and the knowledge of God. Tell them of "the blessing of the Lord," which "maketh rich, and He addeth no sorrow with it." Silver and gold you may have none; but such as you have be sure and give. Learn to consider people. Try and look on things from their standpoint.

Deep calleth unto deep. Psa. 42: 7.

THERE are wonderful harmonies in nature. Voices call to one another across vast spaces. The depths below the firmament call to the heights above. The deep of the ocean calls to the deep of the azure sky. Listen, O my soul, to the mighty voices sounding ever through the universe of God.

THE DEEP OF DIVINE REDEMPTION CALLS TO THE DEEP OF HUMAN NEED. It sometimes seems as though the opposite were true, and as though the cry originated in man; but it is not so. God is always first; and as He looks into hearts stricken and desperate, conscious of unfathomable yearnings, and infinite capacity, He calls aloud, and the depth of his heart appeals to the depth of the heart of man. Would that it might ever answer back!

THE DEEP OF CHRIST'S WEALTH CALLS TO THE DEEP OF THE SAINT'S POVERTY. He looks down upon our attenuated and poverty-stricken experience with an infinite yearning. He cannot endure that we should go through life naked and miserable, poor and blind, when He has got gold, and precious stones, and white raiment. "Hearken, O daughter, and consider. Forsake thy father's house. Come unto Me, and receive from my fulness. Open thy mouth wide, and I will fill it."

THE DEEP OF THE HOLY SPIRIT'S INTERCESSION CALLS TO THE DEEP OF THE CHURCH'S PRAYER. He awakens in us groanings that cannot be uttered, and burdens us with the will of God.

Whatever depths there are in God, they appeal to corresponding depths in us. And whatever be the depths of our sorrow, desire, or necessity, there are correspondences in God from which full supplies may be obtained. Thou hast the pitcher of faith, and the well is deep.

O God, my God! Psa. 43: 4.

WHAT a change within the soul one short hour spent in God's presence will prevail to make! The psalmist is opposed by an ungodly nation, and resisted by a deceitful and unjust man. He mourns because of the oppression of the enemy; he questions whether God has cast him off. Then led by those twin angels, Light and Truth, commissioned and sent forth for that purpose from the presence of God, he enters in thought and spirit within the precincts of the divine Tabernacle, and stands before the Altar. Immediately the clouds break. Putting his puny hand upon the great God, he appropriates all He is and has, as though it were his own, and takes again, in a very ecstasy of realizing faith, his harp, too long silent, and breaks into rapturous melody.

Have you not sometimes groped in the dark, till those two angels have come to lead you also to the altar where the High Priest stands? Then what a change! Your circumstances have not altered, but you have conceived a new idea of what God can be to you. You have said, This God is my God for ever and ever. You have said, O God, MY God! You have laid your hand on God's wealth and called it all your own. You have chided your soul for being disquieted and depressed whilst such a heritage is yours. You have spoken of God, first as the God of your strength; secondly, as the gladness of your joy; thirdly, as the health of your face.

"Why, therefore, should we do ourselves
    this wrong,
Or others—that we are not always strong,
That we are ever overborne with care,
That we should ever weak and heartless be,
Anxious or troubled when with us is prayer,
And joy and strength and courage are with
    Thee?"

Thou art my King, O God: command victories.
Psa. 44: 4 (R.V. marg.).
BEFORE a man can say that God is his King, he must have very definitely consecrated himself to God. The relation of too many believers to Christ falls short of this supreme act of the soul; and in consequence their lives lack directness, power, victory over temptation. My reader, thou hast been sorely tried by overmastering temptations before which thy resolutions have been swept as children's sand-heaps by the tide. Wilt thou quietly consider whether from the very depth of thy being thou hast ever said to God, Thou art my King. The kingship of Jesus is always associated with victory; and just as soon as his supremacy is acknowledged, He will begin to command deliverance and victory.

Behold, thy King cometh to thee, having salvation. Lift up your heads, O ye gates, and the King of Glory shall come in; but He is also the merciful Saviour. Him hath God exalted with his right hand to be a Prince and a Saviour. It is always Prince first. If thou shalt confess with thy mouth Jesus as Lord, thou shalt be saved.

What a battle-shout this is! Whenever temptation is near; when the foe seems about to take the citadel by assault; when heart and flesh quail before the noise of battle—then to look up to the living Christ, and say, Thou art my King, O Son of God: command victory! There is no devil in hell but would flee before that cry of the tempted and tried believer; and God could not be neglectful of such an appeal. Jacob is only a worm; yet he is more than a conqueror when God fights for him. It is thus that Jacob Behmen begins one of his letters: "May the Overcomer, Jesus Christ, through Himself, overcome in us all his enemies."

My work is for a king. Psa. 45: 1 (R.V., marg.).
THIS dignifies the meanest occupation. By this motive the apostles urged their converts to daily duty, slaves though they were in the houses of rich and godless owners. They were taught to look upon their lot as the will of God; and to do service as unto the Lord, and not unto men, seeking the praise of God as their sufficient reward.

As we take in hand the bits of carved work which once stood high in the cathedral roof, but now lie almost hidden by rank vegetation, and consider the exquisite carving, which the artists never thought would be so minutely inspected, we feel that each unknown craftsman did his work for the King. There is no doubt that the religious intention of their work elevated their meanest toils to the level of sacred service. Let us endeavour each day to realize that everything may be done for Jesus which may be done at all. Do you take food? It is that the body may be deft and quick to execute his purposes. Do you rest and seek recreation? It is that your energies may be recuperated, and that the tide of nervous power may return with fresh vigour. Do you manufacture, buy and sell, advise and preach? All may be inspired by the one purpose, that his will may be done, his kingdom come—which is righteousness, peace, and goodwill to men.

Such a life, however, is only possible when the heart overflows, bubbles up and over, with goodly matter. The heart must always be in contact with the fervent love of Christ. It is only as the divine heat passes into us that the affections will boil up and overflow in holy act. Let us make the things about the King before we speak them. Let us give time to muse, that the fire may burn.

He maketh wars to cease. Psa. 46: 9.

"MY soul is among lions, and I dwell among those that are set on fire: even the sons of men, whose words are spears and arrows, and their tongue a sharp sword." Such is the frequent confession of the child of God. Hemmed in by foes, the butt of vehement hate! But the moment comes at length when God arises to deliver. He utters his voice—the earth melts. In the sight the enemy has wrapped up his tents and stolen silently away. War has ceased, and all the land of life lies plain and open.

God makes the wars of the outward life cease, so that as life's afternoon comes the man who had fought his way through overwhelming odds—as a reformer, or inventor, or philanthropist—spends his years amid troops of friends and loving recognition.

God makes the wars of the home cease, so that the disturbing elements pass out, or are transmuted by invincible patience and love.

God makes the wars of the heart cease, so that Satan no longer annoys. The storm dies down, and the river which makes glad the city of God purls quietly through the soul. Sennacherib and his vast array lie as the leaves of autumn, silent in the last sleep.

If as yet God has not made your wars to cease, it is because He knows that you have still strength to fight on. Do not faint in the day of battle. Ponder those great words of Cromwell: "Call not your burden sad or heavy, for if your Heavenly Father sent it (or permitted it) He intended it to be neither." It is through the fight that you are winning experience, strength, the approval of your Captain, and the crown.

He shall choose our inheritance for us. Psa. 47: 4.

"CHOOSE for us, our Father." We say it deliberately. If He were to give us our choice at this moment, though there is no one of us that does not cherish a secret longing too deep for words, we would put it back into his hand and say, "Thou knowest better than words can tell Thee what lies closest to our soul, but we dare not take the opportunity of snatching at it; Thou wilt give it or its equivalent in the sweetest form and at the most opportune hour." Would not this be the wisest attitude for any one of us to assume, believing, as we do, that our Father's wisdom is only outshone by his love?

Wilt thou, O soul of man, standing at the foot of the Hill of God, ask thy Father to choose the track? He knows thy strength and powers of endurance; He knows also thy ardent yearning for the best. Subordinate thy choice to his in all things. Then whatever the difficulties may prove to be, dare to believe that they are less than any that would have opposed thee hadst thou chosen the route for thyself. Never look back; never doubt thy Father's personal interest; the clouds that sweep darkly over thy path may hide Him from thee, but not thee from Him.

And thou, who hast had much experience of God, wilt thou not still say, He shall choose? Thou canst not repent the trust which thou reposedst years ago in his selection. Thou wilt not withdraw thy confidence. For evermore, whatever life may bring here or hereafter, we will cry, He shall choose, He shall choose. As Nicholas Herman said: "Pains and sufferings would be a paradise to me which I should suffer with my God; and the greatest pleasures hell, if I could relish them without Him."

Traverse her palaces. Psa. 48: 13 (R.V.).

THE pious Jew broke into exclamations as he considered the beloved city of his fathers. Beautiful for situation, the joy of the whole earth. In proud confidence he challenged the world of men to walk about Zion, count her towers, and mark her bulwarks. Finally they were to traverse her palaces. But what Jerusalem was to the Jews, God's lovingkindness is to us, as we think of it, in the midst of his temple. Let us consider its beauty and joy, its strength and glory. "How great is his goodness, and how great is his beauty!"

Traverse the rooms in the Palace of God's love—that council-chamber of the eternal foreknowledge where we were chosen in

Christ; this suite of apartments, which began with the unrobing-room of Bethlehem, and ended with the golden stairway of Olivet; those mansions of the Home-land which He is preparing for them that Love Him; the pavilion whither He will lead his bride when He comes to take her to Himself: then look onward to the new heaven and the new earth, where God shall spread his tabernacle over his people, and all our loftiest ideals will be realized for evermore.

Life is a traversing of the successive rooms of the Palace of Love. They are not alike: each has its own beauty; each leads to something better; in each God is All. Some seem to pass through the rooms veiled or blind; others miss seeing the King. But those who dare to look for Him everywhere, find Him. Always our Christ for ever and ever; always our Guide even unto death, and beyond. Always the present opening to something better, as the rosebud to the rose; as the acorn to the oak; as the chrysalis to the butterfly.

Wherefore should I fear in the days of evil?
Psa. 49: 5.

HAVE I not God? At sundry times and in divers manners, He spake to, and succoured his saints. Will He not come to me, and cast around me the soft mantle of his protecting love? And if I love Him, do I need any beside?

"Who that one moment has the least descried Him,
  Dimly and faintly, hidden and afar,
Doth not despise all excellence beside Him,
  Pleasures and powers that are not, and that are?"

Did He not walk with Enoch, and then take him home, before the deluge came? Did He not shut Noah in, with his own hand, that there should be no jeopardy from the overflowing flood? Did He not assure Abram that He was his shield and exceeding great reward, quieting his fears against any possible combination of foes? Did He not preserve his servant Moses from the fury of Pharaoh and the murmurings of Israel? Was not Elijah hidden in the secret of his pavilion from the wrath of Ahab? Did He not send his angel to shut the lions' mouths that they might not hurt Daniel? Were not the coals of the burning fiery furnace as sweet and soft

as forest glades to the feet of the three young confessors? Has God ever forsaken those that trusted Him? Has He ever given them over to the will of their enemies?

Wherefore, then, should I fear in the day of evil? I may be standing on the deck, whilst the ship is beset by icebergs and jagged, splintered rocks; the fog drapes everything, as the way slowly opens through this archipelago of peril: but God is at the helm—why should I fear? Days of evil to others cannot be so to me, for the presence of God transmutes the evil to good.

Our God shall come. Psa. 50: 3.

THE years pass as snowflakes on the river; and as each drops into the mighty past, it cries, God will come! Each Advent season, with its cluster of services, herald-voices, reminiscences and anticipations, lifts the message clear above the turmoil and tumult of mankind, God will come! The disappointments of our fairest hopes, the overcasting of our sunrises, the failures of our politicians, statesmen and counsellors, to effect a permanent, and radical improvement of man's nature, all take up the word, Our God shall come!

"Surely He cometh, and a thousand voices
  Call to the saints and to the deaf and dumb;
Surely He cometh, and the earth rejoices,
  Glad in his coming, who hath sworn, I come."

Dear heart, get thee often to thine oriel window, and look out for the breaking of the day. Did not the Master assure us that He would soon return? Hearken, He saith again to-day, "Surely I come quickly." The little while will soon be over, and He will come first to receive his saints to Himself, and afterwards to come with them to the earth. Why are we disconsolate and dismayed? The perplexities of the Eastern problem, the gradual return of the Jews to Palestine, the despair and lawlessness of men, the unrest of nations, the preparedness on the part of the Church—like so many minute guns at night—keep the heart awake. O, let your eyes flash with the glow of thanksiving! Be glad and strong, confident and calm. Let your loins be girded, and your lamps burning. Through heaven's spaces you shall detect the advent of your God; and when He comes He will break the silence of the ages with words of majesty and might.

Renew a steadfast spirit within me. Psa. 51: 10
(R.V., marg.).

PERHAPS that is our chiefest need: especially so as we gird up our loins for a new stretch of pilgrimage. We do not need nobler ideals. They flash over our souls. We read of Browning kissing, on each anniversary of his wedding, the steps by which his bride went to the marriage altar; and we vow to lift our wedded life higher. We read of Henry Martyn mourning that he had devoted too much time to public work, and too little to private communion with God; and we vow to pray more. We recall the motto written on Green the historian's grave at Mentone, "He died learning"; and we vow that each day shall see some lesson learnt from the great store of Truth. We read those noble words of W. C. Burns, "Oh to have a martyr's heart, if not a martyr's crown"; and we vow to give ourselves absolutely to witness and suffer for Jesus. But, alas! our ideals fade within a few hours, and the withered petals are all that remain. We need the steadfast spirit.

But this God can give us by his Holy Spirit. He can renew our will from day to day, and infuse into us his own unaltering, unalterable purpose. He can make possible, obedience to the apostolic injunction, "Be ye steadfast, unmoveable, always abounding in the work of the Lord." Hear what comfortable words the Apostle Peter saith: "The God of all grace, who called you unto his eternal glory in Christ, after ye have suffered a little while, shall Himself restore, stablish, and settle you." Then we shall move resolutely and unfalteringly onward; like Columbus, undaunted by discouragement, we shall cross unknown seas, till the scent of the land we seek is wafted across the brief intervening distance.

I am like a green olive tree in the house of God.
Psa. 52: 8.

IN its dress of evergreen, the olive is at all times a beautiful object. Many reasons demand that we should resemble it. There are three ways of becoming like a green olive tree, mentioned in this and the following verses:

TRUST IN THE MERCY OF GOD. To trust when the light has burnt to its socket in the house of life, and the heart is as lonely as Job's amid the wreck of his home. To believe that the mercy of God is not clear gone, nor his tender mercies have failed. To know that all is well, that seems most ill. This keeps the heart from withering.

THANKSGIVING. "I will give thee thanks for ever." There is always something to thank God for. When someone condoled with the old slave woman, because she had only two teeth left, she replied quickly, "But I thank Him, honey, all the time, that they are opposite each other." Find out with Paul something to be happy about, even when arraigned before a judge, on trial for your life. "I think myself happy, King Agrippa."

WAITING ON GOD. Not always talking to Him or about Him, but waiting before Him, till the stream runs clear; till the cream rises to the top; till the mists part, and the soul regains its equilibrium. This keeps the soul calm and still. The name of God is good, a wholesome theme for meditation, because it includes his nature. To meditate on it is soul-quieting and elevating. O troubled one, get away to some quiet spot and wait on God! Look away from the wind and waves to the face of Jesus. The divine Name is written on those dear features; and heaven looks forth from those true, deep, tender eyes. The house of God is a safe and sheltered place for his olive trees!

God bringeth back the captivity of his people
Psa. 53: 6.

IT is wonderful to notice the many ways in which God brings us back to Himself. We may have been carried into captivity by a troop of anxieties or a horde of worries; by temptations like the sons of Anak; by pride and other evils, as when David found that the Amalekites had carried off his belongings into captivity. Then God comes to the rescue: sometimes by a drawing felt throughout the soul; sometimes by a little word dropped by another; sometimes by an incident from a biography. Any one of these acts upon us as the sunbeams on frost—there is a meeting and yielding, a desire to get alone, confession of waywardness and wandering, and earnest petitions for renewal of the blessed past. Thus God bringeth back the captivity of his people.

Are you a captive, pining in some distant bondage? It is not surprising that you hang your harp upon the willows, and weep as you remember Zion—how you went with the throng, and even led them to the House of God, with the voice of joy and praise. And as you contrast the past and the present, it is well that your soul is cast down. But when the Lord brings again your captivity, Jacob shall rejoice, and Israel shall be glad.

Would it not be well to look out for your brother Lot if he has been carried off down the long Jordan Plain? Should you not arm and go to his rescue, as Abraham did? Perhaps the Lord would turn your captivity, if you sought to turn the captivity of others; and Melchizedek would meet you with the bread and wine.

"O my God!
Draw me still nearer, closer unto Thee
Till all the hollow of these deep desires
May with Thyself be filled!"

Save me, O God, by thy Name. . . . He hath delivered me out of all trouble. Psa. 54: 1, 7.
THERE are only seven stanzas in this psalm. It is one of the briefer of David's compositions. Written when the Ziphites told of David's hiding-place and compelled him to shift his quarters, perhaps its brevity attests some hasty moment snatched from the hurry and bustle of the necessary flight. It is said that Mr. Gladstone made his memorable Latin version of "Rock of Ages" during an interval of a House of Commons debate. It is worthy of remark that, however hurried David might have been, and however great the responsibility resting upon him, he found time to turn to God for help. He had learnt the secret of abiding in the Divine Presence.

It is said of one, "He was so accustomed to the Divine Presence that he received from it continual succour upon all occasions. It was his continual care to be always with God, and to do nothing, say nothing, which should endanger the perpetual intercourse." But obviously, this frame of mind depended on a previous dedication of himself as a freewill offering to God. There must be no division of interests, if God is to be all. You must consider yourself as a stone before a carver, whereof he is to make a statue—presenting yourself before Him that He may make his perfect image in you and do as He will with your life. You must realize that He has

permitted this interruption of your peace, this intrusion of Ziphite hate. You must look beyond the hand that smites, to the Father who permits. Then the soul will rock itself to rest; and before you have been five minutes with God you will be able to say as David, "He hath delivered me." Be of good cheer; rest on his Name; He will deliver you out of all trouble.

Cast thy burden upon the Lord. Psa. 55: 22.
WE all know the story of the man wearily trudging along the road with the burden on his back, to whom a friend offered a lift in his cart. To the latter's surprise the wayfarer sat beside him with his burden still strapped to his shoulder. "Why do you not put your burden down?" quoth he. "Thank you," was the reply, "I am so obliged at your carrying me that I will not trouble you with my burden also." And so he hugged it still. How many a child of God trusts Him with his soul, but not with his load! Yet if God has undertaken the greater, surely He may be trusted with the less. If He has borne thy sins, He can surely carry thy sorrows.

Thy burden, as the margin suggests, is "that which He hath given thee." Whatever it be—the weight of a church, the pressure of a family, the burden of other souls—thy Father hath given it thee. Give its pressure back to Him, whilst thou retainest the salutary lesson of hourly patience and faith. God imposes burdens, to see what we will do with them. We may carry them to our undoing, or we may cast them on Him for his blessed countenance.

"Oh for the faith to cast our load,
E'en while we pray, upon our God,
Then rise with lightened cheer."

Notice, that if we cast our burden, we must believe He takes it. We must definitely leave it with him, and count as a positive sin the temptation to reconsider it. When you cast your burden, God will take it, and will do more. He will sustain you. He will catch up your burden and you, and bear you all the day long between his shoulders.

Thou hast delivered: . . . wilt not Thou deliver? Psa. 56: 13.
IT has been a wonderful deliverance! The blood and righteousness of Christ have

satisfied the demands of a holy law. Into our souls, dead in trespasses and sins, He has poured the power of an endless life. The very life of God Himself has become resident within us, through the grace of the one Man, Christ Jesus. We cannot be hurt by the second death. We have eaten of the flesh, and drunk of the blood of the Son of Man, and ours is the everlasting life. Death and the grave for ever behind us, whilst before is the city, whose streets are never shadowed by death or crying.

And will not God finish what He has begun? Has He given us life, and will He not give us all that is necessary for right and holy living? Does not the one necessarily involve the other, as the gift of the body involves the bestowment of food and clothing? Have we been saved by Christ's death? Shall we not also be saved by his life? Will it not be for the glory of God that we should walk worthy of the high calling? Trust Him, child of God, whatever the traps and pitfalls, whatever the slipperiness and difficulty of keeping a foothold; believe that He is able to keep you from stumbling, and that his ability is only exceeded by his love. Let your Guide bind you by a strong rope to Himself as you start each morning in his company.

The answer to these reasonings, the fulfilment of our hopes, comes back to us from a verse in Rom. 5, as rendered by combining the suggestions of Dr. Moule, and of Conybeare and Howson, "If, when we were enemies, we were reconciled to God by the death of his Son, much more, being already reconciled, we shall be kept safe by sharing in his life."

God performeth all things for me.
Psa. 57: 2.

IT seemed to David that he was condemned to spend his days in a lion's den; on every side were blasphemy and reproach; his enemies breathed out flames, and their slanders cut like swords. But amid it all he steadily looked away to God, the Most High, who from his elevation would reach down to deliver, and would surely accomplish all that was necessary. It is a marvellous thing to consider that God is literally willing to perform all things in us, and for us, if only we will let Him. The mischief is that most of us insist on performing all things in the energy of our own resolve, in the strength of our own power. We shut God out of our life: and whilst

He is coming to our help, we have forced ourselves, and offered the sacrifice to our own hurt.

Before, therefore, God will perform all things for us, as He did for his servant, we must learn, like him, to wait in his presence that He may teach us our absolute poverty and helplessness; that He may assure us of our need of absolute and unceasing dependence; that He may open our eyes to see the well-spring which Hagar saw on the desert sand. The fixed heart (ver. 7), fixed only upon God, set upon waiting his time, receiving his help, and doing all things according to the inspiration and energy of his Spirit, is absolutely essential.

Awake the dawn, O child of God (8). Give thanks to God: sing his praises (9) let thy aspiration be for his exaltation (5, 11): let thy heart be fixed in its resolve to take deliverance from none other—and He will send forth his twin-angels, Mercy and Truth (3). They will come, even into the lion's den, and save thee from those who would swallow thee up (4).

Verily there is a God that judgeth in the earth
Psa. 58: 11 (R.V.).

THIS is one of the imprecatory psalms, and some are seriously disturbed with what seems an unforgiving spirit on the part of the psalmist. We must remember, however, that he was brought up in a severer school than ours. The cliffs of Sinai are sterner than the undulations of the mountain of Beatitudes. He was impressed more by the righteousness and less by the love of God than we are. The true key to the solution of the difficulty which these words suggest is in the words quoted above, which show his zeal for the character of Jehovah.

We must remember that the great conflict of his time was—why the wicked were permitted to flourish. Their success seemed to suggest that God was indifferent to sin. The book of Job is filled with controversy on the same theme: its chapters are filled with reasonings how God could be just, and allow the wicked to prosper, whilst the righteous suffered sore affliction. The psalmist, therefore, pleads that the wicked should be taken away with a whirlwind, that men may be compelled to admit that there is a God that judgeth. Let wicked men be put to shame and punished, then surely men will seek after righteousness because of the immunity it secures and the blessedness it offers.

Yes, child of God, there is a reward for thee. It is not in vain that thou hast washed thy hands in innocency. But it will not come in the coinage or honour of this age, else it would be evanescent and perishable. God is already giving thee of the eternal and divine —peace, joy, blessedness; and one day thou shalt be fully vindicated.

"Perhaps the cup was broken here
That Heaven's new wine might show
    more clear."

O my Strength, I will wait upon Thee. Unto Thee will I sing praises. Psa. 59: 9, 17.
IN the R.V. this contrast comes out in exquisite beauty. First, the soul waits upon God, its strength; and then to Him who had been its strength, it breaks into praise.

Notice the circumstances in which this psalm was composed. Around the house lurk Saul's emissaries, gathering themselves together against him. At any moment they threaten to break in and murder him upon the psalmist's bed. Michal and he are reduced to their last straits, yet the hunted man finds opportunity to wait upon God. It is not that he asks for aught as a definite gift; but he waits on God Himself, still expectant, eager. There are times when we cannot tell God what He should do; we can only hush our soul, as a mother her babe, and wait patiently until He tells us what He has prepared.

Meditate on these three attributes. He is the God of your mercy, the Fountain from which pure mercy flows, and nothing but mercy; He is your High Tower, whom you may put between yourself and Saul's hate; He is your Strength, not that you receive strength from Him, but that you appropriate Him as your strength. Stay thus musing and resting, until in that very house, pent in and besieged, you shall break into song, singing of God's strength, singing aloud of his mercy in the morning.

There are many beleaguered souls in the world, who have learnt to put God between themselves and their besiegers, and to sing to Him.

"For the glory and the passion of this
    midnight
I praise Thy Name, I give thee thanks,
    O Christ!

Thou hast neither failed me nor forsaken
Through these hard hours with victory
    overpriced;
Now that I too of Thy passion have partaken,
For the world's sake, called—elected—
    sacrificed."

Oh, restore us again! Psa. 60: 1 (R.V.).
CAST off! There is a sense in which that can never be. God will not cast off from salvation any soul of man that has sheltered under the covert of his Almighty wings. He may withdraw the sensible enjoyment and realization of his presence; but He cannot cast off for ever, in the sense of consigning any fugitive to his foes or to the fate he dreads.

And yet there is a sense in which we are cast off, when we have been unbelieving and disobedient. Allowed to take our own way, that we may learn its bitterness; permitted to hunger and thirst, that we may know how evil a thing it is to seek our supreme good anywhere else than in God; given over to the tender mercies of the gods we have chosen, that we may be taught their helplessness. It was thus that God cast off his people. He showed them hard things, and allowed them to reap as they had sown.

But now they cry for restoration. Put us back, they say, into the old place; be to us what Thou wert, and make us to Thee as we were. Restore us again. He did it for Peter, putting him back to the front place in the Apostolic band; for Mark, allowing him, who had gone back in his first missionary journey, to write a Gospel; for Cranmer and many more, who in the first burst of fiery trial shrank back, but to whom He gave more grace. Believe in the restoring grace of Christ, who not only forgives, but puts back the penitent and believing soul where it was before it fell away. Indeed, it has been suggested that the prodigal fares better on his return than those who do not go astray. It is not really so. But there is much music and song when the lost is found and the dead lives.

Lead me to the Rock that is higher than I. Psa. 61: 2.
DAVID is in the wilderness, fleeing from Absalom. It seems to him that he is at the end of the earth. "Love and Longing are potent magnifiers of space." His soul seems

wrapped in gloom; then, from afar, he sees the Rock of his salvation, and asks to be led thither, and set thereon.

Can you not see that rock? All the desert is baking like a furnace. The very pebbles burn the hand like cinders. Nothing can abide the scorching glare but the little green lizards that dart to and fro among the stones. Sunbeams strike like swords on the head of the luckless travellers that dare to brave their glittering edge. But yonder there is a rock, rising high above the shimmering sands, and casting a deep black shadow on one side. Little lichens hide in its crevices, streaks of vegetation are enamelled on its steep surfaces, and at its foot there are even a few rock-plants growing as best they can in the arid soil. That is the higher rock—the rock higher than the traveller's stature. He makes for it; or if he is too faint and overwhelmed, he is led to it, and beneath its gracious shadow finds instant respite and repose. The shadow of a great rock in a weary land!

Jesus will be all this to thee, dear heart. Thou hast got to the end of the earth and of thyself; call out to Christ, and He will bring thee, faint and ready to die, to Himself as the Shadow from the heat. The Man of men can be this for thee, because He is higher than thou art. Higher than I, because of his divine origin; higher, because of his perfect obedience; higher, because of his supreme sufferings; higher, because of his ascension to the right hand of power. Yet his side is scarred and cleft.

My soul waiteth only upon God. Psa. 62: 1 (R.V.).

DR. KAY gives as the literal translation: "Only toward God my soul is in silence"; or, "Only for God waits my soul all hushed." The noises of contending desires, the whispers of earthly hopes, are hushed: and the soul listens.

This is the test of true waiting. Wait before God till the voices, suggestions, and energies of nature become silent. Then only can God realize his uttermost of salvation. This was the secret of Abraham's long trial. He was left waiting till nature was spent, till all expedients proving abortive were surrendered; till all that knew him pitied him for clinging to an impossible dream. But as this great silence fell on him, the evidence of utter helplessness and despair, there arose within

his soul an ever-accumulating faith in the power of God; and there was no obstacle to prevent God realizing all, and beyond all, because all the glory accrued to Himself.

This is why God keeps you waiting. All that is of self and nature must be silenced; one voice after another cease to boast; one light after another be put out; until the soul is shut up to God alone. This process prevails equally in respect to salvation from penalty, deliverance from the power of sin, and our efforts to win souls. O my soul, be silent! Hush thee! Wait thou only upon God! Surrender thy cherished plans and reliances. Only when death has done its perfect work, will He bestow the power of an endless (an indissoluble) life.

"O Lord, my God, do Thou thy holy will!
I will lie still!
I will not stir, lest I forsake thine arm,
And break the charm,
Which lulls me, clinging to my Father's
breast
In perfect rest."

My soul followeth hard after Thee. Psa. 63: 8. THIS is a marvellous saying. Literally rendered, the words are, "cleaves after Thee"— contact and eager pursuit. The metaphor which underlies it is obviously borrowed from the psalmist's familiarity with the wilderness. It is a dry and thirsty land, where no water is: one says that he knows of a secret spring, whose waters are clear and cool, and offers to lead the thirsty one to its margin, lined with mosses and grasses. Instantly the soul starts in pursuit, and follows hard on the footsteps of the pioneer.

So when we are athirst for God, He comes, and, in the person of Jesus, leads us to Himself. He is Guide and Guerdon, Prompter of the impulse, and Promoter of its satisfaction. He excites the desire, offers to show us its sufficient supply, and finally brings us to his own lovingkindness, which is better than life. It becomes us, then, to follow hard after Him. Let us do as Jonathan's armour-bearer, to whom the young prince said, Come up after me. And Jonathan climbed up upon his hands and feet, and his armour-bearer after him, and the Philistines fell before Jonathan, and his armour-bearer slew after him.

Follow hard after Christ, over hedge and ditch, through stubble and gorse, across dyke and brook, sometimes down the steep fall into the hollow, and again breasting the mountain slope in the teeth of the pitiless blast. He has left an example that we should follow his steps. The scent lies lightly; catch it ere it fade. What though the fresh blood marks the track—follow hard! Follow on to apprehend that for which thou wast apprehended. Press toward the mark. Let there be no needless space between the Master and thee.

The righteous shall be glad in the Lord. Psa. 64: 10.

ARE you glad in your Christian life? Gladness is the perquisite of children and childlike hearts, and there is nothing which is more distinctively characteristic of the work of grace in the heart than Christian gladness. The world may simulate it, but it is conscious of its dreary failure. Often faded worldlings will come to the true Christian, saying, What is the secret of your perennial gladness?

The glad heart is conscious of the love of God; knows that it is reconciled through the blood of the cross; realizes that there is nothing between itself and the light of the Father's smile; is conscious of rectitude in intention and tenderness of yearning love and pity. In every difficult circumstance it recognizes the Father's appointment; in every archipelago of rocks it is aware of the presence of God aboard the vessel, holding the helm and keeping the keel in the deepest current.

O souls, get right with God! avail yourselves of the perfect righteousness of Christ; watch that there be nothing between you and Him; walk in the light as He is in the light; cultivate the habit of considering what has been given rather than what has been withheld—and you will find that He will make you glad in proportion to the days in which He has afflicted you, and the years in which you have seen evil. The sad heart tires in a mile. The glad one mounts up with wings as eagles. After his vision Jacob "lifted up his feet, and came to the land of the children of the East" (Gen. 29: 1, R.V.).

"Oh for the joy thy presence gives—
  What peace shall reign when Thou art here!
Thy presence makes this den of thieves
  A calm, delightful house of prayer."

Blessed is the man whom Thou choosest, and causest to approach unto Thee. Psa. 65: 4.

I WOULD be one of those favoured ones, my Saviour. There is nothing that the heart can conceive, which is to be compared with this blessedness. The light of nature, the joy of friendship, the fascination of art and books, can give no such delight as this approach unto Thee, this dwelling in thy courts. But the longer I know myself, the surer I am that Thou must cause me to approach, that Thou must put forth extraordinary means for making me dwell. So cause me to approach that I may dwell.

When thy soul has put up such a prayer as this, be sure that an answer will come. Thou mayest be brought nigh by an invisible but all-penetrating attraction, as when the sun draws the earth, or the magnet the needle: or perhaps God will answer thee by terrible things in righteousness. There will be deep humiliations, solemn heart-searchings, sharp crucifixions, cherished purposes thwarted, the keenest pain, the most searching fire. But through all, there will come a growing tenderness and desire.

It was said by the late Mr. Spurgeon that he was not conscious of spending a quarter of an hour of his waking moments without a distinct recognition of the presence of God. And this will be true of us if we will trust the High Priest to bring us within the vail, and keep us there. He entered that we may enter. He abides that we may abide. He stands in the Holiest that He may cause us to have a place of access among those that stand before the face of God. The anointing which we receive from Him will teach us how to abide. This may well be adopted as a life-prayer: "Cause me to approach, that I may dwell in thy presence."

Thou, O God, hast proved us; Thou hast tried us as silver is tried. Psa. 66: 10.

SILVER is tried by fire, and the heart by pain. "We went through fire." But in the fire thou shalt not be burned; only thy dross shall be removed. The smell of burning shall not pass upon thee, for the form of the Son of God shall be at thy side.

"Be still, and He shall mould thee for his heritage of rest;
The vessel must be shapen for the joys of Paradise.

And if the great Refiner in furnaces of pain
Would do his work more truly, count all
  his dealings gain."

The main end of our life is not to do, but
to become. For this we are being moulded
and disciplined each hour. You cannot
understand why year after year the stern
ordeal is perpetuated; you think the time
is wasted; you are doing nothing. Yes, but
you are situated in the set of circumstances
that gives you the best opportunity for
manifesting, and therefore acquiring, the
qualities in which your character is naturally
deficient. And the Refiner sits patiently beside
the crucible, intent on the process, tempering
the heat, and eager that the scum should pass
off, and his own face become perfectly reflected
in the surface.

Only be satisfied, with Archbishop Leighton,
that nothing can befall thee but what has
first passed concerning thee in the courts of
heaven. And say with the saintly Fletcher:
"I felt the will of my God like unto a soft
pillow, upon which I could lie down and
find rest and safety in all circumstances. Oh,
it is a blessed thing to sink into the will of
God in all things. Absolute resignation to
the Divine will baffles a thousand temptations;
confidence in our Saviour carries us sweetly
through a thousand trials."

*God shall bless us; and all the ends of the earth
     shall fear Him.* Psa. 67: 7.
THIS psalm is full of yearnings for the
salvation of mankind. The selfish desire for
the exclusive blessing of the chosen people
is lost sight of in the catholic yearning that
all the earth should fear Jehovah. Indeed,
this is the ground on which the psalmist rests
his personal claim for the Divine blessing.
It is as though he said, "We only ask for gifts
of grace, that through us they may be transmitted to all mankind." Turn us again, O
God, that times of refreshing may come from
thy presence to all men; our one desire is
that the peoples may praise Thee.

We are reminded of those noble words of
Andrew Fuller, to whom the initiation of
modern missions to the heathen is so largely
due: "We met and prayed for the heathen.
We were drawn out of ourselves. God blessed
us while we tried to be a blessing. Our hearts
were enlarged, and we were baptized into a
deeper sympathy with the soul-saving purposes of the Redeemer."

Are we infected with this noble passion?
Do we echo from our hearts the repeated
prayer of this psalm: "Let all the peoples
praise Thee"? Do we ask for blessing from
our own God, that we may be able to be a
greater blessing to others? It is because God
is "our own God," that we are so anxious to
make Him known. Oh that we might be
carried out to sea on the tide of God's purposes, and yearnings, and pity; and long as
the psalmist did that his saving health might
be known among all nations!

"Whoso hath felt the Spirit of the Highest,
  Cannot confound, nor doubt Him, nor
    deny;
Yea, with one voice, O world, though thou
    deniest,
  Stand thou on that side, for on this am I."

*Blessed be the Lord, who daily beareth our
     burden.* Psa. 68: 19 (R.V.).
NEVER tired or out of patience, that mighty
God, of whose advent the psalmist is so full,
daily bends beneath our burdens, and sets
Himself to help us through crushing difficulties. They are unbearable to us, but to Him
only a very little thing. If He taketh up the
isles as a very little thing, surely your heaviest
burden must be less.

But our mistake is that we do not realize
that God is bearing our burdens. We think
that we must cope with them; we let ourselves
worry, as though we were the loneliest, most
deserted, most pitiable beings in existence,
when all the while God is going beside,
ready to bear our burdens. The burden of
our sins; of our anxieties about ourselves,
and about others; of our frailties and infirmities; the responsibility of keeping us; the
pressure of our daily need—all these rest
daily on our God.

" 'Tis enough that He should care;
    Why should we the burden bear!"

Oh, do not carry your burdens for a single
moment longer; pass them over to Him who
has already taken your eternal interests to
his heart. Only be patient, and wait on Him,
and do not run to and fro seeking for help
from man, or making men your consolers
and confidants. Those who do this have their
reward. But as for you, anoint your head and
wash your face, so as not to excite the pity
of others. "Cast thy burden on the Lord,
and He will sustain thee." But, when it has

been cast, leave it with Him. Refuse to yield to anxious suggestions, and forthwith burst out into a song of thankful confidence. Bless Him! Praise Him! Be glad, and rejoice! When the heart is lightened of its load, it will soar.

Save me, O God: for the waters are come in unto my soul. Psa. 69: 1.

MATTERS sometimes become desperate. For days the waters have been out on the low-lying lands, and slowly rising against the embankment, in the shelter of which some house is situated. Now, however, they have undermined and swept it away. With a crash it has fallen into the yellow foaming waters. A moment's agitation, and then not a trace of it. There is nothing now to keep back the flood, and it comes into the home, rising stealthily up the walls. In the life of the soul such a crisis comes not unfrequently. You have dreaded something, and the cold chill of fear has cast a shudder over you; but surely it could never come to you! There is that protection, that barrier, of position, money, wealthy friends. But one by one these are swept aside, and the waters come ever nearer, till there is nothing between them and the soul. They come in unto the soul.

It is well for a man to be able then to turn to God with the "Save me" of the psalmist. God must have the entire trust of our soul. He takes away all that lies between Him and us, that we may hang on Him, and lie naked and open to Him in our utter helplessness. From the midst of your sorrows, from the deep sin in which you are sinking, from the deep waters that overflow you, cry to God. He knows your foolishness; your sins are not hid from Him. He will stretch out his right hand and catch you, saying, "O thou of little faith, wherefore didst thou doubt?" Then our crying and tears will be turned to joyous shouts. We shall praise the name of God with a song, and magnify Him with thanksgiving; for the Lord heareth the needy, and despiseth not his prisoners (30, 33).

Make haste unto me, O God! Psa. 70: 5.

"MAKE haste!" Our frail patience gives out full often. We think that God is never coming. So many days I have waited for Thee, and as yet there has not been one symptom of thine approach. Why are thy chariots so tardy? Lazarus is dying; a few hours more, and life will have ebbed away. Provisions are failing and water is scarce, and still the enemy is entrenched in proud security. The world scoffs; but Thou comest not down the mountain slope, bringing salvation. Where is the Pentecost of which Thou speakestt? Where thy Second Advent?

But God is making haste. On the wings of every hour, quicker than light leaps from world to world, He is on his way. Delays are not denials, but are necessary to the perfecting of his arrangements. "Lo, I come quickly!" is still true, though nineteen hundred years have passed.

We do not wish the destruction of our enemies, but their salvation. We long that God should be magnified, and souls saved. We yearn for the setting up of the Kingdom of God, which is peace on earth, and blessing. And for this end we desire that God should accelerate his coming. O God, make no tarrying! Thine enemies boast themselves; our spirits faint for fear; men are sinking into perdition. Make haste!

Thy God will not be a moment overdue. When the fourth watch breaks, He will interpose. Not too soon for education; not too late for deliverance. But dare to believe that He is never absent. He is near thee all the while, bending over thee and all men, with tender pity, only waiting till He can see, with infallible wisdom, the best instant to interefore.

Thou which hast showed me many and sore troubles, shalt quicken me again. Psa. 71: 20 (R.V.)

GOD shows us the troubles. We stand beside Him, and the mighty billows break around, but are shivered into myriads of drops. As we ride beside Him in the chariot of salvation, He points out to us the forms of dreaded evils, the ravines, the glaciers, the awful steeps; but it is as though we were cradled in some soft golden cloud which fringes the edge of the precipice, and glides along splintered cliffs where the chamois could not find footing. Look at this, saith our Guide. These are the troubles that overwhelm souls, and drain their life! Behold them, but thou shalt not suffer them! I show you them that you may know how to comfort and help those who have been overwhelmed. Sometimes, as this part of our education is being carried forward, we have to descend into "the lower parts of the earth," pass through subterranean passages, lie buried amongst the dead. But never for a moment is the cord of fellowship and union between God and us strained to breaking; and from the depths God will bring us up again.

Never doubt God. Never say that He has forsaken or forgotten. Never think that He is unsympathetic. He will quicken again. There is always a smooth piece in every skein, however tangled. The longest day at last rings out the evensong. The winter snow lies long, but it goes at last. Be steadfast; your labour is not in vain. God turns again, and comforts. And when He does, the heart which had forgotten its psalmody breaks out in jubilant song, as does the psalmist's.

"I will thank Thee with the lyre, even thy truth, my God;
I will harp unto Thee with the harp, Thou Holy One of Israel;
My lips shall sing aloud when I harp unto Thee,
And my soul which Thou hast redeemed."

Like rain upon the mown grass. Psa. 72: 6.
AMOS speaks of the king's mowings. Our King has many scythes, and is perpetually mowing his lawns. The musical tinkle of the whetstone on the scythe portends the cutting down of myriads of green blades, daisies, and other flowers. Beautiful as they were in the morning, within an hour or two they lie in long, faded rows. Thus in human life we make a brave show, which passes away like the beauty of grass, before the scythe of pain, the shears of disappointment, the sickle of death.

There is no method of obtaining a velvety lawn but by repeated mowings; and there is no way of getting tenderness, evenness, sympathy, but by the passing of God's scythes. How constantly the Word of God compares man to grass, and his glory to its flower! But when grass is mown, and all the tender shoots are bleeding, and desolation reigns where flowers were bursting, it is the most acceptable time for showers of rain falling soft and warm.

O soul, thou hast been mown. Time after time the King has come to thee with his sharp scythe. Thou hast sadly learnt that all flesh is grass, and that the efforts of thy self-life are vain. Where are the kingcups and buttercups of thy pride? They are laid low that thou shouldest bear better crops than ever; and that thou mayest do so, lo, He comes down as spring rain! He comes down; thus you have the miracle of his condescension. He comes down like rain; there you have the manner of his gentle advent. He comes on the mown grass; there is his expectancy, showing that his reason in mowing, followed as it is by the gentle raindrops, lies in the direction of new beauty and use. Do not dread the scythe—it is sure to be followed by the shower.

Only good is God to such as are pure in heart.
    Psa. 73: 1 (R.V., marg.).
GOD is only good. Such is the better rendering of the original. He makes "all things work together for good to them that love Him." However unlike goodness something in your lot may be, turn from the suggestions of sense to the affirmations of faith, and dare to say,

"His every act pure blessing is,
His path unsullied light."

Nothing so glorifies God as when a Cowper, rescued from the border of despair, snatched from committing suicide, dares still to cling to his belief in the goodness of God.

Our faith is sometimes assailed, as Asaph's was, by the anomalies we meet with in the world. The wicked prosper, whilst the waters of a full cup are wrung out to the people of God. The scribes and Pharisees greedily devour widows' houses, and prey on the helpless; whilst earnest merit seeks for work and recognition in vain. It is a strange world, full of contradictions, perplexities, and insoluble questions; but through it all God's children must dare to affirm that He is only good. You do not feel it? Nevertheless, reason, Scripture, experience, demand that you should assert it. The fact is, we have lost the standpoint of vision. The psalmist found these things too painful till he went into the sanctuary of God, and then he understood. Do not take earth as the centre of the universe, but the sun. Do not look at God from circumstances, but at circumstances from God. Live continually with Him: then will mystery become unravelled, and dark problems solved. Above all, be pure in heart, free from the stain of sense, with one purpose. Thou shalt see the soul of good in what seems evil.

Have respect unto the covenant. Psa. 74: 20. What a marvellous ejaculation! Here is a broken heart, pouring out its wail into the ear of God about his sanctuary and city. His adversaries have broken into the sacred precincts, and have hewn down its exquisitely carved work with hammer and hatchet. They were as men who lift up the hatchet against a forest of trees. There is nothing more utterly sad than the lament, "We see not our signs: there is no more any prophet; neither is there any among us that knoweth how long."

But from it all the suppliant rises to a climax of insistent appeal, and bids God have respect unto the covenant, made centuries before with Abraham and his seed. This was an appeal which struck right home to the heart of God. He could not deny Himself.

Here is an attitude in prayer, which can only be taken when the soul has become intimate with God, and come to close grip with Him. When every other reason has been marshalled, and every argument alleged; when still the answer tarries, and the case is desperate, then turn to God, and say, "Thou canst not run back from the terms of the covenant to which Thou hast pledged Thyself. This is included in the bond of agreement. I claim that Thou shouldst do as Thou hast said."

The covenant is set out at length in Heb. 8. It will cover all the exigencies of our lives. And by Gal. 3: 14 we may also place ourselves under the provision of the threefold covenant which God ratified with Abraham. In every trial, when desiring any blessing, when the crashing blows of the adversaries' hatchet are heard, turn to God, and say, "Have respect unto the covenant, of which Jesus is the Mediator and his blood the seal."

He lifteth up. Psa. 75: 7.

THIS is the psalm of uplifts. Against the uplifts of the wicked, described in the fourth verse, the psalmist contrasts the uplifts of God They come neither from E. nor W., but from above. God is the supreme arbiter of human destiny. The horns of the wicked are cut off, and those of the righteous are lifted up, by the interpositions of his Providence: for God is judge.

Are you depressed to-day? Look up to Him, and ask that you may be uplifted into fellowship with the risen glorified Lord. The Ascension of our Lord is the measure and example of our own. Are you lying among the pots? Seek for the wings of the dove, that with flitting pinion you may make your way to the Ark, where the hand awaits to take you in. Have you been in the valley of the shadow of death? Claim that the mighty power which wrought in Christ when God raised Him from the dead, and made Him sit in the heavenlies far above all power and principality, may do as much for you.

This is also true in a temporal sense. Promotions in any direction, to positions of credit, influence, or consideration, are the gift and work of God. To be lifted up to a chief place in his Church, to the stewardship of large wealth, to the exercise of commanding influence, is due to the divine interposition. You do not hold it at the caprice of man, but as the direct bestowment of your Father. Do not fear to lose it because you are true to Him. He expects you to be true to Him. He has put you where you are for no other purpose than that you should realize his purposes among men. "A man can receive nothing, except it have been given him from heaven." But if thou didst receive it, why dost thou glory?

Surely the wrath of man shall praise Thee: the residue shalt Thou restrain.
Psa. 76: 10 (R.V., marg.).

FROM this review of the fate of the foes of Israel, the psalmist comes to this conclusion. He has seen the serried hosts of Sennacherib come up against the city of God, but the warriors have slept their sleep: it was as though the Almighty had snapped the instruments of war across his knee. The wrath of man had been allowed up to a certain point, to bring into clear evidence the greater power of God; and then He had quietly put a term to its further manifestation.

Pharaoh's wrath against Israel only served to make God's mighty arm conspicuous. So with Herod, who took Peter to behead him; and with the high priests who fumed against the early Church. So shall it be with the arch-enemy of all. Christ is mightier than he. All he has done has acted as a foil to our Lord's glorious majesty. What he has wrought against man has only brought out more of the grace and the love of God. So shall it be to the end, when there shall be an eternal limit put to his hellish deeds, for he shall be bound by a great chain and cast into the bottomless pit.

Ah, tried soul, what is permitted to happen in your life will tend ultimately and eternally to the praise and glory of God, if only you will abide in Him, and suffer bravely, nobly, in the grace of Christ. And there always will be a restraint. There will always be a "thus far and no farther." God's faithfulness will not let us be tempted above that we are able. When the lesson is learnt, and the opportunity for the revelation of God is complete, and the tried soul is proved to have won as its reward the crown of life, then God will stay the enemy and avenger, and give spoils more glorious than mountains of prey.

Thy way is in the sea. . . . Thou leddest thy people like a flock. Psa. 77: 19, 20.
THIS is almost the climax of sublimity, because of the contrast of the majesty and gentleness of God. In the first of these verses you have the former. God is described as wading through mighty oceans as a man might ford some tiny stream. The Atlantic with fathomless depths is no more to Him than a brook to us—not so much. But as the brook hides the footmarks which are imprinted on its soft ooze, so are God's footprints hidden. We cannot detect his great and wonderful secrets. We are unable to gauge his reasons. He marches through the ages with steps we cannot track. For his orbit there is no standard of computation.

But dread Him not. This mighty God has the tender heart of a shepherd. He leads his people like a flock; not overdriving, but carrying the lambs in his bosom, and gently leading those that are with young. Mightier than the mightiest, but meeker than the meekest! The Lion of Judah, but the Lamb of Bethlehem! Prince and Saviour; Fellow of Jehovah; and yet the smitten Shepherd of the scattered flock!

Nor is this all. It is a human hand that leads the flock. God does his work through the hands of human and fallible agents. You have not recognized Him; but had your eyes been opened, you would have seen his leading in the gentle hand of that mother, in the strong grasp of that friend, in the trembling fingers of that young girl, in the tiny hand of your little babe. Ah, how many good and tender hands have moulded and fashioned our lives!—but beneath them all there have been the leadings of the great God, convoying us through deep and dark waters to our fold.

Can God? Psa. 78: 19.
OH, fatal question! It shut Israel out of the Land of Promise, and it will do as much for you. Israel had seen the wonderful works of God, cleaving the sea, lighting the night, and giving water from rocks. Yet they questioned God's ability to give bread, and to spread a table in the wilderness. Surely it was a slur on his gracious Providence to suppose that He had begun what He could not complete, and had done so much but could not do all.

But we are in danger of making the same mistake. Though behind us lay the gift of the Cross, the miracles of Resurrection and Ascension, the care exercised by God over our early years, the goodness and mercy of our after lives, we are disposed to say, "Can God?" Can God keep me from yielding to that besetting sin? Can God find me a situation, or provide food for my children? Can God extricate me from this terrible snare in which I am entangled? We look at the difficulties, the many who have succumbed, the surges that are rolling high, the poor devil-possessed child, and we say, If Thou canst do anything, help us!

Nay, nay, there is no If with God; there is no limit to his almightiness but thy unbelief. The words are wrongly placed. Never say again, "Can God?" but God can. Never, If Thou canst; but If I can believe. Never, If Thou canst Thou wilt; but If Thou wilt Thou canst; and Thou wilt, since Thou hast made and redeemed me, and Thou canst not forsake the work of thine own hands. Argue from all the past to the present and future. Fetch arguments for faith from the days that have gone.

"His love in time past forbids me to think
He'll leave me at last in trouble to sink."

How long, O Lord? Psa. 79: 5 (R.V.).
TO us, also, as to this long-suffering Jew, God's dealings seem sometimes interminable. We do not understand why the cloud hangs over us so long, why the pressure of trouble lasts year after year. We cry, "How long, O Lord?" in gusts of impatience; but take care not to hurry God unduly, lest thou force Him to forgo doing his best work in thy life.

This parable helped me; may it help you to be silent, still, and long-suffering. A bar of iron, worth £1, when wrought into horseshoes, is worth £2; if made into needles, it is worth £70; if into penknife blades, it is worth £650; if into springs for watches, it is worth £50,000. What a drilling the poor bar must undergo to be worth this; but the more it is manipulated, the more it is hammered and passed through the fire, and beaten, and pounded, and polished, the greater its value.

So with the Jews. No other nation has passed through such awful trial and discipline as they have; but no other nation was capable of yielding such wealth of service to mankind, nor affording such untold service in the highest regions.

So with ourselves. Those that suffer most are capable of yielding most; and it is through pain that God is getting the most out of us for his glory and the blessing of others. It will be all right some day. We shall see it and be satisfied. Yes, great Father, we would like to be watchsprings. Take no heed of our cry if sometimes we forget ourselves and say, How long?

"Then haste Thee, Lord! Come down
Take thy great power and reign!
But frame Thee first a perfect crown
Of spirits freed from stain."

Turn us again, O God! Psa. 80: 3.
THREE times we have this cry repeated in this psalm. Again and again, and each time with some additional thought, the soul pleads for Restoration (R.V., marg.).

The Master said to Peter: When thou art converted (i.e., turned again) strengthen thy brethren. But Peter did not realize that the Master Himself would need to turn him. He turned his back on his Lord and denied Him; but Jesus turned him back, by that look, that message from his grave mouth, that interview in the garden and on the lake-shore. He turned him facewards to Himself, and caused his face to shine, and Peter was saved.

We can be regenerated only once, but we can be converted many times. The new life is implanted once for all, and it is everlasting, unextinguishable, and permanent; but those who have been born from above, and are undoubtedly children of God, may, beneath the power of some strong fascination, turn aside, may wander in forbidden paths, may get into such a maze as to be walking in the contrary direction to that on which they started. There may even be times when our desire for God is slackened, our appetite for the Bible is lost, our soul is bound and tied with the cords of sin; at such times, let us bemoan ourselves, our folly and impotence, and cry, "Turn us again, O God, and we shall be turned; for

Thou art the Lord our God." He who at first called us to Himself must call us back: He who regenerated, must renew: He who reconciled us to God by his death, must save us by his life. When most dark, and dead, and estranged, cry with Ephraim: "Turn Thou me, and I shall be turned; for Thou art the Lord my God" (Jer. 31: 18).

Thou calledst, . . I delivered; I answered thee in the secret place of thunder. Psa. 81: 7.
SUCH trouble as Israel passed through in the Exodus comes but once in the history of a nation. From the brick-kilns and treasure-cities which they built, God's people called to Him with strong cryings and tears, extorted by insupportable sorrows. Still more did they need to cry for help when they stood between the Egyptians and the waters of the Red Sea. From the beach a nation's call rose to God. Then was their trouble and heart-travail—a nation in throes of pain! Are you in trouble? Call upon God in the day of trouble; He will answer.

God's answers are often in the secret place of thunder. From his pavilion of cloud God spoke in tones of thunder that pealed over the heavily-breaking surf of the Red Sea. Several of the Psalms allude to the thunderstorm that rolled through the night of the passage through the deep. The march of Israel was to the roll of thunder. The peals of heaven's artillery struck dismay into the hearts of the alien; but it was as though the Father was speaking to his children, the people with whom He was in covenant.

God's answer to our prayer is often in thunder-tones that hurtle through the air. By terrible things in righteousness He answers us. When Jesus asked the Father to glorify his name, the quiet reply, "I have . . . and will," which He understood, sounded like thunder to the bystanders. Happy the child who in thunder-claps detects the Father's voice, and in mystic characters of flame reads the Father's handwriting! Whilst, at Sinai, the people trembled at the repeated thunder-peals reverberating above them, Moses went into the thunder-covert where God was. There is no fear in love, because perfect love casteth out the fear that hath torment.

Arise, O God, judge the earth: for Thou shalt inherit all the nations. Psa. 82: 8 (R.V.).
THE judges and magistrates are compared in

this psalm to God, because they exercise something of his power in the right ordering of human society. The Bible always inculcates respect and reverence to properly constituted authority, though it never hesitates to demand of all in authority that they should exercise their high functions impartially. Too often has the high trust been abused, and the psalmist turns with relief to the upright Judge, and comforts himself with the reflection that one day God Himself shall judge the earth, because He shall inherit all the nations.

Christ is the Firstborn and Only Begotten. As such He shall inherit all things. They were made for Him. He is the Heir. He came in his incarnation to claim his inheritance; but his claim was denied. He was cast out of the vineyard and slain; but his claims were not annulled, they remained intact. And during the present age they are being vindicated; and in answer to his appeal He is receiving the heathen for his inheritance, and the uttermost parts of the earth for his possession. One nation after another is becoming his province. The kings of the isles are bringing presents; the kings of Sheba and Seba are offering gifts.

It is great encouragement in missionary work to know that every nation is by right of gift and inheritance our Lord's. He sold his all to purchase it, because his treasure was buried here. It is ours to make it his in fact. It is always easy to work on the line of the divine purpose. God never purposes outside what is practicable and possible for man to realize. Apprehend the purpose of God, and without hesitation claim its realization.

O God, keep not Thou silence; hold not thy peace, and be not still, O God. Psa. 83: 1 (R.V.).
OH that God would break the silence! If He would but say one word! If we might but hear that voice—deep as the sound of many waters, and tender as the call of love—just to say that He was there; that all which we believed was true; that He was satisfied and pleased; that our perplexities would work out right at last! It is so difficult sometimes to go on living day by day without one authoritative word; and we are prone to rebuke Him for silence, that He is still, that He holds his peace. "Be not Thou silent unto me, lest I be like those that go down into the pit."

But God has not kept silence. The Word was manifested. In Him the silence of eternity was broken. And if thou and I are still, if our ear is

purged, and anointed with the blood and oil, if we make a great silence in our heart, we shall hear Him speak.

"Where is thy haunt, Eternal Voice?
  The region of thy choice;
Where, undisturbed by earth, the soul
  Owns thy entire control."

'Tis not where torrents are born, nor amid snow-capped peaks, nor in the break of the surf; but in the heart, weaned from itself, isolated in chambers of sickness, cast among strangers, yearning for tender voices that cannot make themselves heard—there God is no longer still. He breaks the silence. "Comfort ye, comfort ye, my people, saith your God." "It is I; be not afraid." It is always easy to detect God's voice, because it is full of Jesus, who is the Word of God, and it is corroborated by Providence; but the heart must be still, and on the listen!

The Lord God is a sun and shield: the Lord will give grace and glory. Psa. 84: 11.
HOW God suits Himself to our need! In darkness, He is a Sun; in the sultry noon, a Shield; in our earthly pilgrimage He gives grace; when the morning of heaven breaks, He will give glory. He suits Himself to every varying circumstance in life. He becomes what the exigency of the moment requires. And as the psalmist well says, He withholds no good thing from them that walk uprightly. Learn the art of extracting from God the special form of help of which you stand in need.

THE SUN is the source of light and life. With impartial beneficence he scatters his beams on palace and cottage, mountain summit and lowland vale. He is ever pouring out his beams. It is our part only to stand in them, or to open casement or door. God is shining, dear heart. Get out of thyself, and sun thy shivering frame in his untiring love.

A SHIELD may be the shadow of a great rock in the scorching desert, or the canopy of a gourd's growth. Put God between yourself and the sirocco of temptation. Is the noon with its burning heat too much for thee? Hide in the Lord God. The heat shall not smite thee by day, nor the frost by night.

Dost thou need Grace? He is full of it. His grace is sufficient. With both hands He will give and give again; only practise the habit of taking. Grace is the bud of which Glory is the flower. If He has given this, He will not withhold that. If thou knewest the gift of God, thou wouldst be sure that Glory in germ is within thee, waiting only for the summer of Eternity to develop in perfect beauty. "We have had our access by faith into this grace wherein we stand, and we rejoice in hope of the glory of God."

Mercy and truth are met together; righteousness and peace have kissed each other. Psa. 85: 10.
THIS has been fitly called "the bridal of the earth and sky." Mercy is the love that finds its reason in itself, its measure in helplessness and ill-desert. But in God it is always blended with Truth. God must be faithful to his covenant relations, to his Son, to Himself, and to the law which He has instituted. Any display of mercy must be consistent with truth. These are heavenly twins. Where you meet one you will be sure of the other. Jesus was full of grace and truth. The love He brings is consistent with the highest considerations; and by his death it is so arranged that God acts consistently with his holy law in loving and saving the meanest and weakest believer.

RIGHTEOUSNESS has for her twin sister Peace. "The effect of righteousness shall be peace." The King of Righteousness is after that the King of Peace. If you want peace, you must be right with God; and if you would be right with God, you must come to Jesus and become united to Him, who is made unto us the righteousness of God. At the cross these two kissed. The righteousness of God was satisfied, and the peace of man secured.

What a wondrous cross is that on which the Prince of Glory died! The question was—How could God be just, and yet justify the ungodly? How could He uphold the majesty of the moral law, and yet take sinners to his heart? But the answer came clear and satisfying, when the Maker of man took on Himself our sin and gave justice its due. Now see that perfect blending of the divine attributes, and that God is "just, and the Justifier of him that believeth in Jesus." Oh that truth might spring up as the response and echo of our hearts!

Thou, Lord, art good, and ready to forgive. Psa. 86: 5.
WE are blinded by sin, and cannot believe that God is ready to forgive. We think that we must induce Him to forgive, by tears, promises of amendment, religious observances. There is

in every heart such difficulty in understanding the unwearying patience and ever-yearning love of our Heavenly Father. Oh, clasp this word to your heart! Say it over and over again—"Ready to forgive, ready to forgive!" At any moment of the sad history of the prodigal, had he returned, he would have found his old father as ready to forgive as on the day, too long delayed, when he did return. The only pity was that he had not come long before.

You have fallen a hundred times, and are ashamed to come to God again; it seems too much to expect that He will receive you again. But He will, for He is ready to forgive. You feel that your sin is aggravated, because you knew so much better; but it makes no difference to Him, He is as ready to forgive you now, as when first you came. You are disposed to wait a little, till your sin has become more remote, till passion has subsided, till the inscription has faded from the wall; but you might as well go at once, God is as ready to forgive at this moment as at any future time. You are wounding Him greatly by doubting Him. He is ready, waiting, eager to forgive. You have only to call upon Him, and you would discover the plenteousness of his mercy. How ready Jesus ever was to forgive sinners, herein revealing God's heart!

"O Love, Thou deep eternal tide,
How dear are men to Thee!
The Father's heart is opened wide
By Jesus' blood to me."

All my fountains are in Thee. Psa. 87: 7 (R.V.).
"ALL my fresh springs," the Prayer-book version has it. Perennial freshness! This is our portion. We have only to abide in Christ in daily, hourly faith, through the grace of the Holy Spirit, for where that is secured there need be no further effort; naturally, perennially, plentifully, there will arise in us the fountains whose source is God, and the ultimate destination of whose waters are the wildernesses and deserts around.

Do you want freshness in your love? The vintages of other years cannot provide you with the ruddy clusters and the wine of sacrifice required for present-day needs. You want new enthusiasm, tenderness, and interest in those around you. Deepen your union with God by faith and prayer. Your fresh springs are in Him; He will Himself be in you a spring of living water, rising up to everlasting life and love.

Do you want freshness in your views of truth? There are such constant demands made on your teaching powers, that you are sometimes fearful of exhaustion. But if you keep your heart open to God, and your soul perpetually nourished by Scripture, you will find that God's thoughts will come freshly and brightly to you—new as each morning, fresh as spring.

Do you want freshness in your religious life? This, too, is his gift, because the life we live in the flesh is, after all, not our own life, but his. Jesus is in us, the Hope and Fount of the true life. All He wants is to have orifices, channels, openings in the rocky soil, and He will arise in us heavenward and Godward, as fountains in the sunny air. Rise up in us, Thou Blessed One, who art evermore the resurrection and the life!

Incline thine ear unto my cry, for my soul is full of troubles. Psa. 88: 2, 3.

THE psalmist has found the quickest argument before his God. There is nothing that so quickly makes the bell ring in heaven as the touch of a troubled hand. When a man is full of the interests of life, of prosperity, and self-content; when the voices of applause resound on every side; when his house is full of children, and his barn of sheaves, his prayer halts, and God seems far away. But let trouble come—let the waters, swollen by many confluent streams, begin to rise within his soul, so that lover and friend are far away, and he compassed with terror (16, 18), then God bends his ear and heart.

O child of sorrow, do not count that you are cast away! It is true that your Lord cried from his Cross, "Why hast Thou forsaken Me?" but even Him, though laden with the sins of the world, the Father held near his heart. And He has not left you, neither can He.

"The earth and every vassal star,
  All space beyond the soar of angel wings,
Wait on his word; and yet He stays his ear
  For every sigh a suppliant sinner brings."

Try and think of trouble as storing your heart with seeds of joy; as acting upon you as the fire upon the primeval earth, scattering jewels through its crust; or as the glaciers that brought the rich soil into the valleys; or as the husbandman who buries the seeds of spring in the autumn fields. A veiled angel, nothing else!

"But if, impatient, thou let slip thy cross,
Thou wilt not find it in this world again,
Nor in another; here, and here alone,
Is given thee to suffer for God's sake."

Nevertheless my loving-kindness will I not utterly take from him. Psa. 89: 32, 33.

I WAS asked the other day if I believed, as an increasing number were said to do, that each man bears his own sin, and that there is no such thing as the vicarious imputation of the sins of the world to the Lamb of God. I said at once that this idea, so growingly prevalent, would not avail to help men and women like many of those with whom I come in contact, and are deeply dyed. Tell them that they must bear their own sin, and they turn from you in despair. This is what conscience has been reading to them hourly from the stony book of the law. The soul dreads to have to bear its sin, and cries out for propitiation and covering. A dying man said recently, "I have been into the valley of death, and where is my covering?" Men need a covering. It is requisite that help should be laid upon One that is mighty (ver. 19).

We used to distinguish between guilt and secondary consequences of sin. For guilt we must have the transference of the black load of sin to our Saviour. But it is also perfectly true that the nervous or physical system of the drunkard will never be what it might have been. The consequences of wrongdoing must be reaped. God will forgive you, and his loving-kindness will not depart; but He will visit your transgression with the rod, and your iniquity with stripes. But even here his mercy will avail to transform the curse into a blessing, and make myrtles bloom where thistles had flourished. God's love can so transmute these results of sin, that where sin reigned unto death, grace shall reign unto eternal life. But never forget that, when once God has entered into covenant with a soul, He will stand to it, till the heavens be no more.

Oh, satisfy us in the morning with thy mercy. Psa. 90: 14 (R.V.).

IT was towards the close of the desert wanderings that Moses wrote this sublime psalm, all the imagery of which is borrowed from the wilderness. The watch around the camp-fire at night; the rush of the mountain flood; the grass that sprouts so quickly after the rain, and is as quickly scorched; the sigh of the wearied pilgrim (9, R.V., marg.). As the old man looks back on life, he gives it as his experience that the heart which is satisfied with mercy in the morning, never fails to rejoice and be glad all its days.

There is no hour like that of morning prime for fellowship with God. If we would dare to wait before Him for satisfaction then, the filling of that hour would overflow into all other hours. A bright Christian lad, giving his brief testimony for Jesus, recently, told his secret when he said that at his conversion he trusted the Lord with his morning hour; and the way he spoke of it indicated the radiancy of the light that shone for him then.

Perhaps the morning of life was rather in Moses' thought. If so, the old man has prepared a prayer in which successive generations of bright children may join. Young ones, do you want a glad and rejoicing life? Do you want to live by the wells that never dry up or freeze? Seek God's mercy in Jesus Christ our Lord, and the day will never dawn when you will regret having made that choice: nay, every day will be full of rejoicing gladness. I like that record of the holy Columba, at the end of his saintly life, "Angelic in appearance, graceful in speech, holy in work, beloved by all—for a holy joy ever beaming on his face revealed the joy and gladness with which the Holy Spirit filled his inmost soul."

Thou, O Lord, art my refuge.
Psa. 91: 9 (R.V.).

THE structure of this psalm is often obscured. It begins with the announcement on the part of the chorus of the general truth that to dwell in the inner place of fellowship is to abide under the protection of divine Power.

Twice the psalmist speaks. In the second verse we hear him saying:

"I will say of the Lord, He is my refuge and my fortress,
My God in whom I trust."

In the ninth verse he breaks in again:

"For Thou, O Lord, art my refuge."

And each profession on his part is followed by the outburst of the chorus with an enunciation of all the blessings which most certainly will accrue.

In the last three verses God Himself is introduced, assuring his child of all that He is

prepared to do and be. Have you ever said definitely, "O Lord, Thou art my refuge"? Fleeing from all other, have you sheltered in Him from the windy storm and tempest, from the arrow by day, and pestilence by night, from man and devil? You must avow it. Do not only think it, but say it. Keep saying it because it is true, rather than because you feel it to be true. Not only in the midst of sympathizing friends, but in hours of loneliness, desertion, and opposition.

In a farm, in which I am interested, we have an incubator, the artificial heat of which hatches hundreds of little chickens; but there always seems a great lack in their lives—no mother's call or wing. They invariably remind me of those who have not sheltered under the wing of God.

I am anointed with fresh oil.
Psa. 92: 10 (R.V.).

THERE is perennial freshness in God—in the works of nature, in his love, and in the renewal of the soul. Does the eye ever tire of the changeful beauty of the clouds? Though we look out from childhood to old age on the same landscape, there is always something fresh to captivate the roving eye. Think of the unfailing freshness in love—love of woman to man, of mother to child. Think of the freshness of each returning day, of earth in her springtime robe, with the myriads of sweet children, whose laughter is as ringing and their eyes as bright as if the earth were young, instead of being old and weary. And if God can do this for the works of his hands, is there any limit in the freshness which He will communicate to his children?

Each morning bend your heads, ye priests of the Most High, for the fresh anointing for the new ministries that await you. The former grace and strength will not suffice; old texts must be rejuvenated and reminted; old vows must be respoken; the infilling of the Holy Spirit must be as vivid, and may be as definite, as at the first. See to it that you do not rise from your knees till you can say, "I have been, and am, anointed with the fresh oil." And the anointing that ye receive from Him shall abide on you, teaching you how to abide in Him. So you shall bring forth fruit in old age, and in life's winter be full of sap and fervour.

Pastor Harm used to say: Pray diligently. I do not mean your common prayer alone; but pray diligently in your room daily for the

Holy Spirit. How their faces shine, who receive this daily unguent!

The floods have lifted up, O Lord, the floods have lifted up their voice. Psa. 93: 3.

HOW often a man says these words over to himself as he paces the deck of the steamer in mid-Atlantic! There is no commentary to this psalm like that supplied by the break of the waves. Sometimes the voice of the floods is deafening; you cannot hear yourself speak; at other times all night, through the porthole, you hear their musical break beneath. The lifted up voice of the sea gives many notes in the great organ of nature, sometimes the deep bass, at other times the silvery treble. One says to one's self:

"What are the wild waves saying?"

They may be inciting one another to a work of destruction and devastation, roaring in their rage, fretting for supremacy. Why should they endure the presence of man in their wild waste? He is an intruder. The sea-gulls are welcome; they are at home as in their native element, but man has no right.

So do the waves of trouble roar wildly around the bark of our life. There are times when surge on surge rolls in upon the soul, and breaks with boom and roar; but always there floats upon the soul the refrain of this sublime canticle, "Above the voices of many waters the Lord on high is mighty." He sits as King, higher than the spray is tossed, deeper than the fathomless depths, mightier than the strongest billow. Let Him but say, "Peace, be still!" and the greatest storm that ever swept the waves with wild fury sinks into the tranquil sleep of childhood. Or, if we sink beneath the wave, we shall but fall into the hollow of God's hand, where the oceans are cradled.

Blessed is the man whom Thou chastenest . . . that Thou mayest give him rest. Psa. 94: 12, 13.

THE reason of chastening is rest-giving. God chastens us that He may give us rest from the days of adversity. In sorrow we learn lessons which serve us in good stead when others suffer without remedy. In trial-times the child of God falls back upon the lessons his Father taught him out of the black letterbook of pain, and he knows how to comport himself. Thus he finds rest to his soul, rest in the will of God, rest in humble submission to his lot, rest in the wisdom that cannot err, in the love that cannot forget.

God teaches all the scholars in his school. He dares entrust none to an usher. Enter thyself as a scholar in the academy of grace, and thou shalt at once be taught, as all his children are, of God.

There is but one text-book for the whole school. It is always the Law of God. We learn from it when we are babes. In mature life we resort to it at every emergency. In old age we feel we never understood before its meaning or beauty. It is God's "horn-book."

Those who have sat longest under God's tuition profess they know least. Instead of beginning at the lowest class and working up, we begin at the highest, and work down. The grey-heads sit on the infants' forms, and the simplest are the wisest. There is blessedness, not in roaming the fields, but in sitting on the bench and learning what God teaches each soul that will give heed.

Some day, the lessons will be done, the doors thrown open, and the scholars will be dismissed, never to return to the hard bare forms, but to go for holy-days of never-ending gladness in the Father's home.

Unto whom I sware in my wrath that they should not enter into my rest. Psa. 95: 11.

GOD'S Rest has been waiting for man's entrance, since He rested from all the work that He created and made. To all other days there were evening and morning, but not to this. It does not consist in circumstances, or conditions of existence, but in disposition. It does not lie, as sacred poets have too often suggested, beyond the confines of this world— it is now, and here. Canaan is not primarily a type of heaven; but of that blessed experience which is ours when we have passed the Jordan of death to natural impulse or selfish choice, and have elected for evermore to accept, and delight in, the will of God.

Will you not take up this position to-day? To-day! Oh that ye would hear his voice! To hear his voice speaking in the heart, in circumstances, and in nature, and to obey promptly, gladly, blithely—this would bring the soul into the rest that remains unexhausted for the people of God. Are you hardening your heart against some evident duty to which you are called, but which you are evading? Are you hardening your heart to some appeal which comes to you through the ties of kinship and nature? Are you saying, Can God subdue these Canaanites, instead of God can? Beware, for this is the sin of Massah and Meribah, which, being interpreted, means strife. Woe to those that strive with their Maker; let the potsherd strive with the potsherds of the earth.

Everyone comes in the Christian life, once at least, to Kadesh-barnea. On the one hand the land of rest and victory; on the other the desert wastes. The balance, quivering between the two, is turned this way by faith; that by unbelief. Trust God, and rest. Mistrust Him, and the door closes on rest, to open to wanderings, failure, and defeat.

Say among the nations, The Lord reigneth.
     Psa. 96: 10 (R.V.).

TELL it out! The message is too good to warrant silence. That the Lord is King is the secret of jubilation and blessing for all the world.

Nature is glad, because his rule will emancipate her from the thraldom under which she has groaned too long. When the kingdom is established in the hand of the Son of Man, the long travail of creation will be over; the new heavens and earth will have emerged. Therefore the psalmist depicts the outburst of thanksgiving from seas, and fields, and trees. The world of men may be glad also, because the reign of Jesus means equity for the oppressed, equal-handed justice for the poor, peace among the nations.

But, above all, gladness becomes the saints. If the Lord Jesus has become King of your heart, and has brought blessing to you, do not hesitate to give voice to your allegiance. In private, sing unto Him a new song; in public, show forth his salvation, and declare his glory. Tell it out, tell it out! Have you ever seriously considered whether it may not be God's will for you to give up your life to going forth to distant lands, to tell it out that God has made Jesus King, and that He must reign, and that his reign is blessedness?

Probably but a very brief interval remains, during which we can tell it out. Human history has well-nigh fulfilled its six working-days, and approaches its millennial rest; the times of the Gentiles, according to every computation, are nearly fulfilled; the lawlessness, which was to mark the last days, is conspicuously manifest; the bride is rapidly completing her preparation for the marriage-feast—haste then, O heralds of Salvation, prepare in the deserts a highway for our God!

Light is sown for the righteous, and gladness
     for the upright in heart. Psa. 97: 11.

LIGHT means recognition, joy, song. These await such as are clad about with the righteousness of Christ, and are following the paths of righteousness for his Name's sake. Never swerve from the path of the righteous; however trying and dark your present experience may be, it leads to a harvest-home of joy beyond the years.

Sowing is sad work. It is a casting away of precious seed; the flinging far and wide of the treasured stores of the barn; an expenditure of the present for the future. The sower's heart might fail if it pictured the field mice, the rotting rains, the blighting mildew, which have ruined so many hopes, and lie in wait. So the present is your sowing-time; but every moment of trial, each stab of pain, nobly borne, is a seed-germ cast into the furrows, which will certainly bring a blessed recompense of light. You do not realize it, but you are sowing light. Each act of self-denial, in which you cast yourself into the ground to die, is a seed-germ of the harvest of gladness.

Coal is sown light. When the forests in all the glory of their foliage were hurled into the bosom of the primeval earth, and desolation reigned, it seemed a sad waste of the Creator's work. Who could have realized then that God was really sowing the light of winter nights, the fires of factory and forge? Do not be too sad. Harvest will come, though the weeks move slowly.

"All we have willed or hoped or dreamed of
     Good shall exist:
     Not its semblance, but itself; no Beauty,
          nor Good, nor Power,
Whose voice has gone forth, but each
     survives for the melodist,
     When Eternity affirms the conception of
          an hour."

Oh, sing unto the Lord a new song!
     Psa. 98: 1.

COME, my soul, thou must awake to sing a new song. Thou hast dwelt long enough on those old, sad, minor chords of loss and disappointment, of regret for the withered past, of bitter remorse. Surely there is something better, nobler, worthier of thee and thy great Lord. Has He not done, is He not doing, marvellous new things in thy daily experience? Are not his mercies new every morning, and his faithfulness every night? Is not his love always at work spreading thy table for new meals, making thy bed for new slumber, contriving new alleviations and delights? Look out for these till meditation induces thanksgiving.

There is always a new song in heaven, because ever a fresh and deepening appreciation of God. The exploring parties are continually bringing back some fresh and wonderful produce of God's wisdom and grace; and as they hold it up to the admiration of kindred spirits, the exhibition elicits new songs. Through the Church is made known to the principalities and powers of the heavenlies the manifold wisdom of God. The song of redeeming grace can never grow old, even though the same words recur; they resemble the banks of the stream through which waters are passing that never passed before. My soul, listen to the bursting harmonies of creation, seas, floods, hills; they chide thee. Cast off the spirit of heaviness, and don the garment of praise. Perchance thy soul is sluggish and dull. But it should not master thee. The psalmist was master of his soul; and when he bade it bless the Lord, all that was within him broke forth into melodious thanksgiving. Let thy spirit, energized by the Holy Spirit, be regnant over the entire realm of thy inner life.

Samuel among them that call upon his name.
Psa. 99: 6.
EVIDENTLY those that call upon the name of God compose a separate class. There are classes of prophets, pastors, teachers; and there are the mighty wrestlers with God, whose voices are familiar sounds in the divine presence chamber. It is a high honour to be included among them that call upon his name. If you cannot find your place in any other class, perhaps it is here. Possibly you have great gifts of prayer and intercession, which you have never rightly employed, to your own great loss, and the loss of others. Do not wait for God's Angel of Providence to shut you forcibly into a lonely chamber, and compel you to use your great gift.

Samuel's prayers are frequently referred to. At times he would cry unto God all night. He counted it a sin to cease to pray for the people.

His prayers secured the defeat of the Philistines; and the nation sheltered itself in his intercessions. We can never estimate the worth of a good man's prayers; and they lift a man like Samuel, destitute of commanding genius, to stand side by side with Moses in the estimate of Eternity.

In a memorable interview with the late George Müller, he told me some of his wonderful experiences in dealing with a prayer-answering God. Just before he died he heard of the conversion of an old man, for whom he had prayed during fifty years. May not he, and such as he, be remembered in this holy category? Oh to be remembered among those that call on God's name! But always bear in mind the thrice accentuated message of this Psalm (3, 5, 9), that God is holy. It is only as we are cleansed from all filthiness of the flesh and spirit, that we can prevail in intercessory prayer.

We are his; we are his people, and the sheep of his pasture.   Psa. 100: 3 (R.V.).
THE sense of God's proprietorship is the true basis of our consecration. We must realize his rights over us before we can freely give Him his due. Those rights are manifold in their sweet reasonableness; but amongst them all, this of creation is one of the chief. God has a right to us because He has made us.

He made us, as the potter fashions the clay, for a distinct purpose; and surely He has a right to use the vessels of his workmanship for the purpose unto which He has designed them.

He made us, as the builder erects a house for the purpose of inhabiting it; and surely He has a right to occupy every distinct room, and go to and fro in it as He may please.

He made us, as the hand of the weaver makes some textile fabric for wearing; and surely He must not be debarred from the free and unquestioned disposal of that on which He has expended anxiety and time.

We are Christ's by creation, by purchase, by toils and tears, by the gift of the Father. The Good Shepherd owns us, though we do not always acknowledge his ownership, or repay his pains and wounds on our behalf. Look up into his face and say, "I am thine by a myriad ties, and am bound to Thee for evermore. Lead me where Thou wilt; guide me whither Thou choosest; count me as one of thy people; feed me on thy pasture-lands; make as much of me as Thou canst, this side of heaven;

number me with thy saints in glory everlasting."

"With bowed heads and open hearts," says Dr. Westcott, "may we offer ourselves. We can do no more, and we dare do no less."

I will walk within my house with a perfect heart. Psa. 101: 2.

THIS is the hardest place to walk in perfectly. It seems easier to walk perfectly among strangers than in one's own house. But you may rest assured that a man is really no better than he is to his own. You must not gauge your worth by what the outside world thinks and says, but by the estimate of those that see you in the ordinary intercourse of the home.

To be perfectly courteous to those whom you are meeting at every meal; to hold yourself under perfect control when worried by tiny insidious jars, and stung by almost invisible gnats; to maintain always the perfect girding of the loins; to have the head always anointed and the face always washed; to realize God's ideal, love's ideal, and your own. Ah, me! this requires the utmost grace that God can give. To die once is easy; to live always with an undivided heart, this is hard.

Understand that in the home-life God is educating and training you for the greatest victories. There you are learning the deepest lessons in sanctification. You need not run to conventions, sermons, and holiness meetings; if you would resolve to walk in your house with a perfect heart, you would discover how far from perfect you are, and how you are the least of his saints. Seek the perfect heart in your home-life; for then God will come unto you, and dwell beneath your roof, and the story of Bethany would be reduplicated for your household and yourself.

"Perhaps 'a single heart' is never known,
  Save in the yielded life that lives for God
    alone;
  And that is therefore doubted as a dream
  By those who know not the tremendous
    power
  Of all-constraining love."

But Thou art the same. Psa. 102: 27.

THIS psalm is by an anonymous singer. All we know of him is that he was overwhelmed, and poured out his complaint before God. But that lonely, sorrowful heart caught glimpses of God, which it has transmitted to all the world, enriching it for evermore. Sometimes we are led to wander alone in desolate places to catch new visions of the Eternal, hidden from ordinary souls; thus ardent artists are indifferent to peril and privation if they can catch a mountain from some fresh point of vision, and transfer a passing glimpse to their immortal canvas.

This psalm is despairful enough in its earlier passages. The smoke-wreath dissipated in the breeze, the withered grass of the desert, the declining shadow, the chirrup of a lonely sparrow—such are the images that occur naturally enough. But as he sings the man's vision clears. He looks away from the earth-mists to the Eternal God. Here, at least, is the permanent and unchanging. Did He make all things? Then He can unmake them, and be Himself evermore the same. Let the earth vanish like a dream; let the time-sphere be ended; let the very heavens wear out like a moth-eaten garment; let the nearest and dearest pass from our embrace. Thou art the same; Thou art left; Thou remainest. "All that is transitory forsaketh us; but Christ's seal of recognition forsaketh us not even in death, but bringeth us to the joyful heavenly host, unto our eternal fatherland."

The writer to the Hebrews attributes these words to Him who was the brightness of the Father's glory (Heb. 1). We should read the psalm again with this reference in our mind. Our Saviour is God, and He is the unchanging Rock of Ages in whom we may shelter.

But the mercy of the Lord is from everlasting to everlasting. Psa. 103: 17.

NOTE the contrast. Man's frailty against the everlastingness of God's mercy. We are frail as the flower of the field. Each generation of man comes forth like the grass and flowers, which clothe the meadows in spring only to meet the remorseless scythe. But frail as is our physical life, our resolutions and intentions are still more so. One day our soul is covered by the laughing beauty of hope, and faith, and love, kindly thoughts, heavenly aspirations, gracious deeds—the next the whole crop lies smitten and withered.

But God's love does not alter with our alterings, or change with our changes. Does the mother's love fluctuate with the moods of her sick babe? God loves constantly, with an ardent, intense affection, which delivers from dross the heart that is yielded to Him, and secures at last its transformation into his own likeness. If you will let Him, God will yet love you right. Love will make even your tough nature a miracle of beauty. But the friction of the lapidary's wheel and the diamond dust may hurt you a little. Never mind, love is behind it all. There never was a time when He did not love you—his mercy is from everlasting; nor a time when He will love you less—it is to everlasting.

When at last you have found your centre in God's love, a joy will arise within you, which will pour itself forth in blessing, and you will find yourself but one chorister among myriads in heaven and earth. It will appear to you as though angels and hosts in heaven, together with the saints of all the dispensations on earth, compose one vast choir. But none has any right to presume on this mercy, unless the condition of godly fear has been fulfilled.

Who maketh the clouds his chariot.
Psa. 104: 3.

AS I write these words on the bosom of the broad Atlantic, there is little for the eye to rest on but the heaving waters through which we are swiftly cutting our path, and the expanse of sky through which float the great piles of cloud. It is pleasant to think of them as the chariots of God; the heavens beyond are the curtains of his tent; this wind is his swift-stepping messenger; this exquisite light glancing on sky and sea is his garment, hardly dense enough to veil his visible Presence. O Nature, how can we do other than love thee, since the Being of our God is so closely mingled with thy hues and forms!

How often God visits us in a chariot of cloud! We look up and see the looming darkness, and forebode evil. But if we could look down, as from a seat in the heavenlies, we should behold our God sitting within, radiant with golden glory, and hastening to bless. In dry, waterless lands, the rain-bearing clouds are signally the chariots of blessing.

"Ye fearful saints, fresh courage take;
   The clouds ye so much dread
Are big with mercy, and shall break
   In blessings on your head."

When the soul, says one, is born again into the divine light, she becometh a humble, loving, winning creature, that beareth every cross and reproach, that regardeth no insult, either from man or devil, that placeth her love and confidence in the heart of God, full of joy, fed by the Word of God, bathed in a smile of heavenly triumph. But the reason for this is in the absolute confidence that God is in all our life, and that

"The cloud which spreads above,
   And veileth love
Itself is Love."

He was laid in chains of iron.
Psa. 105: 18 (R.V.).

THE margin of the R.V. suggests another rendering: "His soul entered into the iron." May we not yet again turn the sentence round, and say that the iron entered into his soul? When we first meet him, Joseph is a tender, yielding lad, with dreams of rule, but no conspicuous power. Yet he emerges from his captivity well qualified to take the helm of Egypt, just then sore driven and tossed by tempest. How can this striking transformation be accounted for, save that he had taken iron into his moral nature through his painful experiences?

The physician often prescribes an iron tonic for anæmic patients: and what iron is to the outer man that also the captivity of circumstances, deferred hope, and anguish of soul are to the inner. You have been fickle and uncertain of late; dreaming of power, but powerless; yearning for the only good, but greedy of trifles; you must have a course of iron. God wants Iron Dukes, and Iron souls. And there is a process also by which He can turn Iron to Steel. It means high temperature, sudden transitions, and blasts of heavenly air.

"If call'd, like Abraham's child, to climb
   The hill of sacrifice,
Some angel may be there in time—
   Deliverance shall arise!
"Or if some darker lot be good,
   Oh, teach us to endure
The sorrow, pain, or solitude
   That make the spirit pure!"

Life is very mysterious. Indeed, it would be inexplicable unless we believed that God was preparing us for scenes and ministries that lie beyond the vail of sense in the eternal world, where highly-tempered spirits will be required for special service.

He gave them their request; but sent leanness into their soul. Psa. 106: 15.

ISRAEL insisted on being fed, not with manna only, but with flesh. The people complained of their heaven-sent food as too light and unsatisfying. Their gross appetite demanded some heavier diet. So the wind brought down quails, flying a few feet from the ground, within easy reach of club or stick. These they ate ravenously, voraciously, greedily. "The people rose up all that day, and all the night, and all the next day, and gathered the quails." Their pampered bodies were gorged with food. They had their desire, but their souls were starved. "While the flesh was yet between their teeth, ere it was chewed, the anger of the Lord was kindled, and the Lord smote the people with a very great plague." They were buried in the graves of lust.

Generally speaking, the soul and body fare inversely. When the body is pampered with every luxury, the soul starves. The soul thrives best when the body cries out. Probably we all have to choose, not once or twice, in life, whether we will have the full satisfaction of our appetites, and lean souls; or be lean as to our circumstances, while the spirit is keen, alert, and full of vigorous life.

It seems as though the shadow of the eternal were perpetually hiding from us the eternal itself. Those that snatch at the shadow miss the eternal; those who refuse to be satisfied with the shadow, reach the satisfying vision of God; and to find God is to find all in and with Him. Oh, do not seek to impose your will on God; do not insist on anything with too great vehemence; let God choose. Whenever you make request for things which are not definitely promised, ask God not to grant them, except it be for the very best.

Even they shall understand the loving-kindness of the Lord. Psa. 107: 43.

"THE Harvest of a Quiet Eye" is the fascinating title of a fascinating book. When the heart is quiet in God, the eye looks out on the scenes of nature and life around it, and detects everywhere, even where to ordinary men every appearance seems in the contrary direction, the loving-kindness of the Lord. As life advances, and one climbs the hill, one is able to review the path by which life has been directed and controlled. We observe with the wisdom which we have obtained by long experience, and we understand God's reasons for many rebuffs, denials, and bitter disappointments. I believe that we shall one day turn to Him, and say, when we know all, "Thou couldst not have done otherwise. We would not have wished otherwise."

Consider the successive vignettes of this psalm. Love broods over the weary caravan that faints in the desert; visits the prison-house with its captives; watches by our beds of pain; notices each lurch of the tempest-driven vessel; brings the weary hosts from the wilderness into the fruitful soil.

Love is quick to appreciate love. It is natural to a loving heart to find love everywhere. We view all things in hues borrowed from the heart. "He that loveth knoweth God, for God is love; he that loveth not hath not seen Him, neither known Him." Ask therefore for a baptism unto the love of God—this will make you quick to perceive and understand his loving-kindness, where others miss it. Be patient also to await the end of the Lord. And when still the vision tarries, dare to believe that one day, when you know as you are known, you shall understand the loving-kindness that underlay your darkest experiences.

He it is that shall tread down our adversaries. Psa. 108: 13 (R.V.).

THIS is the best way to fight. Keep quietly in fellowship with God; and when the enemy draws nigh, look up to your ever-present Friend, and say, "Now, Lord, now tread down this adversary." When we are observing the conditions which the psalmist enumerates in this psalm, it is easy to do this. Notice what they are.

The heart must be fixed in an attitude of consecration and devotion. We must be awake right early, for fellowship with God, putting on the armour before entering into the battle. We must exalt God in our life and by our lips. Then God will speak in his holiness in our behalf; and when He is for us, who can be against us? Hark to the exultation of the saint. Shechem, Gilead, Manasseh, were famous for their luxuriant fertility, and typify the heavenly graces appropriated by faith. Moab, Edom, Philistia, are synonyms for fierce hostility, and recall our besetting sins, our virulent foes, which fall before us when we are in alliance with the Almighty.

Micah caught sight of this truth, when he said, "The Breaker is gone up before them;

their King is passed on before them, and the Lord at the head of them." Yes, the Shepherd goes before his flock, but the flock must follow Him. We must not be content with the knowledge that all things are ours in Christ, but must enter on their possession and enjoyment. Of what use is it to know that mines of precious ore lie under the broad acres of an estate, unless they are brought to the surface and prepared for the service of man? And we must not let ourselves be robbed of our heritage in Christ, through the hatred of our spiritual foes, when He waits to tread them under his feet and ours.

Let them curse, but bless Thou. Psa. 109: 28. THIS is the Iscariotic psalm. The Apostle Peter quoted it, as applying to Judas, on the occasion of electing a successor to the traitor; but the Church has no desire to appropriate against him or any of her foes the awful anathemas of the psalmist. In reading them we must remember—first, that they may be treated as predictions rather than imprecations, not let, but shall; secondly, that those earlier days had much of the thunder of Sinai and little enough of the tender accents of Calvary; thirdly, that it seemed to the lovers of God all important that wickedness should be punished in this life, as they had very dim conceptions of the next, and it might appear, otherwise, that God was indifferent to moral distinctions.

Men still curse us. It is one of the badges that we belong to the Lord's household, that they call us Beelzebub. The offence of the Cross has not ceased; and if none curse us, we may seriously question whether we are following in the footsteps of the Crucified. We must be baptized into our Saviour's death, and die with Him to all fear of man. Until we are willing to be counted the offscouring of all things, we have not entered into the true significance of baptism into his death, and participation in his risen life. The late George Müller said that he made no progress till he came to this. But when we are willing to forfeit our character, to die to our reputation, to be fools for Christ's sake, then God begins to bless. When men revile, and persecute, and say all manner of evil against us falsely for Christ's sake, God whispers in our heart, "Great is your reward in heaven." You never will know how near and tender God can be, till you are cast out by your kind.

Thy people shall be willing in the day of thy power. Psa. 110: 3. THE literal rendering of the Hebrew is preferable: "Thy people shall be free-will offerings in the day of thy power." When we recall the quotations of the first verse of this psalm in the New Testament, we have no difficulty in understanding what is meant by the day of his power. It is beyond doubt the day of his ascension, of his enthronement at the right hand of the Father, and of the advent of the Holy Spirit.

Whensoever the Holy Spirit is supreme in a church there will be a free-will offering of young hearts and lives. Clad in the priestly garb of stainless purity, pouring forth from the womb of life's young morning, they will scatter themselves over the weary earth like myriads of dewdrops on withered vegetation. The Priest-King has a wonderful fascination for youthful volunteers; and as He is so are they.

Have you become a free-will offering? There is every claim for your entire and devoted service. You have been already included in the Father's gift to the Son; but you must come to Him for yourself. The world has yet to learn what God can do with a soul that is entirely given up to Him. Let Him have your life to shape and mould it, to inspire and infill, to send forth on his errands, to commission for his service. There are no pressed men in our Master's army—all are volunteers. Offer your will to God; say you are willing to be made willing: He can make you willing in this day of his power, as iron is bent in the fierce flame.

"In full and glad surrender we give ourselves
    to Thee,
Thine utterly, and only, and evermore to
    be!
O Son of God, who lovest us, we will be
    Thine alone,
And all we are, and all we have, shalt
    henceforth be Thine own!"

The works of the Lord are great, sought out of all them that have pleasure therein. Psa. 111: 2. THE merchant goes forth to seek goodly pearls. Go forth, O Christian heart, to discover fresh jewels in thy Saviour's character. You will find them in meditation, in converse with other souls, but mainly in the reverent investigation of Scripture.

The theme of the Bible is—the works of the Lord. Its constant affirmation is that they are great; that his work is honour and majesty; that He hath made his wonderful works to be remembered; that He shows his people the power of his works; and that the works of his hands are truth and judgment. Where better could we study or seek them out?

Consider God's works in Creation, as scene after scene is unfolded in the first chapter of Genesis; in destruction, as when the Deluge swept the earth; in redemption, when He led his people out of Egypt; in judgment, when He handed his people over to their enemies; in the holy Incarnation, the Passion, the Resurrection of Jesus, and in the coming of the Paraclete. Seek out these great and wonderful works; trace the references made to them in every part of Scripture; find a holy pleasure in reviewing them in all their wealth of significance.

Kepler, when he first turned his telescope to clustered worlds, exclaimed, "I am thinking over again the first thoughts of God." Oh that the ecstasy of the ardent student of nature might fill our hearts as we direct our thought to the great works of our Saviour-God! But our attitude, like his, must be one of reverence, patience, and dependence on the revealing Spirit. Probably this will be our employment in eternity; ever passing into deeper and fuller appreciation of the works of God, and breaking into more rapturous songs.

He shall not be afraid of evil tidings: his heart is fixed, trusting in the Lord. Psa. 112: 7.

THERE cannot be evil tidings to the soul which has fixed its trust in the Lord. Every messenger that comes post-haste into its presence with despatches brings tidings of what has been permitted or done by our Father; and nothing which is of his ordering or permitting can really injure us. Tidings! tidings! they are always pouring in, by letter, postcard, and telegram. They are presented in the contents bills of every newspaper, and cried by the newsboys in the streets. But the child of God opens each buff-coloured envelope with untrembling hands, and scans the newspaper columns with unblenching eyes. No tidings can be evil to him; his heart is fixed, trusting in the Lord.

But does not the Christian suffer anguish and pain, as others do? Is he stoical and unimpassioned, dull in his emotions, unsympathetic in his affections? Not so; but he refuses to judge things by their appearances. He knows that all things must be working for good on his behalf: in the hieroglyphics he detects his Father's handwriting; in the mysterious figure standing on the shore, veiled in morning mist, he beholds the Lord who died for him. If tidings were to come to you to-day of disease, loss, bereavement, death, they could not be evil if your heart dares to maintain a fixed trust in God; for such trust robs death of its sting, and the grave of its victory. I cannot understand, but I can trust Him. Like the fabled philosopher's stone, faith turns all metals to gold.

> "Know well, my soul, God's hand controls
>   Whate'er thou fearest;
> Round Him in calmest music rolls
>   Whate'er thou hearest."

He maketh the barren woman to keep house, and to be a joyful mother of children. Psa. 113: 9.

THIS is an evident reference to Hannah's psalm of thanksgiving, when she had borne Samuel, and God had taken away her reproach. Her story, and these words, should be a great comfort to those who have never been used in soul-winning. Remember, too, how Sarah received strength by faith to bear a child, because she counted Him faithful that promised. God can make barren souls authors of life to thousands. These are the conditions:

Be content, like Hannah, to cherish a sorrowful spirit. Weep before the Lord. Let your request be poured out before God at Shiloh, with the moving lips, though the voice be inaudible. Ask of God with strong cryings and tears, that He would still the taunts of your adversary. Souls are only born to those who cannot live without them.

Next, look away from all creature help to God's faithful promise, and believe that He can make you to become spiritually productive. Claim this of Him. Believe that of stones He can raise up children. Hold Him to his own word. Remind Him of his promise, "I will make thee exceeding fruitful."

Hannah promised that her child should be given to the Lord; and Samuel, when old enough, was brought to the Temple in pursuance of her vow. We are too apt to take the glory and credit of soul-winning, instead of acknowledging that, as we could not bear them apart from God, so we may not keep them when they are given. Those who, like Hannah, give their Samuels to God, like her can also break forth and sing, "My heart exulteth in the Lord, mine horn is exalted in the Lord; because I rejoice in thy salvation."

Which turned the flint into a fountain of waters.
Psa. 114: 8.

THIS is a miracle which we all need to have wrought in our experience. Our heart is flint, our eyes are dry, our souls fail to respond with tears and regrets to the love of the Pierced One, and to the indictment that charges us with his death. There is little brokenness of heart among God's children; and it is a sad fact that conviction of sin is a comparatively rare experience among the ungodly. This used not to be so. We have read of whole communities being swept with paroxysms of grief and compunction under the preaching of a Finney. His look on one occasion at a scoffing girl smote her to the soul, and led to so deep a work of grace that a whole factory, and then a village, were filled with mourning. I was told of a revival breaking out in a church, and many hearts being made soft because a band of godly elders confessed their unfaithfulness and shortcomings.

Moses struck the rock of flint at the commencement of the wanderings; and was to speak to it, at their close. But in either case the effect was identical; the water gushed from its heart of rock. Use thy cross, O Son of God, Lord of the House in which Moses was but a servant, and smite these hard hearts, that tears may flow freely forth; or speak the word. It is said that every building has a chord, to strike which makes it tremble to its base. Surely there is a chord, a note, a tone, before which our hearts would rend, giving Him tears for his sorrow, anguish for his pain!

"The sacrifices of God are a broken heart: a broken and contrite heart, O God, Thou wilt not despise."

"A broken heart, a fount of tears,
Ask, and it shall not be denied."

They that make them shall be like unto them.
Psa. 115: 8 (R.V.).

THAT men become like their ideals is a commonplace; and that the heathen resemble their deities is notorious. Men first impute to their deities their own vices, as the Greeks and Romans to the gods and goddesses of their Pantheon; and then endeavour to honour them by imitation.

But, in another sense, this is gloriously true of our relation to the Lord Jesus. If we make Him our ideal, and trust Him with all our hearts, his beauty shall dawn upon our face, and we shall be changed into his image, from glory to glory. We know that when He shall be manifested finally we shall be like Him, for we shall see Him as He is; and, in a measure, this process of transformation is taking place in those who see Him by the eye of faith, and are becoming like Him.

We are doing more by our life than by our words. We cannot always speak for Jesus, but we may always live for Him. Of a young girl, lately gone forth as a missionary, who cannot speak a word of the language of the foreign land to which she has gone, I was told the other day that her life, or rather the life of Jesus in her, was exerting a far wider influence than she knew. This is the divine method: look and live; trust and be transfigured; abide in Him, and He shall abide in you.

Auskar, a missionary to the Scandinavians in the ninth century, when asked if he could perform miracles, replied: "If God were indeed to grant that power to me, I would only ask that I might exhibit the miracle of a holy life." But this is the most difficult of all. It is easier to die once for Jesus, than to live always for Him. Yet God's grace is sufficient. He will keep us as stars in his right hand.

Then called I upon the Name of the Lord.
Psa. 116: 4.

WHAT could we do without the resource of prayer? When compassed with the cords of death, and held by trouble and sorrow, what help would there be for us who eschew the methods of self-deliverance which the men of the world do not scruple to employ, if we might not betake ourselves to our knees?

"Nay, but much rather let me late returning,
Bruised of my brethren, wounded from within,
Stoop with sad countenance and blushes burning,
Bitter with weariness and sick with sin.
"Straight to thy presence get me and reveal it,
Nothing ashamed of tears upon thy feet;

Show the sore wound, and beg thine hand
to heal it;
Pour Thee the bitter, pray Thee for the
sweet."

Only let us never forget the immense importance of those five great "ifs":
John 15: 7, which touches our life in Him,
and his in us, in unremitted fellowship.
Matt. 18: 19, which touches our life with
others, that must be clear as crystal.
Matt. 17: 20, which concerns the vigour and
health of our own soul-life.
1 John 5: 14, 15, which demands that we
know God well.
John 14: 14, which winnows out from prayer
all that is inconsistent with the name of Jesus.
Oh for the deep-dwelling life, spent in the
secret place, where earth's voices grow faint,
and God's clear. Such a life is a perpetual
appeal to God's nature for succour—an appeal
which awakens an instant response. "Call unto
Me, and I will answer thee; and will shew thee
great things, and fenced in, which thou
knowest not."

Oh, praise the Lord, all ye nations!
Psa. 117: 1.

THIS is an unwonted summons from Jewish
lips. For the most part the Jews looked with
little sympathy on their Gentile neighbours,
and had no desire that they should laud
Jehovah, save as they became proselytes of
Judaism. But where the love of God is strong
in the heart, it overleaps the bounds of
custom and racial prejudice, and yearns that all
the world should know and love the Saviour.

"If all the world my Saviour knew,
Sure all the world would love Him too."

We all need more of the emancipating power
of the love of Christ, to thaw the icy chains
that hang around us, and bid words flow freely
from our lips to those whom we had been
accustomed to look on as outside the range of
our influence. Oh for the passionate desire
that God should be universally praised and
loved! Oh to be willing to be accounted fools
and enthusiasts, if only we may start to praise,
lips that otherwise had remained sealed and
dumb! Are we doing all we can to kindle the
nations to praise? They cannot praise Him
whom they do not know. It is mere hypocrisy
to bid them praise Him, if we have never
sought to spread, by lip or gift, the mercy and

truth revealed in Jesus our Lord. Oh that each
might ponder the paradox!—

"Christ, alone, can save this world;
But Christ cannot save this world, alone."

What a lesson is given us by Lough Fook, a
Chinese Christian, who, fifteen years ago, was
so touched with the condition of the coolies in
Demerara, as to sell himself into slavery that
he might win them for Christ! He was the
means of two hundred joining the Church
before he died, five years afterwards.

*Bind the sacrifice with cords, even unto the
horns of the altar.* Psa. 118: 27.

IS not this altar his Cross? Shall we not ask to
be bound to it, that we may never be able to
start back from our attitude of consecration?
There are times when life is full of roseate
light, and we choose the Cross; at other times,
when the sky is grey, we shrink from it. It is
well to be bound. Wilt Thou bind us, most
blessed Spirit, and enamour us with the Cross,
and let us never leave it? Bind us with the
scarlet cord of redemption, and the golden
cord of love, and the silver cord of Advent-
hope: so will we not go back from it, or wish
for another lot, than to be the humble partners
with our Lord in his pain and sorrow.

The horns of the altar invite thee. Wilt thou
come? Wilt thou desist from the thinking,
speaking, and willing of thine own selfhood?
Wilt thou place the Cross between thyself and
the world that entices thee? Wilt thou dwell
ever in a spirit of resigned humility, and give
thyself to continual repentance and tears?
Wilt thou love the Cross of our Lord Jesus and
the contempt of the world, and take them as
thy meat and drink? Then thou shalt know the
life that passes through death, and is life
indeed.

How precious are the last lines that David
Livingstone penned in his diary, before his
boys found him kneeling beside his bed, dead,
though in the attitude of prayer, the candle
burning beside him: "My Jesus, my King, my
Life, my All; to Thee I again dedicate myself."
So bind each of us with the cords of love, and
the bands of a man.

Remember Tholuck's motto, which was
adopted by Count Zinzendorf: "I have one
passion, and it is He—only He."

Teach me thy statutes. Psa. 119: 12.

THIS petition occurs many times in the course

of this psalm. It is urged on many pleas: because God is blessed, and therefore must want to lift us to share his blessedness; because the suppliant desires to complete the declaration of God's ways to others; because he is eager to turn them into songs; because the earth is so full of divine mercy; because God is good, and does good. Take this petition as your guide, and follow it through the psalm, and especially trace that recurring word statutes, and you will see how the whole of this splendid ode crystallizes around it.

There is a heavenly wisdom, which can only be acquired from the lips of the Greatest of Teachers, at whose feet Mary sat. It is not to be acquired by the intellect, but by the heart. It will never come by emulation, ambition, or pride; but to those who live a life of perfect love, of deep humility, and of fellowship with the Father, and with his Son Jesus Christ.

Sometimes the pupil wearies of the lesson. Winsome as the Teacher is, the bench is hard, and the horn-book difficult. Outside, the summer land attracts with scent of flower, hum of bee, and frisking squirrel. Yet God loves us too well to let us off till our lesson is learnt. He often turns it back. But some day these statutes shall become our songs in the house of our pilgrimage.

When Elizabeth Fry died at sixty-five, after such a life of Christian philanthropy as few have ever known—for half a century she had been able to affirm that she had never awakened from her sleep, in sickness or in health, by day or by night, without her first waking thought being, "How best may I serve my Lord?"

Woe is me, that I sojourn in Meshech, that I dwell among the tents of Kedar.
Psa. 120: 5 (R.V.).

IT is a bitter experience to have to live where there is no sympathy, but carping criticism and incessant innuendo. A pure-minded friend was recounting to me the other day the anguish he suffered perpetually, because his associates, knowing how acutely he suffered from the least suggestions of impurity, chose to assault his ears continually with abominable expressions. There are souls which have long had their dwelling with those that hate peace. To their least sigh war is the immediate response.

O lily among thorns, this is no new experience! Thy Lord hath been through these paths before thee; see the bent twigs which prove that He has passed this way. But thy loneliness can never be quite as sorrowful as his, for thou hast always Him. And remember, there is a compensation, in that the strict scrutiny of thy foes makes thee ever so much more watchful and prayerful, and drives thee oftener to the bosom of God. One declared to me lately that he had found it easier to live a holy life in a City warehouse than in a Divinity college. Perhaps we gain much more than we know from jealous opposition and criticism.

"Oft in Life's stillest shade reclining,
In desolation unrepining,
Without a hope on earth to find
A mirror in an answering mind,
Meek souls there are who little deem
Their daily strife an Angel's theme."

But as the saintly Samuel Rutherford wrote: "The Cross of Christ is the sweetest burden that I ever bore: it is such a burden as are wings to a bird, and sails to a ship, to carry me forward to my desired heaven."

Shall I lift up mine eyes unto the mountains?
Psa. 121: 1 (marg.).

IT is not high enough to look to mountains. They are deeply rooted and permanent in their sockets. They rise like the pillars of heaven. Rivulets gush from their sides, vineyards drape their terraced slopes, eternal snows cap them with crowns of unsullied purity. The ancients thought that the gods had chosen them for their home, as on Parnassus or Olympus. To their towering steeps the eyes of their votaries were frequently directed to catch the first symptoms of descending help.

But the psalmist forbears to look to soaring mountains for his help. He lifts his eyes above and beyond, to the Lord which made heaven and earth. Thence shall his help come.

We are all tempted to look at the mountains, to the creature rather than the Creator; to wealth, talent, or influence; to things and people beneath the heavens, instead of to Him who dwells above the heavens, in his infinite majesty, and to whom all power is given in heaven and earth.

O unslumbering Keeper! O sleepless Watcher! Shade from heat, shelter from cold, protector from assault, transformer of ill to good, escort when we go out, home when we return! Thou art the complement of our need. We are content to suffer the loss of all things, to find them all in Thee. And therefore we betake ourselves to thy shadow till life's calamities be overpast.

"Nor can the vain toil cease,
Till in the shadowy maze of life we meet
One who can guide our aching, wayward feet
To find Himself, our Way, our Life, our Peace!
In Him the long Unrest is soothed and stilled;
Our hearts are filled!"

For my brethren and companions' sakes, I will now say, Peace be within thee.
Psa. 122: 8.

WHAT the earthly Jerusalem was to the Jews, that the holy Church, the Bride of the Lamb, the heavenly Jerusalem, which descends from God out of heaven, and includes within its limits all holy souls, is to us. Let us pray for its peace and prosperity; let us esteem them above our own good, and let us be glad if our feet stand within its gates.

When the tribes of the Lord go up to give thanks at the remembrance of his holiness, let us go with them. We may be alone in some distant land, or traversing the ocean in the swift steamer, bearing us from the land of religious observances, or confined to the sick chamber: but let us never forget that we belong to the holy mystical Church; let us ascend the staircases of prayer and praise; let us mingle our rivulet of adoring love in the mighty torrent that is setting in towards the throne of God and the Lamb; for we are come to the City of God, to an innumerable company of angels, to the spirits of just men made perfect, and to the blood of sprinkling that speaketh better things than Abel's. Wherever my brethren meet, in whatever section of the Church on earth, so long as they belong to the one Church, the Body of Christ, nothing shall stay me from wishing them prosperity and peace. They may not recognize me here, but five minutes in Heaven will do away with all these earthly estrangements.

When the Church is at peace within herself she flourishes best. "So the Church," we are told, "throughout all Judea, and Galilee, and Samaria, had peace, and was edified." Peace is the condition of up-building and multiplication: but it is only consistent with Truth and Righteousness. First Righteousness, then Peace, then Prosperity.

Unto Thee do I lift up mine eyes, O Thou that sittest in the heavens. Psa. 123: 1 (R.V.).

THESE exquisite Songs of Ascents, prepared for the bands of worshippers as they went up from distant parts of the land to the great annual festivals, are very precious to pilgrim-souls, as from many lands and ages they are gathering home to the throne of the exalted Lamb, who sits at the right hand of God the Father in the highest heavens. And as we journey, we lift up our eyes to his dear face—the face that once was wet with tears and dewed with bloody sweat, but which ere long will shine as the morning when He is anointed with the oil of joy above his fellows. Here is the Old Testament counterpart of the New Testament attitude—looking off unto Jesus.

The slave at the table kept the eye steadfastly fixed on the hand of master or mistress, to obey its least sign and to make it needless to speak. Keep your eye on the pierced hand, child of God; watch its smallest indication; wait patiently until it give some sign. We have too long acted on our own initiative; let us wait on our exalted Lord for the indication of his will. Let us not look askance at the proud, with their contempt, or on the heaving billows of the world's restless strife; but away to those azure depths and beyond, far above all principality, power, might, and dominion, where God hath exalted Him to be a Prince and a Saviour. Let his least gesture be our law.

One day we shall follow the direction of our eyes. Whilst we gaze, we shall be changed; and as we are changed we shall arise to sit with Him on his throne.

"Break up the heavens, O Lord! and far
Through all yon starlight keen,
Draw me, thy bride—a glittering star
In raiment white and clean!"

If it had not been the Lord who was on our side.
Psa. 124: 1.

HERE is an If which cannot be an if. It is never a matter of uncertainty whether the Lord will be on our side or not. For the Lord Jesus in his incarnation and death has taken his place beside us for evermore. He is always on our side, so long as we keep his paths and walk in his ways.

"Though unperceived by mortal sense,
Faith sees Him always near,
A Guide, a Guardian, a Defence;
Then what have you to fear?"

There are in all human lives hours of over-powering anxiety, when we feel as though it were impossible to live another moment—exposed to danger, separated from dear ones, not knowing what an hour may bring forth. Then, as you look up, you find that the Lord is beside you, sharing your anxieties, and affording you his inviolable protection. You cannot descry Him by the eye of sense, but you know Him to be there, and neither man nor devil can prevail against you.

When we look back on life, as the psalmist does here, we become aware of the myriad instances of divine protection. We were not so vividly conscious at the time; we might even have had fits of depression and counted ourselves bereft. But if we narrowly consider the perils from which we have been rescued, when we were about to be swallowed up quick, we become convinced that He was there. In life and death and judgment, Jesus, your Advocate, will ever stand at your side and silence all who would condemn. So that with good courage you may say, "The Lord is my helper; I will not fear: what shall man or devil do unto me!"

"Cast all your care on God! That anchor holds!"

The Lord is round about his people. Psa. 125: 2.
IT is a beautiful conception. Around the chosen city the mountains stood like sentinels, leaving no part without its barrier. So is God around us; and this enables us to understand how his permissions may become his appointments. It is easy to accept pain and disappointment which come to us direct from his hand; but not so when they approach us from the plotting and malevolence of a Judas or Shimei. It is impossible, however, to arrive at a settled peace, so long as we make a distinction between the afflictions which come to us from the divine, and those which visit us from the human; and, indeed, the distinction is untenable. For the assaults of our foes are at least permitted by God, and his permissions are his appointments.

This will become evident, if we clearly apprehend that God is round about us, as a rampart to the city, as an envelope to a letter, as the atmosphere to the configuration of our bodies. If then He chooses, He can pass off from us any arrow that might harm us; but if He opens his environing protection, so as to let it pass through to us, by the time it has traversed the atmosphere of his care, it has become his will for us. Put God between yourself and everything. Many put their anxieties between them and God, and see God as the sun through a fog; mind that you put God between yourself and the entire world of men and things.

In a city on the Continent the custodians keep the regalia without iron bars, on what seems to be an open table—but none would dare to touch one jewel, for all around a powerful stream of electricity is perpetually being poured. Invisible, but potent! Such is the encompassing presence of God.

They that sow in tears shall reap in joy.
Psa. 126: 5.
SOME husbandmen steep their seeds before they sow them. It is well when Christian workers steep their lessons and addresses with their prayers and tears. It is not enough to sow; we may do that lavishly and constantly, but we must add passion, emotion, tender pity, strong cryings and tears, if the second half of the text is to be fulfilled, and we reap in joy.

But what a promise is here! You have sown long and patiently among young or old, sometimes to the point of giving all up in despair; but to give up now would be to miss the harvest and guerdon of all your toils. Be patient, persevere a little longer. God guarantees the harvest. He says, "You shall reap; you shall doubtless come again, bringing your sheaves." Even though you were to die, without reaping, yet in another world you would come again, bringing your sheaves.

We are all sowing tears—tears over our darling Absaloms, tears over our failures and mistakes, tears over our disappointed hopes. But each tear overflowing from a consecrated soul is a seed-germ dropped into God's keeping, and it shall have its reward. He carefully gathers up our tears for his bottle. God is not unrighteous to forget. He guards the buried seed, and stands sponsor for the harvest. No sigh, no tear, no prayer, inspired by the Spirit of God can positively be lost or unproductive. Like your Lord, you shall yet see of the travail of your soul, and be satisfied.

"For while the tired wavelets, vainly breaking,
   Seem here no painful inch to gain,
Far back, through creeks and inlets making,
   Comes silent, flooding in, the main."

He giveth unto his beloved in sleep.
Psa. 127: 2 (R.V., marg.).

ALL day long we may have been fretting and
fuming, running hither and thither, and doing
our little best to build the house and keep the
city. Sometimes we have turned to look to our
faith, to see if that were in good condition,
and sometimes to our friends. But we have not
done much to forward matters. The weight of
our anxiety is unrelieved, the heavy load
presses still. Finally we can hold up no longer;
with one last helpless look to God we fall
back on his everlasting arms, and sleep. We
rest long and deeply, till morning taps at the
window. We spring up relieved; the storm has
ceased, and there, beside us, given whilst we
slept, is the boon we had craved and yearned
for. It has been given unto his beloved in
sleep.

What an emblem of death! We may have
been fretting and worrying all our life, have
attempted much and done little, have questioned God's love and care; then, tired and
heartbroken, we shall fall asleep on the bosom
of Christ, and awake to find the house built,
the New Jerusalem set up, with her gates of
pearl and walls of jasper, and the kingdom of
God come.

Begone, dull, worrying care! let me rest;
sweet Faith and Hope, close mine eyes and still
my heart; Jesus, give me sleep, and in sleeping
give me my heart's desire, that I may awake
and be satisfied. Curtained by eternal
mysteries, guarded by angel watchers, resting
on the lap of mother earth, our bodies (though
not our souls) shall sleep until the sounding of
the Archangel's trump announce the advent of
the new heavens and earth, and we shall awake,
like belated sleepers, to find that God has
been bringing redemption as we slept.

Blessed is every one that feareth the Lord.
Psa. 128: 1.

THE special phase of blessedness here, is that
of the home life. The Jews have always been
distinguished for this. A recent writer,
describing the Jews of the middle ages, says:
"The sanctity of the home was an affectionate
tradition, linking them with a golden chain to
their fathers before them; and amidst the
degradation heaped on them, they were
emancipated in at least one spot on earth, and
learned from their domestic peace to look with
pitiful rather than vindictive eyes upon their
persecutors."

Our religious life, when it is genuine, will
always cast a halo of blessedness on the home.
Not lightly does Wordsworth blend "the
kindred points of heaven and home," for the
man who fears God brings heaven into his
home. We must not be sullen or self-absorbed
there. We must divest ourselves of business
cares and anxieties; of irritation and fretfulness; of the brooding clouds that have
gathered on our faces; we must carefully
maintain the courtesies of home, and be our
sweetest, gladdest, loveliest selves.

What a charming cluster of images! The
wife as a vine twining round the carved trellis-
work of the inner court of the Oriental home—
as though the woman gives the rich wine of
life, which is love, as well as shadowing fertility
and graceful beauty; whilst children as olive
plants are sources of perennial joy. Would you
have such a home? Its key-stone is the fear of
grieving the Spirit of God.

"The work and watching will be very sweet
    Even in an earthly home,
And in such an hour as you think not
    He will come."

*Many a time have they afflicted me: yet they
have not prevailed against me.* Psa. 129: 1, 2.
WHAT a wonder it is that Satan and man do
not prevail against the saint! There is no way
of accounting for it, except in God's election.
Because God has chosen us for Himself, and
redeemed us at great cost, He cannot afford
to hand us over to the will of our enemies. He
may allow our backs to be furrowed by the
heavy scourge, because the servant must be as
his Lord; but He will cut our cords in the day
selected for our execution, and let us go free
from the hand of our foes. So it was with
Peter, and many a time with Paul.

Let us then walk with God. Fellowship with
Him should be the daily bread of our souls. If
we cultivate the fresh sense of fellowship with
Him, we shall not yield to fear, be our foes
never so venomous and their plans never so
insidious. A close walk with God is the sure
way of escaping them. "The man of God sent
unto the king of Israel, saying, Beware that
thou pass not such a place; and the king of
Israel sent to the place that the man of God
told him and warned him of; and he saved
himself not once nor twice."

This daily fellowship is only possible
through the blood of Jesus, by which we draw
nigh unto God; and it can only be maintained

by constant watchfulness in little things. "Let us be very zealous over ourselves for the Lord, watching against the least shyness between the soul and Himself. Where there is much love between friends, a cold look is a matter of complaint." When least inclined to pray, we need to pray the more. When least conscious of Christ's nearness, we need to be most eager, like the old covenanter, to wrestle for access. If the King have not sent for thee these many days, await Him in his court.

There is forgiveness with Thee, that Thou mayest be feared. Psa. 130: 4.

YES, thank God, there is forgiveness, because at his right hand He liveth for evermore who put away sin by the sacrifice of Himself. Forgiveness at any moment for the sins of a life; repeated forgiveness for the sins of every hour; forgiveness instantaneously upon confession. He pardoneth and absolveth all those who truly repent and unfeignedly believe in Him of whom the Gospel speaks. And when God once speaks forgiveness, it can never be unspoken. Fear and doubt and misgiving may question, but cannot revoke it. Based on the Blood of the Covenant, on promises ratified by the most solemn assurances, there is irrevocable forgiveness with God. Weary, sinning, ashamed soul, the fountain of God's forgiveness springs perennially from his heart; as clear and full as when that fountain was first opened for sin and uncleanness. Take it and go your way. Even if there be no rush of emotion, or sense of pardon, yet dare to believe that your cries and tears and confessions have been heard and answered.

Just because God is so ready to forgive, there is wrought within our hearts an ever-deepening dread of giving Him pain. There is forgiveness with Him, that He may be feared. There is a greater fear in the heart of the true child of God of grieving his Father than there is in the unregenerate of the penalty of transgression. The element of fear comes back into our nature, refined and purified through the fires of love. There is no fear in love; and yet love fears with a perpetual dread of giving needless pain. Because God is a consuming fire of tender love, let us serve Him with godly fear.

"What is thy fear, O soul? The fear of that dark place,
Or fear to lose the joy of thy Creator's face?"

Like a weaned child with his mother. Psa. 131: 2 (R.V.).

HOW much the greatest teachers of the world have learnt from little children! Jesus has for evermore set a little child in the midst of us to teach us. It is from the nursery that David got this tender, exquisite conception.

A tender babe has been brought up by the breast, and has loved to nestle to its mother. But the weaning time has come. With Orientals it is often greatly deferred. The little one is impatient of the change, and highly resents the spoon with which he is fed. Vehemently he cries, and fights, and struggles with hand and foot, little knowing that he is resisting a change which is to make him independent, which shall advance his truest life, and shall ultimately bring him back to that mother again, as her stay and blessing. Finally, however, the passion subsides, the sobs die down to little whimpers, a tear still lies upon the cheek to show where the storm had raged; but on the whole the babe is stilled and quieted.

So with us, we have been clinging to the breast of some human help and comfort. Presently the strong, wise hand of God puts us gently from it, and turns us to other sources of consolation. At first we passionately resist with outcry and strife. But the Comforter comes and hushes us as on the very lap of God. He shows us the love which cannot mistake, and, at last, the soul calms, becomes stilled and quieted; with chastened hope it turns to the Lord; it thrives on stronger meat; it leaves behind the life of dependence, and is strengthened with all might unto patience and long-suffering with joy. No longer satisfied with milk, it partakes of strong meat, with exercised sense (*Heb.* 5: 11–14).

Lord, remember David, and all his afflictions. Psa. 132: 1.

THIS psalm commemorates the removal of the Ark to the Temple, newly prepared for its reception by Solomon. David had been dead some years; but as they prepared to fulfil the project on which he had set his heart, the men of the new generation could not forget how he sware unto the Lord, and vowed unto the Mighty One of Jacob. They remembered David. Throughout this psalm his name often recurs. "For thy servant David's sake." "The Lord hath sworn unto David." "The budding of David's horn."

"Shall man remember, and shall God forget?" He would be unrighteous if He were to forget the work of faith and labour of love of his saints. It was in pursuance of his covenant with David that Solomon's Temple at last stood complete. Thus God still bends over the scenes of the life-work of his children. The chapel where a McCheyne pleaded with his congregation; the South Sea Island, where a Williams poured out his blood; the dark forests in which a Brainerd wrestled for his Indians; the great Continent where a Moffat, a Livingstone, a Hannington wrought, prayed, and suffered. He remembers David and all his afflictions. He recalls the prayers, and tears, and travail of soul; and the time comes when the finished structure stands on the site which to them was waste and void. No effort, nor cry, nor prayer of thine goes unheeded. All that thou hast truly desired, purposed, lived for, prepared for, shall yet take shape, and greet thee. There can never be one lost good. Some day a perfect realization of thy dream, which thou shalt descry from heaven's standpoint of vision, will satisfy thee.

It is like the precious oil upon the head.
Psa. 133: 2 (R.V.).

BROTHERLY love binding together kindred hearts is here compared to oil, the chosen symbol of the Holy Spirit, because it is only through his grace that it is possible to love. The love of the brethren is the earthly manifestation of love to God. We have just as much to Him as we have to them; and such love, whether to them or Him, can only be shed abroad in our hearts by the Holy Ghost given unto us. Is love wanting? Seek a baptism of the Holy Ghost. Pentecost meant the most wonderful manifestation of love which the world had ever seen.

The Holy Spirit, as oil, was poured upon the head of our great Aaron as He arose from the waters of baptism, and again when He ascended into the presence of his Father; and it has been descending ever since upon us who are as the skirts of his garments. To the Jew it seemed as though the Hermon range overtowered the land and was able to drop its dews across the intervening distance upon the mountains of Zion. Thus, from the glory of his exaltation, Jesus drops the dew of the Holy Spirit as blessing upon the lowlands of our life—that blessing which is life for evermore.

Our response to it should be the fertility of our heart's and life's activities.

"Ye have," said the apostle, "an unction (anointing) from the Holy One, and ye know all things." Could that assertion be made of us? If not, let us seek it. "He that stablisheth unto Christ, and anointeth, is God." "Serve your God day and night faithfully," says Dr. Goodwin; "walk humbly, and there is a promise of the Holy Ghost to come and fill your hearts. Sue this promise out; wait for it. Rest not in believing only, there is a further assurance to be had."

Bless ye the Lord, all ye which by night stand in the house of the Lord. Psa. 134: 1.

THIS hymn was composed for the night-watch of the Temple, for those that had gone to relieve the Levites who had been in charge during the day. It is to be noticed that these were specially summoned to bless the Lord and lift up their hands. For, after all, is it not they that stand in the house of God by night who are most in need of these exhortations? It seems to us that the sleepless sufferers among us are God's night-watch. When the busy workers are slumbering, they come on duty to bless the Lord, and to seek his blessing on the work of the past day, and the coming one.

It is comparatively easy to bless the Lord in the daytime, when sunshine lies like his smile on nature, and all the world is full of music, and our lives flow on quietly and peacefully. It does not take much grace to bless the Lord then. But when night has draped the earth and hushed the homes of men to solitude, and we stand amid the shadows that lurk around us in the sanctuary, facing the inexplicable mysteries of Providence, of history, of life and death; then the song falters on our lips, and chokes our utterance.

No sooner, however, do we dare to formulate the words of blessing, pursing our lips in the effort, daring to say, by the strong effort of will, what we may not say gladly and easily, there comes back to us, as to this ancient singer, the assurance that the Lord which made heaven and earth shall bless. Is it possible for Him to have made heaven and earth, and not to be able to bless the soul whom He has not created only, but redeemed! He cannot fail to bless those that bless. Indeed, their hearts, like sounding boards, but reflect to Him his own.

Praise Him, O ye servants of the Lord!
Psa. 135: 1.

HERE is an appeal to all of us. We are his servants, we stand in his courts; let us praise Him. There is a distinction between thanksgiving and praise. In that, we render thanks for the great benefits that we have received at his hands; in this, we adore God for all that He is in Himself. Forgetting our own petty interests and concerns, our me and my and mine, we take our stand with angels and archangels and all the host of heaven in crying, Thou art worthy, O holy, holy, holy Lord! Heaven and earth are full of thy great glory. Glory be unto Thee, O God Most High!

We praise Him with our ascriptions of loyal affection, but we praise Him no less when we suffer silently according to the will of God; when we do his commandments, hearkening to the voice of his word; and when we wait for Him to indicate his will, or lead us by a right way.

Oh that life might be one long psalm of praise! Awake my soul, awake psaltery and harp, awake all that is within me! Shall angels praise Thee, my God, and shall I be dumb! Shall song awake to Thee from every copse and bower, from woodland and grove, from the heart of awakening nature, and shall I hold my peace! I praise Thee, I bless Thee, I worship Thee, I magnify Thee, most loving, most holy, most blessed God; my Father, my Redeemer, my Comforter! Every whit of my nature cries, Glory! That thy hand seems to lie heavily on me, and that my soul is pressed and straitened from without, shall not stay me. Yea, if it should be my lot to go from the courts of thy house to the nethermost abyss, I would still ask for grace to fill its unaccustomed spaces with adoring songs!

His mercy endureth for ever. Psa. 136: 26.
TWENTY-SIX times in this Psalm we are told that God's mercy endureth for ever. The psalmist had been reviewing the history of the past. As far back as the Creation his eye had travelled, and all through the stormy, troublous days he could detect the silver thread of mercy. Oh that we had his eyes to see always the love of God! Amid the murky gloom of chaos there is a silver gleam; it is his mercy. When sun and moon appear, there is a brighter light than theirs; it is his mercy. Above the roar of the Red Sea and the rattle of the thunder-storms, are the flute-like notes of his mercy. Through all the strife and horror of the conquest of Canaan there glides the white-robed angel of his mercy. Deeper than the darkest shades of sin, higher than the highest floods of transgression, is the love of God, in the hand of which the round world and all its inhabitants lie, as a drop on the palm. Look back on your life, and say whether you cannot see the thread of mercy linking all its beads.

"A debtor to mercy alone,
Of covenant mercy we sing."

And do you suppose that such mercy is going to fail you? It endureth for ever! You fret and chafe like a restless little child; but you cannot fall out of the arms of God's mercy. Lie still, it canopies you like a mother's face; it breathes about you as a mother's embrace. O love that will not let us go! O mercy that hath neither beginning nor end! O God, who hast loved, who lovest, and who wilt love, when the sun is no more, and the things that are now shall have passed away as a dream! O grace of God, exceeding in thy abundance the highest mountains of our sin!

How shall we sing the Lord's song in a strange land? Psa. 137: 4.

THE Hebrew singers were famous far beyond the limits of Israel. It is not surprising, therefore, that their captors asked of them the songs of Zion, little weening that there was an insuperable incongruity between those holy songs which were associated with the Temple service, and the strange surroundings of idolatrous Babylon. The Lord's song does not befit the strange land. How true this is of the minstrelsy of the heart! Chide it though you may for its silence, it must remain dumb so long as you are carried captive by the powers of evil.

You have ceased singing lately. The joy of your religious life has vanished. You pass through the old routine, but without the exhilaration of former days. Can you not tell the reason? It is not because your circumstances are depressed, though they may be; for Paul and Silas sang praises to God in their prison. Is not disobedience at the root of your songlessness? You have allowed some little rift to come within the lute of your life, which has been slowly widening, and now threatens to silence all. And you never will be able to resume that song until you have put away the evil of your doing, and have returned from the land of the enemy.

The return from Babylon has its duplicate in many a life. In answer to prayer our captivity is turned again as the stream from the south. Delivered out of the land of strangers, we again take up the harp of praise. "The Lord's song" is often more in the heart than on the lips. Remember Jonathan Edwards' description of the lady who afterwards became his wife, whose mind was filled with exceeding sweet delight, and seemed to have someone invisible always communing with her.

The Lord will perfect that which concerneth me.
Psa. 138: 8.

WHAT A COMFORTABLE ASSURANCE! We often despair of ourselves. We awake to see that much on which we have prided ourselves, instead of being gold, silver, and precious stones, was mere wood, hay, and stubble. We discover, as Saul of Tarsus did, that the structure of righteousness which we have been raising is but as dross in the holy eye of God. We find ourselves falling through a bottomless pit of self-despair. Finally, we turn to the Lord Jesus, and say, What we cannot do for ourselves, and what no one can do for us, Thou must undertake. And there steals upon us the comfortable assurance that we have only to be faithful and true to his least prompting, and He will perfect.

WHAT AN ARGUMENT! First, we plead the mercy of God, the patience that endures for ever, never surprised, never surrendering its cherished purpose, never renouncing heart and hope, but always enduring amid rebuffs of neglect and the proud rebellion of self-will. Because thy love is without measure or end, we believe that Thou wilt yet be conqueror, O Christ! Thou wilt have thy way. We despair of ourselves. We hope infinitely in thy mercy.

Secondly, we plead that we are the work of his own hands. Has He done so much, and will He not finish? Has He implanted a hunger that He will not satisfy? Has He led to the point of Pisgah vision, and will He not give the land? A mother might forsake her child, but God cannot forsake those whom He has made the subjects of his thought and care. He cannot have created within us longings and desires that reach to the Infinite, merely to tantalize. "If it were not so, I would have told you." Yes, we shall be perfected, some day, somewhere.

See if there be any way of grief in me.
Psa. 139: 24 (R.V., marg.).

THE A.V. says "wicked way"; but the R.V. marg. gives "way of grief." We may be in a way that causes God grief, even though it is not what men might term a way of wickedness. We may be grieving our blessed Lord more than we know, substituting an ideal religious standard, or absorption in his work, or the conception which our friends persist in holding concerning us, for that direct personal fellowship with Himself, which alone is religion. Ah! How much we may have grieved the Spirit of Christ! Not always consciously. Often in pleading for us, the Lord must needs say, "Forgive; they know not what they do." But we are unwilling that his tender heart should suffer, or his face be overcast with grief, because of our waywardness; therefore we say, "Search us and know us; try us and show us the ways of grief." Be prepared for his revelations, searching and startling.

Lord, that is what we want! We have been going in ways of grief. We desire to go in the way everlasting—the way of eternal life; the way which we shall never need to retrace; the way that touches the deepest life possible to the creature. But we cannot find it for ourselves, nor even see the next step; therefore we stretch out poor, groping hands, and cry, "Lead us, as a woman may lead her blind child. We do not ask to see the distant way. Show us the next thing, and the next, and the next, till thy grief is turned to gladness." May I venture to hope that God will answer my prayer, and lead me in the way everlasting? Certainly! Not only may you hope, you must hope. It is as much your duty to hope always, and for the best things, as to look for forgiveness and grace to help in your time of need.

O God, the strength of my salvation, Thou hast covered my head in the day of battle.
Psa. 140: 7.

ALL day long the fight has waxed fierce against the hardly-pressed soldier. The very sky has seemed darkened with flights of arrows, and the enemy has raged like a tornado amid the reeds on the river's brink. The fiery darts of venomous sarcasm have been like a storm of hail, and yet the lonely warrior has not succumbed. To himself, and to all others, his escape has been marvellous. How could it be accounted for, except that an unseen shield had been around him, covering his head in the day of battle.

Ah, beloved soul, God is not only the strength of thy salvation, but He is also the covert, the panoply, the shield on which the malice of the foe expends itself in vain. Be quiet. Let not thy heart be troubled, neither let it be afraid. No weapon that is formed against thee shall prosper. There is but one matter for which thou needest to care. Always be sure that you are ranged on God's side.

As David anticipated the mischief of violent men who gathered themselves together for war, and sharpened their tongues like a serpent, it was a consolation to look back upon past deliverances. What God had done He would do again, so that the righteous might give thanks, and the upright dwell in his presence. God's covering in the day of battle makes a temple amid its tumult, and the soul dwells there as in the divine Presence Chamber.

"O Holy Lord, who with the children three
    Didst walk the piercing flame,
Help! in these trial hours, which, save to
    Thee, I dare not name;
Nor let these quivering eyes and sickening
    heart
Crumble to dust beneath the tempter's
    dart!"

Let the righteous smite me, it shall be a kindness.
Psa. 141: 5 (R.V.).
DAVID confessed his indebtedness to those who had reproved him. He realized how much he owed them. We ought to consider one another and have a care for each other's growth in grace. It is the duty of every true-hearted child of God to arrest another if he be erring in some way which is inconsistent with the honour of the family. We have to wash one another's feet; and may perform an inestimable benefit in graciously indicating some fly in the ointment of our religious profession.

But perhaps there is nothing which needs greater grace. We are so apt to be censorious, to lord it over the one whom we rebuke, to pride ourselves on our superiority, to be so taken up with another's life, as to miss God's best for ourselves. It is said that some persons wash the saints' feet in scalding water. David says, Let the righteous smite me. You cannot lift a man higher than you are. You must take the beam out of your eye before you can take the mote out of your brother's.

It needs some amount of grace also to accept reproof. The head is rather inclined to refuse it, and to take itself out of the way of the well-meaning adjusting hand. We resent interference. We do not care to be found out. But if, by God's grace, we can and do accept the smiting and reproof, we shall find that they become as fragrant oil. The fresh anointing which you seek in the morning may come not in rapt emotional experiences, but in the straight dealing of some fellow-disciple. Whenever anything is said which finds fault with you and blames you, receive it humbly and tenderly, asking whether it may not contain a message from your Father.

*When my spirit was overwhelmed within me,
then Thou knewest my path.* Psa. 142: 3.
OF course, God knows our path. We were created unto good works which God before prepared that we should walk in them. There is no step in your path which has not been anticipated and ordained by your Heavenly Father. See that path lying across the plain of life, now traversing deserts of sand, or climbing steeps of difficulty, or reaching across lonely steppes. Your heart faints (see R.V., marg.): you say, I cannot take this track; I cannot go through that experience; I cannot bear that strain. Heart and flesh fail. Then it is an infinite solace to look up into the face of the Father, and say, Before I was born, or took the first steps on this path, or essayed to meet its manifold vicissitudes, Thou knewest it; and Thou must have known that it was not too hard, and that there were resources of strength in Thyself sufficient for my day, which the emergency would bring out in a clearer manifestation.

We all have our times of being overwhelmed when the full realization of our grief, and pain, and loneliness rushes over us. The love we can never retrieve; the opportunity we can never recall. Then there is heart-break. But in such dark hours Jesus knows—knows the difficulties which you cannot explain to the dearest; the grave perplexities which you cannot share with your wisest confidant. He can allow for a hesitance, a trepidation, a shrinking back, which to others are unaccountable. He can give credit for the resolution that is sorely tested, and the faith which nearly gives out. He can take into account matters which evade the scrutiny of those who have the best opportunity of judging. What a relief to turn from them to Him, and say, I cannot tell them, but Thou knowest.

In Thy sight shall no man living be justified.
Psa. 143: 2.

THIS is an admission which each must make for himself. Man by nature is very willing to justify himself. The essence of the Pharisees' sin consisted in justifying themselves in the sight of men. But God knows our hearts, and that which is exalted among men is an abomination in the sight of God. We need to have a deeper sense of God's holiness, and of his requirements as set forth in his holy law. We need more particular preaching and teaching. I was interested recently to hear of one who said she did not want to know of God because she did not want to know her own sinfulness. If men did know God, they would be compelled to admit their inability to be just with Him. It is our duty to force the knowledge of God on the unwilling conscience of men.

But probably what we all need as preachers and teachers is to get a glimpse of God's nature, to know what holiness is, and purity, and righteousness, as they exist in the divine nature. We do not know the sinfulness of sin, and cannot enforce it, because we have not come in contact with the burning bliss of the Great White Throne.

We are justified by faith. Directly we are joined to Christ, we stand before the law of God clothed in his righteousness, and accepted not only as forgiven sinners, but as righteous. We know that God will never enter into judgment with us, since we were judged in our Substitute. There will be a judgment of our works, but there can be no condemnation of our persons. It is God that justifies. Who shall condemn? The Master said that the publican who only cried with downcast eyes, "God be propitiated to me, the sinner," went down to his house justified.

My . . . Psa. 144: 1, 2.

NOTICE that repeated My. David had learnt that nothing can take the place of personal dealings with God. Surely he had realized the fulfilment of his own thoughts about dwelling in the House of the Lord all the days of his life, and beholding his beauty. There is a great fear lest many of God's most earnest and devoted children may be losing sight of Jesus in these active days. We allow our work for Christ, our doctrines about Him, and our rules for becoming like Him, to intercept our view of Him. Too seldom do we get so near Him as to be able to talk to Him face to face; or pile word on word in our ineffectual effort to tell Him what we think of Him. One who loved much sang:

"Jesus, Jesus, dearest Lord,
/Forgive me if I say
For very love, thy dearest name,
A thousand times a day."

After all, it is not thoughts about Christ, but Christ Himself that we all need. To know Him in all the various aspects of his character, as Loving-kindness, Fortress, Shield, and Conqueror! Jesus can be the supply of your every need; and as the days pass, you will probably find yourself put into situations which will force you to discover in Him some new aspect, some fresh characteristics, something that would never have appeared to view, till the awful exigency had arisen. Then put out your hand and say My.

Always distinguish between the words attain and obtain. We can never earn his gracious help, either by prayer, or service; but we may claim, appropriate, and take. Learn to put your hand on all spiritual blessings in Christ, and say, Mine.

Thy kingdom is an everlasting kingdom.
Psa. 145: 13.

THESE words are engraven on the door of a mosque in Damascus, which was formerly a Christian church. Originally they were plastered over by stucco; but this has dropped away, and the words stand out clearly defined. They seem to be contradicted by centuries of Mohammedanism; but they are essentially true. Just now the kingdom is in mystery; but soon it will be manifested.

Jesus is gone to the Father to be invested with the kingdom, as a Roman official might have gone from the provinces to Rome for his investiture on the part of the emperor as proconsul or governor. And Daniel tells us that when He comes to the Ancient of Days, He will receive from Him dominion, and glory, and a kingdom that all the peoples, nations, and languages should serve Him; and his dominion is an everlasting dominion which shall not pass away, and his kingdom shall not be destroyed. It shall break in pieces, and consume all other kingdoms. The iron, clay, brass, silver, and gold, shall be broken in pieces, and become like the chaff of summer threshing-floors; but it shall become a great mountain and fill the earth.

We are called to receive a kingdom that cannot be shaken. Each faithful servant is to rule over his allotted cities. We are to reign with Christ for a thousand years in this world, sharing his throne and empire. We have been made kings unto God, and we shall reign for ever and ever.

"Then long Eternity shall greet our bliss
   With an individual kiss;
Then all this earthly grossness quit,
Attir'd with stars, we shall for ever sit,
Triumphing over Death, and chance, and
   Thee, O Time!"

In that very day his thoughts perish. Psa. 146:4
THE R.V. marg. gives the alternative purposes. And surely we all have had reason to notice the vacillation and infirmity of purpose which characterize too many of the sons of men. They promise to visit us every week, in our sickness or bereavement, but after a few months drop off. They pledge themselves to perform certain functions, but get lax, and ultimately the grass grows thick where their feet should have kept it down.

But we have most to complain of ourselves. Who among us has not bitterly to reproach himself for the evanescence of noble resolution—the dying down of earnest purpose? Too often they have been like the early dew and the morning cloud. In the day in which we made them our purposes have perished.

What is the remedy? It is suggested in those memorable words of Jesus, "The water that I shall give him shall become in him a well of water, springing up unto eternal life." When once Jesus has been allowed to do his chosen work in the soul, He opens a subterranean passage to the reservoirs of eternity, along and through which the supplies from God's own heart begin to enter and rise up within the soul. Abide in Him, and the sap of his life will suggest, renew, and reinforce, the purposes of the holy life. Rise up, O well, for ever rise, within hearts that desire a fixed purpose to love God! Infirm of purpose we need never be, whilst God waits to create in us a steadfast spirit (*Psa.* 51:10, R.V., marg.). We must be rooted and grounded in Him. Then will be manifest in us the fruit of the Spirit, which is "love, joy, peace, long-suffering, gentleness, goodness, faith, meekness, self-control" (*Gal.* 5:22, 23. R.V.).

He healeth the broken in heart. . . . He telleth the number of the stars. Psa. 147:3, 4.
HOW wonderful that these two qualities should blend in one Being! That God tells the number of the stars is only what we should expect of Him. They are his flock, lying down on the fields of the heavens; and as a shepherd has a name for each of his charge, so has God for the stars. But that He should be able to bend over one broken heart and bind it with his sympathy and heal its flowing wounds, this is wonderful, amazing, divine.

It is said that in a healthy man the clenched fist is about the size of the heart. So in God, his might is the gauge of his mercy: his hand of his heart. The mountains of his strength show the valleys of his tenderness.

Yet surely it must be so. The stars are after all only things, great masses of matter; whilst hearts are those of living, sentient beings which He made, redeemed, and loves. They are the adornments of his House, whilst broken hearts are his children. Shall He have names for the one and no care for the other? This text is exquisitely illustrated in Jesus. Through Him God made the worlds; and by his pierced hands tears have been wiped and stifling sobs silenced all through the ages. Is your heart bleeding? He knows, He cares, He loves, He bends over and heals with exquisite sensitiveness and skill. Yea, the stars may fall from heaven as untimely figs; the sun burn out as an extinct volcano; but He will never cease to tend and comfort his own.

"There is no sorrow, Lord, too light
   To bring in prayer to Thee;
There is no anxious care too slight
   To wake thy sympathy!"

Stormy wind fulfilling his word. Psa. 148:8.
AS it rushes through the forest, the hurricane tears down the rotten branches, and makes way for the new shoots of the spring; and as it searches out the intricacies of the crowded alleys and courts it bears away the fever germs, and changes the atmosphere. Do not dread it, if you meet it rushing across the ocean and churning up the mighty billows on its way; know it to be your Father's strong servant, intent on fulfilling some errand on which it has been sent.

Stormy winds not unseldom invade our lives. All had been so fair and blessed with us. The south wind, blowing softly, had led us to suppose that we might make for another harbour. But not long afterwards the tempestuous Euroclydon beat down on us, bearing us far out of our course, and threatening us with destruction. But even under those circumstances, dare to trust. That stormy wind cannot separate you from God; for through its mad fury his angels will visit you, his care will surround you, his purpose will be fulfilled of bearing you onward, as the Apostle was borne towards Rome, with its opportunities of witness-bearing (Acts 27).

The great matter to remember is to run before the wind. Let its course be yours. Yield your will to God's will; and even though it bears you far out of your course, dare to believe that it is the quickest and best way of attaining the harbour which God has prepared. There is nothing terrible in fire, or hail, or stormy wind, when we see God behind them.

"O man! hold thee on in courage of soul
  Through the stormy shades of thy worldly way,
And the billows of cloud that around thee roll
Shall sleep in the light of a wondrous day!"

The Lord taketh pleasure in his people.
Psa. 149: 4.

THE Lord watches us more closely than we realize. At each turn, his eye is upon us; and when we manifest some trait of obedience or devotion, it sends a thrill of pleasure through his heart. Of course our standing is always in his grace. We love only because He first loved. Our comeliness is placed on us by our King. And when we are at our best we always need the sprinkling of the precious blood. But still it is the constant teaching of Scripture that we may please God. This was the testimony borne of Enoch before his translation, and the apostle exhorts us to walk worthily of the Lord, unto all pleasing. He tells us not to entangle ourselves in the affairs of this life, that we may please Him who hath chosen us to be his soldiers.

How well it would be if this were the aim of every day, the purpose of every sermon, the motive of every act. It were easy to be baptized in the waters of death, if only on emerging we might stand beneath the open heavens, whilst a voice said, "This is my beloved child, in whom I am well pleased." Let us strive for this. Let our eye be ever fixed on that beloved face, checking any act that might threaten to bedim it, prosecuting all that might bring over it a smile of loving appreciation and thankfulness.

And see how the verse closes: "He will beautify the meek with victory" (R.V., marg.). Not only does God take a personal interest in each step of the obedient soul, but He makes it beautiful, and leads it from victory to victory. This combination is very significant. The victorious are not always meek, and the meek do not generally seem victorious. But it is otherwise when God takes pleasure.

Praise ye the Lord! Hallelujah! Psa. 150: 6.

THE psalter begins with "Blessed," and ends with "Hallelujah." Obedience in walk and conduct leads to blessedness, and this culminates in rapture. The heart that does God's will in this world may not be always happy, but it is always blessed; and when patience has had her perfect work, it will break into such rapture as to need all creation to help its song to perfect and complete expression.

Your life may resemble the psalter with its varying moods, its light and shadow, its sob and smile; but it will end with hallelujahs, if only you will keep true to the will and way and work of the Most Holy.

Your estimate of the world is often pessimistic to the last point; but if you will be still, and let God finish his work perfectly, you will hear all things that have breath joining in the Hallelujah Chorus, and saying, The kingdoms of the world have become those of the Lord and of his Christ.

God is preparing the whole universe to be an orchestra of praise and adoration to his Son. On one occasion a great conductor, amidst the burst of five hundred instruments, is said to have missed the piccolo; and he stayed the entire performance till it chimed in. Nothing can satisfy God till creation's groans are changed to rapture, and the curse, which restrains her songs, is lifted from the face of all nature; but He wants to hear your voice. If you cannot praise Him in the church, praise Him in Nature, "the firmament of his power." If you cannot praise Him for his acts, do so for his excellent greatness. If not with the blare of trumpet, then with the softer lute. If not with the realization of the senses, then in the assurance of faith. Only be sure to praise Him.

The Proverbs

Quiet from fear of evil. Prov. 1: 33.
"WHOSO." This promise is to us all. To the man in the street, as much as for those of us who have been nurtured in Christian homes.
THE EVIL IS TAKEN OUT OF THINGS FOR THOSE WHOSE HEARTS ARE FULL OF GOD. Nothing which God allows to come to us is really evil, except sin. Put away sin from your heart, and let it be filled with Love and Faith, and behold all things will become new. They will lose their evil semblance, because you will look at them with new eyes. Men talk against the March wind; but when they understand that it is cleansing fœtid dens of fever-germs, they regard it as a blessing. Men dread change, anything unwonted or unaccustomed; but when they find that, like the transplanted fruit-tree, they will often attain a greater maturity than when left to one spot of soil, they welcome it. If you look at things apart from God, especially if you anticipate the future without Him, you have good cause for fear; but if you hearken to and obey Him, if you know and love Him, if you abide in God and God in you, you will see that the evil is not in the things or events, but in yourself. Give yourself as alms to God, and lo, all things will become clean to you.

DEATH shall lose its terrors, and become the Father's servant, ushering you into his presence. Pain and suffering shall but cast into relief the stars of divine promise. Poverty will have no pangs, and storm no alarms. You shall become so habituated to find the rarest blessings associated with what men often dread most, that you will be quiet from all fear of evil, and able to look out, with serene and untroubled heart, on a sea of troubles. In fact, it is very doubtful if anything is really evil for those who love God.

If thou seek her as silver, and search for her as for hid treasures, etc. Prov. 2: 4, 5.
THERE is a beautiful illustration of the truth of these words in the life of Justin the Martyr, who died for the Gospel in the second century. As a young man he earnestly sought for truth, specially that which would arm him with self-control. He took up one system of philosophy after another, trying them as a man might explore mine after mine for silver. Finally, he found that every effort was futile.

"All at last did faithless prove,
    And, late or soon, betrayed my love."

At length, wandering in despair on the seashore, he met an aged man, a Christian, who spake as none had ever done to his heart, and pointed him to God in Christ. Beneath those words, that afternoon, he understood the fear of the Lord, and found the knowledge of God.

Thomas longed for evidences of the Resurrection, and Christ came to him. The Chamberlain, as he sat in his chariot reading the book of Esaias the Prophet at chapter 53, was desirous to know the truth, and Philip was sent to him. To Saul of Tarsus, groping in the midnight, there came fuller revelations than ever Gamaliel gave, through Stephen and Ananias, led by the Spirit of God.

But you must be prepared to sacrifice all. He who seeks diamonds, or pearls, or gold, will leave his native land, and what other men hold dear, and centre his whole attention on his quest. Not otherwise must it be with those who would understand the fear of the Lord, and find the knowledge of God. They must be willing to count all things but loss, to sell all they have, in order to buy the field with its treasure-trove.

He shall direct thy paths. Prov. 3: 6.
THY paths! Then, every man's path is distinct for him, and for no other. The paths may lie side by side, but they are different. They have converged; they may diverge. When Peter had been told of the rugged nature of the predestined path which was marked out for him in the Providence of God he turned towards John, his companion and friend, and said to Jesus, "What shall this man do?" The Lord instantly replied, in effect: "That is a matter in which I can brook no interference; it is entirely a matter for my choice and will; if I will, it may be that he shall tarry till I come." WE NEED TO BE DIVINELY DIRECTED. The man who stands above the maze can direct you

through all its labyrinth by the readiest path. God who made thee for thy life, and thy life for thee, can direct thee, and He only.

First: Lean not to thine own understanding.—One is apt to pride oneself on one's far-sighted judgment. We consult our maps and guides and the opinions of fellow-travellers, to find ourselves at fault. We have to learn that our own understanding is not keen enough or wise enough to direct; we must abjure and renounce all dependence on it.

Second: In all thy ways acknowledge Him. —Let thine eye be single; thy one aim to please Him; thy sole motive, his glory. It is marvellous how certainly and delightfully our way opens before us when we no longer look down on it, or around at others, but simply upwards into the face of Christ. "It is a universal law, unalterable as the nature of God, that no created being can be truly holy, useful, or happy, who is knowingly and deliberately out of the divine fellowship, for a single moment."

The light of dawn, that shineth more and more unto the perfect day. Prov. 4: 18 (R.V., marg.).
THIS may be referred to the work of God in the heart. He who commanded light to shine out of darkness hath shined in our hearts, to give the light of the knowledge of the glory of God. A little glimmering ray at first, God's light in the soul grows ever from less to more, revealing Himself and manifesting ourselves, so that we are growingly attracted from the self-life to circle around Him.

But probably it is true also of the graciousness of the believer's life. At first it shows itself in little acts of blessing on children and the poor; but the range of influence is always apt to increase, till what was a glimmer of helpfulness becomes as the sun shining in strength. The Sunday-school teacher becomes the preacher; the visitor among the poor becomes the philanthropist; the witness to the Gospel in the factory is called to witness in the great theatre of the world. See to it that there is a steady obedience to God's least promptings and monitions. Follow on to know the Lord, and to be conformed to his all-wise purpose.

Once again, notice the comparison in its exquisite beauty. Light is so gentle, noiseless, and tender. There is no sound; its voice is not heard. So is the influence of the holy soul. Its life becomes the light of men. As with the angel over the plain of Bethlehem, it sheds a light around those whom it will presently address. Like the Gulf Stream, which changes our climate from northern rigour to the temperate zone, so a holy life gently and irresistibly influences and blesses the world. The world is no worse than it is, not because of the holy words spoken on the Lord's Day, but for the holy lives of obscure saints.

The level path of life. He maketh level all his paths. Prov. 5: 6, 21 (R.V.).
IT is a remarkable expression, "the level path of life"; and there is great comfort in knowing that God is ever before us, levelling our pathway, taking insurmountable obstacles out of the way, so that our feet do not stumble.

It may be that you are facing a great mountain range of difficulty. Before you, obstacles, apparently insuperable, rear themselves like a giant wall to heaven. When you cross the Jordan there is always a Jericho which appears to bar all further advance, and your heart fails. But you are bidden to believe that there is a level path right through those mighty barriers; a pass, as it is called, in mountainous districts. The walking there is easy and pleasant if only you will let yourself be led to it. God has made it, but you must take it. How we dread the thought of those steep cliffs! It seems as though we could never climb them; but if we would only look at the Lord instead of at the hills, if we would look above the hills to Jehovah, we should be able to rest in sure faith that He will show us the level path of life.

Your path is not level, but full of boulders which have rolled down upon and choked it. But may this not be partly due to your mistakes or sins—to your wilfulness and self-dependence? There are sorrows and trials in all lives; but these need not obstruct our progress. The text surely refers to those difficulties which threaten us with their arrest, putting barriers in our way. When Peter reached the iron gate he found it open; when the women reached the sepulchre door they found the stone gone. What an awful indictment against the child of sensual pleasure, "She findeth not the level path of life!"

Bind them continually upon thine heart, tie them about thy neck. Prov. 6: 21.
IF the son addressed here is bidden to thus care for the words of his parents, how much more should we ponder those of God as given us in God's blessed Book.

WHEN THOU WALKEST, IT SHALL LEAD THEE. There is a little circle of friends whom I know of who read this book of Proverbs through every month for practical direction on the path of life. A West-countryman said of this collection of wise words, "If any man shall maister the Book of Proverbs, no man shall maister he." Take for instance the weighty counsels of the first five verses. How many lives would have been saved from bitter anguish and disappointment if only they had been ruled by them! Let every young man also ponder the closing verses. Let us all meditate more constantly on the Word of God.

WHEN THOU SLEEPEST, IT SHALL WATCH THEE. The man who meditates on the Word of God by day will not be troubled by evil dreams at night. Whatever unholy spirits may prowl around his bed, they will be restrained from molesting him whose head is pillowed on some holy word of God. And on awakening, the Angel of Revelation will whisper words of encouragement and love.

AND WHEN THOU AWAKEST, IT SHALL TALK WITH THEE. The heart is accustomed to commune with itself about many things, but when the mind is full of God through his Word, it seems as though the monologue becomes a dialogue. To all our wonderings, fears, questionings, answers come back from the infinite glory in words of Scripture. Some wear amulets about their necks to preserve them; but the Word of God is both a safeguard and choice treasure.

Say unto Wisdom, Thou art my sister; and call Understanding thy kinswoman. Prov. 7: 4.
THIS wisdom might seem to be too unearthly and ethereal to engage our passionate devotion, unless we remember that she was incarnated in Jesus Christ, who, throughout this book, seems forthshadowed in the majestic conception of wisdom. And who shall deny that the most attractive and lovable traits blended in his matchless character as Son of Man and exalted Redeemer.

With what sensitive purity He bent his face to the ground and wrote on the dust, when her accusers brought to Him a woman taken in the act of sin! With what thoughtfulness He sent word to Peter that he was risen, and provided the meal for his weary and wave-drenched sailor friends on the shores of the lake! With what quick intuition He read Mary's desire to anoint Him for the burying!

It was this combination of what is sweet in woman and strong in man, which so deeply satisfied men like Bernard, Rutherford, Fénélon, and thousands more, who have been shut out from the delights of human love, but have found in Jesus the complement of their need, the satisfaction of their hunger and thirst. In Him, for them, was restored the vision of the sweet mother of early childhood; of the angel-sister who went to be with God; of the early love that was never destined to be realized.

Women find in Jesus strength on which to lean their weakness; and men find in Him the tender, thoughtful sympathy to which they can confidently entrust themselves. We are born for the infinite and divine; earthly loves, at their best, are only patterns of things in the heavens. They are priceless; but let us look into them and through them, to behold the unseen and eternal that lie beneath.

The Lord possessed me in the beginning of his way, before his works of old. Prov. 8: 22.
THIS wisdom is not an abstract attribute or quality, but a Person. Whether the ancient writer of these glowing paragraphs realized fully what deep things he was saying when he so depicted her—as one who was brought up with the Father before the world was, as rejoicing in the habitable parts of the earth with the children of men—we cannot positively determine; but we at least may lift the curtain, and see here Christ, who is both the Power and the Wisdom of God. Is not his chosen name the Word of God?

There, in that divine Man, in his gentle love, in his deep and weighty words, in his power to give life to them that find Him, we have the highest embodiment of the wisdom of God, which was before all worlds, and yet stoops to each lowly and obedient heart. It is not enough then for us to seek knowledge and get understanding apart from Jesus; but to seek Him diligently and early, as we are bidden in ver. 17, sure that when we win Him, we shall possess all the wealth of truth and knowledge that we require for this life and the next. He is the Truth and the Life. Truth apart from Him neither nourishes nor inspires.

Would you know the wisdom of God, then be still in heart, wait before God, quieting all your soul before Him; remember that Jesus is near, waiting, longing to impart Himself. Be not content till you have pressed through the words to the Word, through the Scriptures to Him of whom they testify. His delights are with the sons of men. Nothing will fill Him with greater joy than that we should hear Him, watching daily at his gates, and waiting at the posts of his doors.

Whoso is simple, let him turn in hither.
Prov. 9: 4, 16.

TWICE over this invitation is given—first by wisdom, and secondly by the foolish woman. To every young life, in its first setting forth, many voices and inducements speak. Wise, grave voices mingle with siren songs. The strait gate into the narrow way stands side by side with the wide gate that leads into the broad way. The counsels of the father's lips, the tears and prayers of the mother, amid the enticements of sinners, and the blandishments of the world. Here the true Shepherd, there the hireling; here the true Bride, there the apostate Church; here that which condemns the flesh, there that which takes its side.

Life is full of choices. There is no day without them. We are perpetually being reminded of the way in which the Creator introduced lines of division into his earliest work. For it is thus that He proceeds with the work of the new creation within. Repeatedly we hear his voice as He divides the light from the darkness, calling the one Day and the other Night. Would that we ever acted as children of the Light and of the Day, choosing the one and refusing the other! We are always being exercised in this, and our best life depends on the keenness and quickness with which we refuse the evil and choose the good.

Wisdom appeals to conscience. She says nothing at the outset of the sweetness of her service, or the pleasantness of her paths; but bases her appeal on whatsoever things are just, pure, lovely, and of good report. Yet she has rich rewards to those that choose her. Length of days, honour, a heart at leisure from itself, sure satisfaction, the assurance of the favour of God, a sure and certain hope of blessedness for evermore.

He is in the way of life that heedeth correction.
Prov. 10: 17 (R.V.).

IT is a wise prayer, "Correct me, O Lord, but with judgment." Happy is the man whom God correcteth; for whom the Lord loveth He correcteth.

Sometimes God corrects us with rebukes, making our beauty to consume away as a moth before the stroke of illness or physical weakness. At other times we are corrected by the faithful rebuke of a friend, or the question of a little child. And yet again, correction comes to us through the sore discipline of having to reap the results of our sins. Some heed correction; others resist and refuse it. Many get weary of it, and for their sakes it is written, "We have had fathers of our flesh, which corrected us, and we gave them reverence; shall we not much rather be in subjection unto the Father of spirits and live?"

Do not be weary of God's correction, my chastened friend. He does not expose you to the searching trial for his pleasure; but for your profit, and that you may be a partaker of his holiness. Heed correction. Ask why it has come, and what it is designed to teach. Set yourself to learn the lesson quickly. Above all, let us heed more carefully God's Holy Word, which is profitable for correction, as well as for teaching, reproof, and instruction. How often might we have been spared the searching correction of trouble if we had allowed our lives to be pruned by God's Word!

Our behaviour under correction will show whether we are in the Way of Life or not. If the Life of God be truly within us, we will meekly accept and profit by the correction, from whatever source it comes. Otherwise we will murmur and fret, till the wine becomes vinegar, and the milk sour.

There is that scattereth, and yet increaseth.
Prov. 11: 24.

THIS scattering is a conception borrowed from the husbandman. From out of his barns he takes the precious seed, and scatters it broadcast. The child of the city might wonder at his prodigality, little weening that each of the scattered seeds may live in a hundred more, and perpetuate itself for successive autumns.

We are bidden to measure our life by its losses rather than by its gains; by the blood poured out, rather than by its storage in the arteries of life; by its sacrifices, rather than its self-preservation; by its gifts, rather than its accumulations. He is the richest man in the esteem of the world who has gotten most; he is richest in the esteem of heaven who has given most.

And it is so ordered that as we give we get. If we miserly hoard the grain, it is eaten by weevils; if we cast it away it returns to us multiplied. Stagnant water is covered with scum; flowing water is fresh and living. He who gives his five barley loaves and two small fishes into the hands of Jesus sees the people fed and gets twelve baskets over. Tell out all you know, and you will have enough for another meal, and yet another. Set no limit to your gifts of money, time, energy; in the act of giving the whole that you have expended will return to you, and more also. Freely ye have received, freely give; freely give, and freely ye will receive. "He that soweth sparingly shall reap also sparingly; and he that soweth bountifully shall reap also bountifully. . . . And He that supplieth seed to the sower, and bread for food, shall supply and multiply your seed for sowing, and increase the fruits of your righteousness, ye being enriched in everything unto all liberality."

The wicked is snared by the transgression of his lips.   Prov. 12: 13.

IT has been well remarked that God has set many snares in the very constitution and order of the world for the detection and punishment of evil-doers. Amongst others, is the liar's own tongue. Watch a criminal trial, and you will find abundant illustrations of this in the detection of a false witness, who makes statement after statement, which are not only inconsistent with truth, but with each other. Presently he comes to a point, where he falls into one of his own lies, which he had forgotten, and lies, floundering like a wild beast in a snare. It is impossible for a liar to imitate the severe and inflexible majesty of truth. In his endeavour to appear true, he will fall into a trap of his own setting.

But whilst the wicked goes into a snare, the righteous shall come out of trouble. It is not said that he will always escape it. Our Master clearly foretold that all lives which were moulded on the example of his own would pass through similar experiences. For them also the bitter hatred of the world, the title Beelzebub, and at last the cross. "But the just shall come out of trouble." It is not possible that we should be holden by it. We belong to Him who has come out of the great tribulation. Just now we may be following the serried ranks down into the heart of the sea, on either hand the heaped-up billows, and the stars hidden by the pale of thunder-cloud. But He who led us in will lead us out. On yonder bank we shall stand among the victors. That weary hand shall wave the victor's palm; that tired head shall be crowned with light. Listen to the voices that come from that radiant shore: Be of good cheer, I have overcome the world: and, Be thou faithful unto death, and I will give thee a crown of life.

He that guardeth his mouth keepeth his life.
Prov. 13: 3 (R.V.).

WHAT we say influences others, but it has a reflex influence on ourselves. When we speak unadvisedly and impurely, we sow seeds of ill harvests not in others only, but in ourselves, and the very utterance injures us. When, on the other hand, we refuse to give expression to a wrong or unkind thought, we choke and strangle it.

Will each reader and hearer of these words carefully bear this in mind. If you express what is uncharitable or wrong, you gratify the evil nature that is in you, and you strengthen it. If, on the contrary, you refuse to express it, you strike a death-blow at the cursed thing itself. When you guard your mouth you keep your life, because you weaken that which is gnawing insidiously at the root of your life. If there is fire in a room, be sure not to open door or window; for air is its fuel and food. And if a fire is burning within you, be sure not to give it vent. What goes forth from you defiles you. Would you see good days? Refrain your lips from evil.

Perhaps you find yourself unable to guard your mouth. You are only discovering the truth of those terrible words: "The tongue is a fire, the world of iniquity among our members, which defileth the whole body, and setteth on fire the wheel of nature, and is set on fire of hell. . . . The tongue can no man tame; it is a restless evil, full of deadly poison." If man cannot tame it, the Saviour can. Cry to Him then, saying, "Set a watch, O Lord, before my mouth; keep the door of my lips." The fire of God's love will burn out the fire of hell. Hand the bridle, or rudder, as the apostle James calls it, over to Him.

"Take my lips, and let them be
Filled with messages from Thee."

A Tranquil Heart.   Prov. 14: 30 (R.V., marg.).
IF we would have a tranquil heart, we must

resolutely put from us the ambition to get name and reputation among men, to exert wider influence for its own sake, and to amass large accumulation of money. Directly we begin to vie with others, to emulate them, or compare our position and influence with theirs; directly we allow strong desires to roam unchecked through our nature; directly we live on the breath of popular applause, we are like those who step from the pier on a rocking boat—all hope of tranquillity is at an end.

"In God's will," Dante said, "is our peace." When the government is on his shoulder, of its increase and of our peace there is no end. Would you have your peace flow as a river?— then rest in the Lord, be silent unto Him; fret not thyself; turn away from the things that are seen and temporal; set thy face to those that are unseen and eternal. Live in the secret place of the Most High, and hide under the shadow of the Almighty. Say of the Lord that He is thy fortress and high tower. Put God between thyself and everything. Let the one aim of thy life be to please Him, and do the one small piece of work He has entrusted thee with. Look away from all others to Him alone. And learn to look out on others with a tender sympathetic gaze, turning to prayer about them and all things else that might ruffle and sadden. Let all thy requests be made known unto God, so shall his peace keep heart and mind.

"Draw me to Thee, till far within thy rest,
  In stillness of thy peace, thy voice I hear—
For ever quieted upon thy breast,
  So loved, so near."

The prayer of the upright is his delight.
Prov. 15: 8.
WE too seldom consider the pleasure that the prayer of his people gives to God. Often we go to Him with no other thought than to find relief from the pressure of anxiety or sin. We hardly realize that He is looking for our coming because He loves us. Thus nothing delights Him more than the time we consecrate for heartfelt fellowship with Him. Think, O child of God, when next the hour of prayer comes round, that God is waiting for you. Would you cause Him disappointment by curtailing it, and by passing cursorily through a form, when He looks for the fellowship of the soul? Remember how Jesus said, "The Father seeketh such to worship Him."

The prayer which gives God delight is one which is characterized thus: (1) It must be an identification with the prayer of the Lord Jesus. In Him alone can the Father take delight, and in us only as far as we are in the Beloved, and He in us. (2) We must come in full assurance of faith, our hearts sprinkled from an evil conscience, and our lives rid of all known inconsistency and impurity. (3) We must give time for God to speak to us. Rev. Andrew Murray says, "Bow quietly before Him in humble faith and adoration. God is. God is near. God is love, longing to make Himself known." (4) Lie very low before God. Sink down before Him in the lowest dust of self-abasement, reckoning yourself to be nothing. (5) Present yourself to God that He may fulfil through you his own loving purposes.

In the Book of Revelation, we are bidden to behold the Angel of the Covenant mingling much incense with the prayers of all the saints. That incense is the merit of Jesus, which makes our prayers delightful (Rev. 8: 3–5).

Roll thy works unto the Lord, and thy purposes shall be established. Prov. 16: 3 (R.V., marg.).
THERE are four matters which we are to roll upon God—ourselves, as the Messiah in Psa. 22; our burden; our way; and here our works. The genesis of Christian work is on this wise. We become conscious of the uprising of a noble purpose. We are not sure at first whether it is of God or not, till we have taken time to subject it to the winnowing fan of his good Spirit. It is always wise to subject it to the fire of his criticism before it takes shape Even then, however, all is not done. We must. submit our plans before they are executed, our methods by which they are being executed, and the results of the execution, to the infinite wisdom of our Heavenly Father.

What a comfort it is to roll our works upon God! That servant of God who is carrying the responsibilities of a vast missionary enterprise! That preacher with his church and organizations! That promoter of philanthropic and ameliorative agencies! Let them roll their works upon God, and be content to take the subordinate place of acting as his agents and executors. The heart will be light, and the hands free, if only we can learn the blessed secret of imposing the responsibility and anxiety of our efficiency, finance, and success on Jehovah. Roll thy works, and see that they do not roll back again. Put on the arrest of faith to make them keep their position. Reckon that God takes what you give; and when you have let your works go, be sure to cast yourself after them on his patient carefulness. Remember that He desires to work in us to will and to work of his good pleasure. Do not worry, nor fret, nor be always looking for results. Do your best, and leave the rest to Him, who is our rearward. He will follow up your efforts and establish the work of your hands.

He that spareth his words hath knowledge.
Prov. 17: 27 (R.V.).

THE A.V. and R.V. marg. suggest a better rendering, "He that hath knowledge spareth his words." It is a wise thing to say as little as possible to man, and as much as possible to God. The ultimate test of friendship has always seemed to me to be in the ability of true friends to be silent in each other's presence. In silence we best may open the heart to receive the infillings of the divine Spirit. When people are always talking to one another, even though they talk about God, they are liable to lose the first fresh sense of God's presence.

Ordinary conversation greatly weakens character. It is like the perpetual running of a tap which inevitably empties the cistern. It seems to me disastrous when the whole of a summer holiday is spent in contact with friends, however dear, who leave no time for the communing of the soul with itself, nature, and God. We cannot be perpetually in society, speaking to the nearest and dearest, without saying things which will afterwards cause us regret. We shall have spoken too much of ourselves, or too little of Christ, or too much about others; or we shall have allowed the things of the world and sense to bulk too largely. Besides, it is only in silence and thought that our deepest life matures, or the impressions of eternity are realized. If we are always talking, we give no opportunity for the ripening of the soul. Nothing makes the soul more fruitful than to leave it fallow. Who would pick a crop of fruit when first it began to appear on the trees? Live deep. Speak as little as you may. Be slow to speak, and swift to hear.

"Not seldom ceases outward speech awhile,
That the inner, isled in calm, may clearer
sound."

His neighbour cometh and searcheth him out.
Prov. 18: 17 (R.V.).

IT is easy to boast of what we are or are not;

but the real question is as to what others think of us. A Christian lady told me that a little time ago she went to a meeting where one after another arose to say how long they had been without sin. When an opportunity was given, she asked simply if they might be allowed to hear something from those who had lived with the persons that had been so loudly expressing themselves; because she said that she had observed that the opinions of those who shared the same room or home as Christian professors were apt to vary greatly from those of the professors themselves.

It is a grave question for us all—what do our neighbours and associates think of us? Would they credit us with the highest attainments in Christian living? Would they concede the reality and beauty of our characters? After all, may not we be mistaking our ideals for our attainments, and judging ourselves by a lower standard than we apply to others? Might not our wives and sisters, our husbands and brothers, search us? It is so much easier to plead our own cause in a meeting than to stand clear in the searching scrutiny of the home.

And if our neighbours search us, what does God think of us as the fierce light of his eyes scans us and reads our deepest secrets? What should we do were it not for the Blood of Christ? I used to hesitate once to call myself a miserable sinner; but as I know myself better, I begin to feel that it is a reasonable designation. That is what we are by nature, though we have been made by divine grace, children, heirs, joint-heirs with Christ. Job, the righteous man, confessed himself vile when God's light revealed him.

He that hath pity upon the poor lendeth unto the Lord. Prov. 19: 17 (R.V.).

WHAT a revolution would be wrought among us if we really believed this! We are glad to lend to our friends in a temporary strait, especially when we know that our money is safe and will come back to us with a substantial increase. To have an I O U is quite sufficient. But in the light of this text we are taught to look on God as the great Borrower. He comes to us, asking that we will lend to Him. In every needy one who deserves our aid the request of the Almighty may be heard asking a loan.

What mistakes we make! We think we keep what we hold and invest well. But we really keep what we give away. The best investments are the heavenly shares and stocks, which are found in the needs and sorrows of the poor. Will you not, my reader, resolve that you will begin to lend to the Lord in the person of those who need your help, whether for their personal necessities or the work in which they are interested? You are called to be a steward of God's free gifts to you. You must be ready, as his almoner, to deal out his wealth. He will pay you for doing it, by giving you your own present maintenance; and one day He will say, "I was hungry, and you fed Me; thirsty, and you gave Me drink: inherit the place prepared for you."

Just ponder the magnificence of this promise: "His good deed will He pay him again." God will never be in your debt. He is exact and punctilious in his repayment. No man ever dared to do his bidding in respect to any case of need, and found himself the poorer. "Give, and it shall be given to you; good measure, pressed down and running over shall they give into your bosom." Was not Ruth's love to Naomi well compensated?

The spirit of man is the candle of the Lord.
Prov. 20: 27.

SEE that row of unlighted candles, standing in silver sockets, chased and wrought with wondrous skill—such are the souls of men by nature, rich in attainments and generous impulses, highly educated, perhaps, apparently fit for high and glorious work, but they have no light. They are a puzzle to themselves and others. Whilst another, who has none of their powers or advantages, casts a glow on his age, which lingers long after he has gone. He is like a common candle, but lit. The spark from God has ignited his soul.

But remember that while the candle shines with the light of God, it wastes. The slowly-dwindling length shows the amount of the inevitable expenditure. Our Lord said of the Baptist, "He was a burning and shining light." There must be burning before there can be shining; we must suffer in order to serve. It is good to know this, for it gives purpose to pain. "I cried to Thee, O Lord, and unto Thee I made supplication. What profit is there in my blood?" What profit! If we only knew that, the pain might be borne proudly and lightly. Oh, never dare to think of blessing men, except at a cost of blood and tears, that may seem to thee as a guttering candle, the wax of which is flowing down in trickling streams, or curling up in rugged contortions!

"Therefore, O Lord, I will not fail nor falter,
　Nay, but I ask it; nay, but I desire—
Lay on my lips thine embers of the altar,
　Seal with the sting, and furnish with the fire.
"Quick in a moment, infinite for ever,
　Send an arousal better than I pray;
Give me a grace upon the faint endeavour,
　Souls for my hire, and Pentecost to-day."

The heart . . . as the watercourses.
Prov. 21: 1 (R.V.).

MADAME GUYON says that there are three classes of souls that may be compared to rivers flowing towards God as their ocean.

1. Some move on sluggishly and feebly. These are often discouraged, dwell much in the outer and emotional, and fail to seek God with their whole strength.

2. Some proceed decidedly and rapidly. These have large hearts, and are quick in their responses to God's Spirit.

3. Some press on in headlong impetuosity.

This comparison of our hearts to watercourses filled with torrents from the hills is a very beautiful one, and is capable of great expansion.

WATERCOURSES NEED FRESH SUPPLIES OF WATER FROM THE HILLS: and our hearts are in constant need of freshets from the everlasting fountain of God's nature.

WATERCOURSES MUST FULFIL THEIR MINISTRY IN ALL WEATHERS: and we must continue patiently in faith and well-doing, whatever be our circumstances or emotions. If we fail, the whole land will be smitten with drought.

WATERCOURSES END IN MERGING THEIR WATERS WITH THE OCEAN TIDES: so God will one day be all in all.

Will you let God lead your heart whither He will? Just as a husbandman will cut watercourses in different directions to conduct the flow of the water, so will you not let God lead your life? You can be a watercourse: He must give the water. Only be content, like the river-bed, to lie deep hidden beneath the waters; not noticed or thanked by those that stoop to drink the refreshing draughts. It is impossible for the water to pass through you without nourishing your own soul.

Thorns and snares are in the way of the froward.
Prov. 22: 5.

THIS is due to the love of God, shown in the

constitution of the world. It would have been malignity indeed to have placed us in the world without the warning signal of pain to show us where we are wrong, and to sting us when we go astray. By the pitiful mercy of our Creator, pain is the inevitable consequence of the breach of physical and moral law; thus men are shown that they are on the wrong path, and driven back in repentance and rectitude. The Greek motto said: "Pain is therefore gain."

You say that there are many who suffer who are among the holiest and meekest of mankind; and you wonder how it is that those snares have come so plentifully to their share. But you must remember that though an individual may not have broken the law himself in any special sense, yet he inherits broken law. By virtue of his union with a sinful race he reaps a harvest sown by others' sins; and by bearing it meekly and lovingly he enters into union with some aspects of the death of Christ, and fills up that which is behind of his sufferings. When wrong is borne sweetly and uncomplainingly, some froward deed that started long before, and had been cursing the world, is for ever arrested and cancelled; as a cannon ball in a bank of sand.

But, in addition, there are some who suffer according to the will of God. Pain, beneath the touch of the Spirit of God, is in the highest degree disciplinary. As the angels watch the result on a soul of God's sharp ordeal of suffering, they say:

"The keen sanctity,
Which with its effluence, like a glory, clothed
And circled round the Crucified, has seized
And scorched, and shrivelled it."

Be thou in the fear of the Lord all the day long.
Prov. 23: 17.

I ASKED a working man the other day how he fared. His wife, the partner of many years, has died, and there is no one to welcome him on his return from work and prepare for him. His fellow-workmen, younger men, delight in tormenting him and increasing his arduous toils, because they hate his simple godliness. A physical weakness grows upon him distressingly. But he said that he was very happy, because he lived in God. All the way along it was Jesus—Jesus when he woke in the morning; Jesus when he went to bed at night; Jesus when he wrote a letter; Jesus when he went to the butcher's shop to buy his little piece of meat for Sunday—said he, "He made the

beasts; He must know what is good to eat." And when I asked how he managed to maintain this life, he said, "I always ask Him to rouse me up early enough to have a good time in fellowship with the Master." From the way he spoke, he reminded me of the priest's portion of the shoulder and breast as symbolizing the strength and love of the Lord Jesus.

If we are in the love of God we shall be in his fear; for though perfect love casts out fear that hath torment, it introduces the fear that dares not cause needless pain to the Infinite Lover of souls. We fear to tear open his wounds again, to expose his heart to the spear-thrust, or to miss aught of his gracious pains to make us what He wants us to become.

"If ye keep my commandments," the Master said, "ye shall abide in my love." To abide in his fear is equivalent to abiding in his love. They are two sides of the same coin. Only they love who fear. The woman feared Solomon's sword, because the babe was her own.

If thou forbear to deliver them that are drawn unto death. . . . Prov. 24: 11, 12.

CHRIST has greatly added to the convicting power of truth. Before his time men were taught that it was wrong to do wrong; but He taught that it was wrong not to do right. In the Christian church we confess that we have done the things that we ought not to have done—we do this in common with all men that acknowledge the rule of conscience. But we are taught by our Lord, and by such passages as this, to go farther, and confess that we have not done the things that we ought to have done. This is our great and damning crime.

The priest and Levite that did not go to the help of the wounded traveller; the servant who simply did not use the Lord's money; the nations that did not feed, clothe, or visit Him in the persons of the distressed; the virgins who had not oil in their vessels; the trees that did not bear—these Christ held up to shame and everlasting contempt. We cannot ignore the evil around us, and say we are not responsible for it. We cannot shut our eyes and avert our faces from wrongdoing, and tyranny, and oppression. We cannot profess that it is not our business, whosoever else's it may be, without it becoming known to the Searcher of all hearts, who will certainly reckon it against us on the day of account. Not to do is to incur Christ's displeasure.

What a striking illustration is afforded to these words in the Book of Esther! When the young queen was hesitating, Mordecai said very truly: "If thou altogether holdest thy peace at this time, then shall relief and deliverance arise to the Jews from another place; but thou and thy father's house shall perish: and who knoweth whether thou art not come to the kingdom for such a time as this?"

If thine enemy be hungry, give him bread to eat.
Prov. 25: 21, 22.

THE pagan ideal of a manly life was to succeed in doing as much good to your friends, and as much injury to your enemies, as possible. A few exceptions to this rule are recorded; but the wonder at them proves that the sentiments of forgiveness and mercy were foreign to popular morality and public opinion. How different is the teaching of the Bible! and in this have we not an evidence of its divine authority? Our Lord went further even than this noble maxim; He said, "Love your enemies, and pray for them which persecute you."

We are not taught to be entirely indifferent to the moral qualities of actions. The perception of sin and evil is necessary to a holy soul. And it is not required that we should abjure that holy resentment to wrongdoing, to which the apostle alludes when he says, "Be ye angry, and sin not." We must always resent wrong as wrong, though we must carefully eliminate any vindictive feeling towards the wrongdoer.

Do you think that others have wronged you? Pity them; pray for them; seek them out; show them their fault, humbly and meekly; wash their feet; take the mote out of their eye; seek to restore them in a spirit of meekness, remembering that you may be tempted; heap coals of loving-kindness on their heads; bring them if possible into such a broken and tender frame of mind, that they may seek forgiveness at your hand and God's. If you cannot act thus with all the emotion you would feel, do it because it is right, and the emotion will inevitably follow. It was said of Archbishop Leighton, that to do him an injury was to secure his lasting friendship.

For lack of wood the fire goeth out.
Prov. 26: 20 (R.V.).

HOW simple a parable! Of course it must be so. As soon as a fire has reached the end of the material on which it fed, it expires.

THIS IS TRUE OF THE FIRE OF SLANDER. As long as there is an ear to receive, and a tongue to pass on, some piece of malicious slander will continue to circulate. But directly it reaches a hearer who will not whisper it forward, in that direction at least its progress is arrested. Why do you not adopt this role, and urge others to do so? Hear if you must the whisper of the slanderer; but let it stop with you, locked in the secret of your own breast. You may be voted rather uninteresting and stupid by a certain society which thrives in whispered calumnies; but you will save many a heart from being torn and lacerated by unkindness and falsehood.

How graphic that word "whisperer" is! People always tell you to be sure not to tell; it is a way they have, though they do not expect you for a moment to keep the story to yourself. It is the kiss under which they betray. Always tell them that you refuse to be an accomplice in evil. If there is a wrong concerning which you must neither take action nor speak, you had better not defile your ear with it.

THIS IS TRUE OF THE FIRE OF THE HOLY GHOST. You must feed it by your loving obedience, your study of the Word of God, your faith and prayer. Yield yourself more entirely to his possession. Let your spirit, soul, and body, your every act and desire, be as fuel to the Spirit of God. Pile up the wood of continual sacrifice and self-surrender, till the divine fire reaches out its hands toward heaven. Even though the wood, like Elijah's, be drenched with water, God's fire will conquer!

The full soul loatheth an honeycomb.
Prov. 27: 7.

HONEY was not used in sacrifices made by fire unto the Lord. Its luscious taste may have made it an emblem of the pleasures of the world. As bees roam from flower to flower, sipping nectar here and there, so does the heart of the worldling roam over the world for satisfaction; settling nowhere for long, but extracting sweets from a variety of attractive sources.

The best way of combatting worldliness is by satisfying the heart with something better. The full soul loatheth even the honeycomb. When the prodigal gets the fatted calf, he has no further hankering after the husks which the swine eat. The girl who gets real jewels throws away her shams; and the child who has become a man has no taste for childish toys that once seemed all-important. This is the meaning of the old proverb: Love God, and do as you like. Whenever the spirit of worldliness gets into a congregation, you may be sure that the teaching has been defective, and that souls have not been made to sit at the rich banquet of the divine providing.

We are reminded of the words which the psalmist applied to the Word of God: "Sweeter than honey, or the honeycomb." Fill your heart with God and his sacred truth, and the things of the world will lose their charm. Do you know this absorbing love of Jesus? We can at least choose to know it, and present ourselves to the Holy Spirit, that He may shed it abroad in our hearts. Oh to be full! Full of the more abundant life of which the Lord spoke, of the unspeakable joy, of the peace that passeth understanding—in a word, of Jesus, as the chief and best.

He that covereth his transgressions shall not prosper. Prov. 28: 13 (R.V.).

THERE must be confession before forgiveness. This is clearly taught everywhere in God's Word. "If thy brother trespass against thee seven times a day, and seven times a day turn to thee, saying, I repent, thou shalt forgive him." But he must turn and say, I repent. This is the clear condition. You may and must use every method of inducing him to say this; but he must be brought to say it, before it is right to pronounce the gracious formula of absolution. There may be the disposition to forgive, but there cannot be the declaration of forgiveness, until the wrongdoer perceives the wrong and expresses his regret and sorrow.

The prodigal must say to his father, "I have sinned." It is only as we confess our sins, that our merciful High Priest can forgive us our sins and cleanse us from all unrighteousness. Confession is to take God's side against sin. It is the lifting out of one thing after another from heart and life, and holding them for a moment before God, with the acknowledgment that it is our fault, our grievous fault.

There is only one way in which transgressions can be covered: that of which the psalmist speaks, when he says, Blessed is the man whose iniquity is forgiven, whose sin is covered, because hidden under the propitiation of the blood. In Hood's poem, Eugene Aram sought to cover his sin under the leaves of the forest, and beneath the waters of the river. But in vain. So sinners try to cover their sins in vain. But God hath set forth Christ Jesus to be a propitiation—a word which denotes the mercy-seat—the lid that covered the stone slabs on which the finger of God had written the Law.

Where there is no vision. Prov. 29: 18.

WHAT a difference it makes to our teaching and preaching where there is no vision! The people perish for want of seers of those who can say with the apostle, "That which we have seen and heard, declare we unto you also, that ye may have fellowship with us." It is not difficult to know whether a poet or painter has a vision. If he have, there is glow and passion in his work. And it is not more difficult to detect in the accent of the speaker on divine things, whether he is speaking at second-hand, or as the result of direct vision.

This vision of God was vouchsafed to Moses and Elijah and the apostle Paul. Concerning the latter God said, "He shall be a minister and a witness of things which he has seen." This is our only qualification for teaching others; not intellect, nor imagination, nor rhetoric, but to have seen the King and beheld the pattern on the mount. For such a vision, on our part, there must be humility, patience, and faith, a definite withdrawal from the life of sense, and a definite fixedness of gaze on the things that are unseen and eternal. But on God's part there must be revelation. "It pleased God," said the apostle, "to reveal his Son in me, that I might preach Him."

The apostle said, "I could not see for the glory of that light." A party of tourists was divided one dull morning in Switzerland; the majority thought that it was useless to attempt the mountains. A few started, soon got beyond the low-hanging clouds, spent a day in the heights under marvellous skies, and returned at night, radiant, and overflowing with what they had seen. Ah, speaking is easy when one has seen!

Feed me with the food that is needful for me. Prov. 30: 8 (R.V.).

GOD knows what you need for the maintenance of physical life and strength. The body is more than meat, and to have given you this is a pledge that He will give you that. The body is the vehicle and organ of the soul; and since God has given such a wonderful instrument into your custody, He is bound as need arises to furnish needful supplies. He could not expect that you should do what He has arranged should be done in your life, without providing for the repair and maintenance of the wonderful machine through which alone your life-plan can be realized. Trust in his faithfulness. He cannot deny Himself.

But there is other food which is needful. The daily bread of love, of hope, of holy thought, and fellowship. There is other hunger than that of the body. But this also will be provided, according as each day requires. If the human fails, the divine will take its place, and God Himself will become the complement of your need. The Chinese Christians often put on the gravestones of their cemeteries the words, "They shall hunger no more," in allusion to the idea of the Confucians that children must constantly be sending on supplies to maintain their ancestors. And may we not say, with unwavering certainty, of those who have learnt to be satisfied with God, "They shall hunger no more"?

Notice the alternative rendering of the R.V., "The bread of my portion." In God's granaries there is our share of corn already calculated for and provided. Let us ask for and claim it. We have no wish to have more than our share, or to despoil others. As Jesus said, Give us each day the day's supply. O happy child of the great Father, his hired servants have enough and to spare; there is plenty for thee!

The heart of her husband doth safely trust in her. Prov. 31: 11.

THIS alphabetical poem to godly womanhood is one of the gems of Old Testament Scriptures. It should be read from the R.V., that its significant and beautiful touches may be appreciated. Clearly the Hebrew woman was held in high honour, and had as much freedom of action as she enjoys in Christian countries. Herein the contrast was very marked, as against the women of other Oriental nations. But in the whole delineation there is hardly any trait more beautiful than this—absolute trustworthiness. You can see the pair together: the husband comes in from sitting among the elders, his heart weighted with affairs of state, and he seeks her confidence and advice. He has no fear of her betraying his secrets. He can safely trust her.

This surely is the most sacred joy a woman can have. To be consulted, to be trusted, to share the common toils and responsibilities. Who would not work willingly with her hands, and rise while yet night, and engage in ceaseless toils, if only she had the inspiration that trust brings!

"If then your future life should need
    A strength my love can only gain
Through suffering—or my heart be freed
    Only by sorrow from some stain,
Then you shall give, and I will take
This Crown of fire for Love's dear sake."

Can Christ, in like manner, safely trust us? (John 2: 24, R.V.). Can He trust us with his secrets, his interests, his money? Abraham was one whom God could safely trust, and He did trust him as his friend: "Shall I hide from Abraham, . . . for I have known him?" It is required of us also that we be absolutely trustworthy.

Ecclesiastes

All the rivers run into the sea, yet the sea is not full. Eccles. 1: 7 (R.V.).

THE complaint of this chapter is the tiresome monotony of existence. Always the same tedious routine! The jaded soul of the worldling, who has put God out of his life, sees nothing fresh or interesting anywhere, and yawns with weariness. King Solomon had everything that the world could give to make his years rich, glad, and useful. But his heart turned away from God to things, from the only true God to idols, from the spiritual to the sensual, from heaven to earth; and he became a jaded voluptuary, who records his experiences on these pages, to warn coming generations. His words remind us of Byron's lament at his life being in the sere and yellow leaf; of the closing sentence of *Vanity Fair*; and of entries in the journals of the world's greatest wits and courtiers.

All the rivers of earthly joy may be flowing into your heart, but they will never fill it. They may recede, or dry up, or ebb; but if not, still they will never satisfy. The pleasures of this world after a while become monotonous, and pall on our taste. The appetite grows with its food. But in Christ there is perennial interest. The water that He gives rises up to eternal life. In his love and service there is always satisfaction and blessedness. We need not go outside of Him for new delights; and to know Him is to possess a secret which makes all things new.

I know of a gentleman, who has everything that wealth can give, but who is kept in a perpetual state of irritation, because he cannot eradicate the daisies from his lawn. There is a freckle on every flower, a stain on every leaf, a drawback in every lot, that we may be driven to find perfect fruition in God only.

All his days are but sorrows, and his travail is grief. Eccles. 2: 23 (R.V.).

WHAT a glimpse this is into a heart that has put God out! Solomon's power turned away his heart, so that he was not perfect with God, as David, his father. He drifted from God; and plunged into pleasure and laughter; into building and planting; into the pursuit of science and learning. "Whatsoever mine eyes desired I kept not from them. And, behold, all was vanity and a striving after wind" (R.V.). Nothing can satisfy us but God. We were made for Him; and the heart, as Augustine says, must be for ever restless till it finds rest in Him. Thus the shell, brought home from the sea-shore and placed on the shelf, sighs each time you place it to your ear for the ocean whence it came.

We have no need to envy those who prosper in this world, but are without God, and without hope. Their days are sorrows, and their travail is grief, and at night their hearts take no rest. But if we are to avoid their inward anguish, we must avoid their fatal mistake, and learn to take God into our lives. The river of life, which is the Holy Spirit, flows at our feet; but we must stoop to take it freely.

Dr. Gordon records the story of a traveller in Barbary, who saw a beautiful clear spring of water, over which was inscribed the legend, "Drink, and be gone." Robbers infested the region, and were constantly on the track of the traveller, ready to waylay and rob him. Therefore he must snatch the cooling draught and hasten on. Shall we refuse ourselves all pleasure in this world? Shall we write Touch not on every innocent gratification? No; but as soon as we have tasted of the pleasant draught, and lingered long enough to refresh our jaded souls, to hasten to life's serious tasks.

He hath set eternity in their heart. Eccles. 3: 11 (R.V., marg.).

THE Preacher has been enumerating the various extremes and alternatives of existence, and the natural conclusion might seem to be that since each neutralizes the other, it might be as well for a man to do nothing at all. But a deeper thought is suggested. Man is greater than the changes around him; he has eternity in his heart, and therefore all the varied circumstances of human life resemble the wheels of some great machine, the cogs of which turn in different directions, but the effect is a forward motion, and the manufacture of a fabric that will outlive the machinery that made it. We are greater than circumstance, or change, or things. We have the capacity for the Eternal and Infinite. As the sea-shell sighs for the ocean, so our hearts cry out, though sometimes inarticulately, for God, for the living God. Christ said that foxes have holes and the birds their nests, but the Son of Man hath not where to lay his head; and this is true in another sense. The noblest men are those least able to rest anywhere short of God.

God made man in his own image; and nothing more surely attests the greatness of our origin than those faculties of the soul which are capable of yearning for, conceiving, and enjoying the Infinite, the Immortal, and the Divine. And every appetite in nature and grace has its appropriate satisfaction.

Let us come to Him who has the words of eternal life, who is Himself the Bread that endureth unto eternal life. He that cometh to Him shall never hunger; he that believeth in Him shall never thirst.

> "Here would we end our quest;
> Alone are found in Thee
> The life of perfect bliss—the rest
> Of immortality."

Behold, the tears of such as were oppressed.
Eccles. 4: 1.

"DO ye hear the children weeping, O my
brothers,
Ere the sorrow comes with years?
They are leaning their young heads against
their mothers,
But that cannot stop their tears.
The young lambs are bleating in the
meadows;
The young birds are chirping in the nest;
The young fawns are playing with the
shadows;
The young flowers are blowing toward the
west— .
But the young, young children, O my
brothers,
They are weeping bitterly!
They are weeping in the playtime of the
others,
In the country of the free."

It is a sad, sad world, and perhaps must get
sadder yet. It may be that we have not yet
reached the darkest hour. Oh the tears of the
oppressed; the tiny children; the terror-
stricken fugitives from the Turk, the European
trader, and the drunken tyrant of the home!
Through all the centuries tears have flowed,
enough to float a navy.

There need be no difficulty in accounting for
them. Our race has elected the service of sin
and self. Turning our back on God, for whom
we were made, we have turned every one to our
own way, and are inheriting the ancient curse
of travail, tears, thorns, and death. It is quite
true that many suffer innocently and vicarious-
ly, because we are members one of another;
and by the mysterious arrangement of the
Almighty the whole race is bound together by
mysterious but indissoluble cords. In Adam all
die, all suffer, all sorrow and weep, just as in
Christ shall all be made alive. The pain must
last, till the Stronger than the strong comes to
divide the spoils, and set the captives free.

How comforting it is to realize that God
knows our sorrows, puts our tears into his
bottle, is afflicted in all our affliction, and
bears us on his heart.

*To draw nigh to hear is better than to give the
sacrifice of fools.* Eccles. 5: 1 (R.V.).
THIS is certainly half of our business, when we
kneel to pray. It is a drawing nigh to hear. One
has truly said that the closet is not so much
an oratory, in the narrow sense of making

requests, as an observatory, from which we
get new views of God, and new revelations of
Him.

We are all inclined to be rash with our
mouth. We rush into the presence of God,
leave our card as on a morning call, and then
plunge into the eager rush of our life. We have
spoken to Him, but not stayed to hear what He
would say in reply. We have suggested many
things to Him, but have not sought for his
comments, or suggestions, in return. We do
not take time to fix the heart's gaze on the
unseen and eternal, or to abstract our mind
from the voices of the world, so as to hear the
still small voice that speaks in silence and
solitude.

"Only the waters which in perfect stillness
lie
Give back an undistorted image of the
sky."

Keep thy foot; take off the shoes from thy
feet, when entering the Presence-chamber,
whether alone or with others. Walk warily and
reverently; behold! He is near, before whom
angels veil their faces with their wings. Come
into his presence with holy fear. Let there be
no irreverence in demeanour. One writes of the
late Mr. Gladstone, "The House of God
seemed to be to him at all times just what its
name implied; and it is impossible to think of
him at any service missing a response, or
forgetting an 'Amen.' Devotion, earnestness,
and concentrated attention were the regular
attributes of his nature when engaged in
worship. He realized in the simplest fashion
that worship was communing with God."

Under the sun. Eccles. 6: 1.
THE Preacher constantly refers to what is
done under the sun; and is not this the clue to
so much that is puzzling in this book? If your
horizon is limited to what the sun shines on, it
is impossible to get the true standpoint of
vision, or discover the real policy of life. If
this world and the time-day are all, we are
entangled in an inexplicable maze. It is impossible to believe in the existence of a benign
and wise Creator unless there is more than we
can see, larger than we can grasp. We have no
choice but blank materialism, unless we believe
there is someone and something over and
above the sun, and that the sun and his
attendant train of worlds is but a speck in the
vastness of his existence.

O Christian soul, let you and me get beyond the sun, which one day will be no more, to the Lord, who is an everlasting light. Let us sit with Him in the heavenlies, and thence look down upon man and his little life. What inconsiderable atoms do kings and empires appear; even our affliction seems to be but light, and for a moment! Not on this side of the sun, but on that lies our true portion and home, our enduring substance.

In order to live as we should, the sun must be under our feet, a position which is only possible to those who are in Christ Jesus. "I knew a man in Christ," says the Apostle, "caught up into the third heaven, and he heard unspeakable things." Would you be unworldly, seek to become otherworldly. Do you want the sun to grow dim?—ask for the light which is above the brightness of the sun.

Set your affections on those things which are above, where Christ sitteth at the right hand of God.

By the sadness of the countenance the heart is made glad. Eccles. 7: 3 (R.V.).

WHO does not know that our most sorrowful days have been amongst our best? When the face is wreathed with smiles, and we trip lightly over meadows bespangled with spring flowers, our heart is often running to waste. The soul which is always blithe and gay misses the deepest life. It has its reward, and it is satisfied to its measure, though that measure is a very scanty one. But the heart is dwarfed, and the nature, which is capable of the highest heights, the deepest depths, is undeveloped; and life presently burns down to its socket without having known the resonance of the deepest chords of joy. "Blessed are they that mourn."

Stars shine brightest in the long dark nights of winter. The gentians show their fairest bloom amidst almost inaccessible heights of snow and ice. God's promises seem to wait for the pressure of pain to trample out their richest juice as in a wine-press. Sorrow brings us nearest to the Man of Sorrows, and is the surest passport to his loving sympathy. Only those who have sorrowed know how tender his comfort can be. It is only as the door shuts upon the joys of the earth that the window is opened to the blessedness of the unseen and eternal. Let sadness cover your face, Jesus will enter the heart, and make it glad, for the days

in which you have been afflicted, and the years in which you have seen evil.

Is your face sad? Are you passing through bitter and trying experiences? Be of good cheer. Out of the sorrows that make the face sad will come ultimate joy. This affliction is working out a far more exceeding and eternal weight of glory. And the day is not distant when God will wipe tears from off all faces.

The King's word hath power.
Eccles. 8: 4 (R.V.).

WHEN our King speaks it is done. He spoke in creation, and power went with his word to call all things out of nothing. He spoke in his earthly ministry, and power accompanied every word, in giving eyes to the blind and life to the dead. He spoke, and the paralysed had power to walk. He spoke, and the winds dropped, whilst the tumultuous waves were hushed to rest. He spoke, and men knew their sins were forgiven, to be remembered against them no more for ever. He spoke, and the dying thief passed into Paradise.

Whatever He bids you do by his word, be sure that He will enable you to do it by his power. He works in us to will and to work of his good pleasure; that is, He never directs us in any path of obedience or service without furnishing a sufficient supply of grace. Does He bid you renounce some evil habit? The power to renounce it awaits you. Claim it. Does He bid you walk on the water? The power by which to walk only waits for you to claim it. Does He bid you perform irksome duty? There is such transforming power issuing from Him as to make duty a delight, if only you will avail yourself of it. Whenever you are called to stand up to speak the word of your King, be sure to seek and obtain the power—that shall prove your best credential. Take the power of the King with you: it is his signet-ring, by which men will be convinced that you have been entrusted with his word.

"Sustain me, that with Thee I walk these
        waves
    Resisting!—Breathe me upward, Thou in
    me
    Aspiring, Who art the Way, the Truth,
        the Life—
That no Truth henceforth seem indifferent,
No Way to Truth laborious, and no Life,
Not even this life I live, intolerable!"

The race is not to the swift, nor the battle to the strong. Eccles. 9: 11.

THIS is true in another sense than the Preacher meant. His conclusion was that time and chance happen to all alike in the race and battle of life. To us it means that God comes to those who are not swift, but, like Mephibosheth, lame on both feet, and gives them the prize which they could not win; that He bends over those who are not strong, and gives them the victory which they could not procure. The Gospel is full of promise to younger sons, bruised reeds, lame and helpless souls, to babes and sucklings, to those that have no might; whilst it hides its secrets from the wise and prudent, and withholds its rewards from the swift and strong.

YOU ARE NOT SWIFT. Long ago the spring was taken from your life, and the elasticity from your feet. For many years you have lain by the Beautiful Gate, seeing the happy souls pass to the inner shrine, and coming out entranced. You have been content to live on their alms. But better things are in store. He who knows your case will even now give you perfect soundness. Though you cannot win the prize of your high calling by running, it shall be yours by receiving and taking. It is a gift; and though you have not legs you have surely hands.

YOU ARE NOT STRONG. But it is well. Many of us are too strong for God. He has to weaken us by touching the sinew of our thigh. When Jacob went from fighting to clinging, he became a prince with God. Isaiah left it on record that God gives power to the faint, and increases might to those who have no power. And the great Apostle of the Gentiles gloried in his infirmities, because he had discovered that when he was weak then he was strong, since the power of Christ was only perfected in weakness.

If one do not whet the edge, then must he put to more strength. Eccles. 10: 10.

IF this is true, as we know it is, may we not often use it as an appeal to God? There are times with all who work for God, when they are blunt, through much usage. The brain is blunt, and cannot think. The heart is blunt, and cannot feel. The voice is blunt, and has lost its ringing note. How often the evangelist, towards the end of a series of services, feels blunt! Sometimes also there are private sorrows, of which we cannot speak, which

take off the edge. At all such times let us turn to God and say, "Put in more strength. Let thy power be magnified in my weakness. Give more grace, so that thy work shall not suffer." I suppose Paul meant this when he said that he gloried in infirmities, that the power of Christ might rest upon him. Surely more work is done by a blunt edge and divine power, than by a sharp edge and little power.

This, however, does not justify us in seeking to be blunt. And when we are conscious that the edge is going off, it becomes us to seek a fresh whetting. The time is not lost in the harvest-field when the reapers whet their scythes with musical tinkle. A day in the country or a week by the seaside are very pleasant whetstones. Solomon says that friendship, the face of a friend, will sharpen a blunt edge; and full often we have been sharpened and quickened by seasons of holy fellowship. But after all, nothing gives us such a keen edge as the devotional perusal of the divine Word. Let us appropriate the words of the prophet, and each one ask to be made a new sharp threshing-instrument having teeth, that we may thresh the mountains, and make them small, and give our God as little anxiety as possible.

In the morning sow thy seed, and in the evening withhold not thine hand. Eccles. 11: 6.

WE are all tempted to look too much to the winds and clouds. We study the faces of people, their moods and circumstances, and say, "It is not a favourable time to approach them about their souls. He does not look to be a likely case, or in a likely mood." But how do we know? If we are always waiting for favouring conditions, we shall resemble the farmer who is ever looking out for perfect weather, and lets the whole autumn pass without one handful of grain reaching the furrows; or who is always studying the clouds, seeking for a spell of hot summer weather; and presently the chance is gone, and the crop lost.

In fact, we can never tell what God is doing in the secrets of the heart. He may have been prosecuting his deep and wise designs with the souls that appear most untoward and unprepossessing. He may have led them to such a point that they are most eagerly yearning for the hand to lead them into the light. The eunuch in his chariot, might not, from a distance, have seemed specially ripe for the Christian evangelist; but, on coming near, he was discovered to be an inquirer. Saul of Tarsus was the least likely man in all Palestine to be a Christian; but God had been at work with him. Let us dare then to trust God, not looking for winds or sunshine, but scattering everywhere the precious seed of the Gospel.

"Say not, the struggle naught availeth,
    The labour and the wounds are vain;
The enemy faints not, nor faileth,
    And as things have been things remain.
"For while the tired waves, vainly breaking,
    Seem here no painful inch to gain,
Far back, through creeks and inlets making,
    Comes silent, flooding in, the main."

The Preacher sought to find out acceptable words. Eccles. 12: 10.

THE wise preacher or teacher is not content with merely teaching the people knowledge, he will ponder and seek out and set in order the lessons of divine wisdom; and when these are settled, he will go on to find out acceptable words. We must be careful to secure the "apples of gold," and no less careful to place them in the "pictures of silver." Not that we are to make beauty of language an object in itself; but having conceived high and holy thoughts we should give them a worthy expression, so that the Royal word may ride forth in a becoming equipage. It is unfit that the vessels of the sanctuary should be carried only in badger skins; their first covering at least must be "all of blue." If we are stewards in God's household to give his children food, let us serve it up suitably. The linen should be clean, and the table garnished.

Remember, however, that the words of the wise are as goads and nails. They must have points, sometimes to prick to duty, at other times to stick fast in the memory. In every sermon or lesson there should be points. To arrest and compel attention is more important than to please the ear. Do not refine and beautify it to such an extent that there may be nothing left to stir the conscience and lacerate the heart.

Words that best fit the enunciation of God's truth are given from the One Shepherd. We are enriched by Him, not only in all knowledge but in all utterance. He who made the mouth can put his words into the mouth. Ask Him to speak to you, that you may speak in accents borrowed from his tone; for it is not ye that speak, but the Spirit of your Father that speaketh in you.

The Song of Solomon

The King hath brought me into his chambers. S. of Sol. 1: 4.

WE cannot force an entrance into the inner chambers of the love of God. They remind one of the apartments which are reserved for the personal use of the sovereign, and are private from the foot of strangers. All the world is welcome to the State apartments; but only the favoured few to the inner sanctuary. So it is with the love of God. It is open to all the world; but its secret is hidden from the wise and prudent, and revealed to babes.

It is pleasant to think of the chambers of the King opening one from the other in a long and glorious succession, and to imagine each inscribed with its text and adorned with characteristic emblems. The Chamber of Regeneration leading to Assurance; and this to Consecration; and this to the Enduement of the Holy Spirit; and this to the Quiet Heart; and this to a Life of Victory; and this to Abiding Fellowship. Each is a distinct phase of the Christian life; and from one to another the King leads the obedient and loving disciple. At each advance the chambers become more magnificent and delightful, until the last one opens out upon a terrace which looks across the brief space to the City of God.

Will you let the King do this? Then you must begin by enthroning Him in your heart and obeying Him in your life. You must keep his words, that He may manifest Himself unto you as He does not unto the world. Then indeed we shall be glad, and rejoice, and make mention of his love. What if the beauty of our surroundings makes us cry out that we are black as the tents of Kedar! He knew it all before, and will not love us less; nay, He will array us in his own comeliness.

The voice of my Beloved. S. of Sol. 2: 8.
THERE are times when winter rules within,

and the atmosphere is full of rain, and the birds are mute. It does not necessarily argue that we have backslidden; only that the rich, emotional life has for a little died down, as the sap sinks to the earth during the winter's pause.

The first symptom of returning joy is the voice of the Beloved Master. We do not seek Him, but He us. We do not call, but He calls. The voice of spring is heard sounding through our soul. The sweet, clear, tender notes of the Saviour ring melodiously around us, and as we hear them we know that our winter is past, the rain is over and gone, and the flowers and birds are at hand.

Rise up, my love! Rise up from lethargy and sloth; from the low levels on which you have lived; from the earth with its attractions, and the grave with its fetters. And as the command issues from his lips, He gives rising grace. Come away, He cries. There is richer life and wider upon the mountains. Let us climb the heights that beckon us. The voice of Christ is constantly summoning us to fuller experiences, to leave what is behind and below, to press up and on, so that we may know Him and the power of his resurrection.

How appropriate these words are as we may conceive of them being spoken to the expectant Church! After centuries of waiting she shall hear the archangel's trump, and it will be the call of her Beloved to rise up and come away. Then her winter will be past for ever; the unwithering flowers will appear; the time of singing will have come; and the voice of the turtle-dove, significant of affection, will be heard throughout Emmanuel's Land.

I sought Him, but I found Him not.
S. of Sol. 3: 1.

GOD lets us seek, hiding Himself to draw us after Him. How much our race owes to his hidings! He has hidden pearls in the ocean, jewels in the rocks, coal in the earth, fish in the deep. By all these methods He has drawn men forth from lethargy and inaction to strenuous and vigorous lives; so that the gains of their toil have consisted not only in the treasures they have obtained, but in the developed faculties which have come to them in the course of their search.

Is it not so in the spiritual life? Our Lord withdraws Himself, not in anger or disappointment, but that we may be sensible of not having attained, of not being already perfect,

and that we may follow on to know the Lord, and to apprehend something more of that for which we were apprehended. Do not be disappointed, O Christian soul, if some time you should cease to feel the familiar delight in certain hymns, services, books, or teachers. Thy Master has withdrawn Himself from these; but thou wilt find Him further on. Never rest till you have discovered Him in some deeper revelation. The watchmen that go about the city, and who are probably messengers of divine truths, may not help you in your quest; but the Holy Spirit waits to lead you into all truth. Open your heart to Him. It is but a little time, and as you pass from all human teachers you will find Him whom you love, or perhaps be found of Him. Then hold Him, or better, be held by Him. It is a sweet motto, "Teneo et teneor"—"I hold, and am held."

"And not by eastern windows only,
    When daylight comes, comes in the light;
In front, the sun climbs slow, how slowly,
    But westward, look, the land is bright."

Awake, O north wind; and come, thou south; blow upon my garden. S. of Sol. 4: 16.

THE garden of the heart is like one of those old-fashioned gardens, surrounded by high brick walls, prepared for fruit-trees. I have one in my eye as I write, on the south wall of which old apple-trees have bloomed and fruited for generations. The garden is filled with all manner of spices, "spikenard and saffron, calamus and cinnamon, and with all trees of frankincense." Sometimes, however, the spices hang heavily upon the air. They are present, but hardly discernible to the quickest sense. Then the wind is needed to blow through the garden path, that the spices may flow out and pass beyond the barriers to the passers-by.

How often it has happened in the history of the children of God, that those who have known them have never realized the intrinsic excellence and loveliness of their characters until the north wind of sorrow and pain has broken with blustering force upon them. Then suddenly spices of rarest odour have exhaled and been carried afar. How the delicate trees dread the north wind! What a tremor goes through the crowded garden walks when they hear the husbandman calling to the north wind to awake! We all choose the south wind. But remember that the Euroclydon that swept down the ravines of Crete upon the Alexandrian corn-ship brought out spices which had slumbered unknown in the heart of the great apostle. His courage! His patience! His power of inspiring hope amid despair, and breaking bread with thanksgiving! Ah, north wind, thy ministry has been of incalculable worth to all of us. We shiver before thy searching power, but the spices will repay. A vane in Leicestershire is inscribed with GOD IS LOVE. He is so, from whatever quarter the wind blows.

What is thy beloved more than another beloved, that thou dost so adjure us? S. of Sol. 5: 9 (R.V.).
THE daughters of Jerusalem, each of whom had her beloved, could not understand the urgency of this maiden who had lost her beloved. Her anguish at her loss was so extreme, her heart-sickness was so agonizing, her frenzy so bewildering, that they were startled into feeling that he of whom she was bereft was no common lover. There had been times when each of them had been temporarily forlorn; but they knew that they had never suffered like this! The greatness of her pain was the mirror in which they caught a glimpse of the ineffable beauty of the Bridegroom.

Speak of Christ, so that men and women around may be constrained to cry, "Your Beloved excels our beloveds. We cannot speak of them as thou dost of Him. To gain them does not fill us with the same ecstasy, or to lose them with the same woe."

What are the beloveds that men seek after? There is the beloved of worldly success, of human adulation and applause, of art, science, and war. They intoxicate their admirers, but fail to satisfy. Who can say of them that they are chief, and outshine the gold of Ophir, beryl, sapphires, ivory, and cedar, the rarest products of earth, as synonyms for priceless worth? But all these gathered together are poor and unworthy emblems of the peerless beauty of Emmanuel. White in purity, ruddy with the bloodstain, his bushy locks emblematical of immortal youth, his eyes like waterbrooks reflecting the deep azure of the sky and telling of eternal love. Ransack earth for metaphors, and they fall short of the truth. Words fail to express his beauty, his grace, his loveliness: let us try to reflect his glory.

I am my Beloved's, and my Beloved is mine.
S. of Sol. 6: 3.
TO get the full significance of this precious

sentence we should compare it with chap. 2: 16. Remark their parallelism, and their contrast.

"My Beloved is mine, and I am his.
He feedeth his flock among the lilies" (R.V.).

And this:—

"I am my Beloved's, and my Beloved is mine.
He feedeth his flock among the lilies" (R.V.).

In the first of these couplets the Spouse lays the first emphasis on her hold of the Beloved; only secondarily does she congratulate herself that she is his. But in the second couplet her chief thought is that she belongs to Him.

In the earlier stages of Christian life, we think most of what we have in Christ; afterwards we love to dwell on his possession of us. You are his estate, for Him to cultivate and rear successive crops for his praise and glory. You are his jewel, to obtain which He renounced all, and on which He will expend infinite care, cutting your facets, and polishing you to shine brightly in his light. You are his house in which He can dwell, opening out unexpected apartments and passages. You are a member of his body, through which He will fulfil his holy purpose. You are his bride, to win whom He came from afar. You are owned, possessed, inhabited, loved, with a peculiar personal affection. As Keble says: "Thou art thy Saviour's darling; doubt no more."

"As the bridegroom to his chosen,
As the king unto his realm,
As the keep unto the castle,
As the pilot to the helm,
So, Lord, art Thou to me."

I am my Beloved's, and his desire is toward me.
S. of Sol. 7: 10.
THIS is the thankful recognition of the Bride. She knows that she belongs to, that she is loved by, the Bridegroom—that his desire is turned towards her with ineffable longing.

Dear soul, do you realize the desire of your Beloved towards you? You love Him; but He loves you ever so much more. You desire Him; but his desire towards you is as much greater than yours towards Him, as sunlight is more brilliant than moonlight. Know ye not, says James, that the Spirit which He has caused to dwell in us longeth even to envy? Jesus desires all our love, all our energy, all our possessions, that we should be only, always, all for Him. How have we responded to his great desire? Alas, our response has been very uncertain and unsatisfactory. Sometimes we have felt a pure flame answering affection; but it has soon been obscured with clouds of smoke, or has died down for want of oil.

The Lord desires more of our time, that we should withdraw ourselves from the busy rush of the world and the absorbing interests of life, in order to allow Him to commune with us. He desires more of our affection, that He may teach us how to respond to his love. He desires to teach us how to share his riches, as his joint-heirs; how to sit with Him in heavenly places; how to work in the energy of his Spirit. Let us yield ourselves to his desires, and allow Him to effect in us and for us all He desires for us, so that we may give Him delight. "As the bridegroom rejoiceth over the bride, so shall thy God rejoice over thee." If, as Zephaniah says, He is silent in his love, because his love is too strong for speech, we may yield ourselves to it without misgiving.

Who is this that cometh up from the wilderness, leaning upon her Beloved? S. of Sol. 8: 5.
STANDING on the mountainous plateau with which Judea passes into the desert, the daughters of Jerusalem behold the Spouse, coming slowly up from the wilderness, leaning hard upon her Beloved; and in this we have an emblem of the Church, and of each faithful soul. The wilderness can well be taken as an emblem of the experience of believers, who are suffered to hunger and thirst, exposed to be smitten by the sun of temptation, and pacing wearily over the lowlands of a somewhat arduous and monotonous existence.

But the wilderness-life is not destined to be our perpetual experience. We are bidden to come up from it. Life is meant to be an unceasing ascent from strength to strength until we stand in Zion before God. Is your path trying and perilous? Does it seem as though you will never gain the heights that rear themselves before your gaze? Do you feel prepared, like Hagar, to yield to despair and death? See, there is One that goes beside. Turn to regard Him. His hands are as though they had been pierced. He is your Beloved; lean on Him. He gives you his arm to rest upon, and He will sustain you when heart and flesh fail. The wilderness will bring out a tenderness, an all-sufficiency, a readiness of resource, on his part, which you would never have guessed unless your exigencies had become imperative. Be sure of this, lean hard, and believe that

"He will bring thee where the fountains
Fresh and full spring forth above,
Still throughout the endless ages
Serving Him with perfect love."

Isaiah

I will purge away thy dross, and take away all thine alloy. Isa. 1: 25 (R. V., marg.).
THE silver had become dross. Jerusalem, the chosen city, was filled with infidelity, formalism, impurity, and deeds of violence. She had been full of judgment, righteousness had lodged in her; but now, murderers. And this was the reason for the blows that had fallen upon her with such unsparing force. The whole land was now desolate; the cities burned with fire; only a small remnant of the people was left. The prophet, his patriot heart wrung with grief, compares her to a sick man in the last stage of disease, the whole head is sick, and the whole heart faint; from the sole of the foot, even unto the head, there is no soundness in it. Would it not be well for us to search our hearts, and ask whether there may not be some counterpart to this in our declension from our God, and the consequent suffering to which we have been brought? He loves us too well to allow the process of deterioration to go unchecked.

But here the Almighty Lover of his people resolves to bring his hand to the work of entire purging and cleansing. He will no longer simply punish. He will take away the men who had been his adversaries and enemies from the midst of his people, thoroughly purging away the dross and taking away all the tin. There is an immeasurable difference between punishing and refining. It is a great matter for the soul, when God ceases from the one and commences the other; and when we no longer suffer from the results of past sins, but are restored as at the first, and converted as at the beginning.

O House of Jacob, come ye, and let us walk in the light of the Lord. Isa. 2: 5.

TO what a walk are we called! In newness of life: "Like as Christ was raised from the dead to the glory of the Father." In Christ: "As ye have received Christ Jesus the Lord, so walk ye in Him." Like Christ: "He that saith he abideth in Him, ought so to walk even as He walked." By and after the Spirit: "Walk by the Spirit, and ye shall not fulfil the lusts of the flesh." Worthy of God and well pleasing to Him: "Walk worthy of the Lord unto all well-pleasing, being fruitful." In heavenly love, and light, and faith: "Walk in love"; "Walk in the light, as He is in the light"; "Walk by faith, not by sight."

This invitation is primarily addressed to the house of Jacob. Sometimes the elect people are spoken of as Israel; but when Jacob is used, they are reminded of the vein of duplicity and chicanery which lies imbedded in their nature. Such people need specially to "walk in the light of the Lord" until the brooding darkness of their nature is dispelled. You will never succeed in ridding yourself of the self-life, with its jealousies and impurities, until you have learnt to walk in the light of the Lord. Nothing is so hostile to disease and corruption as light and air; believe me, the one way by which we can become sound and strong is to abide in Christ, that He may abide in us.

WALK INVOLVES STEPS. We cannot enjoy the presence of God as a whole unless it governs and illumines every step. We must be perpetually looking into our Father's face and asking where to place the next step. We must have fellowship with Him in all things; then we, who have been darkness, will be light in the Lord, and as we walk in the light we shall become children of light.

I will not be an healer: . . . make me not a ruler of the people. Isa. 3: 7.

GENERALLY men aspire to be rulers; the emolument and honour of the position are infinitely attractive. But the prophet supposes a case in which the people gather round one who has saved a little more than the others from the general wreck, and entreat him to assume the responsibility of directing public affairs. But he refuses, not wishing to be involved in the disasters that have swept the fatherland. Isaiah cites this as the most complete evidence of the desperate situation brought about by wrongdoing.

It is the mark of great deterioration in a religious community when none are forthcoming to take responsibility, none who have power to lead. It is a grave sentence, "I will give children to be their princes, and babes shall rule over them." Never shrink from assuming any responsibility to which God and the church evidently call you. It is an easier life to remain among the stunted undergrowth; but if God calls you to be a forest tree, with fast-spreading branches, humbly accept the opportunity, and fill up its full measure. His grace is sufficient. Better to fail in a great endeavour than to live safely having evaded the divine call. Have you bread and clothing? account yourself God's steward.

What a striking contrast is suggested to the love of Jesus Christ! "He saw that there was no man, . . . therefore his own arm brought salvation." He knew that if He espoused the cause of our lost race, it would involve Him in the bitterest agony and woe. But He steadfastly set his face to the accomplishment of our redemption: He stood up to plead our cause: and He will not lay down his chosen work until He hath brought judgment unto victory.

Over all the glory a canopy. Isa. 4: 5 (R.V.).

THESE twain, the pillar of cloud by day, and the flaming fire by night, were reserved in the wanderings for the tabernacle only; but this promise predicts that they shall be the heritage of each individual home. "The Lord will create over every dwelling-place of Mount Zion, a cloud and smoke by day and the shining of a flaming fire by night" (R.V., marg.). Each family may have its own cloudy pillar to guide, its own illumination through the dark hours, its own canopy from storm and rain and heat. Let this be your comfort: though your family is scattered afar, all the members may dwell in the same pavilion, be directed by the movements of the same pillar-cloud, and enlightened by the glow of the same fire. In God there is no distance; and they who abide in Him live in a dwelling-place which is wide enough to include the world, but narrow enough to draw our hearts into so small a circle that God and we and our loved ones may touch.

There is even more than this suggested in these words. Each holy soul may have all the gracious contents of this promise, because it has become the temple of the indwelling Lord, through the Holy Spirit. For thee there may be the pillar-cloud, arising to guide thy steps through the wilderness world, or settling down with its fleecy folds to rest. For thee, through long dark nights, the pillar of fire—and, indeed, only the darkness can reveal the bright light in the cloud. For thee also the canopy—for it is written, "He shall spread his tabernacle over them" (Rev. 21: 3, Gk.). How God suits Himself to our varying need—now a cloud, again as fire; in the storm a covert, from the heat a shadow. He is always adapting his help to our need.

What could have been done more to my vineyard, that I have not done in it? Isa. 5: 4.

THIS is what the Owner of all souls will say of his dealings with each when the discipline and husbandry of time are over. Each of us is God's vineyard, and for each God has done the best possible. At the end of all things God will have no reason to feel that had He adopted some other method the barren waste of some heart would have brought forth fruit. It will be seen then, Omniscience itself being witness, that every soul of man had the chance of becoming a fruitful vineyard; and if he became the reverse, it was due to no failure in either the wisdom or grace of God.

It is hard to believe this, hard to think that you would not have done better in some other circumstances; but it is nevertheless true that God could not have done better or more. He has trenched for water, gathered out stones which had hindered your fruitfulness, and planted you with slips from the True Vine. There has been the tower of his protection, and the wine-press of suffering! Ah, how eagerly He has looked that you should bring forth grapes! The pity of it is that there has been nothing but the wild growth of nature! But God cannot take the blame for this. He could not have done more than He has done. Alas that we should have so often thwarted Him!

"When I looked." "The Father seeketh," our Saviour said. He comes down the garden path full often, seeking from us the fruits of the Spirit, the grace of prayer and supplication, the plants of his delight. "Let us see," He says, "whether the vine hath budded, and its blossom be opened, and the pomegranates be in flower." Too often it is as when Jesus looked for figs—there was nothing but leaves!

Each one had six wings. Isa. 6: 2.

SERAPHIM signifies "burning ones," to designate their essence, their dazzling appearance, or their intense devotion. But whatever the symbol stands for, they needed the six wings. With twain each seraph covered his face—for reverence, he dare not look upon God. With twain he covered his feet—for humility, he recognized that he was unworthy. With twain he did fly—for service and obedience to the divine commands.

It may be that we are taught that a third part only of our time and energy should be expended in activity; two-thirds to reverent fellowship and communion. Probably with most of us the proportion is in the other direction; and we give two-thirds to flight for God, and one-third only for fellowship with God.

The service that springs from such communion is directed by deep sympathy with the mind of God. The seraph did not wait for the Lord to send him to Isaiah with a live coal from the altar; but spontaneously the son of flame sped to do the required office, as though instinctively he realized that there was nothing else to be done for a man who had confessed himself to be vile. The seraphim have heard that confession made so often, and have so often administered the same restorative to fainting hearts, that they do not need to be directed what to do. They know God's thought before He speaks a word. A notable emblem of this service!

"One cried to another." Holy beings love to stir each other to higher themes, to worthier praise. Thus one bird may awake a woodland into minstrelsy; and one Luther an age. Is your heart full of burning love?—then seek to set others aglow.

Take heed, and be quiet; fear not, neither let thine heart be faint. Isa. 7: 4 (R.V.).

SERIOUS trouble seemed imminent. Two strong peoples were bearing down on Jerusalem, and the heart of the house of David was moved as the trees of the forest are moved with the wind. Fear like this demoralizes men and nations. It unfits them for wise and strong action. Hence the necessity that Isaiah should reassure Ahaz with these words.

They were not sent to him because of his righteousness or virtue, for he was one of the weakest and most idolatrous of the kings of David's line; but because his foes were acting in direct collision with the determined counsel and purpose of God. Such a coalition may be threatening you to-day; but it is in vain for the breakers of human pride and hate to attempt to intrude within limits which God has set around his chosen. Come, my soul, enter thou into thy chamber, and shut thy door about thee! Be quiet! God will fight for you. Be not dismayed; God's purpose cannot be overthrown. Let not thine heart be faint. Lo, a virgin has borne a Son, whose name is Immanuel—God with us. "Fear not: I bring you glad tidings of great joy. To you is born a Saviour."

God Incarnate is the end of fear; and the heart that realizes that He is in the midst, that takes heed to the assurance of his loving presence, will be quiet in the midst of alarm. No weapon that is formed against thee shall prosper, and every tongue that shall rise in judgment against thee thou shalt condemn. Only be patient and be quiet.

"For while the tired waves, vainly breaking,
  Seem here no painful inch to gain,
Far back, through creeks and inlets making,
  Comes silent, flooding in, the main."

The Lord of Hosts, let Him be your fear, and let Him be your dread. Isa. 8: 12, 13.

THE land was panic-stricken for fear of the coalition of Samaria and Damascus. The politicians were seeking the alliance of Assyria, whilst the superstitious had recourse to familiar spirits and wizards. Amid the panic the voice of Isaiah is heard bidding the people fear with only one kind of fear. Not their fear, but the fear of God; not their dread, but his. The apostle Peter quotes these words, when he says, "If ye should suffer for righteousness' sake, blessed are ye; and fear not their fear, neither be troubled; but sanctify in your hearts Christ as Lord" (1 Pet. 3: 15, R.V.).

On the prairies men often fight fire with fire. Against the career of the wall of flame there is but one resource; before it reaches the terrified fugitives they must light a fire to sweep the ground bare, that when the advancing horror reaches the spot there will be no fuel left for it to feed on. So with the heart of man, the only true preservation from fear of our fellows is an overmastering fear of our God. Sanctify Him in your hearts. Let Him be your fear and dread.

It is remarkable that Jacob sware by the Fear of his father Isaac. And this appears to have quieted his heart in the presence of Laban. When the fear of God is strong, the thought of grieving Him, or incurring his just wrath and indignation, is most cogent in warning us from sin! This delivers us from all other fear. One of the greatest sentences a man can utter when tempted to sin or threatened with suffering for the uprightness of his life or the correctness of his creed, is to say simply, quietly, and strongly: "I fear God, and have no other fear." Fear Him: so shall ye be established; so shall ye prosper.

Of the increase of his government and peace there shall be no end. Isa. 9: 7

IS the government of your life upon his shoulder? In olden times the badge of office was worn there, and in some cases a key (22: 22). It was on his shoulder that Aaron bore the names of the tribes. The shoulder is the symbol of strength. It is well when the government of our lives rests on the strong Son of God. It is a blessed day in our experience that witnesses the transference of the rule of life to the Wonderful, the Counsellor, the Mighty God; because all these exalted altitudes of his nature well qualify Him to become the King and Guide of men.

The moment of definitely imposing the government upon the Lord Jesus is generally a marked one in our lives. It stands out as the first of a long series. It is the staple for a chain of successive links, because we are always increasing that government in proportion as we become more familiar with our nature and opportunities, and as new departments of our life open up before us. You were consecrated before marriage, but after you have a home of your own there is a widening of the sphere of Christ's government.

But just in proportion to the increase of his government will be the increase of your peace. As the one extends, so does the other. And he who has extended the dominion of Jesus to the furthest limits of his being, will know most of the peace that passeth understanding. There is Peace where there is Unity; where the soul has but one object to engross its love and aim; where it is able to count on the illimitable stores of its King.

"Yield to the Lord, with simple heart,
All that thou hast and all thou art!
Renounce all strength but strength divine.
And Peace shall be for ever thine!"

Shall the axe boast itself against him that heweth therewith? Isa. 10: 15

THE Assyrian thought that he was acting on his own impulse, and in his pride congratulated himself on his exploits. The prophet reminded him that it was not so. He was only an axe, a saw, a rod, in the hand of the Eternal God whose supremacy he was inclined to challenge and set at nought.

This thought underlay the apostle's reply to those who magnified him against Apollos or Cephas. What are we, he cries, but ministers through whom ye believed, even as God granted to each of us? We are only instruments of God's husbandry, implements through which He fulfils his plans (1 Cor. 3). It dates an era in the life, when we cease to work for God, and allow God to work through us.

Thoughts like these correct alike pride and despondency. Pride, because whatever is the result of our work, we can no more take the credit of it than the pen that wrote the "Paradise Lost" could take to itself the credit of its production. At the best, it is not you, but the grace of God that was with you. You are only a pipe in the organ, but the breath that educed your music was divine. And in despondency it is very helpful to remember that if we are nothing, God is all-sufficient; if we have failed, it is the more needful for Him to exert more power. Throw back the responsibility of all results on God. Only see to it that you are a polished shaft, an unblunted saw, and leave Him to do through you what He will.

> "So, take and use thy work!
> Amend what flaws may lurk,
> What strain o' the stuff, what warpings
> past the aim!
> My times are in thy hand!
> Perfect the cup as plann'd!
> Let age approve of youth, and death
> complete the same!"

And he shall be of quick scent in the fear of the Lord. Isa. 11: 3 (R.V., marg.).

QUICK of scent! This is the prerogative of all who have received the fulness of the Holy Spirit. We all know the great advantage of having a keen scent. Those who can instantly detect an ill-odour are saved from going into places where pestilence and fever lurk in ambush for life. The whiff of ill-odour startles the unwary passer-by, and warns him that influences inimical to health are brooding nigh. Thus he is arrested and saved.

It is a blessed thing when a man's spiritual senses are exercised to discriminate between the good and bad, the healthy and unhealthy, in literature, amusements, fellowship, and many of the questionable or doubtful things which professing Christians permit. There are many of these which appear innocent enough, like some deadly spot of a jungle where miasma and fever breed; but the deadly scent of corruption will instantly be detected by the Spirit-taught spirit, and the child of God, whose senses are exercised to distinguish between good and evil.

The sense of smell is greatly quickened by inhaling pure air, full of ozone and health, such as breathes about the mountain-brow or the ocean wave. If we return from such scenes, we are more sensitive than ever to foul odours. Live with God's Spirit in holy fellowship, so will you become spiritually quick of scent.

The Epistle to the Hebrews tells us that our senses become quick to distinguish between good and evil by reason of use (Heb. 5: 14). In the first stages of Christian living, temptation may have stolen in upon and mastered us before we were aware of its presence. But, as years pass, and we become mature through feeding on the meat of the Gospel we become "quick."

With joy shall ye draw water out of the wells of salvation. Isa. 12: 3

SALVATION IN WELLS. It is a fascinating picture. We remember Elim, for instance, where were twelve springs of water, in Jesus there are wells of salvation and blessedness. Do you want Sympathy? Draw it from his tears. Courage? It resides in our Cœur-de-Lion, the Lion of the tribe of Judah. Purity? It is his life-blood. Peace? He is the Prince of Peace, the Son of Peace. Meekness? He is meek and lowly in heart. Mercifulness? In Him you will obtain it. Prayerfulness? It is his prime characteristic. There is no quality or grace of the soul which has not its well of supply in the divine Manhood of our Lord.

BUT WE MUST DRAW. Thou hast something to draw with, though not to the eye of man. Faith is the bucket, which we let down into the fulness of the divine supply. Not simply the general belief that God does answer prayer, but the specific and particular belief that God has answered the prayer for some special needed grace; and that it is yours. Believe that ye have received. Do not look into the dripping bucket of your faith to see if you have received; dare to believe that you have received whether you get it or not; and go forth to use what you have, sure that in answer to your appeal you have all sufficiency in all things, that you may abound to every good work.

WHAT JOY! There is always joy in some new discovery and acquisition. And oh, the joy of realizing that all the wealth of God's salvation is within our reach; that we may draw for ever without fear of exhaustion; that the Spirit and Bride invite us to end for evermore our thirst, our disquiet, our weary quest!

And Babylon shall be as when God overthrew Sodom and Gomorrah. Isa. 13: 19

THESE prophecies have been fulfilled with marvellous accuracy. It is a pity that so few of our young people in these days study the evidence of prophecy. "Keith's Evidences" would be a wholesome introduction to this marvellous field of investigation; but every year is adding to the store of proof. Unlike the evidence of miracles, that of prophecy increases with every year of increasing distance from the hour that the prediction was given.

There is a God that judgeth in the earth. Nations, as well as individuals, must stand before his judgment bar. Indeed, the judgment of the nations is now in progress. Already before the Son of Man all nations are being gathered, and He is dividing the sheep from among the goats. Men do not see the sentence of the divine Judge put into execution, since the operation of his Providence is so deliberate. But in the landscape of history, as we view it from the eminence of the years, we can detect the condign vengeance of the Almighty on the cruel, rapacious, bloodthirsty kingdom of Babylon. She had served God's purpose, but she had committed such enormous crimes in the process of serving it, that she must be condemned.

The wrongs of the West Indians have, in this generation, been requited upon Spain. It is not possible that modern Turkey should escape. The blood of 100,000 Armenians cries against her from under the altar. But let our beloved country beware! Her opium traffic, her connivance at the sale of firewater to native races, her permission of gross impurity in her streets, her drunkenness, must be telling very heavily against her in the scale of divine justice. "O Jerusalem, Jerusalem!"

The Lord will have compassion on Jacob, and will yet choose Israel. Isa. 14: 1

ISRAEL is the pivot around which the history of the world revolves. We cannot understand the trend of events till we know this. As it was in the days of Isaiah, so it is now. Then the rise and fall of Babylon was conditioned by the history of the people whom her kings so greatly despised. Israel needed punishment, and Babylon was raised up to be the rod of God's vengeance. The precious truths entrusted to Israel needed dissemination throughout the world, and the chosen people were carried captive to Babylon and scattered throughout that vast empire. When seventy years were fulfilled, and the time was ripe for their restoration to their own land, Babylon fell beneath the Medes and Persians, and Cyrus signed the edict for the restoration of Israel.

So, now, it is hardly a matter of doubt that the existing complications of Eastern Europe will never be settled until the chosen people recover the land given by covenant-promise to Abraham, and establish there a free and independent kingdom.

But the practical lesson is, that God bears his people on his heart, and that He is ever engaged in manipulating and governing human affairs for their welfare. He hates putting away. He must keep his promises made to us in Jesus. O backslider, what comfort for thee is here! Israel had surely done her worst to alienate the love of God, and to put herself out of his loving favour. But see how He had compassion and chose her again. Take heart! He will restore thee, as at the first, and bless thee, setting thee again in the old place of favour and privilege. "Return unto Me, and I will return unto you, saith the Lord of hosts."

My heart crieth out for Moab. Isa. 15: 5 (R.V.).

MOAB was once thickly populated, and very fertile. But the country is now strewn with ruins; a few broken shafts of columns alone are standing, and deep wells cut into the heart of rock. That such a civilization should pass so entirely away, leaving no trace behind it, must have seemed most unlikely to the prophet's contemporaries; but these words have been literally fulfilled. So shall others of prophecy be fulfilled; and, indeed, each morning's dawn witnesses some further approach to their accomplishment.

It is to be noticed that the man of God takes no pleasure in these desolations, though Israel and Moab had been perpetually at feud. He speaks of the burden of Moab. Is not this the manner in which we should consider and proclaim the doom of the ungodly? Oh to preach of eternal judgment with wet eyes! Oh to tell men, even weeping, that they are the enemies of the cross of Christ! Oh to know the burdened heart, burdened even to breaking!

This is the only preaching which touches the heart of the unsaved. To announce their doom with metallic voice and unperturbed manner will only harden; but to speak with streaming eyes, and the eloquence of a broken heart, will touch the most callous. It is the broken heart that breaks hearts. Tears start tears. May our merciful High Priest impart to us his compassion and mercies, and lay on our hearts some of his burdens for dying men; that as we behold the cities we may weep, and that there may be a trembling in our voices as we proclaim the fearful woe that awaits the godless and impenitent.

And a throne shall be established in mercy.
Isa. 16: 5 (R.V.).

IN those days thrones were not generally established in mercy; but in blood, and cruelty, and savage might. Addressing Moab, the prophet advises that in the hour of her anguish, when her fugitives gather at the fords of the Arnon, in their mad flight from before the conqueror, they should make peace with their ancient enemies the Jews, and appease their hatred, that the outcasts may find shelter in the Land of Promise. And he goes on to say, that when this should come to pass, their piteous appeal for protection will be generously met, because the throne shall at that time be established in mercy. The ancient causes of enmity will be forgotten; the old feuds will be condoned; and the protection of Israel will be to the trembling crowds of refugees like the shadow of a high rock flung across the sand, when all the land is baking in the noontide glare.

Who can this be that sits on the throne of David, combining mercy with truth, seeking righteousness in his judgment, and swift to act on the behalf of the oppressed? None other than the Prince of the House of David, of whose kingdom there can be no end. Art thou a fugitive, driven from thy nest, and rushing to and fro as a scared and trembling bird (2)? Is the glare of the sun scorching thee? Dost thou stand at the fords of Arnon, with enemies behind, and death in front? Send ye lambs to the Mount of Zion; make peace with her King; invoke his forgiveness and salvation. Remember that though He is a great King, his throne is established in mercy. And his shadow shall be as the night in the midst of the noonday; He will hide the outcast, and will not betray the wanderer (3).

The harvest fleeth away in the day of grief and of desperate sorrow. Isa. 17: 10, 11 (R.V.).

HOW many among us might be addressed in these solemn words! Many are planting pleasant plants, which they hope will one day be beautiful in appearance; whilst from the slips they hope to rear fruit trees. One man is planting his schemes for making a fortune; another is setting slips that should bring him success and renown; yet another is busy in creating a political or religious movement that is intended to benefit mankind. The workers in the village allotment gardens in the early spring are an apt illustration of what politicians, company-mongers, and society-leaders, are attempting in other spheres.

But of what avail are all our preparations, so long as we forget the God of our salvation and are unmindful of the Rock of our strength? We shall never garner the harvest without his help and blessing. The day of grief and desperate sorrow will inevitably visit us, and sweep away all the results of our toils. The co-operation and blessing of God, sought in answer to prayer, cannot be left out of our calculations, if we are to win lasting success.

And is not the reverse also true? Supposing that we remember the God of our salvation, and are ever mindful of the Rock of our strength: may we not infer that our pleasant plants will root themselves, and our slips bear fruit in the coming years to the glory and praise of God, and for the blessing of thirsty wayfarers? "These simple teachings of farm and field knock continually at the doors of our own blessedness, with intent that we may enter therein, and find our home in the will of God, and our permanent lodging under the shadow of the Almighty."

I will be still, and I will behold in my dwelling-place. Isa. 18: 4 (R.V.).

ASSYRIA was marching against Ethiopia, the

people of which are described as tall and smooth. And as the armies advance, God makes no effort to arrest them; it would seem as though they will be allowed to work their will. He is still watching them from his dwelling-place; the sun still shines on them; the dews refresh them. But before the harvest, when the flowers are becoming ripening grapes, the whole of the proud array of Assyria is smitten as easily as when sprigs are cut off by the pruning-hook of the husbandman.

Is not this a marvellous conception of God—being still and watching? His stillness is not acquiescence. His silence is not consent. He is only biding his time, and will arise, in the most opportune moment, and when the designs of the wicked seem on the point of success, to overwhelm them with disaster. As we look out on the evil of the world; as we think of the apparent success of wrongdoing; as we wince beneath the oppression of those that hate us, let us remember these marvellous words about God being still and beholding.

There is, however, another side to this. Jesus beheld his disciples toiling at the oars through the stormy night; and watched, though unseen, the successive steps of the anguish at Bethany, where Lazarus slowly passed through the stages of mortal sickness, till he succumbed and was borne to the rocky tomb. But he was only waiting the moment when He could interpose most effectually. Is He still to thee? He is not unobservant: He is beholding all things: He has his finger on thy pulse, keenly sensitive to all its fluctuations. He will come to save thee when the precise moment has arrived.

Egypt my people, Assyria the work of my hands, Israel my inheritance. Isa. 19: 24, 25
IT is very wonderful to find such expressions in the mouth of a Jew. It shows what an effect that coal of fire had produced on the lips of Isaiah. It had led him to know something of the love of God which overleaps the barriers of nationality and caste, and gives itself to all who humbly seek after Him.

We have here the foreshadowing of an age, yet to be revealed, when the long discipline of God's dealings with men shall be consummated in their conversion to God. What a radiant prospect is thus suggested to us, when the most inveterate enemies of God's Church shall be received into her borders and regarded with the favour that God shows to his people!

Who, standing amid the terrors of the plagues, could ever have supposed that Egypt would be addressed as "my people"? Who could have thought that Assyria, the tyrant persecutor, would ever be called "the work of my hands"? Yet these are the trophies and triumphs of divine grace. Our Shepherd has many sheep, which are not of the Jewish fold: these also He must bring; and there shall be one flock, one Shepherd. Never despair of any, for God's grace abounds over mountains.

But Israel is always his inheritance. There he finds rest and home, for the Lord's portion is his people. Oh to know the riches of the glory of his inheritance in the saints! The soil of our life is poor and thin, the aspect bad, the stones many; but He who chose us will yet vindicate Himself, and if He has to empty heaven of its wealth He will do it rather than fail of his eternal purpose. Naaman asked for two mules' burdens of earth; but Christ can spare more than that, and will, to make the soil of a godly character.

And we, how shall we escape? Isa. 20: 6 (R.V.).
THE argument is as follows—Assyria, according to Isaiah's prophecies, would sweep down on Ethiopia, and take them into captivity; and when this happened, the inhabitants of the coast-line, which we know as Philistia, would have reason to fear indeed. If Ethiopia and Egypt, to whom they looked for aid, could not withstand the mighty northern nation, how hopeless it was for dwellers on the littoral to expect to withstand it by themselves!

The moral is obvious, and it is well pointed by the apostle Peter when he says: "The time is come for judgment to begin at the house of God, and if it begin first with us, what shall be the end of them that obey not the Gospel of God? And if the righteous is scarcely saved, where shall the ungodly and sinner appear?" Scarcely saved! It is as though our salvation tasked the resources of the Eternal God to the uttermost. He had grace and strength enough, but none to spare. Blood and tears and heartbreak were the price with which our redemption was secured! How then will they escape who venture forth into the storm which soon shall break upon our world, apart from the only salvation which can withstand its fury? "If the word spoken by angels was steadfast, and every transgression and disobedience received a just recompense of reward, how shall we escape, if we neglect so great salvation?"

A pious man, when death approached, longed to die in triumph for the conversion of his sons. Instead, his soul was overwhelmed with gloom. But this was used of God to the conversion of the whole family, for they said: If so good a man died in the dark, what will become of us?

Watchman, what of the night? Isa. 21: 11.
ACROSS the desert spaces a voice was heard calling from the land of Esau, calling to the prophet, to know whether the long night of Assyrian oppression was nearly over. He stood on the hills of Zion watching the dawn, as the priests were accustomed to do, that they might give the first signal for the offering of the morning sacrifice. The question, "Watchman, what of the night?" was repeated twice, as if the weary sufferers were at their last gasp.

The prophet's answer was enigmatical. The morning was already on its way; but the night was chasing it, spreading her raven wings in the same sky—"The morning cometh, and also the night." Morning for Israel, but night for Edom; but if Edom would repent, she might come again with her inquiries to find that for her also God had turned the shadow of death into the morning.

Never in the history of the ages have men looked more eagerly towards the Eastern sky, or inquired more persistently, What of the night? What of the night? To those that watch the Eastern sky, standing on the mount of vision afforded by the Word of God, there is but one answer: The morning cometh, but also the night. The morning of millennial glory, and of the bridal chamber; of the taking home of the saints, and the revelation of Jesus Christ: but the night of unutterable sorrow to the servant who knew the Lord's will and did it not, and to the world which would not have this Man to reign over it. Yet if individuals will but turn from darkness to light, and from Satan to God, they will be welcomed, and receive an inheritance amongst the children of the morning. "Come ye again, come" (R.V., marg.).

The key of the house of David will I lay upon his shoulder. Isa. 22: 22.
THE divine Man stands behind the earthly type in these words in majestic beauty. "These things saith He that is holy, He that is true, He that hath the key of David, He that openeth, and none shall shut, and that shutteth and none openeth. Behold, I have set before thee a door opened, which none can shut." Words of incomparable splendour, capable of endless application.

Let Jesus open each day of service, each opportunity of ministry, each door into another soul, each new chamber of life, and knowledge, and opportunity; and remember that He who sets before us open doors is He who knows our works, and that we have but little strength. He will never open a door leading into a passage of life which is too difficult for our strength to tread. The open door will reveal to us possibilities within our reach of which we had not dreamt; and when once a door is opened, though access to it may be beset, as in Bunyan's vision, by armed men, and though strong pressure is brought to bear upon it for its closing, let us dare to persevere against disease and pestilence and opposition, relying on these sublime words, None shall shut. Dear soul, say it to thyself repeatedly, None shall shut.

But the Lord shuts doors. "The Spirit of Jesus suffered them not to go into Bithynia." Down a long corridor of closed doors we may sometimes have to pass. It seems heartbreaking to see doors labelled, Friendship, Love, Home shut against us; but beyond them there is the one unclosed door through which we shall enter into our true life. Oh do not lose heart and hope in useless weeping over the closed doors of the past. Follow Him, who has the keys.

The sea hath spoken. Isa. 23: 4.
ZIDON is bidden to be ashamed because she is suddenly left childless; and this to an Eastern woman was shame indeed. And the prophet, personifying Zidon as the City of the Sea, describes the sea herself as lamenting. It is as though the sea took up Zidon's complaint at the destruction of her children, and spoke in all her multitudinous waves.

With what different tones the sea speaks! Sometimes in the musical breath of her wavelets on the beach; or the long drawl of the shingle in the recession of the retiring billow; or in the rising storm, when the waters lift up their voice; or in the angry roar of the mighty waves far out at sea. Speaking in whispers and in thunder; speaking to itself and to God under the canopy of night! The sea-voices are not the least amongst those of nature. Old Ocean seems to us sometimes like a great organ on which every note of the heart is represented.

And what are the wild waves saying? Listen! "We are his, for He made us; we own his sway, for He once trod our crests; his voice is as the voice of many waters; his thoughts are deep as our profoundest depths; his throne stands beside the sea of glass mingled with fire; his least word is omnipotent over our wildest fury."

But the sea shall one day speak for the last time. The lonely soul of the beloved apostle, which had so often listened to the chime of the Ægean waves around his island prison, rejoiced to know that the sea should one day be no more. No more the speech of the storm; no more the mournful cadence of the retiring wavelet at night telling of separation and loneliness. "The first heaven and the first earth are passed away, and the sea is no more."

From the uttermost part of the earth have we heard songs. Isa. 24: 16.

THIS chapter exceeds in sublimity. The prophet first describes the general desolation about to overtake the world of his time, when, through the ruthless invasions of Nebuchadnezzar, it would become utterly emptied and spoiled. He describes the earth as languishing and fading away, and the high ones of the people languishing (ver. 4). Polluted nature is depicted as groaning in bitter anguish beneath the enormous sins of men, who had transgressed the law, changed the ordinance, and broken the everlasting covenant of their God. All joy is darkened; the mirth of the land is gone.

The scene is changed, and our thought is turned from the judgment and punishment of the wicked, to the blessed lot of the people of God; we are taught to see the Lord of Hosts reigning on Mount Zion and in Jerusalem, and before his ancients gloriously. And all who see it are compelled to confess that it is well with his people who are under such a King. And as that spectacle is beheld by the sons of men, as they compare their misery with the light and joy of the people of God, they lift up their voices and sing. They shall lift up their voice, they shall shout; for the majesty of the Lord, they shall cry aloud from the sea. Where morning lights her fires they shall glorify Him; and from the uttermost parts of the earth songs roll home in a tumult of ecstasy, "Glory, glory to the righteous."

It is a true sentence. Though for our discipline, and to fit us to minister to men, we are often passed through the fiery furnace, yet on the whole it is well with us. Ours is the peace of God; ours the knowledge that love is over all; ours the anticipation of a morning that shall never be overcast.

He will swallow up death in victory. Isa. 25: 8.

IN this ode, which Isaiah prepared for singing when Babylon the first should have fallen, the apostle, taught by the Holy Ghost, saw an anticipation of the triumph of the saints, when the strong bastions of death should be destroyed before the coming of Him who is the resurrection and the life. "This corruptible must put on incorruption, and this mortal must put on immortality." In these words he refers to the first stage in the Second Advent, when the living saints shall be changed, and those who have died shall be raised; and then he proceeds to quote these words, "When this corruptible shall have put on incorruption, and this mortal shall have put on immortality, then shall come to pass the saying that is written, Death is swallowed up in victory."

There can be no doubt that this is Paul's prayer for himself. He says, "We would be clothed upon, that what is mortal may be swallowed up of life." No doubt it would be very delightful! None of the pains of dissolution; no going forth of the unclothed spirit; but the sudden subliming and transfiguring of the mortal, as ice passes into water, or water into vapour. It is not to be wondered at that the prophet adds, "The Lord God will wipe away tears from off all faces." In the rapture of reunion, in the glad embrace of eternity, in the consciousness that death and trouble are for ever behind, and that God has kept his word, we shall forget how to weep!

The prophet also records the triumphant song which will break from myriads of glad spirits, when the hope of the Church will be realized, and her long patience rewarded: "It shall be said in that day, Lo, this is our God: we have waited for Him, we will be glad and rejoice in his salvation."

Thou wilt keep him in perfect peace, whose mind is stayed on Thee. Isa. 26: 3.

THE Hebrew is very significant. "Perfect peace" is Peace, peace. As though the soul dwelt within double doors, like some chambers which we have entered, which had double windows against the noise of the street, and a baize door within the ordinary one to deaden the sound of voices from the next apartment. Understand, dear soul, that it is thy privilege to live inside the double doors of God's loving care. He says to thee, "Peace, peace." If one assurance is not enough, He will follow it with a second and a third. The city is strong, the bulwarks and walls are massive, salvation is appointed and prepared; but the gates do not frown with iron or move heavily on hinges of stone, they open musically and gently.

We remember how, on the evening of his resurrection, our Lord spoke the double peace. Peace, because of his wounds, the peace of the justified; and peace, because He was sending his apostles forth, as the Father had sent Him. The one is the peace of the evening, when we come back to our home, wounded and soiled: the other of the morning, when we dwell in the will of Him who chose our lot and path. His blood and his will—these are the double doors of our peace.

We must see to it that our mind is stayed on God. For mind the margin suggests imagination. It is through our imaginings that we get perturbed and defiled. We anticipate and fancy so many ogres; we harbour such dark forebodings; chambers of imagery are thrown open to such unseemly company; hence our perturbation. Do not imagine, but trust; do not anticipate, but leave God to choose. "Looking forward strains the eyesight; looking upward opens heaven."

Let him take hold of my strength. Isa. 27: 5.
SUCH are the alternatives. You must either resist God's strength, or take hold of it. If the former, it is as though thorns and briars should fight flame. There is no fury in God; He has no desire for the death of the ungodly, but that he should turn from his unrighteousness and live. Yet if the blinded soul persists in flinging itself into collision with Him, it must suffer finally and irretrievably. But notice the double invitation, "Let him take hold of my strength; let him make peace."

Where shall I find his strength? the sinner asks. In the mighty mountains girded with strength; in the arch of the sky; in the break of the ocean wave? No, not in these; but where that dying Man pours out his soul unto death, and is numbered with the transgressors. But surely there is the weakness of God, not the strength! Nay, but it is the strength. The weakness of God is stronger than men. "We preach Christ crucified: to the Jews a stumbling-block, and to Greeks foolishness; but unto them which are called, Christ the power of God."

Come hither, soul of man, the strength of God is in that pierced, transfixed hand. Take hold of it, it will lift thee. In Him God is reconciled; there is nothing to do but take the offered mercy, accept his reconciliation, and be at peace. God is reconciled; be thou reconciled. God has made peace; be thou at peace. God reaches out his hand; take hold of it. God draws nigh; draw nigh to Him. Then He will keep thee, whatever be thy foes or temptation; his protecting strength will interpose between them and thee. He will keep thee night and day (ver. 3).

"Peace, perfect peace, in this dark world of sin?
The blood of Jesus whispers peace within."

A crown of glory, and a diadem of beauty.
Isa. 28: 5.
WHAT many, like the drunkards of Ephraim, as described here, seek in the exhilarating stimulus of wine, God's people seek and find in Himself! Notice the variety of his attributes. There is something for everyone. Are you eager for glory? There is no reputation or fame equal to having his smile, the consciousness of being well pleasing to Him—"He will be a crown of glory." Do you recognize the deformity and unloveliness of your character, and desire beauty? "He will be a diadem of beauty." Do you desire a right judgment in all things, so as to be able to direct large and important undertakings? "He will be a spirit of judgment," when you will be in judgment. Submit your judgment to Him, that He may think through your mind or direct you to a just conclusion. Are there days when the enemy threatens to carry your soul by assault, and is already at the gates? Then turn to Jesus, and He will be your strength. Yes, and in great crises, when evil is predominant, and the citadel of faith and righteousness threatens to be submerged before the weltering chaos, when no other help is near, as you look to the Captain of the Lord's Host, you will suddenly find yourself enabled to roll back the dark battalions, in the very hour of victory.

Let us live in closer fellowship with our glorious Lord. They who receive the abundance of his grace shall reign. Out of his fulness may all receive, and grace for grace. "In that day" on Christ's lips always meant the day of Pentecost; and it is only through the grace of the Holy Spirit that we can avail ourselves of the treasured resources of the Ascended Christ.

"He shall suffice me, for He hath sufficed."

The meek also shall increase their joy in the Lord. Isa. 29: 19.

"BLESSED are the meek," "Blessed are the poor in spirit," said the Lord. What is meekness, and why are meek and poor men so signally blessed with joy? Meekness is different from lowliness and humility. It is our attitude in the presence of our detractors and persecutors—not retaliating, nor opposing force to force, but bowing in silence and submission before high-handed wrong. It was in such a spirit of meekness that Jesus suffered Himself to be led as a lamb to the slaughter; and instead of calling for legions of angels, suffered Caiaphas' armed band to bind Him. This spirit is not natural to us. It is in our nature to retaliate and avenge ourselves. We want to call for fire, or legions of armoured angels from the heaven of God. But this is not the way of peace or joy.

But the Holy Spirit waits to reproduce in us the meekness of Jesus. Then, when you meet all injury and unkindness with an unfailing Christian courtesy, bending like a rush before the storm, to rise when it has passed over, you will have joy. Joy, because God will comfort you: because you have not lost yourself in the heat of passion, but have tried to turn others away from their evil purpose: because your hands could not have vindicated or extricated yourself, as God's have: and because you realize that the passive virtues are stronger, and the patience of Jesus Christ will win the kingdom. Those who fret and fume and storm through life, always standing on their rights, and insisting on being respected and consulted, are in perpetual perturbation. But the meek inherit the earth. All the best comes to them at last. God makes them his special charge. And as they tread the path of Jesus, they share his joy.

Therefore will the Lord wait, that He may be gracious unto you. Isa. 30: 18.

AS long as the people tried to help themselves, sending ambassadors to Egypt, and seeking an alliance against the invader, God could do nothing for them; He could only wait until they returned to simple reliance upon Himself. In returning to trust and rest they would be saved. At first they said No. They were opposed to the idea of simple trust in God. It seemed impossible to believe that if they simply rested on Him He would do better for them than their most strenuous exertions could do for themselves. And all the while God was waiting till every expedient failed, and they were reduced to such a condition that He could step in and save them.

How like this is to much in our lives! It is long before we learn the lesson of returning and rest; of quietness and confidence. We will trust in chariots and horses, and ride upon the swift. It is, of course, right to use the means; but our strong temptation is to put them in the place of God, and trust them. You are trying to save yourself from the just penalty of your sin, from the pursuit of your foes, from perplexing combinations and complications of circumstances; you have been running backwards and forwards, flurried and excited. At how many doors you have knocked to find them closed; and all the while God has been waiting to be gracious to you, waiting till you came to the end of yourself; waiting, till like a spent struggler in the water, you ceased from your mad efforts and cast yourself back upon his strong everlasting love. He is exalted to have mercy; but He is a God of judgment, or literally, of method. He can only save in one way. Blessed are they that wait for Him. The soul that waits for God will always find the God for whom he waits.

As birds flying, so will the Lord of Hosts protect Jerusalem. Isa. 31: 5 (R.V.).

IT was a beautiful conception, for Jerusalem was perched on Mount Zion, as some bird's nest in the cleft of the rocks. Lo! Sennacherib approaches as the hawk, hovering above the fledglings of the nest. But just as the mother-bird gathers her young under her wing, and places herself between her treasures and threatening peril, so would the eternal God spread those wings, under which Ruth came to trust in the old time, over the entire city. To Isaiah there was no cause for fear when Sennacherib's legions were encamped on the mountains of Zion. He, at least, realized that the pinions of Almightiness were between the cowering citizens and the dreaded foe. Warm and safe was such abiding.

How wonderful that Jesus should have appropriated this metaphor, and spoken of Himself as willing to gather Jerusalem under his wing to save her from a more terrible fate! Does it not bespeak his consciousness of Deity that He should hide the people under the shadow of his care?

This may be our daily portion. The Lord of Hosts will be strong as the lion that growls over his prey, undismayed by the multitude of shepherds that shout at him; and He will be sweet and soft and gentle as a mother-bird. Always believe that Jesus stands between you and what you dread. Even now He is passing over you. Do you not hear Him saying, "If you seek Me, let these go their way"? Isaac Pennington, an old follower of George Fox, who had considerable experience of the prisons of his time, said he often felt the healing drop from the wings of Christ. The sense of God's presence and of his power are as two wings, beneath which the believer nestles, till calamities be overpast.

The work of righteousness shall be peace.
Isa. 32: 17.

RIGHTEOUSNESS must precede peace. IN THE GOVERNMENT OF A HOLY GOD. The writer of the Epistle to the Hebrews clearly affirms that Melchizedek, the type of Christ, is first King of Righteousness and then King of Peace. In Rom. 3 the apostle shows how the righteousness of God has been vindicated, and will be imparted to those that believe; and then says, "being justified, . . . let us have peace with God."

IN OUR INNER LIFE. Many seek for peace apart from righteousness. They refuse to adjust some wrong in their lives which calls aloud against them. They refuse to permit the light of God's Spirit to ransack their past, because they are conscious that to do so will expose themselves to the inevitable need of confession and restitution; and as they will not submit to the laying of the foundations of peace, they miss the peace. So far as you know, you must be right, before you can have peace.

IN MEN'S DEALINGS WITH EACH OTHER. Be sure to go to the bottom of disputes and disagreements. There is a right and a wrong in every question. It is always wise to lay the foundations of justice at any cost, assured that peace will inevitably result sooner or later.

Honeyed words will not abide; but just deeds are a permanent basis for a happy and lasting reconciliation.

How blessed that for evermore our peace is secured! The righteous shall never need to leave their peaceful habitation, or to quit their sure dwellings. However it may hail to the downfall of the forest trees, storms shall never drive them from their quiet resting-places, since they are founded upon the righteousness as well as the grace of God.

Be Thou their arm every morning, our salvation also in the time of trouble. Isa. 33: 2.

THIS is an exquisite morning prayer, and the beauty of it is that it is so sweetly unselfish. It begins by appealing for the grace of God, but goes on to ask that He would be as an arm of loving support and deliverance to others, before the suppliant turns back to ask for salvation for himself in time of trouble. "Be Thou their arm; . . . our salvation also." If you want God's arm for yourself, ask that it may be given to someone else. If you want salvation in the time of trouble, pray that God would give his arm for the help of your neighbour.

We all want that arm every morning. The gladdest, fairest day that ever broke for us, or will break, must have been marked, or will be marked, by pitfalls and snares. The path may begin with greensward; but before the evening it will have opened upon stones and steep ascents, and you will need the arm of your Beloved on which to lean. But you will never ask for it in vain. It will be always at hand. Be sure, like the Shulamite, to come up out of the wilderness, leaning on your Beloved. And whatever else you forget in your morning prayer, never forget to ask for the strong, tender arm of God. O woman, bereaved of the strong arm on which thou wert wont to lean, will not this suffice thee!

Is not this a comprehensive prayer for dear ones far away or near? Be their arm, Heavenly Father, to-day. If I may not be there to give the strength of my arm, let thine be their stay, and Thou wilt do better than had been possible, had I been by their side. Then, when the hour of trouble comes, and you ask that He should be your salvation, the glorious Lord will be a place of broad rivers and streams.

The day of the Lord's vengeance, the year of recompense. Isa. 34: 8 (R.V.).

THESE chapters remind us that there is a God

that judgeth in the earth. The tendency of the present day is to reduce all things to the operation of natural law, and to crowd God out of his own world; as though He had no longer as much power as a judge or magistrate to inflict punishment! Here He comes out of the silence of eternity to avenge the wrongs of his people perpetrated upon them by Edom. The Jews could never forget that when they were in the extremity of their conflict with Babylon, Edom rejoiced and said, "Rase it, rase it to the foundation thereof." Now, at length, God would vindicate his people, and punish the proud land whose sins cried to Heaven.

Let us remember that God works not only through natural law, but by sudden manifest interpositions of his providence; and when He arises on behalf of the meek, the result is not only terrible but lasting. It seems as though God's judgment on Edom and other peoples, which has left their lands as desolate scars on the face of the earth, are instances of the permanence of God's decrees, and of their irreversibleness: "The smoke thereof shall go up for ever; from generation to generation it shall be waste; none shall pass through it for ever and ever." It was often told by the Waldenses, how the prince that broke the covenant with them and drove them across the Swiss mountains, died of a broken heart at the death of his first-born.

God does not appear always to avenge the wrongs of his people in the present life. The wicked pass away amid their ill-gotten prosperity, but in the next world their evil deeds come back to roost in their own hearts.

The way of holiness. Isa. 35: 8.
THIS chapter is full of blessed prevision of a state of perfect blessedness, when the curse that has so long brooded over the world shall be removed. Into that sweet and blessed country there is a way from the present: it is the way of holiness.

IT IS A WAY. Our holiness is progressive. Though we may perfectly obey up to the limit of our knowledge, that knowledge is ever on the increase, beckoning our advance. Before us lies the path marked out by the footsteps of Jesus, climbing from strength to strength, and we are called to walk in it.

IT IS A HIGHWAY. That is, it is for everyone that will. It is kept in repair under the King's own orders. There are no toll-gates on its straight line of route. It is like those Roman roads which traversed countries from end to end, and remain to-day imperishable monuments of the skill of their constructors.

IT IS CLOSED AGAINST THE UNCLEAN. The leper of old was forbidden to obstruct the thoroughfare. The unclean soul is equally forbidden to taint that holy way. God's first requirement of us is separation.

THIS WAY IS ALWAYS TRODDEN BY JESUS. "He shall be with them" (R.V., marg.). The holy soul has a divine Companion. For the most part those who tread this way do so as part of a great host; but when the path seems lonely, He goes beside who walked to Emmaus.

IT IS PLAINLY DEFINED. Wayfaring men, though fools, need make no mistake. Be true to the Bible, to the holy instincts of your soul, and above all, to the blessed Comforter who guides all. The way may sometimes be paved with jagged flints; but keep in it, it is safe walking, and it leads home.

They held their peace, and answered him not a word. Isa. 36: 21.
IT was very bitter for Hezekiah and Isaiah that these words of vituperation and abuse were spoken in the open air, the voice of the speaker travelling far enough to be heard by the whole population in Jerusalem. Rabshakeh loudly reminded them that Egypt was a broken reed; then suggested that Hezekiah's recent raid against the idolatry which had grown up in his country must have alienated the God of Israel; then that God Himself had sent him to destroy the land; and lastly, he quoted the long list of conquests that had fallen to the share of his master. What could Hezekiah do against the conqueror of Sepharvaim and other proud cities, which were level with the ground? To all of which the king ordered they should give no reply.

Silence is our best reply to the allegations and taunts of our foes. Be still, O persecuted soul! Hand over thy cause to God. It is useless to argue, even in many cases to give explanations. Be still, and commit thy cause to God. He has heard every word, and will answer. Thus Jesus also held his peace, when falsely accused:

"He stood alone,
Silent amidst their clamour—He whose voice
Of power but late suffic'd to ope the grave!
'Others He saved—Himself He cannot save!'
O mystic silence! how divine thy choice."

But before going into this conflict be sure that, like Hezekiah, thou hast put from thee all that is false and evil. The iconoclasm of the good king which Rabshakeh so curiously mis-interpreted was, after all, his main security. It is necessary that there should be no controversy between God and the soul which He is to defend.

Hezekiah went unto the house of the Lord, and spread the letter before the Lord. Isa. 37: 14. PROBABLY he literally handed in the letter to God, opening it and laying it down in the Holy Place, as though the responsibility of dealing with its contents no longer devolved upon himself.

The post and telegraph are great factors in modern life. They are perpetually bringing to us documents of one kind and another, which involve anxious thought. Sometimes a heavy account for expenditure which has been necessarily and righteously incurred; or a story of wrong-doing on the part of some near relative; or some piteous appeal for help. Indeed, not unseldom, letters like this that Rabshakeh addressed to Hezekiah may fall into our lap. We read with beating hearts, and know not what to say, and finally go into the presence of God and spread it out. Answer it for us, great God, we entreat Thee!

The divine reply came first in the blessed assurance sent through Isaiah; and next when the angel of the Lord "spread his wings on the blast, and breathed on the face of the foe as he passed." Let us more habitually hand over our anxieties and cares to God. God calls us to enter into his rest, i.e., to place Himself and his care between us and all that would hurt or annoy. "Doth God take care for oxen," and will He not care for his children? Is a falling sparrow more to Him than his child? Hath He brought us so far on our journey to put us to shame? Only let us be sure that we have given no just cause for the unkind tone of the letters, or brought ourselves into a false position with respect to those who hate God. Daily exercise yourself to have a conscience void of offence: then, with God on your side, you can face a world in arms.

In love to my soul. Isa. 38: 17. THE R.V. margin is very beautiful. "Thou hast loved my soul from the pit." As though from the pit's mouth and onward there had been one long succession of loving thoughts and words. Or it may be that the love of God has loved us out of the pit of corruption. Let that pit of corruption stand for the evil of our own hearts, the abysmal depths of our selfishness, the lustings and fightings of our flesh. What could have saved us from all these, but the love of God?

THE PATIENCE OF GOD'S LOVE. God's patience has been greatly magnified in us, that He has borne with us so tenderly. If God had been less than infinite, He must long ago have renounced us in despair. Oh, the riches of his long-suffering! He has lingered near the pit of our corruption, drawing us from it with untiring solicitude, even when we have repeatedly cast ourselves back into it with ungrateful per-sistence.

THE SACRIFICES OF GOD'S LOVE. How much He has borne and suffered! The cross, with its shame and spitting, seems to be but a revela-tion, in terms that we can understand, of the pain that lies always on his heart, and of the inestimable cost our sin involves. It is this divine sorrow which purifies us, as we devoutly consider it.

THE PURITY OF GOD'S LOVE. What a contrast between some fœtid pool and the over-arching blue of heaven! Such is God's love as con-trasted with our hate; his sweetness with our chidings, his holiness with our corruption. But his love conquers our sin, and draws us out of the pit. Where sin abounds, his grace much more abounds, and makes us loving and lovely.

"Thou art the victor, Love!"

There is nothing among my treasures that I have not shewed them. Isa. 39: 4. IN the Book of the Chronicles there is a suggestion which shows the hidden evil that lurked beneath Hezekiah's attitude to these Babylonish ambassadors. "Hezekiah ren-dered not again according to the benefit done unto him; for his heart was lifted up, therefore there was wrath upon him." Beyond all other sin, pride is abhorrent to God as the parent of other sins, and it was this accursed principle that prompted Hezekiah to that outburst of ostentation. He did not care to remember that he had nothing which he had not first received, and that at the best he was only a trustee of God's gifts for others. You will remember that by this sin fell the angels. It was when Nebu-chadnezzar surveyed Babylon from the roof of his palace that he was suddenly smitten with madness.

Be very careful to watch against ostentation and the pride from which it springs. The best antidote is the habit of looking from the gifts to the Giver, and to accustom yourself to the position of a steward of the benefits which have been done to you. Oh for more of the spirit of praise and thanksgiving, of adoring gratitude, of grateful love! Not unto us, not unto us, but unto thy name be all the glory, O Lord God. All things come of Thee: wealth, and the power to get it; love, and the qualities that earn it; success, and the health of body and mind so needful to its acquisition. No doubt Hezekiah's sad lapse is intended as a warning to us all. The minuteness with which it is recorded may be intended to impress on us the danger of coquetting with the Babylon around us. It is impossible to do so without becoming ultimately carried into captivity to its corruption.

Comfort ye, comfort ye my people, saith your God. Isa. 40: 1.
THERE is a considerable interval between the preceding chapter and this. The Jews are now nearing the term of their long and bitter sufferings; their fiery trials have done their work.

COMFORT, BECAUSE SIN IS FORGIVEN. "Look to the wounds of Jesus, brother," said Staupitz to Luther. At the foot of the cross alone can sinners be comforted. We need not only the assurance of forgiveness, but some knowledge of the way in which it has been obtained, and the grounds on which it is based. Our hearts are never truly comforted till we learn that God is faithful and just when He forgives.

COMFORT, BECAUSE GOD IS ON HIS WAY TO DELIVER. The imagery is borrowed from the progress of an Oriental prince or conqueror. Great gangs of men are sent to level the ways before him. Be of good cheer, the prophet says; your God shall come with a strong hand. See the mountains become a way; the crooked is made straight and the rough places smooth. The glorious Lord comes to deliver the afflicted from his strong oppressor, and all flesh shall see it together.

COMFORT, BECAUSE THE STRONG DELIVERER HAS A TENDER HEART. He comes as a mighty one, but He feeds his flock like a shepherd. Strong and sweet, mighty and merciful. The Everlasting Father, but the Prince of Peace.

Those arms sustain the universe, but they gather lambs.

COMFORT, BECAUSE HE FAINTS NOT! NEITHER IS WEARY. Others may tire after a while. Physical strength droops and declines. Time seems long. The current may sweep lovers and friends out of our reach, but Thou remainest! "The Creator of the ends of the earth fainteth not, neither is weary."

Look not around thee, for I am thy God.
Isa. 41: 10 (R.V., marg.).
WE are all tempted to look around us, to see who is prepared to stand by and help us. We are apt, like the apostle, to look at the winds and waves. Not so, says our God. Look not around, but look off to Me; look unto Me, and be ye saved, all the ends of the earth.

These exceeding great and precious promises quicken our desire to be able to establish our lineage as belonging to Abraham. We very gladly catch at the apostle's assurance that those who have his faith may claim to be his children. It is good to know that, Gentiles as we are, we may be included in the Israel of God.

Now, troubled soul, look unto these words. They are spoken by one who cannot lie, and spoken for thee. They are as much meant for thee as though they had never been claimed by another; and God is prepared to fulfil them in thy life to the brim. He is with thee at this moment, whilst thou art pondering these words. He is thy God, and will never act unworthily of thy trust. Where thou art weakest and most easily overcome, He will strengthen thee. Where thou needest help, He will give his, so that thy difficult task shall be easily mastered. And when thou art too weary to walk; when no more strength remains in thee; when thou sinkest on the battlefield or the steep hill —He will uphold thee. Dost thou doubt? Behold at his right hand, Jesus sits, thy Lover and Saviour. It is a right hand of righteousness, that can never act unworthily of itself, or fail the trusting soul.

"The steps of faith
Fall on the seeming void—and find
The rock beneath!"

A bruised reed shall He not break, and the smoking flax shall He not quench. Isa. 42: 3.
THIS is characteristic of Jesus Christ. Our great enemy argues so differently. He says, See!

it is but a piece of smouldering tow; blow it out, it is not worth conserving. Jesus says, It is only smouldering, but there is the more reason why I should blow it into a flame. Satan says, That is only a bruised reed, trample it beneath thy feet; Jesus says, Because it is so bruised, it needs very special tenderness, care, and skill, to make anything of it: let Me have it. Satan says, That is only a charred brand plucked out of the fire, cast it back again, it will never be of any use; Jesus answers, It cost Me too much to pluck it out, and I am not going to cast it back again; besides, if there is only a little left of solid wood, it needs the more solicitude to preserve it, and use what there is.

Weakness, weariness, and sin, never fail to draw forth the deepest sympathy from the Lord Jesus. Nothing lays a stronger hold upon Him, or brings Him more swiftly to our side. At home our mother was always sweet but sweetest when we were ill or weary. It almost tempted us to sham, so as to be more coaxed. And Christ's love is like mother's. You need not sham with Him, you are weak and broken enough. But those who are most bruised and struggling get the tenderest manifestations of his love. He resembles the strong man, with muscles like iron, and who stands like a rock, but who will bend in tears and tenderness over his cripple-child.

"It shall be
A Face like my face that receives thee, a Man like to me,
Thou shalt love and be loved by for ever; a Hand like this hand
Shall throw open the gates of new life to thee! See the Christ stand!"

Now thus saith the Lord. Isa. 43: 1, 2.
WHO IS HE THAT SAITH? He that created thee in the womb of time; that has moulded and formed thee in all the varying providences of life; that redeemed thee by his most precious blood; that knows and calls thee by thy name. When Prince Albert died, the Queen cried, in the agony of her grief, "There will be no one now to call me Victoria." Ah, but there is always One who will call his own by name. Simon, Simon!

WHAT DOTH HE PROGNOSTICATE? He foretells that there will be fire through which the ore of character must be passed, and waters which the pilgrim host must traverse. This is inevitable. He is too transparently truthful to engage us without telling the nature of his service.

Through much tribulation we must enter the kingdom.

"The path of sorrow, and that path alone,
Leads to the world where sorrow is unknown."

WHAT DOTH HE PROMISE? In all our lot, God is willing to be our partner and companion. He has called us into fellowship with his Son, and in his faithfulness He will see us through. The waters rise, the night is dark, the ford is hard to find, and footing is insecure; but He is at hand, steadying the feet, and keeping the head above the floods. The fiery furnace is heated sevenfold, so that the strongest soldiers in the armies of the world are consumed by its flame; but one like the Son of Man walks by his faithful witnesses, and makes the burning embers more delightful than the dewy sward of Paradise. The bonds will be burnt, and the captive limbs set free; but no hair of the head shall perish, nor the smell of fire pass on thee.

O Israel, thou shalt not be forgotten of Me.
Isa. 44: 21.
WE think He has forgotten. We lie on our bed of pain, and He sends no chariot to fetch us home. We linger to extreme old age, and are lonely because all the companions of our youth have left our side, and it seems as though He had forgotten to send the ferry-boat across for his child. And the river-brink is cold. We toil all through the night against wind and wave, and it seems inexplicable that the Master tarries so long on the shore. We sit by our dead; and though we sent for Him four days ago, He has not come. We told Him that we had come to our last crust; but as yet no raven has brought us food.

When I was a very little boy, one stormy night, my father, who usually fetched me when the weather was bad, forgot to call for me, and it grew later and later; all the other boys had been sent to bed, and I heard them proposing to send me, and I had never slept outside my father's house. I kept up as long as I could, and then my heart broke. It was only a momentary forgetting, however; for he came for me at last, through miles of storm—and love made amends. But not for a moment can God forget. He is never nearer than when He seems further. He has redeemed. His blood awaits its holy ministry of blotting out sin. He has tied up his heart with us. We are graven upon the palms of his hands.

The dying thief asked to be remembered. And Jesus said in effect: "Remember thee! How could I ever forget thee, who alone couldst speak sustaining words of love and trust in these sad hours? Remember thee! Dost thou ask only to be remembered? I tell thee, when the shadows fall around the holy city, and all these crowds have gone to their homes, thou shalt be with Me in Paradise."

Woe unto him that striveth with his Maker.
Isa. 45: 9.

GOD MOULDS US as a plotter does his clay. In doing this, He comes to a point where our nature seems entrenched in all its might. We can yield everything but this. But not to yield this is to neutralize our yielding in all beside. That is where the soul strives with God. It is the battlefield, the crisis, the crease-line of destiny.

WE MAY STRIVE WITH GOD in two ways, saying, What makest Thou? or, He hath no hands; either by accusing Him of not having a definite purpose, or by alleging that He is not taking the best method of accomplishing it. Have you ever questioned the love, or wisdom, or purpose of God, in the moulding and education of your soul? Or have you questioned the benevolence and wisdom of his methods? To do either of these is disastrous to peace of heart and growth in grace. We must will and dare to believe that God is doing his very best for us, and doing it in the very best way.

THE FATE OF THOSE WHO STRIVE AGAINST THEIR MAKER IS VERY TERRIBLE.

They are counted as potsherds. "Let the potsherd strive with the potsherds of the earth." What is a potsherd? A shred of pottery, which may have been part of a beautiful vase, but now as a broken fragment is good for nothing but the rubbish-heap. See it protruding from the cinders! This is the fate of the castaway, which the apostle feared. The image says nothing as to our eternal destiny, but assures us that we may miss all opportunity of serving the purposes of God. Agree, therefore, with thy divine Adversary quickly, lest He cast thee aside, or touch thee in the sinew of the thigh that shrinks, and thou limp through the remainder of thy days.

I have made, and I will bear. Isa. 46: 4.

WE must not press these words unduly, because we have doubtless warped our original constitution by habits of sin and selfishness, for which we are largely responsible. In these we may look to God for deliverance, but we cannot hold Him responsible.

But there are other attitudes of character and circumstances of life which are the direct result of God's appointment. He allowed us to be born with such a temperament, of such parents, and in such a home. He knew exactly what was to be the climate and colour of the land of our birth. He permitted us to begin our life-race with certain infirmities and disabilities, which have been apparently a great hindrance to our success. He has allowed us to enter a business, or become united in the marriage tie, which seems entirely hostile to our best interests. But all this should only cast us the more upon Him. "He will bear," as He hath borne, our griefs and our sorrows. It is when we touch the lowest depth of our trouble that we most clearly hear Him say, Child, my grace is sufficient for thee; thy weakness is that which the more calls forth my strength; I will turn it for my glory through thy life.

By his grace He bears and upholds us in the circumstances in which He has placed us; and more than this, He bears in patience and love what our wilfulness puts upon Him. He bare our sins in his own body on the tree; and now He bears with our murmurings, petulance, and rebellion.

O God, Thou hast made us, and not we ourselves; we are thy people and the sheep of thy pasture; still bear with our wanderings and sins, we entreat Thee, till Thou hast made us what we would be, and made us meet for thy use.

Come down, and sit in the dust. Isa. 47: 1.

ALL through the history of the chosen people there has been a great antagonist. In the days of the sons of Noah, Babel; in the days of the kingdom, Babylon; in opposition to the Church, Babylon the Great. And deeper than any earthly embodiment, always the spirit of the world, which exalteth itself, and setteth itself against God. Babylon was used by God to execute his purposes on Israel; but she altogether mistook the situation, and attributed her success to her prowess and the might of her arms. She acted with the utmost mercilessness and pride towards the nations of her time; and, therefore, when she had so far fulfilled the divine purpose, her own judgment drew near.

Look at home! To colonize; to civilize heathen races; to make roadways across the ocean, along which the Gospel may travel; to link the whole world by the nerves of telegraph-wires; to give the Bible to every people under heaven—such has been the mission of the Anglo-Saxon race. But how much evil has mingled with it all! Think of the opium traffic, the sale of fire-water, the land-grabbing! Remember the impurity, the drunkenness, the godlessness, which have followed in the track of army and navy! Consider also the way in which our peoples are giving themselves up to pleasure-seeking and luxury, to Sabbath-breaking and irreligion to spiritualism and so-called Christian science! And then ask whether there is not grave cause for apprehension. That Babylon should fall seemed utterly unlikely to the men of Isaiah's time; as unlikely as the fall of the Anglo-Saxon race. But it befell; and she who had sat delicately on the throne, was bidden to do the menial work of a slave.

For mine own sake, for mine own sake, will I do it. Isa. 48: 11.

GOD finds his supreme motive in Himself. Mark how strongly He insists on it. "For my Name's sake will I defer mine anger; and for my praise will I refrain from thee." And in this verse He twice repeats, "for mine own sake." Surely this is a matter for extreme comfort and congratulation.

If God had saved us because of some trait of natural beauty and attractiveness which He beheld in us, He might turn from us when it faded before the touch of years, or the change of our inward temper. The woman whose only claim on attention and homage is in her face—who has no other qualities to command and retain respect, must often dread the inevitable effect of time. It would be therefore a cause of perpetual unrest to us if God's motive were only one of pity or complacency.

But God's motive is his character, his name and nature, the maintenance of his honour in the face of the universe. In the face of the universe of intelligent beings He is too deeply implicated in our salvation to show signs of variableness or the shadow of turning. He did not begin to save us because we were worthy or lovely, but because He would; and therefore He will not give up because we prove ourselves weak and worthless and difficult to save. There are times with us all when we can but cast ourselves on his infinite grace and say, "Save me for thine own Name's sake." And when we have been overcome by sin, it is good to go to Him and say, "Father, I have nothing to plead but thy own nature and name declared in Jesus: for his sake, because Thou hast made a promise to Him, and to me in Him; for thy glory's sake defer thine anger, forgive my sins; save me for thine own Name's sake.

In the shadow of his hand hath He hid me. Isa. 49: 2.

THESE words were addressed to Israel, and must be applied to Him who alone has expressed the true genius and spirit of the Hebrew people, that Prince of the House of David whom we call Master and Lord. And in so far as we belong to and resemble Him, we may claim that God should make these words true of us.

THE MOUTH, LIKE THE SHARP SWORD, recalls the portrait of the Son of Man, out of whose mouth a sharp two-edged sword proceeded. We may well ask that our words should partake of the nature of the Word of God, which is quick and powerful, and sharper than a two-edged sword (Rev. 1: 16).

HIDDEN IN THE SHADOW OF GOD'S HAND is a safe and strong position for the Christian worker. We all need more of the shadow, and we need not fear it when it is cast by his hand. Our life must be hidden with Christ in God, if we shall come forth largely to influence men. Do not be afraid of the shadow, Christian worker.

THE POLISHED SHAFT is one which is free from rust. Nothing removes rust like friction, whether by the file or sand-paper. We have often to submit to the chafe of tiny irritants in order to keep us polished.

IN HIS QUIVER HATH HE HID ME. Always ready for use, within reach of God's hand, waiting to be adjusted to the bowstring, and launched through the air to some joint in the harness; such should be our attitude. But again it is impressed upon us that we must be hidden through long periods of cessation from active use, content with the darkness of the quiver until the moment of our mission has arrived. Then forward, with the might of God's hand thrilling through our souls.

The Lord God hath given me the tongue of them that are taught. Isa. 50: 4 (R.V.).

THIS is a beautiful image. Morning by morning the Lord God draws near his chosen servant and awakens him, calling him by name, giving him some sweet message, and preparing him for the day's errands, duties and sufferings.

THE TONGUE OF THE LEARNER. The sense of the original is somewhat obscured by the use of the word "learned." It should be "disciple": one that learns through being taught. We must be disciples before we can be apostles, and be taught before we teach. We shall never do our best work for God until we accustom ourselves to receive and take his messages; and there is no such time as the early morning for the lowly posture of sitting at the Master's feet to hear his word.

TO HIM THAT IS WEARY. Notice that God's messengers are sent to the weary. There are so many of these in the world that special provision must be made for their sustaining and comfort. God needs a great company of Barnabas's sons of consolation, who having been comforted shall know how to comfort others. No kind of ministry needs such careful preparation as that exercised towards the weary and heavy-laden. To learn how to do this involves some months of lonely suffering.

WAKENED TO HEAR. In softest whispers God draws nigh, uncovering the ear, putting back the locks that might intercept his gentlest accent. Only let us see to it that we are not rebellious, or turn away back. Let not the lowliness of the work, the weary mind, the worry about tiny questions, put us off from this sacred enterprise. And let us not be dissuaded by those who would smite, and pluck out the hair. Neither pride nor fear may deter from this sacred work.

I, even I, am He that comforteth you.
Isa. 51: 12.

IT is related that in the great Indian Mutiny, when some hundreds of English ladies with their children were shut up in the Residency at Lucknow, and threatened by an immense crowd of rebels, a leaf of the Bible, stained with blood, and used as a common piece of wrapping, was brought in to them, and proved to contain these words. It reminded them of God their Maker; and bade them fear no more the fury of the oppressor, or the failure of bread, because the Lord God was at hand to neutralize the tumult and fury of their foes.

In the Lord our Maker we have the only antidote for alarm and sorrow. At this time the cross had not been erected with its precious

revelation of the love of God; and the prophet quotes two of the greatest proofs of God's might—the miracle of Creation, with its overarching heavens and deep-laid foundations of the earth; and that of the deliverance from Egypt.

Go out into nature, behold the might of God written on his glorious works, and then say to yourself, This God is my Father; and He would rather sacrifice worlds of matter, than forget or forsake his child. It were easier for Him to destroy all that He has made, and re-create it in a moment of time, than allow one of his weakest children that trusts in Him to be overwhelmed by trouble. Then go forth and stand at the cross, and remember that it was for thee. Surely He who went to so great expenditure to purchase thee from the power of hell, will not let thee perish before the malice of man. Furious men are but the foam of the breaker which your Deliverer will put aside. The sea may roar, but it cannot overwhelm.

Be ye clean, that bear the vessels of the Lord.
Isa. 52: 11.

THE chosen people are at the end of the seventy years' captivity; the time of their deliverance from Babylon has arrived. Their Almighty Deliverer, throwing back the loose sleeve of his robe, to leave his arm free, makes ready for an unusual exercise of power. There will be no need of haste as when the people fled at night from Egypt. They may not go out with haste, nor go by flight; for their Divine Leader would precede them, and his escort would be their rearguard.

This is the summons to us all who may have been in captivity to Babylon in any form. We are to arise and depart, shaking loose the bonds of our captivity. Let us follow the cloudy pillar of God's presence guiding us continually, and let us not be always looking behind, as though dreading the recurrence of past sins and mistakes. They shall not pursue those whom God has delivered; or, if they do, they shall not overtake. It is an unspeakable comfort to those who have sinned to know that the old temptations and forms of bondage are intercepted by the presence of the Eternal God, just as his cloud intercepted Pharaoh's host.

The one matter about which we must be scrupulously careful is our cleanliness. Of old, Cyrus entrusted Ezra with the holy vessels which Nebuchadnezzar had taken from the temple. Their custodians needed to be holy. We, too, have to bear the sacred trust of God's holy Name and Gospel. His day, his Book, the doctrines of evangelical truth, his honour, are among the vessels which we are to carry through the world. We, too, must be holy, cleansing ourselves of all filthiness of the flesh and spirit; coming out, and not touching the unclean thing.

The Lord hath laid on Him the iniquity of us all. Isa. 53: 6.

THE Lord did it, because He was the Lord, and He took on Himself the iniquity of us all. "Made to meet" is the marginal reading; as though many confluent streams poured their black substances into one foaming maelstrom which filled the heart of the dying Saviour. Well may the apostle Peter recapitulate his work in the matchless, almost monosyllabic sentence, "Who his own self bare our sins in his own body on the tree."

This verse begins and ends with all. We are all alike in having "gone astray." We have not all gone in the same direction, nor all to the same extent. We are not equally far from the fold. But we are all away from it. They say that if sheep can stray, they will; and there is no kind of animal more hopeless and helpless than sheep which have got out of the pen. The ox knoweth his owner, and the ass its master's crib; the dog and cat will make their way home, but the sheep wanders on in small and ever smaller companies, until it is entrapped in the rocks, or devoured by wolves, or harried to death by dogs. Such were we. Panting, driven, chased, weary; but Jesus sought us, and brought us back to the fold, and gave us a name and place among his own. We are returned unto the Shepherd and Bishop of our souls.

But ah, how can we forget the cost we have been to the Shepherd! See ye not the wounds in his hands and feet? Know ye not that his heart was lacerated and broken by the burden of our sins? "Our own way," that has been the curse of our lives, and the agony of our Shepherd. Would that it might be for ever blocked against us, and that we might be led in his own way for his Name's sake!

O Thou afflicted, tossed with tempest, and not comforted. Isa. 54: 11.

FROM his standpoint of vision on the hilltops of glory, He sees the tossings of thy craft. Every billow, every lurch, every rebuff, is discerned and felt by Him. He, too, has sailed through stormy seas, and is acquainted with grief. Not comforted by man, thou shalt be consoled by the divine Comforter. Cast out by thy lovers, thou shalt be gathered to the bosom of God. When the man born blind was cast out of the synagogue, Jesus found him; and He will find thee.

Deep down in the tossing waves, He will lay thy foundations in fair colours, and will spare no stones, however precious, in the elaboration of thy character. Sapphires, rubies, and carbuncles are very resplendent and beautiful, but they are all the children of fire. You cannot have them unless prepared to pay the cost in blood and tears. These jewels are produced of very ordinary ingredients, which have been subjected to tremendous pressure and terrific heat. When next your heart misgives you amid your fiery trials, remember that God is at work making the rubies and carbuncles of your eternal array. You will be well compensated.

There are destructive agencies around us on all hands—the smith with his coals; the waster with his scythe; the destroyer with his weapon —but they are all beneath the mighty hand of God. They cannot overstep the limits He assigns. When a man's ways please the Lord, He maketh even his enemies to be at peace with him. He restrains the wrath of his foes, and surrounds him with a munition of rocks.

The blessings of this chapter are not for the Jews only, but for all the servants of the Lord. It is expressly stated that this is their heritage (ver. 17).

Instead of the thorn shall come up the fir-tree; and instead of the briar the myrtle. Isa. 55: 13.

HERE are the substitutions of grace. It would have been much to root up the thorn, and to cut up the briar, so that the soil should be rid of weeds; but God does more. He substitutes fir-trees for thorns, and myrtles for briars; and He does this for his Name's sake, and as a sign for evermore.

HE WILL DO THIS IN YOUR CHARACTER. There are thorns and briars there; you must confess it to your cost. Now, do not be satisfied with their extermination, but seek that God should substitute their opposites; so that the site of some old evil may be commemorated by the growth of some fair grace. Where the thorn of cynicism and sarcasm grew, there the graceful and sprightly fir of forbearance; where the briar of malice and envy, there the sensitive delicate myrtle of charity. This is the triumph of grace in the believer's heart.

HE WILL DO THIS IN YOUR HOME. You have a thorn in that husband, or a briar in that child. Once you used to look for relief in death. You almost questioned whether you might not hasten yourself out of such terrible and perpetual suffering. It seemed as though you were being scourged with thorns. But God will do much better than this. He is able to transform those trying dispositions. That husband will become your evergreen fir-tree: that child your myrtle.

HE WILL DO THIS IN YOUR TRIALS. There are briars besetting every path that call for earnest care. Many beside Paul have thorns in the flesh. But His grace is sufficient to change our biggest curse into our greatest blessing. Look for this. Ask God to transform the conditions of your life which have cost you excruciating anguish, into sources of benediction.

Even them will I bring to my holy mountain.
Isa. 56: 7.
WHO are these favoured souls? Ah, it is a miracle of grace and comfort to find that they were once, like ourselves, Gentiles after the flesh, separate from Christ, alienated from the commonwealth of Israel, and strangers from the covenant of promise, dug from the same hole of the pit to which we have belonged! And if they were lifted to such holy nearness to God—if this be indeed a true picture of God's dealings with Gentiles, then let us take heart, and ask that not one of these good things should fail in our own experience.

But mark the conditions, as detailed in verse 6. We must be joined to the Lord in an indissoluble covenant; we must minister to Him in daily holy service as his priests; we must love his Name; we must diligently serve Him; we must abide in the Sabbath-keeping of the inner rest of the heart; and we must hold fast by his covenant. These are indispensable conditions to test the calibre and quality of the souls who are admitted to his inner presence. You must conform to them if you would be among those whom God brings in.

To what does God call such souls? To mountains of vision, whence they look out on eternal landscapes, and stand above the taint of this world, its smoke and dust. To joy: He makes them joyful in his house of prayer, for all true prayer has in it the seeds of everlasting joy. To that acceptance which fills the soul with calm and hallowed delight. Such things are within our reach; not too great or high for our feet to attain, because God will bring us in. He gathereth the outcasts; He collects his flock when straying, and leads them up to the dewy pastures of the mountain lawns.

I create the fruit of the lips. Isa. 57: 19.
OUR words should be like fruit. Fruit is the final cause and reason of a tree's culture; and is it not to bear fruit that we have been redeemed and cultivated with infinite solicitude? Fruit reveals the nature of its parent tree; and is there anything that more quickly shows what we are than our talk? "By thy words thou shalt be justified, and by thy words thou shalt be condemned." Fruit, when it is ripe, is sweet to the taste; but beneath these luscious qualities there is always the ultimate design of securing the propagation of the tree through its seed; so beneath the wit, or laughter, or strong common sense of our words, there should be the aim of sowing in others the words of eternal life.

How often, when we get into conversation with comparative strangers or our friends, we are at a loss to turn it into the right channels. Then, let us lift our thoughts to God, and say, Create in me now the right word, which shall refresh and help those whom I address. The answer will always be one of peace. "Peace, peace to him that is far off, and to him that is near." Let our lips ever ring with the silver notes of PEACE, Peace; PEACE, Peace.

Still more in prayer we may claim that God should create the petitions which our lips offer. You feel that you cannot pray as you would. Now, put away the straining and striving which have robbed your quiet times of their blessedness. Kneel before God in the utter stillness of your spirit, and ask Him to create supplications, intercessions, and worship, on your lips. Dare to believe that He is doing this, and be assured that the most broken utterances, which He has created and given, are sweeter to Him than the most ornate ritual.

The Lord shall guide thee continually; and thou shalt be like a watered garden. Isa. 58: 11.
THESE are only a handful of the cluster of promises with which this chapter abounds. Let us ponder them; they are full of comfort. To be

guided continually; to be satisfied when all the world around is athirst; to be fair and attractive to those who see us from day to day; to be as fountains of comfort and joy to the dry and weary land in which we are called to live—are not such blessings good to seek and keep? But there are certain conditions that must be fulfilled. Before we break the seal and appropriate the money within, we must be sure that our name is on the envelope, and that we are intended by the designation.

FIRST, we must undo. If we have injured others by word or act, or if we are still doing so, we must retrace our steps, and so far as possible undo the wrong (ver. 6).

NEXT, we must remember the Lord's words in Matt. 25, and be willing to minister deeds of helpful sympathy to the bodies and souls of men, as though we were doing them to Him (ver. 7).

LASTLY, we must ever remember to maintain within our hearts the spirit of Sabbatic calm and peace. Not fussy, nor anxious, nor fretful and impetuous; but refraining our foot from our own paths and our hand from our own devices; refusing to find our own pleasure, and do our own works. It is only when we are fully resolved to act thus, allowing God to originate all our plans, and to work in us for their accomplishment, that we enter on our heritage of blessedness, or are brought into the enjoyment of the continual guidance and blessing of which we have spoken. Then God will delight in us, and we in Him.

My Spirit . . . and my words . . . shall not depart. Isa. 59: 21.

THIS is a very precious promise, especially to God's ministers and to all who are using their voice and lips in his holy service. These may claim its fulfilment up to the hilt and it is no doubt due to some pious ancestor having claimed these words that there is so often a godly succession of ministers in one family bearing the same honoured name.

But these words are often quoted promiscuously and carelessly. Notice there are two traits of character distinctly noted and specified.

We must receive the Holy Spirit, and we must utter the words which He puts into our lips. They are one, because when the Holy Spirit fills the soul the lips are touched as with a live coal from off the altar. "They were all filled with the Holy Spirit, and began to speak."

Oh, bend your head low beneath the anointing of the great High Priest. Let Him breathe on you, and say, Receive the Holy Spirit; and then go out to be a witness for Him. Thou shalt be taught in the same hour what and how.

It is a marvellous thing that God should enter into covenant with man to keep on blessing his seed for his Word's sake. Yet He does so. He keeps his blessings for thousands of them that love Him and keep his commandments, whilst He punishes only to the third and fourth generation of them that hate Him. Long after you have gone, if only you have earnestly done God's work in the world, He will be gracious to your children and your children's children. Not only, as the poet said, "in a dead man's face" comes out the likeness to one of his ancestors, but in the faces and lives of living men we may trace the influence of their godly forefathers.

Arise, shine; for thy light is come. Isa. 60: 1.

FOR long the night had brooded on Mount Zion, and the beautiful city had sat in the dust desolate and afflicted; but at last the watchers see the sky brightening into the splendour of dawn, and the cry goes forth that the day is at hand, calling her to arise and shine.

Whenever the glory of the Lord rises upon thee, be sure to reflect it. Arise, shine! Arise, to catch as much of it as possible. Shine, that others may catch as much as possible also. Behold as in a glass the glory of the Lord, in long and loving fellowship, till you reflect it in full-orbed glory; and as you reflect it you will be changed into the same image from glory to glory, by the Lord the Spirit. Arise to the highest pinnacle of the mountain to catch the dawn, and then begin to shine with a glory that never shone on sea or shore.

Sometimes Christians seek release from their positions in business or social life, on the plea that they are so uncongenial and ungodly. Yet these are the very circumstances under which Zion is bidden to arise and shine. The darker the staircase, the more need of the candle. Because darkness covers the earth, and gross darkness the people, there is the more need for her towers to gleam with light. The Lord has given us the light of his countenance that we may flash it forward. In loneliness and solitude let us still shine for Jesus, like the stone-white steeple of a church, smitten by a searchlight in the night.

"Yet not in solitude! if Christ anear me
  Waketh Him workers for the great employ!
Oh, not in solitude!—if souls that hear me
  Catch from my joyance the surprise of joy."

The Spirit of the Lord is upon Me.   Isa. 61: 1.
WE can never disassociate those words from
that memorable scene at the Jordan, when,
after the Lord's baptism, the heavens were
opened, and the Spirit, like a dove, rested upon
Him. Forty days of fierce temptation could not
deprive Him of that holy anointing; and He
came to Galilee, stood up in the synagogue of
Nazareth, and announced the anointing He
had received.

If the Master needed it, how much more do
we! If He did not attempt to bind up the
broken-hearted, proclaim liberty to the captives, or the opening of the prison to the
bound; if He would not preach, or comfort, or
communicate joy, until that memorable
unction had been imparted—how absurd it is
for us to attempt similar works without this
anointing!

What a marvellous forecast is here of the
mission of Christ through his Church to the
world during the present age. She is sent to
take up and pass on this blessed ministry.
What a true forecast also of the needs of
mankind! It is as though the Holy Spirit
desired to reveal the salient characteristics of
the great sad world, that it would be full of the
broken-hearted, of captives, prisoners, and
mourners, needing divine assistance and
ministration. Man is so fallen and helpless that
he needs the entire Trinity: The Lord God,
the Father; Me, the Son; and The Spirit, the
Holy Ghost.

When Jesus quoted these words He stopped
at the comma in the second verse, which stood
therefore for at least nineteen hundred years
which intervene between the proclamation of
the year of mercy and of the day of vengeance.
The time for repentance is lengthening out,
since God desires not the sinner's death, but
that he should turn and live.

For Jerusalem's sake I will not rest.   Isa. 62: 1.
        (See also 6 and 7, R.V.).
WE have here the unresting Christ. Day and
night He pleads for the city that crucified Him;
and it is in answer to his supplications that she
will one day arise from her ruins. Is it not also
true that He ever lives to intercede for us,

praying when we are silent, watching when we
sleep? His prayer rises for his people night and
day. Perhaps they would not pray for themselves, if his intercessions did not incite.
Certainly his sifted Simons would drift beyond
hope, if He did not pray for them. Every sinner
has been prayed for to the end of time by
Him who said, "Father, forgive"; and every
saint, by Him who promised to pray the Father
that He would give another Comforter, the
Holy Ghost. The prayers of Jesus hover over
the world like the dove over the weltering
chaos of creation.

Next we have the unresting watchmen (ver.
6). Christ's intercession must be supplemented
by ours—whether for the restoration of the
Jews, or the upbuilding of the Church, or the
salvation of individuals. There must be oneness
of prayer between the Intercessor before the
Throne, and his remembrancers on earth; and
there will be, if the Holy Ghost is allowed to
exercise his chosen ministry of making intercession with us on behalf of the saints according to the will of God.

Lastly, there is the unresting God (ver. 7).
He, too has no rest. The rest of God is crowded
with thought and care for his own. The image
of Buddha presents the conception of an
impassive deity whose one aim is to rid himself
of all that might trouble his repose. In our
God, on the other hand, together with the
perfect serenity and satisfaction of his nature,
there are the eternal tides of desire and gracious
help.

The Spirit of the Lord caused them to rest.
           Isa. 63: 14 (R.V.).
IT is the noonday glare in Palestine. The sun's
rays like spears of flame are striking down
upon the parched sand-wastes, and all the land
burns like a furnace. Away yonder is a sequestered glen, where mosses line the margins of
streamlets and pools, and rich pasture keeps
green in the shadow of the hills. Thither the
cattle descend at noon. As the shadows creep
down the mountain-sides they follow them,
and presently the herd browses on the succu-
lent herbage or reclines beneath the shadows of
the spreading trees, while the brooks purl past
clear and cool. Similarly Isaiah says God
brought his people through the wilderness,
leading them as a horse that might not stumble,
and finally conducted them into the rest of
Canaan.

But how fit an emblem is suggested of our

Father's dealings with us. The scorching sun of temptation shines around us. The glare of publicity, the fever of money-making, the strife of tongues, torment the children of men. But for God's beloved ones there is a secret place by Him, a green and verdant nook, watered by the river of God. Over its portals these words are written: "I will give you rest."

When once we learn to trust our Father's unfailing love, we are caused to rest. Notice that forcible expression: the Spirit of the Lord caused them to rest. Here is a new thought of the omnipotence of love. It can so reveal itself that it almost compels rest. Cause us to lie down, O Lord, we pray Thee! Job speaks of Him as *giving* quietness: and then who can make trouble? Seek quietness as his gift! Lo! there is a place by Him, in the mountain-shadowed valley of his care, where disquieted souls are at peace. Seek it!

Thou meetest him that rejoiceth and worketh righteousness. Isa. 64: 5.

EVEN when visiting judgment upon the unrighteous, God remembers mercy for his people. He meets them as daily Helper and as eternal Saviour. But He always comes towards them down one pathway; and if we would encounter Him, we must tread it. It is the path of waiting expectancy (ver. 4); of rejoicing obedience; of holy remembrance. In these paths He meets us most graciously, working for us, and revealing things which from of old men have not heard, nor perceived by the ear, nor seen.

This meeting of his servants has ever been one of the ways of God. It was his daily habit to meet Adam in the dewy glades of Paradise, and talk with him. As Melchizedek of old met Abraham after a great conflict, so Christ comes upon his people after many a hard duty and severe contest with evil, and ministers heavenly refreshment. As He met Mary at the sepulchre, and Peter in the garden, and the two that walked to Emmaus, and the disciples in the grey dawn by the lake, so He meets us still.

To be thus met by God is a glad Christian experience. At morning prayer it gives strength and joy for the entire day; at eventide it is an inestimable consolation and encouragement. Often Christ will encounter us when treading some lowly path of daily duty, and or ever we are aware, we shall be called up into his chariot. Those whom He meets He will accom-pany in the way; those whom He accompanies He will succour and sustain.

It is very consoling to be told that in these ways of our dear Lord there is continuance (ver. 5). He is not spasmodic nor changeable. On and on for evermore, without the shadow of turning He will meet and bless us.

Behold, I create new heavens and a new earth. Isa. 65: 17.

THE heavens and earth that are now were not produced in their present shape in a day; but through long periods, which are chronicled in the strata of the earth, God was at work building them up. So beneath the scaffolding of history and human affairs it may be that the Creator is already at work laying the founda-tions of the new era which shall soon be un-veiled. But the creation of the new is much more difficult than of the old, because there is so much undoing to be done. Amid the crash of empire, the rock of revolutions, the blood, and tears, and anguish of the present, God is making room for and preparing the new heavens and earth in which dwelleth righteous-ness.

Just think of these exquisite words!— "Never remembered, nor come to mind!" Our bitter sorrows transmuted into such exquisite blessedness that for very joy of heart we shall have no room for remembering what seemed once intolerable. We shall not recall the nights of pain, the years of enforced inactivity, the failures, the partings, the bereavements. The betrothed will forget the long years of waiting. We turn to the Book of Revelation for further particulars, and there learn that the blessed future can only be explained in negatives. What heaven will really be is as yet hidden, that the surprise may be the greater; but it is certain that each of the elements of present distress will be eliminated. No more sorrow, pain, death, curse, tears, or separating sea. Christ will make, is making, all things new; and, best of all, He is making us new to enjoy them.

Oh, blessed condition, in which God will not remember our sins, and we shall not remember the former things, of pain, and sorrow, and death!

As one whom his mother comforteth, so will I comfort you. Isa. 66: 13.

THERE is the mother nature as well as that of the father in God. We are familiar with the thought of the divine Fatherhood; let us not forget the divine Motherhood. All the soft, gentle touches of mother's hand, unlike any other hands; all the tender pleading, yearning affection; all the utter selflessness, that never recks what it expends for the objects of its solicitude, are equally in God. But as men get mad with drink and sin, and refuse the sweet mother-love which would gather them, until worn-out and weary they come back to it wrecked and forlorn, so we have drifted from God's mother-heart, getting to ourselves pain and loss, and missing its exquisite solace. Fools that we are!

Come back to it, children! Like wayward runaway babes, at the end of the long summer's day, who, shamefaced and sorrowful, with their torn clothes and grimy faces, hardly dare present themselves to those tender eyes, and yet have no alternative, and know that they may count on the most tender reception. So come back to Him. He will receive, forgive, cleanse, comfort.

A mother's comfort! Estimate it at its full. Remember how your mother comforted you, as a little child; as a man at the death of your young wife; as a maiden when love had disappointed. How much more God! May we not then address to God's tender heart those most exquisite words:

"Neither love me for
Thine own dear pity's wiping my cheeks dry,
Since one might well forget to weep who bore
Thy comfort long, and lose thy love thereby;
But love me for love's sake, that evermore
Thou mayst love on through love's eternity."

Jeremiah

Then said I, Ah, Lord God! behold, I cannot speak: for I am a child. Jer. 1: 6.

A SENSE of helplessness is of prime importance as a preparation for ministry. Those who count themselves able to speak will never become God's mouthpiece; while those who have no words of their own will be surprised to find how forcible and perennial the stream of holy speech will become through their lips. Though you cannot, He can; and your sense of inability is the condition that the Spirit of your Father should speak through you. Learn to appropriate the Saviour's affirmation, "The words that I speak unto you I speak not of Myself, but the Father that dwelleth in Me doeth the works."

How many of the greatest men have been broken under a sense of their insufficiency! That passage in the life of John Livingstone comes back to me as I write. He had spoken at the yearly communion at Kirk o' Shotts on the Sabbath with marvellous power, and had been requested to preach on the following morning, which he promised to do on condition that his friends should spend the night in prayer. But as he awoke in the morning he was so overwhelmed with the sense of his incompetence that he went three and a half miles out of the town, to be brought back, however, and to preach so marvellously that five hundred souls were converted.

The writer can never forget the comfort that this passage gave him in early boyhood, when he anxiously feared that he never would be able to exercise the ministry of the Gospel. One morning, years ago, when in great anxiety to learn whether his was a true vocation to the Christian ministry, the Bible opened to this page, and he can bear witness that God has been faithful.

Broken cisterns that can hold no water.
Jer. 2: 13.

IN yonder fruitful valley a fountain rises, full of living, sparkling, delicious water. But, see, all the able-bodied inhabitants have left their houses, climbing to the rugged rocks above their homes, and are engaged with incredible labour in hewing them out those rocky cisterns which travellers tell us abound in Eastern lands. The heights resound with the ringing notes of hammer and chisel; for months they labour at their assiduous toils; but when all is done, the cisterns are discovered to be broken by flaws, and to provide but brackish water at the best.

Such is the picture painted from life by Jeremiah; but how truly it represents the spirit of the world! Leaving God, in whom alone man's thirsty spirit can find satisfaction and thirst-quenching, he hath set himself, with infinite labour, to hew out cisterns of gold and silver, cisterns of splendid houses and reputable characters, and lavish alms deeds, cisterns of wisdom and ancient lore. From any of these the hewer thinks he will obtain sufficient supplies to last him for his life. At the best, however, the water is brackish, wanting the sparkle of oxygenated life; hot with the heat of the day.

Jehovah may well ask whether such a spectacle can be matched anywhere else in the world. Heathen peoples are notoriously true to their ancestral faiths and practices. For vast eras the worship of ancestors has been maintained in China, and of fire by the followers of Zoroaster. There is no change in the votive offerings which the poor Hindus of all ages have laid before their impassive deities. "Hath a nation changed their gods, which yet are no gods? But my people have changed their glory for that which doth not profit."

They shall say no more, The ark of the covenant of the Lord. Jer. 3: 16.

THERE was a time in Israel when the Ark of the Covenant of the Lord was the symbol of the national hopes and deliverances. If Israel was smitten before her enemies, it was thither that the people turned for help. On one memorable occasion, they brought from Shiloh the Ark of the Covenant of the Lord of hosts, which dwelleth between the cherubim—and when it came into the camp, all Israel shouted with a great shout, so that the earth rang again; and even the Philistines were afraid. But Jeremiah says that this would never be done in the coming time. Why? Partly because the people would rely more on the spiritual presence than the material emblem, and partly because a new covenant would have been inaugurated, superseding the old.

In all true lives there is something of this. We outgrow our old experiences, and get as far beyond them as they were once beyond anything we had attained. It seems to you that you cannot look for higher heights, more heavenly experiences or deeper insight than you have had. Beware lest you limit God. Your highest water-mark shall be overleapt when the tide comes in again. Wordsworth says Nature was ever singing to the child a more exquisite song, and telling a more wonderful tale. And is not Nature's voice the voice of God? Are not the inexhaustible stores of Nature but an emblem of the still more inex-

haustible stores of Grace? Dare to press on to the things that are before. There is more love than has ever ravished your heart; more joy than has ever shed its ecstasy through your emotions; more utter consecration, closer union; more rapturous insight into the oneness of the Holy Trinity, and our inclusion in its mystic circle.

Break up your fallow ground, and sow not among thorns. Jer. 4: 3.

GOD'S sowing times are often neutralized by the hardness of the soil of our hearts. Caked over by the heavy tread of the passing years, neglected opportunities, and wordly society, even by the beautiful feet of his messengers, they need to be broken up. We sometimes speak of the breaking down of a great convention; but such an experience ought to lead to a breaking up of fallow ground. If this does not accrue from the gracious working of the Holy Spirit, it must be effected by the ploughshare of pain. "Tribulation" is derived from the Latin word for a harrow, tribulum.

In Finney's Revival Sermons there is a great discourse on this text at the beginning of the book. It was the evangelist's wont to open a mission by enumerating the ways by which his hearers' hearts could be laid open to receive the seed of the kingdom. When hearing the Gospel, it is specially necessary to guard our hearers and ourselves against all hardness of heart and contempt of God's Word and commandment.

Our Lord clearly tells us what the thorns are. He says they are the cares, riches, and pleasures of this life (Luke 8: 14). The cares of the poor are as inimical to true religion as the wealth of the rich; and the absorption of the heart in pleasure is as hurtful as either. There is no room on the soil of our nature for more than one absorbing passion. If that be for the glory of Christ, it includes all other desires and pursuits; but if our thoughts are diverted to things or persons apart from Him, there is but little energy left for a strong religious life. O God, fill our hearts with such good crops that there may be no room for thorns!

The sand for the bound of the sea, which it cannot pass. Jer. 5: 22 (R.V., marg.).

WHAT an insignificant atom is a grain of sand! But God has chosen to arrest the advance of the mighty billows by a barrier of sand-grains. Let the ocean chafe as it will, it cannot pass its defined limits. It may destroy the solid masonry of human construction, but it is foiled by a bank of soft sand.

"What cannot his power accomplish for me,
Who makes of soft sand a strong bar to the sea!"

There are many illustrations of this in the history of the Church. The pride of the persecutor has been arrested by the prayers and tears of men, women, and children, who have had no more strength in themselves than a bank of sand-grains, but have succeeded in arresting the might of their foes. The persecutions of the Roman Empire were finally renounced because they actually promoted the cause they were intended to destroy. By the weak things of this world God brings to naught the things that are reckoned mighty.

What a picture of weak submission, of suffering patience, of unresisting gentleness is the sand! What a type of God's hidden ones, whom the world knows not! Out of the mouth of babes and sucklings He ordains strength: out of weakness He makes strong: out of the passive sufferers He makes his strongest ramparts.

"The race of God's anointed priests shall never pass away;
Before his glorious face they stand, and serve Him night and day.
Though reason raves, and unbelief flows on a mighty flood,
There are, and shall be, till the end, the hidden priests of God."

Saying, Peace, peace; when there is no peace.
Jer. 6: 14 (R.V.).
WE spare ourselves, and we are willing to be spared by others. The knife must not cut to the quick; the wound must not be probed to the bottom. We are glad to attend a ministry which is not too searching, dealing with the soul rather than with the spirit; with the intellect rather than with the heart. We are quite prepared that the root and core of our trouble should not be dealt with, if only we may be made presentable to our fellow-creatures as soon as possible. The corrupt matter may still be in the wound, certain to break out again; but we are not desirous that it should be driven forth, if only we may soon regain our comeliness.

In our dealings with God let us reverse all

this, and ask that He will not spare us, or give us anything less than the best. The process may be painful and protracted, but it will be sure. The pressing of the putrid matter from the wound may distress and horrify; but it will make sure work in the end.

"Alas," says Tersteegen, "some never arrive at a thorough knowledge of their inward corruption and their hidden self-love, nor of the perfect, holy, secluded, hidden life in Christ, which is the life of the new creature. Nor do they know the power of the Spirit of Christ, working in his own members, and bringing forth in them the outward life of holiness to God. For all these things are taught to the soul by God, and would never have entered into the thoughts of men; and they have limited themselves within themselves, and enclosed themselves, so to speak, within their own ideal." Let us be warned by these words, and never heal up any wound which God would keep open, till all the evil it was intended to remove has left our system.

The temple of the Lord, the temple of the Lord, the temple of the Lord, are these. Jer. 7: 4.
WHEN Jeremiah threatened Israel with the coming of the king of Assyria, the false prophets minimized the terror of his utterances by pointing to the temple and assuring the people that there was no reason to anticipate the overthrow of their city, since it was the custodian of the holy shrine of Jehovah. "Ye have the temple in your midst, surely then you are a religious people. You cannot be as bad as this pessimistic prophet alleges, and God cannot very well dispense with you."

But men may perform the most sacred rites, and yet perpetrate the grossest crimes. The presence of a temple with all its priests and rites does not necessarily denote holiness; but often the contrary. In Roman Catholic countries, brigands will seek the blessing of heaven on their plans of murder and plunder. Our safety lies not in outward rites, but in amending our ways and doings. Not in having sprung from godly parents, nor in engagedness in holy things, nor in the practice of religious rites, will help come; but in being genuinely right with God. Real religion consists not in temple-rites, but in humility, unselfishness, and godliness. Saul of Tarsus is the type of many who are zealous for religion, but destitute of its power.

"Here on earth a temple stands,
Temple never built with hands;
There the Lord doth fill the place
With the glory of his grace.
Cleansed by Christ's atoning Blood,
Thou art this fair house of God,
Where the soul, a priest in white,
Singeth praises day and night;
Glory of the Love divine,
Filling all this heart of thine."

---

*Is there no balm in Gilead? Is there no physician
there?* Jer. 8: 22.

HOW many of God's children are discouraged!
They have mourned, confessed, and resolved;
but they do not expect to see any great alteration in themselves. They have lost hope. Now,
it is evident that as long as this spirit prevails,
there is very little prospect of improvement.
Discouragement can only bring defeat. One of
the first objects of a physician is always to
awaken hope, for otherwise he knows that his
medicines can profit but little. Now, bethink
you, what is the cause of your failure? Is it in
God? Is there not balm in Gilead? Is there not
a physician there? Why, then, is not the health
of the daughter of my people recovered?

O wounded, sorrowful soul, there is balm in
Gilead, there is a Good Physician. No hurt He
cannot heal, no bleeding He cannot staunch,
no sickness He cannot cure! Why keep lamenting so bitterly, "My bad heart, my bad heart"?
Why speak as though that temper, that pre-
disposition to sin, that habit, were to be lost
only in death? Why be uncomforted? Jesus
can heal all sicknesses, all diseases, among the
people. One touch of the King can heal the
soul of whatsoever disease it has.

Why are you not in health? It is because you
resort to quacks, and not to the divine
Physician; or because you do not bare your
pain to its roots before Him; or because you
refuse to abandon yourself wholly to his
prescriptions and treatment. Dare to search
out and know the cause of ill health; for be
sure it is on your side, not Christ's. Then let
Him treat you as He will. He will prescribe
diet, exercise, fresh air, change of scene. He
may use the knife, but He will do his work as
dexterously and painlessly as possible. "Who
healeth all thy diseases."

---

*Who is he to whom the mouth of the Lord hath
spoken, that he may declare it?* Jer. 9: 12.

A SAINTLY soul has translated these words

into music, which expresses their inner
thought:

"Lord, speak to me, that I may speak
In living echoes of thy tone:
As Thou hast sought, so let me seek
Thy erring children, lost and lone.
"O teach me, Lord, that I may teach
The precious things Thou dost impart:
And wing my words, that they may reach
The hidden depths of many a heart."

With such expressions of the disciples of the
Lord, we should couple his sublime words:
"Be not anxious how or what ye shall speak:
for it shall be given you in that hour what ye
shall speak. For it is not ye that speak, but the
Spirit of your Father that speaketh in you."
And again He said: "What I tell you in the
darkness, speak ye in the light: and what ye
hear in the ear, proclaim upon the housetops."
Often we have run before we were sent. We
have spoken our own message, and it has fallen
flat and powerless. We have elaborated our
sentences with careful art, but they have been
lighter than vanity, for want of the King's
word, in which alone there is power.

Let us amend our ways, and wait on Him
for his word, going forth to speak it with an
authority which can only be obtained when
one has the consciousness of a Thus saith the
Lord. We may have to go into the darkness of
pain and sorrow, or hide in the closet far from
the rush of the world, and the clamour of
human voices; but we shall hear Him speak,
as the prophet Elijah did at Horeb, when the
still, small voice filled the cave with its
thrilling cadence.

---

*The shepherds are become brutish, and have not
inquired of the Lord.* Jer. 10: 21 (R.V.).

THIS is a very solemn indictment; but the pity
of it is that it is true of many shepherds of
flocks in our own land. We must avoid
generalizing too widely; but, on the whole, it is
incontestable that a dwindling flock and
waning cause point to prayerlessness perhaps
on the part of the members, but almost
certainly on the part of the shepherd himself.
And it becomes us to search our hearts to see
how far our prayerlessness may not be hindering the work of God in our own church.

One of the most solemn sermons ever
addressed to ministers is that of Dr. Binney's
on this text; and he shows that the correlative
must also be true, and that where we seek the

Lord we shall prosper, our work shall become successful, and our flock increased. The old Latin motto said that to pray is to labour; and some of the best work in the world has been done by simple prayer. You may be labouring quite as effectively when you are shut within your closet doors as when going to and fro in the world in active Christian endeavour. It is remarkable that whilst Philip was able to preach Jesus, and to bring many to Him, it was needful that the best results of the Gospel could not be realized till Peter and John had come down from Jerusalem to pray for the new converts (Acts viii. 14). Let us ponder and practise the five simple rules given by our sainted brother, George Müller, for prevailing prayer: (1) Not for our own worthiness. (2) Solely through Christ's merits, on the ground of his cross and resurrection. (3) For the glory of God. (4) No sin must be allowed, since this absolutely bars blessing. (5) Be patient: glorify God by waiting on Him.

Then answered I, and said, Amen, O Lord.
Jer. 11: 5.

WHEN God recapitulated his promises in the heart of Jeremiah, even though they involved a curse on those who neutralized his words, there arose from it a deep response. He answered and said, Amen, O Lord. What a remarkable example for us all! By life and lip, by deed and word, when we can understand and when we cannot, when the words are illuminated with blue and gold, when they are as black as the old black-lettered missals, always and everywhere, let us answer, and say, Amen, O Lord. We are irresistibly reminded of our Lord's words, after He had been contemplating the doom of the cities that refused Him, and the mysterious refusal which the wise and prudent accorded to his message. He said solemnly and emphatically, "Yea, Father."

It is an awful thing to read this context, and to remark the sentence to which Jeremiah said Amen. "Cursed be the man that heareth not the words of this covenant." Is it lawful, think you, to infer that the saints will one day acquiesce in God's verdict on the disobedient and ungodly? It may be that we shall be so fully convinced of the mercy of God, which sought the salvation of the lost, and shall see so clearly all the many efforts He made for their arrest, that we shall solemnly and sadly answer and say, Amen, O Lord, to their doom.

But if these words should be read by one who is resisting and disbelieving the love of God that would fain lead him into the land that floweth with milk and honey, let him beware lest his sinful refusal to be saved, his strife against the mercy of God, will one day be so patent that his dearest friend will answer and say, Amen, O Lord.

Righteous art Thou, O Lord: . . . wherefore doth the way of the wicked prosper? Jer. 12: 1.

"I WOULD reason with Thee." Religion is often misrepresented as unreasonable. But there is nothing to warrant the charge. On the contrary, the perpetual note of the Scriptures is, "Come and let us reason together." Doubtless there are many things revealed which never could have been discovered by reason, but there is nothing which may not be apprehended and appreciated by it. Man's reason was made in the image of God's. At present, however, our reasoning faculties are probably in their earliest stage of development, and we are much as infants admitted to some scientific laboratory or library.

God demands that we should use our reason, not only on the facts of nature, but on those revealed in the Bible. He likes us to reason out things with Him. Much better this than to reason against Him. If instead of turning from Him to discuss with each other, men would only turn to Him, there would be given them either an insight into his ways, or grace to wait and trust. Job, Moses, Asaph, and Jeremiah did this; and with them all the same problem troubled them, Why do the wicked prosper?

But there is one fact which can never be questioned. We must always begin our reasoning by saying, "Righteous art Thou, O God." This is a foundation fact which underlies his throne. We cannot question it. By the very conscience which He has put within us, and by the whole trend and drift of his Providence, he has put his Righteousness beyond question. As Abraham said, the Judge of all the earth must do right. But when we grant this, we may proceed to ask how certain facts which are permitted in the world are consistent with it. He may explain: or He may say, Not now, but presently.

That they might be unto Me for a people, and for a name, and for a glory. Jer. 13: 11.

ISRAEL had the opportunity of becoming a

people, a name, and a glory; but they would not. In their declension and refusal God has turned to the Church, largely chosen from among the Gentiles, and in which we by his grace have a part. To us their privileges are offered. Let us gladly avail ourselves of them, and become unto God the people of his inheritance, in whom He may find a welcome and a home. Oh to be a name to Him, so that men may understand and revere Him the better because of what we are! Oh to be a glory to Him, so that He may account us as his choice ornament and jewel! Oh to be as intimately united to Him as the girdle worn on the prophet's loins!

Our hearts misgive us as we write or read. How can such things be? Behold, like that same girdle we have become marred and profitless. Yet, there is one phrase here which is radiant with hope: "As the girdle cleaveth . . . so have I caused to cleave." "Caused to cleave." We are not able to cleave; we have so often tried to, and failed; but now we come in humble eagerness before Him, and say, "Cause us to cleave, O God; cause us to walk in thy ways; cause us to do thy will; cause us to be a people, a name, and a glory unto Thyself."

"O man," Tersteegen said, "whoever you are, stand still for a moment, and think earnestly of the high dignity for which you were created and sent into the world by God. You were not made for time and for passing things, but for God and eternity, and to have your heart filled with God and with the things eternal. Yield yourself up fearlessly to his mighty working, and be still, and welcome Him in his gracious operation in the heart."

Why shouldest Thou be as a man astonied as a mighty man that cannot save? Jer. 14: 9.

A STRONG man may be rendered powerless by a reel of cotton being wound around him. Each thread so brittle, yet all together is irresistible. So a large number of inconsistencies and insincerities may make God powerless to help you, or to work mightily through you to the salvation of others. He may be in the midst of you, and you may be called by his name; great issues for his kingdom and glory may seem at stake; mighty possibilities within your reach; and yet He is as a mighty man that cannot save.

There is might enough in God to save the weakest and sinfullest of his children; and you are unsaved because of the limitations you have placed upon Him. First, you are not absolutely willing to be delivered from your sins. Secondly, you do not entirely believe in his power and will. Thirdly, you have not definitely handed the whole matter over to Him, and believed that He has accepted the charge.

Or—and this is perhaps the deepest reason of all—you have formed your own ideas of divine truth, and of the possible Christian life. And having formed your own conception of the true ideal of Christianity, you have thenceforth lived within the limitations of your ideal, which is bounded by human wisdom and human thought. And so you never come to a thorough knowledge of the indwelling of Christ, or what He is prepared to do for you; or, catching a glimpse of it from afar, you are not sufficiently delivered from the reasonings and workings of your mind to give Him that opportunity for which He waits and yearns. The Lord Jesus could do infinitely more in us, and through us, if we did not hinder. Be sure that the Kingdom of God is within; but you must let it possess you.

If thou return, then will I bring thee again, that thou mayest stand before Me.
Jer. 15: 19 (R.V.).

WHAT a promise for backsliders is this! Here is a soul that had gone away from God's presence, and had ceased to be as his mouth. How long it had been in this castaway condition we need not inquire. It is enough to know that it had dipped beneath the horizon, and been permitted to know the bitter anguish of seeing others do its chosen work. Have you known this? Then these words were written for you; eat them, and let them be unto you the joy and rejoicing of your heart.

Will you return to God? Do you want it to be as in the old time? Tell Him so, and He will bring you again. It will not take Him a second's space to restore you to where you were wont to stand. Dare to believe that you are there again, forgiven, cleansed, sanctified. Live there. Go no more out for ever.

Will you leave what is vile, unworthy, and unholy, casting it away as so much dross, and take forth only the gold, silver, and precious stones, of a holy character? then God will make you his mouth, through which He will speak to saint and sinner. Is not this worth whatever it may cost you? Remember how Peter sinned; but within fifty days he was speaking as the mouth of the Holy Ghost to thousands.

It was thus, also, that Mark was brought again, who forsook the apostle, in his first missionary journey; but he was honoured, as the mouth of the Holy Spirit, to write the Gospel that bears his name.

> "I know not what I am, but only know
> I have had glimpses tongue may never
> speak:
> No more I balance human joy or woe,
> But think of my transgressions, and
> am meek.
> Saviour! forgive the child who sinnèd so—
> His proud heart yields—the tears are on
> his cheek."

O Lord, my strength, and my stronghold, and my refuge in the day of affliction.   Jer. 16: 19 (R.V.).
ONE of the puritans was accustomed to describe prayer as the flight of the lonely man to the only God. There is such prayer here. This man is very lonely. He is like a speckled bird, set on by all the birds of the flock. He looks right and left, but there is no man to care for his soul; then he addresses himself to God in these touching words.

MY STRENGTH. The psalmist spoke of God as the strength of his life. The apostle of love said that little children could overcome the world, because He that was in them was greater and stronger than he that was in the world. "God is the strength of my life; of whom shall I be afraid?"

MY STRONGHOLD. A stronghold is what holds strongly. A keep is that which keeps. We keep God's deposit, which is his Gospel: God keeps our deposit, which is ourselves. And none, man nor devil, can snatch us away.

MY REFUGE IN THE DAY OF AFFLICTION. The night darkening the sky drives the chicks to the hen's wings; so affliction drives us to God. "In the shadow of thy wings will I make my refuge, until these calamities be overpast."

Do you wish to know Him thus? See that you do not burden yourself by your endeavours. God is a Spirit, and within your spirit. You need not ascend into heaven, nor descend into the deep. You need not weary yourself with the reasonings and reflections and questionings of your mind or heart. By these means you will wander further from Him and his knowledge. Be still and know. Enter into the still and peaceful land of inward spiritual fellowship. Commune with your own heart. Be a child

before Him, innocent, unaffected, unrestrained.

Bear no burden on the Sabbath-day, nor bring it in by the gates of Jerusalem.   Jer. 17: 21.
IN the R.V. marg., "take heed to yourselves" is rendered "take heed for your life's sake," as if the matter dealt with in this paragraph closely pertained to the conditions of the best life. And is it not so? Is it not a matter of vital importance that we should keep the eternal Sabbath in our hearts, and suffer no burden to be brought through the gates of the soul? Even if we consider this matter from the lowest aspect, how certain it is that absence of worry and fret promotes length of days! But in the deepest sense we must, like Jeremiah, set a guard at the city portals, and insist that no anxiety should cross our threshold. Do you ask what sentry is strong enough to arrest the intrusion of burden-bearing thoughts? I reply, let the peace of God keep your mind and heart. Meet every anxiety with the one short, strong, sweet answer—God; God will see to it; God will provide.

In verse 24 we are bidden diligently to hearken to God in this matter. It must therefore be within our power. The will can direct the thoughts to what object it chooses. Do not look down, but up; not backward or forward, but God-ward. It is right to think calmly and deliberately about the issues of things; but the allowance of foreboding anxiety is a positive sin against the love of God.

The result is beautiful. Obey God in this, and the King Himself shall enter the gates of your city (ver. 25). Your life will be filled with burnt-offerings and frankincense and thanksgiving (ver. 26). And from the perfect balance and rest of your nature you will be able to look out with equanimity on the storm and change around. We which have believed do enter into the Sabbatism which remaineth.

He made it again.   Jer. 18: 4.
GOD wants to make the very best He can of each of his children. He puts us on his wheel, and subjects us to the discipline which He deems most likely to secure our greatest blessedness and usefulness. But, alas! how often He finds a marred vessel left on his hands when he desired and sought perfect beauty and strength! This is through no failure on his part; but because some bubble of vanity or grit of self-will has hindered Him.

Alas, how many have marred his work! What might we not have been, if only we had perfectly yielded to Him! It is enough to break our hearts to recall all the wasted and misspent years, when He would, but we would not.

When this has been the case, He does not cast us utterly away; but puts us afresh upon the wheel, and "makes us again." If He cannot do what He desired at the first, He will still make the best of us; and the weakness of God is stronger than men. Let God take your life which has hitherto proved a failure; He will make of what remains of it more than men could make with all earthly advantages on their side, and with nothing to hinder its regular development.

Yield yourself afresh to God. Confess that you have marred his work. Humbly ask that He should make you again, as He made again Jacob and Peter and John and Mark. Only be careful in all time to come—first, to give God sufficient opportunity by waiting before Him; and secondly, to be very prompt to obey all that He may impress upon you as being his holy will. There is simply no limit to the progress and development of the soul which is able to meet God with a never-faltering "Yes." Let the lifelike clay in the potter's hands be plastic to its Maker's touch!

A potter's vessel, that cannot be made whole again. Jer. 19: 11.

THESE words were spoken first of the inevitable judgments which were to befall Jerusalem. She who had been a chosen vessel was now to be broken beyond repair.

An earthen vessel is a true emblem of human life, so frail, so brittle. But there is something frailer yet in our resolutions and efforts after holiness. And when once these have failed us, we can never be again what we were. Always the crack, the rivets, the mark of the join.

In Gideon's days there was a light within the earthen vessels; and when these were broken it shone forth. There is, therefore, a breaking of the vessel which is salutary and desirable. And it is of this that Miss Taylor sings:

"Oh to be nothing, nothing!
   Only to lie at his feet,
A broken and emptied vessel,
   For the Master's use made meet."

It reminds me of a piece of pottery I saw in the mountain burn, which was in the water and the water in it. If there be in any one of us a proud and evil disposition, a masterful self-will, which frets for its own way and makes itself strong against God, then indeed we may ask to be so broken as never to be whole again. "Take me—break me—make me," is a very wholesome prayer for us all.

The apostle speaks of the heavenly treasure in the earthen vessel. How wonderful it is that God should put so much of his spiritual ointment into such common and ordinary receptacles! No one detects what is in the saints till they are broken by sickness, pain, trouble; then the house is filled with the odour of the ointment.

I am weary with forbearing and cannot contain. Jer. 20: 9 (R.V.).

THE prophet had looked for marvellous results from his preaching. So great was his consciousness that God's word was on his lips, and his power with him, that he expected by his ministry to arrest the decay of his people. And when, instead of the success he sought, he found himself in the stocks, he was tempted to feel that God had excited hopes which were not destined to be realized. He did not give sufficient weight to man's awful power of resisting and neutralizing God's best designs. We say this reverently, and use human methods of speech.

Yet, on the other hand, as he reviewed the steps by which he had come to act and speak as he did, he felt that he could not have done differently. And though he were suddenly to repress himself, the divine inward impulse would sweep away all his constraints, and assert itself in irresistible might. It was of no use placing the bushel over the light, for the light would burn the bushel; useless to shut in the fire, for the fire would burn through every obstacle to its flames.

What a glorious state of heart to be in! We have sometimes been weary in God's service; but oh, it would be a greater weariness if we were dismissed from it. To speak is an awful responsibility and weight; but not to speak would be impossible. Have you the burning heart? Do you know what it is to feel unable to contain yourself, since the love of Jesus constrains? If not, daily pray that God may light a burning fire in your bones.

"O God! make free
This barren, shackled earth, so deadly
   cold;

Breathe gently forth thy spring, till
    winter flees
In rude amazement!"

Peradventure the Lord will deal with us according to all his wondrous works. Jer. 21: 2 (R.V.).
IT was during the last extremity of the siege that Zedekiah sent this message to Jeremiah. His people and he had postponed their compliance with the warnings and invitations of God's love till the last possible hour, and now they were more eager for immunity from the consequences of their sins than to repent and return to God. The answer was immediate—that matters must now be allowed to take their course. It was, however, added that even now all who dared to act in faith and go out to the besiegers would save their lives.

What a test of faith was here! It seemed as though it were worth while to risk everything and stay in the city rather than venture out to those terrible hosts that were gathered around. But there was no alternative. To stay in the city was certain death; to go forth into what seemed certain death would secure life. Men may reach a certain point in wrongdoing when the disasters their sins have courted are inevitable. As they have sown, they must reap. They have set the rocks rolling, and they must see the devastation wrought on their homes. Yet, even then, there is a way of escape.

Still God pleads with men, as in the 8th verse: "Thus saith the Lord, Behold I set before you the way of life and the way of death. He that abideth in this city shall die by the sword; he that goeth out and falleth away to the Chaldeans shall live." This surely is the exact counterpart of the words which our Lord is recorded as having spoken on four different occasions: "He that loveth his life shall lose it; and he that loseth his life for my sake, the same shall save it." There is a strange reversal of human imaginations at the cross of Christ!

Woe unto him that buildeth his house by unrighteousness. Jer. 22: 13.
THIS denunciation was probably against the king himself. But it has a much fuller reference. He was the godless son of a godly father, whose character is sketched in three particulars. He judged the cause of the poor and needy; it was well with him; it was to know God. But the son had reversed all this. He built his palace of unrighteousness, his

chambers of covetousness; but its width of space could not obliterate the memory of the forced and unpaid labour by which it had been reared. And God would plead and avenge the cause of those oppressed labourers.

When we see the splendid piles of business buildings reared by monopolists who thrive by making existence impossible to smaller but industrious tradesmen; when we hear of the vast fortunes made out of strong drink; or the manipulation of the market by millionaires, that make honest business impossible—we recur to these terrible words. God still arises to avenge the cause of the poor and needy. There is a God who judges in the earth.

In our vast cities it is not easy to trace the incidence of the divine displeasure on a family of wrongdoers. Those who reside in our villages and country towns, and have long memories, could tell of many corroborations in their own knowledge. But there is another side to this. God's children can afford to be generous and openhanded to their employees, because their Father is rich. "He is able to make all grace abound towards us . . . that we may abound." Let us maintain his honour, and his family name, by fair dealing. They who know God, judge the cause of the poor and needy; and for those who do this it is well (ver. 16).

If they had stood in my council. . . .
Jer. 23: 22 (R.V.).
HERE is the cause of so much failure in Christian work—God's servants do not stand in God's council. The previous words explain what is meant by not standing in God's council: "I sent not these prophets, yet they ran; I spake not unto them, yet they prophesied." Alas! these words write our own sentence. Too often we run without being sent, and prophesy because the hour has struck, rather than because the message of God has been given! We do not stand in God's council.

"But if they had stood." . . . We gather, therefore, that the stream of prophetic teaching was not limited to Jeremiah alone. There was no necessary exclusiveness in the divine arrangements. He was chosen, and used as God's agent and medium, because he stood in his council. And the others might have had the same privilege if they had conformed to the same conditions.

Let us claim the positive assurance of this promise. We see where we have fallen short of

God's ideal but we can retrace our steps; we can renounce our fussy activities; refrain from the desire to be always to the front; and wait more absolutely on God for his thoughts, and words, and messages. A Christian worker once complained to George Müller that he had not time enough for the study of the Word and prayer; and the veteran saint asked in reply, whether an hour's less work, with the soul dwelling in the full light of God, and therefore actuated by his impulses, would not be more prosperous and effective than five hours spent under the perpetual fever of our own will and way. Be right with God, and the people shall be caused to hear, and shall be turned.

And they shall be my people, and I will be their God. Jer. 24: 7.

AN heart to know! We know God with our heart, the seat of our moral life, and specially of our affections. As the apostle puts it, it is needful that the eyes of our heart should be opened that we should know. He that loveth not, knoweth not God; for God is love. He that loveth knoweth God, and is known of Him. If there is anything unloving in your nature, it will blur your knowledge of God, as condensed breath on a window-pane will shut out the fairest landscape. But the heart which knows God is his dear gift. Be willing to have it; ask for it, and it shall be yours.

The special aspect in which we are led to know God is as Jehovah—that He is the I AM, the unchanging, ever-loving one; the God who comes down to deliver and save. This is the aspect that we need most. When overcome with failure and sin; when thoroughly discouraged with abortive efforts; when overtaken by some sudden gust of temptation—we need to know that our sin cannot surprise God, or staunch his love, or wear out his patience.

But what a word is this, that we shall be his people and He our God! Oh, infinite God, how canst Thou take such as we are—nay, I will not speak of others, but of myself—such as I am, to be thy own peculiar treasure! I dare not look back on my past, or in upon my heart, but only out and away to thy great mercy; for I am most weak and unworthy. But I will for ever adore Thee for choosing me—not because of aught in myself, but for thy love and mercy's sake. Moreover, Thou hast given me Thyself. What can I want beside Thee? Thou art the strength of my heart, and my portion for ever.

Should ye be utterly unpunished?
Jer. 25: 29 (R.V.).

THIS is a terrible chapter, in which the disasters that were to befall all the surrounding nations are described as a potion presented to each for drinking. If any refuse, the answer is to be given in the words before us, which suggest those of Peter: "The time is come that judgment must begin at the house of God; and if it first begin at us, what shall the end be of them that obey not the Gospel of God?" (1 Peter 4: 17).

God always begins with his own people, because their sins traduce his character and bring it into contempt; and because sinners might otherwise establish a just charge of favouritism against Him. Besides, He loves them so dearly that He is eager to see them rid, as soon as may be, from the blight and parasitism of evil. It is a terrible thing to be an inconsistent child of God; for just in proportion to his love for you will God put forth the most strenuous and unremitting efforts to bring you back to Himself. This thought may arrest you, when you are being led into sinful ways. You will have to come out of them, sooner or later, if you are truly God's child. But the anguish of your extrication will be in proportion to the sinful delight of your self-indulgence.

But if the righteous be scarcely saved, where shall the ungodly and the sinner appear? Even though Babylon had done God service, as the instrument of his chastisement to his own people; yet, because in performing thus she had grossly sinned, she must drink the cup of his wrath. O disobedient and ungodly soul, thou mayest serve God's purpose, yet He will not let thee be unpunished. Your condemnation now for a long time lingereth not.

The Lord sent me to prophesy. . . . Therefore amend your ways and your doings.
Jer. 26: 12, 13.

NATURALLY, Jeremiah was constituted with a very nervous and sensitive disposition. He compares himself to a child that cannot speak; he laments that he had been born into such troublous times. But at the moment of his call it was distinctly promised that he should be made from that day "a defenced city, an iron pillar, and brazen walls, . . . against the kings, princes, priests, and people of the land." Though they should fight against him, they should not prevail (Jer. 1: 18, 19).

What an admirable comment on that promise is presented by this chapter! Here is this timid man standing alone for God against this surging multitude, in which priest and people are merged. Though his life is in the balance, and it might seem necessary to purchase it by absolute silence, he refuses to hold his peace; he insists that God has sent him, and calls on the maddened crowd to amend their ways and return unto Jehovah. Had John the Baptist spoken thus, or John Knox, we had not been surprised. But for this sensitive, retiring man to speak thus is due to the transforming power of the grace of God.

There is hope here for those who are naturally reticent and backward, reserved and timid. Take your nature to God, and ask Him to encrust it with iron and brass. Above all, seek a vivid realization that God is with you. Then open your mouth and speak. Greater is He that is in and with you, than he that is in the world. To have a conviction that God has sent; to know and feel his inspiration thrilling the soul—is utterly essential to strength of purpose and action. When we know that the living Father hath sent us, and is with us, we can stand as a brazen wall.

The nation . . . which will not serve the king of Babylon, will I punish. Jer. 27: 8.

IT may be that, like the people of Israel, you have grossly sinned and violated the bonds of holy fellowship and relationship with God. The result of this not improbably has been some form of chastisement and disaster, which lies heavily on your life. This is what the invasion of the king of Babylon was to Israel and the surrounding nations. Now learn from these striking words that your best attitude is one of humble and reverent submission. Put your neck under the yoke of the king of Babylon. When Samuel told Eli the inevitable results of his negligence to correct and restrain his son, the old man said, "It is the Lord; let Him do what seemeth Him good." Through the infliction of his troubles he discerned the right-ordering and permissive providence of God.

So let it be with you. Accept the deserved chastisement, remembering that "whom the Lord loveth He chasteneth, and scourgeth every son whom He receiveth." Humble yourself under the mighty hand of God. Look beyond the pride and cruelty of man to the permissive providence of your heavenly Father. Set yourself to learn and take well to heart the lessons of the present discipline. It is for a limited period. Do you feel that men meanwhile are going beyond their rights? Avenge not yourself; give place before their wrath; leave the matter with God; vengeance is his—He will recompense.

"To confess ignorance," says a great preacher, "to confess wrong, to admit incapacity, to decline a reputation to which we have no right—these things, and others of the same kind, are often hard and painful, but they are always of the greatest possible value in bracing the character."

Amen: the Lord do so: the Lord perform thy words. . . . Nevertheless. Jer. 28: 6, 7.

THE prophecy of Hananiah of the speedy return of the exiles and the break-up of the power of the king of Babylon was evidently dictated by the desire to win popularity with the people. He spoke in the name of Jehovah, and may even have supposed that his message was divinely given; but his soul was filled with human voices and reasonings, which made him unable to distinguish the still small voice of inspiration. Jeremiah was quite as anxious as he was that his country should be spared further suffering. He uttered a fervent Amen to Hananiah's predictions. Nothing could have given him deeper pleasure than their realization; but standing as he did in the counsels of God, he knew it could not be.

So is it still. Men who follow simply their own thoughts, or are deeply dyed with the spirit of society around, are apt to prophesy smooth things to such as live selfish and worldly lives. "There is no such place as the outer darkness; no such experience as the second death." So they speak. But we know it cannot be. Earnestly as we might wish for it, and say Amen, we know, nevertheless, that it cannot be immaterial how men live, and that wickedness must bring infinite anguish and pain. How terrible will their position be at last, who cried Peace, Peace, when there was none, and encouraged rebellion against the Lord.

There are false prophets still who encourage men in their evil ways, as they paint roseate views of the future, and encourage them to believe that though they sin, the future will not be so dark as they have been led to fear. Hard as it will be for all who perish out of Christ, for these there will be an additional anguish. See Matt. 5: 19.

*Seek the peace of the city, whither I have caused
you to be carried away captives.*   Jer. 29:7.
FOR seventy years the captives must make
themselves at home and happy in Babylon. It
was of no use to scheme and plot a speedier
return. They must work out the predicted
seventy years; and in the meanwhile let them
seek the peace of the great heathen city to
which they had been borne, and pray, not
only for Jerusalem, but for it.

How many who read these lines are captives
in positions against their will and choice.
Servants and governesses in worldly homes;
apprentices and clerks amid uncongenial
associates; travellers in distant towns and
commercial hotels; people in all kinds of
positions in which they would not choose to be.

The natural tendency of all such is to fret,
and begin endeavouring to secure their emancipation and removal. "Let me get away from
this as soon as possible." Or, at least, if
unable to get free, they take as little interest as
possible in their immediate associates, making
themselves cold, and stiff, and inaccessible.
This is not God's way. Wherever you find
yourself, seek the peace and comfort of those
about you. Jesus bade us salute those who do
not salute us, and lift our voices in intercessory
prayer for our oppressors and persecutors.

God had a special purpose in allowing the
captivity of his people into Babylon. It was to
scatter synagogues and the Old Testament, in
preparation for the Gospel. The transportation
of Stundists to Siberia will affect the religious
life of that great tract for all the future. You
are carried into captivity to bring the Gospel to
many who would otherwise never hear of it.
Wherever God shall open the door, leave
behind the bright and genial impression of a
holy, loving personality.

But I will not make a full end of thee.
Jer. 30:11 (R.V.).
THERE is a great difference between the
punishment of the ungodly and the chastisement of God's children. In the former case
there is destruction. The sirocco passes over
the grass, and there is nought left but burnt
and withered stubble. In the latter case there
will be restoration and an aftermath.

Are you just now passing through a season
of chastisement and pain? Take to heart these
tender words: God will not make a full end of
you. It may seem as though nothing will be
left: the furnace is so hot; the stock is cut

down so near to the ground. But God knows
just how much you can bear, and will stay his
hand. "I will not make a full end of thee."

He will correct us with judgment. There is
need for Him to correct us; so much requires
pruning away, and refining. But if He were not
to exercise great judgment, the soul would fail
before Him. This is why we are told that the
Father is the Husbandman. To no other hand
could He entrust this delicate and sacred work:
and while his eye and hand are full of eagerness
to accomplish his purpose, they always move
at the dictate of his judgment. His hand is
always on our pulse.

Chastening also anticipates a blessed
restoration. This chapter has many tender
gleams of hope in it. "I will restore health unto
thee, and I will heal thee of thy wounds, saith
the Lord." "I will turn again the captivity of
Jacob's tents, and have compassion on his
dwelling places." Look forward, poor suffering
one! Beyond the dark clouds light is shining on
the hills. When the discipline is over the Lord
will take you to his care, wash your stripes,
restore comforts to you, and give harvests of
joy.

I have loved thee with an everlasting love.
Jer. 31:3.
WE who by faith are the children of Abraham
may claim and muse upon these sweet and
tender words.

God's love to us is not of to-day or yesterday. It did not originate in any movement of
our heart towards Himself, or even on that day
of days when Jesus died. You must go back
beyond your birth, beyond Calvary and
Bethlehem, beyond the fall of man and the
Garden of Eden, and as you stand looking
out into the immensity of eternity, dare to
believe that you were loved and chosen in
Christ, the object of God's most tender
solicitude and pity.

Does the thought overpower you? Notice the
divine asseveration. Yea, there can be no
doubt about it. Beyond this divine asseveration it is impossible for us to go. By word and
oath God, who cannot lie, has given us strong
assurance that it is even so.

But now see what comes out of this long,
long love. God must have known the worst
about us before He set his love on us; then He
cannot be surprised as, in the work of education, He comes across evils that horrify and
dismay us. He knew all this, and worse. Only

let that love have its way. It is a universal and
invincible solvent. It will yet rid you bit by bit
of these hard and evil elements. The very rocks
shall flow down at his presence.

The R.V. marginal reading gives a further
thought. The fountains of God's love rise in
eternity, and therefore cannot be exhausted by
the demands of time. He will continue his
loving-kindness. Resisted, disappointed, disregarded, his compassions will not fail until
they have overcome and expelled our selfishness, and filled us with the love of God.

I bought the field. Jer. 32: 9.

WHAT could better manifest the heroic
audacity of faith? The Chaldeans infested the
land, and Jeremiah knew by the word of the
Lord that they were destined to hold both it
and the city. And yet at the divine command
he bought a piece of land which was in
possession of the foe, with as much formality
as though he were at once to enter upon its
possession.

He obeyed the divine command, and then
poured out his soul in prayer; nourishing his
faith by the contemplation of the might of
God in creation, for which nothing was too
hard. Surely if God could make the heavens
and the earth by his great power and by his
stretched-out arm, He could easily bring it to
pass that the Chaldeans should recede from the
land, Israel again inhabit it, and the purchase
and tenure of property be unhindered. Faith
made the unseen visible, and the distant near;
and enabled the prophet to take them into his
calculations, and regulate his action in view of
them. Herein the man of faith differs from
others. They base their calculations and actions
upon certain facts and considerations which
are within view of their senses; while he takes
into his estimate a number of other facts and
considerations of which they have no knowledge, and which can only be recognized
through the revelation of God's Spirit.

As that land was purchased, though still in
the enemy's possession—so Israel is God's
possession, though under the bondage of
unbelief; so the bodies of God's saints are his
purchased possession, though now under the
reign of corruption; so does this world belong
to Christ. O man of faith, count on these
things as facts.

Call unto Me, and I will answer thee. Jer. 33: 3.
WE must learn the sacred art of prayer. God
says, "Call unto Me." He likes us to address
Him in prayer. We may surely believe that He
will do the best, but this may degenerate into a
subtle excuse for lethargy; and therefore we
must be stirred by the invitation to call upon
Him. There is no assurance that He will show
us these great and difficult things, unless we
obey the injunction of our text to call on Him.
But be sure and wait before Him until He
teaches you what to pray for. The prayer which
is born of God rises to God from whom it
came with the certainty of an answer.

GOD SEEKS INTERCESSORS. He longs to dispense larger blessings. He longs to reveal his
power and glory as God, his saving grace, his
comfort and peace. But He is limited by the
smallness and fewness of our prayers. He
cannot do what He would for the Church in
the world, because of our unbelief. He cries to
us, Call unto Me, call unto me. Little prayer,
little blessing; more prayer, more blessing;
much prayer, much blessing.

But what a promise is here! We long to see
great things done for God in our churches and
mission halls, in the hearts and lives of our
friends. We long to see the difficult things
unknotted, so that the crooked may be made
straight, and the rough smooth. But all these
things shall be. The impossibilities of your life
are possible to God. The mysteries of your life
can yield their secrets at the summons of God.
The iron gates shall open, the sea divide, the
sepulchres yield their dead. Only get right with
God; only let God have unhindered way
through your life; only dare to believe that
you have already obtained your petition, and
go forward in faith.

*The words of the covenant which they made
before me.* Jer. 34: 18.
THESE are suggested, borrowed from an old
saint's memoirs, as suitable words for a
covenant before God. My Jesus—I own myself
to be thine, my only Saviour and Bridegroom, Christ Jesus. I am thine, wholly and
eternally. I renounce from my heart all right
and authority that Satan unrighteously gave
me over myself, from this day henceforward.

From this sacred hour, remembering how
Thou through thy precious blood didst purchase me for Thyself agonizing even unto
death, and praying till thy blood fell as sweat
to the ground, I desire that I may be thy
treasure and thy bride.

From now and onward, I offer to Thee my

heart and my love, my intellect and my thoughts, my choice and my purpose, my spirit, soul, and body, to be absolutely at thy disposal.

Let thy will henceforth be done in me. Command, rule, and reign in me. I yield myself up without reserve; and I desire, with thy help and power, rather to give up the last drop of this my blood, than knowingly and willingly, in my heart or life, to be untrue and disobedient to Thee. Behold, Thou hast me wholly and completely, sweet Friend of my soul. Thy Spirit be my keeper; thy death my assurance of salvation; thy life my inspiration.

I desire to hold my friendships, my possessions, my gifts and talents at thy disposal, accounting them thy gift to help me fulfil my life-course with better success. Accept me and them, and show how best all may be used in Thee and for Thee. Enable me by thy Holy Spirit to be true to this holy covenant while life shall last; and may I be presented at last, faultless, in thy presence, with exceeding joy.

Jonadab, the son of Rechab, shall not want a man to stand before Me for ever. Jer. 35: 19.
THE point here is the contrast between the strict obedience of the Rechabites to the directions of their ancestors, and the disobedience of Israel to Jehovah. How often is this contrast repeated still! We find men so eager and devoted to the customs and traditions of their families, and so regardless of the yet higher claims of God. It is very wonderful! We should have thought that the temper of mind which bound men to their family traditions would have secured their allegiance to the Almighty. But it is not so, as daily experience proves.

Let us also notice the obvious inference from this chapter. If, because of their obedience to the regulations of Jonadab, the Rechabites should never want a man to stand before God, how much more will obedience to the promptings of God's Spirit secure, through his mercy, a perpetual standing before his face; not only of ourselves, but of our children. Christian parents, you have a perfect right to go to God with this fair deduction from his own words, and say: Give us grace to obey thy commandments, and keep all thy precepts; and do according to all that Thou commandest; and then grant to us to stand before Thee for evermore in thy presence-chamber; and not us only, but our children and children's children.

Let them be a godly seed on earth, ever maintaining sweet recollections of our character and life; and let us be a united family in the presence of thy glory with exceeding joy. How blessed that man is who, like Elijah, stands before God!

"Jesus protects: my fears, be gone!
What can the Rock of Ages move?
Safe in thy arms I lay me down.
Thy everlasting arms of love."

The king cut it with the penknife, and cast it into the fire. Jer. 36: 23 (R.V.).
IT was an audacious and foolish act. Only a fool or a madman could have trifled thus. He did not relish the prophet's words, and so he cut them to pieces; but though he destroyed them, he could not in this way arrest the penalties which they foretold. Indeed, he increased them: "There were added besides unto them many like words." The criminal may tear up the warrant for his arrest; but it will not help his case. The captain may destroy the map which indicates the rocks in his course; but that will not rob them of the cruel fangs with which they will pierce the timbers of his ship. Men may deride and destroy the Bible; but this will not empty the future of hell, or hell of its bitter remorse.

We are all tempted to use the penknife to God's Book. There are passages in it which we do not like; those that cross our favourite notions, our cherished sins. Practically, we eliminate them. We never read them, or we explain them away, or profess to doubt their inspiration. We have no right to set certain passages of Scripture aside because they conflict with our notions of truth or system of theology. The scientific man will not adopt a law while one fact refuses to be included in it. The commercial man will not close his books while a shilling is unaccounted for. Blessed as the habit is of listening for God's voice within, we must never forget the absolute necessity of its corroboration from the words of Scripture.

It is wise, therefore, to read the Scriptures with an open and unbiassed mind, not bringing our preconceptions, like penknives, to cut out what we do not agree with, but meekly inquiring what it may please the Lord our God to speak.

They gave him daily a loaf of bread out of the bakers' street. Jer. 37: 21 (R.V.).
THIS was God's way of caring for his child.

His life was secured to him from the hatred of his foes, and his daily bread, as long as there was any to be had. If you do God's work, you may freely count on Him. He will not fail. In the most unlikely ways your bread shall be given you, and your water shall be sure.

But it may be objected that it is not always so, and that many of God's children are at this very hour suffering the need of many things which are absolutely necessary. But, first, we should have to decide what is really necessary. We might all be deprived of many of the comforts and luxuries of life without detriment. Indeed, it might be better for all of us to undergo something of the weaning and detaching process. But Matt. 6: 32, 33 is always true.

And, moreover, we should have to inquire whether faith had been exercised to seek and obtain their contents. We have God's promises; but we too often fail to plead them. We know that we can only receive the benefits of Christ's Redemption by faith; but we do not see that the same faith is requisite to bring into our hands those other boons which are included in God's guarantees to his children. You have not, child of God, either because you ask for things that would minister simply to appetite and sense; or because you do not exercise the child's privilege of prayer. Perhaps your present privation is intended to teach you the blessedness of prayer. Ask and receive, that your joy may be full.

"Can it be true, the grace He is declaring?
　　Oh, let us trust Him, for his words
　　　　are fair!
Man, what is this, and why art thou
　　despairing?
　　God shall forgive thee all but thy
　　　　despair."

*Obey. . . . So it shall be well with thee, and thy
soul shall live.* Jer. 38: 20 (R.V.).
OF many Christians it can hardly be said that their souls live; they exist, but do not thrive. The food of the soul is in part the Word of God; but in part it is obedience. As we obey we are fed; for our Master said, "My meat is to do the will of Him that sent Me, and to finish his work" (John 4: 34). The same truth is suggested here; if we obey the voice of the Lord, it is well with us, and our soul thrives.

The voice of God speaks from the page of his Word. Let us not accept that to be his voice which does not come to us through Scripture, or is not corroborated by Scripture.

But let us be very careful to obey God's Word, so far as we know it, even when, as in Zedekiah's case, it seems to contradict all the suggestions of prudence and common sense. Better be with God in a minority of one, than have the plaudits of an immense host of godless men.

How well I remember, years ago now, entering the bed-chamber of an eminent saint, one autumn morning, whose diminishing candles told how long he had been feeding on the Word of God. I asked him what had been the subject of his study. He said he had been engaged since four o'clock in discovering all the Lord's positive commandments, that he might be sure that he was not wittingly neglecting any one of them. It is very sad to find how many in the present day are neglecting to observe to do the Lord's precepts—concerning his ordinances, concerning the laying-up of money, the evangelization of the world, and the manifestation of perfect love. They know the Lord's will, and do it not. They appear to think that they are absolved from that "observing to do," which was so characteristic of Deuteronomy. As though Love were not more inexorable than Law!

Because thou hast put thy trust in Me.
Jer. 39: 18.
WHAT will not trust do? It will draw out of God for us the most wonderful exhibitions of his tender and mighty provision on our behalf. Who can put a limit on what God will do for the man who trusts Him? Here was the whole city given up to bloodshed and fire. The utmost confusion prevailed. No quarter was shown to the hapless Jews, pursued from house to house, from street to street, by the brutal soldiery. Yet because Ebed-melech trusted in God, and because he evidenced his faith by his loving care for the prophet, he was not given into the hand of the men of whom he was afraid.

Some who read these words may be greatly afraid. They dwell among lions, among men whose words are a sharp sword. But let them trust in the living God; and, in the meanwhile, go on each day ministering as well as they can to God's Jeremiahs. It is not enough to let down ropes to help them; it is a great sign of the love of God to put some rags to keep the ropes from chafing the tender skin. When God comes to help us, He always combines the strong rope with the old clout. Let us resemble Him in this.

Let us trust Him more. Too many resemble the stone-breaker who came into a vast estate, but was content to live in the lodge. When an old friend came to congratulate him, and see over the property, he said: "There! It is all in those parchments; but I have never been to see for myself what there is." Let us possess our possessions, and learn how much God will do for those who trust Him.

"Oh, could I tell, ye surely would believe it!
    Oh, could I only say what I have seen!
How should I tell, or how can ye receive it—
    How, till He bringeth you where I have
        been?"

The captain of the guard gave him victuals, and a present, and let him go. Jer. 40: 5 (R.V.).
THIS captain seems to have had a remarkable insight into God's dealings with Israel. In verse 3 he speaks quite prophetically; and in this treatment of the prophet he gives every sign of having been admitted into the secret councils of the Most High. He is a comrade of the centurions of the New Testament.

But the interesting matter is the care exercised by God over his servant. During the siege his bread had been given him, and his water had been sure. And now, in spite of all the plottings and devisings against his life, he was the one man of Israel who was treated with respect and provided with an honourable maintenance.

God is able to supply the need of his servants in very remarkable ways; now through ravens, or a widow, and again through a captain of Nebuchadnessar's guard. If we will be all for God, God will be all for us. In the present instance the men who were so eager to save themselves perished in the capture of the city; whilst the one man who sought to do God's will, with a single purpose, not only saved his life, but found all things else added to him.

God would have us live free from care. He made the spirit, and will see that it gets its allowance of sustenance. He made the soul, and knows how much love and culture it requires. He made the body, and will provide for its food and clothing. Do not fear the rough servants whom He employs as the distributors of his gifts. Under the mailed armour a warm heart is beating.

"Give me to trust Thee, Lord,
    In the dark and stormy night,
When morning seems so slow to come,
    And the stars are hid from sight."

Then arose Ishmael . . . and smote Gedaliah . . . with the sword. Jer. 41: 2.
THIS chapter is full of horrible atrocities. Blow on blow befel the already decimated remnant of Jews. Had it not been for Ishmael's ruthless vandalism, the vine of Israel might yet have struck her roots downwards and borne fruit upwards.

We must ask for more of that profound faith which, through all blinding mystery, sees the divine purpose, weaving events and men into its plans, and compelling all to work together for the discipline or aid of his children. "Praise the Lord from the earth, ye dragons, and all deeps; fire, and hail; snow, and vapours; stormy wind fulfilling his word." "Surely the wrath of man shall praise Thee; the remainder of wrath shalt Thou restrain" (Psalms 148: 7, 8; 76: 10).

What a comfort it is to know that all things in heaven, earth, and hell; all demons and men; all Nebuchadnezzars and Ishmaels—are under the control of our heavenly Father! They may hate us with all the power of their evil natures, but they cannot hurt us beyond his permission; and as soon as they have fulfilled what He deemed necessary, they will be withdrawn. There are no second causes for us. We are always dealing first-hand with God, though He may employ many strange servants to bring us his messages.

"A God-inspired Expectation, a Holy Patience, has always been the mark of a true believer, at the most critical periods in the history of the Church and of the individual. She first made hope vocal in the soul of Isaiah; fasted and prayed with Anna in her long widowhood; was at the cross with the mother; at the grave with the Magdalene; and hired the room for Pentecost."

We will obey the voice of the Lord our God, to whom we send thee. Jer. 42: 6.
WHILST the people said this with their lips, they had already set their faces to go into the land of Egypt (vers. 15, 17). It is useless to profess our desire to know God's will, whilst in our secret heart we are determined to follow a certain course, come what may. Indeed it is worse than useless; it is blasphemous. How often do believers ask for prayer that their course may be made clear, when in point of fact they have already decided on it, and are secretly hoping to turn God to their own side! But what a solemn responsibility devolves on

those who are sent to and fro between God and man, as Jeremiah was. He realized that he was sent by the people unto the Lord, and that he was sent back again by the Lord unto the people (ver. 21). He knew, too, that their faces were set on having their own evil way. But he never flinched from declaring the will of God, nor turned to the right or left, to curry favour from man. By nature very timid and sensitive, see how God made him a defenced city, an iron pillar, and brazen walls. Verily he stood in God's council, and caused the people to hear his words. What a contrast to the false prophets of ch. 23!

Compare this statement concerning Gerhard Tersteegen: "His service was always marked by a diffident and retiring spirit, though ever by a courageous valour for the truth. It is recorded that on one occasion, in going with a friend to a meeting where he was expected to give an address, he said, 'I would rather hide myself from all the world than let myself be seen and heard.' But he never swerved a hairbreadth when the honour of God and the testimony of the truth was concerned."

Baruch the son of Neriah setteth thee on against us. Jer. 43: 3.

WHEN men do not like the Word of God, they imagine that someone has set the speaker on against them. A poor woman came to us a few weeks ago, in a terrible condition. She had induced her husband to come to a service, and the address seemed so exactly adapted to him, dealing with his sins in the plainest terms, that nothing could convince him that she had not given the preacher a full and detailed account of his life, and had set the speaker on against him. When they got home he ill-treated her with great cruelty. But that service and her patient suffering were ultimately overruled to work a great change in him.

How strange it is that ungodly men always think the Word of God is against them, whereas they are set against it! The wind would not be so keen in their teeth, if they were not steaming so quickly against it.

But there is a solemn lesson here for us all. Whenever the Word of God makes us wince, or God's messenger presses sorely on us, we are apt to turn aside the point by some superficial and unreasonable excuse. We catch up the first foil we can lay hands on, in order to ward off the missile. We find some excuse to blunt the edge of the sword. It is easy to impute a bad and personal motive. There is always a Baruch the son of Neriah in the question. It is not we who are wrong, but the prophet who is prejudiced against us. As Ahab said of Micaiah, "I hate him, for he doth not prophesy good concerning me, but evil." We can only grow in the divine life by exposing ourselves to the reproofs and searchings of the divine Word; and allowing them their due weight.

Ah, do not this abominable thing that I hate. Jer. 44: 4.

THERE is a personal element in sin. It is not simply a violation of law, the law of the moral universe. It is against our own soul (ver. 7), and, above all, it hurts the holy, loving nature of God, so that his Spirit cries out as in agony, "Oh, do it not!" There is something very pathetic in this cry, extorted by the sin of man from the heart of God. It reminds one of that cry of Jesus, "O faithless and perverse generation, how long shall I be with you, and suffer you?"

If any one suffers very keenly from nervous exhaustion, it seems sometimes almost impossible for him to bear the noise of a child who persists in running heavily overhead. He will adopt a pleading rather than an angry tone: "My child, do not do this again; I cannot bear it." Let us think of God's holy nature as more sensitive to sin than the most highly-strung nerves to noise, and hear Him saying, whenever we are on the point of committing sin, "Oh, do not this abominable thing that I hate."

How greatly God hates sin is taught us in the Cross. In order to put it away He spared not his only-begotten Son, but yielded Him to the bitterness of Calvary.

And how greatly the blessed Son hates it is evident from the bloody sweat of Gethsemane, when the shadow of the great burden of a world's guilt lay upon Him.

And how greatly must the Holy Spirit, whose temple is our body, hate any sin that defiles it! Thus the Holy Trinity, with one voice, pleads with thee, who meditatest evil. Beware of bringing pain into the heart of Infinite Love; but ask that some of God's hate for sin may be yours.

Thou didst say, Woe is me now! . . . but thy life will I give thee. Jer. 45: 3, 5.

TROUBLE is an inevitable part of human

experience. "Man that is born of a woman," we are told, "is of few days and full of trouble." In addition to their share in the common heritage of man, it often falls to the lot of God's saints to suffer specially in connection with his kingdom and glory. They know the fellowship of his sufferings. They sigh and cry for all the abominations which are being wrought in their midst. The very association of Baruch with Jeremiah extorted the groan, "Woe is me now! for the Lord hath added sorrow to my pain."

But out of our sorrow and pain, when borne patiently and trustfully, comes the more abundant life. "Behold, I will bring evil upon all flesh; but thy life will I give unto thee." Pain casts a vail on all our pleasant earthly things, so that we take no further interest in them, and turn our thoughts to the unseen and eternal. Sorrow drives us to the God of all comfort. By the fire our dross is consumed. Through travail of soul the characteristics of godliness are born. "Except a corn of wheat fall into the ground and die, it abides alone; but if it die, it bringeth forth much fruit."

God often reveals ourselves to ourselves till we cry, Woe is me now! When God's light discovers our sins of appetite, of avarice, meanness, and niggardliness; of temper, fretfulness, and peevishness; of lack of conscientiousness, the partial fulfilment of promises, unfaithfulness, and misunderstandings. When we think of the want of constancy, truth, prayer, faith, and love, we are plunged in despair. Woe is me now! But out of all this there springs abundant life, and we rejoice that the great Revealer did not spare.

Fear thou not, O Jacob my servant, saith the Lord; for I am with thee. Jer. 46: 28.

THIS chapter is full of the clash and crash of war. In the most graphic and stirring words, the prophet describes the tide of Egyptian invasion, as its waters toss themselves upon the iron phalanxes of Babylon, like a rockbound coast; to recoil, defeated and broken, into myriads of foam-drops. The result to the great empire of Egypt is disastrous; her gods and kings are not able to save her from her justly-deserved punishment; she drinks the cup of indignation and wrath to her destruction.

But, amid it all, God remembers his people. They, too, are suffering from the results of their sins. And as they hear of all that has befallen greater nations than themselves, they

may well fear that their own fate will no less be irremediable and final. If the great kingdom of Egypt has received its death wound, from which it must slowly bleed to death, what hope can there be for Israel, captive in Babylon, while Canaan lies waste? To such fears God speaks words of tender comfort and reassurance. "Fear not thou, neither be dismayed; I will make a full end of all the nations, but I will not make a full end of thee; I will not leave thee unpunished, but will correct thee in measure; I will save thee from afar."

Oh, blessed words! If we have become the children of God by faith in Jesus; if God has ever entered into covenant with our souls; if He has taken us to be his and to give us his best—then, though we suffer chastisement, we shall not be overwhelmed by it: though we are corrected, diminished, and brought low, God will not make a full end of us: though we are pruned, we shall not be cut down to the ground. We may even look out with a quiet mind on the irretrievable disasters which overtake the ungodly.

O thou sword of the Lord, how long will it be ere thou be quiet? Jer. 47: 6, 7 (R.V.).

O SWORD of the Lord; thou hast wounded us sore! Like a two-edged sword, the Word of God has pierced to the dividing asunder of soul and spirit, of the joints and marrow. How deeply it has penetrated; how sharply it has cut! And even now it cannot rest. The work of discrimination and separation is still going on within us. We are constantly seeing new depths of our own utter worthlessness and evil. Possibilities of our own bad hearts, of which we had not dreamt, arise to confront us; and immediately the divine sword sets itself to hack and hew and cut away the evil growth of selfishness, of which we have caught a glimpse.

There are times in our lives when we cry, "O thou sword of the Lord, how long ere thou be quiet: rest and be still." Will the process of purification and deliverance never be complete? Will not the destructive work of God soon end? The operation has lasted months and years; when will the divine Surgeon lay down the knife? O knife of God, rest thee!

But how can it be quiet seeing that the work is not done? We are not yet rid of the last remains of sin. The wound is not yet probed to the bottom. The roots of the cancerous growth of selfishness have not yet been entirely removed; and if any one of them remains, all the work will have to be done again. How can it be quiet, seeing that God loves us too well to allow us to bear with us into eternity aught that will hinder our perfect fruition of bliss? How can it be quiet, seeing that this is the only world where pain can reach his saints? and He must do his work quickly, ere we reach the land where the sword is placed in its scabbard, and stilled for ever.

Moab hath not been emptied from vessel to vessel.   Jer. 48: 11 (R.V.).

THIS beautiful and appropriate imagery, borrowed from the vineyard, speaks for itself. It would be readily appreciated by the peasant populations that toiled amid the terraced hills of Moab. To prevent scum and sediment, the newly-made wine was emptied from one vessel to another until it reached the condition of perfect fluidity. In Moab's case there had been nothing comparable to this, and therefore the rank, coarse taste remained in him, and he had settled on his lees.

What an insight this affords of God's method with the souls of men! Why these constant removals from town to town; from church to church; from situation to situation? Why this perpetual change and revolution in our plans? Why this incessant going into captivity to irksome and trying circumstances? All this is part of God's manufacture of the wine of life. We must be emptied from vessel to vessel, else we should settle on our lees, and become thick and raw and unpalatable. When the next change comes in your life, do not fear it. The blessed God will see to it that no drop of the precious fluid shall be spilt on the ground. With the tenderest care He conducts the whole operation.

Perhaps there is a counterpart to this incessant change from place to place in the perpetual flux of our emotions. We never feel the same for long together. We are constantly being emptied from one blessed frame into another, not quite so joyous or peaceful. We have to hold the most heavenly emotions with a light hand, not knowing how soon they may have passed. And it is well. Otherwise we should never lose the taste of our proud self-complacency.

Dwell deep.   Jer. 49: 8.

AS originally spoken, these words summoned the people of Edom to seek the shadows of impenetrable forests, and retire into the secrecy of the caves and dens of the rocks. The deeper their hiding place, the better it would be when the storm of invasion swept across the land.

DWELL DEEP IN THE PEACE OF GOD. God's peace is so deep and blessed that it cannot be fathomed or explained; the fugitive into its sacred secrets cannot be followed or dragged forth to perish by the merciless pack of the wolves of care. Men of the world cannot understand that mystery of peace; but the believer knows the way into it, and makes it his hiding-place and pavilion. He sleeps like his Master in the stern, while storms sweep the waters.

DWELL DEEP IN COMMUNION WITH GOD. Hide in God. Get away from the rush and strife around, and go alone into the clear, still depths of his nature. The Rhone loses all its silt in the deep, clear waters of Geneva's lake. A few hasty words of prayer will not avail for this. A day's climb is often necessary before one can reach the heart of the mountains.

DWELL DEEP IN STILLNESS OF SOUL. Do not live on the outside of life, in the outer courts of the temple of the soul. Get within. God awaits thee there. Centre thyself. When the world is full of alarm and harassments, study to be quiet. The soul's health cannot be maintained apart from the observance of times of waiting on God in solitude. The great importance of perseverance in the exercise of prayer and inward retirement may be sufficiently learnt, says one, next to the experience of it, merely from the tempter's artifices and endeavours to allure us from it, and make us neglect it.

They have forgotten their resting-place, their place to lie down in.   Jer. 50: 6 (marg.).

THESE words may often be said of us. A time of emergency arises; the necessity for instant and vigorous action seems overpowering; we fail to see what course to adopt—and immediately we get flurried and excited; we run from one to another; we lose our sleep. All our earnest resolutions to abide in Christ and live in his fellowship are forgotten. We have forgotten our resting-place.

Or we are in the midst of a great campaign of work. From morning to night we are plunged in a mass of calculations and activities. There is no time to take our meals, much less to obtain opportunities for prayer and fellowship with God. Our rooms without, our souls within, are littered with the symptoms of the many absorbing interests which are monopolizing our attention. We have forgotten our resting-place.

Or, perhaps, it is a time of great temptation. Hour after hour the foe returns to the attack. We have done our best to withstand him; but have hit out without precision, have fired at random. Again, we have forgotten our resting-place.

The place where we lie down to rest is under the shadow of the Cross. Whilst we remain there, we are perfectly safe and blessed. Return unto thy rest, O straying sheep! Back to the arms of Jesus, where only such frail ones as thou art are safe.

I knew a man, who had to bear a thousand crosses belonging to others, and who grieved himself into an illness because others did not love God as He deserves, till all at once his own foolishness and sinfulness struck him to the heart. He could do nothing then but cast himself and them into the endless depths of the love of God; and he ended by having rest in his heart, and a song on his lips.

Israel hath not been forsaken, nor Judah of his God, of the Lord of Hosts. Jer. 51: 5.

YES, indeed, our life has been filled with sin against the Holy One of Israel. We see it now. As we look back upon the past with the light of the present reflected upon it, we see how every day has added its quota of transgression. How bitterly we must have grieved the Holy Ghost! How terribly have made the Holy One suffer! Do you wonder that Jesus still appears in heaven as a Lamb as it had been slain!

But He has not forsaken! As again we review our life, how abundant is the evidence that we have not been forsaken. Forsaken!—Then God's right hand would lose its cunning. Forsaken!—Then the tides that flow through the heart of God would have to leap backward. Forsaken!—Then the eternal purposes would have to be frustrated. Forsaken!—Then the divine word would be forfeited, and the divine Son would go without his meed. Sin is mighty; but there is one thing it cannot do, it cannot make God forsake those whom He has adopted into his family. Sin dragged the arch-angel to the pit; but can never wrench the believer out of the hand of God. Sin brought Christ from the throne to the cross; but it can never cause God to leave, or cease to care for, his own.

Does this lead you to presumption? Do you say, Then I may do as I like? Ah, beware! Those that talk thus have not the mark of his children. The child loves with the love that fears to grieve God, more than to be forsaken of Him. "The love of Christ constrains me to forsake these things. I have long enough crucified my beloved Saviour with my sins. His love constrains me to renounce all that grieves Him, and live for Him alone."

Every day a portion until the day of his death, all the days of his life. Jer. 52: 34.

IF the King of Babylon did thus for a captive king, his prisoner, will your heavenly Father do less for you? He created you to need the daily portion, and cannot be oblivious of his own constitution of your nature. You wind up your watch each day, because you know that otherwise it will stop; and God will not be less thoughtful of your constant need of reinforcement. "He knoweth that ye have need of all these things." His faithfulness guarantees that there always will be the portion of good for the body; always the portion of love and light for the soul; always the portion of Holy Spirit quickening for the spirit.

It is easier to die once than to live always. It is not easy to meet the continual demand of recurrent duty; not easy to live a full and strong life, that never dips below the horizon, or sinks in the fountain-basin. But it is possible, when the soul has learnt to leave all care with God, waiting on Him for the supply of all its needs, and esteeming that He is the only really satisfactory portion we need.

"Neither prison-walls, nor locks, nor the cruelty of man," said some imprisoned suffering souls, "can obstruct the issues of the Lord's love nor the manifestation of his presence, which is our joy and comfort, and carries us above all sufferings, and makes days and hours and years pleasant to us; which pass away as a moment, because of the enjoyment of seeing Him with whom a thousand years is but as one day."

Those who can trust God in these directions are not only abundantly satisfied of his great goodness, but are able to send portions to others. Like the disciples, they share out their slender supplies and get twelve baskets full in return.

Lamentations

The Lord is righteous; for I have rebelled against his commandment. Lam. 1: 18.

IN these plaintive elegiacs, Jerusalem, by the mouth of the prophet, laments her fate. But the story of her desolation is mingled with confessions of her sin. She asks boldly if any sorrow could be compared to her sorrow, and then confesses that not one pang or stroke had been in excess of her sin. This is what sorrow does for us all.

Sorrow has been fitly called the mother of all joy. She alone creates the darkness, in which we can distinguish the real meaning of God's dealings, and understand the true nature of our wild wanderings. Her neutral tints subdue the soul's pride, and turn it away from the glare of human ambition. Beneath her teaching we learn to view aright the evanescence of all things human, and to see that the eternal is alone real amid a world of illusions.

"Sweet sorrow, who the earth has ever trod,
  Dreaded and shunned, till, by thy burning kiss,
The heart was fired and flamed serene to God;
  O kind stern friend, we leave thee on Time's shore,
  The only friend of earth whom we shall see no more."

Perhaps your sorrow will be allowed to press on you more and more sorely till you have been led to self-examination, confession of sin, and acknowledgment of the rightness of God's dealings with you. There is an alloy of pride in your nature that must be destroyed. If the fire is not hot enough, its heat must be raised till it suffices. Accept the lesson of your present pain, and rebel no longer.

The waves of unutterable grief may be breaking in succession against the beaten promontory of your faith, and will be followed by the great tenth wave of apparent desertion: but the return-tide of exultant joy is at hand.

The prophets have seen visions for thee of vanity and foolishness. Lam. 2: 14.

THE prophet is addressing Jerusalem— ruined, desolate, and afflicted—the city waste; her children in Babylon. Of course the main question was as to their return from captivity, and deliverance from their yoke. The false prophets were perpetually seeing visions of deliverance that were never fulfilled. Now this kingdom would come to their rescue; now that. But they were empty dreams. The captivity would never be turned, until the iniquity which had led to it had been discovered and put away. But the prophets had no desire or ability to do this. Now this is true of yourself as an individual and as a Christian worker.

AS AN INDIVIDUAL: You are suffering in one way or another: in body, or relative, or circumstance. Your one thought is to obtain deliverance, and your mind is filled with vain dreams of how it is to come. It would be better far to ask God to discover to you any reason for chastisement. If He says nothing, then believe that there is still some wise end in it for yourself or others. But He may indicate some reason for his strokes.

AS A CHRISTIAN WORKER: Your earnest endeavours have failed. You suppose that some new method will bring success. There may be some reason in yourself which will account for all. Ask God to discover it. When you see it in his light, you will be surprised that you never saw it before; and you will cease to wonder that those over whom you have longed have never yielded to the love of God. It is useless to have visions of a lovely and holy life, unless you are willing to have your iniquity discovered and destroyed. Oh for faithful prophet-voices to do their office for us!

Thou drewest near in the day that I called upon Thee: Thou saidst, Fear not. Lam. 3: 57.

JEREMIAH is referring to his own experiences of the dungeon, into which the malice of his foes had plunged him. As he reached its lowest depths, he began to call upon God, and continued to call. His reliance was on the name (i.e., the nature) of God. This is the most potent argument that any soul can employ. Not our faith, but his faithfulness: not our trust, but his trustworthiness. "Act worthily of that great name, which Thou hast taken for Thyself, O God, we beseech Thee."

No sooner was that appeal made than it was heard. "Thou heardest my voice." Notice that the very breathing of the persecuted soul was heard by the Most High. A mother listens for the breathing of her babe in the dark. It will tell her so much. The soft, measured breath, or the labouring, gasping breath. God never hides his ear from our breathing; or from those inarticulate cries, which express, as words could not do, the deep anguish and yearning of the heart. If you cannot speak, cry, sob, or groan, then be still. God can interpret all.

Then He draws nigh. Of course, He is ever nigh. "Nearer than breathing." But He gives a sweet consciousness of his presence. The dark dungeon of bereavement, or sorrow, suddenly becomes luminous with the radiance of the Shekinah; the stillness is broken by the approaching footfall of the Almighty Friend, who is never so near as when lover and friend are unable to help. Oh, how tenderly He draws nigh! Solitude indeed hath charms, for it is our Saviour's opportunity; and the dungeon becomes desirable, for it is the ante-room to the presence-chamber of our King. Happy they who have learned to detect the secret of the Lord, and his whispered Fear not!

Of whom we said, Under his shadow we shall live among the nations. Lam. 4: 20 (R.V.).
THE people tell the sad tale of the pursuit of their foes. Swifter than the eagles, they chased them on the mountains, and laid wait for them in the wilderness. Then they narrate how their king fell into the hands of them who sought his life. He was dear to them as the breath of their nostrils; his person was sacred as the anointed of the Lord; they had thought that even though they were carried into captivity they would find some alleviation to their hardships in dwelling under his protection; they said, "Under his shadow we shall live among the nations." But even he was taken in their pits.

What a likeness and a contrast to our blessed Lord! There is LIKENESS. He is as the breath of our life. As we inhale the air around us, so we expand our souls to drink in of his most blessed nature. We open our mouths, and inhale Him as our vital element; his Spirit for our spirit; his blood for our souls; his resurrection strength for our bodies. He is the Anointed of the Father, who anoints us. Because He is the Christ (Anointed), we are

Christians (anointed ones). His shadow is a most grateful and widespreading one, beneath which we may dwell in safety.

But how great the CONTRAST! Though He was once taken in the pit of Satanic malice and the shadow of death, yet now He liveth to be the shield and protector of his people wherever they are scattered among the nations. He that sitteth on the throne shall spread his tabernacle over them. They shall hunger and thirst no more, neither shall the sun strike them. However far our bodies are from one another, we all dwell beneath the shadow of the Lord, which is as a great rock in a weary land.

Turn Thou us unto Thee, O Lord, and we shall be turned. Renew our days as of old. Lam. 5: 21.
WEARY of chastening, and longing to have again all the blessed enjoyments and privileges of the past, the backslider desires to be right with God, as he used to be. But he is often met with great initial difficulties. He would pray, but cannot; he would feel broken and penitent, but his heart is as hard as the nether millstone; he would take the old pleasure in the service and worship of the Most High, but it evades his grasp. This perplexes and daunts him.

What should be our attitude under such circumstances? There is nothing better than to adopt the cry of the prophet, and ask God to turn the soul, and renew its blessed and holy experiences. There will be no doubt of our being turned, if He turns us.

It is not difficult to recover the attitude, emotions, and work of past days, when we have yielded ourselves absolutely to God, and have cast on Him the responsiblity of making us all that He has taught us to desire. Let Him assign what standard He chooses, there will be no difficulty in our attaining it, if He fulfils in us all the good pleasure of his will, and the work of faith with power.

The happy life is that which does not need to ask for the olden days to be renewed, because it is ever anticipating that it will be better further on, and that the dawn will grow into the perfect day; but where the past was better than the present is, let us ask that God would restore the years that the caterpillar and cankerworm have eaten. Just because God abides for ever, and his throne is from generation to generation, He is able to renew the soul with new pulses of energy and life. Each spring He makes the world as fair as on the morning of creation. "Renew our days as of old."

Ezekiel

When the living creatures went, the wheels went beside them. Ezek. 1: 19 (R.V.).

THESE living creatures, whom Ezekiel afterwards recognized as cherubim, represented the entire round of animate existence. The lion's majestic strength, the patient strength and labour of the ox, the keen vision and aspiring flight of the eagle, combined in perfect proportion in their noble forms. The wheels may represent the round of Providence—what we would call the circle of nature. The point for us to notice is the perfect harmony between the spirit, the living creatures, and the wheels; and from this we learn the deep and sacred lesson, that those who live and walk in the Spirit may count on the co-operation of all animate creatures, and the concurrence of Divine providence. When we live consciously and voluntarily in the centre of the Divine will, we are at the centre of many concentric circles, and all things serve us. All things are ours.

If we would be Spirit-taught and guided, we must die to ourselves, to sin, and to the world; no longer seeking anything for ourselves in this world. If, says Pastor Stockmayer, we have treasure outside of Christ, our heart will hasten to where our treasure lies. Only those who account themselves set loose from the things of this world to serve Christ entirely, amid the things of this world, can distinguish the movements of the Spirit.

Each is guided in a way that he knows; and has the special name written on the white stone. God speaks in the depths of our being, far deeper than the region of our feelings, dispositions, or impressions; and He will make Himself heard, if only we are set to obey Him. Let surrender become the abiding habit of life, and the spiritual hearing will be more and more acute.

Be not afraid of them, neither be afraid of their words. Ezek. 2: 6.

EZEKIEL'S lot was cast in difficult times. His people, to whom he was sent, whether by the Chebar in captivity, or still lingering around their doomed mother-city, were as briars, thorns, and scorpions. Embittered by their many sorrows; convicted by conscience of their guilt before God; compelled to trace a close connection between their sins and their punishment—it was inevitable that they would turn with peculiar dislike on anyone who dared, like Ezekiel, to be an incarnate conscience to them, reminding them of their evil ways, remonstrating, exhorting, pleading.

Many readers of these words are in similar circumstances. Missionaries who are obliged to rebuke, not only the sins of the ungodly, but the inconsistencies of their own converts; ministers at home on whom the burden rests of protesting against popular and fashionable iniquity, or addressing stern words of rebuke to influential but worldly members of their churches; even young clerks or working-men whose life is thrown among the godless and profane, and who seem called upon to lodge their solemn warning against words and ways that are not good. Providing these enter their protest lovingly and tenderly, with no thought of their superiority, with no mere desire to wound and annoy, but to warn the sinner and to uphold the claims of Christ—their mission is a very salutary and necessary one. But it is sure to bring on them a storm of dislike.

At such times there is nothing for us but to abide in the presence of our Master Christ, weeping for the sins we rebuke, interceding for those who revile. Not fearful nor afraid, not flinching from our duty, but ever hearing his sweet reassuring voice.

Eat this roll, and go speak. Ezek. 3: 1.

TO each of us a Hand is put forth; and therein is the roll of the Book. We must feed on it for ourselves. We must find God's words and eat them; they must be the joy and rejoicing of our hearts. It is specially incumbent on those who have to go forth and speak, to open their mouths and eat the roll. There is no greater mistake than to suppose that, because we are constantly handling God's Word for the purpose of teaching and exhorting others, we are therefore feeding on it for ourselves. It is possible to acquire an intellectual knowledge of the truth, while the heart is entirely unaffected. But how far removed is this from that spiritual consideration of God's Word, by virtue of which it yields up its spiritual nutriment to our growth in the divine life.

Sometimes the message we must acquire and give is, like this roll, written within and without with lamentations, and mourning, and woe. It can hardly be otherwise, when we are called to speak to people who are of a hard forehead and a stiff heart. It is very sweet to receive God's messages; but it is bitter to have to deliver them when they proclaim, as they must, the inevitable and disastrous results of sin. Oh that we may not shrink to declare the whole counsel of God, whether rebellious men will hear or forbear. Perhaps there has not been enough of this element in our preaching. All sunshine, the Arabs say, makes the desert. The harvest will fail unless the frost of winter has thoroughly broken up the clods. But whenever we dwell on the sterner aspects of God's truth it must be with bitter tears. "I tell you, even weeping," the apostle said, "that they are enemies of the Cross of Christ."

Then said I, Ah, Lord God! Ezek. 4: 14.
THE prophet was bidden, in a series of striking and significant actions, to show the people the impending fate of their nation and city. Amongst other injunctions there was one so abhorrent to his soul that he craved its mitigation. "Ah, Lord God!" he said, "spare me from this." And God was entreated, and reduced the pressure of the burden proposed to be laid on his servant.

May not the counterpart of this happen in our own experience? We may be feeling that certain trials are insupportable, or certain demands beyond our power to meet. At such hours of bitter anguish it is quite permissible for us to go into the secret place of the Most High and gasp out our complaint, saying, "Ah, Lord God!" God invites us to speak freely with Him thus, and sends gracious mitigations of our griefs. "Ah, Lord God," we say, "let this cup pass from me": and, lo! an angel is sent to strengthen us. "Ah, Lord God," we cry, "this cross is too heavy; this thorn in the flesh too sharp; this diet too nauseous": and immediately there is some response of greater grace or lightened burden.

Oh, suffering child of God, get alone with Him, and talk freely. Do not hesitate to tell Him all that is in thine heart. Remember that Jesus said that the Father Himself loves us.

We may go to that Father-heart, confiding to it how much we are suffering, not for ourselves only, but for their sakes who are dearer to us than life. Oh that they were happy, satisfied, safe! Has the duty become lately more than ever difficult? Has the smart become like a cancer with its venom? Take it to God! It is a sublime moment when the soul dares to plead its cause with God, saying, "Ah, Lord God!"

I will do in thee that which I have not done.
Ezek. 5: 9.
IT is an awful thing when those who have sinned against conspicuous privilege and opportunity come under the rod. Their punishment is infinitely heavier than that of such as have never known. The servant that knows his Lord's will, and does it not, is condemned to be beaten with many stripes. It was because Capernaum had been exalted to heaven that she was cast down to Hades. If an archangel falls, it must be to hell.

The child of God, like Israel, is set in the midst of the nations to testify to pure and undefiled religion; but if he rebels against God's judgments and statutes in doing wickedly, his chastisement is necessarily in proportion to the eminence of his former privileges. God cannot afford to deal lightly with the sin of his own people. Were He to do so, He might be accused of partiality, and they might presume. Well may the author of "Imitation" say, "Esteem not thyself better than others, lest perhaps in the sight of God, who knoweth what is in man, thou be accounted worse than they."

It becomes us to search our hearts to see if we are rejecting any of God's judgments, and refusing to walk in his will, or defiling his sanctuary with detestable things. A small black spot on a white ground is more noticeable than a larger one on a dark ground. A slight inconsistency in his child may lead to very heavy chastisements on the part of the Father in heaven. The nearer a pupil reaches towards perfection, the sterner is his master's discipline. Judgment begins at the house of God. If thou wert not capable of a rich fruitage, He would not take such pains with thee. Humble thyself under his mighty hand: He will exalt thee in due time.

I have been broken with their whorish heart. And they shall loathe themselves. Ezek. 6: 9 (R.V.).
WE never realize what sin is till its passion is

over, and we have time quietly to remember. Oh, the terror of those hours of remembrance and remorse! Sitting in the captivity of its prison, or serving in the heavy bondage of its fetters, the soul has time to review the bitter path by which it has come to such a pass, and the way it has broken the hearts of those who loved and trusted. But the most terrible element in remorse will be the personal one: "Shall remember Me."

One of our great writers depicts a heartless, thoughtless husband standing beside the newly covered-in grave of his wife, and saying, "Ah, Milly, Milly; dost thou hear me? I was not tender enough to thee; but it is too late to alter it now." The wife who has broken away from her husband, bringing desolation on a once happy home, and heartbreak on the one she really loved, will have her time of remorse when she remembers him, and how he was broken by her sin. And she will loathe herself. The child who has given way to fits of ungovernable passion, which have broken up the home, and brought down grey hairs with sorrow to the grave, will loathe itself. Similarly, as we review our past life, and see how we must have grieved the tender Spirit of God, we fall at the feet of Jesus and cover them with tears and kisses.

What a marvellous word is this!—"I have been broken." Our sin can give God the heartbreak, because He loves us so. Indeed, on the Cross the Lord died of a broken heart; of this the issuing stream of blood and water was the sign. O heart of stone, thou too must break and loathe thyself, when thou seest thy Lord broken by thy sin!

Their silver and their gold . . . shall not satisfy their souls. Ezek. 7: 19.

THIS chapter is full of alarms! An end: the end is come! (ver. 2). An evil, an only evil: behold it cometh. An end is come; the end is come (vers. 5, 6). The time is come; the day is near (ver. 7). Behold the day, behold it cometh; thy doom is gone forth (ver. 10). The time is come (ver. 12). At such a crisis, what can silver and gold do? Let not the buyer rejoice, nor the seller mourn. None shall return. The sword is without; pestilence and famine within.

Generally silver and gold stand for much among the children of men; they are the keys to the unlocking of the treasures of life. But when the supreme crises come; when all hands are feeble, and all knees weak as water; when the day of the wrath of the Lord breaks—there is no help in silver and gold; they cannot satisfy or save.

Men forget that they are destined for immortality; and that God hath set Eternity in their hearts. How utterly impotent gold and silver, the things of earth, the abundance of goods which a man may store in his barn, to appease the conscience, or arrest the remorseless hunger of the soul for peace and purity and satisfaction! He is the happiest who is largely independent of these things, and lives a pilgrim life, reckoning that his enduring city is with God, whose treasures are heavenly and incorruptible. It is a great misfortune that professing Christians have failed to realize this. Too many of them are as eager to maintain and extend their establishments, as though life consisted in the abundance of what they possess. So missionary causes dwindle for want of funds; children are drawn into worldly alliances; and worldlings depreciate our holy religion.

Chambers of imagery. Ezek. 8: 12.

WHAT disclosures were these! In the entry to the Temple court stood the great idol, here described as an image of jealousy; because, speaking after the manner of men, it greatly provoked the Eternal Spouse of Israel! The seventy elders engaged in worshipping every form of creeping things and abominable beasts, portrayed on the walls of the secret chambers! The women weeping for Tammuz, whose yearly death and resurrection were celebrated with licentious orgies! The five-and-twenty men with their backs toward the Temple! Is it to be wondered at that God could not spare, nor have pity?

But are there no chambers of imagery in our natures, which were meant to be the sanctuary of the Eternal? Is it quite certain that evil thoughts and imaginations have not imprinted themselves on the walls of the heart? Ah, it may be so. What seems fair and beautiful in the eye of man may be concealing terrible secrets, open only to that of God. In the secret of our hearts, we permit unclean birds to brood; in the darkness of our soul, wild thoughts wander at will. What need there is to adopt the venerable and touching words: "Cleanse the thoughts of our hearts by the inspiration of thy Holy Spirit, that we may perfectly love Thee."

There is deliverance from all this, by the

grace and through the blood of the Lord Jesus. He can save and keep. He can so fill the soul with his presence that sin shall be utterly abhorrent. We may become so sensitive to the least approach of evil as to shelter ourselves in Him, before the first symptom of temptation shall have gained force and volume for its attack. Holy Spirit, keep thine own temple, we pray Thee!

Come not near any man upon whom is the mark; and begin at my sanctuary. Ezek. 9: 6.

ALL these visions were given, as we learn from the first chapter, as Ezekiel was with the earlier groups of Hebrew captives in Babylon. His thoughts were greatly engrossed by what was transpiring in the beloved city among the remnant still residing there. The six men represented judgments yet impending, and the man clothed in linen with the inkhorn, the discriminating righteousness of God's judgments.

Judgment begins with the house of God; with those of us who are called to teach and preach, and bear office in the Church. The six men who had the slaughter-weapons began at the elders, described in the previous chapter, who were before the house. If any such are living in sin, God's judgment must fall first and more heavily on them, because they know better and profess more than others. But let it be remembered always that repentance and the putting away of sin will always avert the sword. "If thou wilt put away thine abominations, then thou shalt not remove."

Amid the scenes of judgment, whether in the Church or the world, there is always a remnant, upon whom is the mark; on Lot in Sodom; on Israel amid the plagues of Egypt; on Rahab in the fall of Jericho; on the 144,000 at the Great Tribulation. They are safe amid the fiery indignation which devours the adversaries. Have we been touched by the blood, sealed by the Spirit, and branded with the mark of the brand of Jesus? Without doubt we have, if we know what it is to sigh and cry for the abominations that are wrought around us, and of which our own nature is capable, except for the grace of God. These are the signs which indicate the humbling, sanctifying work of the Holy Spirit in our hearts.

The glory of the Lord went forth from over the threshold, and stood over the cherubin.
Ezek. 10: 18.

THE gradual withdrawal of God from his house is described in vivid and awful minuteness. In 9: 3, it had gone to the threshold; 10: 4, it had mounted up; 15, the cherubim mounted up; 11: 23, it passes from the city. It is well worth our while to ponder this deep and searching lesson. The light of other days fades but slowly: the year sinks by almost insensible gradations to the fall of the leaf; grey hairs besprinkle our heads without our knowing it; before ever we are aware of it, the train has borne us miles off the main line to the wrong station. So gradually our hearts may backslide. Satan is too knowing to lead us at a single leap into the precipice, but conducts us by a gradual incline. A little less Bible reading; a slight slackening in watchfulness and prayer; an imperceptible drift worldwards.

But turn to 43: 2-4. The glory of the Lord returned to the renovated temple. Like the dawn of a new day; like the sound of many waters, it came, it came. "This," God said, "is the place of my throne; . . . and the house of Israel shall no more defile." Ah, backslider, God will come back to thee again. Thy repentance may be most inadequate; but if it be genuine, if thou dost truly turn to Him from thy sin, thy heart shall again become irradiate with his most blessed of holy light.

Without forcing, these words are also applicable to that coming for which we wait and long; when He who ascended shall descend again to be in us and with us for ever:

"Hark! what a sound, and too divine for hearing,
Stirs on the earth and trembles in the air!
It is the thunder of the Lord's appearing!
It is the music of his peoples' prayer!"

Yet will I be to them a little sanctuary in the countries where they are come. Ezek. 11: 16.

AWAY from the outward ordinances and the material edifice, the exiles would find more than the equivalent in God Himself. He would give them the reality, of which there had been the outward and visible emblems. Amid all their justly-deserved sufferings they would find a deep fountain of spiritual blessing and comfort in God's presence.

TO THOSE WHO ARE DEPRIVED OF THE MEANS OF GRACE. Sufferers in sick rooms, travellers in lonely and distant places, missionaries amongst the heathen. How often to such comes the vision of the country church, when the summer air stole into the open window, bringing the breath of flowers; or of the great City church, with the well-known voice of a beloved minister. They long for these again. But God will be all and more.

TO THOSE WHO CANNOT DERIVE BENEFIT FROM THE SERVICES THEY ATTEND. The clergyman is Ritualistic, or the Free-church minister is broad in his views, and unsympathetic with the deeper moods of the spirit. Still, it may be your duty to attend for example's sake; but whilst waiting before the Lord, He will draw near and become your sanctuary.

TO THOSE WHO ARE EXPOSED TO DANGER AND PERSECUTION. In the olden time the sanctuary was a place of refuge. All who fled thither were in safeguard. So, let the driven soul haste to the folds of the Tabernacle of God's presence. None can pursue it into that secret place. No weapon shall smite; and even envying voices shall die into subdued murmurs.

He that eateth the living bread—that confesseth Jesus to be the Christ—that keepeth his commandments—and that lives in love— dwells in God as his sanctuary, while God dwells in him as His.

The word that I shall speak shall be performed: it shall be no more deferred. Ezek. 12: 25, 28. IN various ways the people of Israel were endeavouring to minimize the effects of Ezekiel's denunciations of judgment. They did not deny that he spoke the word of God; but comforted themselves with the reflection that it was not likely to be fulfilled for some time yet. "The vision that he seeth is for many days to come." God, on the other hand, said, "It shall be no more deferred."

We are all disposed to remove the wonderworking of God to the remote past or the distant future: either that He did miracles or will do them. Heaven touches the earth at this horizon or that; but it is remote from the place where we stand. This is the tendency of our mind; and for this reason we miss the manifestations of God's grace and power, which wait to enrich our lives. Now is the accepted time; now the day of salvation. As Christ is, so are we. There is as much of Divine power and love throbbing around, and within our easy reach, as ever filled the upper room at Pentecost, or shall break on the world in the millennial days. Let us not postpone our appropriation of it. Let us never permit the thought that God is not prepared to fulfil his promises here and now. Let us not lament over the past as having been better than the present can ever be expected to be, nor predict greater days for our children.

It is here that the distinction between fact, faith, and feeling, will help us. We very seldom, indeed, never until Spirit-taught, put these three in their right order. We try to feel that spiritual facts are so, instead of accepting that they are, and daring to act as if they were patent to physical sensations. A spiritual fact is true, even when you do not believe or feel it. Believe! act! and you will come to feel.

Prophesy against the prophets of Israel . . . that prophesy out of their own hearts. Ezek. 13: 2. IT is a great temptation to those of us who are often called to speak for God, to prophesy out of our own heart, to follow our own spirit, and to profess to see what we have not seen. We are apt to say, "The Lord saith," when the Lord hath not sent us. These words of ours always tend towards soothing and pacifying guilty consciences with assurances of peace, peace. You may always tell when a man is speaking from the vanity of his own heart. He glozes over sin, and speaks with bated breath of its consequences.

This is what the Word of God describes as daubing a slight wall with untempered mortar, and sewing pillows on elbows for handfuls of barley and pieces of bread. The daubing makes the wall look as strong as possible, but it cannot save it from collapsing before the overflowing shower of God's judgment and the great hailstones of his wrath. The pillows may save the flesh from chafing, but cannot avert the blows of a broken law. Oh, take care, lest ye give men licence to sin, by the slight views ye circulate of its nature or penalty. Are not these lying divinations? Do they not grieve the heart of the righteous, and strengthen the hands of the wicked? Take care lest the fate of the daubing be the fate also of the false prophets: "The wall is no more; neither they that daubed it."

It is not an easy thing to speak to the prophets. But how necessary that there should be a Prophet to prophets: for these get into the way of supposing that they must be right, whose least word is so reverenced by their people. "You are very fond of preaching," said Dr. Andrew Bonar to one to whom he had been listening. "Yes, doctor; very." "But are you as fond of lost souls?"

Ye shall be comforted concerning the evil that I have brought upon Jerusalem. Ezek. 14: 22.

THE sin of Jerusalem was so heinous that God was constrained to send on her his four sore judgments all at once and together. Each alone was so terrible that Noah, Daniel, and Job, had they been living, would only have succeeded in saving their own souls; but how much more when they befel the land unitedly! But, Jehovah says, ye shall come to know, when you review my work from the vantage-ground of the years, that I have not done without cause (or in vain, marg.) all that I have done (ver. 23). Ye shall be comforted, when a remnant of sons and daughters escapes, who see and acknowledge their sinful ways and deeds.

Those words deserve to be carefully pondered. They seem to contain the very essence of God's thoughts in his dealings with us during the present age. "Ye shall know that I have not done without cause all that I have done" (ver. 23). We do not know the cause of so much that crushes us to the ground. But if we did know it as well as we shall know it some day, we should have no difficulty in reconciling God's dealings with his perfect love.

Yes, some day we shall be comforted! Comforted as to God's meaning in our sorrows and trials! Comforted as to his dealings with our dear ones! Comforted about his government of the whole universe, of which the world is part! We shall see that there was a cause or reason for all God's stern discipline. We shall admit that it was wisely adapted to its end, and achieved it. We are too prone to judge God hastily and superficially, instead of waiting to see the "end of the Lord," when all his reasons and purposes will be explained from the great white throne (see Rev. 15: 3).

What is the vine tree more than any tree? Ezek. 15: 2.

WHAT is the vine good for? Will it bear comparison with the trees of the forest? Do men make chairs, tables, house-roofs out of it? No, they will not make even a pin for hanging vessels on, out of the vine-wood. There is only one use for the vine—to bear fruit. If it fails to do that, it may as well be cast at once to the flames. Then it is still more useless; and as we gather the charred pieces together. we realize that they are hardly worth our care.

So with believers. Like Israel, they are God's vine, created in Christ Jesus unto fruit-bearing.

The one purpose and end of their redemption and salvation is that they should bring forth fruit unto God; and if they fail in this, after having been pruned and enriched in every way, they are cast forth as worthless and unprofitable, and men gather them and cast them into the fire, and they are burned. Savourless salt is good for nothing: fruitless vines are utterly useless: professors who bear no fruit are worse than useless, they cumber the ground. Let us abide in Christ, that He may bear fruit through us. Let us be willing for all the pruning and discipline which God is pleased to send us, that we may bring forth more fruit; but let it ever be borne in mind that fruitfulness does not always mean activity, but the bearing of the sweet fruits of the Spirit, which consist largely in temper and disposition.

Apart from Christ, how helpless and worthless we are! Let us often, and particularly when tempted to vanity, conceit, self-sufficiency, self-satisfaction, remember that we are only vine-branches, of no intrinsic worth, and only useful when the sap of the Vine is passing through us. "What hast thou, that thou didst not receive?" (1 Cor. 4: 7).

Thy beauty . . . was perfect through my comeliness, which I had put upon thee. Ezek. 16: 14.

HOW rich this chapter is in spiritual significance for ourselves! We, too, were born in the land of the Canaanite—our father the first Adam; our mother Eve. There was no beauty in us by nature, but everything to cause abhorrence to the Holy God. And if we are washed and clothed, decked with gold and silver, arrayed in fine linen, silk, and embroidered work, eating fine flour, and honey, and oil, exceedingly beautiful and arrayed in royal estate, it is all of grace—of the exceeding and eternal grace of God. There is nothing of it at all in which we can boast ourselves. Of Him are we in Christ Jesus, through whom we are what we are. We are perfect only through his comeliness which He has put upon us.

First, let us dare to believe that it is so. Accept and value your position. In Christ, we are more than tolerated; we are loved. We are more than forgiven; we are arrayed in fair garments. The King greatly delights in us. In his eyes, and because his beauty is upon us, we are all fair. The joy that the Father has in Jesus, He has in us who are in Him. We may be deeply conscious of our sinnership; but He doth not behold iniquity in Jacob, nor see perverseness in Israel. We need not shrink to take our place even among the holy ones of the Presence chamber, because we are accepted in the Beloved, and clad in his comeliness.

But, next, let us not presume. We have naught of our own. When the temptation tries us to pride ourselves on our goodness; to arrogate to ourselves a special position because of our superiority to others; to assume that we can be independent of our immortal Lover —then let us remember what we were.

All fowl of every wing.   Ezek. 17: 23.

THE cedar is a royal tree. It thrives 6,000 feet above the level of the sea. The concentric rings of one tree showed that it was 3,500 years old. What a contrast between the long-lived, deep-rooted, broad-branched tree, and the little birds that nest among the leaves!

The text suggests that Christ is the cedar, and all kinds of people seek rest in Him, as birds of every wing. Young and old, rich and poor; men high-soaring as the eagle, fierce as the raven, gentle as the dove. The young, just learning to try their wings; the old, weary, and lonely; those who have kept all the commandments from their youth, and those who have broken them all.

It does not matter with what wing we come to Jesus, so long as we come. The practised eye can easily recognize the birds by their flight; each bird has its own wing; so every soul has its own disposition and temperament—one feverish, the other languid and lethargic; one impetuous, the other dilatory; one affectionate and warm, the other cool and shy. But the Lord Jesus knows our frame, and understands us afar off. He does not chide the dove because it cannot breast the storm and face the sun like the eagle. He does not expect the sustained flight of the seagull from the sparrow; or the song of the nightingale from the chaffinch.

Do not imitate another; be yourself. Do not go about the world counting that you are useless and a failure, because you cannot do what is done by others. Learn how to be abased, and how to abound. Only rest in Christ. Out of the windy storm and tempest, make for your roosting-place under the shelter of his wing.

Behold, all souls are mine.   Ezek. 18: 4.

THIS is bed-rock. Let us ever get down to the beginnings of things, when we state God's claims on men. Instead of only pleading with them, let us boldly assert God's claims upon them. All souls are his: of the African as of the European; of the heathen as well as of the Christian born; of the toiling, sorrowing, sinning, as of those that stand in the sunlit circle.

His by right of creation. "He made us, and we are his." Has not a man a claim on all that his hands have made? and has God less? His by right of redemption. To any man we have the privilege of saying, "You have been purchased by the precious blood of Christ." His by the right of his own holy and glorious Nature. Not to own Him and love Him supremely is a gross violation of the eternal fitness of things. The parent has a claim on his child.

Needest thou fear anything, fellow-Christian, since thou art his? Though thou goest forth alone into the wilderness, where there seems no spring, no food; though thou hast no visible means of sustenance through no fault of thine; though thou shalt be called to pass to-day out of this world into the unseen: since thou art God's, is He not responsible for thee? Will an owner allow his house to fall out of repair, or his beasts to lack food and tendance? Will God not tend, maintain, nurture, and cherish thee? Would it not be to his discredit if He were careless of thee, his own? The fact of thy bearing his mark and stamp upon thee is guarantee enough of his obligation to be a God to thee. Let Him do with us as He please. Surely we can perfectly trust Him; He is well within his rights.

This is a lamentation, and shall be for a lamentation.   Ezek. 19: 1 and 14.

THIS chapter is a dirge; first over two kings of the house of David, Jehoahaz and Jehoiachim, who, like wild beasts, had been carried off, the former to Egypt, the latter by the Chaldeans; and then over the whole royal family, described under the figure of a wasted vine, humbled and almost destroyed.

We, too, may lament for the sufferings and sorrows of our King. The Holy Spirit would not have us forget them; because our sin-laden and wounded hearts can only become healed pressing against his wounds who was pierced by the nails and the spear. "Consider Him that endured such contradiction of sinners against Himself"—the agony and bloody sweat; the cross and passion; the scorn and reviling; the contradiction of sinners; and the malice of Satan. And as the full measure of his sufferings is unfolded to us we shall weep and lament; not for Him, but for ourselves and for our children.

That our sins nailed Him to the cross; that our guilt extorted from his heart the cry that He was forsaken; that his prolonged agony was borne in our stead, and borne for nothing else than for love of us; that we have grieved Him so, torn open his wounds, and added to his pains, by our rebellion and ingratitude; that the chastisement of our peace was upon Him, and that we have been healed only by his stripes. Here is subject for lamentation indeed!

But it is strange that the remembrance of all this brings strength, and solace, and peace. As Bunyan says, "He hath given us rest by his sorrow." The bitterness of his sorrows alternately make us sad and blessed. Sad that we brought Him such a heritage of woe: happy that since He has suffered, we are for ever emancipated from what had crushed us.

We will be as the nations, as the families of the countries, to serve wood and stone.
Ezek. 20: 32 (R.V.).

THERE was a tendency among the chosen people to reason thus: Why should we be perpetually reminded of the claims of Jehovah? Why should we not do as we please? Why not do as other nations around, who select their own deities, and do not seem to suffer as we do? Nay, said the Most High, that cannot be. When once I have entered into covenant relations with any, they cannot lightly cast off those sacred bonds. My name and character are too deeply implicated. I must work for my holy Name's sake, that it may not be polluted (vers. 9, 14, 22).

It is a very solemn thing to have become God's children. Sin is not the same in us as in others. In those it may be slightly passed over, but in us it will be visited with many stripes. We cannot sin with impunity, nor do as we list. As far as we go into sin, we shall have to come out of it. The more pleasure we may have had in forbidden paths, the more sharp the anguish through which we shall have to retrace our steps. We cannot be as the nations. We cannot serve wood and stone. We cannot go our own way.

But the thought cuts in two directions; if we are bound to God, He is also bound to us. We may not leave Him, but He CANNOT leave us! He will always be mindful of his covenant. There is one plea with God that never fails:

"Do it for thy great Name's sake." He cannot deny Himself, or allow his honour to be trampled in the mud.

"Yes—howsoe'er I stray and range,
Whate'er I do, Thou dost not change;
I steadier step, when I recall
That, if I slip, Thou dost not fall."

It shall be no more, until He come whose right it is; and I will give it Him. Ezek. 21: 27.

THIS prophecy was directed against Zedekiah and Jerusalem; and predicts the advance of Nebuchadnezzar, who is represented as considering an expedition against them and Ammon. Whatever the king of Judah thought to establish by his wit and power, God would overthrow. Nothing should stand, however carefully constructed, till the Messiah came to take up the kingdom and rule with meekness and righteousness.

I will overturn, overturn, overturn. Our King is always engaged in destruction, that He may the better occupy Himself with construction. He overthrows our cities of brick, that He may build them of marble. He removes the things that can be shaken, as things that are made, that the things which cannot be shaken may remain. He destroyed the institutions of the Old Covenant, that He might substitute the New. This is the inner meaning of the earthquake that so often casts down our lofty towers.

That fortune which you had built up with so much care was overturned, that you might acquire the true riches. That reputation which you had established for integrity and self-restraint was overturned, that you might despair of yourself and avail yourself of the provision made for sinners in Jesus. That friendship was overturned, that you might come to the love of God.

"He took the silver and the gold,
To make me rich in grace;
He quenched earth's lights that I
might see
The shining of his Face."

And God will go on with this overturning work until every high thing that exalts itself against the Lord Jesus is thrown down, and He is enthroned.

I will consume thy filthiness out of thee.
Ezek. 22: 15.

THE idea here, and in the following paragraph, is of the smelting furnace. We are refined by fire. Fire is pain. It is the symbol of all that our nature shrinks from. But affliction is all this. It may be anxiety about money-matters; or the chronic ill-temper of some member of your family; or a random word; or a telegraphic message; or a whispered secret; or anxiety about your health: but your soul is filled with fire—keen, strong, alive, devouring. Do not wonder at this; for only so can you be delivered from your dross and filth.

BUT GOD APPOINTS IT. As much as the process of refining implies the presence of the refiner, the afflictions of the believer imply the presence and purpose of the Lord. The process could not be carried on without Him. We are sure that in every sick chamber where his servant lies, besides the attendant wife or nurse, sits the Great Refiner of silver; closer than close; nearer than near; tenderer than the tenderest. You may not see Him now; but some day when you look back on your present sufferings, you will understand, and say: "I could not have lived through it had not the Master been with me."

THE TRIAL IS A SIGN OF PRECIOUSNESS. You do not cast a stone into the crucible, or winnow chaff, or prune a bramble, or put a cinder in the lap-dog's meal. So, when Jesus subjects us to trial, it is only because, amid all our dross, his keen eye detects the precious gold which cost Him Calvary, and is capable of becoming his ornament of beauty for ever.

"Through the test of sharp distresses,
Those whom Heaven most richly blesses,
For its joys are purified."

I will raise up thy lovers against thee, and bring them against thee on every side. Ezek. 23: 22.
IT is one sign of the revolution that the teaching of Jesus has made, that the imagery of this chapter is foreign to our modes of thought.

Spiritual unfaithfulness is constantly described under metaphors borrowed from the marriage relationship. If the soul wanders from God, He is depicted as the husband in whose heart the fire of jealousy burns; while the soul is compared to a truant wife. In the text quoted above, the analogy is followed still further; and the prophet asserts that it is impossible for us to be always satisfied with the lovers that we have chosen, and that our chastisement for wandering will probably come through their agency.

There is no lack of practical illustration of this. If a Christian choose worldly prosperity, or his own reputation, or any earthly object apart from God, it is through this that he will suffer. The things that he has loved will be raised up against him, just as Israel, that had dallied with Babylon, was carried into captivity to Babylon. Of sinful and forbidden pleasure God will make whips of scorpions by which to drive us back to Himself.

What a light, by force of contrast, is cast on those rapturous words of the apostle, when he tells us that we may be married to that glorious Man, even to Him that was raised from the dead! The soul stands by to see Him die, bathed in tears; but as she beholds Him rise, she is divinely attracted to Him, conscious of a profound affinity, which engrosses and absorbs her being. Nothing will satisfy her then but union with his Spirit. She reckons herself dead to all the old lovers, through the body of Christ, but for ever alive unto Him.

So I spake unto the people in the morning: and at even my wife died. Ezek. 24: 18.
IT was a sudden stroke which befel the prophet's home. In the morning the desire of his eyes was present to care for him, and in the even she had passed away. It is the practice of the Eastern mourner to give vent to heart-rending cries; in his case these were forbidden. He might sigh, but not aloud (R.V.). There was to be no mourning for the dead, neither tears, nor fasting, because his work was to engross him; the needs of the people preponderated over personal anguish; and he was called to set forth in his own reticence the solemn, tearless anguish with which Israel would go into captivity.

We are reminded of the words of the apostle in 1 Cor. 7, that those who had wives should be as though they had none; those that wept as though they wept not; because the time was short, and the fashion of the world was passing away.

In every human experience there are times when the personal must be subordinated to the national and universal. We must choke back our sobs, crush down our almost uncontrollable emotion, preserve a calm and tranquil exterior, that we may devote ourselves more earnestly and continuously to the crying need of others. There is nothing nobler than the self-restraint which anoints the head and washes the face, that it may have leisure from itself to do its life-work, and to press to its bosom those who are suffering around. There was a pretty illustration of this in a recent railway accident, when a little girl, badly hurt, insisted on being cared for last.

"Yet not in solitude! if Christ anear me
 Waketh Him workers for the great employ!
Oh, not in solitude! if souls that hear me
 Catch from my joyance the surprise of joy."

Because Moab and Seir say, Judah is like unto all the nations, therefore behold . . .
Ezek. 25: 8, 9.

IT is a remarkable fact that the Hebrew prophets were such keen politicians in the best sense. They were always watching and interpreting the dealings of God in contemporary history. Mention of Moab and Seir is almost as frequent as of Jerusalem. I remember the saintly Professor Reynolds saying, as he opened the morning paper, "Let us see what our heavenly Father is doing in the world."

As our enemies behold the children of God, they are apt to suppose that there is no difference between them and others. They cannot see the divine environment within which they live, and they suppose that they can easily work their will. They say, Behold these people are like other people; we have but to stretch out our hand, and can spoil them as a boy the nests of spring. Then they discover that they have another to reckon with, and that God will arise to plead the cause of his people and to execute judgment upon their oppressors. Not in vain did He say to Abraham, and through him to all that believe: "I will bless him that blesseth thee, and curse him that curseth thee:" "No weapon that is formed against thee shall prosper."

We must not presume on this. Strong as God is on our behalf towards our enemies, He is equally so within the circle of his household. He will not let others hurt us, but He will not spare his children. He may use others as his rod, just as at certain epochs of their national history He used Moab or Edom. But when the work of refining is done, He will lay the instruments aside, and even punish, if there has been an excess of malice. O child of God, thy privilege and responsibility are immeasurable. Thou art not as others.

Though thou be sought for, yet shalt thou never be found again, saith the Lord God. Ezek. 26: 21.

TYRE, to the world of her age, was what Venice was in the Middle Ages, and London to-day. She was strong in the sea; the carrying trade of the world was in her hands. Carthage, which was able to conflict with Rome, was her daughter; and the coasts of Cornwall were visited by her merchant vessels. In the days of Ezekiel she was a proud and populous city. But the prophet predicted her approaching fall. Her songs would cease; her walls would be overwhelmed in the floods of armed men; and the rocks on which she stood would be as bare as before a fisherman's hut was built on them. And as the prophet anticipates the future, he says that her site would be sought in vain; a prediction so literally fulfilled that it is only of late years that careful research has been able to pronounce where Tyre stood.

This chapter seems to underlie the description given in the Apocalypse of the fall of Babylon, when the mighty angel shall take up a stone, like a great mill-stone, and cast it into the sea; when all human voices shall cease from her vast solitudes, and the grinding of the mill-stone shall be for ever silent. So shall perish every false system; all mere traditionalism and ritualism; all that savours of human pride; all the blandishments and impurities of the unfaithful Church, which sought to turn men's hearts from God.

What a contrast to this are the words of Jeremiah (50: 20): "In those days the iniquity of Israel shall be sought for, and there shall be none; and the sins of Judah, and they shall not be found." Refuse the love of God, and you are doomed; you will leave no enduring record. Trust in Him, and your sins will be blotted out as if they had never been.

The east wind hath broken thee in the heart of the seas. Ezek. 27: 26 (R.V.).

IN this splendid chapter the prophet describes Tyre under the image of one of her own merchant vessels. Looking at it simply as a piece of composition, what an extreme interest there is in this enumeration of the various races which were subject to this mighty city, and the lands from which she drew her supplies! We are reminded of the far-spreading colonies of the Anglo-Saxon race. We can almost hear the noise of her construction in the earlier verses, and see fine linen hoisted as her sail, whilst she is manned and piloted by her statesmen. Heavily laden with the choice merchandise of the East, she sails the seas, independent of the winds of heaven, because the galley slaves toil at treble banks of oars on either side. But their rowing brings her into great waters; she encounters the east wind, which breaks her in the heart of the sea; and in one day, pilots, rowers, men of war, and merchandise, are lost—all brought to silence in the midst of the sea. What a powerful conception of the great ship sinking in silence with all on board! One cry; the waves meet over her; and only a floating spar tells where she sank.

So is it with many a life. The whole world is laid under contribution for its outfit. Bashan, Chittim, Egypt, bring their quota; and to all appearance, as it glides from its stocks upon the sea of life, a fair voyage awaits it, and large exchange of the wares of human industry and thought. But where Christ is not the Pilot, and his Word not the chart, the rowers bring it into great waters, and it is broken by the east wind. O mariner! see to it that Christ is on board; for He only can still the tempest and speak peace, and guide thee out of the great waters.

Thou sealest up the sum, full of wisdom, and perfect in beauty. Ezek. 28: 12.
THE magnificent words of this chapter cannot be applicable merely to Tyre. Behind that mighty city the prophet beheld its Prince, the anointed cherub that covereth (ver. 14); and on further investigation this can only be the prince of the power of the air, who, our Lord says, is also the prince of this world. When he was created he was perfect in his ways, till unrighteousness was found in him (ver. 15). But he was cast out of heaven, when his heart was lifted up (ver. 17). He said, I am God; but as he met in conflict the Son of Man, he learnt his absolute inferiority.

This association of a comity with an evil spirit is not confined to this chapter only. It is a frequent allusion of the Scriptures. For instance, Daniel describes the Prince of Persia as hindering the advent of Gabriel to succour the chosen people: whilst the apostle Paul distinctly attributes the darkness of the world to the wicked spirits in the heavenlies. Without doubt, the same thought underlies the present magnificent apostrophe. And this is such an encouragement to prayer; because from our knees we may affect the balance of power in the heavenlies by the weight of our intercessions.

All through this chapter runs the contrast between the fallen cherub, the patron saint of Zidon, and Jehovah the God of Israel. In the collision between these two, the might of the devil was shown to be a shadow; and his votaries were ashamed and astonished at his impotence to defend them. For us there is blessed significance in this subject. Greater is He that is for us than he that is against us. The last Adam hath stood in the conflict in which the first Adam fell. None shall prevail against us in Him.

I have given him the land of Egypt, . . because they wrought for Me. Ezek. 29: 20 (R.V.).
THE king of Babylon was sent against Tyre. The siege lasted long, and his army suffered great privations. Scorching heat above, and the heavy burdens on their shoulders, made every head bald and every shoulder peal. For this great service he was to be recompensed with the gift of the land of Egypt, because he had wrought God's purpose.

The words quoted above suggest the thought, that though we do not merit anything of God by our service, yet He does not forget our work of faith and labour of love when it is wrought for Him. If He gave Egypt to a heathen king for his service in respect to Tyre, we may also expect Him to bestow a reward on those who have built gold, silver, and precious stones, into his holy temple. The servant who has made his five talents into ten, shall be rewarded with ten cities. Those who have watched and waited through the long night shall be rewarded with special honour in the bridal feast. God will give to us some guerdon for our toils, some prize for our conflict, some token of his favour, which will be all of grace and yet proportionate to the work wrought for Him.

The transference of countries from one sovereign power to another may appear to be only the result of political combinations, or superior armies. "Providence is on the side of the strongest battalions," Napoleon said; and the remark is consistent with man's ordinary way of thinking. But here the prophet withdraws the vail, and shows the fulfilment of the divine purpose, as Egypt comes under the power of the king of Babylon. As we look over the world, how vast are the changes which are passing over it, preparing for Christ's Gospel.

When I shall put my sword into the hand of the king of Babylon. Ezek. 30: 25.
THE emphasis is on the word my. The punish-

ment inflicted by the king of Babylon on Egypt was directly from God; it was his sword in the hand of Nebuchadnezzar (ver. 10). How little the historian of that time realized that there was anything more in the expedition of Babylon against Egypt than the natural ravalry of these two great nations. But the eye of the inspired seer saw that Babylon was the executor of the divine decree.

Very often events and people carry the sword of God, or his rod, which to the natural eye seem to emanate by chance, or by the malice of men. God's chastisements are very real. It is probable that no child of God sins knowingly against the divine order without being chastised. Sometimes the natural consequences of our sins, at other times misfortunes in our circumstances, or the alienation of our friends, make the scourge of small cords by which our souls are taught the bitterness of any way but God's.

Are you undergoing chastisement? Do not regard the human agent with any feeling but of love and pity; do not expend your strength in resistance and threatening; do not faint when you are rebuked: but lie still at the feet of God, receiving meekly the strokes, and thankful that He loves you well enough to take such pains. Thus the bitter discipline will produce the fruits of righteousness which are to the praise and glory of God. Never forget to distinguish between chastisement and punishment. The one is for the child; the other for the rebel. Chastisement we may bear; but the punishment of our sin has been for ever borne by Jesus Christ. Oh, do not call yourself Marah! If you only understood God's way, it would be Naomi.

They . . . that dwelt under his shadow in the midst of the heathen. Ezek. 31: 17.
WHATEVER may be the primary meaning of these words, they have a very blessed application to those who have gone forth, from so many Christian families, into heathen lands. For no choice of their own, and simply in obedience to their King's command, hundreds of our sons and daughters have gone forth to dwell in the midst of the heathen. They have taken up their home amid conditions which they would not have chosen, had it not been for the constraining love of Christ, and the imperative need of dying men; and as fond relatives and friends regard their lot from a distance, they are often filled with anxious

forebodings. May they not be involved in some sudden riot and sacrificed to a frenzy of hate? May not the sanitary conditions and methods of life be seriously detrimental to their health or morals? "Oh, if only I could be there," you sigh.

Hush! Christ is there; as near them as He is to you, casting over them the shadow of his presence, beckoning them to his secret place. He is the shadow of a great Rock in a weary land; or like the canopy of cloud that hovered over the camp of Israel by day, screening it from the torrid glare. Do not fear to trust your loved ones to the immortal Lover, who fainteth not, neither is weary. The hand that would harm is arrested and paralysed when it attempts to penetrate that safe enclosure.

"God is never so far off as even to be near:
    He is within! Our spirit is the home
        He holds most dear.
To think of Him as by our side, is almost
        as untrue
As to remove his throne beyond those
        skies of starry blue;
So all the while I thought myself home-
        less, forlorn, and weary,
Nursing my joy, I walked the earth—
        myself God's sanctuary."

The word of the Lord came unto me, saying:
Ezek. 32: 1, 17.
WE often bring our words to God, without being equally eager to receive his to us. Probably his word often comes to us when we are too engaged to hear it, or because our ear is not anointed and purged. Tennyson used to boast of his power of detecting a bat's shrill scream, which comparatively few can catch. So it is not every child of God that can be still or quick enough to detect the whisper of his small soft voice. When it does come, breaking in through the many voices that fill heart and life, we do well, as Ezekiel did, carefully to mark the days as memorable, writing on the tablet of our heart, "On this day God spake to my soul."

We do well to observe special days in our diary of the years. The day of our conversion or consecration; the day of deliverance from overwhelming trouble; the day when He summoned us to some new duty; the day when Paradise shone around us with its golden sheen. Even Paul recorded, amid his busy life, that day when he was caught up into the third heaven.

Let us invite these divine confidences. Let us fall on our face while God talks with us. Let us be on the outlook lest his invitations are not responded to. Let us address our heavenly Bridegroom in the words of the Song of Songs: "Let me hear thy voice, for sweet is thy voice." Then, though we sleep, our heart will wake; and we shall recognize the voice of our Beloved, as He waits at the door, saying, "Open to Me, my sister, my love, my undefiled." Ah, who shall fathom the confidences that are exchanged when the word of the Lord thus comes to us? But be sure that it will cease, directly we hear, but fail to obey. Humility and obedience are essential.

Then shall they know that a prophet hath been among them. Ezek. 33: 33.

THE people looked on Ezekiel's ministrations as a delightful diversion. They regarded him as one that had a pleasant voice, and could play well on an instrument, and gathered around him with apparent eagerness and devotion. With their mouth they were profuse in expressions of love and admiration; but they had no idea of the weight and worth of his words. They looked only on the beauty of his expressions, without penetrating to the spiritual depth and meaning they contained. But when once his warnings had taken effect, and his predictions had been fulfilled, they would know that he had been something more than a sweet singer, and that there had been a prophet among them.

We do not realize the true worth of God's gifts till they are gone from us never to be recalled. That friendship was grateful and pleasing to the sense; but we did not gauge the true worth of our friend. That opportunity of hearing God's word from the lips of an honoured minister was frittered away in casual criticisms on his manners and gestures, instead of being employed for hearing God's word from his lips. That incident in our life touched us by its outward features only; but we failed to receive the profound lesson it was intended to convey. Alas, so often when the prophet has gone, we realize what he was, and what we have missed!

Let us be more careful to look into the heart of the circumstances and people around us; to ponder deeply the meaning of all that God puts into our lives; to penetrate below the surface to the eternal and divine, which are not far beneath. The vail between us and the Eternal Presence-chamber is as thin and delicate as the walls of our hearts.

I will feed my flock, and I will cause them to lie down, saith the Lord God. Ezek. 34: 15.

IT is perfectly impossible to make sheep lie down unless they are satisfied or free from alarm. When the flocks lie deep in the rich pasture lands, it is because they have eaten to the full, and are quiet from fear of evil. When, therefore, the Shepherd and Bishop of our souls promises that He will so deal with us as to cause us to lie down, He undertakes to fulfil in our life these two conditions.

The Lord Jesus brings us into a good pasture, and causes us to feed in a fat pasture upon the mountains of fellowship, transfiguration, and far-reaching vision. Listen as He cries, "Eat, yea, eat abundantly, O beloved." Our restlessness arises from our refusal to obey his loving invitation to come and dine. We do not read our Bibles enough, or feed on his flesh, or drink his blood. Let us look at the Scriptures as the green pastures; and as we open them let us ask Him to be our guide, and to show us where the food appropriate to our need is to be found.

The Lord Jesus does more. He makes with us a covenant of peace; and even if the evil beasts do not cease out of the land, He so assures us that we can dwell safely in the wilderness and sleep in the woods. He intends that we should be safe in Immanuel's land; that the bonds of our yoke should be broken; and that we should be delivered out of the hands of those who serve themselves of us.

O child of God, be less dependent on people and circumstances! Deal more constantly at first hand with Jesus. Regard Him as your Shepherd; "He maketh to lie down." Rejoice that He the Lord your God is with you, and that the shadowing woods, the mighty mountains, and the stream-watered vales are equally beneath his power and care.

Whereas the Lord was there. Ezek. 35: 10.

LISTEN to the plottings of Mount Seir, waiting until Nebuchadnezzar has dispossessed Israel of their land, and with the fixed intention of entering upon its inheritance. These two nations, says the foe, and these two countries shall be mine. The children of Israel are in captivity in Habor and Gozan; the children of Judah at Babylon. What is there to prevent my entering upon their lands? But Jehovah Shammah, the Lord, was in possession; He was there.

What inspiration this is! How often do our foes plot against us, supposing that we shall fall an easy prey, and that they can divide the spoils without let. But God is there. God is in the heart, holding for Himself that which He redeemed. God is in that bed-chamber of mortal anguish and of long waiting. God is in that home which appears besieged by every kind of misfortune. O foot of the foe, thou shalt not intrude! O might of the foe, thou shalt not prevail! God is in possession! Though there seems nothing to prevent the complete overrunning of the land, the mailed forces of the enemy shall break on the invisible bulwarks of the divine presence.

Jehovah Shammah! That hallows every spot, consecrates every act, invests the meanest believer with transcendent worth, is our buttress against attack, and our glory in the midst. For God to be in the soul is the secret of its holiness, of its persistence in the heavenly way, and of its ultimate triumph over all the power of the adversary. Be sure that He is willing to become all this for you also, O weakest and most helpless man! When the Stronger than the strong is in possession, how safe his goods!

Ye shall shoot forth your branches, and yield your fruit to my people. Ezek. 36: 8.
VERY magnificent is this address to the mountains of Israel. At the moment the prophet spoke they were lying waste, and the people of Idumea were plotting to possess them; but this chapter reiterates the assurance that they should be tilled, sown, and possessed.

It seems to me as though these words may be addressed to desolate hearts that are suffering from heartrending grief. Whereas they were once full of mirth, they are now desolate and lonely. The light of their eyes has departed; the voice that made music is still; the presence that filled the home is gone. Is such your case? Behold, God will do better unto you than at your beginnings, and the old estates shall be apportioned and inherited. Bind this promise to your heart; the desolate land shall be tilled, and they shall say, This land that was desolate has become like the Garden of Eden, and the wastes are inhabited (vers. 34, 35). Do you think that you will never be glad again; that shadow will always lie athwart your path; and that desolation shall hold undisputed empire?

It shall not be so. O desolate mountains, ye shall shoot forth your branches, and yield fruit; and it is near to come.

But before these promises can be realized, you must let your sorrow work to its full result in the purification and sanctification of your heart. Great trouble has been allowed to come that you might know the vanity and evil of your own heart, and be led to claim the promises of verses 25–29. They are exceeding great and precious. Note specially the words, "In the day that I shall have cleansed you from all your iniquities, the wastes shall be builded, and the desolate land tilled" (vers. 33, 34).

Prophesy over these bones. . . . Prophesy unto the wind. Ezek. 37: 4, 9 (R.V.).
THIS is our double office, as servants of God. We are to prophesy to earth and heaven; to man and God. There are some who forget the second of these injunctions, and their work fails of its highest result. When they speak, bones "come together, bone to bone"; there is a stir in the graves of death and corruption; a coming together of the people to hear the word; and in many cases all the appearance of a new life. The flesh comes up and skin covers them above; but (and how fatal is the admission which this but introduces) there is no breath in them. It is clear that no amount of human persuasiveness or oratory can secure the true regeneration of the soul. That which is born of the flesh may be galvanized by the energy of the flesh into the appearance of spiritual life, but it will always remain flesh.

When you have done your best, and have failed of the highest results, prophesy to the Spirit; cry to the four winds, because He may come in the icy north wind of tribulation, or the warm west wind of prosperity; but speak with the certain assurance of, "Thus saith the Lord God: Come!" There is a sense in which the believer has the privilege of commanding the Spirit of God. "Concerning the works of my hands, command ye Me." When you obey the law of a force, the force will obey you; and when you yield utterly and humbly to God, the power of God will answer the summons of your faith.

Even while you are speaking, let your heart be in the attitude of expectancy; and according to your faith, it shall be done unto you. If you cannot go forth to witness or prophesy, let your prayer arise to God like a fountain day and night, that his Spirit may breathe on the slain.

Behold, I am against thee, O Gog, prince of Rosh, Meshech, and Tubal. Ezek. 38: 3 (R.V.).
IT is startling to meet with these three names, which are found in modern maps as Russia, Moscow, and Tobolsk, and to feel that we may be reading words that are shortly coming to pass. So far as we can see, they have not as yet been fulfilled. Within the hearing of the present generation, Russia may resolve to go up to the land of unwalled villages, such as those that abound in Palestine, and may be challenged by the merchants of Tarshish in the far West. Some have even found an allusion to the English standard in the reference to the young lions of verse 13.

The shrewdest among us cannot guess what may await the world in the near future. Peer as we may into the dim mist, we cannot descry the events which are coming upon the earth. But we may be thankful that we have his word of prophecy, to which we "do well to take heed, as unto a light shining in a dark place." It is like the illustrated railway-table, which contains a list of the stations through which we must pass ere we reach the terminus. And as the porters call out the names, and we find that they correspond to the route as detailed on the tables, we come to place more implicit trust in our guide-book, and to count with absolute certainty on our ultimate emergence at our destination. "When ye see these things coming to pass, know ye that He is nigh, even at the doors." In the meanwhile let your loins be girt, and your lamps burning, and ye as those that wait for their Lord.

"Surely He cometh, and a thousand voices
  Shout to the saints, and to the deaf are
    dumb!
Surely He cometh, and the earth rejoices,
  Glad in his coming, who hath sworn, 'I
    come'."

Now will I bring again the captivity of Jacob, and have mercy upon Israel. Ezek. 39: 25.
WE must never overlook the literal significance of this promise. All Israel, insists the apostle of the Gentiles, who never lost his love for his own people, shall be saved. The blindness which has happened to them is only till the fulness of the Gentile contingent to the one Church has been brought in. The gifts and calling of God are without repentance. The covenant made to their fathers cannot be annulled.

But all bringing again must originate in God. The sheep can only wander on, further and further from the foid, ever deeper into the dark mountains; it will never find its way back: if it shall see the fold again, it will be because the shepherd goes after it until he finds it.

Our natural bias is altogether away from God. The pole of our life is aslant from the pole-star. Our natural tendency is to vanity, corruption, and chaos. If God were to withdraw Himself, however slightly, from the natural world, it would revert to the darkness and confusion of its earliest stages; and whenever God is absent from our moral life, there is the natural and inevitable reversion to the original Adam-type. But God is rich in mercy, in neutralizing the effects of our evil nature. He calls us back to Himself; nay, He comes after us, and brings again our captivity for his name's sake. Are you in captivity to evil habits from which you cannot break loose; to evil associations from which you cannot free yourself; to circumstances that shut you in as iron bars? Have you come to an end of your efforts for liberty, finding the more you struggle the more deeply you involve yourself in the close-woven meshes? Then look away to the Lord God, plead his promises, ask Him to remember his holy name, and He will bring you again.

Declare all that thou seest. Ezek. 40: 4.
WE are called to be God's witnesses, beholding the visions of God, and bearing witness to our brethren of what we have seen, tasted, and handled, of the Word of Life. When the city is draped in mist and gloom, the artist takes his portfolio and climbs into the high mountain of vision. He beholds there the crystalline beauty of the unsullied snow; the roseate hues of sunrise and sunset; the heaped magnificence of the glaciers, with their blue depth. Transferring his visions to his canvas, he returns to this lower sphere, and exhibits his picture on the walls of some public gallery, from which it silently witnesses to one of shy Nature's coyest moods. But the passers-by are apt to accuse him of extravagance. Ah, but they have not stood where he stood, or seen what he has beheld! It is thus in divine things also.

God often leads his children into startling and unexpected experiences. They are troubled on every side; bereft of dear ones; deprived of health or property; compelled to pass through the scorching fires of slander, misunderstanding, and temptation. But these are the times when they should set their hearts on all that is being shown, to see the way by which God is leading them; the comfort with which He is comforting them; the help in which He is environing them. They have been brought to these experiences that they may know themselves, and God, and his ways of dealing with his people; and may be able to declare what they have been taught, to the intent that unto the principalities and powers in the heavenlies may be known through the Church the manifold wisdom of God. No vision is for private advantage and jubilation only; declare it all.

He brought me to the Temple, and measured.
Ezek. 41: 1.

THIS is the pattern of an ideal Temple, which was presented in thought to the prophet's mind, as the pattern of the Tabernacle was shown to Moses on the Mount. It is interesting to notice the minute measurements and specifications—even to the ornaments of cherubim and palm trees. We cannot but remember that the plan of our life is also worked out before the face of God, and that we shall live to the best purpose when we make all things according to the pattern shown us on the Mount of Prayer and Vision.

Ever remember to look upward to God's pattern, and do nothing except what He reveals as his will for you; whilst careful to omit nothing that has been prepared for you to say or do. Look up, child of God; look into the plan of your temple-building. The holy places of prayer; the altars of your sacrifice and consecration; the tables of your fellowship; the doors that lead out to work, and open into chambers of pain and suffering; the length and breadth of each; the ornamentation to be chased upon your soul—all, all are fixed. Let your one aim be that God's will for you should be realized in you; and dare to believe that, if only you will yield to Him, He will work out in you that which is well-pleasing in his sight, to whom shall be the glory for ever and ever.

Only remember three rules: (1) Keep your eye directed outwards and upwards, to Christ exalted in the glory. (2) Be careful to maintain the silence of the Sabbath-rest within—rest from your own thoughts and ways. (3) Do not be always speaking of God as having said or shown this or that: let men form their own conclusions.

The priests that are near unto the Lord shall eat the most holy things. Ezek. 42: 13 (R.V.).
EVERY believer is a priest unto God. He may

not exercise his priesthood; but when he was washed from his sins in the blood of the Lamb, he was constituted a priest unto God, even the Father. We are called, not to offer propitiatory sacrifices—there is no need for this, since Jesus when He died offered the one sufficient oblation for the sins of the world—but to present ourselves living sacrifices, to offer up a sacrifice of praise to God continually, and to do good and communicate of our substance to the help of others.

Are you near unto the Lord? Hath He chosen you to stand before Him, and know his will, and hear the word from his mouth? Then most certainly you will often enter into the inner chamber to eat of the most holy things. These are enumerated as the meat-offering, the sin-offering, and the guilt-offering. We must have fellowship with God in his joy over the spotless character and lovely human life of Jesus, which may be compared to fine flour. We must have fellowship in the atoning death of our Substitute; feeding on all the sacred meaning of the wondrous Cross. We must avail ourselves of Jesus as our guilt-offering; making propitiation for our mistakes, negligences, and infirmities (Lev. 2, 4, 5).

If you would be near to God, feed on the work of Jesus; if you are near to God, you cannot live without it. To muse on the propitiatory aspects of the death of Jesus is as necessary for the strength of our inner life as food is to the body. Let us beware of imitating the mistake of Lev. 10: 16–20; and let us be very careful to eat of the wave-breast and the heave-thigh, which stand for the love of Jesus for our affections, and the might of Jesus for our strength (Lev. 10: 14).

Behold, the glory of the Lord filleth the house.
Ezek. 43: 2–7.

AT the beginning of this book (chaps. 9 and 10) we beheld the departure of the Shekinah cloud from the doomed temple. But now, to the new reconstructed temple it returns. So will God shed the sense of his presence through our hearts. We may have grieved Him, and lost it by defiling his holy name, and by the abominations which we have committed. But if we will resolutely put away our unfaithfulness, our coquetting with the world, our tampering with the flesh, He will return and dwell in our midst for ever. Behold, the glory of the Lord will fill the inner shrine of our spirit, and the earth will shine with his glory.

"Heaven above is softer blue;
    Earth beneath is sweeter green;
Something shines in every hue
    Christless eyes have never seen."

There is a very precious promise connected
with the divine return and indwelling: "I will
dwell in the midst of the children of Israel, and
they shall no more defile my holy name"
(ver. 7). Be willing to admit God, and He will
come. "If any man open the door. I will come
in." Whenever God comes He will make the
old sin abhorrent and impossible; and his
indwelling will not be transient and fitful, but
permanent and efficient. "They shall no more
defile."

This is what we need. We cannot have holiness apart from the Holy One. The attribute
may not be divorced from its possessor. But to
the soul that desires holiness, the holy God
comes, and infills, and keeps; so that darkness
cannot intrude on the domain of light, nor
hate on love, nor death on life. Has the
Shekinah left thee? Lo, it returns by the
way it went, and thine earthly life shall shine
again.

I am their inheritance. . . . I am their possession
Ezek. 44: 28.

THESE injunctions for the priests, the Levites,
that keep the charge of the sanctuary, are full
of suggestion to those who have been made
priests to God and the Father. It is for us to
enter into the Holy Place, to come near his
table to minister unto his Father, and to keep
his charge (ver. 16), always remembering that
we need the sin-offering whenever we approach
God (ver. 27). However holy a man becomes,
as the revelation of God's perfect holiness
breaks upon him, there is need to shelter
beneath the blood that was shed.

But when these features of our ministry have
been realized, we have a right to look on God
as our inheritance and possession. How wonderful that in a deep sense we may obtain
supplies of divine help from our fellowship
with God! To follow out the literal comparison of an inheritance would suggest that
as the peasant proprietors of Palestine raised
crops on their lands, so we may obtain, by
prayer and faith, out of the very heart of God,
all things that are needful for life and godliness.

We possess God as the flower the sunlight;
as a babe the mother. All his resources are
placed at our disposal. The seed cast into the
ground immediately begins to take from earth
and air the nutriment of its life, and we have
the same power of deriving from the infinite
fulness of God all that shall make us pure and
strong and gentle. Ours are the unsearchable
riches of Christ; we are made full through the
fulness which God the Father has been pleased
to make dwell in Him. All the resources which
have been placed at his disposal in his
ascension and eternal reign are gifts which He
holds for men. Alas for us that we fail to
possess our possessions!

*And so shalt thou do for every one that
erreth, and for him that is simple.*
Ezek. 45: 20.

A VERY touching provision is here. When the
services of the newly constituted temple were
in full operation, and the priests were performing the usual rites in all the pomp and splendour of their ceremonial on the behalf of all
righteous and godly souls, there was to be
special thought of the erring and simple; for
these two characters a special offering was
made. Perhaps the erring were too hardened
and the simple too obtuse to bring an offering
for themselves; but they were not forgotten.
The blood of the sin-offering was to be placed
on the posts of the house and on the posts of
the gate of the inner court, each seventh day
of the month, on their behalf.

Whenever we draw around the altar of God,
whether in the home or church, we should
remember the erring and simple. If a family
misses from its ranks one erring member, its
prayer and thought are more directed towards
that one than to those that have not gone
astray. Does not the child who is deficient in
its intellect attract more loving care than those
who are able to care for themselves? Should
it be otherwise in God's home? Was it not for
erring Peter that Jesus prayed? Was it not for
Thomas that He made another special visit to
the upper room? Does not the Great Shepherd
gently lead those that are with young? and in
so far as we enter into God's mind, we, too,
shall care for the ignorant and those who are
out of the way.

There is room for all such in the Father's
House—a warm welcome and ample provision.
Like Samuel's words about David, so God
speaks of the most inconspicuous members of
his family, "Send and fetch him; for we will
not sit down till he come hither."

The Prince in the midst of them, when they go in, shall go in. Ezek. 46: 10.

THESE are regulations for ingress and egress in the temple which Ezekiel describes; but we may be pardoned for finding a true and tender thought of the new relationship of Christ and his own.

We, too, go in, to find pasture within the precincts of the fold; to worship in the Holy Place, to get refreshment and strength; as when Jonathan and David met in the wood and strengthened each other's hands in God. On the Lord's Day especially we go in where the seraphim stand around the sapphire throne. But of what avail is it to go in, unless our Prince accompanies us? His presence makes the feast; his company is as sunlight to nature; to hear his voice, to feel the touch of his hand, to sit in his near proximity—this is the bread of life divine.

But there are times when we must go forth; we must leave the transfiguration mount for the valley. The bugle-note rings out in the starry dawn, and tells us that the foe is approaching. The look-out watch calls from the mast-head that the enemies' ships are in view. There is work to be done, suffering borne, difficulty encountered. But when we go forth, our Prince and we shall go forth together (R.V.).

He never puts his sheep forth without going before them. He never thrusts us into the fight without preceding us. If we have to take the way of the Cross, we may always count on seeing Him go first, though we follow Him amazed.

No ascent so steep that we cannot see his form in advance; no stones so sharp that are not flecked with his blood; no fire so intense that One does not go beside us, whose form is like the Son of God; no waters so deep that Emmanuel does not go beside us.

Everything shall live whither the river cometh. Ezek. 47: 9.

THE great need of the world is life. Not more intelligence or activity, but life, and fuller life—life more abundant, life in full tide; the life which is life indeed, the eternal life which was with the Father, and was manifested to the world. Of that life, this river is the emblem. It issues from the throne of God. It ever tends to become fuller and deeper. It becomes finally too mighty to be crossed.

The course of the river of the prophet's vision was due east, to the Arabah, a desert waste, and the Dead Sea, in whose dark, brackish waters no fish can live; but as even these are smitten by the crystal tide, a wonderful change takes place—they are healed, and begin to abound with fish, and fishers stand beside it from Engedi to En-eglaim.

This has been the course of the Gospel of Jesus Christ. Ever since the river of the water of life issued from the Cross it has been deepening and extending, bringing life and beauty into the waste and barren wilderness of the world. The transforming effects of the Gospel on continents and islands, on vast multitudes of men, can be compared to nothing less than the fertilizing effect of a mighty river. Flow on, great sea of God, until all the Dead Sea of sin is swept away before thy beneficent waters!

But chiefly we want this more abundant life within us. Are there no Dead Seas, no marshes, no waste stretches of desert sands? Is there not urgent need that the lengthening out of our days should see a deepening of the river until it rise beyond our depths? We need the ankle-depths of walking to be exchanged for the knee-depths of praying; and these for the loin-depths of perfect purity; and these for the length, depth, breadth, and height of the love of Christ.

The Lord is there. Ezek. 48: 35.

EZEKIEL has in view an ideal city; whether in any material form it is to be realized, we must wait to see. But this shall be its prominent characteristic, that God will be there. A great voice will be heard out of heaven, saying, "Behold, the tabernacle of God is with men, and He will dwell with them, and they shall be his people; and God Himself shall be with them and be their God."

THERE IS COMFORT IN THIS FOR THE SORROWFUL; because where God is, there cannot be sorrow, nor crying, nor pain. God shall wipe away all tears from off all faces. No cypress-trees line the streets of that city; no dirge intrudes upon the glad ascription of praise; no sob or groan is possible.

THERE IS COMFORT FOR FAR-DISSEVERED FRIENDS; for where God is, the centre and goal and home, all his children meet. Back from distant lands and spheres they come; home from the school where they have been taught; back from the voyage; back from the military camp; back from the tour of exploration. The gates stand open to admit to his heart; and that heart is the rendezvous of those who have come out of every nation, and kindred, and tongue, and people—never again to be parted.

THERE IS COMFORT FOR THE DOUBTING AND PERPLEXED. Here, night often reigns over the heart of Thomas and the mind of Mary. Truly devoted souls grope by candle-light, and sometimes they walk in darkness and have no light, learning to walk by faith. But there all mysteries will be unravelled, all problems solved, every question answered; there will be no night, no need of sun or moon, for the glory of God shall lighten it, and the Lamb shall be the lamp thereof.

Daniel

And Daniel continued even unto the first year of King Cyrus. Dan. 1: 21.

IS that wonderful? It may seem so when you consider the uncertainty of Oriental politics, and the feverish haste with which favourites are raised to confidential positions and thrust back again to obscurity. In this very book we have glimpses of the virulence of hatred entertained in the court of Babylon towards Jews, and the mortification with which aspirants for the royal favour found it monopolized by Daniel and his friends. But we cease to wonder when we turn to chap 6: 10, and discover Daniel's habit of kneeling upon his knees three times a day, praying and giving thanks to his God. Prayer is the secret of continuance.

To all deep lives there come moments of serious questioning: Shall I be able to hold out? Shall I always be able to withstand the virulent hate of my foes, and overcome the corruption of my heart? Will it be always possible to meet the strong and imperious demands of duty, and the appeal of those who look to me for help? Amid the changes that the years may bring, will it be possible to maintain my ground? Men are so capricious; events so fluctuating; the sea of human life so unstable. To all such suggestions there is but one reply —prayer is the secret of continuance.

It is a dangerous temptation of the adversary, so writes one of God's hidden ones, when upright minds suffer themselves to be completely cast down by the unbelieving—I had almost said proud—view of their infirmities: in the performance of God's works such ought only to humble themselves, and go forward. He who loves and exercises prayer, will in due time be translated from self unto God: from being a pitcher, filled and emptied, to a river-bed.

Then was the secret revealed in a night vision. Dan. 2: 17, 18, 19.

THIS prayer-meeting, called hurriedly, must have been very intense. There was no knowing whether it might not be interrupted before it was completed by the guards of the palace summoning the supplicants to die. These two or three were gathered in the name of God, in rooms which never before had heard his name. But when their prayers had been offered, such serene peace resulted that Daniel was able to sleep with the utmost composure; and his mind, like a mirror, received upon its placid depths the impression of God's thoughts.

It is a test of prayer having attained its object, when the praying soul feels there is no need to wrestle longer, and the sweet assurance is borne in that God has received our supplication, and that further words are needless. This serenity of heart shows itself in the unruffled calm of the commercial man in a time of panic; in the quietness of the soul under provocation; in the stayedness of the heart on God, while storms sweep earth and sky.

It has been pointed out that there are three New Testament words for prayer to which we do well to take heed. Be sober unto prayer (1 Peter 4: 7). Do not be drunk with worldly vanity, business, or gaiety; but bring a humble, penitent, clear, and sound mind. Be at leisure when you pray (1 Cor. 7: 5). The word means that prayer is not to be hurried; that nothing should interfere with its leisurely enjoyment. Labour at prayer (Col. 1: 29; or 4: 12). As a man labours at his daily work, or strives on the battle-field, or agonizes to preserve a beloved friend from danger. It was thus that Jesus laboured in the Garden of Gethsemane. And it was thus that these faithful souls must have prayed.

Lo, I see four men loose. Dan. 3: 25.

THERE was no doubt about their being bound. Their turbans, mantles, and other garments had bound their limbs so tightly, that when first they reached the furnace they fell down bound in its midst. Whatever else the fire could not do, it at least freed them, so that they walked loose; and the dewy glades of Paradise were not more fragrant and delightful than were those white-hot cinders.

This is what trial has often done for us. We, had become conscious of the binding effect of our own habits which we had permitted as comparatively innocent; but gradually the conviction grew that they were amongst the weights that should be laid aside. Yet they clung to us until some fiery trial befel us, and from that hour, through the grace of the Holy Spirit, we were free. Do not fear the fire. It cannot hurt one hair of your head, or leave the smell of burning on you; but it will eat out the alloy, and gnaw away the iron bands that bound you.

"Beat on, true heart, for ever!
    Shine bright, strong golden chain;
And bless the cleansing fire
And the furnace of living pain."

But Jesus never allows his beloved to walk the fire alone. If it is heated seven times hotter than its wont, this is only the reason for his becoming more real, as our living and glorious Friend. There always goes beside the tried saint, though not always patent even to the eye of the spirit, another whose aspect is that of the Son of God. Reach out thy hands to Him, beloved—He is there. The Refiner not only watches the crucible, He is in it with thee. In all thy affliction He is afflicted.

All his works are truth, and his ways judgment.
Dan. 4: 37.

THIS is the confession of a heathen king; but how true it is, and how well for us, if we dare to affirm, amid all the appearances to the contrary, and all the shrinking of the natural man, that all God's works are truth and his ways righteous, not only in the wide circumference of the heavens, but in the tiny circle of our little life.

The main lesson, let us note it, which this chapter is designed to teach, and which Nebuchadnezzar epitomizes in these words, is the abhorrence with which God regards pride. We are all tempted to walk on the terrace of our palace, and say, "Is not this great Babylon, which I have built by the might of my power and for the glory of my majesty?" But to speak thus is to incur the displeasure of the Most High, who giveth the kingdom to whomsoever He will.

If thou hast achieved a position of wealth and independence and success, do not be proud of it, as though it were all of thy own creating. God gave thee power to get wealth; raised thee to that responsible position as his agent and trustee; and made thy name as one of the great over the earth. Give Him the glory, and be sure to consider thyself only as his steward, entrusted with his property, and continued in thy position for so long a time as thou art faithful in thine administration.

May not that illness, that suspension from active work, that serious deprivation, have been sent to thee, as this madness was permitted to come to the King of Babylon, that thou shouldest know and acknowledge that the heavens do rule? Remember that the watchers and the holy ones still walk the world with viewless footprints, and give in their account.

I have heard of thee, that thou canst make interpretations and dissolve doubts. Dan. 5: 16.

THE perplexed world often turns to the Christian in its hours of anguish and terror. While the foe seems powerless, and the hall of life is full of light and song; while the merry feet chase the flying hours, and mirth is unrestrained; whilst the wine flows freely, and the courtiers whisper flattery—the servant of God may be left in obscurity and neglect, as Daniel by Belshazzar. At such times God Himself is an object of ridicule and scorn. But let a hand come from out the Infinite, and write on the walls of life's palace in words of mystery, then the panic-stricken worldlings cry out for one in whom is the Spirit of the Holy God, and who can decipher the mysterious hieroglyphics, which to conscience forbode only disaster.

At such hours the child of God is kept in perfect peace. How should it be otherwise? He recognizes his Father's handwriting, and can decipher his Father's meaning. Amid the crash of falling kingdoms he is sure of his Father's care. Oblivious of his own interests, he is only anxious to interpret the ways of God, to recall the sinner, and save the State.

The world has more respect for our religion than it cares to admit in its gay moods, and it is noticing us more than we dream. Some day those who treat you with least courtesy will send for you. Only be at peace, and rest in your Father's Spirit. It shall be given you in that same hour what ye should speak. In the meanwhile, do not be surprised if you are led through many mysterious and trying experiences. It is only so that you can get the key to God's secrets, or the clue to his mysteries. Above all, seek for the Spirit of God, that light and understanding and excellent wisdom may be found in thee.

No manner of hurt was found upon him, because he had trusted in his God. Dan 6: 23 (R.V.).
BY faith they shut the mouths of lions. The lions' den is not an old-world experience merely. God's saints still dwell among lions, and fight with wild beasts at Ephesus. Like David, God's people have abundant cause to cry, "They have compassed us in our steps: they set their eyes to cast us down to the earth. He is like a lion that is greedy of his prey, and, as it were, a young lion, lurking in secret places." But still God sends his angel to shut the lions' mouths; still faith surrounds us with his unseen protection. Or, if the lion seems to triumph, it is only in appearance. Was not the martyr Ignatius more than a conqueror when he said:

"I bid all men know that of my own free will I die for God, unless ye should hinder me. I exhort you, be ye not an unseasonable kindness to me. Let me be given to the wild beasts, for through them I can attain unto God. I am God's wheat, and I am ground by the teeth of wild beasts that I may be found pure bread of Christ. Rather entice the wild beasts that they may become my sepulchre, and may leave no part of my body behind; so that I may not, when I am fallen asleep, be burdensome to any one. . . . Now I am beginning to be a disciple. May naught of things visible and things invisible impede me, that I may attain unto Jesus Christ. Come fire, and iron, and grapplings with wild beasts, cuttings, and manglings, crushings of my whole body—only be it mine to attain unto Jesus Christ."

Whether faith closes the mouth of the lion, or gives the soul such an entire deliverance from all fear, it is the same in essence and operation, and shows its heavenly temper with the ease with which it overcomes the world.

There was given Him dominion, and glory, and a kingdom. Dan 7: 14.
JESUS does rule. The kingdom of Christ is no fanciful phrase. The words He spoke, the deeds He did, have shaped the religious life and thought of the civilized world. But this is the lowest ground. He is supreme over all creation. In Him the ancient psalm is fulfilled, "Thou hast put all things under his feet. All sheep and oxen, the fowl of the air, the fish of the sea, and the beasts of the field." The Father hath set Him at his own right hand, far above all principality and power; all angels do his bidding; all demon-powers are beneath his feet. Joseph, our Brother, is King.

But let us never forget that the foundation of his kingdom is his Cross. We want more than the truth, more than a guide to show the way; we need forgiveness, salvation, life: and these are only possible through the death of the Redeemer. Satan offered Him the kingdom when he met Him in the wilderness, and He would not have it on such terms. With face set for Calvary, He went down the mountain to the valley of the shadow of death; and having traversed it, He came to his disciples and said, "All power is given unto Me in heaven and in earth." Thou art the King of Glory, O Christ; for Thou art the Lamb of God that taketh away the sins of the world.

That kingdom is an everlasting one. "All kingdoms will pass away before Christ's as the chaff of the summer threshing-floor." The shaking of the kings and kingdoms of this world has already begun, and is destined to shake to the ground the most stable edifices of human pride; but as we are to receive a kingdom that cannot be moved, let us not be troubled.

Then I rose up, and did the king's business. Dan. 8: 27.
FEW men have been favoured with such visions and revelations as fell to the lot of Daniel. The future, in so many different aspects, was repeatedly unfolded before him, and he saw much that elated and that depressed him. But through it all he steadily did the king's business; so far as he knew, nothing was allowed to suffer or get behind. He would have counted it a great slur on his religious life if it could have been said that his visions and exercises interfered with his service to the king. Probably he did better work because his life was hid with God.

In all this there is much of suggestion and warning. We too must have our secret mount of vision. We too must look across the valley for that blessed hope—the glorious appearing of our great God and Saviour Jesus Christ. We too must have the vision of the evenings and mornings. But that is not enough. We must do our business in the world. Not star-gazing, but following the Star; not always standing at the window, but going to and fro in the King's household, seeing that everyone is at his post, and that the Royal household is properly fed; not always on the mount of transfiguration, but hastening whithersoever the uplifted hand of human need beckons us.

At the same time, it will quicken us to do our business better if we have had a vision. Nothing makes so good a workman as thorough comprehension of his master's purposes. And when Jesus calls us not servants only, but friends, we serve Him with deep appreciation of his thoughts and plans. Our service is more refined, diligent, and intelligent. Get your plan in the mount, and then build.

At the beginning of thy supplications the commandment went forth. Dan 9: 23 (R.V.).
THIS is always so. Directly a God-given prayer is uttered, the commandment goes forth. There is a sense, indeed, in which true prayer is the anticipation in the human heart of the divine intention: "Before they call I will answer; and whilst they are yet speaking I will hear." Does it seem as though your prayer were like a ship lost at sea, which brings no cargo home? Dare to believe that the commandment did go forth, though as yet it has not reached you. It is operating; and before long you shall see the result. "What things soever ye desire, when ye pray, believe that ye have received them." The answer may not have come to hand, but it has been granted. Even if you do not live to see the answer, dare to believe that it is assured.

What a tender address is this—"greatly beloved"! And the margin says "very precious." Is it really so, that we are very precious to God? To those who believe, Christ is precious; but how wonderful that they should be amongst his jewels, who were born of the first Adam, and have cost so much pain and sorrow by their sins! There is no accounting for love. Directly love begins to enumerate the reasons for its attachment, it ceases to be true love. Love knows no law except the drawing of an inward affinity. So Jesus draws near to us. We are very precious to Him. To have our love well compensates Him for all his bitter sorrow.

Let us be very careful not to hurt Him, or give Him needless grief. And when we pray, let it be with the assurance that He bends over us and says, "Thou art greatly beloved; ask what thou wilt." As soon as the child of God says "Father," the whole Godhead is quick to hear his request.

O man greatly beloved, fear not; peace be unto thee, be strong, yea, be strong. Dan. 10: 19.
WHY should we fear? We are loved, greatly beloved; loved to God's uttermost; loved to the gift of his Only-begotten; loved to tears; loved to blood-shedding and death. It is said that Jesus, having loved his own, which were in the world, loved them unto the end; not to the end of his human ministry, but to the uttermost of what love can be (John 8: 1, R.V., marg.).

Why should we fear? Has God done so much, and will He not do all? Has He brought us out of Egypt to let us perish in the wilderness? Is He so careful of the soul, and so careless of all beside? There are mysteries—mysteries of life and death, of sin and sorrow, of this world and the next; but fear not: God is ours, and we are his by immutable and indissoluble ties.

Let us possess ourselves in peace. We cannot understand, but we can trust. We may not know the way we are going, but we can lean back on the heart of our Guide; standing in the cleft of the Rock we can look out in peace on dreaded evils as they pass away together, dismayed and amazed. If only we are acquainted with God, we shall be at peace, and thereby good will come to us. They fear who look at circumstances, and not into God's face.

And we shall be strong—strong to endure; strong to achieve; strong to wait; strong to carry the battle to the gate; strong to set our face like a flint, when the hour strikes for us to go to the cross; strong to be glad when the crowds ebb away from us to follow the dear Master, Christ:

"Be strong to hope, O heart! Though day
  is bright,
The stars can only shine in the dark night.
Be strong, O heart of mine, and look
  towards the light."

The people that do know their God shall be strong, and do exploits. Dan. 11: 32.
DANIEL probably refers to the great perse-

cution under Antiochus, when the followers of Judas Maccabæus, knowing their God, and keeping loyal to Him amidst the general defection, refused to bow before the idols of Syria. These were strong in God's strength, and did exploits never surpassed in the annals of those who have suffered for the truth.

There are many ways of knowing God—through the Bible, in solitary meditation, and pre-eminently in the person of Jesus; but we also come to know Him by the daily experience and intercourse of life. Those who live with you in the same house know and read you in an intimacy of knowledge which no other method can rival. Learn to live with God! Summer and winter with Him! "Abide in Him!"

In the Epistle to the Ephesians there are three prayers, which the apostle was wont to offer for his converts. First, that they might know; next, that they might be strong; lastly, that they might watch unto prayer. All our knowledge of God should be turned to practical use. Few things injure us more than to seek knowledge for its own sake. Know, that you may do.

Then you will be strong to do exploits. When a man is sure of his base of operations; sure that those in the rear of his march will back him up; sure that a strong and wise friend behind him is pledged to his support—his heart is at peace, he can concentrate all his attention and energy on the work that is on hand. He has no care, the Greek word for which means division. When we really know God, and understand how utterly faithful He is to those who venture forth in faith, we can do what others dare not attempt.

Go thou thy way till the end be. Dan. 12: 13.
MAN becomes mystified with the great circle of God's Providence. He tries to follow it, but his eyesight fails; his heart and head grow weary. And God says, It is enough—go thy way till the end be: learn thy lesson; do thy work; tread the predetermined path: it is enough that thou shouldst fulfil thy little day; evening will be here presently, and then thou shalt rest; leave the evolution of my vast schemes to Me; I will bring all right; and "thou shalt stand in thy lot at the end of the days."

THY WAY. For everyone that way is prepared; identical in the main outlines, but special for the footsteps that are destined to tread it. There are three elements, which are almost certainly present—Suffering, the strain of Toil, and Temptation. So long as the blight of the curse lingers on our earth, these will be the ingredients in our cup. But let us go on our way. It is graduated to our steps. God's grace will be sufficient for us.

OUR LOT. What will it be? As Canaan was allotted, so will heaven be. Where shall we stand? Among the overcomers, or the martyrs, or the virgin souls that follow the Lamb whithersoever He goeth, or those that get the victory over the Beast? Or shall our lot be amongst those who have buried their talents, forgotten their oil, and proved disobedient and self-indulgent? "Make us to be numbered with thy saints in glory everlasting."

THOU SHALT REST. Heaven will be to each soul what it most desires, and has missed on earth. To the lonely, Love: to those that hunger and thirst for righteousness, Holiness: to those who have dwelt amid perpetual warring and strife, Peace: to the weary, Rest—and to all the vision of God in Christ.

Hosea

He went and took Gomer, the daughter of Diblaim. Hosea 1: 3.
UNDER the glorious reign of Jeroboam, Israel had become very prosperous; but this period of wealth was one of shameless idolatry, self-indulgence, and oppression of the poor. The people were unfaithful to their marriage covenant with Jehovah; yet He loved them still. With the love that a husband may bear to the woman who is mother of his children, but who has shown herself worthless or abandoned, so God still loved, and wooed, and sought to reclaim. All this was set forth in Hosea's sad personal history.

He married one who was probably well known at the court for her infidelities. Her children's names were all significant. The first was called Jezreel, to indicate their prophetic import; the daughter, "Unpitied"; the third child, "Not My People"; and these children were accustomed, in after years, to go between the prophet and his wife and plead with her. "Plead with your mother, plead."

What a living picture this is of God's relations to ourselves! He has loved us, not because we were pure, and holy, and lovely; for, in fact, He knew that we were the very reverse. But with the clear prevision of our native sin and unfaithfulness, He took us into covenant relationship with Himself. Not because we were good, but to make us so; not because we were faithful, but to lead us to be so. He has given us all kinds of blessings. But, alas, how ill we have requited Him! We have departed from Him, and grossly betrayed His trust; till He has been reluctantly obliged to leave us to ourselves. But He waits to be gracious; and if we repent and turn to Him, He will say to us, Ammi, my people; and Ruhamah, thou hast obtained mercy.

The valley of Achor for a door of hope.
Hosea 2: 15.

WE are familiar with the story of the valley of Achor, where Achan the troubler of Israel was stoned to death. We can almost fancy the long stony valley through which again the house of Israel was made to pass. The prophet foresaw the heavy judgments which were about to fall upon the land, as God took back his corn and wine and flax, and laid waste their vines and fig-trees. It seemed as though the nation were again in the valley of trouble; and as the people take their weary way, dropping with fatigue and privation, behold, a door suddenly opens in the stony wall of flint, through which they pass into a land of corn, and wine, and wifely loyalty to their true husband. Thus the traveller piercing the Alps will, within the space of an hour, leave the northern slopes of ice and snow, and emerge upon the fertile plains of Italy.

It is a beautiful similitude, and one that still has its counterpart in spiritual experience. You, too, are in the valley of Achor—brought there in consequence of your sins; your life is overcast; your heart desolate. Ah, how different it is with you now, compared with those first glad days when you went out after God, in the kindness of your youth, and the love of your espousals! God cannot leave you. He comes and pleads, "Return unto Me; thou art mine." Will you answer his tender pleading with repentance, faith, and prayer? Will you cry, "Oh that it were with me as in the first

days!" Then, immediately, right before you, the door of hope will spring open; and you will pass from winter to summer; from ice to vernal heat. Dare to believe that in your Valley of Achor there is but a door between you and the divine betrothal—only a step.

Afterward shall the children of Israel return, and seek the Lord their God. Hosea 3: 5.

THE unfaithful wife had left husband and children, and sunk into abject poverty and shameful disgrace; but Hosea is bidden to seek her again and bring her to his home. It was a wonderful act of condescending love on his part, to be willing to condone the past and take the poor stricken thing to his well-ordered dwelling. Nothing could have done it but the strong love which had followed her through all her wanderings, refusing to let her go. We cannot certainly affirm that Hosea's love succeeded in making his Guinevere fair and lovely again; but we may cherish the hope that in this his compassionate love was recompensed.

Through the tragedy of the prophet's domestic life, the people were called to see the mystery of the divine faithful love. "The Lord loveth the children of Israel, though they turn unto other gods and love cakes of raisins" (ver. 1, R.V.). The people in their wandering and rebellion had been unfaithful to the marriage vow plighted at Sinai. They had gone after many lovers; but God's redeeming love would not let them go. That love still follows them; and though they have been for so many centuries without king, prince, sacrifice, or temple, they shall doubtless return to God. And is not this marvellous Zionist movement one further step towards the ultimate recognition and reunion?

You, too, have been without king or priest; without tears of penitence, or smiles of conscious acceptance. But the love of God has never ceased to follow you. And now, in your abject need, He seeks you out, and says, "Be for Me only." Will you not come back to the goodness of God in these your latter days?

The Lord hath a controversy with the inhabitants of the land. Hosea 4: 1, 3.

THROUGHOUT the Old Testament the sin of the people and the prosperity or otherwise of their country are closely conjoined. If the people please God, harvests are plentiful, and the seasons of the year pursue their round in unbroken bounty. If the people backslide, the land is smitten. There is probably a much deeper connection than we suppose between the moral condition of our nation and its prosperity. It is at least remarkable that ever since the Indian Government has legalized impurity in India, and has made money out of the vices of Chinamen, that empire has been smitten with drought and pestilence. So with Africa; the injustice with which the natives have been treated has been terribly avenged in the rinderpest which has swept over the land. And may there not be a close connection between the vice, Sabbath-breaking, and drunkenness of Great Britain, and the agricultural distress which has so long driven our people from the open country to life in the cities? It is an awful thing when God has a controversy with the inhabitants of the land. Sin is then terribly avenged.

One noticeable feature with all the prophets is their intense devotion to God on the one hand, and their ardent patriotism on the other. They never scrupled to denounce the sins which were bringing their land to desolation, and to indicate the inevitable result. In the present instance, Hosea turned on the priests and showed how accountable they were for the desolation of the country.

On a wider scale still, we remember that creation groaneth and travaileth in pain because of sin; and its emancipation awaits the advent of the Lord, and the manifestation of his saints (Rom. 8: 21).

I will go and return to my place, till they acknowledge their offence, and seek my face.
Hosea 5: 15.

THE withdrawal of God's countenance and protection involved the exile of Israel from their own land. No weapon formed against them could prosper, so long as they walked with their Almighty Friend; but sin severed them from his care, and cut them adrift to be swept before the storm of the invader.

There is always a "till" in God's withdrawals. He tears that He may heal; goes that He may come; leaves, that He may return so soon as the afflicted soul is led to seek his face. May not this be your lot? You seem deserted by man and God; life is going very hardly with you; thick darkness broods over your soul, and sore affliction devastates your life; yes, and worse is threatened. But is there not an offence somewhere that needs to be acknowledged; a sin that should be confessed?

Search yourself by the suggestions of this chapter. Have you in any way been a snare or a net to other souls, injuring them by your example or conversation (ver. 1)? Have you been unfaithful to your immortal lover, Christ (ver. 3)? Have you become proud of any of God's gifts, or the position to which they have lifted you (ver. 5)? Have you been grasping and fraudulent, like those who secretly remove the landmark to include a little more of their neighbour's lands with their own (ver. 10)? Have you willingly walked after the statutes of Omri (ver. 11, and 1 Kings 16: 25)? Have you gone for help away from God to some unhallowed alliance, such as is represented by King Jareb, the Assyrian, whose alliance Israel sought (ver. 13)? Ask God what controversy He has with you, and put it away. You will be astonished to discover what evils you have been harbouring. But the result will be salutary indeed.

Let us follow on to know the Lord; his going forth is sure as the morning.   Hosea 6: 3 (R.V.).

YOU may always count on God. If there is variation in his relations with us, it is on our side, not on his. Just as surely as we return to Him, we shall find Him running to meet and greet and receive us with a glad welcome.

The exquisite words of the text derive additional beauty when we consider them in the light of modern astronomy. The spot on which we live, when the day is done, slowly turns away from the face of the sun; and as each moment passes, plunges further and further from its wholesome, blessed light. At midnight we look out into the abyss of space in the opposite direction to the solar throne. But the moment when we have reached our furthest from the sun is followed by another, in which we begin to return to the light and glory of the perfect day. So when the soul has reached its furthest from God, it may immediately return to Him. Let us return. Let us know. Let us follow on to know the Lord.

Is there any doubt about our reception? No; there cannot be. Look again at the analogy of the physical night. During our absence the sun has not shifted from his place. We shall find him waiting for us; his going forth is prepared. We have but to pass into his blessed beams, which had not ceased to pour forth through the hours, which to us were so cold and dark. So our God is always waiting for us. He is just where we left Him. In Him can be no variation, neither shadow that is cast by turning. As certainly as we count on the dayspring may we count on God. Move then Godwards, through the dark hours. On the third day—the day of Resurrection—He will burst on your view.

Grey hairs are here and there upon him, yet he knoweth not.   Hosea 7: 9.

SIN in its worst forms was prevalent among the people, and secretly deteriorated their strength. Of this, however, they were unconscious; but imagined that they were as strong as at other times, anticipating long years of national prosperity. They little weened that they had reached the old age of their history, with its attendant decrepitude and helplessness. What a striking illustration of the insidious process of decay, of unconscious deterioration, of the departure of the Samson-might while we wist it not.

But is not this always the case with the initial stages of backsliding, of which this is the most dangerous element, that we are so largely unaware of the change that has come over us? Gradually and almost insensibly we lose our watchfulness over our thoughts; our relish for the society of God's people; our delight in God's house; our interest in the salvation of others; our sensitiveness of conscience as to the conventionalities of trade or society. We do not realize it; we are not specially concerned; we have no idea that the white ant is eating out the substance of our furniture, and the dry-rot undermining the rafters of our house. Strangers are devouring our strength; grey hairs are indicating our decay—to all eyes but our own. We grow grey almost imperceptibly; the strength of our manhood is very slowly undermined; the degrees of spiritual declension are as the fall of the year through the last days of summer. But it need not be if we would regard ourselves in the mirror of God's Word.

"It is strange: but life's currents drift us
     so surely and swiftly on,
That we scarcely notice the changes
     And how many things are gone."

I write for him my law in ten thousand precepts.   Hosea 8: 12 (R.V.).

THE A.V. slightly differs here: "I have written to him the great things of my law, but they were counted as a strange thing." God's will is so all-sided and far-reaching in its scope, that it cannot be contained in one precept or a thousand. It needs ten thousand precepts to set forth its heights, and lengths, and breadths, and to cover all the circumstances of our lives. But how thoughtful God is in anticipating our ten thousand difficulties, perplexities, and questions; and in directing us how He would wish us to act. Anticipating all the steps of our life, God has written ten thousand precepts to guide us.

But what great things have been unfolded to us in the Law of God—using that term to cover the entire compass of revelation! Mysteries which pass the conception of angels have been placed within the reach of men. Our Father has beckoned us to share with Him the sublimest secrets of his government.

Let us not count them as strange things. We often say to one another: "Do not treat me as a stranger." And is not this the sense in which we may get estranged from the word and thought of God—keeping them only for special times; giving them courtly entertainment; but refusing to admit them to the familiarity of daily intercourse? Nothing hurts God more than this! Never perform your daily duties as though God must be shut out from them. If you keep one day sacred, it is that all time may be sanctified: if you keep one place private for prayer and worship, it is that the light which shines there may irradiate all the places of your daily occupation; if you keep one meal for special meditation on the love of Jesus, it is that whether ye eat or drink, or whatever ye do, all should be done for Him.

Ephraim was a watchman with my God.   Hosea 9: 8 (R.V.).

WATCH with God. To watch with God is the privilege of comparatively few. Eight were left outside the garden; to three only did Jesus say, "Come and watch." To watch for the morning star, for the first flowers of the coming spring, for the coming of the Bridegroom, for the setting up of the Kingdom—such is the privilege of those elect souls who are bidden to take their lamps, and go forth to meet the Bridegroom. It is a high honour to be appointed to watch with God the slow evolution of his purpose; to stand on the watch-tower and see what He will say; to be a watchman for the people, a spokesman of their danger when the sword approaches; to be allowed to enter into some of his tears, and yearnings, and prayers, as He beholds the city and weeps over it.

WATCH AGAINST SIN. But we may be displaced from that position of privilege and responsibility as Israel was. We learn that at this time the chosen had deeply corrupted themselves, as in the darkest days of the Judges; and we may fall into similar corruption and rebellion, unless we watch ourselves, whilst we watch with God. Let us watch and pray, lest we enter into temptation. Corruption is always around us in this world of death. Its germs float on every breeze. We need, therefore, to steep ourselves in the antiseptic of the Holy Spirit's grace. This is the true Eucalyptus in which the germs of disease perish.

WATCH UNTO PRAYER. "Prayer," said Phillips Brooks, "is not compelling God's reluctance, but laying hold of God's willingness." It is as though we waited for God's movements to bless us, and taking the stream at the flow, launched our heavy barge upon it, that his power might bear us forward.

Break up your fallow ground; for it is time to seek the Lord. Hosea 10: 12.

THE FALLOW GROUND. There is a great deal of fallow ground in our hearts and lives; it has borne no crops of righteousness. Weeds have covered the unfruitful acres with their rank growth, and have scattered their thistledown into other lots. The rain has fallen and the sun has shone in vain. In some cases our daily business life—in other cases our social life—is a blank, so far as religious usefulness is concerned. God gets no revenue from these barren fallow tracts. But the prophet bids us ascertain what they are, and break up the hard, caked surface by ploughshare and spade.

BREAKING UP THE CLODS. In his great sermon on this text, Finney exhorts to break up the fallow ground by the payment of neglected debts; the putting aside of evil habits; the righting of old wrongs; the forgiveness of old injuries.

IT IS TIME TO SEEK THE LORD. The days are passing over us so rapidly, and we shall be at the end before we are well aware. "It is high time to awake out of sleep; . . . the night is far past, the day is at hand." May not the time past suffice us to have been barren and unfruitful; and shall we not make the best of the time which remains?

HE WILL COME AND RAIN. What a glorious promise! He will come and rain down righteousness. It is parallel to the words of the psalm: "Righteousness hath looked down from heaven." It is certain that righteousness will never spring up in the furrows of our souls unless it has come down to us from the heart of God. In us are only the dark, bare, lifeless clods, lying open in their need: in Him all that is pure, and holy, and righteous—but God waits to rain it down in plentiful showers.

I taught Ephraim to go. Hosea 11: 3.

THIS is very touching. It is one of the sweetest, tenderest words in the Bible—a metaphor borrowed fresh from the nursery. What an epoch it is in the child's life when it first gets upon its feet! The mother sets it there, or it manages to get up by itself. But it dare not walk; it must be taught to go. Sometimes the mother holds the clothes from behind, or reaches out her hands in front, or hovers around the little hesitating figure with outstretched arms to guard against the first sign of tumbling. The lesson is not learnt all at once. Sometimes many a sad fall tutors the venturesome pupil; but the mother is not discouraged. With a kiss and a "never mind" she puts the little one on its feet again, and teaches it to go.

God is teaching us to go. He holds our hands in his; walks beside us with outstretched arms to see that we do not fall to our entire undoing; catches us when we are about to stumble, and picks us up when we have fallen to our hurt. God is never discouraged, any more than the mother is; and the more weak our anklebones and nervous our gait the more care does He expend.

There are stages beyond this. There is the walk that pleases God; the running, when He has enlarged our heart; the mounting up with the wings of eagles. But at the end of life we come back to the going: I will go unto the altar of God, to God my exceeding joy; and upon the harp I will praise Thee, O God, my God.

"I have no help but Thine, nor do I need
    Another arm save Thine to lean upon!
It is enough, my Lord, enough indeed;
    My strength is in thy might, thy might alone!

By his strength he had power with God.
Hosea 12: 3.

JACOB'S strength lay in his weakness. As long as he seemed strong, and was able to oppose force to force, he failed of the highest blessing; but when the sinew of his thigh shrivelled beneath the angel's touch, and was out of joint; when he was in imminent danger of falling helplessly to the ground—he prevailed, and received the name of Israel the Prince.

THE ELOQUENCE OF TEARS. "He wept." There is no record of these tears in Genesis, but we can well understand that they flowed freely. The entire results of Jacob's life—wife, children, and fortune—were at stake. With one fell sweep, Esau on the morrow might reduce him to the loneliness with which he had passed over Jordan years before. God is touched by tears. He puts them in his bottle. He hears the voice of our weeping, and interprets it.

THE POWER OF PRAYER. "He made supplication." "I will not let Thee go unless Thou bless me." Remember how the Syro-Phenician mother cast herself at the Saviour's feet, and pleaded for help. The Lord kept her waiting till her prayer had reached a pitch which only delay could have induced, and then turned to her with the assurance that all she had claimed was hers. You may be kept in the attitude of prayer through the long night, but at daybreak you may receive what you sought.

THE STRENGTH OF WEAKNESS. As long as we can stand and hold our own, we fail of our quest. When we are lamed and broken, and unable to do more than cling, we realize God's hidden stores of blessed help. The sick child elicits most of the mother's love. The last-born babe drags down to the level of its tiny mouth its strong and brawny father.

O death, where are thy plagues? O grave, where is thy destruction? Hosea 13: 14 (R.V.).

THESE words are made familiar to us in the magnificent apostrophe with which Paul's great resurrection chapter closes. They have been recited for centuries over Christian graves.

In their first utterance they record Jehovah's resolve to deliver his people in spite of all their sins. The conflict in the divine heart between hatred of the abominable idolatries by which they were cursed, and his ancient, unalterable love, gives this chapter, and indeed the whole book, its remarkably disjointed character. There is hardly a paragraph which is not marked by abrupt transitions, agitation of speech, appeals, inquiries, expressions of infinite regret. But notwithstanding all, God had given commandment to bless, and He neither could nor would reverse it. Let death

and Hades do their worst against his chosen He was stronger far.

In these intermediate ages these words may be quoted over every Christian's death, whether it be a martyrdom or the quiet yielding up of life. In comparison with the great gain that death brings to those who pass to the "far better" of being with Christ, wherein are we losers by it? Nay, do we not greatly gain?

But the full realization of these words awaits the hour when this corruptible shall put on incorruption, and this mortal shall put on immortality, at the sudden appearance of the Saviour in his advent glory. Then shall be brought to pass the saying which is written, Death is swallowed up in victory. There shall not be a hoof be left behind. Not one of the redeemed shall remain in the prison-house; and even in their bodies, raised in the likeness of Christ, there will be no evidence of the triumph of death or the grave.

I am like a green fir tree. From Me is thy fruit found. Hosea 14: 8.

THIS chapter abounds with picturesque natural imagery. The dew distilling on the parched herbage, as the sign of the Holy Spirit. The blossoming lily, fragile but beautiful, an emblem of the retiring grace and purity of Christian character. The roots of Lebanon, descending far down into the valley, anchoring in its rugged strength, significant of the stability which in each Christian should mingle with grace. The silver beauty of the olive, the cool aromatic breath of the wind that has passed over the snows and slopes of Lebanon, commemorating the beauty and fragrance of the influence of the child of God. The covering shadow, the yellowing corn, the delicious scent of the vine, when it gives a good smell, to denote the gifts and graces of holy living. And finally, all of these summed up in the cry of Ephraim, "I am like a green fir-tree." O child of God, canst thou appropriate this wealth of imagery for thyself? Are the facts which these symbols denote true of thy life? Be not content to be as the lily, seek also to be as the rooted strength of Lebanon; be not satisfied with the similitudes of beauty, seek also those of usefulness. And above all, be an evergreen, never showing signs of autumnal decay.

But, amid it all, remember the caution— "From Me is thy fruit found." Count naught thine own but sin. Thou hast nothing thou didst not receive; thou couldst do nothing apart from Jesus. It is only as thou abidest in Him, and He in thee, that thou canst bring forth any fruit, or be fragrant, or serve any good purpose in the world.

"As some rare perfume in a vase of clay
Pervades it with a fragrance not its own,
So, when Thou dwellest in a mortal soul,
All heaven's own sweetness seems
around it thrown."

Joel

Sanctify a fast, call a solemn assembly, gather the elders, and cry unto the Lord.
Joel 1: 14 (R.V., marg.).

IT was a terrible invasion. The locusts had lighted down upon the land of Israel; so that the seeds rotted under the clods; garners were desolate; the barns were broken down. Despair took hold of the husbandman; and the herds and flocks panted out their anguish. At this juncture the prophet called for a national fast.

Whenever our life is visited by special trials and perplexities, we should withdraw ourselves from common pursuits, and lay bare our heart-secrets, so that we may learn the cause of God's controversy with us. There is a reason and a needs-be; because He does not afflict willingly, or grieve the children of men.

From time to time a call for prayer has issued from the hearts of men closest in touch with heaven. In the middle of the eighteenth century Jonathan Edwards issued such an appeal; and this led to that union of prayer, which played so significant a part in the origination of the great missionary societies. It was notably the effect of that appeal on Sutcliffe, Rylands, Fuller, and Carey, that led to the formation of the Baptist Missionary Society at the close of the eighteenth century.

It may be that a wave of prayer is again about to break over the Church. There are many signs of it. We hear Christian people saying on all hands that they want to get back to God; and surely it would be one of the most significant signs of the unity of the Church and the power of the Holy Spirit, if such a prayer wave were to lift us all on to a new level of intercession for the Church of God and the world around us. We need not wait for the Church to appoint.

I will restore to you the years that the locust hath eaten. Joel 2: 25.

HOW many years of our life have been con-sumed by the locust! Self in one form or another has sorely robbed us of our golden sheaves, reducing them to dust. Self-indulgence, frivolity, wanton spendthriftness of time, and talent, and opportunity, sloth and lethargy, mixed and evil motives, secret sins—what a crew are there! They have played the part of the caterpillar, the cankerworm, and the palmerworm with the green promise and the yellow produce of our lives.

But God waits to forgive; to put away from his mind the memory of the wasted past; to place the crown of a new hope upon our brow —yea, more, to restore to us the years that the locust hath eaten. There shall be a revenue of glory to Him even from those wasted years. Either in the experience they shall have communicated to us for dealing with other men, or in the penitential and broken-hearted temper they shall have begotten in ourselves; those years shall yet yield crops of praise to God, and of fruitfulness to us. And, also, God is prepared so to add his blessing to us, in the present and future, as to give us in each year not only the year's produce, but much more, so that each year will be laden and weighted with the blessing of three or four beside. Where sin abounded, grace shall much more abound. Where we have sown, we shall reap; not thirty-fold only, but a hundred-fold. God is so anxious to give us as large a result as possible to show for our life's work, though we may have sadly wrecked its earlier portions. Did He not restore to Peter at Pentecost what he wasted in the hall of judgment? Did not Paul win harvests for Christ out of the years which preceded his conversion?

I am the Lord your God, dwelling in Zion, my holy mountain. Joel 3: 17.

THIS will be the lot of the chosen people in the millennial age. The Holy God will make the city in which He resides a Holy place. But it is true universally. Wherever the Holy God dwells, there you have holiness—for it is the attribute of his nature, as heat is of fire. Holiness is not It, but He. Do you want it? Then you must invite Him to come.

When God comes into a day, it becomes holy unto Him. When his presence is revealed in a bush, it is holy ground. When He descends on a mountain, the fences are erected, that unhallowed feet may not draw nigh. When He fills a building like Solomon's Temple, the whole is consecrated, and may not be employed for sacrilegious purposes. Best of all, if He dwell in our hearts, they too are rendered holy to Himself.

When the apostle prays that the God of Peace should sanctify us wholly, he goes on to ask that spirit, soul, and body, should be as a temple filled with God. The holy man is he who is God-filled and God-possessed. It is not enough to possess God; we must be possessed by Him. He who has more of God is surely holier than other men; and he is the holiest who has most. Behold, Christ stands at the door and knocks: He longs to come in and abide, never again to depart; He brings with Him the holiness for which He has taught us to yearn.

"Is it true, Ignatius," said the Roman emperor to the Christian martyr, "that you carry about your God within you?" "it is even so," replied the bishop, "for it is written, I will dwell in thee, and walk in thee." And for that answer they cast him to the wild beasts. But what they deemed blasphemy is literally true of the Holy Spirit.

Amos

The words of Amos, who was among the herdmen of Tekoa. Amos 1: 1.

GOD does not hesitate to employ a herdman, if only his heart is pure and devoted to his service. He calls such a one out of the midst of his fellows, designating him for his sacred ministry. And when the fire of God burns within, very common clay becomes luminous and transparent. An ox-goad, a ram's-horn, a sling of stone, will serve his purpose. It is not what a man has, but what he is, that matters.

As we look through this strong book of ancient prophecy, and notice how it abounds with references and imagery peculiar to a herdman's life, we feel that a noble spirit of devotion to God may elevate the meanest employments and dignify the most ordinary subjects. The common incidents of the farm may convey the divine meaning not less than the sacred scenery of the Temple, which was familiar to Ezekiel. There is nothing which is intrinsically common or unclean. We profane things by a profane spirit. But if we view all things from the divine standpoint, we shall find that a sacred light will beat through them, like that which transfigured the coarse garments of Christ so as no fuller on earth could whiten them. The glory streamed through from his heart!

It is comparatively seldom that God calls one of the upper classes of society to conspicuous usefulness. "Behold your calling, brethren, how that not many wise after the flesh, not many mighty, not many noble, are called; but God chose the weak things, . . . the base things, . . . and the things that are despised." Here and there a noble of great authority, a Zinzendorf, a Shaftesbury: but most often fishermen and publicans; Luther, the miner's son, Tersteegen the ribbonweaver, Carey the cobbler.

Behold, I am pressed under you, as a cart is pressed that is full of sheaves. Amos 2: 13.

BEHOLD! This is like the hand which occurs in the margins of old books, to attract the reader's attention. It is God's special call to our heed.

Sin is very burdensome to God: especially the sins enumerated in this context. Look at the story of oppression in the 6th verse; of licentiousness in the 7th; of ingratitude in the 9th; of drunkenness in the 12th. These sins are aggravated when committed by his own people. Just as the groaning wain creaks and cries out under its load, so does the heart of God under our sins. "O Jerusalem, Jerusalem!" Should not we feel more as God does in this respect? Ought not we to bear the burden of sin, as Daniel did for his land and people?

What a fulfilment these words had in the life and death of our blessed Lord! The sheaves of our sins were laid on Him: for the Lord laid on Him the iniquity of us all. As He bore his cross through the streets of Jerusalem; as He lay crushed to the ground in Gethsemane; as He cried, "My God, my God, why hast Thou forsaken Me?"—surely He was like a laden wagon, groaning under an almost insupportable load.

The R.V. gives another sense, which is not so true to the Hebrew, but it should be considered: "I will press you, as a cart presseth" and cuts deep ruts in the road. A discovery is announced of a process of turning silver into gold by a pressure of eighty tons on a square inch, and in very low temperature. Yes, pressure and the chilling effects of persecution, difficulty, and disappointment are God's methods of redeeming us from destruction, and turning our silver into gold. Oh, let us forsake our sins rather than compel Him to employ such an ordeal!

Can two walk together, except they be agreed?
Amos 3: 3.

THIS is the first of seven searching questions, to each of which there is but one answer—Certainly not.

We are conducted, first, to the forest, to the lion's lair, where the roaring indicates that he has certainly secured his prey. There is a cause for those low roars of satisfaction. Then to the moorland, where the bird is suddenly entrapped. But there must have been an intention to entrap it on the part of the fowler, else it had not fallen to his hand. Lastly, to the city, where the panic-stricken crowds cower before some giant evil, such as pestilence, and tremble at the bugle-note of alarm. Here also, whether in the sounding of the trumpet, or the presence of the plague, there is an evident reason. Thus sorrow, causeless, does not come; and whenever it presses on the individual or the State, inquiry should be made whether God has any controversy with those who suffer beneath the stroke.

Often, in answer to such inquiry, it will be discovered that the soul is not in agreement with God; but at some almost imperceptible angle its metals have diverged from the main track of God's wise and holy procedure. And the trouble will remain until the nation or the individual have come back into agreement with God. It is worth our while to make any sacrifices, if only we may get back to God's side.

Whether in marriage, or business, or journeying together, be very sure that you are in perfect accord with your companion before you start. What sorrow might have been saved in thousands of cases, if only there had been stricter comparison of temperaments and methods before starting forth!

Prepare to meet thy God, O Israel.
Amos 4: 12.

THESE words might have rung out in Paradise. When the heat of the day was over, the voice of the Lord might have been heard sounding down the leafy avenues: Prepare, O man, to meet thy God! And the summons must have filled him with ecstasy. As a child to its parent, so must those innocent and happy beings have sped to their Creator.

We, too, hear the summons. Each morning, when we stand ready for the duties of the day, we hear the voice, Prepare to meet Me. Each Lord's Day we wake with this same summons in our heart, and prepare ourselves to meet our God. Each illness, each fluttering of the canvas of our mortality, each premonition of our end, takes up the same appeal, Prepare to meet God. And as we hear the words, we have no dread, no fear. Clothed in Christ's perfect righteousness, arrayed in his beauty, we know that we are accepted; that the love wherewith the Father loves the Son is waiting to greet us.

But there should be a preparedness of heart. We should not rush heedlessly into his presence. We should stimulate our hearts by thoughts like those suggested in the following verse. Stop and remember how great God is: He formed the mountains. How subtle his power: He made the viewless wind, and the Spirit of which it is the emblem. How omniscient his knowledge: He can declare unto man his inmost thought. How absolute his authority: the brightest morning will darken, or the darkest night brighten, as He bids. How vast the circuit of his providence, who steps from Alpine peak to peak. Let me not rush into his presence: He is my Father. But He is the Lord, the God of hosts: I must order my thoughts, and prepare to meet Him.

Seek Him that maketh the Pleiades and Orion.
Amos 5: 8 (R.V.).

THIS chapter resounds with invitations to seek

God. He makes the Pleiades, which usher in the spring: seek Him when life is full of radiant hope and promise, in days of love and joy. But He also makes Orion, the precursor of tempests; be sure, therefore, to seek Him when the sky is overcast and lowering, and when He presses you to enter the boat and face the storm.

He turns the shadow of death into the morning. Thank God for this. There is a turning of death-shadow into morning, when despair gives place to hope; when the dear one begins to revive from sore sickness; when circumstances begin to brighten; and when the perplexity and darkness of this mortal life, with its separations and misunderstandings, shall brighten with the eternal day. Weave thoughts of God into all these glad experiences; but not less so, when He makes the day dark with night. It may be that you will come closest to Him then; as the little child will sit on the far side of the railway carriage from her mother till they enter a tunnel, and then there will be a little startled cry and a rush to the mother's knee.

Sometimes the waters of the sea pour in on the land, engulfing the works of men, and devastating their toils. But amid all such scenes of desolation, the righteous have a secure hiding-place, suggested by the reference to the name Jehovah, with which this verse closes. "The name of the Lord is a strong tower; the righteous runneth into it, and is safe."

"Earth changes, but thy soul and God
    stand sure;
What entered into thee,
That was, is, and shall be;
Time's wheel runs back or stops—Potter
    and clay endure'"

Woe to them that are at ease in Zion!
Amos 6: 1.

A PICTURE is given in the following chapters of the luxury and self-indulgence of the people. Stretched on couches inlaid with ivory, choosing the rarest dainties, accompanying their voices on the lute, and drinking wine from flowing bowls, they were indifferent to the wounds from which the national life-blood was pouring. "They were not grieved for the affliction of Joseph" (ver. 6).

The same behaviour is only too common amongst ourselves. Indeed, this temptation besets us all. If only we are well supplied with the comforts and luxuries of life, we are apt to become thoughtless of the miseries of poverty and misfortune. If our own heaven is secure, we are apt to enwrap ourselves with an atmosphere of satisfaction and composure, without taking sufficiently to heart the needs of the great world of sin and sorrow around.

"The affliction of Joseph" reminds us of the scene at the pit's mouth: how Joseph's brethren sat down to eat bread, whilst their brother was in the pit without water, and then sold him to the travelling merchantmen, to rid their sight of him. But human nature is prone to act thus in every age.

Are we at ease in Zion? Are we using for our own luxurious enjoyment gifts which God entrusted to our care for the world? Are we too indifferent to the fate of those who live in our homes, or pour in great streams of activity along our streets? Are we sleeping in the garden, whilst our Master sweats the bloody sweat? We have but one life to spend; let it be a life in earnest. Let us bethink ourselves of any whom we can help—any who are in affliction, the poor widow, the young wife with the sick husband, the student who is so eager to become a minister.

The latter growth after the king's mowings.
Amos 7: 1.

OUR King has often to mow the grass of the inner life—the daisies and buttercups of experience of which we are so proud, the tall stalks, the flowering grasses. Were He to leave them, the entire growth would become altogether too coarse and rank for use. The lawn on which He loves to walk, with its velvet pile of grass, would become coarse and rough.

Mowing implies death. All the pretty flowers and myriads of blades lie in long swathes of death, presently to be carried away to the rubbish-heap. From myriads of dying flowers the last expiring sigh is being breathed out on the soft spring breeze. We must be prepared to die to our complacent self-content; to our blissful frames and feelings; to our complaints and consolations—if any of them come between us and our King.

But after the King's mowings there is the aftermath. It is said that the tenderest, juiciest shoots appear on lawns which are repeatedly mown. This is what the young lambs love, if they may taste it. And surely there is no such piety as that which follows on the repeated application of God's scythe. When repeated strokes have robbed us of health, friends, money, and favourable circumstances; then we put forth our tenderest shoots of love, and prayer, and consecration. Oh, do not be afraid of the scythe! The King loves thee too well to hurt thee. Be of good heart; thou shalt yet bear an aftermath!

"What do you think of your God now?" asked a well-known sceptic of Silwood of Keswick, who for twenty years suffered agonies. "Since He is able to keep me in perfect peace," was the reply, "amid sufferings like mine, I think of Him more than ever." Here was aftermath indeed!

I will send a famine in the land, . . . of hearing the words of the Lord. Amos 8: 11.
ISRAEL will not listen to God's prophets, and their voices would be silenced. This was a just retribution. As they were not willing to have the word of God, so there should be a famine of that word. The word of God was precious in the days of Samuel, because there was no open vision; so should it be again. And perhaps this privation will one day be meted out to our beloved country. There is a much larger proportion of our population outside than inside our churches; and men proudly eschew God's Word. It may be that the message of the Gospel will almost cease from among them, and be replaced—as in so many instances is now the case—by the dry husks of morality and ceremonialism. Then they shall run to and fro to seek the word of the Lord, and shall not find it.

We may question ourselves, whether we feed enough on God's Word. If we would grow strong, we must feed, not on condiments and sweetmeats, not on tit-bits and scraps, not on versicles and pious sentences; but on the strong meat of the Word, on the doctrines, histories, types of Scripture. Oh for more hunger and thirst for these! Would you have it so? No child will enjoy its meals who is constantly being surfeited with sweets between times. Beware lest you cloy your appetite with the painted sweetmeats of the world.

It is worth notice, that if men have not God,

they will find some substitute. They will swear by the sin of Samaria, and say Thy God, O Dan; thy manner, O Beersheba. This is why palmistry, spiritualism, so-called Christian science, are just now so much in vogue. Man's nature is made for God, and hungers for a substitute.

In that day will I raise up the tabernacle of David that is fallen. Amos 9: 11, 12.
THESE verses were quoted by the grave, white-vestured James in that memorable gathering of the Church to consider the admission of the Gentiles on equal terms with Jews (Acts 15). It is well worth noticing the special turn which the Lord's brother gave to the closing words of the quotation. He reads into it the deeper meaning of the Holy Spirit. The quickening and blessing of the chosen people has always meant the blessing of the world.

It was so, as James says, at Pentecost. The blessing which descended on the hill of Zion passed to all lands. They went everywhere preaching the Gospel, until some began to utter it also to the men of Antioch, and great numbers streamed into the Church (Acts 11); and thence the widening circles broadened out, until Ephesus, Athens, Rome, and distant Spain and Britain were included.

So will it be when the end of the present age has been reached. We, the Church, shall sit with Christ in the heavenlies, occupying the place now held by the devil and his demons, who will no longer be the prince of the power of the air; but the Jews, using that term in its strict sense, having been brought to God, shall be the evangelists and apostles of the world. Then the residue of the Gentiles shall seek unto the Lord. Ponder, specially, the promises of 13th, 14th, and 15th verses; and compare them with Rom. 11: 15, 24, 26.

May we not appropriate them in a spiritual sense, and ask that the days may hasten when the crops shall have no sooner fallen before the sickle, than the ploughmen shall run their shares through the clods; and the vintage shall follow close on the harvest; and men shall be prepared and eager before we begin to speak!

Obadiah

*The house of Jacob shall possess their posses-
sions.* Obadiah 17.

AS long as Edom invaded and annoyed the
house of Jacob, the people were unable to
possess their possessions in peace. No sooner
did the harvest or vintage appear, than their
hereditary foes swooped down to carry off
the fruits of their toils. But Edom's dominion
was to be ended; and then there would be no
cloud in the sky, no barrier to their uninter-
rupted joy.

There are many instances of people not
possessing their possessions. Such are those
who put their plate and valuables into furniture depositories, and for years leave them to
neglect; who have shelves of unread, uncut
books; who do not realize that coal and iron
mines lie under their estates; who never enjoy
the wealth of love and tenderness in their
friends' hearts; who refuse to avail themselves
of resources which are well within their reach.

But too many of God's people are like this.
The Father has caused all his fulness to reside
in the nature of Jesus; He hath given us all
things that pertain unto life and godliness in
Him; He hath blessed us with all spiritual
blessings in Christ Jesus; in our Saviour are
treasures of wisdom, of purity, of prevailing
power, of love and patience. The divine
Merchantman has come to us to give us gold
tried in the fire, white raiment, and eyesalve.
But we go blundering on in our own selfish,
sinful, faltering way. We do not possess our
possessions. We do not call into practical use
the boundless reinforcements awaiting us, at
every hour, within the tiniest beckoning of our
faith. We are like the manufacturer who refuses
to use the steam-power, though it is laid on
into the mill; or the householder who refuses
to touch the button of the electric light.

Jonah

*Jonah rose up to flee unto Tarshish from the
presence of the Lord.* Jonah 1: 3.

HE WENT DOWN TO JOPPA. Sin is always a going
down. Down from the heights of fellowship
with God; down from the life of high and
noble purpose; down from self-restraint and
high endeavour. Yes, and we know we are
going down; that our self-discipline is relaxed;
that our holy separation from the world is
slacker.

HE FOUND A SHIP. Opportunity does not
necessarily indicate either expediency or duty.
Because the ship happened at that moment to
be weighing anchor and the sails to be filled
with a favouring breeze, Jonah might have
argued that his resolution was a right one.
Whether he did or not, there are many times in
our lives when we are disposed to argue that
favouring circumstances indicate the right
course. But it must be remembered that they
never can belie God's summons to the soul to
do his will. The court of conscience is the
supreme court of appeal; and to run away
from known duty cannot be right, though
circumstances seem at first to smile.

HE PAID THE FARE THEREOF. Yes, if we go
opposite to God's will, we always have to pay
for it. The loss of self-respect, the broken peace
of conscience, the deprivation of God's
blessed presence, are part of the fare. And even
when we have paid and lost it all, we fail to
get what we purchased; we are dropped out of
our chosen vessel in mid-ocean; and God
brings us back to land at his own expense, and
in a ship of his own construction. The morning
may be fine, but it is soon overcast: the sky
may be clear at starting, but God sends a
great storm after the runaways to bring them
back to Himself: the ship may seem to be
opportunely leaving the wharf, but disaster
will overtake it.

*I am cast out from before thine eyes; yet I will
look again toward thy holy temple.*
Jonah 2: 4 (R.V.).

THAT is well, O truant soul. Look again from

where thou art! Thou art in the heart of the seas; the flood of sorrow enwraps thee; storms of trouble are sweeping over thee—but look again toward his holy temple. All that sorrow has been sent to bring thee back from thy wanderings, and cause thee to look again. Thou couldest not look so long as thy back was towards the will of God, and thy face towards Tarshish; but now thou art turned again, and art on thy way back, thou mayest look again in the direction of the altar and its sacrifice, the High Priest and his mediation. Look again. Look off unto Jesus, the Author and Finisher of Faith. Do not wait till thou hast come into a better vantage-point for vision, but look again from thy position in the lowest depths.

LOOK AGAIN! GOD INVITES THEE, TOO. Though thou hast turned thy back on Him these many years, He waits to be gracious; his face is wreathed in tenderest, yearning love. One look the least, the most abashed, from the greatest distance, will be eagerly noticed and instantly reciprocated. "They looked unto Him and were lightened"—so wilt thou be. And He will bring up thy life from the pit. Does thy soul faint within thee?—then remember the Lord. Let there be but one yearning desire for Him, and it will come in unto Him as a prayer to his holy temple.

LOOK AGAIN! IN SPITE OF THE REMONSTRANCES OF THINE HEART. "I said." The heart is always saying: I am too vile; I have sinned too deeply; I have gone too far; I have so often fallen and returned, I am ashamed to come again: besides, are there not texts about never forgiveness, and impossible to renew to repentance? I said: Yet, look again!

The word of the Lord came unto Jonah the second time. Jonah 3: 1.

WE must not presume on this, but we may take it to our hearts for their very great comfort. God's word may come to us "the second time." Jonah evaded it the first time; but he was permitted to have a second opportunity of obeying it. Thus it was with Peter; he failed to realize the Lord's ideal in the first great trial of his apostolic career, but the Lord met him on the shores of the lake, and his word came to him a second time.

God is not waiting to notice our first failure and thrust us from his service. He waits, with eager desire, to give us the joy and honour of being fellow-labourers with Himself. He waits

to be gracious. Therefore, when in our madness we refuse to do his bidding, and rush off in another direction, He brings us back, amid bitter experiences, and says, "Go again to Nineveh with the message that I gave thee originally."

How many times He will do this I do not dare to say. He forgives indefinitely, unto seventy times seven; but how often He will re-entrust the sacred message and mission, it is not for me to say. But there is, without doubt, a limit beyond which He cannot go, lest our own character suffer, and the interests of other souls, who may be dissuaded from obedience by our example, should be imperilled.

How wonderful it is that God should employ us at all! Yet it is like his work in nature. He is ever calling men to co-operate with Himself. He lays the coal up in mines, but man must excavate: He puts the flowers in the wilds, but man cultivates them: He gives the water, but man irrigates the fields. So He longs over Nineveh, but summons sinful men to carry his word.

The Lord prepared. Jonah 4: 6, 7, 8.

THIS book is full of this word prepared. We are told that the Lord prepared a great fish, a gourd, a worm, and a sultry east wind.

HE PREPARES THE FISH (chap. 1. 17). When we are at our wits' end, apparently going to destruction, He interposes and arrests our progress, and brings us back again to Himself.

HE PREPARES THE GOURD, that it may come up to be a shadow to our heads, and deliver us from our evil case. The gourd of friendship, of property, of some cherished and successful achievement. Ah, how glad we are for these gourds; though not always sufficiently quick to attribute them to the loving providence of our Heavenly Father.

HE PREPARES THE WORM, AND THE EAST WIND. Jonah would have regarded Nineveh's destruction with equanimity, whilst he mourned over his gourd; and there was no way of awakening him to the true state of the case than by letting worm and east wind do their work. He must be taught that what the gourd was to himself, Nineveh was to God. Yea, it was more; because God had laboured for it, and made it to grow through long centuries (ver. 11).

How often our gourds are allowed to perish, to teach us these deep lessons. In spite of all we can do to keep them green, their leaves turn more and more sere and yellow, until they droop and die. And when they lie prone in the dust, the east wind is let forth from the Almighty hand—the malign breath from which the gourd would have delivered us. O child of God, fainting in the east wind, do not ask to die; but get thee to the blue misty shadow of the great Rock in a weary land; to the Man who is a shadow from the heat.

Micah

The mountains shall be molten under Him, and the valleys shall be cleft. Micah 1: 4.

WE must stay to admire the sublimity of these words. Of course, it is a very human way of describing the movements of the Eternal: but how forcibly the prophet's words suggest the interest of God in human life. He comes out of his place to deliver his own, and to judge the ungodly: to remove obstacles to the fulfilment of his purposes.

Are you looking out to-day on a range of mountains that block your passage and screen off the rays of the sun? Do your difficulties seem to have accumulated till they act as insuperable obstacles to the fulfilment of your most cherished purposes? Perhaps, divided from your friends; hemmed and blocked in from the fair sunny lands of the vineyard and the goldening corn; despairing of tunnelling or scaling the Himalaya and the Alps. It is a sad and drear prospect, enough to daunt the most courageous spirit, and break down the most heroic courage. But look again at this text.

"Behold, the Lord cometh forth out of his place." He steps forth from his pavilion, intent on some great and glorious project. He treads on thy high mountains as on the furrows of a ploughed field. They are nothing to Him. Beneath his tread the mountains melt, and the valleys cleave. Wax melting before the fire is the simple but sublime image of the instant subsidence of whole ranges of difficulty. Wilt thou not walk with Him? Dare to believe that He can make his mountains a way. Who art thou, great mountain before Zerubbabel? Thou shalt become a plain.

"For whom the heart of man shuts out,
   Sometimes the heart of God shuts in;
And fences them all round about
   With silence 'mid the world's loud din."

The breaker is gone up before them. Micah 2: 13 (R.V.).

THE mind of the prophet conceives of the people as captives in a foreign city, surrounded by lofty walls and frowning gates. Like impassable barriers, these lie between them and liberty. There seems no hope of their being able to break forth; but all suddenly a Breaker appears, who, summoning them to follow, breaks through the opposition of armed men and of mighty bulwarks. With resistless might, He breaks his way through; and they that follow Him are described as having broken forth, and passed on to the gate, and gone out thereat. First the Lord, then their king, and then hosts of men.

No finer description could be imagined of the resurrection, which we celebrate as the first day of every week recurs. Looking forth from heaven at the mystery of the resurrection, when the triumphant Lord stepped forth from the restraint of watch, and ward, and stone, and demon hate, and the grim fortress of the grave, the angels might fitly have appropriated these words, "The Breaker is gone up" before his redeemed ones. See! they too are breaking forth, and passing on through the gate—their King passing on before them.

This is also true of every new era of time and novelty of circumstance. Circumstances, like prison walls, may confine us; but our Breaker is always preceding us, breaking down opposition and strong ramparts of apparently impassable difficulty; breaking down the suspicion and hatred of men; breaking down the mailed force of hell. Keep close beside Him, as the armour-bearer behind Jonathan. Let there be no perceptible interspace. The iron gate of the city will open of its own accord, through which you shall pass into perfect liberty.

I truly am full of power by the Spirit of the Lord. Micah 3: 8.

NOTHING needs more of the Spirit of God than the preaching which declares to men their sins. No one is so thoroughly hated as the candid friend. Just because conscience attests the truth of our utterances, the soul of the sinner resents our plain speaking. You may condemn sin generally as much as you like; but when your hand comes near the broken bone, or the diseased flesh, then there is at once a violent outcry. Nothing is more needed in the present day than particular preaching, the careful analysis of motive, the discrimination of shades of wrongdoing; but the ministry of John the Baptist is only possible to those who come in the spirit and power of Elijah.

We need power like that with which the apostles gave witness to Jesus Christ. And it is not difficult to discern when a man is dealing with sin in the power of the eternal God. We need judgment to detect graver and lighter offences, and trace the connection between sin and its consequence. We need might to withstand the opposition we shall inevitably meet.

But all these may be had with the filling of the Holy Ghost, which is the privilege and right of every child of God in this the age of the Holy Ghost. Our ascended Lord received of the Father the fulness of the Spirit, that He might communicate Him to all who believe; but we, in our turn, must receive. Do not be content with a few drops at the bottom of the bucket; ask to stand always beneath the flowing spring and be filled. The disciples were filled suddenly on the day of Pentecost; but they were being filled perpetually (Acts 13: 52, Gr.). The fulness of God for you is only limited by your capacity to receive.

In the latter days it shall come to pass.
Micah 4: 1 (R.V.).

THESE words are repeated in Isa. 2: 2–4. The holy men that wrote the Bible lived upon the inspired words of their predecessors. Amid the dark night this promise of God shone like binary stars.

No doubt they have been fulfilled in the Gospel dispensation. In a deep and true sense it has come to pass that the Lord's house has been established in the top of the mountains, and has been exalted above the hills. The Church is a conspicuous and influential object among the forces of the world; and peoples are flowing towards it. In very many cases whole nations have flung away the religion of their ancestors, and gathered within that Christian temple which has been built upon the foundations of Judaism. Out of Zion there has gone forth the law; and from Jerusalem the Word of the Lord. In Jesus, the Jew is still the centre of the world's vision.

But the full accomplishment of these words waits behind the curtain that is so soon to be rent at the coming of our Lord. Then holy influences will proceed from the chosen people who shall have been led to recognize Christ as their Messiah. From these the Gospel shall go forth unto all the world. Beneath the hallowing influences of that age swords shall be beaten into ploughshares, and spears into pruning hooks; the cannon shall be as obsolete as the tomahawk; the explosives of war shall be stored in museums; whilst schools for training the art of war shall be used as missionary seminaries.

There shall be no war, because there shall be no fear. "None shall make them afraid." And there shall be no fear, because universal love shall reign towards God and man.

And this Man shall be our Peace.
Micah 5: 4, 5 (R.V.).

HE that comes from Bethlehem Ephratah, leaving a trail of light that conducts the eyes of all generations back to the little village, "the least amongst the thousands of Judah," is the Everlasting Jehovah, whose goings forth have been from of old.

What majesty is his! He shall stand amid the swirling waves of change, the shifting quicksands of time, and the drifting cloudwrack of revolution; erect, unchangeable, unmovable. And not He alone, but his flock which has gathered around Him out of the windy storm and tempest. No common majesty mantles that gentle form; it is the majesty of the Name of Jehovah, the glory that He had with the Father before the worlds were.

What tenderness is his! He feeds his flock like a shepherd, and gathers the lambs in his arm. Though He is great to the ends of the earth, He is the Prince of Peace. He makes peace; does his work calmly and tenderly; lays the foundations of peace by yielding his life to the death of the Cross without resistance or complaint.

What strength is his! Strong with the original strength of Deity, with the acquired strength of perfect obedience, with the strength that accrues from the successful prevalence over his foes. His strength is ours, because He loves us perfectly; and it is the boast of the strong to bear the infirmities of the weak, and not to seek its own.

AND THIS MAN IS OUR PEACE. He came and preached peace to them that were far off, and peace to them that were nigh. He has made peace by the Blood of his Cross. He is the Prince of Peace to loyal and loving hearts. He sheds abroad in our hearts his own peace, which the world cannot take away.

Do justly, love mercy, and walk humbly with thy God. Micah 6: 8.

THE perfunctory sacrifices of lambs and rams, rivers of oil, and of tender children, were eagerly practised by the surrounding nations, such as the Moabites, but were abhorrent to God. What to Him is the outward rite without the holy purpose; the child's form of obeisance, apart from filial love! Grave questionings as to the utility of mere ritualism suggested themselves in the old-world religions. It appears that the questions of this chapter were put by Balaam; and the words before us were uttered by the divine Spirit to his heart. But however that may be, it is matter for our adoring gratitude that God has stepped out of the infinite to show us what is good, and what He requires.

TO DO JUSTLY is to preserve the balance of strict equity: if an employer, treating work-people with perfect justice; if a manufacturer or salesman, making and selling what will thoroughly satisfy the just requirements of the purchaser; if an employee, giving an exact equivalent of time and diligence and conscientious labour for money received.

TO LOVE MERCY is to take into consideration all those drawbacks which misfortunes, which enfeebled health, or crushing sorrow may impose on those who owe us service or money, or in some other way are dependent upon us

TO WALK HUMBLY WITH GOD implies constant prayer and watchfulness, familiar yet humble converse, conscientious solicitude, to allow nothing to divert us from his side or to break the holy chain of conversation. We must exchange our monologue, in which we talk with ourselves, for dialogue, in which we talk as we walk with God. Ask Him to make these good things the ordinary tenor of your life.

Rejoice not aga nst me, O mine enemy: when I fall, I shall arise. Micah 7: 8.

THOU art glad, O child of the darkness, that the child of God has fallen into the pit: thou laughest derisively and in scorn. But wait to see the end of the Lord, for He is very pitiful. Thy rock is not as our Rock, and of this thou shalt be the judge. Our God will chastise with many stripes those of his children who persist in wrongdoing. He will withdraw the light of his face. He will permit the backslider to bear his indignation. But He does not keep his anger for ever, or allow the enemy and avenger to wreak all his vengeance. He may use the stripes of the children of men to a certain point; but immediately they exceed it, and take unhallowed license, He steps in and delivers his beloved, enabling the returning and restored soul to use these words.

Wait, O soul; thy God will presently arise to plead thy cause, and execute judgment for thee; do not put forth thine hand to save thyself; wait on Him, He will deliver thee; He will bring thee forth to the light, and thou shalt behold his righteousness in the ordering of thy life. Only acknowledge thy sin; cast thyself on his mercy; and accept what He may appoint by way of chastening.

What an exquisite word is here for those who sit in darkness from any cause: from the waning of human love; the darkening of increasing physical weakness; the withdrawal of beloved faces, one by one, from the family circle. Look unto the Lord; wait for the God of your salvation; when you sit in darkness, He will be a light.

"In darkest shades, if He appear,
My dawning is begun;
He is my soul's sweet morning star,
And He my rising sun."

Nahum

The Lord hath his way in the whirlwind and in the storm. Nahum 1: 3.

GOD'S DEALINGS ARE OFTEN TERRIBLE. He rides on the whirlwind, and wraps Himself in the storm. But the child of God looks beneath the dress to the Father's heart, which beats with as much love when attired thus as when arrayed in the smiles of a summer eve. The whirlwind serves a useful purpose in cleaning the trees of rotten boughs, and searching the corners of fœtid courts; the storm, in deluging the gulleys and drains; the clouds, in forming the fertilizing showers on the thirsty land. God is in it all. God is behind the tempests that sweep over and desolate your life: this is his way; and the clouds that overcast your sky are the pavement of his feet; on our side they seem dark and lowering; but on the other side they are like burnished gold, as He steps across them. Whenever clouds are above, remember that God is at hand. They are the dust of his feet.

GOD'S WAY IS GENERALLY HIDDEN. The clouds as dust conceal Him; but we must not dwell with melancholy foreboding on the clouds, as if they were all. God is behind them, working for us, coming to our rescue, showing Himself strong on our behalf. Whenever the clouds gather over your life, say God cannot be far off—see, the dust He raises in his mighty progress betrays Him.

GOD COUNTS OUR GREAT THINGS AS VERY TRIFLING. A cloud is a great thing to us; it sometimes seems to equal the Alps in magnificence, in height, in girth; but to God it is only as a grain of dust to us. Our difficulties, perplexities, and anxieties, are very little things to Him. With one movement of his hand He could sweep them away, as you can move dust-motes from your table. Trust Him! Your tears are much to Him; your difficulties nothing.

The Lord bringeth again the excellency of Jacob. Nahum 2: 2 (R.V.).

TOO long Nineveh had exerted her malign influence upon the fortunes of the chosen people; that, to use the expressive simile of the eleventh verse, it had resembled a den of lions, whence ravenous beasts prowl forth to devour the villagers. The Assyrians, pouring forth from their mighty metropolis, had devastated the excellency of Jacob, the cry of the land had gone up to Jehovah; and He here declares his determination to quell the enemy and avenger, and to bring again the excellency of the people whom He loved.

It may be that you, too, have been carried into captivity, or devastated by strongly besetting sins; though you pray and yearn for emancipation, still you are kept low by the depredations of the power of evil. But be of good cheer; God is moving to your help. He is against those who are against you; He will bring again your excellency. He resembles the mother, whose child is smitten with smallpox. Does she love it less? Nay, but comes nearer, that they may fight the disease together.

You shall excel in faith when the hindrance is removed. The faith that once characterized you shall arouse with its former vigour, and make an open pathway down which heaven's best blessings may enter your life. At its summons the unseen will become more real than the seen, and God will be all in all. You shall excel also in hope. This is the realizing faculty, accepting the assurances of faith following them as the beacon-lights that guide weary sailors; for hope is more than faith, as the artist is more than the preparer of colours. You shall also excel in love. When self-will looses its hold upon the soul, love springs spontaneously from its soil.

There is no assuaging of thy hurt; thy wound is grievous. Nahum 3: 19 (R.V.).

THIS is one of the greatest chapters in Old Testament prophecy. Nahum the Elkoshite was a man of uncommon power of imagination and force of eloquence. His denunciation of Nineveh is remarkably forcible and eloquent. You can almost hear the crack of the whip, the rattling of wheels, and see the heap of corpses that block the passages. Every traveller, from Layard downwards, has attested the literal fulfilment of these predictions. For Nineveh, from the time of her fall to the present, has been utterly waste. Her hurt has never been assuaged. A scar upon the earth's surface alone marks her site.

From such a spectacle we may well turn to our beloved country, and seriously question whether we are doing all that we can to stay a similar fate. There are many signs that she is being swept along in the same stream as has borne many mighty nations down to ruin. The growing luxury of the rich; the abject poverty of the poor (a child was burned in Whitechapel the other day through the mother having to sell the fire-guard to buy bread); the gross impurity and immorality of our streets; the increasing desecration of the Rest Day; and the overwhelming bill for drink—these things cannot be unpunished. May we not indeed fear that God will soon rise against us? Let us use our influence as citizens, and our prayer as saints, to avert a fate which if it comes will be irretrievable.

Ah, reader, is this thy case? Hast thou an inward hurt, of which no balm or medicine has brought assuagement? Has thou a wound, so grievous that no art has sufficed to heal it? Take it to the Living Saviour. Each of his miracles, in the days of his flesh, has a spiritual counterpart still.

Habakkuk

Art not Thou from everlasting, O Lord my God?
Thou diest not. Hab. 1: 12 (R.V., marg.).
NOTE the attributes of God, which are enumerated in these words. His eternity—He is from everlasting; He is the Holy One—of purer eyes than to behold evil; the Almighty—the Rock. Is it not wonderful that mortals should be permitted to put the possessive pronoun before these wonderful words, and claim this glorious God for themselves! My God; mine Holy One.

But the most remarkable is the reading suggested above by the words, "Thou diest not"; "He only hath immortality." Time cannot lay its hand upon his nature, or death dissolve it. His hair is white, but not with the whiteness of decay, but of unutterable purity. He need not tremble at the summons of man's great last foe. Unchangeable! The same yesterday, to-day, and for ever! The death of death! The destruction of the grave! He dies not.

All this is true; but it is true also that in the person of his Eternal Son He died. He laid down his life, though none took it from Him. He bowed his glorious nature beneath the yoke of death. Because the children were partakers of flesh and blood, He took part in the same, that through death He might destroy death. Though He ever liveth, yet He became obedient unto death, even the death of the Cross.

There are many mysteries like those at which the prophet hints. He holds his peace whilst the wicked swallows up the man that is more righteous than himself. It is the problem of all ages why God should permit it; but whatever be the explanation, it cannot be because He has vacated the throne of the universe, or that his arm is weakened by disease. From everlasting to everlasting He is God.

I will look forth to see what He will speak with
me. Hab. 2: 1 (R.V.).
THE prophet had made his complaint in the preceding chapter; and now he climbs the watch-tower, much as the watchman did who waited for tidings of the battle between Joab and Absalom. He looks forth for God's answer. This, to say the least, is respectful in our dealings with the Almighty. Too often we ask questions, and do not wait for replies; shoot prayer-arrows into the air, without stopping to see where they alight, or what quarry they strike. We are in too great a hurry to take time and trouble for climbing the watch-tower, and awaiting the divine reply.

God still speaks to the waiting soul. Sometimes, there is a direct answer to its perplexity; at others, there is the assurance that the vision is yet for the appointed time, but that it is hastening towards the end. O long-waiting soul, dost thou hear those words? Thou hast been standing long upon the watch-tower. Hope has almost died; but the vision is panting in its haste to be fulfilled. If it tarry, wait for it; because it is already on the way. Every throb of the pendulum brings it nearer. The express train is hurrying towards thee, with its precious freight.

How often God's answers come, and find us gone! We have waited for a while, and, thinking there was no answer, we have gone our way but as we have turned the first corner the post has come in. God's ships touch at our wharves; but there is no one to unload them. His letters lie at the office; but no one calls for them. It is not enough to direct your prayer unto God; look up, and look out, until the blessing alights on your head. When we ask what is according to his will, we receive while we pray.

O Lord, revive Thy work in the midst of the
years. Hab. 3: 2.
WHEN we are oppressed with the state of the Church and the world, as Habakkuk was, there is no resource but to turn to God. It is of

no use to say to our brother, "What shall we do?" Better at once get into the presence of the Almighty. All conferences with flesh and blood are wasted breath, unless there has been a previous one with God.

Note also the unselfishness of the prayer which precedes revival. We must not pray "Revive my work," lest the insidious temptation come in of using the stream of God's blessing to turn our own tiny water-wheels for our own profit. Let us get beyond the narrow limits of our church or section, and ask for a revival of God's work everywhere.

We do not need a new Gospel, but a revival —a revivifying of the old Gospel. If any preach another Gospel than that which the apostles preached, let him be accursed; he is selling bran for wheat; he is filling cartridges with sand. We want nothing but the Gospel of the Cross of Jesus Christ, proclaimed from lips which have received a new baptism of heavenly power.

Note the time. Not at the end of years, but in the midst. This is a prayer for those in middle life. They are apt to think that their power for service has passed its prime, and that the successes of their early days cannot be paralleled. But let them remember that in the midst of the years God can revive his work, and ask for it.

What an argument! "Remember mercy." We cannot appeal to merit, but can lay great stress on mercy. Lord, have mercy on thy Church—revive her; and ere the dispensation close, may she arise for one great work of soul-salvation!

Zephaniah

I will search Jerusalem with candles. Zeph 1: 12.
THE state of things in the chosen city was scandalous. The people worshipped the host of heaven on the housetops; the temple-courts were filled with the priests of idolatry; the court affected foreign dress and manners. Nothing could prevent the invasion of the Chaldeans as ministers of the divine vengeance. These were the terrible guests whom the Almighty had summoned to the feast; and the feast consisted of the spoils of the city (ver. 7).

No sin of his people can escape the notice of God. He searches out the secret evils of our hearts with lighted candles, not for his vision alone, but for ours; that we may know, and abhor them, and put them from us. There is the candle of conscience. The spirit of man is as the candle of the Lord. In some men the candle is present, but not lit: in others it is lit by the power of the divine Spirit; and there is something of the incandescent flame about it then.

There is the candle of outward events. How often does God allow some incident of which we hear in social conversation, or read in the newspaper, to cast a sudden and unexpected light upon some passages in our lives which we have carefully shrouded in darkness. Right into a hidden closet the searchlight falls, saying "thou art the man."

Then there is that candle of his Holy Word. A text or sermon unkindled by the Spirit of God is like an unlighted candle. But when God's Holy Spirit rests on it, interfusing it with fire, then how mighty is its effect! It searches the heart and tries the reins; it reveals to man his thought and the real object of his existence, that he may repent.

It may be ye shall be hid in the day of the Lord's anger. Zeph. 2: 3.
THE name of this prophet means, "Whom God hides or protects." The hidden man invites others to his hiding-place; and shows how we may be hidden in the day of God's anger. It is said that in the centre of the wildest cyclone there is a point of absolute calm: so amid the wildest storms that have swept the face of the world there have always been some of God's hidden ones:

"The secret place, the refuge from the blast,
  The glorious Temple, Lamb of God art Thou;
Our feet shall tread the golden courts at last,
    Our souls have entered now."

"I cannot deny," writes Tersteegen, "the corruptions of the external Church; but I think my dear friend has more necessary things to attend to. Within! Within! With God alone!" There is truth here, though not all the truth. We must have Elijahs as well as Zephaniahs.

Only those may know the hidden life who fulfil the conditions here described. They must be meek; they must work his judgment; they must seek righteousness and meekness. It is the soul that bends before the blast of the terrible ones; that gives place to wrath, not because of pusillanimity, but because of the fear of the Lord; that hands over its cause of alarm and fear to the Most High, which abides in his secret place, and hides under his shadow.

Let us seek these things, and then there will be no maybe in our being hidden. We shall certainly be hidden in the day of the Lord's anger; hidden in the wounds of Jesus, hidden in his heart, hidden in God with Christ, hidden in the fiery glory of his intolerable holiness.

> "Rock of Ages, cleft for me,
> Let me hide myself in Thee!"

The Lord thy God is in the midst of thee, a Mighty One who will save.
Zeph. 3: 17 (R.V.).

IF this announcement is compared with the foregoing verse, it becomes apparent that only those may take its blessed comfort who have made the Lord their King. It is when the Lord, the King of Israel, is in the midst that we cease to fear the incursion of evil. Entire surrender and consecration must precede that deliverance from the power of evil which we all desire in our holiest hours.

O tempted one, who fearest every hour because of the fury of the foe, that seems only waiting to destroy, look no longer upon him, but behold thy glorious Lord. "He will save." Dare to repeat those words again and again, as a sweet refrain. Dare to believe that the battle is not yours, but his. Fear not; nor let thine hands be slack! Do thy work in the world, and let God keep thee.

But God will do more than save the yielded trusting one. He will rejoice over the soul that finds its all in Himself. Such exquisite satisfaction will fill his glorious nature, that it shall be as when the heart can no longer contain itself, and wells over with liquid music. It is much to hear a nightingale sing; more to hear an angel; more to hear some child of Adam redeemed from sin sing the new song: but most to hear the great God break out into song. So a mother sings over her babe. O my God may my life give Thee joy; not grief, nor tears, but a song.

But He does not always express Himself thus. He is sometimes "silent in his love." At such times He does not speak or sing, but broods over the soul that has dared to trust Him. "He will rest in his love." There are times when the heart is too full of blessedness to speak—it has learnt to abide in the secret place. An ocean too full to permit of waves!

Haggai

He that earneth wages earneth wages to put it into a bag with holes. Hag. 1: 6.

IN these words, spoken on their return from captivity, God remonstrates with his people for neglecting the rebuilding of his house, and indicates this as the reason for the failure of their crops, and the profitlessness of their labours. They seemed to put their hard-earned wages into a bag with holes.

How true a description of many in the present day! They work hard, but derive little comfort from their toils. Their homes are bare; their children unkempt; their circumstances meagre. They are always in anxiety. Gambling, drinking, loose and evil company— are indeed bags with holes. But there are other analogies. We sometimes find our days slipping away without accomplishing anything worth mentioning. We have nothing to show for them—nothing accomplished, nothing done. Or we expend time and thought on plans that are apparently well and carefully devised, but they prove abortive and disappointing. All this is like a labourer putting his wages into a bag with holes, and when he reaches home he has nothing to show for his labour.

There is a reason for this loss and failure. What applied to the Jews on their return from captivity, applies still. We have not placed God first. We have run every man to his own house, while His house has lain waste. We have worked from the wrong base of operations. We have not made first things first. If we do not trust in the Lord with all our heart, but lean to our own understanding; if in all our ways we do not acknowledge Him; if our eyes are not single to his interests, we need not be surprised when He calls for a drought upon the land. Let us consider our ways, and amend them.

The latter glory of this house shall be greater than the former. Hag. 2: 8, 9 (R.V.).
THE new Temple was deficient in the splendid adornment which Solomon had lavished on the first. Neither gold, nor silver, nor precious stones garnished its bare walls. But Haggai says that this lack was not due to any failure in the resources of Israel's God. The silver and the gold were his; and if He had chosen He could have poured them without stint into the lap of his people. But He purposely withheld them, that their attention might not be distracted from the spiritual glory which was to make the second Temple more famous than the lavished gold of Parvaim. The latter glory of this house, or the glory of this latter house, shall be greater, saith the Lord of Hosts; and then, as though to indicate that the glory was to be moral and spiritual, the divine voice adds, "And in this place will I give peace."

Dear child of God, it has pleased thy Heavenly Father to withhold from thee both gold and silver. Thou hast just enough to live on, but that is all. With the apostle thou sayest, "Silver and gold have I none." God could have done otherwise for thee; for the silver and gold are his. But He purposely abstained lest thy head should be lifted up; lest thy attention should be so absorbed by these things as to neglect the sure riches; lest the radiance of thy faith, which is more precious than gold tried in the fire, or the beauty of thy meek and quiet spirit, should be obscured by the tawdry sheen of earth's metals.

But peace, and righteousness, and meek humility, are of everlasting work. Cultivate these; let thy life be a Temple whose glory is the indwelling of God; expect that the Desire of all nations should make thee his home, and shine through thee to others.

Zechariah

He stood among the myrtle trees that were in the bottom. Zech. 1: 8.
THE myrtle in a lowland vale is a beautiful emblem of the people of God. They do not aspire to be forest trees, but are content to fill a little space if He be glorified. As the myrtle seeks its home in shady and moist lands, so the believer needs shadow and moisture. God's ideal for us is a lowly plant, fragrant in scent, and graceful in its appearance.

But, however lowly and humble the myrtle might be, the Angel of Jehovah, who could have been none other but the Lord Jesus Himself, was there. At dead of night the prophet beheld Him sitting on a red horse, and attended by a retinue of horsemen, who had come back to Him after walking to and fro in all the earth. The Lord has his throne in the midst of his people, and his servants post over sea and land to do his bidding on their behalf.

And thus the prophet overheard the colloquy. The Lord's inquiry and the Angel's answer were clearly distinguished. He also heard the appeal made by the Redeemer of Israel to the Eternal, as He pleaded that God would avenge his people's cause, and was answered with good and comforting words. The Angel Jehovah who pleaded for Israel (ver. 12) still pleads for his Church: and is similarly answered.

Yes! we are the objects of divine solicitude. Jesus with his bright angels is on our side. Not more really was He with the disciples of old, who were but as myrtles, than He is with us. He is still displeased with those who invade our lives with their cruelties. He is jealous for his people with a great jealousy. He will yet comfort Zion, and choose Jerusalem. However dark your night, dare to believe that the Lord of the Angels has stooped to your myrtle-tree life to help and bless.

I will be unto her a wall of fire round about, and the glory in the midst of her. Zech. 2: 5.
JERUSALEM was to be rebuilt; but it would soon outgrow the narrow boundaries of the walls which Nehemiah and Ezra had reared

with so much care. The multitude of men and cattle would pour over the ramparts as villages spread themselves out over the open country. What then: would there be no wall to arrest the foe and preserve the inhabitants from attack? Yes; there would be one, because the presence of God would be as a wall of fire round about. Nor would this be all, because He would be the glory in the midst (Isaiah 4:5).

How busy some of us are in building walls to our lives—the walls of property; of family alliances; of preparation against all kinds of ill. But the utmost we can do is not enough to defend us against the inevitable perils and dangers of our mortal life. Better far is it to hide within the enfolding, encouraging presence of the Eternal God, which is as a rampart of fire. Can plague or pestilence pass through fire? Travellers light a cordon of fires to surround them with their protection from tigers and wolves; so the soul hides in God. Notice the exquisite similitude—we are safe as "the apple of his eye." What a safe environment is furnished by the brows, lids, lashes, strong frontal bones, and lachrymal water to cleanse each defect. We raise the arm at once to protect the eye. So safe art thou, O weak believer!

But we need not defence only, but illumination; not the fire around alone, but within; not deliverance, but salvation. Where can this be obtained, save in the indwelling of the Son of God, making our hearts so full of his burning purity that sin might be abashed and no sacrilegious foot intrude?

A brand plucked out of the fire. Zech. 3:2.
SUCH is the divine economy, that God makes much of brands, fragments, castaways. What others regard as unworthy of their heed is dear and priceless to the great Lover of souls. The smoking flax, the bruised reed, the woman that was a sinner, the dying thief, the brand plucked from the fire, charred and blackened and almost useless—those whom man rejects as worthless—the base things of the world, and the things that are despised; these are chosen to bring to naught the things that are, so that no flesh should glory in his presence.

Hear the enemy and the Son of Man speaking concerning that smoking brand. The enemy says: It is so worthless and useless, so nearly eaten through with fire, so black and charred— cast it back again into the flame, and take some other. But Jesus says: Because it is so nearly

worthless, because no one else would find any use for it, because all others would fling it back to be consumed—there is the more reason why I should take it in hand: nothing less than divine skill or patience will avail.

And see what He will do for that charred ember. He will take away the filthy garments, clothe with change of raiment, and set the fair mitre of priesthood on his head. From the verge of the pit to the proximity of the throne

"The fair mitre" may fairly be taken to represent a fresh enduement of the Holy Spirit for service. We must receive a new anointing ere we can go into the temple of God, to perform the priestly offices of praying for the people, and of coming forth to bless them. Let us break in on the heavenly ceremonial, pleading for one another that none may be missed, but that on each the fresh mitre may be bestowed.

Two golden spouts. Zech. 4:12 (R.V.).
WHAT a sermon there is in a wick! Sit beside it, and ask how it dares hope to be able to supply light for hours and hours to come. "Will you not soon burn to an end, you wick of lamp?" "No; I do not fear it, since the light does not burn me, though it burns on me. I only bear to it the oil which saturates my texture. I am but the ladder up which it climbs. It is not I, but the oil that is in me, that furnishes the light."

Yes, that is it, and when we anticipate the future, our hearts might well misgive us if we were counting on meeting its demands from our only slender resources. But this is not necessary; we do not give light to the world; we only receive the oil from the Holy Spirit and the spark of his fire; and if we burn steadily through the long, dark hours, it is because we have learned to translate into living beauty those supplies of grace which we receive in fellowship with Jesus.

But how necessary it is that nothing interrupt the flow of oil; that there be no uncleanliness permitted to clog and obstruct the narrow bore of the golden spout of faith. Let us daily see to this; let us watch and pray, that there may be no hindrance or impediment; let us draw from our King-Priest more and more of his grace, to enable us to persevere. It cannot be too often repeated, that it is not what we do for Him, but what He does through us, which really blesses men. Be satisfied then to be only a wick, unseen amid the glory of the light that crowns it, and willing to be consumed by the daily removal of the charred fringe. Delivered to death for Jesus' sake, that the life of Jesus may be manifest in your mortal flesh.

Then said I to the Angel that talked with me, Whither do these bear the ephah? Zech. 5: 10.
THE first vision of this chapter denounces those who had sinned against the first and second tables of the law; the record of their sin would be written in unmistakable syllables, and would consume the houses of evil-doers with dry-rot (ver 4). But the second vision is most consolatory. A woman who symbolizes the wickedness of the land is thrust into an immense ephah, and covered with a leaden weight, and then is borne away from the Holy Land by two women in whose wings are strength and speed. Its destination was Babylon; thence had come the principal forms of iniquity, with which the chosen people were cursed, and thither would they return. But what encouragement to every pious Jew to know that the wickedness which had brought God's judgments on the land was removed beyond recall!

This choice is presented to everyone of us: If we refuse to confess our sin, it eats out our heart and life, as cancer and consumption do the fibre of life. If, on the other hand, we confess, and seek the grace of the Holy Spirit, our iniquity will be purged, and the power of sin broken. With swift and sure salvation will God come to our relief, and the chains that bind shall drop from off us like wreaths of hoarfrost before the sun. What though the tendency and possibility of sin remain yet within us; yet the thrall of wickedness is abolished. However many the dark transgressions of the past, when sought for, they cannot be found; and whatever the temptation without, and the frailty within, we are learning to abhor that which is evil, and cleave to that which is good. So our path mounts up on a stairway of light to the gates of everlasting day. "Awake to righteousness, and sin not."

Behold the Man whose name is The Branch. Zech. 6: 12.
THREE men came from Babylon, where many Jews remained, even after the return under Ezra and Nehemiah; they brought presents to the new-found temple. Their names were Robust; the Goodness of God; God-knows.

Of the gold and silver a double crown was made, and placed on Joshua's head: one circle, as emblem of the priest; the other, of the king—the two signifying the final gathering of Israel's outcasts to the Messiah, who would then be recognized as their true King and Priest. In the Jewish commonwealth it was without precedent for the same man to be both king and priest; but as the time drew nearer the advent of the Lord, revelation concerning his marvellous Person grew in clearness, and the majestic combination of glory in his character became apparent. In his Church Christ is Priest and King, after the order of Melchisedec, and between the two offices is no dispute.

As Branch, He is a scion of David's ancient stock; and through his far-reaching boughs the sap of the eternal purpose breaks into flower and fruit. He sprouted out from his place, Bethlehem, as predicted, and as befitted one of David's line.

As Builder, He began to build the Temple of the Lord, laying its foundations in the blood of his cross. He quarries the stones from the hearts of his people, and superintends the plan of the growing structure, as its Architect. Through the ages tier after tier is being added, though the builders pass: and He will place the top-stone at his second advent. The Temple grows towards completion. Let us ask whether we have been built into its fabric, or left as those huge boulders at Baalbec, shaped for the Temple but never carried beyond the quarry.

When ye fasted and mourned . . . did ye at all fast unto Me, even to Me? Zech. 7: 5.
THE men at Bethel asked this question of the priests; it was answered by the prophet. The fast of the fifth month was in memory of the fall of Jerusalem; that of the seventh commemorated the murder of Gedaliah, when the last blow was struck at Jewish independence. The question was: Should the restored Jews continue these fasts now that the events they recalled were forgotten in the abounding joy of the new state? It was a question of rite and ceremony and outward observance; and the prophet answers in effect: "Ye take much trouble and thought about the observance of a man-constituted religious rite; would that you were really solicitous to practise those virtues, and denounce the vices, which were the theme of so many expostulations and warnings of the older prophets."

God invariably demands a religion which does not consist in outward rites and ceremonies, but is inward and spiritual; and demands true judgment, the showing of mercy and compassion the forsaking of oppression and evil imaginings. This is unpalatable enough to the natural man, who pulls away his shoulder.

On the general question, one would advise that there is no need to observe the sad anniversaries of our sins and their accompanying punishment, if once we are assured of God's free forgiveness. When He forgives and restores, the need for dwelling on the bitter past is over; and we should put off our sackcloth and array ourselves with festal garments. This is a most salutary and necessary lesson. Too many of us are always dwelling beside the graves of the dead past. Each month has an anniversary of something we have lost. "Not looking behind" should be the motto of our Christian life.

Should it also be marvellous in mine eyes, saith the Lord? Zech. 8: 6.

MARVELLOUS! Marvellous! Probably there is no adjective more frequently on our lips than this, in these wonderful years when we are reaping the harvest of centuries of patient sowing, and when any morning the newspapers may announce a discovery which will revolutionize our methods of illumination, or locomotion, or military organization.

The other day we were told that the philosopher's stone was found at last; and that silver can be transformed into gold; to-morrow we may rub our eyes at the marvellous news that the North Pole has been reached. Men resemble the little child led into a toy-shop, or listening to a lecture at the Royal Institute, with open-eyed wonder and open-mouthed exclamation.

But none of these things are wonderful to God; they are but the unravelling of his thoughts, the discovery of his secrets! They are only marvellous to us because we are as yet in the baby stage, waking up to know a little of what a wonderful God He is. Like a little child in Wonderland, man is being led by God from room to room, telling him such wonderful stories of his nature and creative work, as make us continually exclaim, How wonderful!

But there are more wonderful things than these—that rebels should be forgiven, prodigals restored, the sons of darkness changed into children of light, Satan driven out before the Stronger than he, the unclean heart made the pure temple of the holy God. Talk they of marvels in the natural world! These pale before the star of Bethlehem, the sunset of Calvary, and the radiance of the Resurrection morning. And we shall see greater things than these, when we follow on to know through unending ages.

Because of the blood of thy covenant, I have sent forth thy prisoners. Zech. 9: 11.

THE state of the Jews in Palestine is presented under the figure of prisoners, shut up, as Joseph of old, in disused water-pits, from which the water had been drawn off, leaving a miry swamp behind. Jeremiah sank in one of these, almost to suffocation. But all the while they might reasonably be prisoners of hope, not of despair; of hope, because the seventy years had expired; of hope, because the purpose of their captivity had been achieved; of hope, because God had entered into covenant with their fathers, and had ratified it with blood. And, because of this, they would go forth out of the pit.

These words will probably be read by many other prisoners: prisoners of circumstance; prisoners in the hands of strong oppressors; prisoners in the utmost extremity. They fear every day because of the fury of the oppressor, as though he were ready to destroy. Behold, I bring to such of these as are united with the Son of God, good tidings of great joy! God will ever be mindful of his covenant. You may forget, or be utterly unworthy of his continued favour; you may have involved yourself in difficulties of your own making, the consequences of your own sin; but you must never forget that you are bound to God by the blood of an everlasting covenant. In the depth of your despair you may appropriate the psalmist's words, "Remember the covenant!" And He who brought again from the dead the Lord Jesus, the Great Shepherd, will raise you from the dark dungeon, and make you sit with princes. He will certainly chasten, but He will assuredly redeem. Be of good cheer, ye prisoners of hope! According to covenant, God comes down the long corridor to throw open the prison doors.

They shall be as though I had not cast them off: for I am the Lord their God. Zech. 10: 6.

GOD distinguishes, in these words, between

the civil rulers of the people, called shepherds, and the people, his flock. He was determined to interpose on the behalf of his people, and to redeem them from the troubles in which their rulers had involved them. The distinct mention of Judah and Israel foreshadows a more complete restoration than that which had brought them from Babylon; in which Judah alone, with a few other Israelites from the other tribes, participated. This restoration is yet future; but when it comes, it will be so complete that the long history of the centuries shall be obliterated; and both the house of Judah and the house of Joseph will be as though they had never been cast off.

Has thou been cast away from the hand of God—not as far as thy salvation is concerned, but for his purposes of service? Be sure to put away your sin. Ask for rain in the time of the latter rain—the gracious rain of the Holy Spirit; put away the false ideals which you have followed, as Israel false gods; then He will bring you again.

Your sins shall be remembered no more—the deep gulf of separation shall be bridged; the years devoured by the locust shall be restored; the dead past shall bury its dead; the river of the water of life will flow again into the channels which it filled once with music, but have so long been dry; and you shall be as though you had never been cast away. If you take the precious from among the vile, you shall not remove. God not only forgives, but obliterates the memory of past failure and sin. He reposes as much confidence in us as though we had never deceived Him; He treats his prodigals as though they had never gone astray.

I took two staves, the one I called Beauty, and the other I called Bands.   Zech. 11: 7.
THE prophet exercised his office amongst the poor of the land. They gave heed unto him (ver. 11), and recognized that he spoke the word of the Lord. It always has been so; and such people make the best flock, for pastoral oversight.

One day, the prophet appeared amongst these humble folk with two staves: Beauty, to represent the possible excellence of the people whom God loved; Bands, to denote the unity by which the entire nation should have been bound in one. These twain he broke to show, first, that God would be compelled to choose another people to set forth his praise; and,

secondly, that the unity of Israel would be annulled. When his hearers had received these announcements, wrung from his heart, their sole response was to make a collection amongst them in recognition of his pastoral care; and this amounted only to the price of a good bond-servant (Exod. 21: 32). What a miserable return for all the prophet's tears and words!

All this was symbolical of our Lord. He longs for the beauty and unity of his Church. But, alas! how bitterly He has been disappointed! How hopelessly He has snapped his staves! How ungraciously his reward has been meted out to Him! (Matt. 26: 15). The historical counterpart of this scene was afforded in his closing discourses and final betrayal; and its spiritual counterpart is being enacted day by day. O my soul! hast thou missed the beauty and unity He chose for thee? Hast thou esteemed his service of small account? Art thou like the Pharisees, that use the price of blood for the Potter's Field? (Matt. 27: 6, 7, 10). Repent thee, lest the Good Shepherd be compelled to adopt severer methods, and pass thee also through the refining fires.

They shall look upon Me whom they have pierced, and they shall mourn.   Zech. 12: 10.
THE fulfilment of these words is evidently future. A time is undoubtedly coming when the Jews shall recognize that Jesus is their brother. That scene in Joseph's palace, when he made himself known to his brethren, and they looked on him whom they had cast into the pit and mourned with bitter tears, shall be literally enacted before the eyes of the world. The prophet tells us that this great reconciliation will take place, when their foes will be in the siege against Jerusalem; from which we infer that they will be restored to their own land in unbelief, but will be led to recognize Jehovah-Jesus when He comes to their rescue (Rev. 1: 7).

But the interesting point for us to notice is the precise place in which their mourning breaks out with its exceeding great and bitter cry. It is after they have been saved (ver. 7); after they have been engirded with strength; after their foes have been destroyed. Then the sluice-gates of sorrow are opened, and the bitter tears gush forth. They look on Him whom they pierced, and mourn. This is the true place of penitential grief. It was when the woman had been already forgiven that she loved much, and covered the Lord's feet with tears.

Do not chide yourself if your sorrow for sin is meagre and belated. This is quite likely to be the case, until you have deeper experience of the love of your dear Lord. But the more you know Him; the more you gaze on the piercings of his heart, the more you will mourn, as one that is in bitterness for the first-born. Pour on me this grace, O Lord, and give me this brokenness of heart! It was the figure of Christ on the cross that broke down Count Zinzendorf's proud heart.

Awake, O sword, against my Shepherd, and against the man that is my Fellow. Zech. 13: 7. THERE is no uncertainty as to the application of these striking words. On the eve of his death our Lord appropriated them to Himself. To his troubled disciples was He not the Shepherd and they the little flock? (Matt. 26: 31). How well every word suits his lips!

He was a Shepherd, true, steadfast to his Father's charge. There is a special emphasis in the pronoun my: since the Father had given over to his care a number of souls who were his, but whom He committed to the Son with the charge that He should lose none, but raise all of them up at the last day.

But He was more than Shepherd. He was Jehovah's Fellow. From eternity He had dwelt in the bosom of the Father. He counted not equality with God a prize to be grasped at, as though there were any uncertainty about it. It was his native right. To all the deep secrets and purposes of God He was privy: in all the plans of creation, providence, and redemption, He had fellowship. My Shepherd, said the Almighty; and my Fellow. But, O my soul, stand still and wonder; He who was all this became also a man! What an astonishing combination: The man that is "my Fellow"! The mediator between God and man was Himself—man.

But listen to the appeal to the sword of divine justice. It had slept. Even since the sin of Eden it had remained quiet and unavenging. The pledge of the Son to come in the fulness of time met all its demands. But when He came it awoke. He was made sin for us: He bore the penalty of our transgression: He was led as a lamb to the slaughter and slain. And now, O sword of divine Justice, thou hast returned into thy sheath, never again to awake.

In that day shall there be upon the bells of the horses, Holiness unto the Lord. Zech. 14: 20. IN the days which the prophet anticipated, the knowledge and love of God would be universally diffused. The method in which he expresses this is as significant as it is beautiful. Horses were forbidden under the Jewish law, because of the temptations they presented to pride and war; but they would become dedicated to God, and their furniture or trappings would be emblazoned with the same sacred words that shone of old from the high priest's golden frontlet. So, the commonest utensils in the Lord's house would become as sacred vessels.

Such a day ought to be our everyday experience. "Holiness to the Lord" should be written on our commonest and most ordinary actions. The holy emotions and intentions that thirst in our bosoms on the Lord's day and in the Lord's house should always characterize us. Whether we eat, or drink, or whatever we do, we should do all for the glory of God.

Many bells ring in our lives hour by hour: for awakening from our sleep, for meals, for work in the school or factory, for our attendance on those who employ us. There is the bell of call for the surgeon, the clergyman, the man of business. Let us look on each summons, from whatever quarter, as being the call of God, as much so as the recurring duties of the priests in the temple of old; and let us regard each opportunity as a sacred bowl, from which we may pour out some holy libation to the glory of God. We can only live like this when we have consecrated ourselves absolutely to God, and regard our entire life as being marked out in all its details as a sacred plan. It is good also carefully to observe our priestly office, and to remember that we are a holy nation as well as a royal priesthood.

Malachi

Present it now unto thy governor.
Mal. 1: 8 (R.V.).

MALACHI'S special work was in stirring up
the priesthood to their duty, to the proper
maintenance of the Temple services. They
were very careless of these, and treated their
holy duties with great contempt. The special
method adopted seems to have been in the
presentation of the blind, the lame, and sick on
the altar; while the healthy and whole were
reserved for private use. "The table of the
Lord was polluted, and his meat contemptible."
Such unconcealed irreverence and greed could
not pass unrebuked. They are asked to compare their service to God with their service to
man; their sacrifices in the Temple with their
gifts before their governors and rulers. Would
these be pleased, and accept the gift, if they
were treated in the same way as God was?

Professing Christians might sometimes be
addressed in the same terms. When they slip a
copper coin into the collecting-bag, which
they would not think of offering to the butler
in a friend's house; when they give more to
the revenue officer than to the Church or poor;
when they give to the Lord's work whatever
they can spare without loss, and, indeed, are
glad to be rid of; whenever they spend more
time and strength on public duties than on the
calls of Christianity—at such times we might
fairly bid them present it to their governor.

In 10th verse (R.V.) God is heard asking for
someone to close the doors of the Temple. He
would rather this than be mocked by such
heartless rites. It was as though He would
rather that no prayers were offered, no services
maintained, no holy hymn sung—than that
there should be such perfunctory and heartless
worship. Let us be very careful against this
spirit in our daily devotions!

*He walked with me in peace and uprightness, and
did turn many away from iniquity.*
Mal. 2: 6.

THESE inspiring words, especially the last
clause, might well hang in the secret chamber of
every servant of God. They were specially
prized by the sainted R. M. McCheyne, whose
life was a beautiful exemplar of their meaning.

You will notice that covenant dates back to
the righteous zeal of Phinehas for the honour
of God (Num. 25). How well God remembers such things, and writes them in efface-
able characters on the tablets of his memory!
But what a contrast between that noble ancestry and the degenerate successors of Malachi's
days!

Do you want to turn many away from
iniquity? You must walk with God, hourly,
constantly, in blessed and intimate fellowship,
learning from Him who you are to approach,
what line you are to follow in dealing with
them, and the message you are to deliver. You
must expect to come into collision with them:
they are coming in one direction, whilst God
and you will be going in just the reverse. But go
on walking with God; fear his fear; know the
terror of losing his companionship, even for a
moment; be perfectly transparent in speech and
life; let your lips be weighted with his messages only. The result will more than compensate. Yours will be the abundant life, and yours
the peace which is unspeakable; yours will be
the uprightness of soul which carries the
divine radiance on its face, and yours the joy
in arresting the way of transgressors and
sinners.

Plead this promise: "Lord, let me be used to
turn many away from iniquity," and notice
that this most blessed result will accrue much
less from what you say than from what you
are. It was Levi's walk and converse with God,
more even than his words, that produced this
wholesale reformation.

*He shall purify the sons of Levi, and purge them
as gold and silver.* Mal. 3: 3.

IF you are just now in the fire, dear soul, be of
good cheer—it shows at least that you are
silver, and that you are capable of performing
more acceptable service in God's holy
Temple. If it were not so, God would not take
so much pains. He chastens those whom He
loves, and prunes the branches that are already
bearing fruit. What a comfort it is that He
surrenders this work to no other hands than
his own. He may give his angels charge concerning us when we are in danger; but He

keeps our purification beneath his special superintendence.

But notice that He sits. What patience is here! However many years thou mayest have to lie on that couch, He will sit beside thee. The nurses will go off duty, but He never. Love may faint and be weary, and nod into light slumbers; but He never slumbers nor sleeps. Those that were most frequent in attendances may drop off; but He will sit, night and day—when the soul is lonely, and when the room is filled with cheery voices; when the pain is almost unbearable—reach out the hand, you will touch his; breathe the softest sigh, He will answer, "I am here."

And the process will be continued until the scum has passed away, with its rebellion and murmuring, and his dear face shines, sweetly mirrored in its every outline and lineament. Then the fires will die down, and He will bid thee arise to reap the full reward. God is set on reviving the better, holier past, to which some of us revert with tender interest. "It was better with me then than now," we sometimes say. But the tender grace of those days that are dead will come again to the soul, who yields to God's refining. "The offering of Judah and Jerusalem shall be pleasant unto the Lord, as in the days of old."

The Sun of Righteousness shall arise with healing in his wings. Mal. 4: 2.

AT the end of the Old Testament it is meet that the sun should break out. The morning that broke on Paradise was clear enough. It was without clouds. But the sky soon became darkened, and at last veiled, with only here and there a chink of blue sky left. All through the dark succeeding centuries there have been gleams of sunshine to let men know that the sun was shining still. Every precious promise, every solemn type, every holy life, that was bathed in supernatural beauty, was like a shining forth of the sun through the bars of human darkness and sin. But evidently more was in store than Old Testament saints had dreamed; and the time was coming when the reign of type, symbol, and parable, would be succeeded by the clear vision of the face of God.

We live in the days of open vision. Let us go forth and exult. We are to rejoice in every good thing He gives us. As the young calves of the early spring manifest their exuberant life in their caperings and gambols in the pastures, so let us give expression to our joy. Exult because of the clear shining of God's love: exult because the darkness is past, and the true light now shineth: exult because He is coming again, as surely as He came once. Wake up, my soul, take psaltery and harp, and sing. The Bridegroom is at hand. Hark! are those his chariot wheels reverberating through the air? Even so! Lord Jesus, come quickly!

THE NEW TESTAMENT

Matthew

It is He that shall save his people from their sins. Matt. 1: 21 (R.V.).

THIS is the mission of Immanuel. He came, not as the Jews expected, to break the yoke of Cæsar and re-establish the kingdom of David; but to break the yoke of sin, and set up the sinless kingdom of God. The Church has too often misunderstood the object of his advent, as though He meant simply to save from the consequences and results of sin. This were too limited a programme for the Son of God. To cancel the results and leave the bitter cause; to deliver from the penalty, but not from the power, to rescue his people from the grasp of a broken law, but confess Himself unable to deal with the bad virus of the blood—this were to fail. No; dare to take this announcement in its full and glorious meaning, written as it is on the portico of our Saviour's life.

What an admixture of blood flowed through his veins! Let your eye glance through the list of his genealogy. Men and women, notorious for their evil character, lie in the direct line of his descent. This was permitted, that He might fully represent our fallen race; that no sinner, however bad, should be abashed to claim his help; and that it should be clearly shown how powerless sin was to tarnish or taint the holiness of his sinless nature. Made in the likeness of sinful flesh, He knew no sin. The germs of corruption could find no welcome in his heart.

Art thou one of his people? Hast thou accepted his rule, and allied thyself with Him? For if so, He shall save thee. Though possessed with seven devils, He will drive them out.

They offered unto Him gifts, Gold. . . .
Matt. 2: 11 (marg.).

GOLD is for the king. It is meet that Matthew should tell this story: for his is pre-eminently the royal Gospel. Long before the Lord was born, these eastern sages must have been started on their way, whither and to worship whom they knew not: but an ancient prophecy had foretold that to this babe should be offered of the gold of Sheba, and that kings should bring Him the riches of the Gentiles.

How useful this gold was to Joseph in the following months! It helped him to defray the cost of the journey into Egypt and back, and to maintain his precious charges there. The Heavenly Father knew what those needs would be, and met them by anticipation. If you concern yourself in the affairs of his kingdom, and will obey the warnings and directions He gives; if you dare to step out on the path of literal obedience—you will find that God will become responsible and defray all costs. Gold is naught to Him. He can make it out of common dust by a word.

It is sweet to think of all the gold presented to Jesus in after ages. The wealth of the rich, the golden ornaments taken from the person, the tiny pieces of gold which represent the patient saving of the poor—all these have made up the flowing river of which those golden gifts of the Magi were the first trickling drops. Have you given gold to Him, you who know Him, not as the babe only, but as the Man of the Cross; not as man merely, but as the Son of the Highest? You may have given Him copper in abundance, and silver in handfuls; but let your future gifts to Him be of the best. Or, if poverty restrains you, let the philosopher's stone of Love turn the meaner metals to gold.

In those days cometh John the Baptist.
Matt 3: 1.

THE Evangelist is fond of the present tense, "cometh." Yes, these records are true to all time. You tell me that they happened nineteen centuries ago. Certainly but they happened yesterday, and are happening to-day. Remember that He is the same yesterday, to-day, and for ever. He was, and is, and is to come. Christ was born into the world, but He is always being born into the hearts of men in Regeneration. John preceded and announced his advent in the wilderness of Judæa; and He is always preparing his way into the hearts and lives of men. It is doubtful whether Jesus ever comes into the heart of mature manhood without the previous work of a John the Baptist. Of days of conviction of sin, of remorse, of repentance, we may truly say,

"In those days cometh John the Baptist."

John the Baptist is sadly needed to-day. Much of what we call Christianity is but christianized heathenism. It glozes over covetousness, luxurious self-indulgence, compliance with fashion and worldliness; it admits into its high places men who thrive on the oppression of the poor; it condones the oppression of the native races, the sale of opium and spirits, the shameless traffic in impurity; it rears the ideals of the world in the place of the changeless cross of the slain Christ with its divine sorrow and blood. Ah we need that John the Baptist should come with his stern words about the axe, the winnowing-fan, and the fire. Nothing less will avail to prepare the way for a new coming of Christ.

Each age has had its John the Baptist. Now St. Bernard; now Savonarola; now John Knox. With sonorous, ringing voice the herald has prepared the way of the King: "He cometh to judge the world!"

Jesus was led up of the Spirit into the wilderness to be tempted by the devil. Matt. 4: 1.

YESTERDAY, the opened heavens; to-day, the burning cinders of the wilderness of temptation. Then the voice of the Father owning Him as the Well-beloved; now the hiss of the tempter. Then the teeming crowds; now the desert solitude and silence, broken only by the cry of the wild beast. Then the Spirit as a nesting dove, but now as a compelling force. Wherever there is the Christ-life, it passes through these same experiences. The Holy Spirit often anticipates coming trial by granting some great revelation of God; but He who gives the one leads into the other, that the precious bestowments of God's grace may be rendered permanent.

Would you give the bread of life to thousands? You must refuse to use your opportunity to make bread for your own gratification. You cannot use your power for others and for yourself. If you elect to use it for them, you must be content to wait till the Father sends his angels to minister to you. In the meanwhile live by faith on his words.

Would you teach the magnificence of a faith that can trust God to preserve it, though it steps from the mountain brow on to thin air? You must refuse to use it for purposes of ostentation; and wait till God, not Satan, calls.

Would you win the kingdoms of the world? You must obtain them, not by methods which commend themselves to human prudence, but through the death of the cross and the falling into the ground to die. There are two mountains in the Gospel: this, as it opens; that of the Ascension at its close. The valley of death lies between. But the traversing of this valley was necessary, ere Christ could say, "All power is given unto Me in heaven and in earth."

That ye may be sons of your Father which is in heaven. Matt. 5: 45 (R.V.).

WE are made sons by regeneration, through faith in the Son; but we are called to make our calling and election sure—to approve and vindicate our right to that sacred name. We can only do this by showing in word and act that the divine life and principles animate us.

Jesus teaches that the life of God in the hearts of his children will show itself in pure and unaffected love. He says in effect, "God is good: God forgives: God bears with wrong and sin: God loves those who hate Him, blesses those who curse, bestows his favours on the false and unjust, suffers long and is kind; believes, hopes, bears all things. Therefore, if you are his children, do as He does, as I do: follow Me: live as I live: become as a bird, a lily, a little child: be pure, merciful, lowly, gentle, strong in righteousness—and you will be called the sons of God; yours will be the kingdom of heaven."

There were several things the Lord could not say fully in this opening statement. That obedience to his precepts would inevitably conduct them to a cross; that the strength for such a life could only be secured through the coming of the Comforter; that the progress of the Kingdom would be slow and arduous— these things were for the time veiled and hidden. But his main object was to teach that Christianity must be a life after the model of God's. Christian disciple, art thou living this life? Not by a creed, a ritual, a profession; but by living the life, is thy true nature discerned, whether thou art wheat or tare, child or hypocrite. Sometimes we are called to be as the sun, ripening souls by our genial love; at other times we refresh them as rain watering the grass.

Thy Father which is in secret, . . . which seeth in secret. Matt. 6: 18.

HOW fondly Jesus repeats these words (vers. 4, 6, 18). Though compelled to live so much in the public gaze of men, his heart was always sighing for the secret place of fellowship with his Father, who waited for Him there.

Of course, the main object of these paragraphs was to withdraw his disciples from the excessive outwardness of the age in which He spoke, and which necessarily detracted from the singleness, directness, and simplicity of the religious life. It is impossible to perform our religious duties before men, without insensibly considering what impression we are producing, and how far their estimation of us is being enhanced. And in so far as we seek these things, the stream is contaminated with mud and silt, and becomes turbid. We have just as much religious life as we show to God in secret—just that, no less, no more. Whatever is not wrought between thee and God, with no record but his eye, is chaff which the wind driveth away.

Here is a test for our alms, our prayers, and our fasting from sin and self-indulgence. If we do any of these to maintain or increase the consideration that men have of us, they count for nothing in the eye of God. But whatever is done for Him alone will secure his inevitable notice and reward. Dwell on that very definite assurance: "Shall recompense thee." There is no doubt about it. For every petition breathed into his ear; for every sigh and tear; for every abstinence from sin and self—there will be a certain recompense, after the divine measure. Such seeds shall have a prolific harvest. Seek then the secret place, where prying eyes cannot follow, and curious ears cannot overhear.

With what measure ye mete, it shall be measured to you. Matt. 7: 2.
THIS is an invariable principle. Christ did not make it true by saying it; He said it because it was true. There are at least three policies of life—that of the churl, who never gives unless he is compelled; of the niggard, who metes out from the tiniest measure on which he can lay hands; of the bountiful man, who is ever meting out his stores with lavish hand. If he gives, it is to his uttermost; if he loves, it is with all his heart; if he forgives, he crowns the forgiven one with loving kindness; if he puts his hand to constructing aught, every part of it bears trace of the wealth of his taste, and gift, and self-sacrifice.

It might be supposed that such a policy would lead to bankruptcy of resources and speedy impoverishment; and for fear of this most refrain from adopting it. They either do not give, or give stintingly and fearfully. But the remarkable fact is, that when a man is using this large measure towards others, they catch it up and fill it with their bountifulness towards him. They mete out their love and gifts according to the measure of his giving. This is an invariable principle: begin serving men with a miser's hand, and they will do the same to you; begin, on the contrary, by serving men without stint, and they will do the same to you.

Live a royal life, child of God, as becomes such a Father. Give, expecting nothing again, with full measure, pressed down, and running over. Give, not so much money, as love, and tenderness, and human sympathy: give as one who is always receiving from the boundless resources of God. And, provided always that thy motives are pure, it will come back to thee. God will see thee bountifully rewarded.

A man under authority, having soldiers under me. Matt. 8: 9.
THE centurion's faith set Christ marvelling. First, because it was found in such an unlikely place. Here was a Gentile who had come from the West, and was sitting down with Abraham in the Kingdom of God. Secondly, because of its greatness: "I have not found so great faith, no, not in Israel."

This Roman officer applied to our Lord principles with which he was cognizant through his connection with the army. He knew that he had no power over other men in his individual capacity, or apart from his organic connection with the machinery of government. If he said to one man Come; to another Go; to his servant Do this, and his command was immediately obeyed—it was entirely due to his own obedience, in turn, to the authority which was over himself. So long as he obeyed that authority, he represented it; and it passed through him to compel obedience to his commands. This is the principle he applied to our Lord.

He recognized that Jesus of Nazareth was always acting under the authority of his Heavenly Father, and he inferred, therefore, that He could wield the power of God as he could that of Rome. As the authority of the Cæsars flowed through his own yielded life, so the authority of God over diseases, demons, and all else, would flow through Christ's.

What a profound principle is here! Learn to

obey, and you shall rule. Yield yourself absolutely to God, and God's power shall pass through your heart and life. Be under divine authority, and you shall be able to say, Go, come, do this. All things serve the man who serves Jesus Christ. Absolute consecration to God, as a soldier is surrendered to his country, is the condition of power.

Thy faith hath made thee whole. Matt. 9: 22.
WHOLENESS and holiness are identical: the one of the body; the other of the soul. They are closely related to the word Health, and all may be procured through faith. Holiness, wholeness of heart, health—and all by faith. There are three steps to this blessed state—of wholeness of soul.

FIRST, WE MUST BELIEVE THAT IT IS ATTAINABLE. For we never feel morally bound to do, attempt, or choose, what we do not believe to be within our reach. But all questions on the matter are settled for evermore by such words as, "Be ye holy, for I am holy"; and "Thou shalt love the Lord thy God with all thy heart, and with all thy soul, and with all thy mind."

SECOND, WE MUST CONSECRATE OURSELVES TO GOD. In other words, by the help of the Holy Spirit, we must determine and resolve that we will be wholly the Lord's. We must come to a fixed resolve to break off from every known sin; to walk, so far as we know them, in the way of God's commandments; to be and do and suffer all his righteous will. This must be our deliberate resolve for all coming time; and if we are unable to make the resolve, through the frailty of our nature and the strength of our old sins, we must at least tell God that we are willing for this to become our unvacillating attitude.

THIRD, WE MUST BELIEVE, absolutely, that God does accept the consecration we have made, and will do all that He has promised, by infilling us with his Holy Spirit, and working in us that which is pleasing in his sight. Nay, we must not only believe that He will do it, we must ask and claim that He should do it; we must, like this woman, touch Christ and obtain his healing virtue.

What I tell you in the darkness, speak ye in the light. Matt. 10: 27.
THESE striking words are applicable to us all. Our Lord is constantly taking us into the dark, that He may tell us things. Into the dark of the shadowed home, where bereavement has drawn down the blinds; into the dark of the lonely, desolate life, where some infirmity closes us in from the light and stir of life; into the dark of some crushing sorrow and disappointment. Then He tells us his secrets, great and wonderful, eternal and infinite. The eye, which has become dazzled by the glare of earth, becomes able to behold the heavenly constellations; and the ear to detect the undertones of his voice, which is often drowned amid the tumult of earth's strident cries.

But such revelations always imply a corresponding responsibility—that speak ye in the light—that proclaim upon the housetops. We are not meant to linger always in the dark, or stay in the closet; presently we shall be summoned to take our place in the rush and storm of life; and when that moment comes, we are to speak and proclaim what we have learnt.

This gives a new meaning to suffering, the saddest element in which is often its apparent aimlessness. "How useless I am." "What am I doing for the betterment of men?" "Wherefore this waste of the precious spikenard of my soul." Such are the desperate laments of the sufferer. But God has a purpose in it all. He has withdrawn his child to the higher altitudes of fellowship, that he may hear God speaking face to face, and bear the message to his fellows at the mountain foot. Were the forty days wasted that Moses spent on the Mount, or the period spent at Horeb by Elijah, or the years spent in Arabia by Paul?

Blessed is he, whosoever shall not be offended in Me. Matt. 11: 6.
A FRIEND has turned these words into another beatitude—The blessedness of the unoffended. The Baptist was tempted to take offence with Christ, first, because of his long delay in asserting Himself as the promised Messiah; and secondly, because of his apparent indifference to his own welfare. "If He be all that I expected, why does He leave me in this sad plight, extending to me no word of comfort; making no attempt to free me from these dark, damp cells."

Are there not such hours in our lives still? We say, If He really love us and is entrusted with all power, why does He not deliver us from this difficult and irksome condition? Why does He not hurl these prison walls to the ground? Why does He not vindicate and bring me out to the light of life and joy?

But the Lord made no attempt to emancipate his servant; and He seems to be unmindful of our sore straits. All He did for John was to send him materials on which his faith should feed, and rise to a stronger, nobler growth. "Go back," He said in effect to John, "tell him what I can do; he is not mistaken—I have all power, I am the expected King; and if I do not come to his help in the way he expects, it is not through lack of power and willingness, but because of reasons of divine policy and government, to which I must be true. Tell him to trust Me, though I do not deliver him. Assure him of the blessedness which must accrue to those who are not offended at my apparent neglect. I will explain all to him some day." Thus He speaks still. He does not attempt to apologize, or to explain—He only asks our trust; and promises blessedness to those who do not stumble at life's mysteries.

Have ye not read in the law ? . . . If ye had known what this meaneth . . . Matt. 12: 5, 7.
THE Pharisees were great sticklers for rites and ceremonies. Their religion consisted in little else than a perpetual round of outward observances. They believed that they were thus observing and maintaining the ancient Mosaic code. In their judgment, great human necessities, like hunger must be subordinate to their minute exactions. Our Lord, on the other hand, claimed that the laws of God, as written in the nature of man, must have a priority over merely ceremonial enactments. And He showed that his contention was supported by those Scriptures on which they rested their case.

There are two ways of studying Scripture. The one deals with its letter; the other compares Scripture with Scripture, and seeks to fathom its profound and eternal meaning. Do not read as the scribe, but as the Son of Man. Do not rest in the outward rite, but in the spiritual attitude of which the rite was intended to be the expression. Everywhere there is One greater than the Temple; greater than the rigorous exactions of the Jewish Sabbath; greater than the code on which Pharisaism insisted.

All through the Old Testament you may detect the spirit of the New; the mercy in which God delights, the pitiful appreciation of the frailty and hunger of the nature He has made. The New Testament is in accord with the Old of Scripture, and the older Testament of man's nature, as God made it at first.

It is highly important to remember this. The God who redeems is He who created all things by his word, and for his pleasure. Is it likely that He will contradict his original design, and undo what cost Him thought and care? Surely not; He is pledged only to undo the evil which has marred his work.

Unto you it is given to know. Matt. 13: 11.
IN explanation of this statement, our Lord reiterates his favourite saying: "Whosoever hath, to him shall be given, and he shall have abundance." His disciples had already given heed to his words. On the thin soil of their hearts the precious seed had already begun to germinate: and as it throve, it prepared the way for more and more to follow.

In the case of the crowds that pressed around Him, however, there was no such earnest giving heed. They were content with the interest, the beauty and grace, of his nature-teaching, without a thought of its deeper aspects. Hearing, they did not understand; seeing, they did not perceive; face to face with Incarnate Truth, they thought only that He had a pleasant voice, and could play skilfully on the harp.

First, Understand what you hear. Do not be content to have a merely intellectual appreciation of its force or beauty; but open your heart to meditate and ponder it. It is only thus that truth really strikes its roots into the soul, and defies the birds.

Second, Beware of the response of mere emotion. Too many of these receive the word with joy. Their expressions of interest and pleasure are loud and emphatic. Tears course down their cheeks. You think them most hopeful. But it passes like the sunshine and cloud of an April day.

Third, Guard against cares and worldy success. The first, of the poor; the second, of the rich. There is not room in the heart, or nutrition in the soul, for the absorbing pursuit of both earth and heaven, of time and eternity.

Fourth, Practise what you hear. Remember that not the hearers of the word, but the doers of the work, are blessed.

Looking up to heaven, He blessed, and brake, and gave. Matt. 14: 19.
STONEWALL JACKSON was once asked what he meant when he used the expression,

"Instant in prayer." "I will give you," he said, "my idea of it for illustration, if you will allow it, and not think that I am setting myself up as a model for others." On being assured that there would be no misjudgment, he went on to say: "I have so fixed the habit in my own mind, that I never raise a glass of water to my lips without a moment's asking of God's blessing. I never seal a letter without putting a word of prayer under the seal. I never take a letter from the post without a brief sending of my thoughts heavenward. I never change my classes in the section room without a minute's petition on the cadets who go out and those who come in." "And don't you sometimes forget this?" "I think I can say that I scarcely do; the habit has become almost as fixed as breathing."

And if this was the habit of the servant, how much more of the Master. Frequently, in the Gospels, we are told of his heavenward look. It was as though He were always looking up for his Father's smile, direction, and benediction; so that He could be assured that what He was engaged in was in the line of his Father's purpose, and that He might gain the needed power to act and wisdom to speak.

It is only thus that we shall be able to meet the hunger of our times. Our slender stores will not avail for so great a multitude. But if we bring them to Him, and place them in his hands, and look up to heaven for his enablement, we shall break and break again till all have sufficed and left. But this habit can only be maintained by those who go into the mountain of prolonged fellowship.

Be it done unto thee even as thou wilt.
Matt. 15: 28 (R.V.).

THIS was a remarkable permission. It is not often that Christ takes the key to his stores out of the bunch which hangs at his girdle, and entrusts it to a soul, saying in effect, Take what you will. "Of the work of my hands, command ye Me."

1. WE MUST INTERCEDE FOR OTHERS. This woman came for her child. We must always be on our guard when we ask much for self, lest somehow our requests be prompted by self-aggrandisement. If we do ask for power, wisdom, or likeness to Christ, let it be that we may help others better. The apostle says that Christ "loosed us from our sins . . . and made us priests" (Rev. 1: 5, 6, R.V.). We all need this loosing, that we may become intercessors.

2. WE MUST ACCORD CHRIST HIS RIGHT PLACE.

The Canaanitish woman came to Him as the Son of David, and He answered her not a word. She had no claim on Him as such. That He was the Jews' Messiah could not help her. She had given Him that title by courtesy and hearsay. It was necessary that by his silence she should be driven to find Him for herself. When she gave Him a universal title, and said, Lord, help me! worshipping at his feet, she was a step nearer the goal.

3. WE MUST ANSWER HIS AFFIRMATIONS WITH YEA. He told her what she was. She was an alien and outcast. She was not part of the chosen family; she must understand her true position, and take it. And she did. She said, Yea, Lord. If you can perfectly accept God's will, so that it shall take the place of your own; if you will take your place among the dogs beneath the table, you are sure to obtain answers to your prayers—God can let you have your way, because it will be his.

Have mercy on Thee, Lord! this shall never be unto Thee. Matt. 16: 22 (R.V., marg.).

THROUGHOUT his life these words were perpetually flung at the heart of Christ. Spare Thyself this hunger, the devil said in the wilderness, on the threshold of his public ministry; spare Thyself this agonizing death, he said again in the garden, on the eve of the crucifixion.

It is noticeable that the cross was surrounded by voices that repeated the same words. They that passed by it wagged their heads, and said "Thou that destroyest the temple and buildest it in three days, save Thyself." The chief priests mocked Him, with the scribes and elders, and said, "Can He not save Himself?" The soldiers also mocked Him, coming to Him, offering Him vinegar, and saying, "If Thou art the King of the Jews, save Thyself." And one of the malefactors which were hanged railed on Him, saying, "Art not Thou the Christ? save Thyself and us." All these voices spoke after the methods of human wisdom.

This made our Lord turn so quickly on Peter, saying, "Get thee behind Me, Satan: thou art a stumbling-block unto Me." How often are the same words addressed to us: "Pity thyself. Have mercy on your sensitive human nature; do not be too lavish with your money; give yourself a little more licence." But it cannot be. You cannot save others and yourself as well. Those that would follow Jesus in his steps of redemptive help to mankind must deny themselves, take up the cross, and follow Him into rejection, shame, spitting, and the grave. They who have mercy on themselves will never show much to others, or receive much; but the merciful are blessed, because they obtain mercy. Thus mercy is "twice blest; it blesses him that gives, and him that takes."

Behold, there appeared unto them Moses and Elias talking with Him. Matt. 17: 3.

LUKE tells us that they "spake of his decease which He should accomplish at Jerusalem." Moses, as representing the Law, would remind Him that if as God's Lamb He must die, yet as God's Lamb He would redeem countless myriads. Elijah, as representative of the prophets, would dwell on the glory that would accrue to the Father. These thoughts were familiar enough to the mind of our blessed Master; yet they must have gladdened and strengthened Him, as they fell from other lips: the more so when they conversed together on the certain splendour of the resurrection morning that should follow his decease.

And where could there have been found greater subjects than this wondrous death, and his glorious resurrection? Here the attributes of God find their most complete and most harmonious exemplification. Here the problems of human sin and salvation are met and solved. Here the travail of Creation meets with its answer and key. Here are sown the seeds of the new heavens and earth, in which shall dwell righteousness and peace. Here is the point of unity between all ages, all dispensations, all beings, all worlds. Here blend men and angels; departed spirits and the denizens of other spheres; Peter, James, and John, with Moses and Elijah, and all with the great God Himself, whose voice is heard falling in benediction from the opened heaven.

We, too, must often climb the mount of transfiguration in holy reverie; for the nearer we get to the Cross, and the more we meditate upon the decease accomplished at Jerusalem, the closer we shall come into the centre of things; the deeper will be our harmony with ourselves and all other noble spirits and with God Himself.

Go and tell him his fault between thee and him alone. Matt. 18: 15.

"WHERE is thy brother, child?"

"I do not know, Lord; I have not seen or spoken to him these many days; and, as far as I am concerned, I would not mind if I never saw him again; he is as good as lost to me."

"Hast thou wronged him, that this gulf has yawned between you? Remember that I said, if on coming to the altar, thou shouldest remember that thy brother hath some complaint against thee, thou wert to leave thy gift, and seek to be reconciled; then return to offer thy gift."

"Yes, Lord, I remember well. But that is not the case now; my brother has nothing against me; he is in the wrong, not I; he has trespassed against me, not I against him. It is therefore for him to come to me, not for me to go to him."

"Is it likely that he will come to thee?"

"I do not think it is, Lord. He is not one of thy disciples; and it is most unlikely that he will ever cross my threshold to apologize and ask forgiveness."

"Then thou must go to him, and tell him his fault between thee and him alone, and do thy best to win him back."

"But I think he is most likely to put the wrong construction on my going, and to account that I feel myself in the wrong."

"Thou art thy brother's keeper, and thou must win him out of his fault, and lovelessness, and wandering. He is drifting away—not from thee only, but from Me. I know he was in the wrong at first; but thou art in the wrong now, and thou must go and tell him his fault, and try to wash his feet and win him back."

Moses, because of the hardness of your hearts, suffered you. . . . Matt. 19: 8.

THIS is a very profound principle, which is of immense value in dealing with Scripture. There were certain precepts and commands given to Israel, which are not of lasting obligation, because they were stages in their moral discipline and education. It would have been impossible to lift them suddenly from the degradation into which they had sunk in Egypt, to the glorious levels of Isaiah or the Sermon on the Mount: so God's dealings with them were graduated and progressive.

Such were the regulations about a plurality of wives, the keeping of bond-slaves, the treatment of captives, the destruction of their foes. With respect to these, our Lord says, Moses interposed a parenthesis of legislation, which was a stage higher than anything known among the surrounding nations, though it was not God's normal or original code.

What was true of Israel is true of us. We do not realize, in the first stage of our redemption, all that is included in the word "Sin." We are like men enveloped in morning mist, which permits them to descry only the bolder outlines of the cliffs around them, but as yet veils the minuter eminences or depressions. As the mist clears, surrounding objects become ever more distinctly defined: so that we know more of God, we know ourselves better, and realize what sin is, and come to see it where we had never guessed its presence. Thus we condemn to-day what we permitted five years ago. It is interesting to find in these words of Christ the germ of an argument which his apostle used afterwards in the Epistle to the Galatians with such marvellous force. He said the Mosaic dispensation was a parenthesis; but it cannot disannul God's primal institution (Gal. 3: 15–17).

We are able. Matt. 20: 22.

THIS is the cry of youth—ardent, impulsive, self-confident. It does not wait to calculate the ridges and hummocks that lie between it and its goal, but supposes that it will be able to skate the entire distance over the glistening azure-blue ice. Without hesitation it counts on being able to brave all difficulty, surmount all hardship, drink the cup, and be baptized with the baptism.

But these men slept in Gethsemane, forsook the Master when He was arrested, and one of them at least failed Him at the cross. Creature-might cannot carry us in the hour of our greatest peril. We can vaunt ourselves as we may; but we have to learn that we can only follow Christ in his cup and baptism, after we have been endued with the Spirit of Pentecost. I once knew two who said these words to God, when He presented them with the cup of suffering and death. They did not know all it involved; and they confessed afterwards that they could never have stood to their choice, had they not been graciously and repeatedly enabled. But at the end they could not wish it to have been otherwise.

How different were the experiences of these two men! To one the cup and baptism came swiftly, when he fell beneath the beheading axe of Herod (Acts 12: 2); to the other they came in long, long years of sharing in the patience of Jesus Christ. These are different aspects of the same fellowship of suffering—swift death, or long waiting; but in both nearness to Jesus.

We have no right to cherish the assurance of sitting right and left of the throne, if that only means our own power, authority, glory. But if it means nearness to Jesus, we may count on it with the utmost assurance.

All things, whatsoever ye shall ask in prayer, believing, ye shall receive. Matt. 21: 22.

THIS was a very remarkable answer; showing that the Lord, in his human life, was the Author and Finisher of the life of faith. He did not quote his divine power and Godhead as the cause of the withering of the fig-tree; but proceeded to give a lesson on faith, as much as to say that He had wrought the miracle by faith in his Father, and that they could do as He had done, if only they had a similar faith.

Where we get wrong in prayer is that we are so self-willed. We set ourselves to pray for things; we vow to sit up all night to bring God round to our way of thinking; we use strong cryings, tears, and protestations; we endeavour to work ourselves into a frame of faith; we think we believe; we shut the doors of our heart against the tiniest suggestion or suspicion that we do not believe. And then we are surprised if the fig-tree does not wither, or the mountain remove.

Where are we wrong? It is not hard to see. There is too much of self and the energy of the flesh in all this. We can only believe for a thing when we are in such union with God that his thought and purpose can freely flow into us, suggesting what we should pray for, and leading us to that point in which there is a perfect sympathy and understanding between us and the divine mind. Faith is always the product of such a frame as this. Be sure that you are on the line of God's purpose. Wait for Him till the impulses of nature have subsided, and the soul is hushed and still. Then the Spirit will lead you to ask what is in the will of God to give, and you will know instantly that the Spirit intercedes within you according to the will of God.

Thou shalt love the Lord thy God . . . with all thy mind. Matt. 22: 37.

THIS was Adam's blessed privilege in Eden; but he missed it. The love of self took the place of the love of God. It is the aim of our blessed Lord to bring us back to that position. Perfect love is the sunlit peak to which his whole redemption tends. And perfect love would be perfect holiness. If a man were to love God and his neighbour as his first and chief and all-absorbing passion, there would be no room for sin to establish itself in his heart.

But does not this command seem altogether impracticable? It does; and it is impracticable to our mortal flesh. It is high; we cannot attain to it. Yet the very sublimity of the demand is intended to drive us to the Holy Ghost. He sheds abroad the love of God in hearts which are fully yielded to Him. If you desire that this love should be your privilege, lie down low before the flow of the River of Life, and it will fill every gully and inlet of your nature.

But, perhaps you are not of an emotional nature; you cannot gleam and flash, and shed tears, and light up with smiles. You cannot love God with your heart! Then see, the Lord says that you can love Him with your mind, i.e., with your intellect, your choice, you will. Probably this is where you have to begin. Give your mind, your will, your power of choice to God. Make Him first. Ask Him to take the helm of your life, and to control, inspire, and direct its every movement. Crown Him King. And when the will, which is the high priest of your nature, has put its crown of life on the head of Christ, who is God Incarnate, all the emotions and affections and faculties of heart and life will come in to swell the court with their homage and acclaim.

How often would I have gathered thy children together! Matt. 23: 37.
ONLY the greatest artists can make immortal pictures from simple domestic scenes. To detect the imperishable and the infinite in the common and ordinary, and to preserve it in such a form as to arrest the ages, this is the mark of consummate power. But how characteristic of Jesus—a broken bottleskin, a patched garment, a handful of girls shut out of a village feast—these are the subjects which He painted into never-to-be-forgotten pictures. Lord, give us childlike hearts that we may see the secrets that are hidden in common things!

But how this image arrests us! Who has not heard the cluck of the hen when danger was threatening her brood? She is quicker to detect its proximity than her callow young; and she must needs insert herself between it and them. Ah, how often does the rush of life drown the call of Jesus to come under his wing for rest and safety!

Bunyan says that the hen has a variety of calls, some six or eight. Jesus also calls us for different purposes—sometimes to nestle near his heart for fellowship; sometimes for rest. Sometimes He calls us to feast on some rich dainty, to which He has directed us in the Word; and sometimes to hide in the shadow of his wings till dreaded evils pass us by.

Oh that we more often heard and obeyed that warning note! Probably there is never a temptation nor trial which is not thus anticipated and preceded. When passion overcomes you by a sudden rush, you must not impute your failure to any lapse in your Saviour's care. He called you, but you could not hear. "How often!" Who can enumerate the many, many times when we have been summoned by Jesus nearer to Himself, but would not?

The summer is nigh. Matt. 24: 32.
YOU say that it is rather overdue. The nipping winds and morning frosts have held back vegetation so long that it has seemed as if summer would never visit us, spreading her carpet on the earth, and giving her intense hues to stream and lake and sky. But summer is nigh in spite of all prognostications to the contrary, because He is nigh, who is the King of summer, whose presence makes summer. Be sure that He, and therefore it, is nigh, even at the doors.

He is always nigh, and those that love Him realize the perpetual summer of his presence; but his appearing, the parousia, is nigh. Presently the swing doors will be flung wide, and his triumphal procession will sweep into our view. Then the millennial summer of the world will break, and her long winter will be gone for ever. Then the bride will hear Him say: "The winter is over and gone; the time of the singing of birds is come: arise, my fair one, and come."

The rumours of war that frighten the nations; the slackening faith and waning love; the dissemination of the Gospel to all lands; the great movement now in progress in the midst of the ancient people of God; the decrease of conversion work in favour of the preparation of the Bride for the Bridegroom— all these are like the tender shoots of the fig-tree which show that the Lord is at hand. Oh, lonely and sequestered ones, by his appearing, and by our gathering together unto Him, be of good courage, and do the King's work.

Do you want perpetual summer in your

soul? There is only one condition which needs to be fulfilled. You must leave the northern climes to dwell between the Tropics, where the sun is always on the throne of the sky. Thy sun shall no more go down.

He also that had received the one talent came. Matt. 25: 24 (R.V.).

IT is remarkable that the man who had one talent should hide it. If we had been told that he who had five had hidden one we should not have been surprised; but for the man who had only one to hide it!—this is startling; but it is true to life.

The people whose talents and opportunities are very slight and slender are they who are tempted to do nothing at all. "I can do so very little; it will not make much difference if I do nothing: I shall not be missed; my tiny push is not needed to turn the scale." That is the way they talk. They forget that an ounce-weight may turn the scales where hundred-weights are balanced. They do not realize that the last flake of white snow just oversets the gathering avalanche, and sends it into the vales beneath.

Are you one of these slenderly-endowed ones? And are you doing all you can? Are you doing anything? Even though you cannot do much in your isolation, you might join with others and do much. You might invest your little all in the bank of the Church, and trade as part of that heavenly corporation. Oh, disinter your one talent! Be sure you have one; ask the Master where and what it is; place yourself at his disposal. If it is only to carry refreshment to the harvesters—do that. Be thou faithful in thy very little.

We need not wait for the great future, to obtain this multiplication or withdrawal of our talents. They are already waxing or waning in our hands. There are many among us who, as life has progressed, have come into the use of powers of which at first they were perfectly ignorant; whilst others are losing, through misuse, the little they had.

My blood of the covenant. Matt. 26: 28 (R.V.).

THE first covenant was not ratified without blood. For when every commandment had been spoken by Moses, he took the blood of the calves and goats, sprinkled the people, and said, This is the blood of the covenant (Heb. 9: 19, 20). So the second covenant must be ratified by blood; not by that of calves and goats, but by the precious blood of Jesus Himself. He who made the covenant sealed it with his blood, that we might have strong assurance.

But Christ has put the cup which holds the emblem of his blood into our hands, and bids us drink it. What, then, do we mean when at the Supper we lift that sacred cup to our lips? Are we not saying by that significant act, Remember thy covenant? Are we not reminding Jesus that we are relying upon Him to do his part? Are we not pledging ourselves to Him as his own, bound to Him by indissoluble ties, and satisfied with his most blessed service?

Among the most precious promises of the new covenant is that in which God promises to remember our sins no more. Here is the ground which enables God to forgive so freely. The blood has been shed for many unto the remission of sins; the claims of infinite justice have been met; the righteous demands of a broken law satisfied; the barriers have been removed that might have restrained the manifestation of divine love, though they could not obstruct the love. And now we may sit with Christ at his table in his kingdom, not rebels, but welcome guests.

Also among the promises of the new covenant is that in which God promises that we shall be his people, and He our God. This item also is presented by us in humble expectancy, whilst, in expectant faith, we say, Do as Thou hast said.

Him they compelled to go with them, that he might bear His cross. Matt. 27: 32 (R.V.).

IF we may judge from the familiar way in which Mark speaks of the sons of this Cyrenian, who the soldiers brutally compelled to carry our Saviour's cross, we should infer that from this hour he became a Christian. He had little suspected such a thing in the early morning, when he left his lodging to attend to his business; but, being constrained to go to Calvary, he lingered there of his own accord through those anxious hours, and was led to feel that such a sufferer, to whom even Nature paid such homage, was worthy henceforth to receive his loyalty.

But how many of us are carrying our cross because we are compelled! There seems no alternative but to carry the dead weight of our cross with us everywhere, only wishing a hundred times each day that we might have respite. Dear soul, that cross is yet going to be the greatest blessing of your life if it lead you to the Crucified, and you find in Him what will transform it into the ladder which links earth with heaven, swaying beneath angel tread.

If Simon became a Christian, with what rapture must he have reviewed that incident in his life! How easy it would have been to carry the cross had he known Jesus as he came to know Him afterwards! He would have needed no compelling! So if you saw the will of Jesus in your cross, and that you were carrying it with Him, how much easier it would be! But that is so. He is in it. Bear it with Him; out of the cross will fall a shower of flowers.

There is no such thing as chance in our lives. It might have seemed such that Simon was coming into Jerusalem at that moment. It was shown, however, to be part of the Eternal counsel. Dare to believe in the divine purpose which orders your cross.

The angel answered and said unto the women, Fear not ye! Matt. 28: 5.

THE emphasis is on the pronoun ye. The angel meant, As for these sentinels that are quaking in dread and becoming as dead men, it is meet and natural that they should do so. They are strangers to Him whom ye seek, and are set here to do the work of his foes. But there is no need for those that seek Jesus to fear.

ARE YOU SEEKING THE FORGIVENESS OF YOUR SINS THROUGH HIS BLOOD? FEAR NOT YE! Do not fear that they are too many to be forgiven. Do not fear that you have not the right faith. Do not fear that you will find his door shut. Do not fear that He will always be reminding you of what you have cost Him. Do not fear that He will let you drift from Him again. Ye seek the Lord who was crucified. Fear not!

ARE YOU SEEKING A CLOSER IDENTIFICATION WITH HIS DEATH? FEAR NOT! There is no possibility of realizing the life which is life indeed, except through identification with the death and grave of Jesus. We must sink deep down into reunion with Him who lay there as our representative. But as God takes us at our word, and begins to strip us of all we had taken pride in; as the fear of what may be involved crosses our hearts with its chill dread —again we may be assured as we hear the angel say, "Fear not, ye who seek Jesus that was crucified."

AND WHEN AT LAST YOU ARE SEEKING TO FOLLOW HIM THROUGH THE VALLEY OF SHADOW —FEAR NOT! You will never see Him as He is, till this mortal is surrendered, and the house not made with hands entered. But if the heart faints, and the flesh fails, fear not ye, who through that mysterious change seek Jesus that was crucified, but now liveth for evermore at the right hand of God.

Mark

He was with the wild beasts; and the angels ministered unto Him. Mark 1: 13.

IN what different circumstances is the last Adam to the first! He began in a garden which the Lord God had planted; but his great Antitype in a wilderness, the thorns of which spoke of that primal sin. But whereas the first Adam transformed the garden into a wilderness, the last will convert all desert places into gardens —whether they be in the heart, or the world around—so that they shall blossom as the rose.

To Adam the beasts came, that he might name them; but at the coming of the last Adam they were wild. "He was with the wild beasts." Yet they were tame to his pure manhood. "He had dominion over the works of God's hands." On his brow the crown of royalty over the inferior races, which man had lost, was already placed. Is it not also true that holy men still have power over the lower creation? Certainly Francis of Assissi had. And in the ages, yet future, the children shall play, unhurt, amid the wild beasts of the forest.

Again it is true of thee, O son of man, that, like thy Lord, thou art between the wild beasts and the angels. On the one side thou touchest the lower, and on the other the higher. At every moment thou art called to choose between these twain. Thy body calls thee this way, and thy spirit that. Be sure to deny the lower appetites; rule them; be king and lord in the realm of thy soul. Make them crouch around thee, as the lions of Daniel's den. Get thy Lord to master them for thee. Else thou wilt miss the angels of God, who come to encamp around thee, and minister to thee, as one of the heirs of salvation. Was it here that Christ learnt to contrast his homelessness with the lairs of the beasts?

New wine into fresh wine-skins.
Mark 2: 22 (R.V.).

AH, our Lord! Thou hast been speaking of the bridegroom and his coming to the feast. Thou remindest us of the olden comparison of thy love as better than wine, and of thy first miracle at Cana of Galilee. May thy love be poured into our hearts as the fresh juice crushed from the grapes! We have no love of our own to offer Thee; but, oh, pour thy love into hearts that yearn to love Thee with thy love. And let it not be only the memory of the love that was, but the living, fresh enjoyment of the love that is ever new. The new wine of thy love is what we long for, that it may sweep into our hearts as the spring tide along the golden sands, which it frees from their accumulation of debris and waste. Oh for the constraints of thy love—new, fresh, living!

But the Master says, Children, if you have your request, the new wine may refuse to take on with the old shapes; it will make for itself new channels and forms of manifestation; when others fast, you will feast; when others feast, you will be sad. You will be counted eccentric and peculiar. Men will murmur at you, and find fault. They may even cast you out of their churches and social circles.

There is but one answer: Leave us not to ourselves. Permit us not to follow the promptings and suggestions of our undisciplined wills; but provide for us the new wine-skins also. Show us what Thou wouldst have us be and do; and let the methods in which our hearts' devotion shall express itself be so lovely, so befitting, so helpful to the world, and so full of God, that men may recognize thy hand, and adore Thee. Let not thy love be spilled, but stored for the refreshment of others through our lives. Oh, give us love!

He appointed twelve.   Mark 3: 14.

THIS is the threefold work of the Church, and of each disciple.

THAT WE MIGHT BE WITH HIM. The Master dearly loves our company. Let us seek it more. Not necessarily praying, or praising, or learning—but just being quietly with Him. It was said of a holy man, Mons. de Rentz, that his union and converse with God were so wonderful, that after he had spent several hours therein, he found himself in the end as if he had only then begun it, except only that he had then yet more desire to continue it. And at length he arrived to that height that it seemed as though he never ended it at all; being wholly and constantly in inward recollection and application to God. After whose example let us press, that we may enjoy like near approach to God, and our lives be suitably ordered for his glory.

THAT HE MIGHT SEND THEM FORTH TO PREACH. He cannot come forth from the secret chamber of eternity to preach, as once He was wont to do; and therefore He is ever raising up voices, witnesses, lips which He teaches how to speak, and touches with his live coal. Has He not sent you forth, if not by lip yet by life, to bear witness to his love? Like the seraphim, if you have two pairs of wings for reverent modesty, you have at least one pair for flight. Oh, breathe the prayer, Send me.

THAT THEY MIGHT HAVE AUTHORITY OVER DEMONS. The power of Satan is strong; it mastered Adam, but it met more than its match in the Christ-nature. If that nature is regnant in you, you, too, will have power over all the power of the enemy. Nothing shall by any means hurt you, and you will be able to deliver others who have long been held captive.

Cares; . . . Riches; . . . Lusts.   Mark 4: 19.

THERE is enough nutriment in the land for the thorns alone or for the wheat alone, but not for both; and so there is a brief struggle for mastery, in which the sturdy weed prevails against the slender wheat, and chokes it. Nourishment which should go to its support is drained away from it; and though it does not actually expire, it leads a struggling existence, and becomes unfruitful. What are these weeds?

FOR THE POOR MAN—CARES. The Greek word for care is Division. Cares divide our heart, and distract it in many different directions. What shall we eat? What shall we drink? Wherewithal shall we be clothed? How shall we meet our rent and other expenses? It is almost impossible to settle to our prayer, or Bible-study, or Christian work, or to the culture of the soul-life, while questions like these intrude. What shall the poor man do to prevent the word becoming unfruitful? He must take his cares to his Father, and by one act deposit them in his safe keeping. And thereafter, as a care tries to break in on the peace of his heart, he must treat it as a positive temptation, handing it over to God.

FOR THE PROSPEROUS MAN—RICHES. They will distract as much as anxiety does. How much they amount to! Oh, the endless figurings in the brain—how to keep, or invest, or increase. The case for him is to look on all he has as a stewardship for God, deducting only a moderate percentage for himself.

FOR US ALL—LUSTS. Strong and inordinate desires for what may be right in itself, but which we follow with extravagant zest. What is right in itself may become wrong if we put it in God's place, and allow it to monopolize us unduly. Oh, Great Husbandman, root up the thorns by thy Holy Spirit!

Thy daughter is dead: why troublest thou the Master any further? Mark 5: 35.

WHAT hopelessness! They had watched the sweet flower fade, till no colour was left on the pale cheek, and the merry voice was still; and then they thought of the Galilean Teacher: "Why cost Him time and trouble? his visit will be useless now! It was very kind of Him to be willing to come! But it is now of no use! Very kind; but no use."

We go to God in comparatively small trials, and think He can help us. But there are times when we say: It is no use troubling further; we must just bear our trial as well as we can, God Himself cannot help us. Can He give back that twin-soul? Can He restore the love that has died out? Can He undo this unhappy marriage? Can He deliver from that life-long paralysis? Life is extinct; hope is dead; the light has dipped below the horizon. It is no use to trouble God or man. We have no alternative but to suffer till eternity explain the mysteries of time.

But Jesus knows the way out. He says in his sweet undertone, "Fear not! only believe." He has the keys of death. He never would have let things come to this awful pass by his delay unless He had known that, even if the worse came to the worst, all would end well. He has purposely delayed till this, that He might have the better opportunity of showing you what God can do. Fear not! the hand of the Almighty Saviour has yours within its grasp. He will not let you stumble as you go down this dark staircase by his side. Only believe: have faith in Him. All may seem very mys-

terious now, but you will come to see that it was the wisest and best after all. You shall yet clasp to your heart the lost one, arrayed in resurrection beauty.

They told Him all things, whatsoever they had done, and taught. Mark 6: 30 (R.V.).

TALKING things over with Jesus! It is a precious secret! When one has been out in the world, it is delightful to talk over what has happened in the seclusion of the home. We have read of a wife who reserved one room in the house, which no one was permitted to enter but her husband and herself; and there they interchanged their mutual confidences. So it is a blessed habit to talk over everything with Jesus, and to review the events of the past beneath the light of his loving eyes.

"We have had much success, Master," we cry; "the cities were moved; the devils were subject; the crowds followed us everywhere." Ah, children, He seems to say, Those who cry "Hosanna" to-day will cry "Crucify" to-morrow: the real work of God is not done amid congratulating crowds, but in the heart's depths, and in the ante-chamber. See that ye dwell not on the excitement of the outward reception, lest you attribute your success to something in yourselves, and pride yourselves upon it, and become unsuitable for my use. All success comes from above.

"We have been greatly persecuted, and our mission seems to have been a failure, Master," we cry at another time. "Who hath believed our report, and to whom is the arm of the Lord revealed?" Care not for it, the same wise Counsellor replies: I at least am satisfied; I will see to it that your reward is according to your faithfulness, if not to your success; and there shall be a remnant of good soil that shall repay one hundredfold.

Thus his loving words extract the poison from success, and rally us from despondency. Oh, Christian workers, get into the secret of his presence, that He may correct, criticize, or encourage, as He please.

This He said, making all meats clean. Mark 7: 19 (R.V.).

THIS is a remarkable rendering of the Revisers, which has the support of their profound scholarship; and inaugurates an era in the history of the Levitical institutions. Before this hour arrived men were clean if they ate certain kinds of food, and unclean if they ate others. But from this moment, the Evangelist tells us, these outward distinctions were abolished. Henceforth all meats were to be viewed by the followers of Jesus as equally clean. There is, however, need that we should remember two or three things in respect to food. (1) THAT EVERY CREATURE OF GOD IS GOOD, AND NOTHING IS TO BE REFUSED IF IT CAN BE RECEIVED WITH THANKSGIVING. The act of thanksgiving is the test for the fitness and unfitness of food, as the ancient sign was supposed to be when made by the knight over a glass of wine offered by a stranger. Do not touch what you cannot thank God for.

(2) TAKE CARE TO EAT FOR THE NEED OF THE BODY RATHER THAN FOR ITS PLEASURE. There are a great many dainties and luxuries heaped on our tables which we take simply for the pleasure of eating. It is here that we are assailed with temptation, and need to be on our guard. The fact of food being pleasant eating is not in itself sufficient to justify our taking it. It may clog our digestion, and impair our power for thought and prayer and service.

(3) BE MODERATE IN THE AMOUNT YOU EAT. Quite as many over-eat as over-drink. We should always have the girded loin. The majority of the diseases of modern life have been traced to the habit of eating to excess. We are told by eminent authorities that we ought not to rise from table with the sense of having eaten to the full. Let your moderation in this also be known to all men.

He sighed deeply in his spirit. Mark 8: 12.
THIS Evangelist twice over calls attention to the Lord's sighs—in 7: 34, and here. A sigh is one of the most touching and significant tokens of excessive grief! When Nature is too deeply overwrought to remember her necessary inspirations, and has to compensate for their omission by one deep-drawn breath, we sigh, we sigh deeply in our spirit.

LOOKING UP TO HEAVEN, HE SIGHED. As the deaf mute stood before Him—an image of all the closed hearts around Him; of all the inarticulate unexpressed desires; of all the sin and sorrow of mankind—the sensitive heart of Jesus responded with a deep-drawn sigh. But there was simultaneously a heavenward look, which mingled infinite hope in it. If the sigh spoke of his tender sympathy, the look declared his close union with God, by virtue of which He was competent to meet the direst need. Whenever you sigh, look up to heaven. Heaven's light turns tears to jewels!

HE SIGHED DEEPLY. The obdurate and impenetrable hardness of the Pharisees; their wilful misinterpretation of his words and mission; their pride and bigotry—wrung the Lord's heart with bitterness. He turned sorrowfully away. There was no possibility of furnishing help, since on their side there was no desire for it, or belief in Him. Perhaps such sighs still break from his heart, as He views mankind; but through them He is doing his best to bring about the time when all sorrow and sighing shall flee away for ever.

The Son of God, in doing good, would look to heaven and sigh; but his sighs were followed by the touch and word of power. Let us not be content with the sigh of sympathy and regret.

If Thou canst. . . . And Jesus said unto him, If thou canst! Mark 9: 22, 23.
YES, there was an if in this sad case. But the father put it in the wrong place. He put it against Christ's power, "If Thou canst do anything." But it was really on the side of his own ability to believe. If only he believed, all else would be easily possible. Even though his faith were small, it would suffice; the tiniest seed can appropriate the chemical products of the soil, and transmute them into digestible products; the narrowest channel will suffice for the passage of the waters of the whole ocean, if you give time enough. Let us not worry about the greatness or smallness of our faith; the main point is as to whether it is directed towards the living Saviour.

There are many issues to which these words may be applied. If Jesus can save me from the power of sin! No; if thou canst believe, He can. If Jesus can deliver out of a mesh of temptation and perplexity! No; if thou canst believe, He will. If Jesus can revive his work mightily to the upbuilding of his Church and the ingathering of the lost! No; if thou canst believe for it.

Dost thou want that faith? It may be had thus. Look away from difficulty and temptation to Jesus; consider Him; feed thy faith on its native food of promise; familiarize thyself with fellowship with the promises; study what He has done for others: thus thou wilt believe. For every thought of thy little faith take ten thoughts of his faithfulness.

"All things are possible to God,
   To Christ the power of God in man
To me, when I am all subdued,
   When I in Christ am formed again,
And witness from my sins set free,
   All things are possible to me."

And Jesus was going before them.
Mark 10: 32 (R.V.).

THE radiant vision of the Transfiguration was deliberately forsaken, as the Lord took the way of the cross, going to Jerusalem to die. The shadow of his awful exodus had already fallen upon the little group. Behold that resolute figure—the wan face lit up with the fire of an invincible resolve—going in front, climbing the difficult ascent. The apostles cannot keep step with his eager steps, and they fear as an instinctive dread of coming events casts its chilling mantle around them. There was something in their Master they could not understand.

Such moments come to all lives, when Jesus leads us to the cross. How often He asks for a deeper consecration; a more complete crossing of natural inclination for the sake of his Gospel; an intenser purpose. At his bidding we must tear ourselves away from ambitions which had fascinated, and dreams which had allured. We must no longer live on the lower level, however pleasant to flesh and blood, but gird ourselves to go up to Jerusalem.

At such moments He always goes before us. We may not see Him until we begin to follow in the direction of his voice; but so soon as we set ourselves to obey, we become aware of his prevenient grace. He is just in front. He never puts forth his own sheep without going before them. He never asks us to tread a path which has not been trodden by his footsteps. Happy are they who follow Him!

In the first effort to follow Jesus, there may be amazement and not a little fear. The unaccustomed path, the strange look on his face, the shadow of the cross—all dissuade us. But as He dilates on the joy set before Him and us, we learn to think lightly of the difficulties in comparison with the goal.

Jesus answering saith unto them, Have faith in God. Mark 11: 22.

THE margin of the A.V. suggests that this command might be rendered, Have the faith of God. As long as I live I shall remember this text in connection with my first meeting with Hudson Taylor. He was to preach for me on a Sunday morning, now years ago, and gave out this as his text. But he said that he had always interpreted it as dealing rather with God's faith to us than ours to Him; so that it ran thus: Reckon on God's faithfulness.

1. WE MUST BE SURE THAT WE ARE ON GOD'S PLAN. There is a prepared path for us, along which God has stored up all necessary supplies. But if we want those supplies, we must find and follow it. Along the track which He has marked out between this and Home, our Father has erected cairns full of provisions; but we must let his route prevail over our own notions and wishes, if we are to enjoy his preparations.

2. WE MUST BE PREPARED TO WAIT ON HIM. For these things He will be inquired of. Though He knows what we need, He expects our humble request, that we may be perpetually reminded of our entire dependence on Him. He sometimes appears to tarry, to draw out our faith and prayer. But He will never utterly fail.

3. WE MUST WALK WORTHILY OF HIM. God shows Himself strong only on behalf of those whose heart is perfect towards Him. By his enabling grace we must put away the old manner of life, and be renewed in the spirit of our mind, that we may be such whom the great God shall delight to honour. Let such trust Him to the hilt; they will find Him faithful. He will never put us into positions of peril and responsibility, and leave us to take our chance.

He is not the God of the Dead, but the God of the living. Mark 12: 27.

SINCE God spoke of Himself as the God of the patriarchs, centuries after they had been borne to their graves, it stood to reason that they were yet living; and on this ground our Lord met the allegation that there is no life beyond death.

DEATH IS NOT A STATE OR CONDITION, BUT AN ACT. We speak of the dead; but in point of fact there are none such. We should speak of those who have died. They were living up to the moment of death; but they were living quite as much afterwards. Death is like birth, an act, a transition, a passage into a freer life. Never think of a death as a state, but as resembling a bridge which, for a moment, casts its shadow on the express train, which flashes beneath, but does not stay.

ALL OUR DEAR ONES ARE LIVING. As vividly as keenly, as intensely as ever: with all the love and faith and intelligence with which we were wont to associate their beloved personality. It may be that they think of us as only half alive, compared with their own intense and vivid experience of the life which draws its breath from the manifested presence of God. Oh, do not fear that they will cease to recognize, know, or love you! Always it remains true, "Without us they cannot be made perfect."

THOSE WHO LIVE ON EITHER SIDE OF DEATH MAY MEET IN GOD. Those who are present in the body, and those who are absent from it, meet in proportion as they approach God. When we come near Him in thought, and prayer, and love, we are come to the spirits of the just made perfect. God is the glorious centre of all the lines that radiate into all worlds. "Ye are come to God, the Judge of all, . . . and to the spirits of the just made perfect."

Ye know not when the lord of the house cometh. Mark 13: 35 (R.V.).

NO, we know not. It is better that we should not know. But He must be very near. Even has past; the beams of his presence had just died off the world, and the after-glow was still lingering in the ministry of the apostles in the early Church. Midnight is past; it reached its deepest darkness in the middle ages, when only a few holy souls shone like stars in the surrounding gloom. Cock-crow has past; Wickliffe and Luther, and others, heralded the morning. And now the morning is upon us; nay, it is shining more and more unto the perfect day. He must be near, even at the doors. Be ready, O virgin souls, to go forth to meet Him!

But may not these words be interpreted in yet another way? Jesus comes to us in the evening twilight, when the joy of our life seems slowly waning. He comes to us in the deep night of depression, bereavement, and anguish. He comes to us in the hope and expectancy of each new dawn, when we gird ourselves to fresh toils and endeavours. He comes to us in the morning, and satisfies us with his mercy, that we may rejoice and be glad all the day. Only let us watch for his coming, with ears attent to his lightest footfall, his softest whisper. Then, when He shows Himself through the lattice, or softly whispers, "Come away," we shall arise and go forth with Him to the beds of lilies and the gardens of myrrh.

Are we quite sure that we belong to his house? "Whose house are we," says the writer of the Epistle to the Hebrews. But there are conditions: we must be born into it by regeneration; we must walk as becometh saints; we must hold the beginning of our confidence steadfast to the end. Christ is Lord over this house, and his will is law (Heb. 3: 1-9).

But Jesus said, Let her alone. Mark 14: 6.

THE lovers of Jesus are often misunderstood. Those who judge only by a utilitarian standard refuse to acknowledge the worth of their deeds. You might as well despise the electric light because it makes no register on a gas-meter. But when the voices of criticism and jealousy are highest, Jesus steps in and casts the shield of his love around the trembling, disconcerted soul, saying, Let him alone. So He speaks still:

TO SATAN. The adversary stands near to resist and tempt. As Judas criticized Mary, so the Evil One seems at times to pour a perpetual stream of chilling criticism on all we say and do; or he meets us at every turn with some evil suggestion. But Jesus is on the watch, and He will not allow us to be tempted beyond what we are able to bear; but when heart and flesh fail, He will step in and say, Let him (or her) alone.

TO SORROW. We must pass through the fire, and be subjected to the lapidary's wheel; we must drink of His cup, and be baptized with His baptism; we must bear our cross after Him. But He is always on the alert. And whenever the feeble flesh is at an end of its power of endurance, He will step in and say, Let be—it is enough.

TO HUMAN UNKINDNESS. Some of us are called to suffer most from our fellows; our foes belong to our own household; our brother Cain hates us. It is hard to bear. To have one's motives misunderstood and maligned; to lose one's good name; to be an outcast—all this is hard. But God has planted a hedge about us and none may pass through it, except He permit. Even Satan recognizes this, as we learn from the Book of Job.

My God, my God, why hast Thou forsaken Me? Mark 15: 34.

THIS was the darkest hour of the Saviour's human life. Lover and friend stood away from Him; and those for whom his blood was being shed covered Him with contumely and abuse. Let us consider:

HIS QUOTATION OF SCRIPTURE. He is quoting the first verse of Psalm 22, which is truly known as the Psalm of the Cross. It may be that He recited to Himself that wonderful elegy, in which David was to anticipate so minutely the sufferings of his Lord. What meaning there was for those dying lips in the 7th verse: "All they that see Me laugh Me to scorn"; in the 13th: "They gape upon Me"; in the 14th: "All my bones are out of joint"; in the 17th: "I may tell all my bones"; or in the 18th: "They part my garments and cast lots." What sacred feet trod those well-worn steps!

HIS VICARIOUS SUFFERINGS. There is no possible way of understanding, or interpreting, these words, except by believing that He was suffering for sins not his own; that He was being made sin for us; that He was bearing away the sin of the world. It is not for a moment conceivable that the Father could have ever seemed to forsake his well-beloved Son, unless He had stood as the Representative of a guilty race, and during those hours of midday midnight had become the propitiation for the sins of the world.

HIS PERFECT EXAMPLE OF THE WAY OF FAITH. In doing the Father's will, He yielded up his life even to the death of the cross. But amid it all He said, "My God, my God." He still held to the Father with his two hands. And his faith conquered. The clouds broke; the clear heaven appeared; He died with a serene faith. "My God" was exchanged for "Father, into thy hands."

The Lord working with them.   Mark 16: 20.
THIS was the secret of the successes of the early Church. Theirs was the simple commission to preach; but wherever they did so, the Lord confirmed their word with signs following. In Jerusalem, Samaria, Antioch, Rome, and to the uttermost end of the world, wherever these simple men stood up and made their proclamation, their invisible Lord was present, and his Spirit bore witness.

Nothing less than this will account for the marvellous successes of those early preachers. He who sat at the right hand of God in the attitude of majestic rest was always beside them in the intensity of the most untiring work. What was done by them on earth was wrought by Himself. His right hand and his holy arm got Him the victory.

This blessed partnership has never been repealed. Jesus has never withdrawn from the compact; and if we could only dare to count and reckon on Him, we would find that He was co-operating in church, and Sunday-school, and mission-station. There are a few rules to be observed, however, before we can count upon Him thus: (1) We must be clean in heart and life. He cannot identify Himself with those who are consciously delinquent. (2) We must not seek our own glory, but God's, and the pure blessing of men. (3) We must use the word of God as our sword, our lever, our balm, our cordial, our charm. (4) We must be in loving harmony with those who name his name, as He cannot countenance seclusion or uncharitable feeling. (5) We must by faith claim and reckon upon Him—speaking to Him as to the message before it is delivered, relying on Him during its delivery, and conferring with Him about its effect. Not anxious or elated, but at rest.

Luke

Behold the handmaid of the Lord: be it unto me according to thy word.   Luke 1: 38.
THE angel's message meant, for this young, pure-hearted girl, a great deal of misunderstanding and reproach. It was inevitable that clouds would gather around her character, which would sorely perplex the good man to whom she was betrothed. But as soon as she realized that this lot was ordained for her by God she humbly acquiesced, with these model words of patient faith. Let us often say them:

FIRST: TO HIS COMMANDS. God's voice often speaks within our hearts, and no word of his is devoid of power. We must test what seems to be his voice by these three corroborations: First, his Word; second, by the trend of outward circumstances; third, by the advice of Christian people not immediately interested. When these concur, we may take it that God has spoken to us, and whatever the burden of his words we must respond—Be it unto me according to thy word.

SECONDLY: TO THE RESPONSIBILITIES THRUST ON US. It may be a trusteeship for some dying friend; a charge of orphan children; a babe cast on our parentage; an invalid; a difficult and trying piece of Christian enterprise. But whenever it comes on us, imposed by the evident appointment of our Father, notwithstanding the shrinking of our flesh and the fearfulness of our soul, we must say: Be it unto me according to thy word.

THIRDLY: TO ANY BURDEN OF PAIN AND SUFFERING. Are you one whom God has set apart to manifest the power of his grace in suffering and pain? Are you sleepless by night, and helpless by day? Are you likely to spend years in one position, as paralysed or rheumatic? Well, still dare to look up and say: Be it unto me according to thy word.

Glory to God in the highest, and on earth peace. Luke 2: 14.

THESE twain are joined together, and none can sunder them. Do you want peace? your highest aim must be the glory of God. Do you seek God's glory as your highest aim? then, the inevitable result will be the peace that passeth understanding.

GLORY TO GOD IN THE HIGHEST. It was said of the soldiers of the first Napoleon that they were content to die in the ditch if only he rode over them to victory. With their last breath they cried, "Long live the Emperor!" It seemed as though they had lost all thought and care of their own interests, so long as glory accrued to his name. So should it be of us. Higher than our own comfort, or success, or popularity, should be the one thought of the glory of our God. Let Christ be honoured, loved, exalted, at whatever cost to us.

ON EARTH, PEACE. It will come, because when the heart has only one aim to follow, it is delivered from dividing and distracting cares. It will come, because the glory of God is so lofty an aim that it lifts the soul into the atmosphere of the heavenly and eternal world, where peace reigns unbroken. It will come, because we are not greatly troubled by the reverses and alternations of fortune that are incident to all work in this world, since the main object is always secure and beyond fear of failure. What though there be the ebb and flow of the wave, yet the tide is certainly

coming up the shore, and will presently stand at high-water mark.

This peace is said in the R.V. to come only to men in whom God is well pleased. Live to please God, and He will breathe on thee his peace. Seek his glory, and He will make thy heart his home. Do his will, and thereby good shall come to thee.

He shall baptize you with the Holy Ghost, and with fire. Luke 3: 16.

THEY had received the negative, water; they were to receive the positive, fire. Water is not sufficient for natures such as ours. The Baptist pointed to a greater Baptist than himself. Jesus plunges the soul into a baptism of fire.

FIRE CLEANSES. Ore may be mingled with earthly ingredients from which it is imperative to free it. A chisel or pickaxe could not extricate it. But when it is plunged into the furnace, the metal runs out in a molten stream. So our characters are full of impurities and earthly ingredients; but as they are brought into contact with the power of the Holy Spirit, these are eliminated and drop away, and we attain degrees of purity and love which otherwise had made us unserviceable to our dear Lord. Do not seek to rid yourself of these things as a condition of his gracious cleansing, but seek the baptism of the Spirit, and He will free thee; for He is like a consuming fire.

FIRE ILLUMINATES. As the express-train hurries the traveller by night through a district where the smelting furnaces are in full blast, his eyes are arrested by their glow, and the very heavens are lurid with the light, reflected for miles. So when the Spirit comes in power to the soul, He teaches us to know God, and truth, and things hidden from the wise and prudent. The fires that sanctify, illuminate us.

FIRE ENKINDLES. It is contagious. It will spread over an immense area, where inflammable material attracts it. A match may light up a bonfire that will burn for hours. So when the Spirit of God touches a soul, like an unlit candle, it begins to glow; and from it the blessed spark may pass from heart to heart, and church to church, till an entire continent may blaze with heavenly fire.

The Spirit of the Lord is upon Me, because He anointed Me. Luke 4: 18.

AS the Lord emerged from the waters of baptism, the heavens were opened, and the

Spirit in a bodily shape descended upon Him and abode. Then his mouth was opened, and his public ministry commenced. Now He stepped forth into the world, saying:

"The Spirit of the Lord is upon Me,
Because He anointed Me to preach good tidings to the poor:
He hath sent Me to proclaim release to the captives,
And recovering of sight to the blind,
To set at liberty them that are bruised,
To proclaim the acceptable year of the Lord."

The Spirit was given Him without measure, as the power in which He was to cast out devils, preach the Gospel, and glorify his Father by his human life and ministry.

What that scene was in the life of the Lord, Pentecost was for the Church. Then she was anointed for her divine mission among men; the unction of the Holy One rested upon her, to be continued and renewed as the centuries slowly passed. What happened for the Church should take place in the history of each member of it. This anointing is for all, is to be received by faith, and is specially intended to equip us for work. Hast thou had thy share? If not, art thou not making a mistake in attempting God's work without it? If Jesus did not put his hand to this work till He was conscious of his anointing, though He was one with the Holy Spirit in an especial sense, how much less should we! Hast thou known it? Seek it on the threshold of each new enterprise. Be satisfied with nothing less than to be anointed with fresh oil.

He stretched forth his hand, and touched him, saying, I will; be thou clean. Luke 5: 13.
THIS leper, as the physician-evangelist remarks, was full of leprosy. It was a very aggravated case. He lay in the dust before Jesus. What a contrast! Loathsomeness and divine beauty; disease and health; humanity at its worst and best; sinner and Saviour; one of Satan's most miserable victims, and the Almighty Deliverer. So, my reader, if thou art conscious of a heart and life which are full of sin, I would have thee meet thy Saviour now. There is no if about his power—even the leper recognized that. The only doubt was about the Saviour's will: there is, however, no doubt on this score now, since He has healed myriads, and promises healing to all who come.

Throw thyself, then, at his feet, and ask for cleansing.

"He stretched forth his hand, and touched him." No one else would have dared to do as much. To touch that flesh, according to the Levitical code, would induce uncleanness. But Jesus shrank not. On the one hand, He knew that the ceremonial restrictions were abolished in Himself: on the other, He desired to teach that sin cannot defile the divine holiness of the Saviour. Whatever be the stories of sin that are breathed into his ear; whatever the open bruises and putrefying sores which are opened to his touch; whatever the sights and scenes with which He has to cope—none of these can leave a taint of evil in his sinless heart. It would be as impossible for sin to soil Christ as for a plague to contaminate flame. And He will heal thee. Dare to claim it.

"Break up the heavens, O Lord, and far
Through all yon starlight keen
Draw me, thy bride—a glittering star,
In raiment white and clean."

Every one when he is perfected shall be as his Master. Luke 6: 40 (R.V.).
WE ARE NOT PERFECTED YET. There is a great chasm between our highest and our Master's lowest; between where we stop and He begins: between our light, which is twilight at best, and His meridian glory. When we compare ourselves with ourselves, or with our neighbours, our standard is altogether too low; we should compare ourselves with Him, the beloved Master. Job, who was reputed perfect, abhorred himself, and repented in dust and ashes when he had seen God, of whom he had formerly only heard.

BUT WE SHALL BE PERFECTED ONE DAY. That when has a hopeful ring. But to what period does the Master point? Not till sorrow, sanctified by God's grace, has done its work; not till the snow and frost, the light shower and the bitter wind, the earth and sun, have contributed their shares to the desired quota. Not till the perfect image of Jesus has emerged from the sculptured stone; not till the molten metal reflects each lineament of the glorified Lord.

WHEN WE ARE PERFECTED WE SHALL BE AS OUR MASTER. "We shall be like Him, for we shall see Him as He is." It seems altogether too much to expect! To think that we shall be changed into his image; that we shall bear his impress; that we shall be as like Him as Gideon's brethren to Gideon, of whom the princes of Midian testified that they were like the children of a king. Yet it shall be so. The Lord Jesus became like unto us in our low estate, that we should become like Him in his glory. There must ever be the limitation of the creature as compared with Him by whom all things were made. But in our measure there shall be the same perfect beauty—his beauty upon us—for a mountain lake may as perfectly reflect the wide blue heaven as an ocean.

When the Lord saw her, He had compassion on her, and said unto her, Weep not. Luke 7: 13.
NO widow stands by the bier of her only son, no mother by the empty cot of her babe, no lover beside the fading beauty of his beloved— but the Son of Man, unseen but glorious, is at hand, seeing, understanding, touched with compassion, and saying, in his tenderest tones, Weep not!

WEEP NOT: LOVE IS ETERNAL. Hast thou forgotten that there are three things which abide for evermore, the greatest of which is love? Is it likely that those blessed ties which have woven us to others can be snapped by death, which can only touch the body, but is not able to reach the soul? Is not love of God —and can God's love change, and pass away? No; though severed from your sight, the dear ones that are gone are thine to-day, and have not forgotten, but love thee still. Without us they cannot be made perfect.

WEEP NOT: RECOGNITION OF THE BELOVED DEAD IS CERTAIN. Did not Mary and the women, Peter and five hundred more, recognize Jesus after his resurrection? Is He not the same Man? Are we not to be like Him? Recognition went so far, in his case, that the Magdalene recognized the very tones of his voice, when He said Mary, and she answered Rabboni. Yes, though refined and purified, the face thou hast loved shall smile, and the tones that have made thy heart-music shall speak again. Weep not!

WEEP NOT: THEY SHALL RISE AGAIN, NEVER-MORE TO BE SEPARATED. The Lord raised this youth to life; but there had to be another parting, when his mother or he died. But when thy dear ones are reunited to thee, there will be no more partings. There shall be no more sea. Thy heart shall find its mate. Thou and he shall go no more out.

But Jesus said, Some one did touch Me.
Luke 8: 46 (R.V.).
AMID the pressure of the crowd that crushed on Him from all sides, Jesus detected the light touch of one thin hand, which drew from Him healing virtue. We may be very near Christ, and throng Him, without touching; but no one can touch Him, however lightly, without deriving the very grace needed.

We think of Jesus to-day amid the thronging crowds of angels and spirits of the just made perfect. Amid their voices will ours be heard? Amid the pressure of their attendance on his sacred person will He stay to recognize our poor trembling touch? Amid the vast interests that depend on Him, the government of the universe, the holding together and consistence of all things, is there any likelihood of our need asserting itself successfully? See, He is hastening on to raise the dead; there is the daughter of many a Jairus waiting for his summons, in the cemeteries and sleeping places of the dead. Will He stay for me? Yes, always.

There is the touch of prayer and faith. Thou canst never exercise it, however simply, without eliciting an immediate response. The conductor can detect the tiny note of a piccolo in an orchestra; and Christ is moved by a whisper, a sigh, a tear, a touch. There may be a good deal of mistake and superstition, as there was in this woman, who seemed to have thought that virtue clung to his robes; but He will distinguish the soul of holy trust amid many false ingredients. There is also the touch of affection. He knew when the woman crept to kiss his feet. He did not instantly speak of it, but said afterwards, "From the time I came in she hath not ceased to kiss my feet." Not one loving expression from thy heart to his is lost on Him!

Behold, there talked with Him two men, which were Moses and Elijah. Luke 9: 31.
WHAT a spectacle was this, on the slopes of Lebanon, with light transcending that of the moon light shining in the upper heights! And what converse! Possibly that transfiguration was an example of the way in which Adam and all his race might have passed into heaven, had not death come on us all through sin; and therefore it was the greater proof of the love of our dear Lord, when He deliberately turned from all the radiant light and took the way of the cross. His death is here called an exodus: such is the Greek word rendered decease. How much these two great souls, Moses and Elijah, had to say about it: the

one representing the law; the other the prophets.

MOSES would remind Him of the lamb that would be slain before the children of Israel could escape from Egypt; of the rock that must be smitten, before the water could flow forth for the thirsty crowds; of the serpent that must be fixed on the pole, before the dying Israelites could look and live.

ELIJAH would remind the Lord of Psalm 22, beginning with a wail and ending with praise; of Isaiah 33, finishing with a burst of triumph; and many another sacred and familiar pasage.

And after all it was only an exodus, the going forth of his spirit from the Time-sphere to the Eternal; from contact with a very weary world to victory and joy-mending. Lighted by the Shechinah glory; following through the Red Sea of Blood; hastening to the morning, with its vision of enemies strewn dead on the sea-shore. The memory of this talk so far robbed death of its terror, in the heart of one of the disciples at least, that afterwards he described his own death as an exodus (2 Peter 1: 15).

I beheld Satan fallen as lightning from heaven. Luke 10: 18 (R.V.).

THIS was Christ's vision of the effect of his work in man's nature, and on man's behalf. For ages Satan had vaunted his power over man; but now and henceforward the demonnature was to be vanquished by the name and nature of Jesus Christ. "The demons are subject to us in thy name." Whenever you are tempted by the demon of alcohol, of passion, of jealousy, or any other, claim instantly the protection of the Name which is above every name: make the Name and Nature of Jesus your strong tower into which you shall run and be safe: realize all that He stands for: and you will find that the demons will be subject to you. In your life also, Satan will fall from heaven, and be trodden under your feet.

And what is true in your own life is true also of your influence over others. If you dare to live in the risen Christ, you share his empire and all the fruits of his victory over Satan. He gives you authority over serpents and scorpions, and over all the power of the enemy. The Christ nature within you becomes the dominant, triumphant power to which all power must ultimately yield. Dare to use it. In conflict with the demon spirits that haunt so many lives; in antagonizing the giant forces that are so strongly entrenched in our natural life, the ravages of vice—be sure to rely, not on numbers or organization, but on the name of Jesus, used not as a charm, but as representing his living and ascended might.

And let it be carefully noted that as the success of these disciples over a few demons in the villages and towns of Israel reacted on the balance of power in the heavenlies so there is no victory won anywhere by any lonely disciple, or handful of disciples, that does not react on the entire battlefield.

Lord, teach us to pray. Luke 11: 1.

IT was a wise and good request, prompted by the Saviour's own practice. He did not, in the first instance, command his disciples to pray; but He gave Himself to the blessed practice of prayer, and this made them eager to learn and practise the holy art. This is the best way of inculcating new and holy habits on those who surround us. Do not begin by exhorting them; but by living before them a life so holy, so unselfish, so consecrated and devout, that they shall spontaneously approach you, saying, "Give us your secret; tell us how we may do and become as you." It is a holy life which constitutes our best pulpit.

We should daily ask the Master to teach us to pray. Each time we kneel in prayer we may well preface our petitions with the sentence: "We know not what we should pray for as we ought; but by thy Holy Spirit, Lord, teach us to pray." And probably the Lord's answer will fall into suggestions, borrowed from the form and model of prayer which He gave his disciples. It has been called the Lord's Prayer; it should be called the Disciples'.

Address prayer to the Father, through the Son. Do not be selfish in prayer; but look out on the needs of others, incorporating them in every petition—us, we, our. Remember, you are speaking to your Father, and that his honour and glory should have a paramount and foremost place. If you desire first the hallowing of his name, and the coming of his kingdom, all your personal needs and desires will fall easily and naturally into their place, which will be a comparatively subordinate one. You will need forgiveness as often and as regularly as your daily bread. Be, also, direct and definite in prayer.

Be not anxious. Luke 12: 11 (R.V.).

SO often through this discourse the Lord

refers to anxiety. "Be not anxious how or what ye shall answer" (ver. 11). "Which of you by being anxious can add?" (ver. 25). "Why are ye anxious?" (ver. 26). There must have been a great strain on the crowds who listened to Him; and there was every likelihood of the strain becoming even greater for his disciples as the years passed on. So, also, the characteristic of our age is anxious strain.

But the heart of Jesus was always at peace. His life was calm amid the storms of life; as the coral-island, with its fronded palms and lagoons of still water, is peaceful amid the storm-tossed ocean, because of the protection of its reef. The surf breaks there, but does not intrude further. The secrets of Jesus were the perpetual presence of God in his soul, and his never-faltering faith in the loving, careful providence of God in all the experiences of his chequered life.

Can we not have this? We may if we are willing to pay the price. If we will resign or surrender our will utterly to Him; if we will tear down every vail that might hide his face, and throw open our whole being to his in-dwelling and use; if we will cease scheming, planning, devising, and fall back on the abso-lute care and arrangements of God; if we will learn to reckon on God as absolutely as on any resourceful human friend; if we will dare to believe that God holds Himself responsible for the sustenance and equipment for duty of all who absolutely seek his glory—then

"Our lives shall be full of sunshine,
     And the cares that infest the day
Shall fold up their tents like the Arabs,
     And as silently steal away."

Enter in by the narrow door. Luke 13: 24 (R.V.). THE question which the disciples asked was for their gratification and curiosity. Men have always been curious to know what will be the numerical result of the Redeemer's work. But to such questions the Lord has no reply. He was only eager that none of those whom He loved should miss the full measure of blessed-ness that was within his reach; therefore He bade each be sure of entering the narrow door, so narrow that there is no room to carry through it the love of self, the greed of gain, the thirst for the applause and rewards of the world.

We may be saved from the penalty of sin by one single glance at the Saviour, who lived, and died, and lives for evermore; but we cannot be saved in the deepest meaning of the word, in the sense of being delivered from the love and power of sin, unless we are willing to enter through a door, so constructed and strait, that it seems impossible to effect an entrance. Art thou willing for this, willing to leave behind thy amassed and hardly-gained treasures, thy luggage and impedimenta, thy jewels and gewgaws, thy certificate of merit and creden-tials, thy notions of self-importance, the weights which thou hast carried so long, the pillows with which thou art always sparing thyself from the stern realities and efforts of a noble life? If thou art willing for this, and prepared to strive, even to the rending of thyself asunder, then thou shalt be saved from the love and tyranny of that wild, dark power, which, hitherto, has always dragged thee down-wards.

It is not enough to eat and drink of the blessed memorial supper, nor to listen to the voice of Jesus teaching in his Church. Many may do all this, and yet never be included in the Kingdom of Heaven.

He cannot be my disciple. Luke 14: 26, 27, 33. THREE times Christ repeats these solemn words; and it may be that earnest men have done injury to his cause, which they desired to serve, by omitting these stringent conditions in their Gospel invitations. It is quite true that whosoever will may come and take; that whosoever believeth in Him shall never perish; that the door of mercy stands open wide. But it is equally true that the faith that saves must pass such tests as these; and if it does not, it is not of the quality which can bear the soul through the swelling billows of the river of death. These three tests may be classified thus:

SEPARATION. It sometimes happens in the disciple's life that Christ's work lies in one direction, whilst the blessed ties of home lie in another. Tender voices call; loving hands reach out to hold him. Here the plough is waiting in its furrow; there the hearth with its tender memory and association. At such times, for the true man, there can be but one choice.

CRUCIFIXION. Everyone has his own cross—some one thing in which the will of God crosses his will. Jesus made that cross, and bids us take it up and bear it after Himself. Yet how many evade it, flee from it, postpone it. They think they can follow Him apart from it; but it is impossible. We can only follow the

Crucified when we bear each his own cross. And to shrink from it shows that we are not disciples.

RENUNCIATION. All we have must be gladly yielded when Christ asks for it. If the accumulation of a life be on one scale and Christ in the other, we must choose Christ, come what may to the rest, or we must abandon our title to discipleship.

He would not go in.   Luke 15: 28.
THE elder brother is the dark contrast which heightens the glowing picture of the repentant prodigal; as the gargoyle does the beauty of the angel faces on the cathedral font.

When we look at sin, not in its theological aspects, but in its everyday clothes, we find that it divides itself into two kinds. We find that there are sins of the body and sins of the disposition; or, more narrowly, sins of the passions, including all forms of lust and selfishness, and sins of the temper. The prodigal is the instance in the New Testament of sins of passion—the elder brother of sins of temper. Now we might be disposed to think that the prodigal is the worse sinner of these two; but it is at least worthy of remark that as the story ends, we see him found, forgiven, restored; whilst the elder brother is still outside the house, and an absentee from the feast. Does Christ mean that the ill-tempered murmuring of the Pharisee is more hopeless than the passion of the publican and sinner? We must not press the thought too far; but we may at least ask whether we are harbouring, beneath a very respectable, moral exterior, the spirit of the elder brother, who plods daily to work, and is accounted a paragon of filial dutifulness, but is left without the door.

One has made a careful analysis of the ingredients that went to make up that one spiteful speech; they come out thus: jealousy, anger, pride, uncharity, cruelty, self-righteousness, sulkiness, touchiness, doggedness. "His speech, like the bubble escaping to the surface of the pool, betrays the rottenness beneath." Let us carefully read our hearts, lest there be any trace of this spirit in ourselves, when others are pressing into the kingdom with joy.

That which is another's.   Luke 16: 12.
OUR Lord is speaking of money and its use.

HE DESCRIBES MONEY. It is so associated with unrighteousness that He speaks of it as the unrighteous mammon. It was as though the inveterate moneymaker, who will get money at all costs, was an idolater, prostrating himself daily in the temple of the heathen deity who bore that name. In his judgment, also, it is a very little thing (ver. 10). We only know how little when we compared it with the immortal qualities of a lowly character. At least, it is not the true riches (ver. 11). Moreover, it is not our own—it is clearly another's—God's (ver. 12). We have nothing that we have not received.

HE INDICATES THE MAIN USE OF MONEY. It is God's; but He puts it into our hands to watch the use we will make of it, before He entrusts to us the true riches of eternity—just as you will test a child with a toy watch before you dare place in his hands a real one. If he is destructive of the one, you hesitate to hand him the other; whilst if he is careful, you feel able to consign to his care some family heirloom. So God is testing men by giving them money, that He may know how far to trust them in the mart of the New Jerusalem.

HE AROUSES US TO FIDELITY—care for God's interests as much as the wasteful and unfaithful steward cared for his own. He used his master's money to secure a welcome to the debtor's houses when he lost his situation. But God has so arranged it, that if you use his money aright, you shall not only win his approbation, but his interests will be so coincident with yours, that when the world fades from view, those whom you have helped for God's sake shall welcome you to heaven.

The kingdom of God cometh not with observation.   Luke 17: 20.
THE Kingdom is "in mystery" just now. It is hidden from mortal eye, because the King Himself is withdrawn from the visible sphere. The creation groans and travails for its manifestation. He must be manifested before we can be manifested with Him in glory. In the meanwhile, it is not without, but within; not compelling human attention, but pervading human hearts. Let us remember this when we are lamenting the slow progress of Christianity in the world. It appears to recede almost as quickly as it advances; what it gains in one place it loses in another. If heathen lands are receiving Christ, are not the populations of Christian lands departing from Him? Stay; you cannot tell! It is useless to argue! There may be much more good working than you know. For every bold confessor there are pro-

bably seven thousand who have not bowed to Baal.

WHEN WE ARE TEMPTED TO ESTIMATE OUR SUCCESS BY NUMERICAL RESULTS. When our church is crowded; our roll of communicants constantly augmented; and the money revenue large—we are disposed to think that the cause of Christ is really advancing in our midst. It may be so. But sometimes, where numbers are scant and difficulties many, a yet deeper and more lasting result is being achieved.

WHEN WE ARE LAMENTING THE APPARENT SLOWNESS OF OUR GROWTH IN GRACE. You do not feel as you would; nay, to judge by your emotional life you fear lest you are positively receding in the divine life; you think that the quality and quantity of your fruit unto God is decreasing. Stay; the deepest work is not always the most obvious. Before the mole appears above the wave, years of work have been expended where no eye can see; but every stone tells in the result.

Hear what the unjust judge saith. Luke 18: 6.
THE force of this parable lies in its succession of vivid contrasts, which rise to an irresistible climax.

THE JUDGE IS UNJUST. He neither fears God nor regards man. His one idea is to extort as much money as he can from the prisoners who desire to get out of gaol, and from those that want to keep them in, or put others to share their fate. But God is our Father, unimpeachable in his integrity, and only eager to promote our welfare.

THE JUDGE HAD NO PERSONAL INTEREST IN THE CLAIMANT. She had no personal attraction for him. Had she been possessed of property, he might have cared more. But now he looked on her as a pest that plagued and worried him. But we are God's elect, over whom his tender heart yearns. Did He not choose us before all the worlds unto his glory?

THE JUDGE ANSWERED THE WIDOW'S CRY JUST TO SAVE HIMSELF TROUBLE. Whenever he went to his seat, there she was. Though he had refused to hear her a score of times, there was her voice again, as clear and penetrating as ever. She had been forcibly hurried from his presence by his officials, and she had been borne screaming and remonstrating into the rear; but she never knew herself defeated. At last he could bear it no longer, and gave orders that her patrimony should be restored.

And will not God do as much, as, generation after generation, He sees his Church, like a widowed soul, oppressed by the great enemy and avenger? As He hears the cries of martyrs and saints; the perpetual prayer, Come, Lord Jesus; the insolent boast of the foe—will He not arise and avenge? Yes, verily, speedily! But it may seem long to us, because one thousand years with Him are as one day.

They said, The Lord hath need of him.
Luke 19: 34.
OH, could I hear Thee say as much of me, my blessed Lord! Here, where two ways meet, I have been standing long, waiting for a purpose worthy to fill my soul, and task the powers that are, as yet, only in the first burst of young life.

Thou needest much and many in thy great redemptive work. The boat to cross the lake; the line to catch the fish; the bread and fish to feed the crowds; the baskets to gather up the fragments; the chalice to hold the wine; the dish to hold the sop; the little child to be the text for thy sermon; the clay for the blind man's eyes; the tender women to minister of their substance; the apostles to preach thy Gospel. Canst Thou not find a niche for me also?

Thou requirest undivided loyalty. Born of the Virgin's womb, laid in death where man's dust had never come, Thou must have a colt on which none had ever sat. I cannot give Thee a heart which has never known another; but I profess to Thee that there is no rival now. Thou mayest have all. Thine is the Kingdom.

Thou requirest patience and humility. But these, also, Thou hast taught. I have waited patiently till this glad hour, and am quieted and humbled like a weaned child. No longer do I seek great things for myself. It is enough for me to be and do anything, if only Thou shalt be glorified.

THOU REQUIREST, PERHAPS, BUT ONE BRIEF SERVICE. To serve Thee always with increasing fervour would be my choice; but if Thou needest only one brief, glad hour of ministry, like that the good Ananias did to thy Church when he ministered to Saul, then be it so. To prepare for it, and revert to it, would be my satisfaction in having lived.

Whose image and superscription hath it?
Luke 20: 24.
OUR Lord more than once compared men to

coins. He spoke of the woman who lost one piece of silver, and searched till she had found it. The analogy might be carried out in many particulars; for as the ore passes through the crucible, and many another process, before it is stamped with the image of the sovereign, so do souls experience many fiery trials ere they can receive and keep the impression of heaven's mint, which is the face of Jesus.

WHOSE IMAGE DOST THOU BEAR? Is there a clear-cut outline of the features of Christ, so manifest that those who touch and handle you are irresistibly reminded of Him; or have the features of your King, which were once clear-cut, become effaced?

WHOSE IS THY SUPERSCRIPTION? IS A.D. THERE? the year in which you were born into the kingdom of God, the year of our Lord, the year of your eternal life? Is "Dei gratia" there? (By the grace of God). So that all the while those who know you magnify the exceeding riches of his love as manifested in you. Is "Christus Rex" there? (Christ the King). Are you absolutely Christ's—to serve and to obey? Is "Fid. Def." there? (Defender of the Faith). Do you keep the deposit of Christ's holy Gospel, as you look to Him to keep the deposit which you have committed to Him? Is the lion on the quarterings?—speaking of the strength of the Lion of Judah imparted to your soul. Is the harp amongst them?—indicating the subjection of every string of your life to his finger. Is the crown there?—indicating how absolutely you have placed the empire of your nature upon the brow of your Lord. Then weave together the rose of Sharon and the lily of the valley as the symbol of his reign.

Watch ye at every season, making supplication. Luke 21: 36 (R.V.).
LET us never release the girdle from around our loins, nor throw ourselves listlessly upon the bank to drink, whilst the enemy may be stealing up against the wind. It is the art of our great enemy to fill the air with the heavy breath of the poppy; that, like the lotus-eaters of the old legend we may be indisposed for the perils and toils of our onward journey.

WATCH YE IN THE SEASON OF FESTIVITY. When merry voices fill the chamber with mirth, and jokes pass; old stories are retold; quaint anecdotes circulated—remember to look frequently up into the Master's face, to discover if aught has covered it with shame, or filled it with regret. Let not your heart be overcharged with surfeiting drunkenness.

WATCH YE IN HOURS OF STRESS AND ANXIETY. These will come between the soul and Christ, oppressing us with anxious care, leading us to think too much of the things which are seen and transient, and filling our hearts with dismay, as though the future would find us orphans and homeless, because the storm had swept away some few gatherings of the earth's perishable stores. When stocks are falling, business declining, competition increasing—Watch! Make supplication! Stand before the Son of Man as those whom He cannot forget or forsake.

WATCH YE IN SEASONS OF TENDER LOVE. We wear armour abroad, but when we come within the closed door of the home, and our hearts expand beneath the genial warmth of kindred natures, how apt we are to cry, Now, surely, we may unbend, ungird, and let nature have free course. But the Master says, Watch ye at every season; and He reminds us that we never cease to stand before the Son of Man.

Simon, Simon, behold Satan asked to have you that he might sift you as wheat. Luke 22: 31.
THE Master apparently did not pray that temptation should be withheld. The quick eye of his affection had discerned the tempter's approach. His quick ear had detected Satan's request of the Father; as though he said, "Let me have the chance for one brief hour, and I will show that these men, so far from being gold, silver, and precious stones, are only wood, hay, and stubble." But though He knew all this, the Master did not request that the winnowing wind should be withheld. Why? Because temptation is part of the present order of the world. Why it is so we cannot tell; that it is so we know assuredly. Why the Almighty permitted the evil one to intrude into paradise, and to assail every single soul of woman born, that has passed to years of consciousness, we shall probably never understand until mystery drops from our eyes in the meridian light of heaven. We only are sure that the permission of temptation is not inconsistent with His almightiness or beneficence.

BECAUSE TEMPTATION TESTS CHARACTER AND REVEALS US TO OURSELVES AND TO ONE ANOTHER. Was it not well that Peter should know how weak he was; that he might become truly penitent and converted? Was it not befitting that Judas should be exposed before the

Day of Pentecost? Was it not best that the foundation stones of the Church should be well tested? It is better to learn our weakness now and here than at the Judgment-seat.

But if Satan tempts, our Advocate pleads. He anticipates the advent of temptation by storing up his prayers. He warns the soul when the hawk begins to hover. If He may not arrest temptation, He will at least ask that our faith may not fail; and will seek us out as He did Peter.

Verily, I say unto thee, To-day shalt thou be with Me in Paradise. Luke 23: 43.

TO-DAY!—Dost thou ask Me to remember thee at some distant moment, when the kingdom of which I am now laying the foundations shall have become the all-conquering kingdom of the world? Thou needest not wait so long. I say unto thee that this very day, when yonder sun now scorching above our heads is sinking in the west, and the shadows lie long from our crosses, and the people have gone to their homes, thou shalt be with Me, where the sun shall no more be thy light by day, nor the moon by night, but the Lord shall be thy everlasting light.

THOU SHALT BE WITH ME. Dost thou ask only to be remembered; that I should give thee the glance of a thought; that I shall recall thy voice and face for a brief moment? Thou shalt be with Me, for I will await thee on the confines of my home. The throngs which escort Me shall behold thee by my side, and when I sit upon my sapphire throne I will give thee to sit beside Me, the one who, in my mortal anguish, trod the vale of the shadow, and who, with Me, shall tread the paths of light and glory.

IN PARADISE. I am here regaining Paradise. All that was lost is being recovered. Within a few hours it will be mine to give; within a few hours its key will be in my hand; within a few hours thou shalt walk with Me there in the cool of the day, and the angel that drove out Adam shall keep watch lest the Serpent enter to molest.

VERILY, I SAY UNTO THEE. All this is fixed and certain. I say "verily" to thee because the Father hath said "verily" to Me. Oh, trembling soul, who hast fled for refuge, to lay hold upon the hope set before thee, thou mayest have strong encouragement from my Word and death.

Crucified, and the third day rise again.
Luke 24: 7.

THESE are the two poles of Christian life—Death and Resurrection. That which was true in the history of our Lord must have its counterpart in our own experiences. That Jesus died and rose again is not only the dual basis of justification, but it is the dual basis of sanctification. Did He die? Then we must arm ourselves with the same mind. The crucifixion was not finished on Calvary; it has continued through all ages, and will continue unto the end; not in its mediatorial and atoning aspect, but with the view of each man denying himself and taking up his cross to follow daily. So also we are perpetually leaving the things of time and sense where Christ left his grave-clothes, and are pressing up and on in the wake of his resurrection and ascension.

It is a solemn question, how far we are participating in this daily dying and daily rising. "Be not conformed to this world; but be ye transformed. Mortify your members which are upon the earth; seek those things which are above. If one died for all, then all died; that they which live should not henceforth live unto themselves, but unto Him who died for them and rose again."

It is not that the old nature dies, but that we die to it. As a matter of experience and walk, the results will be very similar from either of these ways of stating the fact. But it is true to Scripture and experience also to speak of reckoning ourselves to be dead indeed unto sin—that is, the root-principle which so often fruits in sins. Reckon that the grave of Christ lies between thee and the solicitations of the world, the flesh, and the devil. Deem thyself dead to thyself. All this, however, is only possible through the Holy Spirit.

John

Thou shalt see greater things than these.
John 1: 50.

GOD'S dealings with us are always on an

ascending scale. If we see clearly the lowest rung in the heavenly ladder, whilst we behold, the vail of mist will part, and we shall see the next above it, and then the next, and, in due order, the next; and so the steps that slope away through darkness up to God will always be beckoning to greater and yet greater things.

Have you known Christ as the Word? He is more; both Spirit and Life.

Has He become flesh? You shall behold Him glorified with the glory He had before the worlds.

Have you known Him as Alpha, before all? He is also Omega.

Have you met John? You shall meet One so much greater, that the latchet of his shoes the Baptist shall deem himself unworthy to unloose.

Do you know the baptism by water? You shall be baptized by fire.

Have you beheld the Lamb on the Cross? You shall behold Him in the midst of the throne.

Have you seen the Spirit descend as a dove on one head? You shall see Him come as a fire upon an unnumbered multitude.

Have you followed the Christ to the slight booth in the Jordan Valley? You shall enter with Him into mansions of eternal glory.

Do you acknowledge Him as King of Israel? You shall hear the acclamations that salute Him as King of the worlds.

Live up to all you know, and you shall know more. Be all you can, and you shall become more. Do all that your two talents permit, and you will find yourself ruler over four cities.

Thou hast kept the good wine until now.
John 2: 10.

THE world gives its best first. As youth and beauty are ushered into the banqueting-room of life, the world spreads the table with its best. The zest of enjoyment is keen in those young days, but it is soon satiated; the delicacies with which the table is spread pall, and the appetite, unduly stimulated at the first, demands coarser and more passionate delights to stimulate. At last the table is served with provision, from which, in the first days, the banqueters would have turned away disgusted.

But if you let the King lead you into his banqueting house, beneath his banner of love you will find yourself feeding on dainties which never satiate nor pall—which whet the appetite and give the taste a more delicate appreciation of the vintages of heaven.

YOU MAY SAY THIS OF THE WORD OF GOD. At the beginning of Christian life it is full of meaning and inspiration; but as the years pass, and we realize ever more of its helpfulness, we repeat the refrain, "Thou hast kept the best until now!"

YOU MAY SAY THIS OF CHRISTIAN LOVE. Let two love in Christ, and instead of their affection waning, as so often happens in the world, they will discover that the fellowship, which began in comradeship, will end in a sacramental meal; truest, purest, deepest enjoyment being kept for Paradise.

YOU MAY SAY IT OF HEAVEN. Neither hath eye seen nor heart conceived the things, even now and here, that God has prepared for those that love Him. But so soon as the redeemed spirit shall awaken in the uncreated glory of God's presence, it will exclaim, "The half was never told; Thou hast kept the best until now." At every moment and always God is giving his best.

A man can receive nothing, except it have been given him from heaven. John 3: 27 (R.V.).

AFTER six months of marvellous ministry, in which the Baptist had seen the whole land at his feet, had gathered a band of disciples, and introduced the Messiah to the Jewish people, he found the crowds dwindling. His disciples viewed with feelings of chagrin the transference of popular interest from their master to Him of whom he had borne witness.

WHAT JOHN THE BAPTIST MEANT BY IT. He realized that the crowds, the hushed attention, the swift response, the power of speech, the message, the deep repentance, the office of morning star heralding the Dayspring from on high, had been the gift of God. He had nothing which he had not received; he would have received nothing, except God had given it to him. Whether these things went or came was a matter altogether beyond his control. His part was to receive and use what God gave; and then return to Him, at his bidding, the saved talent. This forbade alike pride and despondency.

WHAT WE MAY LEARN BY IT. Humility and peace. Humility. Is this the time of your prosperity? Crowds wait on your words; mighty movements circle around you; glorious results follow on your plans! Do not be puffed up. Boast not yourself. "Who maketh thee to differ? and what hast thou that thou didst not receive? but if thou didst receive it, why dost thou glory, as if thou hadst not received it?"

Peace. If it is not due to your lethargy or sloth that the crowds have ebbed away, and that the tide of conversions has dropped below its former level, be at peace. These are things which the Holy Spirit worketh, dividing to each one severally even as He will.

If thou knewest the gift of God. . . .
John 4: 10.

THERE are wonderful contrasts here! He who gives rest sits weary on the well-head; He who was the Jews' Messiah utters his deepest lessons to a woman of Samaria; He that gives living water asks for water from the dark, cool depths that lay beneath them.

GOD'S BEST THINGS ARE GIFTS. Light, air, natural beauty, elasticity of the spirits, the sense of vigorous health, human love, and, above all, his only begotten and beloved Son. Among all other gifts is there one to be compared to this? The living spring of eternal life, which Jesus opens up in our hearts, and which so greatly differs from the pit of outward ordinance, is an altogether unspeakable bestowment. Nothing can purchase it. If a man would give all the substance of his house for it, it would be utterly contemned. It must be received as a gift, or not at all.

GOD'S GIFTS MUST BE ASKED FOR. "Thou wouldest have asked, and He would have given." This is the law of Heaven. Prayer is a necessary link between the divine hand that gives and the human heart that receives. We have not, because we ask not. There is nothing in our Lord's words of the dreamy and languid pietism which refuses to ask because it will not dictate to the perfect wisdom of God.

IF WE HAD FULLER KNOWLEDGE WE SHOULD PRAY MORE. "If thou knewest . . . thou wouldest ask." If thou knewest who He is that stands beside thee, in thy hours of private prayer—if thou knewest all the possibilities of the life of prayer—if thou knewest what gains would accrue to thee on thy knees, thou wouldest give thyself to prayer, as though it were the main object of thy life.

The Father loveth the Son, and showeth Him
all things that Himself doeth.   John 5: 20.

HEAVEN stands open to me, my Lord, in these deep and holy words. Through the open door I see the source of the golden light that shone around thy earthly life, and detect the secret of the music that ever sounded around thy path, as the music of the golden bells when Aaron passed to and fro.

The Father loved Thee, not only because Thou wert his Son, dwelling in his bosom, but because Thou wert his obedient Servant. And I would inherit a similar love; not only the love of my adoption, but of service; for Thou saidst, "If a man love Me, he will keep my word, and my Father will love him."

The Father was ever showing Thee what He was doing in the unseen and eternal depths. Indeed, it seemed that Thou wert more occupied in beholding the things which were unseen than those which were seen. Thine eye was ever on the dial-plate of eternity, and thine ear attent to the note of the tide on its shore. Thou didst nothing that was not in the pattern shown Thee on the mount of fellowship; but whatever was wrought there Thou didst here. Teach me to live like this.

Thy Father led Thee to ever greater works. First the daughter of Jairus, then Lazarus; first the Sermon on the Mount, then the prophecies of the closing days; first the Mountain of Transfiguration, then of Ascension. So would I be led forward, from Cana to Calvary; from Bethlehem to Bethany; from Jerusalem to the uttermost part of the world. Ever greater things, because with profounder humility and deeper insight into the meaning of thy death. Deeper and therefore higher; nearer thy cross, and therefore reaching further.

For Him the Father, even God, hath sealed.
John 6: 27 (R.V.).

THE seal is the mark of authentication. The Book of Esther often refers to the importance of the royal seal as giving validity and authenticity to documents to which it was appended. So at the waters of Jordan God authenticated our Lord; first by the voice that spake from heaven, and secondly by the holy anointing that came upon his head, setting Him apart for holy service. What the Father did for his Son, He does for his sons. "He that stablisheth us with you into Christ, and anointed us, is God, who also sealed us." In other words, God waits to authenticate us to ourselves and to the world, as his beloved children, in whom He is well pleased.

THE CONDITIONS OF SEALING. In the case of our Lord there was entire subjection to the Father's will, although it involved his leaving the blessed home of Nazareth and identifying Himself with the sins and sorrows of men, by baptism in waters where they had confessed their sins. We, too, must be prepared to obey utterly, even to death.

THE AGENT OF SEALING. The Spirit descended and abode upon Him; He was filled with the Spirit, and returned in his power to Galilee. We, too, are sealed by the Holy Spirit of promise; who stamps us with the die of our Saviour's image and superscription. Simultaneously with his gracious work upon us, we may detect his loving voice within us, witnessing with our spirits that we are children of God.

THE EFFECT OF SEALING. Secrecy, safety, and assurance. Secrecy, Song of Sol. 4: 12. Safety, Matt. 27: 65, 66. Assurance, Rom. 8: 15, 16, 17. There is also a daily assimilation, though we know it not, to the glorious likeness of our Lord; so that those who see us bear witness that his name is on us.

The Spirit was not given; because Jesus was not yet glorified. John 7: 39 (R.V.).

CALVARY must precede the Ascension, and both must come before Pentecost. The glorified Lord was the text on which the Spirit was to discourse, and the text must be complete before the sermon can commence. Moreover, it was only when our Lord had ascended to the right hand of the Father, that He could receive or transmit the divine Comforter. It was needful for Him to be by the right hand of God exalted, before He could ask for and receive, and shed forth the Holy Spirit of promise. The one Paraclete must finish his work, and be withdrawn, ere the other could come to take up and finish his work on earth. The Son must sit down on the throne, or the Spirit could not descend to sit on each of the disciples.

But there is a deep inner lesson for us all in these words. We sometimes wonder why we have not received the Spirit and why our lives are not channels through which He pours in mighty rivers to make desert hearts and lives blossom and sing. How gladly would we part with all beside, if we might be conscious that not tiny streamlets, not one river of holy influence merely, but that rivers were issuing from us as the waters from the temple threshold!

Is not the reason to be sought in our neglect to glorify Christ? We have never yet abandoned ourselves to Him, content to live the branch-life, with no other aim than to realize the one purpose of his most blessed life, the glorifying of the Father. We have never seriously made it

our life-purpose to glorify the Lord Jesus. There has been no triumphal entry into our hearts, no enthronisation, no challenge to the gates of our soul that they should lift themselves up to admit the King of Glory.

If ye abide in my word. John 8: 31 (R.V.).

1. WE SHALL BE APPROVED AS CHRIST'S DISCIPLES. "Then are ye truly my disciples." Of some the Master asks, "Why call ye Me, Lord, Lord, and do not the things which I say?" And He drives these from Him, saying, "I never knew you." His words are the supreme test—the fire which detects the ore; the winnowing-fan that finds out the wheat. Our treatment of our Lord's words discriminates us: He that hath my commandments, and keepeth them, is he that loveth Me.

2. WE SHALL KNOW THE TRUTH. God teaches us differently from men. They deal in peradventures and surmises; He with certainties—"Ye shall know the truth." They talk about the truth; He gives us the thing itself, and we know because we possess. They deal with circumstances and externals; He with the heart and root of matters. They give to the mind and soul; He to the spirit. We know the truth, because the Truth is in us, and we are in the Truth. "We know that the Son of God is come, and hath given us an understanding, that we know Him that is true, and we are in Him that is true."

3. WE SHALL BE FREE. "The truth shall make you free." Just as we are free from the terrors which belief in witchcraft and ghosts was wont to breed, because we know that the spirits of the dead do not haunt dark and dangerous places; just as we no longer fear the fatuous light over the marsh, or the death-tick, because science has attributed these to natural causes; so, as Jesus teaches us the truth about God, and the future, and the forgiveness of sins, and the broken power of Satan, and the impotence of death, we are delivered from the bondage of fear and walk with God in perfect peace.

We must work the works of Him that sent Me. John 9: 4 (R.V.).

IS not this exceedingly tender and beautiful? The Lord does not hesitate to describe Himself as specially designated to do a certain work. In every part of this Gospel He speaks of Himself as the sent One; but He graciously conjoins his disciples and friends in it, saying, We must work. It is as though He said, "I have a designated work which must needs be done; but I cannot do it alone. We must do it, you and I, together."

FELLOWSHIP WITH GOD THE FATHER IS THE LAW OF ALL INDUSTRY. Every crop that goldens in the summer wind is due to the summons of the God of Nature to the husbandman, "Come and let us work together, thou and I." Every achievement in factory or mill of textile fabrics is due to the combination of the divine laws and the human agency. We must work, is God's constant appeal.

FELLOWSHIP WITH THE SON IS THE LAW OF THE KINGDOM. We have been called into the fellowship or partnership of the Son of God. He does not say, Go, but come; not, Do this, but, Let us do it. He has set his heart on the glory of the Father, and He calls us to co-operate with Him in bringing back men to God. In some way we must contribute to the final result on which Christ has set his heart.

FELLOWSHIP WITH THE HOLY SPIRIT IS THE LAW OF ALL SUCCESSFUL SERVICE. The closing words of the benediction that refer to the communion of the Holy Spirit are specially significant. "We are witnesses, and so is also the Holy Ghost." The Spirit and the Bride say Come. As Peter began to speak, the Holy Ghost fell. Oh for pure hands and a clean heart, that we may be worthy of this divine confederacy!

John did no miracle; but all things that John spake of this Man were true.   John 10: 41.

THIS is full of rare interest and beauty. John the Baptist had been dead some two years at least, and the memory of good men is apt quickly to pass from the mind of their contemporaries, especially when they are eclipsed by some greater successor. Who thinks of the morning star when the sun has risen! But as the crowds came back again on the spot so closely identified with Christ's forerunner, he was recalled to mind; and they used of him the words ascribed to them in our text.

YOUR LIFE MAY BE WITHOUT MIRACLE. It may pass on with nothing to distinguish it above the lives of myriads around. There is no sensation-making note in your voice; no extraordinary intellectual calibre in your mind; no aptitude for wielding vast influence over the crowds. The years pass on with even monotony. Life is one dead level.

BUT MIND YOU SPEAK TRUE WORDS OF JESUS CHRIST. Point to Him and say, Behold the Lamb of God! Say of Him, This is He that baptizeth with the Holy Ghost. Announce Him as the Bridegroom, and be content to be the Bridegroom's friend. Say that He has his winnowing-fan and axe in hand. Be careless what men think of your accent, your gestures, your way of stating the truth; but go on bearing witness to what you have known, tasted, and handled of the Word of Life.

AFTER YOUR DEATH, YOUR WORDS MAY COME TO MIND AGAIN, AND BE THE MEANS OF BRINGING SOULS TO THE LAMB OF GOD. As corn-seeds, buried in mummy-cases, now bloom on English soil, so may words be carried in the memory through long years, and bear fruit after the speaker's death. What an epitaph for the grave of a Christian minister or teacher!

Said I not unto thee, that, if thou believedst, thou shouldest see the glory of God?
John 11: 40 (R.V.).

YES, we shall see the glory of God. We shall see the graves give up their dead—not only at the last day, but now. Thousands around us are dead in trespasses and sins, in which they walk according to the course of this world. Alas! more than this, they stink in the putridity of their lives and speech. Around their graves gather their friends and relatives, bathed in tears, but unable to arrest the progress of decay. But, if we will believe, we shall see the glory of God.

But how shall we believe for this? It seems easy for some to believe. The Marys who sit at the Lord's feet, feeding on his words, find the life and light of faith in his beloved presence. But others, like Martha, are distracted with so many things, that faith seems impossible. And this is the very point where this story is so abundantly helpful. Jesus must have the co-operation and sympathy of someone's faith before this miracle could be wrought—and these He found, not in Mary, as we might have expected, but in Martha, the harassed housewife.

In educating Martha to this stupendous act of faith, (1) The Lord gave her a distinct promise: "Thy brother shall rise again." (2) He drew her attention from his words to Himself, who lay beneath and behind them: "I am the Resurrection and the Life." (3) He forced her to confess her faith. To express it would confirm and increase it: "Believest thou this?" (4) He compelled her to act on the faith He had created, by allowing the bystanders to remove the stone. All her soul woke up as she remarked these preparations for her brother's resurrection. She believed; and in her faith gave the Lord the pivot on which his leverage might rest.

Except a grain of wheat fall into the earth and die, it abideth by itself alone. John 12 : 24 (R.V.).
THE East came to the cradle; the West to the Cross. Sunrise becomes the Orient; sunset the Occident wave. These were not Hellenist Jews, but pure-blooded Greeks, whose life and philosophy were in the present, in as much joy as nature, art, and amusement could yield. It was startling to be met with the grave announcement of death. But how wise to send them to read that earliest divine book of Nature. Hear the parable of the corn of wheat,

ITS LONELINESS. Before sowing, it is by itself alone. It lies on the barn floor, beside myriads more, but there is no vital contact between it and them. They are just so many isolated units: as foreign to each other as the stars, between which millions of dividing miles intervene. So if you save your life, nursing it in selfishness, dreading and avoiding all that savours of self-denial and self-giving, you will be utterly and drearily lonely.

THE FALLING INTO THE GROUND TO DIE. If we compare ourselves to a corn of wheat, we may say that the seed-germ cannot bury itself; but it can choose burial. It can be willing to be cast forth. It is not a pleasant experience for the little seed. As soon as it finds itself entombed, it is seized upon by chemical agents, which pierce and tear its delicate waterproof sheath, and eat their way to its vitals. Death is no child's-play.

THE FRUIT-BEARING. Presently the rootlet shoots downward, the tiny frond upward, and, almost without knowing it, the stalk begins to blossom and bear fruit, which, with every sowing, reduplicates itself. Such may your life become, if you will let God have his way. Via Crucis, via lucis: the way of the cross is the way of light.

Thou canst not follow Me now; but thou shalt follow afterwards. John 13 : 36, 37 (R.V.).
HEAVEN DESIRED. We often say it. When the pressure of life seems unbearable; when the door opens just wide enough to admit our dearest, and shuts before we can follow; when we want to see Him whom we love—we find ourselves using Peter's words again : "Why not now?"

HEAVEN DELAYED. "Thou canst not follow Me now." The emphasis is on the cannot. It is as though the Master said, "The hindrance is not in some arbitrary edict of divine power, but in the infinite knowledge and wisdom that cannot err." Peter was not fit to go. There were lessons of the utmost importance waiting for him to acquire in the near future. He must learn to know himself, and Christ, and the grace of the Holy Spirit. When he proudly vaunted that he would lay down his life for Jesus, he gave incontestable evidence that he did not know himself; and there was every reason to think that he was similarly deceived when he supposed that he was fit to quit earth's discipline, and enter on heaven's blessed enjoyment. He must exchange his own strivings and resolvings for the gracious indwelling of the Spirit of Pentecost; he must learn the glorious energy of the indwelling Saviour; he must be girded by another, and carried whither he would not; and only then would the time of his putting off of the tabernacle of the body arrive.

HEAVEN GUARANTEED. "Thou shalt follow afterwards." There could be no doubt about it, since Jesus had said it; and often, in after days, these words must have been as a cordial, "Thou shalt follow afterwards." But what the Master said to Peter He says to each who believes, Thou shalt follow Me afterwards, "unto fountains of waters of life."

Believe also in Me. John 14 : 1.
WERE we less familiar with these words, we should be more startled by their immeasurable meaning. One who seems a man asks all men to give Him precisely the same faith and confidence that they give to God. He would not abate his claims, though He was the humblest and meekest of men. And the irresistible conclusion is forced on us, that He was and knew Himself to be "God manifest in the flesh."

1. FAITH IN JESUS IS THE CURE OF HEART TROUBLE. It is of little use to say, "Let not your heart be troubled," unless you can add "Trust Christ." Only if we can trust can we be still. Only if we can shift the responsibility of our life on the care of our never-failing Redeemer can weeping be exchanged for radiant and unspeakable joy.

2. FAITH IN JESUS CONDUCTS TO THE KNOW-

LEDGE OF GOD. "Believe Me that I am in the Father, and the Father in Me." Philip said, "Show us the Father." Jesus answered, "Believe, and thou dost behold." The world says, Seeing is believing; Jesus says, Believing is seeing. The true way to know God is, not by arguing about or seeking to verify his existence by intellectual processes, but by obeying the precepts of Jesus; following the footsteps of Jesus; holding fellowship with Jesus.

3. FAITH IN JESUS WILL MAKE OUR LIVES THE CHANNEL THROUGH WHICH HE CAN WORK. "He that believeth on Me, the works," etc. (vers. 12–14). The Gospels are included in the one clause; the Acts and all the marvels of the following ages in the other. Jesus is always the worker; and the man who yields himself most utterly to Him in obedience and faith, will become the channel through which He will work most mightily.

Abide in Me, and I in you. John 15: 4.
THE unity between the Lord and his members is beautifully set forth in this exquisite parable; which was perhaps suggested by the swaying of a vine in the evening air, as they essayed to go from the upper room towards Gethsemane. In certain conservatories the pliant branches are trained along roof or wall for vast distances; yet one life pervades the whole plant, from the rugged root to the furthest twig and leaf and cluster. Thus there is one holy life pervading all who have belonged, or shall belong, to Jesus. They live because He lives. His life is theirs.

We are in Christ by grace; but we need to realize and accentuate the union by meditation and prayer. Waiting more absolutely for his impulses in intercession and action. Being silent for Him to speak. Drawing on Him by the constant appeal of faith which becomes as natural as breathing. Looking away to Him for his commendation. Seeking only his verdict on what may have been said and done. So closely joined to Him, that He may produce in and through us whatever fruit He will for the refreshment of men and the glory of God.

We are in Christ for ever, so far as our standing is concerned; but we may be "taken away," so far as our opportunities of ministry are concerned. How many of us have failed to be what He desired, so that He has had to bestow elsewhere the luxury of ministering to Him!

We are in Christ, not because we hold Him, but because He holds us; therefore we must expect the Father's pruning. Yet do not dread the knife. It is his Word, wielded by a Father's hand; and if we will yield to the golden pruning-knife of the Word, we shall escape the iron one of sorrow.

In that day. John 16: 23, 26.
THRICE in these closing words the Master refers to that day (see John 14: 20). Without doubt He refers to the Day of Pentecost, and the era it would introduce.

THE HOLY SPIRIT REVEALS THE RELATION BETWEEN THE FATHER AND THE SON (14: 20). And this not as a matter of speculation merely, but for our holy living. The model of our union with Jesus is his union with the Father. As He is in his Father in perpetual and most blessed union, so are we to be in Him.

THE HOLY SPIRIT'S PRESENCE ANSWERS OUR QUESTIONS. "Ye shall ask Me no question" (16: 23, R.V., marg.). Whilst the Lord was with them, they were constantly breaking in on Him with their questions: "Lord, are there few that be saved?" "Wilt Thou at this time restore the kingdom?" "When shall these things be?" This is always the symptom of the earliest stage of the religious life—perpetual questioning and worrying. But when the Spirit comes, his presence is the sufficient answer. He does not teach our intellects to know the truth, but gives the truth to our hearts. We need not question, because we see; we possess; we can taste and handle for ourselves.

THE HOLY SPIRIT'S INDWELLING TEACHES US HOW TO PRAY. "In that day, ye shall ask in my name" (16: 26). To pray in Christ's name is to let his nature pray in and through our lips. Of course such prayer prevails. The one condition of successful prayer is to bring yourself into a line with the thoughts of God, to breathe his spirit, to be swayed by his impulses; this is only possible through the gracious operation of the Spirit of God. Has the blessed day of Pentecost broken upon you? Do you live in its light? Have you received all it was meant to bring you?

Father, the hour is come; glorify thy Son, that the Son may glorify Thee. John 17: 1 (R.V.).
IN one form or another we are constantly asking the Father to glorify us. Glorify me, O Father, we cry, by giving me the largest congregation in the town; by commencing a great

revival in my mission, by increasing my spiritual power, so that I shall be greatly sought after. Of course, we do not state our reasons quite so concisely; but this is really what we mean. And then we wonder why the answer tarries. Is it not because our Father dare not trust us with glory? He knows that we would become proud and self-conscious; that we would ascribe our success to the strength of our arm and the swiftness of our foot. Nothing would be more harmful to our Christian growth. But when we desire glory only that we may be able better to glorify Jesus, then there will be no stint in what He will confer on us. Glory, like a golden river, will pour into our hearts and lives.

Oh for this absorbing passion for the glory of Jesus! To be able to pray "Thy kingdom come," without reference to our share in securing its advent. To be as glad when another scores a great success, as though it had been ourselves who had won the laurels. To pray as eagerly for the success of others as of ourselves. Here is an ideal which seems inaccessible, as it ridicules all our natural attempts to win it. To be pleased to suffer, to fail, to be counted nothing and nobody, if only our dear Lord is extolled, exalted, and made very high— is this possible?

Do you choose it? Then be of good cheer. This is the hunger which God has promised to satisfy. He never shows you your lack of a grace without pledging Himself thereby to realize it for you. Yes, this blessed experience shall come even to you. You shall be taught the blessed lesson of perfect love.

Jesus answered, My kingdom is not of this world. John 18: 36.
WELL might Pilate ask if Jesus was a king. Thou poor, weary, rejected Nazarene, art Thou a king? A strange contrast, surely, to the Herod that built those halls of judgment! Thy people, at least, fail to recognize thy royalty! But Jesus did not abate his claims. "Thou sayest that I am," He answered, "a king." And as the ages have passed they have substantiated his claim.

THE ORIGIN OF HIS KINGDOM. "My kingdom is not of this world." The Lord did not mean, as his words have been too often interpreted, that his kingdom had nothing to do with this world; but that it did not originate here. The "of" means out of. Jesus is King, not by earthly descent, or human right, but by the purpose and counsel of the Father, who said, "Thou art my Son; this day have I begotten Thee: yet will I set my King upon my holy hill of Zion."

THE METHOD OF ITS PROMULGATION. It is not spread by armed force. His servants do not fight. They are priests clad in the white robes of immaculate purity, and bearing aloft their banner with the inscription, "Blessed are the peacemakers." Like their Master, they bear witness to the truth; and as they do so those who are of the truth are attracted to the Lord, as steel filings to the magnet.

THERE IS TRUE ROYALTY IN BEARING WITNESS TO THE TRUTH. Humbly we may appropriate our Master's words: to this end were we born, and of this cause are we left in the world, that in every act and word we might bear witness to the Truth. As we do so, we manifest a royalty which is not of human gift or descent, but which has been communicated by the reception of the Christ-nature, through the regenerating grace of the Holy Ghost.

When Jesus had received the vinegar, He said, It is finished. John 19: 30.
COMPARING the Gospels, we discover that these words were said "with a loud voice." It was the shout of a conqueror, who has fought through a long and terrible day, but greets victory as evening closes in.

FINISHED, THE LONG LINE OF SACRIFICIAL RITE. From the gates of Eden the blood of sacrifice had begun to flow, augmented by the confluent streams of the years. From that moment, however, not another drop need be shed. The types were finished now that the Antitype had been realized.

FINISHED, HIS FULFILMENT OF PROPHECY. How contradictory some had seemed! Ancient of Days, yet a babe; the Mighty God, yet marred of visage, and led to the slaughter; Son of God, yet scion of David's stock; ruling in the midst of enemies, yet a bruised and broken Sufferer. But all of them, even to the last pathetic intimation of his dying thirst, fulfilled.

FINISHED, HIS MORTAL LIFE. Never again to be weary, hungered, tempted, buffeted, or to bear the contradiction of sinners. Never again to sweat the bloody sweat, or bear the accumulated faults of men. Nevermore to die.

FINISHED, A WORLD'S REDEMPTION. He had wrought out and brought in a perfect salvation. The world, so far as God could make it so, was already reconciled. Sin was put away.

FINISHED, THE PERFECT OBEDIENCE. He alone of all born of woman was able to say that there was nothing which the Father had asked that He had not given; nothing that the Father had imposed that He had not gladly borne. He had finished the work given Him to do.

Jesus saith unto her, Mary. John 20: 16.
MANY had called her by that name. She had been wont to hear it many times a day from many lips; but only One had spoken it with that intonation. In his mouth its familiar syllables had a sweetness and tenderness which lingered in her heart; as the fragrance of the Rumanian rose-valley clings for many a day to the clothes of those who have entered it.

Her eyes had deceived her. Startled by the sudden glad expression which had passed over the features of the angels, who sat sentry in the sepulchre, she had turned herself back to see the source from which the radiance had gleamed; but even with that hint to help her, she had failed to recognize her Lord. But her ear could not mistake; the voice carried immediate recognition.

We sigh sometimes for "the touch of a vanished hand and the sound of a voice that is still"; but we shall hear those voices again. Our mortal body is to be fashioned according to the body of Christ's resurrection; and evidently in that body there were the old familiar tones. May we not, therefore, certainly infer that the voices which welcome us on the other side will be those that hushed us with their lullabies when we were babes; asked us for our love and assured us of theirs when we attained maturity; whispered their dying messages in our ears, and sent us their Godspeed as we went down into the river.

The Master knows our names, and calls his own followers by them. There is one response, which He waits to elicit—one which alone will satisfy Him; one in which the love and devotion of a life may be summed up. Like Mary, let us turn and say to Him: Rabboni! that is, Master!

That disciple therefore whom Jesus loved saith unto Peter, It is the Lord. John 21: 7 (R.V.).
THIS miracle was also a parable. When we go fishing apart from Jesus, we may indeed toil all the night and take nothing. But when through the darkness Jesus comes, and speaks to us across the wave, and tells us where to let down the nets; when we are in blessed partnership with Himself; when, though we see Him not, we obey his slightest promptings—then the nets are filled to their uttermost.

THOSE WHO ARE LOVED, LOVE. It was the consciousness that Jesus loved him which made John the Apostle of Love. Love casts such a wondrous spell over its objects, that they begin to shine in its rays and reflect them. Nothing will make a coal glow with heat but to plunge it into the heart of the fire. Do you want to love the Lord Jesus?—dwell on his love to you.

THOSE WHO LOVE CHRIST SEE HIM. Not Peter, the man of eager action, but John, the man of devoted love, saw the Master amid the haze that lay on the lake shore. Love will penetrate every disguise; will detect Him by the slightest sign; will strip from our eyes the film that sense and sin draw over them. If you loved Him more, you would see his hand in that disappointment, that crushing sorrow.

THOSE WHO SEEK CHRIST CANNOT KEEP IT TO THEMSELVES. They must tell it out to their next companion, with beating heart and thrilling speech. John said unto Peter, It is the Lord. How often has the affirmation of a pensive, quiet heart been the torch to ignite all the soul of another, who was more fitted to execute than plan. Is not this what we may all experience as we draw near to eternity? Shall we not see Jesus standing on the shore, with preparations beyond all thought, to welcome us as we arrive from the night cruise?

The Acts

Ye shall be my witnesses. Acts 1: 8 (R.V.).
HOW different this function, entrusted to the apostles, to that assumed by the self-styled priests of our time, who claim the power to repeat the sacrifice of Calvary, and to absolve the penitent from his sins! The Master did not say that his followers were to become sacrificing priests, but witnesses to what He had done and would do.

LOOKING TO JESUS IS THE CONDITION OF

WITNESS-BEARING. How else can we bear witness of Him? As we behold Him we shall reflect Him; and as we reflect Him we shall be changed into the same image from glory to glory, as by the Lord the Spirit (2 Cor. 3: 18, R.V.). It will not involve strenuous effort to witness to Jesus, if we are living in fellowship with Him. Light is self-revealing. In infinitesimal touches and expressions the light we are catching from Him will gleam forth, and men will unconsciously be led to believe in Him who has made us what we are.

WITNESS-BEARING MUST SPREAD THROUGH SUCCESSIVE CIRCLES OF INFLUENCE like the circling wavelets from a stone flung into the midst of a calm mountain lake. Some think they could witness in the uttermost ends of the earth, but they neglect the Jerusalem of the home. Those who begin here will be led almost unconsciously forward to the Judæa of their relatives, and the Samaria of their near neighbourhood, and so to the further boundary.

FOR WITNESSING WE HAVE SUPREME POWER. If even your testimony is demanded, claim the power for the emergency. It is certainly at hand, and within reach. The hand of faith, the opened heart, may surely receive not a power, an attribute merely, but the Spirit, whose attribute of power certainly accompanies Him. Not It, but He.

He hath poured forth this, which ye see and hear. Acts 2: 33 (R.V.).
WHAT a sublime commencement! As Jacob's heart revived, and he was assured that Joseph lived when he saw the waggons that his sons had sent, so the heart of the Church revived when the Spirit came. It was the promised sign that the Master had reached the Father's throne, and was fulfilling the unforgotten promise that He would ask the Father for another Paraclete to fill his place, and abide until He should come again in glory.

It was as though, when the Son ascended on high, leading captivity captive, He passed through all heavens, till He came where no creature had ever come, or could come. There He prayed the Father, as He had said. It was as though He spoke thus: "Father, I have glorified Thee on the earth; I have finished the work which Thou gavest Me to do."

And the Father answered: "Thou art my beloved Son, in whom I am well pleased. Ask of Me, . . . and I will give Thee."

It was as if He said: "Father, I ask nothing for Myself; for all thine are mine, and mine are thine. But for others I ask that I may have the power of giving to my own the same anointing and power which Thou gavest Me when I stood on the threshold of my work. I was then filled with the Spirit; grant unto Me the power to fill the hearts of all who believe with that same Spirit. It was in the power of that Spirit that I wrought, died, and rose; let my Church be quickened and endued with the same sacred power."

And it pleased the Father that in Him all the fulness of the Godhead should dwell, bodily. And the glorified body of Jesus became the reservoir of the divine fulness, from which we all might receive.

Whom they laid daily at the door of the temple which is called Beautiful. Acts 3: 2 (R.V.).
IS not this thyself? Thou art of the Israel of God. There is no doubt of thy name being enrolled in the pedigree of elect and regenerate souls; but thou art lame, needing to be carried by the strong support of minister and friend; never able to leap, and walk, and praise God; and at the best only able to reach the outer side of the Beautiful Gate that conducts to the richest, gladdest life. Through that gate of entire consecration there come snatches of holy melody; glimpses of white-vestured souls; visions of ideals of life which thou hast not attained: but thou art excluded, condemned to live on the alms of those that enter. How great the pity! Why shouldest thou not have the very best that God can give?

But look up! expect to receive something; open thine ears to hear and thine heart to receive immediately strength, just where thou lackest it most sorely. The feet and ankle-bones of this helpless cripple only needed strength; they were perfectly formed, but paralysed. Similarly thine ideals of Christian living are true and accurate, but thou art deficient in power. Thou must receive strength.

But this strength can only be had by union with the risen Lord. His name (that is, his nature) alone can make thee strong, and give thee perfect soundness in the presence of those who have hitherto only pitied thy weakness. Believe in Him! All that have ever risen up to obey his lead have had perfect health and strength. Open thine heart to receive them. Claim and appropriate the power and grace of the Holy Spirit. The Spirit of Life which is in Christ Jesus shall make thee free from the law of sin and death, from weakness and failure.

They were all filled with the Holy Ghost.
Acts 4: 31.

THEY had been filled on the Day of Pentecost, and Peter had been suddenly and mightily infilled for his encounter with the Sanhedrim (ver. 8); but here again they were all privileged, whilst in the attitude of prayer and praise, to be once more most blessedly infilled. From this we gather that we may claim repeated fillings of the Holy Spirit.

But let us remember that it is not necessary for the place to be shaken, or for the air to be filled with the outward phenomena of Pentecost as the necessary condition of this heavenly gift. Mr. Fletcher reminds us that the Lord may be pleased to come softly to our help. He may make an end of our corruption by helping us to sink gently to unknown depths of meekness. Like Naaman, we are full of prejudices. We expect that the Penecostal gift will come to us with as much ado, pomp, and bustle, as the Syrian general looked for. But the blessed Paraclete often disconcerts all these preconceived notions. When we are looking for the hurricane, He comes as the zephyr. When we are expecting the torrent to pour into and fill the well, He fills it by single drops.

But the results will always be the same—great boldness in witness-bearing, much liberty in prayer and praise; great grace and beauty of character; self-denying love for those in need; great power through union with the risen Lord. If the second chapter of this book had been lost from the first MS., we must still have inferred something like the Pentecost. In no other way could we have accounted for the marvellous change which passed over the followers of Jesus, delivering them from the cowardice, wrangling, and prejudices of former days. Oh for a similar transforming experience for us all!

Thou hast not lied unto men, but unto God.
Acts 5: 4.

ACHAN, Belshazzar, and Ananias, met the same fate, because of their persistent use of devoted things. When once we have devoted aught to God, He counts it as his own, and strikes down the hand that would abase it to common and profane use. The Lord our God is a jealous God; He will brook no perversion of his rights. Beware that you take back nothing which you have laid on God's altar, least of all yourself.

Each gathering of believers is endowed with mystic and extraordinary importance, because the Lord, through the Eternal Spirit, is literally present. The true President is not the minister, however distinguished by his gift or grace, but the divine Spirit Himself; and any sin against the Church is really against Him. It is this divine presence that invests a gathering of the simplest, humblest believers with such unique importance. It is this which gives them the mysterious binding and loosing power, which is recognized and ratified in heaven. Behind Peter was the real Head of the Church; and so with every faithful minister. Honour the Personality, the Presidency, and Deity of the Holy Spirit, as set forth in this narrative.

Dr. Gordon told me on one occasion that he had in his church a man who, like a very crooked stick, obstructed all its work. He spoke to him alone, and before his brethren; but to no purpose. Then he bethought himself; and remembered that not himself, nor his church officials, was the true Head of the Church, but Christ and the power of the Holy Spirit. He therefore handed the whole matter over to the divine Spirit, as the Executive of the Godhead. In a fortnight this man had left the city, and necessarily ceased the obstruction in which he had persisted.

We will give ourselves continually to prayer.
Acts 6: 4.

IF ever there was a sacred work, it was that of caring for these poor widows; and yet the apostles felt that even such duties might interfere with the continual ministry of intercession. No doubt they always lived in the atmosphere and spirit of prayer, but they rightly felt that this was not enough either for them or their work. So they sought a division of labour, that while some specially served tables and ministered the alms of the church, others might be set free for steadfast continuance in prayer. This would keep the communication with the King on the throne clear and fresh, would draw down the power and blessing of the heavenly world, and be the means of procuring wisdom and strength for their great responsibilities.

There are many courses of usefulness open to each of us in this world, and we must choose the one, not only most suited to our idiosyncrasies, but in which we can best serve our day and generation. It may be that in our incessant activities we are neglecting the one method by which we may contribute most largely to the coming of our Father's kingdom. Notice that word give. It is as though the Spirit of prayer were seeking natures so pure, so devoted, that without hindrance He might form Himself into them. Give yourself to Him for this!

"In that day," said our Lord, speaking of the Day of Pentecost, "ye shall ask in my name." It is only when we are full of the Holy Spirit that we can experience the true power to plead with God, and use the name of Christ so effectively as to receive the richest blessings for ourselves and others. Much prayer, much blessing; little prayer, little blessing; no prayer, no blessing. "The Word of God increased."

Being full of the Holy Ghost. Acts 7: 55.
THE blessed characteristic of Stephen lay in his being perpetually full of the Holy Ghost. It is said of others, even Peter, that they were filled, as though they needed some special and over-mastering inducement for special service. But Stephen is more than once described as full (6: 5), as though he were always kept brimming, like a lake from the hills.

THOSE WHO ARE FULL OF THE HOLY SPIRIT ARE ALWAYS LOOKING STEADFASTLY UPWARDS. They look not at the things which are seen, but at those which are not seen. Across the valleys, they catch sight of the Delectable Mountains, rising like the Himalaya above the plains of India. Whilst others look around for help, they lift up their eyes to the hills whence cometh their help; and to them heaven stands always open.

THOSE WHO ARE FULL OF THE HOLY SPIRIT SEE AND ARE TRANSFIGURED BY THE GLORY OF GOD. What wonder that those who sat in the Council beheld Stephen's face, as it had been the face of an angel. The light that shone there was not as when Jesus was transfigured—in that case, the light of the Shechinah broke out from within—but here the glory of God shone from the open door of Heaven. So the sunrise smites the highest peaks.

THOSE WHO ARE FULL OF THE HOLY GHOST SEE THE LORD JESUS, IN HIS GLORY, AS THEIR PRIEST. It is the special work of the Holy Spirit to direct the gaze to Jesus. Those who are full of the Spirit may hardly be aware of his gracious presence, but they are keenly alive to their Lord's. The Spirit takes of the things of Jesus, and reveals them to the loving and obedient; specially those that concern his priestly work on the cross and in heaven.

The same is desert. Acts 8: 26 (R.V.).
DESERT means uninhabited. It seemed a strange providence that took Philip thither. He had been chosen to the honourable office of deacon, and there was probably plenty of work to do in connection with the scattered Church. Moreover, he had just completed a most successful mission in Samaria, where the multitude had given heed with one accord to the things he had spoken; but now he was suddenly landed in these lonely solitudes, where only chance travellers could be encountered. Did he not count it strange, and wish to get home to his four little daughters (Acts 21: 9)?

There are many deserts in life! The solitude of a new country, in which you do not know the language. The solitude of a sick-chamber, in which the earnest worker suddenly discovers the limitations of physical weakness. The solitude of suspicion and dislike, which contrast strangely with some large and devoted circle. Thither God brings us not infrequently. No flower can thrive in unbroken light.

But in every solitude, if we wait patiently on the Lord, there are opportunities of service. There is always some inquiring soul in need of the precise help we can give. There is an old story of some monks to whom the Book of Revelation was being read. At the end each was asked to choose the promise he loved best. One said I will take this, "God shall wipe away all tears." Another chose, "To him that overcometh I will give to sit on my throne." The third replied, "I would choose, 'His servants shall serve Him'." This latter was Thomas à Kempis, who afterwards wrote "The Imitation."

"Not caring how to serve Thee much,
But to please Thee perfectly."

*The Church had peace, being edified; and . . .
was multiplied.* Acts 9: 31 (R.V.).
THE CHURCH grew not simply by addition, but by multiplication. Three added to three make six; three multiplied by three, nine. That is the Pentecost ratio of increase. These are the conditions of Church growth:

FIRST, THERE MUST BE PEACE. Let us

endeavour to keep the unity of the Spirit in the bond of peace. As far as it lies in our power, let each of us live peaceably with all men. Let all bitterness, and wrath, and anger, and clamour, and railing, be put away out of our hearts, with all malice, and let us be kind one to another, tender-hearted, and imitating God the great Peacemaker.

NEXT, THE CHURCH MUST BE EDIFIED. We must build ourselves up on our most holy faith. And, indeed, such growth in grace and the knowledge of God is almost inevitable where the Holy Ghost breaks up the reign of apathy and stagnation. When its foundations are deeply laid in righteousness and peace, the City of God arises into the pure air.

Moreover, the members of such a Christian community must walk in the fear of the Lord. To walk means the daily plodding, routine life—full of commonplaces, somewhat prosaic —but always ruled by the fear of grieving the heart that was pierced on Calvary. Lastly, we must walk in the comfort of the Holy Ghost, or, as the words might be rendered, in the paracletism of the Paraclete. The Holy Spirit is our Advocate, Teacher, Guide; and we should habitually dwell in his radiant and helpful environment. What a difference there is between seaweeds and sea flowers expanding in their rock-surrounded aquariums, and the same when taken into common air! Such is the contrast wrought by the Spirit.

He lodgeth with one Simon, a tanner.
Acts 10: 6.

THIS lodging must have been somewhat distasteful to the apostle; not only because of its insalubrious odours, but because of the association with death that rendered him liable to the ceremonial pollution which a religious Jew, as Peter was, peculiarly dreaded. Probably he was only driven to it by the sternest necessity. But was it not remarkable that he who had been the chief apostle of the Church, and who had but recently come from a most successful tour, should suddenly be isolated from all his happy and holy associations, and be stranded for many days in the tanner's house (9: 43)?

Yet such dealings on the part of the Lord with his servant are easy of explanation. We are all apt to substitute work for God instead of communion with Him. We become strong in our own strength; elated with success; puffed up by the adulation of our friends. It is

needful, therefore, that we be withdrawn from the madding crowd and the career of unbroken prosperity; that the glare of the sun should be tempered, and confidence in ourselves be brought low. There is only one resort. To be hidden in the quiver; to become dependent on the widow-woman of Zarephath; to spend forty years in the desert till the passionate impulses of our own life subside; to go apart into Arabia; to spend the slowly-moving weeks in the tanner's house.

Whilst Peter waited, he maintained his habits of prayer; left his heart open to the impressions and teachings of the Holy Spirit; awaited the next movements of the cloudy pillar; set himself to acquire lessons which, though subversive of his past experience, reacted on his whole after-life; and from his retirement went forth to unlock a new era.

He was a good man. Acts 11: 24.

THIS is the Holy Spirit's verdict on the character and life of Barnabas. Very different to the magniloquent inscriptions on the tombs of warriors and statesmen; but it were better to deserve this at the lips of the Master than to have the longest list of titles ever appended to a mortal's name. For a good man like this some would even dare to die. The characteristics of this good man were these:

HE COULD SEE THE GOOD IN MOVEMENTS OUTSIDE HIS OWN CHURCH-ORDER. The Church at Antioch originated, as this paragraph proves, in the preaching of a number of unknown, unordained refugees, who were fleeing from the iron hand of persecution. All we know of them is that they were men of Cyprus and Cyrene. They had broken through the barrier of the ages by preaching to the Gentiles, great numbers of whom had been saved. The Church in Jerusalem was somewhat suspicious of this new departure, and sent Barnabas to report; but when he came he was forthwith convinced of its genuineness, saw the evidence of the hand of the Lord, and was glad. No jealousy, nor narrow bigotry, nor suspicion, warped his judgment.

HE WAS WILLING THAT ANOTHER SHOULD SHARE WITH HIMSELF THE JOYS OF HARVEST. He went off to Tarsus to seek his old acquaintance, and perhaps fellow-student, Paul, and for a whole year the two wrought side by side in living fellowship, and taught much people.

HE WAS EAGER THAT PEOPLE SHOULD BE ADDED TO THE LORD. Too often good men seek a following for themselves, and rejoice in those who are added to their church or organization. This is not the noblest style of work. It is better far to imitate the Baptist who was content to be the Bridegroom's friend.

The Iron Gate. Acts 12: 10.

THERE are iron gates before most of us. We are not specially anxious about the first or second ward, but ah, that iron gate! The iron gate of supreme difficulty; of a parent's prohibition against entering the mission-field; of some obstinate circumstance which seems to forbid the execution of our plans; of some barred and locked prohibition; of death at the end of all. It may be that in his strange bewilderment, between waking and sleeping, Peter anticipated this iron gate with a good deal of dread. That at least would bar his progress; but lo, it opened of its own accord! So shall it be with many of the evils that we anticipate.

Not before we come to them, but at the moment of reaching them; when heart and flesh threaten to fail—in the dim light we shall find them standing open, set back for us to pass. The tram-line is not cleared from end to end before the tram starts. Were the driver to wait for this, he would never start at all. But as he comes to each van, or drag, or carriage, it moves, and allows him a free course; or, if it seems dilatory, his whistle hastens it. Thus, when we arise to follow the angel of God's purpose, who has suddenly entered the dark cell of our life, we shall discover that apparently insuperable difficulties, which we have long dreaded, shall open to us, and allow us to pass; when we come to the object we have dreaded most, we shall find it gone.

Let there be plenty of prayer, "prayer without ceasing." Let there be prompt obedience to the angel's touch and summons; the willingness to gird the relaxed loins, and follow; and as you go through life, you will find yourself escorted by an invisible Companion, who holds the key to all doors.

Separate Me Barnabas and Saul for the work whereunto I have called them. Acts 13: 2.

THE Holy Spirit, as the representative of the ascended Lord, is supreme in the Church. It is his sovereign voice that summons his chosen workers to undertake missionary or home enterprise. Dr. Ryland, who at first opposed Carey's idea of going to India, said afterwards, "I believe God Himself infused into the mind of Carey that solicitude for the salvation of the heathen which cannot be fairly traced to any other source." And the same is true of all missionaries. The true call is always of the divine Spirit. Whom He wills to call, He calls. Whom He calls, He separates. Whom He separates, He endows and sends forth.

But, divine and absolute though the selection is, the Spirit seeks the concurrence of the Church. It was in answer to the Church's prayer for direction that the Spirit designated Barnabas and Saul for the great work of world-evangelization; and it was when the Church had fasted and prayed, and had offered these two to God as their wave-offering, that they were sent forth by the Holy Ghost. Thus the Spirit and the Bride co-operate.

In determining whether you have been called by the Holy Spirit to be a missionary, you must certainly call in the advice of Christian friends, and specially of the church with which you worship. If the Spirit of God is in you and them, they will ratify the movements of your heart. It is right, too, to consider whether you have been specially gifted and qualified for the work. In this also, the advice of the Church is most valuable. Of course, the Church herself must fast, i.e., be separate from known evil and indulgence, that she may hear God's voice, and be able to advise her children.

Granting signs and wonders to be done by their hands. Acts 14: 3 (R.V.).

THERE is no source of encouragement more fruitful of help than the co-witness and co-working of the Holy Spirit. Those who are filled with the Spirit are called into communion, i.e., partnership, with Him in his work. Whilst they work from the outside, He works from within; whilst they sow the seed, He waters it abundantly. We must be very careful to be such in character and teaching that He may co-operate with us. Our hands must be very clean, if He, with an infinite condescension, is to grant signs and wonders to be wrought by them. But when we work with Him, and He with us, the results are beyond measure astonishing, and his alone.

"We are now seven years in this land," wrote one of Gossner's missionaries from the land of the Kohls in India; "but through these long years it was but trial of our patience and endurance. . . . Everything seemed to be in vain, and many said the mission was useless. Then the Lord Himself kindled a fire before our eyes; and it seized not only single souls, but spread from village to village; and from every side the question was borne to us, What shall we do? How shall we be saved? And I thought it was no more a heathen land I was in, but a Christian, and at home."

DEUS HABET HORAS ET MORAS, says the old proverb. God has his seasons and delays. We do not at once see the result of our sowings, toils, and tears; but we are conscious that our work is with our God—we know that we have our petitions, and we rejoice in hope. We must go on uttering "the word of his grace"— the grace that chooses such rebels to be his children; that cleanses them from sin; that restores and keeps and sanctifies.

They rehearsed. Acts 15: 4, 12 (R.V.).
THERE is a difference between those two assertions. They are in exquisite harmony, but each contributes a different note. In the first we have the co-operation of the Holy Spirit with every faithful worker whom He sends forth; so that, while the servant speaks to the outward ear, the Lord simultaneously addresses the heart. In the second, we have the work of the Holy Spirit wrought through a yielded life which has become his pure channel and mouth-piece. This is his twofold ministry.

HIS WITNESS WITH US. As we speak of Jesus crucified, risen, ascended, the blessed Spirit convicts men of sin, righteousness, and judgment. To every faithful word of testimony there is a deep resonant affirmation from this hidden but mighty Co-operant. If we say, "Behold the Lamb of God!" He adds, "He takes away the sin of the world." If we say, "He died in weakness," the Spirit adds, "He was raised in power." If we say, "Repent and believe the Gospel," He adds, "Now is the accepted time. The Holy Ghost saith To-day." If the Bride says Come, the Spirit joins his voice to hers.

HIS WITNESS THROUGH US. "The word which ye hear," said our Lord, "is not mine, but the Father's who sent Me." And that which was his glory may be ours also. We speak not of ourselves. This is the secret of a fruitful life—to be the yielded channel; the cleansed vessel; the bugle at the castle gate on which the King may sound his summons; the lute on whose strings the divine hand may play. Oh, be sure that the most lasting work in this world is only possible when we can say with Paul that we will not boast of anything save what Christ has wrought through us to make men obedient to the Gospel.

A certain woman named Lydia. . . . The Keeper of the prison. Acts 16: 14, 27.
THESE are typical cases, put here in juxtaposition for the teaching and comfort of believers in every age. Each of them needed Christ, and each was brought into his true light; but each came in a different way. Lydia's heart opened as a flower beneath the touch of the sun, so gradually and imperceptibly that it was impossible to say the precise moment of her new life. The jailer came to Christ suddenly, startlingly, amid the crash of an earthquake. The one was drawn by love; the other driven by fear. A distinguished missionary says, "The Lord awakened me with a kiss"—it was so that Lydia's heart was won. Another tells us that the Lord sprang on him like a lion—it was thus with the jailer.

LYDIA. Do not always be looking out for signs and manifestations, for marked experiences. We do not notice the lines of longitude and latitude as we cross the ocean of life. Without knowing it, your character may be in the process of transfiguration. By insensible gradations the work of God may be proceeding in your heart. The tide is rising daily by tiny wavelets that appear to recede as fast as they advance. Do not measure progress by experiences; only be yielded to God, and let Him do his will.

THE JAILER. Do not undervalue the influence of fear. There are some natures that never will be awakened unless they are startled by being brought face to face with the consequences of sin. If men will not come by the highest motives, be thankful that they come by any. Remember it is not belief about Christ, about his death or resurrection, but trust in Him as a living Person, that saves from the power and penalty of sin. "Believe in the Lord Jesus Christ." He is a living Person. Trust Him now.

It behoved the Christ to suffer. Acts 17: 3 (R.V.).
THIS is what our Lord was constantly insisting upon during the closing days of his earthly ministry. "Behoved it not," He asked, "the Christ to suffer these things, and to enter into

his glory?" The Jewish nation rejected Him because his conception of Messianic power was so foreign to theirs; but in doing so, doomed themselves to rejection from the purposes of God, at least during the present dispensation.

It behoved Him, that He might be a merciful and faithful High Priest. How could He have sympathized with the anguish of human hearts, if He had not drunk deeply of the cup of sorrow? How could He have led his flock through the thorny brake, if He had not gone to and fro with his bare feet? In that He hath suffered, He is able to succour.

It behoved Him, that He might be the sacrifice for sin. The conscience demands that forgiveness should be consistent with righteousness. It was necessary, therefore, if Jesus was to bring us forgiveness, that He should be prepared to make reparation and atonement for sin. He must shed his blood, that He may cleanse his people from their sins: He must be willing to be their scapegoat; He must offer Himself without spot to God, that He may cleanse our consciences from dead works to serve the living God.

It behoved Him, that He might reign for evermore. It is a fundamental principle in God's universe, that suffering, humbly and resignedly borne, leads to royalty and reigning. He who can stoop most profoundly can rise to reign most gloriously. As is the descent, so is the ascent. In proportion to the submission to take the form of a servant is the exaltation to the right hand of power.

A certain Jew named Aquila, . . . with his wife Priscilla. Acts 18: 2.

IT is a striking spectacle to see Paul, on his entrance to Corinth, with which his name was to be so remarkably associated, looking around, probably in the Jewish quarter, for manual employment, that he might be sure of his bread. Similarity of craft introduced him to Aquila and his wife Priscilla, who had been recently expelled from Rome by the imperial edict. At this time they were in unbelief, but were apparently converted by the words the apostle addressed to them as they sat together over their daily toil.

How eager Paul was, not only to preach the Gospel to the crowds that thronged the gay and sunny streets of Corinth, but to win individual souls for his Master's kingdom. Some are eager enough in this holy quest, when they occupy the pulpit, and are conscious of many

eyes being fixed upon them; but they are careless of the individual souls cast in their way. Not so was it with the Master, who went out of his way to find one Samaritan woman, and stopped beneath the tree to call down one publican. Not so was it with Philip, who spoke to the eunuch as eagerly as to Samaria. Not so was it with the apostle, who was as intense in his endeavours for a jailer, a Lydia, a Timothy, as for the crowds that were going to destruction.

Is not this God's secret test? If we are not careful about the ones and twos, He will not use us to the crowds. Indeed, it is the experience we obtain in dealing with individuals that equips us for multitudes. The way in which the kingdom of God comes ordinarily is, "One by one." How much might be done if each Christian workman would seek to win his neighbour!

Did ye receive the Holy Ghost when ye believed? Acts 19: 2 (R.V.).

THIS was Paul's first question of these twelve disciples. He knew perfectly well that they could not have believed without the special grace of the Holy Spirit; but now he asked if at the moment of regeneration and conversion they received Him. Obviously, his question implied his belief that there was a special enduement of the Spirit of God for a consecrated and useful life over and above his initial work on the soul.

It is a question which is in these words addressed to every Christian reader. You have believed in Christ through the ministry of the Spirit; but did you at that or any subsequent moment receive the infilling and unction of the Pentecostal Spirit? You may not be able to point to some marked manifestation; but are you conscious of those fruits which are the invariable accompaniments of that supreme gift? If not, learn to receive, and receive now.

In how many instances might this inquiry be met by the reply which the apostle received: "Nay, we did not so much as hear whether the Holy Ghost was given." John the Baptist clearly foretold that Christ would baptize with the Holy Ghost and with fire; but in his days Pentecost was still more than three years away, and these, his disciples, had never heard that the last days foretold by God had already been inaugurated. Alas that it should be possible after these centuries for many Christian people to be in ignorance of the special glory and characteristic of this age, and be content to live without seeking for themselves all that Pentecost means! Ephesus was moved in every avenue of her corporate life, and the worship of Diana imperilled—and all because twelve men received the fulness of the Spirit.

Take heed unto yourselves, and to all the flock. Acts 20: 28 (R.V.).

THERE are many lessons in this verse.

(1) The Christian worker must not neglect his own soul. He must take heed to himself, as well as to the flock. Our temptation is to neglect our close walk with God in our eagerness to save others.

(2) The overseer, elder, or bishop, is not set over the flock, but is in it. Note the force of the Greek, as given in R.V.: the flock in the which they are made bishops. So to the end of life the most eminent of God's servants must remember that he is but a saved sinner, needing the blood and righteousness of Christ as much as the weakest of his flock; and he also must lie down in green pastures, and be led beside still waters.

(3) The office of the minister is given by the Holy Ghost. It is He who lays on him the burden of souls, and equips him for his work. He, too, is willing to direct and use. How awful and solemn the responsibility! Woe be to us if we exercise our ministry only for the eye and ear of our fellow-men!

(4) Notice that the Church is distinctly asserted to be God's. "Feed the Church of God." We are his people and the sheep of his pasture. His by choice, by purchase, by the drawing of the Holy Ghost. We must get a right understanding of this doctrine of the Church, that she has been taken out of the world to be God's peculiar possession and delight.

(5) The purchase money of the Church is here said to be God's own blood. It is a remarkable expression. It stands alone in the Word of God, but brings out very distinctly the thought that the entire Godhead achieved man's redemption in the offering of the Cross. We are dear to God, and must give Him the benefit of his great expenditure!

And kneeling down on the beach, we prayed, and bade each other farewell. Acts 21: 5 (R.V.).

IT is thus that Christians say farewell. On their knees, within sound of the breaking wave-lets, men, women, and children, gathered in a weeping circle around the servant of God, who had been to so many of them the apostle of a new life. There is no attitude more befitting than this, at times when the heartstrings are strained to cracking, and it seems as though the sacrifice were too great for trembling hands to place on the altar of God.

But it is thus that Christians never say farewell. The relationship which is founded in the love of God cannot be broken. Of such friendship there is no past or future, but always a blessed present tense. What has been, is, and will be. And as severed hearts meet in prayer, though the bodies may be divided by hundreds of miles of sea and land, there is no separation. They are one in the Father's presence, eternally, indissolubly, and blessedly one.

When we are called to part from those whom we love better than ourselves, let us kneel down and pray; let us abide alike in the attitude and exercise of unceasing intercession; let us realize that space and time are mere accidents of being, and not essential; let us be sure that they who are near the King must be near to all who, in heaven or on earth, are nearest Him also. For such there is "no more sea."

It is easier, for the most part, to go on board ship, than to turn home again. There are the interest and excitement of new scenes and people to divert the traveller. But how grey is the common landscape from which the light of the dear presence is withdrawn! God alone can comfort the bereaved.

The God of our fathers hath appointed thee to know his will. Acts 22: 14 (R.V.).

THE will of God is general and particular. We may know it generally from the book of creation, the ten commandments, the beatitudes, and the conscience. But, in addition to this, God has a particular will for each of his children. The moon shines on the sea, but there is a special path of moonbeams to the spot where you stand, where you should be born, live, and die; what you should accomplish by your life; with what souls you should be brought into contact.

God comes still, as He did to Paul, with a great summons, calling his own from the midst of their fellows, and entrusting to them the sacred prerogative of knowing, seeing, and hearing. Happy are they who are prepared to arise at once, leave all, and follow. To them it will be given, as to Paul, to know the mysteries of the kingdom of heaven, so as to unfold them to others.

You have been appointed to know his will—be sure of this; and if as yet it is not clearly made known, adopt these precautions: (1) Carefully remove all your preconceptions and prejudices, so that your mind and heart can be a tablet for God to write on. (2) Set aside much time for waiting on God, in the study of his Holy Word. (3) Let the glory of Jesus be the supreme consideration with you. (4) Do not run to and fro, asking your friends and companions what they would recommend. (5) Wait the Lord's leisure, nor dare to act unless you are sure that you are in the line of his purpose. (6) Mark the trend of his providence, for it will certainly corroborate his inner voice. (7) When you have once made up your mind in faith and prayer, dare to act, and never look back. He will not let you be ashamed.

Brethren, I have lived before God in all good conscience until this day. Acts 23: 1 (R.V.).
CONSCIENCE is what one knows with oneself. That at least is an exact translation of this Latin word. It is a man coming to himself, facing himself, looking deep into his own eyes as he stands before the mirror of God's truth. There are varieties of conscience—the weak conscience, which is ever questioning; the defiled conscience, which has a consciousness of neglected duty or unforgiven sin; the morbid conscience, which is perpetually discussing infinitesimal niceties, and splitting hairs. In contrast with these is the good conscience, of which the apostle speaks.

We have to live with our conscience, and if it is disquieted and restless, we find that it will make life almost unbearable. Like the restless sea, it frets and foams through the dark hours; and is always casting up the bitter memories and sad regrets of bygone days. As it was with King Ahab, so it is with all who have sinned against conscience, they get the vineyard of Naboth; but with it they get Elijah, standing like an incarnate conscience at the door, and taking pleasure and enjoyment from their possession.

Paul could not have made this statement unless he had been very accurate and careful in his daily walk and conversation; but he tells us that he perpetually exercised himself to have a conscience void of offence toward God and man. Let us subject ourselves to a similar discipline, and often expose ourselves to the searching scrutiny of the Holy Spirit, so that we may say with the apostle, "My conscience also bearing me witness in the Holy Ghost" (Acts 24: 16; Rom. 9: 1).

It is a marvellous experience to stand before God; but how much more so to live before Him!

After the Way which they call a sect, so serve I the God of our fathers. Acts 24: 14 (R.V.).
FOR want of a better term by which to set forth Christianity—whether by friend or foe is immaterial—the new principle which it represented was called the Way.

"Saul asked for letters to Damascus, that if he found any that were of the Way, he might bring them bound to Jerusalem" (Acts 9: 2, R.V.). At Ephesus some were "disobedient, speaking evil of the Way before the multitude" (19: 9). "About that time there arose no small stir concerning the Way" (19: 23). "Felix had more exact knowledge concerning the Way" (24: 22). "I persecuted this Way unto the death" (22: 4).

It is a beautiful and significant phrase. Christ is Himself the Way. He has opened the way to God. Through the heavens He passed in his ascension, leaving behind Him at every step a way by which we may travel till every one of us appears in Zion before God. In Christ we have found the way to the Father, and have learnt a rule of life. The word Methodist is closely akin to this. The followers of Wesley have been obeying on a new method which their illustrious founder opened.

"Men of the Way"; such is the designation by which Christians should be known. They are pilgrims and strangers, wayfarers, having no abiding city, but always passing on. We may say of them as the psalmist did of the pilgrim hosts that went up yearly to worship at the feast, "Blessed is the man whose strength is in Thee; in whose heart are the highways to Zion" (Psa. 84: 5, R.V.). And is not this the Way that Isaiah spoke of when he said, "An highway shall be there, and a way, and it shall be called the way of holiness" (Isa. 35: 8–10)?

One Jesus, who was dead, whom Paul affirmed to be alive. Acts 25: 19.
FESTUS talked lightly enough about Jesus. It was only a question in his mind of some Jewish superstition hardly worth debating.

What did it matter to him or his imperial master whether Jesus were alive or dead? And was it not a fact that he was dead, crucified under Pontius Pilate? How little Festus realized the importance of that death, not to the Jews alone, but to himself! How little he understood that his own continued life was due to that death of which he spoke so lightly! Generations of luxury and years of self-indulgence had blunted his perception: as for all religious questions—they were mere superstition! And with respect to religious enthusiasm, as it appeared in Paul, he could find in his own history nothing that could account for or explain it.

Contrast with this sated worldling—a flatterer, an office-seeker, prepared to sell his soul for gold—the noble apostle whose character stands out in unsullied light. Though Christ had died, according to the Scriptures, he knew that He had risen, and was alive for evermore. His faith did not go back to the cross, but rose perpetually to the throne. He who was dead, was living for evermore; sharing His servant's sorrows, and supplying hourly grace for his every need.

He affirmed that He was alive. On the abundant testimony of those who had spoken with Him after his resurrection; on the strength of his own vision when Jesus had laid an arrest on him hard by Damascus; because of the mighty works that emanated from his hand; because of the daily fellowship which brought him into the presence of his Lord, in spite of clanking chain and iron bar—he affirmed that Jesus was alive.

I was not disobedient unto the heavenly vision.
                    Acts 26: 19.

TO us, also, the heavenly visions come. On our summer holidays, rising between us and some soaring Alp, or meeting us in our walk beside the gently-breaking sea; on beds of pain and in chambers of watching; visions of the risen Lord; visions of his infinite grief and pain which we have caused; visions of the possibilities of our life as a minister and witness of the things which we have seen; visions of results far down the vista wherein dark souls should become light, slaves emancipated, the defiled saintly. Ah, visions of God! ye leave an indelible impression that moulds and ennobles all after-years! Pitiable the soul to which visions of a holier, sweeter life never come, or, if they come, are never seen.

The one important matter is our treatment of them. We may indolently refuse to follow the beckoning hand and obey the voice that calls. We may return to our evil courses and follow the devices and desires of our own hearts. We may cling to the prison cell, instead of following the angel that strikes us on our side, and bids us go forth into freedom. And if so, like Balaam, we shall become spiritually blind, and fail to see visions that the dumb creatures recognize, and that would fain arrest us in our perilous career.

On the other hand, if we will obey the vision, we shall not only retain the impression, and feel its prolonged and enthralling power, but shall receive still further manifestations of the will of God. "A witness both of the thing wherein thou hast seen Me, and of the things wherein I will appear unto thee." To those who love and obey Him, He is ever drawing near with fresh and deeper thoughts of the Father.

There stood by me this night an angel of God,
    saying, Fear not, Paul! Acts 27: 23, 24.

YES, the angels of God can find their way through the murkiest air, and alight on the most weather-beaten vessel that ever ploughed its difficult way through the stormy seas. Wheresoever thou art, O child of God. God's angels have their eyes fixed lovingly on thee; and in a moment, if it were God's will to give thee eyes, thou wouldest behold them.

"How oft do they their silver bowers leave,
    To come to succour us that succour want!
How oft do they with golden pinions cleave
    The flitting skyes, like flying pursuivant,
    Against fowle feandes to ayd us militant!
They for us fight, they watch and dewly ward,
    And their bright squadrons round about us plant!
And all for love, and nothing for reward:
Oh, why should Heavenly God to men have such regard?"

But if, like Paul, we would have the angel ministry, with their assurances against fear, like him we must be able to comply with two conditions—of being owned and being loyal.

WHOSE I AM. We are His by creation, by purchase, by consecration. That sentiment of being owned, which in the case of slaves is inimical to the highest development, is the elementary condition of our truest growth and well-being. We belong to One who is infinitely worthy. We cannot do as we would with ourselves. We may not take our own course.

WHOM I SERVE. The word rendered serve is the deepest and most expressive term that Paul could employ of the prostration of the soul at the feet of God. It is employed of the glorified, who serve Him day and night in his temple, and of whom it is said that his servants shall do Him service. The heavenly life begins here; and following its course, angels minister to us, and the stars in their courses fight for us.

And he abode two whole years in his own hired dwelling, etc. Acts 28: 30, 31 (R.V.).
THUS, abruptly, does this fifth Gospel close. It has been well said that a close so abrupt suggests a continuance and a sequel. The curtain of silence falls when Paul's life is not brought to a close, and his work at Rome is still in process; and does not this indicate the design of the Holy Spirit that we should believe that the book of the Acts of the Apostles is never complete, but is really conterminous with the present age? Thus, every generation of every life adds its own gold link to the chain, which reaches from the upper chamber in the earthly Jerusalem to the bridal chamber of the New Jerusalem, uniting in one glorious succession all in whom Jesus continues by the Spirit to speak and work.

When the late Bishop of Ripon read of the labours and sufferings of John Williams in the South Seas, he laid down the narrative, exclaiming, "This is the twenty-ninth chapter of the Acts of the Apostles." May we not rather say the five hundredth or five thousandth? Between the stories of Paul and of John Williams, you must insert thousands which have been recorded of God's remembrancing angels alone, as well as those which are filling our shelves with missionary romance and biography, more interesting than novels, more wonderful than dreams.

"The book is left incomplete, as it always will be while one believer is left to teach and preach those things concerning the Lord Jesus Christ, and to fill up that which is behind of the afflictions of Christ in his own flesh for his body's sake, which is the Church." And the question arises, Have you wrought or suffered for Jesus in such wise as to add some verses to those chapters, which are now being written by angel scribes?

Romans

Therein is the righteousness of God revealed from faith in faith. Rom. 1: 17.
IT is important to understand this verse, because it is the key to the Epistle. In the deepest sense, righteousness stands for two things—first, our standing before God; and next, our personal character—our position and our condition—what we are in Jesus, and what we are in ourselves by the Holy Spirit. Hooker, therefore, well expresses the truth when he says, "The righteousness with which we shall be clothed in the world to come, is both perfect and inherent; that wherewith we are justified is perfect, but not inherent; that by which we are sanctified is inherent, but not perfect." The term righteousness, therefore, covers justification and sanctification, whereof the former is treated in the first five chapters of this Epistle; and to this we confine ourselves.

There is a difference between forgiveness and justification. By forgiveness the sinner may be reinstated in the confidence of Him whom he has wronged; by justification he is declared righteous according to law, and thereby commended to the confidence and respect of all men.

Justification is our position through the wonderful grace of God, and by virtue of the finished work of Christ, which is imputed to all who believe. All that He is, is reckoned to us who are in Him. We are not merely forgiven, great and wonderful as that act of love and grace would be; but we are dealt with as though we had never sinned. Instead, therefore, of the law being against us, as we deserve, it is on our side, defending and protecting us. Our salvation actually rests on law. We may claim it as an absolute right. And all this because of God's infinite grace: because, in the person of Jesus, He has perfectly met, and satisfied, the claims of his holy but broken law.

The law written in their hearts, their conscience bearing witness therewith. Rom. 2: 15 (R.V.).
THIS is a great announcement, and shows

how God can judge men who have never heard of the Bible or the Decalogue. The latter is engraven on their hearts, and is witnessed to by conscience.

Conscience is an original faculty. We are no more called upon to investigate its origin than the mathematician to inquire how the mind can add, or multiply, or divide; or than the artist to ask why we can appreciate the beautiful. It is part of the make-up and constitution of our moral nature. The word ought lies behind conscience, investing it with the certainty and irresistibleness of the throne of God.

Conscience is the judgment-seat of God set up within our nature. You may always know when conscience speaks. She never hesitates, or questions, or pronounces on the expediency of a course; but, as any case is presented to her, she pronounces absolutely and directly upon it as right or wrong. And as she speaks, she anticipates the verdict of the great white throne.

Doubtless conscience may be impaired in its action by long neglect, or by the determined preference of human maxims as our rule of action; but it is always liable to resurrection when the voice of God is sounding. The office of the minister, like "Old Mortality" in the story, is to go through the world, chisel in hand, clearing the inscriptions of the law from the grit of growth which has rendered them almost illegible in too many cases. The Prince, in the old fairy story, sounded a blast at the gate of the Sleeping Palace, and broke the spell, so that all its inmates sprang up into alert vitality; and similarly the Spirit of God, through the Truth, appeals to the human conscience, which is his ally in the heart of man.

That He might be just, and the Justifier.
Rom. 3: 26.

THIS verse is often quoted as though the word yet must be inserted to bring out its meaning. "Just, and yet the Justifier." The marvel of a just God justifying sinful men is thus strongly accentuated. Of course, this is a true thought and marvellous. But it is not the precise idea of the apostle, when he says that the just God is the Justifier of those that have faith in Jesus. He means that the very justice of God has come on our side, and that his love may have its unhindered way, not only consistently with his justice, but because of it.

This is the heart of the Gospel. Jesus has stood as our representative. He has borne our sin, in its curse and penalty; has met the claims of a broken law, and satisfied the demands of infinite righteousness. To have done this in our name and on our behalf not only makes us free from any penalty which might otherwise have accrued, but gives us a claim—the claim of the righteous—on all those blessings which the righteous government of God has to bestow.

Directly we become one with Jesus by a living faith, we stand possessed of all that He has done and is. In Him we have already suffered all that the holy law of God could demand as the just penalty of our sins. In Him we have lain in the grave, paying the uttermost farthing that could be exacted. In Him we have been liberated from the prison-house, and have passed into the presence and welcome of God. We may claim, therefore, that the law of God should make for us, as once it made against us. We are saved not only by the grace, but by the justice of God. He is faithful to his Son and just to the law, when He forgives us our sins.

He staggered not ta the promise of God through unbelief. Rom. 4: 20.

IT was a marvellous promise that this childless pair should have a child, and become progenitors of a great nation, so that the stars of the heavenly vault and the sand-grains on the ocean-shore should not be more numerous. And it was enough to stagger any man to be told of it. But Abraham staggered not. How was this?

IT DID NOT ARISE FROM IGNORING THE DIFFICULTIES THAT OBSTRUCTED ITS REALIZATION. He might have done so. Whenever the natural obstacles arose in his mind, he might have ignored them. But this, according to the R.V. rendering of the previous verse, was not Abraham's policy. He quietly and deliberately considered the enormous difficulties that lay in the path of the divine purpose, and in spite of them "he staggered not."

BUT HIS UNSTAGGERING FAITH AROSE FROM HIS GREAT THOUGHTS OF HIM WHO HAD PROMISED. He kept saying to himself, He is able, He is able. He knew that God would not have said what He could not perform. He knew that the God of nature was Lord of the nature He had made. He knew that no word of the Almighty could be destitute of power.

He fed his faith by cherishing lofty and profound thoughts of God's infinite resources. There rang in his heart the assurance, I am El Shaddai.

It is remarkable that, throughout Abraham's life God was continually giving new glimpses into his own glorious nature. With every temptation, call to obedience, or demand for sacrifice, a new and deeper revelation was entwined. This fed his faith, and gave it unstaggering strength. Child of God, feed thy faith on Promise. For every look at your difficulties, take ten at what thy God is.

They which receive abundance of grace ... shall reign in life. Rom. 5: 17.

ALL God's dealings with us are on the same principle. As we received Christ Jesus the Lord, so we must walk in Him. Whether it be justification or sanctification; whether reconciliation or reigning in life that is under consideration—the same mighty principles underlie and control the divine gifts and our participation in them. We receive reconciliation as a gift at the beginning of our Christian life, and we have to receive all else by the same medium to the end. For ever and for ever we have just to wait till God fill us, as the flower-cups that are now filled with sunshine and now with dew or rain.

YOU HAVE ALREADY RECEIVED THE RECONCILIATION (ver. 11). Unable to earn it by your own endeavours, you were at last content to receive it as a free gift placed into your open hand; now you have to maintain the same position with respect to all the spiritual gifts that you need for the maintenance of a godly life, and to enable you to reign. Faith—simple, open-handed, heaven-regarding faith —is the one unchanging law of the holy life.

"Trusting Jesus, that is all."

THIS REIGNING IN LIFE IS NOT TO BE RELEGATED TO THE UNSEEN AND FUTURE. It is meant to be our present experience. He hath made us kings to God, even the Father. We are called to the royalty of men, the abundance, the freedom, the consciousness of power and victory, which we are wont to associate with those who reign. To reign in the ordinary life of the home, the shop, the counting-house—such is our high calling in Christ Jesus. And it may be ours if we receive "abundance of grace" of the one Man, Jesus Christ.

Present yourselves unto God. Rom. 6: 13 (R.V.).

WE must choose. On the one hand stands sin, filling the market-place with its appeals, and bidding for us; on the other hand, God in the person of his Son. For it is well known that to whomsoever we yield ourselves to obey, his servants we shall be. Sin wants us, not only to work its fell results by us, but to curse and ruin us; whilst God wants to bless us with eternal life.

We may not be able to forecast or to arrange many things in our lives, which are difficult and perplexing; and at first it is not wise to discuss our attitude or action with respect to them. The first and most momentous question which presses for immediate solution is, whether we are prepared to present our members—brain, voice, hand, heart—to God; that through them He may fulfil his good purpose.

The argument is a very cogent one. The apostle tells us that we have been delivered from death; that in Jesus Christ we have been brought back to stand on the resurrection side of the grave. For such a wondrous deliverance, he exclaims, there is only one adequate return. Present yourselves to be the slaves of your Redeemer. Surely none of us would resemble the rich man, who was saved from drowning by a brave sailor, and offered him half-a-crown in recompense!

In this way also we shall be delivered from sin. Merely to resist and refuse it, is not enough; we shall not get perfect freedom so. But if we turn to God with a full purpose of heart, and give Him possession, we shall be delivered from the dominion of evil, because the responsibility of our emancipation and perfecting will rest on Him to whom we have yielded spirit, soul, and body.

O wretched man that I am! Rom. 7: 24.

THIS chapter is very full of the personal pronoun. Me and I are the pivot around which its argument revolves. The strenuous efforts which the soul makes, not so much to justify as to sanctify itself, to realize its ideal, to walk worthy of the Lord, are well-pleasing, and are described by a master hand.

Is there one of us who has not read these words repeatedly, and in desperation? They have been so exactly true. We have longed with passionate sincerity that a new man might arise in us to free us from our old man, and make us the men we fain would be. We have been conscious of a subtle force mastering our struggles, like the serpents overcoming Laocoon and his sons; we have realized that a corrupting carcase was bound to our backs, as to the Roman criminals of old, filling the air with miasma, and poisoning our life. We have cried bitterly, O wretched man, who shall deliver?

The key to the plaintive moan of this chapter consists in this. It is the result of the endeavour to live a holy life apart from the power of the indwelling Saviour, and independently of the grace of the Holy Spirit. All such efforts are sure to end in wretchedness. We can no more sanctify ourselves than we can justify. Deliverance from the power of sin is the gift of God's grace, as forgiveness is. And it is only when we have come to the very end of all our strivings and resolvings, and have abandoned ourselves to the Saviour, that He should do in us and for us what we cannot do for ourselves, that we are led to cry, "I thank God through Jesus Christ our Lord."

"All things are possible to God;
   To Christ, the power of God in men,
To me, when I am all subdued,
   When I, in Christ, am born again."

The Spirit Himself maketh intercession with groanings. Rom. 8: 26 (R.V.).
THERE is a threefold groaning here.

CREATION GROANS (22). The sufferings of the dumb animals, under the brutal tyranny of man; in hard service; in the torture chambers of vivisectionists; to yield pleasure; to give food; or to provide dress—must fill the ear of Heaven with groans. The sighs of myriads of acres, condemned to bear the poisonous poppy or the barley for the manufacture of spirit, must be heard across the broad expanse of space. There is a discord, an oppression, a vanity in the universe around us, which constantly betrays the secret oppression of evil. Goethe said that Nature seemed to him to be like a captive maiden crying aloud for release.

THE SAINTS GROAN (23). We wait for our adoption, for the manifestation of our sonship, for the redemption of our bodies from the last remnants of the fall; and as we wait, we groan beneath the pressure of the present, the weight of mortality, and with eager desire for the blessed advent of the Lord.

THE SPIRIT GROANS (26). The pressure of sin and sorrow in our world is heavy for Him to

bear, and He sighs bitterly, as Jesus did when He stood face to face with the grave of his dead friend.

But these groans portend life, not death. They are full of hope, not despair. They are the pangs of birth, not the throes of death. Out of the agony of the present the new heavens and earth are being born.

"Unto you is given
To watch for the coming of His feet
Who is the Glory of our blessed Heaven.
The work and watching will be very sweet,
Even in an earthly home;
And in such an hour as you think not
   He will come."

Jacob I loved, but Esau I hated.
Rom. 9: 13 (R.V.).
THE apostle is dealing here, not with individuals as such, but with peoples and nations. For instance, Isaac stands for the entire Jewish race—Abraham's seed (ver. 7). He is dealing with the question, why it was that God chose Israel and rejected Edom; chose Jacob and rejected Esau: and he shows that the ultimate decision of their destinies lay in the purpose of God, according to election. The one was elect to be a channel of immense blessing to the world; whilst the other was rejected.

But we must always associate the divine foreknowledge with the divine choice. "Whom He did foreknow, He also did predestinate." We must regard Jacob and Esau, not as individual personalities merely, but as the founders of nations. For God's purpose in the building-up of the chosen people, Jacob the methodical and far-seeing, was more suited than Esau the free-lance, the rover, the child of impulse and passion. And, besides, there were religious aptitudes and capacities within him, of which Esau gave no sign or trace. This does not solve the entire mystery, perhaps; but only casts it a degree or two further back. Still, it ought to be considered. Like a candle, it casts a slender ray on to the black abyss. In any case, is it not certain that God's choice did alight on him who was most suited to serve the divine purpose?

It may be that God is wanting to execute his purpose through you. Take heed. Still the savoury dish steams on the desert air, and appeals to the appetite of our natures; and we are strongly tempted to forgo the unseen and eternal for a moment's gratification. See to it that for one morsel of meat you do not sell your birthright.

If thou shalt confess with thy mouth Jesus as Lord, etc. Rom. 10: 9 (R.V.).
SALVATION here is evidently to be taken in its most extended meaning. It stands even more for the deliverance of the soul from the love and dominion of sin than for the removal of its justly-incurred penalty. That we should be pure in heart, holy in thought, consecrated in life, with all the range of our nature controlled by his indwelling Spirit—such is the divine intention with respect to us, as suggested by this deep, great word Salvation. But there are two conditions, on our compliance with which this saving power is realized.

WE MUST CONFESS JESUS AS LORD. Throughout Scripture there is a close connection between Christ's Royalty and his Saviourship. "Behold, thy King cometh to thee, . . . having salvation;" "Him hath God set forth to be a Prince and a Saviour." "Melchizedek, king of Salem, priest of God Most High, . . . made like unto the Son of God, abideth a priest continually." We shall never know Christ as a Saviour from inbred sin until we have definitely and absolutely enthroned Him in our hearts. A physician is not content with healing outbreaks of disease and fever when they occur; but claims leave to examine all the arrangements of the house, so as to deal with the sources of the mischief.

WE MUST ALSO STEADFASTLY BELIEVE IN THE RESURRECTION. The risen Lord, sitting at the right hand of God, in all the vigour of an indissoluble life: still working in the world, and energizing the hearts of his own; entering to indwell, to fill, to unite with his own eternal life—such is the vision offered to our faith. Let us look away to Him with a persistent, unwavering gaze, until sin ceases to attract us, and Satan finds a Stronger in possession.

Of Him, and through Him, and to Him, are all things. Rom. 11: 36.
THIS verse reminds us of those lagoons of perfectly still clear water, of which travellers tell. So clear, that it is easily possible to look into their translucent depths to where the submarine foliage waves! So deep, that the ordinary measuring line fails to plumb them! All these words are monosyllables. A child

just learning to read could easily spell them out. But who shall exhaust their meaning?

OF HIM. The entire scheme of redemption; the marvellous history of the chosen people, with which this chapter is occupied; the universe of matter, all are included in the all things that have emanated out of God. No one has been his counsellor, or given aught to Him. From all created things, which are as the stream, let us climb to Him, who is their fountain, source, and origin; and in Him let us learn to fill our own souls to the very brim.

THROUGH HIM. Through Jesus Christ, the Mediator, God has poured the entire grace and wealth of his nature to bless and help us. There is no good thing that does not come to us through the mediation of the Second Person of the Holy Trinity. Through Him He made the worlds. Through Him we have received the reconciliation. Through Him, also, all grace is made to abound towards us. Never forget to magnify the Lord Jesus as the source of all your supply.

TO HIM. Creation, Providence, Redemption, are all tending back to God. The tide is setting in towards the throne. A revenue of glory shall yet accrue from all that has happened within the parenthesis of time. Every whit in the great temple shall one day say "Glory!"

Present your bodies a living sacrifice, holy, acceptable to God. Rom. 12: 1.
TO present carries us back to chapter 6. We might almost say that the intervening chapters, after the manner of the apostle, are one prolonged digression or parenthesis, and that he classes all the great things with which he has been treating as among the mercies of God, and as reasons for our entire consecration. Every disclosure of God's grace towards us is an argument for our complete surrender to his will and power.

We are called on to present our bodies as instruments of righteousness, because all true regimen of the inner life immediately affects the body in all its members; and, conversely, the consecration of the body reacts upon and affects the temper of the soul. It would be well for you to take Miss Havergal's hymn, with its enumeration of the various parts of the body, and offer and present yourself, to be from this day and forward, wholly for God. Only believe that He is more anxious for this than words can tell, because He loves you so, and that He accepts immediately what you offer.

Such consecration must be living; that is, it must enter into all our life, being holy, well-pleasing to God, and rational. It is not only reasonable when we consider the relation we sustain to Him, but it should engage all our intelligence and reasoning faculties. And when it is made, and the soul is becoming duly transfigured in its exercise, we begin to prove that God's will, which once we dreaded, is also good, well-pleasing, and perfect. When we look at God's will from a distance, and before consecration, it seems impossible. It is only when we begin to obey, that we can say:

"Thou sweet beloved will of God."

Put ye on the Lord Jesus Christ. Rom. 13: 14. THIS verse is ever memorable from its association with the life of Augustine, who says: "Thus was I sick and tormented in mind, bitterly accusing myself, and rolling and turning about in my chain, till it might be wholly broken."

At length, rushing into the garden, groaning in spirit, "all my bones were crying out, soul-sick was I and grievously tormented. I said to myself, 'Be it done now; be it done now.' And a voice said, 'Why standest thou in thyself, and so standest not? Cast thyself upon Him. Fear not; He will not withdraw Himself, to let thee fall. He will receive, and will heal thee. Stop thine ears against those unclean members of thine, which are upon the earth, that they may be mortified.'"

Then arose a mighty tempest, bringing a heavy downpour of tears. "I cast myself under a certain fig-tree, and gave vent to my tears, and the floods of mine eyes brake forth. Why not now? Why not this hour make an end of my uncleanness? And, lo! from the neighbouring house I heard a voice as of a boy or girl, I know not which, singing and oft repeating, 'Take and read; take and read!' Checking the torrent of my tears, I arose, interpreting it to be a divine command to open the Book and read the first chapter I could find. I seized; I opened, and in silence read the passage on which mine eyes fell: 'Not in rioting and drunkenness, not in chambering and wantonness, not in strife and envying. But put ye on the Lord Jesus Christ, and make not provision for the flesh, to fulfil the lusts thereof.' No further would I read; nor was there need, for instantly all my heart was flooded with a light of peace, all the sadness of doubt melted away!"

He that herein serveth Christ is well-pleasing to God, and approved of men. Rom. 14: 18 (R.V.). DEAN HOWSON renders this verse thus: "He who lives in these things as Christ's bondsman is well-pleasing to God, and cannot be condemned by men." There are two rules, therefore, to be observed by us when we consider our behaviour in that great border-land which lies between the dark and light, the clearly wrong and clearly right. We are all conscious of habits and tastes, of inclinations towards certain forms of amusement and recreation, of methods of life, which do not contravene any distinct law of God, but are certainly open to question. It is such things that fall within the scope of these two principles.

FIRST, WE MUST ALWAYS REMEMBER THAT WE ARE CHRIST'S BONDSERVANTS. Let us look then, every day and hour, and as to the mental habit, every moment, upon Jesus Christ as our Master. Saintly George Herbert chose that to be, as it were, his best-beloved aspect of his Saviour; "My Master, Jesus." "An oriental fragrancy, my Master." Let us do the same. Let us wear the word next the heart, next the will; nay, let it sink into the very springs of both, deeper every day. And as each fresh question arises in our life, let us stand close beside Him, noticing the expression of His face, asking Him what He would desire, and always reckoning that the least suggestion of his preference is law. "None of us liveth to himself: for, whether we live, we live unto the Lord."

SECOND, WE MUST ALWAYS BEAR IN MIND THE SPIRITUAL LIFE OF OTHERS. We are to put no stumbling-block, or occasion for falling, in another's way. It is good neither to eat flesh, nor drink wine, nor to do any other thing, whereby our brother is made to stumble. Let us each of us please his neighbour for good ends, to build him up; for Christ pleased not Himself.

I will not dare to speak of any things save those that Christ wrought through me.
Rom. 15: 18 (R.V.).
ALL things that have not sprung from the indwelling and inworking power of Christ, are probably valueless in the sight of God.

As the apostle dared not record them in this book, so probably they are not recorded in God's book. They lack the one principle or germ of life. Our Lord said, Separate from Me ye can do nothing; and probably, therefore, whatever we do out of living union with Him amounts to nothing.

These words are a window into the apostle's inner life. He was ever looking to the Lord to work through him, in the power of the Holy Ghost. He had nothing, therefore, to boast of, as he reviewed his labours; the impulse in which they originated, and the success with which they were crowned, were alike attributable to the Son of God, who had been revealed and formed within.

Let us so yield ourselves to Him, that the great Master may fulfil through us also all the good pleasure of his will.

Let us wait before Him in earnest expectancy, till the foundation of his purpose begins to arise within us; and let us receive from Him the gracious power of which to realize his plans. "I cannot," one may say, "give that tract; speak to that fellow-traveller; witness for Christ on that ship or in that shop; stand up in that pulpit and preach." No, perhaps not. But you can let Christ do these things through you.

"So others shall
Take patience, labour, to their heart and land,
From thy land and thy heart and thy brave cheer,
And God's grace fructify through thee to all.
The least flower with a brimming cup may stand
And share its dew-drop with another near."

Quartus the brother. Rom. 16: 23 (R.V.).
THAT is all we know about him. The others whose names are written here are more or less famous. Tertius wrote the Epistle; Gaius was evidently a man of influence; Erastus was the treasurer of the city, and so on. But Quartus was just a humble, simple Christian, who had no handle to his name, save his brotherliness and his desire to assure his Roman brethren, whom probably he had never seen, of his love to them. "So he begs a little corner in Paul's letter, and gets it; and there, in his little niche, like some statue of a forgotten saint scarce seen amidst the glories of a great cathedral, 'Quartus the brother' stands to all time."

WHAT A LESSON IN HUMILITY! Seekest thou great things for thyself? seek them not. Be content to live and die unknown, except for the love that breathes through thy life, not to those of thine own circle merely, but for those across the sea, with whom thou wouldst fain strike hands. Thy one joy, that thou hast been born into the family of God. Thy creed, that all regenerate souls, of every name and sect, are members of the same family, children of the same Father, and therefore one in ties of peculiar tenderness and strength.

WHAT A REVELATION this slight reference is to the new binding forces of the Gospel! At the Advent the world was split by great gulfs of national hatred; fierce enmities of race, language, and religion; wide separations far profounder than anything that we know. And then the Gospel came, which began to gather men of every race into one family, in Jesus Christ, the Divine Elder-brother; and from this, uniting influences of brotherhood began to permeate the world.

1 Corinthians

Called unto the fellowship of his Son Jesus Christ our Lord. 1 Cor. 1: 9.
THE word for fellowship is the same that is employed in Luke 5: 10, of James and John being partners with Simon. We have been called into partnership with the Son of God, in his redemptive purposes, his love and tears for men, and ultimately in his triumph and glory. He has entered into partnership with man, and we are now summoned into partner-

ship with Him through the communion of the Holy Ghost. In the words of the apostle, "our fellowship [or partnership] is with the Father, and with his Son Jesus Christ our Lord."

How fruitful of comfort is the thought that Christ's interests are ours, and that we are at liberty to draw upon his resources to the uttermost. Suppose a poor clerk were to be summoned from his desk into the counting-house of a Rothschild, and informed that from that moment he was taken into partnership with the firm: would it not be less of an honour than this which has fallen to our lot? Association with millionaires in money-making were infinitely less desirable than association with the Son of God in world-saving. And would that poor clerk feel any anxiety as to his share in meeting the immense liabilities of the concern? However great they might be, he would know that the resources of the firm were adequate, and he would be able to sleep easily at night, though millions were due on the morrow. Child of God, cannot thy Father meet all his Son's engagements?

The call to this partnership is from the Father. It is He who has chosen us for this high honour of co-operating with his Son. Will He have led us into such an association, and leave us to be overwhelmed by the difficulties of the situation He has created? It cannot be! He will supply all our need.

God hath revealed them unto us by his Spirit.
1 Cor. 2: 10.

EYES of my soul, ye have no need to wait until the vail of the flesh that screens off the beatific vision has been rent in twain by the mighty hands of the Angel of Death, ere ye behold the land that floweth with milk and honey!

EARS of my heart, ye need not remain dull and listless till the peal of the archangel's trumpet thrill you, and summon you to the music of the harpers harping on their harps or the chime of the glassy sea.

HEART of mine, be expectant! Awake! Lo, there shall come into thee, penetrating, pervading, filling thy every recess, all those blessed things which God hath prepared for them that love Him. They shall enter thee, as a retinue of knights might enter a beleaguered castle to make it strong against any possible combination of the foe.

Only I must love God. Through Isaiah I am taught that I must wait for Him (Isa. 64: 4); here I learn that I must love. For love is quick to know. He that loveth knoweth God. It was the apostle whom Jesus loved that beheld Him on the margin of the lake. It is to the warm, tender atmosphere of loving hearts that the unchecked, ungrieved Spirit unfolds his secrets. Let me, therefore, bathe myself in the gracious atmosphere of my Saviour's presence, never going outside its genial glow, never falling behind his going forth, until I am entrusted, through the Spirit, with the deep things of God.

"God only knows the love of God;
Oh that it now were shed abroad
In this poor stony heart!
For love I sigh, for love I pine,
This only portion, Lord, be mine—
Be mine this better part!"

Let every man take heed how he buildeth.
1 Cor. 3: 10.

A FITTING illustration of the Christian life for the people of Corinth, famed for its architecture. We are all builders, whether we choose or not! We may be temple-builders! Each heart, each life, each character, may become a temple of the Holy Spirit.

Every act we do, every word we utter, the way in which we spend any moments of our time, is either a fragment of gold, silver, and precious stones, or of wood, hay, and stubble, built into the rising structure of the erection entrusted to our skill and pains. It does not so much matter what we do, but how we do it. Every time we perform any action with the best motives and spirit, we deposit a tiny grain of gold-dust; whenever, on the other hand, we do aught after a slovenly, superficial, and careless manner, we weave into the structure of character a material which will yield as inevitably in the hour of temptation as wood, hay, and stubble before flame.

We sometimes, at the end of the day, reviewing the past hours, bitterly lament that we have done nothing in the way of character-building. "There is nothing to show for this day," we say mentally to ourselves. Ah! but there is. Every moment has left its record on your heart. Every act has left you confirmed in a good habit or in a bad one. The soul-life has not halted for a second; one has been growing to moral health, or towards decrepitude, consumption, and decay. If not gold, then wood; if not silver, then hay; if not costly stones, then stubble.

We shall not be saved on account of our works. The only thing that can secure salvation is the being built into God's foundation, the Rock Christ Jesus. But we shall be rewarded according to the manner in which we have built up the structure.

He that judgeth me is the Lord.   1 Cor. 4: 4.

THERE are four courts of trial.

First: Man's judgment.—It is significantly spoken of as man's "day." Our conduct is narrowly scrutinized and weighed by many eyes which we know not of, but which are fixed on every act and word—the eyes of our neighbours, associates, fellow-workpeople, servants. They are ever reasoning about us, comparing our lives with our professions, partly with the view of excusing themselves, if there is any gross inconsistency. But, after all, their verdict need not greatly move us. It is only for a day.

Second: The judgment of fellow-Christians. —We are perpetually being summoned before the court of the church circle to which we belong; not always because we are inconsistent with our professions, but whenever we over-step the pace at which the majority is slowly moving. To be too zealous, too eager, too earnest, too particular, will, in some Christian communities, expose to a great deal of adverse criticism. But we have not to look right and left to get the sentence of our fellow-believers when we are clearly prompted by the Spirit of God.

Third: The judgment of conscience.—"I judge not mine own self." We are all apt to arraign ourselves at our own bar, and pass verdicts which are altogether favourable, because we compare ourselves with characters and standards inferior to ourselves. It is a great mistake to judge yourself, for even if you score a favourable verdict—if you know nothing against yourself—it is liable to be reversed by the decisions of the Supreme Court.

Fourth: The Lord's judgment.—The Lord will come, bringing to light the hidden things of darkness, and making manifest the counsels of the heart.

Christ our passover is sacrificed for us; therefore let us keep the feast. 1 Cor. 5: 7, 8.

AT the time of the first Passover, outside, as the ominous midnight hour approached, Egypt gave herself up to her usual life. "They ate and drank; they married and gave in marriage." But within their homes, the children of Israel stood around their tables, their loins girt, their staves in their hands, with unleavened bread packed up with their kneading-troughs in their clothes, waiting for the signal to depart. The Passover Lamb had been sacri-ficed; its blood was on the door; whilst its flesh, roast with fire, was being eaten. For seven days, all leavened bread had been put away out of the houses of the chosen people,

because leaven, in the Bible, is the symbol of the working of the corrupt principle.

THE BELIEVER SHOULD LOOK BACK. The Paschal Lamb was sacrificed for us on the cross. Though He had done no sin, and was without blemish, yet He was slain for us without the gates of the city. He made there a sufficient sacrifice, satisfaction, oblation, for the sins of the whole world.

THE BELIEVER SHOULD LOOK AROUND. With lighted candle, search the heart of your house, that there may be no speck or mote of leaven. Let us keep the perpetual feast of the Christian life, not with old leaven, nor with the leaven of malice and wickedness, but with the unleavened bread of sincerity and truth.

THE BELIEVER SHOULD LOOK ON. Soon we shall hear the midnight trumpet sound, "Arise and depart, for this is not your rest!" and we shall go forth from Egypt, where we have suffered, and toiled, and been misunderstood; where also our Lord was crucified. It is but a little while (how little, how little!) and He that shall come will come, and will not tarry.

Know ye not that your body is the temple of the Holy Ghost which is in you? 1 Cor. 6: 19.

THIS is a sentence which should be deeply pondered; every clause is significant. We evidently should know its deep and solemn meaning. Apparently it is one of the common-places of our holy religion. This knowledge, however, should not be merely that of the intellect, but born out of the deep musing of the heart.

THE HOLY TEMPLE. Built up of the dust of the earth, our bodies are rarer than the most glorious structures that ever the sun shone on, because they are meant to be the shrine and home of God. Jesus spake of the Temple of his Body; and if He was so zealous for his Father's House that He drove out the unholy traffickers, and refused to allow a vessel to be carried through the courts, should we not be equally careful? We are the custodians of the divine residence; let us be very careful that there be nothing to offend or trouble the celestial Inmate.

THE DIVINE INMATE. Too often He is grieved, and driven to occupy the most secret shrine, concealed and hidden beneath the heavy vail of our inconsistency and unbelief. He is not driven out by our sins, but driven in. Whenever, on the contrary, we put away our sin, and walk in the light as He is in the light; whenever the vail is rent and the whole heart thrown open to Him—He comes in power to occupy every part of our being, so that there is no part dark, and the very body becomes transfigured.

THE GREAT PRICE. Bought as any slave standing in the market-place for sale! Ransomed from the direst slave-master to the dearest Lord! The price—not corruptible things, as silver and gold—but precious blood! Our life is henceforth not our own, but his.

Let every man, wherein he is called, therein abide with God. 1 Cor. 7: 24.

STRONG temptations to restlessness beset the early Christians. The great change through which they had passed from heathenism to Christ threatened to dissolve all the ties by which they had been held, in the home, the business, and the State. Very necessary and wholesome, therefore, was the apostle's advice. Stay as you are, until God clearly leads you into something else—only with this difference, whatever be the vocation of your life, therein abide with God. Paul was only careful that the thought of God should penetrate their entire existence; all else would come right in time; and he was only anxious that they should be laid hold of by that central, vivifying, transmuting influence.

PRACTISE THE PRESENCE OF GOD. A godly brother used to say that we should establish ourselves in a sense of God's presence by an act of the will, which put aside wandering, frivolous, and evil thoughts, and that we should be continually conversing with Him; that we ought to give ourselves up to God, making Him the end of all our actions, and seeking our only satisfaction in doing his will; and that even the set times of prayer should not greatly differ from other times, because all were equally filled with God.

SUCH A SENSE EQUALIZES OUR LOT. The slave realizes that he is God's free man; the master that he is God's slave. The poor are enriched, and the rich are convicted to their poverty. So this holy brother said that, in his business in the kitchen (to which naturally he had a great aversion), having accustomed himself to do everything there for the love of God and with prayer, he had found everything easy, and was very well pleased to continue in the same post so long as it was God's will.

If meat maketh my brother to stumble, I will eat no flesh for evermore. 1 Cor. 8: 13 (R.V.).

THERE are two principles for our guidance in doubtful and debatable questions. FIRST, THE LAW OF CONSCIENCE. The apostle does not hesitate to say that the scruples of the weaker brethren were unquestionably needless. Idols have no real existence, and the presentation of food in their presence before it is eaten is a matter of complete indifference. "If we eat, we are not the better; if we eat not, we are not the worse." At the same time, if a man were not able to reach this high standard, and still believed that an idol had a real existence, and that it was wrong for him to partake of food which had been offered to it, he must abide by that decision, and must on no account force himself to more liberal action. His conscience might be misinformed, and he should take every means of bringing it to a more healthy condition; but if it still remained stationary, he must accept its ruling.

SECONDLY, THE LAW OF CHARITY. We must consider one another. No one liveth to himself. We are members of the body of Christ, and have no right to injure any who are so closely allied with us, and on whose healthy existence our own materially depends. If, then, we see that certain other souls are constantly being caused to stumble, because of what we do; not simply surprised and startled, but actually made to sin; trying to do as we do, but as often as they attempt it, falling short; unable to take our steep path without falling; always brought into condemnation when in our company; there is no alternative—for their sakes we must forgo what is innocent and pleasant to ourselves. It may be a daily glass of wine, or attendance at some form of amusement, or some evil habit—but the love of Christ forbids.

Lest I myself should be a castaway. 1 Cor. 9: 27.

IS it for one moment to be supposed that Paul really feared being cast away from the love and presence of God into the outer darkness with its weeping and gnashing of teeth? Surely not! Had he not said unmistakably that nothing could avail to separate him from the love of God which was in Jesus Christ! No, it is impossible to think such a thing. He knew too well that none of Christ's members can be amputated; none of his sheep perish.

"The soul that to Jesus has fled for repose,
  He will not, He cannot, desert to its foes;
  That soul, though all hell should endeavour
    to take,
  He'll never—no, never—no, never forsake."

But when the apostle speaks of being a castaway, he means that he feared lest, after having proclaimed the rules of the contest to others, he should himself fail shamefully of the prize. And what was that prize? Certainly not forgiveness, nor eternal life; because these are not procured by any efforts of our own. These are not the prizes of agility or strength, but the gift of God, through Jesus Christ our Lord. What, then, is the prize? The context reveals it. It is surely the guerdon of winning souls; the blessed joy and crown of bringing to Jesus those who had otherwise never known Him.

But we may fall short of this. We may set others to do what we fail to do. We may appear before Christ with handfuls of withered leaves. We may yet be rejected. Esau missed the crown of his birthright; Moses the Promised Land; Saul the founding of a line of kings. We may miss utterly and irretrievably. God help us to watch and pray, and bring the body into subjection!

The profit of the many, that they may be saved.
1 Cor. 10: 33.

PROBABLY the world has never seen a more enthusiastic soul-winner than the great apostle. If he visits a strange town, he will cast out the demon from a possessed girl. If he takes up tent-making, beside an unbelieving Jew and his wife, he will before long have won each for Christ. If he is cast into prison, he will have baptized the gaoler before dawn. If he stands before a judge, he will almost persuade him to be a Christian. If he is a prisoner in a hired house, he will speak to all who come to him, and win a runaway slave like Onesimus to Christ, and make him profitable to Philemon. Always and everywhere, he sets himself to win souls.

Here, also, we see how this one passion ruled his behaviour in all things. He was willing to yield to men in matters where only his own comfort, but not his conscience, was concerned. He sought to please all men in all things; not seeking his own profit, but "the profit of the many, that they may be saved."

Oh for more of this sacred passion!—such as inspired, for instance, the Moravians to expatriate themselves for the sake of the lepers of Table Bay!

A woman at the Presbyterian hospital at Canton, hearing of Christ, and loving Him, asked:

"How long can I live if I remain in the hospital?"

"Four months."

"And how long if I go home?"

"Two months," replied the doctor.

"I am going home," she said.

"But," urged the doctor, "you will lose half your life."

"Do you not think I would be glad to give half my life for the sake of telling my people of Jesus?"

And she went home.

Eateth and drinketh judgment unto himself, if he discern not the body. 1 Cor. 11: 29 (R.V.).

HOW many humble and earnest souls this verse, as rendered in the A.V., has kept from the blessed enjoyment of the Lord's Table! They did not understand the nature of the sin which the apostle was describing; they were terrified by the word damnation, and they felt that it were better to forgo the privilege than risk the peril.

The difficulties will, however, largely disappear, when we understand the disorders that disgraced the Corinthian Church, and which arose from the abuses of the love-feast which preceded the Lord's Supper. At that repast each disciple was expected to put the provisions he had brought with him into a common stock, from which all shared alike. But at Corinth, the rich and their friends ate of their luxuries; whilst the poor were allowed to go without. After such an introduction, the Church could not approach the Lord's Table with that appreciation of the solemnity and tenderness of the ordinance which could alone consist with the holy memories of the betrayal night.

The eating and drinking unworthily arose from not discerning the Body. This does not refer to the Lord's Body which was broken for us; but to his Body the Church. "The bread which we break, is it not a communion of the body of Christ, seeing that we, who are many, are one bread, one body?" (1 Cor. 10: 16, 17). We eat and drink unworthily when we fail to discern that the poor, and weak, and simple, who belong to Jesus, belong also to us; that they are members with us; and that we are bound to share our gifts and graces with them for the glory of our common Lord. The one thing which disqualifies us from joining in this feast of dying love is our refusal to feel and manifest love to all in the Body.

*No man can say that Jesus is the Lord, but by
the Holy Ghost.* 1 Cor. 12: 3.

JESUS is Saviour, but is He Lord? Hast thou
yielded to Him the Lordship? Nothing short of
this will give thee true peace and power. Thou
must be brought to say with the psalmist,
"Other lords beside Thee have had dominion
over me; but by Thee only will I make mention
of thy name."

Jesus must be Lord of thy heart; every affection must be brought under his most wise and
loving control. He must be Lord of thy home,
so that no conversation may be indulged, no
recreation set afoot, no society entertained,
which is inconsistent with his character and
claims. He must be Lord of thy business and its
returns, so that thou shalt live in perpetual
communication with Him, along the lines of
the Heavenly Telephone; and in the use of
all its proceeds He must have the supreme
voice. He must be Lord of thy plans. It is for
Him to say Go, or Come, or Do this. That
was a true message which Ahasuerus sent
through the good Ezra to the Jewish people:
"Whatsoever is commanded by the God of
heaven, let it be done exactly for the house
of the God of heaven." I like that word
exactly.

But this perpetual recognition of the Lordship of Jesus is only possible to those who have
yielded their entire nature to the gracious
influences of the Holy Spirit, who loves to
glorify Christ. Dost thou seek the attitude of
consecration which thus honours thy Lord?
Then let the Holy Spirit work it for thee!
Wouldst thou have it maintained? Let Him
maintain it! And if thou askest thyself, whether
thou hast received the Pentecostal endowment,
be sure that thou hast, if with all thine heart
thou sayest that Jesus Christ is Lord, to the
blory of God the Father. This is the certain
test.

The greatest of these is love.
1 Cor. 13: 13 (R.V.).

WHAT a light must have shone on the
apostle's face as he broke into this exquisite
idyll, this perfect poem of love! The change in
tone and rhythm must have caused his
amanuensis to look suddenly up into his
master's face, and lo! it was as the face of an
angel. Why is love greatest?

BECAUSE IT IS THE CROWN OF THE OTHER TWO,
AND INCLUDES THEM. Faith is the root; hope is
the stem; love the perfect flower. You may
have faith without hope, and hope without

love; but you cannot have love apart from
faith and hope.

BECAUSE IT IS LIKEST GOD. God's nature is not
specially characterized by faith, because there
is no uncertainty with his perfect knowledge;
nor by hope, because there is no future to his
eternal existence. But God is love; and to love
is to resemble Him.

BECAUSE IT WILL IMMEASURABLY OUTLAST THE
OTHER TWO. Human knowledge, at best but
the spellings of babes, will vanish in the perfect
light of heaven. Eloquence will seem like the
lispings of infancy. Prophecies will have no
place, because all the landscape of the future
will be revealed. Faith and hope will be lost in
realization. Love only is for ever.

BECAUSE LOVE BRINGS THE PUREST RAPTURE.
"Where is heaven?" asked a wealthy Christian
of his minister. "I will tell you where it is," was
the quick reply: "if you will go to the store, and
buy £10 worth of provisions and necessaries,
and take them to that poor widow on the hillside, who has three of her children sick. She is
poor, and a member of the Church. Take a
nurse, and someone to cook the food. When
you get there, read the twenty-third Psalm, and
kneel by her side and pray. Then you will find
out where heaven is."

*There are, it may be, so many kinds of voices in
the world.* 1 Cor. 14: 10 (R.V.).

THERE ARE THE VOICES OF NATURE. The deep
bass of the ocean wave booming along the
shore; the crash of the ice; the silver choirs of
the stars; the song of bird, hum of bee, shrill
trumpet of gnat, the rustle of the leaves, the
patter of the rain, the chorus of the hailstones
—how varied, and charming, and musical! No
doubt if we could listen to all these from a
distance we should detect perfect chords.

THERE ARE THE VOICES OF HUMAN LIFE. First,
the mother's; then of the brothers and sisters
of our home (and sad is the lot of the lonely
child which has none); then of the teacher, the
minister, the friend, the lover, not one could
be spared; not one that has not a significance;
not one to whose words we shall not do well to
give heed.

THERE ARE THE VOICES OF OUR DAILY LOT.
Now we are called to experience joy, now
sorrow, now gain, and now loss; now of the
harsh reprimand of disaster; now of the tender
assurances of sunny hours. Behind all these
God is speaking. Listen, therefore, heedfully to
all, and try to acquire the lesson He is longing

to inculcate. What is He saying to you, by your circumstances, at this moment? Is it in tones of pleading, of remonstrance, of blame?

"Where is thy favoured haunt, Eternal Voice,
The region of thy choice,
Where, undisturbed by sin and earth, the soul
Owns thy entire control?
"'Tis then we hear the voice of God within,
Pleading with care and sin:
'Child of my Love,
How have I wearied thee?'"

Christ hath been raised from the dead, the first-fruits of them that are asleep.
1 Cor. 15: 20 (R.V.).

WORDS which are altogether transcendent! How they thrill us and inspire! What memories they recall! How impossible it is not to feel their majesty. Surely no brain nor lip of man had begotten them! They bear the mint-mark of heaven.

On the day that Jesus arose, the firstfruit sheaf of the barley harvest was being waved by the High Priest in the Temple, as the representative of the myriads that stood stacked amid the stubble of the fields. It was the specimen sheaf—representative, pattern, and pledge of all the rest. The risen Christ is the pattern and pledge of what his people will be when their bodies shall be fashioned anew in the likeness of his resurrection.

HE IS PATTERN. His body bore the same general outlines as before; so will theirs. It was recognizable by those who had known and loved Him, even to the tones of his voice; so will it be with theirs. It was the ethereal and pliant instrument of his spirit; so will theirs be. It could no more return to corruption; no more will theirs. It was invulnerable to disease and pain; such an experience awaits them too.

HE IS PLEDGE. He does not stand alone. He is united to us by a myriad indissoluble ties. What the power of God did for Him it will do for us. Those that sleep in Jesus God will bring with Him, and we that are alive and remain shall be caught up. There shall not a hoof be left behind. Not one purchased body of a saint, however obscure or unworthy, shall be excepted from the effect of the voice of the archangel and the trump of God. Meanwhile, in the kindly embrace of Mother Earth, like the seed-germs of a vast harvest, the resurrection principle in the bodies of the saints awaits the resurrection signal.

If any man loveth not the Lord, let him be anathema. 1 Cor. 16: 22 (R.V.).

THIS sentence reminds us of the saintly Samuel Rutherford, of whose Letters the holy Richard Baxter said: "Hold off the Bible, such a book the world never saw." And the late revered and beloved C. H. Spurgeon said of them: "When we are dead and gone, let the world know that Spurgeon held Rutherford's Letters to be the nearest thing to inspiration which can be found in all the writings of mere men."

Take this extract, because it indicates how you may come to love the Lord Jesus as he did:

"Strive to make prayer, and reading, and holy company, and holy conference, your delight; and when delight cometh in, you shall, by little and little, find the sweetness of Christ, till at length your soul be over head and ears in Christ's sweetness. Then shall you be taken up to the top of the mountain with the Lord, to know the delights of spiritual love, and the glory and excellency of a seen, revealed, felt, and embraced Christ; and then you shall not be able to loose yourself off from Christ, and to bind your soul to old lovers; then, and never till then, are all the paces, motions, and wheels of your soul in a right tune and in a spiritual temper.

"But if this world and the lusts thereof be your delight, I know not what Christ can make of you; you cannot be metal for a vessel of glory and mercy. My desire is that my Lord would give me broader and deeper thoughts to feed myself with wondering at his love. I would I could weigh it, but I have no balance for it. When I have worn my tongue to the stump in praising Christ, I have done nothing to Him. What remaineth then, but that my debt to the love of Christ lie unpaid for all eternity!"

2 Corinthians

Who comforteth us in all our affliction, that we may be able to comfort. 2 Cor. 1: 4 (R.V.).
CHILD of God, think it not strange concerning the fiery trial which tries thee, as though some strange thing had happened. Rejoice, inasmuch as it is a sure sign that thou art on the right track. All the saints have gone by this road, notably the writer of this Epistle.

Its keyword is affliction, because written amid afflictions so great that the apostle despaired of life. It is steeped in affliction, as a handkerchief with the flowing blood of a fresh wound. But in this passage the apostle has built himself a little chamber of comfort, the stones of which were quarried from the pit of his own sorrow. He blesses God, who had led him into affliction to teach him the art of comfort, that by observing how God comforted, he might become proficient in the art.

The world is full of comfortless hearts—orphan children crying in the night. Our God pities them, and would comfort them through thee. But ere thou undertake this lofty ministry thou must be trained, and thou must therefore pass through the very trials that they are exposed to. Now watch how God comforts thee. Keep a diary, if thou wilt, of his procedure. Ponder in thine heart the length of each splint, the folds of each bandage, the ministration of each opiate, cordial, or drug. This will have a twofold effect, in turning thy thoughts from thy miseries to thy mercies, and in taking away the sense of useless and aimless existence.

There is evidently scope for comfort even in heaven, for it is said that God will wipe away tears from all faces. Oh thou that art sorrowful even unto death, be sure that some day the Comforter will get the victory over thy sorest griefs.

We are a sweet savour of Christ unto God.
2 Cor. 2: 15 (R.V.).
THE idea is borrowed from an ancient Roman triumph, which to the eyes of the world of that day was the most glorious spectacle which the imagination could conceive. The apostle compares himself first to one of the prisoners led in long chains behind the conqueror's chariot; then to a servant bearing incense; and lastly to the incense itself that rose all along the line of the procession.

Nothing touches the sense more quickly than sweet odours, unless it be noxious ones; and they almost instantly recall some scene of the past with which they were indissolubly associated. For instance, the scent of new-mown hay will carry us off to merry scenes in the far away days of childhood. Thus the apostle wished that his life might be a sweet perfume, floating on the air, reminding men, and above all reminding God, of Christ. It was as though he said, "I desire so to live that I may perpetually remind God of the obedience, sacrifice, and devotion of the Lord Jesus, so that my words and deeds may recall to His heart similar ones in the earthly life of Jesus."

A sweet savour of Christ! It does not consist so much in what we do, but in our manner of doing it; not so much in our words or deeds, as in an indefinable sweetness, tenderness, courtesy, unselfishness, and desire to please others to their edification. It is the breath and fragrance of a life hidden with Christ in God, and deriving its aroma from fellowship with Him. Wrap the habits of your soul in the sweet lavender of your Lord's character.

The secret of abounding joy in self-sacrifice is the happy consciousness, such as Enoch had, that we have pleased God. To have this is to secure deliverance from self-consciousness.

Beholding as in a glass (A.V.). *Reflecting as a mirror* (R.V.). 2 Cor. 3: 18.
MOSES veiled his face, and the veiled lawgiver was characteristic of the dispensation he inaugurated. It was a partial revelation, gleaming through a vail, expressing truths in rites and types and symbols. But Christ has torn away the vail, removed the fences of the mount of vision, and revealed to babes the deepest secrets of God's heart. The apostle's phrase is characteristic of Christianity, "Behold, I show you (i.e., unveil) a mystery."

THE OBJECT OF VISIONS. "The glory of the Lord." Concerning which we may accept the statement of a trustworthy commentator, that the reference is not to the incomprehensible, incommunicable lustre of the absolute divine perfectness; but to that glory which, as John says, tabernacled in the Lord Jesus Christ, full of grace and truth—the glory of loving, pitying words and lovely deeds; the glory of faultless and complete manhood; the glory of God in the face of Jesus Christ.

THE NATURE OF THE VISION. "We behold." It is true that we cannot see. "Whom, not having seen, ye love." But it is also true that the heart has eyes, by which it looks away unto Jesus. "Seeing is believing" is a familiar proverb among men; but "believing is seeing" is a true aphorism of the spirit which clings to the Lord by its faith and love.

THE EFFECT OF THE VISION. First, we reflect. The beauty of his face glancing on ours will be mirrored, as a man's eye will contain a tiny miniature picture of what he is beholding. Then we shall be changed. If you try to represent Jesus in your character and behaviour, you will become transfigured into his likeness. Love makes like. Imitation produces assimilation. Reflect and resemble.

While we look . . . at the things which are not seen. 2 Cor. 4: 18.
WE are here bidden to look through the things which are seen; to consider them as the glass window through which we pass to that which is behind and beyond. You do not waste your time by admiring the frame or casket of some rare jewel, but penetrate to the jewel itself; so, day by day, look through the material and transient to the eternal purpose, the divine idea, the deep that lieth under.

"All visible things," said Carlyle, "are emblems. What thou seest is not there on its own account; strictly speaking, is not there at all. Matter exists only spiritually, and to represent some idea and body it forth." This is an exaggerated way of stating the old saying, "Everything that is, is double." Both, however, illustrate the affirmation of the text.

Look for God's thought in all the incidents, circumstances, and objects of your daily life. Do not stop at the outward; penetrate to the inward and eternal. Beneath that bitter physical suffering there are stores of divine fortitude and grace. Beneath that trying dispensation there are celestial compensations. Beneath those sweet family ties there are suggestions of love and friendship, which can never grow old or pass away. Beneath the letter of Scripture is the spirit; beneath the ordinance, oneness with the loving Saviour; beneath the world of nature, the processes of the eternal husbandry.

When such is the attitude of the soul, afflictions, that might otherwise have weighed as heavy, become light; and those that drag through long and tedious years, seem but for a moment. And without exception, they all go to produce that receptivity of character that can contain the far more exceeding and eternal weight of glory.

All things are of God. 2 Cor. 5: 18.
OF here is equivalent to out of. All the precious contents of the Gospel have emanated from the heart of God; so that we may say with the psalmist, "All my springs are in Thee."

That we have a building, a house not made with hands, eternal in the heavens, to which to go when the earthly house of this tabernacle is broken up; that it is possible for the mortal to be swallowed up in the descending glory of the Second Advent; that we have received the Spirit as earnest of our future glory; that we shall be one day at home with the Lord; that One died for all that the dominion of the self-life should be destroyed, and that they should henceforth live, not to themselves, but to Him; that it is possible to become a new creation in Christ; that God is already reconciled to the world of men, and is only waiting for them to be reconciled to Him; that He hath committed to men the ministry of reconciliation, and commissioned them to be his ambassadors; that it is possible for us to be the righteousness of God in Jesus—all these things have issued from his heart of love.

Oh for a soul as wide as the utmost circle of the highest heaven that containeth all, to contain his love! Oh, world's wonder! Oh, what a sight to be up in heaven, in "the fair orchard of Paradise!" But the very greatness of his provisions will make our doom the greater, if we refuse or ignore them. The men who made light of the king's invitation had their city burnt. This is the terror of the Lord; and our duty is to beseech men not to put away the reconciliation which God offers. Let the "all things" of your life be of God's direction, impulse, and inspiration.

As deceivers, and yet true. 2 Cor. 6: 8.
THIS is the first clause in one of the most

wonderful series of paradoxes in all literature. Let us class together these different conceptions of the apostle, as held by those who judged him by his outward and inward life respectively.

JUDGED FROM THE VIEW-POINT OF THIS AGE he was a deceiver, intent on some purpose of his own, misleading and hoodwinking his converts. In the annals of this world he was utterly unknown, and there was no attempt to chronicle his doings or record his words. His life seemed to the gay and worldy a prolonged death, whilst to his close associates and friends it was a perpetual chastening. Very sorrowful, very poor, very destitute—such was his appearance as seen from the outside. And many must have turned from it and felt thankful that the lines had fallen to them in pleasanter places.

JUDGED FROM THE VIEW-POINT OF ETERNITY he was known to be true, and building the temple of truth. By every new dying to the world around, his inner life was being recruited, deepened, and purified. His sufferings were chastening and pruning him, that he might bear more fruit. Amid his outward griefs he was ever drinking at the wells of purest joy; amid his poverty he was enriching the world with the most precious wealth; amid his utter destitution he was handling the imperishable riches of eternity.

The monks of Chartreux, when they first erected their monastery, made all their windows look in on the small inner court, but had none commanding the sublime mountains and glaciers around. So, too, many lives are always contemplating the trifles of earth's court-yard! Oh that such would take into their view the unseen and eternal!

Let us cleanse ourselves from all defilement.
2 Cor. 7: 1 (R.V.).

THE closing paragraph of the previous chapter tells us what this defilement stands for; and in the enumeration note the increasing bonds of approximation which each word indicates. An unequal yoke in ill-matched intercourse with unbelievers leads to fellowship, and this to communion, and this again to concord, and this to partnership; whilst the culmination of the entire series is agreement, and the yielding up of the body for the possession and indwelling of idols. Let us beware of the beginning of this awful approximation. It is impossible to stand still; and they who think lightly of marrying an unbeliever may in the end hear words like those which watchers heard spoken in the doomed temple on the night before it fell into the hands of Titus. "There was, as it were, the rushing of wings, and voices were heard saying, Let us depart."

There is not only defilement of the flesh, but of the spirit. It is not enough to avoid the gross sins of the outward life. Those of the inner temple and disposition are equally abhorrent to the holiness of God. We must come out and be separate from the latter as well as the former, or we shall never realize what God means when He promises to receive us, and to be a Father to us.

The word cleanse is very decisive in the Greek. It calls for sudden, decisive action; and if you answer, that sin is too closely interwoven with your nature to be thus summarily disposed of, remember that God demands our will only. Directly we are perfectly willing and eager, He steps in and does all the rest. At unknown depths the Spirit of God is at work within us; let us work out what He works in, that we may be welcomed to God's heart.

See that ye abound in this grace also.
2 Cor. 8: 7.

THE grace of liberality is as much a gift of God as faith, or utterance, or knowledge, or love. This is implied in our text, and distinctly stated in the first verse, where the apostle says that he desires to make known the grace of God, which had been given to the churches of Macedonia, so that they were able in their deep poverty to abound in riches of liberality. In the ninth verse we learn that this grace first dwelt in our blessed Lord, who, though He was rich, for our sakes became poor, that we through his poverty might become rich. If yours is a grudging, niggard nature, be sure to appropriate the royal nature of the Lord Jesus, that it may fill and possess you.

Probably there is no greater test of our true religion than our behaviour in giving. How few, comparatively, give in proportion to their income! How few give systematically! How few have learnt the joy and luxury of giving, so that they abound therein!

This arises partly because they do not realize that they are stewards of God's property, and that He expects them to devote all they own to Him, keeping back only a necessary percentage for themselves and their families, as a steward might who was farming an estate for his absent master. And partly it arises from mistrust of

God, and the fear that some day there may be a sudden falling off of supplies. Oh that each reader would consider that all is God's, and begin by always giving a certain proportion of every pound, so as to be sure of not robbing God of his own. Pray day and night that you may abound in this grace also; and then, in faith that God is answering your prayer, begin to do violence to your churlish, niggard nature. What though it protest—Give!

He that supplieth seed to the sower and bread for food. 2 Cor. 9: 10 (R.V.).

IN every harvest there is a twofold object. First, the supply of seed for the next autumn's sowing, and then of food for those that sow or reap; so in the spiritual sphere God will not fail either sowers or reapers.

ALL SOWERS MUST EAT. However much wheat has passed through the sower's hands, he is not fed thereby. At night he returns hungry to his home. So we, who are engaged in the work of God, cannot live on what we do for the world around. After the most fruitful day of service, we need to take our Bibles and feed our famished souls by meditation and prayer. We must not mistake the glow and exhilaration of the sanctuary for nourishment. They are rather a stimulant. Therefore we may expect God to increase the fruits of our righteousness. Shall Boaz cause handfuls on purpose to fall for Ruth, and shall not God supply our need? Will the Father not provide bread to those who are engaged in tilling his fields?

ALL EATERS SHOULD SOW. It would never do for the farmer to live on all the produce of his fields. He must sow a certain proportion of his grain. And nothing is more foreign to the genius of true religion than to be always nursing and ministering to oneself; eating the fine wheat of the Gospel, but not sowing it in other hearts; consuming the consolations of the divine Spirit, but not endeavouring to pass them on to others. Oh ye who have eaten bountifully, sow bountifully; else ye shall suffer the results of spiritual repletion and indigestion. And note this precious assurance, that God will supply seed for daily and weekly sowing for the congregation and the class; and that He will multiply it when sown.

Bringing every thought into . . . the obedience of Christ. 2 Cor. 10: 5.

THE apostle is planning a campaign; his words glow with the fire of military enthusiasm: but, as one has eloquently said, the weapons of his warfare are not carnal; the standard under which he fights is a more sacred sign than that of Cæsar; the territory he invades is more difficult of conquest than any which kept the conquerors of the world at bay. He sees rising before him the lofty fortresses of hostile error; they must be reduced or razed. Every mountain fastness to which the enemy can retreat must be scaled and destroyed; and every thought of the soul, which is hostile to the authority of the divine Truth, must become a prisoner of war in the camp of Christ.

Be sure to distinguish between the proper use of the intellect by the man who recognizes its necessary limitations and uses it in the humble and reverent inquiry after truth, and that undue exaltation of the intellect, which sets itself on high as the ultimate judge of truth, or which roams wildly, unheeding the divine control. There are vain thoughts, sensual thoughts, cynical and self-reliant thoughts, sceptical thoughts, proud thoughts, wandering and wayward thoughts; but the apostle says that, however strongly they fortify themselves against Christ, they should and must be brought into captivity. Paul once thought he ought to do many things contrary to Jesus, but became his humble disciple.

The intellect has its province, but faith has hers; and while the intellect tends to exalt man, faith humbles him and leads him captive in the chains of love. We must come with absolute obedience to Christ, that every vail may be torn away, and whatever blurs the clear surface of the mirroring intellect may be removed.

In perils. 2 Cor. 11: 26.

THIS enumeration was made before the imprisonment at Cæsarea and the voyage to Rome. How little do we know of Paul's life, after all! Every victory was hardly fought for and dearly won.

THESE SUFFERINGS ATTEST THE TRUTH OF CHRISTIANITY. Whenever a doubt crosses your mind with respect to the Resurrection, or any other Gospel fact, say to yourself, Paul knew everything that could be said against it. He was in the secrets of the Sanhedrim; and if he believed it, we certainly may. And he had nothing to gain by his witness. It was to his great loss, and the shattering of his position in Israel, that he became a Christian.

THESE SUFFERINGS APPROVE THE GENUINENESS OF PAUL'S CHARACTER. This age is athirst for biography; it loves to read the story of its great men; but sometimes we ask whether they are just as real and good and pure as we have been led to hope. There is one life at least about which no such inquiry can be raised. The severest tests may be applied to this diamond, but it shines only the brighter —a very Koh-i-noor, "A mountain of light."

THESE SUFFERINGS APPROVE THE POWER OF THE HOLY SPIRIT. Such love had He inspired toward the Blessed Lord in the heart of the apostle, that he counted the loss of all things gain, and the uncounted sorrows of his lot as light and but for a moment, if only he might win Christ, and know Him, and be found in Him. You cannot explain a life like this apart from the mighty power and indwelling of the Holy Spirit. What a puzzle the Christian presents to the world! I remember how a poor child of fashion and sin kept asking me once, "What do you Christians get?" It was quite impossible to explain.

When I am weak, then am I strong.
2 Cor. 12: 10.

WE need not discuss the nature of Paul's thorn in the flesh. It is enough that he calls it "a stake," as though he had been impaled. It must have, therefore, been very painful. It must also have been physical, because he could not have prayed thrice for the removal of a moral taint, and been refused. It came from Satan, permitted by God, as in the case of Job, to buffet his servant. It is not unlikely that he suffered from weak eyes, or some distressing form of ophthalmia; hence the eagerness of the Galatian converts to give him their eyes (see Gal. 4: 15).

God does not take away our thorns, but He communicates sufficient grace. He always answers prayer, though not as we expect. Let the music of these tender words soar unto thee, poor sufferer! "My grace is sufficient even for thee." Sufficient when friends forsake, and foes pursue; sufficient to make thee strong against an infuriated crowd and a tyrannical judge; sufficient for excessive physical exertion and spiritual conflict; sufficient to enable thee to do as much work, and even more, than if health and vigour were not impaired, because the very weakness of our nature is the chosen condition under which God will manifest the strength of his.

Do not sit down before that mistaken marriage, that uncongenial business, that physical weakness, as though thy life must be a failure; but take in large reinforcements of that divine grace which is given to the weak and to those who have no might. It is clear that Paul had reached such a condition, that it was a matter of deep congratulation to him to be deficient in much that men hold dear, and to have what most men dread. He rejoiced in all that diminished creature-might and strengthened his hold on God.

The Communion of the Holy Ghost.
2 Cor. 13: 14.

HOW often these words are uttered without any real appreciation of their depth of meaning! The word communion signifies having in common. It is used of our fellowship with one another (1 Cor. 10: 16) and with God (1 John 1: 3). The bond of such fellowship is always through the Holy Spirit. As the ocean unites all lands, and is the medium through which they are able to exchange commodities, so does the blessed Spirit unite the Persons of the Blessed Trinity to each other, and us to them, and secures that oneness for which our Saviour prayed.

How wonderful it is to have the privilege of this divine fellowship! That we need never be alone again; that we can at any moment turn to Him for advice and direction; that we may draw on his resources for the supply of every need; that it is impossible to exhaust or even tax his willingness to counsel and succour; that there is no kind of service or suffering into which He is not prepared to enter with us! Surely, if we would but give ourselves time to realize this marvellous fact, there would be no room for the despondency which at times threatens to deprive us of heart and hope.

Of course, we must be very careful of the tender sensibilities and holy disposition of our divine Confederate. We cannot ruthlessly grieve Him by our harshness or impurity at one moment, and turn to Him for his succour and direction at the next. Such divine union as lies within our reach certainly demands on our part watchfulness, a tender conscience, a yielded and pliant will, a heart which has no other love, no affection nor idol inconsistent with the Spirit's fellowship.

Galatians

It was the good pleasure of God . . . to reveal his Son to me. Gal. 1: 15, 16 (R.V.).

IF you have truly believed in the Son of God, it is certain that He, by the Spirit, has taken up his abode in your heart. But perhaps He is hidden in the deeps of your nature, as the young Joash in the heart of the Temple. He is, therefore, unable to exert that influence on your inner thought and outward life that He should. Is it not befitting that you should ask the Father to reveal his Son in you? He has been revealed to you as the divine Substitute, but not in you as the source and spring of holiness.

Beneath the body with its physical existence, and the mind with the play of intellect, lies the spirit of man, like the most holy place in the Temple of old. That is the shrine in which the Shechinah of Christ's presence shines, and in which we can hold fellowship with Him face to face. Alas, that so heavy a vail of unbelief, of absorption in the world around us, of inattention, hangs between Him and us! Would that the strong hands which rent the vail in twain when our Saviour died would rend in twain all that deprives us of this inspiring and most helpful vision of the Son, so that we might anticipate the eternal years!

But such revelations are only given that we may better help others. Not for selfish enjoyment, but for ministering help. Hence the apostle says, "that I might preach Him among the Gentiles." Be pleased, O Father, to give us that revelation, that we may speak as those who have seen the great sight, and need no further conference with flesh and blood! Then, like the apostles of old, we shall go forth among men, saying, "We cannot but speak the things which we have seen and heard."

I have been crucified with Christ; yet I live. Gal. 2: 20 (R.V.).

CLEARLY Paul intends us to understand that the life of which he was the centre had been nailed to the Saviour's cross, and that Christ's life had been substituted for it. Some have spoken of this real life of Christ in the soul as being mystical and untrue; but there can be no kind of doubt that it is the constant affirmation of the New Testament.

DEATH, THE GATE OF LIFE. It is obviously so in nature. Once each year nature lies down in its grave, sleeps in unbroken repose, and steps forth again with the glory of a freshly-renewed beauty. Often the overclouding of one faculty has been the signal of the quickening of all the rest. The blind Milton becomes the author of the *Paradise Lost*. Death of a twin-soul will often give to the survivor a new impulse towards a spiritual and transfigured affection. We cannot be possessed by the self-life and the Christ-life at the same moment. and wherever, by God's grace, we erect the cross and assign our own life to its nails, the Spirit of Christ will breathe life and power.

IN THE FLESH, BUT NOT AFTER THE FLESH. We live our life in the flesh, as aforetime, doing the duties of our ordinary existence with careful precision; but we are no longer controlled by the selfish principle which too long dominated us. The attraction of earth is overborne by the mighty drawing of the eternal and unseen. The rush of the whirlpool is unable to prevail over the throb of the steam-propeller within.

NOT I. Yet loved and ransomed by the Son of God, each of us is distinct to his loving eye. He does not bulk us all together as a mass, but singles each out for the gift of Himself, his prayers, his blood, his ceaseless thought.

That we might receive the promise of the Spirit through faith. Gal. 3: 14.

"THE promise of the Spirit" is the invariable term for the special Pentecostal gift; and this is to be equally received by faith as the forgiveness of sins and eternal life. To me this text once came as a perfect revelation. It was the clue to unravel perplexity, the point around which truth held long in solution suddenly crystallized. Before this verse spoke to my heart it had been my constant endeavour to feel the Spirit's presence as the sign of my having received; but now it became clear that one might receive by simple faith God's very richest communications, even though the emotion tarried long.

The stages have been thus specified:

THERE IS SUCH A BLESSING. Yes; there can be no doubt of this; for it pleased the Father that the fulness of the Holy Spirit should dwell in Jesus, that He might communicate Him to each member of his Church.

IT IS FOR ME. At Pentecost Peter said, This promise is for as many as the Lord our God shall call.

I HAVE NOT RECEIVED. It is very important to realize what your standing is. Paul's first inquiry of the Ephesians was to ascertain this.

I WOULD GIVE ANYTHING IF IT MIGHT BE MINE. Because of the life, and love, and power it would bring into your life, and the immense increase of power over others, there is no sacrifice you should be unwilling to make.

I DO NOW IN HUMBLE FAITH RECEIVE. There may be no coronet of flame, nor rush of wind, nor flash of joy; but if we have put ourselves in the right attitude towards God, and opened our hearts to receive—He who taught us to hunger and thirst must have bestowed.

Until Christ be formed in you. Gal. 4: 19.
CHRIST is in us, if we truly believe in Him, as the sap in the vine, the air in the lung, the steam in the engine; but He may not be formed in us.

Is it not possible that the indefinable sensation of joy and pain, of yearning and unfulfilled desire, are all attributable to this deep-seated process? Christ is being formed within our hearts, dispossessing the old evil self-life, and taking its place.

"O Jesus Christ, grow Thou in me,
  And all things else recede;
My heart be daily nearer Thee,
  From sin be daily freed.
"Make this poor self grow less and less,
  Be thou my life and aim;
Oh, make me daily through thy grace
  More meet to bear thy name."

The mention of travail in this connection suggests that this in-forming of Christ does not take place apart from suffering. And probably it is at times when we are in a furnace of pain that the Christ in us grows most quickly. "When my pain became unbearable," says one, "I became conscious that there is a part of our being which no physical pain, and no mental anguish, can disturb. And there came to me such a sense of God—so enfolding, so assuring, so satisfying—that I could as well doubt the shining of the sun." The Comforter

had come—Christ was being formed within.

In the egg, when first laid, there is a tiny point of life amid the thick, viscous fluid; but this gradually increases, while the other diminishes, and at last there is hardly a trace of this left, and the chick is formed, the egg-shell is broken, and the tiny feathered thing steps forth. The chick is formed in the shell.

Ye may not do the things that ye would.
Gal. 5: 17 (R.V.).
THIS is a notable rendering of the R.V., which throws a flood of light on the entire passage. The A.V. has it, "Ye cannot do"; it is more correct to say, "Ye may not do." It is always possible to go back and to fall under the tyrannous power of the evil self principle, the flesh, either in its more debased or refined form; but as long as we are led by the Spirit, live in the Spirit, and walk in the Spirit, He energizes against the flesh, keeping it in the place of death, and allowing the life of Christ to work freely.

In Christian ethics there must be, first, a definite willingness to surrender ourselves to his death. Secondly, there must be a perpetual yielding to the indwelling grace and power of the Holy Spirit. He will deal with the self-life in the deep abysses of your nature. When the antiseptic influence of carbolic acid is in the atmosphere it counteracts the microbes of disease, so that they cannot do as otherwise they would in infecting healthy bodies with disease. An eminent surgeon told me the other day that he was accustomed to boil his operating instruments in antiseptic mixture, that they might not carry microbes to the open wounds. Oh that those of us who are used as instruments by God would take heed!

When the baleful effect of the self-life is arrested, the fruits of the Spirit appear naturally and easily. Note the distinction between work, in which there is effort, and fruit, which swells so imperceptibly and silently on the branch—pressed out from within. Each of these fruits is a variation of the first, which is love. Joy is love on wings; peace, with the wings folded; long-suffering, love in the sick-room; goodness, in business; meekness, in society; self-control, in the regimen of habit for the sake of others.

Let no man trouble me: for I bear branded on my body the marks of Jesus. Gal. 6: 17 (R.V.).
AS a slave was branded with the initials of his

owner, so was Paul. It was his pride to count himself the slave of Jesus, and to regard the scars which had eaten into his flesh as the brand-marks of his Master. Why should men try to deflect him from his course, when he was so absolutely implicated in the service of the one great Master, Christ?

THE SERVICE OF JESUS. It is founded in his blood, by which He purchased us to be his own; but it must be accepted by the glad consent of the will. We must awake each morning as his property, take his commands for the day, and lie down at night, only satisfied when He has said, Well done! We must own to ourselves that we have no personal rights, no locked rooms, no kind of reserve.

THE BRAND OF JESUS. The dislike which our religion engenders; the losses to which principle compels; the averted look, the distant manner on the part of those who could not make enough of us when we lived the life of the world—these are as much his brand, the brand of his Cross, as the weals of recent scourgings on the apostle's flesh.

THE PEACE OF JESUS. "Let no man trouble me." My heart has cast her anchor; my soul her foundation; my life her aim. If He is satisfied, I am content, though the world is in arms. If He is with me, I have good company, though all forsake. The Master said, "Trouble her not."

"Lord, as thy temple's portals close
    Behind the outward-parting throng,
So shut my spirit in repose;
    So bind it here, thy flock among:
The fickle wanderer else will stray
Back to the world's wide-parted way."

W. E. Gladstone.

Ephesians

Sealed with the Holy Spirit of promise.
Eph. 1: 13 (R.V.).

POSSESSED. The saints have been purchased at great cost by the precious blood of the Son of God. Not only their spirits, but their bodies, have been bought with an infinite expenditure. Is it not a wonderful thought that God should have thought it worth his while to expend so much on us! But since He has done it, we cannot suppose that He will not make all He can of us! He will bring his estate under cultivation; there will be no corner of it that will not yield Him produce.

TO BE REDEEMED. Our bodies are owned by God, but they are not yet entirely redeemed. And if we should die before the Lord's advent, they will return to their mother earth, possessed but not redeemed. Hence the apostle says that we are waiting for our adoption—to wit, the redemption of our body (Rom. 8: 23). We are under the sentence of corruption for Adam's sin; but we are to be redeemed.

SEALED. In Ezekiel's day a mark was set on the foreheads of the men that sighed and cried for sin (Ezek. 9: 4); and in the Apocalypse we read of the sealing of God's servants (Rev. 7: 2, 3). For sealing there are needed the softened wax; the imprint of the beloved face; the steady pressure. Would that the Spirit might impress the face of our dear Lord on our softened hearts, that they may keep it for evermore!

THIS SEALING IS AN EARNEST OF OUR INHERITANCE. The eternal future is all unknown, yet we may guess at it, because the work of the Spirit within us is the first fruits—the grapes of Eshcol, showing what the vintage will be; the earnest-penny, which is the pledge as well as part of the entire payment; the first streak of the coming day.

We are his workmanship. Eph. 2: 10.

THE Greek word might be literally rendered his poem. As the metre varies in the poems of a laureate, so does the course of one life differ from another; but God has a thought, a plan, a purpose for each. This lyric, that heroic, another dramatic.

CREATED FOR GOOD WORKS. How carefully the apostle defines the true position of works in the divine life. In the foregoing verses he insists that we are not saved by our works, that none should boast; but, as though to meet the objection that his system was inconsistent with holy living, he affirms that the whole intention of God was that we should manifest our new life in Christ by the holy life in which it fruits. We were created in Him unto good works. Whatever good works may be demanded of you, dare to believe that you were created in Christ Jesus to do them. There is a perfect adjustment between the two.

THE GOOD WORKS PREPARED. Our new creation in Christ Jesus and the preparation of our life-work are due to the same mind. God who made us has prepared our path for us. It may lie up hill or down dale; may be lined with grassy sward or be full of jagged stones; may be short with the years of childhood or long with those of old age; may consist in lying on a couch to suffer or in strenuous activity—but every yard has been prepared.

OUR DAILY WALK. We have not to cut or make our path; but simply to follow it, one step at a time. And when the heart or flesh fails, when the way seems too difficult, or the door too strait—we must look always unto Jesus, who has gone along the same track, asking that his righteousness may go before us, and set us in the way of his steps (Psa. 85: 13, R.V.).

To make all men see what is the dispensation of the mystery. Eph. 3: 9 (R.V.).

THIS chapter is parallel with Col. 2. To the stewardship of the apostle Paul two mysteries were entrusted, with the intention that he should unravel and explain them to our race.

THE MYSTERY. A mystery is a hidden secret. The word does not imply that there is no solution, but that the solution has not yet been communicated. God has many secrets, which unfold as the ages are ripe for them, but not before. This secret, which was hid in the divine heart from all ages, was that the Gentiles are on an equality with the Jews in the Church. Under the old covenant they were alienated from the commonwealth of Israel, and strangers from the covenants of promise; but under the new they are fellow-heirs, fellow-members, and fellow-partakers of the blessings of the Gospel.

THE STEWARDSHIP OF THE MYSTERY. The apostle felt that whatever had been communicated to him was not for himself alone, but for all his fellow-disciples. Hence he was ever accounting himself a steward of the mysteries of God (1 Cor. 4: 1). This is the clue, also, to his assertion that he was a debtor to all men for Christ's sake. What was given him was on deposit for others. See to it that you count nothing you possess or know as your own; look on all as a sacred trust.

THE EXERCISE OF HIS STEWARDSHIP. "To preach unto the Gentiles the unsearchable riches of Christ, and to make all men know." It is not enough to proclaim, as a herald might; we must stay with the dull of wit and slow of thought, elaborating, explaining, and insisting, till we have made them see what a Saviour Jesus is, and how rich the soul may be that uses his unsearchable wealth.

He also descended first into the lower parts of the earth. Eph. 4: 9.

WE fill a cup or bucket from the bottom upwards. And Jesus obeyed a universal law when, in his desire to fill all things, He first descended into the place of a servant, the death of the cross, the lowly bed of a borrowed grave, and thence into the abyss of Hades. "He descended into hell," by which we mean, of course, Hades, the place of disembodied spirits. If we would sit with Him in the heavenlies, we too must be subordinated to the same law. We must also descend.

THERE IS THE LOW PLACE OF CONTRITION FOR SIN. We must go thither; lying in the dust before God; placing the leper's covering on our lips; smiting on our breasts. Be willing that the Spirit of God should reveal all the selfishness, the subtlety, the impurity, of your heart. Let your cry ever be that God would not spare your eyes and heart from the pain of knowing what you are in his sight. From this low place you shall ascend to the bosom of God. "Blessed are they that mourn."

THERE IS THE LOW PLACE OF HUMILITY. Be willing to take the lowest place with no mock modesty, but because you have learnt to esteem others better than yourself. Humble yourself under the mighty hand of God. Be willing to perform lowly deeds of service to your brethren and sisters in Christ. Reckon that you have not attained. Ascribe all that is good in you to the grace of God. God giveth peace to the humble; He raiseth up the poor out of the dust.

THERE IS THE LOW PLACE OF DEATH. The more we are delivered to the death of Jesus the more will his life be manifested in our mortal flesh. Life through death, ascent after descent, the glory after the cross of shame. "If it die, it bringeth forth much fruit."

Be ye therefore imitators of God, as beloved children. Eph. 5: 1 (R.V.).

CHILDREN mostly resemble their father.

There is often an unmistakable family likeness, which compels the most casual observer to exclaim, "The very image of his father." Oh that in each of us there might be that which would make men think of God!

PUT AWAY YOUR FORMER MANNER OF LIFE (4: 22). The old man stands for the collection of habits, sayings, and doings which characterized our unregenerate days. The apostle says that they are to be put away suddenly, instantly. Evidently this is possible, or such a command would not be issued. Men speak of a gradual reformation, and advise the piecemeal discontinuance of evil. God, on the contrary, bids us treat the evil past as a company of soldiers would bandits and outlaws. There is the greater reason for this, as the old man waxeth corrupt. Even Martha could not bear the opening of her brother's vault.

BE RENEWED IN THE SPIRIT OF YOUR MIND (4: 23). We are reminded of Rom. 12: 2. The mind needs to be brought into daily, hourly contact with God's thoughts, as contained in Scripture, that it may be renewed; else our constant association with the men and women of the world, their maxims and practices, will inevitably and sorrowfully deteriorate it. The only source of daily renewal is fellowship with God.

PUT ON THE NEW MAN. Of this the apostle affirms that it is according to God, and has been created. Our Lord created this beauteous dress when He rose from the dead. The day of resurrection was one of creation. All the habits and dispositions of a holy, godlike life have been prepared for us in Him, and await our appropriation; and as they are according to God, so soon as we put them on we shall become imitators of God as dear children.

Praying at all seasons in the Spirit.
Eph. 6: 18.

THE dying Monod regretted he had not prayed more. We should pray at all seasons. Prayer is never out of place. There is no conceivable circumstance in life where it would be inappropriate to pray. At the wedding or the funeral; as we engage in work or finish it; whether the wind blow from the cold north or the balmy south—it is wise and right to pray. "Prayer and provender," the old proverb says, "hinder no man."

We should pray in the Spirit. Reversing the order of the words, but bringing in their true meaning, we might say, "Let the Spirit pray in the soul." It is well in prayer to wait until the scum of our own choice and desire has passed off, that the yearnings of the Holy Spirit may arise and manifest themselves. We need to be in the Spirit, not only on the Lord's Day, but always, that He may be mightily in us, teaching us the will of God.

We should pray unselfishly. "For all saints," said the apostle, "and for me."

We should watch. Do not give runaway knocks. Stand at God's door till it opens. Be on the alert. Wait on the watch-tower. Many of God's ships pass in the night, and many of his gifts arrive at the wharf when those to whom they were consigned are asleep or gone.

We should persevere. God keeps us waiting that He may test and humble us, and know what is in our heart. Delays are his winnowing fan, discriminating between the chaff and the wheat. What we asked so vehemently we did not ask wisely. When we pray according to his heart, He graciously sustains us. Persevere; you do not know how near you are to the blessing you have sought for years.

Philippians

To you it hath been granted in the behalf of Christ . . . to suffer. Phil. 1: 29 (R.V.).

THE child of God is often called to suffer, because nothing will convince onlookers of the reality and power of true religion as suffering will do, when it is borne with Christian resignation and fortitude. And how great the compensations are!

He can keep in such perfect peace. He can make lonely times, when no one is near the couch, to be so full of sweet fellowship and communion. He can put such strong, soft hands under the tired limbs, resting them. He can give refreshment to the spirit when the body is deprived of sleep.

Everyone cannot be trusted with suffering. All could not stand the fiery ordeal. They would speak rashly and complainingly. So the Master has to select with careful scrutiny the branches which can stand the knife; the jewels which can bear the wheel. It is given to some to preach, to others to work, but to others to suffer. Accept it as a gift from his hand. Look up and take each throb of pain, each hour of agony, as his gift. Dare to thank Him for it. Look inside the envelope of pain for the message it enfolds. It is a rough packing-case, but there is treasure in it.

And can you not minister to other sufferers? Can you not dictate letters of comfort, or pray for them, or devise little alleviations and surprises for those who have not what you have? Suffering is on Christ's behalf; it must, then, be intended as part of that great ministry for the world in which He, with his saints, is engaged. There is a sense in which all suffering, borne in the spirit of Calvary, helps men, not in the way of atonement or propitiation, of course, but by the exhibition of the power of God's grace in the sufferer.

He was full of heaviness, because that ye had heard that he had been sick. Phil. 2: 26.
SOME have identified Epaphroditus here with Epaphras in the Epistle to the Colossians. Here he is represented as sorrowful, even to agony, because his friends had heard of his illness, and he would have wished that no one should be burdened on his account. But in the other epistle he is represented as always striving for the saints in prayer.

It is very beautiful to discover his unwillingness to have his sickness published. When we are in trouble it is best not to speak much of it, save to God. "Only inexperienced sufferers are voluble; those familiar with the secrets of anguish are silent." Let us anoint the head, and wash the face, that we may not appear unto men to fast, but to the Father who is in secret; and our Father who seeth in secret will Himself reward openly. The Comforter will draw near, will whisper his own consolations, and amid much sorrow we shall be calm and strong.

But with Epaphras there was probably another thought. He knew that the Philippians were bearing a very heavy load of sorrow. It was a hard and difficult fight for them, as for him. And with much generosity he was most unwilling that the news of his illness should add a feather-weight to their grief.

This eagerness to conceal pain, lest it should add sorrow to those who already have almost as much as they can bear, is very characteristic of noble souls. And we may quote here Robert Hall's words, on recovering from a keen

paroxysm of anguish: "I have not complained, have I, sir? No, and I will not complain." How much of God's strength and comfort we miss in our incessant endeavour to secure the support which notoriety for pain and privation may bring from our fellows!

The working whereby He is able even to subject all things unto Himself. Phil. 3: 21 (R.V.).
WHAT cannot He do? From the dust of mother Earth He was able to build up man in the image of God, in the first creation; and from the dust to which death shall again reduce us He will build up again our bodies in the likeness of his resurrection body. The formless clay shall be obliged to yield to his voice, his touch; and if He can do this, what can He not do?

There may be sins within your heart that have long resisted control. Do with them as you will, they still defy you. So long have they been entrenched within the citadel of your soul that, like the Jebusites in the days of David, they laugh you to scorn. But if you will hand over the conflict to Jesus, He will subdue them; He will bring them under his strong, subjecting hand. Be of good cheer. What you cannot do, He can. Whenever the old temptation arises, directly you are aware of it, lift your heart instantly to Jesus, and reckon on Him to cope with it in your behalf. The Lord will fight for you, whilst you shall hold your peace.

So with other difficulties in your life. The raising of a noble nature and character within you; the calling of souls, by your voice, from the death of sin to a life of righteousness; the bringing forth of a fair and well-ordered work from one which seems mere chaos and ruin— all such things are within the scope of this wonderful text. They must be easy to Him who from the dust of death can raise a body ethereal enough to be the home and vehicle of the new celestial life, which shall unfold into perfect beauty in his presence. Repeat the words until the rhythm charms away your doubts, "He is able to subject all things unto Himself."

In nothing be anxious. Phil. 4: 6 (R.V.).
BLACK care! It has always been among men, and perhaps more so to-day than ever, when the pressure of life is heavier and the constraint of circumstances more imperious. Are there not hours in which the clouds gather

densely over the Ark of God, and the stoutest hearts tremble? Is it easy for even the Christian soul to look on a family of little ones, sleeping soundly, and know that they will certainly awake hungry for food, of which the cupboard is bare, and have no tinge of anxiety?

It is at such times that the apostle bids us pray. "Make your requests known unto God." We have not to agonize before Him, as though, like the priests of Baal, who cried and cut themselves, we shall move Him by our anguish. Calmly, quietly, simply, make your requests known. Take your burden into his presence and lay it down there. He is your Father. He who made the body, and gave it you, will see to the supply of its needs. Your health, your children, the condition of his Church, are dear to Him who notices a falling sparrow, and by whom the very hairs of your head are all numbered.

We shall not escape life's discipline. We may expect to abound here, and to be abased there But amid all, Peace, God's white-winged sentinel-angel, shall come down to keep the heart with its affections, the mind with its thoughts. Worry, unrest, anxiety will stand without, as the noise of the street breaks in vain on the double windows of the city counting-house, whilst the child of God learns humbly and patiently the lesson of his Father's love. Careful for nothing; prayerful and thankful in everything.

Colossians

The riches of the glory of this mystery . . . which is Christ in you, the hope of glory. Col. 1: 27.
THE only son of a widow runs off to sea when quite a lad. She must needs work for her living, and takes lodgers in her little home. After years have passed, a bronzed and bearded sailor comes to her door for accommodation, which she gladly affords at an agreed price. She has no idea who has come to dwell beneath her roof—it is a secret, a mystery.

By-and-by, one day as they are sitting at the mid-day meal, a remark, a gesture, startles her; she looks hard into the stranger's face, recognizes him, and, with a cry, rushes into his arms and weeps out on his bosom her joy: "My son, my son, what deceived my old eyes, that I didn't know thee!" That is the glory of the mystery, which breaks in smiles and kisses.

Then he says, "Mother, how hard life has gone with you; your hands are hard with toil. But see, I have plenty of money, and you shall go shares in all. I will take a nice little home, and you shall live there, to keep it as long as you live, and never have to do a stroke of hard toil." That is the riches of the glory of the mystery.

So at your conversion Jesus came into your heart to abide. Too long He has been unrecognized; but of late you have been made aware of the nature and worth of your Heavenly Friend. The mystery has broken in light. Henceforth, realize that all his riches are yours, to be shared and enjoyed; that all your needs may be fully met, even to the abundance of his unsearchable riches; and that there may be an end for ever to all the weary sense of inability and incompetence to meet the inevitable demands of daily living. Christ is in you; let his life within reach out its hands to the life of glory above.

As therefore ye received Christ Jesus the Lord, so walk in Him. Col. 2: 6 (R.V.).
WHEN we were first brought to Jesus, we received Him into our hearts by faith. Throwing open the door, we bade Him be welcome; and He came in never to depart again. Though he was viewless as the wind, and silent as light, He came. And there was a perfume as of myrrh, aloes, and cassia; like that which fills the ivory palaces of eternity.

Now the apostle says that all our after Christian life is to be lived on the same principle. The holy life is not an attainment, but an attitude. Holiness is not an acquirement of which we may make a boast, but an openness of soul towards the Lord Jesus, as of a window unshuttered and uncurtained to the light. The believer is never independent of Jesus; but at every moment he is receiving out of his fulness, and grace upon grace. He does not receive his qualities and attributes as things apart from the Lord Jesus; but receiving Him, he obtains them. The holy man is he who has learned the art of receiving Jesus; the holier, who has a greater capacity, through humility and faith; the holiest, he who can receive most of the life of the Son of God.

Our daily life is here compared to a walk. We cannot choose it. There is no alternative but to take what God has marked out for you; though you may choose your atmosphere, or, to use a modern word, your environment. Every step may be taken in Christ; rooted in Him as a tree in rich soil; builded up as a house on a rock; inhaling his very breath as the life of life. And whatever the need may be which the exigencies of the path suggest, there is always an abundant supply in the Lord Jesus, in whom all treasures are hid. He teaches us that we may know; He indwells that we may be.

Let the peace of God rule in your hearts, to the which also ye are called.   Col. 3: 15.
THE peace of God is the peace of the divine nature—the very tranquillity which prevails in the heart of the God of Peace. It was of this that Jesus spoke when He said, "My peace I give unto you"; for his own being was filled and blessed with it during his earthly career. In each of us may be a sea of glass, reflecting on its pellucid and tranquil bosom the untroubled calm and rest, which are unspeakable because eternal and divine. "The Lord of peace Himself give you peace always."

There are three things against which we must ever be on our guard, lest they rob us of our peace. First, unconfessed sin; second, worry; third, the permission of an unrebuked selfish principle. As on the Sabbath the good Nehemiah carefully excluded the Tyrian fishwives from Jerusalem, lest they should mar its spirit of rest by their cries and traffic, so we must preserve an unbroken Sabbath-keeping within. "There remaineth therefore a Sabbath rest for the people of God."

The apostle says, Let it rule. The Greek word means arbitrate. Whenever there is a doubtful issue to be decided, and by one course your peace may be disturbed, whilst by another it may be maintained, choose those things that make for peace, whether for yourselves or others. Let God's peace act as umpire.

At the same time, this does not mean peace at any price. When the cause of truth is assailed, or the rights of others invaded, we must stand up boldly and strongly for Righteousness. Then the effect of Righteousness will be Peace. Melchizedek was first King of Righteousness, and after that King of Peace.

Always striving for you in his prayers . . . he hath much labour for you.   Col. 4: 12, 13 (R.V.).
THIS is a very beautiful epitaph on a good man's life. He had come from Colosse with tidings for the apostle; but amid all the crowding interests of his visit to Rome his heart was with his friends, and he sought to help them, as we may all help dear ones far away.

He strove for them in prayer. It was no runaway knock that he gave; no light breathing of desire; no formal mention of their names: but it seemed as though he were a wrestler, whose muscles stood out like whipcord as he agonized for the prize. He laboured. We shall never know, till we stand in the clear light of heaven, how much has been wrought in the world by prayer. Here, at least, there is mention of a man's labours. Probably the work on the results of which we are wont to pride ourselves is due less to us than we suppose, and more to unrecognized fellow-labourers.

There is a pretty legend which tells of the dream of a great preacher who was marvellously used of God, and inclined to magnify himself and his gifts; but who was instructed by an angel of God that his success was entirely attributable to a poor widow, who sat regularly in the free seats at the foot of his pulpit, and who never ceased to pray for him. May the writer ask of any who receive benefit from these words to labour and strive for him in prayer to God.

Let us be careful to mingle much intercession with all our prayers, especially on the behalf of missionaries and lonely workers in foreign lands, that they may realize that we are actually working and labouring beside them, though many thousands of miles intervene.

1 Thessalonians

To wait for his Son from heaven. 1 Thess. 1: 10.
OH blessed hope! Is it not wonderful that each of the chapters of this Epistle brims over with the glad anticipation of the Master's quick return!

We should never lose this spirit of eager longing and waiting. It hath the promise of the life that now is, as of that which is to come. It lifts above the darkness of the present age; links the present with the great future; comforts us amid bereavement with the hope of speedy reunion; quickens us to watchfulness and consecration by the thought of the shortening of our opportunities; leads us to purify ourselves as He is pure, to gird our loins and trim our lamps.

Notice how closely the apostle combines the service of the living and true God, herein distinguishing Him from the dumb, dead stones of heathen idolatries, with this waiting for his Son from heaven. It has been alleged that the hope of the Second Advent is a dreamy, mystical sentiment, which disqualifies one for the active fulfilment of the duties of life. Nothing could be further from the truth. Those who cherish that anticipation, who awake in the morning, saying, "Perhaps it will be to-day"; who go to their sleep whispering to their hearts, "Perchance I shall be changed into his likeness in a moment as I sleep and wake in my resurrection body"—these are among the most devoted, strenuous, and successful workers of the Church. They are not recognized in the daily or religious Press; but God knows and honours them.

"Oh, blessed Hope! With this elate,
Let not our hearts be desolate;
But strong in faith and patience, wait
Until He come."

*What is our hope, or joy, or crown of glorying?
Are not even ye?* 1 Thess. 2: 19.
THE tender heart of the apostle suffered keenly in his enforced absence from these beloved converts. He had cherished them as a nurse her children; he would have gladly imparted to them his own soul. Not once nor twice he had sought to see them again, but

had been hindered by malign spiritual forces that were very real to him. He found comfort, however, in the thought that, at the Lord's coming, they and he would be reunited, and that they would be his joy, as now they were his hope. Now they lit his hope to an intenser passion; then they would intensify his joy to a more exquisite fulness.

But there is a further thought. The souls whom he had won for Jesus were to constitute his crown. It was as though they would be woven into a wreath like that given to the ancient athlete, and placed on his brow as he emerged from the terrific conflict of his life— not to be worn there, but cast forthwith at the feet of his Lord. What an incentive was this! Each soul plucked from the enemy would be another jewel for the Master's crown, and herein a fresh source of heavenly blessedness to himself.

I remember Mr. Spurgeon telling of an old Christian woman in his almshouses, who persisted in saying loving thoughts about her beloved pastor to his face, at which he greatly demurred. He feared that she was making more of him than of Christ. But she said sweetly, "It is written in the Song, 'Thou, O Solomon, must have a thousand, and those that keep the fruit two hundred'; so, dear pastor, you must have your two hundred." Yes, it will be so; we shall partake with Jesus of the fish that we have caught; we shall have fellowship in his exceeding joy over the saved.

*No man should be moved by these afflictions; for
. . . we are appointed thereunto.* 1 Thess. 3: 3.
WE all love the sunshine, but the Arabs have a proverb that "all sunshine makes the desert"; and it is a matter for common observation that the graces of Christian living are more often apparent in the case of those who have passed through great tribulation. God desires to get as rich crops as possible from the soil of our natures. There are certain plants of the Christian life, such as meekness, gentleness, kindness, humility, which cannot come to perfection if the sun of prosperity always shines.

We often shrank from the lessons set us at school, and looked out of the windows, longing for the hour of release. But now how thankful we are for the tutors and governors, appointed by our parents, who kept us steadily at our tasks. We feel almost kindly to the schoolmaster or mistress that we dreaded. And, similarly, one day we shall be glad for those hard lessons acquired from the horn-book of pain. "We have had fathers of our flesh to chasten us, and we gave them reverence: shall we not much rather be in subjection unto the Father of spirits, who chastens for our profit, and live?"

The tears of those who suffer according to the will of God are spiritual lenses and windows of agate. As the weights of the clock or the ballast in the vessel are necessary for their right ordering, so is trouble in the soul-life. The sweetest scents are only obtained by tremendous pressure; the fairest flowers grow amid Alpine snow-solitudes; the rarest gems have suffered longest from the lapidary's wheel; the noblest statues have borne most blows of the chisel. All, however, is under law. Nothing happens that has not been appointed with consummate care and foresight.

Sorrow not, even as the rest, which have no hope.
1 Thess. 4: 13 (R.V.).

NATURE will have her due. Tears will fall, and hearts seem near to breaking. Nowhere does God chide the tears of natural affection; how could He, since it is written that "Jesus wept"? But He sets Himself to extract their bitterness. Sorrow you may, and must; but not as without hope.

THOSE WHO DIE IN CHRIST ARE WITH HIM. They are said to sleep, not because they are unconscious, but because their decease was as devoid of terror as an infant's slumbers. Believers have all died once in Christ, and it was necessary to find a word which, whilst significant of death, was not death, in order to describe the moment of our farewell to this world and birth into the next. This word was furnished by Death's twin-sister Sleep. The catacombs are covered with the brief significant sentence, Obdormivit in Christo (He slept in Christ). But just as in sleep the spirit is conscious, of which dreams bear witness, so in the last sleep. Absent from the body, we shall be present with the Lord.

THOSE WHO DIE IN CHRIST WILL COME WITH HIM. They are now waiting around Him till He give the final order for the whole heavenly cortège, which has been collecting for ages, to move. The holy angels will accompany; but the beloved saints shall ride in the chariots of God as the bride beside the bridegroom.

THOSE WHO DIE IN CHRIST SHALL BE FOR EVER REUNITED WITH US WHO WAIT FOR HIM AND THEM. They shall come with Him. "God will bring them." We, on the other hand, if we are living at that supreme moment, shall be changed and caught up to meet Him and them; and then, all one in Christ, we shall be for ever with Him, to go no more out.

The God of Peace Himself sanctify you wholly.
1 Thess. 5: 23, 24 (R.V.).

OUR God has set Himself the work of our sanctification. As the Greek indicates, He looks upon us as his inheritance, and He will not rest until He has brought every acre of territory under cultivation. It is is not enough that briars and thistles should be exterminated; they must be replaced by the rare growth of Christian virtue, which is Christ.

THE WORK OF SANCTIFICATION IS QUIET AND SILENT. It is wrought by the God of Peace. The mightiest forces of nature are stilled; and when God comes with power into the human spirit there is often no hurricane, tempest, fire, or earthquake, but the thrilling whisper of the still, small voice. Do not be afraid, as though God would treat you roughly. So long as peaceful, gentle methods will effect his purpose, He will gladly employ them.

THE WORK IS ALSO GRADUAL. We are not made faultless, but preserved blameless; i.e., we are kept from known sin, preserved from incurring perpetual self-reproach. "There is no condemnation." I saw the other day the love-letter of a little boy to his father. It was anything but faultless; but the father, at least, did not count it worthy of blame, since he carried it next his heart. So we are not to be faultless, as judged by God's perfect standard, till we are presented before the presence of his glory; but we may be blameless up to our acquaintance with the divine will.

THE WORK IS FROM WITHIN OUTWARDS. Notice the order—spirit, soul, body. The Shechinah of his presence shines in the holy of holies, and thence pours over into the holy place, and so into the outer court, until the very curtains of the body are irradiated with its light. He will do it.

2 Thessalonians

That the name of our Lord Jesus may be glorified in you. 2 Thess. 1: 12 (R.V.).

WILL you, dear Christian soul, enter into a solemn compact with the Holy Spirit that you will live for this as your supreme purpose, namely, to glorify the name (i.e., the character) of the Lord Jesus? This is his supreme purpose and aim throughout the present age. He seeks the glory of Jesus with the same persistent patience as Jesus sought the glory of his Father, and longs for our fellowship and co-operation. Nothing gratifies the Holy Spirit more than to welcome into partnership those who love the Lord Jesus with a consuming passion, and are prepared to glorify Him, at whatever cost to themselves.

It has made a great difference to my life since I responded to the call of the Spirit, as though He said directly, as once through his servant, "Oh, magnify the Lord with me, and let us exalt his Name together." One has now a worthy object always in view, whether in speaking or keeping silence; in acting or suffering; in life or death—that the Lord Jesus may be magnified.

Does this seem too high an aim? Then ponder the gracious assurance that the Lord will fulfil every desire of goodness (ver. 11). He first instils the desire, and then realizes it; first suggests the outline plan, and then fills in the colours. Take your desires for goodness to Him, and trust Him, in all faithfulness, to realize and fulfil them. They are like the chalice which the child brings to the lake-side impure, indeed, but capable of being rinsed; and the father, taking it from his hand, plunges it into the pellucid waters, that cleanse and fill to the brim. Thank God for every desire of goodness! But be not content till that which you desire is in actual possession; for He who prompts the desire is well able to fulfil it.

God hath from the beginning chosen you to salvation. 2 Thess. 2: 13.

FROM the beginning! Who shall compute the contents of the vast unknown abyss, which is comprehended in that phrase? The beginning of creation was preceded by the anticipation of Redemption, and the love of God to all who were one with Christ.

GOD'S AIM AND PURPOSE. SALVATION. Not simply our deliverance from the penalty, but from the power of all besetting sin; so that we may be delivered from the fear of our enemies, and serve Him in holiness and righteousness all our days. This He is prepared to give to us; but we must claim it by faith.

GOD'S CHOICE. Whom He did foreknow He also did predestinate. From all eternity He saw those who would be attracted to Jesus by a divine affinity, and these were included in his gift to the Son. "Thine they were, and Thou gavest them Me, and they have kept thy word." We must not presume on the eternal choice; but we may be very grateful that the tendencies emanating from the fall are met, in mid-flow, by the grace and choice of the Almighty.

GOD'S METHOD. THROUGH SANCTIFICATION OF THE SPIRIT. The Holy Ghost sets us apart from sin, and consecrates us to God. "Know ye not that your body is the temple of the Holy Ghost, which is in you, which ye have of God, and ye are not your own? For ye are bought with a price." Our sanctification is not the property of our soul, but its possession of the Holy One; not an attribute, but a Person. And belief of the truth. Let the Word of God dwell in you richly. Hide it in your heart, that you may be kept from sin. We are sanctified by the truth in so far as we expose our hearts to its entrance and rule. We are cleansed by the washing of water through the Word.

The Lord direct your hearts into the love of God, and into the patient waiting for Christ.
2 Thess. 3: 5.

"DIRECT" might be rendered "make straight." It is used of the apostle's own coming to these beloved converts in 1 Thess. 3: 11. It is as though he asked that their hearts might travel easily and swiftly along the road which leads into the love of God, and the patience which untiring, waits for Christ.

THE LOVE OF GOD. We urgently need, for many reasons, to be brought into the love of

God. Only so can our selfishness be conquered and expelled; only so can we become like God in our daily life and conversation; only this is the complete evidence to the world that our holy religion is true; only thus shall we have power to influence the lost and fallen; only so can we know God, "for he that loveth not, knoweth not God." But how can we learn to love? God alone can teach us and guide our way into this sacred art. His Holy Spirit must fill our hearts with his love; we must ever claim and receive it as our power for daily self-sacrifice, and we must be prepared to take every opportunity of sharing the love of God in unselfishness and thoughtfulness for those with whom we come in contact.

THE PATIENCE OF CHRIST. Thus the original might be rendered; and the beloved disciple confesses himself a brother and companion in the patience of Jesus Christ (Rev. 1: 9). We all know something of this. Longing for answers to prayers that are still delayed; yearning for the realization of hopes and ideals of which God's Spirit has spoken to us; waiting for the manifestation of the sons of God. May we be led into something of that sublime faith and patience with which Jesus sits, until all things are put under Him, and He is satisfied.

1 Timothy

Sinners, of whom I am chief. 1 Tim. 1: 15.
IF the elephant can go safely over the swaying bridge, the horse and mule can; and the apostle seems to glory that in the very beginning of the progress of the Gospel through the world it had laid hold of and converted himself, because if he had been saved, anyone might be. As men have been brought under conviction, in successive ages, it has been a profound consolation to learn that the chief of sinners has been in heaven for eighteen hundred years. In him first Jesus Christ showed forth "all long-suffering, for a pattern to them which should hereafter believe."

Without doubt Paul never forgot the excess of his hatred and persecutions towards the infant Church. But probably he alludes here also to the deepening consciousness of unworthiness and sinfulness which accompanies all progress towards the knowledge and love of God. This phase of experience may be accounted for thus. The true saint of God, though certain of forgiveness, reviews his past sins in the light of that purity of which he is ever obtaining truer perceptions, and thus recognizes shades of evil in them which a slighter knowledge of God had failed to reveal. He also feels himself a greater sinner than others, because he supposes that God cannot have treated another with the same forbearance and mercy as have been extended to himself; and the greater the love the more heinous the transgression. And in addition, as subtler forms of temptation are suggested to him, and to everyone, he knows that there are kindred susceptibilities within him, even though they are abhorred and resisted. It is beneath the pressure of such thoughts that he recognizes his uttermost indebtedness to the grace of God.

That supplications, prayers, intercessions, and giving of thanks be made for all men.
1 Tim. 2: 1.
A LIFE is revealed here of which many of us know practically nothing. We do not feel the absolute necessity of being much alone in the presence of God, not so much for ourselves, as for others; and this sad neglect of inter-cessory prayer, which we all deplore, really points to a lack of the divine life, since if that were mightily within us we should inevitably feel its throb and pulse in this direction. This comes out clearly in the words that follow.

Intercession is necessary that we may know the secrets of a quiet, peaceable, and godly life (ver. 2).

Such intercession for others is good and acceptable in the sight of God our Saviour (ver. 3). And the word translated good might be rendered beautiful.

IT IS CONSONANT WITH THE DIVINE PURPOSE, for God wishes to have all men saved (ver. 4). If, then, his Spirit is within us, we, too, shall long that men should be saved and come to the knowledge of the truth. Our hearts will be filled with a divine tenderness of yearning which will find vent in strong cryings and tears. It is only thus we can live in harmony with the divine purpose. One writes: "When I think of this, I feel I must pray. Oh, how near it brings to God to pray in the Spirit, and leads me to see that no pressure of duty among men can free us from the absolute need of much prayer."

Such intercession is in profound union with the mediation of our Lord (vers. 5, 6). As the great High Priest, He ever liveth to intercede; and in our little measure we, too, as members of a holy priesthood, must blend our supplications, prayers, intercessions, and giving of thanks with his (1 Peter 2: 5).

Without controversy great is the mystery of godliness. 1 Tim. 3: 16.

IT is more than likely that this is a fragment of one of the earliest hymns of the Church. In her hymns, and maintenance of the ordinances, she thus becomes the pillar and ground of the truth. The words "mystery of godliness" are probably a general heading which is further unfolded and expanded in the six following sentences, which may have been sung antiphonally:

"God was manifest in the flesh,
Justified in the Spirit.
Seen of angels,
Preached unto the Gentiles.
Believed on in the world,
Received up into glory."

THE EXTREMES OF MANIFESTATION. The Eternal Word was manifested in the flesh. But it was not simply a physical manifestation; we cannot forget the descent of the Holy Spirit at his baptism, or the authentication of his words which the Spirit gave in signs and wonders, and convinced hearts, and converted lives.

THE EXTREMES OF CREATED INTELLIGENCE. Angels worship Him; and Gentiles, sunk in heathen darkness, hear the story of his wondrous love. Jesus is the centre of all worlds: from heaven's bright spaces they come to Him on the one hand; from earth's dark sins they come on the other. In Him meet angels and men.

THE EXTREMES OF SPACE. Glory is above: "He was received up into glory." The world is but a speck, a mote in the beam of eternity. How great the space between the two! But the feet of our Emmanuel have trodden its low pavement, and He has now taken to Himself his former glory. Like Jacob's ladder, He links earth with the throne of God.

Every creature of God is good ... if it be received with thanksgiving. 1 Tim. 4: 4.

WE must be very careful in applying these words. Intoxicating liquor, for instance, is sometimes described as "a good creature of God." But surely that term is not legitimate. Whatever grounds there may be for defending its use, can this text be alleged as one? For there is a great deal of human manipulation in its preparation. Before it reaches our lips, it is greatly altered by the process of fermentation. It can hardly be called God's good creature.

When we are quite sure that we are dealing with one of God's pure and unadulterated gifts, such as human love, friendship, the beauties of nature, wholesome food, fresh young spirits, the innocent mirth of the Christmas home-gathering; we must distinguish between God's gifts and our abuse of them; between his creation and our distortion of it. There are things in our lives which are not his creation or gift, and which we must resolutely refuse and put away. There are others which come to us clearly and absolutely from his hand.

REJOICE IN EVERY GOOD THING WHICH THE LORD GIVES. Rejoice! Do not enjoy things as though under the sword of Damocles, suspended by a thread.

BE CAREFUL TO MAINTAIN THE SPIRIT OF THANKSGIVING AND PRAYER. What you can thank God for or use in his name and for his glory; what lifts you from the gift to the Giver, or is capable of being prayed over, with no shadow of misgiving, is innocent and healthy.

WATCH ONLY AGAINST THE INTRUSION OF SELF. Whatever you place between yourself and God, or rest on apart from God, or make the aim and centre of your life, is hurtful and must pass through the fire. The way to rid yourself of its poison is to insist on making it a subject of thanksgiving.

She that is a widow indeed, and desolate, trusteth in God. 1 Tim. 5: 5.

ART thou desolate indeed, because the light of thine eyes has passed from view, leaving thee immeasurably lonely? Dear soul, do not look down into the grave which has received the precious mortal frame, but up into the face of God.

He lent thee thy beloved. From the time of the first knitting of soul with soul he was but a loan for a specified time; and wouldst thou not rather have had him for so short a time than not at all? Wouldst thou not have said, had God asked thee, "I would rather have a year or a month of such love as his than none?" Do not be angry because God has done as He always intended.

Besides, that beloved one is still thine. Thy love so entered into his heart that it could not be eradicated, though ages should pass. Do not suppose that death is so mighty a magician as to alter the very nature of those who pass for a moment beneath his wand.

And God will care for thee. Trust Him for society, that thou be not lonely; for the provision of what is necessary to thy support; and for the protecting love which thy shrinking nature calls for. Thy Maker will be thy husband.

Wouldst thou be comforted, continue in prayers and supplications for others night and day. Cease to shut thyself up with thy sorrow, and go out to minister comfort to those who sorrow as without hope. A Hindoo story tells of a bereaved mother, who was advised to obtain a handful of corn from a house where there was no trouble, and was so occupied in seeking it, and in comforting the inmates of the various homes she visited, that her own grief was assuaged.

Nor trust in uncertain riches, but in the living God. 1 Tim. 6: 17.

THE contrast here is very beautiful. Men, for the most part, look to riches to supply them with all they need richly to enjoy; but the postle says that it is beyond all comparison better to look away from dead coin to a living Person, who takes pleasure in giving liberally without upbraiding.

HERE IS A REBUKE. Suppose you had your cellars filled with gold coin, would you not think yourself secure against all possible need and care? Almost certainly you would. But you ought to be even more at rest, since you have neither silver nor gold, and only your Heavenly Father's hand.

HERE IS A CONTRAST. Riches are uncertain at the best. A man in these difficult days finds it easier to gain money than to hold it. He who is rich to-day may awake to-morrow to find that some sudden turn of the market has made him poor. But God is not uncertain. He is the same yesterday, to-day, and for ever. His covenants are certainties.

HERE IS AN APPEAL. Trust in the living God with as much restfulness as others in their lands and revenues, and be almost glad if God takes away from you what you have clung to so tenaciously, that you may drop securely into his everlasting arms. You smile at the story of the lady who was told by the captain that he had done all he could for the vessel, and they must now look to the Almighty; and who replied, "O captain, has it come to that?" But you may be nearer akin to her spirit than you suppose!

HERE IS AN ASSURED DESTINY. Those who trust in riches are pierced through with many sorrows, and are caught in the maelstrom, which drowns souls in perdition; they who trust in the Lord are as Mount Zion, which cannot be removed.

2 Timothy

He is able to keep my deposit. . . . The good deposit, keep.
2 Tim. 1: 12, 14 (R.V., marg.).

THERE is a double deposit here, and the comparison comes out clear and marked in the Greek. When we give our most precious treasure into the custodianship of Jesus, He turns to honour us by entrusting his own treasure to our care. Oh that we might be as eager to keep that which He entrusts to us, as He is that which we entrust to Him; so that He might be able to say of us, "I know them in whom I have trusted, and am persuaded that

they will never fail to do whatever needs to be done for my honour and glory."

OUR DEPOSIT WITH CHRIST. What is the true policy of life? How can I best spend these few years to the best advantage? What is there beyond, and beyond? Such questions come to all earnest souls, and greatly trouble them, till they entrust the keeping of their souls and the direction of their lives into the hands of the faithful Saviour. We feel sure that He has the words of eternal life, and that all power is given to Him in heaven and on earth. At first there is something of a venture—we trust Him;

next, there is the knowledge which comes from experience—we know Him; lastly, there is strong confidence—we are persuaded that He is able.

CHRIST'S DEPOSIT WITH US. And what is this? 1 Tim. 6: 20, 14, and 4: 16, suggest the answer. To every believer Jesus hands the custody of his honour, his Gospel, his Father's glory, his holy day, the ordinances which He bequeathed to the Church. As Ezra charged the priests to bear safely through the desert march the sacred vessels, so our Captain charges us, and throughout the whole Bible rings the injunction: "Be ye clean, ye that bear the vessels of the Lord."

Meet for the Master's use. 2 Tim. 2: 21.
THIS I would be, O Lord, clay though I am. Be Thou my potter. Make of me what Thou canst and by what process Thou wilt, only let me be what Thou canst use.

Art thou able to drink the cup that I drink of, and be baptized with the baptism that I am baptized with?

By thy grace I am able. Let me die with Thee; lie in the grave of obscurity and neglect; be counted as the off-scouring of all things; be broken on the edge of thy wheel; pass through the fire of thy hottest kiln—only let me be one whom Thou choosest and usest, constantly in thy hand; dipped down often into the brimming well, and back to thy dear lips, or to the lips of whom Thou lovest.

The spirit is willing, my child, but the flesh is weak.

I know it, I know it, Lord. But I desire to die to the weakness of the flesh, its ache, its tears, its faintness, that I may live in the Spirit. Is not thy grace sufficient? Is not thy strength perfected in weakness? Is not the residue of the Spirit with Thee, to give without measure? Heed not my weak cryings, but perfect that which concerneth me. Only make me a vessel that Thou canst use.

He that would be great, let him be as he that doth serve.

I understand Thee, Master. Thou wouldst winnow my heart, and rid me of all that is proud and selfish. It is true that in the time past I have sought great things for myself: but that is gone now: I am but a weaned babe: my only desire is for Thee, for thy glory, for the magnifying of thy name: my one cry to be often, always, in thy hand.

All Scripture is given by inspiration of God.
2 Tim. 3: 16.
LITERALLY the words stand, All Scripture, God-breathed and profitable. It is a remarkable expression, reminding of the early record, "God breathed into his nostrils the breath of life, and he became a living soul." The breath of God has entered these holy words, and they live.

THIS MAKES SCRIPTURE FRAGRANT. I write these words beneath the leafy shadow of an oak-tree, on a ridge of hill commanding the Weald of Kent. The summer breeze is hurrying past. Since it left the southern sea it has passed over miles of fragrant country, imbibing the sweet scents of flower gardens, orchards, and hop-gardens; lading it with perfume, which makes it an ecstasy to inhale. Ah, fragrant breeze, how thou remindest me of those holy thoughts which are wafted to me from the orchards of Paradise, whensoever I open the sacred Word!

THIS MAKES IT REFRESHING. On this hot summer day the heat would be overpowering but for this delightful breeze, which fans the cheek and cools the atmosphere. The current is always changing, hence the refreshment. And the Word of God is always fresh and interesting, because the Spirit of God is perpetually passing into and through it, bringing his own life to us, and through us to the world.

THIS MAKES IT BEAUTIFUL. The effect of the wind, in the music of the leaves above, the swaying of the grasses at my feet, the rustling of yonder golden corn across the beaten footpath, adds an element of incomparable delight. There is new meaning, movement, music, in it all. And it is only as the divine breath breathes through apostles and prophets, that, like great organ-pipes, they become resonant with heavenly music.

The Lord Jesus Christ, who shall judge the quick and the dead at his appearing. 2 Tim. 4: 1.
PROFESSOR RENDEL HARRIS reminds us that an early piece of Christian literature, called the Second Epistle of Clement, opens with these words: "Brethren, we ought to think of Jesus Christ as God, as the Judge of quick and dead. And we ought not to think meanly of our salvation; for when we think meanly of Him, meanly also do we expect to receive." In the view of this holy soul there was a very deep and necessary connection between creed and character. Those who esteem

Him most worthily will derive most from Him.

LARGE THOUGHTS OF CHRIST ARE NECESSARY TO HOLINESS. Unless we think of Christ as the Ideal Man, in whom there was no flaw or stain, how can we make Him the model of our daily life? Unless we think of Him as the Son of God, able to subdue all things to Himself, how can we dare to hope to become like Him? "I should die, O my Lord," cried a saint in a moment of religious ecstasy, "if I thought that I should fail of loving Thee with all my heart."

LARGE THOUGHTS OF CHRIST ARE NECESSARY TO PRAYER. He that cometh to God must believe that He is, and that He is the Rewarder. Bethink thee well before thou openest thy lips in the first entreaty, who He is whom thou addressest, and forthwith great and far-reaching petitions will naturally form themselves within thine heart.

LARGE THOUGHTS OF CHRIST ARE NECESSARY FOR CHRISTIAN WORK. The solid belief that Christ has redeemed our race, and that the Father has given Him the kingdom over all the world, is absolutely necessary before there can be any enthusiastic effort on our part to make Him King and secure for Him actually the kingdom, the power, and the glory.

Titus

According to the faith of God's elect, and the knowledge of the truth. Titus 1: 1 (R.V.).

THESE seem to have been the two guiding stars of the apostle's life—faith and knowledge. Some are afraid of the conjunction. The men of faith are afraid of science, and the men of science often despise faith. But they are not antagonistic.

FAITH. The faith that inspires all elect souls is one and the same. In some there may be more, in others less; but its attitude towards God and its phases of experience, trial, and triumph, are the same in all who believe. In addition to this, the general facts and truths on which our faith lays hold, and from which it extracts its nourishment, are the same: and it is a comfort to know that these have been passed on from age to age from the earliest days, and that we are called to believe in them, and hold them fast.

KNOWLEDGE OF THE TRUTH. We need not fear or shun knowledge, which is simply the exploring and discovery of the ways and thoughts of God. "Let knowledge grow from more to more." Only let her always concern herself with the great facts and methods of God's universe, rather than with human speculation and fancy. There is a distinction between knowledge and wisdom. The one may be only intellectual; the other is always moral. Those who pretend to know are not always wise; but the wise always know.

GODLINESS. True knowledge will make you godly, reverent, devout; filling you with the Spirit of God within, and with likeness to God without. It is only as you are godly, that you will really be wise and know things that are hidden from the wise and prudent. True knowledge leads to godliness, and godliness back to knowledge.

Who gave Himself for us, that He might redeem us from all iniquity. Titus 2: 14.

AFTER all that we have professed and learnt, how hard it is to believe that God intends just what He says! When the Holy Spirit says all, He clearly means ALL. And we are, therefore, taught that the death of Jesus was intended, not for our forgiveness and justification merely, but for our sanctification, and our deliverance from the power of all our besetting sins. The text does not promise freedom from temptation; but from all yielding to habits, dispositions, and tempers of soul which have ruthlessly tyrannized over us as Egypt over Israel.

Jesus died for thee, O child of God, that having been set free from the bondage of all iniquity thou mightest live soberly as regards the use of the world, righteously towards thy fellows, and godly towards the Almighty, and "looking for that blessed hope." The grace of God has appeared; his glory will appear. There has been an Epiphany of the one; there shall be as certainly an Epiphany of the other. Many awaited the first; more shall await the second. The one was in humiliation; the other shall be in glory: the one was as a Babe; the other shall be in the glory of the divine Man.

But till then we are called to wait with garments unspotted from the world, and hearts delivered from the love and power of human sin.

Let us teach the world that God has something tangible and practicable to give—not for the next life only, but for this. We are taught by that gentle school-mistress, the Grace of God, to live—soberly, as regards our personal life; righteously, in relation to others; godly, in our attitude towards God. Wesley says, "Until you press believers to accept full salvation now, you must not look for any revival."

The kindness and love of God our Saviour toward man appeared. Titus 3: 4.

THE emphasis must surely rest on appeared. Kindness and love towards man were always in the heart of God, but they were not clearly revealed. They might have been perceived in the order of nature and human life; but there are stormy winds as well as zephyrs in the one—and in the other deaths as well as births; knells of hope as well as marriage peals. But in Jesus the true heart of God towards man was manifested. It is thus in human life.

AT FIRST GOD BLESSED US ANONYMOUSLY. In Cowper's memoirs we read how Theodora, his cousin, pursued him throughout his sad life with her gifts; but they always came without indication of their source. As the poet unwrapped his new-come treasure, he would say, "Dear Anonymous has come again; God bless him." So, through years of thoughtless childhood, and afterwards in opening youth, we were the recipients of myriads of gifts contrived with the most exquisite skill to give us pleasure; but we did not trace them to their source. They were from God.

SINCE THEN HIS GRACE AND LOVING-KINDNESS HAVE APPEARED. We have had eyes to see, and hearts to understand. The Anonymous Benefactor is now recognized as our Father and Friend. We no longer praise our earthly loves for our cornfields and vineyards, but our Heavenly Spouse (Hosea 2). In the breaking of the bread we have recognized the Son of God, and we know now who it was that walked with us along the path of life, and why our hearts burned.

> "Oh, to grace how great a debtor
> Daily I'm constrained to be!
> Let that grace, Lord, like a fetter,
> Bind my wandering heart to Thee."

Philemon

My very heart. Philemon 12 (R.V.).

THIS fragment of ancient letter-writing gives us a model of the way in which our commonest or most prosaic dealings, and our letters, even on business matters may breathe the spirit of Christ. It also illustrates the relation in which we stand to Jesus Christ. What Onesimus was to Paul and Philemon combined, that we are to our Lord.

WHAT WAS ONESIMUS TO PAUL? His child, whom he had begotten in his bonds. He had probably been discovered by some of his companions in the purlieus of Rome, where criminals concealed themselves from justice, and abandoned characters gave vent to the wildest passions. Or, having heard that the apostle, whom he had so often met in his master's house, was residing in his own hired house in Rome, the runaway slave had found him out, when in the extremity of hunger. In either case he had now become dear as the apostle's heart; had learnt to minister to him in his bonds; had proved more than a servant —a brother beloved. O Thou who hast redeemed us from our sins, may we be all this to Thee!

WHAT WAS ONESIMUS TO PHILEMON? He had been unprofitable; and we have been. He was sent back; and we have returned to the Shepherd and Bishop of our souls. He had been a servant, henceforth he should be a beloved brother; and we are no longer servants, but friends. He had grievously wronged his master; but his sin had been forgiven, and so covered by over-abounding grace, that it would bring him into a position of greater privilege and blessing than ever before. In this man's sin and restoration we see ourselves. Where our sin abounded, grace has much more abounded, through the tender pity of Him who had put our defalcations to his own account.

Hebrews

Thou art the same. Heb. 1: 12.

THOU ART THE SAME, WHEN CONTRASTED WITH NATURE. The solid bases of the hills were laid in their sockets by thy hands. The blue tapestry of the sky was woven by thy fingers; and it is as easy for Thee to lay it aside and substitute new heavens as for us to lay aside a worn-out dress and take another. And as the change of dress does not affect the nature of the wearer, neither will all the changes of creation or nature affect the power of thine hand or the tenderness of thy heart. Thou art the same!

THOU ART THE SAME, WHEN CONTRASTED WITH MEN. They come and go. The great ones of the past—Abraham, Moses, David, Elijah—stood with Thee for a moment on the earth, and then passed into the great silence. Augustine, Luther, Calvin, Knox, wrought for Thee and with Thee, and passed away. Our own teachers and friends have not been suffered to continue by reason of death. One by one they have passed from us; but Thou art the same, and thy years shall not fail!

THOU ART THE SAME, WHEN CONTRASTED WITH OUR OWN MOODS AND IMPULSES. They are too fitful; like the morning dew; like the evening wind. Sometimes we feel we could die for Thee; at other times we sleep amid thy sorrows. Emotions, resolutions, methods of thought and action, are permanent only in their changefulness. But Thou art the same— changeless and timeless, our Rock of Ages, our impregnable Fortress and Home!

This was the import of the Burning Bush which flamed out on the hillside in the dark night, but did not burn to the ground. Steadily, constantly, fiercely, the fire shone, but needed no fuel from the tree—symbol of the I AM.

A merciful and faithful High Priest. Heb. 2: 17.

THE priesthood of Jesus stretches like the sky from the horizon of the past to that of the eternal future. It covers all we know of Him.

IN THE DAYS THAT PRECEDED HIS INCARNATION. We are told that the priesthood of Melchizedek was made like that of the Son of God (Heb. 7: 3), from which it is clear that all the apparatus of priesthood within and without the Jewish system was some faint imagining forth of the priestly mediation and intercession of the Saviour. The eternal temple was reared, the incense of intercession ascended, the sacrifice of the Lamb was slain, before the first thin spiral of smoke rose from Moriah's summit.

IN THE DAYS OF HIS EARTHLY MINISTRY. At the Passover, when the High Priest had finished the sacred rites, he came forth to the people, and said, "Now ye are clean." In John 15: 3 Jesus addressed his disciples in the same words. His authority to forgive sins; his quick sympathy, and likeness to his brethren; his frequent prayers; his intercessions for sinners, as when He pleaded for his crucifiers; his intercessions for the tempted, as when He prayed for Peter; his intercessions for his own, as in the matchless John 17; his reference to the shedding of blood; the whole circumstances of his death—show his priestly attitude, which culminated in his passing within the vail.

IN THE DAYS OF THE PRESENT DISPENSATION. The divine apostle tells us that he saw Christ clothed in a vesture to the foot, and employs this specific word for high-priestly dress. He saw Him engaged in priestly ministry; and in a subsequent vision tells us that he saw Him mingle much incense with the prayer of saints and present them before God.

Consider . . . Jesus. Heb. 3: 1.

WHO ARE TO CONSIDER HIM? "Holy brethren." Because we are the brethren of Jesus, we must consider our Brother. Because we are brethren with all, whom He brothers, we should emulate the saints of all ages in their eager gaze at Christ. We must possess the holiness without which none can see the Lord, and we must live in holy love with all who bear the name of Christ. Do you lack either of these? This is the reason why your eyes are blinded. Step out of the mist into the clear prospect:

"A step,
A single step, shall free you from the skirts
Of the blind vapour, and open to your view
Glory beyond all glory ever seen
By waking sense or by the dreaming soul."

WHAT RIGHT HAVE THEY TO CONSIDER HIM? Because they are "partakers of a heavenly calling." They have turned from the world, from the fascinations of the sin and the flesh; they are seeking the heavenly city, the New Jerusalem. Surely such have a right, given them of grace, to live in daily personal vision of their King!

IN WHAT ASPECTS SHOULD THEY CONSIDER HIM? As Apostle, whom God has sent out of his bosom to man, and whom man sends back to God. As Priest, who was in all points tempted like as we are, yet without sin, who bears our needs and sins and sorrows on his heart. As the Son, compared with whom Moses was but a servant. As Creator, by whom all things were made, and without whom was not anything made. As the Head of the household of those who believe. As the All-faithful One, who will never resign his charge. Consider Jesus in each of these aspects, and rejoice in Him.

There remaineth, therefore, a Sabbath rest for the people of God. Heb. 4: 9 (R.V.).
THERE IS A REST FOR WEARY SOULS. God speaks of it as his Rest. He entered it, we are told, when He had finished his work, and beheld it to be very good; and ever since the door has been standing open for the travel-stained, weary children of men to enter it. To every other creation-day there were evening and morning, but not to this; it partakes of the nature of eternity in its timeless bliss.

LET US REJOICE THAT THIS REST REMAINETH. Of course, the Sabbath, which was and is a type of it, could not exhaust it. And Canaan, with its sweet plains and cessation of the wilderness wanderings, could not completely fulfil it; because centuries after it had been given through Joshua, in the Psalms God spoke of yet another day, as though his rest were still future.

THE REST MAY BE A PRESENT EXPERIENCE. The word "remaineth" has diverted the thoughts of commentators who have supposed it referred to heaven. There is rest, sweet rest, there. But "remaineth" means "unexhausted, unrealized, by aught which has taken place." The rest is for us here and now. "We which have believed do enter into rest." Where is it? In the bosom of Christ: "Come unto Me, and I will give you rest." It is in ploughing the furrow of daily duty—"Take my yoke; ... and find rest."

THIS REST IS COMPATIBLE WITH GREAT ACTIVITY. He that enters into the divine rest is not reduced to quietism. On the seventh day the Creator rested from creation; but He works in providence. Jesus, on the seventh day, rested from Calvary; but He pleads in heaven. Cease from your own works, after a similar fashion; abandon your restless planning and striving; by the grace of the Holy Spirit better service will be produced.

Senses exercised to discern good and evil.
Heb. 5: 14.
IT is difficult to exaggerate the value of the physical senses. Take, for instance, that of scent. It is the means of exquisite enjoyment, conveying to us the perfume of garden or field; and it secures us against serious perils that lie in wait for our unwary footsteps. By the order of God's providence, hurtful substances exhale noxious and forbidding odours, by reason of which we are warned from going into their close proximity.

The soul also is endowed with senses. How important a part our spiritual senses may play in the regimen of the inner life! If we are quick to discern good and evil, we may welcome the one and avoid the other with ever-increasing readiness. We may receive the blessing of the one when still afar off, and avoid the curse of the other when only threatening us.

The army which is ill served by its scouts stands a much worse chance than if it were forewarned when an attack was advancing. The foremost ranks of the foe may be over the ramparts, and engaged in the heart of the fortress, before there has been time for preparation. Oh, to detect temptation, when still it is only a thought, a suggestion, a faint shadow on the sky!

We may sharpen our senses by use. When I was in the tea-trade, my sense of touch and taste and smell became acute to discern quite minute differences. We need a similar acuteness in discerning good and evil. May our hearts become most sensitive to all that might lead to temptation, so that we may deal with the tempter in the very earliest suggesions of evil. Lord, make us quick of scent in the fear of the Lord (Isa. 11: 3, R.V.).

It is impossible to renew again to repentance, the while ... Heb. 6: 6 (R.V., marg.).
THE writer of this Epistle is eager to lead his readers from first principles to that strong meat

which was befitting for those of mature growth; and, as he proceeds to do so, it was as though he were arrested by a sudden thought of some who had recently fallen away from the faith.

In the awful stress of trial which accompanied the fall of Jerusalem, the Hebrew Christians, who were still dwelling in Palestine, were strongly tempted to apostatise. Some, indeed, had done so. But can we really consider that they ever were true Christians? They went out, because they had never been truly of. They had been enlightened as to the doctrines of Christianity; but the enlightenment had been of their head rather than of their heart. They had tasted of the heavenly hopes, anticipations, and joys of the Gospel message, without really belonging to the Household of Faith. But, notwithstanding all, they had gone back.

It is impossible to renew such to repentance, whilst they go on living as they do, crucifying the Son of God by their vicious and cowardly course of action, and putting Him to an open shame. Notice that whilst, suggested by Bishop Westcott, of the margin of the R.V. It is the solution of the great difficulty which has perplexed many timid souls. The impossibility of renewal is only for those who persist in their evil ways. Abandon your sins, and God will restore you to your old place.

It cannot be too clearly emphasized that this text does not say that backsliders cannot be restored to the favour and forgiveness of God; but that they cannot be restored so long as they cling to the things which had been the sources of their declension.

After the power of an indissoluble life.
Heb. 7: 16 (R.V., marg.).

THIS chapter is a veritable Psalm of Life. It overflows with the message of the Easter morning. Throughout its verses it is witnessed that He liveth; that He ever liveth; that He liveth after the power of an indissoluble life.

Remember all that was done to dissolve and loose it. Satan spoke to his chief captains, Sepulchre and Corruption, and bade them hold his Prisoner fast. The Sanhedrim affixed their seal, set the watch, and made the grave as secure as possible. But it was all in vain. His body could not see corruption. His life defied death. All through the Greek mythology there is the wail of infinite sorrow. Laocoon and his sons strangled by the folds of the mighty serpent: day always mastered by night: the year with its wealth of life descending to the abyss. Strive as man might, he would be mastered at last, the primeval night reign once more. But all this is altered in Jesus. He is Priest after the power of an indissoluble life.

And, what is more, that life may be communicated to us by the Holy Spirit. It is not only true that He ever liveth; but also that because He lives, and as He lives, we shall live also. In the first creation God breathed into Adam the breath of his life, and he became a living soul; but in the second creation Christ breathes into us the spirit of his life, and our spirit is filled with a property which it had not previously, and in which the sons of men have no share. "The first man Adam became a living soul. The last Adam became a life-giving spirit." "He that is joined to the Lord is one spirit." See to it that you deny your own life, so that his life may become evermore regnant within you.

In that He saith, A new covenant, He hath made the first old. Heb. 8: 13.

THERE had been a manifest decay and vanishing away of the first Tabernacle or Temple with its rites and services. At the time when these words were written there were evident symptoms of the approaching collapse of the whole system of which pious Jews had been wont to boast. But the Holy Spirit reassures their failing hearts.

It is well, He seems to say, that these should vanish from the earth; that men may be certified that the old covenant, of which they were the sign and seal, has also gone—gone never to be recalled. Thereupon, the very natural inquiry was suggested: If the old covenant has decayed and vanished away, what is the agreement or arrangement under which we are living now? To this inquiry the present chapter is an answer.

Those who believe in Christ are still in covenant relationship with God. A new covenant has been set up, which indeed is as old as the everlasting hills. It is the covenant of love; the covenant which says very little of what man does, and much of the I WILLS of Jehovah; a covenant which was entered into between God and his Son, standing as Mediator; a covenant which has been sealed with priceless blood.

The provisions of that covenant are enumerated in the foregoing verses: that God will engrave his law on mind and heart, and take us to be his people and be our God, and remember our sins no more. As the decay of the symbols of the Old Testament indicated that it was vanishing, so the ever-fresh beauty of the supper of our Lord, as it was practised in the first Church, witnessed to the permanence of the New Testament.

Unto them that look for Him shall He appear. Heb. 9: 28.

THERE is an evident parallel intended between the first and second Advent, and especially in the manner of looking for it. At the first Advent there were many who were definitely looking for and hastening to that day. Simeon was waiting for the consolation of Israel; and Anna spoke of the infant Lord to those who were expecting redemption in Israel. To look for the consolation and to look for the redemption were the two articles in that early creed. And presently this quiet, patient waiting broke out into the rapturous song of the *Nunc Dimittis*.

But all Jews were not looking for that blessed Hope, the appearance of the Grace of God. When our Lord came, the leading teacher of Judaism was Philo, and he not only had no Messianic hopes of his own, but discouraged them in other people. He conceded that there might be a return of Jewish national life; but he had no expectation of it being under the leadership of the Christ.

It has been truly remarked that this eager looking for the Advent has always been the mark of the living Church. "Ye turned," said the apostle, "unto God from idols . . . to wait for his Son from heaven." And again he said, "A crown of righteousness which the Lord, the righteous Judge, shall give unto me in that day; and not to me only, but to all them that love his appearing."

As it was with the first Advent it shall be with the second. The Son of God will come at a time and in a manner for which men are not prepared; and only the elect, who may have been contemned and despised by the world at large, will discern Him, and go forth to meet Him in the air.

He taketh away the first, that He may establish the second. Heb. 10: 9.

THE meaning of this is clear. In the old covenant the stress was laid on the outward rite; but in the new covenant, for burnt-offerings and sacrifices for sin are substituted first the entire devotion and consecration of the blessed Lord to his Father's will; and next, ours in Him.

It is very noticeable that by the offering of the cross, in which the Saviour's yielded will culminated, we are said to have been sanctified, consecrated, or set apart once for all (ver. 10). The thought there is, evidently, that our Saviour's death has implicated us for evermore; and that his Church, whom He represented in that supreme act, is for ever pledged to be dead unto the world and sin.

But still later we learn that He hath perfected for ever them that are sanctified (ver. 14). The change of tense surely indicates that what was accomplished for us in the purpose of God when Jesus died, must be accomplished in us by the operation of the Holy Spirit. Every time, therefore, our will is brought into more perfect union with that of God, a further step is taken towards that glorious elevation which Jesus made ours in the death of the cross.

And if you would have an incentive to this, remember how Jesus promised that all who would do the will of God should be reckoned members of the holy family (Matt. 12: 46–50). Are you a member of that family? You may be, and sit only on the outer circle, for the constituent members are always altering their position towards the central Christ; now advancing towards the inner heart, now receding. Oh, see to it that you are not only within the holy circle of the will of God, but that you are near the golden centre where Jesus is seated.

They without us should not be made perfect. Heb. 11: 40.

THIS chapter proves that the saints of all ages are essentially one. There is a link which unites them; a thrill which passes from hand to hand around the circle. One theme for many voices; one attitude for many faces; one inspiration for many hearts. The saints that lived before the Advent and those that have lived since are one in their faith in the living God, making the unseen visible, the distant near, and seeing the eternal through the transient and ephemeral.

And now heaven waits. Its joys are not complete, its rapture not full. The blessed are blessed; but there is yet a margin between what they are and what they will be—between what they enjoy, and what they may enjoy. The choir is not full, and the anthem cannot be fully rendered till our voices blend in it. There is a pause, a halt, an expectancy, an incompleteness, till we come. Your dear ones want you to be there. They have not gone far into the heart of God's bliss, but are lingering near the gate till you have joined them.

From Switzerland your friends write you to say it is perfectly beautiful, but "it will be better when you join us; we are reserving the best excursions till you arrive; we are incomplete without you; make haste." It is thus that the blessed await us. The spirit of Heaven is well represented by the courtesy of the old prophet, who would not sit down to meat with Jesse and his sons, till David, the youngest, had come thither also. And when the whole family is gathered, there will be a perfecting indeed, from which no element shall be wanting.

Oh rapture of eternal joy! We stretch out our hands in yearning desire, and doing so touch other hands reached towards ours!

Ye are come unto Mount Zion. Heb. 12: 22.
THESE poor Hebrew Christians, outcast from their Temple, and soon to see their beloved city vanish from the earth, were sore at heart. What a contrast was presented by the bare room in which they celebrated the simple supper and the splendid Temple with its magnificent rites! What a tiny rill their hymns were, compared with the mighty torrent of Temple psalmody! What a handful of worshippers, compared with the multitudes that congregated from all the world! Sometimes it seemed as though the contrast were unbearable.

Then said the Holy Ghost, lift up your eyes and see. Ye are not the lonely, isolated handful ye suppose. Every time you offer your prayer and sing your hymns ye are joining with the spirits of the perfected just, with numberless holy angels, and with vast multitudes in heaven and on earth who are ever adoring Christ. You climb the temple of Worship, of which the steps are prayers and the gates praise, and as you do so, on either hand go myriads of happy and holy spirits; and those surely are specially near whom you "have loved long since and lost awhile."

What special blessing these thoughts will bring to the bedridden, who for many years have not entered the courts of God's house; to the aged, and lonely, and exiled! We never worship God alone. As soon as we begin to pray, we say, Our Father which art in heaven, forgive our sins; give us our daily bread. We need not die to pass within thy gates, O Jerusalem, city of God! Already we tread thy golden pavement, and hear the music of the waters of life, and press to our wounds the leaves of thy tree.

Make you perfect in every good work to do his will. Heb. 13: 21.
TO perfect is to adjust, to put in joint, to articulate us with the living Saviour. It may be described as a surgical operation. Too many of those who are in the Body of Christ are not in living articulate union with Him. Hence the writer asks that we may be properly jointed with Christ.

THE AGENT OF THIS PROCESS. The God of Peace. Let us not be afraid of Him, as though He must use some terrible anguish, some heartrending grief. He will not shrink from this, if all other methods fail; but He prefers to achieve his purpose by gentle, tender, peaceful means. He is the God of the summer evening; of the bursting spring; of the slumber of the little babe.

THE GUARANTEE THAT HE WILL PERFORM THIS PROCESS. He brought again from the dead our Lord Jesus, that Great Shepherd of the sheep; and surely the power which achieved that bringing again is capable of any demand that may be made on it. Will He do so much for the Shepherd, and neglect the flock? Will He give Him the victory, and forsake those for whom He won it? In bringing the Shepherd did He not pledge Himself by the most solemn sanctions to do all that needed doing for the weakest of his sheep?

THE OBJECT OF THIS PROCESS. He adjusts us, that all which is well pleasing in his sight may be readily fulfilled in and through our yielded natures. When the helmsman is right with the captain, the boat will naturally take the course that the captain selects. When the machinery is adjusted with the motive power, the pulse of the piston will be felt away at the furthest loom with the smallest amount of leakage and the largest of result.

James

Unspotted from the world. James 1: 27.
"THE white flower of a blameless life!" The view of pure and undefiled religion presented in this definition was characteristic of James, surnamed the Just, who was revered even by the Jews for his austere piety, and whose vesture of simple white was emblematic of his stainless character. Whatever may be our views about the doctrines of Christianity, we must see to it that their outcome be in pure and holy living. Orthodoxy of view is utterly worthless unless it be combined with orthodoxy of life. This was the side of truth on which James insisted.

What a beautiful conception is here! The unspotted life! No book is like the Bible in its conception of sin; indeed, we owe to it the thought of sin, and its evil in the sight of God. But there is no book with so lofty an ideal of what life may become when it is yielded to the grace of Christ. A cleansed heart, and an unspotted robe; no sin allowed and permitted in the soul, and no evil habit allowed to dominate and enthral the life.

But how is it to be ours? (1) Put the grave of Christ between you and your former life, and so reckon that you are dead to all solicitations that would induce you to live according to the lusts and passions that dominate the rest of the Gentiles. (2) Seek by use to exercise your spiritual senses, that you may be quick to discern the first and most distant approach of temptation, that so it may find you hidden in the risen living Saviour. (3) Let the blood of Jesus be instantly applied, so that you may be immediately cleansed from the least spot that may have defiled your dress. (4) Keep away your eyes, and speech, and feet, from all scenes and society that have a defiling influence.

Hath not God chosen the poor of this world?
James 2: 5.
THERE is nothing that men dread more than poverty. They will break every commandment in the Decalogue rather than be poor. But it is God's chosen lot. He had one opportunity only of living our life, and He chose to be born of parents too poor to present more than two

doves at his presentation in the temple. All his life was spent among the poor. His chosen apostles and friends were, with few exceptions, poor. He lived on charity, rode in triumph on a borrowed steed, ate his last meal in a borrowed room, and lay in a borrowed grave. "Hath not God chosen the poor of this world?" Why is poverty so dear to God?

IT IS IN HARMONY WITH THE SPIRIT OF THE GOSPEL. The world-spirit aggrandises itself with the abundance of its possessions. Its children vie with each other in luxury and display. The spirit of Christ, on the other hand, chooses obscurity, lowliness, humility; and with these poverty is close akin.

IT COMPELS TO SIMPLER FAITH IN GOD. The rich man may trust Him; but the poor man must. There is so much temptation to the well-to-do classes to interpose their wealth between themselves and the pressure of daily need; but the poor man has no fortress in which to hide, except the two strong arms of God. He waits on Him for his daily bread, and gathers the manna falling straight from the sky.

IT GIVES MORE OPPORTUNITIES OF SERVICE. The rich are waited on, and pay for servants to wait on those they love. The poor, on the contrary, are called to minister to one another, at every meal, and in all the daily round of life. Herein they become like Him who was, and is, as one that serveth, and who became poor, that through his poverty we might be rich.

If any man offend not in word, the same is a perfect man. James 3: 2.
THINK of the sins of speech! How innumerable they are! When we see them in the light of this chapter, we can understand the holy Isaiah saying, "Woe is me, for I am undone; because I am a man of unclean lips, and I dwell in the midst of a people of unclean lips; for mine eyes have seen the King."

THE SINS OF SPEECH ABOUT OURSELVES. The tongue boasteth great things. We are all apt to be vain, boastful, exaggerated. We tell stories that redound to our own credit; contrive to focus attention on our own words and deeds; and even in delivering God's messages manage to let it be seen that we have a clearer insight into truth or a closer familiarity with God than our fellows.

THE SINS OF SPEECH ABOUT OTHERS. "We break the law of courtesy, and become harsh, insolent, and uncivil; or the law of purity, and repeat stories that leave a stain; or the law of truth, and practise insincerity, equivocation, and dissimulation; or the law of kindness, and are harsh and implacable to those who are beneath us in station. Or in our desire to stand well with others we are guilty of flattery, servility, time-serving, and the like."

THE SINS OF SPEECH IN CONNECTION WITH GOD'S WORK. We disparage other workers; compliment them to their faces on addresses they have delivered, and disparage them behind their backs; pass criticisms which take away the effect which their words had otherwise exercised over others; contrive to indicate one defect in which was otherwise a perfect achievement. Alas for us! How greatly we need to offer the prayer of the psalmist: Set a watch, O God, upon our lips!

The Spirit . . . yearneth for us even unto jealous envy. James 4: 5 (R.V., marg.).

A VERY deep and remarkable verse! The apostle is contending against the worldliness which was so rife among the believers he was addressing. They were set on pleasure; they sought the friendship of the world, and became unfaithful to their divine Lover; they were proud and high-minded. He went so far as to speak of them as adulterers and adulteresses; and then adopting a gentler, pleading tone, he says, "You are grieving the gentle Holy Spirit who has come to dwell within you, who yearns with a jealous envy to possess your entire nature for Himself."

The Spirit of God dwells within thee, O believer in Jesus Christ. If a man have not the Spirit of God, he is none of his; and since thou art undoubtedly one of us, thou hast most certainly the Holy Spirit. But the mistake of thy life consists in this, that He hath not thee. Some part of thy heart is given, but not all; and this causes Him the most intense pain, resembling that which we suffer from jealousy.

No keener pain is possible to the heart of man than to have good reason for the belief that a loved one is not wholly true; that there has been an alienation of affection which was once whole and entire; that another is receiving a part at least of the heart's devotion. The fire and screw are light in comparison with our anguish then; but, this is what the Spirit of God suffers when we share between Him and the world that love which should be all his own. "I, the Lord thy God am a jealous God," is as true as when first spoken from Sinai. The person of Jesus Christ must be the Sun of our system, though that system may include many planets beside.

The effectual fervent prayer of a righteous man availeth much. James 5: 16.

IT might be rendered literally: "Very strong is the supplication of a righteous man, energizing." When a man is right with God, not regarding iniquity in his heart, nor seeking aught for his own pleasure, the energy of the divine Spirit moves mightily within him, and his prayers become very strong. They recall the Master's, with their strong cryings and tears.

THE RIGHTEOUS MAN FINDS RELIEF FOR SUFFERING IN PRAYER. "Is any among you suffering? let him pray." There are sorrows we cannot tell to our dearest. Surges of grief sweep over us for which we have no words. Life is a stern fight for us all; and each heart knows its own bitterness. But there is always one resort: we can pour out our sorrows into the ear of our compassionate and merciful High Priest.

THE RIGHTEOUS MAN PRAYS THE PRAYER OF FAITH. The prayer of faith is that which is so sure of the divine answer that it knows that it has received it, though there is no appearance of its having been granted to the sense. We can only pray that prayer when we have asked what is in God's will to bestow. But righteous men cannot always pray thus, because they do not know the Lord's will on matters not recorded in this book. There are some sicknesses which are unto death, and we cannot pray the prayer of faith for these. If you cannot pray the prayer of faith, take medicine, and use the best means in your reach.

THE RIGHTEOUS MAN CAN AFFECT THE WHOLE HISTORY OF HIS FATHERLAND BY HIS PRAYERS. It was so with Elijah, as we learn here. It was so with John Knox, whose prayers were more dreaded by Mary of Scots than the armies of Philip.

1 Peter

An inheritance incorruptible and undefiled, and that fadeth not away. 1 Pet. 1: 4.

YES, it is an inheritance. It is a free gift, and yet we have a right to it. We do not ask for it—we were born into its blessed privilege. The child that lies in yonder cradle, over which the coronet is emblazoned, may claim his broad ancestral estates simply by right of birth: and it is on that tenure that the saints hold heaven. By God's great mercy we have been begotten again.

Oh, blessed heritage! Incorruptible! The gnawing tooth of decay cannot injure it. Moth and rust cannot consume, nor thieves break through to steal. No spendthrift hand can scatter or over-spend its treasures. Undefiled! Not a stain in its pure robes; not a freckle on its leaves; not a taint of miasma on its atmosphere. Into the city entereth nothing that defileth, or worketh abomination, or maketh a lie. That fadeth not away! To use the Greek word, it is amaranthine. Some of the fairest hopes that ever blessed human vision; the most delightful friendships; the most perfect dreams of delight, have faded and withered before our eyes. That never can.

IT IS KEPT FOR US, and we are kept for it. It is reserved in heaven for you.

"I have a heritage of joy,
  That yet I must not see;
The hand that bled to make it mine,
  Is keeping it for me."

WHO BY THE POWER OF GOD ARE GUARDED THROUGH FAITH. The idea is that we are being brought through an enemy's country under a strong escort—as the women and children from Lucknow, between the double line of English soldiers, till they were safe from the onset of the Sepoys. We are not in heaven yet; but we are as safe as if we were.

Who his own self bare our sins in his own body on the tree. 1 Pet. 2: 24.

HE CAME INTO THE SINNER'S WORLD. Himself sinless, He took our nature. Accustomed to the pure atmosphere of his own bright home, He allowed his ears and eyes to be assailed by sounds and sights beneath which they must have smarted. His blessed feet trod among the dust of death, the mounds of graves, and the traps that men laid to catch Him. And all for love of us.

HE LIVED THE SINNER'S LIFE. Not a sinner's life, but the ordinary life of men. He wrought in the carpenter's shed; attended wedding festivals, and heartrending funerals; ate, and drank, and slept. He sailed in the boat with his fisher-friends; sat wearied at the well-head; and was hungry with the sharp morning air.

HE SYMPATHIZED WITH THE SINNER'S GRIEFS. In their affliction He was afflicted. He often groaned, and sighed, and wept. When leprosy with its sores, bereavement with its heart-rending loneliness, dumbness and deafness, and devil-possession, came beneath his notice, they elicited the profoundest response from his sympathetic heart.

HE DIED THE SINNER'S DEATH. He was wounded for our transgressions. He was treated as the scapegoat, the leper, the sin-offering of the human family. The iniquities of us all met in Him, as the dark waters of the streets pour into one whirling pool. He stood as our substitute, sacrifice, and satisfaction: the guilt, and curse, and penalty of a broken law borne and exhausted in his suffering nature.

HE IS PREPARING THE SINNER'S HOME. "I go to prepare a place for you"; and no mother was ever more intent on preparing his bedroom for her sailor-boy on his return, than Jesus on preparing heaven.

Fear not their fear, neither be troubled.
1 Pet. 3: 14 (R.V.).

IT was a time of very real and fiery trial when Peter wrote these words. Persecution was already beginning with the House of God. The first mutterings of the awful storm which was to break in Nero's terrible atrocities were making themselves heard throughout the Roman world. The intention of this Epistle, therefore, was to encourage these scattered saints, that they might not be overwhelmed.

Some who read these words may need similar comfort.

Remember, beloved fellow-believers, that Jesus has suffered; your Lord and Master has trodden these thorns before you. See, they are flecked with his blood. Would you not desire to be fellow-partaker with Him in his sorrow, that you may share his glory? It is only in suffering that we can properly identify ourselves with the great anguish of the world, or learn to comfort or pray for others. And, probably, none know the innermost tenderness and companionship of Jesus like those who daily fill up that which is behind of his sufferings. Besides, their fear is much worse in anticipation than in actual experience. Probably God entirely delivers his martyrs from those physical tortures which to onlookers might seem unbearable.

This has been the perpetual testimony of the Armenian refugees. Miss Codrington's story of her experiences in China, and Dr. Baedeker's statement of what he has learnt in his wide experience amid the refugees and imprisoned saints in all parts of Europe support and confirm the same conclusion. Sanctify Jesus Christ in your heart as Lord and King. Maintain a good conscience; do not be turned aside for fear of man; and when you come to suffer, you will find the fire has lost its sting.

Arm yourselves with the same mind.
1 Pet. 4: 1.

THE Church was redeemed in a baptism of pain: for her members to suffer, and by suffering to overcome the world, is to fulfil the forecast which Jesus gave when He said, "In the world ye shall have tribulation; be of good cheer, I have overcome the world." Arm yourselves with this mind; put on this thought, this resolution, this purpose; determine that suffering at least shall never daunt you.

THE REASON FOR DONNING THIS ARMOUR. Here we have no continuing city. In the death of Jesus we suffered in the flesh, and ceased from our connection with the world which cast Him out: and, as suffering is meted out to us, we become increasingly convinced that we can have no fellowship with its sins. The pain which the world allots to the followers of Jesus widens the chasm between them and it, pulls down the old nests in which their affections once built, and makes them more determined than ever to follow their Lord.

THE CHOICE WHICH THIS ARMOUR INVOLVES. No more the lusts of men, but the will of God. Never again to work the desire of the Gentiles, but to live according to God. Not henceforth to bow before the bondage of evil habit, but with erect and upright gaze to behold the face of Christ—such is the choice. Will you not now make it at this solemn moment, as you stand on this watershed between the two continents—here of the morning, there of the midnight? Follow the King, cost what it may.

THE NATURE OF THE ARMOUR. It is the armour of Light: in which Christ's nature was encased, and on which all the shafts of man and devil broke into splinters. No weapon that was ever manufactured can prevail against its heavenly temper.

After that ye have suffered a little while.
1 Pet. 5: 10 (R.V.).

SUCH a little while! In the Epistle to the Hebrews (10: 37, R.V.) it is called a very little while. The late Dr. Gordon loved to read it, Yet a little while, how little, how little! which is the literal rendering of the Greek. A little while! compared with the eternal years; with the far more exceeding and eternal weight of glory; with the compensations which await us in the Home of God. Though our life were one long agony, it would seem but as yesterday when it is past; a dream, or a sleepless watch in the night, when the morning breaks.

There is a limitation to our suffering. It is only for a little while; but every moment has been fixed by the immutable purpose and love of God. The hour of darkness is timed with an exact measurement. You shall not suffer one moment more than is absolutely necessary for your perfecting of God's glory; and for every moment there is an ample supply of grace.

But remember also that in Christ God has called you to his Eternal Glory. You heard that call years ago, and have been following it through days of evil and nights of pain. But the gifts and calling of God are without repentance, and He is waiting to fulfil his eternal purpose. What a banquet that will be when God will satisfy the expectations of those whom He has called to partake of it!

And the suffering is being used in ways you little understand to perfect, stablish, and strengthen you. It is from sick chambers and torture-rooms that God brings forth his veteran hosts in the day of battle. Think not so much of affliction as of the love of Christ, and the blessedness of being like Him and with Him for ever.

2 Peter

An entrance shall be ministered unto you abundantly. 2 Pet. 1: 11.

THERE are two ways of entering a port. A ship may come in, waterlogged and crazy, just kept afloat by continual working at the pumps; or it may enter with every sail set, her pennon floating at the mast-head. The latter is what the apostle desires for himself and those whom he addresses. He desired that an entrance abundant should be ministered unto them.

An abundant entrance is really a choral entrance. The idea may be illustrated from the entrance of a Roman conqueror to his city, whence he had been sent out to war. Amid the crowds of spectators, the procession climbed slowly to the capital, while sweet incense was poured on the air, and music raised her sweetest and most inspiring strains. Will your entrance into heaven be like that? Will you enter it, saved so as by fire, or to receive a reward? Will you come unrecognized and unknown, or be welcomed by scores and hundreds to whom you have been the means of blessing, and who will wait you? Will your coming make music right through the home of God? This is the meaning of the choral entrance. It reminds us of those words of Christ about the friends whom we have made by the right use of money welcoming us into eternal habitations.

The conditions on which that choral welcome will be afforded are clearly enunciated here. Look back to verses 5, 6 (R.V.). There the identical word of the choir occurs again, translated "supply." It is as though these eight Christian graces composed the octave choir, and that our diligence in acquiring and cultivating these will be rewarded hereafter by the choral welcome into the eternal kingdom of the Lord Jesus. Wherefore give diligence.

The Lord knoweth how to deliver the godly. 2 Pet. 2: 9.

THE following authentic story will best illustrate and enforce this text. I give it as it was given to me by a friend who had verified the circumstances during a visit to Blankenburg. A godly Lutheran pastor, Sander, of Elberfeld, had been compelled to rebuke an evil-liver for some gross sin, and had thereby attracted to himself his malicious hate; and the man vowed to repay him. One night the pastor was called to visit a house that could only be reached by passing over a plank which bridged an impetuous torrent. Nothing seemed easier to his enemy than to conceal himself on the bank till the man of God was returning from the opposite end of the plank, to meet him in the middle, throw him into the deep and turbid stream, leaving it to be surmised that in the darkness he had simply lost his foothold. When, however, from his hiding-place he caught sight of the pastor's figure in the dim light, he was surprised to see that he was not alone, but accompanied by another. There were two figures advancing towards him across the narrow plank, and he did not dare attempt his murderous deed. And as they passed his hiding-place, the one whom he did not know cast such a glance towards him as convinced him of the sinfulness of the act he had contemplated, and began a work in his heart which led to his conversion.

When converted, he sought out the pastor, to confess to him the murderous intention which had so nearly mastered him, and said: "It would have been your death had you not been accompanied." "What do you mean?" said the other; "I was absolutely alone." "Nay," said he, "there were two." Then the pastor knew that God had sent his angel, as He sent him to bring Lot out of Sodom.

One day is with the Lord as a thousand years. 2 Pet. 3: 8.

THERE is no succession of time with God: no past, no future; He dwells in the eternal present, as I AM. As we may look down from a lofty mountain on a stream in the valley beneath, tracing it from its source to its fall into the ocean, and feeling that each part of it is equally distant from the spot where we stand, so must time appear to the Eternal; who was, and is, and is to come.

ONE DAY IS AS A THOUSAND YEARS. He could do in a single day, if He chose, what He has at other times taken a thousand years to accomplish. Do not say that He will require so long to do this or that—to restore or convert the Jews; to introduce the millennial age; to undo the effects of the Curse, and fill the years with blessing. Do not say that He must have as long to make the second heavens and earth as the first. Do not say that the overthrow of the empire of darkness, and the conversion of multitudes to God, can only be achieved by the processes which are now in vogue. All this could be changed in a moment, in the twinkling of an eye; and between sunrise and sunset God could effect the work of a thousand ordinary years.

A THOUSAND YEARS AS ONE DAY. Periods that seem so long to our finite minds are not so to God. A thousand years in our reckoning is but a day in his. You say it is nearly two thousand years ago since Jesus died, or at least that we are in the evening of the second thousand. But in God's reckoning, the Cross, the Grave, the Resurrection, took place in the morning of yesterday. Take wider views of God's horizon; believe in his mighty march throughout the centuries; He takes up the isles as a very little thing, and the centuries are the beats of the minute-hand.

1 John

If we say, . . . but if we walk.
1 John 1: 6, 7.

IN three marked passages, the beloved apostle guards against what men are apt to say, and indicates to them what it would be better for them to substitute in thought and speech.

MEN ARE APT TO SAY THAT THEY HAVE FELLOWSHIP WITH CHRIST, AND YET CONTINUE TO WALK IN DARKNESS. It arises sometimes from their desire to stand well with their fellows, or because they do not realize how much darkness is still in their lives. But whichever be the cause, they lie and do not the truth. It is better to walk quietly in the light, so far as we have it; and thus we shall secure his blessed fellowship, and his blood will be continually cleansing us from sin, removing all hindrance on Christ's side to the free communication of his choicest gifts.

AGAIN, MEN ARE APT TO SAY THAT THEY HAVE NO SIN (ver. 8). It is a profound mistake on their part, arising from defective ideas of what sin is, or from self-ignorance. If they realized what God's standard of holiness and sinlessness is; if they understood that sin consists in coming short of his glory as much as in distinct violation of his will; if they knew that there may be sin in motive as much as in act, and even in want of love—they would not speak thus. As it is, they deceive themselves, though no one else. It is better to confess our sins and seek cleansing, even for those of ignorance, in the precious blood of Jesus.

AGAIN, MEN ARE APT TO SAY THAT THEY HAVE NOT SINNED. Though they have fallen below their own standard, they do not like to admit it,

and cling tenaciously to their position of having got beyond the range of sinning. Much better to admit it, and obtain forgiveness through the one Advocate with the Father, Jesus Christ the Righteous.

The world passeth away, and the lust thereof.
1 John 2: 17.

THE world stands for the entire system of human interests by which we are surrounded. It does not refer to what God made by his creative fiat and moulding hands, but to the shows, fashions, and pursuits of men. It is used here in the sense in which the devil took Jesus into an exceeding high mountain, and showed Him all the kingdoms of the world and the glory of them, and said, "It hath been delivered unto me, and to whomsoever I will, I give it."

The word used of its evanescence is a remarkably interesting one. It is that employed of the rapid change in some scenic display or performance. A moment ago the stage was full of life and colour; but it is suddenly deserted, and the actors and actresses have put off their splendid dresses, and are habited in mean and common attire. Or we might compare the passing away of the world to the dying colour of the sunset. The tempter offers us some bait, some outward object which appeals to the eye of the body or the mind, and we reach out towards it; but as we grasp it, it is gone. We have caught at a soap-bubble, have journeyed after a mirage, have hunted the will-o'-the-wisp. So unsubstantial and fleeting are the things with which the men of this world try to appease their immortal appetite.

But it is to be noticed that the desire for these things is even more evanescent than the things themselves. The apostle says that the lust thereof passeth away. The power of enjoyment dies away. The eye is sated with spectacles; the mind with constant change.

How great the contrast!—"He that doeth the will of God abideth for ever."

Beloved, now are we children of God.
1 John 3: 2 (R.V.).

IT is our privilege, not only to be children, but to know that we are such. "Such we are" (ver. 1, R.V.). The world knows us not; but God knows us, and we know Him, and we know that we are his sons and daughters, through regeneration and faith. How do we know?

WE BELIEVE HIS WORD (John 1: 12). By faith we have received Him, we do trust in his name; then, by the authority of that text, if there were no other, we may claim to have been born into the divine household.

WE HAVE THE WITNESS OF THE SPIRIT (Gal. 4: 6). The fact that our hearts look to God as Father, and appeal to Him with the infant's cry, Abba, is a proof that we are born again. Do not look for an audible voice in your heart, but notice whether the thought of the fatherly love of God towards you is not becoming more familiar and precious. It is not the perception of your childship, but of his fatherhood, which will reassure you.

WE ARE LED BY THE SPIRIT. If we are led by the Spirit, we shall love the things we once hated, and hate those we once loved. Our choices, tastes, methods of life, habits, and companionships, will undergo a radical alteration.

WE LOVE THE PEOPLE OF GOD (1 John 4: 7, R.V.). The converse is also true, that he who is begotten of God loveth.

WE DO NOT PRESUMPTUOUSLY AND HABITU-ALLY YIELD TO KNOWN SIN (1 John 3: 9, R.V.). The apostle is not speaking of some isolated act into which a man may fall under unexpected temptation, but of habitual courses of inconsistency and wrongdoing. Test yourselves, therefore, whether ye are indeed born again.

We have known and believed the love that God hath to us. 1 John 4: 16.

LIFE is one long education in various phases and aspects of love. First as a child, then as a friend, then as a lover, as wife or husband, as father or mother. We are perpetually being allowed to sit in some higher form for the progress of this divine study. For to love is to live. To be loved is to drink of the sweetest cordial that can be prepared from the vintages of earth. And all is intended to help us to understand better the nature of God, who is love. As each new experience enters our life, we should consider a fresh facet or angle to break up and reveal to us the glory of God's love. We should say to ourselves, Now I understand and know more accurately than before how God feels, and what his love is.

THE APOSTLE SAYS WE HAVE KNOWN THE LOVE OF GOD. Indeed, it is so. Through years of life, each of which has been filled with the most various experiences, but filled also to the brim with proofs of God's tender loving-kindness, we have had innumerable proofs of his love, for

"E'en the cloud that spreads above, and
    veileth Love,
    Itself is Love."

THE APOSTLE SAYS WE MUST BELIEVE GOD'S LOVE. Standing on the sure foundation of what we have proved God to be in the past, we may look on the present and future with perfect faith. We have known Him too well to doubt Him now. We have known, and now we believe. He has made no mistakes. He is making none. He has done the best, and is doing it. We do not understand his dealings, but we know Him who is behind the mystery of Providence, and can hear Him saying: "It is all right, only trust Me. Fear not! it is I."

We know that we have. 1 John 5: 15.

THIS Epistle is full of certainty. It rings with the words we know. And in these words we are taught that we may be certain in the region of prayer. Probably there is no region of the Christian life concerning which there is more uncertainty than this of prayer. Perhaps this is also the reason why there is so little prayer. Men doubt the use of spending time in shooting arrows, a very small percentage of which seem to strike the target.

THE FIRST CONDITION IN TRUE PRAYER IS TO BE SURE THAT IT IS ACCORDING TO THE WILL OF GOD. It is not difficult to do this when we base prayer on a promise. And this is what we should do to secure definiteness and assurance. There is nothing that pleases our Father more in his praying children than that they should bring his promises to Him for fulfilment, saying, "Do as Thou hast said." But in cases where there is no promise to guide us we shall discover his will as we pray.

THE NEXT CONDITION IS TO BELIEVE THAT GOD IS LISTENING. We need not pray long to know this. Only be quiet and silent before Him, and a blessed sense, induced by the Holy Spirit, will pervade your heart and mind, that you are literally speaking into the ear and heart of your Heavenly Father, who is listening as intently as if He had nothing else to attend to in all the universe.

THE THIRD CONDITION IS TO BE SURE THAT THE THING WE ASKED IS GRANTED. It may not have come to hand, and it may not come in the precise form in which we sought it; but it is ours. We must dare to believe that we have that petition, labelled with our name, consigned to us, perhaps started on its way to us, although it may take years to come.

2 John

This is love, that we should walk after his commandments. 2 John 6 (R.V.).

HERE is a solution to many difficulties, and given so easily and naturally by this beloved elder to the elect lady and her children. He had been laying much emphasis on truth, and combining truth and love in an exquisite unity. Probably we can never love perfectly, till we are perfectly true. If you examine yourself in the feelings of distance and dislike which you have towards some individual, it is almost certain that you will come on some want of transparency and sincerity in your dealings with him. It is also the case that if we put away all insincerity, and want of consecration, as between us and God, we shall come to love God more perfectly.

What deep, sweet rhythm of meaning there is in the first three verses of this letter! One reads them over and over again. Oh that grace, mercy, and peace, may be with us, from God the Father, and from Jesus Christ, the Son of the Father, in truth and love.

The difficulty that you feel is that you do not love enough. You would like to love with a strong, undying flame, burning steadily towards Jesus Christ, cleansing you with its heat, constraining you with its love. But perhaps you fail to distinguish between love and the emotion of love. They are not the same. We may love without being directly conscious of love, or being able to estimate its strength and passion. Here is the solution to many of our questionings: They love who obey.

It is recorded of Dr. Chalmers that when a Scotch girl applied to be admitted to the sacrament, her testimony was so halting that it seemed as though she must stand back; but as she was leaving his room she turned back and said, "I canna speak for the Lord Jesus, but I could dee for Him."

3 John

For the sake of the Name they went forth. 3 John 7 (R.V.).

THE beloved elder is anxious about some travelling evangelists, who had gone forth to visit the churches; and is commending them to the care of Gaius. He was to set them forward in a manner that should be worthy of God. This is a high standard for our entertainment of brethren and strangers withal. It would save us from niggardliness and stint, for God is never miserly or meagre. It would equally save us from ostentation, since in God there is perfect simplicity. It would pervade our behaviour with the most perfect grace. But notice, in respect of these evangelists:

THEIR MOTIVE. "For the sake of the Name." It is not needful to say whose Name. There is one Name above every name, in which whatever we do is to be done. To teach the meaning hidden in that Name; to unfold its sweetness and power; to exert its spell over souls that had never felt its magnetism; to glorify it and make it honoured and beloved—this was their one thought and aim. Oh that we were animated by the same gracious motive!

THEIR DELICACY. They would take nothing of the Gentiles. It seemed to them incongruous to go for alms and maintenance to those who do not love their Lord. Besides, could not He maintain his own servants? They certainly would not have sanctioned the means that modern Christians adopt of getting money from the ungodly.

THEIR WELCOME. We ought to welcome all such; and in doing so we may be fellow-helpers with them and with the truth. It is a very beautiful act to link ourselves with God's honoured servants by prayer and sympathy, that we may be counted their fellow-helpers and companions.

Jude

Keep yourselves in the love of God. Jude 21. THERE is a strong current running. If you keep in its main stream, it will bear you gently but irresistibly forward; but there are so many side-currents, that we must be very careful not to be swept out of it. You are in it by grace, now keep in it.

BUILD YOURSELVES ON YOUR MOST HOLY FAITH. Build, not on your emotions; nor on your conceptions of what may be right or wrong; nor on your experience—but on the strong and massive outlines of the faith once delivered to the saints (ver. 3). We may well contend for it, if it is to yield the foundation of our spiritual upbuilding. In other words, you must come back, again and yet again, to the teachings of the Word of God, and specially of the life of Jesus.

PRAY IN THE HOLY SPIRIT. Wait at the divine foot-stool until your prayers are indicted by Him, and the spring arises from the depths of God. And whensoever you feel the inward movement of God's Spirit, yield to it. He will correct and prune from your prayers all that should not be in them. He will lead you out in intercession for others, and for the glory of Christ, of which you did not know yourself capable. To pray in the Holy Spirit is to let the Holy Spirit pray in you.

LOOK FOR THE MERCY OF OUR LORD JESUS CHRIST. Always be on the outlook. Let your soul stand on tiptoe in anticipation of his coming. Let yours be the words of the Canticles, "I sleep, but my heart waketh; it is the voice of my Beloved, that knocketh, saying, Open to Me, my sister; my love, my undefiled." The heart that waits for Jesus, will not have to wait in vain. And even in the act of waiting, it will be kept in the love of God, which is also eternal life.

Revelation

I am the First and the Last. Rev. 1: 11. IT is true, O Son of God. Thou art! The First in order of Being, and last in the full completeness of thy glory.

FIRST IN RESPECT OF TIME, for Thou art the everlasting Father—Father and Creator of the ages; and when time shall be no more, Thou wilt last for ever. From everlasting to everlasting Thou art God. Thy years shall not fail.

FIRST IN RESPECT TO CREATION. Thou wast before all things; thine was an age prior to the creation of matter; all things were made by Thee: and when the heavens and earth that are now have passed away for ever; when the elements shall have melted with fervent heat; when the sun shall be burnt out and the stars wane—Thou wilt still be the last, able to bring into being new heavens and a new earth.

FIRST IN THE ORDER OF REDEMPTION. God first loved us. From before the foundation of the world, Thou wert the Lamb slain; before the foundation of the world we were chosen in Thee. First in the love that resolved to redeem;

first in the mystery of thine incarnation, lowest in the depth of thy descent unto death, and in the resurrection through which Thou becamest the First-born among the dead; first to open the way within the vail, to bear our nature risen before the throne, and to inaugurate for man the life of resurrection-power.

FIRST IN RESPECT TO THE EXPERIENCE OF THINE ELECT. None is to be compared with Thee, Thou Prince of the kings of the earth. Their Alpha, their Beginning, the Day-star of their Hope, the Dawn of their Life, the Origin of all that is good and blessed in their life; whom they take to be their Ideal, their Goal, their Aim, their Omega, their End.

I will give him a white stone. Rev. 2: 17.

THERE is every reason to suppose that this white stone is a diamond, and that it stands for the Urim and Thummim stone, which the high priest wore in his breast-plate, and which he consulted for the oracles of God. It probably darkened with the divine No, and grew lustrous with Yes.

THE BELIEVER MAY HAVE DIRECT KNOWLEDGE OF THE WILL OF GOD. You may have your white stone. If only your heart is right with God, you may know his will for your path, not only by the pillared cloud of outward circumstances, but by the inner bearing of the heart. By a quick intuition you may know what God's mind is, both when you kneel in prayer and when you are called on to act. Only the surface of the inner life must be unruffled and pure; there must be no anxious agitation, no blurring miasma of sin.

EACH REVELATION OF GOD'S WILL CARRIES WITH IT A DEEPER KNOWLEDGE OF HIMSELF. On the Urim stone were engraven the mystic characters of the divine name. On these no eye but Aaron's might rest; so, deep in our heart, these revelations of God's nature are given, which are direct and special for each loving and obedient soul. Eye hath not seen nor heart conceived what God says to his children about life and death, and Himself, and their relationship, and the glorious future.

SUCH REVELATIONS ARE IN PROPORTION TO OUR OVERCOMING LIFE. If you are perpetually yielding to sin and impurity, and being trodden down by the heel of passion, such communications from the Infinite will be rare and indistinct. To him that overcometh, not once for all, but perpetually, shall be made the revelations of God.

I will make . . . a pillar in the Temple of my God. Rev. 3: 12.

All who lived on the seaboard of Asia Minor were familiar with the vast and beautiful temples, in which Oriental lavishness and Greek art combined to realize the utmost magnificence. Their ruins strew the deserted sites of former cities to this day. The Lord therefore used familiar imagery in this promise. A column hewn from its rocky bed, richly sculptured, and conveyed to the rising temple-structure!

STABILITY. "Shall go no more out." God Himself shall establish, strengthen, and settle, the soul which trusts Him, and is willing to follow at all costs where He leads. He will make such a one to be as Jachin or Boaz, the two mighty pillars which Solomon erected in the Temple court, their names signifying establishment and strength. There is no spectacle more inspiring than to behold the steadfastness of the soul that wavers and swerves not, but stands to its post, though all nature rocks.

RESPONSIBILITY. The pillar bears up some part of the structure; and it is Christ's good pleasure to call us to share with Him the weight of ministering to his Church. As you show yourself true and faithful, God will allow you to bear up the common life of his people by ministering comfort, direction, encouragement, to such as could not stand by themselves.

BEAUTY. The mediæval architects and masons took great pleasure in their designs. In many cases each pillar is sculptured as to its capital in its own fashion. There is infinite variety and beauty in the patterns. So Jesus is cutting deep into us the name of his Father and Himself, and making us bear new revelations to the world. Do not shrink from the deep cutting of his chisel.

A door opened in heaven. Rev. 4: 1.

YOU must remember that John was in the isle of Patmos, a lone, rocky, inhospitable prison, for the Word of God and the testimony of Jesus. And yet to him, under such circumstances—separated from all the loved ones of Ephesus; debarred from the worship of the Church; condemned to the companionship of uncongenial fellow-captives—were vouchsafed these visions. For him, also, a door was opened.

We are reminded of Jacob, exiled from his father's house, who laid himself down in a desert place to sleep, and in whose dreams beheld a ladder which united earth with heaven, and at the top stood God.

Not to these only, but to many more, doors have been opened into heaven; when, so far as this world was concerned, it seemed as though their circumstances were altogether unlikely for such revelations. To prisoners and captives; to constant sufferers, bound by iron chains of pain to sick couches; to lonely pilgrims and wanderers; to women detained from the Lord's house by the demands of home; to domestic servants, missing the blessed opportunities of the sanctuary—how often has the door been opened in heaven. And what has not Nature been to some of us! How often in a country glade, the first flower of spring, a bird's warble, a gleam of light chequering the path, has been as a door opened in heaven!

There are conditions. You must know what it is to be in the Spirit; you must be pure in heart, and obedient in life; you must be willing to count all things but loss for the excellency of the knowledge of Jesus Christ. Then, when God is all in all to us, when we live, move, and have our being in his favour, to us also will the door be opened.

In the midst of the throne stood a Lamb as it had been slain. Rev. 5: 6.

IT is a marvellous combination, but how reassuring! Not the throne without the Lamb, else sinners dare not venture nigh: not the Lamb without the throne, or we might question his victory, his omnipotence to succour and save. No; but the throne with the Lamb, the Lamb and the throne, the Lamb in its very midst.

How does the Lamb come there? Surely meekness, humility, gentle submissiveness to an irresistible lot, are not the virtues that win thrones! Perhaps not in man's world, but they do in God's. In the eternal world the passive virtues are stronger than the active; sufferers wield more might than wrestlers; to yield is to overcome; to be vanquished is to conquer. It is because He was God's Lamb that He is now God's Anointed King, having seven horns for his omnipotence, seven eyes for omniscience, and seven spirits sent into all the world for omnipresence.

But see: the marks of suffering, of agony and death, of sacrifice, are stamped upon his flesh. "A Lamb as it had been slain." The redeemed ones that stand around tell the story;

He purchased and cleansed them by his blood; He is worthy to fill the throne and rule for ever. He who could make Himself the supreme sacrifice and offering for the sins of the world is worthy to be the world's King. The angels corroborate their verdict. In concentric rings they stand around the throne in their massed myriads. From ten thousand times ten thousand clear voices the acclamation rings out, Thou art worthy!

Take the scroll of history, of empire, of our lives, O gentle, holy, victorious, mighty Lamb. Break the seals, and unroll it page by page. All must be well that passes beneath thy tender and mighty hand.

Come! Rev. 6: 7.

THE A.V. reads, Come and see. The R.V., with the majority of Greek MSS., drops the last two words, and puts the simple word come into the lips of the four living creatures. Indeed, that word rings through the corridors of this book like a clarion. Come, Son of God! Come, according to thy plighted word! Come, for creation travails in pain together until now! Come restore thine ancient people, and bring in the golden age! Come! Take to Thyself thy great power, and reign! The time is ripe! Midnight has faded into dawn, and dawn is lightening fast to day!

The ages which are characterized by the bloodless victories of civilization and peace are incomplete without Thee; and as the white horse issues forth; men are not satisfied with the abundance of this world's goods, there is still an unsatisfied yearning which says, Come.

The ages most saturated with blood—the blood of men, shed by the hands of men, where harvests grow rank because the soil has been so richly fertilized by blood and tears— need Thee sorely; and as the red horse comes forth, sad Mother Earth, who has received so many mangled bodies to her bosom, bids Thee come.

The ages, filled with plague, pestilence, and famine, wherein beasts multiply about the homes of men, because there is no hand to keep them back, since men have perished from the earth, as the livid horses go forth, cry, Come.

And listen to the cry of thy martyrs, from beneath the altar. Is it not time to arrest the heavy hand of the persecutor, and avenge their blood? Then come, and add to all thy other crowns, the crown of all the earth!

The Lamb shall guide them unto fountains of waters of life. Rev. 7: 17 (R.V.).

WE do not live until we have been born again. The moment of regeneration is the first moment of life. All the years before are as though they had never been. But from the moment we receive the life of the eternal God into our being, we begin an endless progression.

THE ENTRANCE OF THAT LIFE MAKES US LAMBS IN THE FLOCK OF THE GOOD SHEPHERD. We no longer resist, or fight, or boast in things of which we should be ashamed. We become pure, sweet, gentle, lowly, and submissive. We are willing to lay down our lives for others. We follow the way of the cross without murmur or complaint. Every time we eat of that bread and drink of the cup we witness to the world our desire to absorb more and more of the lamb-like nature of the Son of God. Hence, it is said, the Lamb shall lead, shall shepherd, shall tend us as his flock.

THE LIFE WHICH GOD HAS IMPLANTED YEARNS FOR SATISFACTION. As a parched flock desires the crystal streams that purl over the pebbles, so the flock of God in this life and the next cry out for God, for the living God. Nothing will satisfy God's lambs and sheep but God Himself. And this is satisfied in Jesus. In Him the eternal God comes near to us; we follow Him without fear.

AND IN THAT LIFE THERE IS ETERNAL PROGRESSION. Jesus leads us from one fountain to another, from one well to the next; always deeper into the heart of heaven, always further towards the very centre of all things, which is God. We shall always be satisfied; but our capacity will constantly enlarge, and it will become necessary to give us fuller manifestations, according to his own promise (John 17: 26, R.V.).

That He should add it unto the prayers of all saints. Rev. 8: 3.

EACH series of seven, whether of the candlesticks, the seals, the trumpets, or the vials, is introduced by some appropriate and suggestive appearance of Christ. Here, for instance, the seven trumpets are restrained until this inspiring vision of the Redeemer is delineated as an imperishable fresco on the wall of Scripture.

It is not startling that He assumes here the appearance of an angel. This was his frequent guise in the ages which preceded his incarnation. And as to the priestly function here ascribed to Him, they are his habitual practice and wont throughout the present dispensation. He appears in the presence of God on our behalf. He has gone within the vail to make intercession for us. Such a Priest becomes us who is a minister of the sanctuary, and of the true tabernacle which the Lord has pitched, and not man. And since it is necessary that, as High Priest, He should have somewhat to offer, there is given to Him the praises, prayers, and gifts of the saints, that He should mingle them with the much incense of his own merit, and present them at the golden altar which is before the throne. Whenever we approach God in the name of Jesus we are really appealing to Him on the ground of that presentation, of that much incense, and the prevalence of that intercession.

Our prayers appear at times too utterly unworthy to bring to God. How can we dare to believe that they can be acceptable to the Holy God! Granted! It is all true. But never forget the much incense which is added to each petition; and remember that Christ gave Himself unto God, and is perpetually giving Himself, for us, an offering and a sacrifice, for an odour of a sweet smell.

Only such men as have not the seal of God on their foreheads. Rev. 9: 4 (R.V.).

THIS reference carries us back to chap. 7, with its sublime description of the angel ascending from the sunrise, having the seal of the living God. He had cried with a great voice to the four angels, to whom it was given to hurt the earth and the sea (7: 3).

The seal of God! Whatever that means in this pictorial or hieroglyphic book, we know what it means throughout the Epistles. The sealed have no doubt about their personal acceptance with God. They have set their seal to God, and He to them. They realize that they belong to Him in bonds of ownership which neither life nor death can dissolve. They bear upon their lives the impression of his image and superscription. They go to and fro about the world under the protecting escort of his high angels, who are commissioned to bring them safely to their Father's home. They have been anointed as kings and priests.

What a remarkable inference may be derived from the prohibition of the previous chapter, and the immunity accorded to the sealed ones in this! If the hordes of horsemen are withheld from touching the servants of God, whom the Angel sealed, we may infer, when no such caution is uttered about our lives, and no such immunity secured, that God has allowed pain, and sorrow, and death to hurt us for some sufficient reason—one which we shall be able to appreciate when we stand in his light. If He who has power to withhold the power of the adversary does not withhold it, the assaults which make our frail craft tremble from stem to stern must be his appointment and choice for us, and we must dare to look up into his face, and say, It is the Lord, let Him do what seemeth Him good.

Time no longer. Rev. 10: 6.

TIME is but an incident in the procession of eternity: a wreath of cloud on its expanse; a throb of its pendulum; a drop in its multitudinous ocean. There was a moment when it began; there shall be another of its pause and cessation.

But we may look for this expiration of the Time Ages without alarm. We have already received the germ of the eternal life, which existed before time began, and will last when it has fulfilled its course. "The witness is this, that God gave unto us eternal life, and this life is in his Son. He that hath the Son hath the life." We are the children of eternity; our eternal life dates from the moment of our regeneration; we know not how it befel, but we awoke in the time sphere to discover that we were objects of an eternal love, and that we are destined to a life which will outlast the universe of matter. From everlasting to everlasting Thou art God; and Thou hast made us partakers of thy divine nature, who art, and wast, and art to come!

The margin suggests another rendering, that there should be no longer delay for the finishing of the mystery of God. From times eternal God has been elaborating his secret purpose, which surely must include the overruling of evil for good; the vindication of his permission of evil; and the final restitution of all things. For long that mystery has remained unfinished. God has not told his deep design. To many questionings He has given no reply. But the moment is at hand when the mystery of God will be finished, and the draping vail will be removed. Then, beloved, but not before, you will understand. Then you shall see the end from the beginning; and in God's light, see light.

There was seen in his Temple the Ark of his Covenant. Rev. 11: 19 (R.V.).

WE are constantly encountering evidences that the Bible is one. Its writers are as various in their styles and characteristics as their respective ages; but they keep striking the same notes, and making allusion to the same objects. We have not heard of the Ark for centuries. Now we suddenly meet with it in a description of the coronation of the Son of Man. He has taken his great power and reigned. The kingdoms of the world have become his. The portals of the temple of God have been thrown open, and within is seen the Ark of the Covenant.

GOD WILL NEVER FORGET HIS COVENANT. When once He has pledged Himself to a nation or an individual, to Abraham or Israel, or to Christ and his seed, He will infallibly stand to it. All traces of his faithfulness may elude the eye of the earthly watchers, obliterated by the storms of sorrow that sweep the world; the very emblems of the covenant may have passed from human custody; and the time may be long—but at the destined hour the parted vail will reveal the Ark of the Covenant, as though to show that the victory of Christ was the fulfilment of that ancient pledge.

THE COVENANT, WHICH MEANS BLESSING TO GOD'S CHILDREN, IS FRAUGHT WITH TERROR TO HIS ENEMIES. "There followed lightnings, and voices, and thunders, and an earthquake, and great hail." It was so of old, when the ark brought deliverance to Israel, but disaster to Philistia. The savour of life and of death; the pillar of cloud which was light, and midnight darkness; the "Come, ye blessed," and "Depart, ye cursed"—these alternatives are presented to us all.

They overcame him because of the blood of the Lamb. Rev. 12: 11.

THE overcoming and casting-out of Satan is the theme of the Book. First he overcomes; then he is overcome. Overcome first by Christ; and secondly by those who belong to Christ. Cast out from Heaven to the heavenly places or the air, of which as prince he wields the power. Cast out from there into the earth. Cast out thence into the bottomless pit. Cast out thence into the lake of fire. Such are the stages of the overthrow of the adversary of God and man.

Though Satan has no access to the presence of God now that the risen Saviour has entered there by virtue of his own blood, yet he may accuse us to our own conscience:

"I hear the accuser roar
  Of ills that I have done:
 I know them well, and thousands more;
  Jehovah findeth none."

How are such accusations to be met? By the blood of the Lamb, and by the word of our testimony. There is no force so potent as the witness of the saints for truth, purity, and spirituality. Oh that there were more of this, by life and lip! Oh that there were more unswerving loyalty to the King, who before Pontius Pilate witnessed a good confession!

For when this is so Satan gives back. The darkness cannot withstand the light. Victory is assured to those who love not their life unto the death, in their steadfast obedience to the truth. Then the fruit of the tree of life, immunity from the second death, the hidden manna, the white stone, the morning star, the confession before the angels of God, and the pillar in the temple of Eternity!

That no man should be able to buy or to sell, save he that hath the mark. Rev. 13: 17.
FROM many hints dropped from time to time by business men it would seem as though the time described in these words is already being inaugurated. Christian men are finding it increasingly difficult to carry on their businesses without adopting a lower standard than that of the sanctuary. Tradespeople are strongly tempted to adopt two prices, adulterate, or sell beneath their samples. Workmen are hardly put to it when association with their fellows threatens to involve them in movements from which in their secret souls they revolt. How much business is done over the glass of wine or in the public-house!

Under these circumstances, Christians must resolve:

FIRST, THAT THEY WILL NOT TRIFLE WITH THEIR CONSCIENCE, BUT WILL DARE IN ALL RESPECTS TO OBEY THE LAW OF CHRIST. For everyone there is an inevitable choice to be made and maintained, whether a clear conscience or a fortune is to hold the first place in their business career. At many a subsequent crisis the decision may be tested; but the peril of reversing it will become always less.

SECOND, MEN MUST BE CONTENT TO BEAR POVERTY AS PART OF THE CROSS OF CHRIST. We admire and canonize the martyrs, but are strangely unwilling to face the disgrace of poverty, the dens and caves of the earth, which they endured for principle. Our religion will cost us something, or we may fairly question its vitality and worth. What a man will not suffer for he does not value.

THIRD, CHRISTIAN PEOPLE SHOULD TEACH THEIR CHILDREN THE NOBILITY OF FRUGALITY, SIMPLICITY, AND CONTENTMENT. There would be fewer hearts broken by prodigals if we lived as though Christian life did not consist in our possessions, but in God.

The firstfruits unto God and unto the Lamb.
Rev. 14: 4.
WHAT a word is here! The apostle points to the radiant throng, grouped around Christ as his bodyguard of personal attendants. We had just beheld in the previous chapter the mighty legions mustering under the prince of darkness, and which furnish a strange contrast to this galaxy of strength and beauty. And as we wonder and admire, we are told that they are but as the firstfruit sheaf of the mighty harvest to be reaped from the earth.

By examining the firstfruit sheaf, we are able to tell the nature and quality of all the other sheaves that stand in the harvest-field under the golden autumn light. It is by studying the characteristics of these happy and holy spirits that we may learn what we shall be, and what the whole body of the elect shall be one day. Let us consider their number, their character, and their occupation.

THEIR NUMBER. "With Him, a hundred and forty-four thousand." But if this vast multitude is only a sheaf, what will not the entire harvest be but a multitude which none shall be able to compute?

THEIR CHARACTER. Stamped indelibly with the name of God and of the Lamb; singing a new song, which only redeemed hearts can learn and redeemed lips utter; virgin souls, clad in stainless purity, with no lie in their mouths, and no blemish in their lives; purchased from among men to follow the Lamb. Such are they before the throne.

THEIR OCCUPATION. Adoration: they sing a new song. Loyal obedience and companionship: they follow the Lamb whithersoever He goeth. They cannot claim aught to themselves. Their whole story is told in the announcement that they were purchased—purchased by the blood of the Lamb they love.

Righteous and true are thy ways, Thou King of the ages. Rev. 15: 3 (R.V.).

THIS is the scene of the deliverance from Pharaoh on the shores of the Red Sea, translated into the imagery and language of eternity. The hosts of God shall emerge ere long from their long oppressions; by suffering they shall conquer; they shall come off victorious from the beast, and from his image, and from the number of his name. Behind them shall be spread out the sea of time, so calm and still, so hushed from all its tumult and storm, that it shall seem to be like sheets of glass; and as the morning of eternity breaks, it shall be drenched with fire. Fire here is probably an emblem of the holiness and the judgments of God.

Israel broke into rapturous thanksgiving, as the people saw their enemies dead upon the shore. "Sing unto the Lord, for He hath triumphed gloriously!" But those triumphant notes, though chanted by an entire nation, shall be as a whisper compared with that song which shall break in thunder from the saints of all the ages. Those who were brought up under the dispensation of Moses, and the followers of the Lamb in the present dispensation, together with all holy souls who have overcome, shall constitute one vast choir.

But search the song of Moses as you will, you will fail to find one note that equals this in sublimity. Here are the saints of God, trained in distinguishing the niceties of righteous and holy government and behaviour, enabled from their vantage-ground in eternity to survey the entire history of the divine dealings, adoring Him as King of the Ages, and acknowledging that all his ways had been righteous and true. What a confession! What an acknowledgment!

Behold, I come as a thief. Blessed is he that watcheth. Rev. 16: 15.

THE Second Advent will come on men generally suddenly and unexpectedly. When they say, Peace and safety, then sudden destruction shall overtake them, as travail a woman with child, and they shall not escape. With the rapidity of the lightning flash; with the suddenness of a flood or avalanche; with the surprise of the midnight robber—Christ will come. When men are asleep, when every bolt and fastening refuses admittance, when the streets are still and hushed, behold the Judge will stand before the door.

As Lightfoot, quoted by Dr. Macduff, suggests, the allusion may be to a Jewish custom in the service of the temple. Twenty-four wards or companies were appointed night by night to guard the various entrances to the sacred courts. One individual was appointed as captain or marshal over the others, called the "Man of the Mountain of the House of God." His duty was to go round the various gates during the night to see that his subordinates were faithful to their charge. Preceded as he was by men bearing torches, it was expected that each wakeful sentinel should hail his appearance with the password, "Thou Man of the Mountains of the House, peace be unto thee!" If through unwatchfulness and slumber this were neglected, the offender was beaten with the staff of office, his garments were burnt, and he was branded with shame.

It was in contrast with these slumbering Levites that Jesus pronounces a blessing on his own people who watch and keep their garments, and are saved from the reproach of spiritual nakedness. Let us, therefore, wait for the promise of his coming, looking for and hasting unto the coming of the day of God.

Drunken with the blood of the saints, and with the blood of the martyrs of Jesus. Rev. 17: 6.

PAGAN and papal Rome have had to contend with an unbroken line of the witnesses of Jesus. In the words of an exiled Huguenot, "Since the birth of anti-Christianity, there have not been wanting those who have cried against its errors and idolatries." They have been called by various names—Paulicians, Waldenses, Albigenses, Wicliffites, Lollards, Lutherans, Zwinglians, Pietists, and Schismatics; but God never left Himself without witness. They might all have adopted the symbol and motto of one of them, "A lighted candle in a candlestick," with the words, "The light shineth in darkness."

But how terribly has the vision of the text been verified! Think of the persecutions under the Emperors, when the entire empire was filled with fire and sword. Take the single instance of the Empress Theodora, who slaughtered and drowned one hundred thousand of these Paulician Christians. During the thirteenth, fourteenth, and fifteenth centuries, Romanism, then in the plenitude of its power, gathered itself for a great, determined, and persistent effort to crush out all that opposed its supremacy, and to clear Christendom of heresy. And wherever any revival of true religion took place, or any confessors of Christ could be found, they were hunted, if possible, to death.

We have not yet resisted unto blood, in the strife against the sin and evil of our time. It is not that the world or the professing Church loves us better, but, probably, we are deficient in the spirit that lived in the martyr's breast. O Spirit of the living God, kindle that flame of love again which shall make us willing to suffer the loss of all, even of life, for the sake of Jesus!

Come forth, My people, out of her.
Rev. 18: 4 (R.V.).

WE cannot be surprised to find that God has people in the midst of Babylon. Probably in the most corrupt days there has always been a remnant of seven thousand who have not bowed the knee or kissed the hand to Baal. It is the presence of true, though benighted, piety which has perpetuated the existence of organizations which are an offence and a stumbling-block. But their presence in such company cannot be tolerated.

It is often argued that we should stay in the midst of churches and bodies whose sins and follies we deplore, in the hope of saving them for God and man. And such reasoning has a good deal of force in the first stages of declension. A strong protest may arrest error. A vigorous policy may stop the gangrene. But as time advances, and the whole body becomes infected and diseased; when the protests have been disregarded, and the arguments trampled underfoot; when the majority have clearly taken up their position against the truth; when her sins have reached up to heaven, and the plagues are about to befall—there is need for another policy; we have no alternative but to come out and be separate, and not touch unclean thing. "Let us, therefore, go forth unto Him without the camp, bearing his reproach."

The place from which we can exert the strongest influence for good is not from within, but from without. Lot lost all influence of his life in Sodom; but Abraham, from the heights of Mamre, was able to exert a mighty influence on its history. Obadiah might hide the prophets of God by fifties in a cave; but Elijah, from the Mount of Carmel, was able to exterminate the priests of Baal, and call back again the people's hearts to God.

Blessed are they which are bidden to the marriage supper of the Lamb. Rev. 19: 9 (R.V.).

AT the epoch described in the text we behold the Church of Christ unveiled and visible to heaven and earth. She has laid aside her weeds of sorrow, her ashen garments, her evidences of persecution and rejection, and stands forth a monument of grace, the masterpiece of Christ, the joy of the Bridegroom's heart. There will be no churches then, but one Church, which will contain within her borders the believing ones of all the churches.

The marriage supper, it has been truly said, is the arrival of that epoch which the redeemed of every age have anticipated. It has been the longed-for day of patriarchs, the glowing prediction of prophets, the burden of songs, the hope of the Church, the era for which creation groans and the sons of God pray.

But there must be a present character to fit us for this future felicity. Who are they that are thus called to the marriage supper? They are of every kindred, nation, people, and tongue, who have accepted the promises and invitations of the everlasting Gospel, and have washed their robes and made them white in the blood of the Lamb. Let us now pass on that invitation; let him that heareth say Come. Let us go forth into the highways and hedges and compel men to come in, that God's feast may be furnished with guests. Let us not be content with the first refusal, or the second; but with eager persistency press on men the urgency of these closing hours of opportunity, remembering that, when once the Master of the house has risen up and shut to the door, it will be hopeless and impossible to secure an entrance. "Now is the accepted time; now is the day of salvation."

A great white throne. Rev. 20: 11.

GREAT, because of the great causes that will be decided there; the great destinies that will impinge; the great God who will sit there; the great eternity which will be decided for good or bad.

WHITE, because of its immaculate purity. Sir Walter Raleigh, involved in a network of malice, and unjustly condemned to die, turned from the earthly court in which he had suffered vile insult and cruel wrong to the thought of heaven's unimpeachable truth. Whilst being ferried from Westminster to his dark cell in the Tower, which we visit with hushed footsteps and bated breath, he wrote by lamplight of

> "Heaven's bribeless hall,
> Where no corrupted voices brawl,
> No conscience molten into gold,
> No forged accuser bought or sold,
> No cause deferred, no vain spent journey—
> For Christ is there, the King's Attorney."

A THRONE, because a King will sit there, the Son of Man, the Son of God. What a change is here! He that hung upon the cross in shame, shall sit upon the throne in glory. He who stood condemned before the earthly tribunal, shall decide the destinies of the race and reveal the principles of the divine government.

But that judgment will not affect those who have fled to the refuge of his wounds. These cannot come into judgment. Let us always distinguish between the judgment of the world-spirit, when Jesus died; the judgment of sin on the cross; the judgment which awaits each believer as to the use he has made of his talents, and the work he has done in the world, and finally, the last great judgment which has to do with those who have refused the love and light of God, and have voluntarily cast in their lot with Satan.

The sea is no more. Rev. 21: 1 (R.V.).
ALL through this book we hear the clash of the waves. Throughout there is the voice of many waters. But when there dawns on the eye of the seer the bright and blessed time, which is yet to come; when the new heavens and earth appear, this is among the chief attractions of that glorious world—that there is no more sea. The sea is a characteristic emblem of this age, but not of the next.

THERE SHALL BE NO MORE PAINFUL MYSTERY. To the Jew there was a double mystery in the sea—that which lay in its sunless caves, and that which lay beyond the rim of the horizon; and because there was mystery there was dread and alarm. We, too, live on the shores of mystery, and float above it, with only a plank between it and us. But there we shall know as we are known; our questions answered; our problems solved.

THERE SHALL BE NO MORE REBELLIOUS POWER. The sea is the emblem of untamed power. Lashed into yeasty foam it drives the great ships before it and eats into the land. Men cry,

Let us break his bands asunder, and cast away his cords. But God laughs at them. Remember the motto that England struck on its medal to celebrate the destruction of the Armada: "The Lord blew upon them, and they were scattered." And so shall it be one day when all proud opposition to his will is vanquished.

THERE SHALL BE NO MORE DISQUIET AND UNREST. Life is like a voyage over the sea—now miles of calm, then days of storm; now monotonous and slow progress, then the awful stress of peril and threatening death. Outside of Christ life is like the troubled sea, when it cannot rest, but casts up mire and dirt. But yonder there will be unbroken peace and rest.

His servants shall serve Him; and see his face; his name shall be in their foreheads.
Rev. 22: 3, 4.
THESE are the three elements in heavenly bliss:

SERVICE. In the disciples' prayer the Lord taught us that the will of God is done there. Not that there is any breach in its perfect rest. Activity there will be, as easy and natural as the play of the bees among the limes, or of minnows in the pool. There will be no strain, no effort, no exhaustion. To stay those ministries which the blessed render to Him would be intolerable pain. They would be weary with forbearing, and could not stay.

VISION. "They shall see his face." Here, through a glass darkly; there, face to face. Here, as when the two walked to Emmaus, and knew not their Companion, though their burning hearts might have told them the secret; there, as when their eyes were opened, and they knew Him (though He will not vanish from our sight). Oh, what a glad surprise!

TRANSFIGURATION. "His name shall be in their foreheads." The name of God is the totality of the divine perfection and beauty, and the bearing of his name on their foreheads indicates that they are becoming like Him, whilst they see Him as He is.

There the Bible closes its record, finding man in a garden, leaving him in a city; demonstrating that where sin reigned unto death, there much more grace reigned through righteousness unto eternal life, giving man a more exalted and blessed lot than Adam enjoyed in the cool of the day in Eden.